PETERSON'S COLLEGE & UNIVERSITY ALMANAC

COMPLETE INFORMATION ON 1,700 REGIONALLY ACCREDITED COLLEGES AND UNIVERSITIES

Peterson's
Princeton, New Jersey

About Peterson's

Peterson's is the country's largest educational information/communications company, providing the academic, consumer, and professional communities with books, software, and online services in support of lifelong education access and career choice. Well-known references include Peterson's annual guides to private schools, summer programs, colleges and universities, graduate and professional programs, financial aid, international study, adult learning, and career guidance. Peterson's Web site at petersons.com is the only comprehensive—and most heavily traveled—education resource on the Internet. The site carries all of Peterson's fully searchable major databases and includes financial aid sources, test-prep help, job postings, direct inquiry and application features, and specially created Virtual Campuses for every accredited academic institution and summer program in the U.S. and Canada that offers in-depth narratives, announcements, and multimedia features.

Visit Peterson's Education Center on the Internet (World Wide Web) at www.petersons.com

Editorial inquiries concerning this book should be addressed to the editor at Peterson's, P.O. Box 2123, Princeton, New Jersey 08543-2123.

ISBN 1-56079-970-6

Production Editor: Joe Emanski
Research Director: Kimberly Hoeritz
Compositor: Gary Rozmierski
Programmer: Sean Conway

Printed in the United States of America

10 9 8 7 6 5 4 3 2

CONTENTS

CHAPTER 1

A Guide to Good Four-Year Colleges

by Ernest L. Boyer, edited by Paul Boyer

When you think of college you probably imagine the cliché or Hollywood image: a campus filled with ivy-covered buildings, students socializing in the academic quad, or the faint sounds of a professor's voice coming from an open window. Despite this stereotypical picture of what college might look like on the surface, there is no single model of a "good college." Missions and circumstances vary greatly from one campus to another. Each of the approximately 2,000 four-year colleges and universities has something different to offer its students. And with college costs rising, you want to be assured that you will get the best value out of the college investment. This makes choosing the right college even more difficult. It may help to know that despite all the differences among colleges, there are characteristics commonly shared by reputable schools that you should consider in your search.

Although these standards can be used to evaluate any college, you should narrow your list prior to the "test of quality" and put these questions to the schools on your final list. First consider other facts that may be important to you, such as location or size. As you work through the list, you will find that a great deal of this information can be uncovered by reading this book as well as the individual college's literature. But you will need to look further, to discuss these items with your guidance counselor, representatives from the colleges, and other advisers in order to come up with the most complete review of a particular school.

Some Common Measures of Quality

Every college should be guided by a clear and vital mission. It should understand its unique role in higher education and present itself honestly to prospective students through its literature and other information outlets. An institution cannot be all things to all people, however, so choices must be made and priorities assigned. What shows the strength of an institution is whether it has clearly defined its focus and, beyond that, whether it has successfully turned those goals into a living purpose for the campus. Of course, you also need to determine if the college's mission matches up with your own goals and values. At the very least, you need to know that you will be comfortable at a college and that it will deliver the type of educational experience you're seeking.

The quality of the undergraduate college is measured largely by the extent of its cooperation with high schools and by its willingness to smooth the transition of students into college. The way you are recruited by a college helps to shape your expectations of that college. A good college conducts its recruitment and selection with the best interests of the students in mind and should, therefore, try to learn more about you than simply your test scores and class rank.

Beyond the admissions process it is important for a college to continue to demonstrate commitment to you by taking steps to make you feel at home. The first few weeks on campus are a major rite of passage and may have a significant influence on your entire undergraduate experience. In short, you will want to determine whether the freshman year is viewed as something special and whether the college has a well-planned orientation program that addresses the particular concerns of the new student.

Since students need guidance throughout their entire education, a college of quality has a year-round program of academic advising and personal counseling, structured to serve all undergraduates, including part-time and commuting students. You will want to find out if the faculty is available to freshmen to talk about their disciplines and whether they give guidance to young students as they consider career choices. A college worthy of commendation works as hard at holding students as it does at getting them to the campus in the first place. You may wish to investigate a college's retention rate over the past five years and find out whether or not it offers guidance programs for students who are having trouble. These are all measures of a college's dedication to its students.

A Planned, Yet Flexible, Curriculum

At a good college, the academic major will broaden rather than restrict the perspective, presenting, in effect, an enriched major. An enriched major will answer three essential questions: What are the history and traditions of the field to be examined? What are the social and economic implications to be pursued? What are the ethical and moral issues within the specialty that need to be confronted? Rather than dividing the undergraduate experience into separate camps—general versus specialized education—the curriculum at a college of high quality will bring the two together. Therefore, it's important to determine if the college has a coherent general education sequence—an integrated core—rather than a more loosely connected distribution arrangement. This core academic program should provide not only for an integration of the separate academic principles but also for their application and relationship to life. All colleges impose requirements for graduation, including a set number of credits and some predetermined courses within a major. But within this set of general expectations, there is also room for flexibility. Increasingly, innovative colleges are recognizing the needs and skills of older students, encouraging individual learning, giving credit for experience, and helping students to craft their own unique majors. Students should not all have to march on to graduation in four years if they have interests, skills, and needs that are not acknowledged by a traditional degree program. New types of students are enrolling, and the location of learning has moved beyond the campus—to the home, the workplace, and around the world. In recognition of this trend, an effective college designs programs that meet new patterns and creates ways to both extend and encourage diversity on the campus.

The Classroom Climate

The undergraduate experience, at its best, also means encouraging students to be active rather than passive learners. In measuring the quality of a college, you should ask if the institution has a climate that encourages independent, self-directed study, where teaching is perceived as more than just lecturing. If a college encourages small discussion sessions in which students work together on group assignments, it may indicate dedication to the undergraduate curriculum. In addition, if undergraduate courses are taught by the most respected and most gifted teachers on campus, it speaks further to this commitment.

Indeed, the strength of the faculty plays a leading role in determining the quality of the undergraduate experience. Students and parents have become increasingly concerned with the balance of time that faculty members spend on research and publishing requirements versus lecturing or advising. To uncover how an institution views this balance, you should ask if good teaching is valued equally with research and if it is an important criterion for tenure and promotion. It's important to know if the college recognizes that some faculty members are great teachers, others great researchers, and still others a blend of both. The central qualities that make for successful teaching are the ones that can be simply stated: command of the material to be taught, a contagious enthusiasm for the play of ideas, optimism about the potential of one's students, and sensitivity, integrity, and warmth as a human being. At a good college, this combination is present in the classroom.

Devoting Resources to Learning

An institution of high quality is one that supports its mission of learning both financially and philosophically. In doing so, a college should allot ample funds to its library and other educational resources. In terms of its use, you should determine if the library is more than just a study hall and if students are encouraged to spend at least as much time with library resources as they spend in classes. These resources should primarily serve the interests of undergraduate research and not be dominated by narrow scholarly interests of faculty members or graduate students. In addition, computers offer great potential for learning on campus. Some colleges now require that you purchase a computer before coming to campus. Others make terminals available to all students in common areas. Particularly if you are looking to advance in computer-related fields, or if you are inclined toward furthering your computer skills, you will want to know if campus terminals are linked to wider networks (including the Internet) and if the college connects technology, the library, and the classroom, letting each resource do what it does best and encouraging students to engage in creative, independent learning.

The Campus Culture

A college campus is also a community. A high-quality college will work to make the time spent outside of the classroom as meaningful as the time spent in class. The high-quality college sees academic and nonacademic functions as related and arranges events ranging from lecture series and concerts to sports and student organizations to reinforce the curriculum. These campuswide activities, intended for both faculty and students, should encourage community, sustain college traditions, and stimulate both social and cultural interaction. Because much learning occurs outside the classroom, it is important to know how accessible faculty members are to their students—not only through office hours but also elsewhere on the campus, at social or extracurricular functions. In this setting, the academic campus transcends the classroom and is viewed as a place for learning. Beyond the structured programs, the campus culture extends into the residence halls and other social areas on campus. Residential living can be one of the most chaotic parts of campus life, yet it has the potential of being one of the most rewarding. It is a good idea to find out if residence halls also promote a sense of community through organized activities and informal learning.

A Final Word of Advice

In the end, a high-quality college is concerned about outcomes. It asks questions about student development that go beyond the evaluation of skill. But a good college will avoid measuring that which matters least and will focus on the need for students to think clearly, to be well informed, to integrate their knowledge, and to apply what they have learned.

The impact of college extends beyond graduation, and a college of quality will provide placement guidance to its students and follow their careers. These students will be well equipped to put their work in context and adequately prepared to move from one intellectual challenge to another. The undergraduate experience will also have prepared students to see beyond the narrow boundaries of their own interests and discover global connections. The college succeeds as its graduates are inspired by a larger vision, using their newfound knowledge to form values and advance the common good.

When you make your college contacts and campus visits, you now know what questions to ask and what to look for in order to make an informed decision. In doing so, however, you should always take into account your specific goals and you'll find that some colleges will immediately fall from your list. In the end, the important thing to remember is that a college of high quality is one that will prepare you for a productive career but will also offer you values and principles that you can apply beyond graduation day.

CHAPTER 2

Narrowing Your List: How This Almanac Can Help

In the preceding article, "A Guide to Good Four-Year Colleges," you were presented with several points to consider when evaluating the quality of a particular college. There are other factors to consider, in addition, that don't necessarily point to the overall quality of the education you might receive but that heavily influence your final choice. Among the many criteria you might use are the location, size, cost, entrance selectivity, or diversity of an institution. Rather than flipping through the thousands of pages in this guide to find the perfect college, you might first consider other means of narrowing your search. By answering some of the following types of questions: "What part of the country do you want to be in?" "Do you prefer an urban or rural setting?" or "Are you looking for a small, intimate environment or a college with a large student body?" you will be able to develop a personalized list of criteria. By compiling that list of questions and answers, you will soon arrive at a list of things that you'll need to research for each college under consideration.

This guide, with its special search features and easy-to-use college profiles, is designed to provide you with the data you'll need to single out colleges for "the final list." In addition to using resources such as this one, don't underestimate the guidance of your parents, high school counselor, friends, and alumni of the institutions you are considering. Be sure to carefully review the college's viewbook and recruiting literature and make use of the campus visit, especially as a screening tool for your narrowed list.

Considering Your Options

If you have a very specific idea of what you want out of a college education, you will have an easier time compiling your list of prospective colleges. By considering some of the following criteria, you will soon find that your initial list of perhaps fifty colleges has been narrowed to a more reasonable number.

1. **Location**. For some students, staying close to home might be a priority. Or, venturing all the way across the country might be something you've always wanted to do and college seems like the perfect time to do it. Likewise, you may know that city life is not for you; therefore, you would like to limit your search to suburban or even rural colleges. Whatever the reason, the location of a college often plays a key role in the college selection process.
2. **Entrance Difficulty**. Many students will look to a college's entrance difficulty as an indication of whether or not they will be admitted. For instance, if you have an excellent academic record, you might wish to primarily consider those colleges that are highly selective. Although entrance difficulty does not necessarily translate into quality of education, it does often indicate whether a college is highly sought-after.
3. **Education Costs**. As the price tag for higher education continues to rise, cost becomes an increasingly important factor when selecting a college. Certainly it is necessary to consider your family's resources when choosing a list of schools to which you might apply. On the other hand, avoid eliminating colleges that you might otherwise consider based solely on cost. You may be able to obtain the necessary financial aid to allow you to enroll in your higher-priced college of choice.
4. **Most Popular Recent Majors**. Despite all of the other factors that might influence your selection, certainly one of the most important is whether a college offers a program in your academic area of interest. Or, conversely, if you have not selected a program at the onset, you will want to find a college with a broad enough selection to satisfy your eventual choice.

Beyond these major factors, you will undoubtedly uncover other criteria that will strongly influence your choice of where to attend college. Questions about a particular institution's size, the diversity of its student body, or special academic programs or services may weigh heavily in the decision process. The straightforward format of the College Profiles makes it easy to gather the facts on all of these points and more, providing you with the answers you need to make the most informed choice. The following paragraph describes in detail the data that are contained within these features.

How Hard Is It to Get In?

The five levels of entrance difficulty, as defined below, are based on the percentage of applicants who were accepted for fall 1996 freshman admission (or, in the case of upper-level schools, for entering-class admission) and on the high school class rank and standardized test scores of the accepted freshmen who actually enrolled in fall 1996. The colleges were asked to select the level that most closely corresponds to their entrance difficulty, according to the guidelines below, to assist prospective students in assessing their chances for admission. Canadian colleges, specialized schools of art and music, upper-level schools, and other institutions for which high school class rank or standardized test scores do not apply as admission criteria were asked to select the level that best indicates their entrance difficulty as compared to other institutions of the same type that use similar admission criteria. The listing of schools in this index is based on the overall entrance difficulty level for all or most applicants at each institution.

The five levels of entrance difficulty are as follows:

1. **Most difficult:** More than 75% of the freshmen were in the top 10% of their high school class and scored over 1250 on the SAT I (verbal and mathematical combined) or over 29 on the ACT (composite); about 30% or fewer of the applicants were accepted.
2. **Very difficult:** More than 50% of the freshmen were in the top 10% of their high school class and scored over 1150 on the SAT I or over 26 on the ACT; about 60% or fewer of the applicants were accepted.
3. **Moderately difficult:** More than 75% of the freshmen were in the top half of their high school class and scored over 900 on the SAT I or over 18 on the ACT; about 85% or fewer of the applicants were accepted.
4. **Minimally difficult:** Most freshmen were not in the top half of their high school class and scored somewhat below 900 on the SAT I or below 19 on the ACT; up to 95% of the applicants were accepted.
5. **Noncompetitive:** Virtually all applicants were accepted regardless of high school rank or test scores.

Profile Highlights

Campus setting: Designated as urban (located within a major city), suburban (a residential area within commuting distance of a major city), small town (a small but compactly settled area not within commuting distance of a major city), or rural (a remote and sparsely populated area).

Total enrollment: The number of matriculated undergraduate and (if applicable) graduate students, both full-time and part-time, as of fall 1994. If the institution is a subunit of a university, the total university enrollment is given along with the unit enrollment (if there are graduate students).

Freshmen: Figures are given for the number of freshmen (or, for upper-level institutions, the number of entering students) who enrolled, the number of students who applied for admission, and the percentage of those accepted.

Faculty: The school's estimate of the ratio of matriculated undergraduate students to faculty members teaching undergraduate courses.

Application Deadline: Deadlines and dates for notification of acceptance or rejection are given either as specific dates or as rolling and continuous. Rolling means that applications are processed as they are received, and qualified students are accepted as long as there are openings. Continuous notification means that applicants are notified of acceptance or rejection as applications are processed up until the date indicated or the actual beginning of classes.

Tuition: The average basic tuition for an academic year is presented as a dollar amount.

Housing: Indicates whether on-campus housing is available.

Undergraduates: Percentages are given of undergraduates who are women, part-time students, 25 or older, Native American (Indian, Eskimo, Polynesian), Hispanic, African American, and Asian American.

Most popular recent majors: The 1996 graduating class's highest-enrolled majors.

Class size: The number of undergraduate courses offered in the 1995–96 academic year and the average class size for required undergraduate courses.

Advanced Placement: Credit toward a degree awarded for acceptable scores on some or all College Board Advanced Placement tests.

Accelerated degree program: Students may earn a bachelor's degree in three academic years.

Self-designed majors: Students may design their own program of study based on individual interests.

Honors program: Unusually challenging academic program for superior students.

Summer session for credit: Summer courses through which students may make up degree work or accelerate their program.

Part-time degree programs: Students may earn a degree without having to attend classes full-time; part-time degree programs may be offered for students attending regular-session classes (daytime) or evening, weekend, or summer classes.

External degree programs: Students may earn a degree through a program that (1) requires no more than 25% of the degree credit to be earned through campus-located instruction, (2) grants credit for documented extra-institutional and experiential learning, and (3) emphasizes off-campus self-directed study.

Adult/continuing education programs: Courses offered for nontraditional students who are currently working or are returning to formal education.

Cooperative (co-op) education programs: Formal arrangement with off-campus employers allowing students to combine work and study in order to gain degree-related experience, usually extending the time required to complete a degree.

Internships: College-arranged work experience for which students earn academic credit.

Contact: The name, title, mailing address, and telephone number of the person to contact for further information are given at the end of the profile. Toll-free telephone numbers may also be included. The admission office fax number and e-mail address may be provided for the use of prospective students.

How Schools Get Into This Guide

The profiles of the colleges and universities include all the U.S. schools that appear in *Peterson's Guide to Four-Year Colleges 1998*. The term "four-year college" is the commonly used designation for institutions that grant the baccalaureate, since four years is the normal duration of the traditional undergraduate curriculum. However, some bachelor's programs may be completed in three years, others require five years, and, of course, part-time programs may take a considerably longer period. Also included are upper-level institutions that award the baccalaureate but require that entering students have at least two years of previous college-level credit and thus normally require an additional two years to complete a degree program.

Accreditation

To be included in this guide, an institution must have full accreditation or candidate-for-accreditation (preaccreditation) status granted by an institutional or specialized accrediting body recognized by the U.S. Department of Education or the Council on Postsecondary Accreditation. Recognized institutional accrediting bodies, which consider each institution as a whole, are the following: the six regional associations of schools and colleges (Middle States, New England, North Central, Northwest, Southern, and Western), each of which is responsible for a specified portion of the United States and its territories; the Accrediting Association of Bible Colleges (AABC); the Accrediting Council for Independent Colleges and Schools (ACICS); the Accrediting Commission of Career Schools/Colleges of Technology (ACCSCT); The Distance Education and Training Council (DETC); and the Transnational Association of Christian Schools (TRACS). Program registration by the New York State Board of Regents is considered to be the equivalent of institutional accreditation, since the Board requires that all programs offered by an institution meet its standards before recognition is granted. A Canadian institution must be chartered and authorized to grant degrees by the provincial government, affiliated with a chartered institution, or accredited by a recognized U.S. accrediting body. This guide also includes institutions outside the United States, the U.S. territories, and Canada that are accredited by recognized U.S. accrediting bodies. There are recognized specialized accrediting bodies in more than forty different fields, each of which is authorized to accredit specific programs in its particular field. This can serve as the equivalent of institutional accreditation for specialized institutions that offer programs in one field only (schools of art, music, optometry, theology, etc.). For a full explanation of the accrediting process and complete information on recognized accrediting bodies, the reader should refer to *Peterson's Register of Higher Education*.

Research Procedures

The data contained in the college indexes and college profiles were collected between fall 1996 and spring 1997 through Peterson's Annual

Survey of Undergraduate Institutions. Questionnaires were sent to the more than 1,900 colleges and universities that meet the criteria for inclusion outlined above. All data included in this edition have been submitted by officials (usually admission and financial aid officers, registrars, or institutional research personnel) at the schools themselves. In addition, the great majority of institutions that submitted data were contacted directly by Peterson's editorial staff to verify unusual figures, resolve discrepancies, and obtain additional data. All usable information received in time for publication has been included. The omission of any particular item from an index or profile listing signifies that the item is either not applicable to that institution or that data were not available. Because of the comprehensive editorial review that takes place in our offices and because all material comes directly from college officials, we have every reason to believe that the information presented in this guide is accurate. However, students should check with a specific college or university at the time of application to verify such figures as tuition and fees, which may have changed since the publication of this volume.

For Further Information

If you would like in-depth information about the colleges of your choice, refer to Peterson's Web site at http://www.petersons.com/ugrad. Articles including "Considering College Quality" and "The Application Essay" provide further tips on applying to college.

CHAPTER 3

A Guide to Financing a College Education

by Don M. Betterton, Director of Undergraduate Aid, Princeton University

Given the lifelong benefit of a college degree (college graduates are projected to earn in a lifetime $600,000 more than those with only a high school diploma), higher education is a very worthwhile investment. However, it is also an expensive one made even harder to manage by cost increases that have outpaced both inflation and gains in family income. This reality of higher education economics means that parental concern about how to pay college costs is a dilemma that shows no sign of getting easier.

Because of the high cost involved (even the most inexpensive four-year education at a public institution costs about $10,000 a year), good information about college budgets and strategies for reducing the "sticker price" is essential. In the following chapter you will learn valuable information about the four main sources of aid—federal, state, college, and private. Before you learn about the various programs, however, it will be helpful if you have an overview of how the college financial aid system operates and what long-range financing strategies are available.

Financial Aid

Financial aid refers to money that is awarded to a student, usually in a "package" that consists of a scholarship (also called grant or gift aid), a student loan, and a campus job.

College Costs and Qualifying for Need-Based Aid

The starting point for organizing a plan to pay for your college education is making a good estimate of the yearly cost. The profiles give you an estimate of tuition, but there are other costs to consider. *Peterson's*

College Money Handbook is an excellent resource to make this first step of determining total costs easy for you.

The next step is to evaluate whether or not you are likely to qualify for financial aid based on need. This step is critical, since more than 90 percent of the yearly total of $50 billion in student aid is awarded only after a determination is made that the family lacks sufficient financial resources to pay the full cost of college on its own. To judge your chance of receiving need-based aid, it is necessary to estimate an Expected Family Contribution (EFC) according to a government formula known as the Federal Methodology, also found in the *College Money Handbook*.

Applying for Need-Based Aid

Because the federal government provides about 75 percent of all aid awarded, the application and need evaluation process is controlled by Congress and the U.S. Department of Education. The application used is the Free Application for Federal Student Aid (FAFSA). The FAFSA is your "passport" to receiving your share of the billions of dollars awarded annually in need-based aid. If you think you might qualify for aid, pick up a FAFSA from the high school guidance office after mid-November, 1997. The form will ask for 1997 financial data and it should be filed after January 1, 1998, in time to meet the earliest college or state scholarship deadline. Within two to four weeks after you submit the form, you will receive a summary of the FAFSA information, which is called the Student Aid Report (SAR). The SAR will give you an estimated expected family contribution and will also allow you to make corrections to the data you submitted.

Students can apply for 1997–98 federal student aid over the Internet using the interactive FAFSA on the Web. The 1998–99 FAFSA and an interactive renewal application will be available in December 1997. FAFSA on the Web can be accessed at http://www.fafsa.ed.gov/ with Netscape Navigator 3.0 or higher. It can be used with any computer, including Macintosh and UNIX.

Many colleges feel that the federal aid system (FAFSA and FM) does not collect or evaluate information thoroughly enough to be used to award their institutional funds. These colleges have made an arrangement with the College Scholarship Service, a branch of the College Board, to establish a separate application system to meet their needs. The application is called the Financial Aid PROFILE, and the means of need determination is known as the Institutional Methodology (IM). (When used, the PROFILE is always in addition to the FAFSA; it does not replace it.) If you apply for financial aid at one of the approximately 400 colleges that use PROFILE, the admission material will state that the PROFILE is required in addition to the FAFSA. You should read the information carefully and file the PROFILE to meet the earliest deadline among the colleges involved. Before you can receive the PROFILE form, however, you must register, providing enough basic information so the PROFILE package can be designed specifically for you. Also, while the FAFSA is free, there is a charge for the PROFILE.

Many colleges provide the option to apply for early-decision admission. If you apply for this before January 1, which is prior to when FAFSA can be is used, follow the college's instructions. Many colleges use either PROFILE or their own application form for early admission candidates.

Awarding Aid

About the same time you receive the SAR, the colleges you list will receive the FAFSA information so they can calculate a financial aid award in a package that typically includes aid from at least one of the major sources—federal, state, college, or private. In addition, the award will probably consist of a combination of scholarship or grant, loan, and campus job. These last two pieces—loan and job—are called self-help aid because they require effort on the part of the student. Scholarships or grants are outright gifts that have no such obligation.

When you receive an award letter from a college, it is important that you understand each part of the package so that you can determine your true costs. For example: How much is gift aid? What are the interest rate and repayment terms of the student loan? How many hours per week does the campus job require? There should be an enclosure with the award letter that answers these kinds of questions. If not, make a list of your questions and call or visit the financial aid office.

Once you understand the terms of each item in the award letter, you should turn your attention to the "bottom line"—how much you will have to pay for each college to which you are admitted. In addition to understanding the aid award, you must have a good estimate of the college budget so that you can accurately calculate how much you and your family will have to contribute (often an aid package does not cover the entire need). If you think that what the college expects you and your family to pay is too high, you should contact the college's financial aid office and ask whether additional aid is available. Many colleges, private high-cost colleges in particular, have a service perspective—they are willing to work with families to help make education at their colleges affordable. If there is still a gap between the expected contribution and what you feel you can pay from income and savings, you are left with two choices. One option is to attend a college where paying your share of the bill will not be a problem. (This assumes that an affordable option was included on the original list of colleges, a wise admission application strategy.) The second is to look into an alternate method of financing, including loans and tuition payment plans. A loan can bring the yearly cost down to a manageable level by spreading payments over a number of years. A tuition payment plan is essentially a short-term loan and allows you to pay the cost over ten to twelve months. It is an option for families who have the resources available but need help with managing their cash-flow.

Aid Not Based on Need

Whether or not you qualify for a need-based award, it is always worthwhile to look into merit, or non-need, scholarships from sources such as foundations, agencies, religious groups, and service organizations. If you aren't eligible for need-based aid, merit scholarships are the only form of gift aid available. If you later qualify for a need-based award, a merit scholarship can be quite helpful in providing additional resources when the aid does not fully cover the costs. Even if the college meets 100 percent of need, a merit scholarship can benefit the student by reducing the self-help (loan and job) portion of an award.

In searching for outside merit-based scholarships, keep in mind that there are relatively few awards (compared to those that are need-based) and most of them are highly competitive. Use the following checklist when investigating merit scholarships.

- Take advantage of any scholarships for which you are automatically eligible based on employer benefits, military service, association or church membership, other affiliations, or student or parent attributes (ethnic background, nationality, etc.). Company or union tuition remissions are the most common examples of these awards.
- Look for other awards for which you might be eligible based on the characteristics and affiliations indicated above, but where there is a selection process and an application is required. Computerized searches are available on the Internet. Scholarship directories, such as *Peterson's Scholarships, Grants & Prizes,* which details some 2,200

scholarship programs, are useful resources and can be found in bookstores, high school guidance offices, or public libraries.

- Look into national scholarship competitions. High school guidance counselors usually know about these scholarships. Examples of these awards are the National Merit Scholarship, Coca Cola Scholarship, Aid Association for Lutherans, Westinghouse Science Talent Search, and the U.S. Senate Youth Program. *Winning Money for College* (Peterson's, 2nd ed., 1997) provides detailed profiles of fifty of the most lucrative and prestigious competitions open to high school students.
- ROTC (Reserve Officers' Training Corps) scholarships are offered by the Army, Navy, Air Force, and Marine Corps. A full ROTC scholarship can cover virtually all tuition, fees, and textbook costs. Acceptance of an ROTC scholarship entails a commitment to take a military science course and to serve for a specific number of years as an officer in the sponsoring branch of the service. ROTC is not available at every college. Competition is heavy, and preference may be given to students in certain fields of study, such as nursing, engineering, science, or business. Contact an armed services recruiter or a high school guidance counselor for further information.
- Investigate community scholarships. The high school guidance counselor usually has a list of these awards, and announcements are published in the town newspaper. Most common are awards given by service organizations such as the American Legion, Rotary International, and the local women's club.
- If you are strong academically (for example, a National Merit Commended Scholar or better) or are very talented in fields such as athletics or performing/creative arts, you may want to consider colleges that offer their own merit awards to gifted students they wish to enroll.

In addition to merit scholarships, there are loan and job opportunities for students who do not qualify for need-based aid. Some of the organizations that sponsor scholarships—for example, the Air Force Aid Society—also provide loans.

Work opportunities during the academic year are another type of assistance that is not restricted to aid recipients. Many colleges, after assigning jobs to students on aid, will open campus positions to all students looking for work. In addition, there are usually off-campus employment opportunities available to everyone.

Financing Your College Education

In this section, "financing" means arranging for the use of resources to pay balances due to the college over and above payments from the primary sources of aid—scholarships, student loans, and jobs. Financing strategies are important because the high cost of a college education today often requires you, whether you receive aid or not, to think about stretching the payment for college beyond the four-year period of enrollment. For high-cost colleges, it is not unreasonable to think about a 10-4-10 plan: ten years of saving; four years of paying college bills out of current income, savings, and borrowing; and ten years to repay a loan.

Savings

Although saving for college is always a good idea, many families are unclear about its advantages. Families do not save for two reasons. First, after expenses have been covered, many families do not have much money to set aside. An affordable but regular savings plan through a payroll deduction is usually the answer to the problem of spending your entire paycheck every month.

The second reason that saving for college is not a high priority is the belief that the financial aid system penalizes a family by lowering aid eligibility. The Federal Methodology of need determination is very kind to savers. In fact, savings are ignored completely for those that earn less than $50,000.

A sensible savings plan is important because of the financial advantage of saving compared to borrowing. The amount of money students borrow for college is now greater than the amount they receive in grants and scholarships. With loans becoming so widespread, savings should be carefully considered as an alternative to borrowing. Your incentive for saving is that a dollar saved is a dollar not borrowed.

Borrowing

Once you've calculated your "bottom-line" parental contribution and determined that the amount is not affordable out of your current income and assets, the most likely alternative is borrowing. First determine if you are eligible for a Subsidized Federal Stafford or Direct Loan. Because no interest is due while a student attends college, these are the most favorable loans. If you are not eligible, look into the Unsubsidized

Stafford or Direct Loan, which does not require a needs test but where the interest is due each year. The freshman year limit (either Subsidized or Unsubsidized) is $2625.

After you have taken out the maximum amount of student loans, the next step is to look into parental loans. The federal government's parent loan program is called the PLUS loan and is the standard against which other loans are judged. A local bank that participates in the PLUS program can give you a schedule of monthly repayments per $1000 borrowed. Use this repayment figure to compare other parental loans available through commercial lenders (including home equity loans), state programs, or colleges themselves. Choose the one that offers the best terms after all up-front costs, tax advantages, and the amount of monthly payments are considered.

Creditworthiness

If you will be borrowing to pay for your college education, making sure you qualify for a loan is critical. For the most part, that means your credit record must be free of default or delinquency. You can check your credit history with a credit bureau and clean up any adverse information that appears.

Making Financial Aid Work For You

This overview is intended to provide you with a road map to help you think about financing strategies and navigate through the complexities of the financial aid process. For further information about the process, consult *Peterson's College Money Handbook*. Use the parental contribution tables in conjunction with the college cost worksheet to estimate need eligibility. If there is any chance you could qualify for aid, complete the FAFSA (and PROFILE if required). At the same time look into merit scholarships. Finally, check out the terms of PLUS and parental loan options. The key is to understand the financial aid system and to follow the best path for you. The result of good information and good planning should be that you will receive your fair share of the billions of dollars available each year and that the cost of college will not prevent you from attending.

CHAPTER 4

Federal Financial Aid Programs

There are a number of sources of financial aid available to students: the federal government, state governments, private lenders, foundations and private agencies, and the institutions themselves. In addition, there are three different forms of aid: grants, earnings, and loans.

The federal government is the single largest source of financial aid for students, accounting for about 74 percent of the $50 billion available annually. Presently, there are two federal grant programs—the Federal Pell Grant and the Federal Supplemental Educational Opportunity Grant (FSEOG); three loan programs—the Federal Perkins Loan, the Federal Direct Loan, and the Federal Stafford Loan; and a work program that helps colleges provide jobs for students, the Federal Work-Study (FWS).

The two grants, Federal Work-Study, Federal Perkins Loan, and two other loan programs—the Subsidized Federal Direct Loan and the Subsidized Federal Stafford Loan—are awarded to students with demonstrated financial need. Interest on the loans is paid by the government during the time the student is in school. For the Federal Unsubsidized Direct Loan and Federal Unsubsidized Stafford Loan, the interest begins to accrue as soon as the money is received. There is also a parental loan (PLUS) available under the Direct or Stafford programs.

Federal Pell Grant

The Federal Pell Grant is the largest grant program; more than 5 million students receive awards annually. This grant is intended to be the base, or starting point, of assistance for lower-income families. Eligibility for a Federal Pell Grant depends on the Expected Family Contribution (EFC). The amount you receive will depend on your EFC, the cost of education at the college or university you will attend, and whether you attend full-time or part-time. The highest award depends on how much the program is funded. The maximum for 1997–98 was $2700.

Federal Supplemental Educational Opportunity Grant (FSEOG)

As its name implies, the Federal Supplemental Educational Opportunity Grant (FSEOG) provides additional need-based federal grant money to supplement the Federal Pell Grant. Each participating college is given funds to award to especially needy students. The maximum award is $4000 per year, but the amount you receive depends on the college's policy, the availability of FSEOG funds, the total cost of education, and the amount of other aid awarded.

Federal Work-Study (FWS)

This program provides jobs for students who need financial aid for their educational expenses. The salary is paid by funds from the federal government and the college (or the employer). You work on an hourly basis in jobs on or off campus and must be paid at least the federal minimum wage. You may earn only up to the amount awarded, which depends on the calculated financial need and the total amount of money available to the college.

Federal Perkins Loan

This loan is a low-interest (5 percent) loan for students with exceptional financial need. Federal Perkins Loans are made through the college's financial aid office. That is, the college is the lender. Students may borrow a maximum of $3000 per year for up to five years of undergraduate study. They may take up to ten years to repay the loan, beginning nine months after they graduate, leave school, or drop below half-time status. No interest accrues while they are in school, and, under certain conditions (e.g., they teach in low-income areas, work in law enforcement, are full-time nurses or medical technicians, serve as Peace Corps or VISTA volunteers, etc.), some or all of the loan can be canceled or payments deferred.

Federal Stafford Loan

A Federal Stafford Loan may be borrowed from a participating commercial lender such as a bank, credit union, or savings and loan association. The interest rate varies annually, up to a maximum of 8.25 percent. If you qualify for a need-based, subsidized Federal Stafford Loan, the interest is paid by the federal government while you are enrolled in school. There is also an unsubsidized Federal Stafford Loan not based on need for which you are eligible regardless of your family income.

The maximum amount dependent students may borrow in any one year is $2625 for freshmen, $3500 for sophomores, and $5500 for juniors and seniors, with a maximum of $23,000 for the total undergraduate program. The maximum amount independent students can borrow is $6625 for freshmen (no more than $2625 in subsidized Stafford Loans), $7500 for sophomores (no more than $3500 in subsidized Stafford Loans), and $10,500 for juniors and seniors (no more than $5500 in subsidized Stafford Loans). Borrowers must pay a 4 percent fee, which is deducted from the loan proceeds.

To apply for a Federal Stafford Loan, you must first complete a FAFSA to determine eligibility for a subsidized loan, then a separate loan application that is submitted to a lender. The financial aid office can help in selecting a lender, or you can contact your state department of higher education to find a participating lender.

If you qualify for a subsidized Federal Stafford Loan, you do not have to pay interest while in school. For an unsubsidized Federal Stafford Loan, you will be responsible for paying the interest from the time the loan is established. However, some lenders will permit borrowers to delay making payments and will add the interest to the loan. Once the repayment period starts, borrowers of both subsidized and unsubsidized Federal Stafford Loans will have to pay a combination of interest and principal monthly for up to a ten-year period.

Federal PLUS Loan

The Federal PLUS loan is a loan for parents of dependent students. There is no needs test to qualify, and the loans are made by participating lenders. The loan has a variable interest rate that cannot exceed 9 percent. There is no specific yearly limit; you can borrow up to the cost of your education less other financial aid received. Repayment begins sixty days after the money is advanced. A 4 percent fee is subtracted from the proceeds. Parent borrowers must generally have a good credit record to qualify for Federal PLUS Loans.

The PLUS loan is processed under either the Direct or Stafford system, depending on the type of loan program for which the college has contracted.

Federal Direct Student Loans

The Federal Direct Student Loan is a relatively new program that is basically the same as the Federal Stafford Loan. The difference is that the U.S. Department of Education is the lender rather than a bank. Not all colleges participate in this program, and if your college does not, you can still apply for a Federal Stafford Loan.

Many of the terms of the Federal Direct Student Loan are similar to those of the Federal Stafford Loan. In particular, the interest rate, loan maximums, deferments, and cancellation benefits are the same. However, under the terms of the Federal Direct Student Loan, students have a choice of repayment plans. They may choose either a fixed monthly payment for ten years; a different fixed monthly payment for twelve to thirty years at a rate that varies with the loan balance; or a variable monthly payment for up to twenty-five years that is based on a percentage of income. Students cannot receive both a Federal Direct Student Loan and a Federal Stafford Loan for the same period of time, but may receive both in different enrollment periods.

National and Community Service Plan

The National and Community Service Plan is a program for a limited number of students. Participants work in a public or private nonprofit agency providing service to the community in one of four priority areas: education, human services, the environment, and public safety. In exchange, they earn a stipend of between $7400 and $14,800 a year for living expenses and up to $4725 for up to two years to apply toward college expenses. Students can work either before, during, or after they go to college and can use the funds to pay either current educational expenses or repay federal student loans. Speak to a college financial aid officer for more details about this program and any other new initiatives available to students.

PROFILES

This section contains quick-reference profiles of colleges and universities, covering such items as background information, entrance difficulty, academic programs, and contact information. The data in each of these profiles, collected from fall 1996 to spring 1997, come solely from Peterson's Annual Survey of undergraduate institutions, which was sent to deans or admissions officers at each institution. The profiles are organized first by region and then by state and arranged alphabetically within those sections by the official names of the institutions.

Delaware

DELAWARE STATE UNIVERSITY

DOVER, DELAWARE

Entrance Moderately difficult **General** State-supported, comprehensive, coed **Setting** 400-acre small-town campus **Enrollment** 3,328 **Faculty** 14:1 **Application deadline** 6/1 **Freshmen** 69% accepted **Housing** Yes **Tuition** $2970 **Undergraduates** 58% women, 20% part-time, 25% 25 or older, 0% Native American, 1% Hispanic, 72% black, 1% Asian or Pacific Islander **Most popular recent majors** Business administration/commerce/management, education, social work **Academic program** Advanced placement, accelerated degree program, self-designed majors, honors program, summer session, adult/continuing education programs, internships **Contact** Mr. Jethro C. Williams, Director of Admissions, Delaware State University, Dover, DE 19901-2277. Telephone: 302-739-4917. Fax: 302-739-5309.

GOLDEY-BEACOM COLLEGE

WILMINGTON, DELAWARE

Entrance Moderately difficult **General** Independent, comprehensive, coed **Setting** 27-acre suburban campus **Enrollment** 1,600 **Faculty** 23:1 **Application deadline** Rolling **Freshmen** 82% accepted **Housing** Yes **Tuition** $7200 **Undergraduates** 66% women, 52% part-time, 43% 25 or older, 1% Native American, 4% Hispanic, 12% black, 6% Asian or Pacific Islander **Most popular recent majors** Business administration/commerce/management, accounting, computer information systems **Academic program** Average class size 28, advanced placement, accelerated degree program, tutorials, honors program, summer session, internships **Contact** Mr. Kevin McIntyre, Director of Admissions, Goldey-Beacom College, Wilmington, DE 19808-1999. Telephone: 302-998-8814 Ext. 266. Fax: 302-996-5408.

UNIVERSITY OF DELAWARE

NEWARK, DELAWARE

Entrance Moderately difficult **General** State-related, coed **Setting** 1,000-acre small-town campus **Enrollment** 18,115 **Faculty** 15:1 **Application deadline** 3/1 **Freshmen** 69% accepted **Housing** Yes **Tuition** $4574 **Undergraduates** 58% women, 9% part-time, 11% 25 or older, 1% Native American, 2% Hispanic, 5% black, 3% Asian or Pacific Islander **Most popular recent majors** Biology/biological sciences, elementary education, business administration/commerce/management **Academic program** Advanced placement, accelerated degree program, self-designed majors, tutorials, honors program, summer session, adult/continuing education programs, internships **Contact** Dr. John C. Cavanaugh, Interim Associate Provost, Admissions/Student Financial Services, University of Delaware, Newark, DE 19716. Telephone: 302-831-8123. Fax: 302-831-6905.

WESLEY COLLEGE

DOVER, DELAWARE

Entrance Moderately difficult **General** Independent United Methodist, 4-year, coed **Setting** 20-acre small-town campus **Enrollment** 1,325 **Faculty** 19:1 **Application deadline** Rolling **Freshmen** 85% accepted **Housing** Yes **Tuition** $11,665 **Undergraduates** 52% women, 39% part-time, 34% 25 or older, 1% Native American, 1% Hispanic, 13% black, 3% Asian or Pacific Islander **Most popular recent majors** Business administration/commerce/management, accounting, elementary education **Academic program** Average class size 22, advanced placement, accelerated degree program, tutorials, summer session, adult/continuing education programs, internships **Contact** Mr. Brian D. Best, Director of Admissions, Wesley College, Dover, DE 19901. Telephone: 302-736-2400. Fax: 302-736-2301.

WILMINGTON COLLEGE

NEW CASTLE, DELAWARE

Entrance Noncompetitive **General** Independent, comprehensive, coed **Setting** 13-acre suburban campus **Enrollment** 5,500 **Faculty** 22:1 **Application deadline** Rolling **Freshmen** 100% accepted **Tuition** $5750 **Undergraduates** 55% women, 65% part-time, 60% 25 or older, 0% Native American, 3% Hispanic, 17% black, 1% Asian or Pacific Islander **Academic program** Accelerated degree program, tutorials, summer session, adult/continuing education programs, internships **Contact** Mr. Michael Lee, Dean of Admissions, Financial Aid and Marketing, Wilmington College, New Castle, DE 19720-6491. Telephone: 302-328-9407 Ext. 105. Fax: 302-328-5902.

District of Columbia

AMERICAN UNIVERSITY

WASHINGTON, DISTRICT OF COLUMBIA

Entrance Moderately difficult **General** Independent Methodist, coed **Setting** 77-acre suburban campus **Enrollment** 11,285 **Faculty** 14:1 **Application deadline** 2/1 **Freshmen** 79% accepted

Housing Yes **Tuition** $18,555 **Undergraduates** 60% women, 11% part-time, 1% Native American, 6% Hispanic, 6% black, 5% Asian or Pacific Islander **Most popular recent majors** International studies, communication, political science/government **Academic program** Advanced placement, self-designed majors, honors program, summer session, adult/continuing education programs, internships **Contact** Mr. Stephen Pultz, Director of Admissions, American University, Washington, DC 20016-8001. Telephone: 202-885-6000. Fax: 202-885-6014.

THE CATHOLIC UNIVERSITY OF AMERICA
WASHINGTON, DISTRICT OF COLUMBIA

Entrance Moderately difficult **General** Independent, coed, affiliated with Roman Catholic Church **Setting** 155-acre urban campus **Enrollment** 5,974 **Faculty** 10:1 **Application deadline** 2/15 **Freshmen** 67% accepted **Housing** Yes **Tuition** $17,110 **Undergraduates** 55% women, 12% part-time, 14% 25 or older, 0% Native American, 6% Hispanic, 9% black, 4% Asian or Pacific Islander **Most popular recent majors** Nursing, political science/government, architecture **Academic program** Advanced placement, accelerated degree program, self-designed majors, tutorials, honors program, summer session, adult/continuing education programs, internships **Contact** Ms. Katherine S. Lafrance, Associate Dean of Admissions, The Catholic University of America, Cardinal Station Post Office, Washington, DC 20064. Telephone: 202-319-5305. Fax: 202-319-6533.

THE CORCORAN SCHOOL OF ART
WASHINGTON, DISTRICT OF COLUMBIA

Entrance Moderately difficult **General** Independent, 4-year, specialized, coed **Setting** 7-acre urban campus **Enrollment** 340 **Application deadline** Rolling **Freshmen** 53% accepted **Housing** Yes **Tuition** $12,800 **Undergraduates** 52% women, 0% part-time, 28% 25 or older, 1% Native American, 6% Hispanic, 12% black, 11% Asian or Pacific Islander **Most popular recent majors** Art/fine arts, graphic arts, photography **Academic program** Advanced placement, tutorials, summer session, adult/continuing education programs, internships **Contact** Mr. Mark Sistek, Director of Admissions, The Corcoran School of Art, 500 17th Street, NW, Washington, DC 20006-4804. Telephone: 202-639-1814 Ext. 700. Fax: 202-639-1830.

GALLAUDET UNIVERSITY
WASHINGTON, DISTRICT OF COLUMBIA

Entrance Moderately difficult **General** Independent, coed **Setting** 100-acre urban campus **Enrollment** 2,034 **Application deadline** 5/15 **Freshmen** 71% accepted **Housing** Yes **Tuition** $6283 **Undergraduates** 55% women, 5% part-time, 20% 25 or older, 1% Native American, 5% Hispanic, 6% black, 4% Asian or Pacific Islander **Most popular recent majors** Psychology, business administration/commerce/management, biology/biological sciences **Academic program** Advanced placement, accelerated degree program, honors program, summer session, adult/continuing education programs, internships **Contact** Ms. Deborah E. DeStefano, Director of Admissions, Gallaudet University, 800 Florida Avenue, NE, Washington, DC 20002-3625. Telephone: 202-651-5750. Fax: 202-651-5774.

GEORGETOWN UNIVERSITY
WASHINGTON, DISTRICT OF COLUMBIA

Entrance Most difficult **General** Independent Roman Catholic (Jesuit), coed **Setting** 110-acre urban campus **Enrollment** 12,629 **Application deadline** 1/10 **Freshmen** 23% accepted **Housing** Yes **Tuition** $21,405 **Undergraduates** 52% women, 5% part-time, 4% 25 or older, 1% Native American, 6% Hispanic, 6% black, 8% Asian or Pacific Islander **Most popular recent majors** International relations, political science/government, English **Academic program** Advanced placement, self-designed majors, tutorials, honors program, summer session, adult/continuing education programs, internships **Contact** Mr. Charles A. Deacon, Dean of Undergraduate Admissions, Georgetown University, 37th and O Street, NW, Washington, DC 20057. Telephone: 202-687-3600. Fax: 202-687-5084.

THE GEORGE WASHINGTON UNIVERSITY
WASHINGTON, DISTRICT OF COLUMBIA

Entrance Very difficult **General** Independent, coed **Setting** 36-acre urban campus **Enrollment** 18,986 **Faculty** 14:1 **Application deadline** 2/1 **Freshmen** 58% accepted **Housing** Yes **Tuition** $20,640 **Undergraduates** 55% women, 7% part-time, 7% 25 or older, 1% Native American, 4% Hispanic, 7% black, 12% Asian or Pacific Islander **Most popular recent majors** International studies, biology/biological sciences, psychology **Academic program** Average class size 27, advanced placement, accelerated degree program, self-designed majors, tutorials, honors program, summer session, adult/continuing education programs, internships **Contact** Mr. Frederic A. Siegel, Assistant Vice-President, Enrollment Management, The George Washington University, Office of Undergraduate Admissions, Washington, DC 20052. Telephone: 202-994-6040. Fax: 202-994-0325.

HOWARD UNIVERSITY

WASHINGTON, DISTRICT OF COLUMBIA

Entrance Moderately difficult **General** Independent, coed **Setting** 242-acre urban campus **Enrollment** 10,332 **Application deadline** 4/1 **Freshmen** 48% accepted **Housing** Yes **Tuition** $8985 **Undergraduates** 60% women, 38% part-time, 18% 25 or older, 90% black, 1% Asian or Pacific Islander **Most popular recent majors** Political science/government, psychology, radio and television studies **Academic program** Advanced placement, tutorials, honors program, summer session, adult/continuing education programs, internships **Contact** Mr. Avon Dennis, Director of Admissions, Howard University, 2400 Sixth Street, NW, Washington, DC 20059-0002. Telephone: 202-806-2750.

MOUNT VERNON COLLEGE

WASHINGTON, DISTRICT OF COLUMBIA

Entrance Minimally difficult **General** Independent, comprehensive, women only **Setting** 26-acre urban campus **Enrollment** 600 **Faculty** 15:1 **Application deadline** Rolling **Freshmen** 75% accepted **Housing** Yes **Tuition** $16,410 **Undergraduates** 30% part-time, 19% 25 or older, 0% Native American, 5% Hispanic, 18% black, 3% Asian or Pacific Islander **Most popular recent majors** Business administration/commerce/management, communication, interior design **Academic program** Advanced placement, accelerated degree program, self-designed majors, tutorials, honors program, summer session, adult/continuing education programs, internships **Contact** Ms. Susan Knight, Director of Admissions, Mount Vernon College, 2100 Foxhall Road, NW, Washington, DC 20007. Telephone: 202-625-4682.

SOUTHEASTERN UNIVERSITY

WASHINGTON, DISTRICT OF COLUMBIA

Entrance Noncompetitive **General** Independent, comprehensive, coed **Setting** 1-acre urban campus **Enrollment** 610 **Application deadline** Rolling **Freshmen** 90% accepted **Tuition** $5850 **Undergraduates** 58% women, 83% part-time, 50% 25 or older, 0% Native American, 1% Hispanic, 75% black, 20% Asian or Pacific Islander **Most popular recent majors** Business administration/commerce/management, accounting **Academic program** Advanced placement, accelerated degree program, tutorials, honors program, summer session, adult/continuing education programs, internships **Contact** Mr. Jack Flinter, Director of Admissions, Southeastern University, 501 I Street, SW, Washington, DC 20024-2788. Telephone: 202-265-5343 Ext. 212.

STRAYER COLLEGE

WASHINGTON, DISTRICT OF COLUMBIA

Entrance Minimally difficult **General** Proprietary, comprehensive, coed **Setting** Urban campus **Enrollment** 8,172 **Faculty** 25:1 **Application deadline** Rolling **Tuition** $7650 **Undergraduates** 57% women, 66% part-time, 78% 25 or older, 1% Native American, 5% Hispanic, 39% black, 5% Asian or Pacific Islander **Most popular recent majors** Computer information systems, business administration/commerce/management, accounting **Academic program** Average class size 29, advanced placement, accelerated degree program, tutorials, summer session, adult/continuing education programs, internships **Contact** Mr. Michael Williams, Campus Coordinator, Strayer College, 1025 15th Street, NW, Washington, DC 20005. Telephone: 202-408-2400. Fax: 202-289-1831.

TRINITY COLLEGE

WASHINGTON, DISTRICT OF COLUMBIA

Entrance Moderately difficult **General** Independent Roman Catholic, comprehensive, women only **Setting** 26-acre urban campus **Enrollment** 1,453 **Application deadline** 3/1 **Freshmen** 73% accepted **Housing** Yes **Tuition** $12,490 **Undergraduates** 60% part-time, 59% 25 or older, 0% Native American, 5% Hispanic, 46% black, 3% Asian or Pacific Islander **Most popular recent majors** Business administration/commerce/management, political science/government, psychology **Academic program** Average class size 17, advanced placement, accelerated degree program, self-designed majors, tutorials, summer session, adult/continuing education programs, internships **Contact** Ms. Susan Grogan Ikerd, Dean of Enrollment Management, Trinity College, 125 Michigan Avenue, NE, Washington, DC 20017-1094. Telephone: 202-884-9400. Fax: 202-939-5134.

UNIVERSITY OF THE DISTRICT OF COLUMBIA

WASHINGTON, DISTRICT OF COLUMBIA

Entrance Noncompetitive **General** District-supported, comprehensive, coed **Setting** 28-acre urban campus **Enrollment** 7,464 **Application deadline** 8/1 **Tuition** $2360 **Undergraduates** 57% women, 63% part-time, 56% 25 or older, 3%

Hispanic, 72% black, 2% Asian or Pacific Islander **Academic program** Accelerated degree program, honors program, summer session, adult/continuing education programs, internships **Contact** Office of Recruitment and Admissions, University of the District of Columbia, 4200 Connecticut Avenue, NW, Washington, DC 20008-1175. Telephone: 202-274-5010.

Maryland

BALTIMORE HEBREW UNIVERSITY

BALTIMORE, MARYLAND

Entrance Moderately difficult **General** Independent, comprehensive, specialized, coed **Setting** 2-acre urban campus **Enrollment** 334 **Faculty** 12:1 **Application deadline** Rolling **Freshmen** 90% accepted **Tuition** $3620 **Undergraduates** 65% women, 55% part-time, 90% 25 or older, 0% Native American, 0% Hispanic, 1% black, 0% Asian or Pacific Islander **Most popular recent major** Judaic studies **Academic program** Advanced placement, accelerated degree program, tutorials, honors program, summer session, adult/continuing education programs **Contact** Dr. George Berlin, Dean, Baltimore Hebrew University, 5800 Park Heights Avenue, Baltimore, MD 21215-3996. Telephone: 410-578-6912.

BOWIE STATE UNIVERSITY

BOWIE, MARYLAND

Entrance Minimally difficult **General** State-supported, comprehensive, coed **Setting** 312-acre small-town campus **Enrollment** 5,067 **Faculty** 18:1 **Application deadline** 4/1 **Freshmen** 34% accepted **Housing** Yes **Tuition** $3357 **Undergraduates** 66% women, 31% part-time, 34% 25 or older, 1% Native American, 1% Hispanic, 83% black, 2% Asian or Pacific Islander **Most popular recent majors** Business administration/commerce/management, elementary education, psychology **Academic program** Advanced placement, accelerated degree program, tutorials, honors program, summer session, adult/continuing education programs, internships **Contact** Ms. Hope Ransom, Director of Undergraduate Admissions, Bowie State University, Bowie, MD 20715-3318. Telephone: 301-464-6565.

CAPITOL COLLEGE

LAUREL, MARYLAND

Entrance Minimally difficult **General** Independent, comprehensive, specialized, coed **Setting** 52-acre suburban campus **Enrollment** 709 **Faculty** 14:1 **Application deadline** Rolling **Freshmen** 75% accepted **Housing** Yes **Tuition** $9252 **Undergraduates** 15% women, 46% part-time, 46% 25 or older, 1% Native American, 4% Hispanic, 32% black, 6% Asian or Pacific Islander **Most popular recent majors** Electronics engineering technology, electrical engineering, computer engineering **Academic program** Advanced placement, accelerated degree program, summer session, adult/continuing education programs **Contact** Mr. Anthony Miller, Director of Admissions, Capitol College, Laurel, MD 20708-9759. Telephone: 301-953-3200.

COLLEGE OF NOTRE DAME OF MARYLAND

BALTIMORE, MARYLAND

Entrance Moderately difficult **General** Independent Roman Catholic, comprehensive, women only **Setting** 58-acre suburban campus **Enrollment** 3,237 **Faculty** 15:1 **Application deadline** 2/15 **Freshmen** 83% accepted **Housing** Yes **Tuition** $13,365 **Undergraduates** 3% part-time, 1% Native American, 3% Hispanic, 15% black, 5% Asian or Pacific Islander **Most popular recent majors** Business administration/commerce/management, education, communication **Academic program** Advanced placement, accelerated degree program, self-designed majors, tutorials, honors program, summer session, adult/continuing education programs, internships **Contact** Ms. Theresa C. Boer, Director of Admissions and Enrollment Management, College of Notre Dame of Maryland, Baltimore, MD 21210-2476. Telephone: 410-532-5330. Fax: 410-435-6287.

COLUMBIA UNION COLLEGE

TAKOMA PARK, MARYLAND

Entrance Minimally difficult **General** Independent Seventh-day Adventist, 4-year, coed **Setting** 19-acre suburban campus **Enrollment** 1,163 **Faculty** 13:1 **Application deadline** 8/1 **Freshmen** 79% accepted **Housing** Yes **Tuition** $11,790 **Undergraduates** 63% women, 52% part-time, 36% 25 or older, 0% Native American, 7% Hispanic, 43% black, 7% Asian or Pacific Islander **Most popular recent majors** Business administration/commerce/management, nursing **Academic program** Advanced placement, self-designed majors, summer session, adult/continuing education programs, internships **Contact** Mrs. Sheila Burnette, Director of Admissions, Columbia Union College, Takoma Park, MD 20912-7794. Telephone: 301-891-4503.

COPPIN STATE COLLEGE
BALTIMORE, MARYLAND

Entrance Moderately difficult **General** State-supported, comprehensive, coed **Setting** 33-acre urban campus **Enrollment** 3,643 **Faculty** 17:1 **Application deadline** 7/15 **Freshmen** 55% accepted **Housing** Yes **Tuition** $3624 **Undergraduates** 73% women, 37% part-time, 50% 25 or older, 1% Native American, 1% Hispanic, 93% black, 1% Asian or Pacific Islander **Most popular recent majors** Business administration/commerce/management, nursing, psychology **Academic program** Advanced placement, honors program, summer session, adult/continuing education programs, internships **Contact** Mr. Allen Mosley, Director of Admissions, Coppin State College, 2500 West North Avenue, Baltimore, MD 21216-3698. Telephone: 410-383-5990. Fax: 410-333-7094.

FROSTBURG STATE UNIVERSITY
FROSTBURG, MARYLAND

Entrance Moderately difficult **General** State-supported, comprehensive, coed **Setting** 260-acre small-town campus **Enrollment** 5,418 **Faculty** 17:1 **Application deadline** Rolling **Freshmen** 85% accepted **Housing** Yes **Tuition** $3544 **Undergraduates** 50% women, 9% part-time, 13% 25 or older, 1% Native American, 1% Hispanic, 8% black, 1% Asian or Pacific Islander **Most popular recent majors** Business administration/commerce/management, education, criminal justice **Academic program** Advanced placement, accelerated degree program, tutorials, honors program, summer session, adult/continuing education programs, internships **Contact** Mr. Edgerton Deuel II, Director of Admissions, Frostburg State University, Frostburg, MD 21532-2302. Telephone: 301-687-4201. Fax: 301-687-7074.

GOUCHER COLLEGE
BALTIMORE, MARYLAND

Entrance Moderately difficult **General** Independent, comprehensive, coed **Setting** 287-acre suburban campus **Enrollment** 1,303 **Faculty** 10:1 **Application deadline** 2/1 **Freshmen** 87% accepted **Housing** Yes **Tuition** $18,525 **Undergraduates** 71% women, 6% part-time, 5% 25 or older, 0% Native American, 3% Hispanic, 8% black, 4% Asian or Pacific Islander **Most popular recent majors** English, business administration/commerce/management, psychology **Academic program** Average class size 20, advanced placement, accelerated degree program, self-designed majors, tutorials, honors program, summer session, adult/continuing education programs, internships **Contact** Mr. Carlton E. Surbeck III, Director of Admissions, Goucher College, Baltimore, MD 21204-2794. Telephone: 410-337-6100. Fax: 410-337-6123.

GRIGGS UNIVERSITY
SILVER SPRING, MARYLAND

Entrance Minimally difficult **General** Independent Seventh-day Adventist, 4-year, specialized, coed **Setting** Suburban campus **Enrollment** 497 **Application deadline** Rolling **Undergraduates** 100% part-time **Academic program** Accelerated degree program, summer session, adult/continuing education programs, internships **Contact** Ms. Eva Michel, Enrollment Officer, Griggs University, PO Box 4437, Silver Spring, MD 20914-4437. Telephone: 301-680-6593. Fax: 301-680-6577.

HOOD COLLEGE
FREDERICK, MARYLAND

Entrance Moderately difficult **General** Independent, comprehensive, primarily women, affiliated with United Church of Christ **Setting** 50-acre urban campus **Enrollment** 1,870 **Faculty** 10:1 **Application deadline** 3/31 **Freshmen** 84% accepted **Housing** Yes **Tuition** $16,418 **Undergraduates** 95% women, 11% part-time, 38% 25 or older, 0% Native American, 5% Hispanic, 13% black, 3% Asian or Pacific Islander **Most popular recent majors** Business administration/commerce/management, education, biology/biological sciences **Academic program** Average class size 15, advanced placement, accelerated degree program, self-designed majors, tutorials, honors program, summer session, adult/continuing education programs, internships **Contact** Ms. Meg Miller, Acting Director of Admissions, Hood College, 401 Rosemont Avenue, Frederick, MD 21701-8575. Telephone: 301-696-3400.

JOHNS HOPKINS UNIVERSITY
BALTIMORE, MARYLAND

Entrance Most difficult **General** Independent, coed **Setting** 140-acre urban campus **Enrollment** 4,979 **Faculty** 10:1 **Application deadline** 1/1 **Freshmen** 40% accepted **Housing** Yes **Tuition** $21,675 **Undergraduates** 39% women, 0% part-time, 0% 25 or older, 1% Native American, 3% Hispanic, 6% black, 23% Asian or Pacific Islander **Most popular recent majors** Biology/biological sciences, biomedical engineering, international studies **Academic program** Advanced placement, accelerated degree program, self-designed majors, tutorials, summer session, adult/continuing education programs, internships **Contact** Mr.

Paul White, Director of Undergraduate Admissions, Johns Hopkins University, 3400 North Charles Street, Baltimore, MD 21218-2699. Telephone: 410-516-7247.

LOYOLA COLLEGE

BALTIMORE, MARYLAND

Entrance Moderately difficult **General** Independent Roman Catholic (Jesuit), comprehensive, coed **Setting** 65-acre suburban campus **Enrollment** 6,245 **Faculty** 14:1 **Application deadline** 1/15 **Freshmen** 71% accepted **Housing** Yes **Tuition** $16,560 **Undergraduates** 55% women, 4% part-time, 4% 25 or older, 0% Native American, 2% Hispanic, 4% black, 2% Asian or Pacific Islander **Most popular recent majors** Business administration/commerce/management, psychology, biology/biological sciences **Academic program** Advanced placement, honors program, summer session, internships **Contact** Mr. William Bossemeyer, Director of Admissions, Loyola College, Baltimore, MD 21210-2699. Telephone: 410-617-2000 Ext. 2252. Fax: 410-617-2176.

MARYLAND INSTITUTE, COLLEGE OF ART

BALTIMORE, MARYLAND

Entrance Moderately difficult **General** Independent, comprehensive, specialized, coed **Setting** 12-acre urban campus **Enrollment** 1,064 **Faculty** 6:1 **Application deadline** Rolling **Freshmen** 67% accepted **Housing** Yes **Tuition** $16,760 **Undergraduates** 53% women, 2% part-time, 7% 25 or older, 1% Native American, 6% Hispanic, 5% black, 7% Asian or Pacific Islander **Most popular recent majors** Art/fine arts, illustration, painting/drawing **Academic program** Advanced placement, self-designed majors, honors program, summer session, adult/continuing education programs, internships **Contact** Ms. Theresa Lynch Bedoya, Dean of Admissions and Financial Aid, Maryland Institute, College of Art, 1300 Mount Royal Avenue, Baltimore, MD 21217-4192. Telephone: 410-225-2294.

MORGAN STATE UNIVERSITY

BALTIMORE, MARYLAND

Entrance Moderately difficult **General** State-supported, coed **Setting** 130-acre urban campus **Enrollment** 5,889 **Faculty** 18:1 **Application deadline** Rolling **Freshmen** 47% accepted **Housing** Yes **Tuition** $3412 **Undergraduates** 59% women, 14% part-time, 27% 25 or older, 0% Native American, 2% Hispanic, 94% black, 2% Asian or Pacific Islander **Most popular recent majors** Electrical engineering, accounting, biology/biological sciences **Academic program** Advanced placement, accelerated degree program, tutorials, honors program, summer session, adult/continuing education programs, internships **Contact** Ms. Chelseia Harold-Miller, Director of Admission and Recruitment, Morgan State University, Cold Spring Lane and Hillen Road, Baltimore, MD 21251. Telephone: 410-319-3000.

MOUNT SAINT MARY'S COLLEGE AND SEMINARY

EMMITSBURG, MARYLAND

Entrance Moderately difficult **General** Independent Roman Catholic, comprehensive, coed **Setting** 1,400-acre rural campus **Enrollment** 1,884 **Faculty** 15:1 **Application deadline** 3/1 **Freshmen** 78% accepted **Housing** Yes **Tuition** $15,650 **Undergraduates** 53% women, 9% part-time, 10% 25 or older, 0% Native American, 2% Hispanic, 5% black, 2% Asian or Pacific Islander **Most popular recent majors** Business administration/commerce/management, sociology **Academic program** Average class size 20, advanced placement, self-designed majors, tutorials, honors program, summer session, adult/continuing education programs, internships **Contact** Mr. John Gill, Director of Admissions, Mount Saint Mary's College and Seminary, Emmitsburg, MD 21727-7799. Telephone: 301-447-5214.

PEABODY CONSERVATORY OF MUSIC OF THE JOHNS HOPKINS UNIVERSITY

BALTIMORE, MARYLAND

Entrance Very difficult **General** Independent, comprehensive, specialized, coed **Setting** Urban campus **Enrollment** 637 **Faculty** 3:1 **Application deadline** 2/1 **Freshmen** 51% accepted **Housing** Yes **Tuition** $19,775 **Undergraduates** 54% women, 3% part-time, 6% 25 or older, 2% Hispanic, 3% black, 14% Asian or Pacific Islander **Most popular recent majors** Stringed instruments, piano/organ, voice **Academic program** Average class size 15, advanced placement, accelerated degree program, tutorials, honors program, summer session, internships **Contact** Mr. David Lane, Director of Admissions, Peabody Conservatory of Music of The Johns Hopkins University, 1 East Mount Vernon Place, Baltimore, MD 21202-2397. Telephone: 410-659-8110.

ST. JOHN'S COLLEGE
ANNAPOLIS, MARYLAND

Entrance Moderately difficult **General** Independent, comprehensive, coed **Setting** 36-acre small-town campus **Enrollment** 516 **Faculty** 8:1 **Application deadline** Rolling **Freshmen** 84% accepted **Housing** Yes **Tuition** $21,180 **Undergraduates** 43% women, 1% part-time, 5% 25 or older, 1% Native American, 5% Hispanic, 2% black, 4% Asian or Pacific Islander **Academic program** Average class size 16, tutorials **Contact** Mr. John Christensen, Director of Admissions, St. John's College, PO Box 2800, Annapolis, MD 21404. Telephone: 410-263-2371 Ext. 222.

ST. MARY'S COLLEGE OF MARYLAND
ST. MARY'S CITY, MARYLAND

Entrance Very difficult **General** State-supported, 4-year, coed **Setting** 275-acre rural campus **Enrollment** 1,478 **Faculty** 14:1 **Application deadline** 1/15 **Freshmen** 58% accepted **Housing** Yes **Tuition** $6575 **Undergraduates** 58% women, 4% part-time, 8% 25 or older, 0% Native American, 2% Hispanic, 10% black, 4% Asian or Pacific Islander **Most popular recent majors** Biology/biological sciences, economics, psychology **Academic program** Average class size 20, advanced placement, self-designed majors, tutorials, honors program, summer session, adult/continuing education programs, internships **Contact** Mr. Richard Edgar, Director of Admissions, St. Mary's College of Maryland, Admissions Office, St. Mary's City, MD 20686. Telephone: 301-862-0292. Fax: 301-862-0906.

ST. MARY'S SEMINARY AND UNIVERSITY
BALTIMORE, MARYLAND

Entrance Difficulty N/R **General** Independent Roman Catholic, upper-level, coed **Setting** Urban campus **Enrollment** 222 **Freshmen** 100% accepted **Housing** Yes **Tuition** $9055 **Contact** Director of Recruitment, St. Mary's Seminary and University, 5400 Roland Avenue, Baltimore, MD 21210-1994. Telephone: 410-323-3100.

SALISBURY STATE UNIVERSITY
SALISBURY, MARYLAND

Entrance Moderately difficult **General** State-supported, comprehensive, coed **Setting** 140-acre small-town campus **Enrollment** 5,308 **Faculty** 16:1 **Application deadline** 3/1 **Freshmen** 49% accepted **Housing** Yes **Tuition** $3842 **Undergraduates** 58% women, 12% part-time, 19% 25 or older, 1% Native American, 1% Hispanic, 7% black, 1% Asian or Pacific Islander **Most popular recent majors** Elementary education, business administration/commerce/management, communication **Academic program** Advanced placement, accelerated degree program, self-designed majors, honors program, summer session, adult/continuing education programs, internships **Contact** Mrs. Jane H. Dané, Dean of Admissions and Financial Aid, Salisbury State University, Salisbury, MD 21801-6837. Telephone: 410-543-6161.

SOJOURNER-DOUGLASS COLLEGE
BALTIMORE, MARYLAND

Entrance Minimally difficult **General** Independent, 4-year, coed **Setting** 15-acre urban campus **Enrollment** 433 **Faculty** 10:1 **Application deadline** Rolling **Freshmen** 85% accepted **Tuition** $4090 **Undergraduates** 80% women, 18% part-time, 95% 25 or older, 0% Native American, 1% Hispanic, 99% black, 0% Asian or Pacific Islander **Academic program** Accelerated degree program, self-designed majors, honors program, summer session, adult/continuing education programs, internships **Contact** Ms. Diana Samuels, Manager, Office of Admissions, Sojourner-Douglass College, 500 North Caroline Street, Baltimore, MD 21205-1814. Telephone: 410-276-0306 Ext. 249. Fax: 410-675-1810.

TOWSON STATE UNIVERSITY
TOWSON, MARYLAND

Entrance Moderately difficult **General** State-supported, comprehensive, coed **Setting** 321-acre suburban campus **Enrollment** 15,105 **Faculty** 16:1 **Application deadline** 5/1 **Freshmen** 69% accepted **Housing** Yes **Tuition** $4120 **Undergraduates** 59% women, 23% part-time, 24% 25 or older, 0% Native American, 2% Hispanic, 9% black, 3% Asian or Pacific Islander **Most popular recent majors** Communication, business administration/commerce/management, psychology **Academic program** Advanced placement, accelerated degree program, self-designed majors, tutorials, honors program, summer session, adult/continuing education programs, internships **Contact** Ms. Angel Jackson, Director of Admissions, Towson State University, Towson, MD 21252-7097. Telephone: 410-830-3333.

UNITED STATES NAVAL ACADEMY
ANNAPOLIS, MARYLAND

Entrance Very difficult **General** Federally supported, 4-year, coed **Setting** 329-acre small-town campus **Enrollment** 4,000 **Faculty** 7:1 **Application deadline** 3/20 **Freshmen** 18% accepted **Housing** Yes **Tuition** $0 **Undergraduates** 14% women, 0% part-time, 0% 25 or older, 1% Native American, 6% Hispanic, 7% black, 4% Asian or Pacific Islander **Most popular recent majors** Political science/government, aerospace engineering, oceanography **Academic program** Advanced placement, tutorials, honors program, summer session **Contact** Capt. John W. Renard, Retd., Dean of Admissions, United States Naval Academy, Annapolis, MD 21402-5000. Telephone: 410-293-4336. Fax: 410-293-4348.

UNIVERSITY OF BALTIMORE
BALTIMORE, MARYLAND

Entrance Noncompetitive **General** State-supported, upper-level, coed **Setting** 49-acre urban campus **Enrollment** 4,361 **Faculty** 16:1 **Freshmen** 92% accepted **Tuition** $3804 **Undergraduates** 54% women, 58% part-time, 72% 25 or older, 3% Native American, 1% Hispanic, 26% black, 2% Asian or Pacific Islander **Most popular recent majors** Business administration/commerce/management, criminal justice, interdisciplinary studies **Academic program** Advanced placement, self-designed majors, honors program, summer session, adult/continuing education programs, internships **Contact** Ms. Janenne Corcoron, Associate Director of Admissions, University of Baltimore, 1420 North Charles Street, Baltimore, MD 21201-5779. Telephone: 410-837-4777.

UNIVERSITY OF MARYLAND BALTIMORE COUNTY
BALTIMORE, MARYLAND

Entrance Moderately difficult **General** State-supported, coed **Setting** 500-acre suburban campus **Enrollment** 9,932 **Faculty** 14:1 **Application deadline** 3/15 **Freshmen** 61% accepted **Housing** Yes **Tuition** $4570 **Undergraduates** 51% women, 27% part-time, 27% 25 or older, 1% Native American, 2% Hispanic, 15% black, 13% Asian or Pacific Islander **Most popular recent majors** Psychology, computer information systems **Academic program** Advanced placement, accelerated degree program, self-designed majors, tutorials, honors program, summer session, adult/continuing education programs, internships **Contact** Mr. Tom Taylor, Director of Admissions, University of Maryland Baltimore County, Baltimore, MD 21228-5398. Telephone: 410-455-2291. Fax: 410-455-1094.

UNIVERSITY OF MARYLAND COLLEGE PARK
COLLEGE PARK, MARYLAND

Entrance Moderately difficult **General** State-supported, coed **Setting** 3,773-acre suburban campus **Enrollment** 31,471 **Application deadline** 2/15 **Freshmen** 61% accepted **Housing** Yes **Tuition** $4460 **Undergraduates** 48% women, 12% part-time, 16% 25 or older, 1% Native American, 5% Hispanic, 14% black, 14% Asian or Pacific Islander **Most popular recent majors** Criminal justice, psychology, political science/government **Academic program** Advanced placement, accelerated degree program, self-designed majors, tutorials, honors program, summer session, adult/continuing education programs, internships **Contact** Dr. Linda Clement, Director of Admissions, University of Maryland College Park, College Park, MD 20742. Telephone: 301-314-8385. Fax: 301-3149693.

UNIVERSITY OF MARYLAND EASTERN SHORE
PRINCESS ANNE, MARYLAND

Entrance Moderately difficult **General** State-supported, coed **Setting** 620-acre rural campus **Enrollment** 3,166 **Faculty** 18:1 **Application deadline** Rolling **Freshmen** 75% accepted **Housing** Yes **Tuition** $3240 **Undergraduates** 58% women, 15% part-time, 13% 25 or older, 1% Hispanic, 76% black, 1% Asian or Pacific Islander **Academic program** Advanced placement, accelerated degree program, self-designed majors, honors program, summer session, adult/continuing education programs, internships **Contact** Mrs. Edwina Morse, Assistant Director of Admissions, University of Maryland Eastern Shore, Princess Anne, MD 21853. Telephone: 410-651-6411. Fax: 410-651-7922.

UNIVERSITY OF MARYLAND UNIVERSITY COLLEGE
COLLEGE PARK, MARYLAND

Entrance Noncompetitive **General** State-supported, comprehensive, coed **Setting** Suburban campus **Enrollment** 33,435 **Application deadline** Rolling **Tuition** $5430 **Undergraduates** 56% women, 89% part-time, 87% 25 or older, 1% Native American, 3% Hispanic, 27% black, 5% Asian or Pacific Islander **Most popular recent majors** Business administration/commerce/management, computer management, computer information systems **Academic program** Advanced placement, accelerated degree program, summer session, adult/continuing education programs **Contact** Mr. Gary Thornhill, Director of Undergraduate Enrollment Service, University of Maryland University College, College Park, MD 20742-1600. Telephone: 301-985-7265. Fax: 301-985-7364.

VILLA JULIE COLLEGE
STEVENSON, MARYLAND

Entrance Moderately difficult **General** Independent, comprehensive, coed **Setting** 60-acre suburban campus **Enrollment** 1,866 **Faculty** 15:1 **Application deadline** 7/15 **Freshmen** 81% accepted **Housing** Yes **Tuition** $9240 **Undergraduates** 81% women, 39% part-time, 37% 25 or older, 0% Native American, 1% Hispanic, 14% black, 2% Asian or Pacific Islander **Most popular recent majors** Computer information systems, nursing **Academic program** Average class size 18, advanced placement, self-designed majors, tutorials, honors program, summer session, adult/continuing education programs, internships **Contact** Mr. Mark Hergan, Director of Admissions, Villa Julie College, Stevenson, MD 21153. Telephone: 410-486-7001.

WASHINGTON BIBLE COLLEGE
LANHAM, MARYLAND

Entrance Moderately difficult **General** Independent nondenominational, 4-year, specialized, coed **Setting** 63-acre suburban campus **Enrollment** 319 **Faculty** 12:1 **Application deadline** Rolling **Freshmen** 58% accepted **Housing** Yes **Tuition** $5220 **Undergraduates** 43% women, 58% part-time, 62% 25 or older, 0% Native American, 2% Hispanic, 42% black, 7% Asian or Pacific Islander **Academic program** Advanced placement, accelerated degree program, summer session, adult/continuing education programs, internships **Contact** Ms. Mary S. Holliker, Admissions Office Manager, Washington Bible College, Lanham, MD 20706-3599. Telephone: 301-552-1400 Ext. 212. Fax: 301-552-2775.

WASHINGTON COLLEGE
CHESTERTOWN, MARYLAND

Entrance Moderately difficult **General** Independent, comprehensive, coed **Setting** 120-acre small-town campus **Enrollment** 1,009 **Faculty** 12:1 **Application deadline** 2/15 **Freshmen** 84% accepted **Housing** Yes **Tuition** $18,250 **Undergraduates** 57% women, 1% part-time, 3% 25 or older, 1% Native American, 2% Hispanic, 5% black, 2% Asian or Pacific Islander **Most popular recent majors** English, psychology, business administration/commerce/management **Academic program** Average class size 11, advanced placement, self-designed majors, tutorials, internships **Contact** Mr. Kevin Coveney, Vice President for Admissions, Washington College, Chestertown, MD 21620-1197. Telephone: 410-778-7700. Fax: 410-778-7287.

WESTERN MARYLAND COLLEGE
WESTMINSTER, MARYLAND

Entrance Moderately difficult **General** Independent, comprehensive, coed **Setting** 160-acre small-town campus **Enrollment** 2,592 **Faculty** 13:1 **Application deadline** 3/15 **Freshmen** 83% accepted **Housing** Yes **Tuition** $16,850 **Undergraduates** 54% women, 5% part-time, 8% 25 or older, 1% Native American, 1% Hispanic, 5% black, 1% Asian or Pacific Islander **Most popular recent majors** Sociology, physical education, biology/biological sciences **Academic program** Average class size 19, advanced placement, self-designed majors, tutorials, honors program, summer session, adult/continuing education programs, internships **Contact** Ms. M. Martha O'Connell, Director of Admissions, Western Maryland College, Westminster, MD 21157-4390. Telephone: 410-857-2230. Fax: 410-857-2729.

New Jersey

BLOOMFIELD COLLEGE
BLOOMFIELD, NEW JERSEY

Entrance Minimally difficult **General** Independent, 4-year, coed, affiliated with Presbyterian Church (U.S.A.) **Setting** 12-acre suburban campus **Enrollment** 2,054 **Faculty** 17:1 **Application deadline** Rolling **Freshmen** 59% accepted **Housing** Yes **Tuition** $9650 **Undergraduates** 69% women, 34% part-time, 44% 25 or older, 0% Native American, 13% Hispanic, 49% black, 4% Asian or Pacific Islander **Most popular recent majors** Business administration/commerce/management, nursing, criminal justice **Academic program** Advanced placement, accelerated degree program, self-designed majors, tutorials, honors program, summer session, adult/continuing education programs, internships **Contact** Office of Admission, Bloomfield College, Park Place, Bloomfield, NJ 07003-9981. Telephone: 201-748-9000 Ext. 230. Fax: 201-748-0916.

CALDWELL COLLEGE
CALDWELL, NEW JERSEY

Entrance Moderately difficult **General** Independent Roman Catholic, comprehensive, coed **Setting** 100-acre suburban campus **Enrollment** 1,750 **Faculty** 12:1 **Application deadline** Rolling

Freshmen 67% accepted **Housing** Yes **Tuition** $10,800 **Undergraduates** 69% women, 49% part-time, 52% 25 or older, 0% Native American, 6% Hispanic, 10% black, 3% Asian or Pacific Islander **Most popular recent majors** Business administration/commerce/management, psychology, elementary education **Academic program** Advanced placement, accelerated degree program, tutorials, honors program, summer session, adult/continuing education programs, internships **Contact** Mr. Raymond Sheenan, Director of Admissions, Caldwell College, Caldwell, NJ 07006-6195. Telephone: 201-228-4424 Ext. 220.

CAMDEN COLLEGE OF ARTS AND SCIENCES

SEE RUTGERS, THE STATE UNIVERSITY OF NEW JERSEY, CAMDEN COLLEGE OF ARTS AND SCIENCES

CENTENARY COLLEGE

HACKETTSTOWN, NEW JERSEY

Entrance Moderately difficult **General** Independent, comprehensive, coed, affiliated with United Methodist Church **Setting** 42-acre suburban campus **Enrollment** 968 **Faculty** 13:1 **Application deadline** Rolling **Freshmen** 84% accepted **Housing** Yes **Tuition** $13,120 **Undergraduates** 78% women, 48% part-time, 53% 25 or older, 1% Native American, 2% Hispanic, 5% black, 1% Asian or Pacific Islander **Most popular recent majors** Business administration/commerce/management, education, equestrian studies **Academic program** Average class size 20, advanced placement, self-designed majors, tutorials, summer session, internships **Contact** Mr. Dennis Kelly, Vice President for Enrollment Management, Centenary College, Hackettstown, NJ 07840-2100. Telephone: 908-852-4696. Fax: 908-852-3454.

THE COLLEGE OF NEW JERSEY

TRENTON, NEW JERSEY

Entrance Very difficult **General** State-supported, comprehensive, coed **Setting** 255-acre suburban campus **Enrollment** 6,704 **Faculty** 14:1 **Application deadline** 3/1 **Freshmen** 45% accepted **Housing** Yes **Tuition** $4925 **Undergraduates** 61% women, 11% part-time, 13% 25 or older, 1% Native American, 5% Hispanic, 6% black, 6% Asian or Pacific Islander **Most popular recent majors** Elementary education, biology/biological sciences, English **Academic program** Average class size 25, advanced placement, tutorials, honors program, summer session, internships **Contact** Director of Admissions, The College of New Jersey, Trenton, NJ 08650-4700. Telephone: 609-771-2131.

COLLEGE OF SAINT ELIZABETH

MORRISTOWN, NEW JERSEY

Entrance Moderately difficult **General** Independent Roman Catholic, comprehensive, primarily women **Setting** 188-acre suburban campus **Enrollment** 1,694 **Faculty** 9:1 **Application deadline** Rolling **Freshmen** 83% accepted **Housing** Yes **Tuition** $13,060 **Undergraduates** 93% women, 63% part-time, 61% 25 or older, 1% Native American, 9% Hispanic, 9% black, 2% Asian or Pacific Islander **Most popular recent majors** Business administration/commerce/management, psychology, education **Academic program** Average class size 17, advanced placement, accelerated degree program, self-designed majors, honors program, summer session, adult/continuing education programs, internships **Contact** Ms. Donna Yamanis, Dean of Admissions and Financial Aid, College of Saint Elizabeth, Morristown, NJ 07960-6989. Telephone: 201-605-7700. Fax: 201-605-7755.

COOK COLLEGE

SEE RUTGERS, THE STATE UNIVERSITY OF NEW JERSEY, COOK COLLEGE

DOUGLASS COLLEGE

SEE RUTGERS, THE STATE UNIVERSITY OF NEW JERSEY, DOUGLASS COLLEGE

DREW UNIVERSITY

MADISON, NEW JERSEY

Entrance Very difficult **General** Independent, coed, affiliated with United Methodist Church **Setting** 186-acre suburban campus **Enrollment** 2,174 **Faculty** 11:1 **Application deadline** 2/15 **Freshmen** 73% accepted **Housing** Yes **Tuition** $21,396 **Undergraduates** 59% women, 4% part-time, 4% 25 or older, 1% Native American, 6% Hispanic, 3% black, 7% Asian or Pacific Islander **Most popular recent majors** Political science/government, psychology, English **Academic program** Advanced placement, self-designed majors, honors program, summer session, adult/continuing education programs, internships **Contact** Mr. Roberto Noya, Dean of Admissions for the College of Liberal Arts, Drew University, Madison, NJ 07940-1493. Telephone: 201-408-3739. Fax: 201-408-3939.

FAIRLEIGH DICKINSON UNIVERSITY

TEANECK AND MADISON, NEW JERSEY

Entrance Moderately difficult **General** Independent, comprehensive, coed **Setting** 125-acre suburban campus **Enrollment** 6,934 **Application deadline** Rolling **Freshmen** 65% accepted **Housing** Yes **Tuition** $14,712 **Undergraduates** 55% women, 32% part-time, 34% 25 or older, 1% Native American, 7% Hispanic, 12% black, 4% Asian or Pacific Islander **Most popular recent majors** Business administration/commerce/management, psychology, nursing **Academic program** Advanced placement, accelerated degree program, self-designed majors, tutorials, honors program, summer session, adult/continuing education programs, internships **Contact** Ms. Dale Herold, Dean of Enrollment Management, Fairleigh Dickinson University, Teaneck, NJ 07666-1914. Telephone: 201-692-7300.

FELICIAN COLLEGE

LODI, NEW JERSEY

Entrance Moderately difficult **General** Independent Roman Catholic, comprehensive, coed **Setting** 27-acre suburban campus **Enrollment** 1,250 **Faculty** 15:1 **Application deadline** Rolling **Freshmen** 73% accepted **Housing** Yes **Tuition** $9932 **Undergraduates** 88% women, 46% part-time, 53% 25 or older, 0% Native American, 11% Hispanic, 5% black, 8% Asian or Pacific Islander **Most popular recent majors** Nursing, education **Academic program** Average class size 21, ESL program, advanced placement, self-designed majors, tutorials, honors program, summer session, adult/continuing education programs, internships **Contact** Ms. Susan M. Chalfin, Director of Admissions, Felician College, Lodi, NJ 07644. Telephone: 201-778-1029. Fax: 201-778-4111.

GEORGIAN COURT COLLEGE

LAKEWOOD, NEW JERSEY

Entrance Moderately difficult **General** Independent Roman Catholic, comprehensive, primarily women **Setting** 150-acre suburban campus **Enrollment** 1,919 **Faculty** 11:1 **Application deadline** 8/1 **Freshmen** 94% accepted **Housing** Yes **Tuition** $11,116 **Undergraduates** 91% women, 30% part-time, 40% 25 or older, 1% Native American, 4% Hispanic, 5% black, 1% Asian or Pacific Islander **Most popular recent majors** Psychology, business administration/commerce/management, accounting **Academic program** Average class size 17, advanced placement, tutorials, summer session, adult/continuing education programs, internships **Contact** Mrs. Nancy Hazelgrove, Director of Admissions, Georgian Court College, Lakewood, NJ 08701-2697. Telephone: 908-364-2200 Ext. 760. Fax: 908-364-4442.

JERSEY CITY STATE COLLEGE

JERSEY CITY, NEW JERSEY

Entrance Moderately difficult **General** State-supported, comprehensive, coed **Setting** 17-acre urban campus **Enrollment** 7,450 **Faculty** 18:1 **Application deadline** 4/1 **Freshmen** 49% accepted **Housing** Yes **Tuition** $3048 **Undergraduates** 60% women, 36% part-time, 43% 25 or older, 0% Native American, 26% Hispanic, 19% black, 10% Asian or Pacific Islander **Most popular recent majors** Business administration/commerce/management, criminal justice, computer science **Academic program** Advanced placement, accelerated degree program, tutorials, honors program, summer session, adult/continuing education programs, internships **Contact** Mr. Samuel T. McGhee, Director of Admissions, Jersey City State College, 2039 Kennedy Boulevard, Jersey City, NJ 07305-1957. Telephone: 201-200-3234. Fax: 201-200-2044.

KEAN COLLEGE OF NEW JERSEY

UNION, NEW JERSEY

Entrance Moderately difficult **General** State-supported, comprehensive, coed **Setting** 151-acre urban campus **Enrollment** 10,404 **Faculty** 19:1 **Application deadline** 6/15 **Housing** Yes **Tuition** $3669 **Undergraduates** 63% women, 35% part-time, 37% 25 or older, 0% Native American, 18% Hispanic, 17% black, 6% Asian or Pacific Islander **Most popular recent majors** Accounting, business administration/commerce/management **Academic program** Accelerated degree program, honors program, summer session, adult/continuing education programs, internships **Contact** Mr. Audley Bridges, Director of Admissions, Kean College of New Jersey, 1000 Morris Avenue, Union, NJ 07083. Telephone: 908-527-2195. Fax: 908-355-5143.

LIVINGSTON COLLEGE

SEE RUTGERS, THE STATE UNIVERSITY OF NEW JERSEY, LIVINGSTON COLLEGE

MASON GROSS SCHOOL OF THE ARTS

SEE RUTGERS, THE STATE UNIVERSITY OF NEW JERSEY, MASON GROSS SCHOOL OF THE ARTS

MONMOUTH UNIVERSITY

WEST LONG BRANCH, NEW JERSEY

Entrance Moderately difficult **General** Independent, comprehensive, coed **Setting** 138-acre suburban campus **Enrollment** 5,110 **Faculty** 17:1

Application deadline 4/1 **Freshmen** 85% accepted **Housing** Yes **Tuition** $14,442 **Undergraduates** 57% women, 19% part-time, 24% 25 or older, 0% Native American, 4% Hispanic, 5% black, 2% Asian or Pacific Islander **Most popular recent majors** Business administration/commerce/management, communication, education **Academic program** Average class size 23, advanced placement, accelerated degree program, self-designed majors, tutorials, honors program, summer session, adult/continuing education programs, internships **Contact** Ms. Christine Benol, Associate Director of Undergraduate Admission, Monmouth University, West Long Branch, NJ 07764-1898. Telephone: 908-571-3456.

MONTCLAIR STATE UNIVERSITY
UPPER MONTCLAIR, NEW JERSEY

Entrance Moderately difficult **General** State-supported, comprehensive, coed **Setting** 200-acre suburban campus **Enrollment** 12,993 **Faculty** 15:1 **Application deadline** 3/1 **Freshmen** 46% accepted **Housing** Yes **Tuition** $3694 **Undergraduates** 62% women, 30% part-time, 33% 25 or older, 1% Native American, 14% Hispanic, 11% black, 5% Asian or Pacific Islander **Most popular recent majors** Business administration/commerce/management, psychology, home economics **Academic program** Advanced placement, accelerated degree program, honors program, summer session, adult/continuing education programs, internships **Contact** Dr. Alan L. Buechler, Director of Admissions, Montclair State University, Upper Montclair, NJ 07043-1624. Telephone: 201-655-4444. Fax: 201-893-5455.

NEWARK COLLEGE OF ARTS AND SCIENCES
SEE RUTGERS, THE STATE UNIVERSITY OF NEW JERSEY, NEWARK COLLEGE OF ARTS AND SCIENCES

NEW JERSEY INSTITUTE OF TECHNOLOGY
NEWARK, NEW JERSEY

Entrance Moderately difficult **General** State-supported, coed **Setting** 45-acre urban campus **Enrollment** 7,837 **Faculty** 14:1 **Application deadline** 4/1 **Freshmen** 67% accepted **Housing** Yes **Tuition** $5466 **Undergraduates** 19% women, 32% part-time, 35% 25 or older, 1% Native American, 13% Hispanic, 13% black, 18% Asian or Pacific Islander **Most popular recent majors** Engineering technology, electrical engineering, mechanical engineering **Academic program** Average class size 25, advanced placement, tutorials, honors program, summer session, adult/continuing education programs, internships **Contact** Ms. Kathy Kelly, Director of Admissions, New Jersey Institute of Technology, University Heights, Newark, NJ 07102-1982. Telephone: 201-596-3300. Fax: 201-802-1854.

PRINCETON UNIVERSITY
PRINCETON, NEW JERSEY

Entrance Most difficult **General** Independent, coed **Setting** 600-acre suburban campus **Enrollment** 6,340 **Faculty** 5:1 **Application deadline** 1/2 **Freshmen** 12% accepted **Housing** Yes **Tuition** $22,920 **Undergraduates** 46% women, 0% part-time, 0% 25 or older, 1% Native American, 6% Hispanic, 7% black, 12% Asian or Pacific Islander **Most popular recent majors** History, political science/government, economics **Academic program** Advanced placement, accelerated degree program, self-designed majors, tutorials, adult/continuing education programs **Contact** Mr. Fred A. Hargadon, Dean of Admission, Princeton University, Princeton, NJ 08544-1019. Telephone: 609-258-3060.

RAMAPO COLLEGE OF NEW JERSEY
MAHWAH, NEW JERSEY

Entrance Moderately difficult **General** State-supported, comprehensive, coed **Setting** 300-acre suburban campus **Enrollment** 4,001 **Faculty** 17:1 **Application deadline** 3/15 **Freshmen** 50% accepted **Housing** Yes **Tuition** $4206 **Undergraduates** 56% women, 33% part-time, 40% 25 or older, 0% Native American, 6% Hispanic, 9% black, 3% Asian or Pacific Islander **Most popular recent majors** Business administration/commerce/management, psychology, communication **Academic program** Average class size 22, advanced placement, accelerated degree program, self-designed majors, tutorials, honors program, summer session, adult/continuing education programs, internships **Contact** Ms. Nancy Jaeger, Director of Admissions, Ramapo College of New Jersey, Mahwah, NJ 07430-1681. Telephone: 201-529-7600. Fax: 201-529-7508.

THE RICHARD STOCKTON COLLEGE OF NEW JERSEY
POMONA, NEW JERSEY

Entrance Very difficult **General** State-supported, comprehensive, coed **Setting** 1,600-acre suburban campus **Enrollment** 5,512 **Faculty** 18:1 **Application deadline** 5/1 **Freshmen** 48% accepted **Housing** Yes **Tuition** $3776 **Undergraduates** 57% women, 15% part-time, 24% 25 or older, 1% Native American, 4% Hispanic, 8% black, 3% Asian or Pacific Islander **Most popular recent**

majors Business administration/commerce/management, environmental sciences, criminal justice **Academic program** Average class size 23, advanced placement, accelerated degree program, self-designed majors, tutorials, honors program, summer session, adult/continuing education programs, internships **Contact** Mr. Salvatore Catalfamo, Dean of Enrollment Management, The Richard Stockton College of New Jersey, Pomona, NJ 08240-9988. Telephone: 609-652-4261. Fax: 609-652-4958.

RIDER UNIVERSITY

LAWRENCEVILLE, NEW JERSEY

Entrance Moderately difficult **General** Independent, comprehensive, coed **Setting** 340-acre suburban campus **Enrollment** 4,640 **Faculty** 13:1 **Application deadline** Rolling **Freshmen** 85% accepted **Housing** Yes **Tuition** $15,410 **Undergraduates** 59% women, 30% part-time, 18% 25 or older, 1% Native American, 4% Hispanic, 6% black, 4% Asian or Pacific Islander **Most popular recent majors** Elementary education, accounting, business administration/commerce/management **Academic program** Average class size 25, advanced placement, tutorials, honors program, summer session, adult/continuing education programs, internships **Contact** Mr. Thomas Kelly, Dean of Admissions and Financial Aid, Rider University, Lawrenceville, NJ 08648-3001. Telephone: 609-896-5042. Fax: 609-895-6645.

ROWAN UNIVERSITY

GLASSBORO, NEW JERSEY

Entrance Moderately difficult **General** State-supported, comprehensive, coed **Setting** 200-acre small-town campus **Enrollment** 9,213 **Faculty** 16:1 **Application deadline** 3/15 **Freshmen** 43% accepted **Housing** Yes **Tuition** $4241 **Undergraduates** 57% women, 18% part-time, 24% 25 or older, 1% Native American, 5% Hispanic, 10% black, 3% Asian or Pacific Islander **Most popular recent majors** Business administration/commerce/management, elementary education, communication **Academic program** Average class size 23, advanced placement, accelerated degree program, tutorials, honors program, summer session, adult/continuing education programs, internships **Contact** Mr. Marvin G. Sills, Director of Admissions, Rowan University, Glassboro, NJ 08028-1701. Telephone: 609-256-4200.

RUTGERS, THE STATE UNIVERSITY OF NEW JERSEY, CAMDEN COLLEGE OF ARTS AND SCIENCES

CAMDEN, NEW JERSEY

Entrance Moderately difficult **General** State-supported, 4-year, coed **Setting** 25-acre urban campus **Enrollment** 47,812 **Faculty** 14:1 **Application deadline** 12/15 **Freshmen** 57% accepted **Housing** Yes **Tuition** $5190 **Undergraduates** 61% women, 21% part-time, 31% 25 or older, 1% Native American, 7% Hispanic, 15% black, 6% Asian or Pacific Islander **Most popular recent majors** Psychology, accounting, sociology **Academic program** Average class size 33, advanced placement, self-designed majors, tutorials, honors program, summer session, internships **Contact** Ms. Diane W. Harris, Associate Director of University Undergraduate Admissions, Rutgers, The State University of New Jersey, Camden College of Arts and Sciences, PO Box 2101, New Brunswick, NJ 08903-2101. Telephone: 908-445-3770. Fax: 908-445-0237.

RUTGERS, THE STATE UNIVERSITY OF NEW JERSEY, COLLEGE OF ENGINEERING

PISCATAWAY, NEW JERSEY

Entrance Very difficult **General** State-supported, 4-year, specialized, coed **Setting** 2,695-acre small-town campus **Enrollment** 47,812 **Faculty** 10:1 **Application deadline** 12/15 **Freshmen** 72% accepted **Housing** Yes **Tuition** $5817 **Undergraduates** 20% women, 3% part-time, 7% 25 or older, 1% Native American, 7% Hispanic, 8% black, 24% Asian or Pacific Islander **Most popular recent majors** Mechanical engineering, electrical engineering, civil engineering **Academic program** Average class size 45, advanced placement, self-designed majors, tutorials, honors program, summer session, internships **Contact** Ms. Diane W. Harris, Associate Director of University Undergraduate Admissions, Rutgers, The State University of New Jersey, College of Engineering, PO Box 2101, New Brunswick, NJ 08903-2101. Telephone: 908-445-3770. Fax: 908-445-0237.

RUTGERS, THE STATE UNIVERSITY OF NEW JERSEY, COLLEGE OF NURSING

NEWARK, NEW JERSEY

Entrance Moderately difficult **General** State-supported, 4-year, specialized, coed **Setting** 34-acre urban campus **Enrollment** 47,812 **Faculty** 9:1 **Application deadline** 12/15 **Freshmen** 26% accepted **Housing** Yes **Tuition** $5130 **Undergraduates** 90% women, 8% part-time, 22% 25 or older, 0% Native American, 11% Hispanic, 17%

black, 24% Asian or Pacific Islander **Academic program** Advanced placement, tutorials, honors program, summer session **Contact** Ms. Diane W. Harris, Associate Director of University Undergraduate Admissions, Rutgers, The State University of New Jersey, College of Nursing, PO Box 2101, New Brunswick, NJ 08903-2101. Telephone: 908-445-3770. Fax: 908-445-0237.

RUTGERS, THE STATE UNIVERSITY OF NEW JERSEY, COLLEGE OF PHARMACY

PISCATAWAY, NEW JERSEY

Entrance Most difficult **General** State-supported, comprehensive, specialized, coed **Setting** 2,695-acre small-town campus **Enrollment** 47,812 **Faculty** 16:1 **Application deadline** 12/15 **Freshmen** 39% accepted **Housing** Yes **Tuition** $5817 **Undergraduates** 62% women, 1% part-time, 8% 25 or older, 1% Native American, 6% Hispanic, 5% black, 43% Asian or Pacific Islander **Academic program** Average class size 45, advanced placement, tutorials, honors program, summer session, internships **Contact** Ms. Diane W. Harris, Associate Director of University Undergraduate Admissions, Rutgers, The State University of New Jersey, College of Pharmacy, PO Box 2101, New Brunswick, NJ 08903-2101. Telephone: 908-445-3770. Fax: 908-445-0237.

RUTGERS, THE STATE UNIVERSITY OF NEW JERSEY, COOK COLLEGE

NEW BRUNSWICK, NEW JERSEY

Entrance Very difficult **General** State-supported, 4-year, coed **Setting** 2,695-acre small-town campus **Enrollment** 47,812 **Faculty** 16:1 **Application deadline** 12/15 **Freshmen** 61% accepted **Housing** Yes **Tuition** $5817 **Undergraduates** 50% women, 10% part-time, 11% 25 or older, 1% Native American, 6% Hispanic, 5% black, 12% Asian or Pacific Islander **Most popular recent majors** Environmental sciences, biology/biological sciences, business economics **Academic program** Average class size 45, advanced placement, self-designed majors, tutorials, honors program, summer session, internships **Contact** Ms. Diane W. Harris, Associate Director of University Undergraduate Admissions, Rutgers, The State University of New Jersey, Cook College, PO Box 2101, New Brunswick, NJ 08903-0231. Telephone: 908-445-3770. Fax: 908-445-0237.

RUTGERS, THE STATE UNIVERSITY OF NEW JERSEY, DOUGLASS COLLEGE

NEW BRUNSWICK, NEW JERSEY

Entrance Moderately difficult **General** State-supported, 4-year, women only **Setting** 2,695-acre small-town campus **Enrollment** 47,812 **Faculty** 17:1 **Application deadline** 12/15 **Freshmen** 71% accepted **Housing** Yes **Tuition** $5349 **Undergraduates** 6% part-time, 7% 25 or older, 1% Native American, 7% Hispanic, 12% black, 14% Asian or Pacific Islander **Most popular recent majors** Psychology, English, political science/government **Academic program** Average class size 45, advanced placement, self-designed majors, tutorials, honors program, summer session, adult/continuing education programs, internships **Contact** Ms. Diane W. Harris, Associate Director of University Undergraduate Admissions, Rutgers, The State University of New Jersey, Douglass College, PO Box 2101, New Brunswick, NJ 08903-0270. Telephone: 908-445-3770. Fax: 908-445-0237.

RUTGERS, THE STATE UNIVERSITY OF NEW JERSEY, LIVINGSTON COLLEGE

NEW BRUNSWICK, NEW JERSEY

Entrance Moderately difficult **General** State-supported, 4-year, coed **Setting** 2,695-acre small-town campus **Enrollment** 47,812 **Faculty** 17:1 **Application deadline** 12/15 **Freshmen** 60% accepted **Housing** Yes **Tuition** $5382 **Undergraduates** 39% women, 6% part-time, 6% 25 or older, 1% Native American, 8% Hispanic, 13% black, 16% Asian or Pacific Islander **Most popular recent majors** Psychology, economics, criminal justice **Academic program** Average class size 45, advanced placement, self-designed majors, tutorials, honors program, summer session, internships **Contact** Ms. Diane W. Harris, Associate Director of University Undergraduate Admissions, Rutgers, The State University of New Jersey, Livingston College, PO Box 2101, New Brunswick, NJ 08903. Telephone: 908-445-3770. Fax: 908-445-0237.

RUTGERS, THE STATE UNIVERSITY OF NEW JERSEY, MASON GROSS SCHOOL OF THE ARTS

NEW BRUNSWICK, NEW JERSEY

Entrance Moderately difficult **General** State-supported, comprehensive, coed **Setting** 2,695-acre small-town campus **Enrollment** 47,812 **Faculty** 11:1 **Application deadline** 12/15 **Freshmen** 23% accepted **Housing** Yes **Tuition** $5347 **Undergraduates** 54% women, 3% part-time, 8% 25 or older, 1% Native American, 6% Hispanic, 7% black, 8% Asian or Pacific Islander **Most popular recent majors** Art/fine arts, music, theater arts/drama **Academic program** Advanced placement, tutorials, honors program, summer session **Contact** Ms. Diane W. Harris, Associate Director of University Undergraduate Admissions, Rutgers,

The State University of New Jersey, Mason Gross School of the Arts, PO Box 2101, New Brunswick, NJ 08903-0270. Telephone: 908-445-3770. Fax: 908-445-0237.

RUTGERS, THE STATE UNIVERSITY OF NEW JERSEY, NEWARK COLLEGE OF ARTS AND SCIENCES

NEWARK, NEW JERSEY

Entrance Moderately difficult **General** State-supported, 4-year, coed **Setting** 34-acre urban campus **Enrollment** 47,812 **Faculty** 15:1 **Application deadline** 12/15 **Freshmen** 52% accepted **Housing** Yes **Tuition** $5151 **Undergraduates** 53% women, 16% part-time, 21% 25 or older, 1% Native American, 21% Hispanic, 18% black, 16% Asian or Pacific Islander **Most popular recent majors** Accounting, biology/biological sciences, psychology **Academic program** Average class size 30, advanced placement, self-designed majors, tutorials, honors program, summer session, adult/continuing education programs, internships **Contact** Ms. Diane E. Harris, Associate Director of University Undergraduate Admissions, Rutgers, The State University of New Jersey, Newark College of Arts and Sciences, PO Box 2101, New Brunswick, NJ 08903-2101. Telephone: 908-445-3770. Fax: 908-445-0237.

RUTGERS, THE STATE UNIVERSITY OF NEW JERSEY, RUTGERS COLLEGE

NEW BRUNSWICK, NEW JERSEY

Entrance Very difficult **General** State-supported, 4-year, coed **Setting** 2,695-acre small-town campus **Enrollment** 47,812 **Faculty** 17:1 **Application deadline** 12/15 **Freshmen** 52% accepted **Housing** Yes **Tuition** $5386 **Undergraduates** 51% women, 4% part-time, 3% 25 or older, 1% Native American, 10% Hispanic, 7% black, 19% Asian or Pacific Islander **Most popular recent majors** Psychology, political science/government, biology/biological sciences **Academic program** Average class size 45, advanced placement, self-designed majors, tutorials, honors program, summer session, internships **Contact** Ms. Diane W. Harris, Associate Director of University Undergraduate Admissions, Rutgers, The State University of New Jersey, Rutgers College, PO Box 2101, New Brunswick, NJ 08903-2101. Telephone: 908-445-3770. Fax: 908-445-0237.

RUTGERS, THE STATE UNIVERSITY OF NEW JERSEY, UNIVERSITY COLLEGE–CAMDEN

CAMDEN, NEW JERSEY

Entrance Moderately difficult **General** State-supported, 4-year, coed **Setting** 25-acre urban campus **Enrollment** 47,812 **Faculty** 14:1 **Application deadline** 12/15 **Freshmen** 70% accepted **Undergraduates** 54% women, 54% part-time, 59% 25 or older, 1% Native American, 2% Hispanic, 16% black, 4% Asian or Pacific Islander **Most popular recent majors** Psychology, English, computer science **Academic program** Average class size 33, advanced placement, self-designed majors, tutorials, honors program, summer session, internships **Contact** Ms. Diane W. Harris, Associate Director of University Undergraduate Admissions, Rutgers, The State University of New Jersey, University College–Camden, PO Box 2101, New Brunswick, NJ 08903-2101. Telephone: 908-445-3770. Fax: 908-445-0237.

RUTGERS, THE STATE UNIVERSITY OF NEW JERSEY, UNIVERSITY COLLEGE–NEWARK

NEWARK, NEW JERSEY

Entrance Moderately difficult **General** State-supported, 4-year, coed **Setting** 34-acre urban campus **Enrollment** 47,812 **Faculty** 15:1 **Application deadline** 12/15 **Freshmen** 73% accepted **Undergraduates** 54% women, 62% part-time, 56% 25 or older, 1% Native American, 16% Hispanic, 32% black, 12% Asian or Pacific Islander **Most popular recent majors** Accounting, criminal justice, business administration/commerce/management **Academic program** Average class size 30, advanced placement, self-designed majors, tutorials, honors program, summer session, adult/continuing education programs, internships **Contact** Ms. Diane W. Harris, Associate Director of University Undergraduate Admissions, Rutgers, The State University of New Jersey, University College–Newark, PO Box 2101, New Brunswick, NJ 08903-2101. Telephone: 908-445-3770. Fax: 908-445-0237.

RUTGERS, THE STATE UNIVERSITY OF NEW JERSEY, UNIVERSITY COLLEGE–NEW BRUNSWICK

NEW BRUNSWICK, NEW JERSEY

Entrance Moderately difficult **General** State-supported, 4-year, coed **Setting** 2,694-acre small-town campus **Enrollment** 47,812 **Faculty** 17:1 **Application deadline** 7/19 **Freshmen** 64% accepted **Undergraduates** 54% women, 78% part-time, 71% 25 or older, 1% Native American, 5% Hispanic, 7% black, 8% Asian or Pacific Islander **Most popular recent majors** Psychology, English, computer science **Academic program** Average class size 45, advanced placement, self-designed majors, tutorials, honors program, summer session, adult/continuing education programs, internships **Contact** Ms. Loretta Daniel,

Director of Admissions, Rutgers, The State University of New Jersey, University College–New Brunswick, New Brunswick, NJ 08903. Telephone: 908-932-7276. Fax: 908-932-8767.

SAINT PETER'S COLLEGE
JERSEY CITY, NEW JERSEY

Entrance Moderately difficult **General** Independent Roman Catholic (Jesuit), comprehensive, coed **Setting** 10-acre urban campus **Enrollment** 3,863 **Faculty** 15:1 **Application deadline** Rolling **Freshmen** 83% accepted **Housing** Yes **Tuition** $14,214 **Undergraduates** 58% women, 31% part-time, 27% 25 or older, 0% Native American, 21% Hispanic, 13% black, 8% Asian or Pacific Islander **Most popular recent majors** Business administration/commerce/management, accounting, elementary education **Academic program** Average class size 24, advanced placement, accelerated degree program, self-designed majors, tutorials, honors program, summer session, adult/continuing education programs, internships **Contact** Mr. Michael A. Worlds, Director of Admissions, Saint Peter's College, 2641 Kennedy Boulevard, Jersey City, NJ 07306-5997. Telephone: 201-915-9213. Fax: 201-432-5860.

SETON HALL UNIVERSITY
SOUTH ORANGE, NEW JERSEY

Entrance Moderately difficult **General** Independent Roman Catholic, coed **Setting** 58-acre suburban campus **Enrollment** 8,518 **Faculty** 15:1 **Application deadline** 3/1 **Freshmen** 80% accepted **Housing** Yes **Tuition** $14,470 **Undergraduates** 54% women, 13% part-time, 16% 25 or older, 0% Native American, 9% Hispanic, 12% black, 5% Asian or Pacific Islander **Most popular recent majors** Communication, nursing, accounting **Academic program** Average class size 30, advanced placement, accelerated degree program, tutorials, honors program, summer session, adult/continuing education programs, internships **Contact** Mr. Gregg A. Meyer, Director of Admissions, Seton Hall University, South Orange, NJ 07079-2697. Telephone: 201-761-9332. Fax: 201-761-9452.

STEVENS INSTITUTE OF TECHNOLOGY
HOBOKEN, NEW JERSEY

Entrance Very difficult **General** Independent, coed **Setting** 55-acre urban campus **Enrollment** 3,382 **Faculty** 9:1 **Application deadline** 3/1 **Freshmen** 64% accepted **Housing** Yes **Tuition** $19,360 **Undergraduates** 22% women, 0% part-time, 0% Native American, 11% Hispanic, 7% black, 25% Asian or Pacific Islander **Most popular recent majors** Electrical engineering, mechanical engineering, civil engineering **Academic program** Average class size 20, advanced placement, accelerated degree program, tutorials, honors program, summer session, internships **Contact** Mrs. Maureen P. Weatherall, Dean of Undergraduate Admissions and Financial Aid, Stevens Institute of Technology, Castle Point on Hudson, Hoboken, NJ 07030. Telephone: 201-216-5194. Fax: 201-216-8348.

THOMAS EDISON STATE COLLEGE
TRENTON, NEW JERSEY

Entrance Noncompetitive **General** State-supported, comprehensive, coed **Setting** 2-acre urban campus **Enrollment** 8,585 **Freshmen** 100% accepted **Tuition** $2100 **Undergraduates** 41% women, 100% part-time, 97% 25 or older, 1% Native American, 3% Hispanic, 8% black, 2% Asian or Pacific Islander **Most popular recent majors** Social science, humanities, liberal arts/general studies **Academic program** Advanced placement, accelerated degree program, self-designed majors, summer session, adult/continuing education programs **Contact** Ms. Janice Toliver, Director of Admissions Services, Thomas Edison State College, 101 West State Street, Trenton, NJ 08608-1176. Telephone: 609-984-1150. Fax: 609-989-9321.

TRENTON STATE COLLEGE
SEE THE COLLEGE OF NEW JERSEY

WESTMINSTER CHOIR COLLEGE OF RIDER UNIVERSITY
PRINCETON, NEW JERSEY

Entrance Moderately difficult **General** Independent, comprehensive, specialized, coed **Setting** 23-acre small-town campus **Enrollment** 398 **Faculty** 7:1 **Application deadline** Rolling **Freshmen** 22% accepted **Housing** Yes **Tuition** $15,430 **Undergraduates** 57% women, 3% part-time, 0% Native American, 4% Hispanic, 7% black, 6% Asian or Pacific Islander **Most popular recent majors** Music education, sacred music, voice **Academic program** Advanced placement, honors program, summer session, adult/continuing education programs, internships **Contact** Mr. Stephen B. Milbauer, Assistant Director of Admissions, Westminster Choir College of Rider University, Princeton, NJ 08540-3899. Telephone: 609-921-7144 Ext. 103. Fax: 609-921-2538.

WILLIAM PATERSON COLLEGE OF NEW JERSEY
WAYNE, NEW JERSEY

Entrance Moderately difficult **General** State-supported, comprehensive, coed **Setting** 250-acre small-town campus **Enrollment** 8,941 **Application deadline** 5/15 **Freshmen** 47% accepted **Housing** Yes **Tuition** $3786 **Undergraduates** 59% women, 26% part-time, 26% 25 or older, 11% Hispanic, 9% black, 3% Asian or Pacific Islander **Most popular recent majors** Business administration/commerce/management, psychology, communication **Academic program** Advanced placement, accelerated degree program, tutorials, honors program, summer session, adult/continuing education programs, internships **Contact** Mr. Leo DeBartolo, Director of Admissions, William Paterson College of New Jersey, Wayne, NJ 07470-8420. Telephone: 973-595-2906. Fax: 973-595-2910.

Pennsylvania

ACADEMY OF THE NEW CHURCH COLLEGE
SEE BRYN ATHYN COLLEGE OF THE NEW CHURCH

ALBRIGHT COLLEGE
READING, PENNSYLVANIA

Entrance Moderately difficult **General** Independent, 4-year, coed, affiliated with United Methodist Church **Setting** 110-acre suburban campus **Enrollment** 1,193 **Faculty** 12:1 **Application deadline** 2/15 **Freshmen** 85% accepted **Housing** Yes **Tuition** $18,310 **Undergraduates** 53% women, 8% part-time, 2% 25 or older, 1% Native American, 3% Hispanic, 5% black, 3% Asian or Pacific Islander **Most popular recent majors** Business administration/commerce/management, biology/biological sciences, psychology **Academic program** Average class size 25, advanced placement, accelerated degree program, self-designed majors, tutorials, honors program, summer session, internships **Contact** Mr. Gregory E. Eichhorn, Director of Admissions, Albright College, Reading, PA 19612-5234. Telephone: 610-921-7512. Fax: 610-921-7530.

ALLEGHENY COLLEGE
MEADVILLE, PENNSYLVANIA

Entrance Very difficult **General** Independent, 4-year, coed, affiliated with United Methodist Church **Setting** 254-acre small-town campus **Enrollment** 1,846 **Faculty** 12:1 **Application deadline** 2/15 **Freshmen** 71% accepted **Housing** Yes **Tuition** $19,360 **Undergraduates** 54% women, 1% part-time, 1% 25 or older, 1% Native American, 1% Hispanic, 3% black, 2% Asian or Pacific Islander **Most popular recent majors** Psychology, biology/biological sciences, political science/government **Academic program** Advanced placement, accelerated degree program, self-designed majors, tutorials, internships **Contact** Ms. Gayle Pollock, Director of Admissions, Allegheny College, Meadville, PA 16335. Telephone: 814-332-4351. Fax: 814-337-0431.

ALLEGHENY UNIVERSITY OF THE HEALTH SCIENCES
PHILADELPHIA, PENNSYLVANIA

Entrance Moderately difficult **General** Independent, coed **Setting** Urban campus **Enrollment** 3,154 **Faculty** 12:1 **Application deadline** Rolling **Freshmen** 30% accepted **Housing** Yes **Tuition** $4060 **Undergraduates** 74% women, 43% part-time, 90% 25 or older, 1% Native American, 3% Hispanic, 14% black, 7% Asian or Pacific Islander **Most popular recent majors** Physician's assistant studies, nursing **Academic program** ESL program, Advanced placement, tutorials, honors program, summer session **Contact** Ms. Paula Greenberg, Director of Admissions, School of Health Sciences/Humanities, Allegheny University of the Health Sciences, 201 North 15th Street, Mail Stop 506, Philadelphia, PA 19102-1192. Telephone: 215-762-4293.

ALLENTOWN COLLEGE OF ST. FRANCIS DE SALES
CENTER VALLEY, PENNSYLVANIA

Entrance Moderately difficult **General** Independent Roman Catholic, comprehensive, coed **Setting** 300-acre suburban campus **Enrollment** 2,158 **Faculty** 14:1 **Application deadline** 8/1 **Freshmen** 81% accepted **Housing** Yes **Tuition** $11,750 **Undergraduates** 54% women, 34% part-time, 1% Native American, 3% Hispanic, 1% black, 1% Asian or Pacific Islander **Most popular recent majors** Accounting, theater arts/drama, nursing **Academic program** Average class size 18, advanced placement, accelerated degree program, tutorials, honors program, summer session, adult/continuing education programs, internships **Contact** Mr. James McCarthy, Director of Admissions, Allentown College of St. Francis de Sales, Center Valley, PA 18034-9568. Telephone: 610-282-1100 Ext. 1205.

ALVERNIA COLLEGE
READING, PENNSYLVANIA

Entrance Moderately difficult **General** Independent Roman Catholic, 4-year, coed **Setting** 85-acre suburban campus **Enrollment** 1,347 **Faculty** 14:1 **Application deadline** Rolling **Freshmen** 77% accepted **Housing** Yes **Tuition** $11,320 **Undergraduates** 65% women, 29% part-time, 44% 25 or older, 2% Hispanic, 2% black, 1% Asian or Pacific Islander **Most popular recent majors** Business administration/commerce/management, education, criminal justice **Academic program** ESL program, Advanced placement, accelerated degree program, tutorials, summer session, adult/continuing education programs, internships **Contact** Ms. Karin Allmendinger, Director of Admission, Alvernia College, Reading, PA 19607-1799. Telephone: 610-796-8220. Fax: 610-796-8336.

BAPTIST BIBLE COLLEGE OF PENNSYLVANIA
CLARKS SUMMIT, PENNSYLVANIA

Entrance Minimally difficult **General** Independent Baptist, comprehensive, coed **Setting** 143-acre suburban campus **Enrollment** 820 **Faculty** 19:1 **Application deadline** Rolling **Freshmen** 72% accepted **Housing** Yes **Tuition** $7530 **Undergraduates** 60% women, 8% part-time, 7% 25 or older, 1% Native American, 1% Hispanic, 1% black, 1% Asian or Pacific Islander **Academic program** Advanced placement, summer session, internships **Contact** Ms. Amy Yvonne Terrell, Applications Coordinator, Baptist Bible College of Pennsylvania, PO Box 800, Clarks Summit, PA 18411-1297. Telephone: 717-586-2400 Ext. 376. Fax: 717-585-9400.

BEAVER COLLEGE
GLENSIDE, PENNSYLVANIA

Entrance Moderately difficult **General** Independent, comprehensive, coed, affiliated with Presbyterian Church (U.S.A.) **Setting** 55-acre suburban campus **Enrollment** 2,567 **Application deadline** Rolling **Freshmen** 73% accepted **Housing** Yes **Tuition** $15,840 **Undergraduates** 67% women, 29% part-time, 32% 25 or older, 0% Native American, 2% Hispanic, 10% black, 3% Asian or Pacific Islander **Most popular recent majors** Biology/biological sciences, art/fine arts, psychology **Academic program** Advanced placement, accelerated degree program, self-designed majors, tutorials, honors program, summer session, adult/continuing education programs, internships **Contact** Mr. Mark Lapreziosa, Director of Admissions, Beaver College, Glenside, PA 19038-3295. Telephone: 215-572-2910. Fax: 215-572-4049.

BLOOMSBURG UNIVERSITY OF PENNSYLVANIA
BLOOMSBURG, PENNSYLVANIA

Entrance Moderately difficult **General** State-supported, comprehensive, coed **Setting** 192-acre small-town campus **Enrollment** 7,438 **Faculty** 17:1 **Application deadline** Rolling **Freshmen** 68% accepted **Housing** Yes **Tuition** $4278 **Undergraduates** 62% women, 6% part-time, 10% 25 or older, 0% Native American, 1% Hispanic, 2% black, 1% Asian or Pacific Islander **Most popular recent majors** Elementary education, business administration/commerce/management, early childhood education **Academic program** ESL program, Advanced placement, honors program, summer session, adult/continuing education programs, internships **Contact** Mr. Christopher Keller, Director of Admissions, Bloomsburg University of Pennsylvania, Ben Franklin Building, Room 10, Bloomsburg, PA 17815-1905. Telephone: 717-389-4316.

BRYN ATHYN COLLEGE OF THE NEW CHURCH
BRYN ATHYN, PENNSYLVANIA

Entrance Noncompetitive **General** Independent Swedenborgian, comprehensive, coed **Setting** 130-acre small-town campus **Enrollment** 145 **Application deadline** Rolling **Freshmen** 98% accepted **Housing** Yes **Tuition** $4920 **Undergraduates** 47% women, 12% part-time, 1% Hispanic, 2% black, 2% Asian or Pacific Islander **Academic program** Advanced placement, accelerated degree program, self-designed majors, tutorials, internships **Contact** Mr. Dan Synnestvedt, Director of Admissions, Bryn Athyn College of the New Church, Bryn Athyn, PA 19009-0717. Telephone: 215-938-2503. Fax: 215-938-2658.

BRYN MAWR COLLEGE
BRYN MAWR, PENNSYLVANIA

Entrance Most difficult **General** Independent, women only **Setting** 135-acre suburban campus **Enrollment** 1,886 **Faculty** 9:1 **Application deadline** 1/15 **Freshmen** 58% accepted **Housing** Yes **Tuition** $21,430 **Undergraduates** 3% part-time, 3% 25 or older, 1% Native American, 3% Hispanic, 4% black, 18% Asian or Pacific Islander **Most popular recent majors** History, political science/government, English **Academic program** Average class size 10, advanced placement, accelerated degree program, self-designed majors, tutorials, honors program, summer session, adult/continuing education programs **Contact** Ms. Nancy Monnich, Director of Admissions and Financial Aid, Bryn Mawr College, Bryn Mawr, PA 19010-2899. Telephone: 610-526-5152. Fax: 610-526-7471.

BUCKNELL UNIVERSITY

LEWISBURG, PENNSYLVANIA

Entrance Very difficult **General** Independent, comprehensive, coed **Setting** 300-acre small-town campus **Enrollment** 3,573 **Faculty** 13:1 **Application deadline** 1/1 **Freshmen** 49% accepted **Housing** Yes **Tuition** $21,210 **Undergraduates** 50% women, 1% part-time, 1% 25 or older, 0% Native American, 2% Hispanic, 2% black, 4% Asian or Pacific Islander **Most popular recent majors** Biology/biological sciences, economics, English **Academic program** Advanced placement, accelerated degree program, self-designed majors, honors program, summer session, internships **Contact** Mr. Mark D. Davies, Director of Admissions, Bucknell University, Lewisburg, PA 17837. Telephone: 717-524-1101. Fax: 717-524-3760.

CABRINI COLLEGE

RADNOR, PENNSYLVANIA

Entrance Moderately difficult **General** Independent Roman Catholic, comprehensive, coed **Setting** 112-acre suburban campus **Enrollment** 2,042 **Faculty** 13:1 **Application deadline** Rolling **Freshmen** 88% accepted **Housing** Yes **Tuition** $13,200 **Undergraduates** 71% women, 38% part-time, 40% 25 or older, 1% Native American, 2% Hispanic, 5% black, 2% Asian or Pacific Islander **Most popular recent majors** Education, business administration/commerce/management, communication **Academic program** Advanced placement, accelerated degree program, self-designed majors, tutorials, honors program, summer session, adult/continuing education programs, internships **Contact** Ms. Laurie Turns, Director of Admissions, Cabrini College, Radnor, PA 19087-3698. Telephone: 610-902-8552. Fax: 610-902-8309.

CALIFORNIA UNIVERSITY OF PENNSYLVANIA

CALIFORNIA, PENNSYLVANIA

Entrance Moderately difficult **General** State-supported, comprehensive, coed **Setting** 148-acre small-town campus **Enrollment** 5,636 **Faculty** 18:1 **Application deadline** 7/30 **Freshmen** 83% accepted **Housing** Yes **Tuition** $4475 **Undergraduates** 51% women, 13% part-time, 21% 25 or older, 1% Native American, 1% Hispanic, 5% black, 1% Asian or Pacific Islander **Most popular recent majors** Education, business administration/commerce/management, accounting **Academic program** Advanced placement, accelerated degree program, honors program, summer session, adult/continuing education programs, internships **Contact** Mr. Norman Hasbrouck, Dean of Enrollment Management and Academic Services, California University of Pennsylvania, Third Street, California, PA 15419-1394. Telephone: 412-938-4404. Fax: 412-938-4138.

CARLOW COLLEGE

PITTSBURGH, PENNSYLVANIA

Entrance Moderately difficult **General** Independent Roman Catholic, comprehensive, primarily women **Setting** 13-acre urban campus **Enrollment** 2,339 **Faculty** 13:1 **Application deadline** Rolling **Freshmen** 79% accepted **Housing** Yes **Tuition** $11,708 **Undergraduates** 92% women, 55% part-time, 66% 25 or older, 1% Native American, 1% Hispanic, 13% black, 1% Asian or Pacific Islander **Most popular recent majors** Nursing, communication, business administration/commerce/management **Academic program** Average class size 15, ESL program, advanced placement, accelerated degree program, self-designed majors, tutorials, honors program, summer session, adult/continuing education programs, internships **Contact** Ms. Carol Descak, Director of Admissions, Carlow College, 3333 Fifth Avenue, Pittsburgh, PA 15213-3165. Telephone: 412-578-6059. Fax: 412-578-6668.

CARNEGIE MELLON UNIVERSITY

PITTSBURGH, PENNSYLVANIA

Entrance Very difficult **General** Independent, coed **Setting** 103-acre urban campus **Enrollment** 7,758 **Faculty** 10:1 **Application deadline** 1/15 **Freshmen** 47% accepted **Housing** Yes **Tuition** $20,375 **Undergraduates** 32% women, 2% part-time, 1% 25 or older, 1% Native American, 4% Hispanic, 4% black, 17% Asian or Pacific Islander **Most popular recent majors** Electrical engineering, industrial administration, architecture **Academic program** Advanced placement, accelerated degree program, self-designed majors, honors program, summer session, adult/continuing education programs, internships **Contact** Mr. Michael Steidel, Director of Admissions, Carnegie Mellon University, 5000 Forbes Avenue, Pittsburgh, PA 15213-3891. Telephone: 412-268-2082. Fax: 412-268-7838.

CEDAR CREST COLLEGE
ALLENTOWN, PENNSYLVANIA

Entrance Moderately difficult **General** Independent, comprehensive, primarily women, affiliated with United Church of Christ **Setting** 84-acre suburban campus **Enrollment** 1,699 **Faculty** 12:1 **Application deadline** Rolling **Freshmen** 77% accepted **Housing** Yes **Tuition** $15,820 **Undergraduates** 94% women, 48% part-time, 37% 25 or older, 0% Native American, 1% Hispanic, 2% black, 2% Asian or Pacific Islander **Most popular recent majors** Biology/biological sciences, psychology, nursing **Academic program** Advanced placement, accelerated degree program, self-designed majors, tutorials, honors program, summer session, adult/continuing education programs, internships **Contact** Ms. Judith A. Neyhart, Vice President for Enrollment Management, Cedar Crest College, Allentown, PA 18104-6196. Telephone: 610-740-3780. Fax: 610-740-3786.

CHATHAM COLLEGE
PITTSBURGH, PENNSYLVANIA

Entrance Moderately difficult **General** Independent, comprehensive, primarily women **Setting** 34-acre urban campus **Enrollment** 801 **Faculty** 9:1 **Application deadline** Rolling **Freshmen** 87% accepted **Housing** Yes **Tuition** $15,340 **Undergraduates** 12% part-time, 25% 25 or older, 1% Hispanic, 9% black, 1% Asian or Pacific Islander **Most popular recent majors** Psychology, English, biology/biological sciences **Academic program** Advanced placement, accelerated degree program, self-designed majors, tutorials, honors program, summer session, adult/continuing education programs, internships **Contact** Dr. Annette Giovengo, Acting Vice President for Admissions, Chatham College, Woodland Road, Pittsburgh, PA 15232-2826. Telephone: 412-365-1290. Fax: 412-365-1609.

CHESTNUT HILL COLLEGE
PHILADELPHIA, PENNSYLVANIA

Entrance Moderately difficult **General** Independent Roman Catholic, comprehensive, women only **Setting** 45-acre suburban campus **Enrollment** 1,340 **Faculty** 9:1 **Application deadline** Rolling **Freshmen** 83% accepted **Housing** Yes **Tuition** $13,148 **Undergraduates** 46% part-time, 22% 25 or older, 0% Native American, 6% Hispanic, 21% black, 3% Asian or Pacific Islander **Most popular recent majors** Elementary education, early childhood education, English **Academic program** Advanced placement, accelerated degree program, self-designed majors, honors program, summer session, adult/continuing education programs, internships **Contact** Sr. Margaret Anne Birtwistle, SSJ, Director of Admissions, Chestnut Hill College, Philadelphia, PA 19118-2695. Telephone: 215-248-7001. Fax: 215-248-7056.

CHEYNEY UNIVERSITY OF PENNSYLVANIA
CHEYNEY, PENNSYLVANIA

Entrance Minimally difficult **General** State-supported, comprehensive, coed **Setting** 275-acre suburban campus **Enrollment** 1,360 **Faculty** 12:1 **Application deadline** Rolling **Freshmen** 71% accepted **Housing** Yes **Tuition** $4023 **Undergraduates** 50% women, 4% part-time, 15% 25 or older, 0% Native American, 1% Hispanic, 98% black, 1% Asian or Pacific Islander **Most popular recent majors** Education, social science, business administration/commerce/management **Academic program** Summer session, adult/continuing education programs, internships **Contact** Ms. Sharon Cannon, Director of Admissions, Cheyney University of Pennsylvania, Cheyney, PA 19319. Telephone: 610-399-2275. Fax: 610-399-2099.

CLARION UNIVERSITY OF PENNSYLVANIA
CLARION, PENNSYLVANIA

Entrance Minimally difficult **General** State-supported, comprehensive, coed **Setting** 100-acre rural campus **Enrollment** 5,886 **Faculty** 18:1 **Application deadline** Rolling **Freshmen** 89% accepted **Housing** Yes **Tuition** $4622 **Undergraduates** 61% women, 10% part-time, 19% 25 or older, 0% Native American, 0% Hispanic, 4% black, 0% Asian or Pacific Islander **Most popular recent majors** Elementary education, secondary education, communication **Academic program** Advanced placement, accelerated degree program, tutorials, honors program, summer session, adult/continuing education programs, internships **Contact** Mr. John S. Shropshire, Dean of Enrollment Management and Academic Records, Clarion University of Pennsylvania, Clarion, PA 16214. Telephone: 814-226-2306. Fax: 814-226-2030.

COLLEGE MISERICORDIA
DALLAS, PENNSYLVANIA

Entrance Moderately difficult **General** Independent Roman Catholic, comprehensive, coed **Setting** 100-acre small-town campus **Enrollment** 1,736 **Faculty** 13:1 **Application deadline** Rolling **Freshmen** 61% accepted **Housing** Yes **Tuition** $13,830 **Undergraduates** 73% women, 24% part-time, 23% 25 or older, 0% Native American, 1% Hispanic, 1% black, 1% Asian or Pacific Islander **Most popular recent majors** Physical therapy, occupational therapy, elementary education **Academic program** Average class size 28, ESL program, advanced placement, accelerated degree program, self-designed majors, honors program, summer session, adult/continuing education programs, internships **Contact** Ms. Jane Dessoye, Executive Director of Admissions and Financial Aid, College Misericordia, Dallas, PA 18612-1098. Telephone: 717-674-6460. Fax: 717-675-2441.

THE CURTIS INSTITUTE OF MUSIC
PHILADELPHIA, PENNSYLVANIA

Entrance Most difficult **General** Independent, comprehensive, specialized, coed **Setting** Urban campus **Enrollment** 165 **Application deadline** 1/15 **Freshmen** 7% accepted **Tuition** $695 **Undergraduates** 52% women, 0% part-time **Academic program** Advanced placement, accelerated degree program **Contact** Mr. Christopher Hodges, Admissions Officer, The Curtis Institute of Music, 1726 Locust Street, Philadelphia, PA 19103-6107. Telephone: 215-893-5262.

DELAWARE VALLEY COLLEGE
DOYLESTOWN, PENNSYLVANIA

Entrance Moderately difficult **General** Independent, 4-year, coed **Setting** 600-acre suburban campus **Enrollment** 1,380 **Faculty** 18:1 **Application deadline** Rolling **Freshmen** 73% accepted **Housing** Yes **Tuition** $14,929 **Undergraduates** 50% women, 30% part-time, 29% 25 or older, 0% Native American, 1% Hispanic, 2% black, 1% Asian or Pacific Islander **Most popular recent majors** Business administration/commerce/management, ornamental horticulture, animal sciences **Academic program** Advanced placement, tutorials, honors program, summer session, adult/continuing education programs, internships **Contact** Mr. Stephen W. Zenko, Director of Admissions, Delaware Valley College, Doylestown, PA 18901-2697. Telephone: 215-345-1500 Ext. 2211. Fax: 215-345-5277.

DICKINSON COLLEGE
CARLISLE, PENNSYLVANIA

Entrance Very difficult **General** Independent, 4-year, coed **Setting** 103-acre suburban campus **Enrollment** 1,709 **Faculty** 10:1 **Application deadline** 2/15 **Freshmen** 83% accepted **Housing** Yes **Tuition** $21,600 **Undergraduates** 56% women, 0% part-time, 0% 25 or older, 0% Native American, 2% Hispanic, 2% black, 3% Asian or Pacific Islander **Most popular recent majors** English, political science/government, psychology **Academic program** Average class size 18, advanced placement, accelerated degree program, self-designed majors, tutorials, summer session, adult/continuing education programs, internships **Contact** Mr. R. Russell Shunk, Dean of Admissions, Dickinson College, PO Box 1773, Carlisle, PA 17013-2896. Telephone: 717-245-1231. Fax: 717-245-1442.

DREXEL UNIVERSITY
PHILADELPHIA, PENNSYLVANIA

Entrance Moderately difficult **General** Independent, coed **Setting** 38-acre urban campus **Enrollment** 9,590 **Faculty** 12:1 **Application deadline** 3/1 **Freshmen** 74% accepted **Housing** Yes **Tuition** $16,114 **Undergraduates** 33% women, 25% part-time, 23% 25 or older, 1% Native American, 2% Hispanic, 10% black, 10% Asian or Pacific Islander **Most popular recent majors** Electrical engineering, accounting, finance/banking **Academic program** Advanced placement, tutorials, honors program, summer session, adult/continuing education programs, internships **Contact** Mr. Gary Hamme, Dean of Enrollment Management and Career Services, Drexel University, Room 220, Philadelphia, PA 19104-2875. Telephone: 215-895-2400. Fax: 215-895-5939.

DUQUESNE UNIVERSITY
PITTSBURGH, PENNSYLVANIA

Entrance Moderately difficult **General** Independent Roman Catholic, coed **Setting** 40-acre urban campus **Enrollment** 9,400 **Faculty** 16:1 **Application deadline** 7/1 **Freshmen** 65% accepted **Housing** Yes **Tuition** $14,066 **Undergraduates** 57% women, 16% part-time, 17% 25 or older, 1% Native American, 2% Hispanic, 4% black, 3% Asian or Pacific Islander **Most popular recent majors** Health science, business administration/commerce/management, pharmacy/pharmaceutical sciences **Academic program** Average class size 33, advanced placement, accelerated degree program, self-designed majors, tutorials, honors program, summer session, adult/continuing education programs, internships **Contact** Office of Admissions, Duquesne University, 600 Forbes Avenue, Pittsburgh, PA 15282-0001. Telephone: 412-396-6220. Fax: 412-396-5644.

EASTERN COLLEGE
ST. DAVIDS, PENNSYLVANIA

Entrance Moderately difficult **General** Independent American Baptist, comprehensive, coed **Setting** 107-acre small-town campus **Enrollment**

2,348 **Faculty** 15:1 **Application deadline** Rolling **Freshmen** 88% accepted **Housing** Yes **Tuition** $12,700 **Undergraduates** 67% women, 20% part-time, 41% 25 or older, 1% Native American, 2% Hispanic, 12% black, 1% Asian or Pacific Islander **Most popular recent majors** Business administration/commerce/management, elementary education, nursing **Academic program** Advanced placement, accelerated degree program, self-designed majors, tutorials, honors program, summer session, adult/continuing education programs, internships **Contact** Mr. Mark Seymour, Director for Enrollment Management, Eastern College, St. Davids, PA 19087-3696. Telephone: 610-341-5967. Fax: 610-341-1723.

EAST STROUDSBURG UNIVERSITY OF PENNSYLVANIA
EAST STROUDSBURG, PENNSYLVANIA

Entrance Moderately difficult **General** State-supported, comprehensive, coed **Setting** 183-acre small-town campus **Enrollment** 5,552 **Faculty** 19:1 **Application deadline** 3/1 **Freshmen** 67% accepted **Housing** Yes **Tuition** $4322 **Undergraduates** 57% women, 13% part-time, 18% 25 or older, 0% Native American, 3% Hispanic, 2% black, 1% Asian or Pacific Islander **Most popular recent majors** Elementary education, physical education, business administration/commerce/management **Academic program** Average class size 40, advanced placement, accelerated degree program, self-designed majors, honors program, summer session, adult/continuing education programs, internships **Contact** Mr. Alan T. Chesterton, Director of Admission, East Stroudsburg University of Pennsylvania, East Stroudsburg, PA 18301-2999. Telephone: 717-422-3542.

EDINBORO UNIVERSITY OF PENNSYLVANIA
EDINBORO, PENNSYLVANIA

Entrance Moderately difficult **General** State-supported, comprehensive, coed **Setting** 585-acre small-town campus **Enrollment** 7,178 **Faculty** 17:1 **Application deadline** Rolling **Freshmen** 78% accepted **Housing** Yes **Tuition** $4193 **Undergraduates** 57% women, 16% part-time, 20% 25 or older, 1% Native American, 1% Hispanic, 5% black, 1% Asian or Pacific Islander **Most popular recent majors** Elementary education, criminal justice, psychology **Academic program** Advanced placement, accelerated degree program, self-designed majors, honors program, summer session, adult/continuing education programs, internships **Contact** Mr. Terrence Carlin, Assistant Vice President for Admissions, Edinboro University of Pennsylvania, Edinboro, PA 16444. Telephone: 814-732-2761.

ELIZABETHTOWN COLLEGE
ELIZABETHTOWN, PENNSYLVANIA

Entrance Moderately difficult **General** Independent, 4-year, coed, affiliated with Church of the Brethren **Setting** 185-acre small-town campus **Enrollment** 1,728 **Faculty** 15:1 **Application deadline** Rolling **Freshmen** 74% accepted **Housing** Yes **Tuition** $16,930 **Undergraduates** 66% women, 12% part-time, 0% Native American, 1% Hispanic, 2% black, 2% Asian or Pacific Islander **Most popular recent majors** Business administration/commerce/management, education, communication **Academic program** Average class size 23, advanced placement, summer session, adult/continuing education programs, internships **Contact** Mr. Gordon Mck. Bateman, Dean of Admissions and Enrollment Management, Elizabethtown College, Elizabethtown, PA 17022-2298. Telephone: 717-361-1365. Fax: 717-361-1365.

FRANKLIN AND MARSHALL COLLEGE
LANCASTER, PENNSYLVANIA

Entrance Very difficult **General** Independent, 4-year, coed **Setting** 125-acre suburban campus **Enrollment** 1,822 **Faculty** 11:1 **Application deadline** 2/1 **Freshmen** 59% accepted **Housing** Yes **Tuition** $27,570 **Undergraduates** 48% women, 3% part-time, 1% 25 or older, 1% Native American, 3% Hispanic, 3% black, 6% Asian or Pacific Islander **Most popular recent majors** Political science/government, English, biology/biological sciences **Academic program** Advanced placement, accelerated degree program, self-designed majors, tutorials, summer session, internships **Contact** Mr. Peter W. VanBuskirk, Dean of Admissions, Franklin and Marshall College, PO Box 3003, Lancaster, PA 17604-3003. Telephone: 717-291-3953. Fax: 717-291-4389.

GANNON UNIVERSITY
ERIE, PENNSYLVANIA

Entrance Moderately difficult **General** Independent Roman Catholic, comprehensive, coed **Setting** 13-acre urban campus **Enrollment** 3,327 **Faculty** 13:1 **Application deadline** Rolling **Freshmen** 76% accepted **Housing** Yes **Tuition** $11,694 **Undergraduates** 57% women, 16% part-time, 23% 25 or older, 1% Hispanic, 3% black, 2% Asian or Pacific Islander **Most popular recent majors** Biology/biological sciences, criminal justice, elementary education **Academic program**

Average class size 24, advanced placement, accelerated degree program, tutorials, honors program, summer session, adult/continuing education programs, internships **Contact** Ms. Beth Nemenz, Director of Admissions, Gannon University, University Square, Erie, PA 16541. Telephone: 814-871-7240. Fax: 814-871-5803.

GENEVA COLLEGE

BEAVER FALLS, PENNSYLVANIA

Entrance Moderately difficult **General** Independent, comprehensive, coed, affiliated with Reformed Presbyterian Church of North America **Setting** 55-acre suburban campus **Enrollment** 1,782 **Faculty** 18:1 **Application deadline** Rolling **Freshmen** 84% accepted **Housing** Yes **Tuition** $11,534 **Undergraduates** 53% women, 15% part-time, 1% Native American, 1% Hispanic, 14% black, 1% Asian or Pacific Islander **Most popular recent majors** Elementary education, business administration/commerce/management, biology/biological sciences **Academic program** Average class size 35, advanced placement, accelerated degree program, self-designed majors, tutorials, honors program, summer session, adult/continuing education programs, internships **Contact** Mr. David Layton, Director of Admissions, Geneva College, Beaver Falls, PA 15010-3599. Telephone: 412-847-6500. Fax: 412-847-6776.

GETTYSBURG COLLEGE

GETTYSBURG, PENNSYLVANIA

Entrance Very difficult **General** Independent, 4-year, coed **Setting** 200-acre small-town campus **Enrollment** 2,000 **Faculty** 12:1 **Application deadline** 2/15 **Freshmen** 66% accepted **Housing** Yes **Tuition** $22,430 **Undergraduates** 50% women, 1% part-time, 1% 25 or older, 1% Native American, 2% Hispanic, 3% black, 3% Asian or Pacific Islander **Most popular recent majors** Business administration/commerce/management, political science/government, psychology **Academic program** Average class size 20, advanced placement, accelerated degree program, self-designed majors, tutorials, honors program, adult/continuing education programs, internships **Contact** Mr. Delwin K. Gustafson, Dean of Admissions, Gettysburg College, Gettysburg, PA 17325-1411. Telephone: 717-337-6100. Fax: 717-337-6145.

GRATZ COLLEGE

MELROSE PARK, PENNSYLVANIA

Entrance Noncompetitive **General** Independent Jewish, comprehensive, specialized, coed **Setting** 28-acre suburban campus **Enrollment** 104 **Faculty** 3:1 **Application deadline** Rolling **Freshmen** 100% accepted **Tuition** $6900 **Undergraduates** 68% women, 58% part-time, 89% 25 or older, 0% Native American, 0% Hispanic, 0% black, 0% Asian or Pacific Islander **Academic program** Summer session, adult/continuing education programs **Contact** Ms. Evelyn Klein, Director of Admissions, Gratz College, Melrose Park, PA 19027. Telephone: 215-635-7300. Fax: 215-635-7320.

GROVE CITY COLLEGE

GROVE CITY, PENNSYLVANIA

Entrance Very difficult **General** Independent Presbyterian, comprehensive, coed **Setting** 150-acre small-town campus **Enrollment** 2,329 **Faculty** 21:1 **Application deadline** 2/15 **Freshmen** 48% accepted **Housing** Yes **Tuition** $6576 **Undergraduates** 49% women, 1% part-time, 1% 25 or older, 0% Native American, 0% Hispanic, 0% black, 1% Asian or Pacific Islander **Most popular recent majors** Business administration/commerce/management, mechanical engineering, elementary education **Academic program** Average class size 64, advanced placement, self-designed majors, summer session, internships **Contact** Mr. Jeffrey C. Mincey, Director of Admissions, Grove City College, Grove City, PA 16127-2104. Telephone: 412-458-2100.

GWYNEDD-MERCY COLLEGE

GWYNEDD VALLEY, PENNSYLVANIA

Entrance Moderately difficult **General** Independent Roman Catholic, comprehensive, coed **Setting** 170-acre suburban campus **Enrollment** 1,721 **Faculty** 13:1 **Application deadline** 7/1 **Freshmen** 55% accepted **Housing** Yes **Tuition** $12,280 **Undergraduates** 82% women, 61% part-time, 67% 25 or older, 1% Native American, 2% Hispanic, 6% black, 6% Asian or Pacific Islander **Most popular recent majors** Nursing, business administration/commerce/management, elementary education **Academic program** Advanced placement, accelerated degree program, tutorials, honors program, summer session, adult/continuing education programs, internships **Contact** Ms. Jacqueline Williams, Director of Admissions, Gwynedd-Mercy College, Gwynedd Valley, PA 19437-0901. Telephone: 215-641-5510. Fax: 215-641-5556.

HAHNEMANN UNIVERSITY

SEE ALLEGHENY UNIVERSITY OF THE HEALTH SCIENCES

HAVERFORD COLLEGE

HAVERFORD, PENNSYLVANIA

Entrance Most difficult **General** Independent, 4-year, coed **Setting** 216-acre suburban campus **Enrollment** 1,137 **Faculty** 10:1 **Application deadline** 1/15 **Freshmen** 35% accepted **Housing** Yes **Tuition** $21,740 **Undergraduates** 52% women, 0% part-time, 1% 25 or older, 5% Hispanic, 5% black, 8% Asian or Pacific Islander **Most popular recent majors** Biology/biological sciences, history, English **Academic program** Average class size 19, advanced placement, accelerated degree program, self-designed majors, tutorials **Contact** Ms. Delsie Phillips, Director of Admissions, Haverford College, Haverford, PA 19041-1392. Telephone: 610-896-1350. Fax: 610-896-1338.

HOLY FAMILY COLLEGE

PHILADELPHIA, PENNSYLVANIA

Entrance Moderately difficult **General** Independent Roman Catholic, comprehensive, coed **Setting** 47-acre suburban campus **Enrollment** 2,590 **Faculty** 11:1 **Application deadline** Rolling **Freshmen** 78% accepted **Tuition** $10,620 **Undergraduates** 76% women, 51% part-time, 48% 25 or older, 1% Hispanic, 4% black, 2% Asian or Pacific Islander **Most popular recent majors** Nursing, elementary education, business administration/commerce/management **Academic program** Advanced placement, accelerated degree program, tutorials, honors program, summer session, adult/continuing education programs, internships **Contact** Ms. Linda DiSandro, Associate Director of Admissions, Holy Family College, Philadelphia, PA 19114-2094. Telephone: 215-637-3050.

IMMACULATA COLLEGE

IMMACULATA, PENNSYLVANIA

Entrance Moderately difficult **General** Independent Roman Catholic, comprehensive, primarily women **Setting** 400-acre suburban campus **Enrollment** 2,391 **Faculty** 12:1 **Application deadline** Rolling **Freshmen** 91% accepted **Housing** Yes **Tuition** $12,115 **Undergraduates** 88% women, 62% part-time, 76% 25 or older, 0% Native American, 1% Hispanic, 4% black, 1% Asian or Pacific Islander **Most popular recent majors** Psychology, business administration/commerce/management, biology/biological sciences **Academic program** Average class size 20, advanced placement, accelerated degree program, self-designed majors, honors program, summer session, adult/continuing education programs, internships **Contact** Mr. Ken R. Rasp, Dean of Enrollment Management, Immaculata College, Immaculata, PA 19345-0900. Telephone: 610-647-4400. Fax: 610-251-1668.

INDIANA UNIVERSITY OF PENNSYLVANIA

INDIANA, PENNSYLVANIA

Entrance Moderately difficult **General** State-supported, coed **Setting** 341-acre small-town campus **Enrollment** 13,680 **Faculty** 19:1 **Application deadline** Rolling **Freshmen** 63% accepted **Housing** Yes **Tuition** $4204 **Undergraduates** 54% women, 7% part-time, 13% 25 or older, 1% Native American, 1% Hispanic, 5% black, 1% Asian or Pacific Islander **Most popular recent majors** Criminology, elementary education, accounting **Academic program** Advanced placement, accelerated degree program, honors program, summer session, adult/continuing education programs, internships **Contact** Mr. William Nunn, Dean of Admissions, Indiana University of Pennsylvania, 216 Pratt Hall, Indiana, PA 15705. Telephone: 412-357-2230.

JUNIATA COLLEGE

HUNTINGDON, PENNSYLVANIA

Entrance Moderately difficult **General** Independent, 4-year, coed **Setting** 850-acre small-town campus **Enrollment** 1,161 **Faculty** 13:1 **Application deadline** Rolling **Freshmen** 85% accepted **Housing** Yes **Tuition** $17,260 **Undergraduates** 53% women, 3% part-time, 3% 25 or older, 0% Native American, 1% Hispanic, 1% black, 1% Asian or Pacific Islander **Most popular recent majors** Business administration/commerce/management, education, natural sciences **Academic program** Advanced placement, accelerated degree program, self-designed majors, tutorials, honors program, summer session, adult/continuing education programs, internships **Contact** Mr. David Hawsey, Dean of Enrollment, Juniata College, Huntingdon, PA 16652-2119. Telephone: 814-641-3420 Ext. 420. Fax: 814-641-3100.

KING'S COLLEGE

WILKES-BARRE, PENNSYLVANIA

Entrance Moderately difficult **General** Independent Roman Catholic, comprehensive, coed **Setting** 48-acre suburban campus **Enrollment** 2,279 **Faculty** 17:1 **Application deadline** Rolling

Freshmen 74% accepted **Housing** Yes **Tuition** $14,000 **Undergraduates** 51% women, 19% part-time, 22% 25 or older, 0% Native American, 1% Hispanic, 2% black, 1% Asian or Pacific Islander **Most popular recent majors** Accounting, communication, business administration/commerce/management **Academic program** Average class size 22, advanced placement, self-designed majors, tutorials, honors program, summer session, adult/continuing education programs, internships **Contact** Mr. Daniel P. Conry, Dean of Admissions, King's College, Wilkes-Barre, PA 18711-0801. Telephone: 717-826-5858. Fax: 717-826-5971.

KUTZTOWN UNIVERSITY OF PENNSYLVANIA

KUTZTOWN, PENNSYLVANIA

Entrance Moderately difficult **General** State-supported, comprehensive, coed **Setting** 325-acre small-town campus **Enrollment** 7,843 **Faculty** 19:1 **Application deadline** Rolling **Freshmen** 73% accepted **Housing** Yes **Tuition** $4219 **Undergraduates** 58% women, 12% part-time, 12% 25 or older, 1% Native American, 2% Hispanic, 3% black, 1% Asian or Pacific Islander **Most popular recent majors** Marketing/retailing/merchandising, early childhood education **Academic program** Average class size 30, advanced placement, accelerated degree program, self-designed majors, tutorials, honors program, summer session, adult/continuing education programs, internships **Contact** Ms. Valerie Reidout, Interim Director of Admissions, Kutztown University of Pennsylvania, Kutztown, PA 19530. Telephone: 610-683-4060. Fax: 610-683-1375.

LAFAYETTE COLLEGE

EASTON, PENNSYLVANIA

Entrance Very difficult **General** Independent, 4-year, coed, affiliated with Presbyterian Church (U.S.A.) **Setting** 110-acre suburban campus **Enrollment** 2,185 **Faculty** 11:1 **Application deadline** 1/1 **Freshmen** 62% accepted **Housing** Yes **Tuition** $21,202 **Undergraduates** 44% women, 9% part-time, 1% Native American, 2% Hispanic, 4% black, 4% Asian or Pacific Islander **Most popular recent majors** Biology/biological sciences, business economics, psychology **Academic program** Advanced placement, accelerated degree program, self-designed majors, tutorials, honors program, summer session, adult/continuing education programs, internships **Contact** Dr. Gary Ripple, Director of Admissions, Lafayette College, Easton, PA 18042-1798. Telephone: 610-250-5100. Fax: 610-250-5355.

LANCASTER BIBLE COLLEGE

LANCASTER, PENNSYLVANIA

Entrance Minimally difficult **General** Independent nondenominational, comprehensive, coed **Setting** 100-acre suburban campus **Enrollment** 682 **Faculty** 14:1 **Application deadline** Rolling **Freshmen** 98% accepted **Housing** Yes **Tuition** $8550 **Undergraduates** 54% women, 25% part-time, 30% 25 or older, 1% Hispanic, 1% black, 2% Asian or Pacific Islander **Academic program** Average class size 45, advanced placement, summer session, adult/continuing education programs, internships **Contact** Mrs. Joanne Roper, Director of Admissions, Lancaster Bible College, Lancaster, PA 17601-5036. Telephone: 717-569-8271. Fax: 717-560-8213.

LA ROCHE COLLEGE

PITTSBURGH, PENNSYLVANIA

Entrance Minimally difficult **General** Independent, comprehensive, coed, affiliated with Roman Catholic Church **Setting** 80-acre suburban campus **Enrollment** 1,641 **Application deadline** Rolling **Freshmen** 91% accepted **Housing** Yes **Tuition** $10,400 **Undergraduates** 67% women, 47% part-time, 52% 25 or older, 1% Native American, 1% Hispanic, 3% black, 1% Asian or Pacific Islander **Most popular recent majors** Nursing, business administration/commerce/management, psychology **Academic program** Advanced placement, tutorials, honors program, summer session, adult/continuing education programs, internships **Contact** Mr. Brett Freshour, Director of Enrollment Services, La Roche College, Pittsburgh, PA 15237-5898. Telephone: 412-367-9300 Ext. 185. Fax: 412-367-9368.

LA SALLE UNIVERSITY

PHILADELPHIA, PENNSYLVANIA

Entrance Moderately difficult **General** Independent Roman Catholic, comprehensive, coed **Setting** 100-acre urban campus **Enrollment** 5,130 **Faculty** 14:1 **Application deadline** 4/1 **Freshmen** 80% accepted **Housing** Yes **Tuition** $14,850 **Undergraduates** 54% women, 28% part-time, 2% 25 or older, 0% Native American, 3% Hispanic, 6% black, 4% Asian or Pacific Islander **Most popular recent majors** Accounting, (pre)medicine sequence, communication **Academic program** Advanced placement, accelerated degree program, self-designed majors, tutorials, honors program, summer session, adult/continuing education programs, internships **Contact** Mr. Christopher P. Lydon, Director of Admission and Financial Aid, La Salle University, 1900 West Olney Avenue, Philadelphia, PA 19141-1199. Telephone: 215-951-1500. Fax: 215-951-1488.

LEBANON VALLEY COLLEGE
ANNVILLE, PENNSYLVANIA

Entrance Moderately difficult **General** Independent United Methodist, 4-year, coed **Setting** 200-acre small-town campus **Enrollment** 1,879 **Faculty** 15:1 **Application deadline** Rolling **Freshmen** 75% accepted **Housing** Yes **Tuition** $15,936 **Undergraduates** 60% women, 22% part-time, 22% 25 or older, 1% Native American, 1% Hispanic, 2% black, 2% Asian or Pacific Islander **Most popular recent majors** Business administration/commerce/management, elementary education, biology/biological sciences **Academic program** Advanced placement, accelerated degree program, self-designed majors, honors program, summer session, adult/continuing education programs, internships **Contact** Mr. William J. Brown, Dean of Admission and Financial Aid, Lebanon Valley College, Annville, PA 17003-0501. Telephone: 717-867-6181. Fax: 717-867-6124.

LEHIGH UNIVERSITY
BETHLEHEM, PENNSYLVANIA

Entrance Very difficult **General** Independent, coed **Setting** 1,600-acre suburban campus **Enrollment** 6,275 **Faculty** 11:1 **Application deadline** 1/15 **Freshmen** 54% accepted **Housing** Yes **Tuition** $21,350 **Undergraduates** 38% women, 5% part-time, 1% 25 or older, 1% Native American, 2% Hispanic, 3% black, 5% Asian or Pacific Islander **Most popular recent majors** Mechanical engineering, civil engineering, accounting **Academic program** Advanced placement, accelerated degree program, self-designed majors, tutorials, honors program, summer session, adult/continuing education programs, internships **Contact** Mrs. Lorna Hunter, Dean of Admissions and Financial Aid, Lehigh University, Bethlehem, PA 18015-3094. Telephone: 610-758-3100. Fax: 610-758-4361.

LINCOLN UNIVERSITY
LINCOLN UNIVERSITY, PENNSYLVANIA

Entrance Minimally difficult **General** State-related, comprehensive, coed **Setting** 442-acre rural campus **Enrollment** 1,810 **Faculty** 11:1 **Application deadline** Rolling **Freshmen** 64% accepted **Housing** Yes **Tuition** $4180 **Undergraduates** 59% women, 5% part-time, 5% 25 or older, 0% Native American, 1% Hispanic, 94% black, 1% Asian or Pacific Islander **Academic program** Advanced placement, accelerated degree program, self-designed majors, honors program, summer session, adult/continuing education programs, internships **Contact** Dr. Robert Laney Jr., Director of Admissions, Lincoln University, Lincoln University, PA 19352. Telephone: 610-932-8300 Ext. 306.

LOCK HAVEN UNIVERSITY OF PENNSYLVANIA
LOCK HAVEN, PENNSYLVANIA

Entrance Moderately difficult **General** State-supported, comprehensive, coed **Setting** 135-acre small-town campus **Enrollment** 3,549 **Faculty** 19:1 **Application deadline** Rolling **Freshmen** 76% accepted **Housing** Yes **Tuition** $4062 **Undergraduates** 55% women, 8% part-time, 11% 25 or older **Most popular recent majors** Education, health science, biology/biological sciences **Academic program** Advanced placement, accelerated degree program, self-designed majors, tutorials, honors program, summer session, adult/continuing education programs, internships **Contact** Mr. James Reeser, Interim Director of Admission, Lock Haven University of Pennsylvania, Lock Haven, PA 17745-2390. Telephone: 717-893-2027. Fax: 717-893-2201.

LYCOMING COLLEGE
WILLIAMSPORT, PENNSYLVANIA

Entrance Moderately difficult **General** Independent United Methodist, 4-year, coed **Setting** 35-acre small-town campus **Enrollment** 1,489 **Faculty** 13:1 **Application deadline** 4/1 **Freshmen** 75% accepted **Housing** Yes **Tuition** $16,160 **Undergraduates** 55% women, 6% part-time, 10% 25 or older, 1% Native American, 2% Hispanic, 2% black, 1% Asian or Pacific Islander **Most popular recent majors** Psychology, biology/biological sciences, business administration/commerce/management **Academic program** Advanced placement, accelerated degree program, self-designed majors, tutorials, honors program, summer session, internships **Contact** Mr. James Spencer, Dean of Admissions and Financial Aid, Lycoming College, Williamsport, PA 17701-5192. Telephone: 717-321-4026. Fax: 717-321-4337.

MANSFIELD UNIVERSITY OF PENNSYLVANIA
MANSFIELD, PENNSYLVANIA

Entrance Moderately difficult **General** State-supported, comprehensive, coed **Setting** 205-acre small-town campus **Enrollment** 2,897 **Freshmen** 61% accepted **Housing** Yes **Tuition** $4454 **Undergraduates** 58% women, 16% part-time, 13% 25 or older, 1% Native American, 1% Hispanic, 4% black, 1% Asian or Pacific Islander **Most popular recent majors** Criminal justice, elementary education, business administration/commerce/management **Academic program** Advanced placement, accelerated degree program, self-designed majors, honors program, summer session, adult/continuing education programs, internships **Contact** Mr. Brian D. Barden, Interim Director of Enrollment Services, Mansfield University of Pennsylvania, Beecher House, Mansfield, PA 16933. Telephone: 717-662-4813.

MARYWOOD COLLEGE
SCRANTON, PENNSYLVANIA

Entrance Moderately difficult **General** Independent Roman Catholic, comprehensive, coed **Setting** 115-acre suburban campus **Enrollment** 2,926 **Faculty** 12:1 **Application deadline** Rolling **Freshmen** 75% accepted **Housing** Yes **Tuition** $13,649 **Undergraduates** 75% women, 19% part-time, 26% 25 or older, 1% Native American, 2% Hispanic, 1% black, 1% Asian or Pacific Islander **Most popular recent majors** Elementary education, graphic arts, business administration/commerce/management **Academic program** Average class size 25, advanced placement, accelerated degree program, self-designed majors, honors program, summer session, adult/continuing education programs, internships **Contact** Mr. Fred R. Brooks Jr., Director of Admissions, Marywood College, Scranton, PA 18509-1598. Telephone: 717-348-6234. Fax: 717-348-1817.

MEDICAL COLLEGE OF PENNSYLVANIA AND HAHNEMANN UNIVERSITY
SEE ALLEGHENY UNIVERSITY OF THE HEALTH SCIENCES

MERCYHURST COLLEGE
ERIE, PENNSYLVANIA

Entrance Moderately difficult **General** Independent Roman Catholic, comprehensive, coed **Setting** 88-acre suburban campus **Enrollment** 2,712 **Faculty** 20:1 **Application deadline** Rolling **Freshmen** 76% accepted **Housing** Yes **Tuition** $12,942 **Undergraduates** 53% women, 20% part-time, 17% 25 or older, 1% Native American, 2% Hispanic, 6% black, 2% Asian or Pacific Islander **Most popular recent majors** Business administration/commerce/management, archaeology, music **Academic program** Advanced placement, accelerated degree program, self-designed majors, tutorials, honors program, summer session, adult/continuing education programs, internships **Contact** Mr. Andrew Roth, Dean of Enrollment Services, Mercyhurst College, Erie, PA 16546. Telephone: 814-824-2241. Fax: 814-824-2438.

MESSIAH COLLEGE
GRANTHAM, PENNSYLVANIA

Entrance Moderately difficult **General** Independent, 4-year, coed, affiliated with Brethren in Christ Church **Setting** 350-acre small-town campus **Enrollment** 2,517 **Faculty** 15:1 **Application deadline** Rolling **Freshmen** 85% accepted **Housing** Yes **Tuition** $12,990 **Undergraduates** 61% women, 4% part-time, 6% 25 or older, 1% Native American, 2% Hispanic, 1% black, 2% Asian or Pacific Islander **Most popular recent majors** Nursing, elementary education, biology/biological sciences **Academic program** Average class size 26, ESL program, advanced placement, accelerated degree program, self-designed majors, tutorials, honors program, summer session, adult/continuing education programs, internships **Contact** Mr. William G. Strausbaugh, Vice President for Enrollment Management, Messiah College, Grantham, PA 17027. Telephone: 717-691-6000. Fax: 717-796-5374.

MILLERSVILLE UNIVERSITY OF PENNSYLVANIA
MILLERSVILLE, PENNSYLVANIA

Entrance Moderately difficult **General** State-supported, comprehensive, coed **Setting** 250-acre small-town campus **Enrollment** 7,474 **Faculty** 17:1 **Application deadline** Rolling **Freshmen** 55% accepted **Housing** Yes **Tuition** $4422 **Undergraduates** 59% women, 19% part-time, 16% 25 or older, 0% Native American, 2% Hispanic, 6% black, 2% Asian or Pacific Islander **Most popular recent majors** Elementary education, business administration/commerce/management, biology/biological sciences **Academic program** Average class size 25, advanced placement, tutorials, honors program, summer session, adult/continuing education programs, internships **Contact** Mr. Darrell Davis, Director of Admissions, Millersville University of Pennsylvania, Millersville, PA 17551-0302. Telephone: 717-872-3371.

MOORE COLLEGE OF ART AND DESIGN
PHILADELPHIA, PENNSYLVANIA

Entrance Moderately difficult **General** Independent, 4-year, specialized, women only **Setting** 3-acre urban campus **Enrollment** 385 **Faculty** 8:1 **Application deadline** Rolling **Freshmen** 73% accepted **Housing** Yes **Tuition** $14,422 **Undergraduates** 10% part-time, 10% 25 or older, 0% Native American, 3% Hispanic, 5% black, 9% Asian or Pacific Islander **Most popular recent majors** Art/fine arts, fashion design and technology, graphic arts **Academic program** Average class size 20, tutorials, honors program, summer session, adult/continuing education programs, internships **Contact** Ms. Karina Dayich, Director of Admissions, Moore College of Art and Design, 20th and the Parkway, Philadelphia, PA 19103. Telephone: 215-568-4515 Ext. 1105. Fax: 215-568-8017.

MORAVIAN COLLEGE
BETHLEHEM, PENNSYLVANIA

Entrance Moderately difficult **General** Independent, comprehensive, coed, affiliated with Moravian Church **Setting** 80-acre suburban campus **Enrollment** 1,952 **Faculty** 14:1 **Application deadline** 3/1 **Freshmen** 80% accepted **Housing** Yes **Tuition** $17,276 **Undergraduates** 51% women, 2% part-time, 2% 25 or older, 2% Hispanic, 1% black, 1% Asian or Pacific Islander **Most popular recent majors** Business administration/commerce/management, psychology, biology/biological sciences **Academic program** Average class size 22, advanced placement, accelerated degree program, self-designed majors, honors program, summer session, adult/continuing education programs, internships **Contact** Mr. Bernard Story, Dean of Admissions and Financial Aid, Moravian College, Bethlehem, PA 18018-6650. Telephone: 610-861-1320. Fax: 610-861-3956.

MOUNT ALOYSIUS COLLEGE
CRESSON, PENNSYLVANIA

Entrance Minimally difficult **General** Independent Roman Catholic, 4-year, coed **Setting** 125-acre rural campus **Enrollment** 1,012 **Faculty** 9:1 **Application deadline** Rolling **Freshmen** 54% accepted **Housing** Yes **Tuition** $9190 **Undergraduates** 71% women, 6% part-time, 40% 25 or older, 2% black, 1% Asian or Pacific Islander **Most popular recent majors** Nursing, occupational therapy, business administration/commerce/management **Academic program** Advanced placement, summer session, adult/continuing education programs, internships **Contact** Ms. Sylvia Ghezzi Hirsch, Dean of Enrollment Management/Director of Admissions, Mount Aloysius College, 7373 Admiral Highway, Cresson, PA 16630. Telephone: 814-886-6383. Fax: 814-886-2978.

MUHLENBERG COLLEGE
ALLENTOWN, PENNSYLVANIA

Entrance Very difficult **General** Independent, 4-year, coed, affiliated with Lutheran Church **Setting** 75-acre suburban campus **Enrollment** 1,953 **Faculty** 13:1 **Application deadline** 2/15 **Freshmen** 67% accepted **Housing** Yes **Tuition** $18,660 **Undergraduates** 53% women, 7% part-time, 4% 25 or older, 0% Native American, 2% Hispanic, 2% black, 4% Asian or Pacific Islander **Most popular recent majors** Biology/biological sciences, psychology, English **Academic program** Average class size 30, advanced placement, accelerated degree program, self-designed majors, tutorials, honors program, summer session, adult/continuing education programs, internships **Contact** Mr. Christopher Hooker-Haring, Dean of Admissions, Muhlenberg College, Allentown, PA 18104-5586. Telephone: 610-821-3245. Fax: 610-821-3234.

NEUMANN COLLEGE
ASTON, PENNSYLVANIA

Entrance Moderately difficult **General** Independent Roman Catholic, comprehensive, coed **Setting** 22-acre suburban campus **Enrollment** 1,142 **Faculty** 8:1 **Application deadline** Rolling **Freshmen** 79% accepted **Tuition** $12,870 **Undergraduates** 78% women, 50% part-time, 58% 25 or older, 1% Native American, 2% Hispanic, 7% black, 3% Asian or Pacific Islander **Most popular recent majors** Nursing, liberal arts/general studies, education **Academic program** Average class size 22, advanced placement, tutorials, honors program, summer session, adult/continuing education programs, internships **Contact** Mr. Mark Osborn, Director of Admissions and Financial Aid, Neumann College, Aston, PA 19014-1298. Telephone: 610-361-5215.

PENNSYLVANIA COLLEGE OF OPTOMETRY
PHILADELPHIA, PENNSYLVANIA

Entrance Moderately difficult **General** Independent, upper-level, specialized, coed **Setting** 13-acre urban campus **Enrollment** 609 **Faculty** 10:1 **Freshmen** 33% accepted **Housing** Yes **Tuition** $20,300 **Undergraduates** 0% part-time **Contact** Mr. Robert E. Horne, Director of Admissions, Pennsylvania College of Optometry, 1200 West Godfrey Avenue, Philadelphia, PA 19141-3323. Telephone: 215-276-6200.

PENNSYLVANIA STATE UNIVERSITY ABINGTON COLLEGE
ABINGTON, PENNSYLVANIA

Entrance Moderately difficult **General** State-related, 4-year, coed **Setting** 45-acre small-town campus **Enrollment** 3,262 **Faculty** 25:1 **Application deadline** Rolling **Freshmen** 82% accepted **Tuition** $5682 **Undergraduates** 52%

women, 34% part-time, 16% 25 or older, 0% Native American, 3% Hispanic, 10% black, 7% Asian or Pacific Islander **Academic program** Advanced placement, summer session, adult/continuing education programs, internships **Contact** Mr. Robert McCaig, Admissions Officer, Pennsylvania State University Abington College, Abington, PA 19001-3918. Telephone: 215-881-7600 Ext. 266.

PENNSYLVANIA STATE UNIVERSITY ALTOONA COLLEGE

ALTOONA, PENNSYLVANIA

Entrance Moderately difficult **General** State-related, 4-year, coed **Setting** 81-acre suburban campus **Enrollment** 3,475 **Application deadline** Rolling **Freshmen** 92% accepted **Housing** Yes **Tuition** $5682 **Undergraduates** 47% women, 12% part-time, 10% 25 or older, 0% Native American, 2% Hispanic, 3% black, 1% Asian or Pacific Islander **Academic program** Advanced placement, summer session, adult/continuing education programs, internships **Contact** Ms. Fredina Ingold, Admissions Officer, Pennsylvania State University Altoona College, Altoona, PA 16601-3760. Telephone: 814-949-5466.

PENNSYLVANIA STATE UNIVERSITY AT ERIE, THE BEHREND COLLEGE

ERIE, PENNSYLVANIA

Entrance Very difficult **General** State-related, comprehensive, coed **Setting** 714-acre suburban campus **Enrollment** 3,207 **Faculty** 19:1 **Application deadline** Rolling **Freshmen** 74% accepted **Housing** Yes **Tuition** $5832 **Undergraduates** 37% women, 15% part-time, 10% 25 or older, 1% Native American, 1% Hispanic, 3% black, 2% Asian or Pacific Islander **Most popular recent majors** Business administration/commerce/management, engineering (general), psychology **Academic program** Advanced placement, honors program, summer session, adult/continuing education programs, internships **Contact** Ms. Mary-Ellen Madigan, Admissions Director, Pennsylvania State University at Erie, The Behrend College, Erie, PA 16563. Telephone: 814-898-6100.

PENNSYLVANIA STATE UNIVERSITY BERKS–LEHIGH VALLEY COLLEGE

READING, PENNSYLVANIA

Entrance Moderately difficult **General** State-related, 4-year, coed **Setting** 241-acre suburban campus **Enrollment** 2,423 **Faculty** 27:1 **Application deadline** Rolling **Freshmen** 88% accepted **Housing** Yes **Tuition** $5654 **Undergraduates** 40% women, 19% part-time, 11% 25 or older, 0% Native American, 3% Hispanic, 3% black, 3% Asian or Pacific Islander **Academic program** Advanced placement, summer session, adult/continuing education programs, internships **Contact** Mr. John W. Gemmell, Admissions Officer, Pennsylvania State University Berks–Lehigh Valley College, Reading, PA 19610-6009. Telephone: 610-320-4864.

PENNSYLVANIA STATE UNIVERSITY HARRISBURG CAMPUS OF THE CAPITAL COLLEGE

MIDDLETOWN, PENNSYLVANIA

Entrance Moderately difficult **General** State-related, comprehensive, coed **Setting** 218-acre small-town campus **Enrollment** 3,417 **Faculty** 14:1 **Freshmen** 84% accepted **Housing** Yes **Tuition** $5832 **Undergraduates** 52% women, 41% part-time, 35% 25 or older, 2% Hispanic, 3% black, 3% Asian or Pacific Islander **Academic program** Advanced placement, summer session, adult/continuing education programs **Contact** Dr. Thomas Streveler, Director of Enrollment Services, Pennsylvania State University Harrisburg Campus of the Capital College, Middletown, PA 17057-4898. Telephone: 717-948-6250.

PENNSYLVANIA STATE UNIVERSITY SCHUYLKILL CAMPUS OF THE CAPITAL COLLEGE

SCHUYLKILL HAVEN, PENNSYLVANIA

Entrance Moderately difficult **General** State-related, 4-year, coed **Setting** 42-acre small-town campus **Enrollment** 988 **Faculty** 20:1 **Application deadline** Rolling **Freshmen** 90% accepted **Housing** Yes **Tuition** $5654 **Undergraduates** 59% women, 31% part-time, 16% 25 or older, 1% Native American, 1% Hispanic, 7% black, 2% Asian or Pacific Islander **Academic program** Advanced placement, summer session, adult/continuing education programs, internships **Contact** Mr. Jerry Bowmanky, Director of Student Programs and Services, Pennsylvania State University Schuylkill Campus of the Capital College, Schuylkill Haven, PA 17972-2208. Telephone: 717-385-6252.

PENNSYLVANIA STATE UNIVERSITY UNIVERSITY PARK CAMPUS

STATE COLLEGE, PENNSYLVANIA

Entrance Very difficult **General** State-related, coed **Setting** 5,448-acre small-town campus **En-**

rollment 39,782 **Faculty** 19:1 **Application deadline** Rolling **Freshmen** 46% accepted **Housing** Yes **Tuition** $5832 **Undergraduates** 45% women, 6% part-time, 3% 25 or older, 1% Native American, 2% Hispanic, 3% black, 5% Asian or Pacific Islander **Most popular recent majors** Engineering (general), science, business administration/commerce/management **Academic program** Advanced placement, self-designed majors, honors program, summer session, adult/continuing education programs, internships **Contact** Dr. John J. Romano, Vice Provost for Enrollment Management and Administration, Pennsylvania State University University Park Campus, University Park, PA 16802-1503. Telephone: 814-865-5471.

PHILADELPHIA COLLEGE OF BIBLE
LANGHORNE, PENNSYLVANIA

Entrance Moderately difficult **General** Independent nondenominational, comprehensive, coed **Setting** 105-acre suburban campus **Enrollment** 1,187 **Faculty** 16:1 **Application deadline** Rolling **Freshmen** 99% accepted **Housing** Yes **Tuition** $9120 **Undergraduates** 51% women, 13% part-time, 34% 25 or older, 1% Native American, 2% Hispanic, 15% black, 3% Asian or Pacific Islander **Most popular recent majors** Biblical studies, education, social work **Academic program** Advanced placement, summer session, adult/continuing education programs, internships **Contact** Mrs. Fran Emmons, Director of Admissions Services, Philadelphia College of Bible, Langhorne, PA 19047-2990. Telephone: 215-702-4239. Fax: 215-752-5812.

PHILADELPHIA COLLEGE OF PHARMACY AND SCIENCE
PHILADELPHIA, PENNSYLVANIA

Entrance Moderately difficult **General** Independent, coed **Setting** 25-acre urban campus **Enrollment** 2,021 **Faculty** 13:1 **Application deadline** Rolling **Freshmen** 68% accepted **Housing** Yes **Tuition** $13,290 **Undergraduates** 63% women, 1% part-time, 5% 25 or older, 0% Native American, 1% Hispanic, 4% black, 18% Asian or Pacific Islander **Most popular recent majors** Pharmacy/pharmaceutical sciences, physical therapy, biology/biological sciences **Academic program** Advanced placement, summer session, internships **Contact** Mr. Louis L. Hegyes, Director of Admission, Philadelphia College of Pharmacy and Science, 600 South 43rd Street, Philadelphia, PA 19104-4495. Telephone: 215-596-8810. Fax: 215-895-1100.

PHILADELPHIA COLLEGE OF TEXTILES AND SCIENCE
PHILADELPHIA, PENNSYLVANIA

Entrance Moderately difficult **General** Independent, comprehensive, coed **Setting** 100-acre suburban campus **Enrollment** 3,402 **Faculty** 20:1 **Application deadline** Rolling **Freshmen** 81% accepted **Housing** Yes **Tuition** $13,466 **Undergraduates** 63% women, 5% part-time, 30% 25 or older, 0% Native American, 2% Hispanic, 10% black, 5% Asian or Pacific Islander **Most popular recent majors** Fashion merchandising, marketing/retailing/merchandising, fashion design and technology **Academic program** Advanced placement, accelerated degree program, honors program, summer session, adult/continuing education programs, internships **Contact** Mr. Guy Brignola, Director of Admissions, Philadelphia College of Textiles and Science, Philadelphia, PA 19144-5497. Telephone: 215-951-2800. Fax: 215-951-2907.

POINT PARK COLLEGE
PITTSBURGH, PENNSYLVANIA

Entrance Moderately difficult **General** Independent, comprehensive, coed **Setting** Urban campus **Enrollment** 2,297 **Faculty** 15:1 **Application deadline** Rolling **Freshmen** 77% accepted **Housing** Yes **Tuition** $11,406 **Undergraduates** 63% women, 47% part-time, 61% 25 or older, 0% Native American, 1% Hispanic, 14% black, 1% Asian or Pacific Islander **Most popular recent majors** Electrical engineering technology, business administration/commerce/management, communication **Academic program** Advanced placement, accelerated degree program, self-designed majors, summer session, adult/continuing education programs, internships **Contact** Ms. Michele Lawrence, Associate Director of Admissions and Financial Aid, Point Park College, 201 Wood Street, Pittsburgh, PA 15222-1984. Telephone: 412-392-3430. Fax: 412-391-1980.

ROBERT MORRIS COLLEGE
MOON TOWNSHIP, PENNSYLVANIA

Entrance Moderately difficult **General** Independent, comprehensive, coed **Setting** 230-acre suburban campus **Enrollment** 4,907 **Faculty** 20:1 **Application deadline** Rolling **Freshmen** 97% accepted **Housing** Yes **Tuition** $8339 **Undergraduates** 51% women, 38% part-time, 43% 25 or older, 1% Native American, 1% Hispanic, 7% black, 1% Asian or Pacific Islander **Most popular recent majors** Accounting, business administration/commerce/management, marketing/retailing/

merchandising **Academic program** Average class size 22, advanced placement, accelerated degree program, tutorials, honors program, summer session, adult/continuing education programs, internships **Contact** Mr. James R. Welsh, Dean of Enrollment Management, Robert Morris College, Moon Township, PA 15108-1189. Telephone: 412-262-8265. Fax: 412-262-8619.

ROSEMONT COLLEGE
ROSEMONT, PENNSYLVANIA

Entrance Moderately difficult **General** Independent Roman Catholic, comprehensive, women only **Setting** 56-acre suburban campus **Enrollment** 846 **Faculty** 8:1 **Application deadline** Rolling **Freshmen** 67% accepted **Housing** Yes **Tuition** $13,340 **Undergraduates** 20% part-time, 6% 25 or older, 2% Hispanic, 7% black, 5% Asian or Pacific Islander **Most popular recent majors** Psychology, English, political science/government **Academic program** Average class size 15, advanced placement, accelerated degree program, self-designed majors, tutorials, honors program, summer session, adult/continuing education programs, internships **Contact** Admissions Office, Rosemont College, Rosemont, PA 19010-1699. Telephone: 610-526-2966. Fax: 610-527-1041.

ST. CHARLES BORROMEO SEMINARY, OVERBROOK
WYNNEWOOD, PENNSYLVANIA

Entrance Moderately difficult **General** Independent Roman Catholic, comprehensive, specialized, men only **Setting** 77-acre suburban campus **Enrollment** 515 **Faculty** 5:1 **Application deadline** 7/1 **Freshmen** 100% accepted **Housing** Yes **Tuition** $6700 **Undergraduates** 0% part-time, 45% 25 or older, 0% Native American, 6% Hispanic, 1% black, 8% Asian or Pacific Islander **Academic program** Average class size 14, advanced placement, accelerated degree program, tutorials, honors program, summer session, adult/continuing education programs **Contact** Rev. Gregory J. Parlante, Director of Vocation Office for Diocean Priesthood, St. Charles Borromeo Seminary, Overbrook, 100 East Wynnewood Road, Wynnewood, PA 19096. Telephone: 610-667-5778.

SAINT FRANCIS COLLEGE
LORETTO, PENNSYLVANIA

Entrance Moderately difficult **General** Independent Roman Catholic, comprehensive, coed **Setting** 600-acre rural campus **Enrollment** 1,886 **Application deadline** Rolling **Freshmen** 71% accepted **Housing** Yes **Tuition** $13,928 **Undergraduates** 55% women, 5% part-time, 15% 25 or older, 1% Hispanic, 2% black, 1% Asian or Pacific Islander **Most popular recent majors** Business administration/commerce/management, accounting, elementary education **Academic program** Advanced placement, accelerated degree program, self-designed majors, honors program, summer session, adult/continuing education programs, internships **Contact** Ms. Dana Bear, Interim Dean of Enrollment Management, Saint Francis College, PO Box 600, Loretto, PA 15940-0600. Telephone: 814-472-3100. Fax: 814-472-3044.

SAINT JOSEPH'S UNIVERSITY
PHILADELPHIA, PENNSYLVANIA

Entrance Moderately difficult **General** Independent Roman Catholic (Jesuit), comprehensive, coed **Setting** 60-acre suburban campus **Enrollment** 6,963 **Faculty** 17:1 **Application deadline** Rolling **Freshmen** 69% accepted **Housing** Yes **Tuition** $16,025 **Undergraduates** 55% women, 30% part-time, 0% Native American, 3% Hispanic, 9% black, 2% Asian or Pacific Islander **Most popular recent majors** Food marketing, psychology, accounting **Academic program** Average class size 22, advanced placement, accelerated degree program, self-designed majors, tutorials, honors program, summer session, adult/continuing education programs, internships **Contact** Mr. David Conway, Dean of Enrollment Management, Saint Joseph's University, Philadelphia, PA 19131-1395. Telephone: 610-660-1300.

SAINT VINCENT COLLEGE
LATROBE, PENNSYLVANIA

Entrance Moderately difficult **General** Independent Roman Catholic, 4-year, coed **Setting** 100-acre suburban campus **Enrollment** 1,215 **Faculty** 14:1 **Application deadline** Rolling **Freshmen** 85% accepted **Housing** Yes **Tuition** $13,461 **Undergraduates** 50% women, 13% part-time, 12% 25 or older, 1% Native American, 1% Hispanic, 2% black, 1% Asian or Pacific Islander **Most popular recent majors** Psychology, biology/biological sciences, accounting **Academic program** Advanced placement, accelerated degree program, self-designed majors, tutorials, honors program, summer session, adult/continuing education programs, internships **Contact** Rev. Earl J. Henry, OSB, Dean of Admission and Financial Aid, Saint Vincent College, Latrobe, PA 15650. Telephone: 412-537-4540. Fax: 412-537-4554.

SETON HILL COLLEGE
GREENSBURG, PENNSYLVANIA

Entrance Moderately difficult **General** Independent Roman Catholic, comprehensive, primarily women **Setting** 200-acre small-town campus **Enrollment** 929 **Faculty** 14:1 **Application deadline** 8/1 **Freshmen** 91% accepted **Housing** Yes **Tuition** $12,640 **Undergraduates** 93% women, 23% part-time, 13% 25 or older, 1% Native American, 3% Hispanic, 4% black, 2% Asian or Pacific Islander **Most popular recent majors** Psychology, family and consumer studies, English **Academic program** Average class size 16, advanced placement, accelerated degree program, self-designed majors, tutorials, honors program, summer session, adult/continuing education programs, internships **Contact** Ms. Barbara C. Hinkle, Vice President for Enrollment Services, Seton Hill College, Greensburg, PA 15601. Telephone: 412-838-4218. Fax: 412-830-4611.

SHIPPENSBURG UNIVERSITY OF PENNSYLVANIA
SHIPPENSBURG, PENNSYLVANIA

Entrance Moderately difficult **General** State-supported, comprehensive, coed **Setting** 200-acre rural campus **Enrollment** 6,683 **Faculty** 16:1 **Application deadline** Rolling **Freshmen** 70% accepted **Housing** Yes **Tuition** $4344 **Undergraduates** 54% women, 5% part-time, 7% 25 or older, 1% Native American, 1% Hispanic, 3% black, 1% Asian or Pacific Islander **Most popular recent majors** Elementary education, criminal justice, accounting **Academic program** Advanced placement, accelerated degree program, tutorials, honors program, summer session, internships **Contact** Mr. Joseph Cretella, Dean of Admissions, Shippensburg University of Pennsylvania, 1871 Old Main Drive, Shippensburg, PA 17257-2299. Telephone: 717-532-1231.

SLIPPERY ROCK UNIVERSITY OF PENNSYLVANIA
SLIPPERY ROCK, PENNSYLVANIA

Entrance Moderately difficult **General** State-supported, comprehensive, coed **Setting** 611-acre rural campus **Enrollment** 7,291 **Faculty** 20:1 **Application deadline** 5/1 **Freshmen** 79% accepted **Housing** Yes **Tuition** $4302 **Undergraduates** 57% women, 12% part-time, 16% 25 or older, 1% Native American, 1% Hispanic, 4% black, 1% Asian or Pacific Islander **Most popular recent majors** Education, business administration/commerce/management **Academic program** Advanced placement, accelerated degree program, tutorials, honors program, summer session, adult/continuing education programs, internships **Contact** Dr. Duncan M. Sargent, Director of Admissions, Slippery Rock University of Pennsylvania, Slippery Rock, PA 16057. Telephone: 412-738-2015.

SUSQUEHANNA UNIVERSITY
SELINSGROVE, PENNSYLVANIA

Entrance Moderately difficult **General** Independent, 4-year, coed, affiliated with Lutheran Church **Setting** 210-acre small-town campus **Enrollment** 1,568 **Faculty** 15:1 **Application deadline** 3/1 **Freshmen** 76% accepted **Housing** Yes **Tuition** $18,350 **Undergraduates** 54% women, 1% part-time, 1% 25 or older, 0% Native American, 2% Hispanic, 2% black, 1% Asian or Pacific Islander **Most popular recent majors** Communication, business administration/commerce/management, biology/biological sciences **Academic program** Average class size 25, advanced placement, accelerated degree program, self-designed majors, tutorials, honors program, summer session, adult/continuing education programs, internships **Contact** Mr. Richard Ziegler, Director of Admissions, Susquehanna University, Selinsgrove, PA 17870-1001. Telephone: 717-372-4260.

SWARTHMORE COLLEGE
SWARTHMORE, PENNSYLVANIA

Entrance Most difficult **General** Independent, 4-year, coed **Setting** 330-acre suburban campus **Enrollment** 1,437 **Faculty** 9:1 **Application deadline** 1/1 **Freshmen** 30% accepted **Housing** Yes **Tuition** $22,000 **Undergraduates** 54% women, 1% part-time, 0% 25 or older, 1% Native American, 7% Hispanic, 7% black, 11% Asian or Pacific Islander **Most popular recent majors** Biology/biological sciences, economics, political science/government **Academic program** Average class size 18, advanced placement, self-designed majors, tutorials, honors program, internships **Contact** Office of Admissions, Swarthmore College, Swarthmore, PA 19081-1397. Telephone: 610-328-8300. Fax: 610-328-8673.

TALMUDICAL YESHIVA OF PHILADELPHIA
PHILADELPHIA, PENNSYLVANIA

Entrance Moderately difficult **General** Independent-religious, 4-year, specialized, men only **Setting** 3-acre urban campus **Enrollment** 121 **Faculty** 15:1 **Application deadline** 7/15 **Freshmen** 75% accepted **Housing** Yes **Tuition** $5080 **Undergraduates** 0% part-time, 0% 25 or older,

0% Native American, 0% Hispanic, 0% black, 0% Asian or Pacific Islander **Academic program** ESL program, Tutorials, honors program, internships **Contact** Rabbi Shmuel Kamenetsky, Co-Dean, Talmudical Yeshiva of Philadelphia, 6063 Drexel Road, Philadelphia, PA 19131-1296. Telephone: 215-473-1212.

TEMPLE UNIVERSITY

PHILADELPHIA, PENNSYLVANIA

Entrance Moderately difficult **General** State-related, coed **Setting** 76-acre urban campus **Enrollment** 25,469 **Faculty** 24:1 **Application deadline** 5/1 **Freshmen** 71% accepted **Housing** Yes **Tuition** $6040 **Undergraduates** 55% women, 17% part-time, 28% 25 or older, 1% Native American, 3% Hispanic, 25% black, 12% Asian or Pacific Islander **Most popular recent majors** Business administration/commerce/management, education **Academic program** Advanced placement, accelerated degree program, self-designed majors, honors program, summer session, adult/continuing education programs, internships **Contact** Dr. Timm Rinehart, Acting Director of Admissions, Temple University, 1801 N. Broad St, Philadelphia, PA 19122-6096. Telephone: 215-204-8556. Fax: 215-204-5694.

THIEL COLLEGE

GREENVILLE, PENNSYLVANIA

Entrance Moderately difficult **General** Independent, 4-year, coed, affiliated with Evangelical Lutheran Church in America **Setting** 135-acre rural campus **Enrollment** 985 **Faculty** 11:1 **Application deadline** Rolling **Freshmen** 84% accepted **Housing** Yes **Tuition** $13,355 **Undergraduates** 57% women, 12% part-time, 14% 25 or older, 1% Native American, 1% Hispanic, 6% black, 1% Asian or Pacific Islander **Most popular recent majors** Business administration/commerce/management, nursing, communication **Academic program** Advanced placement, accelerated degree program, tutorials, honors program, summer session, adult/continuing education programs, internships **Contact** Mr. Stephen Eidson, Executive Director of Enrollment Management, Thiel College, Greenville, PA 16125-2181. Telephone: 412-589-2176. Fax: 412-589-2013.

THOMAS JEFFERSON UNIVERSITY

PHILADELPHIA, PENNSYLVANIA

Entrance Moderately difficult **General** Independent, upper-level, specialized, coed **Setting** 13-acre urban campus **Enrollment** 1,175 **Faculty** 9:1 **Freshmen** 27% accepted **Housing** Yes **Tuition** $14,920 **Undergraduates** 79% women, 22% part-time, 65% 25 or older, 0% Native American, 3% Hispanic, 5% black, 5% Asian or Pacific Islander **Most popular recent majors** Nursing, physical therapy, occupational therapy **Academic program** Advanced placement, accelerated degree program, adult/continuing education programs, internships **Contact** Associate Director of Admissions, Thomas Jefferson University, Edison Building, Suite 1610, 130 South Ninth Street, Philadelphia, PA 19107. Telephone: 215-503-8890.

UNIVERSITY OF PENNSYLVANIA

PHILADELPHIA, PENNSYLVANIA

Entrance Most difficult **General** Independent, coed **Setting** 260-acre urban campus **Enrollment** 21,171 **Faculty** 5:1 **Application deadline** 1/1 **Freshmen** 30% accepted **Housing** Yes **Tuition** $22,250 **Undergraduates** 50% women, 7% part-time, 11% 25 or older, 1% Native American, 4% Hispanic, 6% black, 17% Asian or Pacific Islander **Most popular recent majors** Finance/banking, history, communication **Academic program** Advanced placement, accelerated degree program, self-designed majors, tutorials, honors program, summer session, adult/continuing education programs, internships **Contact** Mr. Willis J. Stetson Jr., Dean of Admissions, University of Pennsylvania, 1 College Hall, Levy Park, Philadelphia, PA 19104. Telephone: 215-898-7507.

UNIVERSITY OF PITTSBURGH

PITTSBURGH, PENNSYLVANIA

Entrance Moderately difficult **General** State-related, coed **Setting** 132-acre urban campus **Enrollment** 25,479 **Faculty** 14:1 **Application deadline** Rolling **Freshmen** 67% accepted **Housing** Yes **Tuition** $6164 **Undergraduates** 53% women, 20% part-time, 21% 25 or older, 1% Native American, 1% Hispanic, 9% black, 4% Asian or Pacific Islander **Most popular recent majors** Business administration/commerce/management, psychology, speech/rhetoric/public address/debate **Academic program** Advanced placement, self-designed majors, honors program, summer session, adult/continuing education programs, internships **Contact** Dr. Betsy A. Porter, Director of Admissions and Financial Aid, University of Pittsburgh, Bruce Hall, Second Floor, Pittsburgh, PA 15260. Telephone: 412-624-7488. Fax: 412-648-8815.

UNIVERSITY OF PITTSBURGH AT BRADFORD
BRADFORD, PENNSYLVANIA

Entrance Moderately difficult **General** State-related, 4-year, coed **Setting** 145-acre small-town campus **Enrollment** 1,274 **Faculty** 14:1 **Application deadline** Rolling **Freshmen** 91% accepted **Housing** Yes **Tuition** $6108 **Undergraduates** 54% women, 27% part-time, 14% 25 or older, 1% Native American, 1% Hispanic, 3% black, 1% Asian or Pacific Islander **Most popular recent majors** Business administration/commerce/management, psychology, communication **Academic program** Advanced placement, accelerated degree program, self-designed majors, tutorials, summer session, adult/continuing education programs, internships **Contact** Ms. Roxie Vanderpoel, Office Manager, University of Pittsburgh at Bradford, Bradford, PA 16701-2812. Telephone: 814-362-7555. Fax: 814-362-7578.

UNIVERSITY OF PITTSBURGH AT GREENSBURG
GREENSBURG, PENNSYLVANIA

Entrance Moderately difficult **General** State-related, 4-year, coed **Setting** 165-acre small-town campus **Enrollment** 1,381 **Faculty** 18:1 **Application deadline** 8/1 **Freshmen** 74% accepted **Housing** Yes **Tuition** $6074 **Undergraduates** 50% women, 21% part-time, 30% 25 or older, 0% Native American, 0% Hispanic, 1% black, 1% Asian or Pacific Islander **Most popular recent majors** Business administration/commerce/management, psychology, accounting **Academic program** Advanced placement, accelerated degree program, self-designed majors, tutorials, summer session, adult/continuing education programs, internships **Contact** Mr. John R. Sparks, Director of Admissions and Financial Aid, University of Pittsburgh at Greensburg, Greensburg, PA 15601-5860. Telephone: 412-836-9880. Fax: 412-836-9901.

UNIVERSITY OF PITTSBURGH AT JOHNSTOWN
JOHNSTOWN, PENNSYLVANIA

Entrance Moderately difficult **General** State-related, 4-year, coed **Setting** 650-acre suburban campus **Enrollment** 3,143 **Faculty** 20:1 **Application deadline** Rolling **Freshmen** 85% accepted **Housing** Yes **Tuition** $6154 **Undergraduates** 52% women, 16% part-time, 1% 25 or older, 1% Native American, 1% Hispanic, 2% black, 1% Asian or Pacific Islander **Most popular recent majors** Business economics, elementary education, biology/biological sciences **Academic program** Advanced placement, accelerated degree program, self-designed majors, summer session, adult/continuing education programs, internships **Contact** Mr. James F. Gyure, Director of Admissions, University of Pittsburgh at Johnstown, 133 Biddle Hall, Johnstown, PA 15904-2990. Telephone: 814-269-7050. Fax: 814-269-7044.

UNIVERSITY OF SCRANTON
SCRANTON, PENNSYLVANIA

Entrance Moderately difficult **General** Independent Roman Catholic (Jesuit), comprehensive, coed **Setting** 50-acre urban campus **Enrollment** 4,906 **Faculty** 14:1 **Application deadline** 3/1 **Freshmen** 67% accepted **Housing** Yes **Tuition** $16,080 **Undergraduates** 57% women, 12% part-time, 11% 25 or older, 0% Native American, 2% Hispanic, 1% black, 2% Asian or Pacific Islander **Most popular recent majors** Biology/biological sciences, accounting, communication **Academic program** Advanced placement, accelerated degree program, self-designed majors, tutorials, honors program, summer session, adult/continuing education programs, internships **Contact** Rev. Bernard R. McIlhenny, SJ, Dean of Admissions, University of Scranton, Scranton, PA 18510-4622. Telephone: 717-941-7540. Fax: 717-941-6369.

UNIVERSITY OF THE ARTS
PHILADELPHIA, PENNSYLVANIA

Entrance Moderately difficult **General** Independent, comprehensive, coed **Setting** Urban campus **Enrollment** 1,399 **Faculty** 9:1 **Application deadline** Rolling **Freshmen** 81% accepted **Housing** Yes **Tuition** $15,070 **Undergraduates** 50% women, 4% part-time, 11% 25 or older, 1% Native American, 4% Hispanic, 10% black, 4% Asian or Pacific Islander **Most popular recent majors** Dance, illustration, art/fine arts **Academic program** Advanced placement, tutorials, summer session, adult/continuing education programs, internships **Contact** Ms. Barbara Elliott, Director of Admission, University of the Arts, Broad and Pine Streets, Philadelphia, PA 19102-4944. Telephone: 215-732-4832. Fax: 215-875-5458.

URSINUS COLLEGE
COLLEGEVILLE, PENNSYLVANIA

Entrance Very difficult **General** Independent, 4-year, coed, affiliated with United Church of Christ **Setting** 140-acre suburban campus **Enrollment** 1,196 **Faculty** 12:1 **Application deadline** 2/15 **Freshmen** 81% accepted **Housing** Yes **Tuition** $17,380 **Undergraduates** 53% women, 1% part-time, 1% 25 or older, 1% Native American, 1% Hispanic, 4% black, 4% Asian or Pacific Islander **Academic program** Average class size 18, advanced placement, accelerated degree program, self-designed majors, tutorials, honors program, summer session, adult/continuing education programs, internships **Contact** Mr. Richard G. Di Feliciantonio, Vice President for Enrollment, Ursinus College, Collegeville, PA 19426-1000. Telephone: 610-409-3200. Fax: 610-489-0627.

VALLEY FORGE CHRISTIAN COLLEGE
PHOENIXVILLE, PENNSYLVANIA

Entrance Minimally difficult **General** Independent, 4-year, specialized, coed, affiliated with Assemblies of God **Setting** 77-acre small-town campus **Enrollment** 479 **Faculty** 16:1 **Application deadline** 8/15 **Housing** Yes **Tuition** $6560 **Undergraduates** 42% women, 8% part-time, 22% 25 or older, 1% Native American, 3% Hispanic, 3% black, 6% Asian or Pacific Islander **Academic program** Advanced placement, summer session, adult/continuing education programs, internships **Contact** Mr. James Barco, Executive Director of Enrollment Management, Valley Forge Christian College, 1401 Charlestown Road, Phoenixville, PA 19460. Telephone: 610-935-0450.

VILLANOVA UNIVERSITY
VILLANOVA, PENNSYLVANIA

Entrance Moderately difficult **General** Independent Roman Catholic, comprehensive, coed **Setting** 222-acre suburban campus **Enrollment** 10,182 **Faculty** 13:1 **Application deadline** 1/15 **Freshmen** 65% accepted **Housing** Yes **Tuition** $18,670 **Undergraduates** 50% women, 6% part-time, 1% 25 or older, 1% Native American, 2% Hispanic, 2% black, 3% Asian or Pacific Islander **Most popular recent majors** Accounting, nursing, political science/government **Academic program** Advanced placement, accelerated degree program, tutorials, honors program, summer session, adult/continuing education programs, internships **Contact** Mr. Stephen Merritt, Director of Undergraduate Admission, Villanova University, Villanova, PA 19085-1699. Telephone: 610-519-4000. Fax: 610-519-6450.

WASHINGTON AND JEFFERSON COLLEGE
WASHINGTON, PENNSYLVANIA

Entrance Moderately difficult **General** Independent, 4-year, coed **Setting** 40-acre small-town campus **Enrollment** 1,128 **Faculty** 11:1 **Application deadline** 2/1 **Freshmen** 86% accepted **Housing** Yes **Tuition** $18,000 **Undergraduates** 46% women, 1% part-time, 1% Native American, 1% Hispanic, 3% black, 2% Asian or Pacific Islander **Academic program** Advanced placement, accelerated degree program, self-designed majors, tutorials, honors program, summer session, internships **Contact** Mr. Thomas P. O'Connor, Director of Admissions, Washington and Jefferson College, Washington, PA 15301-4801. Telephone: 412-223-6025. Fax: 412-223-5271.

WAYNESBURG COLLEGE
WAYNESBURG, PENNSYLVANIA

Entrance Moderately difficult **General** Independent, comprehensive, coed, affiliated with Presbyterian Church (U.S.A.) **Setting** 30-acre small-town campus **Enrollment** 1,288 **Faculty** 16:1 **Application deadline** Rolling **Freshmen** 78% accepted **Housing** Yes **Tuition** $10,550 **Undergraduates** 52% women, 7% part-time, 13% 25 or older, 1% Hispanic, 3% black, 1% Asian or Pacific Islander **Most popular recent majors** Business administration/commerce/management, nursing, English **Academic program** Advanced placement, tutorials, honors program, summer session, adult/continuing education programs, internships **Contact** Mrs. Robin L. Moore, Dean of Admissions, Waynesburg College, Waynesburg, PA 15370-1222. Telephone: 412-852-3333. Fax: 412-627-6416.

WEST CHESTER UNIVERSITY OF PENNSYLVANIA
WEST CHESTER, PENNSYLVANIA

Entrance Moderately difficult **General** State-supported, comprehensive, coed **Setting** 547-acre small-town campus **Enrollment** 11,261 **Faculty** 17:1 **Application deadline** Rolling **Freshmen** 61% accepted **Housing** Yes **Tuition** $4162 **Undergraduates** 59% women, 18% part-time, 19% 25 or older, 1% Native American, 2% Hispanic, 8% black, 2% Asian or Pacific Islander **Most popular recent majors** Education, marketing/retailing/merchandising, criminal justice **Academic program** Advanced placement, accelerated degree program, self-designed majors, tutorials, honors program, summer session, adult/continuing education programs, internships **Contact** Ms. Marsha Haug, Director of Admissions, West Chester University of Pennsylvania, 100 West Rosedale Avenue, West Chester, PA 19383. Telephone: 610-436-3411.

WESTMINSTER COLLEGE
NEW WILMINGTON, PENNSYLVANIA

Entrance Moderately difficult **General** Independent, comprehensive, coed, affiliated with Presbyterian Church (U.S.A.) **Setting** 300-acre small-town campus **Enrollment** 1,584 **Faculty** 16:1 **Application deadline** Rolling **Freshmen** 88% accepted **Housing** Yes **Tuition** $14,650 **Undergraduates** 60% women, 10% part-time, 1% 25 or older, 1% Native American, 1% Hispanic, 2% black, 1% Asian or Pacific Islander **Most popular recent majors** Business administration/commerce/management, elementary education, history **Academic program** Advanced placement, accelerated degree program, self-designed majors, honors program, summer session, adult/continuing education programs, internships **Contact** Mr. R. Dana Paul, Director of Admissions, Westminster College, New Wilmington, PA 16172-0001. Telephone: 412-946-7100. Fax: 412-946-7171.

WIDENER UNIVERSITY
CHESTER, PENNSYLVANIA

Entrance Moderately difficult **General** Independent, comprehensive, coed **Setting** 110-acre suburban campus **Enrollment** 8,150 **Faculty** 12:1 **Application deadline** Rolling **Freshmen** 83% accepted **Housing** Yes **Tuition** $14,380 **Undergraduates** 48% women, 40% part-time, 16% 25 or older, 1% Native American, 2% Hispanic, 14% black, 4% Asian or Pacific Islander **Academic program** Average class size 27, advanced placement, accelerated degree program, self-designed majors, tutorials, honors program, summer session, adult/continuing education programs, internships **Contact** Dr. Michael L. Mahoney, Vice President of Admissions and Student Services, Widener University, One University Place, Chester, PA 19013-5792. Telephone: 610-499-4126. Fax: 610-499-4676.

WILKES UNIVERSITY
WILKES-BARRE, PENNSYLVANIA

Entrance Moderately difficult **General** Independent, comprehensive, coed **Setting** 25-acre urban campus **Enrollment** 2,800 **Faculty** 13:1 **Application deadline** Rolling **Freshmen** 78% accepted **Housing** Yes **Tuition** $15,091 **Undergraduates** 49% women, 25% part-time, 23% 25 or older, 1% Hispanic, 2% black, 1% Asian or Pacific Islander **Most popular recent majors** Business administration/commerce/management, psychology, engineering (general) **Academic program** Advanced placement, accelerated degree program, self-designed majors, honors program, summer session, adult/continuing education programs, internships **Contact** Mr. Joe DeMelfi, Associate Dean of Admissions, Wilkes University, 170 South Franklin St, PO Box 111, Wilkes-Barre, PA 18766-0002. Telephone: 717-831-4400. Fax: 717-831-4904.

WILSON COLLEGE
CHAMBERSBURG, PENNSYLVANIA

Entrance Moderately difficult **General** Independent, 4-year, women only, affiliated with Presbyterian Church (U.S.A.) **Setting** 262-acre small-town campus **Enrollment** 283 **Faculty** 8:1 **Application deadline** Rolling **Freshmen** 94% accepted **Housing** Yes **Tuition** $12,750 **Undergraduates** 10% part-time, 17% 25 or older, 1% Native American, 1% Hispanic, 6% black, 2% Asian or Pacific Islander **Most popular recent majors** Veterinary sciences, equestrian studies, behavioral sciences **Academic program** Average class size 15, advanced placement, self-designed majors, tutorials, summer session, adult/continuing education programs, internships **Contact** Ms. Karen L. Jewell, Director of Admissions, Wilson College, Chambersburg, PA 17201-1285. Telephone: 717-262-2002. Fax: 717-264-1578.

YORK COLLEGE OF PENNSYLVANIA
YORK, PENNSYLVANIA

Entrance Moderately difficult **General** Independent, comprehensive, coed **Setting** 80-acre suburban campus **Enrollment** 5,046 **Faculty** 17:1 **Application deadline** Rolling **Freshmen** 71% accepted **Housing** Yes **Tuition** $6100 **Undergraduates** 57% women, 33% part-time, 15% 25 or older, 0% Native American, 1% Hispanic, 2% black, 1% Asian or Pacific Islander **Most popular recent majors** Nursing, elementary education, law enforcement/police sciences **Academic program** Advanced placement, accelerated degree program, self-designed majors, tutorials, summer session, adult/continuing education programs, internships **Contact** Mrs. Nancy L. Spataro, Director of Admissions, York College of Pennsylvania, York, PA 17405-7199. Telephone: 717-846-7788.

Virginia

AMERICAN MILITARY UNIVERSITY
MANASSAS PARK, VIRGINIA

Entrance Difficulty N/R **General** Proprietary, upper-level, coed **Enrollment** 1,000 **Faculty** 20:1 **Freshmen** 100% accepted **Tuition** $4835 **Undergraduates** 25% women, 100% part-time, 100% 25 or older, 0% Native American, 0% Hispanic, 0% black, 0% Asian or Pacific Islander **Contact** Director of Undergraduate Admissions, American Military University, Manassas Park, VA 22111-5211. Telephone: 703-330-5398.

AVERETT COLLEGE
DANVILLE, VIRGINIA

Entrance Moderately difficult **General** Independent Baptist, comprehensive, coed **Setting** 25-acre suburban campus **Enrollment** 2,540 **Faculty** 10:1 **Application deadline** 8/15 **Freshmen** 86% accepted **Housing** Yes **Tuition** $12,500 **Undergraduates** 56% women, 49% part-time, 64% 25 or older, 2% Hispanic, 17% black, 5% Asian or Pacific Islander **Most popular recent majors** Business administration/commerce/management, education **Academic program** Average class size 15, advanced placement, accelerated degree program, self-designed majors, tutorials, honors program, summer session, adult/continuing education programs, internships **Contact** Mr. Gary Sherman, Dean of Enrollment and Management, Averett College, Danville, VA 24541-3692. Telephone: 804-791-5660. Fax: 804-791-5637.

BLUEFIELD COLLEGE
BLUEFIELD, VIRGINIA

Entrance Moderately difficult **General** Independent Southern Baptist, 4-year, coed **Setting** 85-acre small-town campus **Enrollment** 758 **Faculty** 16:1 **Application deadline** Rolling **Freshmen** 93% accepted **Housing** Yes **Tuition** $9100 **Undergraduates** 52% women, 10% part-time, 28% 25 or older, 1% Native American, 1% Hispanic, 5% black, 1% Asian or Pacific Islander **Most popular recent majors** Business administration/commerce/management, education, psychology **Academic program** ESL program, Advanced placement, tutorials, honors program, summer session, adult/continuing education programs, internships **Contact** Office of Admissions, Bluefield College, 3000 College Drive, Bluefield, VA 24605-1799. Telephone: 540-326-4214. Fax: 540-326-4288.

BRIDGEWATER COLLEGE
BRIDGEWATER, VIRGINIA

Entrance Moderately difficult **General** Independent, 4-year, coed, affiliated with Church of the Brethren **Setting** 190-acre small-town campus **Enrollment** 1,033 **Faculty** 14:1 **Application deadline** Rolling **Freshmen** 83% accepted **Housing** Yes **Tuition** $13,270 **Undergraduates** 56% women, 2% part-time, 3% 25 or older, 1% Native American, 1% Hispanic, 5% black, 1% Asian or Pacific Islander **Most popular recent majors** Business administration/commerce/management, psychology, biology/biological sciences **Academic program** Average class size 25, advanced placement, accelerated degree program, tutorials, summer session, adult/continuing education programs, internships **Contact** Mr. Brian C. Hildebrand, Dean for Enrollment Management, Bridgewater College, Bridgewater, VA 22812-1599. Telephone: 540-828-2501 Ext. 5358. Fax: 540-828-5481.

CHRISTENDOM COLLEGE
FRONT ROYAL, VIRGINIA

Entrance Moderately difficult **General** Independent Roman Catholic, comprehensive, coed **Setting** 100-acre small-town campus **Enrollment** 213 **Faculty** 10:1 **Application deadline** Rolling **Freshmen** 91% accepted **Housing** Yes **Tuition** $10,545 **Undergraduates** 51% women, 2% part-time, 6% 25 or older, 0% Native American, 2% Hispanic, 0% black, 2% Asian or Pacific Islander **Most popular recent majors** History, literature, theology **Academic program** Average class size 25, advanced placement, accelerated degree program, summer session, internships **Contact** Mr. Paul Heisler, Director of Admissions, Christendom College, Front Royal, VA 22630-5103. Telephone: 540-636-2900 Ext. 290. Fax: 540-636-1655.

CHRISTOPHER NEWPORT UNIVERSITY
NEWPORT NEWS, VIRGINIA

Entrance Moderately difficult **General** State-supported, comprehensive, coed **Setting** 113-acre suburban campus **Enrollment** 4,558 **Faculty** 19:1 **Application deadline** 8/1 **Freshmen** 82% accepted **Housing** Yes **Tuition** $3466 **Undergraduates** 60% women, 36% part-time, 38% 25 or older, 1% Native American, 2% Hispanic, 18% black, 2% Asian or Pacific Islander **Most popular recent majors** Business administration/commerce/management, political science/government, accounting **Academic program** Average class size 25, advanced placement, accelerated degree program, self-designed majors, tutorials, honors program, summer session, adult/continuing education programs, internships **Contact** Mr. Robert J. LaVerriere, Acting Director of Admissions, Christopher Newport University, Newport News, VA 23606-2998. Telephone: 757-594-7015. Fax: 757-594-7713.

CLINCH VALLEY COLLEGE OF THE UNIVERSITY OF VIRGINIA
WISE, VIRGINIA

Entrance Moderately difficult **General** State-supported, 4-year, coed **Setting** 350-acre small-town campus **Enrollment** 1,387 **Faculty** 22:1 **Application deadline** 8/15 **Freshmen** 82% accepted **Housing** Yes **Tuition** $3258 **Undergradu-**

ates 50% women, 27% part-time, 42% 25 or older, 0% Native American, 1% Hispanic, 4% black, 1% Asian or Pacific Islander **Most popular recent majors** Business administration/commerce/management, psychology, history **Academic program** Advanced placement, self-designed majors, tutorials, honors program, summer session, adult/continuing education programs, internships **Contact** Ms. Courtney Kilgore, Director of Enrollment Management, Clinch Valley College of the University of Virginia, Wise, VA 24293. Telephone: 540-328-0102. Fax: 540-328-0251.

COLLEGE OF WILLIAM AND MARY
WILLIAMSBURG, VIRGINIA

Entrance Very difficult **General** State-supported, coed **Setting** 1,200-acre small-town campus **Enrollment** 7,722 **Faculty** 10:1 **Application deadline** 1/15 **Freshmen** 48% accepted **Housing** Yes **Tuition** $5032 **Undergraduates** 59% women, 3% part-time, 3% 25 or older, 1% Native American, 2% Hispanic, 7% black, 7% Asian or Pacific Islander **Most popular recent majors** Business administration/commerce/management, biology/biological sciences, English **Academic program** Average class size 25, advanced placement, accelerated degree program, self-designed majors, tutorials, honors program, summer session **Contact** Ms. Virginia Carey, Dean of Admission, College of William and Mary, Williamsburg, VA 23187-8795. Telephone: 757-221-4223.

COMMUNITY HOSPITAL OF ROANOKE VALLEY–COLLEGE OF HEALTH SCIENCES
ROANOKE, VIRGINIA

Entrance Moderately difficult **General** Independent, 4-year, specialized, coed **Setting** Urban campus **Enrollment** 561 **Faculty** 11:1 **Application deadline** 7/31 **Freshmen** 42% accepted **Housing** Yes **Tuition** $4500 **Undergraduates** 76% women, 54% part-time, 66% 25 or older, 6% black, 2% Asian or Pacific Islander **Most popular recent majors** Nursing, physical therapy, occupational therapy **Academic program** Average class size 15, advanced placement, summer session, adult/continuing education programs, internships **Contact** Ms. Ruth Robertson, Registrar, Community Hospital of Roanoke Valley–College of Health Sciences, PO Box 13186, Roanoke, VA 24031-3186. Telephone: 540-985-8481.

EASTERN MENNONITE UNIVERSITY
HARRISONBURG, VIRGINIA

Entrance Moderately difficult **General** Independent Mennonite, comprehensive, coed **Setting** 92-acre small-town campus **Enrollment** 1,150 **Faculty** 13:1 **Application deadline** 8/1 **Freshmen** 92% accepted **Housing** Yes **Tuition** $12,120 **Undergraduates** 61% women, 10% part-time, 19% 25 or older, 0% Native American, 2% Hispanic, 4% black, 2% Asian or Pacific Islander **Most popular recent majors** Education, biology/biological sciences, nursing **Academic program** Advanced placement, self-designed majors, honors program, summer session, adult/continuing education programs, internships **Contact** Mrs. Ellen B. Miller, Director of Admissions, Eastern Mennonite University, Harrisonburg, VA 22801-2462. Telephone: 540-732-4118. Fax: 540-432-4444.

EMORY & HENRY COLLEGE
EMORY, VIRGINIA

Entrance Moderately difficult **General** Independent United Methodist, 4-year, coed **Setting** 150-acre rural campus **Enrollment** 917 **Faculty** 14:1 **Application deadline** Rolling **Freshmen** 86% accepted **Housing** Yes **Tuition** $11,572 **Undergraduates** 49% women, 3% part-time, 5% 25 or older, 0% Native American, 0% Hispanic, 5% black, 1% Asian or Pacific Islander **Most popular recent majors** Business administration/commerce/management, English, education **Academic program** Advanced placement, self-designed majors, tutorials, summer session, internships **Contact** Dr. Jean-Marie Luce, Dean of Admissions and Financial Aid, Emory & Henry College, Emory, VA 24327-0947. Telephone: 540-944-6133. Fax: 540-944-6935.

FERRUM COLLEGE
FERRUM, VIRGINIA

Entrance Minimally difficult **General** Independent United Methodist, 4-year, coed **Setting** 720-acre rural campus **Enrollment** 1,075 **Faculty** 14:1 **Application deadline** Rolling **Freshmen** 74% accepted **Housing** Yes **Tuition** $10,750 **Undergraduates** 44% women, 6% part-time, 10% 25 or older, 1% Native American, 1% Hispanic, 13% black, 1% Asian or Pacific Islander **Most popular recent majors** Business administration/commerce/management, psychology, history **Academic program** Average class size 23, advanced placement, self-designed majors, tutorials, summer session, internships **Contact** Ms. Leslie Shipp, Associate Director of Admissions, Ferrum College, Ferrum, VA 24088-9001. Telephone: 540-365-4290. Fax: 540-365-4266.

GEORGE MASON UNIVERSITY
FAIRFAX, VIRGINIA

Entrance Moderately difficult **General** State-supported, coed **Setting** 677-acre suburban campus **Enrollment** 24,368 **Faculty** 17:1 **Application deadline** 2/1 **Freshmen** 69% accepted **Housing** Yes **Tuition** $4296 **Undergraduates** 56% women, 29% part-time, 29% 25 or older, 1% Native American, 5% Hispanic, 8% black, 15% Asian or Pacific Islander **Most popular recent majors** Business administration/commerce/management, psychology, English **Academic program** Advanced placement, accelerated degree program, self-designed majors, tutorials, summer session, adult/continuing education programs, internships **Contact** Mr. John C. Carter, Associate Director of Admissions, George Mason University, Finley Building, Fairfax, VA 22030-4444. Telephone: 703-993-2421.

HAMPDEN-SYDNEY COLLEGE
HAMPDEN-SYDNEY, VIRGINIA

Entrance Moderately difficult **General** Independent Presbyterian, 4-year, men only **Setting** 820-acre rural campus **Enrollment** 956 **Faculty** 13:1 **Application deadline** 3/1 **Freshmen** 89% accepted **Housing** Yes **Tuition** $15,074 **Undergraduates** 0% part-time, 0% 25 or older, 0% Native American, 1% Hispanic, 4% black, 2% Asian or Pacific Islander **Most popular recent majors** Economics, history, political science/government **Academic program** Average class size 16, advanced placement, accelerated degree program, tutorials, honors program, summer session, internships **Contact** Ms. Anita H. Garland, Dean of Admissions, Hampden-Sydney College, PO Box 667, Hampden-Sydney, VA 23943-0667. Telephone: 804-223-6120. Fax: 804-223-6346.

HAMPTON UNIVERSITY
HAMPTON, VIRGINIA

Entrance Moderately difficult **General** Independent, comprehensive, coed **Setting** 210-acre urban campus **Enrollment** 6,035 **Faculty** 16:1 **Application deadline** 3/15 **Freshmen** 72% accepted **Housing** Yes **Tuition** $8948 **Undergraduates** 61% women, 21% part-time, 19% 25 or older, 1% Native American, 1% Hispanic, 85% black, 1% Asian or Pacific Islander **Most popular recent majors** Accounting, biology/biological sciences, psychology **Academic program** Advanced placement, tutorials, honors program, summer session, adult/continuing education programs, internships **Contact** Mr. Leonard M. Jones Jr., Director of Admissions, Hampton University, Hampton, VA 23668. Telephone: 757-727-5328. Fax: 757-727-5084.

HOLLINS COLLEGE
ROANOKE, VIRGINIA

Entrance Moderately difficult **General** Independent, comprehensive, women only **Setting** 475-acre suburban campus **Enrollment** 1,030 **Faculty** 9:1 **Application deadline** 2/15 **Freshmen** 81% accepted **Housing** Yes **Tuition** $15,320 **Undergraduates** 6% part-time, 9% 25 or older, 1% Native American, 2% Hispanic, 4% black, 2% Asian or Pacific Islander **Most popular recent majors** English, psychology, biology/biological sciences **Academic program** Average class size 15, advanced placement, accelerated degree program, self-designed majors, tutorials, honors program, adult/continuing education programs, internships **Contact** Mrs. Stuart Trinkle, Director of Admissions, Hollins College, Roanoke, VA 24020-1688. Telephone: 540-362-6401. Fax: 540-362-6642.

JAMES MADISON UNIVERSITY
HARRISONBURG, VIRGINIA

Entrance Very difficult **General** State-supported, comprehensive, coed **Setting** 472-acre small-town campus **Enrollment** 12,963 **Faculty** 19:1 **Application deadline** 1/15 **Freshmen** 63% accepted **Housing** Yes **Tuition** $4148 **Undergraduates** 55% women, 4% part-time, 4% 25 or older, 1% Native American, 2% Hispanic, 5% black, 4% Asian or Pacific Islander **Most popular recent majors** Psychology, biology/biological sciences, English **Academic program** Average class size 25, advanced placement, accelerated degree program, honors program, summer session, adult/continuing education programs, internships **Contact** Mrs. Roxie Shabazz, Director of Admissions, James Madison University, Office of Admissions, Harrisonburg, VA 22807. Telephone: 540-568-6147.

LIBERTY UNIVERSITY
LYNCHBURG, VIRGINIA

Entrance Minimally difficult **General** Independent nondenominational, comprehensive, coed **Setting** 160-acre suburban campus **Enrollment** 5,581 **Faculty** 28:1 **Application deadline** 8/15 **Freshmen** 73% accepted **Housing** Yes **Tuition** $7680 **Undergraduates** 51% women, 4% part-time, 7% 25 or older, 1% Native American, 2% Hispanic, 8% black, 3% Asian or Pacific Islander **Most popular recent majors** Business administration/commerce/management, psychology, education **Academic program** Advanced placement, accelerated degree program, self-designed majors, tutorials, honors program, summer session, internships **Contact** Mrs. Holly Honeycutt, Associate Director of Admissions, Liberty University, Lynchburg, VA 24502. Telephone: 804-582-2158.

LONGWOOD COLLEGE
FARMVILLE, VIRGINIA

Entrance Moderately difficult **General** State-supported, comprehensive, coed **Setting** 154-acre small-town campus **Enrollment** 3,023 **Faculty** 14:1 **Application deadline** 2/15 **Freshmen** 76% accepted **Housing** Yes **Tuition** $4416 **Undergraduates** 67% women, 13% part-time, 11% 25 or older, 1% Hispanic, 10% black, 1% Asian or Pacific Islander **Most popular recent majors** Business administration/commerce/management, education, psychology **Academic program** Average class size 25, advanced placement, accelerated degree program, tutorials, honors program, summer session, adult/continuing education programs, internships **Contact** Mr. Robert J. Chonko, Director of Admissions, Longwood College, Farmville, VA 23909-1800. Telephone: 804-395-2060. Fax: 804-395-2635.

LYNCHBURG COLLEGE
LYNCHBURG, VIRGINIA

Entrance Moderately difficult **General** Independent, comprehensive, coed, affiliated with Christian Church (Disciples of Christ) **Setting** 214-acre suburban campus **Enrollment** 1,842 **Faculty** 13:1 **Application deadline** Rolling **Freshmen** 86% accepted **Housing** Yes **Tuition** $15,615 **Undergraduates** 64% women, 14% part-time, 19% 25 or older, 0% Native American, 1% Hispanic, 12% black, 1% Asian or Pacific Islander **Most popular recent majors** Education, business administration/commerce/management, communication **Academic program** Advanced placement, accelerated degree program, tutorials, honors program, summer session, adult/continuing education programs, internships **Contact** Ms. Mari Normyle, Director of Enrollment, Lynchburg College, Lynchburg, VA 24501-3199. Telephone: 804-544-8300. Fax: 804-544-8653.

MARY BALDWIN COLLEGE
STAUNTON, VIRGINIA

Entrance Moderately difficult **General** Independent, comprehensive, primarily women, affiliated with Presbyterian Church (U.S.A.) **Setting** 54-acre small-town campus **Enrollment** 2,132 **Faculty** 12:1 **Application deadline** Rolling **Freshmen** 81% accepted **Housing** Yes **Tuition** $13,360 **Undergraduates** 92% women, 1% part-time, 0% 25 or older, 0% Native American, 3% Hispanic, 7% black, 3% Asian or Pacific Islander **Most popular recent majors** Business administration/commerce/management, psychology, art/fine arts **Academic program** Average class size 19, advanced placement, accelerated degree program, self-designed majors, tutorials, honors program, adult/continuing education programs, internships **Contact** Ms. Patricia N. LeDonne, Dean of Admissions & Financial Aid, Mary Baldwin College, Staunton, VA 24401. Telephone: 540-887-7019. Fax: 540-886-6634.

MARYMOUNT UNIVERSITY
ARLINGTON, VIRGINIA

Entrance Moderately difficult **General** Independent, comprehensive, coed, affiliated with Roman Catholic Church **Setting** 21-acre suburban campus **Enrollment** 3,845 **Faculty** 16:1 **Application deadline** Rolling **Freshmen** 74% accepted **Housing** Yes **Tuition** $12,770 **Undergraduates** 75% women, 36% part-time, 49% 25 or older, 0% Native American, 5% Hispanic, 13% black, 6% Asian or Pacific Islander **Most popular recent majors** Nursing, business administration/commerce/management, interior design **Academic program** Average class size 16, advanced placement, accelerated degree program, self-designed majors, honors program, summer session, adult/continuing education programs, internships **Contact** Mr. Chris E. Domes, Dean of Admissions, Marymount University, Arlington, VA 22207-4299. Telephone: 703-284-1500. Fax: 703-522-0349.

MARY WASHINGTON COLLEGE
FREDERICKSBURG, VIRGINIA

Entrance Very difficult **General** State-supported, comprehensive, coed **Setting** 176-acre small-town campus **Enrollment** 3,745 **Faculty** 18:1 **Application deadline** 2/1 **Freshmen** 55% accepted **Housing** Yes **Tuition** $3556 **Undergraduates** 65% women, 15% part-time, 6% 25 or older, 0% Native American, 2% Hispanic, 6% black, 3% Asian or Pacific Islander **Most popular recent majors** Business administration/commerce/management, psychology, English **Academic program** Advanced placement, accelerated degree program, self-designed majors, tutorials, summer session, adult/continuing education programs, internships **Contact** Dr. Martin A. Wilder Jr., Vice President for Admissions and Financial Aid, Mary Washington College, 1301 College Avenue, Fredericksburg, VA 22401-5358. Telephone: 540-654-2000.

NORFOLK STATE UNIVERSITY
NORFOLK, VIRGINIA

Entrance Moderately difficult **General** State-supported, comprehensive, coed **Setting** 130-acre urban campus **Enrollment** 8,352 **Faculty** 22:1 **Application deadline** Rolling **Freshmen** 95% accepted **Housing** Yes **Tuition** $3000 **Undergraduates** 62% women, 14% part-time, 87% black **Academic program** ESL program, Advanced placement, accelerated degree program, honors program, summer session, adult/continuing education programs, internships **Contact** Dr. Frank W. Cool, Director of Admissions, Norfolk State University, 2401 Corprew Avenue, Norfolk, VA 23504-3907. Telephone: 757-683-8391.

OLD DOMINION UNIVERSITY
NORFOLK, VIRGINIA

Entrance Moderately difficult **General** State-supported, coed **Setting** 186-acre urban campus **Enrollment** 11,400 **Faculty** 10:1 **Application deadline** 5/1 **Freshmen** 81% accepted **Housing** Yes **Tuition** $4250 **Undergraduates** 55% women, 31% part-time, 42% 25 or older, 2% Native American, 2% Hispanic, 19% black, 6% Asian or Pacific Islander **Most popular recent majors** Psychology, interdisciplinary studies, nursing **Academic program** Advanced placement, accelerated degree program, self-designed majors, tutorials, honors program, summer session, adult/continuing education programs, internships **Contact** Ms. Patty Cavender, Assistant Vice President for Enrollment Services, Old Dominion University, 5215 Hampton Boulevard, Norfolk, VA 23529. Telephone: 757-683-3637. Fax: 757-683-5357.

RADFORD UNIVERSITY
RADFORD, VIRGINIA

Entrance Moderately difficult **General** State-supported, comprehensive, coed **Setting** 177-acre small-town campus **Enrollment** 8,270 **Faculty** 16:1 **Application deadline** 4/1 **Freshmen** 80% accepted **Housing** Yes **Tuition** $4344 **Undergraduates** 57% women, 8% part-time, 11% 25 or older, 0% Native American, 2% Hispanic, 4% black, 2% Asian or Pacific Islander **Most popular recent majors** Interdisciplinary studies, criminal justice, psychology **Academic program** Average class size 23, advanced placement, accelerated degree program, self-designed majors, tutorials, honors program, summer session, adult/continuing education programs, internships **Contact** Dr. David Kraus, Director of Admissions and Records, Radford University, PO Box 6903, Radford, VA 24142. Telephone: 540-831-5371. Fax: 540-831-5138.

RANDOLPH-MACON COLLEGE
ASHLAND, VIRGINIA

Entrance Moderately difficult **General** Independent United Methodist, 4-year, coed **Setting** 110-acre suburban campus **Enrollment** 1,101 **Faculty** 11:1 **Application deadline** 3/1 **Freshmen** 81% accepted **Housing** Yes **Tuition** $15,990 **Undergraduates** 50% women, 4% part-time, 1% 25 or older, 1% Native American, 1% Hispanic, 4% black, 1% Asian or Pacific Islander **Most popular recent majors** Business economics, psychology, English **Academic program** Average class size 22, advanced placement, accelerated degree program, tutorials, honors program, summer session, internships **Contact** Mr. John C. Conkright, Dean of Admissions and Financial Aid, Randolph-Macon College, Ashland, VA 23005-5505. Telephone: 804-752-7305. Fax: 804-752-4707.

RANDOLPH-MACON WOMAN'S COLLEGE
LYNCHBURG, VIRGINIA

Entrance Moderately difficult **General** Independent Methodist, 4-year, women only **Setting** 100-acre suburban campus **Enrollment** 698 **Faculty** 9:1 **Application deadline** 3/1 **Freshmen** 89% accepted **Housing** Yes **Tuition** $16,230 **Undergraduates** 7% part-time, 10% 25 or older, 0% Native American, 3% Hispanic, 5% black, 3% Asian or Pacific Islander **Most popular recent majors** Psychology, political science/government, English **Academic program** Average class size 17, advanced placement, accelerated degree program, self-designed majors, tutorials, honors program, summer session, adult/continuing education programs, internships **Contact** Mr. James Duffy, Senior Associate Director of Admissions, Randolph-Macon Woman's College, Lynchburg, VA 24503-1526. Telephone: 804-947-8100.

ROANOKE COLLEGE
SALEM, VIRGINIA

Entrance Moderately difficult **General** Independent, 4-year, coed, affiliated with Evangelical Lutheran Church in America **Setting** 68-acre suburban campus **Enrollment** 1,694 **Faculty** 14:1 **Application deadline** 3/1 **Freshmen** 83% accepted **Housing** Yes **Tuition** $15,570 **Undergraduates** 58% women, 12% part-time, 10% 25 or older, 1% Native American, 1% Hispanic, 3% black, 2% Asian or Pacific Islander **Most popular recent majors** Business administration/commerce/

management, sociology, English **Academic program** Average class size 20, advanced placement, accelerated degree program, honors program, summer session, adult/continuing education programs, internships **Contact** Mr. Michael C. Maxey, Vice President of Admissions, Roanoke College, Salem, VA 24153-3794. Telephone: 540-375-2270.

SAINT PAUL'S COLLEGE
LAWRENCEVILLE, VIRGINIA

Entrance Minimally difficult **General** Independent Episcopal, 4-year, coed **Setting** 75-acre small-town campus **Enrollment** 666 **Faculty** 17:1 **Freshmen** 72% accepted **Housing** Yes **Tuition** \$7260 **Undergraduates** 57% women, 6% part-time, 1% 25 or older, 0% Native American, 0% Hispanic, 95% black, 0% Asian or Pacific Islander **Most popular recent majors** Business administration/commerce/management, biology/biological sciences, sociology **Academic program** Honors program, summer session, adult/continuing education programs, internships **Contact** Mrs. Mary Ransom, Director of Admissions and Recruitment, Saint Paul's College, Lawrenceville, VA 23868-1202. Telephone: 804-848-3984.

SHENANDOAH UNIVERSITY
WINCHESTER, VIRGINIA

Entrance Moderately difficult **General** Independent United Methodist, comprehensive, coed **Setting** 70-acre small-town campus **Enrollment** 1,871 **Faculty** 12:1 **Application deadline** Rolling **Freshmen** 81% accepted **Housing** Yes **Tuition** \$14,400 **Undergraduates** 65% women, 18% part-time, 26% 25 or older, 1% Native American, 1% Hispanic, 6% black, 1% Asian or Pacific Islander **Most popular recent majors** Nursing, music, business administration/commerce/management **Academic program** Advanced placement, accelerated degree program, summer session, adult/continuing education programs, internships **Contact** Mr. Michael Carpenter, Director of Admissions, Shenandoah University, 1460 University Drive, Winchester, VA 22601-5195. Telephone: 540-665-4581. Fax: 540-665-4627.

SWEET BRIAR COLLEGE
SWEET BRIAR, VIRGINIA

Entrance Moderately difficult **General** Independent, 4-year, women only **Setting** 3,300-acre rural campus **Enrollment** 734 **Faculty** 8:1 **Application deadline** 2/15 **Freshmen** 91% accepted **Housing** Yes **Tuition** \$15,795 **Undergraduates** 2% part-time, 4% 25 or older, 1% Native American, 2% Hispanic, 6% black, 3% Asian or Pacific Islander **Most popular recent majors** Biology/biological sciences, political science/government, English **Academic program** Advanced placement, accelerated degree program, self-designed majors, tutorials, honors program, adult/continuing education programs, internships **Contact** Ms. Nancy E. Church, Dean of Admissions, Sweet Briar College, PO Box B, Sweet Briar, VA 24595. Telephone: 804-381-6142. Fax: 804-381-6152.

UNIVERSITY OF RICHMOND
UNIVERSITY OF RICHMOND, VIRGINIA

Entrance Very difficult **General** Independent, comprehensive, coed, affiliated with Baptist General Association of Virginia **Setting** 350-acre suburban campus **Enrollment** 4,366 **Faculty** 11:1 **Application deadline** 2/1 **Freshmen** 50% accepted **Housing** Yes **Tuition** \$17,570 **Undergraduates** 50% women, 3% part-time, 1% Native American, 2% Hispanic, 4% black, 3% Asian or Pacific Islander **Most popular recent majors** Business administration/commerce/management, biology/biological sciences, political science/government **Academic program** Average class size 19, advanced placement, accelerated degree program, self-designed majors, tutorials, honors program, summer session, adult/continuing education programs, internships **Contact** Ms. Pamela Spence, Dean of Admissions, University of Richmond, University of Richmond, VA 23173. Telephone: 804-289-8640. Fax: 804-287-6003.

UNIVERSITY OF VIRGINIA
CHARLOTTESVILLE, VIRGINIA

Entrance Most difficult **General** State-supported, coed **Setting** 1,136-acre suburban campus **Enrollment** 17,959 **Faculty** 14:1 **Application deadline** 1/2 **Freshmen** 33% accepted **Housing** Yes **Tuition** \$4790 **Undergraduates** 53% women, 1% part-time, 2% 25 or older, 0% Native American, 2% Hispanic, 11% black, 10% Asian or Pacific Islander **Most popular recent majors** Business administration/commerce/management, biology/biological sciences, psychology **Academic program** Advanced placement, accelerated degree program, self-designed majors, tutorials, honors program, summer session, adult/continuing education programs, internships **Contact** Mr. John A. Blackburn, Dean of Admission, University of Virginia, Charlottesville, VA 22903. Telephone: 804-982-3200. Fax: 804-924-3587.

VIRGINIA COMMONWEALTH UNIVERSITY
RICHMOND, VIRGINIA

Entrance Moderately difficult **General** State-supported, coed **Setting** 101-acre urban campus **Enrollment** 21,681 **Application deadline** 2/1 **Freshmen** 82% accepted **Housing** Yes **Tuition** $4111 **Undergraduates** 59% women, 21% part-time, 27% 25 or older, 1% Native American, 2% Hispanic, 21% black, 8% Asian or Pacific Islander **Most popular recent majors** Psychology, nursing, English **Academic program** Average class size 27, advanced placement, accelerated degree program, self-designed majors, honors program, summer session, adult/continuing education programs, internships **Contact** Counseling Staff, Virginia Commonwealth University, 821 West Franklin Street, Box 842526, Richmond, VA 23284-9005. Telephone: 804-828-1222. Fax: 804-828-1899.

VIRGINIA INTERMONT COLLEGE
BRISTOL, VIRGINIA

Entrance Minimally difficult **General** Independent, 4-year, coed, affiliated with Baptist Church **Setting** 27-acre small-town campus **Enrollment** 769 **Faculty** 12:1 **Application deadline** Rolling **Freshmen** 81% accepted **Housing** Yes **Tuition** $10,850 **Undergraduates** 73% women, 19% part-time, 52% 25 or older, 1% Native American, 1% Hispanic, 2% black, 1% Asian or Pacific Islander **Most popular recent majors** Business administration/commerce/management, social work, photography **Academic program** Average class size 30, advanced placement, summer session, adult/continuing education programs, internships **Contact** Ms. Robin B. Cozart, Director of Admissions, Virginia Intermont College, Bristol, VA 24201-4298. Telephone: 540-669-6101 Ext. 287. Fax: 540-669-5763.

VIRGINIA MILITARY INSTITUTE
LEXINGTON, VIRGINIA

Entrance Moderately difficult **General** State-supported, 4-year, primarily men **Setting** 133-acre small-town campus **Enrollment** 1,218 **Faculty** 12:1 **Application deadline** 4/1 **Freshmen** 78% accepted **Housing** Yes **Tuition** $6380 **Undergraduates** 0% part-time, 0% 25 or older, 1% Native American, 2% Hispanic, 6% black, 3% Asian or Pacific Islander **Most popular recent majors** Economics, history, civil engineering **Academic program** Average class size 20, advanced placement, accelerated degree program, tutorials, honors program, summer session **Contact** Maj. Tom Mortenson, Associate Director of Admissions, Virginia Military Institute, Admissions Office, Lexington, VA 24450. Telephone: 540-464-7211. Fax: 540-464-7746.

VIRGINIA POLYTECHNIC INSTITUTE AND STATE UNIVERSITY
BLACKSBURG, VIRGINIA

Entrance Moderately difficult **General** State-supported, coed **Setting** 2,600-acre small-town campus **Enrollment** 24,812 **Faculty** 17:1 **Application deadline** 2/1 **Freshmen** 81% accepted **Housing** Yes **Tuition** $4147 **Undergraduates** 41% women, 3% part-time, 3% 25 or older, 0% Native American, 1% Hispanic, 5% black, 6% Asian or Pacific Islander **Most popular recent majors** Psychology, mechanical engineering, marketing/retailing/merchandising **Academic program** Advanced placement, accelerated degree program, tutorials, honors program, summer session, adult/continuing education programs, internships **Contact** Office of Undergraduate Admissions, Virginia Polytechnic Institute and State University, 104 Burruss Hall, Blacksburg, VA 24061-0202. Telephone: 540-231-6267. Fax: 540-231-3242.

VIRGINIA STATE UNIVERSITY
PETERSBURG, VIRGINIA

Entrance Minimally difficult **General** State-supported, comprehensive, coed **Setting** 236-acre suburban campus **Enrollment** 4,014 **Application deadline** Rolling **Freshmen** 78% accepted **Housing** Yes **Tuition** $3307 **Undergraduates** 58% women, 9% part-time, 0% 25 or older, 0% Native American, 0% Hispanic, 94% black, 0% Asian or Pacific Islander **Most popular recent majors** Business administration/commerce/management, accounting, psychology **Academic program** Advanced placement, accelerated degree program, honors program, summer session, adult/continuing education programs, internships **Contact** Ms. Lisa Winn, Director of Admissions, Virginia State University, PO Box 9018, Petersburg, VA 23806-0001. Telephone: 804-524-5902. Fax: 804-524-5055.

VIRGINIA UNION UNIVERSITY
RICHMOND, VIRGINIA

Entrance Moderately difficult **General** Independent Baptist, comprehensive, coed **Setting** 72-acre urban campus **Enrollment** 1,551 **Faculty** 16:1 **Application deadline** Rolling **Freshmen** 94% accepted **Housing** Yes **Tuition** $8980 **Undergraduates** 58% women, 4% part-time, 0% Native American, 1% Hispanic, 98% black, 0% Asian or Pacific Islander **Most popular recent majors**

Business administration/commerce/management, criminology, biology/biological sciences **Academic program** Average class size 16, advanced placement, tutorials, honors program, summer session, adult/continuing education programs, internships **Contact** Mr. Gil Powell, Director of Admissions, Virginia Union University, 1500 North Lombardy Street, Richmond, VA 23220-1170. Telephone: 804-257-5881.

VIRGINIA WESLEYAN COLLEGE
NORFOLK, VIRGINIA

Entrance Moderately difficult **General** Independent United Methodist, 4-year, coed **Setting** 300-acre urban campus **Enrollment** 1,460 **Faculty** 13:1 **Application deadline** Rolling **Freshmen** 88% accepted **Housing** Yes **Tuition** $13,400 **Undergraduates** 65% women, 26% part-time, 35% 25 or older, 1% Native American, 2% Hispanic, 7% black, 3% Asian or Pacific Islander **Most popular recent majors** Business administration/commerce/management, communication, education **Academic program** Advanced placement, accelerated degree program, self-designed majors, tutorials, honors program, summer session, adult/continuing education programs, internships **Contact** Dr. Martha E. Rogers, Vice President for Enrollment Management, Dean of Admissions, Virginia Wesleyan College, 1584 Wesleyan Drive, Norfolk, VA 23502-5599. Telephone: 804-455-3208. Fax: 804-461-5238.

WASHINGTON AND LEE UNIVERSITY
LEXINGTON, VIRGINIA

Entrance Most difficult **General** Independent, comprehensive, coed **Setting** 322-acre small-town campus **Enrollment** 2,006 **Faculty** 10:1 **Application deadline** 1/15 **Freshmen** 34% accepted **Housing** Yes **Tuition** $16,195 **Undergraduates** 41% women, 0% part-time, 1% 25 or older, 0% Native American, 1% Hispanic, 2% black, 2% Asian or Pacific Islander **Most popular recent majors** History, economics, business administration/commerce/management **Academic program** Advanced placement, accelerated degree program, self-designed majors, tutorials, honors program, internships **Contact** Mr. William M. Hartog, Dean of Admissions and Financial Aid, Washington and Lee University, Lexington, VA 24450. Telephone: 540-463-8710. Fax: 540-463-8062.

WORLD COLLEGE
VIRGINIA BEACH, VIRGINIA

Entrance Noncompetitive **General** Proprietary, 4-year, specialized, primarily men **Setting** Suburban campus **Enrollment** 562 **Application deadline** Rolling **Undergraduates** 4% women, 100% part-time, 92% 25 or older, 4% Native American, 6% Hispanic, 9% black, 3% Asian or Pacific Islander **Academic program** Accelerated degree program, adult/continuing education programs **Contact** Ms. Kristen Tanner, Administrative Assistant, World College, Virginia Beach, VA 23455-2500. Telephone: 804-464-4600.

West Virginia

ALDERSON-BROADDUS COLLEGE
PHILIPPI, WEST VIRGINIA

Entrance Moderately difficult **General** Independent, comprehensive, coed, affiliated with Baptist Church **Setting** 170-acre rural campus **Enrollment** 740 **Faculty** 11:1 **Application deadline** Rolling **Freshmen** 99% accepted **Housing** Yes **Tuition** $12,215 **Undergraduates** 59% women, 5% part-time, 33% 25 or older, 1% Native American, 1% Hispanic, 3% black, 2% Asian or Pacific Islander **Most popular recent majors** Physician's assistant studies, nursing, secondary education **Academic program** Advanced placement, self-designed majors, tutorials, honors program, summer session, internships **Contact** Mr. Eric A. Ruf, Director of Admissions, Alderson-Broaddus College, Campus Box 216, Philippi, WV 26416. Telephone: 304-457-1700 Ext. 310.

APPALACHIAN BIBLE COLLEGE
BRADLEY, WEST VIRGINIA

Entrance Minimally difficult **General** Independent Baptist, 4-year, specialized, coed **Setting** 110-acre small-town campus **Enrollment** 291 **Faculty** 14:1 **Application deadline** Rolling **Housing** Yes **Tuition** $5510 **Undergraduates** 46% women, 23% part-time, 7% 25 or older, 1% Native American, 1% Hispanic, 2% black, 2% Asian or Pacific Islander **Academic program** Advanced placement, adult/continuing education programs, internships **Contact** Mrs. Rita Pritt, Director of Admissions, Appalachian Bible College, Bradley, WV 25818. Telephone: 304-877-6428 Ext. 202.

BETHANY COLLEGE
BETHANY, WEST VIRGINIA

Entrance Moderately difficult **General** Independent, 4-year, coed, affiliated with Christian Church (Disciples of Christ) **Setting** 1,600-acre rural campus **Enrollment** 761 **Faculty** 13:1 **Application deadline** Rolling **Freshmen** 80% accepted **Housing** Yes **Tuition** $17,349 **Undergraduates** 52%

women, 5% part-time, 1% 25 or older, 0% Native American, 1% Hispanic, 4% black, 2% Asian or Pacific Islander **Most popular recent majors** Communication, psychology, business administration/commerce/management **Academic program** Advanced placement, accelerated degree program, self-designed majors, tutorials, honors program, summer session, internships **Contact** Mr. Gary R. Forney, Vice President for Enrollment Management, Bethany College, Bethany, WV 26032. Telephone: 304-829-7611.

BLUEFIELD STATE COLLEGE
BLUEFIELD, WEST VIRGINIA

Entrance Noncompetitive **General** State-supported, 4-year, coed **Setting** 45-acre small-town campus **Enrollment** 2,609 **Faculty** 18:1 **Application deadline** Rolling **Freshmen** 65% accepted **Tuition** $2044 **Undergraduates** 57% women, 38% part-time, 35% 25 or older, 1% Native American, 1% Hispanic, 8% black, 1% Asian or Pacific Islander **Most popular recent majors** Business administration/commerce/management, nursing, education **Academic program** Advanced placement, summer session, adult/continuing education programs, internships **Contact** Mr. John C. Cardwell, Director of Admissions and Enrollment Management, Bluefield State College, Bluefield, WV 24701-2198. Telephone: 304-327-4065. Fax: 304-327-7747.

THE COLLEGE OF WEST VIRGINIA
BECKLEY, WEST VIRGINIA

Entrance Noncompetitive **General** Independent, 4-year, coed **Setting** 4-acre suburban campus **Enrollment** 1,983 **Faculty** 18:1 **Application deadline** Rolling **Freshmen** 100% accepted **Housing** Yes **Tuition** $3360 **Undergraduates** 70% women, 30% part-time, 57% 25 or older, 1% Native American, 1% Hispanic, 6% black, 1% Asian or Pacific Islander **Academic program** Advanced placement, accelerated degree program, self-designed majors, tutorials, summer session, adult/continuing education programs, internships **Contact** Ms. Terri Williams, Admissions Coordinator, The College of West Virginia, Beckley, WV 25802-2830. Telephone: 304-253-7351 Ext. 334. Fax: 304-253-0789 Ext. 386.

CONCORD COLLEGE
ATHENS, WEST VIRGINIA

Entrance Minimally difficult **General** State-supported, 4-year, coed **Setting** 100-acre rural campus **Enrollment** 2,357 **Faculty** 22:1 **Application deadline** Rolling **Freshmen** 93% accepted **Housing** Yes **Tuition** $2310 **Undergraduates** 59% women, 29% part-time, 11% 25 or older, 0% Native American, 1% Hispanic, 5% black, 1% Asian or Pacific Islander **Most popular recent majors** Education, business administration/commerce/management, tourism and travel **Academic program** Advanced placement, accelerated degree program, honors program, summer session **Contact** Mr. Joseph P. Bagnoli, Director of Admissions, Concord College, Athens, WV 24712-1000. Telephone: 304-384-5248. Fax: 304-384-9044.

DAVIS & ELKINS COLLEGE
ELKINS, WEST VIRGINIA

Entrance Moderately difficult **General** Independent Presbyterian, 4-year, coed **Setting** 170-acre small-town campus **Enrollment** 732 **Faculty** 13:1 **Application deadline** Rolling **Freshmen** 91% accepted **Housing** Yes **Tuition** $10,780 **Undergraduates** 60% women, 13% part-time, 21% 25 or older, 0% Native American, 0% Hispanic, 3% black, 3% Asian or Pacific Islander **Most popular recent majors** Business administration/commerce/management, education, psychology **Academic program** Average class size 25, advanced placement, accelerated degree program, self-designed majors, tutorials, honors program, summer session, adult/continuing education programs, internships **Contact** Mr. Kevin Chenoweth, Director of Admissions, Davis & Elkins College, Elkins, WV 26241-3996. Telephone: 304-637-1301. Fax: 304-637-1419.

FAIRMONT STATE COLLEGE
FAIRMONT, WEST VIRGINIA

Entrance Minimally difficult **General** State-supported, 4-year, coed **Setting** 80-acre small-town campus **Enrollment** 6,555 **Faculty** 23:1 **Application deadline** 6/15 **Freshmen** 99% accepted **Housing** Yes **Tuition** $2040 **Undergraduates** 55% women, 33% part-time, 29% 25 or older, 1% Native American, 1% Hispanic, 3% black, 1% Asian or Pacific Islander **Most popular recent majors** Criminal justice, accounting, education **Academic program** Average class size 30, advanced placement, accelerated degree program, honors program, summer session, adult/continuing education programs, internships **Contact** Dr. John G. Conaway, Director of Admissions, Fairmont State College, Fairmont, WV 26554. Telephone: 304-367-4141.

GLENVILLE STATE COLLEGE
GLENVILLE, WEST VIRGINIA

Entrance Moderately difficult **General** State-supported, 4-year, coed **Setting** 331-acre rural campus **Enrollment** 2,179 **Faculty** 13:1 **Application deadline** 8/1 **Freshmen** 38% accepted **Housing** Yes **Tuition** $1956 **Undergraduates** 56% women, 26% part-time, 28% 25 or older, 1% Native American, 1% Hispanic, 3% black, 1% Asian or Pacific Islander **Most popular recent majors** Business administration/commerce/management, education, behavioral sciences **Academic program** Advanced placement, accelerated degree program, self-designed majors, summer session, adult/continuing education programs **Contact** Dr. Phillip Cottrill, Registrar/Director of Enrollment Management, Glenville State College, 200 High Street, Glenville, WV 26351-1200. Telephone: 304-462-7361 Ext. 152. Fax: 304-462-8619.

MARSHALL UNIVERSITY
HUNTINGTON, WEST VIRGINIA

Entrance Minimally difficult **General** State-supported, comprehensive, coed **Setting** 70-acre urban campus **Enrollment** 11,066 **Faculty** 20:1 **Application deadline** Rolling **Freshmen** 90% accepted **Housing** Yes **Tuition** $2184 **Undergraduates** 52% women, 24% part-time, 27% 25 or older, 1% Native American, 1% Hispanic, 4% black, 1% Asian or Pacific Islander **Most popular recent majors** Elementary education, criminal justice, psychology **Academic program** Average class size 24, ESL program, advanced placement, accelerated degree program, tutorials, honors program, summer session, adult/continuing education programs, internships **Contact** Dr. James W. Harless, Admissions Director, Marshall University, 400 Hal Greer Boulevard, Huntington, WV 25755-2020. Telephone: 304-696-3160. Fax: 304-696-3135.

SALEM-TEIKYO UNIVERSITY
SALEM, WEST VIRGINIA

Entrance Moderately difficult **General** Independent, comprehensive, coed **Setting** 100-acre rural campus **Enrollment** 867 **Faculty** 15:1 **Application deadline** Rolling **Freshmen** 76% accepted **Housing** Yes **Tuition** $12,106 **Undergraduates** 40% women, 2% part-time, 6% 25 or older, 2% Hispanic, 9% black, 2% Asian or Pacific Islander **Academic program** Advanced placement, accelerated degree program, summer session, internships **Contact** Ms. Billie Hudson, Assistant Director of Admissions, Salem-Teikyo University, PO Box 500, Salem, WV 26426-0500. Telephone: 304-782-5279.

SHEPHERD COLLEGE
SHEPHERDSTOWN, WEST VIRGINIA

Entrance Moderately difficult **General** State-supported, 4-year, coed **Setting** 320-acre small-town campus **Enrollment** 3,845 **Faculty** 14:1 **Application deadline** 2/1 **Freshmen** 64% accepted **Housing** Yes **Tuition** $2228 **Undergraduates** 60% women, 36% part-time, 33% 25 or older, 1% Native American, 2% Hispanic, 6% black, 1% Asian or Pacific Islander **Most popular recent majors** Business administration/commerce/management, education, nursing **Academic program** Average class size 30, advanced placement, accelerated degree program, honors program, summer session, adult/continuing education programs, internships **Contact** Mr. Karl L. Wolf, Director of Admissions, Shepherd College, Shepherdstown, WV 25443-3210. Telephone: 304-876-5212. Fax: 304-876-5765.

THE UNIVERSITY OF CHARLESTON
CHARLESTON, WEST VIRGINIA

Entrance Moderately difficult **General** Independent, comprehensive, coed **Setting** 40-acre urban campus **Enrollment** 1,424 **Faculty** 11:1 **Application deadline** Rolling **Freshmen** 79% accepted **Housing** Yes **Tuition** $11,600 **Undergraduates** 69% women, 37% part-time, 39% 25 or older, 1% Native American, 1% Hispanic, 3% black, 1% Asian or Pacific Islander **Most popular recent majors** Health science, business administration/commerce/management, education **Academic program** ESL program, Advanced placement, accelerated degree program, self-designed majors, tutorials, summer session, adult/continuing education programs, internships **Contact** Mr. Alan Liebrecht, Director of Admissions, The University of Charleston, 2300 MacCorkle Avenue, SE, Charleston, WV 25304-1099. Telephone: 304-357-4800. Fax: 304-357-4715.

WEST LIBERTY STATE COLLEGE
WEST LIBERTY, WEST VIRGINIA

Entrance Minimally difficult **General** State-supported, 4-year, coed **Setting** 290-acre rural campus **Enrollment** 2,412 **Faculty** 18:1 **Application deadline** 8/1 **Freshmen** 95% accepted **Housing** Yes **Tuition** $2120 **Undergraduates** 55% women, 11% part-time, 16% 25 or older, 1% Hispanic, 3% black **Most popular recent majors** Business administration/commerce/management, education, criminal justice **Academic program** Advanced placement, self-designed majors, honors program, summer session, adult/continuing education programs, internships **Contact** Mr. Paul Milam, Director of Admissions, West Liberty State College, West Liberty, WV 26074. Telephone: 304-336-8076. Fax: 304-336-8285.

WEST VIRGINIA INSTITUTE OF TECHNOLOGY

WEST VIRGINIA— SEE WEST VIRGINIA UNIVERSITY INSTITUTE OF TECHNOLOGY

WEST VIRGINIA STATE COLLEGE

INSTITUTE, WEST VIRGINIA

Entrance Minimally difficult **General** State-supported, 4-year, coed **Setting** 90-acre suburban campus **Enrollment** 4,545 **Faculty** 18:1 **Application deadline** 8/11 **Freshmen** 99% accepted **Housing** Yes **Tuition** $2184 **Undergraduates** 55% women, 39% part-time, 40% 25 or older, 0% Native American, 1% Hispanic, 13% black, 1% Asian or Pacific Islander **Most popular recent majors** Business administration/commerce/management, elementary education, criminal justice **Academic program** Advanced placement, accelerated degree program, summer session, adult/continuing education programs, internships **Contact** Mr. L. Robin Green, Associate Director of Admissions, West Virginia State College, WVSC, Campus Box 188, PO Box 1000, Institute, WV 25112-1000. Telephone: 304-766-3221. Fax: 304-766-4158.

WEST VIRGINIA UNIVERSITY

MORGANTOWN, WEST VIRGINIA

Entrance Moderately difficult **General** State-supported, coed **Setting** 541-acre small-town campus **Enrollment** 21,743 **Faculty** 17:1 **Application deadline** Rolling **Freshmen** 89% accepted **Housing** Yes **Tuition** $2336 **Undergraduates** 47% women, 7% part-time, 9% 25 or older, 1% Native American, 1% Hispanic, 4% black, 2% Asian or Pacific Islander **Most popular recent majors** Accounting, journalism **Academic program** Advanced placement, accelerated degree program, self-designed majors, tutorials, honors program, summer session, adult/continuing education programs, internships **Contact** Ms. Evie Brantmayer, Interim Director of Admissions and Records, West Virginia University, Box 6009, Morgantown, WV 26506-6009. Telephone: 304-293-2121 Ext. 511. Fax: 304-293-3080.

WEST VIRGINIA UNIVERSITY INSTITUTE OF TECHNOLOGY

MONTGOMERY, WEST VIRGINIA

Entrance Noncompetitive **General** State-supported, comprehensive, coed **Setting** 200-acre small-town campus **Enrollment** 2,486 **Faculty** 18:1 **Application deadline** Rolling **Freshmen** 99% accepted **Housing** Yes **Tuition** $2370 **Undergraduates** 35% women, 1% Native American, 1% Hispanic, 4% black, 2% Asian or Pacific Islander **Most popular recent majors** Electrical engineering, mechanical engineering, accounting **Academic program** Advanced placement, accelerated degree program, self-designed majors, tutorials, summer session, adult/continuing education programs, internships **Contact** Ms. Donna Darlington, Director of Admissions, West Virginia University Institute of Technology, Montgomery, WV 25136. Telephone: 304-442-3167.

WEST VIRGINIA WESLEYAN COLLEGE

BUCKHANNON, WEST VIRGINIA

Entrance Moderately difficult **General** Independent, comprehensive, coed, affiliated with United Methodist Church **Setting** 80-acre small-town campus **Enrollment** 1,592 **Faculty** 15:1 **Application deadline** Rolling **Freshmen** 85% accepted **Housing** Yes **Tuition** $15,775 **Undergraduates** 54% women, 7% part-time, 11% 25 or older, 1% Native American, 1% Hispanic, 5% black, 1% Asian or Pacific Islander **Most popular recent majors** Business administration/commerce/management, biology/biological sciences, education **Academic program** Advanced placement, accelerated degree program, self-designed majors, honors program, summer session, adult/continuing education programs, internships **Contact** Mr. Robert N. Skinner II, Director of Admission, West Virginia Wesleyan College, Buckhannon, WV 26201. Telephone: 304-473-8510. Fax: 304-472-2571.

WHEELING JESUIT UNIVERSITY

WHEELING, WEST VIRGINIA

Entrance Moderately difficult **General** Independent Roman Catholic (Jesuit), comprehensive, coed **Setting** 70-acre suburban campus **Enrollment** 1,527 **Faculty** 14:1 **Application deadline** Rolling **Freshmen** 88% accepted **Housing** Yes **Tuition** $14,200 **Undergraduates** 57% women, 26% part-time, 15% 25 or older, 0% Native American, 2% Hispanic, 2% black, 1% Asian or Pacific Islander **Most popular recent majors** Business administration/commerce/management, psychology, biology/biological sciences **Academic program** Average class size 35, ESL program, advanced placement, self-designed majors, tutorials, honors program, summer session, adult/continuing education programs, internships **Contact** Ms. Carol Loncar, Director of Admissions, Wheeling Jesuit University, Wheeling, WV 26003-6295. Telephone: 304-243-2359.

Illinois

AMERICAN CONSERVATORY OF MUSIC

CHICAGO, ILLINOIS

Entrance Moderately difficult **General** Independent, comprehensive, specialized, coed **Setting** Urban campus **Enrollment** 117 **Faculty** 4:1 **Application deadline** Rolling **Freshmen** 84% accepted **Tuition** $8575 **Undergraduates** 46% women, 31% part-time, 71% 25 or older, 1% Native American, 5% Hispanic, 21% black, 41% Asian or Pacific Islander **Most popular recent majors** Music, piano/organ, voice **Academic program** Accelerated degree program, tutorials, summer session, adult/continuing education programs, internships **Contact** Ms. Mary Ellen Newsom, Registrar, American Conservatory of Music, 36 South Wabash Avenue, Suite 800, Chicago, IL 60603-2901. Telephone: 312-263-4161.

THE ART INSTITUTE OF ILLINOIS

SEE ILLINOIS INSTITUTE OF ART

AUGUSTANA COLLEGE

ROCK ISLAND, ILLINOIS

Entrance Moderately difficult **General** Independent, 4-year, coed, affiliated with Evangelical Lutheran Church in America **Setting** 115-acre suburban campus **Enrollment** 2,214 **Faculty** 13:1 **Application deadline** 4/1 **Freshmen** 76% accepted **Housing** Yes **Tuition** $15,300 **Undergraduates** 59% women, 2% part-time, 4% 25 or older, 1% Native American, 2% Hispanic, 3% black, 2% Asian or Pacific Islander **Most popular recent majors** Business administration/commerce/management, biology/biological sciences, English **Academic program** ESL program, Advanced placement, tutorials, honors program, summer session, internships **Contact** Mr. Martin Sauer, Director of Admissions, Augustana College, Rock Island, IL 61201-2296. Telephone: 309-794-7341. Fax: 309-794-7431.

AURORA UNIVERSITY

AURORA, ILLINOIS

Entrance Moderately difficult **General** Independent, comprehensive, coed **Setting** 26-acre suburban campus **Enrollment** 2,016 **Application deadline** Rolling **Freshmen** 72% accepted **Housing** Yes **Tuition** $11,310 **Undergraduates** 59% women, 50% part-time, 58% 25 or older, 0% Native American, 5% Hispanic, 12% black, 4% Asian or Pacific Islander **Most popular recent majors** Nursing, business administration/commerce/management, social work **Academic program** Advanced placement, self-designed majors, honors program, summer session, adult/continuing education programs, internships **Contact** Mr. Frank Johnson, Assistant Dean of Admissions and Financial Aid, Aurora University, 347 South Gladstone Avenue, Aurora, IL 60506-4892. Telephone: 630-896-1975.

BARAT COLLEGE

LAKE FOREST, ILLINOIS

Entrance Moderately difficult **General** Independent Roman Catholic, 4-year, coed **Setting** 30-acre suburban campus **Enrollment** 757 **Application deadline** Rolling **Freshmen** 77% accepted **Housing** Yes **Tuition** $12,570 **Undergraduates** 67% women, 49% part-time, 39% 25 or older, 0% Native American, 5% Hispanic, 13% black, 4% Asian or Pacific Islander **Most popular recent majors** Business administration/commerce/management, psychology, education **Academic program** Advanced placement, accelerated degree program, self-designed majors, tutorials, summer session, adult/continuing education programs, internships **Contact** Mr. Douglas Schacke, Director of Admissions, Barat College, Lake Forest, IL 60045-3297. Telephone: 847-295-4260. Fax: 847-234 1084.

BENEDICTINE UNIVERSITY

LISLE, ILLINOIS

Entrance Moderately difficult **General** Independent Roman Catholic, comprehensive, coed **Setting** 108-acre suburban campus **Enrollment** 2,579 **Faculty** 16:1 **Application deadline** Rolling **Freshmen** 86% accepted **Housing** Yes **Tuition** $12,330 **Undergraduates** 56% women, 26% part-time, 27% 25 or older, 1% Native American, 4% Hispanic, 6% black, 11% Asian or Pacific Islander **Most popular recent majors** Biology/biological sciences, education, business economics **Academic program** Advanced placement, accelerated degree program, tutorials, honors program, summer session, adult/continuing education programs, internships **Contact** Undergraduate Admissions Office, Benedictine University, Lisle, IL 60532-0900. Telephone: 630-829-6300. Fax: 630-960-1126.

BLACKBURN COLLEGE

CARLINVILLE, ILLINOIS

Entrance Moderately difficult **General** Independent Presbyterian, 4-year, coed **Setting** 80-acre small-town campus **Enrollment** 576 **Faculty** 15:1 **Application deadline** Rolling **Freshmen** 74% accepted **Housing** Yes **Tuition** $7510 **Under-**

graduates 49% women, 4% part-time, 6% 25 or older, 1% Native American, 1% Hispanic, 6% black, 2% Asian or Pacific Islander **Most popular recent majors** Business administration/commerce/management, elementary education, biology/biological sciences **Academic program** Advanced placement, accelerated degree program, self-designed majors, honors program, internships **Contact** Mr. John Malin, Director of Admissions, Blackburn College, Carlinville, IL 62626-1498. Telephone: 217-854-3231 Ext. 4252. Fax: 217-854-3713.

BLESSING-RIEMAN COLLEGE OF NURSING
QUINCY, ILLINOIS

Entrance Moderately difficult **General** Independent, 4-year, specialized, primarily women **Setting** 1-acre small-town campus **Enrollment** 183 **Application deadline** Rolling **Freshmen** 47% accepted **Housing** Yes **Tuition** $9200 **Undergraduates** 90% women, 16% part-time, 27% 25 or older, 0% Native American, 2% Hispanic, 2% black, 1% Asian or Pacific Islander **Academic program** Advanced placement, summer session, adult/continuing education programs, internships **Contact** Ms. Sharon Wharton, Director of Admissions, Blessing-Rieman College of Nursing, Quincy, IL 62305-7005. Telephone: 217-228-5520 Ext. 6961.

BRADLEY UNIVERSITY
PEORIA, ILLINOIS

Entrance Moderately difficult **General** Independent, comprehensive, coed **Setting** 65-acre urban campus **Enrollment** 5,900 **Faculty** 14:1 **Application deadline** Rolling **Freshmen** 89% accepted **Housing** Yes **Tuition** $12,690 **Undergraduates** 52% women, 11% part-time, 11% 25 or older, 1% Native American, 2% Hispanic, 5% black, 2% Asian or Pacific Islander **Most popular recent majors** Communication, psychology, nursing **Academic program** Advanced placement, accelerated degree program, self-designed majors, tutorials, honors program, summer session, adult/continuing education programs, internships **Contact** Executive Director of Enrollment Management, Bradley University, 1501 West Bradley Avenue, Peoria, IL 61625-0002. Telephone: 309-677-1000.

CHICAGO STATE UNIVERSITY
CHICAGO, ILLINOIS

Entrance Moderately difficult **General** State-supported, comprehensive, coed **Setting** 161-acre urban campus **Enrollment** 9,412 **Faculty** 30:1 **Application deadline** Rolling **Freshmen** 43% accepted **Housing** Yes **Tuition** $2496 **Undergraduates** 69% women, 36% part-time, 44% 25 or older, 0% Native American, 4% Hispanic, 86% black, 1% Asian or Pacific Islander **Most popular recent majors** Computer science, business administration/commerce/management, nursing **Academic program** Advanced placement, accelerated degree program, self-designed majors, honors program, summer session, adult/continuing education programs, internships **Contact** Ms. Annie Epps, Director of Admissions, Chicago State University, 95th Street at King Drive, Chicago, IL 60628. Telephone: 773-995-2513.

COLLEGE OF ST. FRANCIS
JOLIET, ILLINOIS

Entrance Moderately difficult **General** Independent Roman Catholic, comprehensive, coed **Setting** 16-acre suburban campus **Enrollment** 1,500 **Faculty** 11:1 **Application deadline** 7/1 **Freshmen** 69% accepted **Housing** Yes **Tuition** $11,950 **Undergraduates** 54% women, 29% part-time, 27% 25 or older, 6% Hispanic, 7% black, 1% Asian or Pacific Islander **Most popular recent majors** Business administration/commerce/management, communication, elementary education **Academic program** Advanced placement, accelerated degree program, tutorials, summer session, adult/continuing education programs, internships **Contact** Ms. Carol Koziol, Assistant Director of Admissions, College of St. Francis, Joliet, IL 60435-6188. Telephone: 815-740-3400. Fax: 815-740-4285.

COLUMBIA COLLEGE
CHICAGO, ILLINOIS

Entrance Noncompetitive **General** Independent, comprehensive, coed **Setting** Urban campus **Enrollment** 8,066 **Faculty** 7:1 **Application deadline** Rolling **Freshmen** 90% accepted **Housing** Yes **Tuition** $8598 **Undergraduates** 48% women, 26% part-time, 28% 25 or older, 1% Native American, 11% Hispanic, 20% black, 7% Asian or Pacific Islander **Most popular recent majors** Film and video production, art/fine arts, radio and television studies **Academic program** Average class size 15, advanced placement, self-designed majors, tutorials, summer session, adult/continuing education programs, internships **Contact** Mr. Terry Miller, Director of Admissions and Recruitment, Columbia College, 600 South Michigan Avenue, Chicago, IL 60605-1997. Telephone: 312-663-1600 Ext. 133.

CONCORDIA UNIVERSITY
RIVER FOREST, ILLINOIS

Entrance Moderately difficult **General** Independent, comprehensive, coed, affiliated with Lutheran Church–Missouri Synod **Setting** 40-acre suburban campus **Enrollment** 2,107 **Faculty** 17:1 **Application deadline** Rolling **Freshmen** 94% accepted **Housing** Yes **Tuition** $11,571 **Undergraduates** 68% women, 18% part-time, 13% 25 or older, 0% Native American, 4% Hispanic, 8% black, 4% Asian or Pacific Islander **Most popular recent majors** Education, nursing, psychology **Academic program** Advanced placement, accelerated degree program, honors program, summer session, adult/continuing education programs, internships **Contact** Mr. Kurt Schick, Director of Admission, Concordia University, River Forest, IL 60305-1499. Telephone: 708-209-3100. Fax: 708-209-3176.

DEPAUL UNIVERSITY
CHICAGO, ILLINOIS

Entrance Moderately difficult **General** Independent Roman Catholic, coed **Setting** 36-acre urban campus **Enrollment** 17,294 **Faculty** 16:1 **Application deadline** 8/15 **Freshmen** 78% accepted **Housing** Yes **Tuition** $13,488 **Undergraduates** 59% women, 38% part-time, 45% 25 or older, 1% Native American, 11% Hispanic, 13% black, 7% Asian or Pacific Islander **Most popular recent majors** Accounting, finance/banking, communication **Academic program** Advanced placement, accelerated degree program, self-designed majors, tutorials, honors program, summer session, adult/continuing education programs, internships **Contact** Ms. Ellen Cohen, Director of Undergraduate Admission, DePaul University, 1 East Jackson Boulevard, Chicago, IL 60604-2287. Telephone: 312-362-8300. Fax: 312-362-5322.

DEVRY INSTITUTE OF TECHNOLOGY
ADDISON, ILLINOIS

Entrance Minimally difficult **General** Proprietary, 4-year, coed **Setting** 14-acre suburban campus **Enrollment** 3,468 **Faculty** 34:1 **Application deadline** Rolling **Freshmen** 76% accepted **Tuition** $6968 **Undergraduates** 21% women, 39% part-time, 46% 25 or older, 0% Native American, 6% Hispanic, 7% black, 4% Asian or Pacific Islander **Most popular recent majors** Computer information systems, electronics engineering technology, electrical and electronics technologies **Academic program** Advanced placement, accelerated degree program, summer session, adult/continuing education programs **Contact** Ms. Tash Uray, Director of Admissions, DeVry Institute of Technology, Addison, IL 60101-6106. Telephone: 630-953-2000.

DEVRY INSTITUTE OF TECHNOLOGY
CHICAGO, ILLINOIS

Entrance Minimally difficult **General** Proprietary, 4-year, coed **Setting** 17-acre urban campus **Enrollment** 3,192 **Faculty** 32:1 **Application deadline** Rolling **Freshmen** 82% accepted **Tuition** $6968 **Undergraduates** 29% women, 38% part-time, 46% 25 or older, 0% Native American, 21% Hispanic, 30% black, 11% Asian or Pacific Islander **Most popular recent majors** Computer information systems, electrical and electronics technologies **Academic program** Advanced placement, accelerated degree program, summer session, adult/continuing education programs **Contact** Mr. Hamed Shibly, Director of Admissions, DeVry Institute of Technology, 3300 North Campbell Avenue, Chicago, IL 60618-5994. Telephone: 773-929-6550.

DR. WILLIAM M. SCHOLL COLLEGE OF PODIATRIC MEDICINE
CHICAGO, ILLINOIS

Entrance Moderately difficult **General** Independent, upper-level, specialized, coed **Setting** Urban campus **Enrollment** 392 **Freshmen** 43% accepted **Tuition** $19,310 **Undergraduates** 27% women, 0% part-time, 64% 25 or older, 1% Native American, 2% Hispanic, 4% black, 13% Asian or Pacific Islander **Academic program** Honors program, adult/continuing education programs **Contact** Dr. Howard M. Bers, Associate Dean for Student Affairs, Dr. William M. Scholl College of Podiatric Medicine, 1001 North Dearborn Street, Chicago, IL 60610-2856. Telephone: 312-280-2899. Fax: 312-280-2997.

DOMINICAN UNIVERSITY
RIVER FOREST, ILLINOIS

Entrance Moderately difficult **General** Independent Roman Catholic, comprehensive, coed **Setting** 30-acre suburban campus **Enrollment** 1,818 **Faculty** 12:1 **Application deadline** Rolling **Freshmen** 80% accepted **Housing** Yes **Tuition** $12,950 **Undergraduates** 72% women, 27% part-time, 24% 25 or older, 0% Native American, 11% Hispanic, 8% black, 2% Asian or Pacific Islander **Most popular recent majors** Business administration/commerce/management, accounting, psychology **Academic program** Advanced placement, self-designed majors, tutorials, honors program, summer session, adult/continuing education programs, internships **Contact** Ms. Hildegarde Schmidt, Dean of Admissions and Financial Aid, Dominican University, River Forest, IL 60305-1099. Telephone: 708-524-6800. Fax: 708-366-5360.

EASTERN ILLINOIS UNIVERSITY
CHARLESTON, ILLINOIS

Entrance Moderately difficult **General** State-supported, comprehensive, coed **Setting** 320-acre small-town campus **Enrollment** 11,711 **Faculty** 15:1 **Application deadline** Rolling **Freshmen** 76% accepted **Housing** Yes **Tuition** $2916 **Undergraduates** 57% women, 9% part-time, 10% 25 or older, 2% Hispanic, 5% black, 1% Asian or Pacific Islander **Most popular recent majors** Elementary education, liberal arts/general studies, psychology **Academic program** Advanced placement, tutorials, honors program, summer session, adult/continuing education programs, internships **Contact** Mr. Dale W. Wolf, Director of Admissions, Eastern Illinois University, 600 Lincoln Avenue, Charleston, IL 61920-3099. Telephone: 217-581-2223. Fax: 217-581-7060.

EAST-WEST UNIVERSITY
CHICAGO, ILLINOIS

Entrance Minimally difficult **General** Independent, 4-year, coed **Setting** Urban campus **Enrollment** 334 **Faculty** 12:1 **Application deadline** Rolling **Freshmen** 95% accepted **Tuition** $6960 **Undergraduates** 47% women, 3% part-time, 34% 25 or older, 0% Native American, 8% Hispanic, 53% black, 27% Asian or Pacific Islander **Most popular recent majors** Business administration/commerce/management, electrical and electronics technologies, computer science **Academic program** Summer session **Contact** Mrs. Mettha M. Green, Director of Admissions, East-West University, 816 South Michigan Avenue, Chicago, IL 60605-2103. Telephone: 312-939-0111. Fax: 312-939-0083.

ELMHURST COLLEGE
ELMHURST, ILLINOIS

Entrance Moderately difficult **General** Independent, 4-year, coed, affiliated with United Church of Christ **Setting** 38-acre suburban campus **Enrollment** 2,701 **Faculty** 13:1 **Application deadline** 8/1 **Freshmen** 69% accepted **Housing** Yes **Tuition** $11,900 **Undergraduates** 66% women, 33% part-time, 44% 25 or older, 1% Native American, 4% Hispanic, 6% black, 3% Asian or Pacific Islander **Most popular recent majors** Business administration/commerce/management, nursing, education **Academic program** Advanced placement, accelerated degree program, tutorials, honors program, summer session, adult/continuing education programs, internships **Contact** Mr. John Hopkins, Dean of Admission, Elmhurst College, 190 Prospect, Elmhurst, IL 60126-3296. Telephone: 630-617-3400. Fax: 630-617-5501.

EUREKA COLLEGE
EUREKA, ILLINOIS

Entrance Moderately difficult **General** Independent, 4-year, coed, affiliated with Christian Church (Disciples of Christ) **Setting** 112-acre small-town campus **Enrollment** 486 **Faculty** 12:1 **Application deadline** Rolling **Freshmen** 80% accepted **Housing** Yes **Tuition** $13,950 **Undergraduates** 50% women, 6% 25 or older, 0% Native American, 1% Hispanic, 4% black, 1% Asian or Pacific Islander **Most popular recent majors** Education, business administration/commerce/management, athletic training **Academic program** Average class size 20, advanced placement, self-designed majors, tutorials, honors program, internships **Contact** Ms. Susan R. Jordan, Dean of Admissions and Financial Aid, Eureka College, Eureka, IL 61530-0128. Telephone: 309-467-6350. Fax: 309-467-6576.

FINCH UNIVERSITY OF HEALTH SCIENCES/ THE CHICAGO MEDICAL SCHOOL
NORTH CHICAGO, ILLINOIS

Entrance Moderately difficult **General** Independent, upper-level, specialized, coed **Setting** 50-acre suburban campus **Enrollment** 1,440 **Faculty** 3:1 **Freshmen** 19% accepted **Tuition** $10,907 **Undergraduates** 69% women, 14% part-time, 52% 25 or older, 1% Native American, 1% Hispanic, 0% black, 8% Asian or Pacific Islander **Academic program** Advanced placement, tutorials, summer session, adult/continuing education programs, internships **Contact** Ms. Dana Frederick, Admissions Officer/Office Manager, Finch University of Health Sciences/The Chicago Medical School, North Chicago, IL 60064-3037. Telephone: 847-578-8601. Fax: 847-578-3284.

GOVERNORS STATE UNIVERSITY
UNIVERSITY PARK, ILLINOIS

Entrance Minimally difficult **General** State-supported, upper-level, coed **Setting** 750-acre suburban campus **Enrollment** 6,082 **Faculty** 16:1 **Freshmen** 78% accepted **Tuition** $2278 **Undergraduates** 64% women, 67% part-time, 55% 25 or older, 1% Native American, 3% Hispanic, 23% black, 2% Asian or Pacific Islander **Most popular**

recent majors Business administration/commerce/management, elementary education, nursing **Academic program** Advanced placement, self-designed majors, honors program, summer session, adult/continuing education programs, internships **Contact** Ms. Dora Hubbard, Registrar, Governors State University, University Park, IL 60466. Telephone: 708-534-4500. Fax: 708-534-8951.

GREENVILLE COLLEGE
GREENVILLE, ILLINOIS

Entrance Moderately difficult **General** Independent Free Methodist, 4-year, coed **Setting** 12-acre small-town campus **Enrollment** 910 **Faculty** 14:1 **Application deadline** Rolling **Freshmen** 71% accepted **Housing** Yes **Tuition** $12,586 **Undergraduates** 53% women, 6% part-time, 12% 25 or older, 1% Native American, 2% Hispanic, 5% black, 2% Asian or Pacific Islander **Most popular recent majors** Education, business administration/commerce/management, biology/biological sciences **Academic program** Average class size 50, advanced placement, accelerated degree program, self-designed majors, tutorials, honors program, summer session, adult/continuing education programs, internships **Contact** Mr. Kent Krober, Director of Admissions, Greenville College, Greenville, IL 62246-0159. Telephone: 618-664-1840 Ext. 4402. Fax: 618-664-9841.

HARRINGTON INSTITUTE OF INTERIOR DESIGN
CHICAGO, ILLINOIS

Entrance Noncompetitive **General** Proprietary, 4-year, specialized, coed **Setting** Urban campus **Enrollment** 330 **Faculty** 11:1 **Application deadline** Rolling **Freshmen** 100% accepted **Tuition** $9949 **Undergraduates** 85% women, 44% part-time, 65% 25 or older, 0% Native American, 6% Hispanic, 9% black, 5% Asian or Pacific Islander **Academic program** Adult/continuing education programs **Contact** Ms. Wendy Davidson, Director of Admissions, Harrington Institute of Interior Design, 410 South Michigan Avenue, Chicago, IL 60605-1496. Telephone: 312-939-4975. Fax: 312-939-8005.

HEBREW THEOLOGICAL COLLEGE
SKOKIE, ILLINOIS

Entrance Moderately difficult **General** Independent Jewish, 4-year, specialized, men only, coordinate with Anne M. Blitstein Teachers Institute of the Hebrew Theological College **Setting** 13-acre suburban campus **Enrollment** 135 **Application deadline** Rolling **Freshmen** 92% accepted **Housing** Yes **Tuition** $6500 **Academic program** Accelerated degree program **Contact** Office of Admissions, Hebrew Theological College, Skokie, IL 60077-3263. Telephone: 847-674-7750.

ILLINOIS BENEDICTINE COLLEGE
SEE BENEDICTINE UNIVERSITY

ILLINOIS COLLEGE
JACKSONVILLE, ILLINOIS

Entrance Moderately difficult **General** Independent interdenominational, 4-year, coed **Setting** 62-acre small-town campus **Enrollment** 905 **Faculty** 15:1 **Application deadline** 8/15 **Freshmen** 88% accepted **Housing** Yes **Tuition** $9500 **Undergraduates** 55% women, 2% part-time, 4% 25 or older, 0% Native American, 0% Hispanic, 2% black, 2% Asian or Pacific Islander **Most popular recent majors** Business administration/commerce/management, biology/biological sciences, education **Academic program** Advanced placement, accelerated degree program, tutorials, summer session, internships **Contact** Mr. Gale Vaughn, Director of Enrollment, Illinois College, Jacksonville, IL 62650-2299. Telephone: 217-245-3030. Fax: 217-245-3034.

ILLINOIS COLLEGE OF OPTOMETRY
CHICAGO, ILLINOIS

Entrance Very difficult **General** Independent, upper-level, specialized, coed **Setting** 5-acre urban campus **Enrollment** 600 **Faculty** 6:1 **Freshmen** 33% accepted **Housing** Yes **Tuition** $21,223 **Academic program** Summer session, internships **Contact** Dr. Mark Colip, Director of Student Services and Admissions, Illinois College of Optometry, 3241 South Michigan Avenue, Chicago, IL 60616-3816. Telephone: 312-225-1700. Fax: 312-225-3405.

THE ILLINOIS INSTITUTE OF ART
CHICAGO, ILLINOIS

Entrance Minimally difficult **General** Proprietary, 4-year, coed **Setting** Urban campus **Enrollment** 600 **Application deadline** Rolling **Freshmen** 95% accepted **Tuition** $9984 **Undergraduates** 70% women, 30% part-time, 30% 25 or older, 0% Native American, 9% Hispanic, 35% black, 11% Asian or Pacific Islander **Most popular recent majors** Computer graphics, fashion design and technology, graphic arts **Academic program** Advanced placement, accelerated degree program, summer session, adult/continuing education programs, internships **Contact** Ms. Jan Anton, Director of Admissions, The Illinois Institute of Art, 350 North Orleans, 136, Chicago, IL 60654. Telephone: 312-280-3500. Fax: 312-280-3528.

ILLINOIS INSTITUTE OF TECHNOLOGY
CHICAGO, ILLINOIS

Entrance Very difficult **General** Independent, coed **Setting** 120-acre urban campus **Enrollment** 6,287 **Faculty** 12:1 **Application deadline** Rolling **Freshmen** 67% accepted **Housing** Yes **Tuition** $16,460 **Undergraduates** 23% women, 27% part-time, 29% 25 or older, 0% Native American, 8% Hispanic, 11% black, 13% Asian or Pacific Islander **Most popular recent majors** Electrical engineering, mechanical engineering, architecture **Academic program** Advanced placement, accelerated degree program, self-designed majors, tutorials, summer session, internships **Contact** Dr. Carole L. Snow, Dean of Admission, Illinois Institute of Technology, IIT Center, Chicago, IL 60616. Telephone: 312-567-3025. Fax: 312-567-6939.

ILLINOIS STATE UNIVERSITY
NORMAL, ILLINOIS

Entrance Moderately difficult **General** State-supported, coed **Setting** 850-acre urban campus **Enrollment** 19,409 **Faculty** 21:1 **Freshmen** 78% accepted **Housing** Yes **Tuition** $4004 **Undergraduates** 56% women, 10% part-time, 12% 25 or older, 0% Native American, 2% Hispanic, 9% black, 2% Asian or Pacific Islander **Most popular recent majors** Elementary education, accounting, special education **Academic program** Advanced placement, accelerated degree program, self-designed majors, honors program, summer session, internships **Contact** Mr. Steve Adams, Director of Admissions, Illinois State University, Normal, IL 61790-2200. Telephone: 309-438-2181.

ILLINOIS WESLEYAN UNIVERSITY
BLOOMINGTON, ILLINOIS

Entrance Very difficult **General** Independent, 4-year, coed **Setting** 63-acre suburban campus **Enrollment** 1,928 **Faculty** 13:1 **Application deadline** Rolling **Freshmen** 61% accepted **Housing** Yes **Tuition** $17,490 **Undergraduates** 53% women, 1% part-time, 1% 25 or older, 1% Native American, 1% Hispanic, 3% black, 4% Asian or Pacific Islander **Most popular recent majors** Business administration/commerce/management, English, biology/biological sciences **Academic program** Advanced placement, accelerated degree program, self-designed majors, honors program, summer session, internships **Contact** Mr. James R. Ruoti, Dean of Admissions, Illinois Wesleyan University, Bloomington, IL 61702-2900. Telephone: 309-556-3031. Fax: 309-556-3411.

INTERNATIONAL ACADEMY OF MERCHANDISING & DESIGN, LTD.
CHICAGO, ILLINOIS

Entrance Minimally difficult **General** Proprietary, 4-year, coed **Setting** Urban campus **Enrollment** 758 **Faculty** 14:1 **Application deadline** Rolling **Freshmen** 99% accepted **Tuition** $9270 **Undergraduates** 82% women, 65% part-time, 48% 25 or older, 1% Native American, 13% Hispanic, 24% black, 6% Asian or Pacific Islander **Most popular recent majors** Fashion merchandising, fashion design and technology, interior design **Academic program** Advanced placement, summer session, adult/continuing education programs, internships **Contact** Ms. Vanessa Bell, Director of Admissions, International Academy of Merchandising & Design, Ltd., One North State Street, Chicago, IL 60602-9736. Telephone: 312-541-3900. Fax: 312-828-9405.

JUDSON COLLEGE
ELGIN, ILLINOIS

Entrance Moderately difficult **General** Independent Baptist, 4-year, coed **Setting** 80-acre suburban campus **Enrollment** 933 **Application deadline** 8/15 **Freshmen** 77% accepted **Housing** Yes **Tuition** $11,350 **Undergraduates** 55% women, 17% part-time, 18% 25 or older, 1% Native American, 5% Hispanic, 5% black, 1% Asian or Pacific Islander **Most popular recent majors** Education, business administration/commerce/management, graphic arts **Academic program** Average class size 25, advanced placement, accelerated degree program, tutorials, honors program, adult/continuing education programs, internships **Contact** Mr. Matthew Osborne, Director of Enrollment Services, Judson College, Elgin, IL 60123-1498. Telephone: 847-695-2500 Ext. 2310. Fax: 847-695-0216.

KENDALL COLLEGE
EVANSTON, ILLINOIS

Entrance Moderately difficult **General** Independent United Methodist, 4-year, coed **Setting** 1-acre suburban campus **Enrollment** 500 **Faculty** 15:1 **Application deadline** Rolling **Housing** Yes **Tuition** $10,128 **Undergraduates** 45% women, 34% part-time, 45% 25 or older, 1% Native American, 5% Hispanic, 6% black, 5% Asian or Pacific Islander **Most popular recent majors** Culinary arts, liberal arts/general studies, business administration/commerce/management **Academic program** Advanced placement, self-designed majors, tutorials, summer session, internships **Contact** Ms. Jennifer McDermott, Director of Enrollment Management, Kendall College, Evanston, IL 60201-2899. Telephone: 847-866-1304. Fax: 847-866-1320.

KNOX COLLEGE
GALESBURG, ILLINOIS

Entrance Very difficult **General** Independent, 4-year, coed **Setting** 70-acre small-town campus **Enrollment** 1,134 **Faculty** 12:1 **Application deadline** 2/15 **Freshmen** 82% accepted **Housing** Yes **Tuition** $18,393 **Undergraduates** 54% women, 3% part-time, 2% 25 or older, 1% Native American, 4% Hispanic, 5% black, 5% Asian or Pacific Islander **Most popular recent majors** Political science/government, biology/biological sciences, English **Academic program** ESL program, Advanced placement, self-designed majors, tutorials, internships **Contact** Mr. Paul Steenis, Director of Admissions, Knox College, Admissions Office, Box K-148, Galesburg, IL 61401. Telephone: 309-341-7100. Fax: 309-341-7070.

LAKE FOREST COLLEGE
LAKE FOREST, ILLINOIS

Entrance Very difficult **General** Independent, comprehensive, coed **Setting** 110-acre suburban campus **Enrollment** 1,106 **Faculty** 11:1 **Application deadline** 3/1 **Freshmen** 80% accepted **Housing** Yes **Tuition** $19,560 **Undergraduates** 53% women, 3% part-time, 2% 25 or older, 1% Native American, 5% Hispanic, 6% black, 4% Asian or Pacific Islander **Most popular recent majors** Psychology, English, business economics **Academic program** Average class size 19, advanced placement, accelerated degree program, self-designed majors, tutorials, summer session, adult/continuing education programs, internships **Contact** Mr. William G. Motzer Jr., Director of Admissions, Lake Forest College, Lake Forest, IL 60045-2399. Telephone: 847-735-5000. Fax: 847-735-6271.

LAKEVIEW COLLEGE OF NURSING
DANVILLE, ILLINOIS

Entrance Moderately difficult **General** Independent, upper-level, specialized, coed **Setting** Small-town campus **Enrollment** 111 **Freshmen** 99% accepted **Tuition** $7099 **Undergraduates** 94% women, 45% part-time, 33% 25 or older, 0% Native American, 4% Hispanic, 3% black, 2% Asian or Pacific Islander **Academic program** Summer session **Contact** Ms. Beverly Shelton, Director of Admissions and Advisement, Lakeview College of Nursing, Danville, IL 61832. Telephone: 217-443-5238. Fax: 217-431-4015.

LEWIS UNIVERSITY
ROMEOVILLE, ILLINOIS

Entrance Moderately difficult **General** Independent, comprehensive, coed, affiliated with Roman Catholic Church **Setting** 600-acre small-town campus **Enrollment** 4,310 **Faculty** 17:1 **Application deadline** Rolling **Freshmen** 85% accepted **Housing** Yes **Tuition** $12,416 **Undergraduates** 43% women, 39% part-time, 46% 25 or older, 1% Native American, 5% Hispanic, 13% black, 3% Asian or Pacific Islander **Most popular recent majors** Nursing, business administration/commerce/management, criminal justice **Academic program** Average class size 25, ESL program, advanced placement, accelerated degree program, self-designed majors, tutorials, summer session, adult/continuing education programs, internships **Contact** Mr. Don St. Clair, Director of Admissions, Lewis University, Romeoville, IL 60446. Telephone: 815-838-0500 Ext. 5470. Fax: 815-838-9456.

LINCOLN CHRISTIAN COLLEGE
LINCOLN, ILLINOIS

Entrance Moderately difficult **General** Independent, 4-year, coed, affiliated with Christian Churches and Churches of Christ **Setting** 227-acre small-town campus **Enrollment** 580 **Faculty** 17:1 **Application deadline** Rolling **Freshmen** 86% accepted **Housing** Yes **Tuition** $5884 **Undergraduates** 50% women, 16% part-time, 21% 25 or older, 0% Native American, 1% Hispanic, 1% black, 1% Asian or Pacific Islander **Most popular recent majors** Ministries, religious education, elementary education **Academic program** Advanced placement, summer session, adult/continuing education programs, internships **Contact** Ms. Patsy Wilson, Assistant Director of Admissions, Lincoln Christian College, Lincoln, IL 62656-2167. Telephone: 217-732-3168 Ext. 2218. Fax: 217-732-5914.

LOYOLA UNIVERSITY CHICAGO
CHICAGO, ILLINOIS

Entrance Moderately difficult **General** Independent Roman Catholic (Jesuit), coed **Setting** 105-acre urban campus **Enrollment** 13,759 **Faculty** 13:1 **Application deadline** 4/1 **Freshmen** 86%

accepted **Housing** Yes **Tuition** $16,054 **Undergraduates** 63% women, 30% part-time, 7% 25 or older, 1% Native American, 8% Hispanic, 7% black, 13% Asian or Pacific Islander **Most popular recent majors** Psychology, biology/biological sciences, nursing **Academic program** Advanced placement, accelerated degree program, honors program, summer session, adult/continuing education programs, internships **Contact** Mr. Robert Blust, Director of Admissions, Loyola University Chicago, 820 North Michigan Avenue, Chicago, IL 60611-2196. Telephone: 312-915-6500.

MACMURRAY COLLEGE
JACKSONVILLE, ILLINOIS

Entrance Moderately difficult **General** Independent United Methodist, 4-year, coed **Setting** 60-acre small-town campus **Enrollment** 669 **Faculty** 12:1 **Application deadline** 7/15 **Freshmen** 76% accepted **Housing** Yes **Tuition** $11,400 **Undergraduates** 58% women, 7% part-time, 10% 25 or older, 1% Native American, 4% Hispanic, 6% black **Most popular recent majors** Special education, nursing, business administration/commerce/management **Academic program** Advanced placement, tutorials, honors program, summer session, internships **Contact** Dr. Edwin R. Hockett, Dean of Admissions, MacMurray College, Jacksonville, IL 62650. Telephone: 217-479-7056. Fax: 217-245-0405.

MCKENDREE COLLEGE
LEBANON, ILLINOIS

Entrance Moderately difficult **General** Independent, 4-year, coed, affiliated with United Methodist Church **Setting** 65-acre small-town campus **Enrollment** 1,787 **Faculty** 13:1 **Application deadline** Rolling **Freshmen** 91% accepted **Housing** Yes **Tuition** $10,400 **Undergraduates** 61% women, 38% part-time, 48% 25 or older, 1% Hispanic, 9% black, 1% Asian or Pacific Islander **Most popular recent majors** Business administration/commerce/management, nursing, elementary education **Academic program** Average class size 25, advanced placement, accelerated degree program, self-designed majors, tutorials, honors program, summer session, internships **Contact** Mrs. Sue Cordon, Dean of Admissions, McKendree College, Lebanon, IL 62254-1299. Telephone: 618-537-4481 Ext. 6830. Fax: 618-537-6259.

MENNONITE COLLEGE OF NURSING
BLOOMINGTON, ILLINOIS

Entrance Moderately difficult **General** Independent interdenominational, upper-level, specialized, coed **Setting** 2-acre urban campus **Enrollment** 200 **Faculty** 9:1 **Freshmen** 54% accepted **Housing** Yes **Tuition** $8834 **Undergraduates** 91% women, 6% part-time, 43% 25 or older, 0% Native American, 2% Hispanic, 3% black, 1% Asian or Pacific Islander **Academic program** ESL program, Advanced placement, tutorials, summer session, internships **Contact** Mrs. Mary Ann Watkins, Director of Admissions and Financial Aid, Mennonite College of Nursing, 804 North East Street, Bloomington, IL 61701. Telephone: 309-829-0718. Fax: 309-829-0765.

MILLIKIN UNIVERSITY
DECATUR, ILLINOIS

Entrance Moderately difficult **General** Independent, 4-year, coed, affiliated with Presbyterian Church (U.S.A.) **Setting** 45-acre suburban campus **Enrollment** 1,930 **Faculty** 14:1 **Application deadline** Rolling **Freshmen** 85% accepted **Housing** Yes **Tuition** $14,079 **Undergraduates** 57% women, 4% part-time, 7% 25 or older, 1% Hispanic, 5% black, 1% Asian or Pacific Islander **Most popular recent majors** Nursing, elementary education, business administration/commerce/management **Academic program** Advanced placement, self-designed majors, tutorials, honors program, summer session, adult/continuing education programs, internships **Contact** Mr. Lin Stoner, Dean of Admission, Millikin University, 1184 West Main Street, Decatur, IL 62522. Telephone: 217-424-6210. Fax: 217-424-3993.

MONMOUTH COLLEGE
MONMOUTH, ILLINOIS

Entrance Moderately difficult **General** Independent, 4-year, coed, affiliated with Presbyterian Church **Setting** 40-acre small-town campus **Enrollment** 998 **Faculty** 14:1 **Application deadline** 5/1 **Freshmen** 78% accepted **Housing** Yes **Tuition** $14,630 **Undergraduates** 60% women, 1% part-time, 3% 25 or older, 0% Native American, 2% Hispanic, 1% black, 1% Asian or Pacific Islander **Most popular recent majors** Business administration/commerce/management, education, biology/biological sciences **Academic program** Average class size 20, ESL program, advanced placement, self-designed majors, tutorials, honors program, summer session, internships **Contact** Mr. Richard Valentine, Vice President for Enrollment, Monmouth College, Monmouth, IL 61462-1998. Telephone: 309-457-2131. Fax: 309-457-2141.

MOODY BIBLE INSTITUTE
CHICAGO, ILLINOIS

Entrance Moderately difficult **General** Independent nondenominational, comprehensive, coed **Setting** 25-acre urban campus **Enrollment** 1,553 **Faculty** 18:1 **Application deadline** 3/1 **Freshmen** 76% accepted **Housing** Yes **Tuition** $830 **Undergraduates** 41% women, 4% part-time, 20% 25 or older, 2% Hispanic, 2% black, 4% Asian or Pacific Islander **Most popular recent majors** Biblical studies, ministries, communication **Academic program** Advanced placement, summer session, adult/continuing education programs, internships **Contact** Administrator of Admissions, Moody Bible Institute, 820 North LaSalle Boulevard, Chicago, IL 60610. Telephone: 312-329-4267. Fax: 312-329-8987.

NAES COLLEGE
CHICAGO, ILLINOIS

Entrance Noncompetitive **General** Independent, 4-year, coed **Enrollment** 87 **Application deadline** Rolling **Freshmen** 100% accepted **Tuition** $4340 **Undergraduates** 75% women, 20% part-time, 97% 25 or older, 94% Native American, 0% black, 0% Asian or Pacific Islander **Academic program** Advanced placement, accelerated degree program, self-designed majors, summer session **Contact** Ms. Christine Redcloud, Registrar, NAES College, Chicago, IL 60659-3813. Telephone: 773-761-5000. Fax: 773-761-3808.

THE NATIONAL COLLEGE OF CHIROPRACTIC
LOMBARD, ILLINOIS

Entrance Moderately difficult **General** Independent, upper-level, specialized, coed **Setting** 32-acre suburban campus **Enrollment** 900 **Faculty** 8:1 **Freshmen** 71% accepted **Housing** Yes **Tuition** $10,504 **Undergraduates** 31% women, 0% part-time, 39% 25 or older, 1% Native American, 2% Hispanic, 3% black, 5% Asian or Pacific Islander **Academic program** Tutorials, summer session, adult/continuing education programs, internships **Contact** Ms. Julie Talarico, Director of Admissions, The National College of Chiropractic, Lombard, IL 60148-4583. Telephone: 630-629-2000 Ext. 6572.

NATIONAL-LOUIS UNIVERSITY
EVANSTON, ILLINOIS

Entrance Moderately difficult **General** Independent, coed **Setting** 12-acre suburban campus **Enrollment** 7,430 **Faculty** 13:1 **Application deadline** Rolling **Freshmen** 76% accepted **Housing** Yes **Tuition** $11,250 **Undergraduates** 72% women, 17% part-time, 69% 25 or older, 1% Native American, 8% Hispanic, 18% black, 4% Asian or Pacific Islander **Most popular recent majors** Business administration/commerce/management, behavioral sciences, elementary education **Academic program** Average class size 13, advanced placement, accelerated degree program, tutorials, honors program, summer session, adult/continuing education programs, internships **Contact** Mr. Randall Berd, Director of Student Enrollment, National-Louis University, 1000 Capitol Drive, Wheeling, IL 60090. Telephone: 847-465-0575 Ext. 5151.

NORTH CENTRAL COLLEGE
NAPERVILLE, ILLINOIS

Entrance Moderately difficult **General** Independent United Methodist, comprehensive, coed **Setting** 56-acre suburban campus **Enrollment** 2,623 **Faculty** 14:1 **Application deadline** Rolling **Freshmen** 84% accepted **Housing** Yes **Tuition** $13,845 **Undergraduates** 54% women, 19% part-time, 27% 25 or older, 1% Native American, 3% Hispanic, 4% black, 3% Asian or Pacific Islander **Most popular recent majors** Business administration/commerce/management, psychology, communication **Academic program** Average class size 18, ESL program, advanced placement, accelerated degree program, self-designed majors, tutorials, honors program, summer session, adult/continuing education programs, internships **Contact** Ms. Marguerite Waters, Dean of Admission, North Central College, Naperville, IL 60566-7063. Telephone: 630-637-5802.

NORTHEASTERN ILLINOIS UNIVERSITY
CHICAGO, ILLINOIS

Entrance Minimally difficult **General** State-supported, comprehensive, coed **Setting** 67-acre urban campus **Enrollment** 10,035 **Faculty** 20:1 **Application deadline** 7/1 **Freshmen** 69% accepted **Tuition** $2142 **Undergraduates** 60% women, 45% part-time, 42% 25 or older, 1% Native American, 23% Hispanic, 13% black, 11% Asian or Pacific Islander **Most popular recent majors** Accounting, elementary education **Academic program** Advanced placement, self-designed majors, tutorials, honors program, summer session, adult/continuing education programs **Contact** Ms. Miriam Rivera, Director of Admissions and Records, Northeastern Illinois University, 5500 North St. Louis Avenue, Chicago, IL 60625-4699. Telephone: 773-794-2853. Fax: 773-794-6243.

Northern Illinois University

NORTHERN ILLINOIS UNIVERSITY
DE KALB, ILLINOIS

Entrance Moderately difficult **General** State-supported, coed **Setting** 589-acre small-town campus **Enrollment** 21,609 **Faculty** 17:1 **Application deadline** 8/1 **Freshmen** 74% accepted **Housing** Yes **Tuition** $3933 **Undergraduates** 54% women, 12% part-time, 16% 25 or older, 5% Hispanic, 10% black, 7% Asian or Pacific Islander **Most popular recent majors** Communication, education, accounting **Academic program** Advanced placement, accelerated degree program, self-designed majors, honors program, summer session, adult/continuing education programs, internships **Contact** Dr. Robert Burk, Director of Admissions, Northern Illinois University, De Kalb, IL 60115-2854. Telephone: 815-753-0446.

NORTH PARK UNIVERSITY
CHICAGO, ILLINOIS

Entrance Moderately difficult **General** Independent, comprehensive, coed, affiliated with Evangelical Covenant Church **Setting** 30-acre urban campus **Enrollment** 1,815 **Faculty** 16:1 **Application deadline** Rolling **Freshmen** 72% accepted **Housing** Yes **Tuition** $13,990 **Undergraduates** 62% women, 20% part-time, 26% 25 or older, 1% Native American, 8% Hispanic, 6% black, 10% Asian or Pacific Islander **Most popular recent majors** Business administration/commerce/management, nursing, psychology **Academic program** Advanced placement, accelerated degree program, self-designed majors, tutorials, honors program, summer session, adult/continuing education programs, internships **Contact** Office of Admissions, North Park University, 3225 West Foster Avenue, Chicago, IL 60625-4895. Telephone: 773-244-5500. Fax: 773-583-0858.

NORTHWESTERN UNIVERSITY
EVANSTON, ILLINOIS

Entrance Very difficult **General** Independent, coed **Setting** 231-acre suburban campus **Enrollment** 12,213 **Faculty** 12:1 **Application deadline** 1/1 **Freshmen** 32% accepted **Housing** Yes **Tuition** $19,218 **Undergraduates** 53% women, 1% part-time, 1% 25 or older, 1% Native American, 3% Hispanic, 6% black, 18% Asian or Pacific Islander **Most popular recent majors** Economics, political science/government, engineering (general) **Academic program** Advanced placement, accelerated degree program, self-designed majors, tutorials, honors program, summer session, adult/continuing education programs, internships **Contact** Ms. Carol Lunkenheimer, Director of Admissions, Northwestern University, 1801 Hinman Avenue, Evanston, IL 60208. Telephone: 847-491-7271.

OLIVET NAZARENE UNIVERSITY
KANKAKEE, ILLINOIS

Entrance Moderately difficult **General** Independent, comprehensive, coed, affiliated with Church of the Nazarene **Setting** 168-acre suburban campus **Enrollment** 2,256 **Faculty** 16:1 **Application deadline** 8/1 **Freshmen** 99% accepted **Housing** Yes **Tuition** $10,166 **Undergraduates** 55% women, 15% part-time, 10% 25 or older, 1% Native American, 1% Hispanic, 6% black, 1% Asian or Pacific Islander **Academic program** Advanced placement, accelerated degree program, self-designed majors, summer session, adult/continuing education programs, internships **Contact** Rev. John Mongerson, Director of Admissions, Olivet Nazarene University, Kankakee, IL 60901-0592. Telephone: 815-939-5203.

PRINCIPIA COLLEGE
ELSAH, ILLINOIS

Entrance Moderately difficult **General** Independent Christian Science, 4-year, coed **Setting** 2,800-acre rural campus **Enrollment** 533 **Faculty** 7:1 **Application deadline** 5/1 **Freshmen** 91% accepted **Housing** Yes **Tuition** $14,112 **Undergraduates** 55% women, 2% part-time, 4% 25 or older, 0% Native American, 2% Hispanic, 1% black, 1% Asian or Pacific Islander **Most popular recent majors** Biology/biological sciences, environmental sciences, business administration/commerce/management **Academic program** Average class size 10, advanced placement, accelerated degree program, self-designed majors, honors program, adult/continuing education programs, internships **Contact** Ms. Martha Green Quirk, Director of Admissions and Enrollment, Principia College, Elsah, IL 62028-9799. Telephone: 618-374-5181. Fax: 618-374-4000.

QUINCY UNIVERSITY
QUINCY, ILLINOIS

Entrance Moderately difficult **General** Independent Roman Catholic, comprehensive, coed **Setting** 75-acre small-town campus **Enrollment** 1,141 **Faculty** 11:1 **Application deadline** Rolling **Freshmen** 71% accepted **Housing** Yes **Tuition** $12,410 **Undergraduates** 50% women, 6% part-time, 7% 25 or older, 1% Native American, 2% Hispanic, 6% black, 1% Asian or Pacific Islander **Most popular recent majors** Elementary education, communication, psychology **Academic**

program ESL program, Advanced placement, accelerated degree program, self-designed majors, tutorials, honors program, summer session, adult/continuing education programs, internships **Contact** Mr. Jeff Van Camp, Director of Admissions, Quincy University, Quincy, IL 62301-2699. Telephone: 217-222-8020 Ext. 5215. Fax: 217-228-5479.

ROBERT MORRIS COLLEGE
CHICAGO, ILLINOIS

Entrance Minimally difficult **General** Independent, 4-year, coed **Setting** Urban campus **Enrollment** 3,734 **Faculty** 20:1 **Application deadline** Rolling **Freshmen** 60% accepted **Tuition** $9750 **Undergraduates** 76% women, 10% part-time, 29% 25 or older, 28% Hispanic, 40% black, 3% Asian or Pacific Islander **Most popular recent majors** Accounting, business administration/commerce/management, secretarial studies/office management **Academic program** Advanced placement, tutorials, honors program, summer session, adult/continuing education programs, internships **Contact** Ms. Jean Norris, Dean of Admissions, Robert Morris College, 180 North LaSalle Street, Chicago, IL 60601-2592. Telephone: 312-836-4635.

ROCKFORD COLLEGE
ROCKFORD, ILLINOIS

Entrance Moderately difficult **General** Independent, comprehensive, coed **Setting** 130-acre suburban campus **Enrollment** 1,309 **Faculty** 9:1 **Application deadline** Rolling **Freshmen** 77% accepted **Housing** Yes **Tuition** $14,750 **Undergraduates** 70% women, 27% part-time, 41% 25 or older, 1% Native American, 4% Hispanic, 6% black, 1% Asian or Pacific Islander **Most popular recent majors** Education, business administration/commerce/management, psychology **Academic program** Average class size 15, advanced placement, self-designed majors, tutorials, honors program, summer session, adult/continuing education programs, internships **Contact** Mr. Paul Hartzog, Associate Director of Admission, Rockford College, Rockford, IL 61108-2393. Telephone: 815-226-4050. Fax: 815-226-4119.

ROOSEVELT UNIVERSITY
CHICAGO, ILLINOIS

Entrance Moderately difficult **General** Independent, comprehensive, coed **Setting** Urban campus **Enrollment** 6,663 **Faculty** 13:1 **Application deadline** 8/15 **Freshmen** 92% accepted **Housing** Yes **Tuition** $11,030 **Undergraduates** 62% women, 65% part-time, 74% 25 or older, 1% Native American, 9% Hispanic, 27% black, 4% Asian or Pacific Islander **Most popular recent majors** Accounting, social science, psychology **Academic program** Advanced placement, accelerated degree program, self-designed majors, honors program, summer session, adult/continuing education programs, internships **Contact** Admission Counselors, Roosevelt University, Office of Admissions, Chicago, IL 60605-1394. Telephone: 312-341-3515.

ROSARY COLLEGE
SEE DOMINICAN UNIVERSITY

RUSH UNIVERSITY
CHICAGO, ILLINOIS

Entrance Moderately difficult **General** Independent, upper-level, coed **Setting** 35-acre urban campus **Enrollment** 1,474 **Faculty** 6:1 **Freshmen** 60% accepted **Housing** Yes **Tuition** $10,254 **Undergraduates** 86% women, 54% 25 or older, 0% Native American, 6% Hispanic, 10% black, 12% Asian or Pacific Islander **Contact** Ms. Phyllis Peterson, Director of College Admission Services, Rush University, 1653 West Congress Parkway, Chicago, IL 60612-3832. Telephone: 312-942-7100. Fax: 312-942-2219.

SAINT ANTHONY COLLEGE OF NURSING
ROCKFORD, ILLINOIS

Entrance Moderately difficult **General** Independent Roman Catholic, upper-level, specialized, coed **Setting** 17-acre urban campus **Enrollment** 81 **Faculty** 9:1 **Freshmen** 56% accepted **Tuition** $10,400 **Undergraduates** 87% women, 5% part-time, 45% 25 or older, 0% Native American, 2% Hispanic, 1% black, 1% Asian or Pacific Islander **Academic program** Advanced placement, summer session **Contact** Ms. Cathy Mueller, Student Services Assistant, Saint Anthony College of Nursing, 5658 East State Street, Rockford, IL 61108-2468. Telephone: 815-395-5089.

SAINT FRANCIS MEDICAL CENTER COLLEGE OF NURSING
PEORIA, ILLINOIS

Entrance Moderately difficult **General** Independent Roman Catholic, upper-level, specialized, coed **Setting** Urban campus **Enrollment** 152 **Freshmen** 100% accepted **Housing** Yes **Tuition** $8355 **Undergraduates** 86% women, 30% part-time, 50% 25 or older, 0% Native American, 1% Hispanic, 3% black, 4% Asian or Pacific Islander **Academic program** Advanced placement, summer session **Contact** Mrs. Janice Farquharson, Director of Admissions and Registrar, Saint Francis Medical Center College of Nursing, 511 Greenleaf Street, Peoria, IL 61603-3783. Telephone: 309-655-2596.

ST. JOHN'S COLLEGE
SPRINGFIELD, ILLINOIS

Entrance Difficulty N/R **General** Independent Roman Catholic, upper-level, specialized, primarily women **Setting** Urban campus **Enrollment** 114 **Faculty** 6:1 **Freshmen** 37% accepted **Housing** Yes **Tuition** $6798 **Undergraduates** 93% women, 5% part-time, 35% 25 or older, 0% Native American, 0% Hispanic, 4% black, 1% Asian or Pacific Islander **Academic program** Average class size 45 **Contact** Ms. Nancy Cobetto, Student Development Officer, St. John's College, 421 North Ninth Street, Springfield, IL 62702-5317. Telephone: 217-525-5628.

SAINT JOSEPH COLLEGE OF NURSING
SEE COLLEGE OF ST. FRANCIS

SAINT XAVIER UNIVERSITY
CHICAGO, ILLINOIS

Entrance Moderately difficult **General** Independent Roman Catholic, comprehensive, coed **Setting** 55-acre urban campus **Enrollment** 4,200 **Faculty** 16:1 **Application deadline** 8/1 **Freshmen** 83% accepted **Housing** Yes **Tuition** $12,560 **Undergraduates** 73% women, 43% part-time, 44% 25 or older, 8% Hispanic, 13% black, 1% Asian or Pacific Islander **Most popular recent majors** Business administration/commerce/management, nursing, education **Academic program** ESL program, Advanced placement, self-designed majors, summer session, adult/continuing education programs, internships **Contact** Sr. Evelyn McKenna, Director of Admissions, Saint Xavier University, 3700 West 103rd Street, Chicago, IL 60655-3105. Telephone: 773-298-3050. Fax: 773-298-3076 Ext. 3050.

SANGAMON STATE UNIVERSITY
SEE UNIVERSITY OF ILLINOIS AT SPRINGFIELD

SCHOOL OF THE ART INSTITUTE OF CHICAGO
CHICAGO, ILLINOIS

Entrance Moderately difficult **General** Independent, comprehensive, specialized, coed **Setting** 1-acre urban campus **Enrollment** 2,012 **Faculty** 12:1 **Application deadline** Rolling **Freshmen** 76% accepted **Housing** Yes **Tuition** $17,160 **Undergraduates** 58% women, 14% part-time, 24% 25 or older, 1% Native American, 7% Hispanic, 5% black, 7% Asian or Pacific Islander **Academic program** Advanced placement, self-designed majors, tutorials, summer session, internships **Contact** Director of Admissions, School of the Art Institute of Chicago, 37 South Wabash, Chicago, IL 60603-3103. Telephone: 312-899-5219. Fax: 312-263-0141.

SHIMER COLLEGE
WAUKEGAN, ILLINOIS

Entrance Moderately difficult **General** Independent, 4-year, coed **Setting** 3-acre suburban campus **Enrollment** 130 **Faculty** 7:1 **Application deadline** 8/10 **Freshmen** 63% accepted **Housing** Yes **Tuition** $13,800 **Undergraduates** 52% women, 5% part-time, 30% 25 or older, 0% Native American, 8% Hispanic, 11% black, 3% Asian or Pacific Islander **Most popular recent majors** Humanities, social science, natural sciences **Academic program** Average class size 8, accelerated degree program, self-designed majors, tutorials, summer session, adult/continuing education programs, internships **Contact** Mr. Marc Hoffman, Assistant Director of Admissions, Shimer College, Waukegan, IL 60079-0500. Telephone: 847-249-7175. Fax: 847-249-7171.

SOUTHERN ILLINOIS UNIVERSITY AT CARBONDALE
CARBONDALE, ILLINOIS

Entrance Moderately difficult **General** State-supported, coed **Setting** 1,128-acre small-town campus **Enrollment** 21,863 **Faculty** 13:1 **Application deadline** Rolling **Freshmen** 72% accepted **Housing** Yes **Tuition** $3260 **Undergraduates** 42% women, 12% part-time, 31% 25 or older, 1% Native American, 2% Hispanic, 13% black, 2% Asian or Pacific Islander **Most popular recent majors** Vocational education, industrial engineering technology, aviation administration **Academic program** Advanced placement, accelerated degree program, tutorials, honors program, summer session, adult/continuing education programs, internships **Contact** Mr. Thomas McGinnis, Director of Admissions, Southern Illinois University at Carbondale, Carbondale, IL 62901-6806. Telephone: 618-536-4405.

SOUTHERN ILLINOIS UNIVERSITY AT EDWARDSVILLE
EDWARDSVILLE, ILLINOIS

Entrance Moderately difficult **General** State-supported, comprehensive, coed **Setting** 2,660-

acre suburban campus **Enrollment** 11,151 **Faculty** 15:1 **Application deadline** 8/4 **Freshmen** 85% accepted **Housing** Yes **Tuition** $2276 **Undergraduates** 58% women, 26% part-time, 31% 25 or older, 0% Native American, 1% Hispanic, 13% black, 2% Asian or Pacific Islander **Most popular recent majors** Business administration/commerce/management, nursing, elementary education **Academic program** Average class size 21, advanced placement, accelerated degree program, honors program, summer session, adult/continuing education programs, internships **Contact** Mr. Gene Magac, Director of School and College Relations, Southern Illinois University at Edwardsville, Edwardsville, IL 62026-0001. Telephone: 618-692-3705. Fax: 618-692-2081.

TRINITY CHRISTIAN COLLEGE
PALOS HEIGHTS, ILLINOIS

Entrance Moderately difficult **General** Independent interdenominational, 4-year, coed **Setting** 53-acre suburban campus **Enrollment** 619 **Faculty** 12:1 **Application deadline** 8/15 **Freshmen** 94% accepted **Housing** Yes **Tuition** $11,700 **Undergraduates** 63% women, 8% part-time, 7% 25 or older, 1% Native American, 2% Hispanic, 4% black, 2% Asian or Pacific Islander **Most popular recent majors** Business administration/commerce/management, education, nursing **Academic program** Advanced placement, tutorials, adult/continuing education programs, internships **Contact** Mr. David Lageveen, Director of Admissions, Trinity Christian College, Palos Heights, IL 60463-0929. Telephone: 708-239-4709. Fax: 708-385-5665.

TRINITY COLLEGE
SEE TRINITY INTERNATIONAL UNIVERSITY

TRINITY INTERNATIONAL UNIVERSITY
DEERFIELD, ILLINOIS

Entrance Moderately difficult **General** Independent, coed, affiliated with Evangelical Free Church of America **Setting** 108-acre suburban campus **Enrollment** 2,160 **Faculty** 16:1 **Application deadline** Rolling **Freshmen** 93% accepted **Housing** Yes **Tuition** $12,630 **Undergraduates** 52% women, 10% part-time, 26% 25 or older, 1% Native American, 3% Hispanic, 11% black, 3% Asian or Pacific Islander **Most popular recent majors** Education, ministries, business administration/commerce/management **Academic program** Advanced placement, self-designed majors, honors program, summer session, adult/continuing education programs, internships **Contact** Mr. Brian Medaglia, Director of Admissions, Trinity International University, Deerfield, IL 60015-1284. Telephone: 847-317-7000. Fax: 847-317-7081.

UNIVERSITY OF CHICAGO
CHICAGO, ILLINOIS

Entrance Most difficult **General** Independent, coed **Setting** 203-acre urban campus **Enrollment** 12,117 **Faculty** 6:1 **Application deadline** 1/1 **Freshmen** 58% accepted **Housing** Yes **Tuition** $22,476 **Undergraduates** 46% women, 1% part-time, 1% 25 or older, 0% Native American, 5% Hispanic, 4% black, 27% Asian or Pacific Islander **Most popular recent majors** Economics, biology/biological sciences, English **Academic program** Average class size 25, advanced placement, accelerated degree program, self-designed majors, tutorials, summer session, adult/continuing education programs, internships **Contact** Mr. Theodore O'Neill, Dean of Admissions, University of Chicago, 1116 East 59th Street, Chicago, IL 60637-1513. Telephone: 773-702-8650. Fax: 773-702-4199.

UNIVERSITY OF ILLINOIS AT CHICAGO
CHICAGO, ILLINOIS

Entrance Moderately difficult **General** State-supported, coed **Setting** 200-acre urban campus **Enrollment** 24,583 **Faculty** 14:1 **Application deadline** 6/9 **Freshmen** 63% accepted **Housing** Yes **Tuition** $3898 **Undergraduates** 54% women, 16% part-time, 20% 25 or older, 1% Native American, 17% Hispanic, 10% black, 20% Asian or Pacific Islander **Most popular recent majors** Psychology, accounting, nursing **Academic program** Advanced placement, accelerated degree program, self-designed majors, honors program, summer session, adult/continuing education programs, internships **Contact** Ms. Marge Gockel, Associate Director for Undergraduate Admissions, University of Illinois at Chicago, PO Box 5220, Chicago, IL 60680-5220. Telephone: 312-996-4350.

UNIVERSITY OF ILLINOIS AT SPRINGFIELD
SPRINGFIELD, ILLINOIS

Entrance Minimally difficult **General** State-supported, upper-level, coed **Setting** 746-acre suburban campus **Enrollment** 4,611 **Faculty** 15:1 **Freshmen** 80% accepted **Housing** Yes **Tuition** $2220 **Undergraduates** 65% women, 57% part-time, 66% 25 or older, 3% Native American, 1% Hispanic, 7% black, 1% Asian or Pacific Islander **Most popular recent majors** Business administration/commerce/management, psychology, criminal justice **Academic program** Self-designed majors, tutorials, summer session, adult/continuing education programs, internships **Contact** Office of Enrollment Services, University of Illinois at Springfield, Springfield, IL 62794-9243. Telephone: 217-786-6626.

UNIVERSITY OF ILLINOIS AT URBANA–CHAMPAIGN
CHAMPAIGN, ILLINOIS

Entrance Very difficult **General** State-supported, coed **Setting** 1,470-acre small-town campus **Enrollment** 36,164 **Faculty** 14:1 **Application deadline** 1/1 **Freshmen** 70% accepted **Housing** Yes **Tuition** $4186 **Undergraduates** 46% women, 3% part-time, 4% 25 or older, 1% Native American, 5% Hispanic, 7% black, 13% Asian or Pacific Islander **Most popular recent majors** Biology/biological sciences, psychology, electrical engineering **Academic program** Average class size 31, advanced placement, accelerated degree program, self-designed majors, tutorials, honors program, summer session, internships **Contact** Ms. Tammy Bouseman, Assistant Director of Admissions, University of Illinois at Urbana-Champaign, 10 Henry Administration Building, Urbana, IL 61820-5711. Telephone: 217-333-0302.

VANDERCOOK COLLEGE OF MUSIC
CHICAGO, ILLINOIS

Entrance Moderately difficult **General** Independent, comprehensive, specialized, coed **Setting** 1-acre urban campus **Enrollment** 175 **Faculty** 6:1 **Application deadline** Rolling **Freshmen** 85% accepted **Housing** Yes **Tuition** $9650 **Undergraduates** 40% women, 2% part-time, 16% 25 or older, 2% Native American, 4% Hispanic, 24% black, 1% Asian or Pacific Islander **Academic program** Average class size 20, advanced placement, summer session, adult/continuing education programs, internships **Contact** Ms. Ami Bartz, Admissions Counselor, VanderCook College of Music, 3140 South Federal, Chicago, IL 60616-3886. Telephone: 312-225-6288. Fax: 312-225-5211.

WESTERN ILLINOIS UNIVERSITY
MACOMB, ILLINOIS

Entrance Moderately difficult **General** State-supported, comprehensive, coed **Setting** 1,050-acre small-town campus **Enrollment** 12,184 **Faculty** 15:1 **Application deadline** 8/10 **Freshmen** 69% accepted **Housing** Yes **Tuition** $2885 **Undergraduates** 49% women, 16% part-time, 21% 25 or older, 1% Native American, 3% Hispanic, 7% black, 1% Asian or Pacific Islander **Most popular recent majors** Law enforcement/police sciences, elementary education, communication **Academic program** Advanced placement, accelerated degree program, self-designed majors, tutorials, honors program, summer session, adult/continuing education programs, internships **Contact** Ms. Karen Helmers, Director of Admissions, Western Illinois University, Macomb, IL 61455-1390. Telephone: 309-298-3157. Fax: 309-298-3111.

WEST SUBURBAN COLLEGE OF NURSING
OAK PARK, ILLINOIS

Entrance Moderately difficult **General** Independent, 4-year, specialized, coed **Setting** 10-acre suburban campus **Enrollment** 229 **Application deadline** Rolling **Freshmen** 81% accepted **Housing** Yes **Tuition** $11,930 **Undergraduates** 91% women, 30% part-time, 30% 25 or older, 4% Hispanic, 13% black, 12% Asian or Pacific Islander **Academic program** Advanced placement, tutorials, summer session **Contact** Mr. Edward Pryor, Director of Admission, West Suburban College of Nursing, Oak Park, IL 60302. Telephone: 708-763-6530. Fax: 708-383-8783.

WHEATON COLLEGE
WHEATON, ILLINOIS

Entrance Very difficult **General** Independent nondenominational, comprehensive, coed **Setting** 80-acre suburban campus **Enrollment** 2,697 **Faculty** 15:1 **Application deadline** 2/1 **Freshmen** 52% accepted **Housing** Yes **Tuition** $13,780 **Undergraduates** 50% women, 2% part-time, 6% 25 or older, 1% Native American, 3% Hispanic, 2% black, 6% Asian or Pacific Islander **Most popular recent majors** Literature, music, psychology **Academic program** Average class size 28, advanced placement, self-designed majors, summer session, internships **Contact** Mr. Dan Crabtree, Director of Admissions, Wheaton College, Wheaton, IL 60187-5593. Telephone: 630-752-5011.

Indiana

ANDERSON UNIVERSITY
ANDERSON, INDIANA

Entrance Moderately difficult **General** Independent, comprehensive, coed, affiliated with Church of God **Setting** 100-acre suburban campus **Enrollment** 2,136 **Faculty** 14:1 **Application deadline** 8/25 **Freshmen** 77% accepted **Housing** Yes **Tuition** $12,700 **Undergraduates** 58% women, 12% part-time, 17% 25 or older, 1% Native American, 1% Hispanic, 5% black, 1% Asian or Pacific Islander **Most popular recent majors** Elementary education, social work, nursing **Academic program** Advanced placement, accelerated degree program, self-designed majors, tutorials, summer session, adult/continuing education programs, internships **Contact** Mr. Jim King, Director of Admissions, Anderson University, Anderson, IN 46012-3495. Telephone: 317-641-4080. Fax: 317-641-3851.

BALL STATE UNIVERSITY
MUNCIE, INDIANA

Entrance Moderately difficult **General** State-supported, coed **Setting** 955-acre suburban campus **Enrollment** 18,594 **Faculty** 17:1 **Application deadline** Rolling **Freshmen** 89% accepted **Housing** Yes **Tuition** $3414 **Undergraduates** 54% women, 11% part-time, 11% 25 or older, 1% Native American, 1% Hispanic, 5% black, 1% Asian or Pacific Islander **Most popular recent majors** Elementary education, liberal arts/general studies, journalism **Academic program** Advanced placement, accelerated degree program, tutorials, honors program, summer session, adult/continuing education programs, internships **Contact** Mrs. Elaine Cotner, Director of Admissions, Ball State University, Office of Admissions, Muncie, IN 47306-1099. Telephone: 317-285-8300. Fax: 317-285-1632.

BETHEL COLLEGE
MISHAWAKA, INDIANA

Entrance Moderately difficult **General** Independent, comprehensive, coed, affiliated with Missionary Church **Setting** 65-acre suburban campus **Enrollment** 1,467 **Faculty** 18:1 **Application deadline** 8/1 **Freshmen** 81% accepted **Housing** Yes **Tuition** $11,100 **Undergraduates** 66% women, 36% part-time, 42% 25 or older, 0% Native American, 1% Hispanic, 10% black, 1% Asian or Pacific Islander **Most popular recent majors** Elementary education, nursing, psychology **Academic program** ESL program, Advanced placement, accelerated degree program, summer session, adult/continuing education programs, internships **Contact** Mr. Steve Matteson, Dean of Admissions, Bethel College, Mishawaka, IN 46545-5591. Telephone: 219-257-3339 Ext. 319. Fax: 219-257-3326.

BUTLER UNIVERSITY
INDIANAPOLIS, INDIANA

Entrance Moderately difficult **General** Independent, comprehensive, coed **Setting** 290-acre urban campus **Enrollment** 3,932 **Faculty** 15:1 **Application deadline** 8/15 **Freshmen** 85% accepted **Housing** Yes **Tuition** $15,570 **Undergraduates** 61% women, 3% part-time, 5% 25 or older, 0% Native American, 1% Hispanic, 4% black, 2% Asian or Pacific Islander **Most popular recent majors** Pharmacy/pharmaceutical sciences, elementary education, secondary education **Academic program** Average class size 18, advanced placement, accelerated degree program, tutorials, honors program, summer session, adult/continuing education programs, internships **Contact** Ms. Carroll Davis, Director of Admission, Butler University, 4600 Sunset Avenue, Indianapolis, IN 46208-3485. Telephone: 317-940-8100. Fax: 917-940-9972.

CALUMET COLLEGE OF SAINT JOSEPH
WHITING, INDIANA

Entrance Minimally difficult **General** Independent Roman Catholic, 4-year, coed **Setting** 260-acre suburban campus **Enrollment** 1,018 **Faculty** 15:1 **Application deadline** Rolling **Freshmen** 71% accepted **Tuition** $6293 **Undergraduates** 66% women, 59% part-time, 72% 25 or older, 1% Native American, 16% Hispanic, 21% black, 1% Asian or Pacific Islander **Most popular recent majors** Business administration/commerce/management, accounting, computer information systems **Academic program** Accelerated degree program, self-designed majors, tutorials, honors program, summer session, adult/continuing education programs, internships **Contact** Mr. Kevin Goldberg, Acting Director of Admissions, Calumet College of Saint Joseph, Whiting, IN 46394-2195. Telephone: 219-473-4215. Fax: 219-473-4259.

DEPAUW UNIVERSITY
GREENCASTLE, INDIANA

Entrance Moderately difficult **General** Independent, 4-year, coed, affiliated with United Methodist Church **Setting** 175-acre small-town campus **Enrollment** 2,147 **Faculty** 12:1 **Application deadline** 2/15 **Freshmen** 81% accepted **Housing** Yes **Tuition** $17,050 **Undergraduates** 55% women, 1% part-time, 1% 25 or older, 1% Native American, 3% Hispanic, 7% black, 2% Asian or Pacific Islander **Most popular recent majors** Communication, economics, biology/biological sciences **Academic program** Average class size 23, advanced placement, self-designed majors, tutorials, honors program, internships **Contact** Ms. Madeline Eagon, Dean of Admission and Financial

Aid, DePauw University, Greencastle, IN 46135-1772. Telephone: 317-658-4006. Fax: 317-658-4007.

EARLHAM COLLEGE
RICHMOND, INDIANA

Entrance Moderately difficult **General** Independent, 4-year, coed, affiliated with Society of Friends **Setting** 800-acre small-town campus **Enrollment** 1,005 **Faculty** 11:1 **Application deadline** 2/15 **Freshmen** 83% accepted **Housing** Yes **Tuition** $18,618 **Undergraduates** 57% women, 2% part-time, 0% 25 or older, 1% Native American, 1% Hispanic, 5% black, 3% Asian or Pacific Islander **Most popular recent majors** Biology/biological sciences, English, psychology **Academic program** Advanced placement, accelerated degree program, self-designed majors, tutorials, adult/continuing education programs, internships **Contact** Mr. Michael Oligmueller, Dean of Admissions, Earlham College, 801 National Road West, Richmond, IN 47374. Telephone: 765-983-1600. Fax: 765-983-1560.

FRANKLIN COLLEGE OF INDIANA
FRANKLIN, INDIANA

Entrance Moderately difficult **General** Independent, 4-year, coed, affiliated with American Baptist Churches in the U.S.A. **Setting** 74-acre small-town campus **Enrollment** 874 **Faculty** 12:1 **Application deadline** 8/1 **Freshmen** 86% accepted **Housing** Yes **Tuition** $12,360 **Undergraduates** 55% women, 6% part-time, 2% 25 or older, 0% Native American, 1% Hispanic, 1% black, 1% Asian or Pacific Islander **Most popular recent majors** Education, journalism, business administration/commerce/management **Academic program** Average class size 17, advanced placement, accelerated degree program, tutorials, honors program, summer session, internships **Contact** Mr. Bruce Stephen Richards, Dean of Admissions and Financial Aid, Franklin College of Indiana, 501 East Monroe Street, Franklin, IN 46131-2598. Telephone: 317-738-8062. Fax: 317-738-8274.

GOSHEN COLLEGE
GOSHEN, INDIANA

Entrance Moderately difficult **General** Independent Mennonite, 4-year, coed **Setting** 135-acre small-town campus **Enrollment** 1,014 **Faculty** 12:1 **Application deadline** Rolling **Freshmen** 88% accepted **Housing** Yes **Tuition** $11,450 **Undergraduates** 57% women, 12% part-time, 17% 25 or older, 1% Native American, 4% Hispanic, 1% black, 1% Asian or Pacific Islander **Most popular recent majors** Business administration/commerce/management, nursing, elementary education **Academic program** Advanced placement, accelerated degree program, self-designed majors, tutorials, summer session, adult/continuing education programs, internships **Contact** Ms. Martha Lehman, Director of Admissions, Goshen College, Goshen, IN 46526-4794. Telephone: 219-535-7535. Fax: 219-535-7609.

GRACE COLLEGE
WINONA LAKE, INDIANA

Entrance Moderately difficult **General** Independent, 4-year, coed, affiliated with Fellowship of Grace Brethren Churches **Setting** 160-acre small-town campus **Enrollment** 645 **Faculty** 16:1 **Application deadline** 8/1 **Freshmen** 80% accepted **Housing** Yes **Tuition** $9820 **Undergraduates** 59% women, 9% part-time, 10% 25 or older, 0% Native American, 1% Hispanic, 2% black, 1% Asian or Pacific Islander **Most popular recent majors** Elementary education, psychology, business administration/commerce/management **Academic program** Average class size 30, advanced placement, accelerated degree program, summer session, internships **Contact** Mr. Ron Henry, Dean of Enrollment, Grace College, Winona Lake, IN 46590-1294. Telephone: 219-372-5128. Fax: 219-372-5265.

HANOVER COLLEGE
HANOVER, INDIANA

Entrance Moderately difficult **General** Independent Presbyterian, 4-year, coed **Setting** 630-acre rural campus **Enrollment** 1,051 **Faculty** 11:1 **Application deadline** 3/1 **Freshmen** 71% accepted **Housing** Yes **Tuition** $10,085 **Undergraduates** 52% women, 1% part-time, 1% 25 or older, 0% Native American, 1% Hispanic, 1% black, 1% Asian or Pacific Islander **Most popular recent majors** Business administration/commerce/management, psychology, English **Academic program** Average class size 16, advanced placement, accelerated degree program, tutorials, honors program, internships **Contact** Mr. Kenneth Moyer Jr., Director of Admissions, Hanover College, Box 108, Hanover, IN 47243-0108. Telephone: 812-866-7021. Fax: 812-866-2164.

HUNTINGTON COLLEGE
HUNTINGTON, INDIANA

Entrance Moderately difficult **General** Independent, comprehensive, coed, affiliated with Church of the United Brethren in Christ **Setting** 200-acre small-town campus **Enrollment** 726 **Faculty** 14:1 **Application deadline** 8/15 **Freshmen** 90% accepted **Housing** Yes **Tuition** $12,180 **Undergraduates** 51% women, 9% part-time, 15% 25 or older, 0% Native American, 0% Hispanic, 2% black, 1% Asian or Pacific Islander **Most popular recent majors** Elementary education, business administration/commerce/management, theology **Academic program** Advanced placement, accelerated degree program, self-designed majors, tutorials, summer session, adult/continuing education programs, internships **Contact** Mr. Jeff Berggren, Executive Director of Admissions and Financial Aid, Huntington College, Huntington, IN 46750-1299. Telephone: 219-356-6000 Ext. 1016. Fax: 219-356-9448.

INDIANA INSTITUTE OF TECHNOLOGY

FORT WAYNE, INDIANA

Entrance Moderately difficult **General** Independent, 4-year, coed **Setting** 25-acre urban campus **Enrollment** 1,321 **Application deadline** 8/1 **Freshmen** 87% accepted **Housing** Yes **Tuition** $10,850 **Undergraduates** 20% women, 40% part-time, 5% 25 or older, 0% Native American, 5% Hispanic, 20% black, 5% Asian or Pacific Islander **Most popular recent majors** Engineering (general), business administration/commerce/management, accounting **Academic program** Advanced placement, tutorials, summer session, adult/continuing education programs, internships **Contact** Mrs. Diane L. Maldeney, Registrar, Indiana Institute of Technology, 1600 East Washington Boulevard, Fort Wayne, IN 46803-1297. Telephone: 219-422-5561 Ext. 265. Fax: 219-422-7696.

INDIANA STATE UNIVERSITY

TERRE HAUTE, INDIANA

Entrance Moderately difficult **General** State-supported, coed **Setting** 91-acre suburban campus **Enrollment** 10,934 **Faculty** 15:1 **Application deadline** 8/15 **Freshmen** 88% accepted **Housing** Yes **Tuition** $3196 **Undergraduates** 51% women, 18% part-time, 16% 25 or older, 1% Native American, 1% Hispanic, 8% black, 1% Asian or Pacific Islander **Most popular recent majors** Elementary education, criminology, nursing **Academic program** Average class size 25, advanced placement, accelerated degree program, tutorials, honors program, summer session, adult/continuing education programs, internships **Contact** Ms. Leah Bell, Director of Admissions, Indiana State University, Terre Haute, IN 47809-1401. Telephone: 812-237-2121. Fax: 812-237-4292.

INDIANA UNIVERSITY BLOOMINGTON

BLOOMINGTON, INDIANA

Entrance Moderately difficult **General** State-supported, coed **Setting** 1,800-acre small-town campus **Enrollment** 34,700 **Faculty** 17:1 **Application deadline** 2/15 **Freshmen** 83% accepted **Housing** Yes **Tuition** $3929 **Undergraduates** 54% women, 6% part-time, 6% 25 or older, 0% Native American, 2% Hispanic, 4% black, 3% Asian or Pacific Islander **Most popular recent majors** Liberal arts/general studies, business administration/commerce/management, education **Academic program** Advanced placement, accelerated degree program, self-designed majors, tutorials, honors program, summer session, adult/continuing education programs, internships **Contact** Mr. Robert Magee, Director of Admissions, Indiana University Bloomington, 300 North Jordan Avenue, Bloomington, IN 47405. Telephone: 812-855-0661.

INDIANA UNIVERSITY EAST

RICHMOND, INDIANA

Entrance Noncompetitive **General** State-supported, 4-year, coed **Setting** 194-acre small-town campus **Enrollment** 2,302 **Faculty** 12:1 **Application deadline** Rolling **Freshmen** 100% accepted **Tuition** $2849 **Undergraduates** 68% women, 59% part-time, 47% 25 or older, 1% Native American, 1% Hispanic, 3% black, 1% Asian or Pacific Islander **Most popular recent majors** Nursing, elementary education, liberal arts/general studies **Academic program** Advanced placement, tutorials, summer session, adult/continuing education programs, internships **Contact** Ms. Susanna Tanner, Admissions Counselor, Indiana University East, 2325 Chester Boulevard, Richmond, IN 47374-1289. Telephone: 765-973-8415. Fax: 765-973-8388.

INDIANA UNIVERSITY KOKOMO

KOKOMO, INDIANA

Entrance Minimally difficult **General** State-supported, comprehensive, coed **Setting** 51-acre small-town campus **Enrollment** 2,965 **Faculty** 18:1 **Application deadline** 8/5 **Freshmen** 99% accepted **Tuition** $2890 **Undergraduates** 70% women, 55% part-time, 51% 25 or older, 1% Native American, 1% Hispanic, 3% black, 1% Asian or Pacific Islander **Most popular recent majors** Nursing, business administration/commerce/management, elementary education **Academic program** Advanced placement, tutorials, honors program, summer session, adult/continuing education programs, internships **Contact** Dr. Jack

Tharp, Vice Chancellor of Student Services, Indiana University Kokomo, Kokomo, IN 46904-9003. Telephone: 317-455-9360.

INDIANA UNIVERSITY NORTHWEST
GARY, INDIANA

Entrance Minimally difficult **General** State-supported, comprehensive, coed **Setting** 27-acre urban campus **Enrollment** 5,149 **Faculty** 14:1 **Application deadline** Rolling **Freshmen** 53% accepted **Tuition** $2895 **Undergraduates** 67% women, 52% part-time, 49% 25 or older, 0% Native American, 9% Hispanic, 24% black, 1% Asian or Pacific Islander **Most popular recent majors** Business administration/commerce/management, accounting, nursing **Academic program** Advanced placement, accelerated degree program, honors program, summer session, adult/continuing education programs, internships **Contact** Mr. William D. Lee, Director of Admissions, Indiana University Northwest, 3400 Broadway, Gary, IN 46408-1197. Telephone: 219-980-6991. Fax: 219-980-6624.

INDIANA UNIVERSITY–PURDUE UNIVERSITY FORT WAYNE
FORT WAYNE, INDIANA

Entrance Minimally difficult **General** State-supported, comprehensive, coed **Setting** 412-acre urban campus **Enrollment** 10,749 **Faculty** 20:1 **Application deadline** 8/1 **Freshmen** 99% accepted **Tuition** $3321 **Undergraduates** 57% women, 56% part-time, 44% 25 or older, 1% Hispanic, 3% black **Academic program** Self-designed majors, honors program, summer session, adult/continuing education programs, internships **Contact** Mr. Karl F. Zimmerman, Director of Admissions, Indiana University–Purdue University Fort Wayne, 2101 Coliseum Boulevard East, Fort Wayne, IN 46805-1499. Telephone: 219-481-6812.

INDIANA UNIVERSITY–PURDUE UNIVERSITY INDIANAPOLIS
INDIANAPOLIS, INDIANA

Entrance Moderately difficult **General** State-supported, coed **Setting** 370-acre urban campus **Enrollment** 27,011 **Faculty** 16:1 **Application deadline** Rolling **Freshmen** 88% accepted **Housing** Yes **Tuition** $3441 **Undergraduates** 60% women, 48% part-time, 43% 25 or older, 0% Native American, 1% Hispanic, 10% black, 2% Asian or Pacific Islander **Most popular recent majors** Nursing, liberal arts/general studies, elementary education **Academic program** Advanced placement, accelerated degree program, tutorials, honors program, summer session, adult/continuing education programs, internships **Contact** Dr. Alan Crist, Director of Admissions, Indiana University–Purdue University Indianapolis, Cavanaugh Hall Room 129, Indianapolis, IN 46202-5143. Telephone: 317-274-4591.

INDIANA UNIVERSITY SOUTH BEND
SOUTH BEND, INDIANA

Entrance Moderately difficult **General** State-supported, comprehensive, coed **Setting** 40-acre suburban campus **Enrollment** 7,544 **Faculty** 14:1 **Application deadline** 7/1 **Freshmen** 78% accepted **Tuition** $2985 **Undergraduates** 62% women, 55% part-time, 50% 25 or older, 1% Native American, 1% Hispanic, 6% black, 1% Asian or Pacific Islander **Academic program** Accelerated degree program, honors program, summer session, adult/continuing education programs **Contact** Mr. Esker E. Ligon, Director of Admissions, Indiana University South Bend, South Bend, IN 46634-7111. Telephone: 219-237-IUSB. Fax: 219-237-4834.

INDIANA UNIVERSITY SOUTHEAST
NEW ALBANY, INDIANA

Entrance Minimally difficult **General** State-supported, comprehensive, coed **Setting** 177-acre suburban campus **Enrollment** 5,396 **Faculty** 19:1 **Application deadline** Rolling **Freshmen** 99% accepted **Tuition** $2895 **Undergraduates** 62% women, 51% part-time, 40% 25 or older, 1% Native American, 1% Hispanic, 2% black, 1% Asian or Pacific Islander **Most popular recent majors** Business administration/commerce/management, education **Academic program** Advanced placement, accelerated degree program, tutorials, summer session, adult/continuing education programs, internships **Contact** Mr. David B. Campbell, Director of Admissions, Indiana University Southeast, New Albany, IN 47150-6405. Telephone: 812-941-2212.

INDIANA WESLEYAN UNIVERSITY
MARION, INDIANA

Entrance Moderately difficult **General** Independent Wesleyan, comprehensive, coed **Setting** 132-acre small-town campus **Enrollment** 5,069 **Faculty** 17:1 **Application deadline** Rolling **Freshmen** 72% accepted **Housing** Yes **Tuition** $10,722 **Undergraduates** 61% women, 14% part-time, 20% 25 or older, 0% Native American, 2% Hispanic, 2% black, 1% Asian or Pacific Islander **Most popular recent majors** Nursing, psychology, ministries

Academic program Advanced placement, accelerated degree program, self-designed majors, honors program, summer session, adult/continuing education programs, internships **Contact** Ms. Gaytha Holloway, Director of Admissions, Indiana Wesleyan University, Marion, IN 46953-4999. Telephone: 317-677-2138. Fax: 317-677-2333.

MANCHESTER COLLEGE
NORTH MANCHESTER, INDIANA

Entrance Moderately difficult **General** Independent, comprehensive, coed, affiliated with Church of the Brethren **Setting** 125-acre small-town campus **Enrollment** 1,054 **Faculty** 13:1 **Application deadline** Rolling **Freshmen** 81% accepted **Housing** Yes **Tuition** $12,660 **Undergraduates** 48% women, 4% part-time, 6% 25 or older, 1% Native American, 2% Hispanic, 3% black, 1% Asian or Pacific Islander **Most popular recent majors** Accounting, education, social work **Academic program** Average class size 21, advanced placement, accelerated degree program, self-designed majors, tutorials, honors program, summer session, internships **Contact** Dr. David McFadden, Vice President for Enrollment Management, Manchester College, North Manchester, IN 46962-1225. Telephone: 219-982-5055. Fax: 219-982-6868.

MARIAN COLLEGE
INDIANAPOLIS, INDIANA

Entrance Moderately difficult **General** Independent Roman Catholic, 4-year, coed **Setting** 114-acre urban campus **Enrollment** 1,304 **Faculty** 12:1 **Application deadline** 8/15 **Freshmen** 56% accepted **Housing** Yes **Tuition** $12,458 **Undergraduates** 73% women, 28% part-time, 35% 25 or older, 0% Native American, 1% Hispanic, 13% black, 2% Asian or Pacific Islander **Most popular recent majors** Nursing, business administration/commerce/management, education **Academic program** Advanced placement, accelerated degree program, tutorials, honors program, summer session, adult/continuing education programs **Contact** Dr. Brent Smith, Dean for Enrollment Management and Admissions, Marian College, 3200 Cold Spring Road, Indianapolis, IN 46222-1997. Telephone: 317-929-0321.

MARTIN UNIVERSITY
INDIANAPOLIS, INDIANA

Entrance Noncompetitive **General** Independent, comprehensive, coed **Setting** 5-acre urban campus **Enrollment** 649 **Faculty** 11:1 **Application deadline** Rolling **Freshmen** 48% accepted **Tuition** $8370 **Undergraduates** 73% women, 33% part-time, 80% 25 or older, 0% Native American, 1% Hispanic, 84% black, 1% Asian or Pacific Islander **Most popular recent majors** Business administration/commerce/management, drug and alcohol/substance abuse counseling **Academic program** ESL program, Advanced placement, accelerated degree program, self-designed majors, honors program, summer session, adult/continuing education programs, internships **Contact** Ms. Brenda Shaheed, Director of Enrollment Management, Martin University, 2171 Avondale Place, PO Box 18567, Indianapolis, IN 46218-3867. Telephone: 317-543-3238. Fax: 317-543-3257.

OAKLAND CITY UNIVERSITY
OAKLAND CITY, INDIANA

Entrance Minimally difficult **General** Independent General Baptist, comprehensive, coed **Setting** 20-acre rural campus **Enrollment** 1,087 **Faculty** 15:1 **Application deadline** Rolling **Freshmen** 96% accepted **Housing** Yes **Tuition** $7966 **Undergraduates** 46% women, 6% part-time, 1% Native American, 1% Hispanic, 2% black, 1% Asian or Pacific Islander **Most popular recent majors** Education, interdisciplinary studies, business administration/commerce/management **Academic program** Average class size 15, ESL program, advanced placement, accelerated degree program, summer session, adult/continuing education programs **Contact** Mr. H. B. Harris, Director of Admissions, Oakland City University, Oakland City, IN 47660-1099. Telephone: 812-749-1222. Fax: 812-749-1233.

PURDUE UNIVERSITY
WEST LAFAYETTE, INDIANA

Entrance Moderately difficult **General** State-supported, coed **Setting** 1,579-acre suburban campus **Enrollment** 35,156 **Faculty** 16:1 **Application deadline** Rolling **Freshmen** 90% accepted **Housing** Yes **Tuition** $3352 **Undergraduates** 43% women, 8% part-time, 8% 25 or older, 0% Native American, 2% Hispanic, 4% black, 4% Asian or Pacific Islander **Most popular recent majors** Communication, mechanical engineering, civil engineering **Academic program** Advanced placement, accelerated degree program, self-designed majors, tutorials, honors program, summer session, adult/continuing education programs, internships **Contact** Office of Admissions, Purdue University, Schleman Hall, West Lafayette, IN 47907-1080. Telephone: 765-494-1776.

PURDUE UNIVERSITY CALUMET
HAMMOND, INDIANA

Entrance Noncompetitive **General** State-supported, comprehensive, coed **Setting** 167-acre urban campus **Enrollment** 9,402 **Faculty** 29:1 **Application deadline** Rolling **Freshmen** 85% accepted **Tuition** $3088 **Undergraduates** 56% women, 57% part-time, 47% 25 or older, 1% Native American, 10% Hispanic, 11% black, 4% Asian or Pacific Islander **Most popular recent majors** Engineering (general), nursing, business administration/commerce/management **Academic program** Advanced placement, honors program, summer session, adult/continuing education programs, internships **Contact** Mr. Paul McGuinness, Director of Admissions, Purdue University Calumet, 173rd and Woodmar Avenue, Hammond, IN 46323-2094. Telephone: 219-989-2289. Fax: 219-989-2775.

PURDUE UNIVERSITY NORTH CENTRAL
WESTVILLE, INDIANA

Entrance Noncompetitive **General** State-supported, comprehensive, coed **Setting** 264-acre rural campus **Enrollment** 3,399 **Faculty** 14:1 **Application deadline** 8/6 **Freshmen** 90% accepted **Tuition** $2979 **Undergraduates** 62% women, 57% part-time, 52% 25 or older, 1% Native American, 2% Hispanic, 4% black, 1% Asian or Pacific Islander **Most popular recent majors** Business administration/commerce/management, nursing, liberal arts/general studies **Academic program** Average class size 25, ESL program, advanced placement, self-designed majors, tutorials, honors program, summer session, adult/continuing education programs, internships **Contact** Ms. Cathy Buckman, Director of Admissions, Purdue University North Central, Westville, IN 46391-9543. Telephone: 219-785-5458. Fax: 219-785-5538.

ROSE-HULMAN INSTITUTE OF TECHNOLOGY
TERRE HAUTE, INDIANA

Entrance Very difficult **General** Independent, comprehensive, coed **Setting** 130-acre rural campus **Enrollment** 1,574 **Application deadline** Rolling **Freshmen** 70% accepted **Housing** Yes **Tuition** $16,968 **Undergraduates** 12% women, 0% part-time, 0% 25 or older, 1% Native American, 1% Hispanic, 2% black, 3% Asian or Pacific Islander **Most popular recent majors** Mechanical engineering, electrical engineering, chemical engineering **Academic program** Average class size 25, advanced placement, honors program, summer session, adult/continuing education programs, internships **Contact** Mr. Charles G. Howard, Dean of Admissions, Rose-Hulman Institute of Technology, Terre Haute, IN 47803-3920. Telephone: 812-877-8213. Fax: 812-877-8941.

SAINT FRANCIS COLLEGE
FORT WAYNE, INDIANA

Entrance Moderately difficult **General** Independent Roman Catholic, comprehensive, coed **Setting** 73-acre suburban campus **Enrollment** 954 **Faculty** 13:1 **Application deadline** Rolling **Freshmen** 80% accepted **Housing** Yes **Tuition** $10,710 **Undergraduates** 71% women, 35% part-time, 39% 25 or older, 1% Native American, 3% Hispanic, 4% black, 2% Asian or Pacific Islander **Most popular recent majors** Business administration/commerce/management, education, nursing **Academic program** Advanced placement, tutorials, honors program, summer session, adult/continuing education programs, internships **Contact** Mr. Scott Flanagan, Director of Admissions, Saint Francis College, Fort Wayne, IN 46808-3994. Telephone: 219-434-3279.

SAINT JOSEPH'S COLLEGE
RENSSELAER, INDIANA

Entrance Minimally difficult **General** Independent Roman Catholic, comprehensive, coed **Setting** 340-acre small-town campus **Enrollment** 876 **Faculty** 15:1 **Application deadline** Rolling **Freshmen** 85% accepted **Housing** Yes **Tuition** $12,950 **Undergraduates** 54% women, 18% part-time, 11% 25 or older, 0% Native American, 3% Hispanic, 5% black, 0% Asian or Pacific Islander **Most popular recent majors** Business administration/commerce/management, secondary education, biology/biological sciences **Academic program** Average class size 18, advanced placement, accelerated degree program, self-designed majors, tutorials, honors program, summer session, internships **Contact** Mr. Frank Bevec, Director of Admissions, Saint Joseph's College, PO Box 890, Rensselaer, IN 47978-0850. Telephone: 219-866-6170. Fax: 219-866-6122.

SAINT MARY-OF-THE-WOODS COLLEGE
SAINT MARY-OF-THE-WOODS, INDIANA

Entrance Moderately difficult **General** Independent Roman Catholic, comprehensive, women only **Setting** 67-acre rural campus **Enrollment** 1,266 **Application deadline** 8/15 **Freshmen** 86% accepted **Housing** Yes **Tuition** $12,975 **Undergraduates** 67% part-time, 50% 25 or older, 1% Native American, 4% Hispanic, 5% black, 2% Asian or Pacific Islander **Academic program** Advanced placement, accelerated degree program, self-designed majors, summer session, adult/continuing education programs, internships **Contact** Ms. Marcia DeAngelo, Director of Admission, Saint Mary-of-the-Woods College, Guerin Hall, Saint Mary-of-the-Woods, IN 47876. Telephone: 812-535-5106. or Telephone: 812-535-5105. Fax: 812-535-5215.

SAINT MARY'S COLLEGE
NOTRE DAME, INDIANA

Entrance Moderately difficult **General** Independent Roman Catholic, 4-year, women only **Setting** 275-acre suburban campus **Enrollment** 1,474 **Faculty** 11:1 **Application deadline** 3/1 **Freshmen** 82% accepted **Housing** Yes **Tuition** $15,652 **Undergraduates** 3% part-time, 1% 25 or older, 1% Native American, 4% Hispanic, 1% black, 1% Asian or Pacific Islander **Most popular recent majors** Business administration/commerce/management, elementary education, communication **Academic program** Advanced placement, accelerated degree program, self-designed majors, tutorials, internships **Contact** Ms. Mary Pat Nolan, Director of Admission, Saint Mary's College, Notre Dame, IN 46556. Telephone: 219-284-4587. Fax: 219-284-4716.

SAINT MEINRAD COLLEGE
SAINT MEINRAD, INDIANA

Entrance Moderately difficult **General** Independent Roman Catholic, 4-year, men only **Setting** 250-acre rural campus **Enrollment** 104 **Faculty** 4:1 **Application deadline** Rolling **Freshmen** 55% accepted **Housing** Yes **Tuition** $8175 **Undergraduates** 4% part-time, 10% 25 or older, 0% Native American, 6% Hispanic, 7% black, 4% Asian or Pacific Islander **Most popular recent majors** Philosophy, psychology, history **Academic program** Advanced placement, accelerated degree program, tutorials, honors program **Contact** Rev. Jonathan Fassero, Assistant Director of Enrollment, Saint Meinrad College, Saint Meinrad, IN 47577. Telephone: 812-357-6575.

TAYLOR UNIVERSITY
UPLAND, INDIANA

Entrance Very difficult **General** Independent interdenominational, 4-year, coed **Setting** 250-acre rural campus **Enrollment** 1,866 **Faculty** 18:1 **Application deadline** Rolling **Freshmen** 65% accepted **Housing** Yes **Tuition** $13,484 **Undergraduates** 52% women, 2% part-time, 1% Native American, 1% Hispanic, 2% black, 2% Asian or Pacific Islander **Most popular recent majors** Business administration/commerce/management, elementary education, psychology **Academic program** Average class size 25, ESL program, advanced placement, accelerated degree program, self-designed majors, tutorials, honors program, summer session, internships **Contact** Mr. Stephen R. Mortland, Director of Admissions, Taylor University, 500 West Reade Avenue, Upland, IN 46989-1001. Telephone: 317-998-5134.

TAYLOR UNIVERSITY, FORT WAYNE CAMPUS
FORT WAYNE, INDIANA

Entrance Moderately difficult **General** Independent interdenominational, 4-year, coed **Setting** 32-acre suburban campus **Enrollment** 404 **Faculty** 11:1 **Application deadline** Rolling **Freshmen** 89% accepted **Housing** Yes **Tuition** $11,420 **Undergraduates** 61% women, 24% part-time, 24% 25 or older, 0% Native American, 1% Hispanic, 7% black, 1% Asian or Pacific Islander **Most popular recent majors** Ministries, elementary education, psychology **Academic program** Average class size 14, advanced placement, self-designed majors, tutorials, summer session, internships **Contact** Mr. Charles Belknap, Interim Director of Admissions, Taylor University, Fort Wayne Campus, 1025 West Rudisill Boulevard, Fort Wayne, IN 46807-2197. Telephone: 219-456-2111 Ext. 2274. Fax: 219-456-2119.

TRI-STATE UNIVERSITY
ANGOLA, INDIANA

Entrance Moderately difficult **General** Independent, 4-year, coed **Setting** 400-acre small-town campus **Enrollment** 1,146 **Faculty** 13:1 **Application deadline** 6/1 **Freshmen** 85% accepted **Housing** Yes **Tuition** $11,100 **Undergraduates** 28% women, 10% part-time, 20% 25 or older, 1% Native American, 1% Hispanic, 4% black, 1% Asian or Pacific Islander **Most popular recent majors** Mechanical engineering, electrical engineering, elementary education **Academic program** Average class size 25, advanced placement, accelerated degree program, self-designed majors, tutorials, summer session, adult/continuing education programs, internships **Contact** Mr. Kim Bryan, Director of Admissions, Tri-State University, Angola, IN 46703-1764. Telephone: 219-665-4139. Fax: 219-665-4292.

UNIVERSITY OF EVANSVILLE
EVANSVILLE, INDIANA

Entrance Moderately difficult **General** Independent, comprehensive, coed, affiliated with United

Methodist Church **Setting** 75-acre suburban campus **Enrollment** 3,185 **Faculty** 13:1 **Application deadline** 2/15 **Freshmen** 91% accepted **Housing** Yes **Tuition** $13,880 **Undergraduates** 53% women, 9% part-time, 2% 25 or older, 0% Native American, 1% Hispanic, 3% black, 1% Asian or Pacific Islander **Most popular recent majors** Accounting, electrical engineering, elementary education **Academic program** Advanced placement, tutorials, honors program, summer session, adult/continuing education programs, internships **Contact** Ms. Jennifer Garner, Director of Undergraduate Admission, University of Evansville, Evansville, IN 47722-0002. Telephone: 812-479-2468. Fax: 812-479-2320.

UNIVERSITY OF INDIANAPOLIS
INDIANAPOLIS, INDIANA

Entrance Moderately difficult **General** Independent, comprehensive, coed, affiliated with United Methodist Church **Setting** 60-acre suburban campus **Enrollment** 3,861 **Faculty** 13:1 **Application deadline** 8/15 **Freshmen** 89% accepted **Housing** Yes **Tuition** $12,990 **Undergraduates** 67% women, 47% part-time, 1% Native American, 1% Hispanic, 7% black, 1% Asian or Pacific Islander **Most popular recent majors** Nursing, physical therapy, elementary education **Academic program** Average class size 20, advanced placement, self-designed majors, tutorials, honors program, summer session, adult/continuing education programs, internships **Contact** Mr. Mark T. Weigand, Director of Admissions, University of Indianapolis, Indianapolis, IN 46227-3697. Telephone: 317-788-3216. Fax: 317-788-3300.

UNIVERSITY OF NOTRE DAME
NOTRE DAME, INDIANA

Entrance Most difficult **General** Independent Roman Catholic, coed **Setting** 1,250-acre suburban campus **Enrollment** 9,927 **Faculty** 12:1 **Application deadline** 1/5 **Freshmen** 40% accepted **Housing** Yes **Tuition** $19,947 **Undergraduates** 44% women, 0% part-time, 1% 25 or older, 1% Native American, 6% Hispanic, 3% black, 4% Asian or Pacific Islander **Most popular recent majors** Accounting, political science/government, finance/banking **Academic program** Advanced placement, accelerated degree program, tutorials, honors program, summer session, adult/continuing education programs **Contact** Mr. Kevin M. Rooney, Director of Admissions, University of Notre Dame, Notre Dame, IN 46556. Telephone: 219-631-7505.

UNIVERSITY OF SOUTHERN INDIANA
EVANSVILLE, INDIANA

Entrance Noncompetitive **General** State-supported, comprehensive, coed **Setting** 300-acre suburban campus **Enrollment** 7,763 **Faculty** 18:1 **Application deadline** 8/15 **Freshmen** 98% accepted **Housing** Yes **Tuition** $2705 **Undergraduates** 60% women, 32% part-time, 34% 25 or older, 1% Native American, 1% Hispanic, 3% black, 1% Asian or Pacific Islander **Most popular recent majors** Business administration/commerce/management, elementary education **Academic program** Average class size 24, advanced placement, summer session, adult/continuing education programs, internships **Contact** Mr. Timothy K. Buecher, Director of Admissions and Enrollment Services, University of Southern Indiana, Evansville, IN 47712-3590. Telephone: 812-464-1765. Fax: 812-465-7154.

VALPARAISO UNIVERSITY
VALPARAISO, INDIANA

Entrance Moderately difficult **General** Independent, comprehensive, coed, affiliated with Lutheran Church–Missouri Synod **Setting** 310-acre small-town campus **Enrollment** 3,472 **Faculty** 12:1 **Application deadline** Rolling **Freshmen** 85% accepted **Housing** Yes **Tuition** $15,060 **Undergraduates** 56% women, 10% part-time, 12% 25 or older, 1% Native American, 3% Hispanic, 4% black, 2% Asian or Pacific Islander **Most popular recent majors** Nursing, business administration/commerce/management, elementary education **Academic program** Average class size 25, advanced placement, accelerated degree program, self-designed majors, honors program, summer session, adult/continuing education programs, internships **Contact** Ms. Karen Foust, Director of Admissions, Valparaiso University, Valparaiso, IN 46383-6493. Telephone: 219-464-5011. Fax: 219-464-5381.

WABASH COLLEGE
CRAWFORDSVILLE, INDIANA

Entrance Moderately difficult **General** Independent, 4-year, men only **Setting** 50-acre small-town campus **Enrollment** 824 **Faculty** 10:1 **Application deadline** 3/1 **Freshmen** 69% accepted **Housing** Yes **Tuition** $15,700 **Undergraduates** 1% part-time, 0% 25 or older, 1% Native American, 4% Hispanic, 4% black, 3% Asian or Pacific Islander **Academic program** Advanced placement, accelerated degree program, self-designed majors, tutorials **Contact** Mr. John Carroll, Director of Admissions, Wabash College, Crawfordsville, IN 47933-0352. Telephone: 317-361-6225. Fax: 317-361-6437.

Iowa

ALLEN COLLEGE OF NURSING
WATERLOO, IOWA

Entrance Moderately difficult **General** Independent, 4-year, coed **Setting** 20-acre suburban campus **Enrollment** 244 **Faculty** 14:1 **Freshmen** 89% accepted **Housing** Yes **Tuition** $3647 **Undergraduates** 93% women, 21% part-time, 1% Native American, 1% Hispanic, 2% black, 1% Asian or Pacific Islander **Academic program** Average class size 45, advanced placement, tutorials, summer session **Contact** Ms. Lois Hagedorn, Technician, Allen College of Nursing, Waterloo, IA 50703. Telephone: 319-235-3649.

BRIAR CLIFF COLLEGE
SIOUX CITY, IOWA

Entrance Moderately difficult **General** Independent Roman Catholic, 4-year, coed **Setting** 70-acre suburban campus **Enrollment** 1,116 **Faculty** 14:1 **Application deadline** Rolling **Freshmen** 82% accepted **Housing** Yes **Tuition** $11,880 **Undergraduates** 70% women, 39% part-time, 35% 25 or older, 1% Native American, 2% Hispanic, 2% black, 1% Asian or Pacific Islander **Most popular recent majors** Business administration/commerce/management, nursing, elementary education **Academic program** Advanced placement, accelerated degree program, self-designed majors, tutorials, summer session, adult/continuing education programs, internships **Contact** Ms. Laurie Grothaus, Director of Admissions, Briar Cliff College, Sioux City, IA 51104-2100. Telephone: 712-279-5496. Fax: 712-279-5410.

BUENA VISTA UNIVERSITY
STORM LAKE, IOWA

Entrance Moderately difficult **General** Independent, comprehensive, coed, affiliated with Presbyterian Church (U.S.A.) **Setting** 60-acre small-town campus **Enrollment** 1,173 **Faculty** 15:1 **Application deadline** Rolling **Freshmen** 91% accepted **Housing** Yes **Tuition** $14,848 **Undergraduates** 54% women, 4% part-time, 6% 25 or older, 0% Native American, 1% Hispanic, 1% black, 3% Asian or Pacific Islander **Most popular recent majors** Business administration/commerce/management, education, science **Academic program** Average class size 25, advanced placement, self-designed majors, tutorials, honors program, summer session, adult/continuing education programs, internships **Contact** Mr. Mike Frantz, Director of Admissions, Buena Vista University, Storm Lake, IA 50588. Telephone: 712-749-2235. Fax: 712-749-2037.

CENTRAL COLLEGE
PELLA, IOWA

Entrance Moderately difficult **General** Independent, 4-year, coed, affiliated with Reformed Church in America **Setting** 133-acre small-town campus **Enrollment** 1,299 **Faculty** 11:1 **Application deadline** Rolling **Freshmen** 86% accepted **Housing** Yes **Tuition** $12,802 **Undergraduates** 59% women, 2% part-time, 1% 25 or older, 0% Native American, 2% Hispanic, 1% black, 1% Asian or Pacific Islander **Most popular recent majors** Business administration/commerce/management, elementary education, liberal arts/general studies **Academic program** Average class size 20, advanced placement, self-designed majors, tutorials, honors program, summer session, internships **Contact** Mr. John Olsen, Director of Admission, Central College, Pella, IA 50219-1999. Telephone: 515-628-5285. Fax: 515-628-5316.

CLARKE COLLEGE
DUBUQUE, IOWA

Entrance Moderately difficult **General** Independent Roman Catholic, comprehensive, coed **Setting** 55-acre urban campus **Enrollment** 1,082 **Faculty** 12:1 **Application deadline** Rolling **Freshmen** 76% accepted **Housing** Yes **Tuition** $12,439 **Undergraduates** 66% women, 34% part-time, 32% 25 or older, 1% Native American, 2% Hispanic, 2% black, 1% Asian or Pacific Islander **Most popular recent majors** Physical therapy, nursing, business administration/commerce/management **Academic program** Advanced placement, self-designed majors, honors program, summer session, adult/continuing education programs, internships **Contact** Mr. John Foley, Director of Admissions, Clarke College, 1550 Clarke Drive, Dubuque, IA 52001-3198. Telephone: 319-588-6316. Fax: 319-588-6789.

COE COLLEGE
CEDAR RAPIDS, IOWA

Entrance Moderately difficult **General** Independent, comprehensive, coed, affiliated with Presbyterian Church **Setting** 55-acre urban campus **Enrollment** 1,247 **Faculty** 12:1 **Application deadline** 3/1 **Freshmen** 90% accepted **Housing** Yes **Tuition** $16,320 **Undergraduates** 54%

women, 16% part-time, 7% 25 or older, 0% Native American, 1% Hispanic, 2% black, 2% Asian or Pacific Islander **Most popular recent majors** Business administration/commerce/management, psychology, biology/biological sciences **Academic program** Advanced placement, accelerated degree program, self-designed majors, tutorials, honors program, summer session, adult/continuing education programs, internships **Contact** Mr. Dennis Trotter, Dean of Admissions and Financial Aid, Coe College, 1220 1st Avenue, NE, Cedar Rapids, IA 52402-5070. Telephone: 319-399-8500. Fax: 319-399-8816.

CORNELL COLLEGE
MOUNT VERNON, IOWA

Entrance Moderately difficult **General** Independent Methodist, 4-year, coed **Setting** 129-acre small-town campus **Enrollment** 1,105 **Faculty** 13:1 **Application deadline** 3/1 **Freshmen** 82% accepted **Housing** Yes **Tuition** $17,840 **Undergraduates** 60% women, 1% part-time, 2% 25 or older, 1% Native American, 3% Hispanic, 3% black, 1% Asian or Pacific Islander **Most popular recent majors** Psychology, English, biology/biological sciences **Academic program** Average class size 16, advanced placement, accelerated degree program, self-designed majors, tutorials, adult/continuing education programs, internships **Contact** Ms. Janel Sutkus, Acting Dean of Admissions and Enrollment Management, Cornell College, Mount Vernon, IA 52314-1098. Telephone: 319-895-4477. Fax: 319-895-4451.

DIVINE WORD COLLEGE
EPWORTH, IOWA

Entrance Minimally difficult **General** Independent Roman Catholic, 4-year, primarily men **Setting** 28-acre rural campus **Enrollment** 113 **Faculty** 4:1 **Application deadline** 7/15 **Freshmen** 29% accepted **Housing** Yes **Tuition** $7800 **Undergraduates** 2% women, 2% part-time, 50% 25 or older, 0% Native American, 10% Hispanic, 3% black, 81% Asian or Pacific Islander **Academic program** Average class size 9, advanced placement **Contact** Brother Dennis Newton, SVD, Director of Admissions, Divine Word College, Epworth, IA 52045-0380. Telephone: 319-876-3353 Ext. 249. Fax: 319-876-3407.

DORDT COLLEGE
SIOUX CENTER, IOWA

Entrance Moderately difficult **General** Independent Christian Reformed, comprehensive, coed **Setting** 55-acre small-town campus **Enrollment** 1,269 **Faculty** 15:1 **Application deadline** 8/1 **Freshmen** 94% accepted **Housing** Yes **Tuition** $11,450 **Undergraduates** 49% women, 2% part-time, 5% 25 or older, 0% Native American, 1% Hispanic, 0% black, 1% Asian or Pacific Islander **Most popular recent majors** Education, business administration/commerce/management, engineering (general) **Academic program** Self-designed majors, tutorials, honors program, summer session, internships **Contact** Mr. Quentin Van Essen, Director of Admissions, Dordt College, Sioux Center, IA 51250-1697. Telephone: 712-722-6081. Fax: 712-722-1967.

DRAKE UNIVERSITY
DES MOINES, IOWA

Entrance Moderately difficult **General** Independent, coed **Setting** 120-acre suburban campus **Enrollment** 5,376 **Faculty** 12:1 **Application deadline** Rolling **Freshmen** 93% accepted **Housing** Yes **Tuition** $14,880 **Undergraduates** 60% women, 14% part-time, 12% 25 or older, 1% Native American, 2% Hispanic, 4% black, 5% Asian or Pacific Islander **Most popular recent majors** Pharmacy/pharmaceutical sciences, advertising, marketing/retailing/merchandising **Academic program** Advanced placement, accelerated degree program, self-designed majors, honors program, summer session, internships **Contact** Mr. Thomas F. Willoughby, Dean of Admission, Drake University, Des Moines, IA 50311-4516. Telephone: 515-271-3181. Fax: 515-271-2831.

EMMAUS BIBLE COLLEGE
DUBUQUE, IOWA

Entrance Noncompetitive **General** Independent nondenominational, 4-year, coed **Setting** 22-acre small-town campus **Enrollment** 236 **Faculty** 16:1 **Application deadline** 8/1 **Freshmen** 100% accepted **Housing** Yes **Tuition** $2270 **Undergraduates** 51% women, 3% part-time, 14% 25 or older, 0% Native American, 5% Hispanic, 3% black, 2% Asian or Pacific Islander **Academic program** Advanced placement, accelerated degree program, tutorials, internships **Contact** Mr. Philip K. Leverentz, Registrar/Director of Admissions, Emmaus Bible College, Dubuque, IA 52001-3097. Telephone: 319-588-8000 Ext. 262. Fax: 319-588-1216.

FAITH BAPTIST BIBLE COLLEGE AND THEOLOGICAL SEMINARY
ANKENY, IOWA

Entrance Minimally difficult **General** Independent, comprehensive, coed, affiliated with General Association of Regular Baptist Churches **Setting** 52-acre small-town campus **Enrollment** 306 **Faculty** 16:1 **Application deadline** 8/1 **Freshmen** 88% accepted **Housing** Yes **Tuition** $6694 **Undergraduates** 54% women, 9% part-time, 5% 25 or older, 1% Native American, 1% Hispanic, 1% black, 1% Asian or Pacific Islander **Most popular recent majors** Elementary education, pastoral studies, biblical studies **Academic program** Advanced placement, summer session, adult/continuing education programs, internships **Contact** Mr. Tim Nilius, Vice President of Enrollment and Constituent Services, Faith Baptist Bible College and Theological Seminary, Ankeny, IA 50021-2152. Telephone: 515-964-0601 Ext. 238. Fax: 515-964-1638.

GRACELAND COLLEGE
LAMONI, IOWA

Entrance Moderately difficult **General** Independent Reorganized Latter Day Saints, comprehensive, coed **Setting** 169-acre small-town campus **Enrollment** 1,260 **Faculty** 15:1 **Application deadline** 5/1 **Freshmen** 63% accepted **Housing** Yes **Tuition** $10,860 **Undergraduates** 54% women, 9% part-time, 17% 25 or older, 1% Native American, 3% Hispanic, 4% black, 3% Asian or Pacific Islander **Most popular recent majors** Nursing, business administration/commerce/management, education **Academic program** Average class size 28, advanced placement, self-designed majors, tutorials, honors program, summer session, adult/continuing education programs, internships **Contact** Ms. Bonita A. Booth, Dean of Admissions, Graceland College, Lamoni, IA 50140. Telephone: 515-784-5118. Fax: 515-784-5480.

GRAND VIEW COLLEGE
DES MOINES, IOWA

Entrance Noncompetitive **General** Independent, 4-year, coed, affiliated with Evangelical Lutheran Church in America **Setting** 25-acre urban campus **Enrollment** 1,468 **Faculty** 15:1 **Application deadline** Rolling **Freshmen** 88% accepted **Housing** Yes **Tuition** $11,410 **Undergraduates** 66% women, 32% part-time, 40% 25 or older, 1% Native American, 1% Hispanic, 4% black, 3% Asian or Pacific Islander **Most popular recent majors** Business administration/commerce/management, nursing, education **Academic program** ESL program, Advanced placement, accelerated degree program, self-designed majors, tutorials, honors program, summer session, internships **Contact** Ms. Lori Hanson, Director of Admissions, Grand View College, 1200 Grandview Avenue, Des Moines, IA 50316-1599. Telephone: 515-263-2810.

GRINNELL COLLEGE
GRINNELL, IOWA

Entrance Very difficult **General** Independent, 4-year, coed **Setting** 95-acre small-town campus **Enrollment** 1,314 **Faculty** 10:1 **Application deadline** 2/1 **Freshmen** 73% accepted **Housing** Yes **Tuition** $17,568 **Undergraduates** 55% women, 0% part-time, 1% 25 or older, 0% Native American, 4% Hispanic, 4% black, 4% Asian or Pacific Islander **Most popular recent majors** Biology/biological sciences, English, history **Academic program** Advanced placement, accelerated degree program, self-designed majors, tutorials, internships **Contact** Mr. Vincent Cuseo, Director of Admission, Grinnell College, Grinnell, IA 50112-0807. Telephone: 515-269-3600. Fax: 515-269-4800.

HAMILTON TECHNICAL COLLEGE
DAVENPORT, IOWA

Entrance Noncompetitive **General** Proprietary, 4-year, coed **Setting** Urban campus **Enrollment** 350 **Faculty** 20:1 **Application deadline** Rolling **Freshmen** 100% accepted **Tuition** $5250 **Undergraduates** 27% women, 0% part-time, 1% Native American, 3% Hispanic, 4% black **Academic program** Accelerated degree program **Contact** Mrs. Maryanne Hamilton, School Director of Admissions, Hamilton Technical College, 1011 East 53rd Street, Davenport, IA 52807-2653. Telephone: 319-386-3570 Ext. 16. Fax: 319-386-6756.

IOWA STATE UNIVERSITY OF SCIENCE AND TECHNOLOGY
AMES, IOWA

Entrance Moderately difficult **General** State-supported, coed **Setting** 1,736-acre suburban campus **Enrollment** 24,899 **Faculty** 13:1 **Application deadline** Rolling **Freshmen** 90% accepted **Housing** Yes **Tuition** $2766 **Undergraduates** 43% women, 9% part-time, 13% 25 or older, 0% Native American, 2% Hispanic, 3% black, 2% Asian or Pacific Islander **Most popular recent majors** Finance/banking, mechanical engineering, elementary education **Academic program** Advanced placement, accelerated degree program, self-designed majors, tutorials, honors program, summer session, adult/continuing education programs, internships **Contact** Mr. Phil Caffrey, Associate Director for Freshman Admissions, Iowa

State University of Science and Technology, Ames, IA 50011-2010. Telephone: 515-294-5836. Fax: 515-294-2592.

IOWA WESLEYAN COLLEGE
MOUNT PLEASANT, IOWA

Entrance Moderately difficult **General** Independent United Methodist, 4-year, coed **Setting** 60-acre small-town campus **Enrollment** 794 **Faculty** 12:1 **Application deadline** 8/15 **Freshmen** 83% accepted **Housing** Yes **Tuition** $11,640 **Undergraduates** 62% women, 44% part-time, 51% 25 or older, 0% Native American, 2% Hispanic, 8% black, 2% Asian or Pacific Islander **Most popular recent majors** Business administration/commerce/management, elementary education, nursing **Academic program** Average class size 22, advanced placement, self-designed majors, tutorials, summer session, adult/continuing education programs, internships **Contact** Mr. Donald Hapward, Director of Admissions, Iowa Wesleyan College, Mount Pleasant, IA 52641-1398. Telephone: 319-385-6231.

LORAS COLLEGE
DUBUQUE, IOWA

Entrance Moderately difficult **General** Independent Roman Catholic, comprehensive, coed **Setting** 60-acre suburban campus **Enrollment** 1,815 **Faculty** 13:1 **Application deadline** Rolling **Freshmen** 82% accepted **Housing** Yes **Tuition** $12,660 **Undergraduates** 52% women, 14% part-time, 2% 25 or older, 0% Native American, 0% Hispanic, 3% black **Most popular recent majors** Business administration/commerce/management, social science, education **Academic program** Advanced placement, accelerated degree program, self-designed majors, tutorials, honors program, summer session, adult/continuing education programs, internships **Contact** Ms. Joan Williams, Assistant Director of Admissions, Loras College, 1450 Alta Vista, Dubuque, IA 52004-0178. Telephone: 319-588-7236. Fax: 319-588-7964.

LUTHER COLLEGE
DECORAH, IOWA

Entrance Moderately difficult **General** Independent, 4-year, coed, affiliated with Evangelical Lutheran Church in America **Setting** 800-acre small-town campus **Enrollment** 2,409 **Faculty** 13:1 **Application deadline** 6/1 **Freshmen** 93% accepted **Housing** Yes **Tuition** $15,630 **Undergraduates** 59% women, 3% part-time, 4% 25 or older, 1% Hispanic, 1% black, 2% Asian or Pacific Islander **Most popular recent majors** Biology/biological sciences, business administration/commerce/management, elementary education **Academic program** Advanced placement, self-designed majors, tutorials, honors program, summer session, internships **Contact** Dr. David Sallee, Dean for Enrollment Management, Luther College, Decorah, IA 52101-1045. Telephone: 319-387-1287. Fax: 319-387-2159.

MAHARISHI UNIVERSITY OF MANAGEMENT
FAIRFIELD, IOWA

Entrance Moderately difficult **General** Independent, coed **Setting** 262-acre small-town campus **Enrollment** 1,025 **Faculty** 10:1 **Application deadline** 8/1 **Freshmen** 70% accepted **Housing** Yes **Tuition** $13,976 **Undergraduates** 45% women, 75% part-time, 85% 25 or older, 1% Native American, 1% Hispanic, 2% black, 3% Asian or Pacific Islander **Most popular recent majors** Business administration/commerce/management, literature, art/fine arts **Academic program** Advanced placement, tutorials, honors program, adult/continuing education programs, internships **Contact** Mr. Brad Mylett, Director of Admissions, Maharishi University of Management, 1000 North 4th Street, Fairfield, IA 53557. Telephone: 515-472-7000 Ext. 1110. Fax: 515-472-1179.

MARYCREST INTERNATIONAL UNIVERSITY
DAVENPORT, IOWA

Entrance Moderately difficult **General** Independent, comprehensive, coed **Setting** 30-acre urban campus **Enrollment** 905 **Faculty** 11:1 **Application deadline** Rolling **Freshmen** 72% accepted **Housing** Yes **Tuition** $11,436 **Undergraduates** 74% women, 61% part-time, 35% 25 or older, 1% Native American, 3% Hispanic, 4% black, 1% Asian or Pacific Islander **Most popular recent majors** Business administration/commerce/management, nursing, elementary education **Academic program** Average class size 18, self-designed majors, summer session, adult/continuing education programs, internships **Contact** Mr. Tim McDonough, Acting Chief Admissions Officer, Marycrest International University, 1607 West 12th Street, Davenport, IA 52804-4096. Telephone: 319-327-9609. Fax: 319-326-9250.

MORNINGSIDE COLLEGE
SIOUX CITY, IOWA

Entrance Moderately difficult **General** Independent United Methodist, comprehensive, coed **Setting** 27-acre suburban campus **Enrollment** 1,137

Faculty 14:1 **Application deadline** Rolling **Freshmen** 94% accepted **Housing** Yes **Tuition** $11,612 **Undergraduates** 66% women, 17% part-time, 25% 25 or older, 1% Native American, 1% Hispanic, 3% black, 4% Asian or Pacific Islander **Most popular recent majors** Business administration/commerce/management, education, biology/biological sciences **Academic program** Average class size 20, advanced placement, accelerated degree program, self-designed majors, tutorials, summer session, adult/continuing education programs, internships **Contact** Ms. Lora Vander Zwaag, Director of Admissions, Morningside College, Sioux City, IA 51106-1751. Telephone: 712-274-5111.

MOUNT MERCY COLLEGE

CEDAR RAPIDS, IOWA

Entrance Moderately difficult **General** Independent Roman Catholic, 4-year, coed **Setting** 36-acre suburban campus **Enrollment** 1,131 **Faculty** 12:1 **Application deadline** 8/15 **Freshmen** 87% accepted **Housing** Yes **Tuition** $11,860 **Undergraduates** 70% women, 42% part-time, 38% 25 or older, 1% Native American, 1% Hispanic, 1% black, 1% Asian or Pacific Islander **Most popular recent majors** Business administration/commerce/management, elementary education, nursing **Academic program** Advanced placement, accelerated degree program, self-designed majors, tutorials, honors program, summer session, adult/continuing education programs, internships **Contact** Dr. Alex Popovics, Vice President for Enrollment Management, Mount Mercy College, Cedar Rapids, IA 52402-4797. Telephone: 319-363-8213 Ext. 1221. Fax: 319-363-5270.

MOUNT ST. CLARE COLLEGE

CLINTON, IOWA

Entrance Minimally difficult **General** Independent Roman Catholic, 4-year, coed **Setting** 124-acre small-town campus **Enrollment** 515 **Faculty** 11:1 **Application deadline** 8/15 **Freshmen** 87% accepted **Housing** Yes **Tuition** $11,640 **Undergraduates** 65% women, 22% part-time, 34% 25 or older, 1% Native American, 1% Hispanic, 8% black, 1% Asian or Pacific Islander **Most popular recent majors** Liberal arts/general studies, education, business administration/commerce/management **Academic program** ESL program, Advanced placement, self-designed majors, tutorials, honors program, summer session, adult/continuing education programs, internships **Contact** Ms. Waunita M. Sullivan, Director of Enrollment, Mount St. Clare College, Clinton, IA 52732-3998. Telephone: 319-242-4153. Fax: 319-242-2003.

NORTHWESTERN COLLEGE

ORANGE CITY, IOWA

Entrance Moderately difficult **General** Independent, 4-year, coed, affiliated with Reformed Church in America **Setting** 45-acre rural campus **Enrollment** 1,160 **Faculty** 16:1 **Application deadline** Rolling **Freshmen** 96% accepted **Housing** Yes **Tuition** $11,300 **Undergraduates** 56% women, 3% part-time, 3% 25 or older, 0% Native American, 1% Hispanic, 1% black, 1% Asian or Pacific Islander **Most popular recent majors** Business administration/commerce/management, elementary education, biology/biological sciences **Academic program** Average class size 40, advanced placement, accelerated degree program, self-designed majors, tutorials, honors program, summer session, internships **Contact** Mr. Ronald K. DeJong, Director of Admissions, Northwestern College, 101 College Lane, Orange City, IA 51041-1996. Telephone: 712-737-7000. Fax: 712-737-7164.

ALMER COLLEGE OF CHIROPRACTIC

DAVENPORT, IOWA

Entrance Moderately difficult **General** Independent, comprehensive, specialized, coed **Setting** 3-acre urban campus **Enrollment** 1,922 **Faculty** 13:1 **Application deadline** Rolling **Freshmen** 87% accepted **Tuition** $13,905 **Undergraduates** 27% women, 5% part-time, 62% 25 or older, 1% Native American, 1% Hispanic, 1% black, 3% Asian or Pacific Islander **Academic program** Summer session, internships **Contact** Ms. Alana Callender, Director of Admissions, Palmer College of Chiropractic, 1000 Brady Street, Davenport, IA 52803-5287. Telephone: 319-326-9656.

ST. AMBROSE UNIVERSITY

DAVENPORT, IOWA

Entrance Moderately difficult **General** Independent Roman Catholic, comprehensive, coed **Setting** 11-acre urban campus **Enrollment** 2,680 **Faculty** 16:1 **Application deadline** Rolling **Freshmen** 85% accepted **Housing** Yes **Tuition** $12,300 **Undergraduates** 57% women, 20% part-time, 36% 25 or older, 3% Hispanic, 4% black **Most popular recent majors** Business administration/commerce/management, biology/biological sciences, communication **Academic program** ESL program, Advanced placement, accelerated degree program, self-designed majors, tutorials, summer session, adult/continuing education programs, internships **Contact** Mr. Patrick O'Connor, Dean of Admissions, St. Ambrose University, 518 West Locust Street, Davenport, IA 52803-2898. Telephone: 319-333-6300. Fax: 319-383-8791.

SIMPSON COLLEGE
INDIANOLA, IOWA

Entrance Moderately difficult **General** Independent United Methodist, 4-year, coed **Setting** 63-acre small-town campus **Enrollment** 1,805 **Faculty** 14:1 **Application deadline** Rolling **Freshmen** 84% accepted **Housing** Yes **Tuition** $13,095 **Undergraduates** 56% women, 31% part-time, 29% 25 or older, 1% Native American, 1% Hispanic, 1% black, 1% Asian or Pacific Islander **Most popular recent majors** Business administration/commerce/management, accounting, biology/biological sciences **Academic program** Advanced placement, accelerated degree program, self-designed majors, tutorials, honors program, summer session, adult/continuing education programs, internships **Contact** Mr. John Kellogg, Vice President of Enrollment and Planning, Simpson College, Indianola, IA 50125-1297. Telephone: 515-961-1624. Fax: 515-961-1498.

TEIKYO MARYCREST UNIVERSITY
SEE MARYCREST INTERNATIONAL UNIVERSITY

TEIKYO WESTMAR UNIVERSITY
SEE WESTMAR UNIVERSITY

UNIVERSITY OF DUBUQUE
DUBUQUE, IOWA

Entrance Moderately difficult **General** Independent Presbyterian, comprehensive, coed **Setting** 56-acre suburban campus **Enrollment** 954 **Faculty** 14:1 **Application deadline** 8/15 **Freshmen** 85% accepted **Housing** Yes **Tuition** $12,640 **Undergraduates** 45% women, 16% part-time, 37% 25 or older, 1% Native American, 1% Hispanic, 3% black, 1% Asian or Pacific Islander **Most popular recent majors** Education, aviation administration, environmental sciences **Academic program** Advanced placement, accelerated degree program, self-designed majors, tutorials, summer session, adult/continuing education programs, internships **Contact** Mr. Clifford D. Bunting, Dean of Admissions and Records, University of Dubuque, Dubuque, IA 52001-5050. Telephone: 319-589-3200. Fax: 319-556-8633.

THE UNIVERSITY OF IOWA
IOWA CITY, IOWA

Entrance Moderately difficult **General** State-supported, coed **Setting** 1,900-acre small-town campus **Enrollment** 27,921 **Faculty** 15:1 **Application deadline** 5/15 **Freshmen** 86% accepted **Housing** Yes **Tuition** $2760 **Undergraduates** 54% women, 15% part-time, 13% 25 or older, 1% Native American, 2% Hispanic, 2% black, 4% Asian or Pacific Islander **Most popular recent majors** Psychology, English, finance/banking **Academic program** Advanced placement, accelerated degree program, self-designed majors, tutorials, honors program, summer session, adult/continuing education programs, internships **Contact** Mr. Michael Barron, Director of Admissions, The University of Iowa, Iowa City, IA 52242. Telephone: 319-335-3847. Fax: 319-335-1535.

UNIVERSITY OF NORTHERN IOWA
CEDAR FALLS, IOWA

Entrance Moderately difficult **General** State-supported, comprehensive, coed **Setting** 940-acre small-town campus **Enrollment** 12,957 **Faculty** 17:1 **Application deadline** Rolling **Freshmen** 84% accepted **Housing** Yes **Tuition** $2752 **Undergraduates** 58% women, 12% part-time, 12% 25 or older, 1% Hispanic, 2% black, 1% Asian or Pacific Islander **Most popular recent majors** Elementary education, accounting, biology/biological sciences **Academic program** Average class size 54, advanced placement, accelerated degree program, self-designed majors, summer session, adult/continuing education programs, internships **Contact** Mr. Clark Elmer, Director of Enrollment Management and Admissions, University of Northern Iowa, Cedar Falls, IA 50614. Telephone: 319-273-2281. Fax: 319-273-2888.

UNIVERSITY OF OSTEOPATHIC MEDICINE AND HEALTH SCIENCES
DES MOINES, IOWA

Entrance Most difficult **General** Independent, upper-level, coed **Setting** 20-acre urban campus **Enrollment** 1,350 **Faculty** 20:1 **Freshmen** 8% accepted **Tuition** $10,070 **Undergraduates** 50% women, 50% 25 or older, 2% Native American, 2% Hispanic, 2% black, 2% Asian or Pacific Islander **Academic program** Advanced placement, internships **Contact** Dr. Dennis Bates, Director of Admissions, University of Osteopathic Medicine and Health Sciences, 3200 Grand Avenue, Des Moines, IA 50312-4104. Telephone: 515-271-1450. Fax: 515-271-1532.

UPPER IOWA UNIVERSITY
FAYETTE, IOWA

Entrance Moderately difficult **General** Independent, comprehensive, coed **Setting** 80-acre rural campus **Enrollment** 695 **Faculty** 18:1 **Application deadline** Rolling **Freshmen** 74% accepted

Housing Yes **Tuition** $9750 **Undergraduates** 40% women, 5% part-time, 8% 25 or older, 1% Native American, 2% Hispanic, 12% black, 1% Asian or Pacific Islander **Most popular recent majors** Business administration/commerce/management, biology/biological sciences, education **Academic program** Advanced placement, accelerated degree program, self-designed majors, tutorials, summer session, adult/continuing education programs, internships **Contact** Mr. Kent McElvania, Vice President for Enrollment Management, Upper Iowa University, Box 1859, Fayette, IA 52142-1857. Telephone: 319-425-5281. Fax: 319-425-5277.

WARTBURG COLLEGE
WAVERLY, IOWA

Entrance Moderately difficult **General** Independent Lutheran, 4-year, coed **Setting** 118-acre small-town campus **Enrollment** 1,467 **Faculty** 15:1 **Application deadline** Rolling **Freshmen** 87% accepted **Housing** Yes **Tuition** $13,610 **Undergraduates** 57% women, 8% part-time, 5% 25 or older, 0% Native American, 1% Hispanic, 7% black, 1% Asian or Pacific Islander **Most popular recent majors** Education, business administration/commerce/management, biology/biological sciences **Academic program** Average class size 27, advanced placement, accelerated degree program, self-designed majors, tutorials, summer session, internships **Contact** Mr. Doug Bowman, Director of Admissions, Wartburg College, Waverly, IA 50677-1033. Telephone: 319-352-8264. Fax: 319-352-8579.

WESTMAR UNIVERSITY
LE MARS, IOWA

Entrance Moderately difficult **General** Independent, 4-year, coed **Setting** 63-acre small-town campus **Enrollment** 633 **Faculty** 20:1 **Application deadline** Rolling **Freshmen** 76% accepted **Housing** Yes **Tuition** $10,276 **Undergraduates** 31% women, 16% part-time, 22% 25 or older, 0% Native American, 2% Hispanic, 8% black, 1% Asian or Pacific Islander **Most popular recent majors** Business administration/commerce/management, elementary education, human services **Academic program** Advanced placement, accelerated degree program, self-designed majors, tutorials, honors program, summer session, internships **Contact** Mr. Brian F. Atchison, Dean for Enrollment Management, Westmar University, 1002 3rd Avenue, SE, Le Mars, IA 51031-2697. Telephone: 712-546-2070 Ext. 2617. Fax: 712-546-2080.

WILLIAM PENN COLLEGE
OSKALOOSA, IOWA

Entrance Moderately difficult **General** Independent, 4-year, coed, affiliated with Society of Friends **Setting** 40-acre rural campus **Enrollment** 472 **Freshmen** 79% accepted **Housing** Yes **Tuition** $11,490 **Undergraduates** 40% women, 13% part-time, 25% 25 or older, 2% Hispanic, 5% black, 1% Asian or Pacific Islander **Most popular recent majors** Elementary education, physical education, accounting **Academic program** Advanced placement, accelerated degree program, self-designed majors, tutorials, summer session, adult/continuing education programs, internships **Contact** Mr. Eric Otto, Director of Admissions, William Penn College, Oskaloosa, IA 52577-1799. Telephone: 515-673-1012. Fax: 515-673-1396.

Kansas

BAKER UNIVERSITY
BALDWIN CITY, KANSAS

Entrance Moderately difficult **General** Independent United Methodist, comprehensive, coed **Setting** 26-acre small-town campus **Enrollment** 2,508 **Application deadline** Rolling **Freshmen** 80% accepted **Housing** Yes **Tuition** $10,900 **Undergraduates** 53% women, 3% part-time, 1% 25 or older, 4% Hispanic, 6% black, 3% Asian or Pacific Islander **Most popular recent majors** Business administration/commerce/management, psychology **Academic program** Advanced placement, accelerated degree program, tutorials, honors program, summer session, adult/continuing education programs, internships **Contact** Mr. Jody Johnson, Vice President for Enrollment Management, Baker University, Baldwin City, KS 66006-0065. Telephone: 913-594-6451. Fax: 913-594-8372.

BARCLAY COLLEGE
HAVILAND, KANSAS

Entrance Noncompetitive **General** Independent, 4-year, coed, affiliated with Society of Friends **Setting** 13-acre rural campus **Enrollment** 106 **Faculty** 12:1 **Application deadline** 9/1 **Freshmen** 88% accepted **Housing** Yes **Tuition** $5000 **Undergraduates** 59% women, 5% part-time, 23% 25 or older, 2% Native American, 2% Hispanic, 0% black, 4% Asian or Pacific Islander **Academic program** Average class size 15, advanced placement, accelerated degree program, self-designed majors, tutorials, internships **Contact** Mr. Sean O'Connor, Director of Admissions, Barclay College, Haviland, KS 67059-0288. Telephone: 316-862-5252 Ext. 41. Fax: 316-862-5403.

BENEDICTINE COLLEGE
ATCHISON, KANSAS

Entrance Moderately difficult **General** Independent Roman Catholic, comprehensive, coed **Setting** 225-acre small-town campus **Enrollment** 964 **Faculty** 12:1 **Application deadline** 8/15 **Freshmen** 99% accepted **Housing** Yes **Tuition** $10,650 **Undergraduates** 46% women, 22% part-time, 12% 25 or older, 1% Native American, 6% Hispanic, 4% black, 4% Asian or Pacific Islander **Most popular recent majors** Business administration/commerce/management, elementary education, biology/biological sciences **Academic program** Average class size 22, advanced placement, accelerated degree program, self-designed majors, tutorials, honors program, summer session, internships **Contact** Mr. Alan Mitchler, Dean of Enrollment Management, Benedictine College, Atchison, KS 66002-1499. Telephone: 913-367-5340 Ext. 2475.

BETHANY COLLEGE
LINDSBORG, KANSAS

Entrance Moderately difficult **General** Independent Lutheran, 4-year, coed **Setting** 80-acre small-town campus **Enrollment** 685 **Faculty** 13:1 **Application deadline** Rolling **Freshmen** 62% accepted **Housing** Yes **Tuition** $9980 **Undergraduates** 49% women, 11% part-time, 12% 25 or older, 1% Native American, 2% Hispanic, 3% black, 2% Asian or Pacific Islander **Most popular recent majors** Business economics, education, psychology **Academic program** Advanced placement, accelerated degree program, self-designed majors, tutorials, summer session, internships **Contact** Mrs. Louise Cummings-Simmons, Dean of Admissions and Financial Aid, Bethany College, Lindsborg, KS 67456-1897. Telephone: 913-227-3311 Ext. 111. Fax: 913-227-2860.

BETHEL COLLEGE
NORTH NEWTON, KANSAS

Entrance Moderately difficult **General** Independent, 4-year, coed, affiliated with General Conference Mennonite Church **Setting** 60-acre small-town campus **Enrollment** 618 **Faculty** 12:1 **Application deadline** 8/15 **Freshmen** 89% accepted **Housing** Yes **Tuition** $10,290 **Undergraduates** 60% women, 14% part-time, 20% 25 or older, 1% Native American, 5% Hispanic, 3% black, 1% Asian or Pacific Islander **Most popular recent majors** Nursing, education, business administration/commerce/management **Academic program** Average class size 16, advanced placement, accelerated degree program, self-designed majors, tutorials, summer session, adult/continuing education programs, internships **Contact** Mr. Michael Lamb, Director of Admissions, Bethel College, North Newton, KS 67117. Telephone: 316-283-2500 Ext. 230. Fax: 316-284-5286.

EMPORIA STATE UNIVERSITY
EMPORIA, KANSAS

Entrance Noncompetitive **General** State-supported, comprehensive, coed **Setting** 207-acre small-town campus **Enrollment** 5,772 **Faculty** 18:1 **Application deadline** Rolling **Freshmen** 100% accepted **Housing** Yes **Tuition** $1900 **Undergraduates** 61% women, 9% part-time, 29% 25 or older, 1% Native American, 2% Hispanic, 3% black, 1% Asian or Pacific Islander **Most popular recent majors** Elementary education, accounting, psychology **Academic program** Advanced placement, accelerated degree program, self-designed majors, honors program, summer session, adult/continuing education programs, internships **Contact** Mr. Karl Kandt, Coordinator of Student Recruitment, Emporia State University, Emporia, KS 66801-5087. Telephone: 316-341-5465.

FORT HAYS STATE UNIVERSITY
HAYS, KANSAS

Entrance Noncompetitive **General** State-supported, comprehensive, coed **Setting** 200-acre small-town campus **Enrollment** 5,540 **Faculty** 17:1 **Application deadline** Rolling **Freshmen** 98% accepted **Housing** Yes **Tuition** $1993 **Undergraduates** 54% women, 29% part-time, 20% 25 or older, 1% Native American, 2% Hispanic, 1% black, 3% Asian or Pacific Islander **Most popular recent majors** Elementary education, physical education, nursing **Academic program** Advanced placement, accelerated degree program, summer session, adult/continuing education programs, internships **Contact** Mr. Joey Linn, Director of Admissions, Fort Hays State University, Hays, KS 67601-4099. Telephone: 913-628-4222. Fax: 913-628-4010.

FRIENDS UNIVERSITY
WICHITA, KANSAS

Entrance Moderately difficult **General** Independent, comprehensive, coed **Setting** 46-acre urban campus **Enrollment** 2,169 **Application deadline** Rolling **Freshmen** 84% accepted **Housing** Yes **Tuition** $9975 **Undergraduates** 56% women, 2% part-time, 14% 25 or older, 1% Native American, 6% Hispanic, 6% black, 1% Asian or Pacific Islander **Most popular recent majors** Business administration/commerce/management, psychology, education **Academic program** Advanced placement, accelerated degree program, self-designed majors, honors program, summer session, adult/continuing education programs, internships **Contact** Mr. Tony Meyers, Director of Undergraduate Admissions, Friends University, 2100 University, Wichita, KS 67213. Telephone: 316-261-5842.

KANSAS NEWMAN COLLEGE

WICHITA, KANSAS

Entrance Minimally difficult **General** Independent Roman Catholic, comprehensive, coed **Setting** 53-acre urban campus **Enrollment** 1,989 **Faculty** 14:1 **Application deadline** Rolling **Freshmen** 52% accepted **Housing** Yes **Tuition** $9000 **Undergraduates** 73% women, 48% part-time, 64% 25 or older, 2% Native American, 4% Hispanic, 6% black, 1% Asian or Pacific Islander **Most popular recent majors** Business administration/commerce/management, elementary education **Academic program** Advanced placement, accelerated degree program, honors program, summer session, adult/continuing education programs, internships **Contact** Mr. Thomas C. Green, Dean of Enrollment Management, Kansas Newman College, 3100 McCormick Avenue, Wichita, KS 67213-2084. Telephone: 316-942-4291 Ext. 144. Fax: 316-942-4483.

KANSAS STATE UNIVERSITY

MANHATTAN, KANSAS

Entrance Noncompetitive **General** State-supported, coed **Setting** 668-acre suburban campus **Enrollment** 20,325 **Faculty** 15:1 **Application deadline** Rolling **Freshmen** 69% accepted **Housing** Yes **Tuition** $2467 **Undergraduates** 46% women, 16% part-time, 13% 25 or older, 1% Native American, 2% Hispanic, 3% black, 2% Asian or Pacific Islander **Most popular recent majors** Journalism, animal sciences, elementary education **Academic program** Advanced placement, accelerated degree program, honors program, summer session, adult/continuing education programs, internships **Contact** Mr. Richard N. Elkins, Director of Admissions, Kansas State University, Manhattan, KS 66506. Telephone: 913-532-6250.

KANSAS WESLEYAN UNIVERSITY

SALINA, KANSAS

Entrance Moderately difficult **General** Independent United Methodist, comprehensive, coed **Setting** 28-acre urban campus **Enrollment** 700 **Faculty** 11:1 **Application deadline** Rolling **Freshmen** 72% accepted **Housing** Yes **Tuition** $10,400 **Undergraduates** 63% women, 30% part-time, 35% 25 or older, 1% Native American, 3% Hispanic, 7% black, 2% Asian or Pacific Islander **Most popular recent majors** Education, business administration/commerce/management, nursing **Academic program** Average class size 22, advanced placement, accelerated degree program, self-designed majors, tutorials, honors program, summer session, adult/continuing education programs, internships **Contact** Ms. Muriel Morgenthaller, Office Manager-Admissions, Kansas Wesleyan University, 100 East Claflin, Salina, KS 67401-6196. Telephone: 913-827-5541 Ext. 1291. Fax: 913-827-0927.

MANHATTAN CHRISTIAN COLLEGE

MANHATTAN, KANSAS

Entrance Minimally difficult **General** Independent, 4-year, coed, affiliated with Christian Churches and Churches of Christ **Setting** 10-acre small-town campus **Enrollment** 281 **Faculty** 14:1 **Freshmen** 81% accepted **Housing** Yes **Tuition** $5620 **Undergraduates** 51% women, 26% part-time, 9% 25 or older, 0% Native American, 0% Hispanic, 2% black, 2% Asian or Pacific Islander **Most popular recent majors** Religious education, ministries **Academic program** ESL program, Advanced placement, self-designed majors, summer session, internships **Contact** Mr. John Poulson, Vice President for Admissions, Manhattan Christian College, Manhattan, KS 66502-4081. Telephone: 913-539-3571 Ext. 30. Fax: 913-539-0832.

MCPHERSON COLLEGE

MCPHERSON, KANSAS

Entrance Moderately difficult **General** Independent, 4-year, coed, affiliated with Church of the Brethren **Setting** 26-acre small-town campus **Enrollment** 474 **Faculty** 10:1 **Application deadline** Rolling **Housing** Yes **Tuition** $9970 **Undergraduates** 52% women, 24% part-time, 26% 25 or older, 1% Native American, 4% Hispanic, 4% black, 1% Asian or Pacific Islander **Most popular recent majors** Business administration/commerce/management, elementary education, accounting **Academic program** Advanced placement, self-designed majors, tutorials, summer session, adult/continuing education programs, internships **Contact** Mr. Frederick Schmidt, Director of Admission, McPherson College, McPherson, KS 67460-3899. Telephone: 316-241-0731.

MIDAMERICA NAZARENE COLLEGE

OLATHE, KANSAS

Entrance Minimally difficult **General** Independent, comprehensive, coed, affiliated with Church of the Nazarene **Setting** 112-acre suburban campus **Enrollment** 1,394 **Faculty** 17:1 **Application deadline** 8/1 **Freshmen** 100% accepted **Housing** Yes **Tuition** $9256 **Undergraduates** 56% women, 9% part-time, 33% 25 or older, 2% Native American, 3% Hispanic, 4% black, 1% Asian or Pacific Islander **Most popular recent majors** Human resources, elementary education, nursing **Academic program** Advanced placement, accelerated degree program, summer session, adult/continuing education programs, internships **Contact** Mr. Dennis Troyer, Admissions Counselor, MidAmerica Nazarene College, Olathe, KS 66062-1899. Telephone: 913-782-3750 Ext. 481.

OTTAWA UNIVERSITY
OTTAWA, KANSAS

Entrance Moderately difficult **General** Independent American Baptist, comprehensive, coed **Setting** 60-acre small-town campus **Enrollment** 575 **Faculty** 17:1 **Application deadline** Rolling **Freshmen** 67% accepted **Housing** Yes **Tuition** $8990 **Undergraduates** 49% women, 8% part-time, 14% 25 or older, 2% Native American, 2% Hispanic, 5% black, 1% Asian or Pacific Islander **Most popular recent majors** Elementary education, business administration/commerce/management, biology/biological sciences **Academic program** Average class size 30, advanced placement, accelerated degree program, self-designed majors, tutorials, summer session, internships **Contact** Mr. Steve Koberlein, Director of Admissions, Ottawa University, Ottawa, KS 66067-3399. Telephone: 913-242-5200 Ext. 5558.

PITTSBURG STATE UNIVERSITY
PITTSBURG, KANSAS

Entrance Noncompetitive **General** State-supported, comprehensive, coed **Setting** 233-acre small-town campus **Enrollment** 6,426 **Faculty** 18:1 **Application deadline** Rolling **Freshmen** 86% accepted **Housing** Yes **Tuition** $2016 **Undergraduates** 54% women, 11% part-time, 19% 25 or older, 2% Native American, 3% Hispanic, 3% black, 3% Asian or Pacific Islander **Most popular recent majors** Business administration/commerce/management, elementary education, engineering technology **Academic program** Advanced placement, self-designed majors, tutorials, honors program, summer session, adult/continuing education programs, internships **Contact** Ms. Ange Peterson, Director of Admissions and Retention, Pittsburg State University, Pittsburg, KS 66762-5880. Telephone: 316-235-4252. Fax: 316-232-7515.

SAINT MARY COLLEGE
LEAVENWORTH, KANSAS

Entrance Moderately difficult **General** Independent Roman Catholic, comprehensive, coed **Setting** 240-acre suburban campus **Enrollment** 678 **Faculty** 12:1 **Application deadline** Rolling **Freshmen** 96% accepted **Housing** Yes **Tuition** $10,350 **Undergraduates** 73% women, 38% part-time, 1% Native American, 5% Hispanic, 15% black, 1% Asian or Pacific Islander **Most popular recent majors** Business administration/commerce/management, elementary education **Academic program** Advanced placement, self-designed majors, honors program, summer session, adult/continuing education programs, internships **Contact** Mr. John Horn, Director of Admissions, Saint Mary College, Leavenworth, KS 66048-5082. Telephone: 913-682-5151 Ext. 6118.

SOUTHWESTERN COLLEGE
WINFIELD, KANSAS

Entrance Moderately difficult **General** Independent United Methodist, comprehensive, coed **Setting** 70-acre small-town campus **Enrollment** 649 **Faculty** 13:1 **Application deadline** 8/1 **Freshmen** 96% accepted **Housing** Yes **Tuition** $9260 **Undergraduates** 53% women, 24% part-time, 34% 25 or older, 1% Native American, 3% Hispanic, 6% black, 2% Asian or Pacific Islander **Most popular recent majors** Nursing, elementary education, biology/biological sciences **Academic program** Average class size 20, advanced placement, self-designed majors, tutorials, honors program, summer session, adult/continuing education programs, internships **Contact** Ms. Brenda D. Hicks, Director of Admissions, Southwestern College, Winfield, KS 67156-2499. Telephone: 316-221-8236. Fax: 316-221-8344.

STERLING COLLEGE
STERLING, KANSAS

Entrance Minimally difficult **General** Independent Presbyterian, 4-year, coed **Setting** 46-acre small-town campus **Enrollment** 674 **Faculty** 14:1 **Application deadline** Rolling **Freshmen** 72% accepted **Housing** Yes **Tuition** $10,076 **Undergraduates** 52% women, 36% part-time, 29% 25 or older, 1% Native American, 3% Hispanic, 9% black, 1% Asian or Pacific Islander **Most popular recent majors** Education, business administration/commerce/management, behavioral sciences **Academic program** Advanced placement, honors program, summer session, internships **Contact** Mr. Dennis W. Dutton, Director of Admissions, Sterling College, Sterling, KS 67579-0098. Telephone: 316-278-4364. Fax: 316-278-3188.

TABOR COLLEGE
HILLSBORO, KANSAS

Entrance Moderately difficult **General** Independent Mennonite Brethren, 4-year, coed **Setting** 26-acre small-town campus **Enrollment** 500 **Application deadline** Rolling **Freshmen** 67% accepted **Housing** Yes **Tuition** $10,560 **Undergraduates** 49% women, 6% part-time, 14% 25 or older, 1% Native American, 2% Hispanic, 3% black, 1% Asian or Pacific Islander **Most popular recent majors** Business administration/commerce/management, social science, elementary education **Academic program** Average class size 27, advanced placement, self-designed majors, tutorials, honors program, summer session, adult/continuing education programs, internships **Contact** Mr. Glenn Lygrisse, Vice President for Enrollment Management, Tabor College, Hillsboro, KS 67063. Telephone: 316-947-3121 Ext. 1723. Fax: 316-947-2607.

UNIVERSITY OF KANSAS
LAWRENCE, KANSAS

Entrance Moderately difficult **General** State-supported, coed **Setting** 1,000-acre suburban campus **Enrollment** 27,407 **Faculty** 14:1 **Application deadline** 4/1 **Freshmen** 62% accepted **Housing** Yes **Tuition** $2451 **Undergraduates** 51% women, 11% part-time, 11% 25 or older, 1% Native American, 2% Hispanic, 3% black, 3% Asian or Pacific Islander **Most popular recent majors** Journalism, psychology, biology/biological sciences **Academic program** Advanced placement, accelerated degree program, self-designed majors, tutorials, honors program, summer session, adult/continuing education programs, internships **Contact** Mr. Alan Cerveny, Director of Admissions, University of Kansas, 126 Strong Hall, Lawrence, KS 66045-1910. Telephone: 913-864-3911.

WASHBURN UNIVERSITY OF TOPEKA
TOPEKA, KANSAS

Entrance Noncompetitive **General** City-supported, comprehensive, coed **Setting** 160-acre urban campus **Enrollment** 6,248 **Faculty** 18:1 **Application deadline** 8/6 **Freshmen** 98% accepted **Housing** Yes **Tuition** $3150 **Undergraduates** 61% women, 44% part-time, 50% 25 or older, 2% Native American, 5% Hispanic, 7% black, 4% Asian or Pacific Islander **Most popular recent majors** Business administration/commerce/management, education, communication **Academic program** Advanced placement, self-designed majors, honors program, summer session, adult/continuing education programs, internships **Contact** Mr. Allen Dickes, Dean of Enrollment Management, Washburn University of Topeka, Topeka, KS 66621. Telephone: 913-231-1010 Ext. 1812. Fax: 913-231-1089.

WICHITA STATE UNIVERSITY
WICHITA, KANSAS

Entrance Noncompetitive **General** State-supported, coed **Setting** 335-acre urban campus **Enrollment** 14,264 **Faculty** 15:1 **Application deadline** Rolling **Freshmen** 76% accepted **Housing** Yes **Tuition** $2489 **Undergraduates** 53% women, 52% part-time, 40% 25 or older, 1% Native American, 3% Hispanic, 7% black, 5% Asian or Pacific Islander **Most popular recent major** Business administration/commerce/management **Academic program** Average class size 23, advanced placement, accelerated degree program, self-designed majors, tutorials, honors program, summer session, adult/continuing education programs, internships **Contact** Ms. Christine Schneikart-Luebbe, Director of Admissions, Wichita State University, 1845 North Fairmount, Wichita, KS 67260. Telephone: 316-978-3085. Fax: 316-978-3795.

Michigan

ADRIAN COLLEGE
ADRIAN, MICHIGAN

Entrance Moderately difficult **General** Independent, 4-year, coed, affiliated with United Methodist Church **Setting** 100-acre small-town campus **Enrollment** 1,049 **Faculty** 16:1 **Application deadline** 8/15 **Freshmen** 89% accepted **Housing** Yes **Tuition** $12,830 **Undergraduates** 49% women, 8% part-time, 61% 25 or older, 3% Native American, 1% Hispanic, 7% black, 1% Asian or Pacific Islander **Most popular recent majors** Business administration/commerce/management, biology/biological sciences **Academic program** Advanced placement, self-designed majors, tutorials, honors program, summer session, adult/continuing education programs, internships **Contact** Mr. George Wolf, Director of Admissions and Enrollment Management, Adrian College, Adrian, MI 49221-2575. Telephone: 517-265-5161 Ext. 4326. Fax: 517-265-3331.

ALBION COLLEGE
ALBION, MICHIGAN

Entrance Moderately difficult **General** Independent Methodist, 4-year, coed **Setting** 225-acre small-town campus **Enrollment** 1,527 **Faculty** 13:1 **Application deadline** Rolling **Freshmen** 92% accepted **Housing** Yes **Tuition** $16,806 **Undergraduates** 51% women, 1% part-time, 1% 25 or older, 1% Hispanic, 5% black, 2% Asian or Pacific Islander **Most popular recent majors** Economics, biology/biological sciences, English **Academic program** Advanced placement, self-designed majors, tutorials, honors program, summer session, internships **Contact** Mr. Evan Lipp, Director of Admissions, Albion College, Albion, MI 49224-1831. Telephone: 517-629-0321. Fax: 517-629-0569.

ALMA COLLEGE
ALMA, MICHIGAN

Entrance Moderately difficult **General** Independent Presbyterian, 4-year, coed **Setting** 100-acre small-town campus **Enrollment** 1,363 **Faculty** 14:1 **Application deadline** Rolling **Freshmen** 90% accepted **Housing** Yes **Tuition** $13,823 **Undergraduates** 55% women, 4% part-time, 2% 25 or older, 1% Native American, 1% Hispanic, 1% black, 1% Asian or Pacific Islander **Most popular recent majors** Business administration/commerce/management, physical fitness/exercise science, biology/biological sciences **Academic program** Average class size 23, advanced placement, accelerated degree program, self-designed majors, tutorials, honors program, summer session, adult/continuing education programs, internships **Contact** Mr. John Seveland, Vice President for Enrollment and Student Affairs, Alma College, Alma, MI 48801-1599. Telephone: 517-463-7139.

ANDREWS UNIVERSITY
BERRIEN SPRINGS, MICHIGAN

Entrance Moderately difficult **General** Independent Seventh-day Adventist, coed **Setting** 1,650-acre small-town campus **Enrollment** 3,133 **Application deadline** Rolling **Freshmen** 34% accepted **Housing** Yes **Tuition** $11,577 **Undergraduates** 55% women, 17% part-time, 26% 25 or older, 1% Native American, 8% Hispanic, 17% black, 10% Asian or Pacific Islander **Academic program** Advanced placement, accelerated degree program, self-designed majors, tutorials, honors program, summer session, adult/continuing education programs, internships **Contact** Dr. Dean Hunt, Vice President for Enrollment Services, Andrews University, Berrien Springs, MI 49104. Telephone: 616-471-3203.

AQUINAS COLLEGE
GRAND RAPIDS, MICHIGAN

Entrance Moderately difficult **General** Independent Roman Catholic, comprehensive, coed **Setting** 107-acre suburban campus **Enrollment** 2,385 **Faculty** 16:1 **Application deadline** Rolling **Freshmen** 92% accepted **Housing** Yes **Tuition** $12,950 **Undergraduates** 66% women, 34% part-time, 36% 25 or older, 1% Native American, 3% Hispanic, 6% black, 1% Asian or Pacific Islander **Most popular recent majors** Business administration/commerce/management, English, psychology **Academic program** Average class size 25, advanced placement, accelerated degree program, self-designed majors, tutorials, honors program, summer session, adult/continuing education programs, internships **Contact** Ms. Karen Lucas, Applications Secretary, Aquinas College, Grand Rapids, MI 49506-1799. Telephone: 616-732-4460. Fax: 616-459-2563.

BAKER COLLEGE OF AUBURN HILLS
AUBURN HILLS, MICHIGAN

Entrance Noncompetitive **General** Independent, 4-year, coed **Setting** 7-acre urban campus **Enrollment** 905 **Faculty** 17:1 **Application deadline** Rolling **Freshmen** 100% accepted **Tuition** $5850 **Undergraduates** 77% women, 49% part-time, 41% 25 or older, 0% Native American, 3% Hispanic, 13% black, 1% Asian or Pacific Islander **Most popular recent major** Business administration/commerce/management **Academic program** Average class size 17, advanced placement, accelerated degree program, summer session, internships **Contact** Mr. John Tomaszewski, Admission Advisor, Baker College of Auburn Hills, 1500 University Drive, Auburn Hills, MI 48326-1586. Telephone: 810-340-0600.

BAKER COLLEGE OF CADILLAC
CADILLAC, MICHIGAN

Entrance Noncompetitive **General** Independent, 4-year, coed **Setting** 40-acre small-town campus **Enrollment** 743 **Faculty** 20:1 **Application deadline** Rolling **Freshmen** 100% accepted **Tuition** $5850 **Undergraduates** 79% women, 46% part-time, 56% 25 or older, 0% Native American, 0% Hispanic, 0% black **Most popular recent majors** Accounting, medical assistant technologies, business administration/commerce/management **Academic program** Average class size 18, advanced placement, summer session, internships **Contact** Ms. Candace Baldwin, Director of Admissions, Baker College of Cadillac, Cadillac, MI 49601-9169. Telephone: 616-775-8458.

BAKER COLLEGE OF FLINT
FLINT, MICHIGAN

Entrance Noncompetitive **General** Independent, 4-year, coed **Setting** 30-acre urban campus

Enrollment 4,039 **Faculty** 25:1 **Application deadline** Rolling **Freshmen** 100% accepted **Housing** Yes **Tuition** $5850 **Undergraduates** 72% women, 43% part-time, 53% 25 or older, 1% Native American, 2% Hispanic, 13% black, 1% Asian or Pacific Islander **Most popular recent majors** Business administration/commerce/management, health services administration, accounting **Academic program** Average class size 25, advanced placement, accelerated degree program, summer session, internships **Contact** Mr. Mark Heaton, Director of Admissions, Baker College of Flint, 1050 West Bristol Road, Flint, MI 48507-5508. Telephone: 810-766-4015.

BAKER COLLEGE OF MOUNT CLEMENS
CLINTON TOWNSHIP, MICHIGAN

Entrance Noncompetitive **General** Independent, 4-year, coed **Setting** Urban campus **Enrollment** 1,081 **Faculty** 16:1 **Application deadline** Rolling **Freshmen** 100% accepted **Tuition** $5850 **Undergraduates** 88% women, 48% part-time, 42% 25 or older, 1% Native American, 2% Hispanic, 9% black, 1% Asian or Pacific Islander **Most popular recent major** Business administration/commerce/management **Academic program** Average class size 35, advanced placement, summer session, internships **Contact** Ms. Annette M. Looser, Director of Admissions, Baker College of Mount Clemens, 34950 Little Mack, Clinton Township, MI 48035-4701. Telephone: 810-791-6610.

BAKER COLLEGE OF MUSKEGON
MUSKEGON, MICHIGAN

Entrance Noncompetitive **General** Independent, 4-year, coed **Setting** 15-acre urban campus **Enrollment** 1,711 **Faculty** 19:1 **Application deadline** Rolling **Freshmen** 100% accepted **Housing** Yes **Tuition** $5850 **Undergraduates** 75% women, 41% part-time, 26% 25 or older, 1% Native American, 3% Hispanic, 8% black, 1% Asian or Pacific Islander **Most popular recent majors** Drafting and design, marketing/retailing/merchandising, accounting **Academic program** Average class size 20, advanced placement, accelerated degree program, summer session, adult/continuing education programs, internships **Contact** Ms. Kathy Jacobson, Director of Admissions, Baker College of Muskegon, 123 East Apple Avenue, Muskegon, MI 49442-3497. Telephone: 616-726-4904 Ext. 305. Fax: 616-728-1417.

BAKER COLLEGE OF OWOSSO
OWOSSO, MICHIGAN

Entrance Noncompetitive **General** Independent, 4-year, coed **Setting** 32-acre small-town campus **Enrollment** 1,812 **Faculty** 20:1 **Application deadline** Rolling **Freshmen** 100% accepted **Housing** Yes **Tuition** $5850 **Undergraduates** 70% women, 34% part-time, 40% 25 or older, 1% Native American, 2% Hispanic, 1% black, 1% Asian or Pacific Islander **Most popular recent majors** Radiological technology, accounting, secretarial studies/office management **Academic program** Advanced placement, accelerated degree program, tutorials, summer session, adult/continuing education programs, internships **Contact** Mr. Bruce A. Lundeen, Director of Admissions, Baker College of Owosso, Owosso, MI 48867-4400. Telephone: 517-723-5251 Ext. 454.

BAKER COLLEGE OF PORT HURON
PORT HURON, MICHIGAN

Entrance Noncompetitive **General** Independent, 4-year, coed **Setting** 10-acre urban campus **Enrollment** 837 **Faculty** 20:1 **Application deadline** Rolling **Freshmen** 100% accepted **Tuition** $5850 **Undergraduates** 83% women, 47% part-time, 47% 25 or older, 2% Native American, 0% Hispanic, 2% black, 2% Asian or Pacific Islander **Most popular recent majors** Accounting, medical records services, secretarial studies/office management **Academic program** Average class size 20, advanced placement, accelerated degree program, summer session, internships **Contact** Ms. Kimberly Hall, Assistant Director of Admissions, Baker College of Port Huron, 3403 Lapeer Road, Port Huron, MI 48060-2597. Telephone: 810-985-7000.

CALVIN COLLEGE
GRAND RAPIDS, MICHIGAN

Entrance Moderately difficult **General** Independent, comprehensive, coed, affiliated with Christian Reformed Church **Setting** 370-acre suburban campus **Enrollment** 4,051 **Faculty** 16:1 **Application deadline** Rolling **Freshmen** 97% accepted **Housing** Yes **Tuition** $12,250 **Undergraduates** 56% women, 8% part-time, 6% 25 or older, 0% Native American, 1% Hispanic, 1% black, 2% Asian or Pacific Islander **Most popular recent majors** Education, business administration/commerce/management, engineering (general) **Academic program** Advanced placement, self-designed majors, tutorials, honors program, summer session, adult/continuing education programs, internships **Contact** Mr. Dale D. Kuiper, Director of Admissions, Calvin College, Grand Rapids, MI 49546-4388. Telephone: 616-957-6106.

CENTER FOR CREATIVE STUDIES—COLLEGE OF ART AND DESIGN
DETROIT, MICHIGAN

Entrance Moderately difficult **General** Independent, 4-year, specialized, coed **Setting** 11-acre urban campus **Enrollment** 921 **Faculty** 10:1 **Application deadline** Rolling **Freshmen** 76% accepted **Housing** Yes **Tuition** $13,750 **Undergraduates** 40% women, 34% part-time, 26% 25 or older, 1% Native American, 3% Hispanic, 12% black, 4% Asian or Pacific Islander **Most popular recent majors** Graphic arts, industrial design, art/fine arts **Academic program** Advanced placement, tutorials, summer session, internships **Contact** Ms. Marlene Kenney, Office Manager, Center for Creative Studies—College of Art and Design, 201 East Kirby, Detroit, MI 48202-4034. Telephone: 313-872-3118 Ext. 204. Fax: 313-872-8377.

CENTRAL MICHIGAN UNIVERSITY
MOUNT PLEASANT, MICHIGAN

Entrance Moderately difficult **General** State-supported, coed **Setting** 854-acre small-town campus **Enrollment** 16,597 **Faculty** 17:1 **Application deadline** Rolling **Freshmen** 77% accepted **Housing** Yes **Tuition** $2973 **Undergraduates** 58% women, 8% part-time, 11% 25 or older, 1% Native American, 1% Hispanic, 3% black, 1% Asian or Pacific Islander **Most popular recent majors** Psychology, marketing/retailing/merchandising, accounting **Academic program** Advanced placement, accelerated degree program, self-designed majors, honors program, summer session, adult/continuing education programs, internships **Contact** Mrs. Betty J. Wagner, Director of Admissions, Central Michigan University, Mount Pleasant, MI 48859. Telephone: 517-774-3076. Fax: 517-774-3537.

CLEARY COLLEGE
YPSILANTI, MICHIGAN

Entrance Noncompetitive **General** Independent, 4-year, specialized, coed **Setting** 22-acre small-town campus **Enrollment** 782 **Faculty** 15:1 **Application deadline** Rolling **Freshmen** 100% accepted **Tuition** $7290 **Undergraduates** 65% women, 69% part-time, 70% 25 or older, 0% Native American, 1% Hispanic, 22% black, 1% Asian or Pacific Islander **Most popular recent major** Business administration/commerce/management **Academic program** Average class size 15, accelerated degree program, summer session, adult/continuing education programs **Contact** Mr. Tim Olszewski, Director of Admissions and Marketing Services, Cleary College, Ypsilanti, MI 48197-1788. Telephone: 517-548-2670 Ext. 2213. Fax: 313-483-0090.

CONCORDIA COLLEGE
ANN ARBOR, MICHIGAN

Entrance Moderately difficult **General** Independent, 4-year, coed, affiliated with Lutheran Church–Missouri Synod **Setting** 234-acre suburban campus **Enrollment** 601 **Faculty** 11:1 **Application deadline** Rolling **Freshmen** 100% accepted **Housing** Yes **Tuition** $11,850 **Undergraduates** 64% women, 8% part-time, 46% 25 or older, 0% Native American, 1% Hispanic, 11% black, 2% Asian or Pacific Islander **Most popular recent majors** Education, business administration/commerce/management, social science **Academic program** Average class size 25, advanced placement, self-designed majors, tutorials, summer session, adult/continuing education programs, internships **Contact** Mr. Don Vogt, Vice President, Student Services, Concordia College, Ann Arbor, MI 48105-2797. Telephone: 313-995-7322 Ext. 7311. Fax: 313-995-4610.

CORNERSTONE COLLEGE
GRAND RAPIDS, MICHIGAN

Entrance Moderately difficult **General** Independent Baptist, 4-year, coed **Setting** 132-acre suburban campus **Enrollment** 1,082 **Faculty** 18:1 **Application deadline** Rolling **Freshmen** 89% accepted **Housing** Yes **Tuition** $9450 **Undergraduates** 55% women, 13% part-time, 7% 25 or older, 0% Native American, 1% Hispanic, 1% black, 1% Asian or Pacific Islander **Most popular recent majors** Business administration/commerce/management, biblical studies, psychology **Academic program** Advanced placement, honors program, summer session, adult/continuing education programs, internships **Contact** Mr. Rick Newberry, Executive Director of Enrollment Management, Cornerstone College, Grand Rapids, MI 49505-5897. Telephone: 616-222-1426. Fax: 616-949-0875.

DAVENPORT COLLEGE OF BUSINESS
GRAND RAPIDS, MICHIGAN

Entrance Noncompetitive **General** Independent, 4-year, coed **Setting** 5-acre urban campus **Enrollment** 2,719 **Faculty** 19:1 **Application deadline** Rolling **Freshmen** 100% accepted **Housing** Yes **Tuition** $8508 **Undergraduates** 70% women, 62% part-time, 56% 25 or older, 1% Native American, 2% Hispanic, 6% black, 2% Asian or Pacific Islander **Most popular recent majors**

Business administration/commerce/management, accounting **Academic program** Advanced placement, accelerated degree program, tutorials, summer session, adult/continuing education programs, internships **Contact** Ms. Colleen Wolfe, Director of Admissions, Davenport College of Business, 415 East Fulton, Grand Rapids, MI 49503. Telephone: 616-732-1200.

DAVENPORT COLLEGE OF BUSINESS, KALAMAZOO CAMPUS

KALAMAZOO, MICHIGAN

Entrance Noncompetitive **General** Independent, 4-year, primarily women **Setting** 5-acre suburban campus **Enrollment** 1,200 **Faculty** 18:1 **Application deadline** Rolling **Freshmen** 100% accepted **Tuition** $8418 **Undergraduates** 80% women, 60% part-time, 74% 25 or older, 1% Native American, 2% Hispanic, 12% black, 1% Asian or Pacific Islander **Most popular recent majors** Secretarial studies/office management, business administration/commerce/management, accounting **Academic program** Tutorials, summer session, adult/continuing education programs, internships **Contact** Ms. Brigid Hansen, Admissions Director, Davenport College of Business, Kalamazoo Campus, 4123 West Main Street, Kalamazoo, MI 49006-2791. Telephone: 616-382-2835 Ext. 35.

DAVENPORT COLLEGE OF BUSINESS, LANSING CAMPUS

LANSING, MICHIGAN

Entrance Noncompetitive **General** Independent, 4-year, coed **Setting** 2-acre suburban campus **Enrollment** 1,218 **Faculty** 17:1 **Application deadline** 9/15 **Freshmen** 100% accepted **Tuition** $8418 **Undergraduates** 78% women, 69% part-time, 73% 25 or older, 1% Native American, 4% Hispanic, 16% black, 2% Asian or Pacific Islander **Most popular recent majors** Business administration/commerce/management, secretarial studies/office management **Academic program** Advanced placement, accelerated degree program, self-designed majors, tutorials, summer session, adult/continuing education programs, internships **Contact** Ms. Susan Backofen, Dean, Davenport College of Business, Lansing Campus, Lansing, MI 48933-2197. Telephone: 517-484-2600 Ext. 256. Fax: 517-484-9719.

DETROIT COLLEGE OF BUSINESS

DEARBORN, MICHIGAN

Entrance Noncompetitive **General** Independent, 4-year, coed **Setting** 17-acre suburban campus **Enrollment** 3,374 **Faculty** 13:1 **Application deadline** Rolling **Freshmen** 100% accepted **Tuition** $8526 **Undergraduates** 77% women, 52% part-time, 59% 25 or older, 1% Native American, 3% Hispanic, 47% black, 1% Asian or Pacific Islander **Most popular recent majors** Accounting, business administration/commerce/management, secretarial studies/office management **Academic program** Advanced placement, tutorials, summer session, internships **Contact** Ms. Lynda Menard, Director of Admissions, Detroit College of Business, 4801 Oakman Boulevard, Dearborn, MI 48126-3799. Telephone: 313-581-4400. Fax: 313-581-1985.

DETROIT COLLEGE OF BUSINESS–FLINT

FLINT, MICHIGAN

Entrance Noncompetitive **General** Independent, 4-year, coed **Setting** 1-acre suburban campus **Enrollment** 943 **Faculty** 12:1 **Application deadline** Rolling **Freshmen** 100% accepted **Tuition** $6321 **Undergraduates** 80% women, 39% part-time, 69% 25 or older, 1% Native American, 1% Hispanic, 40% black, 0% Asian or Pacific Islander **Most popular recent major** Business administration/commerce/management **Academic program** Advanced placement, tutorials, summer session **Contact** Ms. Wilma Collins, Director of Admissions, Detroit College of Business–Flint, Flint, MI 48504-1700. Telephone: 810-789-2200. Fax: 810-789-2266.

DETROIT COLLEGE OF BUSINESS, WARREN CAMPUS

WARREN, MICHIGAN

Entrance Noncompetitive **General** Independent, 4-year, coed **Setting** 9-acre suburban campus **Enrollment** 2,041 **Faculty** 21:1 **Application deadline** Rolling **Freshmen** 100% accepted **Tuition** $8526 **Undergraduates** 75% women, 58% part-time, 59% 25 or older, 0% Native American, 1% Hispanic, 32% black, 1% Asian or Pacific Islander **Most popular recent major** Business administration/commerce/management **Academic program** Advanced placement, tutorials, summer session **Contact** Ms. Diane Ranik, Director of Admissions, Detroit College of Business, Warren Campus, Warren, MI 48092-5209. Telephone: 810-558-8700. Fax: 810-558-7868.

EASTERN MICHIGAN UNIVERSITY

YPSILANTI, MICHIGAN

Entrance Moderately difficult **General** State-supported, comprehensive, coed **Setting** 460-acre suburban campus **Enrollment** 22,541 **Faculty** 20:1 **Application deadline** 7/31 **Fresh-**

men 74% accepted **Housing** Yes **Tuition** $3529 **Undergraduates** 58% women, 34% part-time, 32% 25 or older, 1% Native American, 2% Hispanic, 13% black, 2% Asian or Pacific Islander **Most popular recent majors** Elementary education, business administration/commerce/management, psychology **Academic program** Advanced placement, accelerated degree program, self-designed majors, tutorials, honors program, summer session, adult/continuing education programs, internships **Contact** Ms. Judy Benfield-Tatum, Director of Admissions, Eastern Michigan University, Ypsilanti, MI 48197. Telephone: 313-487-3060. Fax: 313-487-1484.

FERRIS STATE UNIVERSITY
BIG RAPIDS, MICHIGAN

Entrance Minimally difficult **General** State-supported, comprehensive, coed **Setting** 600-acre small-town campus **Enrollment** 9,495 **Faculty** 17:1 **Application deadline** Rolling **Freshmen** 97% accepted **Housing** Yes **Tuition** $3665 **Undergraduates** 42% women, 23% part-time, 27% 25 or older, 1% Native American, 1% Hispanic, 9% black, 2% Asian or Pacific Islander **Most popular recent majors** Business administration/commerce/management, criminal justice, pharmacy/pharmaceutical sciences **Academic program** Advanced placement, accelerated degree program, summer session, adult/continuing education programs, internships **Contact** Mr. Don Mullens, Interim Dean of Enrollment Services, Ferris State University, PRK 110, Big Rapids, MI 49307-2742. Telephone: 616-592-2100. Fax: 616-592-2978.

GMI ENGINEERING & MANAGEMENT INSTITUTE
FLINT, MICHIGAN

Entrance Very difficult **General** Independent, comprehensive, coed **Setting** 45-acre suburban campus **Enrollment** 3,225 **Faculty** 12:1 **Application deadline** Rolling **Freshmen** 74% accepted **Housing** Yes **Tuition** $13,696 **Undergraduates** 19% women, 0% part-time, 2% 25 or older, 1% Native American, 2% Hispanic, 5% black, 6% Asian or Pacific Islander **Most popular recent majors** Mechanical engineering, electrical engineering, manufacturing engineering **Academic program** Average class size 25, advanced placement, tutorials, honors program **Contact** Mr. Phillip D. Lavender, Director of Admissions, GMI Engineering & Management Institute, Flint, MI 48504-4898. Telephone: 810-762-7865. Fax: 810-762-9837.

GRACE BIBLE COLLEGE
GRAND RAPIDS, MICHIGAN

Entrance Minimally difficult **General** Independent, 4-year, coed, affiliated with Grace Gospel Fellowship **Setting** 16-acre suburban campus **Enrollment** 143 **Faculty** 10:1 **Application deadline** 7/15 **Freshmen** 63% accepted **Housing** Yes **Tuition** $6500 **Undergraduates** 56% women, 13% part-time, 12% 25 or older, 0% Native American, 1% Hispanic, 1% black, 2% Asian or Pacific Islander **Most popular recent majors** Liberal arts/general studies, human services, business administration/commerce/management **Academic program** Advanced placement, internships **Contact** Miss Linda K. Siler, Registrar, Grace Bible College, Grand Rapids, MI 49509-1921. Telephone: 616-538-2330. Fax: 616-538-0599.

GRAND VALLEY STATE UNIVERSITY
ALLENDALE, MICHIGAN

Entrance Moderately difficult **General** State-supported, comprehensive, coed **Setting** 900-acre small-town campus **Enrollment** 14,662 **Faculty** 22:1 **Application deadline** 7/26 **Freshmen** 85% accepted **Housing** Yes **Tuition** $3348 **Undergraduates** 59% women, 22% part-time, 21% 25 or older, 1% Native American, 2% Hispanic, 5% black, 2% Asian or Pacific Islander **Most popular recent majors** Health science, business administration/commerce/management, psychology **Academic program** Average class size 30, ESL program, advanced placement, accelerated degree program, honors program, summer session, adult/continuing education programs, internships **Contact** Mr. William Eilola, Director of Admissions, Grand Valley State University, Allendale, MI 49401-9403. Telephone: 616-895-2025. Fax: 616-895-2000.

GREAT LAKES CHRISTIAN COLLEGE
LANSING, MICHIGAN

Entrance Moderately difficult **General** Independent, 4-year, coed, affiliated with Church of Christ **Setting** 50-acre suburban campus **Enrollment** 140 **Faculty** 8:1 **Application deadline** 8/1 **Freshmen** 84% accepted **Housing** Yes **Tuition** $4658 **Undergraduates** 45% women, 9% part-time, 36% 25 or older, 0% Native American, 1% Hispanic, 3% black, 0% Asian or Pacific Islander **Most popular recent majors** Ministries, religious education **Academic program** Advanced placement, adult/continuing education programs, internships **Contact** Mr. Ray Maurer, Director of Admissions, Great Lakes Christian College, 6211 West Willow Highway, Lansing, MI 48917-1299. Telephone: 517-321-0242. Fax: 517-321-5902.

HILLSDALE COLLEGE
HILLSDALE, MICHIGAN

Entrance Very difficult **General** Independent, 4-year, coed **Setting** 200-acre small-town campus **Enrollment** 1,163 **Faculty** 12:1 **Application deadline** Rolling **Freshmen** 81% accepted **Housing** Yes **Tuition** $12,680 **Undergraduates** 51% women, 3% part-time, 1% 25 or older **Most popular recent majors** Business administration/commerce/management, biology/biological sciences, education **Academic program** Average class size 20, ESL program, advanced placement, accelerated degree program, tutorials, honors program, summer session, internships **Contact** Mr. Jeffrey S. Lantis, Director of Admissions, Hillsdale College, Hillsdale, MI 49242-1298. Telephone: 517-437-7341 Ext. 2327. Fax: 517-437-3923.

HOPE COLLEGE
HOLLAND, MICHIGAN

Entrance Moderately difficult **General** Independent, 4-year, coed, affiliated with Reformed Church in America **Setting** 45-acre small-town campus **Enrollment** 2,849 **Faculty** 13:1 **Application deadline** Rolling **Freshmen** 92% accepted **Housing** Yes **Tuition** $14,878 **Undergraduates** 58% women, 7% part-time, 1% 25 or older, 0% Native American, 1% Hispanic, 1% black, 2% Asian or Pacific Islander **Most popular recent majors** Business administration/commerce/management, chemistry, biology/biological sciences **Academic program** Average class size 35, advanced placement, self-designed majors, tutorials, summer session, internships **Contact** Office of Admissions, Hope College, 69 East 10th Street, Holland, MI 49422-9000. Telephone: 616-395-7850. Fax: 616-395-7130.

KALAMAZOO COLLEGE
KALAMAZOO, MICHIGAN

Entrance Very difficult **General** Independent, 4-year, coed **Setting** 60-acre suburban campus **Enrollment** 1,302 **Faculty** 11:1 **Application deadline** 2/15 **Freshmen** 94% accepted **Housing** Yes **Tuition** $17,976 **Undergraduates** 58% women, 0% part-time, 1% 25 or older, 1% Native American, 1% Hispanic, 3% black, 6% Asian or Pacific Islander **Most popular recent majors** Economics, biology/biological sciences, English **Academic program** Advanced placement, tutorials, adult/continuing education programs, internships **Contact** Ms. Jennifer Earle, Records Manager, Kalamazoo College, Mandelle Hall, Kalamazoo, MI 49006-3295. Telephone: 616-337-7166. Fax: 616-337-7390.

KENDALL COLLEGE OF ART AND DESIGN
GRAND RAPIDS, MICHIGAN

Entrance Minimally difficult **General** Independent, 4-year, specialized, coed **Setting** Urban campus **Enrollment** 527 **Faculty** 11:1 **Application deadline** Rolling **Freshmen** 72% accepted **Tuition** $10,550 **Undergraduates** 52% women, 33% part-time, 36% 25 or older, 1% Native American, 2% Hispanic, 4% black, 2% Asian or Pacific Islander **Most popular recent majors** Communication, illustration, interior design **Academic program** Average class size 25, advanced placement, tutorials, summer session, adult/continuing education programs, internships **Contact** Ms. Amy Packard, Director of Admissions, Kendall College of Art and Design, 111 Division Avenue North, Grand Rapids, MI 49503. Telephone: 616-451-2787 Ext. 109.

LAKE SUPERIOR STATE UNIVERSITY
SAULT SAINTE MARIE, MICHIGAN

Entrance Moderately difficult **General** State-supported, comprehensive, coed **Setting** 121-acre small-town campus **Enrollment** 3,392 **Faculty** 19:1 **Application deadline** 8/12 **Freshmen** 94% accepted **Housing** Yes **Tuition** $3742 **Undergraduates** 50% women, 20% part-time, 24% 25 or older, 5% Native American, 1% Hispanic, 1% black, 1% Asian or Pacific Islander **Most popular recent majors** Business administration/commerce/management, engineering technology, criminal justice **Academic program** Advanced placement, accelerated degree program, self-designed majors, tutorials, honors program, summer session, adult/continuing education programs, internships **Contact** Mr. Bruce R. Johnson, Director of Admissions, Lake Superior State University, Sault Sainte Marie, MI 49783-1699. Telephone: 906-635-2231. Fax: 906-635-6669.

LAWRENCE TECHNOLOGICAL UNIVERSITY
SOUTHFIELD, MICHIGAN

Entrance Moderately difficult **General** Independent, comprehensive, coed **Setting** 110-acre suburban campus **Enrollment** 3,916 **Faculty** 9:1 **Application deadline** 8/11 **Freshmen** 80% accepted **Housing** Yes **Tuition** $9140 **Undergraduates** 24% women, 60% part-time, 4% 25 or older, 1% Native American, 1% Hispanic, 10% black, 3% Asian or Pacific Islander **Academic program** Advanced placement, self-designed majors, summer session, adult/continuing education programs, internships **Contact** Mr. Kevin Pollock, Director of Admissions, Lawrence Technological University, Southfield, MI 48075-1058. Telephone: 810-204-3160. Fax: 810-204-3727.

MADONNA UNIVERSITY
LIVONIA, MICHIGAN

Entrance Moderately difficult **General** Independent Roman Catholic, comprehensive, coed **Setting** 49-acre suburban campus **Enrollment** 3,972 **Faculty** 18:1 **Application deadline** Rolling **Freshmen** 81% accepted **Housing** Yes **Tuition** $5940 **Undergraduates** 76% women, 62% part-time, 69% 25 or older, 1% Native American, 2% Hispanic, 11% black, 2% Asian or Pacific Islander **Most popular recent majors** Business administration/commerce/management, nursing, criminal justice **Academic program** Advanced placement, accelerated degree program, honors program, summer session, adult/continuing education programs, internships **Contact** Mr. Louis E. Brohl III, Director of Admissions and Marketing, Madonna University, 36600 Schoolcraft Road, Livonia, MI 48150-1173. Telephone: 313-432-5339. Fax: 313-591-0156.

MARYGROVE COLLEGE
DETROIT, MICHIGAN

Entrance Moderately difficult **General** Independent Roman Catholic, comprehensive, primarily women **Setting** 50-acre urban campus **Enrollment** 2,510 **Faculty** 17:1 **Application deadline** 8/15 **Freshmen** 52% accepted **Housing** Yes **Tuition** $9056 **Undergraduates** 87% women, 56% part-time, 70% 25 or older, 0% Native American, 1% Hispanic, 80% black, 1% Asian or Pacific Islander **Most popular recent majors** Social work, education, business administration/commerce/management **Academic program** Average class size 15, advanced placement, self-designed majors, summer session, internships **Contact** Ms. Carla Mathews, Director of Admissions, Marygrove College, 8425 West McNichols Road, Detroit, MI 48221-2599. Telephone: 313-862-5200 Ext. 570. Fax: 313-864-6670.

MICHIGAN CHRISTIAN COLLEGE
ROCHESTER HILLS, MICHIGAN

Entrance Minimally difficult **General** Independent, 4-year, coed, affiliated with Church of Christ **Setting** 83-acre suburban campus **Enrollment** 363 **Faculty** 13:1 **Application deadline** Rolling **Freshmen** 75% accepted **Housing** Yes **Tuition** $6120 **Undergraduates** 51% women, 17% part-time, 16% 25 or older, 0% Native American, 2% Hispanic, 9% black, 1% Asian or Pacific Islander **Most popular recent majors** Business administration/commerce/management, human services, ministries **Academic program** Advanced placement, accelerated degree program, tutorials, summer session, adult/continuing education programs, internships **Contact** Mr. Elton Albright, Dean of Enrollment Services, Michigan Christian College, Rochester Hills, MI 48307-2764. Telephone: 810-651-5800 Ext. 6005. Fax: 810-650-6060.

MICHIGAN STATE UNIVERSITY
EAST LANSING, MICHIGAN

Entrance Moderately difficult **General** State-supported, coed **Setting** 5,000-acre small-town campus **Enrollment** 41,545 **Application deadline** 7/30 **Freshmen** 81% accepted **Housing** Yes **Tuition** $4789 **Undergraduates** 52% women, 14% part-time, 7% 25 or older, 1% Native American, 2% Hispanic, 8% black, 4% Asian or Pacific Islander **Most popular recent majors** Psychology, accounting, finance/banking **Academic program** Advanced placement, self-designed majors, tutorials, honors program, summer session, adult/continuing education programs, internships **Contact** Dr. William H. Turner, Director of Admissions, Michigan State University, East Lansing, MI 48824-1020. Telephone: 517-355-8332.

MICHIGAN TECHNOLOGICAL UNIVERSITY
HOUGHTON, MICHIGAN

Entrance Moderately difficult **General** State-supported, coed **Setting** 240-acre small-town campus **Enrollment** 6,195 **Faculty** 15:1 **Application deadline** Rolling **Freshmen** 94% accepted **Housing** Yes **Tuition** $3936 **Undergraduates** 26% women, 8% part-time, 10% 25 or older, 1% Native American, 1% Hispanic, 2% black, 1% Asian or Pacific Islander **Most popular recent majors** Mechanical engineering, electrical engineering, civil engineering **Academic program** Average class size 26, advanced placement, self-designed majors, tutorials, summer session, internships **Contact** Ms. Nancy Rehling, Director of Undergraduate Admissions, Michigan Technological University, 1400 Townsend Drive, Houghton, MI 49931-1295. Telephone: 906-487-2335. Fax: 906-487-3343.

NORTHERN MICHIGAN UNIVERSITY
MARQUETTE, MICHIGAN

Entrance Minimally difficult **General** State-supported, comprehensive, coed **Setting** 300-acre small-town campus **Enrollment** 8,034 **Faculty** 20:1 **Application deadline** Rolling **Freshmen** 92% accepted **Housing** Yes **Tuition** $3092

Undergraduates 54% women, 18% part-time, 25% 25 or older, 2% Native American, 1% Hispanic, 1% black, 1% Asian or Pacific Islander **Most popular recent majors** Education, business administration/commerce/management, nursing **Academic program** Average class size 21, advanced placement, accelerated degree program, self-designed majors, tutorials, summer session, adult/continuing education programs, internships **Contact** Mr. James G. Gadzinski, Associate Director of Admissions, Northern Michigan University, Marquette, MI 49855-5301. Telephone: 906-227-2650. Fax: 906-227-1747.

NORTHWOOD UNIVERSITY

MIDLAND, MICHIGAN

Entrance Moderately difficult **General** Independent, comprehensive, coed **Setting** 435-acre small-town campus **Enrollment** 1,549 **Application deadline** Rolling **Freshmen** 49% accepted **Housing** Yes **Tuition** $10,889 **Undergraduates** 37% women, 5% part-time, 7% 25 or older, 0% Native American, 2% Hispanic, 10% black, 1% Asian or Pacific Islander **Most popular recent majors** Marketing/retailing/merchandising, accounting, business administration/commerce/management **Academic program** Advanced placement, accelerated degree program, honors program, summer session, adult/continuing education programs, internships **Contact** Dr. David Long, Dean of Admissions, Northwood University, Midland, MI 48640-2398. Telephone: 517-837-4273. Fax: 517-837-4104.

OAKLAND UNIVERSITY

ROCHESTER, MICHIGAN

Entrance Moderately difficult **General** State-supported, coed **Setting** 1,444-acre suburban campus **Enrollment** 13,965 **Faculty** 18:1 **Application deadline** 8/1 **Freshmen** 84% accepted **Housing** Yes **Tuition** $3734 **Undergraduates** 64% women, 39% part-time, 27% 25 or older, 1% Native American, 1% Hispanic, 6% black, 2% Asian or Pacific Islander **Most popular recent majors** Psychology, biology/biological sciences, nursing **Academic program** Average class size 29, advanced placement, accelerated degree program, self-designed majors, tutorials, honors program, summer session, internships **Contact** Mr. Robert E. Johnson, Associate Vice President for Enrollment Management, Oakland University, 101 North Foundation Hall, Rochester, MI 48309-4401. Telephone: 810-370-3360. Fax: 810-370-4462.

OLIVET COLLEGE

OLIVET, MICHIGAN

Entrance Moderately difficult **General** Independent, 4-year, coed, affiliated with Congregational Christian Church **Setting** 92-acre rural campus **Enrollment** 831 **Faculty** 15:1 **Application deadline** 9/1 **Freshmen** 83% accepted **Housing** Yes **Tuition** $12,660 **Undergraduates** 42% women, 7% part-time, 13% 25 or older, 1% Native American, 3% Hispanic, 12% black, 2% Asian or Pacific Islander **Most popular recent majors** Business administration/commerce/management, education, psychology **Academic program** Average class size 20, advanced placement, accelerated degree program, self-designed majors, tutorials, honors program, summer session, internships **Contact** Mr. Bernie McConnell, Director of Admissions, Olivet College, Olivet, MI 49076-9701. Telephone: 616-749-7635.

REFORMED BIBLE COLLEGE

GRAND RAPIDS, MICHIGAN

Entrance Moderately difficult **General** Independent-religious, 4-year, specialized, coed **Setting** 27-acre suburban campus **Enrollment** 181 **Faculty** 13:1 **Application deadline** Rolling **Freshmen** 96% accepted **Housing** Yes **Tuition** $6736 **Undergraduates** 50% women, 25% part-time, 36% 25 or older, 1% Native American, 3% Hispanic, 2% Asian or Pacific Islander **Academic program** Average class size 22, advanced placement, accelerated degree program, tutorials, summer session, adult/continuing education programs, internships **Contact** Mr. David De Boer, Director of Admissions, Reformed Bible College, Grand Rapids, MI 49505-9749. Telephone: 616-222-3000. Fax: 616-222-3045.

SACRED HEART MAJOR SEMINARY

DETROIT, MICHIGAN

Entrance Moderately difficult **General** Independent Roman Catholic, comprehensive, specialized, coed **Setting** 24-acre urban campus **Enrollment** 92 **Faculty** 5:1 **Application deadline** 7/31 **Freshmen** 50% accepted **Housing** Yes **Tuition** $5180 **Undergraduates** 38% women, 34% part-time, 86% 25 or older, 0% Native American, 1% Hispanic, 1% black, 0% Asian or Pacific Islander **Academic program** Average class size 10, advanced placement, honors program **Contact** Rev. Earl Boyea, Dean of Studies, Sacred Heart Major Seminary, 2701 Chicago Boulevard, Detroit, MI 48206. Telephone: 313-883-8556.

SAGINAW VALLEY STATE UNIVERSITY
UNIVERSITY CENTER, MICHIGAN

Entrance Moderately difficult **General** State-supported, comprehensive, coed **Setting** 782-acre rural campus **Enrollment** 7,338 **Faculty** 34:1 **Application deadline** Rolling **Freshmen** 92% accepted **Housing** Yes **Tuition** $3448 **Undergraduates** 60% women, 42% part-time, 25% 25 or older, 1% Native American, 4% Hispanic, 6% black, 1% Asian or Pacific Islander **Most popular recent majors** Business administration/commerce/management, elementary education, criminal justice **Academic program** Advanced placement, accelerated degree program, self-designed majors, tutorials, honors program, summer session, internships **Contact** Mr. James P. Dwyer, Director of Admissions, Saginaw Valley State University, University Center, MI 48710. Telephone: 517-790-4200. Fax: 517-790-0180.

SAINT MARY'S COLLEGE
ORCHARD LAKE, MICHIGAN

Entrance Moderately difficult **General** Independent Roman Catholic, 4-year, coed **Setting** 120-acre suburban campus **Enrollment** 350 **Faculty** 11:1 **Application deadline** Rolling **Freshmen** 52% accepted **Housing** Yes **Tuition** $6330 **Undergraduates** 57% women, 50% part-time, 40% 25 or older, 0% Native American, 1% Hispanic, 11% black, 1% Asian or Pacific Islander **Most popular recent majors** Communication, (pre)medicine sequence, business administration/commerce/management **Academic program** Advanced placement, tutorials, adult/continuing education programs, internships **Contact** Ms. Deborah Graczyk, Director of Admissions, Saint Mary's College, Orchard Lake, MI 48324-1623. Telephone: 810-683-0507.

SIENA HEIGHTS COLLEGE
ADRIAN, MICHIGAN

Entrance Moderately difficult **General** Independent Roman Catholic, comprehensive, coed **Setting** 140-acre small-town campus **Enrollment** 2,002 **Faculty** 14:1 **Application deadline** Rolling **Freshmen** 94% accepted **Housing** Yes **Tuition** $10,700 **Undergraduates** 58% women, 35% part-time, 8% 25 or older, 1% Native American, 3% Hispanic, 6% black, 1% Asian or Pacific Islander **Academic program** Average class size 35, advanced placement, accelerated degree program, self-designed majors, tutorials, honors program, summer session, adult/continuing education programs, internships **Contact** Mr. Frank J. Hribar, Associate Dean of Admissions and Financial Aid, Siena Heights College, Adrian, MI 49221-1796. Telephone: 517-264-7131. Fax: 517-264-7704.

SPRING ARBOR COLLEGE
SPRING ARBOR, MICHIGAN

Entrance Moderately difficult **General** Independent Free Methodist, comprehensive, coed **Setting** 70-acre small-town campus **Enrollment** 1,069 **Faculty** 17:1 **Application deadline** Rolling **Freshmen** 99% accepted **Housing** Yes **Tuition** $10,686 **Undergraduates** 61% women, 21% part-time, 24% 25 or older, 0% Native American, 1% Hispanic, 3% black, 1% Asian or Pacific Islander **Most popular recent majors** Business administration/commerce/management, English, physical education **Academic program** Advanced placement, self-designed majors, honors program, summer session, adult/continuing education programs, internships **Contact** Mr. Steve Schippers, Director of Enrollment Services, Spring Arbor College, Spring Arbor, MI 49283-9799. Telephone: 517-750-1200 Ext. 1470. Fax: 517-750-1604.

UNIVERSITY OF DETROIT MERCY
DETROIT, MICHIGAN

Entrance Moderately difficult **General** Independent Roman Catholic (Jesuit), coed **Setting** 70-acre urban campus **Enrollment** 7,284 **Faculty** 14:1 **Application deadline** 8/15 **Freshmen** 77% accepted **Housing** Yes **Tuition** $12,986 **Undergraduates** 66% women, 51% part-time, 52% 25 or older, 1% Native American, 2% Hispanic, 39% black, 2% Asian or Pacific Islander **Most popular recent majors** Nursing, engineering (general), architecture **Academic program** Advanced placement, accelerated degree program, self-designed majors, tutorials, honors program, summer session, adult/continuing education programs, internships **Contact** Dr. Robert Johnson, Dean of Enrollment Management, University of Detroit Mercy, PO Box 19900, Detroit, MI 48219-0900. Telephone: 313-993-1245.

UNIVERSITY OF MICHIGAN
ANN ARBOR, MICHIGAN

Entrance Very difficult **General** State-supported, coed **Setting** 2,871-acre suburban campus **Enrollment** 36,525 **Faculty** 13:1 **Application deadline** 2/1 **Freshmen** 68% accepted **Housing** Yes **Tuition** $5888 **Undergraduates** 50% women, 7% part-time, 4% 25 or older, 1% Native American, 5% Hispanic, 9% black, 12% Asian or Pacific Islander **Most popular recent majors** Psychology, mechanical engineering, biology/

biological sciences **Academic program** Advanced placement, accelerated degree program, self-designed majors, tutorials, honors program, summer session, adult/continuing education programs, internships **Contact** Mr. Ted Spencer, Director of Undergraduate Admissions, University of Michigan, Ann Arbor, MI 48109-1316. Telephone: 313-764-7433. Fax: 313-936-0740.

UNIVERSITY OF MICHIGAN–DEARBORN
DEARBORN, MICHIGAN

Entrance Moderately difficult **General** State-supported, comprehensive, coed **Setting** 210-acre suburban campus **Enrollment** 8,324 **Faculty** 21:1 **Application deadline** Rolling **Freshmen** 77% accepted **Tuition** $4040 **Undergraduates** 54% women, 44% part-time, 31% 25 or older, 1% Native American, 2% Hispanic, 7% black, 4% Asian or Pacific Islander **Most popular recent majors** Mechanical engineering, electrical engineering, psychology **Academic program** Accelerated degree program, self-designed majors, honors program, summer session, adult/continuing education programs, internships **Contact** Ms. Carol S. Mack, Director of Admissions, University of Michigan-Dearborn, 4901 Evergreen Road, Dearborn, MI 48128-1491. Telephone: 313-593-5100.

UNIVERSITY OF MICHIGAN–FLINT
FLINT, MICHIGAN

Entrance Moderately difficult **General** State-supported, comprehensive, coed **Setting** 42-acre urban campus **Enrollment** 6,236 **Faculty** 25:1 **Application deadline** 8/21 **Freshmen** 93% accepted **Tuition** $3559 **Undergraduates** 58% women, 49% part-time, 33% 25 or older, 1% Native American, 2% Hispanic, 10% black, 1% Asian or Pacific Islander **Most popular recent majors** Business administration/commerce/management, education **Academic program** Advanced placement, accelerated degree program, self-designed majors, honors program, summer session, adult/continuing education programs **Contact** Dr. Virginia R. Allen, Vice Chancellor for Student Services and Enrollment, University of Michigan–Flint, Flint, MI 48502-2186. Telephone: 810-762-3434.

WALSH COLLEGE OF ACCOUNTANCY AND BUSINESS ADMINISTRATION
TROY, MICHIGAN

Entrance Noncompetitive **General** Independent, upper-level, coed **Setting** 20-acre suburban campus **Enrollment** 3,428 **Faculty** 21:1 **Tuition** $6849 **Undergraduates** 61% women, 84% part-time, 71% 25 or older, 0% Native American, 1% Hispanic, 4% black, 2% Asian or Pacific Islander **Most popular recent majors** Accounting, finance/banking, business administration/commerce/management **Academic program** Summer session, adult/continuing education programs **Contact** Ms. Mary Cay Slecman, Director of Admissions, Walsh College of Accountancy and Business Administration, Troy, MI 48007-7006. Telephone: 810-689-8282 Ext. 211. Fax: 810-524-2520.

WAYNE STATE UNIVERSITY
DETROIT, MICHIGAN

Entrance Moderately difficult **General** State-supported, coed **Setting** 203-acre urban campus **Enrollment** 31,185 **Application deadline** 8/1 **Freshmen** 81% accepted **Housing** Yes **Tuition** $3399 **Undergraduates** 60% women, 51% part-time, 43% 25 or older, 1% Native American, 2% Hispanic, 28% black, 5% Asian or Pacific Islander **Most popular recent majors** Psychology, elementary education, accounting **Academic program** Advanced placement, accelerated degree program, tutorials, honors program, summer session, adult/continuing education programs, internships **Contact** Mr. Michael Wood, Associate Director, Wayne State University, 656 West Kirby Street, Detroit, MI 48202. Telephone: 313-577-7928.

WESTERN MICHIGAN UNIVERSITY
KALAMAZOO, MICHIGAN

Entrance Moderately difficult **General** State-supported, coed **Setting** 451-acre urban campus **Enrollment** 25,699 **Faculty** 17:1 **Application deadline** Rolling **Freshmen** 82% accepted **Housing** Yes **Tuition** $3332 **Undergraduates** 54% women, 22% part-time, 17% 25 or older, 1% Native American, 2% Hispanic, 7% black, 1% Asian or Pacific Islander **Most popular recent majors** Marketing/retailing/merchandising, sociology, education **Academic program** Average class size 25, advanced placement, accelerated degree program, self-designed majors, tutorials, honors program, summer session, adult/continuing education programs, internships **Contact** Office of Admissions, Western Michigan University, Office of Admissions and Orientation, Kalamazoo, MI 49008. Telephone: 616-387-6000.

WILLIAM TYNDALE COLLEGE
FARMINGTON HILLS, MICHIGAN

Entrance Minimally difficult **General** Independent-religious, 4-year, coed **Setting** 28-acre suburban campus **Enrollment** 512 **Faculty** 6:1 **Application deadline** Rolling **Freshmen** 100% accepted **Housing** Yes **Tuition** $6000 **Undergraduates** 52% women, 38% part-time, 71% 25 or older, 1% Native American, 0% Hispanic, 29% black, 1% Asian or Pacific Islander **Most popular recent majors** Biblical studies, psychology, music **Academic program** Advanced placement, accelerated degree program, tutorials, summer session, adult/continuing education programs, internships **Contact** Office of Admissions, William Tyndale College, 37500 West Twelve Mile Road, Farmington Hills, MI 48331. Telephone: 810-553-7200. Fax: 810-553-5963.

Minnesota

AUGSBURG COLLEGE

MINNEAPOLIS, MINNESOTA

Entrance Moderately difficult **General** Independent Lutheran, comprehensive, coed **Setting** 23-acre urban campus **Enrollment** 2,862 **Faculty** 15:1 **Application deadline** 5/1 **Freshmen** 82% accepted **Housing** Yes **Tuition** $13,996 **Undergraduates** 54% women, 8% part-time, 20% 25 or older, 2% Native American, 2% Hispanic, 4% black, 5% Asian or Pacific Islander **Most popular recent majors** Business administration/commerce/management, education, communication **Academic program** Average class size 25, advanced placement, accelerated degree program, self-designed majors, tutorials, honors program, summer session, adult/continuing education programs, internships **Contact** Ms. Sally Daniels, Director of Admissions, Augsburg College, 2211 Riverside Avenue, Minneapolis, MN 55454-1351. Telephone: 612-330-1001. Fax: 612-330-1649.

BEMIDJI STATE UNIVERSITY

BEMIDJI, MINNESOTA

Entrance Moderately difficult **General** State-supported, comprehensive, coed **Setting** 83-acre small-town campus **Enrollment** 4,019 **Faculty** 20:1 **Application deadline** 8/15 **Freshmen** 68% accepted **Housing** Yes **Tuition** $2925 **Undergraduates** 53% women, 14% part-time, 23% 25 or older, 4% Native American, 1% Hispanic, 1% black, 1% Asian or Pacific Islander **Most popular recent majors** Elementary education, business administration/commerce/management, industrial engineering technology **Academic program** Advanced placement, accelerated degree program, honors program, summer session, adult/continuing education programs, internships **Contact** Mr. Paul Muller, Associate Director of Admissions, Bemidji State University, Bemidji, MN 56601-2699. Telephone: 218-755-2040. Fax: 218-755-2074.

BETHEL COLLEGE

ST. PAUL, MINNESOTA

Entrance Moderately difficult **General** Independent, comprehensive, coed, affiliated with Baptist General Conference **Setting** 231-acre suburban campus **Enrollment** 2,584 **Faculty** 15:1 **Application deadline** Rolling **Freshmen** 81% accepted **Housing** Yes **Tuition** $13,840 **Undergraduates** 60% women, 6% part-time, 1% Native American, 1% Hispanic, 1% black, 2% Asian or Pacific Islander **Most popular recent majors** Education, nursing, business administration/commerce/management **Academic program** Advanced placement, self-designed majors, honors program, summer session, adult/continuing education programs, internships **Contact** Mr. John C. Lassen, Director of Admissions, Bethel College, St. Paul, MN 55112-6999. Telephone: 612-638-6436.

CARLETON COLLEGE

NORTHFIELD, MINNESOTA

Entrance Very difficult **General** Independent, 4-year, coed **Setting** 955-acre small-town campus **Enrollment** 1,698 **Faculty** 10:1 **Application deadline** 1/15 **Freshmen** 50% accepted **Housing** Yes **Tuition** $22,985 **Undergraduates** 50% women, 0% part-time, 0% 25 or older, 1% Native American, 4% Hispanic, 3% black, 9% Asian or Pacific Islander **Most popular recent majors** Biology/biological sciences, English, political science/government **Academic program** Advanced placement, accelerated degree program, self-designed majors, tutorials **Contact** Mr. Paul Thiboutot, Dean of Admissions, Carleton College, Northfield, MN 55057-4001. Telephone: 507-646-4190. Fax: 507-646-4526.

COLLEGE OF ASSOCIATED ARTS

SEE COLLEGE OF VISUAL ARTS

COLLEGE OF SAINT BENEDICT

SAINT JOSEPH, MINNESOTA

Entrance Moderately difficult **General** Independent Roman Catholic, 4-year, women only, coordinate with Saint John's University (MN) **Setting** 315-acre small-town campus **Enrollment** 1,958 **Faculty** 13:1 **Application deadline** Rolling **Freshmen** 92% accepted **Housing** Yes **Tuition** $13,996 **Undergraduates** 4% part-time, 5% 25 or older, 1% Native American, 1% Hispanic, 1% black, 2% Asian or Pacific Islander **Most popular recent majors** Education, nursing, biology/biological sciences **Academic program** Average class size 21, advanced placement, self-designed majors, tutorials, honors program, adult/continuing education programs, internships **Contact** Ms. Mary Milbert, Director of Admissions, College of Saint Benedict, Saint Joseph, MN 56374. Telephone: 320-363-5308. Fax: 320-363-5010.

COLLEGE OF ST. CATHERINE

ST. PAUL, MINNESOTA

Entrance Moderately difficult **General** Independent Roman Catholic, comprehensive, women only **Setting** 110-acre urban campus **Enrollment** 2,695 **Faculty** 14:1 **Application deadline** 8/15 **Freshmen** 90% accepted **Housing** Yes **Tuition** $13,702 **Undergraduates** 24% part-time, 43% 25 or older, 1% Native American, 2% Hispanic, 2% black, 4% Asian or Pacific Islander **Most popular recent majors** Business administration/commerce/management, nursing, occupational therapy **Academic program** Advanced placement, accelerated degree program, self-designed majors, honors program, summer session, adult/continuing education programs, internships **Contact** Ms. Mary Docken, Associate Dean of Admissions, College of St. Catherine, 2004 Randolph Avenue, St. Paul, MN 55105-1789. Telephone: 612-690-6505. Fax: 612-690-6024.

COLLEGE OF ST. SCHOLASTICA

DULUTH, MINNESOTA

Entrance Moderately difficult **General** Independent, comprehensive, coed, affiliated with Roman Catholic Church **Setting** 160-acre suburban campus **Enrollment** 2,101 **Faculty** 13:1 **Application deadline** Rolling **Freshmen** 92% accepted **Housing** Yes **Tuition** $13,995 **Undergraduates** 74% women, 9% part-time, 19% 25 or older, 2% Native American, 1% Hispanic, 1% black, 1% Asian or Pacific Islander **Most popular recent majors** Nursing, business administration/commerce/management, health services administration **Academic program** Average class size 19, advanced placement, self-designed majors, tutorials, honors program, summer session, adult/continuing education programs, internships **Contact** Ms. Rebecca Urbanski-Junkert, Vice President for Admissions and Financial Aid, College of St. Scholastica, Duluth, MN 55811-4199. Telephone: 218-723-6053. Fax: 218-723-6290.

COLLEGE OF VISUAL ARTS

ST. PAUL, MINNESOTA

Entrance Minimally difficult **General** Independent, 4-year, specialized, coed **Setting** 2-acre urban campus **Enrollment** 203 **Faculty** 6:1 **Application deadline** Rolling **Freshmen** 93% accepted **Tuition** $9400 **Undergraduates** 51% women, 9% part-time, 20% 25 or older, 1% Native American, 4% Hispanic, 1% black, 4% Asian or Pacific Islander **Most popular recent majors** Commercial art, illustration, art/fine arts **Academic program** Average class size 18, advanced placement, tutorials, summer session, internships **Contact** Ms. Sherry A. Essen, Director of Admissions, College of Visual Arts, 344 Summit Avenue, St. Paul, MN 55102-2124. Telephone: 612-224-3416.

CONCORDIA COLLEGE

MOORHEAD, MINNESOTA

Entrance Moderately difficult **General** Independent, 4-year, coed, affiliated with Evangelical Lutheran Church in America **Setting** 120-acre suburban campus **Enrollment** 2,928 **Faculty** 14:1 **Application deadline** Rolling **Freshmen** 93% accepted **Housing** Yes **Tuition** $12,145 **Undergraduates** 62% women, 2% part-time, 2% 25 or older, 1% Native American, 1% Hispanic, 1% black, 2% Asian or Pacific Islander **Most popular recent majors** Business administration/commerce/management, biology/biological sciences, psychology **Academic program** Advanced placement, tutorials, honors program, summer session, adult/continuing education programs, internships **Contact** Mr. Lee E. Johnson, Director of Admissions, Concordia College, 901 8th Street South, Moorhead, MN 56562. Telephone: 218-299-3004. Fax: 218-299-3947.

CONCORDIA COLLEGE

ST. PAUL, MINNESOTA

Entrance Minimally difficult **General** Independent, comprehensive, coed, affiliated with Lutheran Church–Missouri Synod **Setting** 37-acre urban campus **Enrollment** 1,259 **Faculty** 19:1 **Application deadline** 8/15 **Freshmen** 94% accepted **Housing** Yes **Tuition** $11,980 **Undergraduates** 59% women, 15% part-time, 40% 25 or older, 1% Native American, 1% Hispanic, 6% black, 6% Asian or Pacific Islander **Most popular recent majors** Education, business administration/commerce/management, early childhood education **Academic program** Average class size 18, advanced placement, accelerated degree program, self-designed majors, tutorials, summer session, adult/continuing education programs, internships **Contact** Mr. Tim Utter, Director of Admissions, Concordia College, 275 Syndicate Street North, St. Paul, MN 55104-5494. Telephone: 612-641-8230. Fax: 612-659-0207.

CROWN COLLEGE
ST. BONIFACIUS, MINNESOTA

Entrance Minimally difficult **General** Independent, comprehensive, coed, affiliated with The Christian and Missionary Alliance **Setting** 193-acre suburban campus **Enrollment** 629 **Faculty** 14:1 **Application deadline** Rolling **Freshmen** 98% accepted **Housing** Yes **Tuition** $9335 **Undergraduates** 54% women, 8% part-time, 20% 25 or older, 0% Native American, 3% Hispanic, 1% black, 6% Asian or Pacific Islander **Most popular recent majors** Elementary education, ministries, child care/child and family studies **Academic program** Average class size 24, advanced placement, summer session, adult/continuing education programs, internships **Contact** Mr. L. Marshall Hauger, Vice President of Enrollment Services, Crown College, St. Bonifacius, MN 55375-9001. Telephone: 612-446-4141. Fax: 612-446-4149.

DR. MARTIN LUTHER COLLEGE
SEE MARTIN LUTHER COLLEGE

GUSTAVUS ADOLPHUS COLLEGE
ST. PETER, MINNESOTA

Entrance Very difficult **General** Independent, 4-year, coed, affiliated with Evangelical Lutheran Church in America **Setting** 309-acre small-town campus **Enrollment** 2,376 **Faculty** 13:1 **Application deadline** 4/1 **Freshmen** 81% accepted **Housing** Yes **Tuition** $16,140 **Undergraduates** 55% women, 2% part-time, 0% 25 or older, 0% Native American, 1% Hispanic, 2% black, 3% Asian or Pacific Islander **Most popular recent majors** Psychology, biology/biological sciences, political science/government **Academic program** Advanced placement, accelerated degree program, self-designed majors, tutorials, honors program, summer session, internships **Contact** Mr. Mark Anderson, Director of Admissions, Gustavus Adolphus College, St. Peter, MN 56082-1498. Telephone: 507-933-7676.

HAMLINE UNIVERSITY
ST. PAUL, MINNESOTA

Entrance Moderately difficult **General** Independent, comprehensive, coed, affiliated with United Methodist Church **Setting** 50-acre urban campus **Enrollment** 3,335 **Faculty** 13:1 **Application deadline** Rolling **Freshmen** 84% accepted **Housing** Yes **Tuition** $14,854 **Undergraduates** 58% women, 9% part-time, 7% 25 or older, 1% Native American, 1% Hispanic, 3% black, 5% Asian or Pacific Islander **Most popular recent majors** Psychology, political science/government, English **Academic program** Average class size 19, advanced placement, self-designed majors, tutorials, honors program, summer session, adult/continuing education programs, internships **Contact** Dr. Louise Cummings-Simmons, Dean of Undergraduate Admissions, Hamline University, 1536 Hewitt Avenue, St. Paul, MN 55104-1284. Telephone: 612-641-2207. Fax: 612-641-2458.

MACALESTER COLLEGE
ST. PAUL, MINNESOTA

Entrance Very difficult **General** Independent Presbyterian, 4-year, coed **Setting** 53-acre urban campus **Enrollment** 1,797 **Faculty** 11:1 **Application deadline** 1/15 **Freshmen** 55% accepted **Housing** Yes **Tuition** $18,758 **Undergraduates** 57% women, 5% part-time, 2% 25 or older, 1% Native American, 4% Hispanic, 4% black, 6% Asian or Pacific Islander **Most popular recent majors** Psychology, English, history **Academic program** Advanced placement, self-designed majors, tutorials, honors program, internships **Contact** Mr. William M. Shain, Dean of Admissions, Macalester College, 1600 Grand Avenue, St. Paul, MN 55105-1899. Telephone: 612-696-6357. Fax: 612-696-6724.

MANKATO STATE UNIVERSITY
MANKATO, MINNESOTA

Entrance Moderately difficult **General** State-supported, comprehensive, coed **Setting** 303-acre small-town campus **Enrollment** 12,695 **Application deadline** Rolling **Freshmen** 87% accepted **Housing** Yes **Tuition** $2896 **Undergraduates** 52% women, 16% part-time, 21% 25 or older, 1% Hispanic, 1% black, 2% Asian or Pacific Islander **Most popular recent majors** Business administration/commerce/management, education, accounting **Academic program** Advanced placement, accelerated degree program, self-designed majors, honors program, summer session, adult/continuing education programs, internships **Contact** Dr. Gerald Wuori, Director of Admissions, Mankato State University, PO Box 8400, MSU 55, Mankato, MN 56002-8400. Telephone: 507-389-1822.

MARTIN LUTHER COLLEGE
NEW ULM, MINNESOTA

Entrance Moderately difficult **General** Independent, 4-year, coed, affiliated with Wisconsin Evangelical Lutheran Synod **Setting** 50-acre small-town campus **Enrollment** 817 **Faculty** 9:1 **Application deadline** 5/1 **Freshmen** 98% accepted **Housing** Yes **Tuition** $4465 **Undergraduates** 47% women, 1% part-time, 6% 25 or older, 0% Native American, 1% Hispanic, 1% black, 1% Asian or Pacific Islander **Most popular recent majors** Elementary education, pastoral studies **Academic program** Advanced placement, summer session, internships **Contact** Prof. John Sebald, Associate Director of Admissions, Martin Luther College, New Ulm, MN 56073-3965. Telephone: 507-354-8221 Ext. 280. Fax: 507-354-8225.

MAYO SCHOOL OF HEALTH-RELATED SCIENCES

ROCHESTER, MINNESOTA

Entrance Difficulty N/R **General** Independent, comprehensive **Enrollment** 307 **Tuition** $1000 **Financial Aid** 44% applied for aid, 100% of those who applied for aid were judged to have need, 100% of those were aided. Average percent of need met: 100%. Non-need awards available; for 1996, a total of 14 non-need awards were made. Required forms: institutional, FAFSA. Financial aid deadline: continuous.

METROPOLITAN STATE UNIVERSITY

ST. PAUL, MINNESOTA

Entrance Moderately difficult **General** State-supported, comprehensive, coed **Setting** Urban campus **Enrollment** 5,245 **Faculty** 9:1 **Application deadline** Rolling **Freshmen** 73% accepted **Tuition** $2570 **Undergraduates** 64% women, 73% part-time, 86% 25 or older, 1% Native American, 1% Hispanic, 8% black, 4% Asian or Pacific Islander **Most popular recent majors** Liberal arts/general studies, accounting, nursing **Academic program** Self-designed majors, summer session, adult/continuing education programs, internships **Contact** Ms. Cindy Olson, Registrar, Metropolitan State University, 700 East 7th Street, St. Paul, MN 55106-5000. Telephone: 612-772-7776.

MINNEAPOLIS COLLEGE OF ART AND DESIGN

MINNEAPOLIS, MINNESOTA

Entrance Moderately difficult **General** Independent, comprehensive, specialized, coed **Setting** 7-acre urban campus **Enrollment** 567 **Faculty** 11:1 **Application deadline** Rolling **Freshmen** 83% accepted **Housing** Yes **Tuition** $15,810 **Undergraduates** 43% women, 22% part-time, 25% 25 or older, 1% Native American, 2% Hispanic, 2% black, 7% Asian or Pacific Islander **Most popular recent majors** Commercial art, art/fine arts **Academic program** Self-designed majors, tutorials, summer session, adult/continuing education programs, internships **Contact** Ms. Rebecca Haas, Director of Admissions, Minneapolis College of Art and Design, 2501 Stevens Avenue South, Minneapolis, MN 55404-4347. Telephone: 612-874-3760. Fax: 612-874-3704.

MINNESOTA BIBLE COLLEGE

ROCHESTER, MINNESOTA

Entrance Noncompetitive **General** 0005410011, 4-year, coed, affiliated with Christian Churches and Churches of Christ **Setting** 40-acre urban campus **Enrollment** 116 **Faculty** 11:1 **Application deadline** 8/15 **Freshmen** 93% accepted **Housing** Yes **Tuition** $4960 **Undergraduates** 48% women, 18% part-time, 28% 25 or older, 0% Native American, 2% Hispanic, 3% black, 6% Asian or Pacific Islander **Academic program** Advanced placement, self-designed majors, tutorials, internships **Contact** Ms. Tay J. Schield, Director of Admissions, Minnesota Bible College, 920 Mayowood Road, SW, Rochester, MN 55902-2275. Telephone: 507-288-4563 Ext. 246.

MOORHEAD STATE UNIVERSITY

MOORHEAD, MINNESOTA

Entrance Moderately difficult **General** State-supported, comprehensive, coed **Setting** 118-acre urban campus **Enrollment** 6,194 **Faculty** 18:1 **Application deadline** 8/7 **Freshmen** 96% accepted **Housing** Yes **Tuition** $2881 **Undergraduates** 62% women, 20% part-time, 22% 25 or older, 1% Native American, 1% Hispanic, 1% black, 1% Asian or Pacific Islander **Most popular recent majors** Education, business administration/commerce/management, accounting **Academic program** Advanced placement, self-designed majors, tutorials, honors program, summer session, adult/continuing education programs, internships **Contact** Ms. Jean Lange, Director of Admissions, Moorhead State University, Owens Hall, Moorhead, MN 56563-0002. Telephone: 218-236-2548. Fax: 218-236-2168.

NATIONAL COLLEGE–ST. PAUL CAMPUS

ST. PAUL, MINNESOTA

Entrance Noncompetitive **General** Proprietary, 4-year, coed **Setting** 1-acre urban campus **Enrollment** 310 **Application deadline** Rolling **Freshmen** 100% accepted **Tuition** $8160 **Undergraduates** 52% women, 40% part-time, 55% 25 or older, 2% Native American, 3% Hispanic, 28% black, 22%

Asian or Pacific Islander **Most popular recent majors** Business administration/commerce/management, accounting, computer information systems **Academic program** Average class size 14, accelerated degree program, tutorials, summer session, internships **Contact** Ms. Collette A. Garrity, Vice President, National College–St. Paul Campus, 1380 Energy Lane, St. Paul, MN 55108-9952. Telephone: 612-644-1265. Fax: 612-644-0690.

NORTH CENTRAL BIBLE COLLEGE

MINNEAPOLIS, MINNESOTA

Entrance Noncompetitive **General** Independent, 4-year, coed, affiliated with Assemblies of God **Setting** 7-acre urban campus **Enrollment** 1,008 **Faculty** 18:1 **Application deadline** Rolling **Freshmen** 93% accepted **Housing** Yes **Tuition** $7707 **Undergraduates** 50% women, 18% part-time, 27% 25 or older, 1% Native American, 2% Hispanic, 4% black, 1% Asian or Pacific Islander **Most popular recent majors** Pastoral studies, ministries, elementary education **Academic program** Advanced placement, self-designed majors, summer session, adult/continuing education programs, internships **Contact** Ms. Aimee Cheek, Admissions Secretary, North Central Bible College, 910 Elliot Avenue South, Minneapolis, MN 55404-1322. Telephone: 612-343-4401. Fax: 612-343-4778.

NORTHWESTERN COLLEGE

ST. PAUL, MINNESOTA

Entrance Moderately difficult **General** Independent nondenominational, 4-year, coed **Setting** 95-acre suburban campus **Enrollment** 1,362 **Faculty** 16:1 **Application deadline** 8/15 **Freshmen** 75% accepted **Housing** Yes **Tuition** $13,140 **Undergraduates** 59% women, 3% part-time, 10% 25 or older, 1% Native American, 1% Hispanic, 1% black, 2% Asian or Pacific Islander **Most popular recent majors** Elementary education, business administration/commerce/management, music **Academic program** ESL program, Advanced placement, summer session, adult/continuing education programs, internships **Contact** Mr. Ralph D. Anderson, Dean of Admissions, Northwestern College, 3003 Snelling Avenue N, St. Paul, MN 55113-1598. Telephone: 612-631-5111. Fax: 612-631-5680.

OAK HILLS BIBLE COLLEGE

BEMIDJI, MINNESOTA

Entrance Minimally difficult **General** Independent interdenominational, 4-year, coed **Setting** 180-acre rural campus **Enrollment** 174 **Faculty** 8:1 **Freshmen** 57% accepted **Housing** Yes **Tuition** $7680 **Undergraduates** 60% women, 22% part-time, 20% 25 or older, 1% Native American, 1% Hispanic, 1% black, 0% Asian or Pacific Islander **Most popular recent majors** Biblical studies, ministries **Academic program** Advanced placement, tutorials, honors program, internships **Contact** Mrs. Monica Bush, Admissions Director, Oak Hills Bible College, Bemidji, MN 56601-8832. Telephone: 218-751-8670 Ext. 230. Fax: 218-751-8825 Ext. 284.

PILLSBURY BAPTIST BIBLE COLLEGE

OWATONNA, MINNESOTA

Entrance Noncompetitive **General** Independent Baptist, 4-year, coed **Setting** 14-acre small-town campus **Enrollment** 197 **Faculty** 8:1 **Application deadline** 8/27 **Freshmen** 100% accepted **Housing** Yes **Tuition** $5200 **Undergraduates** 51% women, 9% part-time, 0% Native American, 1% Hispanic, 2% black, 3% Asian or Pacific Islander **Most popular recent majors** Biblical studies, education, business administration/commerce/management **Academic program** Advanced placement, accelerated degree program, self-designed majors, summer session, adult/continuing education programs, internships **Contact** Mr. Paul Rumsey, Director of Admissions, Pillsbury Baptist Bible College, Owatonna, MN 55060-3097. Telephone: 507-451-2710 Ext. 279. Fax: 507-451-6459.

ST. CLOUD STATE UNIVERSITY

ST. CLOUD, MINNESOTA

Entrance Moderately difficult **General** State-supported, comprehensive, coed **Setting** 82-acre suburban campus **Enrollment** 14,048 **Faculty** 22:1 **Application deadline** 5/1 **Freshmen** 87% accepted **Housing** Yes **Tuition** $2904 **Undergraduates** 51% women, 15% part-time, 16% 25 or older, 1% Native American, 1% Hispanic, 1% black, 1% Asian or Pacific Islander **Most popular recent majors** Elementary education, psychology, communication **Academic program** Advanced placement, accelerated degree program, self-designed majors, tutorials, honors program, summer session, adult/continuing education programs, internships **Contact** Mr. Sherwood Reid, Director of Admissions, St. Cloud State University, St. Cloud, MN 56301-4498. Telephone: 320-255-2244.

SAINT JOHN'S UNIVERSITY

COLLEGEVILLE, MINNESOTA

Entrance Moderately difficult **General** Independent Roman Catholic, comprehensive, men only, coordinate with College of Saint Benedict **Setting** 2,400-acre rural campus **Enrollment** 1,796 **Faculty** 13:1 **Application deadline** Rolling **Freshmen** 87% accepted **Housing** Yes **Tuition** $14,758 **Undergraduates** 4% part-time, 3% 25 or older, 1% Native American, 1% Hispanic, 1% black, 2% Asian or Pacific Islander **Most popular recent majors** Business administration/commerce/management, biology/biological sciences, accounting **Academic program** Average class size 21, advanced placement, self-designed majors, tutorials, honors program, internships **Contact** Ms. Mary Milbert, Director of Admissions, Saint John's University, PO Box 7155, Collegeville, MN 56321. Telephone: 320-363-2196. Fax: 320-363-3206.

SAINT MARY'S UNIVERSITY OF MINNESOTA
WINONA, MINNESOTA

Entrance Moderately difficult **General** Independent Roman Catholic, comprehensive, coed **Setting** 350-acre small-town campus **Enrollment** 9,321 **Faculty** 13:1 **Application deadline** Rolling **Freshmen** 88% accepted **Housing** Yes **Tuition** $12,495 **Undergraduates** 53% women, 3% part-time, 5% 25 or older, 1% Native American, 1% Hispanic, 1% black, 2% Asian or Pacific Islander **Most popular recent majors** Marketing/retailing/merchandising, criminal justice, biology/biological sciences **Academic program** Average class size 24, advanced placement, accelerated degree program, self-designed majors, tutorials, honors program, summer session, adult/continuing education programs, internships **Contact** Mr. Anthony M. Piscitiello, Vice President for Admission, Saint Mary's University of Minnesota, Winona, MN 55987-1399. Telephone: 507-457-1700. Fax: 507-457-1633.

ST. OLAF COLLEGE
NORTHFIELD, MINNESOTA

Entrance Very difficult **General** Independent Lutheran, 4-year, coed **Setting** 350-acre small-town campus **Enrollment** 2,959 **Faculty** 11:1 **Application deadline** Rolling **Freshmen** 77% accepted **Housing** Yes **Tuition** $16,500 **Undergraduates** 58% women, 3% part-time, 2% 25 or older, 1% Native American, 1% Hispanic, 1% black, 3% Asian or Pacific Islander **Most popular recent majors** Biology/biological sciences, economics, English **Academic program** Advanced placement, accelerated degree program, self-designed majors, tutorials, summer session, adult/continuing education programs, internships **Contact** Ms. Barbara Lundberg, Director of Admissions, St. Olaf College, Northfield, MN 55057-1098. Telephone: 507-646-3025. Fax: 507-646-3549.

SOUTHWEST STATE UNIVERSITY
MARSHALL, MINNESOTA

Entrance Moderately difficult **General** State-supported, comprehensive, coed **Setting** 216-acre small-town campus **Enrollment** 2,900 **Faculty** 19:1 **Application deadline** Rolling **Freshmen** 90% accepted **Housing** Yes **Tuition** $2980 **Undergraduates** 56% women, 40% part-time, 10% 25 or older, 1% Native American, 1% Hispanic, 2% black, 1% Asian or Pacific Islander **Most popular recent majors** Business administration/commerce/management, education, accounting **Academic program** Advanced placement, accelerated degree program, self-designed majors, honors program, summer session, adult/continuing education programs, internships **Contact** Mr. Richard Shearer, Director of Admissions, Southwest State University, Marshall, MN 56258-3306. Telephone: 507-537-6286.

UNIVERSITY OF MINNESOTA, CROOKSTON
CROOKSTON, MINNESOTA

Entrance Noncompetitive **General** State-supported, 4-year, coed **Setting** 95-acre rural campus **Enrollment** 937 **Application deadline** Rolling **Freshmen** 100% accepted **Housing** Yes **Tuition** $4251 **Undergraduates** 58% women, 45% part-time, 27% 25 or older, 1% Native American, 1% Hispanic, 1% black, 1% Asian or Pacific Islander **Most popular recent majors** Natural resource management, business administration/commerce/management, aviation technology **Academic program** Average class size 35, advanced placement, tutorials, summer session, adult/continuing education programs, internships **Contact** Mr. Russ Kreager, Director of Admissions and Enrollment Manager, University of Minnesota, Crookston, Crookston, MN 56716-5001. Telephone: 218-281-6510 Ext. 8569. Fax: 218-281-8050.

UNIVERSITY OF MINNESOTA, DULUTH
DULUTH, MINNESOTA

Entrance Moderately difficult **General** State-supported, comprehensive, coed **Setting** 250-acre suburban campus **Enrollment** 7,501 **Faculty** 19:1 **Application deadline** 2/1 **Freshmen** 85% accepted **Housing** Yes **Tuition** $4187 **Undergraduates** 48% women, 8% part-time, 11% 25 or older, 1% Native American, 1% Hispanic, 1% black, 2% Asian or Pacific Islander **Most popular recent majors** Business administration/commerce/management, criminology, biology/biological sciences **Academic program** Advanced placement, self-designed majors, tutorials, honors program, summer session, adult/continuing education programs, internships **Contact** Mr. Russell Kreager, Assistant Director of Admissions, University of Minnesota, Duluth, Duluth, MN 55812-2496. Telephone: 218-726-7171. Fax: 218-726-6144.

UNIVERSITY OF MINNESOTA, MORRIS
MORRIS, MINNESOTA

Entrance Moderately difficult **General** State-supported, 4-year, coed **Setting** 130-acre small-town campus **Enrollment** 1,970 **Faculty** 16:1 **Application deadline** 3/15 **Freshmen** 84% accepted **Housing** Yes **Tuition** $4554 **Undergraduates** 57% women, 4% part-time, 5% 25 or older, 5% Native American, 2% Hispanic, 4% black, 3% Asian or Pacific Islander **Most popular recent majors** Business economics, English, biology/biological sciences **Academic program** Advanced placement, accelerated degree program, self-designed majors, tutorials, honors program, summer session, adult/continuing education programs, internships **Contact** Mr. Rodney M. Oto, Director of Admissions and Financial Aid, University of Minnesota, Morris, Morris, MN 56267. Telephone: 320-589-6035. Fax: 320-589-1673.

UNIVERSITY OF MINNESOTA, TWIN CITIES CAMPUS
MINNEAPOLIS, MINNESOTA

Entrance Moderately difficult **General** State-supported, coed **Setting** 2,000-acre urban campus **Enrollment** 37,018 **Faculty** 15:1 **Application deadline** Rolling **Freshmen** 55% accepted **Housing** Yes **Tuition** $4090 **Undergraduates** 51% women, 17% part-time, 16% 25 or older, 1% Native American, 2% Hispanic, 4% black, 9% Asian or Pacific Islander **Most popular recent majors** Business administration/commerce/management, psychology, mechanical engineering **Academic program** ESL program, Advanced placement, accelerated degree program, self-designed majors, tutorials, honors program, summer session, adult/continuing education programs, internships **Contact** Dr. Wayne Sigler, Director of Admissions, University of Minnesota, Twin Cities Campus, 240 Williamson, Minneapolis, MN 55455-0213. Telephone: 612-625-2006. Fax: 612-626-1693.

UNIVERSITY OF ST. THOMAS
ST. PAUL, MINNESOTA

Entrance Moderately difficult **General** Independent Roman Catholic, coed **Setting** 78-acre urban campus **Enrollment** 10,324 **Faculty** 17:1 **Application deadline** Rolling **Freshmen** 91% accepted **Housing** Yes **Tuition** $14,660 **Undergraduates** 52% women, 17% part-time, 17% 25 or older, 0% Native American, 2% Hispanic, 3% black, 4% Asian or Pacific Islander **Most popular recent majors** Business administration/commerce/management, sociology, communication **Academic program** Advanced placement, self-designed majors, honors program, summer session, adult/continuing education programs, internships **Contact** Ms. Marla Friederichs, Director of Admissions, University of St. Thomas, Mail #32F-1, 2115 Summit Avenue, St. Paul, MN 55105-1096. Telephone: 612-962-6150. Fax: 612-962-6160.

WINONA STATE UNIVERSITY
WINONA, MINNESOTA

Entrance Moderately difficult **General** State-supported, comprehensive, coed **Setting** 40-acre small-town campus **Enrollment** 7,500 **Faculty** 21:1 **Application deadline** Rolling **Freshmen** 65% accepted **Housing** Yes **Tuition** $3116 **Undergraduates** 58% women, 15% part-time, 10% 25 or older, 1% Native American, 1% Hispanic, 2% black, 2% Asian or Pacific Islander **Most popular recent majors** Business administration/commerce/management, liberal arts/general studies, nursing **Academic program** Average class size 26, advanced placement, accelerated degree program, self-designed majors, tutorials, honors program, summer session, adult/continuing education programs, internships **Contact** Dr. J. A. Mootz, Director of Admissions, Winona State University, Winona, MN 55987-5838. Telephone: 507-457-5100. Fax: 507-457-5620.

Missouri

AVILA COLLEGE
KANSAS CITY, MISSOURI

Entrance Moderately difficult **General** Independent Roman Catholic, comprehensive, coed **Setting** 50-acre suburban campus **Enrollment** 1,275 **Faculty** 12:1 **Application deadline** Rolling **Freshmen** 90% accepted **Housing** Yes **Tuition** $10,800 **Undergraduates** 74% women, 37% part-time, 44% 25 or older, 1% Native American, 3% Hispanic, 9% black, 2% Asian or Pacific Islander **Most popular recent majors** Business administration/commerce/management, nursing, elementary education **Academic program** Average class size 19, advanced placement, accelerated degree program, tutorials, summer session, adult/continuing education programs, internships **Contact** Mr. Todd H. Moore, Director of Admissions, Avila College, Kansas City, MO 64145-1698. Telephone: 816-942-8400 Ext. 3500. Fax: 816-942-3362.

BAPTIST BIBLE COLLEGE
SPRINGFIELD, MISSOURI

Entrance Noncompetitive **General** Independent Baptist, comprehensive, coed **Setting** 38-acre campus **Enrollment** 893 **Application deadline** Rolling **Freshmen** 99% accepted **Housing** Yes **Tuition** $2528 **Undergraduates** 46% women, 7% part-time, 1% Native American, 1% Hispanic, 1% black, 2% Asian or Pacific Islander **Academic program** Summer session, internships **Contact** Dr. Joseph Gleason, Director of Admissions, Baptist Bible College, Springfield, MO 65803-3498. Telephone: 417-268-6000 Ext. 2219. Fax: 417-831-8029.

BEREAN UNIVERSITY OF THE ASSEMBLIES OF GOD
SPRINGFIELD, MISSOURI

Entrance Noncompetitive **General** Independent, comprehensive, specialized, coed, affiliated with Assemblies of God **Enrollment** 999 **Freshmen** 99% accepted **Tuition** $2208 **Undergraduates** 99% part-time, 25% 25 or older **Most popular recent majors** Biblical studies, theology **Academic program** Advanced placement, accelerated degree program, honors program, internships **Contact** Mr. Stephen M. Kersting, Registrar, Berean University of the Assemblies of God, Springfield, MO 65802-1805. Telephone: 417-862-2781 Ext. 2321. Fax: 417-862-5318.

CALVARY BIBLE COLLEGE AND THEOLOGICAL SEMINARY
KANSAS CITY, MISSOURI

Entrance Minimally difficult **General** Independent-religious, comprehensive, coed **Setting** 55-acre suburban campus **Enrollment** 317 **Faculty** 10:1 **Application deadline** Rolling **Freshmen** 80% accepted **Housing** Yes **Tuition** $4570 **Undergraduates** 43% women, 30% part-time, 34% 25 or older, 1% Native American, 1% Hispanic, 3% black, 1% Asian or Pacific Islander **Most popular recent majors** Elementary education, pastoral studies, secondary education **Academic program** Advanced placement, accelerated degree program, self-designed majors, summer session, adult/continuing education programs, internships **Contact** Mr. Brian Krause, Director of Admissions, Calvary Bible College and Theological Seminary, Kansas City, MO 64147-1341. Telephone: 816-322-0110 Ext. 1326.

CENTRAL BIBLE COLLEGE
SPRINGFIELD, MISSOURI

Entrance Very difficult **General** Independent, 4-year, specialized, coed, affiliated with Assemblies of God **Setting** 82-acre suburban campus **Enrollment** 976 **Faculty** 20:1 **Application deadline** Rolling **Freshmen** 99% accepted **Housing** Yes **Tuition** $4750 **Undergraduates** 43% women, 10% part-time, 18% 25 or older, 1% Native American, 3% Hispanic, 1% black, 2% Asian or Pacific Islander **Most popular recent majors** Biblical studies, ministries, pastoral studies **Academic program** Advanced placement, summer session, internships **Contact** Mrs. Eunice A. Bruegman, Director of Admissions and Records, Central Bible College, Springfield, MO 65803-1096. Telephone: 417-833-2551 Ext. 1184. Fax: 417-833-5141.

CENTRAL CHRISTIAN COLLEGE OF THE BIBLE
MOBERLY, MISSOURI

Entrance Noncompetitive **General** Independent, 4-year, coed, affiliated with Christian Churches and Churches of Christ **Setting** 40-acre small-town campus **Enrollment** 135 **Faculty** 10:1 **Application deadline** Rolling **Housing** Yes **Tuition** $4495 **Undergraduates** 49% women, 16% part-time, 14% 25 or older, 0% Native American, 0% Hispanic, 1% black, 0% Asian or Pacific Islander **Academic program** Self-designed majors, internships **Contact** Mr. Troy Titus, Director of Admissions, Central Christian College of the Bible, Moberly, MO 65270-1997. Telephone: 816-263-3900.

CENTRAL METHODIST COLLEGE
FAYETTE, MISSOURI

Entrance Moderately difficult **General** Independent Methodist, comprehensive, coed **Setting** 52-acre small-town campus **Enrollment** 1,152 **Faculty** 12:1 **Application deadline** Rolling **Freshmen** 90% accepted **Housing** Yes **Tuition** $10,220 **Undergraduates** 57% women, 12% part-time, 10% 25 or older, 0% Native American, 1% Hispanic, 7% black, 1% Asian or Pacific Islander **Most popular recent majors** Business administration/commerce/management, biology/biological sciences, physical education **Academic program** Accelerated degree program, self-designed majors, tutorials, honors program, summer session, internships **Contact** Mr. David Heinger, Vice President for Student Enrollment, Central Methodist College, Fayette, MO 65248-1198. Telephone: 816-248-3391 Ext. 251.

CENTRAL MISSOURI STATE UNIVERSITY
WARRENSBURG, MISSOURI

Entrance Moderately difficult **General** State-supported, comprehensive, coed **Setting** 1,166-acre small-town campus **Enrollment** 10,770 **Faculty** 17:1 **Application deadline** Rolling **Freshmen** 77% accepted **Housing** Yes **Tuition** $2728 **Undergraduates** 53% women, 19% part-time, 22% 25 or older, 1% Native American, 1% Hispanic, 7% black, 1% Asian or Pacific Islander **Most popular recent majors** Elementary education, criminal justice, aviation technology **Academic program** Advanced placement, accelerated degree program, self-designed majors, tutorials, honors program, summer session, adult/continuing education programs, internships **Contact** Mrs. Delores Hudson, Director of Admissions, Central Missouri State University, Warrensburg, MO 64093. Telephone: 816-543-4290. Fax: 816-543-8517.

COLLEGE OF THE OZARKS
POINT LOOKOUT, MISSOURI

Entrance Moderately difficult **General** Independent Presbyterian, 4-year, coed **Setting** 1,000-acre small-town campus **Enrollment** 1,525 **Faculty** 14:1 **Application deadline** Rolling **Freshmen** 19% accepted **Housing** Yes **Tuition** $150 **Undergraduates** 53% women, 15% part-time, 11% 25 or older, 1% Native American, 1% Hispanic, 1% black, 1% Asian or Pacific Islander **Most popular recent majors** Education, business administration/commerce/management, psychology **Academic program** Average class size 35, advanced placement, accelerated degree program, self-designed majors, tutorials, honors program, summer session, internships **Contact** Mrs. Janet Miller, Admissions Secretary, College of the Ozarks, Point Lookout, MO 65726. Telephone: 417-334-6411 Ext. 4217. Fax: 417-335-2618.

COLUMBIA COLLEGE
COLUMBIA, MISSOURI

Entrance Moderately difficult **General** Independent, comprehensive, coed, affiliated with Christian Church (Disciples of Christ) **Setting** 29-acre small-town campus **Enrollment** 855 **Faculty** 10:1 **Application deadline** Rolling **Freshmen** 76% accepted **Housing** Yes **Tuition** $9244 **Undergraduates** 56% women, 20% part-time, 21% 25 or older, 0% Native American, 2% Hispanic, 6% black, 2% Asian or Pacific Islander **Most popular recent majors** Business administration/commerce/management, art/fine arts, education **Academic program** Advanced placement, accelerated degree program, self-designed majors, honors program, summer session, adult/continuing education programs, internships **Contact** Director of Admissions, Columbia College, Columbia, MO 65216-0002. Telephone: 573-875-7352. Fax: 573-875-7506.

CONCEPTION SEMINARY COLLEGE
CONCEPTION, MISSOURI

Entrance Noncompetitive **General** Independent Roman Catholic, 4-year, primarily men **Setting** 30-acre rural campus **Enrollment** 64 **Faculty** 3:1 **Application deadline** 7/31 **Housing** Yes **Tuition** $7184 **Undergraduates** 7% women, 12% part-time, 35% 25 or older, 0% Native American, 4% Hispanic, 13% Asian or Pacific Islander **Academic program** Advanced placement **Contact** Fr. Daniel Petsche, OSB, Director of Admissions, Conception Seminary College, Conception, MO 64433-0502. Telephone: 816-944-2806. Fax: 816-944-2829.

CULVER-STOCKTON COLLEGE
CANTON, MISSOURI

Entrance Moderately difficult **General** Independent, 4-year, coed, affiliated with Christian Church (Disciples of Christ) **Setting** 143-acre rural campus **Enrollment** 1,031 **Faculty** 16:1 **Application deadline** Rolling **Freshmen** 91% accepted **Housing** Yes **Tuition** $9200 **Undergraduates** 65% women, 11% part-time, 13% 25 or older, 2% black, 1% Asian or Pacific Islander **Most popular recent majors** Nursing, business administration/commerce/management, elementary education **Academic program** Average class size 27, advanced placement, accelerated degree program, self-designed majors, tutorials, honors program, summer session, adult/continuing education programs, internships **Contact** Ms. Betty A. Smith, Dean of Admissions, Culver-Stockton College, Canton, MO 63435-1299. Telephone: 217-231-6461. Fax: 217-231-6612.

DEACONESS COLLEGE OF NURSING
ST. LOUIS, MISSOURI

Entrance Moderately difficult **General** Independent, 4-year, specialized, coed, affiliated with United Church of Christ **Setting** 15-acre urban campus **Enrollment** 380 **Application deadline** Rolling **Freshmen** 75% accepted **Housing** Yes **Tuition** $7560 **Undergraduates** 88% women, 21% part-time, 22% 25 or older, 0% Native American, 1% Hispanic, 11% black, 2% Asian or Pacific Islander **Academic program** Advanced placement, summer session **Contact** Ms. Barbara Bizer, Student Services Coordinator, Deaconess College of Nursing, 6150 Oakland Avenue, St. Louis, MO 63139-3215. Telephone: 314-768-3044.

DEVRY INSTITUTE OF TECHNOLOGY
KANSAS CITY, MISSOURI

Entrance Minimally difficult **General** Proprietary, 4-year, coed **Setting** 12-acre urban campus **Enrollment** 2,130 **Faculty** 28:1 **Application deadline** Rolling **Freshmen** 75% accepted **Tuition** $6968 **Undergraduates** 22% women, 26% part-time, 47% 25 or older, 0% Native American, 2% Hispanic, 11% black, 2% Asian or Pacific Islander **Most popular recent majors** Telecommunications, computer information systems, electrical and electronics technologies **Academic program** Advanced placement, accelerated degree program, summer session, adult/continuing education programs **Contact** Mr. Michael Thompson, Director of Admissions, DeVry Institute of Technology, 11224 Holmes Road, Kansas City, MO 64131-3698. Telephone: 816-941-2810.

DRURY COLLEGE
SPRINGFIELD, MISSOURI

Entrance Moderately difficult **General** Independent, comprehensive, coed **Setting** 60-acre urban campus **Enrollment** 1,620 **Faculty** 11:1 **Application deadline** Rolling **Freshmen** 93% accepted **Housing** Yes **Tuition** $10,060 **Undergraduates** 54% women, 4% part-time, 5% 25 or older, 0% Native American, 1% Hispanic, 1% black, 1% Asian or Pacific Islander **Most popular recent majors** Business administration/commerce/management, communication, behavioral sciences **Academic program** Advanced placement, accelerated degree program, tutorials, honors program, summer session, adult/continuing education programs, internships **Contact** Mr. Michael Thomas, Director of Admissions, Drury College, 900 North Benton Avenue, Springfield, MO 65802-3791. Telephone: 417-873-7205. Fax: 417-873-7529.

EVANGEL COLLEGE
SPRINGFIELD, MISSOURI

Entrance Moderately difficult **General** Independent, 4-year, coed, affiliated with Assemblies of God **Setting** 80-acre urban campus **Enrollment** 1,574 **Faculty** 18:1 **Application deadline** 8/15 **Freshmen** 91% accepted **Housing** Yes **Tuition** $8065 **Undergraduates** 58% women, 8% part-time, 2% 25 or older, 1% Native American, 1% Hispanic, 5% black **Most popular recent majors** Business administration/commerce/management, education, communication **Academic program** Advanced placement, summer session **Contact** Mr. David I. Schoolfield, Executive Director of Enrollment, Evangel College, 1111 North Glenstone, Springfield, MO 65802-2191. Telephone: 417-865-2811 Ext. 7202. Fax: 417-865-9599.

FONTBONNE COLLEGE
ST. LOUIS, MISSOURI

Entrance Moderately difficult **General** Independent Roman Catholic, comprehensive, coed **Setting** 13-acre suburban campus **Enrollment** 1,882 **Application deadline** 8/1 **Freshmen** 84% accepted **Housing** Yes **Tuition** $10,150 **Undergraduates** 71% women, 20% part-time, 40% 25 or older, 1% Native American, 1% Hispanic, 12% black, 1% Asian or Pacific Islander **Most popular recent majors** Business administration/commerce/management, education **Academic program** Advanced placement, self-designed majors, honors program, summer session, adult/continuing education programs, internships **Contact** Ms. Peggy Musen, Associate Dean for Enrollment Management, Fontbonne College, St. Louis, MO 63105-3098. Telephone: 314-889-1400.

HANNIBAL-LAGRANGE COLLEGE
HANNIBAL, MISSOURI

Entrance Moderately difficult **General** Independent Southern Baptist, 4-year, coed **Setting** 110-acre small-town campus **Enrollment** 1,050 **Faculty** 15:1 **Application deadline** Rolling **Freshmen** 70% accepted **Housing** Yes **Tuition** $7590 **Undergraduates** 62% women, 41% part-time, 28% 25 or older, 1% Native American, 1% Hispanic, 2% black, 1% Asian or Pacific Islander **Most popular recent majors** Education, business administration/commerce/management **Academic program** Average class size 24, advanced placement, self-designed majors, honors program, summer session, adult/continuing education programs, internships **Contact** Mr. Raymond Carty, Dean of Enrollment Management, Hannibal-LaGrange College, Hannibal, MO 63401-1940. Telephone: 573-221-3113. Fax: 573-221-6594.

HARRIS-STOWE STATE COLLEGE
ST. LOUIS, MISSOURI

Entrance Minimally difficult **General** State-supported, 4-year, coed **Setting** 8-acre urban campus **Enrollment** 1,723 **Application deadline** Rolling **Freshmen** 66% accepted **Tuition** $2528 **Undergraduates** 71% women, 45% part-time, 50% 25 or older, 1% Native American, 1% Hispanic, 71% black **Academic program** Accelerated degree program, summer session **Contact** Ms. Valerie

A. Beeson, Director of Admissions and Academic Advisement, Harris-Stowe State College, 3026 Laclede Avenue, St. Louis, MO 63103-2136. Telephone: 314-340-3300. Fax: 314-340-3322.

JEWISH HOSPITAL COLLEGE OF NURSING AND ALLIED HEALTH

ST. LOUIS, MISSOURI

Entrance Moderately difficult **General** Independent, comprehensive, primarily women **Setting** Urban campus **Enrollment** 449 **Faculty** 10:1 **Application deadline** Rolling **Freshmen** 69% accepted **Housing** Yes **Tuition** $8680 **Undergraduates** 89% women, 48% part-time, 70% 25 or older, 0% Native American, 1% Hispanic, 5% black, 2% Asian or Pacific Islander **Most popular recent major** Nursing **Academic program** Average class size 20, advanced placement, tutorials, summer session **Contact** Ms. Constance J. Stohlman, Chief Admissions Officer, Jewish Hospital College of Nursing and Allied Health, 306 South Kingshighway, St. Louis, MO 63110-1091. Telephone: 314-454-7057. Fax: 314-454-5239.

KANSAS CITY ART INSTITUTE

KANSAS CITY, MISSOURI

Entrance Moderately difficult **General** Independent, 4-year, specialized, coed **Setting** 12-acre urban campus **Enrollment** 598 **Faculty** 12:1 **Application deadline** Rolling **Freshmen** 70% accepted **Housing** Yes **Tuition** $16,320 **Undergraduates** 44% women, 3% part-time, 96% 25 or older, 1% Native American, 5% Hispanic, 2% black, 3% Asian or Pacific Islander **Academic program** Average class size 20, advanced placement, summer session, adult/continuing education programs, internships **Contact** Mr. Gerald Valet, Admissions Office Supervisor, Kansas City Art Institute, 4415 Warwick Boulevard, Kansas City, MO 64111-9738. Telephone: 816-931-5224.

LINCOLN UNIVERSITY

JEFFERSON CITY, MISSOURI

Entrance Noncompetitive **General** State-supported, comprehensive, coed **Setting** 152-acre small-town campus **Enrollment** 2,979 **Faculty** 15:1 **Application deadline** 8/1 **Freshmen** 90% accepted **Housing** Yes **Tuition** $2076 **Undergraduates** 60% women, 38% part-time, 35% 25 or older, 1% Native American, 1% Hispanic, 25% black, 1% Asian or Pacific Islander **Most popular recent majors** Nursing, elementary education, business administration/commerce/management **Academic program** Advanced placement, accelerated degree program, self-designed majors, tutorials, honors program, summer session, adult/continuing education programs, internships **Contact** Mr. Mohammed Khaleel, Admissions Officer III, Lincoln University, Jefferson City, MO 65102. Telephone: 573-681-5024.

LINDENWOOD COLLEGE

ST. CHARLES, MISSOURI

Entrance Moderately difficult **General** Independent Presbyterian, comprehensive, coed **Setting** 200-acre suburban campus **Enrollment** 4,293 **Faculty** 17:1 **Application deadline** Rolling **Freshmen** 55% accepted **Housing** Yes **Tuition** $10,150 **Undergraduates** 58% women, 7% part-time, 38% 25 or older, 1% Native American, 1% Hispanic, 58% black, 1% Asian or Pacific Islander **Most popular recent majors** Business administration/commerce/management, communication, education **Academic program** Advanced placement, accelerated degree program, self-designed majors, tutorials, honors program, summer session, adult/continuing education programs, internships **Contact** Dr. David R. Williams, Dean of Admissions and Financial Aid, Lindenwood College, St. Charles, MO 63301-1695. Telephone: 314-949-4935. Fax: 314-949-4910.

LOGAN COLLEGE OF CHIROPRACTIC

CHESTERFIELD, MISSOURI

Entrance Moderately difficult **General** Independent, upper-level, specialized, coed **Setting** 100-acre suburban campus **Enrollment** 1,054 **Faculty** 13:1 **Application deadline** Rolling **Freshmen** 75% accepted **Tuition** $8974 **Undergraduates** 27% women, 0% part-time, 50% 25 or older, 1% Native American, 1% Hispanic, 2% black, 4% Asian or Pacific Islander **Academic program** Advanced placement, adult/continuing education programs, internships **Contact** Mr. Melvin Reynolds, Dean of Admissions, Logan College of Chiropractic, Chesterfield, MO 63006-1065. Telephone: 314-227-2100 Ext. 156. Fax: 314-227-9338.

MARYVILLE UNIVERSITY OF SAINT LOUIS

ST. LOUIS, MISSOURI

Entrance Moderately difficult **General** Independent, comprehensive, coed **Setting** 130-acre suburban campus **Enrollment** 3,196 **Faculty** 14:1 **Application deadline** Rolling **Freshmen** 81% accepted **Housing** Yes **Tuition** $10,910 **Undergraduates** 71% women, 54% part-time, 56% 25 or older, 1% Native American, 1% Hispanic, 4% black, 1% Asian or Pacific Islander **Most popular recent majors** Business administration/commerce/

management, nursing, accounting **Academic program** Average class size 15, advanced placement, accelerated degree program, tutorials, honors program, summer session, adult/continuing education programs, internships **Contact** Dr. Martha Wade, Dean of Admissions and Enrollment Management, Maryville University of Saint Louis, St. Louis, MO 63141-7299. Telephone: 314-529-9350. Fax: 314-542-9085.

MESSENGER COLLEGE
JOPLIN, MISSOURI

Entrance Moderately difficult **General** Independent-religious, 4-year, coed **Setting** 16-acre small-town campus **Enrollment** 93 **Application deadline** 9/1 **Freshmen** 95% accepted **Housing** Yes **Tuition** $2880 **Undergraduates** 40% women, 11% part-time **Academic program** Honors program, internships **Contact** Mrs. Gwen Minor, Registrar, Messenger College, Joplin, MO 64803. Telephone: 417-624-7070.

MISSOURI BAPTIST COLLEGE
ST. LOUIS, MISSOURI

Entrance Moderately difficult **General** Independent Southern Baptist, 4-year, coed **Setting** 65-acre suburban campus **Enrollment** 2,423 **Faculty** 20:1 **Application deadline** Rolling **Freshmen** 75% accepted **Housing** Yes **Tuition** $8450 **Undergraduates** 60% women, 69% part-time, 12% 25 or older, 1% Native American, 1% Hispanic, 9% black, 1% Asian or Pacific Islander **Most popular recent majors** Elementary education, business administration/commerce/management, religious education **Academic program** Advanced placement, accelerated degree program, summer session, internships **Contact** Mrs. Gloria Vertrees, Director of Enrollment Management, Missouri Baptist College, St. Louis, MO 63141-8698. Telephone: 314-434-1115 Ext. 4111.

MISSOURI SOUTHERN STATE COLLEGE
JOPLIN, MISSOURI

Entrance Moderately difficult **General** State-supported, 4-year, coed **Setting** 350-acre small-town campus **Enrollment** 5,258 **Faculty** 27:1 **Application deadline** 8/16 **Freshmen** 99% accepted **Housing** Yes **Tuition** $2384 **Undergraduates** 56% women, 35% part-time, 36% 25 or older, 3% Native American, 1% Hispanic, 1% black, 1% Asian or Pacific Islander **Most popular recent majors** Business administration/commerce/management, education, law enforcement/police sciences **Academic program** Average class size 27, advanced placement, accelerated degree program, honors program, summer session, adult/continuing education programs, internships **Contact** Mr. Richard D. Humphrey, Director of Admission, Missouri Southern State College, Joplin, MO 64801-1595. Telephone: 417-625-9537. Fax: 417-659-4429 Ext. 537.

MISSOURI TECHNICAL SCHOOL
ST. LOUIS, MISSOURI

Entrance Moderately difficult **General** Proprietary, 4-year, specialized, coed **Setting** Suburban campus **Enrollment** 231 **Application deadline** Rolling **Tuition** $7396 **Undergraduates** 14% women **Academic program** Advanced placement, accelerated degree program, tutorials, internships **Contact** Mr. Bob Honaker, Director of Admissions, Missouri Technical School, St. Louis, MO 63132-1716. Telephone: 314-569-3600. Fax: 314-569-1167.

MISSOURI VALLEY COLLEGE
MARSHALL, MISSOURI

Entrance Moderately difficult **General** Independent, 4-year, coed, affiliated with Presbyterian Church **Setting** 140-acre small-town campus **Enrollment** 1,214 **Faculty** 20:1 **Application deadline** Rolling **Freshmen** 82% accepted **Housing** Yes **Tuition** $10,300 **Undergraduates** 38% women, 4% part-time, 10% 25 or older, 2% Native American, 2% Hispanic, 14% black, 1% Asian or Pacific Islander **Most popular recent majors** Business administration/commerce/management, education, psychology **Academic program** Average class size 20, advanced placement, accelerated degree program, self-designed majors, tutorials, summer session, adult/continuing education programs, internships **Contact** Ms. Debbie Bultman, Admissions, Missouri Valley College, Marshall, MO 65340-3197. Telephone: 816-831-4114. Fax: 816-831-4039.

MISSOURI WESTERN STATE COLLEGE
ST. JOSEPH, MISSOURI

Entrance Noncompetitive **General** State-supported, 4-year, coed **Setting** 744-acre suburban campus **Enrollment** 5,109 **Faculty** 18:1 **Application deadline** 7/30 **Freshmen** 99% accepted **Housing** Yes **Tuition** $2534 **Undergraduates** 62% women, 29% part-time, 31% 25 or older, 1% Native American, 2% Hispanic, 7% black, 1% Asian or Pacific Islander **Most popular recent majors** Criminal justice, nursing, elementary education **Academic program** Advanced placement, accelerated degree program, honors program, summer session, adult/continuing education programs, internships **Contact** Mr. Howard McCauley, Director of Admissions, Missouri Western State College, St. Joseph, MO 64507-2294. Telephone: 816-271-4267. Fax: 816-271 5833.

NATIONAL COLLEGE
KANSAS CITY, MISSOURI

Entrance Noncompetitive **General** Proprietary, 4-year, coed **Setting** 1-acre urban campus **Enrollment** 156 **Application deadline** Rolling **Freshmen** 95% accepted **Tuition** $8400 **Undergraduates** 49% women, 23% part-time, 97% 25 or older, 0% Native American, 3% Hispanic, 51% black, 3% Asian or Pacific Islander **Most popular recent majors** Business administration/commerce/management, computer information systems **Academic program** Tutorials, summer session **Contact** Ms. Tanya Carr, Director of Admissions, National College, 4200 Blue Ridge Boulevard, Kansas City, MO 64133-1612. Telephone: 816-353-4554. Fax: 816-353-1176.

NORTHEAST MISSOURI STATE UNIVERSITY
SEE TRUMAN STATE UNIVERSITY

NORTHWEST MISSOURI STATE UNIVERSITY
MARYVILLE, MISSOURI

Entrance Moderately difficult **General** State-supported, comprehensive, coed **Setting** 240-acre small-town campus **Enrollment** 6,154 **Faculty** 27:1 **Application deadline** Rolling **Freshmen** 91% accepted **Housing** Yes **Tuition** $2713 **Undergraduates** 55% women, 47% part-time, 7% 25 or older, 1% Native American, 1% Hispanic, 2% black, 1% Asian or Pacific Islander **Academic program** Advanced placement, accelerated degree program, tutorials, summer session, internships **Contact** Mr. Roger Pugh, Dean of Enrollment Management, Northwest Missouri State University, Maryville, MO 64468-6001. Telephone: 816-562-1562. Fax: 816-562-1121.

OZARK CHRISTIAN COLLEGE
JOPLIN, MISSOURI

Entrance Noncompetitive **General** Independent Christian, 4-year, coed **Setting** 110-acre suburban campus **Enrollment** 661 **Faculty** 20:1 **Application deadline** 8/15 **Freshmen** 100% accepted **Housing** Yes **Tuition** $4025 **Undergraduates** 44% women, 12% part-time, 30% 25 or older, 1% Native American, 1% Hispanic, 1% black, 1% Asian or Pacific Islander **Academic program** Summer session, adult/continuing education programs, internships **Contact** Mr. James Marcum, Director of Admissions, Ozark Christian College, Joplin, MO 64801-4804. Telephone: 417-624-2518 Ext. 260.

PARK COLLEGE
PARKVILLE, MISSOURI

Entrance Moderately difficult **General** Independent, comprehensive, coed, affiliated with Reorganized Church of Jesus Christ of Latter Day Saints **Setting** 800-acre suburban campus **Enrollment** 1,207 **Faculty** 14:1 **Application deadline** 8/1 **Freshmen** 74% accepted **Housing** Yes **Tuition** $4410 **Undergraduates** 63% women, 32% part-time, 32% 25 or older, 1% Native American, 5% Hispanic, 11% black, 2% Asian or Pacific Islander **Most popular recent majors** Business administration/commerce/management, criminal justice, elementary education **Academic program** Average class size 25, advanced placement, self-designed majors, honors program, summer session, adult/continuing education programs, internships **Contact** Mr. Randy Condit, Director of Admissions, Park College, Parkville, MO 64152-4358. Telephone: 816-741-2000 Ext. 6215. Fax: 816-746-6423.

RESEARCH COLLEGE OF NURSING–ROCKHURST COLLEGE
KANSAS CITY, MISSOURI

Entrance Moderately difficult **General** Independent, comprehensive, specialized, coed **Setting** 66-acre urban campus **Enrollment** 274 **Application deadline** 6/30 **Freshmen** 78% accepted **Housing** Yes **Tuition** $12,150 **Undergraduates** 92% women, 17% part-time, 11% 25 or older, 0% Native American, 4% Hispanic, 9% black, 1% Asian or Pacific Islander **Academic program** Average class size 30, advanced placement, honors program **Contact** Mrs. Leslie A. Mendenhall, Assistant Director of Admissions, Research College of Nursing–Rockhurst College, 2316 East Meyer Boulevard, Kansas City, MO 64132. Telephone: 816-501-4100. Fax: 816-501-4588.

ROCKHURST COLLEGE
KANSAS CITY, MISSOURI

Entrance Moderately difficult **General** Independent Roman Catholic (Jesuit), comprehensive, coed **Setting** 35-acre urban campus **Enrollment** 2,866 **Faculty** 11:1 **Application deadline** Rolling **Freshmen** 91% accepted **Housing** Yes **Tuition** $11,790 **Undergraduates** 58% women, 23% part-time, 18% 25 or older, 1% Native American, 4% Hispanic, 6% black, 2% Asian or Pacific Islander **Most popular recent majors** Nursing, psychology, biology/biological sciences **Aca-**

demic program Advanced placement, accelerated degree program, tutorials, honors program, summer session, adult/continuing education programs, internships **Contact** Mr. Jack Reichmeier, Director of Admissions, Rockhurst College, 1100 Rockhurst Road, Kansas City, MO 64110-2561. Telephone: 816-501-4100. Fax: 816-501-4588.

ST. LOUIS CHRISTIAN COLLEGE

FLORISSANT, MISSOURI

Entrance Minimally difficult **General** Independent Christian, 4-year, coed **Setting** 20-acre suburban campus **Enrollment** 176 **Faculty** 11:1 **Application deadline** 7/1 **Freshmen** 85% accepted **Housing** Yes **Tuition** $4703 **Undergraduates** 41% women, 18% part-time, 50% 25 or older, 0% Native American, 0% Hispanic, 14% black **Most popular recent majors** Ministries, religious education, liberal arts/general studies **Academic program** Average class size 20, ESL program, advanced placement, accelerated degree program, tutorials, adult/continuing education programs, internships **Contact** Ms. Wanda Reed, Registrar, St. Louis Christian College, 1360 Grandview Drive, Florissant, MO 63033-6499. Telephone: 314-837-6777 Ext. 1500. Fax: 314-837-8291.

ST. LOUIS COLLEGE OF PHARMACY

ST. LOUIS, MISSOURI

Entrance Moderately difficult **General** Independent, comprehensive, specialized, coed **Setting** 5-acre urban campus **Enrollment** 832 **Faculty** 12:1 **Application deadline** Rolling **Freshmen** 87% accepted **Housing** Yes **Tuition** $11,600 **Undergraduates** 62% women, 5% part-time, 15% 25 or older, 0% Native American, 1% Hispanic, 2% black, 10% Asian or Pacific Islander **Academic program** Advanced placement, tutorials, summer session, adult/continuing education programs, internships **Contact** Ms. Lisa Boeschen, Director of Admissions, St. Louis College of Pharmacy, 4588 Parkview Place, St. Louis, MO 63110-1088. Telephone: 314-367-8700 Ext. 1072. Fax: 314-367-2784.

SAINT LOUIS UNIVERSITY

ST. LOUIS, MISSOURI

Entrance Moderately difficult **General** Independent Roman Catholic (Jesuit), coed **Setting** 279-acre urban campus **Enrollment** 10,572 **Faculty** 14:1 **Application deadline** Rolling **Freshmen** 76% accepted **Housing** Yes **Tuition** $15,050 **Undergraduates** 54% women, 11% part-time, 19% 25 or older, 1% Native American, 2% Hispanic, 9% black, 4% Asian or Pacific Islander **Most popular recent majors** (pre)law sequence, business administration/commerce/management, education **Academic program** Average class size 22, advanced placement, accelerated degree program, self-designed majors, tutorials, honors program, summer session, adult/continuing education programs, internships **Contact** Ms. Patsy Brooks, Credential Evaluator for Undergraduate Admissions, Saint Louis University, 221 North Grand Boulevard, St. Louis, MO 63103-2097. Telephone: 314-977-2500. Fax: 314-977-7136.

SAINT LUKE'S COLLEGE

KANSAS CITY, MISSOURI

Entrance Difficulty N/R **General** Independent Episcopal, upper-level, coed **Setting** 3-acre urban campus **Enrollment** 108 **Faculty** 8:1 **Application deadline** 12/15 **Freshmen** 26% accepted **Housing** Yes **Tuition** $7070 **Undergraduates** 88% women, 11% part-time, 80% 25 or older, 1% Hispanic, 6% black, 3% Asian or Pacific Islander **Academic program** Average class size 50, tutorials, summer session **Contact** Ms. Marsha Thomas, Director, Admissions and Records, Saint Luke's College, 4426 Wornall Road, Kansas City, MO 64111. Telephone: 816-932-2073.

SOUTHEAST MISSOURI STATE UNIVERSITY

CAPE GIRARDEAU, MISSOURI

Entrance Moderately difficult **General** State-supported, comprehensive, coed **Setting** 800-acre small-town campus **Enrollment** 8,200 **Faculty** 18:1 **Application deadline** 7/15 **Freshmen** 90% accepted **Housing** Yes **Tuition** $3100 **Undergraduates** 56% women, 19% part-time, 19% 25 or older, 1% Native American, 1% Hispanic, 5% black, 1% Asian or Pacific Islander **Most popular recent majors** Business administration/commerce/management, education, communication **Academic program** Advanced placement, accelerated degree program, self-designed majors, tutorials, honors program, summer session, adult/continuing education programs, internships **Contact** Mr. Jay Goff, Assistant Director of Admissions, Southeast Missouri State University, Cape Girardeau, MO 63701-4799. Telephone: 573-651-2590.

SOUTHWEST BAPTIST UNIVERSITY

BOLIVAR, MISSOURI

Entrance Moderately difficult **General** Independent Southern Baptist, comprehensive, coed **Setting** 152-acre small-town campus **Enrollment** 3,096 **Faculty** 18:1 **Application deadline** 9/6 **Freshmen** 66% accepted **Housing** Yes **Tuition**

$8332 **Undergraduates** 65% women, 30% part-time, 31% 25 or older, 1% Native American, 1% Hispanic, 1% black, 1% Asian or Pacific Islander **Most popular recent majors** Nursing, elementary education, business administration/commerce/management **Academic program** Advanced placement, accelerated degree program, honors program, summer session, adult/continuing education programs, internships **Contact** Mr. Ronn Ramey, Senior Director, Admissions and Student Financial Planning, Southwest Baptist University, 1600 University Avenue, Bolivar, MO 65613-2597. Telephone: 417-326-1822. Fax: 417-326-1514.

SOUTHWEST MISSOURI STATE UNIVERSITY
SPRINGFIELD, MISSOURI

Entrance Moderately difficult **General** State-supported, comprehensive, coed **Setting** 183-acre suburban campus **Enrollment** 15,535 **Faculty** 18:1 **Application deadline** 8/1 **Freshmen** 94% accepted **Housing** Yes **Tuition** $3060 **Undergraduates** 55% women, 21% part-time, 10% 25 or older, 1% Native American, 1% Hispanic, 3% black, 1% Asian or Pacific Islander **Most popular recent majors** Elementary education, psychology, marketing/retailing/merchandising **Academic program** Advanced placement, accelerated degree program, self-designed majors, tutorials, honors program, summer session, adult/continuing education programs, internships **Contact** Ms. Jill Duncan, Acting Director of Admissions, Southwest Missouri State University, Springfield, MO 65804-0094. Telephone: 417-836-5517. Fax: 417-836-6334.

STEPHENS COLLEGE
COLUMBIA, MISSOURI

Entrance Moderately difficult **General** Independent, 4-year, women only **Setting** 244-acre urban campus **Enrollment** 789 **Faculty** 11:1 **Application deadline** 7/31 **Freshmen** 95% accepted **Housing** Yes **Tuition** $14,830 **Undergraduates** 38% part-time, 8% 25 or older, 1% Native American, 4% Hispanic, 8% black, 1% Asian or Pacific Islander **Most popular recent majors** Fashion merchandising, theater arts/drama, business administration/commerce/management **Academic program** Advanced placement, accelerated degree program, self-designed majors, tutorials, summer session, adult/continuing education programs, internships **Contact** Ms. Annabelle Smith, Director of Admissions, Stephens College, Box 2121, Columbia, MO 65215-0002. Telephone: 573-876-7207. Fax: 573-876-7237.

TRUMAN STATE UNIVERSITY
KIRKSVILLE, MISSOURI

Entrance Moderately difficult **General** State-supported, comprehensive, coed **Setting** 140-acre small-town campus **Enrollment** 6,261 **Faculty** 16:1 **Application deadline** 3/1 **Freshmen** 72% accepted **Housing** Yes **Tuition** $3274 **Undergraduates** 57% women, 5% part-time, 3% 25 or older, 0% Native American, 2% Hispanic, 4% black, 2% Asian or Pacific Islander **Most popular recent majors** Business administration/commerce/management, biology/biological sciences, psychology **Academic program** Average class size 22, advanced placement, accelerated degree program, honors program, summer session, internships **Contact** Mr. Brad Chambers, Co-director of Admissions, Truman State University, 205 McClain Hall, Kirksville, MO 63501-4221. Telephone: 816-785-4114. Fax: 816-785-7456.

UNIVERSITY OF MISSOURI–COLUMBIA
COLUMBIA, MISSOURI

Entrance Moderately difficult **General** State-supported, coed **Setting** 1,348-acre small-town campus **Enrollment** 22,483 **Faculty** 19:1 **Application deadline** 5/1 **Freshmen** 90% accepted **Housing** Yes **Tuition** $4280 **Undergraduates** 53% women, 9% part-time, 7% 25 or older, 1% Native American, 1% Hispanic, 6% black, 3% Asian or Pacific Islander **Most popular recent majors** Business administration/commerce/management, engineering (general), education **Academic program** Advanced placement, accelerated degree program, self-designed majors, tutorials, honors program, summer session, adult/continuing education programs, internships **Contact** Ms. Georgeanne Porter, Director of Undergraduate Admissions, University of Missouri–Columbia, Columbia, MO 65211. Telephone: 573-882-7786. Fax: 573-882-7887.

UNIVERSITY OF MISSOURI–KANSAS CITY
KANSAS CITY, MISSOURI

Entrance Moderately difficult **General** State-supported, coed **Setting** 191-acre urban campus **Enrollment** 10,298 **Faculty** 10:1 **Application deadline** Rolling **Freshmen** 60% accepted **Housing** Yes **Tuition** $4278 **Undergraduates** 56% women, 36% part-time, 38% 25 or older, 1% Native American, 3% Hispanic, 10% black, 5% Asian or Pacific Islander **Most popular recent majors** Biology/biological sciences, liberal arts/general studies, psychology **Academic program** Advanced placement, accelerated degree program, self-designed majors, honors program, summer session, adult/continuing education programs, internships **Contact** Mr. Melvin C. Tyler, Director of Admissions, University of Missouri–Kansas City, 5100 Rockhill Road, Kansas City, MO 64110-2499. Telephone: 816-235-1111. Fax: 816-235-1717.

UNIVERSITY OF MISSOURI–ROLLA
ROLLA, MISSOURI

Entrance Very difficult **General** State-supported, coed **Setting** 284-acre small-town campus **Enrollment** 5,264 **Faculty** 14:1 **Application deadline** 7/1 **Freshmen** 97% accepted **Housing** Yes **Tuition** $4384 **Undergraduates** 25% women, 12% part-time, 10% 25 or older, 1% Native American, 2% Hispanic, 3% black, 3% Asian or Pacific Islander **Most popular recent majors** Mechanical engineering, electrical engineering, civil engineering **Academic program** Advanced placement, accelerated degree program, tutorials, honors program, summer session, adult/continuing education programs **Contact** Dr. Edward Hornsey, Director of Admissions and Financial Aid, University of Missouri–Rolla, 102 Parker Hall, Rolla, MO 65401-0249. Telephone: 573-341-4164.

UNIVERSITY OF MISSOURI–ST. LOUIS
ST. LOUIS, MISSOURI

Entrance Moderately difficult **General** State-supported, coed **Setting** 250-acre suburban campus **Enrollment** 23,344 **Faculty** 10:1 **Application deadline** Rolling **Freshmen** 72% accepted **Housing** Yes **Tuition** $4323 **Undergraduates** 60% women, 55% part-time, 44% 25 or older, 1% Native American, 1% Hispanic, 13% black, 3% Asian or Pacific Islander **Most popular recent majors** Education, business administration/commerce/management, psychology **Academic program** Advanced placement, accelerated degree program, self-designed majors, tutorials, honors program, summer session, adult/continuing education programs, internships **Contact** Mr. Donald Morris, Acting Director of Admissions, University of Missouri–St. Louis, Woods Hall, St. Louis, MO 63121-4499. Telephone: 314-516-5460. Fax: 314-516-5310.

WASHINGTON UNIVERSITY
ST. LOUIS, MISSOURI

Entrance Very difficult **General** Independent, coed **Setting** 169-acre suburban campus **Enrollment** 10,767 **Faculty** 7:1 **Application deadline** 1/15 **Freshmen** 51% accepted **Housing** Yes **Tuition** $21,210 **Undergraduates** 49% women, 8% part-time, 2% 25 or older, 1% Native American, 2% Hispanic, 6% black, 12% Asian or Pacific Islander **Most popular recent majors** Engineering (general), psychology, business administration/commerce/management **Academic program** Average class size 17, advanced placement, accelerated degree program, self-designed majors, tutorials, summer session, adult/continuing education programs, internships **Contact** Ms. Nanette Clift, Director of Recruitment, Washington University, Campus Box 1089, 1 Brookings Drive, St. Louis, MO 63130-4899. Telephone: 314-935-6000. Fax: 314-935-4290.

WEBSTER UNIVERSITY
ST. LOUIS, MISSOURI

Entrance Moderately difficult **General** Independent, comprehensive, coed **Setting** 47-acre suburban campus **Enrollment** 12,319 **Faculty** 16:1 **Application deadline** 8/1 **Freshmen** 80% accepted **Housing** Yes **Tuition** $10,860 **Undergraduates** 66% women, 50% part-time, 55% 25 or older, 1% Native American, 2% Hispanic, 10% black, 1% Asian or Pacific Islander **Most popular recent majors** Business administration/commerce/management, nursing, communication **Academic program** Advanced placement, accelerated degree program, self-designed majors, tutorials, summer session, adult/continuing education programs, internships **Contact** Mr. Niel DeVasto, Director of Admission, Webster University, 470 East Lockwood Avenue, St. Louis, MO 63119-3194. Telephone: 314-968-7000. Fax: 314-968-7115.

WESTMINSTER COLLEGE
FULTON, MISSOURI

Entrance Moderately difficult **General** Independent, 4-year, coed, affiliated with Presbyterian Church **Setting** 65-acre small-town campus **Enrollment** 653 **Faculty** 12:1 **Application deadline** Rolling **Freshmen** 89% accepted **Housing** Yes **Tuition** $11,940 **Undergraduates** 45% women, 2% part-time, 1% 25 or older, 2% Native American, 2% Hispanic, 2% black, 3% Asian or Pacific Islander **Most popular recent majors** Business administration/commerce/management, political science/government, English **Academic program** Average class size 20, advanced placement, accelerated degree program, self-designed majors, tutorials, honors program, summer session, adult/continuing education programs, internships **Contact** Ms. Carole Reynolds, Associate Dean of Admissions, Westminster College, Fulton, MO 65251-1299. Telephone: 573-592-1251. Fax: 573-592-1255.

WILLIAM JEWELL COLLEGE
LIBERTY, MISSOURI

Entrance Moderately difficult **General** Independent Baptist, 4-year, coed **Setting** 700-acre small-town campus **Enrollment** 1,172 **Faculty** 13:1 **Application deadline** Rolling **Freshmen** 87% accepted **Housing** Yes **Tuition** $11,850 **Undergraduates** 61% women, 4% part-time, 8% 25 or older, 1% Native American, 1% Hispanic, 2% black, 1% Asian or Pacific Islander **Most popular recent majors** Business administration/commerce/management, nursing, elementary education **Academic program** Advanced placement, accelerated degree program, self-designed majors, tutorials, honors program, summer session, adult/continuing education programs, internships **Contact** Mr. David Maltby, Dean of Enrollment Development, William Jewell College, Liberty, MO 64068-1843. Telephone: 816-781-7700 Ext. 5570. Fax: 816-415-5027.

WILLIAM WOODS UNIVERSITY
FULTON, MISSOURI

Entrance Moderately difficult **General** Independent, comprehensive, coed, affiliated with Christian Church (Disciples of Christ) **Setting** 160-acre small-town campus **Enrollment** 1,151 **Application deadline** Rolling **Freshmen** 83% accepted **Housing** Yes **Tuition** $12,200 **Undergraduates** 87% women, 31% part-time, 40% 25 or older, 0% Native American, 1% Hispanic, 3% black, 1% Asian or Pacific Islander **Most popular recent majors** Business administration/commerce/management, education, paralegal studies **Academic program** Advanced placement, accelerated degree program, self-designed majors, tutorials, honors program, summer session, adult/continuing education programs, internships **Contact** Ms. Mary Hawk, Dean of Admission, William Woods University, Fulton, MO 65251-1098. Telephone: 373-592-4221.

Nebraska

BELLEVUE UNIVERSITY
BELLEVUE, NEBRASKA

Entrance Minimally difficult **General** Independent, comprehensive, coed **Setting** 19-acre urban campus **Enrollment** 2,600 **Faculty** 27:1 **Application deadline** Rolling **Tuition** $3650 **Undergraduates** 52% women, 37% part-time, 80% 25 or older, 1% Native American, 2% Hispanic, 5% black, 1% Asian or Pacific Islander **Most popular recent majors** Business administration/commerce/management, accounting, management information systems **Academic program** Advanced placement, accelerated degree program, tutorials, summer session, adult/continuing education programs **Contact** Ms. Sharon Thonen, Director of Admissions, Bellevue University, 1000 Galvin Road South, Bellevue, NE 68005-3098. Telephone: 402-293-3767. Fax: 402-293-2020.

CHADRON STATE COLLEGE
CHADRON, NEBRASKA

Entrance Noncompetitive **General** State-supported, comprehensive, coed **Setting** 281-acre small-town campus **Enrollment** 2,983 **Faculty** 20:1 **Application deadline** Rolling **Freshmen** 100% accepted **Housing** Yes **Tuition** $2148 **Undergraduates** 55% women, 22% part-time, 15% 25 or older, 2% Native American, 2% Hispanic, 1% black, 1% Asian or Pacific Islander **Most popular recent majors** Business administration/commerce/management, education **Academic program** Advanced placement, honors program, summer session, adult/continuing education programs, internships **Contact** Ms. Terie Dawson, Director of Enrollment Management, Chadron State College, Chadron, NE 69337. Telephone: 308-432-6263. Fax: 308-432-6229.

CLARKSON COLLEGE
OMAHA, NEBRASKA

Entrance Moderately difficult **General** Independent, comprehensive, coed, affiliated with Episcopal Church **Setting** 3-acre urban campus **Enrollment** 570 **Faculty** 12:1 **Application deadline** Rolling **Freshmen** 61% accepted **Housing** Yes **Tuition** $9248 **Undergraduates** 86% women, 40% part-time, 56% 25 or older, 1% Native American, 2% Hispanic, 3% black, 1% Asian or Pacific Islander **Most popular recent major** Nursing **Academic program** Average class size 15, advanced placement, accelerated degree program, self-designed majors, tutorials, summer session, adult/continuing education programs, internships **Contact** Mr. Jeffrey S. Beals, Director of Enrollment Management, Clarkson College, 101 South 42nd Street, Omaha, NE 68131-2739. Telephone: 402-552-2551. Fax: 402-552-6057.

COLLEGE OF SAINT MARY
OMAHA, NEBRASKA

Entrance Moderately difficult **General** Independent Roman Catholic, 4-year, women only **Setting** 25-acre suburban campus **Enrollment** 1,069 **Faculty** 11:1 **Application deadline** Rolling **Freshmen** 81% accepted **Housing** Yes **Tuition**

$11,814 **Undergraduates** 45% part-time, 44% 25 or older, 1% Native American, 1% Hispanic, 2% black, 1% Asian or Pacific Islander **Most popular recent majors** Nursing, business administration/commerce/management, paralegal studies **Academic program** Average class size 25, advanced placement, tutorials, summer session, adult/continuing education programs, internships **Contact** Ms. Sheila K. Haggas, Vice President of Enrollment Services, College of Saint Mary, Omaha, NE 68124-2377. Telephone: 402-399-2407.

CONCORDIA COLLEGE
SEWARD, NEBRASKA

Entrance Moderately difficult **General** Independent, comprehensive, coed, affiliated with Lutheran Church–Missouri Synod **Setting** 120-acre small-town campus **Enrollment** 951 **Faculty** 9:1 **Application deadline** Rolling **Freshmen** 84% accepted **Housing** Yes **Tuition** $10,650 **Undergraduates** 55% women, 9% part-time, 8% 25 or older, 1% Native American, 1% Hispanic, 1% black, 1% Asian or Pacific Islander **Most popular recent majors** Education, business administration/commerce/management, commercial art **Academic program** Advanced placement, self-designed majors, honors program, summer session, adult/continuing education programs, internships **Contact** Mr. Don Vos, Director of Admission, Concordia College, Seward, NE 68434-1599. Telephone: 402-643-7233. Fax: 402-643-4073.

CREIGHTON UNIVERSITY
OMAHA, NEBRASKA

Entrance Moderately difficult **General** Independent Roman Catholic (Jesuit), coed **Setting** 85-acre urban campus **Enrollment** 6,158 **Faculty** 14:1 **Application deadline** Rolling **Freshmen** 92% accepted **Housing** Yes **Tuition** $12,756 **Undergraduates** 59% women, 15% part-time, 5% 25 or older, 1% Native American, 3% Hispanic, 3% black, 8% Asian or Pacific Islander **Most popular recent majors** Nursing, psychology, finance/banking **Academic program** Advanced placement, accelerated degree program, tutorials, honors program, summer session, adult/continuing education programs, internships **Contact** Ms. Laurie R. Vinduska, Director of Admissions, Creighton University, 2500 California Plaza, Omaha, NE 68178-0001. Telephone: 402-280-2703. Fax: 402-280-2685.

DANA COLLEGE
BLAIR, NEBRASKA

Entrance Moderately difficult **General** Independent, 4-year, coed, affiliated with Evangelical Lutheran Church in America **Setting** 150-acre small-town campus **Enrollment** 614 **Faculty** 12:1 **Application deadline** 8/1 **Freshmen** 91% accepted **Housing** Yes **Tuition** $11,580 **Undergraduates** 54% women, 7% part-time, 8% 25 or older, 0% Native American, 1% Hispanic, 2% black, 1% Asian or Pacific Islander **Most popular recent majors** Elementary education, business administration/commerce/management, social work **Academic program** Average class size 19, advanced placement, tutorials, honors program, summer session, adult/continuing education programs, internships **Contact** Mr. John Schueth, Director of Admissions, Dana College, Blair, NE 68008-1099. Telephone: 402-426-7222. Fax: 402-426-7386.

DOANE COLLEGE
CRETE, NEBRASKA

Entrance Moderately difficult **General** Independent, comprehensive, coed, affiliated with United Church of Christ **Setting** 300-acre small-town campus **Enrollment** 1,795 **Faculty** 13:1 **Application deadline** 8/1 **Freshmen** 90% accepted **Housing** Yes **Tuition** $11,450 **Undergraduates** 52% women, 3% part-time, 3% 25 or older, 0% Native American, 1% Hispanic, 2% black, 0% Asian or Pacific Islander **Most popular recent majors** Education, business administration/commerce/management, sociology **Academic program** Advanced placement, accelerated degree program, self-designed majors, tutorials, honors program, summer session, adult/continuing education programs, internships **Contact** Mr. Dan Kunzman, Dean of Admissions, Doane College, Crete, NE 68333-2430. Telephone: 402-826-8242. Fax: 402-826-8600.

GRACE UNIVERSITY
OMAHA, NEBRASKA

Entrance Moderately difficult **General** Independent nondenominational, comprehensive, coed **Setting** Urban campus **Enrollment** 468 **Faculty** 14:1 **Application deadline** Rolling **Freshmen** 92% accepted **Housing** Yes **Tuition** $7484 **Undergraduates** 48% women, 26% part-time, 1% Native American, 2% Hispanic, 5% black, 0% Asian or Pacific Islander **Academic program** Advanced placement, accelerated degree program, tutorials, summer session, adult/continuing education programs, internships **Contact** Ms. Terri L. Thomas, Director of Admissions, Grace University, Ninth and William, Omaha, NE 68108. Telephone: 402-449-2831. Fax: 402-341-9587.

HASTINGS COLLEGE
HASTINGS, NEBRASKA

Entrance Moderately difficult **General** Independent Presbyterian, comprehensive, coed **Setting** 88-acre small-town campus **Enrollment** 1,107 **Faculty** 13:1 **Application deadline** 7/15 **Freshmen** 94% accepted **Housing** Yes **Tuition** $11,368 **Undergraduates** 53% women, 4% part-time, 9% 25 or older, 0% Native American, 2% Hispanic, 2% black, 1% Asian or Pacific Islander **Most popular recent majors** Business administration/commerce/management, education, psychology **Academic program** Average class size 25, advanced placement, accelerated degree program, self-designed majors, tutorials, honors program, summer session, adult/continuing education programs, internships **Contact** Mr. Michael Karloff, Director of Admissions, Hastings College, 720 North Turner Avenue, Hastings, NE 68902-0269. Telephone: 402-461-7316. Fax: 402-463-3002.

MIDLAND LUTHERAN COLLEGE
FREMONT, NEBRASKA

Entrance Moderately difficult **General** Independent Lutheran, 4-year, coed **Setting** 27-acre small-town campus **Enrollment** 1,062 **Faculty** 15:1 **Application deadline** Rolling **Freshmen** 92% accepted **Housing** Yes **Tuition** $12,250 **Undergraduates** 55% women, 12% part-time, 12% 25 or older, 1% Native American, 1% Hispanic, 6% black, 1% Asian or Pacific Islander **Most popular recent majors** Business administration/commerce/management, education, nursing **Academic program** Advanced placement, self-designed majors, tutorials, summer session, internships **Contact** Mr. Roland R. Kahnk, Vice President for Enrollment Services, Midland Lutheran College, Fremont, NE 68025-4200. Telephone: 402-721-5487 Ext. 6500. Fax: 402-721-0250.

NEBRASKA CHRISTIAN COLLEGE
NORFOLK, NEBRASKA

Entrance Minimally difficult **General** Independent, 4-year, coed, affiliated with Christian Churches and Churches of Christ **Setting** 85-acre small-town campus **Enrollment** 141 **Faculty** 16:1 **Application deadline** Rolling **Freshmen** 80% accepted **Housing** Yes **Tuition** $4510 **Undergraduates** 50% women, 5% part-time, 12% 25 or older, 0% Native American, 1% black, 1% Asian or Pacific Islander **Academic program** Internships **Contact** Mr. Jerry Hopkins, Director of Admissions, Nebraska Christian College, Norfolk, NE 68701-2458. Telephone: 402-371-5960.

NEBRASKA METHODIST COLLEGE OF NURSING AND ALLIED HEALTH
OMAHA, NEBRASKA

Entrance Moderately difficult **General** Independent, 4-year, primarily women **Setting** 5-acre urban campus **Enrollment** 380 **Faculty** 10:1 **Application deadline** 4/1 **Freshmen** 88% accepted **Housing** Yes **Tuition** $8320 **Undergraduates** 90% women, 42% part-time, 45% 25 or older, 1% Native American, 1% Hispanic, 2% black, 2% Asian or Pacific Islander **Most popular recent major** Nursing **Academic program** Advanced placement, tutorials, summer session, internships **Contact** Ms. Deann Clyde-Sterner, Director of Admissions, Nebraska Methodist College of Nursing and Allied Health, 8501 West Dodge Road, Omaha, NE 68114-3426. Telephone: 402-354-4922.

NEBRASKA WESLEYAN UNIVERSITY
LINCOLN, NEBRASKA

Entrance Moderately difficult **General** Independent United Methodist, 4-year, coed **Setting** 50-acre suburban campus **Enrollment** 1,562 **Faculty** 13:1 **Application deadline** 3/15 **Freshmen** 99% accepted **Housing** Yes **Tuition** $11,220 **Undergraduates** 61% women, 12% part-time, 11% 25 or older, 0% Native American, 2% Hispanic, 2% black, 1% Asian or Pacific Islander **Most popular recent majors** Business administration/commerce/management, biology/biological sciences, psychology **Academic program** Average class size 23, advanced placement, summer session, adult/continuing education programs, internships **Contact** Mr. Ken Sieg, Director of Admissions, Nebraska Wesleyan University, Lincoln, NE 68504-2796. Telephone: 402-465-2218. Fax: 402-465-2179.

PERU STATE COLLEGE
PERU, NEBRASKA

Entrance Noncompetitive **General** State-supported, comprehensive, coed **Setting** 103-acre rural campus **Enrollment** 1,800 **Faculty** 16:1 **Application deadline** Rolling **Freshmen** 57% accepted **Housing** Yes **Tuition** $2145 **Undergraduates** 50% women, 31% part-time, 29% 25 or older, 1% Native American, 2% Hispanic, 2% black, 1% Asian or Pacific Islander **Most popular recent majors** Business administration/commerce/management, education, psychology **Academic program** Average class size 25, advanced placement, tutorials, honors program, summer session, adult/continuing education programs, internships **Contact** Mr. Louis T. Levy, Director of Admissions, Peru State College, Peru, NE 68421. Telephone: 402-872-3815 Ext. 2221.

UNION COLLEGE
LINCOLN, NEBRASKA

Entrance Noncompetitive **General** Independent Seventh-day Adventist, 4-year, coed **Setting** 26-acre suburban campus **Enrollment** 553 **Faculty** 10:1 **Application deadline** Rolling **Freshmen** 90% accepted **Housing** Yes **Tuition** $9926 **Undergraduates** 55% women, 23% part-time, 1% Native American, 5% Hispanic, 2% black, 2% Asian or Pacific Islander **Most popular recent majors** Nursing, business administration/commerce/management, education **Academic program** Average class size 18, advanced placement, accelerated degree program, self-designed majors, summer session, adult/continuing education programs, internships **Contact** Mr. Timothy J. Simon, Director of Enrollment Services, Union College, Lincoln, NE 68506-4300. Telephone: 402-486-2504. Fax: 402-486-2895.

UNIVERSITY OF NEBRASKA AT KEARNEY
KEARNEY, NEBRASKA

Entrance Moderately difficult **General** State-supported, comprehensive, coed **Setting** 235-acre small-town campus **Enrollment** 7,620 **Faculty** 19:1 **Application deadline** 8/1 **Freshmen** 96% accepted **Housing** Yes **Tuition** $2332 **Undergraduates** 54% women, 17% part-time, 17% 25 or older, 2% Hispanic, 1% black **Most popular recent majors** Business administration/commerce/management, elementary education, criminal justice **Academic program** Advanced placement, honors program, summer session, adult/continuing education programs, internships **Contact** Ms. Denice Archer, Assistant Director of Admissions, University of Nebraska at Kearney, Kearney, NE 68849-0001. Telephone: 308-865-8526. Fax: 308-865-8987.

UNIVERSITY OF NEBRASKA AT OMAHA
OMAHA, NEBRASKA

Entrance Minimally difficult **General** State-supported, coed **Setting** 88-acre urban campus **Enrollment** 15,000 **Faculty** 22:1 **Application deadline** Rolling **Freshmen** 96% accepted **Tuition** $2328 **Undergraduates** 52% women, 41% part-time, 49% 25 or older, 3% Hispanic, 7% black, 2% Asian or Pacific Islander **Most popular recent majors** Business administration/commerce/management, education, psychology **Academic program** Advanced placement, self-designed majors, honors program, summer session, adult/continuing education programs, internships **Contact** Mr. John Flemming, Director of Admissions, University of Nebraska at Omaha, 60th and Dodge Streets, Omaha, NE 68182. Telephone: 402-554-2709. Fax: 402-554-3472.

UNIVERSITY OF NEBRASKA–LINCOLN
LINCOLN, NEBRASKA

Entrance Moderately difficult **General** State-supported, coed **Setting** 616-acre urban campus **Enrollment** 23,887 **Faculty** 13:1 **Application deadline** 6/30 **Freshmen** 83% accepted **Housing** Yes **Tuition** $2713 **Undergraduates** 46% women, 13% part-time, 12% 25 or older, 1% Native American, 2% Hispanic, 2% black, 4% Asian or Pacific Islander **Most popular recent majors** Psychology, biology/biological sciences, business administration/commerce/management **Academic program** Advanced placement, accelerated degree program, self-designed majors, tutorials, honors program, summer session, adult/continuing education programs, internships **Contact** Ms. Lisa Schmidt, Director of Admissions, University of Nebraska–Lincoln, 14th and R Streets, Lincoln, NE 68588-0417. Telephone: 402-472-2030. Fax: 402-472-8189.

UNIVERSITY OF NEBRASKA MEDICAL CENTER
OMAHA, NEBRASKA

Entrance Moderately difficult **General** State-supported, upper-level, coed **Setting** 51-acre urban campus **Enrollment** 2,718 **Freshmen** 22% accepted **Tuition** $2572 **Undergraduates** 82% women, 9% part-time, 1% Native American, 2% Hispanic, 2% black, 2% Asian or Pacific Islander **Most popular recent majors** Nursing, physician's assistant studies, medical technology **Academic program** Tutorials, adult/continuing education programs, internships **Contact** Ms. Jo Wagner, Assistant Director of Academic Records, University of Nebraska Medical Center, 600 South 42nd Street, Omaha, NE 68198-4230. Telephone: 402-559-6468. Fax: 402-559-6796.

WAYNE STATE COLLEGE
WAYNE, NEBRASKA

Entrance Noncompetitive **General** State-supported, comprehensive, coed **Setting** 128-acre small-town campus **Enrollment** 3,828 **Faculty** 23:1 **Application deadline** Rolling **Freshmen** 99% accepted **Housing** Yes **Tuition** $2140 **Undergraduates** 57% women, 12% part-time, 14% 25 or older, 3% Native American, 1% Hispanic, 2% black, 1% Asian or Pacific Islander **Most popular**

recent majors Business administration/commerce/management, education, criminal justice **Academic program** Average class size 28, honors program, summer session, adult/continuing education programs, internships **Contact** Mr. Robert Zetocha, Director of Admissions, Wayne State College, Wayne, NE 68787. Telephone: 402-375-7234. Fax: 402-375-7204.

YORK COLLEGE
YORK, NEBRASKA

Entrance Moderately difficult **General** Independent, 4-year, coed, affiliated with Church of Christ **Setting** 44-acre small-town campus **Enrollment** 452 **Faculty** 10:1 **Application deadline** Rolling **Freshmen** 68% accepted **Housing** Yes **Tuition** $6565 **Undergraduates** 52% women, 7% part-time, 12% 25 or older, 1% Native American, 2% Hispanic, 2% black, 1% Asian or Pacific Islander **Most popular recent majors** Elementary education, business administration/commerce/management, English **Academic program** Average class size 15, advanced placement, honors program, summer session, adult/continuing education programs, internships **Contact** Mr. Steddon Sikes, Admissions Director, York College, York, NE 68467-2699. Telephone: 402-363-5668. Fax: 402-363-5623.

North Dakota

DICKINSON STATE UNIVERSITY
DICKINSON, NORTH DAKOTA

Entrance Noncompetitive **General** State-supported, 4-year, coed **Setting** 100-acre small-town campus **Enrollment** 1,701 **Faculty** 16:1 **Application deadline** 8/19 **Freshmen** 100% accepted **Housing** Yes **Tuition** $2096 **Undergraduates** 58% women, 15% part-time, 25% 25 or older, 2% Native American, 1% Hispanic, 1% black, 1% Asian or Pacific Islander **Most popular recent majors** Business administration/commerce/management, education, nursing **Academic program** Advanced placement, self-designed majors, honors program, summer session, adult/continuing education programs, internships **Contact** Ms. Deb Hourigan, Interim Coordinator of Student Recruitment, Dickinson State University, Dickinson, ND 58601-4896. Telephone: 701-227-2175. Fax: 701-227-2006.

JAMESTOWN COLLEGE
JAMESTOWN, NORTH DAKOTA

Entrance Moderately difficult **General** Independent Presbyterian, 4-year, coed **Setting** 107-acre small-town campus **Enrollment** 1,094 **Faculty** 19:1 **Application deadline** Rolling **Freshmen** 96% accepted **Housing** Yes **Tuition** $8770 **Undergraduates** 53% women, 7% part-time, 9% 25 or older, 1% Native American, 0% Hispanic, 1% black, 2% Asian or Pacific Islander **Most popular recent majors** Nursing, business administration/commerce/management, history **Academic program** Advanced placement, accelerated degree program, self-designed majors, honors program, summer session, adult/continuing education programs, internships **Contact** Mrs. Carol Schmeichel, Dean of Students, Jamestown College, Jamestown, ND 58405. Telephone: 701-252-3467 Ext. 2563. Fax: 701-253-4318.

MAYVILLE STATE UNIVERSITY
MAYVILLE, NORTH DAKOTA

Entrance Noncompetitive **General** State-supported, 4-year, coed **Setting** 60-acre rural campus **Enrollment** 680 **Application deadline** Rolling **Freshmen** 100% accepted **Housing** Yes **Tuition** $1920 **Undergraduates** 49% women, 6% part-time, 15% 25 or older, 1% Native American, 1% Hispanic, 1% black, 1% Asian or Pacific Islander **Most popular recent majors** Elementary education, business administration/commerce/management, computer information systems **Academic program** Advanced placement, summer session, adult/continuing education programs, internships **Contact** Mr. Ronald G. Brown, Director of Admissions, Mayville State University, Mayville, ND 58257-1299. Telephone: 701-786-2301.

MEDCENTER ONE COLLEGE OF NURSING
BISMARCK, NORTH DAKOTA

Entrance Moderately difficult **General** Independent, upper-level, specialized, primarily women **Setting** 15-acre small-town campus **Enrollment** 83 **Faculty** 7:1 **Freshmen** 47% accepted **Housing** Yes **Tuition** $2815 **Undergraduates** 92% women, 10% part-time, 25% 25 or older, 0% Hispanic, 0% black, 0% Asian or Pacific Islander **Academic program** Honors program, summer session, internships **Contact** Dr. Louis Rigley, Director, Student Services, Medcenter One College of Nursing, 512 North 7th Street, Bismarck, ND 58501-4494. Telephone: 701-224-6833.

MINOT STATE UNIVERSITY
MINOT, NORTH DAKOTA

Entrance Minimally difficult **General** State-supported, comprehensive, coed **Setting** 103-acre small-town campus **Enrollment** 3,602 **Faculty** 19:1 **Application deadline** Rolling **Fresh-**

men 99% accepted **Housing** Yes **Tuition** $2139 **Undergraduates** 63% women, 15% part-time, 30% 25 or older, 4% Native American, 1% Hispanic, 1% black, 1% Asian or Pacific Islander **Most popular recent majors** Business administration/commerce/management, education, criminal justice **Academic program** Advanced placement, accelerated degree program, self-designed majors, tutorials, honors program, summer session, adult/continuing education programs, internships **Contact** Ms. Lisa Beltz, Admissions Adviser, Minot State University, Minot, ND 58707-0002. Telephone: 701-858-3350. Fax: 701-839-6933.

NORTH DAKOTA STATE UNIVERSITY

FARGO, NORTH DAKOTA

Entrance Moderately difficult **General** State-supported, coed **Setting** 2,100-acre urban campus **Enrollment** 9,688 **Faculty** 19:1 **Application deadline** Rolling **Freshmen** 77% accepted **Housing** Yes **Tuition** $2566 **Undergraduates** 42% women, 14% part-time, 14% 25 or older, 1% Native American, 1% Hispanic, 1% black, 1% Asian or Pacific Islander **Most popular recent majors** Business administration/commerce/management, electrical engineering, pharmacy/pharmaceutical sciences **Academic program** Advanced placement, accelerated degree program, self-designed majors, honors program, summer session, adult/continuing education programs, internships **Contact** Dr. Kate Haugen, Director of Admission, North Dakota State University, University Station, Fargo, ND 58105. Telephone: 701-231-8643. Fax: 701-231-7050.

TRINITY BIBLE COLLEGE

ELLENDALE, NORTH DAKOTA

Entrance Noncompetitive **General** Independent, 4-year, coed, affiliated with Assemblies of God **Setting** 28-acre rural campus **Enrollment** 329 **Faculty** 14:1 **Application deadline** Rolling **Freshmen** 100% accepted **Housing** Yes **Tuition** $6078 **Undergraduates** 50% women, 8% part-time, 21% 25 or older, 3% Native American, 5% Hispanic, 0% black, 1% Asian or Pacific Islander **Most popular recent majors** Biblical studies, psychology, ministries **Academic program** Advanced placement, accelerated degree program, tutorials, summer session, internships **Contact** Mr. Clyde Kallal, Director of Admissions, Trinity Bible College, 50 South 6th Avenue, Ellendale, ND 58436-7150. Telephone: 701-349-3621 Ext. 2045. Fax: 701-349-5443.

UNIVERSITY OF MARY

BISMARCK, NORTH DAKOTA

Entrance Moderately difficult **General** Independent Roman Catholic, comprehensive, coed **Setting** 107-acre small-town campus **Enrollment** 2,016 **Faculty** 18:1 **Application deadline** Rolling **Freshmen** 90% accepted **Housing** Yes **Tuition** $7740 **Undergraduates** 61% women, 20% part-time, 39% 25 or older, 6% Native American, 0% Hispanic, 1% black, 1% Asian or Pacific Islander **Most popular recent majors** Nursing, business administration/commerce/management, elementary education **Academic program** Advanced placement, accelerated degree program, tutorials, summer session, adult/continuing education programs, internships **Contact** Mrs. MaryBeth Storey, Director of Admissions, University of Mary, 7500 University Drive, Bismarck, ND 58504-9652. Telephone: 701-255-7500 Ext. 429. Fax: 701-255-7687.

UNIVERSITY OF NORTH DAKOTA

GRAND FORKS, NORTH DAKOTA

Entrance Moderately difficult **General** State-supported, coed **Setting** 570-acre small-town campus **Enrollment** 11,300 **Faculty** 15:1 **Application deadline** 7/1 **Freshmen** 73% accepted **Housing** Yes **Tuition** $2946 **Undergraduates** 49% women, 12% part-time, 29% 25 or older, 3% Native American, 1% Hispanic, 1% black, 1% Asian or Pacific Islander **Most popular recent majors** Aerospace sciences, accounting, business administration/commerce/management **Academic program** Average class size 33, advanced placement, accelerated degree program, self-designed majors, honors program, summer session, adult/continuing education programs, internships **Contact** Ms. Donna Bruce, Associate Director of Admissions, University of North Dakota, Box 8382, Grand Forks, ND 58202. Telephone: 701-777-3821. Fax: 701-777-2696.

VALLEY CITY STATE UNIVERSITY

VALLEY CITY, NORTH DAKOTA

Entrance Noncompetitive **General** State-supported, 4-year, coed **Setting** 55-acre small-town campus **Enrollment** 1,121 **Faculty** 15:1 **Application deadline** Rolling **Freshmen** 94% accepted **Housing** Yes **Tuition** $1893 **Undergraduates** 48% women, 25% part-time, 25% 25 or older, 2% Native American, 1% Hispanic, 1% black, 1% Asian or Pacific Islander **Most popular recent majors** Elementary education, business administration/commerce/management, human resources **Academic program** Accelerated degree program, self-designed majors, tutorials, summer session, adult/continuing education programs, internships **Contact** Mr. LaMonte Johnson, Director of Admissions, Valley City State University, Valley City, ND 58072. Telephone: 701-845-7101. Fax: 701-845-7245.

Ohio

ANTIOCH COLLEGE

YELLOW SPRINGS, OHIO

Entrance Moderately difficult **General** Independent, 4-year, coed **Setting** 100-acre small-town campus **Enrollment** 640 **Faculty** 9:1 **Application deadline** 2/1 **Freshmen** 74% accepted **Housing** Yes **Tuition** $18,487 **Undergraduates** 60% women, 4% 25 or older, 1% Native American, 4% Hispanic, 6% black, 3% Asian or Pacific Islander **Academic program** Advanced placement, self-designed majors **Contact** Ms. Debby Campbell, Data Entry Clerk, Antioch College, 795 Livermore Street, Yellow Springs, OH 45387-1697. Telephone: 513-767-6400. Fax: 513-767-6473.

ART ACADEMY OF CINCINNATI

CINCINNATI, OHIO

Entrance Moderately difficult **General** Independent, comprehensive, specialized, coed **Setting** 184-acre urban campus **Enrollment** 168 **Application deadline** 8/15 **Freshmen** 76% accepted **Tuition** $10,925 **Undergraduates** 48% women, 15% part-time, 30% 25 or older, 5% black, 2% Asian or Pacific Islander **Academic program** Average class size 17, advanced placement, self-designed majors, tutorials, summer session, adult/continuing education programs, internships **Contact** Ms. Sarah Colby, Dean of Enrollment Services, Art Academy of Cincinnati, 1125 Saint Gregory Street, Cincinnati, OH 45202-1700. Telephone: 513-562-8745. Fax: 513-562-8778.

ASHLAND UNIVERSITY

ASHLAND, OHIO

Entrance Moderately difficult **General** Independent, comprehensive, coed, affiliated with Brethren Church **Setting** 98-acre small-town campus **Enrollment** 5,733 **Faculty** 16:1 **Application deadline** Rolling **Freshmen** 95% accepted **Housing** Yes **Tuition** $13,601 **Undergraduates** 57% women, 24% part-time, 29% 25 or older, 1% Native American, 1% Hispanic, 4% black, 1% Asian or Pacific Islander **Most popular recent majors** Marketing/retailing/merchandising, education **Academic program** Average class size 15, advanced placement, accelerated degree program, honors program, summer session, adult/continuing education programs, internships **Contact** Mr. Carl A. Gerbasi Jr., Vice President of Enrollment Management, Ashland University, Ashland, OH 44805-3702. Telephone: 419-289-5054. Fax: 419-289-5333.

BALDWIN-WALLACE COLLEGE

BEREA, OHIO

Entrance Moderately difficult **General** Independent Methodist, comprehensive, coed **Setting** 56-acre suburban campus **Enrollment** 4,621 **Faculty** 14:1 **Application deadline** Rolling **Freshmen** 84% accepted **Housing** Yes **Tuition** $13,275 **Undergraduates** 62% women, 31% part-time, 29% 25 or older, 0% Native American, 1% Hispanic, 5% black, 2% Asian or Pacific Islander **Most popular recent majors** Business administration/commerce/management, education, English **Academic program** Advanced placement, accelerated degree program, self-designed majors, tutorials, honors program, summer session, adult/continuing education programs, internships **Contact** Mrs. Julie Baker, Director of Undergraduate Admission, Baldwin-Wallace College, Berea, OH 44017-2088. Telephone: 216-826-2222.

BLUFFTON COLLEGE

BLUFFTON, OHIO

Entrance Moderately difficult **General** Independent Mennonite, comprehensive, coed **Setting** 65-acre small-town campus **Enrollment** 1,090 **Faculty** 15:1 **Application deadline** 5/31 **Freshmen** 88% accepted **Housing** Yes **Tuition** $11,835 **Undergraduates** 54% women, 11% part-time, 10% 25 or older, 1% Native American, 1% Hispanic, 9% black, 1% Asian or Pacific Islander **Most popular recent majors** Business administration/commerce/management, education, social science **Academic program** Advanced placement, accelerated degree program, self-designed majors, tutorials, honors program, summer session, adult/continuing education programs, internships **Contact** Mr. Michael Hieronimus, Dean of Admissions, Bluffton College, Bluffton, OH 45817-1196. Telephone: 419-358-3254. Fax: 419-358-3323.

BOWLING GREEN STATE UNIVERSITY

BOWLING GREEN, OHIO

Entrance Moderately difficult **General** State-supported, coed **Setting** 1,338-acre small-town campus **Enrollment** 17,564 **Faculty** 18:1 **Application deadline** Rolling **Freshmen** 83% accepted **Housing** Yes **Tuition** $4422 **Undergraduates** 57% women, 8% part-time, 7% 25 or older, 0% Native American, 2% Hispanic, 3% black, 1% Asian or Pacific Islander **Most popular recent majors** Elementary education, marketing/retailing/merchandising, biology/biological sciences **Academic program** Advanced placement, accelerated degree program, self-designed majors, tutorials, honors program, summer session, adult/continuing education programs, internships **Contact** Mr. Michael D. Walsh, Director of Admissions, Bowling Green State University, Bowling Green, OH 43403. Telephone: 419-372-2086.

BRYANT AND STRATTON COLLEGE
CLEVELAND, OHIO

Entrance Moderately difficult **General** Proprietary, 4-year, coed **Setting** Urban campus **Enrollment** 339 **Application deadline** Rolling **Freshmen** 80% accepted **Housing** Yes **Tuition** $6960 **Undergraduates** 20% women, 50% 25 or older, 5% Hispanic, 40% black, 2% Asian or Pacific Islander **Most popular recent major** Electronics engineering technology **Academic program** Advanced placement, accelerated degree program, adult/continuing education programs **Contact** Ms. Vanetta McClain, Associate Director of Admissions, Bryant and Stratton College, 1700 East 13th Street, Cleveland, OH 44114-3203. Telephone: 216-771-1700. Fax: 216-771-1700.

CAPITAL UNIVERSITY
COLUMBUS, OHIO

Entrance Moderately difficult **General** Independent, comprehensive, coed, affiliated with Evangelical Lutheran Church in America **Setting** 48-acre suburban campus **Enrollment** 4,035 **Faculty** 13:1 **Application deadline** Rolling **Freshmen** 83% accepted **Housing** Yes **Tuition** $14,760 **Undergraduates** 62% women, 2% part-time, 6% 25 or older, 0% Native American, 1% Hispanic, 8% black, 2% Asian or Pacific Islander **Most popular recent majors** Nursing, elementary education, psychology **Academic program** Average class size 20, advanced placement, self-designed majors, summer session, adult/continuing education programs, internships **Contact** Ms. Beth Heiser, Director of Admission, Capital University, Columbus, OH 43209-2394. Telephone: 614-236-6101. Fax: 614-236-6820.

CASE WESTERN RESERVE UNIVERSITY
CLEVELAND, OHIO

Entrance Very difficult **General** Independent, coed **Setting** 128-acre urban campus **Enrollment** 9,970 **Faculty** 8:1 **Application deadline** 2/1 **Freshmen** 79% accepted **Housing** Yes **Tuition** $17,940 **Undergraduates** 42% women, 15% part-time, 8% 25 or older, 1% Native American, 2% Hispanic, 6% black, 12% Asian or Pacific Islander **Most popular recent majors** Psychology, mechanical engineering, biomedical engineering **Academic program** Average class size 40, advanced placement, accelerated degree program, self-designed majors, tutorials, honors program, summer session, adult/continuing education programs, internships **Contact** Mr. William T. Conley, Dean of Undergraduate Admissions, Case Western Reserve University, 10900 Euclid Avenue, Cleveland, OH 44106. Telephone: 216-368-4450. Fax: 216-368-5111.

CEDARVILLE COLLEGE
CEDARVILLE, OHIO

Entrance Moderately difficult **General** Independent Baptist, 4-year, coed **Setting** 293-acre rural campus **Enrollment** 2,509 **Faculty** 17:1 **Application deadline** Rolling **Freshmen** 87% accepted **Housing** Yes **Tuition** $9312 **Undergraduates** 54% women, 3% part-time, 3% 25 or older, 1% Native American, 1% Hispanic, 1% black, 1% Asian or Pacific Islander **Most popular recent majors** Elementary education, nursing, biology/biological sciences **Academic program** Advanced placement, accelerated degree program, honors program, summer session, internships **Contact** Mr. Stuart Zaharek, Associate Director of Admissions, Cedarville College, PO Box 601, Cedarville, OH 45314-0601. Telephone: 937-766-7700.

CENTRAL STATE UNIVERSITY
WILBERFORCE, OHIO

Entrance Minimally difficult **General** State-supported, comprehensive, coed **Setting** 60-acre rural campus **Enrollment** 1,976 **Application deadline** 6/15 **Freshmen** 66% accepted **Housing** Yes **Tuition** $3318 **Undergraduates** 11% part-time, 18% 25 or older, 0% Native American, 1% Hispanic, 93% black, 1% Asian or Pacific Islander **Most popular recent majors** Business administration/commerce/management, computer science, education **Academic program** Self-designed majors, honors program, summer session, adult/continuing education programs, internships **Contact** Ms. Sharon K. Hope, Acting Director of Admissions and Enrollment Management, Central State University, Wilberforce, OH 45384. Telephone: 937-376-6348. Fax: 937-376-6648.

CINCINNATI BIBLE COLLEGE AND SEMINARY
CINCINNATI, OHIO

Entrance Minimally difficult **General** Independent, comprehensive, coed, affiliated with Church of Christ **Setting** 40-acre urban campus **Enrollment** 848 **Faculty** 24:1 **Application deadline** 8/10 **Freshmen** 98% accepted **Housing** Yes **Tuition** $5944 **Undergraduates** 42% women, 20% part-time, 20% 25 or older, 1% Native American, 1% Hispanic, 4% black, 1% Asian or Pacific Islander **Most popular recent majors** Education, ministries, sacred music **Academic program** Average class size 20, advanced placement, tutorials, summer session, adult/continuing education programs, internships **Contact** Mr. Philip G. Coleman, Director of Admissions, Cincinnati Bible College and Seminary, 2700 Glenway Avenue, Cincinnati, OH 45204-1799. Telephone: 513-244-8141. Fax: 513-244-8140.

CINCINNATI COLLEGE OF MORTUARY SCIENCE
CINCINNATI, OHIO

Entrance Minimally difficult **General** Independent, 4-year, specialized, coed **Setting** 10-acre urban campus **Enrollment** 145 **Application deadline** Rolling **Freshmen** 81% accepted **Tuition** $9075 **Undergraduates** 40% women, 0% part-time, 35% 25 or older, 0% Native American, 1% Hispanic, 8% black, 0% Asian or Pacific Islander **Academic program** Advanced placement, summer session, adult/continuing education programs **Contact** Dr. Dan Flory, President, Cincinnati College of Mortuary Science, 645 West North Bend Road, Cincinnati, OH 45224-1462. Telephone: 513-761-2020. Fax: 513-761-3333.

CIRCLEVILLE BIBLE COLLEGE
CIRCLEVILLE, OHIO

Entrance Noncompetitive **General** Independent, 4-year, coed, affiliated with Churches of Christ in Christian Union **Setting** 40-acre small-town campus **Enrollment** 203 **Faculty** 10:1 **Application deadline** Rolling **Housing** Yes **Tuition** $5892 **Undergraduates** 43% women, 19% part-time, 0% 25 or older, 0% Native American, 1% Hispanic, 3% black, 1% Asian or Pacific Islander **Most popular recent majors** Ministries, guidance and counseling, education **Academic program** Average class size 18, advanced placement, self-designed majors, tutorials, honors program, summer session, internships **Contact** Rev. Matt Taylor, Director of Enrollment, Circleville Bible College, Circleville, OH 43113-9487. Telephone: 614-477-7701.

CLEVELAND COLLEGE OF JEWISH STUDIES
BEACHWOOD, OHIO

Entrance Noncompetitive **General** Independent, comprehensive, coed **Setting** 2-acre suburban campus **Enrollment** 75 **Faculty** 10:1 **Application deadline** Rolling **Tuition** $4950 **Undergraduates** 65% women, 90% part-time, 99% 25 or older, 0% Native American, 0% Hispanic, 0% black, 0% Asian or Pacific Islander **Academic program** Summer session, internships **Contact** Ms. Linda L. Rosen, Registrar, Cleveland College of Jewish Studies, 26500 Shaker Boulevard, Beachwood, OH 44122-7116. Telephone: 216-464-4050 Ext. 101.

CLEVELAND INSTITUTE OF ART
CLEVELAND, OHIO

Entrance Moderately difficult **General** Independent, 5-year, specialized, coed **Setting** 488-acre urban campus **Enrollment** 513 **Faculty** 10:1 **Application deadline** Rolling **Freshmen** 81% accepted **Housing** Yes **Tuition** $13,434 **Undergraduates** 46% women, 10% part-time, 17% 25 or older, 0% Native American, 4% Hispanic, 6% black, 4% Asian or Pacific Islander **Most popular recent majors** Industrial design, painting/drawing, graphic arts **Academic program** Advanced placement, self-designed majors, tutorials, honors program, summer session, adult/continuing education programs, internships **Contact** Office of Admissions, Cleveland Institute of Art, 11141 East Boulevard, Cleveland, OH 44106-1700. Telephone: 216-421-7418. Fax: 216-421-7438.

CLEVELAND INSTITUTE OF MUSIC
CLEVELAND, OHIO

Entrance Very difficult **General** Independent, comprehensive, specialized, coed **Setting** 488-acre urban campus **Enrollment** 354 **Faculty** 10:1 **Application deadline** 12/15 **Freshmen** 48% accepted **Housing** Yes **Tuition** $17,029 **Undergraduates** 50% women, 0% part-time, 3% 25 or older, 0% Native American, 3% Hispanic, 4% black, 4% Asian or Pacific Islander **Academic program** Advanced placement, accelerated degree program, summer session **Contact** Mr. William Fay, Director of Admissions, Cleveland Institute of Music, 11021 East Boulevard, Cleveland, OH 44106-1776. Telephone: 216-795-3107.

CLEVELAND STATE UNIVERSITY
CLEVELAND, OHIO

Entrance Noncompetitive **General** State-supported, coed **Setting** 70-acre urban campus **Enrollment** 15,522 **Faculty** 18:1 **Application deadline** 8/1 **Freshmen** 98% accepted **Housing** Yes **Tuition** $3524 **Undergraduates** 55% women, 33% part-time, 44% 25 or older, 0% Native American, 3% Hispanic, 18% black, 3% Asian or Pacific Islander **Most popular recent majors** Accounting, psychology, communication **Academic program** Advanced placement, accelerated degree program, self-designed majors, tutorials, summer session, adult/continuing education programs, internships **Contact** Mr. David Norris, Director of Admissions, Cleveland State University, East 24th and Euclid Avenue, Cleveland, OH 44115. Telephone: 216-687-3763.

COLLEGE OF MOUNT ST. JOSEPH
CINCINNATI, OHIO

Entrance Moderately difficult **General** Independent Roman Catholic, comprehensive, coed **Setting** 75-acre suburban campus **Enrollment** 2,205 **Faculty** 15:1 **Application deadline** 8/15 **Freshmen** 80% accepted **Housing** Yes **Tuition** $11,950 **Undergraduates** 74% women, 45% part-time, 34% 25 or older, 1% Native American, 1% Hispanic, 7% black, 1% Asian or Pacific Islander **Most popular recent majors** Business administration/commerce/management, nursing, liberal arts/general studies **Academic program** Average class size 20, advanced placement, accelerated degree program, self-designed majors, tutorials, honors program, summer session, adult/continuing education programs, internships **Contact** Mr. Edward Eckel, Director of Admission, College of Mount St. Joseph, Cincinnati, OH 45233-1670. Telephone: 513-244-4302. Fax: 513-244-4629.

THE COLLEGE OF WOOSTER
WOOSTER, OHIO

Entrance Moderately difficult **General** Independent, 4-year, coed, affiliated with Presbyterian Church (U.S.A.) **Setting** 320-acre small-town campus **Enrollment** 1,650 **Faculty** 11:1 **Application deadline** 2/15 **Freshmen** 90% accepted **Housing** Yes **Tuition** $19,300 **Undergraduates** 52% women, 0% part-time, 1% 25 or older, 0% Native American, 1% Hispanic, 5% black, 1% Asian or Pacific Islander **Most popular recent majors** History, psychology, biology/biological sciences **Academic program** Average class size 22, advanced placement, self-designed majors, summer session, internships **Contact** Dr. W. A. Hayden Schilling, Dean of Admissions, The College of Wooster, Wooster, OH 44691. Telephone: 330-263-2270. Fax: 330-263-2594.

COLUMBUS COLLEGE OF ART AND DESIGN
COLUMBUS, OHIO

Entrance Moderately difficult **General** Independent, 4-year, specialized, coed **Setting** 7-acre urban campus **Enrollment** 1,494 **Faculty** 9:1 **Application deadline** Rolling **Freshmen** 64% accepted **Housing** Yes **Tuition** $11,880 **Undergraduates** 45% women, 29% part-time, 11% 25 or older, 1% Native American, 2% Hispanic, 5% black, 3% Asian or Pacific Islander **Most popular recent majors** Illustration, art/fine arts, advertising **Academic program** ESL program, Advanced placement, summer session, internships **Contact** Mr. Thomas E. Green, Director of Admissions, Columbus College of Art and Design, 107 North Ninth Street, Columbus, OH 43215-1758. Telephone: 614-224-9101.

DAVID N. MYERS COLLEGE
CLEVELAND, OHIO

Entrance Minimally difficult **General** Independent, 4-year, coed **Setting** Urban campus **Enrollment** 1,178 **Faculty** 11:1 **Application deadline** 9/1 **Freshmen** 100% accepted **Tuition** $7500 **Undergraduates** 71% women, 45% part-time, 63% 25 or older, 0% Native American, 3% Hispanic, 41% black, 0% Asian or Pacific Islander **Most popular recent majors** Business administration/commerce/management, accounting **Academic program** Advanced placement, accelerated degree program, tutorials, summer session, adult/continuing education programs, internships **Contact** Marketing Department, David N. Myers College, 112 Prospect Avenue, Cleveland, OH 44115-1096. Telephone: 216-696-9000.

THE DEFIANCE COLLEGE
DEFIANCE, OHIO

Entrance Moderately difficult **General** Independent, comprehensive, coed, affiliated with United Church of Christ **Setting** 150-acre small-town campus **Enrollment** 826 **Faculty** 13:1 **Application deadline** 8/15 **Freshmen** 80% accepted **Housing** Yes **Tuition** $13,475 **Undergraduates** 52% women, 29% part-time, 40% 25 or older, 1% Native American, 3% Hispanic, 5% black, 1% Asian or Pacific Islander **Most popular recent majors** Elementary education, criminal justice, business administration/commerce/management **Academic program** Advanced placement, self-designed majors, tutorials, summer session, adult/

continuing education programs, internships **Contact** Mr. Eric Stockard, Vice President of Enrollment Management, The Defiance College, Defiance, OH 43512-1610. Telephone: 419-783-4010. Fax: 419-784-0426.

DENISON UNIVERSITY

GRANVILLE, OHIO

Entrance Moderately difficult **General** Independent, 4-year, coed **Setting** 1,200-acre small-town campus **Enrollment** 2,017 **Faculty** 12:1 **Application deadline** 2/1 **Freshmen** 82% accepted **Housing** Yes **Tuition** $20,250 **Undergraduates** 52% women, 1% part-time, 1% 25 or older, 0% Native American, 2% Hispanic, 4% black, 3% Asian or Pacific Islander **Most popular recent majors** English, psychology, economics **Academic program** Average class size 18, advanced placement, self-designed majors, tutorials, honors program, internships **Contact** Ms. Pennie Miller, Communications Coordinator, Denison University, Box H, Granville, OH 43023. Telephone: 614-587-6618. Fax: 614-587-6306.

DEVRY INSTITUTE OF TECHNOLOGY

COLUMBUS, OHIO

Entrance Minimally difficult **General** Proprietary, 4-year, coed **Setting** 21-acre urban campus **Enrollment** 2,647 **Faculty** 34:1 **Application deadline** Rolling **Freshmen** 71% accepted **Tuition** $6968 **Undergraduates** 23% women, 28% part-time, 36% 25 or older, 0% Native American, 1% Hispanic, 18% black, 2% Asian or Pacific Islander **Most popular recent majors** Computer information systems, electronics engineering technology, electrical and electronics technologies **Academic program** Advanced placement, accelerated degree program, summer session, adult/continuing education programs **Contact** Ms. Jody Wasmer, Director of Admissions, DeVry Institute of Technology, 1350 Alum Creek Drive, Columbus, OH 43209-2764. Telephone: 614-253-1525 Ext. 700.

DYKE COLLEGE

SEE DAVID N. MYERS COLLEGE

ETI TECHNICAL COLLEGE

SEE BRYANT AND STRATTON COLLEGE

FRANCISCAN UNIVERSITY OF STEUBENVILLE

STEUBENVILLE, OHIO

Entrance Moderately difficult **General** Independent Roman Catholic, comprehensive, coed **Setting** 100-acre suburban campus **Enrollment** 1,927 **Faculty** 15:1 **Application deadline** 6/30 **Freshmen** 88% accepted **Housing** Yes **Tuition** $11,370 **Undergraduates** 60% women, 13% part-time, 0% Native American, 4% Hispanic, 1% black, 2% Asian or Pacific Islander **Most popular recent majors** Theology, business administration/commerce/management, psychology **Academic program** Advanced placement, accelerated degree program, tutorials, honors program, summer session, adult/continuing education programs, internships **Contact** Mrs. Margaret Weber, Director of Admissions, Franciscan University of Steubenville, Steubenville, OH 43952-6701. Telephone: 614-283-6226.

FRANKLIN UNIVERSITY

COLUMBUS, OHIO

Entrance Noncompetitive **General** Independent, comprehensive, coed **Setting** 14-acre urban campus **Enrollment** 4,049 **Faculty** 18:1 **Application deadline** Rolling **Freshmen** 100% accepted **Tuition** $5066 **Undergraduates** 59% women, 72% part-time, 74% 25 or older, 1% Native American, 1% Hispanic, 13% black, 2% Asian or Pacific Islander **Most popular recent majors** Business administration/commerce/management, accounting, marketing/retailing/merchandising **Academic program** Average class size 22, advanced placement, accelerated degree program, self-designed majors, tutorials, summer session, adult/continuing education programs, internships **Contact** Ms. Linda M. Steele, Vice President for Students and Alumni, Franklin University, 201 South Grant Avenue, Columbus, OH 43215-5399. Telephone: 614-341-6230. Fax: 614-224-0434.

GOD'S BIBLE SCHOOL AND COLLEGE

CINCINNATI, OHIO

Entrance Minimally difficult **General** Independent interdenominational, 4-year, coed **Setting** 14-acre urban campus **Enrollment** 176 **Faculty** 11:1 **Application deadline** Rolling **Freshmen** 100% accepted **Housing** Yes **Tuition** $3850 **Undergraduates** 51% women, 15% part-time, 18% 25 or older, 0% Native American, 0% Hispanic, 2% black, 0% Asian or Pacific Islander **Most popular recent majors** Ministries, religious education, liberal arts/general studies **Academic program** Average class size 60, advanced placement, summer session, internships **Contact** Mr. Fred Wingham, Director of Admissions, God's Bible School and College, 1810 Young Street, Cincinnati, OH 45210-1599. Telephone: 513-721-7944 Ext. 269. Fax: 513-721-3971.

HEIDELBERG COLLEGE
TIFFIN, OHIO

Entrance Moderately difficult **General** Independent, comprehensive, coed, affiliated with United Church of Christ **Setting** 110-acre small-town campus **Enrollment** 1,386 **Faculty** 12:1 **Application deadline** 8/1 **Freshmen** 89% accepted **Housing** Yes **Tuition** $15,594 **Undergraduates** 50% women, 24% part-time, 34% 25 or older, 1% Native American, 2% Hispanic, 3% black, 1% Asian or Pacific Islander **Most popular recent majors** Business administration/commerce/management, biology/biological sciences, education **Academic program** Average class size 14, advanced placement, accelerated degree program, honors program, summer session, adult/continuing education programs, internships **Contact** Mr. David Rhodes, Dean of Admission, Heidelberg College, Tiffin, OH 44883-2462. Telephone: 419-448-2334. Fax: 419-448-2334.

HIRAM COLLEGE
HIRAM, OHIO

Entrance Very difficult **General** Independent, 4-year, coed, affiliated with Christian Church (Disciples of Christ) **Setting** 110-acre rural campus **Enrollment** 800 **Faculty** 11:1 **Application deadline** 3/15 **Freshmen** 87% accepted **Housing** Yes **Tuition** $16,514 **Undergraduates** 54% women, 0% Native American, 1% Hispanic, 8% black, 1% Asian or Pacific Islander **Most popular recent majors** Biology/biological sciences, elementary education, business administration/commerce/management **Academic program** Average class size 15, advanced placement, accelerated degree program, self-designed majors, tutorials, summer session, adult/continuing education programs, internships **Contact** Mr. Monty L. Curtis, Vice President for Admission and College Relations, Hiram College, Hiram, OH 44234-0067. Telephone: 330-569-5169. Fax: 330-569-5944.

JOHN CARROLL UNIVERSITY
UNIVERSITY HEIGHTS, OHIO

Entrance Moderately difficult **General** Independent Roman Catholic (Jesuit), comprehensive, coed **Setting** 60-acre suburban campus **Enrollment** 4,197 **Faculty** 10:1 **Application deadline** Rolling **Freshmen** 89% accepted **Housing** Yes **Tuition** $13,883 **Undergraduates** 52% women, 5% part-time, 7% 25 or older, 0% Native American, 1% Hispanic, 4% black, 3% Asian or Pacific Islander **Most popular recent majors** Communication, psychology, biology/biological sciences **Academic program** Average class size 22, advanced placement, accelerated degree program, self-designed majors, tutorials, honors program, summer session, adult/continuing education programs, internships **Contact** Mr. Thomas P. Fanning, Director of Admission, John Carroll University, University Heights, OH 44118-4581. Telephone: 216-397-4294. Fax: 216-397-3098.

KENT STATE UNIVERSITY
KENT, OHIO

Entrance Moderately difficult **General** State-supported, coed **Setting** 1,200-acre small-town campus **Enrollment** 20,600 **Faculty** 17:1 **Application deadline** 3/15 **Freshmen** 88% accepted **Housing** Yes **Tuition** $4460 **Undergraduates** 57% women, 17% part-time, 18% 25 or older, 1% Native American, 1% Hispanic, 6% black, 1% Asian or Pacific Islander **Academic program** Advanced placement, self-designed majors, tutorials, honors program, summer session, adult/continuing education programs, internships **Contact** Ms. Kari Johnston, Graduate Assistant, Kent State University, 161 Michael Schwartz Center, Kent, OH 44242-0001. Telephone: 330-672-2444. Fax: 330-672-2499.

KENYON COLLEGE
GAMBIER, OHIO

Entrance Very difficult **General** Independent, 4-year, coed **Setting** 800-acre rural campus **Enrollment** 1,547 **Faculty** 10:1 **Application deadline** 2/15 **Freshmen** 67% accepted **Housing** Yes **Tuition** $22,850 **Undergraduates** 54% women, 1% part-time, 0% 25 or older, 1% Native American, 3% Hispanic, 4% black, 4% Asian or Pacific Islander **Most popular recent majors** English, history, psychology **Academic program** Advanced placement, self-designed majors, tutorials, honors program, internships **Contact** Mr. John W. Anderson, Dean of Admissions, Kenyon College, Gambier, OH 43022-9623. Telephone: 614-427-5776. Fax: 614-427-2634.

LAKE ERIE COLLEGE
PAINESVILLE, OHIO

Entrance Moderately difficult **General** Independent, comprehensive, coed **Setting** 57-acre small-town campus **Enrollment** 622 **Faculty** 13:1 **Application deadline** 8/1 **Freshmen** 87% accepted **Housing** Yes **Tuition** $13,750 **Undergraduates** 69% women, 42% part-time, 0% Native American, 1% Hispanic, 3% black, 0% Asian or Pacific Islander **Most popular recent majors** Business administration/commerce/management, elementary education, accounting **Academic pro-**

gram Average class size 15, advanced placement, accelerated degree program, self-designed majors, tutorials, summer session, adult/continuing education programs, internships **Contact** Ms. Mary Ann Kalbaugh, Director of Admissions, Lake Erie College, Painesville, OH 44077-3389. Telephone: 216-639-7879. Fax: 216-352-3533.

LOURDES COLLEGE
SYLVANIA, OHIO

Entrance Moderately difficult **General** Independent Roman Catholic, 4-year, coed **Setting** 90-acre suburban campus **Enrollment** 1,540 **Faculty** 14:1 **Application deadline** Rolling **Freshmen** 86% accepted **Tuition** $8100 **Undergraduates** 82% women, 70% part-time, 70% 25 or older, 1% Native American, 1% Hispanic, 5% black, 1% Asian or Pacific Islander **Most popular recent majors** Business administration/commerce/management, nursing, occupational therapy **Academic program** Advanced placement, accelerated degree program, self-designed majors, tutorials, summer session, adult/continuing education programs, internships **Contact** Ms. Beth Tanesky, Director of Admissions, Lourdes College, Sylvania, OH 43560-2898. Telephone: 419-885-5291 Ext. 299. Fax: 419-882-3987.

MALONE COLLEGE
CANTON, OHIO

Entrance Moderately difficult **General** Independent, comprehensive, coed, affiliated with Evangelical Friends Church–Eastern Region **Setting** 78-acre suburban campus **Enrollment** 2,069 **Faculty** 14:1 **Application deadline** 7/1 **Freshmen** 88% accepted **Housing** Yes **Tuition** $11,651 **Undergraduates** 62% women, 12% part-time, 26% 25 or older, 1% Native American, 1% Hispanic, 5% black, 1% Asian or Pacific Islander **Most popular recent majors** Business administration/commerce/management, nursing, elementary education **Academic program** Average class size 27, advanced placement, accelerated degree program, self-designed majors, tutorials, summer session, adult/continuing education programs, internships **Contact** Mr. Leland J. Sommers, Dean of Admissions, Malone College, Canton, OH 44709-3897. Telephone: 330-471-8145. Fax: 330-454-6977.

MARIETTA COLLEGE
MARIETTA, OHIO

Entrance Moderately difficult **General** Independent, comprehensive, coed **Setting** 120-acre small-town campus **Enrollment** 1,256 **Faculty** 15:1 **Application deadline** 4/15 **Freshmen** 90% accepted **Housing** Yes **Tuition** $16,150 **Undergraduates** 47% women, 1% part-time, 6% 25 or older, 1% Native American, 1% Hispanic, 1% black, 1% Asian or Pacific Islander **Most popular recent majors** Business administration/commerce/management, communication, education **Academic program** Average class size 20, advanced placement, accelerated degree program, self-designed majors, tutorials, honors program, summer session, adult/continuing education programs, internships **Contact** Ms. Marke Vickers, Director of Admission, Marietta College, Marietta, OH 45750-4000. Telephone: 614-376-4600. Fax: 614-376-8888.

THE MCGREGOR SCHOOL OF ANTIOCH UNIVERSITY
YELLOW SPRINGS, OHIO

Entrance Noncompetitive **General** Independent, upper-level, coed **Setting** 100-acre small-town campus **Enrollment** 1,057 **Freshmen** 100% accepted **Tuition** $9408 **Undergraduates** 60% women, 62% part-time, 99% 25 or older, 1% Native American, 3% Hispanic, 10% black, 1% Asian or Pacific Islander **Most popular recent majors** Business administration/commerce/management, labor studies, human services **Academic program** Average class size 15, advanced placement, accelerated degree program, tutorials, summer session, adult/continuing education programs, internships **Contact** Ms. Terri J. Haney, Director of Admissions and Community Relations, The McGregor School of Antioch University, Yellow Springs, OH 45387-1609. Telephone: 937-767-6325. Fax: 937-767-6461.

MIAMI UNIVERSITY
OXFORD, OHIO

Entrance Moderately difficult **General** State-related, coed **Setting** 1,900-acre small-town campus **Enrollment** 16,103 **Faculty** 17:1 **Application deadline** 1/31 **Freshmen** 72% accepted **Housing** Yes **Tuition** $5512 **Undergraduates** 55% women, 6% part-time, 4% 25 or older, 1% Native American, 1% Hispanic, 3% black, 2% Asian or Pacific Islander **Most popular recent majors** Marketing/retailing/merchandising, elementary education, zoology **Academic program** Average class size 25, advanced placement, accelerated degree program, self-designed majors, tutorials, honors program, summer session, adult/continuing education programs, internships **Contact** Dr. James S. McCoy, Associate Vice President for Enrollment Services, Miami University, Oxford, OH 45056. Telephone: 513-529-2531.

MOUNT CARMEL COLLEGE OF NURSING
COLUMBUS, OHIO

Entrance Difficulty N/R **General** Independent, 4-year **Tuition** $6296 **Financial Aid** 90% applied for aid, 78% of those who applied for aid were judged to have need, 100% of those were aided. Average amount received per student (from all sources): $6200. Non-need awards available; for 1996, a total of 53 non-need awards were made. Required forms: institutional, FAFSA. Financial aid (priority) deadline: 3/1.

MOUNT UNION COLLEGE
ALLIANCE, OHIO

Entrance Moderately difficult **General** Independent United Methodist, 4-year, coed **Setting** 105-acre suburban campus **Enrollment** 1,731 **Faculty** 16:1 **Application deadline** Rolling **Freshmen** 86% accepted **Housing** Yes **Tuition** $14,290 **Undergraduates** 49% women, 1% part-time, 1% 25 or older, 1% Native American, 1% Hispanic, 5% black, 1% Asian or Pacific Islander **Most popular recent majors** Business administration/commerce/management, education, biology/biological sciences **Academic program** Average class size 19, advanced placement, accelerated degree program, self-designed majors, tutorials, honors program, summer session, adult/continuing education programs, internships **Contact** Mr. Greg King, Director of Admissions and Enrollment Management, Mount Union College, Alliance, OH 44601-3993. Telephone: 330-823-2590. Fax: 330-821-0425.

MOUNT VERNON NAZARENE COLLEGE
MOUNT VERNON, OHIO

Entrance Moderately difficult **General** Independent Nazarene, comprehensive, coed **Setting** 210-acre small-town campus **Enrollment** 1,685 **Faculty** 18:1 **Application deadline** 6/15 **Freshmen** 94% accepted **Housing** Yes **Tuition** $9977 **Undergraduates** 59% women, 6% part-time, 7% 25 or older, 1% Hispanic, 1% black, 1% Asian or Pacific Islander **Most popular recent majors** Social science, business administration/commerce/management, education **Academic program** Advanced placement, tutorials, honors program, summer session, adult/continuing education programs, internships **Contact** Rev. Bruce Oldham, Director of Admissions and Student Recruitment, Mount Vernon Nazarene College, Mount Vernon, OH 43050-9509. Telephone: 614-397-1244 Ext. 4510.

MUSKINGUM COLLEGE
NEW CONCORD, OHIO

Entrance Moderately difficult **General** Independent, comprehensive, coed, affiliated with Presbyterian Church (U.S.A.) **Setting** 215-acre small-town campus **Enrollment** 1,411 **Faculty** 15:1 **Application deadline** 6/1 **Freshmen** 82% accepted **Housing** Yes **Tuition** $10,785 **Undergraduates** 49% women, 6% part-time, 4% 25 or older, 1% Native American, 1% Hispanic, 3% black, 2% Asian or Pacific Islander **Most popular recent majors** Business administration/commerce/management, elementary education, secondary education **Academic program** Average class size 22, advanced placement, accelerated degree program, self-designed majors, tutorials, summer session, adult/continuing education programs, internships **Contact** Mr. Doug Kellar, Director of Admission, Muskingum College, New Concord, OH 43762. Telephone: 614-826-8137. Fax: 614-826-8404.

NOTRE DAME COLLEGE OF OHIO
SOUTH EUCLID, OHIO

Entrance Moderately difficult **General** Independent Roman Catholic, comprehensive, women only **Setting** 53-acre suburban campus **Enrollment** 644 **Faculty** 8:1 **Application deadline** Rolling **Freshmen** 90% accepted **Housing** Yes **Tuition** $12,150 **Undergraduates** 60% part-time, 62% 25 or older, 0% Native American, 2% Hispanic, 28% black, 1% Asian or Pacific Islander **Most popular recent majors** Business administration/commerce/management, elementary education, biology/biological sciences **Academic program** Advanced placement, accelerated degree program, summer session, adult/continuing education programs, internships **Contact** Mrs. Karen Poelking, Dean of Admission, Notre Dame College of Ohio, South Euclid, OH 44121-4293. Telephone: 216-381-1680 Ext. 239. Fax: 216-381-3802.

OBERLIN COLLEGE
OBERLIN, OHIO

Entrance Very difficult **General** Independent, 4-year, coed **Setting** 440-acre small-town campus **Enrollment** 2,861 **Faculty** 12:1 **Application deadline** 1/15 **Freshmen** 65% accepted **Housing** Yes **Tuition** $22,438 **Undergraduates** 58% women, 2% part-time, 1% 25 or older, 1% Native American, 4% Hispanic, 7% black, 9% Asian or Pacific Islander **Most popular recent majors** English, history, biology/biological sciences **Academic program** Advanced placement, accelerated degree program, self-designed majors, tutorials, honors program, internships **Contact** Ms. Debra Chermonte, Director of College Admissions, Oberlin College, Oberlin, OH 44074-1090. Telephone: 216-775-8411.

OHIO DOMINICAN COLLEGE

COLUMBUS, OHIO

Entrance Moderately difficult **General** Independent Roman Catholic, 4-year, coed **Setting** 62-acre urban campus **Enrollment** 1,883 **Faculty** 17:1 **Application deadline** Rolling **Housing** Yes **Tuition** $9350 **Undergraduates** 66% women, 37% part-time, 43% 25 or older, 1% Native American, 2% Hispanic, 15% black, 1% Asian or Pacific Islander **Most popular recent majors** Business administration/commerce/management, elementary education, criminal justice **Academic program** Advanced placement, self-designed majors, honors program, summer session, adult/continuing education programs, internships **Contact** Ms. Vicki Thompson-Campbell, Director of Admissions, Ohio Dominican College, 1216 Sunbury Road, Columbus, OH 43219-2099. Telephone: 614-251-4500. Fax: 614-252-0776.

OHIO NORTHERN UNIVERSITY

ADA, OHIO

Entrance Moderately difficult **General** Independent United Methodist, comprehensive, coed **Setting** 260-acre small-town campus **Enrollment** 2,931 **Faculty** 13:1 **Application deadline** 8/15 **Freshmen** 90% accepted **Housing** Yes **Tuition** $18,870 **Undergraduates** 51% women, 3% part-time, 4% 25 or older, 1% Hispanic, 2% black, 1% Asian or Pacific Islander **Most popular recent majors** Pharmacy/pharmaceutical sciences, mechanical engineering, elementary education **Academic program** Advanced placement, tutorials, summer session, internships **Contact** Ms. Karen Condeni, Dean of Admissions and Financial Aid, Ohio Northern University, Ada, OH 45810-1599. Telephone: 419-772-2260. Fax: 419-772-2313.

THE OHIO STATE UNIVERSITY

COLUMBUS, OHIO

Entrance Moderately difficult **General** State-supported, coed **Setting** 3,303-acre urban campus **Enrollment** 48,352 **Faculty** 14:1 **Application deadline** 2/15 **Freshmen** 85% accepted **Housing** Yes **Tuition** $3660 **Undergraduates** 47% women, 15% part-time, 15% 25 or older, 1% Native American, 2% Hispanic, 7% black, 5% Asian or Pacific Islander **Most popular recent majors** Psychology, communication, accounting **Academic program** Advanced placement, accelerated degree program, self-designed majors, tutorials, honors program, summer session, adult/continuing education programs, internships **Contact** Ms. Lori Faur, Assistant Director, Financial Aid/Operations/Admissions, The Ohio State University, 3rd Floor, Lincoln Tower, Columbus, OH 43210. Telephone: 614-292-3980. Fax: 614-292-4818.

THE OHIO STATE UNIVERSITY AT MARION

MARION, OHIO

Entrance Noncompetitive **General** State-supported, 4-year, coed **Setting** 180-acre small-town campus **Enrollment** 1,312 **Faculty** 16:1 **Application deadline** 7/1 **Freshmen** 97% accepted **Tuition** $3570 **Undergraduates** 55% women, 30% part-time, 33% 25 or older, 1% Native American, 1% Hispanic, 6% black, 1% Asian or Pacific Islander **Academic program** Advanced placement, accelerated degree program, tutorials, honors program, summer session, adult/continuing education programs **Contact** Ms. Becky Vanderlind, Admissions Counselor and Staff Assistant, The Ohio State University at Marion, Marion, OH 43302-5695. Telephone: 614-389-6786.

THE OHIO STATE UNIVERSITY–LIMA CAMPUS

LIMA, OHIO

Entrance Noncompetitive **General** State-supported, 4-year, coed **Setting** 565-acre small-town campus **Enrollment** 1,281 **Faculty** 18:1 **Application deadline** 7/1 **Freshmen** 94% accepted **Tuition** $3570 **Undergraduates** 54% women, 23% part-time, 26% 25 or older, 1% Native American, 1% Hispanic, 3% black, 1% Asian or Pacific Islander **Academic program** Advanced placement, accelerated degree program, tutorials, honors program, summer session, adult/continuing education programs **Contact** Ms. Garlene Penn, Director of Admissions, The Ohio State University–Lima Campus, Lima, OH 45804-3576. Telephone: 419-221-1641.

OHIO STATE UNIVERSITY–MANSFIELD CAMPUS

MANSFIELD, OHIO

Entrance Noncompetitive **General** State-supported, 4-year, coed **Setting** 593-acre small-town campus **Enrollment** 1,343 **Faculty** 21:1 **Application deadline** 7/1 **Freshmen** 94% accepted **Tuition** $3570 **Undergraduates** 61% women, 36% part-time, 24% 25 or older, 1% Native American, 1% Hispanic, 4% black, 1% Asian or Pacific Islander **Academic program** Advanced placement, accelerated degree program, tutorials, honors program, summer session, adult/continuing education programs **Contact** Mr. Henry D. Thomas, Coordinator of Admissions and Financial Aid, Ohio State University–Mansfield Campus, Mansfield, OH 44906-1547. Telephone: 419-755-4226.

OHIO STATE UNIVERSITY–NEWARK CAMPUS
NEWARK, OHIO

Entrance Noncompetitive **General** State-supported, 4-year, coed **Setting** 101-acre small-town campus **Enrollment** 1,611 **Faculty** 18:1 **Application deadline** 7/1 **Freshmen** 97% accepted **Tuition** $3570 **Undergraduates** 59% women, 29% part-time, 24% 25 or older, 1% Native American, 1% Hispanic, 2% black, 1% Asian or Pacific Islander **Academic program** Advanced placement, accelerated degree program, tutorials, honors program, summer session, adult/continuing education programs **Contact** Ms. Ann Donahue, Coordinator of Admissions, Ohio State University–Newark Campus, Newark, OH 43055-1797. Telephone: 614-366-9333.

OHIO UNIVERSITY
ATHENS, OHIO

Entrance Moderately difficult **General** State-supported, coed **Setting** 1,700-acre small-town campus **Enrollment** 18,997 **Faculty** 18:1 **Application deadline** 2/1 **Freshmen** 73% accepted **Housing** Yes **Tuition** $4275 **Undergraduates** 53% women, 6% part-time, 7% 25 or older, 1% Native American, 1% Hispanic, 4% black, 1% Asian or Pacific Islander **Most popular recent majors** Biology/biological sciences, journalism, elementary education **Academic program** Average class size 21, advanced placement, accelerated degree program, self-designed majors, tutorials, honors program, summer session, adult/continuing education programs, internships **Contact** Mr. N. Kip Howard, Director of Admissions, Ohio University, Athens, OH 45701-2979. Telephone: 614-593-4100. Fax: 614-593-0560.

OHIO UNIVERSITY–CHILLICOTHE
CHILLICOTHE, OHIO

Entrance Noncompetitive **General** State-supported, 4-year, coed **Setting** 124-acre small-town campus **Enrollment** 1,565 **Application deadline** 9/1 **Freshmen** 100% accepted **Tuition** $3102 **Undergraduates** 63% women, 45% part-time, 40% 25 or older, 0% Native American, 0% Hispanic, 3% black, 0% Asian or Pacific Islander **Most popular recent majors** Elementary education, nursing, business administration/commerce/management **Academic program** Advanced placement, accelerated degree program, self-designed majors, tutorials, summer session, adult/continuing education programs **Contact** Mr. Richard R. Whitney, Director of Student Services, Ohio University–Chillicothe, Chillicothe, OH 45601-0629. Telephone: 614-774-7242. Fax: 614-774-7214.

OHIO UNIVERSITY–EASTERN
ST. CLAIRSVILLE, OHIO

Entrance Noncompetitive **General** State-supported, 4-year, coed **Setting** 300-acre rural campus **Enrollment** 1,050 **Application deadline** Rolling **Freshmen** 99% accepted **Tuition** $3102 **Undergraduates** 60% women, 35% part-time, 32% 25 or older, 1% Native American, 1% Hispanic, 2% black, 1% Asian or Pacific Islander **Academic program** Advanced placement, accelerated degree program, self-designed majors, summer session, adult/continuing education programs **Contact** Mr. Barry Hess, Director of Student Services, Ohio University–Eastern, St. Clairsville, OH 43950-9724. Telephone: 614-695-1720 Ext. 213.

OHIO UNIVERSITY–LANCASTER
LANCASTER, OHIO

Entrance Noncompetitive **General** State-supported, comprehensive, coed **Setting** 360-acre small-town campus **Enrollment** 1,500 **Faculty** 13:1 **Application deadline** Rolling **Freshmen** 100% accepted **Tuition** $3102 **Undergraduates** 59% women, 54% part-time, 46% 25 or older, 1% Native American, 1% Hispanic, 1% black, 1% Asian or Pacific Islander **Academic program** Advanced placement, accelerated degree program, self-designed majors, tutorials, summer session, adult/continuing education programs **Contact** Dr. Scott Shepherd, Director of Student Services, Ohio University–Lancaster, Lancaster, OH 43130-1097. Telephone: 614-654-6711 Ext. 209.

OHIO UNIVERSITY–ZANESVILLE
ZANESVILLE, OHIO

Entrance Noncompetitive **General** State-supported, comprehensive, coed **Setting** 169-acre small-town campus **Enrollment** 1,195 **Faculty** 18:1 **Application deadline** Rolling **Freshmen** 100% accepted **Tuition** $3117 **Undergraduates** 68% women, 43% part-time, 43% 25 or older, 0% Native American, 0% Hispanic, 2% black, 0% Asian or Pacific Islander **Most popular recent majors** Nursing, elementary education, liberal arts/general studies **Academic program** Advanced placement, self-designed majors, summer session, adult/continuing education programs **Contact** Mr. Matt Melvin, Assistant Director of Student Services, Ohio University-Zanesville, Zanesville, OH 43701-2695. Telephone: 614-453-0762. Fax: 614-453-6161.

OHIO WESLEYAN UNIVERSITY
DELAWARE, OHIO

Entrance Very difficult **General** Independent United Methodist, 4-year, coed **Setting** 200-acre small-town campus **Enrollment** 1,815 **Faculty** 13:1 **Application deadline** 3/1 **Freshmen** 85% accepted **Housing** Yes **Tuition** $19,140 **Undergraduates** 52% women, 3% part-time, 2% 25 or older, 1% Native American, 1% Hispanic, 3% black, 2% Asian or Pacific Islander **Most popular recent majors** Psychology, biology/biological sciences, economics **Academic program** Average class size 18, advanced placement, self-designed majors, tutorials, honors program, summer session, internships **Contact** Mr. Douglas C. Thompson, Dean of Admission, Ohio Wesleyan University, Delaware, OH 43015. Telephone: 614-368-3020. Fax: 614-368-3314.

OTTERBEIN COLLEGE
WESTERVILLE, OHIO

Entrance Moderately difficult **General** Independent United Methodist, comprehensive, coed **Setting** 140-acre suburban campus **Enrollment** 2,526 **Faculty** 13:1 **Application deadline** 4/20 **Freshmen** 86% accepted **Housing** Yes **Tuition** $14,997 **Undergraduates** 59% women, 32% part-time, 30% 25 or older, 1% Native American, 1% Hispanic, 5% black, 2% Asian or Pacific Islander **Most popular recent majors** Business administration/commerce/management, accounting, elementary education **Academic program** Advanced placement, accelerated degree program, self-designed majors, honors program, summer session, adult/continuing education programs, internships **Contact** Ms. Cass Johnson, Director of Admissions, Otterbein College, Westerville, OH 43081. Telephone: 614-823-1500. Fax: 614-823-1200.

PONTIFICAL COLLEGE JOSEPHINUM
COLUMBUS, OHIO

Entrance Minimally difficult **General** Independent Roman Catholic, comprehensive, primarily men **Setting** 100-acre suburban campus **Enrollment** 130 **Faculty** 3:1 **Application deadline** Rolling **Freshmen** 86% accepted **Housing** Yes **Tuition** $7170 **Undergraduates** 7% women, 6% part-time, 16% 25 or older, 0% Native American, 8% Hispanic, 0% black, 2% Asian or Pacific Islander **Most popular recent majors** Philosophy, literature, psychology **Academic program** ESL program, Advanced placement, tutorials, internships **Contact** Ms. Barbara Couts, Secretary for Admissions, Pontifical College Josephinum, Columbus, OH 43235-1498. Telephone: 614-885-5585 Ext. 436.

SHAWNEE STATE UNIVERSITY
PORTSMOUTH, OHIO

Entrance Noncompetitive **General** State-supported, 4-year, coed **Setting** 500-acre small-town campus **Enrollment** 3,505 **Faculty** 13:1 **Application deadline** Rolling **Freshmen** 100% accepted **Housing** Yes **Tuition** $3063 **Undergraduates** 63% women, 24% part-time, 41% 25 or older, 1% Native American, 1% Hispanic, 4% black, 1% Asian or Pacific Islander **Most popular recent majors** Health science, elementary education, business administration/commerce/management **Academic program** Average class size 20, advanced placement, self-designed majors, summer session, adult/continuing education programs, internships **Contact** Ms. Suzanne Shelpman, Director of Admission and Retention, Shawnee State University, Portsmouth, OH 45662-4344. Telephone: 614-355-2610 Ext. 610.

TIFFIN UNIVERSITY
TIFFIN, OHIO

Entrance Minimally difficult **General** Independent, comprehensive, coed **Setting** 108-acre small-town campus **Enrollment** 1,151 **Faculty** 19:1 **Application deadline** Rolling **Freshmen** 85% accepted **Housing** Yes **Tuition** $9210 **Undergraduates** 50% women, 34% part-time, 24% 25 or older, 0% Native American, 1% Hispanic, 8% black, 1% Asian or Pacific Islander **Most popular recent majors** Business administration/commerce/management, accounting, criminal justice **Academic program** Advanced placement, accelerated degree program, summer session, adult/continuing education programs, internships **Contact** Mr. Ron Schumacher, Director of Admissions, Tiffin University, Tiffin, OH 44883-2161. Telephone: 419-448-3425. Fax: 419-447-9605.

THE UNION INSTITUTE
CINCINNATI, OHIO

Entrance Moderately difficult **General** Independent, coed **Setting** Urban campus **Enrollment** 2,016 **Faculty** 18:1 **Application deadline** 10/9 **Freshmen** 73% accepted **Tuition** $7296 **Undergraduates** 61% women, 34% part-time, 95% 25 or older, 2% Native American, 11% Hispanic, 29% black, 1% Asian or Pacific Islander **Most popular recent majors** Business administration/commerce/management, criminal justice, psychology **Academic program** Advanced placement, self-designed majors, tutorials, summer session, adult/continuing education programs **Contact** Mr. Michael Robertson, Associate Registrar, The Union Institute, 440 East McMillan Street, Cincinnati, OH 45206-1925. Telephone: 513-861-6400. Fax: 513-861-0779.

UNIVERSITY OF AKRON
AKRON, OHIO

Entrance Noncompetitive **General** State-supported, coed **Setting** 170-acre urban campus **Enrollment** 24,252 **Faculty** 20:1 **Application deadline** 8/25 **Freshmen** 100% accepted **Housing** Yes **Tuition** $3625 **Undergraduates** 55% women, 44% part-time, 37% 25 or older, 1% Native American, 1% Hispanic, 12% black, 2% Asian or Pacific Islander **Most popular recent majors** Elementary education, accounting, marketing/retailing/merchandising **Academic program** Average class size 27, advanced placement, accelerated degree program, self-designed majors, tutorials, honors program, summer session, adult/continuing education programs, internships **Contact** Ms. Connie Murray, Senior Associate Director of Admissions, University of Akron, 381 Buchtel Common, Akron, OH 44325-2001. Telephone: 330-972-6428.

UNIVERSITY OF CINCINNATI
CINCINNATI, OHIO

Entrance Moderately difficult **General** State-supported, coed **Setting** 137-acre urban campus **Enrollment** 19,139 **Faculty** 19:1 **Application deadline** Rolling **Freshmen** 85% accepted **Housing** Yes **Tuition** $4359 **Undergraduates** 48% women, 17% part-time, 16% 25 or older, 0% Native American, 1% Hispanic, 9% black, 4% Asian or Pacific Islander **Most popular recent majors** Business administration/commerce/management, engineering and applied sciences, education **Academic program** ESL program, Accelerated degree program, self-designed majors, honors program, summer session, adult/continuing education programs **Contact** Mr. James Williams, Director of Admissions, University of Cincinnati, Mail Location 91, 100 Edwards Center, Cincinnati, OH 45221-0091. Telephone: 513-556-1100.

UNIVERSITY OF DAYTON
DAYTON, OHIO

Entrance Moderately difficult **General** Independent Roman Catholic, coed **Setting** 110-acre suburban campus **Enrollment** 10,320 **Faculty** 15:1 **Application deadline** Rolling **Freshmen** 90% accepted **Housing** Yes **Tuition** $14,180 **Undergraduates** 50% women, 9% part-time, 6% 25 or older, 0% Native American, 2% Hispanic, 3% black, 1% Asian or Pacific Islander **Most popular recent majors** Business administration/commerce/management, education, communication **Academic program** Advanced placement, accelerated degree program, self-designed majors, tutorials, honors program, summer session, adult/continuing education programs, internships **Contact** Mr. Myron H. Achbach, Director of Admission, University of Dayton, Dayton, OH 45469-1611. Telephone: 937-229-4411. Fax: 937-229-4545.

THE UNIVERSITY OF FINDLAY
FINDLAY, OHIO

Entrance Moderately difficult **General** Independent, comprehensive, coed, affiliated with Church of God **Setting** Small-town campus **Enrollment** 3,743 **Faculty** 19:1 **Application deadline** Rolling **Freshmen** 78% accepted **Housing** Yes **Tuition** $13,112 **Undergraduates** 53% women, 22% part-time, 31% 25 or older, 1% Native American, 4% Hispanic, 9% black, 3% Asian or Pacific Islander **Most popular recent majors** Business administration/commerce/management, (pre)veterinary medicine sequence, environmental sciences **Academic program** Average class size 35, advanced placement, self-designed majors, tutorials, honors program, summer session, adult/continuing education programs, internships **Contact** Dr. Mary Ellen Klein, Dean of Enrollment Management, The University of Findlay, 1000 N. Main Street, Findlay, OH 45840-3653. Telephone: 419-424-4640. Fax: 419-424-4822.

UNIVERSITY OF RIO GRANDE
RIO GRANDE, OHIO

Entrance Noncompetitive **General** Independent, comprehensive, coed **Setting** 170-acre rural campus **Enrollment** 2,057 **Faculty** 18:1 **Application deadline** Rolling **Freshmen** 94% accepted **Housing** Yes **Tuition** $2394 **Undergraduates** 60% women, 18% part-time, 21% 25 or older, 1% Native American, 0% Hispanic, 2% black, 0% Asian or Pacific Islander **Most popular recent majors** Education, business administration/commerce/management, nursing **Academic program** Average class size 18, advanced placement, accelerated degree program, self-designed majors, tutorials, honors program, summer session, adult/continuing education programs, internships **Contact** Mr. Mark F. Abell, Executive Director of Admissions, University of Rio Grande, Rio Grande, OH 45674. Telephone: 614-245-5353 Ext. 207. Fax: 614-245-9220.

UNIVERSITY OF TOLEDO
TOLEDO, OHIO

Entrance Noncompetitive **General** State-supported, coed **Setting** 407-acre suburban campus **Enrollment** 21,692 **Faculty** 18:1 **Application deadline** Rolling **Freshmen** 97% accepted **Housing** Yes **Tuition** $3952 **Undergraduates** 53% women, 21% part-time, 31% 25 or older, 1% Native American, 2% Hispanic, 13% black, 2% Asian or Pacific Islander **Most popular recent majors** Communication, marketing/retailing/merchandising **Academic program** Advanced placement, accelerated degree program, self-designed majors, tutorials, honors program, summer session, adult/continuing education programs, internships **Contact** Mr. Kent Hopkins, Director of Admissions, University of Toledo, Toledo, OH 43606-3398. Telephone: 419-530-8888. Fax: 419-530-4504.

URBANA UNIVERSITY
URBANA, OHIO

Entrance Moderately difficult **General** Independent Swedenborgian, 4-year, coed **Setting** 128-acre small-town campus **Enrollment** 1,179 **Faculty** 16:1 **Application deadline** Rolling **Freshmen** 79% accepted **Housing** Yes **Tuition** $10,530 **Undergraduates** 49% women, 19% part-time, 20% 25 or older, 1% Native American, 1% Hispanic, 25% black **Most popular recent majors** Business administration/commerce/management, education, liberal arts/general studies **Academic program** Average class size 17, advanced placement, accelerated degree program, self-designed majors, honors program, summer session, adult/continuing education programs, internships **Contact** Mr. Robert Allen, Vice President of Enrollment Management, Urbana University, Urbana, OH 43078-2091. Telephone: 513-484-1356. Fax: 513-484-1389.

URSULINE COLLEGE
PEPPER PIKE, OHIO

Entrance Minimally difficult **General** Independent Roman Catholic, comprehensive, primarily women **Setting** 112-acre suburban campus **Enrollment** 1,312 **Faculty** 14:1 **Application deadline** Rolling **Freshmen** 84% accepted **Housing** Yes **Tuition** $12,128 **Undergraduates** 95% women, 44% part-time, 58% 25 or older, 1% Native American, 1% Hispanic, 18% black, 1% Asian or Pacific Islander **Most popular recent majors** Nursing, psychology, business administration/commerce/management **Academic program** Advanced placement, self-designed majors, summer session, adult/continuing education programs, internships **Contact** Mr. Dennis L. Giacomino, Director of Admissions, Ursuline College, Pepper Pike, OH 44124-4398. Telephone: 216-449-4203. Fax: 216-449-2235.

WALSH UNIVERSITY
NORTH CANTON, OHIO

Entrance Moderately difficult **General** Independent Roman Catholic, comprehensive, coed **Setting** 58-acre small-town campus **Enrollment** 1,381 **Faculty** 19:1 **Application deadline** Rolling **Freshmen** 53% accepted **Housing** Yes **Tuition** $10,680 **Undergraduates** 55% women, 25% part-time, 46% 25 or older, 0% Native American, 1% Hispanic, 5% black, 1% Asian or Pacific Islander **Most popular recent majors** Business administration/commerce/management, nursing, education **Academic program** Average class size 19, advanced placement, accelerated degree program, self-designed majors, tutorials, honors program, summer session, adult/continuing education programs, internships **Contact** Br. Doug Swartz, Director of Admissions, Walsh University, North Canton, OH 44720-3396. Telephone: 330-490-7172. Fax: 330-490-7165.

WILBERFORCE UNIVERSITY
WILBERFORCE, OHIO

Entrance Minimally difficult **General** Independent, 4-year, coed, affiliated with African Methodist Episcopal Church **Setting** 125-acre rural campus **Enrollment** 897 **Faculty** 12:1 **Application deadline** 6/1 **Freshmen** 25% accepted **Housing** Yes **Tuition** $8060 **Undergraduates** 64% women, 1% part-time, 10% 25 or older, 0% Native American, 0% Hispanic, 96% black **Academic program** Advanced placement, tutorials, honors program **Contact** Mr. Kenneth C. Christmon, Director of Admissions, Wilberforce University, Wilberforce, OH 45384. Telephone: 937-376-2911 Ext. 789. Fax: 937-376-4751.

WILMINGTON COLLEGE
WILMINGTON, OHIO

Entrance Moderately difficult **General** Independent Friends, 4-year, coed **Setting** 1,465-acre small-town campus **Enrollment** 1,092 **Faculty** 17:1 **Application deadline** Rolling **Freshmen** 84% accepted **Housing** Yes **Tuition** $12,500 **Undergraduates** 55% women, 3% part-time, 7% 25 or older, 0% Native American, 1% Hispanic, 3% black,

1% Asian or Pacific Islander **Most popular recent majors** Education, business administration/commerce/management, agricultural sciences **Academic program** Average class size 22, advanced placement, self-designed majors, tutorials, honors program, summer session, adult/continuing education programs, internships **Contact** Dr. Lawrence T. Lesick, Dean of Admission and Financial Aid, Wilmington College, Wilmington, OH 45177. Telephone: 513-382-6661 Ext. 265. Fax: 513-382-7077.

WITTENBERG UNIVERSITY
SPRINGFIELD, OHIO

Entrance Moderately difficult **General** Independent, 4-year, coed, affiliated with Evangelical Lutheran Church **Setting** 71-acre suburban campus **Enrollment** 2,000 **Faculty** 14:1 **Application deadline** 3/15 **Freshmen** 87% accepted **Housing** Yes **Tuition** $19,140 **Undergraduates** 54% women, 2% part-time, 1% 25 or older, 1% Native American, 2% Hispanic, 7% black, 2% Asian or Pacific Islander **Most popular recent majors** Business administration/commerce/management, biology/biological sciences, education **Academic program** ESL program, Advanced placement, accelerated degree program, self-designed majors, tutorials, honors program, summer session, adult/continuing education programs, internships **Contact** Mr. Kenneth G. Benne, Dean of Admissions, Wittenberg University, Springfield, OH 45501-0720. Telephone: 937-327-6314 Ext. 6366. Fax: 937-327-6379.

WRIGHT STATE UNIVERSITY
DAYTON, OHIO

Entrance Minimally difficult **General** State-supported, coed **Setting** 557-acre suburban campus **Enrollment** 15,697 **Faculty** 20:1 **Application deadline** 9/1 **Freshmen** 90% accepted **Housing** Yes **Tuition** $3708 **Undergraduates** 55% women, 27% part-time, 31% 25 or older, 1% Native American, 1% Hispanic, 7% black, 2% Asian or Pacific Islander **Most popular recent majors** Accounting, nursing, psychology **Academic program** Advanced placement, self-designed majors, honors program, summer session, adult/continuing education programs, internships **Contact** Mr. Ken Davenport, Director of Undergraduate Admissions, Wright State University, Dayton, OH 45435. Telephone: 937-775-5700.

XAVIER UNIVERSITY
CINCINNATI, OHIO

Entrance Moderately difficult **General** Independent Roman Catholic, comprehensive, coed **Setting** 100-acre suburban campus **Enrollment** 6,423 **Faculty** 14:1 **Application deadline** Rolling **Freshmen** 95% accepted **Housing** Yes **Tuition** $13,650 **Undergraduates** 59% women, 22% part-time, 0% Native American, 1% Hispanic, 8% black, 2% Asian or Pacific Islander **Most popular recent majors** Business administration/commerce/management, education, communication **Academic program** Average class size 22, advanced placement, accelerated degree program, honors program, summer session, adult/continuing education programs, internships **Contact** Mr. Raymond Kennelly, Director of Admissions, Xavier University, Cincinnati, OH 45207-5311. Telephone: 513-745-3301. Fax: 513-745-4319.

YOUNGSTOWN STATE UNIVERSITY
YOUNGSTOWN, OHIO

Entrance Noncompetitive **General** State-supported, comprehensive, coed **Setting** 130-acre urban campus **Enrollment** 12,801 **Application deadline** 8/15 **Housing** Yes **Tuition** $3558 **Undergraduates** 53% women, 25% part-time, 30% 25 or older, 1% Native American, 1% Hispanic, 8% black, 1% Asian or Pacific Islander **Most popular recent majors** Criminal justice, elementary education, accounting **Academic program** Advanced placement, accelerated degree program, self-designed majors, honors program, summer session, adult/continuing education programs, internships **Contact** Ms. Marie D. Cullen, Director of Admissions, Youngstown State University, One University Plaza, Youngstown, OH 44555-0002. Telephone: 330-742-3150. Fax: 330-742-1998.

Oklahoma

BARTLESVILLE WESLEYAN COLLEGE
BARTLESVILLE, OKLAHOMA

Entrance Minimally difficult **General** Independent, 4-year, coed, affiliated with Wesleyan Church **Setting** 127-acre small-town campus **Enrollment** 571 **Application deadline** Rolling **Freshmen** 53% accepted **Housing** Yes **Tuition** $8100 **Undergraduates** 62% women, 34% part-time, 40% 25 or older, 7% Native American, 2% Hispanic, 2% black, 1% Asian or Pacific Islander **Most popular recent majors** Business administration/commerce/management, education, behavioral sciences **Academic program** Advanced placement, self-designed majors, summer session, adult/continuing education programs, internships **Contact** Mr. Jere Johnson, Enrollment Services Administrator, Bartlesville Wesleyan College, Bartlesville, OK 74006-6299. Telephone: 918-335-6219. Fax: 918-335-6229.

CAMERON UNIVERSITY
LAWTON, OKLAHOMA

Entrance Minimally difficult **General** State-supported, comprehensive, coed **Setting** 160-acre suburban campus **Enrollment** 5,231 **Faculty** 14:1 **Application deadline** Rolling **Freshmen** 94% accepted **Housing** Yes **Tuition** $1760 **Undergraduates** 59% women, 39% part-time, 52% 25 or older, 5% Native American, 6% Hispanic, 16% black, 3% Asian or Pacific Islander **Most popular recent majors** Business administration/commerce/management, education, computer information systems **Academic program** Average class size 50, advanced placement, honors program, summer session, adult/continuing education programs **Contact** Ms. Zoe Du Rant, Director of Admissions, Cameron University, Lawton, OK 73505-6377. Telephone: 405-581-2288. Fax: 405-581-5514.

EAST CENTRAL UNIVERSITY
ADA, OKLAHOMA

Entrance Moderately difficult **General** State-supported, comprehensive, coed **Setting** 140-acre small-town campus **Enrollment** 4,369 **Faculty** 20:1 **Application deadline** 8/21 **Freshmen** 95% accepted **Housing** Yes **Tuition** $1724 **Undergraduates** 60% women, 26% part-time, 40% 25 or older, 14% Native American, 1% Hispanic, 3% black, 1% Asian or Pacific Islander **Most popular recent majors** Elementary education, physical education, nursing **Academic program** Advanced placement, accelerated degree program, tutorials, honors program, summer session, adult/continuing education programs, internships **Contact** Ms. Pamla Armstrong, Registrar, East Central University, Ada, OK 74820-6899. Telephone: 405-332-8000. Fax: 405-521-6516.

HILLSDALE FREE WILL BAPTIST COLLEGE
MOORE, OKLAHOMA

Entrance Noncompetitive **General** Independent Free Will Baptist, 4-year, coed **Setting** 40-acre suburban campus **Enrollment** 147 **Faculty** 10:1 **Application deadline** Rolling **Freshmen** 100% accepted **Housing** Yes **Tuition** $4535 **Undergraduates** 37% women, 34% part-time, 20% 25 or older, 6% Native American, 1% Hispanic, 7% black, 0% Asian or Pacific Islander **Most popular recent majors** Biblical studies, elementary education, ministries **Academic program** Average class size 20, advanced placement, accelerated degree program, tutorials, summer session, internships **Contact** Ms. Pam Thompson, Director of Financial Aid/Admissions, Hillsdale Free Will Baptist College, Moore, OK 73160. Telephone: 405-794-6661 Ext. 233. Fax: 405-794-6663.

LANGSTON UNIVERSITY
LANGSTON, OKLAHOMA

Entrance Minimally difficult **General** State-supported, comprehensive, coed **Setting** 40-acre rural campus **Enrollment** 4,008 **Faculty** 25:1 **Application deadline** Rolling **Freshmen** 62% accepted **Housing** Yes **Tuition** $1482 **Undergraduates** 48% women, 6% part-time, 20% 25 or older, 2% Native American, 1% Hispanic, 61% black **Academic program** Advanced placement, accelerated degree program, honors program, summer session, adult/continuing education programs, internships **Contact** Ms. La Cressa Trice, Admission Counselor, Langston University, Langston, OK 73050-0838. Telephone: 405-466-3428. Fax: 405-466-3381.

MID-AMERICA BIBLE COLLEGE
OKLAHOMA CITY, OKLAHOMA

Entrance Noncompetitive **General** Independent, 4-year, coed, affiliated with Church of God **Setting** 145-acre suburban campus **Enrollment** 512 **Application deadline** Rolling **Freshmen** 98% accepted **Housing** Yes **Tuition** $4684 **Undergraduates** 44% women, 16% part-time, 25% 25 or older, 2% Native American, 2% Hispanic, 8% black, 1% Asian or Pacific Islander **Most popular recent majors** Religious studies, liberal arts/general studies, behavioral sciences **Academic program** Advanced placement, accelerated degree program, summer session, adult/continuing education programs, internships **Contact** Mr. Scott Ethridge, Director of Student Recruitment, Mid-America Bible College, Oklahoma City, OK 73170-4504. Telephone: 405-691-3800 Ext. 107.

NORTHEASTERN STATE UNIVERSITY
TAHLEQUAH, OKLAHOMA

Entrance Moderately difficult **General** State-supported, comprehensive, coed **Setting** 160-acre small-town campus **Enrollment** 8,735 **Application deadline** 8/1 **Freshmen** 91% accepted **Housing** Yes **Tuition** $1650 **Undergraduates** 54% women, 32% part-time, 17% Native American, 1% Hispanic, 8% black **Most popular recent majors** Education, business administration/commerce/management, criminal justice **Academic program** Advanced placement, tutorials, honors program, summer session, adult/continuing education programs, internships **Contact** Director of Admissions and Registrar, Northeastern State University, Tahlequah, OK 74464-2399. Telephone: 918-456-5511 Ext. 2200. Fax: 918-458-2342.

NORTHWESTERN OKLAHOMA STATE UNIVERSITY

ALVA, OKLAHOMA

Entrance Moderately difficult **General** State-supported, comprehensive, coed **Setting** 70-acre small-town campus **Enrollment** 1,790 **Faculty** 19:1 **Application deadline** Rolling **Freshmen** 99% accepted **Housing** Yes **Tuition** $1650 **Undergraduates** 56% women, 27% part-time, 28% 25 or older, 3% Native American, 2% Hispanic, 3% black, 1% Asian or Pacific Islander **Most popular recent major** Elementary education **Academic program** Advanced placement, tutorials, summer session, adult/continuing education programs **Contact** Mr. S. L. White, Director of Pre-Admissions, Northwestern Oklahoma State University, 709 Oklahoma Boulevard, Alva, OK 73717-2799. Telephone: 405-327-8545. Fax: 405-327-1881.

OKLAHOMA BAPTIST UNIVERSITY

SHAWNEE, OKLAHOMA

Entrance Moderately difficult **General** Independent Southern Baptist, comprehensive, coed **Setting** 125-acre small-town campus **Enrollment** 2,361 **Faculty** 14:1 **Application deadline** 8/1 **Freshmen** 95% accepted **Housing** Yes **Tuition** $7656 **Undergraduates** 54% women, 26% part-time, 20% 25 or older, 5% Native American, 2% Hispanic, 3% black, 1% Asian or Pacific Islander **Most popular recent majors** Education, business administration/commerce/management, nursing **Academic program** Average class size 27, advanced placement, self-designed majors, tutorials, honors program, summer session, internships **Contact** Mr. Michael Cappo, Dean of Admissions, Oklahoma Baptist University, Shawnee, OK 74801-2558. Telephone: 405-878-2033.

OKLAHOMA CHRISTIAN UNIVERSITY OF SCIENCE AND ARTS

OKLAHOMA CITY, OKLAHOMA

Entrance Noncompetitive **General** Independent, comprehensive, coed, affiliated with Church of Christ **Setting** 200-acre suburban campus **Enrollment** 1,562 **Faculty** 15:1 **Application deadline** Rolling **Freshmen** 91% accepted **Housing** Yes **Tuition** $8278 **Undergraduates** 47% women, 10% part-time, 2% Native American, 2% Hispanic, 5% black, 3% Asian or Pacific Islander **Most popular recent majors** Business administration/commerce/management, elementary education, biology/biological sciences **Academic program** Average class size 25, advanced placement, accelerated degree program, honors program, summer session, internships **Contact** Mr. Kyle Ray, Director of Admissions, Oklahoma Christian University of Science and Arts, Box 11000, Oklahoma City, OK 73136-1100. Telephone: 405-425-5050. Fax: 405-425-5208.

OKLAHOMA CITY UNIVERSITY

OKLAHOMA CITY, OKLAHOMA

Entrance Moderately difficult **General** Independent United Methodist, comprehensive, coed **Setting** 65-acre urban campus **Enrollment** 4,696 **Faculty** 14:1 **Application deadline** Rolling **Freshmen** 82% accepted **Housing** Yes **Tuition** $8512 **Undergraduates** 52% women, 26% part-time, 35% 25 or older, 4% Native American, 2% Hispanic, 5% black, 2% Asian or Pacific Islander **Most popular recent majors** Business administration/commerce/management, dance, communication **Academic program** Average class size 21, advanced placement, self-designed majors, honors program, summer session, adult/continuing education programs, internships **Contact** Mr. Keith Hackett, Vice President of Admissions, Oklahoma City University, 2501 North Blackwelder, Oklahoma City, OK 73106-1402. Telephone: 405-521-5050.

OKLAHOMA PANHANDLE STATE UNIVERSITY

GOODWELL, OKLAHOMA

Entrance Noncompetitive **General** State-supported, 4-year, coed **Setting** 40-acre rural campus **Enrollment** 1,366 **Faculty** 16:1 **Application deadline** Rolling **Freshmen** 100% accepted **Housing** Yes **Tuition** $1653 **Undergraduates** 53% women, 18% part-time, 25% 25 or older, 2% Native American, 7% Hispanic, 1% black, 1% Asian or Pacific Islander **Most popular recent majors** Agricultural education, business administration/commerce/management, elementary education **Academic program** Advanced placement, accelerated degree program, tutorials, summer session, adult/continuing education programs, internships **Contact** Ms. Melissa Worth, Admissions Counselor, Oklahoma Panhandle State University, Goodwell, OK 73939-0430. Telephone: 405-349-2611 Ext. 311. Fax: 405-349-2302.

OKLAHOMA STATE UNIVERSITY
STILLWATER, OKLAHOMA

Entrance Moderately difficult **General** State-supported, coed **Setting** 840-acre small-town campus **Enrollment** 19,201 **Faculty** 22:1 **Application deadline** Rolling **Freshmen** 96% accepted **Housing** Yes **Tuition** $1708 **Undergraduates** 46% women, 11% part-time, 16% 25 or older, 7% Native American, 2% Hispanic, 3% black, 2% Asian or Pacific Islander **Most popular recent majors** Education, management information systems, marketing/retailing/merchandising **Academic program** Average class size 45, advanced placement, accelerated degree program, self-designed majors, tutorials, honors program, summer session, adult/continuing education programs, internships **Contact** High School and College Relations, Oklahoma State University, Stillwater, OK 74078. Telephone: 405-744-5358. Fax: 405-744-5285.

ORAL ROBERTS UNIVERSITY
TULSA, OKLAHOMA

Entrance Moderately difficult **General** Independent interdenominational, coed **Setting** 500-acre urban campus **Enrollment** 3,761 **Faculty** 16:1 **Application deadline** Rolling **Freshmen** 53% accepted **Housing** Yes **Tuition** $9934 **Undergraduates** 55% women, 7% part-time, 19% 25 or older, 1% Native American, 6% Hispanic, 22% black, 3% Asian or Pacific Islander **Most popular recent majors** Business administration/commerce/management, telecommunications, elementary education **Academic program** ESL program, Advanced placement, accelerated degree program, self-designed majors, honors program, summer session, adult/continuing education programs, internships **Contact** Mr. Shawn Nichols, Director of Admissions, Oral Roberts University, 7777 South Lewis Avenue, Tulsa, OK 74171-0001. Telephone: 918-495-6518. Fax: 918-495-6222.

PHILLIPS UNIVERSITY
ENID, OKLAHOMA

Entrance Moderately difficult **General** Independent, comprehensive, coed, affiliated with Christian Church (Disciples of Christ) **Setting** 35-acre small-town campus **Enrollment** 613 **Faculty** 13:1 **Application deadline** Rolling **Freshmen** 85% accepted **Housing** Yes **Tuition** $7105 **Undergraduates** 51% women, 22% part-time, 21% 25 or older, 2% Native American, 5% Hispanic, 7% black, 2% Asian or Pacific Islander **Most popular recent majors** Business administration/commerce/management, education, health science **Academic program** Average class size 16, advanced placement, accelerated degree program, self-designed majors, tutorials, summer session, adult/continuing education programs, internships **Contact** Ms. DeeDee Moss, Administrative Assistant of Admissions, Phillips University, Enid, OK 73701-6439. Telephone: 405-548-2203. Fax: 405-237-1607.

SOUTHEASTERN OKLAHOMA STATE UNIVERSITY
DURANT, OKLAHOMA

Entrance Moderately difficult **General** State-supported, comprehensive, coed **Setting** 176-acre small-town campus **Enrollment** 3,831 **Faculty** 20:1 **Application deadline** 8/15 **Freshmen** 84% accepted **Housing** Yes **Tuition** $1709 **Undergraduates** 54% women, 19% part-time, 30% 25 or older, 32% Native American, 1% Hispanic, 4% black, 1% Asian or Pacific Islander **Most popular recent majors** Elementary education, criminal justice, business administration/commerce/management **Academic program** Advanced placement, accelerated degree program, honors program, summer session, adult/continuing education programs, internships **Contact** Ms. Debra Hemphill, Director of Admissions and Records, Southeastern Oklahoma State University, Durant, OK 74701-0609. Telephone: 405-924-0121 Ext. 2381. Fax: 405-920-7472.

SOUTHERN NAZARENE UNIVERSITY
BETHANY, OKLAHOMA

Entrance Noncompetitive **General** Independent Nazarene, comprehensive, coed **Setting** 40-acre suburban campus **Enrollment** 1,828 **Faculty** 17:1 **Application deadline** 8/15 **Freshmen** 100% accepted **Housing** Yes **Tuition** $8222 **Undergraduates** 58% women, 10% part-time, 21% 25 or older, 2% Native American, 5% Hispanic, 4% black, 1% Asian or Pacific Islander **Most popular recent majors** Education, (pre)medicine sequence, business administration/commerce/management **Academic program** Advanced placement, accelerated degree program, self-designed majors, summer session, adult/continuing education programs, internships **Contact** Ms. Tollya Spindle, Director of Admissions, Southern Nazarene University, Bethany, OK 73008-2694. Telephone: 405-491-6324. Fax: 405-491-6381.

SOUTHWESTERN COLLEGE OF CHRISTIAN MINISTRIES
BETHANY, OKLAHOMA

Entrance Minimally difficult **General** Independent, comprehensive, specialized, coed, affiliated with Pentecostal Holiness Church **Setting** 7-acre small-town campus **Enrollment** 222 **Faculty** 10:1 **Application deadline** Rolling **Freshmen** 84% accepted **Housing** Yes **Tuition** $4324 **Undergraduates** 55% women, 25% part-time, 20% 25 or older, 6% Native American, 2% Hispanic, 5% black, 2% Asian or Pacific Islander **Academic program** Advanced placement, summer session, internships **Contact** Mr. John Wheeler, Director of Admissions, Southwestern College of Christian Ministries, PO Box 340, Bethany, OK 73008-0340. Telephone: 405-789-7661.

SOUTHWESTERN OKLAHOMA STATE UNIVERSITY
WEATHERFORD, OKLAHOMA

Entrance Moderately difficult **General** State-supported, comprehensive, coed **Setting** 73-acre small-town campus **Enrollment** 4,506 **Faculty** 19:1 **Application deadline** 8/15 **Freshmen** 99% accepted **Housing** Yes **Tuition** $1584 **Undergraduates** 56% women, 12% part-time, 21% 25 or older, 4% Native American, 2% Hispanic, 3% black, 3% Asian or Pacific Islander **Most popular recent majors** Pharmacy/pharmaceutical sciences, elementary education, accounting **Academic program** Average class size 30, advanced placement, accelerated degree program, tutorials, summer session, adult/continuing education programs, internships **Contact** Mr. Bob Klaassen, Registrar/Director of Admissions, Southwestern Oklahoma State University, Weatherford, OK 73096-3098. Telephone: 405-774-3777. Fax: 405-772-5447.

UNIVERSITY OF BIBLICAL STUDIES AND SEMINARY
BETHANY, OKLAHOMA

Entrance Noncompetitive **General** Independent interdenominational, comprehensive, coed **Setting** 1-acre small-town campus **Enrollment** 1,400 **Tuition** $2325 **Undergraduates** 15% women, 85% part-time, 90% 25 or older **Contact** Mr. Paul Leach, Recruiting Coordinator, University of Biblical Studies and Seminary, Bethany, OK 73008. Telephone: 405-495-2526. Fax: 405-495-2521.

UNIVERSITY OF CENTRAL OKLAHOMA
EDMOND, OKLAHOMA

Entrance Minimally difficult **General** State-supported, comprehensive, coed **Setting** 200-acre suburban campus **Enrollment** 14,481 **Faculty** 21:1 **Application deadline** Rolling **Freshmen** 94% accepted **Housing** Yes **Tuition** $1716 **Undergraduates** 58% women, 35% part-time, 36% 25 or older, 4% Native American, 2% Hispanic, 6% black, 2% Asian or Pacific Islander **Most popular recent majors** Liberal arts/general studies, elementary education, nursing **Academic program** Average class size 31, advanced placement, accelerated degree program, honors program, summer session, adult/continuing education programs, internships **Contact** Ms. Evelyn Wilson, Dean of Enrollment Services, University of Central Oklahoma, Edmond, OK 73034-5209. Telephone: 405-341-2980.

UNIVERSITY OF OKLAHOMA
NORMAN, OKLAHOMA

Entrance Moderately difficult **General** State-supported, coed **Setting** 3,200-acre suburban campus **Enrollment** 20,026 **Application deadline** 7/15 **Freshmen** 88% accepted **Housing** Yes **Tuition** $2126 **Undergraduates** 45% women, 16% part-time, 16% 25 or older, 7% Native American, 3% Hispanic, 7% black, 5% Asian or Pacific Islander **Most popular recent majors** Management information systems, accounting, psychology **Academic program** Advanced placement, accelerated degree program, self-designed majors, tutorials, honors program, summer session, adult/continuing education programs, internships **Contact** Mr. J. P. Audus, Director of Prospective Student Services, University of Oklahoma, 407 West Boyd, Norman, OK 73019. Telephone: 405-325-2151. Fax: 405-325-7478.

UNIVERSITY OF OKLAHOMA HEALTH SCIENCES CENTER
OKLAHOMA CITY, OKLAHOMA

Entrance Moderately difficult **General** State-supported, upper-level, coed **Setting** 200-acre urban campus **Enrollment** 2,757 **Tuition** $2271 **Undergraduates** 72% women, 9% part-time, 45% 25 or older, 8% Native American, 3% Hispanic, 2% black, 7% Asian or Pacific Islander **Most popular recent majors** Nursing, pharmacy/pharmaceutical sciences, physical therapy **Academic program** Advanced placement, honors program, summer session, internships **Contact** Dr. Willie V. Bryan, Vice Provost for Educational Services and Registrar, University of Oklahoma Health Sciences Center, PO Box 26901, Oklahoma City, OK 73190. Telephone: 405-271-2655. Fax: 405-271-2480.

UNIVERSITY OF SCIENCE AND ARTS OF OKLAHOMA
CHICKASHA, OKLAHOMA

Entrance Moderately difficult **General** State-supported, 4-year, coed **Setting** 75-acre small-town campus **Enrollment** 1,523 **Faculty** 22:1 **Application deadline** Rolling **Freshmen** 91% accepted **Housing** Yes **Tuition** $1604 **Undergraduates** 65% women, 27% part-time, 42% 25 or older, 10% Native American, 1% Hispanic, 4% black, 0% Asian or Pacific Islander **Most popular recent majors** Business administration/commerce/management, elementary education, speech pathology and audiology **Academic program** Average class size 42, advanced placement, accelerated degree program, self-designed majors, tutorials, honors program, summer session, adult/continuing education programs, internships **Contact** Dr. Tim McElroy, Registrar and Director of Admissions and Records, University of Science and Arts of Oklahoma, Chickasha, OK 73018-0001. Telephone: 405-224-3140 Ext. 205. Fax: 405-521-6244.

UNIVERSITY OF TULSA
TULSA, OKLAHOMA

Entrance Moderately difficult **General** Independent, coed, affiliated with Presbyterian Church **Setting** 100-acre urban campus **Enrollment** 4,236 **Faculty** 11:1 **Application deadline** Rolling **Freshmen** 83% accepted **Housing** Yes **Tuition** $12,940 **Undergraduates** 52% women, 10% part-time, 21% 25 or older, 6% Native American, 3% Hispanic, 7% black, 2% Asian or Pacific Islander **Most popular recent majors** Psychology, chemical engineering, accounting **Academic program** Advanced placement, self-designed majors, honors program, summer session, adult/continuing education programs, internships **Contact** Mr. John C. Corso, Associate VP for Administration/Dean of Admission, University of Tulsa, 600 South College Avenue, Tulsa, OK 74104-3189. Telephone: 918-631-2307. Fax: 918-631-3172.

South Dakota

AUGUSTANA COLLEGE
SIOUX FALLS, SOUTH DAKOTA

Entrance Moderately difficult **General** Independent, comprehensive, coed, affiliated with Evangelical Lutheran Church in America **Setting** 100-acre urban campus **Enrollment** 1,750 **Faculty** 12:1 **Application deadline** Rolling **Freshmen** 92% accepted **Housing** Yes **Tuition** $13,112 **Undergraduates** 65% women, 8% part-time, 5% 25 or older, 1% Native American, 1% Hispanic, 1% black, 1% Asian or Pacific Islander **Most popular recent majors** Biology/biological sciences, education, business administration/commerce/management **Academic program** Advanced placement, accelerated degree program, self-designed majors, tutorials, honors program, summer session, adult/continuing education programs, internships **Contact** Mr. Robert A. Preloger, Vice President of Enrollment, Augustana College, 2001 South Summit, Sioux Falls, SD 57197. Telephone: 605-336-5516. Fax: 605-336-5518.

BLACK HILLS STATE UNIVERSITY
SPEARFISH, SOUTH DAKOTA

Entrance Minimally difficult **General** State-supported, comprehensive, coed **Setting** 123-acre small-town campus **Enrollment** 2,866 **Faculty** 21:1 **Application deadline** Rolling **Freshmen** 99% accepted **Housing** Yes **Tuition** $2878 **Undergraduates** 58% women, 18% part-time, 30% 25 or older, 4% Native American, 1% Hispanic, 1% black, 1% Asian or Pacific Islander **Most popular recent majors** Education, business administration/commerce/management **Academic program** Average class size 25, ESL program, advanced placement, summer session, internships **Contact** Ms. Judy Berry, Assistant Director of Admissions, Black Hills State University, Spearfish, SD 57799-9502. Telephone: 605-642-6343.

DAKOTA STATE UNIVERSITY
MADISON, SOUTH DAKOTA

Entrance Minimally difficult **General** State-supported, 4-year, coed **Setting** 40-acre rural campus **Enrollment** 1,231 **Faculty** 15:1 **Application deadline** Rolling **Freshmen** 91% accepted **Housing** Yes **Tuition** $3027 **Undergraduates** 59% women, 34% part-time, 12% 25 or older, 1% black, 1% Asian or Pacific Islander **Most popular recent majors** Business administration/commerce/management, education, computer information systems **Academic program** Advanced placement, honors program, summer session, internships **Contact** Ms. Katy O'Hara, Admissions Secretary, Dakota State University, Madison, SD 57042-1799. Telephone: 605-256-5139. Fax: 605-256-5316.

DAKOTA WESLEYAN UNIVERSITY
MITCHELL, SOUTH DAKOTA

Entrance Moderately difficult **General** Independent United Methodist, comprehensive, coed **Setting** 40-acre small-town campus **Enrollment** 710 **Faculty** 15:1 **Application deadline** 8/26 **Freshmen** 75% accepted **Housing** Yes **Tuition** $8825 **Undergraduates** 62% women, 22% part-time, 16% 25 or older, 4% Native American, 1% Hispanic, 3% black, 1% Asian or Pacific Islander **Most popular recent majors** Nursing, business administration/

commerce/management, education **Academic program** Accelerated degree program, self-designed majors, tutorials, honors program, summer session, adult/continuing education programs, internships **Contact** Ms. Laura Miller, Director of Admissions, Dakota Wesleyan University, Office of Admissions, Mitchell, SD 57301-4398. Telephone: 605-995-2650. Fax: 605-995-2699.

HURON UNIVERSITY
HURON, SOUTH DAKOTA

Entrance Minimally difficult **General** Proprietary, comprehensive, coed **Setting** 15-acre small-town campus **Enrollment** 476 **Faculty** 9:1 **Application deadline** Rolling **Freshmen** 70% accepted **Housing** Yes **Tuition** $6300 **Undergraduates** 49% women, 20% part-time, 33% 25 or older, 1% Native American, 1% Hispanic, 2% black, 1% Asian or Pacific Islander **Most popular recent majors** Business administration/commerce/management, education, nursing **Academic program** Advanced placement, accelerated degree program, self-designed majors, honors program, summer session, adult/continuing education programs, internships **Contact** Mr. Richard Shelton, Director of Admissions, Huron University, Huron, SD 57350-2798. Telephone: 605-352-9465. Fax: 605-352-7421.

MOUNT MARTY COLLEGE
YANKTON, SOUTH DAKOTA

Entrance Moderately difficult **General** Independent Roman Catholic, comprehensive, coed **Setting** 80-acre small-town campus **Enrollment** 936 **Faculty** 20:1 **Application deadline** 8/15 **Freshmen** 70% accepted **Housing** Yes **Tuition** $9168 **Undergraduates** 68% women, 31% part-time, 27% 25 or older, 1% Native American, 2% Hispanic, 1% black, 1% Asian or Pacific Islander **Most popular recent majors** Business administration/commerce/management, nursing, education **Academic program** Advanced placement, accelerated degree program, self-designed majors, tutorials, honors program, summer session, adult/continuing education programs, internships **Contact** Ms. JoEllen Lindner, Acting Director of Admission, Mount Marty College, Yankton, SD 57078-3724. Telephone: 605-668-1545. Fax: 605-668-1607.

NATIONAL COLLEGE
RAPID CITY, SOUTH DAKOTA

Entrance Noncompetitive **General** Proprietary, 4-year, coed **Setting** 8-acre urban campus **Enrollment** 621 **Faculty** 20:1 **Application deadline** Rolling **Freshmen** 99% accepted **Housing** Yes **Tuition** $8475 **Undergraduates** 60% women, 30% part-time, 48% 25 or older, 5% Native American, 1% Hispanic, 3% black, 7% Asian or Pacific Islander **Most popular recent majors** Business administration/commerce/management, accounting, computer information systems **Academic program** Average class size 15, advanced placement, accelerated degree program, tutorials, summer session, adult/continuing education programs, internships **Contact** Mr. Blake Faulkner, Vice President and Director of Admissions and Marketing, National College, PO Box 1780, Rapid City, SD 57709-1780. Telephone: 605-394-4800. Fax: 605-394-4871.

NATIONAL COLLEGE–SIOUX FALLS BRANCH
SIOUX FALLS, SOUTH DAKOTA

Entrance Noncompetitive **General** Proprietary, 4-year, coed **Setting** Urban campus **Enrollment** 326 **Faculty** 10:1 **Application deadline** Rolling **Freshmen** 100% accepted **Tuition** $7920 **Undergraduates** 52% women, 44% part-time, 76% 25 or older, 2% Native American, 1% Hispanic, 1% black, 1% Asian or Pacific Islander **Most popular recent majors** Business administration/commerce/management, management information systems, computer information systems **Academic program** Advanced placement, accelerated degree program, tutorials, summer session, adult/continuing education programs, internships **Contact** Ms. Joan Meyer, Director of Admissions, National College–Sioux Falls Branch, 2801 South Kiwanis Avenue, Suite 100, Sioux Falls, SD 57105-4293. Telephone: 605-334-5430.

NORTHERN STATE UNIVERSITY
ABERDEEN, SOUTH DAKOTA

Entrance Minimally difficult **General** State-supported, comprehensive, coed **Setting** 52-acre small-town campus **Enrollment** 2,634 **Faculty** 18:1 **Application deadline** 9/1 **Freshmen** 97% accepted **Housing** Yes **Tuition** $2704 **Undergraduates** 64% women, 18% part-time, 25% 25 or older, 2% Native American, 0% Hispanic, 1% black, 1% Asian or Pacific Islander **Most popular recent majors** Business administration/commerce/management, elementary education, sociology **Academic program** Advanced placement, accelerated degree program, self-designed majors, honors program, summer session, adult/continuing education programs, internships **Contact** Mr. Steve Ochsner, Director, Admissions, Northern State University, Aberdeen, SD 57401-7198. Telephone: 605-626-2544. Fax: 605-626-3022.

OGLALA LAKOTA COLLEGE
KYLE, SOUTH DAKOTA

Entrance Noncompetitive **General** State and locally supported, comprehensive, coed **Setting** Rural campus **Enrollment** 882 **Application deadline** Rolling **Freshmen** 100% accepted **Tuition** $1330 **Undergraduates** 70% women, 55% part-time, 70% 25 or older, 86% Native American, 0% Hispanic, 1% black, 0% Asian or Pacific Islander **Most popular recent majors** Elementary education, business administration/commerce/management, human services **Academic program** Accelerated degree program, summer session, adult/continuing education programs, internships **Contact** Miss Billi K. Hornbeck, Registrar, Oglala Lakota College, Kyle, SD 57752-0490. Telephone: 605-455-2321 Ext. 236. Fax: 605-455-2787.

PRESENTATION COLLEGE
ABERDEEN, SOUTH DAKOTA

Entrance Noncompetitive **General** Independent Roman Catholic, 4-year, primarily women **Setting** 100-acre small-town campus **Enrollment** 422 **Faculty** 8:1 **Application deadline** Rolling **Freshmen** 100% accepted **Housing** Yes **Tuition** $6968 **Undergraduates** 79% women, 32% part-time, 44% 25 or older, 12% Native American, 1% Hispanic, 2% black **Most popular recent majors** Nursing, social work, radiological technology **Academic program** Average class size 15, advanced placement, tutorials, summer session, internships **Contact** Ms. Brenda Schmitt, Director of Admissions, Presentation College, Aberdeen, SD 57401-1299. Telephone: 605-225-0420 Ext. 492.

SINTE GLESKA UNIVERSITY
ROSEBUD, SOUTH DAKOTA

Entrance Noncompetitive **General** Independent, comprehensive, coed **Setting** 52-acre rural campus **Enrollment** 698 **Application deadline** 8/20 **Freshmen** 100% accepted **Tuition** $1980 **Undergraduates** 70% women, 39% part-time, 70% 25 or older, 75% Native American, 0% Hispanic, 0% black, 0% Asian or Pacific Islander **Most popular recent majors** Education, business administration/commerce/management, human services **Academic program** Honors program, summer session, adult/continuing education programs **Contact** Mr. Michael Benge, Director of Student Services, Sinte Gleska University, Rosebud, SD 57570-0490. Telephone: 605-747-2263. Fax: 605-747-2098.

SOUTH DAKOTA SCHOOL OF MINES AND TECHNOLOGY
RAPID CITY, SOUTH DAKOTA

Entrance Moderately difficult **General** State-supported, coed **Setting** 120-acre suburban campus **Enrollment** 2,218 **Faculty** 16:1 **Application deadline** Rolling **Freshmen** 75% accepted **Housing** Yes **Tuition** $3378 **Undergraduates** 32% women, 23% part-time, 2% Native American, 1% Hispanic, 1% black, 1% Asian or Pacific Islander **Most popular recent majors** Interdisciplinary studies, mechanical engineering, civil engineering **Academic program** Advanced placement, self-designed majors, summer session **Contact** Mr. Robert Austin, Admissions Manager, South Dakota School of Mines and Technology, Rapid City, SD 57701-3995. Telephone: 605-394-2400. Fax: 605-394-6721 Ext. 2400.

SOUTH DAKOTA STATE UNIVERSITY
BROOKINGS, SOUTH DAKOTA

Entrance Moderately difficult **General** State-supported, coed **Setting** 260-acre small-town campus **Enrollment** 8,350 **Faculty** 17:1 **Application deadline** Rolling **Freshmen** 93% accepted **Housing** Yes **Tuition** $2912 **Undergraduates** 52% women, 5% part-time, 1% Native American, 1% Hispanic, 1% black, 1% Asian or Pacific Islander **Most popular recent majors** Economics, nursing, sociology **Academic program** Advanced placement, accelerated degree program, honors program, summer session, adult/continuing education programs, internships **Contact** Ms. Michelle Kuebler, Assistant Director of Admissions, South Dakota State University, PO Box 2201, Brookings, SD 57007. Telephone: 605-688-4121. Fax: 605-688-6384.

UNIVERSITY OF SIOUX FALLS
SIOUX FALLS, SOUTH DAKOTA

Entrance Moderately difficult **General** Independent American Baptist, comprehensive, coed **Setting** 22-acre suburban campus **Enrollment** 947 **Faculty** 14:1 **Application deadline** Rolling **Freshmen** 92% accepted **Housing** Yes **Tuition** $10,750 **Undergraduates** 56% women, 29% part-time, 40% 25 or older, 1% Native American, 1% Hispanic, 2% black, 1% Asian or Pacific Islander **Most popular recent majors** Business administration/commerce/management, education, behavioral sciences **Academic program** Advanced placement, accelerated degree program, self-designed majors, honors program, summer session, adult/continuing education programs, internships **Contact** Mr. Terry Okken, Director of Admissions, University of Sioux Falls, Sioux Falls, SD 57105-1699. Telephone: 605-331-6600. Fax: 605-331-6615.

UNIVERSITY OF SOUTH DAKOTA
VERMILLION, SOUTH DAKOTA

Entrance Moderately difficult **General** State-supported, coed **Setting** 216-acre small-town campus **Enrollment** 7,028 **Faculty** 15:1 **Application deadline** Rolling **Freshmen** 98% accepted **Housing** Yes **Tuition** $3012 **Undergraduates** 56% women, 2% part-time, 3% Native American, 1% Hispanic, 1% black, 1% Asian or Pacific Islander **Most popular recent majors** Business administration/commerce/management, biology/biological sciences, psychology **Academic program** Advanced placement, accelerated degree program, self-designed majors, tutorials, honors program, summer session, internships **Contact** Ms. Paula Tacke, Director of Admissions, University of South Dakota, Vermillion, SD 57069-2390. Telephone: 605-677-5434. Fax: 605-677-5073.

Wisconsin

ALVERNO COLLEGE
MILWAUKEE, WISCONSIN

Entrance Moderately difficult **General** Independent Roman Catholic, comprehensive, women only **Setting** 46-acre suburban campus **Enrollment** 2,191 **Faculty** 13:1 **Application deadline** 8/1 **Freshmen** 65% accepted **Housing** Yes **Tuition** $9722 **Undergraduates** 42% part-time, 67% 25 or older, 1% Native American, 7% Hispanic, 18% black, 2% Asian or Pacific Islander **Most popular recent majors** Nursing, business administration/commerce/management, communication **Academic program** Average class size 17, advanced placement, tutorials, summer session, adult/continuing education programs, internships **Contact** Mr. Owen Smith, Director of Admissions, Alverno College, Milwaukee, WI 53234-3922. Telephone: 414-382-6100. Fax: 414-382-6354.

BELLIN COLLEGE OF NURSING
GREEN BAY, WISCONSIN

Entrance Moderately difficult **General** Independent, 4-year, specialized, primarily women **Setting** Urban campus **Enrollment** 194 **Faculty** 10:1 **Application deadline** Rolling **Freshmen** 78% accepted **Tuition** $8592 **Undergraduates** 88% women, 8% part-time, 33% 25 or older, 1% Native American, 1% Hispanic, 0% black, 1% Asian or Pacific Islander **Academic program** Advanced placement, summer session **Contact** Ms. Teresa Halcsik, Vice President for Support Services, Bellin College of Nursing, 725 South Webster Ave, PO Box 23400, Green Bay, WI 54305-3400. Telephone: 414-433-3673.

BELOIT COLLEGE
BELOIT, WISCONSIN

Entrance Very difficult **General** Independent, 4-year, coed **Setting** 65-acre small-town campus **Enrollment** 1,273 **Faculty** 11:1 **Application deadline** Rolling **Freshmen** 70% accepted **Housing** Yes **Tuition** $19,050 **Undergraduates** 57% women, 8% part-time, 3% 25 or older, 1% Native American, 2% Hispanic, 4% black, 2% Asian or Pacific Islander **Most popular recent majors** Anthropology, biology/biological sciences, English **Academic program** Average class size 17, advanced placement, self-designed majors, tutorials, summer session, internships **Contact** Mr. Alan G. McIvor, Vice President of Enrollment Services, Beloit College, Beloit, WI 53511-5596. Telephone: 608-363-2500.

CARDINAL STRITCH COLLEGE
MILWAUKEE, WISCONSIN

Entrance Moderately difficult **General** Independent Roman Catholic, comprehensive, coed **Setting** 40-acre suburban campus **Enrollment** 5,526 **Faculty** 17:1 **Application deadline** Rolling **Freshmen** 78% accepted **Housing** Yes **Tuition** $10,130 **Undergraduates** 73% women, 15% part-time, 73% 25 or older, 1% Native American, 3% Hispanic, 11% black, 2% Asian or Pacific Islander **Most popular recent majors** Business administration/commerce/management, education, nursing **Academic program** Average class size 17, advanced placement, accelerated degree program, tutorials, summer session, adult/continuing education programs, internships **Contact** Mr. David Wegener, Director of Admissions, Cardinal Stritch College, Milwaukee, WI 53217-3985. Telephone: 414-352-5400 Ext. 444.

CARROLL COLLEGE
WAUKESHA, WISCONSIN

Entrance Moderately difficult **General** Independent Presbyterian, 4-year, coed **Setting** 52-acre suburban campus **Enrollment** 2,464 **Faculty** 16:1 **Application deadline** Rolling **Freshmen** 88% accepted **Housing** Yes **Tuition** $13,890 **Undergraduates** 66% women, 32% part-time, 20% 25 or older, 0% Native American, 2% Hispanic, 3% black, 1% Asian or Pacific Islander **Most popular recent majors** Business administration/commerce/

management, nursing, communication **Academic program** Advanced placement, accelerated degree program, self-designed majors, tutorials, honors program, summer session, adult/continuing education programs, internships **Contact** Mr. James V. Wiseman III, Vice President of Enrollment, Carroll College, Waukesha, WI 53186-5593. Telephone: 414-524-7221. Fax: 414-524-7139.

CARTHAGE COLLEGE
KENOSHA, WISCONSIN

Entrance Moderately difficult **General** Independent, comprehensive, coed, affiliated with Evangelical Lutheran Church in America **Setting** 72-acre suburban campus **Enrollment** 2,164 **Faculty** 15:1 **Application deadline** Rolling **Freshmen** 93% accepted **Housing** Yes **Tuition** $15,365 **Undergraduates** 58% women, 29% part-time, 34% 25 or older, 1% Native American, 2% Hispanic, 4% black, 1% Asian or Pacific Islander **Most popular recent majors** Business administration/commerce/management, education, social science **Academic program** Advanced placement, accelerated degree program, self-designed majors, tutorials, honors program, summer session, adult/continuing education programs, internships **Contact** Mr. Mark S. Kopenske, Assistant Vice President for Enrollment, Carthage College, Kenosha, WI 53140-1994. Telephone: 414-551-6000. Fax: 414-551-5762.

COLUMBIA COLLEGE OF NURSING
MILWAUKEE, WISCONSIN

Entrance Moderately difficult **General** Independent, 4-year, specialized, coed **Setting** Urban campus **Enrollment** 373 **Application deadline** Rolling **Freshmen** 80% accepted **Housing** Yes **Tuition** $14,610 **Undergraduates** 92% women, 43% part-time, 40% 25 or older, 1% Native American, 2% Hispanic, 3% black, 2% Asian or Pacific Islander **Academic program** Average class size 20, advanced placement, tutorials, honors program, summer session **Contact** Mr. James Wiseman, Dean of Admissions, Columbia College of Nursing, Carroll College, 100 North East Avenue, Waukesha, WI 53186. Telephone: 414-524-7220.

CONCORDIA UNIVERSITY WISCONSIN
MEQUON, WISCONSIN

Entrance Moderately difficult **General** Independent, comprehensive, coed, affiliated with Lutheran Church–Missouri Synod **Setting** 155-acre suburban campus **Enrollment** 3,659 **Faculty** 17:1 **Application deadline** 8/15 **Freshmen** 73% accepted **Housing** Yes **Tuition** $10,760 **Undergraduates** 52% women, 21% part-time, 8% 25 or older, 1% Native American, 0% Hispanic, 8% black, 1% Asian or Pacific Islander **Most popular recent majors** Education, nursing, business administration/commerce/management **Academic program** Average class size 25, advanced placement, self-designed majors, tutorials, summer session, adult/continuing education programs, internships **Contact** Mr. Kenneth Gaschk, Dean of Admissions, Concordia University Wisconsin, Mequon, WI 53097-2402. Telephone: 414-243-5700 Ext. 305. Fax: 414-243-4351.

EDGEWOOD COLLEGE
MADISON, WISCONSIN

Entrance Moderately difficult **General** Independent Roman Catholic, comprehensive, coed **Setting** 55-acre urban campus **Enrollment** 2,032 **Faculty** 15:1 **Application deadline** Rolling **Freshmen** 80% accepted **Housing** Yes **Tuition** $10,280 **Undergraduates** 73% women, 35% part-time, 42% 25 or older, 1% Native American, 1% Hispanic, 1% black, 2% Asian or Pacific Islander **Most popular recent majors** Nursing, business administration/commerce/management, education **Academic program** ESL program, Advanced placement, self-designed majors, tutorials, honors program, summer session, adult/continuing education programs, internships **Contact** Mr. Kevin C. Kucera, Dean of Admissions and Financial Aid, Edgewood College, 855 Woodrow Street, Madison, WI 53711-1998. Telephone: 608-257-4861 Ext. 2294.

LAKELAND COLLEGE
SHEBOYGAN, WISCONSIN

Entrance Moderately difficult **General** Independent, comprehensive, coed, affiliated with United Church of Christ **Setting** 240-acre rural campus **Enrollment** 928 **Faculty** 15:1 **Application deadline** Rolling **Freshmen** 87% accepted **Housing** Yes **Tuition** $11,230 **Undergraduates** 54% women, 12% part-time, 15% 25 or older, 0% Native American, 2% Hispanic, 6% black, 8% Asian or Pacific Islander **Most popular recent majors** Business economics, education, psychology **Academic program** Advanced placement, tutorials, honors program, summer session, adult/continuing education programs, internships **Contact** Mr. Leo Gavrilos, Director of Admissions, Lakeland College, Sheboygan, WI 53082-0359. Telephone: 414-565-1217. Fax: 414-565-1206.

LAWRENCE UNIVERSITY
APPLETON, WISCONSIN

Entrance Very difficult **General** Independent, 4-year, coed **Setting** 84-acre small-town campus **Enrollment** 1,218 **Faculty** 11:1 **Application deadline** 2/1 **Freshmen** 61% accepted **Housing** Yes **Tuition** $19,620 **Undergraduates** 53% women, 7% part-time, 4% 25 or older, 1% Native American, 2% Hispanic, 1% black, 4% Asian or Pacific Islander **Most popular recent majors** Biology/biological sciences, English, psychology **Academic program** Advanced placement, self-designed majors, tutorials, honors program, internships **Contact** Mr. Steven T. Syverson, Dean of Admissions and Financial Aid, Lawrence University, Appleton, WI 54912-0599. Telephone: 414-832-6500. Fax: 414-832-6782.

MARANATHA BAPTIST BIBLE COLLEGE
WATERTOWN, WISCONSIN

Entrance Noncompetitive **General** Independent Baptist, comprehensive, coed **Setting** 60-acre small-town campus **Enrollment** 700 **Faculty** 13:1 **Application deadline** Rolling **Housing** Yes **Tuition** $5976 **Undergraduates** 51% women, 9% part-time, 9% 25 or older, 1% Hispanic, 1% black, 1% Asian or Pacific Islander **Most popular recent majors** Education, biblical studies, business administration/commerce/management **Academic program** Average class size 60, tutorials, summer session, internships **Contact** Mr. Michael Shellman, Director of Admissions, Maranatha Baptist Bible College, Watertown, WI 53094. Telephone: 414-261-9300 Ext. 308. Fax: 414-261-9109.

MARIAN COLLEGE OF FOND DU LAC
FOND DU LAC, WISCONSIN

Entrance Moderately difficult **General** Independent Roman Catholic, comprehensive, coed **Setting** 50-acre small-town campus **Enrollment** 2,432 **Faculty** 14:1 **Application deadline** Rolling **Freshmen** 90% accepted **Housing** Yes **Tuition** $11,370 **Undergraduates** 60% women, 30% part-time, 35% 25 or older, 1% Native American, 2% Hispanic, 2% black, 3% Asian or Pacific Islander **Most popular recent majors** Business administration/commerce/management, nursing, education **Academic program** Advanced placement, accelerated degree program, self-designed majors, tutorials, summer session, adult/continuing education programs, internships **Contact** Ms. Carol A. Reichenberger, Vice President for Enrollment Services, Marian College of Fond du Lac, Fond du Lac, WI 54935-4699. Telephone: 414-923-7650.

MARQUETTE UNIVERSITY
MILWAUKEE, WISCONSIN

Entrance Moderately difficult **General** Independent Roman Catholic (Jesuit), coed **Setting** 80-acre urban campus **Enrollment** 10,539 **Faculty** 15:1 **Application deadline** Rolling **Housing** Yes **Tuition** $14,064 **Undergraduates** 53% women, 8% part-time, 1% Native American, 4% Hispanic, 4% black, 5% Asian or Pacific Islander **Most popular recent majors** Business administration/commerce/management, electrical engineering, civil engineering **Academic program** Advanced placement, accelerated degree program, self-designed majors, tutorials, honors program, summer session, adult/continuing education programs, internships **Contact** Mr. Raymond A. Brown, Dean of Admissions, Marquette University, PO Box 1881, Milwaukee, WI 53201-1881. Telephone: 414-288-7302.

MILWAUKEE INSTITUTE OF ART AND DESIGN
MILWAUKEE, WISCONSIN

Entrance Moderately difficult **General** Independent, 4-year, specialized, coed **Setting** Urban campus **Enrollment** 518 **Application deadline** Rolling **Freshmen** 74% accepted **Housing** Yes **Tuition** $14,620 **Undergraduates** 41% women, 13% part-time, 27% 25 or older, 2% Native American, 5% Hispanic, 3% black, 3% Asian or Pacific Islander **Academic program** Advanced placement, summer session, adult/continuing education programs, internships **Contact** Ms. Mary Schopp, Executive Director of Enrollment Services, Milwaukee Institute of Art and Design, 273 East Erie Street, Milwaukee, WI 53202. Telephone: 414-291-8070.

MILWAUKEE SCHOOL OF ENGINEERING
MILWAUKEE, WISCONSIN

Entrance Moderately difficult **General** Independent, comprehensive, coed **Setting** 12-acre urban campus **Enrollment** 2,957 **Faculty** 13:1 **Application deadline** Rolling **Freshmen** 91% accepted **Housing** Yes **Tuition** $13,305 **Undergraduates** 16% women, 32% part-time, 5% 25 or older, 1% Native American, 1% Hispanic, 4% black, 2% Asian or Pacific Islander **Most popular recent majors** Electrical engineering, mechanical engineering, architectural engineering **Academic program** Advanced placement, summer session, adult/continuing education programs, internships **Contact** Ms. Jennie Goran, Director of Admissions, Milwaukee School of Engineering, 1025 North Broadway, Milwaukee, WI 53202-3109. Telephone: 414-277-7238. Fax: 414-277-7475.

MOUNT MARY COLLEGE
MILWAUKEE, WISCONSIN

Entrance Moderately difficult **General** Independent Roman Catholic, comprehensive, women only **Setting** 80-acre suburban campus **Enrollment** 1,287 **Faculty** 11:1 **Application deadline** 8/15 **Freshmen** 85% accepted **Housing** Yes **Tuition** $10,740 **Undergraduates** 38% part-time, 45% 25 or older, 0% Native American, 2% Hispanic, 8% black, 2% Asian or Pacific Islander **Most popular recent majors** Occupational therapy, education, business administration/commerce/management **Academic program** Advanced placement, accelerated degree program, self-designed majors, honors program, summer session, adult/continuing education programs, internships **Contact** Mrs. Mary Jane Reilly, Director of Admission, Mount Mary College, Milwaukee, WI 53222-4597. Telephone: 414-258-4810 Ext. 360. Fax: 414-256-1205.

MOUNT SENARIO COLLEGE
LADYSMITH, WISCONSIN

Entrance Minimally difficult **General** Independent, 4-year, coed **Setting** 110-acre small-town campus **Enrollment** 431 **Faculty** 12:1 **Application deadline** 8/20 **Freshmen** 68% accepted **Housing** Yes **Tuition** $8980 **Undergraduates** 31% women, 59% part-time, 33% 25 or older, 2% Native American, 2% Hispanic, 9% black, 4% Asian or Pacific Islander **Most popular recent majors** Criminal justice, business administration/commerce/management, education **Academic program** Accelerated degree program, self-designed majors, tutorials, summer session, adult/continuing education programs, internships **Contact** Mr. Max M. Waits, Admissions Consultant, Mount Senario College, Ladysmith, WI 54848-2128. Telephone: 715-532-5511 Ext. 110. Fax: 715-532-7690.

NORTHLAND COLLEGE
ASHLAND, WISCONSIN

Entrance Moderately difficult **General** Independent, 4-year, coed, affiliated with United Church of Christ **Setting** 130-acre small-town campus **Enrollment** 879 **Faculty** 16:1 **Application deadline** 8/1 **Freshmen** 94% accepted **Housing** Yes **Tuition** $12,365 **Undergraduates** 56% women, 9% part-time, 17% 25 or older, 4% Native American, 3% Hispanic, 1% black, 1% Asian or Pacific Islander **Most popular recent majors** Biology/biological sciences, education **Academic program** Advanced placement, accelerated degree program, self-designed majors, honors program, summer session, adult/continuing education programs, internships **Contact** Mr. James L. Miller, Dean of Student Development and Enrollment, Northland College, Ashland, WI 54806-3925. Telephone: 715-682-1224. Fax: 715-682-1258.

RIPON COLLEGE
RIPON, WISCONSIN

Entrance Moderately difficult **General** Independent, 4-year, coed **Setting** 250-acre small-town campus **Enrollment** 734 **Faculty** 10:1 **Application deadline** 3/15 **Freshmen** 88% accepted **Housing** Yes **Tuition** $17,580 **Undergraduates** 50% women, 3% part-time, 1% 25 or older, 1% Native American, 2% Hispanic, 2% black, 2% Asian or Pacific Islander **Most popular recent majors** History, English, biology/biological sciences **Academic program** Advanced placement, accelerated degree program, self-designed majors, tutorials, internships **Contact** Mr. Paul J. Weeks, Vice President and Dean of Admission, Ripon College, Ripon, WI 54971. Telephone: 414-748-8102.

ST. NORBERT COLLEGE
DE PERE, WISCONSIN

Entrance Moderately difficult **General** Independent Roman Catholic, comprehensive, coed **Setting** 86-acre suburban campus **Enrollment** 2,122 **Faculty** 15:1 **Application deadline** Rolling **Freshmen** 89% accepted **Housing** Yes **Tuition** $14,434 **Undergraduates** 59% women, 4% part-time, 5% 25 or older, 1% Native American, 1% Hispanic, 1% black, 1% Asian or Pacific Islander **Most popular recent majors** Business administration/commerce/management, elementary education, communication **Academic program** Average class size 30, advanced placement, accelerated degree program, self-designed majors, tutorials, honors program, summer session, internships **Contact** Mr. Craig Wesley, Dean of Admission, St. Norbert College, 100 Grant Street, Office of Admission, De Pere, WI 54115-2099. Telephone: 414-403-3005.

SILVER LAKE COLLEGE
MANITOWOC, WISCONSIN

Entrance Minimally difficult **General** Independent Roman Catholic, comprehensive, coed **Setting** 30-acre rural campus **Enrollment** 1,144 **Fac-**

ulty 10:1 **Application deadline** 8/31 **Freshmen** 92% accepted **Housing** Yes **Tuition** $9630 **Undergraduates** 66% women, 59% part-time, 71% 25 or older, 1% Native American, 2% Hispanic, 0% black, 1% Asian or Pacific Islander **Most popular recent majors** Business administration/commerce/management, elementary education **Academic program** Self-designed majors, summer session, adult/continuing education programs, internships **Contact** Ms. Sandra Schwartz, Director of Admissions, Silver Lake College, Manitowoc, WI 54220-9319. Telephone: 414-684-5955 Ext. 175. Fax: 414-684-7082.

UNIVERSITY OF WISCONSIN–EAU CLAIRE

EAU CLAIRE, WISCONSIN

Entrance Moderately difficult **General** State-supported, comprehensive, coed **Setting** 333-acre urban campus **Enrollment** 10,503 **Faculty** 19:1 **Application deadline** 3/1 **Freshmen** 85% accepted **Housing** Yes **Tuition** $2574 **Undergraduates** 60% women, 13% part-time, 11% 25 or older, 1% Native American, 1% Hispanic, 1% black, 2% Asian or Pacific Islander **Most popular recent majors** Nursing, elementary education, accounting **Academic program** Average class size 29, advanced placement, honors program, summer session, adult/continuing education programs, internships **Contact** Mr. Roger GroeneWold, Director of Admissions, University of Wisconsin–Eau Claire, PO Box 4004, Eau Claire, WI 54702-4004. Telephone: 715-836-5415. Fax: 715-836-2380.

UNIVERSITY OF WISCONSIN–GREEN BAY

GREEN BAY, WISCONSIN

Entrance Moderately difficult **General** State-supported, comprehensive, coed **Setting** 700-acre suburban campus **Enrollment** 5,220 **Faculty** 19:1 **Application deadline** 2/1 **Freshmen** 89% accepted **Housing** Yes **Tuition** $2545 **Undergraduates** 63% women, 18% part-time, 22% 25 or older, 2% Native American, 1% Hispanic, 1% black, 2% Asian or Pacific Islander **Most popular recent majors** Business administration/commerce/management, human development, psychology **Academic program** Average class size 50, advanced placement, accelerated degree program, self-designed majors, tutorials, summer session, adult/continuing education programs, internships **Contact** Mr. Myron Van de Ven, Director of Admissions, University of Wisconsin–Green Bay, Green Bay, WI 54311-7001. Telephone: 414-465-2111. Fax: 414-465-2032.

UNIVERSITY OF WISCONSIN–LA CROSSE

LA CROSSE, WISCONSIN

Entrance Moderately difficult **General** State-supported, comprehensive, coed **Setting** 119-acre suburban campus **Enrollment** 9,046 **Faculty** 20:1 **Application deadline** Rolling **Freshmen** 81% accepted **Housing** Yes **Tuition** $2635 **Undergraduates** 57% women, 9% part-time, 13% 25 or older, 1% Native American, 1% Hispanic, 1% black, 1% Asian or Pacific Islander **Most popular recent majors** Biology/biological sciences, business administration/commerce/management, elementary education **Academic program** Advanced placement, accelerated degree program, honors program, summer session, adult/continuing education programs, internships **Contact** Mr. Tim Lewis, Director of Admissions, University of Wisconsin–La Crosse, La Crosse, WI 54601-3742. Telephone: 608-785-8576.

UNIVERSITY OF WISCONSIN–MADISON

MADISON, WISCONSIN

Entrance Very difficult **General** State-supported, coed **Setting** 1,050-acre urban campus **Enrollment** 39,826 **Faculty** 12:1 **Application deadline** 2/1 **Freshmen** 78% accepted **Housing** Yes **Tuition** $3040 **Undergraduates** 51% women, 3% part-time, 4% 25 or older, 1% Native American, 4% Hispanic, 4% black, 5% Asian or Pacific Islander **Most popular recent majors** Political science/government, mechanical engineering, history **Academic program** Advanced placement, accelerated degree program, self-designed majors, tutorials, honors program, summer session, adult/continuing education programs, internships **Contact** Office of Admissions, University of Wisconsin–Madison, 140 Peterson Office Building, 750 University Avenue, Madison, WI 53706-1490. Telephone: 608-262-3961. Fax: 608-262-1429.

UNIVERSITY OF WISCONSIN–MILWAUKEE

MILWAUKEE, WISCONSIN

Entrance Moderately difficult **General** State-supported, coed **Setting** 90-acre urban campus **Enrollment** 21,877 **Application deadline** 6/30 **Freshmen** 81% accepted **Housing** Yes **Tuition** $3104 **Undergraduates** 55% women, 32% part-time, 36% 25 or older, 1% Native American, 3% Hispanic, 8% black, 3% Asian or Pacific Islander **Academic program** Advanced placement, accelerated degree program, self-designed majors, honors program, summer session, adult/continuing education programs, internships **Contact** Ms. Beth Weckmueller, Director of Admissions, University of Wisconsin-Milwaukee, PO Box 413, Milwaukee, WI 53201-0413. Telephone: 414-229-6164.

UNIVERSITY OF WISCONSIN–OSHKOSH

OSHKOSH, WISCONSIN

Entrance Moderately difficult **General** State-supported, comprehensive, coed **Setting** 192-acre suburban campus **Enrollment** 10,382 **Faculty** 19:1 **Application deadline** Rolling **Freshmen** 49% accepted **Housing** Yes **Tuition** $2419 **Undergraduates** 57% women, 15% part-time, 20% 25 or older, 1% Native American, 1% Hispanic, 1% black, 2% Asian or Pacific Islander **Most popular recent majors** Nursing, marketing/retailing/merchandising, elementary education **Academic program** Advanced placement, accelerated degree program, self-designed majors, tutorials, honors program, summer session, adult/continuing education programs, internships **Contact** Mr. Rick Hillman, Associate Director of Admissions, University of Wisconsin-Oshkosh, Oshkosh, WI 54901-3551. Telephone: 414-424-0202.

UNIVERSITY OF WISCONSIN–PARKSIDE

KENOSHA, WISCONSIN

Entrance Moderately difficult **General** State-supported, comprehensive, coed **Setting** 700-acre suburban campus **Enrollment** 4,254 **Faculty** 14:1 **Application deadline** 8/1 **Freshmen** 80% accepted **Housing** Yes **Tuition** $2523 **Undergraduates** 56% women, 39% part-time, 35% 25 or older, 1% Native American, 3% Hispanic, 5% black, 1% Asian or Pacific Islander **Most popular recent majors** Business administration/commerce/management, psychology, biology/biological sciences **Academic program** Advanced placement, accelerated degree program, summer session, adult/continuing education programs, internships **Contact** Mr. Charles Murphy, Director of Admissions, University of Wisconsin-Parkside, Kenosha, WI 53141-2000. Telephone: 414-595-2355.

UNIVERSITY OF WISCONSIN–PLATTEVILLE

PLATTEVILLE, WISCONSIN

Entrance Moderately difficult **General** State-supported, comprehensive, coed **Setting** 380-acre small-town campus **Enrollment** 4,998 **Faculty** 20:1 **Application deadline** Rolling **Freshmen** 88% accepted **Housing** Yes **Tuition** $2591 **Undergraduates** 35% women, 10% part-time, 18% 25 or older, 1% Native American, 1% Hispanic, 1% black, 2% Asian or Pacific Islander **Most popular recent majors** Mechanical engineering, criminal justice, business administration/commerce/management **Academic program** Advanced placement, accelerated degree program, self-designed majors, tutorials, honors program, summer session, adult/continuing education programs, internships **Contact** Dr. Richard Schumacher, Dean of Admissions and Enrollment Management, University of Wisconsin-Platteville, 1 University Plaza, Platteville, WI 53818-3099. Telephone: 608-342-1125.

UNIVERSITY OF WISCONSIN–RIVER FALLS

RIVER FALLS, WISCONSIN

Entrance Moderately difficult **General** State-supported, comprehensive, coed **Setting** 225-acre suburban campus **Enrollment** 5,359 **Faculty** 17:1 **Application deadline** Rolling **Freshmen** 80% accepted **Housing** Yes **Tuition** $2565 **Undergraduates** 59% women, 16% part-time, 22% 25 or older, 1% Native American, 1% Hispanic, 1% black, 1% Asian or Pacific Islander **Most popular recent majors** Business administration/commerce/management, agricultural business, elementary education **Academic program** Average class size 30, advanced placement, accelerated degree program, self-designed majors, tutorials, honors program, summer session, adult/continuing education programs, internships **Contact** Mr. Alan Tuchtenhagen, Director of Admissions, University of Wisconsin-River Falls, River Falls, WI 54022-5001. Telephone: 715-425-3500. Fax: 715-425-4487.

UNIVERSITY OF WISCONSIN–STEVENS POINT

STEVENS POINT, WISCONSIN

Entrance Moderately difficult **General** State-supported, comprehensive, coed **Setting** 335-acre small-town campus **Enrollment** 8,360 **Faculty** 19:1 **Application deadline** Rolling **Freshmen** 77% accepted **Housing** Yes **Tuition** $2522 **Undergraduates** 53% women, 10% part-time, 17% 25 or older, 1% Native American, 1% Hispanic, 1% black, 1% Asian or Pacific Islander **Most popular recent majors** Elementary education, business administration/commerce/management, biology/biological sciences **Academic program** Advanced placement, self-designed majors, honors program, summer session, adult/continuing education programs, internships **Contact** Dr. David Eckholm, Director of Admissions, University of Wisconsin-Stevens Point, Stevens Point, WI 54481-3897. Telephone: 715-346-2441.

UNIVERSITY OF WISCONSIN–STOUT

MENOMONIE, WISCONSIN

Entrance Moderately difficult **General** State-supported, comprehensive, coed **Setting** 120-acre small-town campus **Enrollment** 7,322 **Fac-**

ulty 21:1 **Application deadline** Rolling **Freshmen** 94% accepted **Housing** Yes **Tuition** $2619 **Undergraduates** 48% women, 11% part-time, 17% 25 or older, 1% Native American, 1% Hispanic, 1% black, 2% Asian or Pacific Islander **Most popular recent majors** Hotel and restaurant management, industrial engineering technology, business administration/commerce/management **Academic program** Advanced placement, accelerated degree program, tutorials, summer session, adult/continuing education programs, internships **Contact** Mr. Richard Lowery, Associate Director Admissions, University of Wisconsin-Stout, Menomonie, WI 54751. Telephone: 715-232-1411.

UNIVERSITY OF WISCONSIN–SUPERIOR

SUPERIOR, WISCONSIN

Entrance Moderately difficult **General** State-supported, comprehensive, coed **Setting** 230-acre small-town campus **Enrollment** 2,647 **Faculty** 12:1 **Application deadline** Rolling **Freshmen** 84% accepted **Housing** Yes **Tuition** $2465 **Undergraduates** 51% women, 26% part-time, 21% 25 or older, 2% Native American, 1% Hispanic, 1% black, 3% Asian or Pacific Islander **Most popular recent majors** Business administration/commerce/management, education, art/fine arts **Academic program** Advanced placement, accelerated degree program, self-designed majors, tutorials, honors program, summer session, adult/continuing education programs, internships **Contact** Ms. Lorraine Washa, Student Application Contact, University of Wisconsin–Superior, Superior, WI 54880-2873. Telephone: 715-394-8230. Fax: 715-394-8454.

UNIVERSITY OF WISCONSIN–WHITEWATER

WHITEWATER, WISCONSIN

Entrance Moderately difficult **General** State-supported, comprehensive, coed **Setting** 385-acre small-town campus **Enrollment** 10,398 **Faculty** 21:1 **Application deadline** Rolling **Freshmen** 83% accepted **Housing** Yes **Tuition** $2586 **Undergraduates** 55% women, 15% part-time, 10% 25 or older, 1% Native American, 2% Hispanic, 3% black, 1% Asian or Pacific Islander **Most popular recent majors** Business administration/commerce/management, accounting, marketing/retailing/merchandising **Academic program** Advanced placement, self-designed majors, honors program, summer session, adult/continuing education programs, internships **Contact** Mr. Irv Madsen, Executive Director of Admissions, University of Wisconsin–Whitewater, Whitewater, WI 53190-1790. Telephone: 414-472-1440. Fax: 414-472-1515.

VITERBO COLLEGE

LA CROSSE, WISCONSIN

Entrance Moderately difficult **General** Independent Roman Catholic, comprehensive, coed **Setting** 5-acre urban campus **Enrollment** 1,914 **Faculty** 14:1 **Application deadline** Rolling **Freshmen** 90% accepted **Housing** Yes **Tuition** $11,150 **Undergraduates** 74% women, 23% part-time, 32% 25 or older, 1% Native American, 1% Hispanic, 1% black, 2% Asian or Pacific Islander **Most popular recent majors** Nursing, business administration/commerce/management, elementary education **Academic program** Advanced placement, accelerated degree program, self-designed majors, summer session, adult/continuing education programs, internships **Contact** Dr. Roland Nelson, Director of Admissions, Viterbo College, 815 South Ninth Street, La Crosse, WI 54601-4797. Telephone: 608-796-3010. Fax: 608-796-3020.

WISCONSIN LUTHERAN COLLEGE

MILWAUKEE, WISCONSIN

Entrance Moderately difficult **General** Independent, 4-year, coed, affiliated with Wisconsin Evangelical Lutheran Synod **Setting** 16-acre suburban campus **Enrollment** 401 **Faculty** 11:1 **Application deadline** 9/1 **Freshmen** 93% accepted **Housing** Yes **Tuition** $11,000 **Undergraduates** 62% women, 10% part-time, 8% 25 or older, 0% Native American, 0% Hispanic, 0% black, 0% Asian or Pacific Islander **Most popular recent majors** Communication, psychology, business administration/commerce/management **Academic program** Advanced placement, self-designed majors, tutorials, summer session, internships **Contact** Mr. Joel Mischke, Dean of Enrollment Services, Wisconsin Lutheran College, Milwaukee, WI 53226-4699. Telephone: 414-443-8611. Fax: 414-443-8514.

Connecticut

ALBERTUS MAGNUS COLLEGE

NEW HAVEN, CONNECTICUT

Entrance Moderately difficult **General** Independent Roman Catholic, comprehensive, coed **Setting** 55-acre urban campus **Enrollment** 1,177 **Faculty** 13:1 **Application deadline** Rolling **Freshmen** 47% accepted **Housing** Yes **Tuition** $17,224 **Undergraduates** 59% women, 30% part-time, 60% 25 or older, 1% Native American, 3% Hispanic, 14% black, 1% Asian or Pacific Islander **Most popular recent majors** Business economics, psychology, English **Academic program** Advanced placement, accelerated degree program, self-designed majors, tutorials, honors program, summer session, adult/continuing education programs, internships **Contact** Ms. Maureen Morrison, Associate Dean of Admissions, Albertus Magnus College, 700 Prospect Street, New Haven, CT 06511-1189. Telephone: 203-773-8501. Fax: 203-785-8652.

CENTRAL CONNECTICUT STATE UNIVERSITY

NEW BRITAIN, CONNECTICUT

Entrance Moderately difficult **General** State-supported, comprehensive, coed **Setting** 176-acre suburban campus **Enrollment** 9,520 **Faculty** 17:1 **Application deadline** 5/1 **Freshmen** 67% accepted **Housing** Yes **Tuition** $3614 **Undergraduates** 55% women, 27% part-time, 31% 25 or older, 1% Native American, 5% Hispanic, 7% black, 2% Asian or Pacific Islander **Most popular recent majors** Elementary education, accounting, psychology **Academic program** Advanced placement, self-designed majors, tutorials, honors program, summer session, adult/continuing education programs, internships **Contact** Ms. Charlotte Bisson, Director of Admissions, Central Connecticut State University, New Britain, CT 06050-4010. Telephone: 860-832-2278.

CHARTER OAK STATE COLLEGE

NEWINGTON, CONNECTICUT

Entrance Noncompetitive **General** State-supported, 4-year, coed **Setting** Small-town campus **Enrollment** 1,252 **Undergraduates** 50% women, 100% part-time, 97% 25 or older, 1% Native American, 3% Hispanic, 5% black, 1% Asian or Pacific Islander **Academic program** Advanced placement, accelerated degree program, self-designed majors **Contact** Mr. Paul Morganti, Director of Admissions, Charter Oak State College, 66 Cedar Street, Newington, CT 06111-2646. Telephone: 860-666-4595.

CONNECTICUT COLLEGE

NEW LONDON, CONNECTICUT

Entrance Very difficult **General** Independent, comprehensive, coed **Setting** 702-acre suburban campus **Enrollment** 1,918 **Faculty** 11:1 **Application deadline** 1/15 **Freshmen** 43% accepted **Housing** Yes **Tuition** $28,475 **Undergraduates** 58% women, 4% part-time, 3% 25 or older, 1% Native American, 3% Hispanic, 6% black, 4% Asian or Pacific Islander **Most popular recent majors** Psychology, English, biology/biological sciences **Academic program** Advanced placement, accelerated degree program, self-designed majors, tutorials, honors program, summer session, adult/continuing education programs, internships **Contact** Mr. Lee A. Coffin, Dean of Admissions, Connecticut College, New London, CT 06320-4196. Telephone: 860-439-2202. Fax: 860-439-4301.

EASTERN CONNECTICUT STATE UNIVERSITY

WILLIMANTIC, CONNECTICUT

Entrance Moderately difficult **General** State-supported, comprehensive, coed **Setting** 174-acre small-town campus **Enrollment** 4,590 **Faculty** 17:1 **Application deadline** 5/1 **Freshmen** 80% accepted **Housing** Yes **Tuition** $3594 **Undergraduates** 53% women, 33% part-time, 35% 25 or older, 1% Native American, 6% Hispanic, 10% black, 1% Asian or Pacific Islander **Most popular recent majors** Business administration/commerce/management, education, psychology **Academic program** Advanced placement, accelerated degree program, self-designed majors, tutorials, honors program, summer session, adult/continuing education programs, internships **Contact** Ms. Kimberly Crone, Director of Admissions and Enrollment Management, Eastern Connecticut State University, Willimantic, CT 06226-2295. Telephone: 860-465-5286.

FAIRFIELD UNIVERSITY

FAIRFIELD, CONNECTICUT

Entrance Moderately difficult **General** Independent Roman Catholic (Jesuit), comprehensive, coed **Setting** 200-acre suburban campus **Enrollment** 5,111 **Faculty** 13:1 **Application deadline** 2/15 **Freshmen** 71% accepted **Housing** Yes **Tuition** $18,310 **Undergraduates** 52% women, 0% part-time, 1% 25 or older, 1% Native American, 4% Hispanic, 2% black, 4% Asian or Pacific Islander

Most popular recent majors English, psychology, nursing **Academic program** Average class size 24, advanced placement, tutorials, honors program, summer session, adult/continuing education programs, internships **Contact** Ms. Mary Spiegel, Acting Dean of Admission, Fairfield University, Fairfield, CT 06430-5195. Telephone: 203-254-4100. Fax: 203-254-4199.

HARTFORD COLLEGE FOR WOMEN
HARTFORD, CONNECTICUT

Entrance Moderately difficult **General** Independent, 4-year, women only **Setting** 13-acre suburban campus **Enrollment** 250 **Faculty** 8:1 **Application deadline** Rolling **Freshmen** 69% accepted **Housing** Yes **Tuition** $14,415 **Undergraduates** 50% part-time, 44% 25 or older, 5% Hispanic, 14% black, 2% Asian or Pacific Islander **Most popular recent majors** Liberal arts/general studies, legal studies, women's studies **Academic program** Advanced placement, accelerated degree program, self-designed majors, tutorials, honors program, summer session, adult/continuing education programs, internships **Contact** Ms. Gwendolyn Gardner, Director of Admissions, Hartford College for Women, Hartford, CT 06105-2299. Telephone: 860-768-5600. Fax: 860-233-5493.

HOLY APOSTLES COLLEGE AND SEMINARY
CROMWELL, CONNECTICUT

Entrance Noncompetitive **General** Independent Roman Catholic, comprehensive, coed **Setting** Small-town campus **Enrollment** 125 **Faculty** 4:1 **Application deadline** Rolling **Freshmen** 100% accepted **Housing** Yes **Tuition** $5030 **Undergraduates** 43% women, 86% part-time, 95% 25 or older, 0% Native American, 0% Hispanic, 5% black, 0% Asian or Pacific Islander **Most popular recent majors** Religious studies, philosophy, social science **Academic program** Accelerated degree program, adult/continuing education programs, internships **Contact** Rev. Raymond Halliwell, MSA, Director of Admissions, Holy Apostles College and Seminary, 33 Prospect Hill Road, Cromwell, CT 06416-2005. Telephone: 860-632-3030. Fax: 860-632-0176.

LYME ACADEMY OF FINE ARTS
OLD LYME, CONNECTICUT

Entrance Moderately difficult **General** Independent, 4-year, specialized, coed **Setting** 3-acre small-town campus **Enrollment** 67 **Application deadline** Rolling **Freshmen** 83% accepted **Tuition** $8690 **Undergraduates** 60% women, 25% part-time, 50% 25 or older, 0% Native American, 3% Hispanic, 1% black, 0% Asian or Pacific Islander **Most popular recent major** Painting/drawing **Academic program** Average class size 16, summer session **Contact** Ms. Michelle M. Raiti, Admissions, Lyme Academy of Fine Arts, Old Lyme, CT 06371. Telephone: 860-434-5232 Ext. 104. Fax: 860-434-8725.

PAIER COLLEGE OF ART, INC.
HAMDEN, CONNECTICUT

Entrance Minimally difficult **General** Proprietary, 4-year, specialized, coed **Setting** 3-acre suburban campus **Enrollment** 259 **Faculty** 6:1 **Application deadline** Rolling **Freshmen** 64% accepted **Tuition** $10,595 **Undergraduates** 49% women, 44% part-time, 42% 25 or older, 1% Native American, 4% Hispanic, 2% black, 2% Asian or Pacific Islander **Academic program** Average class size 12, advanced placement, honors program, summer session, adult/continuing education programs, internships **Contact** Mr. Daniel Paier, Dean of Admissions, Paier College of Art, Inc., Hamden, CT 06514-3902. Telephone: 203-287-3031.

QUINNIPIAC COLLEGE
HAMDEN, CONNECTICUT

Entrance Moderately difficult **General** Independent, comprehensive, coed **Setting** 200-acre suburban campus **Enrollment** 5,117 **Faculty** 15:1 **Application deadline** 2/15 **Freshmen** 55% accepted **Housing** Yes **Tuition** $14,880 **Undergraduates** 60% women, 19% part-time, 12% 25 or older, 1% Native American, 3% Hispanic, 5% black, 2% Asian or Pacific Islander **Most popular recent majors** Physical therapy, accounting, occupational therapy **Academic program** Average class size 25, advanced placement, accelerated degree program, self-designed majors, honors program, summer session, adult/continuing education programs, internships **Contact** Ms. Joan Isaac Mohr, Vice President and Dean of Admissions, Quinnipiac College, Hamden, CT 06518-1904. Telephone: 203-281-8600. Fax: 203-281-8906.

SACRED HEART UNIVERSITY
FAIRFIELD, CONNECTICUT

Entrance Moderately difficult **General** Independent Roman Catholic, comprehensive, coed **Setting** 56-acre suburban campus **Enrollment** 5,545 **Faculty** 14:1 **Application deadline** 4/15 **Freshmen** 85% accepted **Housing** Yes **Tuition** $13,475 **Undergraduates** 55% women, 7% 25 or older, 0% Native American, 6% Hispanic, 5% black, 3% Asian or Pacific Islander **Most popular recent**

majors Business administration/commerce/management, communication, psychology **Academic program** Advanced placement, accelerated degree program, tutorials, honors program, summer session, adult/continuing education programs, internships **Contact** Ms. Karen N. Pagliuco, Dean of Undergraduate Admissions, Sacred Heart University, Fairfield, CT 06432-1000. Telephone: 203-371-7880. Fax: 203-371-7889.

SAINT JOSEPH COLLEGE
WEST HARTFORD, CONNECTICUT

Entrance Moderately difficult **General** Independent Roman Catholic, comprehensive, primarily women **Setting** 84-acre suburban campus **Enrollment** 1,922 **Faculty** 12:1 **Application deadline** 5/1 **Freshmen** 87% accepted **Housing** Yes **Tuition** $14,490 **Undergraduates** 94% women, 48% part-time, 15% 25 or older, 0% Native American, 4% Hispanic, 8% black, 2% Asian or Pacific Islander **Most popular recent majors** Nursing, social work, special education **Academic program** Average class size 15, advanced placement, accelerated degree program, self-designed majors, honors program, summer session, adult/continuing education programs, internships **Contact** Ms. Mary C. Demo, Director of Admissions, Saint Joseph College, West Hartford, CT 06117-2700. Telephone: 860-232-4571 Ext. 360. Fax: 860-233-5695.

SOUTHERN CONNECTICUT STATE UNIVERSITY
NEW HAVEN, CONNECTICUT

Entrance Moderately difficult **General** State-supported, comprehensive, coed **Setting** 168-acre urban campus **Enrollment** 11,412 **Faculty** 19:1 **Application deadline** 7/1 **Freshmen** 71% accepted **Housing** Yes **Tuition** $3568 **Undergraduates** 56% women, 29% part-time, 23% 25 or older, 1% Native American, 4% Hispanic, 10% black, 2% Asian or Pacific Islander **Academic program** Advanced placement, accelerated degree program, honors program, summer session, adult/continuing education programs, internships **Contact** Ms. Sharon Brennan, Director of Admissions, Southern Connecticut State University, 501 Crescent Street, New Haven, CT 06515-1355. Telephone: 203-392-5644.

TEIKYO POST UNIVERSITY
WATERBURY, CONNECTICUT

Entrance Minimally difficult **General** Independent, 4-year, coed **Setting** 70-acre suburban campus **Enrollment** 1,550 **Application deadline** Rolling **Freshmen** 82% accepted **Housing** Yes **Tuition** $12,260 **Undergraduates** 70% women, 50% part-time, 62% 25 or older, 0% Native American, 2% Hispanic, 5% black, 1% Asian or Pacific Islander **Academic program** Average class size 16, ESL program, advanced placement, accelerated degree program, self-designed majors, tutorials, honors program, summer session, adult/continuing education programs, internships **Contact** Ms. Jane LaRocco, Senior Associate Director of Admission, Teikyo Post University, Waterbury, CT 06723-2540. Telephone: 203-596-4520. Fax: 203-756-5810.

TRINITY COLLEGE
HARTFORD, CONNECTICUT

Entrance Very difficult **General** Independent, comprehensive, coed **Setting** 96-acre urban campus **Enrollment** 2,134 **Faculty** 10:1 **Application deadline** 1/15 **Freshmen** 46% accepted **Housing** Yes **Tuition** $22,470 **Undergraduates** 49% women, 10% part-time, 9% 25 or older, 0% Native American, 5% Hispanic, 5% black, 5% Asian or Pacific Islander **Most popular recent majors** History, psychology, English **Academic program** Advanced placement, accelerated degree program, self-designed majors, tutorials, summer session, adult/continuing education programs, internships **Contact** Mr. Larry Dow, Director of Admissions, Trinity College, 300 Summit Street, Hartford, CT 06106-3100. Telephone: 860-297-2180. Fax: 860-297-2287.

UNITED STATES COAST GUARD ACADEMY
NEW LONDON, CONNECTICUT

Entrance Very difficult **General** Federally supported, 4-year, coed **Setting** 110-acre suburban campus **Enrollment** 807 **Faculty** 9:1 **Application deadline** 12/15 **Freshmen** 22% accepted **Housing** Yes **Tuition** $0 **Undergraduates** 27% women, 0% part-time, 0% 25 or older, 1% Native American, 7% Hispanic, 5% black, 5% Asian or Pacific Islander **Most popular recent majors** Marine engineering, business administration/commerce/management, marine sciences **Academic program** Tutorials, honors program, summer session **Contact** Capt. R. W. Thorne, Director of Admissions, United States Coast Guard Academy, New London, CT 06320-4195. Telephone: 860-444-8500. Fax: 860-444-8289.

UNIVERSITY OF BRIDGEPORT
BRIDGEPORT, CONNECTICUT

Entrance Moderately difficult **General** Independent, comprehensive, coed **Setting** 86-acre urban campus **Enrollment** 2,142 **Faculty** 10:1 **Application deadline** 4/1 **Freshmen** 83% accepted **Housing** Yes **Tuition** $13,695 **Undergraduates** 53% women, 25% part-time, 34% 25 or older, 7% Hispanic, 15% black, 3% Asian or Pacific Islander **Most popular recent majors** Liberal arts/general studies, dental services, business administration/commerce/management **Academic program** Average class size 15, ESL program, advanced placement, accelerated degree program, self-designed majors, tutorials, honors program, summer session, adult/continuing education programs, internships **Contact** Dr. Suzanne Dale Wilcox, Dean of Admissions and Financial Aid, University of Bridgeport, 380 University Avenue, Bridgeport, CT 06601. Telephone: 203-576-4552. Fax: 203-576-4941.

UNIVERSITY OF CONNECTICUT

STORRS, CONNECTICUT

Entrance Moderately difficult **General** State-supported, coed **Setting** 4,000-acre rural campus **Enrollment** 15,541 **Faculty** 14:1 **Application deadline** 3/1 **Freshmen** 67% accepted **Housing** Yes **Tuition** $5096 **Undergraduates** 50% women, 9% part-time, 9% 25 or older, 1% Native American, 4% Hispanic, 4% black, 6% Asian or Pacific Islander **Most popular recent majors** Psychology, English, political science/government **Academic program** Advanced placement, accelerated degree program, self-designed majors, honors program, summer session, adult/continuing education programs, internships **Contact** Dr. Ann L. Huckenbeck, Director of Admissions, University of Connecticut, 2131 Hillside Road, U-88, Storrs, CT 06269. Telephone: 860-486-3137. Fax: 860-486-1476.

UNIVERSITY OF HARTFORD

WEST HARTFORD, CONNECTICUT

Entrance Moderately difficult **General** Independent, comprehensive, coed **Setting** Suburban campus **Enrollment** 7,068 **Faculty** 11:1 **Application deadline** Rolling **Freshmen** 82% accepted **Housing** Yes **Tuition** $17,320 **Undergraduates** 52% women, 23% part-time, 18% 25 or older, 0% Native American, 3% Hispanic, 6% black, 2% Asian or Pacific Islander **Academic program** Advanced placement, self-designed majors, honors program, summer session, adult/continuing education programs, internships **Contact** Mr. Richard Zeiser, Director of Admissions, University of Hartford, West Hartford, CT 06117-1500. Telephone: 860-768-4296. Fax: 860-768-4961.

UNIVERSITY OF NEW HAVEN

WEST HAVEN, CONNECTICUT

Entrance Moderately difficult **General** Independent, comprehensive, coed **Setting** 78-acre suburban campus **Enrollment** 5,438 **Faculty** 11:1 **Application deadline** 9/1 **Freshmen** 84% accepted **Housing** Yes **Tuition** $13,100 **Undergraduates** 37% women, 47% part-time, 1% Native American, 4% Hispanic, 8% black, 2% Asian or Pacific Islander **Most popular recent majors** Business administration/commerce/management, mechanical engineering, criminal justice **Academic program** Advanced placement, self-designed majors, honors program, summer session, adult/continuing education programs, internships **Contact** Mr. Steve Briggs, Dean of Admissions and Financial Aid, University of New Haven, West Haven, CT 06516-1916. Telephone: 203-932-7088.

WESLEYAN UNIVERSITY

MIDDLETOWN, CONNECTICUT

Entrance Most difficult **General** Independent, coed **Setting** 120-acre small-town campus **Enrollment** 3,279 **Faculty** 11:1 **Application deadline** 1/1 **Freshmen** 32% accepted **Housing** Yes **Tuition** $23,340 **Undergraduates** 52% women, 1% part-time, 1% 25 or older, 0% Native American, 7% Hispanic, 8% black, 11% Asian or Pacific Islander **Most popular recent majors** English, political science/government, history **Academic program** Advanced placement, accelerated degree program, self-designed majors, tutorials, adult/continuing education programs, internships **Contact** Ms. Barbara-Jan Wilson, Dean of Admissions and Financial Aid, Wesleyan University, Middletown, CT 06459-0260. Telephone: 860-685-3000. Fax: 860-685-3001.

WESTERN CONNECTICUT STATE UNIVERSITY

DANBURY, CONNECTICUT

Entrance Moderately difficult **General** State-supported, comprehensive, coed **Setting** 340-acre urban campus **Enrollment** 5,607 **Application deadline** 5/1 **Freshmen** 61% accepted **Housing** Yes **Tuition** $3626 **Undergraduates** 58% women, 39% part-time, 29% 25 or older, 1% Native American, 4% Hispanic, 5% black, 3% Asian or Pacific Islander **Academic program** Advanced placement, accelerated degree program, self-designed majors, honors program, summer session, adult/continuing education programs, internships **Contact** Mr. Patrick Quinn, Director of Admissions, Western Connecticut State University, 181 White Street, Danbury, CT 06810-6885. Telephone: 203-837-9000.

YALE UNIVERSITY
NEW HAVEN, CONNECTICUT

Entrance Most difficult **General** Independent, coed **Setting** 200-acre urban campus **Enrollment** 11,047 **Faculty** 6:1 **Application deadline** 12/31 **Freshmen** 18% accepted **Housing** Yes **Tuition** $23,100 **Undergraduates** 49% women, 1% part-time, 1% 25 or older, 1% Native American, 7% Hispanic, 7% black, 17% Asian or Pacific Islander **Most popular recent majors** History, English, biology/biological sciences **Academic program** Advanced placement, accelerated degree program, self-designed majors, tutorials, honors program, summer session, adult/continuing education programs **Contact** Admissions Director, Yale University, PO Box 208234, New Haven, CT 06520. Telephone: 203-432-9300. Fax: 203-432-9392.

Maine

BATES COLLEGE
LEWISTON, MAINE

Entrance Most difficult **General** Independent, 4-year, coed **Setting** 109-acre suburban campus **Enrollment** 1,672 **Faculty** 11:1 **Application deadline** 1/15 **Freshmen** 36% accepted **Housing** Yes **Tuition** $28,650 **Undergraduates** 52% women, 0% part-time, 1% 25 or older, 1% Native American, 2% Hispanic, 2% black, 4% Asian or Pacific Islander **Most popular recent majors** Biology/biological sciences, English, economics **Academic program** Advanced placement, accelerated degree program, self-designed majors, tutorials, honors program, internships **Contact** Mr. Wylie L. Mitchell, Dean of Admissions, Bates College, 23 Campus Avenue, Lewiston, ME 04240-6028. Telephone: 207-786-6000. Fax: 207-786-6025.

BOWDOIN COLLEGE
BRUNSWICK, MAINE

Entrance Most difficult **General** Independent, 4-year, coed **Setting** 110-acre small-town campus **Enrollment** 1,581 **Faculty** 11:1 **Application deadline** 1/1 **Freshmen** 29% accepted **Housing** Yes **Tuition** $22,905 **Undergraduates** 51% women, 1% part-time, 1% Native American, 3% Hispanic, 2% black, 7% Asian or Pacific Islander **Most popular recent majors** Political science/government, biology/biological sciences, history **Academic program** Average class size 17, advanced placement, accelerated degree program, self-designed majors, tutorials **Contact** Dr. Richard E. Steele, Dean of Admissions, Bowdoin College, Brunswick, ME 04011-2546. Telephone: 207-725-3190. Fax: 207-725-3003.

COLBY COLLEGE
WATERVILLE, MAINE

Entrance Most difficult **General** Independent, 4-year, coed **Setting** 714-acre small-town campus **Enrollment** 1,764 **Faculty** 11:1 **Application deadline** 1/15 **Freshmen** 31% accepted **Housing** Yes **Tuition** $29,190 **Undergraduates** 52% women, 0% part-time, 0% 25 or older, 1% Native American, 3% Hispanic, 2% black, 6% Asian or Pacific Islander **Academic program** Advanced placement, self-designed majors, tutorials, honors program, internships **Contact** Mr. Parker J. Beverage, Dean of Admissions and Financial Aid, Colby College, Waterville, ME 04901. Telephone: 207-872-3168. Fax: 207-872-3474.

COLLEGE OF THE ATLANTIC
BAR HARBOR, MAINE

Entrance Very difficult **General** Independent, comprehensive, coed **Setting** 25-acre small-town campus **Enrollment** 254 **Faculty** 9:1 **Application deadline** 3/1 **Freshmen** 71% accepted **Housing** Yes **Tuition** $17,066 **Undergraduates** 67% women, 8% part-time, 5% 25 or older, 2% Hispanic, 1% black, 1% Asian or Pacific Islander **Most popular recent majors** Environmental sciences, public affairs and policy studies, environmental studies **Academic program** Average class size 16, advanced placement, accelerated degree program, self-designed majors, tutorials, internships **Contact** Mr. Steve Thomas, Director of Admission and Student Services, College of the Atlantic, Bar Harbor, ME 04609-1198. Telephone: 207-288-5015 Ext. 233. Fax: 207-288-4126.

HUSSON COLLEGE
BANGOR, MAINE

Entrance Moderately difficult **General** Independent, comprehensive, coed **Setting** 170-acre suburban campus **Enrollment** 1,946 **Faculty** 20:1 **Application deadline** 9/1 **Freshmen** 87% accepted **Housing** Yes **Tuition** $8800 **Undergraduates** 60% women, 48% part-time, 23% 25 or older, 1% Native American, 1% Hispanic, 1% black, 1% Asian or Pacific Islander **Most popular recent majors** Business administration/commerce/management, nursing, accounting **Academic program** Average class size 40, advanced placement, tutorials, honors program, summer session, adult/continuing education programs, internships **Contact** Mrs. Jane Goodwin, Director of Admissions, Husson College, Bangor, ME 04401-2999. Telephone: 207-941-7100. Fax: 207-941-7988.

MAINE COLLEGE OF ART
PORTLAND, MAINE

Entrance Moderately difficult **General** Independent, 4-year, specialized, coed **Setting** Urban campus **Enrollment** 316 **Faculty** 10:1 **Application deadline** Rolling **Freshmen** 88% accepted **Housing** Yes **Tuition** $15,005 **Undergraduates** 58% women, 10% part-time, 24% 25 or older, 1% Native American, 1% Hispanic, 1% black, 3% Asian or Pacific Islander **Most popular recent majors** Jewelry and metalsmithing, sculpture, graphic arts **Academic program** Average class size 15, advanced placement, self-designed majors, tutorials, summer session, adult/continuing education programs, internships **Contact** Ms. Pamela Hartford, Administrative Assistant, Maine College of Art, 75 Spring Street, Portland, ME 04101-3987. Telephone: 207-775-3052. Fax: 207-772-5069.

MAINE MARITIME ACADEMY
CASTINE, MAINE

Entrance Moderately difficult **General** State-supported, comprehensive, coed **Setting** 35-acre small-town campus **Enrollment** 665 **Faculty** 10:1 **Application deadline** 7/1 **Freshmen** 77% accepted **Housing** Yes **Tuition** $4656 **Undergraduates** 12% women, 0% part-time, 5% 25 or older, 1% Native American, 1% Hispanic, 1% black **Most popular recent majors** Marine engineering, maritime sciences **Academic program** Advanced placement, tutorials, summer session, adult/continuing education programs, internships **Contact** Mr. Jeffrey C. Wright, Director of Admissions, Maine Maritime Academy, Castine, ME 04420. Telephone: 207-326-2215. Fax: 207-326-2515.

SAINT JOSEPH'S COLLEGE
STANDISH, MAINE

Entrance Moderately difficult **General** Independent, comprehensive, coed, affiliated with Roman Catholic Church **Setting** 330-acre small-town campus **Enrollment** 1,105 **Faculty** 16:1 **Application deadline** Rolling **Freshmen** 90% accepted **Housing** Yes **Tuition** $11,710 **Undergraduates** 60% women, 32% part-time, 2% 25 or older, 0% Native American, 1% Hispanic, 2% black, 2% Asian or Pacific Islander **Most popular recent majors** Nursing, business administration/commerce/management, elementary education **Academic program** Average class size 22, advanced placement, accelerated degree program, tutorials, honors program, summer session, adult/continuing education programs, internships **Contact** Mr. Fredric V. Stone, Director of Admissions, Saint Joseph's College, Standish, ME 04084-5263. Telephone: 207-893-7741. Fax: 207-893-7861.

THOMAS COLLEGE
WATERVILLE, MAINE

Entrance Minimally difficult **General** Independent, comprehensive, coed **Setting** 70-acre small-town campus **Enrollment** 842 **Faculty** 15:1 **Application deadline** Rolling **Freshmen** 96% accepted **Housing** Yes **Tuition** $11,200 **Undergraduates** 62% women, 32% part-time, 42% 25 or older, 1% Native American, 1% Hispanic, 1% black, 1% Asian or Pacific Islander **Most popular recent majors** Accounting, business administration/commerce/management, marketing/retailing/merchandising **Academic program** ESL program, Advanced placement, summer session, adult/continuing education programs, internships **Contact** Mr. Robert Callahan, Associate Director of Admissions, Thomas College, Waterville, ME 04901-5097. Telephone: 207-873-0771. Fax: 207-877-0114.

UNITY COLLEGE
UNITY, MAINE

Entrance Moderately difficult **General** Independent, 4-year, coed **Setting** 205-acre rural campus **Enrollment** 512 **Faculty** 14:1 **Application deadline** Rolling **Freshmen** 89% accepted **Housing** Yes **Tuition** $10,950 **Undergraduates** 40% women, 1% part-time, 3% 25 or older, 0% Native American, 0% Hispanic, 0% black, 0% Asian or Pacific Islander **Academic program** Advanced placement, accelerated degree program, self-designed majors, honors program, summer session, internships **Contact** Dr. John M. B. Craig, Vice President and Dean for Admissions, Unity College, P.O. Box 532, Unity, ME 04988. Telephone: 207-948-3131 Ext. 222. Fax: 207-948-5626.

UNIVERSITY OF MAINE
ORONO, MAINE

Entrance Moderately difficult **General** State-supported, coed **Setting** 3,298-acre small-town campus **Enrollment** 9,928 **Faculty** 14:1 **Application deadline** 2/1 **Freshmen** 77% accepted **Housing** Yes **Tuition** $4339 **Undergraduates** 52% women, 24% part-time, 34% 25 or older, 2%

Native American, 1% Hispanic, 1% black, 2% Asian or Pacific Islander **Most popular recent majors** Business administration/commerce/management, elementary education, nursing **Academic program** Average class size 25, advanced placement, accelerated degree program, self-designed majors, honors program, summer session, adult/continuing education programs, internships **Contact** Ms. Joyce Henckler, Director of Enrollment Management, University of Maine, Orono, ME 04469-5713. Telephone: 207-581-1561. Fax: 207-581-1213.

UNIVERSITY OF MAINE AT FARMINGTON

FARMINGTON, MAINE

Entrance Moderately difficult **General** State-supported, 4-year, coed **Setting** 50-acre small-town campus **Enrollment** 2,391 **Faculty** 16:1 **Application deadline** 4/15 **Freshmen** 74% accepted **Housing** Yes **Tuition** $3520 **Undergraduates** 69% women, 11% part-time, 21% 25 or older, 1% Native American, 1% Hispanic, 1% black, 1% Asian or Pacific Islander **Most popular recent majors** Elementary education, interdisciplinary studies, secondary education **Academic program** Average class size 30, advanced placement, accelerated degree program, self-designed majors, tutorials, honors program, summer session, internships **Contact** Mr. James G. Collins, Associate Director of Admissions, University of Maine at Farmington, Farmington, ME 04938-1911. Telephone: 207-778-7050. Fax: 207-778-8182.

UNIVERSITY OF MAINE AT FORT KENT

FORT KENT, MAINE

Entrance Moderately difficult **General** State-supported, 4-year, coed **Setting** 52-acre rural campus **Enrollment** 767 **Application deadline** Rolling **Freshmen** 96% accepted **Housing** Yes **Tuition** $3140 **Undergraduates** 61% women, 42% part-time, 33% 25 or older, 1% Native American, 0% Hispanic, 1% black, 1% Asian or Pacific Islander **Most popular recent majors** Nursing, education, social science **Academic program** ESL program, Advanced placement, self-designed majors, honors program, summer session, internships **Contact** Mr. Jerald R. Nadeau, Director of Admissions, University of Maine at Fort Kent, Fort Kent, ME 04743-1292. Telephone: 207-834-7600. Fax: 207-834-7609.

UNIVERSITY OF MAINE AT MACHIAS

MACHIAS, MAINE

Entrance Moderately difficult **General** State-supported, 4-year, coed **Setting** 42-acre rural campus **Enrollment** 915 **Faculty** 16:1 **Application deadline** Rolling **Freshmen** 83% accepted **Housing** Yes **Tuition** $3225 **Undergraduates** 63% women, 40% part-time, 3% Native American, 0% Hispanic, 1% black **Most popular recent majors** Business administration/commerce/management, environmental studies, behavioral sciences **Academic program** Advanced placement, accelerated degree program, self-designed majors, honors program, summer session, adult/continuing education programs, internships **Contact** Mr. David Baldwin, Director of Admissions, University of Maine at Machias, Machias, ME 04654-1321. Telephone: 207-255-1318. Fax: 207-255-4864.

UNIVERSITY OF MAINE AT PRESQUE ISLE

PRESQUE ISLE, MAINE

Entrance Minimally difficult **General** State-supported, 4-year, coed **Setting** 150-acre small-town campus **Enrollment** 1,347 **Faculty** 15:1 **Application deadline** Rolling **Freshmen** 84% accepted **Housing** Yes **Tuition** $3215 **Undergraduates** 57% women, 29% part-time, 48% 25 or older, 2% Native American, 1% Hispanic, 2% black, 1% Asian or Pacific Islander **Most popular recent majors** Education, liberal arts/general studies, business administration/commerce/management **Academic program** Advanced placement, accelerated degree program, self-designed majors, honors program, summer session, adult/continuing education programs, internships **Contact** Mr. Brian Manter, Assistant Director of Admissions, University of Maine at Presque Isle, Presque Isle, ME 04769-2888. Telephone: 207-768-9536. Fax: 207-768-9608.

UNIVERSITY OF NEW ENGLAND

BIDDEFORD, MAINE

Entrance Moderately difficult **General** Independent, comprehensive, coed **Setting** 410-acre small-town campus **Enrollment** 1,892 **Faculty** 19:1 **Application deadline** Rolling **Freshmen** 66% accepted **Housing** Yes **Tuition** $14,085 **Undergraduates** 70% women, 6% part-time, 15% 25 or older, 1% Asian or Pacific Islander **Most popular recent majors** Occupational therapy, physical therapy, nursing **Academic program** Advanced placement, accelerated degree program, self-designed majors, summer session, adult/continuing education programs, internships **Contact** Ms. Patricia Cribby, Dean of Admissions, University of New England, Hills Beach Road, Biddeford, ME 04005-9526. Telephone: 207-283-0171 Ext. 2240.

University of Southern Maine

UNIVERSITY OF SOUTHERN MAINE
PORTLAND, MAINE

Entrance Moderately difficult **General** State-supported, comprehensive, coed **Setting** 126-acre suburban campus **Enrollment** 9,966 **Faculty** 15:1 **Application deadline** Rolling **Freshmen** 78% accepted **Housing** Yes **Tuition** $3938 **Undergraduates** 60% women, 45% part-time, 46% 25 or older, 1% Native American, 1% Hispanic, 1% black, 1% Asian or Pacific Islander **Most popular recent majors** Nursing, business administration/commerce/management, English **Academic program** Average class size 25, advanced placement, self-designed majors, tutorials, honors program, summer session, adult/continuing education programs, internships **Contact** Ms. Debbie Jordan, Director of Admissions, University of Southern Maine, 37 College Avenue, Gorham, ME 04038. Telephone: 207-780-5670. Fax: 207-780-5640.

WESTBROOK COLLEGE
SEE UNIVERSITY OF NEW ENGLAND

Massachusetts

AMERICAN INTERNATIONAL COLLEGE
SPRINGFIELD, MASSACHUSETTS

Entrance Moderately difficult **General** Independent, comprehensive, coed **Setting** 58-acre urban campus **Enrollment** 1,986 **Faculty** 16:1 **Application deadline** Rolling **Freshmen** 77% accepted **Housing** Yes **Tuition** $11,244 **Undergraduates** 52% women, 17% part-time, 9% 25 or older, 5% Hispanic, 13% black, 2% Asian or Pacific Islander **Most popular recent majors** Criminal justice, accounting, nursing **Academic program** Advanced placement, accelerated degree program, tutorials, honors program, summer session, adult/continuing education programs, internships **Contact** Mr. Peter J. Miller, Dean of Admissions, American International College, 1000 State Street, Springfield, MA 01109-3189. Telephone: 413-747-6201. Fax: 413-737-2803.

AMHERST COLLEGE
AMHERST, MASSACHUSETTS

Entrance Most difficult **General** Independent, 4-year, coed **Setting** 964-acre small-town campus **Enrollment** 1,607 **Faculty** 10:1 **Application deadline** 12/31 **Freshmen** 20% accepted **Housing** Yes **Tuition** $23,027 **Undergraduates** 47% women, 0% part-time, 1% 25 or older, 1% Native American, 9% Hispanic, 7% black, 12% Asian or Pacific Islander **Most popular recent majors** English, psychology, political science/government **Academic program** Self-designed majors, tutorials, honors program **Contact** Ms. Jane E. Reynolds, Dean of Admission, Amherst College, Amherst, MA 01002. Telephone: 413-542-2328. Fax: 413-542-2040.

ANNA MARIA COLLEGE
PAXTON, MASSACHUSETTS

Entrance Moderately difficult **General** Independent Roman Catholic, comprehensive, coed **Setting** 180-acre rural campus **Enrollment** 1,927 **Faculty** 15:1 **Application deadline** Rolling **Freshmen** 88% accepted **Housing** Yes **Tuition** $12,240 **Undergraduates** 60% women, 51% part-time, 10% 25 or older, 1% Native American, 2% Hispanic, 2% black, 2% Asian or Pacific Islander **Most popular recent majors** Criminal justice, business administration/commerce/management, elementary education **Academic program** Advanced placement, accelerated degree program, self-designed majors, tutorials, honors program, summer session, adult/continuing education programs, internships **Contact** Ms. Christine L. Soverow, Director of Admissions, Anna Maria College, Box, Paxton, MA 01612. Telephone: 508-849-3360.

ART INSTITUTE OF BOSTON
BOSTON, MASSACHUSETTS

Entrance Moderately difficult **General** Independent, 4-year, specialized, coed **Setting** Urban campus **Enrollment** 461 **Faculty** 13:1 **Application deadline** Rolling **Freshmen** 90% accepted **Housing** Yes **Tuition** $11,770 **Undergraduates** 53% women, 32% part-time, 27% 25 or older, 0% Native American, 2% Hispanic, 2% black, 4% Asian or Pacific Islander **Most popular recent majors** Illustration, commercial art, photography **Academic program** Average class size 14, advanced placement, self-designed majors, tutorials, honors program, summer session, adult/continuing education programs, internships **Contact** Ms. Diana Arcadipone, Dean of Admissions, Art Institute of Boston, 700 Beacon Street, Boston, MA 02215-2598. Telephone: 617-262-1223 Ext. 304. Fax: 617-437-1226.

ASSUMPTION COLLEGE
WORCESTER, MASSACHUSETTS

Entrance Moderately difficult **General** Independent Roman Catholic, comprehensive, coed **Setting** 150-acre suburban campus **Enrollment** 2,596 **Faculty** 17:1 **Application deadline** 3/1 **Freshmen** 72% accepted **Housing** Yes **Tuition** $14,845

Undergraduates 60% women, 1% part-time, 2% 25 or older, 1% Native American, 4% Hispanic, 1% black, 2% Asian or Pacific Islander **Most popular recent majors** Human resources, business administration/commerce/management, psychology **Academic program** Advanced placement, self-designed majors, tutorials, honors program, summer session, adult/continuing education programs, internships **Contact** Mr. Thomas E. Dunn, Vice President for Enrollment Management, Assumption College, Worcester, MA 01615-0005. Telephone: 508-767-7285.

ATLANTIC UNION COLLEGE
SOUTH LANCASTER, MASSACHUSETTS

Entrance Moderately difficult **General** Independent Seventh-day Adventist, comprehensive, coed **Setting** 314-acre small-town campus **Enrollment** 642 **Faculty** 11:1 **Application deadline** 8/1 **Freshmen** 94% accepted **Housing** Yes **Tuition** $12,000 **Undergraduates** 51% women, 20% part-time, 26% Hispanic, 30% black, 4% Asian or Pacific Islander **Most popular recent majors** Elementary education, business administration/commerce/management, nursing **Academic program** Advanced placement, tutorials, honors program, summer session, adult/continuing education programs, internships **Contact** Ms. Julie Lee, Associate Director for Enrollment Management, Atlantic Union College, South Lancaster, MA 01561-1000. Telephone: 508-368-2255. Fax: 508-368-2015.

BABSON COLLEGE
WELLESLEY, MASSACHUSETTS

Entrance Very difficult **General** Independent, comprehensive, specialized, coed **Setting** 450-acre suburban campus **Enrollment** 3,270 **Faculty** 11:1 **Application deadline** 2/1 **Freshmen** 45% accepted **Housing** Yes **Tuition** $19,675 **Undergraduates** 37% women, 0% part-time, 1% 25 or older, 0% Native American, 5% Hispanic, 3% black, 7% Asian or Pacific Islander **Most popular recent majors** Finance/banking, business administration/commerce/management, marketing/retailing/merchandising **Academic program** Advanced placement, accelerated degree program, self-designed majors, tutorials, honors program, summer session, internships **Contact** Dr. Charles Nolan, Dean of Undergraduate Admission, Babson College, Office of Undergraduate Admission, Mustard Hall, Babson Park, MA 02157-0310. Telephone: 617-239-5522. Fax: 617-239-4006.

BAY PATH COLLEGE
LONGMEADOW, MASSACHUSETTS

Entrance Moderately difficult **General** Independent, 4-year, women only **Setting** 32-acre suburban campus **Enrollment** 608 **Faculty** 17:1 **Application deadline** Rolling **Freshmen** 78% accepted **Housing** Yes **Tuition** $11,800 **Undergraduates** 28% part-time, 40% 25 or older, 0% Native American, 3% Hispanic, 5% black, 1% Asian or Pacific Islander **Most popular recent majors** Business administration/commerce/management, early childhood education, occupational therapy **Academic program** Average class size 25, advanced placement, self-designed majors, tutorials, honors program, summer session, adult/continuing education programs, internships **Contact** Ms. Caron T. Hobin, Dean of Enrollment Services, Bay Path College, 588 Longmeadow Street, Longmeadow, MA 01106-2292. Telephone: 413-567-0621 Ext. 333. Fax: 413-567-0501.

BECKER COLLEGE–LEICESTER CAMPUS
LEICESTER, MASSACHUSETTS

Entrance Minimally difficult **General** Independent, 4-year, coed **Setting** 75-acre small-town campus **Enrollment** 378 **Application deadline** Rolling **Freshmen** 85% accepted **Housing** Yes **Tuition** $10,130 **Undergraduates** 80% women, 9% part-time, 25% 25 or older, 2% Native American, 3% Hispanic, 5% black, 4% Asian or Pacific Islander **Most popular recent major** Veterinary technology **Academic program** Average class size 15, advanced placement, self-designed majors, summer session, adult/continuing education programs, internships **Contact** Mr. Brian Davis, Dean of Admissions, Becker College–Leicester Campus, 61 Sever Street, Worcester, MA 01615. Telephone: 508-791-9241 Ext. 245. or Telephone: 508-791-9241 Ext. 445. Fax: 508-892-0330.

BECKER COLLEGE–WORCESTER CAMPUS
WORCESTER, MASSACHUSETTS

Entrance Minimally difficult **General** Independent, 4-year, coed **Setting** Urban campus **Enrollment** 905 **Faculty** 15:1 **Application deadline** Rolling **Freshmen** 66% accepted **Housing** Yes **Tuition** $10,130 **Undergraduates** 65% women, 20% part-time, 25% 25 or older, 1% Native American, 5% Hispanic, 3% black, 2% Asian or Pacific Islander **Most popular recent majors** Physical therapy, nursing, criminal justice **Academic program** Advanced placement, honors program, adult/continuing education programs, internships **Contact** Mr. Brian Davis, Dean of Admissions, Becker College–Worcester Campus, 61 Sever Street, Worcester, MA 01615-0071. Telephone: 508-791-9241 Ext. 245. Fax: 508-831-7505.

BENTLEY COLLEGE
WALTHAM, MASSACHUSETTS

Entrance Moderately difficult **General** Independent, comprehensive, coed **Setting** 110-acre suburban campus **Enrollment** 6,169 **Faculty** 18:1 **Application deadline** 2/15 **Freshmen** 66% accepted **Housing** Yes **Tuition** $16,495 **Undergraduates** 45% women, 34% part-time, 25% 25 or older, 0% Native American, 3% Hispanic, 3% black, 6% Asian or Pacific Islander **Most popular recent majors** Accounting, marketing/retailing/merchandising, finance/banking **Academic program** Average class size 30, advanced placement, accelerated degree program, self-designed majors, honors program, summer session, adult/continuing education programs, internships **Contact** Ms. JoAnn McKenna, Director of Admissions, Bentley College, Waltham, MA 02154-4705. Telephone: 617-891-2244. Fax: 617-891-3414.

BERKLEE COLLEGE OF MUSIC
BOSTON, MASSACHUSETTS

Entrance Moderately difficult **General** Independent, 4-year, specialized, coed **Setting** Urban campus **Enrollment** 2,809 **Faculty** 9:1 **Application deadline** 3/1 **Freshmen** 75% accepted **Housing** Yes **Tuition** $14,340 **Undergraduates** 20% women, 13% part-time, 15% 25 or older, 1% Native American, 7% Hispanic, 5% black, 4% Asian or Pacific Islander **Academic program** Advanced placement, accelerated degree program, self-designed majors, summer session **Contact** Ms. Emily Woolf Economou, Director of Admissions, Berklee College of Music, 1140 Boylston Street, Boston, MA 02215-3693. Fax: 617-536-2632.

BOSTON ARCHITECTURAL CENTER
BOSTON, MASSACHUSETTS

Entrance Noncompetitive **General** Independent, 5-year, coed **Setting** Urban campus **Enrollment** 623 **Faculty** 6:1 **Application deadline** Rolling **Freshmen** 92% accepted **Tuition** $5310 **Undergraduates** 24% women, 16% part-time, 67% 25 or older, 3% Hispanic, 2% black, 3% Asian or Pacific Islander **Academic program** Advanced placement, tutorials, summer session, adult/continuing education programs, internships **Contact** Ms. Ellen Driscoll, Admissions Coordinator, Boston Architectural Center, 320 Newbury Street, Boston, MA 02115-2795. Telephone: 617-536-3170. Fax: 617-536-5829.

BOSTON COLLEGE
CHESTNUT HILL, MASSACHUSETTS

Entrance Very difficult **General** Independent Roman Catholic (Jesuit), coed **Setting** 240-acre suburban campus **Enrollment** 14,830 **Faculty** 15:1 **Application deadline** 1/10 **Freshmen** 41% accepted **Housing** Yes **Tuition** $20,307 **Undergraduates** 53% women, 0% 25 or older, 5% Hispanic, 4% black, 8% Asian or Pacific Islander **Most popular recent majors** Finance/banking, English, political science/government **Academic program** Advanced placement, accelerated degree program, self-designed majors, tutorials, honors program, summer session, adult/continuing education programs, internships **Contact** Mr. John L. Mahoney Jr., Director of Undergraduate Admission, Boston College, Chestnut Hill, MA 02167-9991. Telephone: 617-552-3100.

BOSTON CONSERVATORY
BOSTON, MASSACHUSETTS

Entrance Moderately difficult **General** Independent, comprehensive, specialized, coed **Setting** Urban campus **Enrollment** 452 **Application deadline** Rolling **Freshmen** 45% accepted **Housing** Yes **Tuition** $15,925 **Undergraduates** 69% women, 11% part-time, 1% Native American, 3% Hispanic, 5% black, 2% Asian or Pacific Islander **Academic program** Advanced placement, summer session, adult/continuing education programs **Contact** Mr. Richard Wallace, Director of Enrollment, Boston Conservatory, 8 The Fenway, Boston, MA 02215. Telephone: 617-536-6340 Ext. 116. Fax: 617-536-3176.

BOSTON UNIVERSITY
BOSTON, MASSACHUSETTS

Entrance Very difficult **General** Independent, coed **Setting** 123-acre urban campus **Enrollment** 29,664 **Faculty** 13:1 **Application deadline** 1/15 **Freshmen** 53% accepted **Housing** Yes **Tuition** $22,278 **Undergraduates** 57% women, 3% part-time, 3% 25 or older, 1% Native American, 6% Hispanic, 4% black, 14% Asian or Pacific Islander **Most popular recent majors** Business administration/commerce/management, social science, communication **Academic program** ESL program, Advanced placement, self-designed majors, tutorials, honors program, summer session, adult/continuing education programs, internships **Contact** Ms. Kelly Walter, Associate Director of Admissions, Boston University, 121 Bay State Road, Boston, MA 02215. Telephone: 617-353-2300. Fax: 617-353-9695.

BRADFORD COLLEGE
BRADFORD, MASSACHUSETTS

Entrance Moderately difficult **General** Independent, 4-year, coed **Setting** 75-acre small-town campus **Enrollment** 568 **Faculty** 12:1 **Application deadline** Rolling **Freshmen** 78% accepted **Housing** Yes **Tuition** $16,315 **Undergraduates** 63% women, 6% part-time, 14% 25 or older, 1% Native American, 5% Hispanic, 6% black, 2% Asian or Pacific Islander **Most popular recent majors** Psychology, art/fine arts, marketing/retailing/merchandising **Academic program** Advanced placement, accelerated degree program, self-designed majors, tutorials, honors program, summer session, adult/continuing education programs, internships **Contact** Mr. William Dunfey, Dean of Admissions, Bradford College, Bradford, MA 01835. Telephone: 508-372-7161 Ext. 271. Fax: 508-521-0480.

BRANDEIS UNIVERSITY
WALTHAM, MASSACHUSETTS

Entrance Very difficult **General** Independent, coed **Setting** 250-acre suburban campus **Enrollment** 4,219 **Faculty** 10:1 **Application deadline** 2/1 **Freshmen** 53% accepted **Housing** Yes **Tuition** $22,851 **Undergraduates** 55% women, 2% part-time, 2% 25 or older, 1% Native American, 3% Hispanic, 3% black, 9% Asian or Pacific Islander **Most popular recent majors** Political science/government, English, psychology **Academic program** Average class size 16, advanced placement, self-designed majors, tutorials, summer session, adult/continuing education programs, internships **Contact** Mr. Michael Kalafatas, Director of Admissions, Brandeis University, Waltham, MA 02254-9110. Telephone: 781-736-3500. Fax: 781-736-3536.

BRIDGEWATER STATE COLLEGE
BRIDGEWATER, MASSACHUSETTS

Entrance Moderately difficult **General** State-supported, comprehensive, coed **Setting** 235-acre suburban campus **Enrollment** 8,711 **Faculty** 22:1 **Application deadline** 3/1 **Freshmen** 69% accepted **Housing** Yes **Tuition** $3372 **Undergraduates** 59% women, 18% part-time, 22% 25 or older, 0% Native American, 2% Hispanic, 4% black, 1% Asian or Pacific Islander **Most popular recent majors** Business administration/commerce/management, physical education, psychology **Academic program** Average class size 30, advanced placement, self-designed majors, tutorials, honors program, summer session, adult/continuing education programs, internships **Contact** Mr. James F. Plotner Jr., Associate Dean of Academic Admissions, Admission Office, Bridgewater State College, Bridgewater, MA 02325-0001. Telephone: 508-697-1237. Fax: 508-697-1746.

CLARK UNIVERSITY
WORCESTER, MASSACHUSETTS

Entrance Moderately difficult **General** Independent, coed **Setting** 50-acre urban campus **Enrollment** 2,732 **Faculty** 11:1 **Application deadline** 2/1 **Freshmen** 79% accepted **Housing** Yes **Tuition** $20,940 **Undergraduates** 58% women, 2% part-time, 2% Hispanic, 4% black, 5% Asian or Pacific Islander **Most popular recent majors** Psychology, political science/government, business administration/commerce/management **Academic program** Advanced placement, accelerated degree program, self-designed majors, tutorials, honors program, summer session, adult/continuing education programs, internships **Contact** Mr. Harold M. Wingood, Dean of Admissions, Clark University, 950 Main Street, Worcester, MA 01610-1477. Telephone: 508-793-7431.

COLLEGE OF OUR LADY OF THE ELMS
CHICOPEE, MASSACHUSETTS

Entrance Moderately difficult **General** Independent Roman Catholic, comprehensive, women only **Setting** 32-acre suburban campus **Enrollment** 1,133 **Faculty** 12:1 **Application deadline** Rolling **Freshmen** 93% accepted **Housing** Yes **Tuition** $12,950 **Undergraduates** 45% part-time, 15% 25 or older, 0% Native American, 4% Hispanic, 5% black, 1% Asian or Pacific Islander **Most popular recent majors** Nursing, social work, education **Academic program** Advanced placement, accelerated degree program, self-designed majors, tutorials, summer session, adult/continuing education programs, internships **Contact** Ms. Cori L. Nevers, Director of Admissions, College of Our Lady of the Elms, Chicopee, MA 01013-2839. Telephone: 413-592-3189. Fax: 413-592-4871.

COLLEGE OF THE HOLY CROSS
WORCESTER, MASSACHUSETTS

Entrance Very difficult **General** Independent Roman Catholic (Jesuit), 4-year, coed **Setting** 174-acre suburban campus **Enrollment** 2,636 **Faculty** 12:1 **Application deadline** 1/15 **Freshmen** 44% accepted **Housing** Yes **Tuition** $21,080 **Undergraduates** 52% women, 0% part-time, 0% 25 or older, 0% Native American, 3% Hispanic, 3% black, 3% Asian or Pacific Islander **Most popular recent majors** English, psychology, history **Academic program** Advanced placement, accelerated degree program, self-designed majors, tutorials, honors program, internships **Contact** Ms. Ann Bowe McDermott, Director of Admissions, College of the Holy Cross, Worcester, MA 01610. Telephone: 508-793-2443. Fax: 508-793-3888.

CURRY COLLEGE
MILTON, MASSACHUSETTS

Entrance Moderately difficult **General** Independent, comprehensive, coed **Setting** 120-acre suburban campus **Enrollment** 1,909 **Application deadline** 4/1 **Freshmen** 86% accepted **Housing** Yes **Tuition** $15,700 **Undergraduates** 48% women, 40% part-time, 13% 25 or older, 0% Native American, 1% Hispanic, 4% black, 1% Asian or Pacific Islander **Most popular recent majors** Business administration/commerce/management, communication, nursing **Academic program** Advanced placement, accelerated degree program, self-designed majors, tutorials, honors program, summer session, adult/continuing education programs, internships **Contact** Ms. Janet Cromie Kelly, Dean of Admissions and Financial Aid, Curry College, Milton, MA 02186-9984. Telephone: 617-333-2210. Fax: 617-333-6860.

EASTERN NAZARENE COLLEGE
QUINCY, MASSACHUSETTS

Entrance Moderately difficult **General** Independent, comprehensive, coed, affiliated with Church of the Nazarene **Setting** 15-acre suburban campus **Enrollment** 844 **Faculty** 12:1 **Application deadline** Rolling **Freshmen** 78% accepted **Housing** Yes **Tuition** $11,440 **Undergraduates** 57% women, 4% part-time, 7% 25 or older, 0% Native American, 2% Hispanic, 5% black, 4% Asian or Pacific Islander **Most popular recent majors** Business administration/commerce/management, education, psychology **Academic program** Average class size 45, advanced placement, accelerated degree program, tutorials, summer session, adult/continuing education programs, internships **Contact** Mr. Martin Trice, Vice President of Enrollment Services, Eastern Nazarene College, Quincy, MA 02170-2999. Telephone: 617-745-3711. Fax: 617-745-3490.

ELMS COLLEGE
SEE COLLEGE OF OUR LADY OF THE ELMS

EMERSON COLLEGE
BOSTON, MASSACHUSETTS

Entrance Moderately difficult **General** Independent, comprehensive, coed **Setting** Urban campus **Enrollment** 3,441 **Faculty** 15:1 **Application deadline** 2/1 **Freshmen** 67% accepted **Housing** Yes **Tuition** $17,826 **Undergraduates** 66% women, 8% part-time, 6% 25 or older, 1% Native American, 3% Hispanic, 3% black, 2% Asian or Pacific Islander **Most popular recent majors** Communication, theater arts/drama, public relations **Academic program** Average class size 35, advanced placement, self-designed majors, tutorials, honors program, summer session, adult/continuing education programs, internships **Contact** Mr. Gerald P. Doyle, Director of Admission, Emerson College, 100 Beacon Street, Boston, MA 02116-1511. Telephone: 617-824-8600.

EMMANUEL COLLEGE
BOSTON, MASSACHUSETTS

Entrance Moderately difficult **General** Independent Roman Catholic, comprehensive, women only **Setting** 16-acre urban campus **Enrollment** 1,564 **Faculty** 10:1 **Application deadline** Rolling **Freshmen** 84% accepted **Housing** Yes **Tuition** $14,550 **Undergraduates** 60% part-time, 55% 25 or older, 1% Native American, 3% Hispanic, 8% black, 4% Asian or Pacific Islander **Academic program** Advanced placement, accelerated degree program, summer session, adult/continuing education programs, internships **Contact** Ms. Barbara Mitchell, Associate Director of Admissions, Emmanuel College, 400 The Fenway, Boston, MA 02115. Telephone: 617-735-9715. Fax: 617-735-9801.

ENDICOTT COLLEGE
BEVERLY, MASSACHUSETTS

Entrance Minimally difficult **General** Independent, comprehensive, coed **Setting** 150-acre suburban campus **Enrollment** 902 **Faculty** 11:1 **Application deadline** Rolling **Freshmen** 84% accepted **Housing** Yes **Tuition** $13,344 **Undergraduates** 66% women, 3% part-time, 14% 25 or older, 0% Native American, 2% Hispanic, 2% black, 7% Asian or Pacific Islander **Most popular recent majors** Nursing, psychology, education **Academic program** Advanced placement, self-designed majors, tutorials, honors program, summer session, adult/continuing education programs, internships **Contact** Mr. Thomas J. Redman, Vice President of Admissions and Financial Aid, Endicott College, Beverly, MA 01915-2096. Telephone: 508-921-1000. Fax: 508-927-0084.

FITCHBURG STATE COLLEGE
FITCHBURG, MASSACHUSETTS

Entrance Moderately difficult **General** State-supported, comprehensive, coed **Setting** 45-acre small-town campus **Enrollment** 3,701 **Faculty** 12:1 **Application deadline** Rolling **Freshmen** 59% accepted **Housing** Yes **Tuition** $3346 **Undergraduates** 59% women, 19% part-time, 18% 25 or older, 1% Native American, 3% Hispanic, 5% black, 2% Asian or Pacific Islander **Most popular**

recent majors Business administration/commerce/management, communication, nursing **Academic program** Average class size 20, advanced placement, accelerated degree program, self-designed majors, honors program, summer session, adult/continuing education programs, internships **Contact** Mr. James Dupont, Director of Admissions, Fitchburg State College, Fitchburg, MA 01420-2697. Telephone: 508-665-3534. Fax: 508-665-3693.

FRAMINGHAM STATE COLLEGE
FRAMINGHAM, MASSACHUSETTS

Entrance Moderately difficult **General** State-supported, comprehensive, coed **Setting** 73-acre suburban campus **Enrollment** 5,155 **Faculty** 15:1 **Application deadline** 3/15 **Freshmen** 73% accepted **Housing** Yes **Tuition** $3150 **Undergraduates** 64% women, 35% part-time, 20% 25 or older, 1% Native American, 3% Hispanic, 3% black, 3% Asian or Pacific Islander **Most popular recent majors** Business administration/commerce/management, psychology, elementary education **Academic program** Average class size 23, advanced placement, self-designed majors, honors program, summer session, adult/continuing education programs, internships **Contact** Dr. Philip M. Dooher, Dean of Admissions and Enrollment Services, Framingham State College, Framingham, MA 01701-9101. Telephone: 508-626-4500. Fax: 508-626-4017.

GORDON COLLEGE
WENHAM, MASSACHUSETTS

Entrance Moderately difficult **General** Independent Christian, comprehensive, coed **Setting** 300-acre small-town campus **Enrollment** 1,259 **Faculty** 15:1 **Application deadline** Rolling **Freshmen** 85% accepted **Housing** Yes **Tuition** $15,150 **Undergraduates** 63% women, 4% part-time, 3% 25 or older, 0% Native American, 2% Hispanic, 2% black, 3% Asian or Pacific Islander **Most popular recent majors** English, psychology, biology/biological sciences **Academic program** Average class size 21, advanced placement, self-designed majors, tutorials, honors program, internships **Contact** Mrs. Pamela B. Lazarakis, Dean of Admissions, Gordon College, 255 Grapevine Road, Wenham, MA 01984-1899. Telephone: 508-927-2300 Ext. 4217. Fax: 508-524-3704.

HAMPSHIRE COLLEGE
AMHERST, MASSACHUSETTS

Entrance Moderately difficult **General** Independent, 4-year, coed **Setting** 800-acre rural campus **Enrollment** 1,068 **Faculty** 11:1 **Application deadline** 2/1 **Freshmen** 70% accepted **Housing** Yes **Tuition** $23,780 **Undergraduates** 56% women, 0% part-time, 4% 25 or older, 1% Native American, 3% Hispanic, 5% black, 3% Asian or Pacific Islander **Most popular recent majors** Art/fine arts, biology/biological sciences, film studies **Academic program** Average class size 17, advanced placement, self-designed majors, internships **Contact** Ms. Audrey Smith, Director of Admissions, Hampshire College, Amherst, MA 01002. Telephone: 413-582-5471. Fax: 413-582-5631.

HARVARD UNIVERSITY
CAMBRIDGE, MASSACHUSETTS

Entrance Most difficult **General** Independent, coed **Setting** 380-acre urban campus **Enrollment** 18,310 **Faculty** 8:1 **Application deadline** 1/1 **Freshmen** 11% accepted **Housing** Yes **Tuition** $22,802 **Undergraduates** 44% women, 0% part-time, 1% 25 or older, 1% Native American, 7% Hispanic, 8% black, 19% Asian or Pacific Islander **Most popular recent majors** Economics, biology/biological sciences, political science/government **Academic program** Advanced placement, accelerated degree program, self-designed majors, tutorials, honors program, summer session, adult/continuing education programs **Contact** Office of Admissions and Financial Aid, Harvard University, Byerly Hall, 8 Garden Street, Cambridge, MA 02138. Telephone: 617-495-1551.

HEBREW COLLEGE
BROOKLINE, MASSACHUSETTS

Entrance Noncompetitive **General** Independent Jewish, comprehensive, specialized, coed **Setting** 3-acre suburban campus **Faculty** 3:1 **Application deadline** Rolling **Tuition** $10,590 **Undergraduates** 80% part-time, 0% Native American, 0% Hispanic, 0% black, 0% Asian or Pacific Islander **Academic program** Tutorials, summer session, adult/continuing education programs, internships **Contact** Mrs. Norma Frankel, Registrar, Hebrew College, Brookline, MA 02146-5495. Telephone: 617-278-4944. Fax: 617-734-9769.

HELLENIC COLLEGE
BROOKLINE, MASSACHUSETTS

Entrance Minimally difficult **General** Independent Greek Orthodox, 4-year, coed **Setting** 52-acre suburban campus **Enrollment** 64 **Faculty** 6:1 **Application deadline** Rolling **Freshmen** 69% accepted **Housing** Yes **Tuition** $7900 **Undergraduates** 29% women, 3% part-time, 14% 25 or older, 0% Native American, 1% Hispanic, 3% black,

0% Asian or Pacific Islander **Most popular recent majors** Religious studies, elementary education, human development **Academic program** Average class size 20, ESL program, advanced placement, tutorials, summer session **Contact** Dr. John Klentos, Director of Admissions and Records, Hellenic College, 50 Goddard Avenue, Brookline, MA 02146-7496. Telephone: 617-731-3500 Ext. 260.

LASELL COLLEGE
NEWTON, MASSACHUSETTS

Entrance Minimally difficult **General** Independent, 4-year, women only **Setting** 50-acre suburban campus **Enrollment** 679 **Faculty** 10:1 **Application deadline** Rolling **Freshmen** 80% accepted **Housing** Yes **Tuition** $14,000 **Undergraduates** 18% part-time, 24% 25 or older, 0% Native American, 6% Hispanic, 8% black, 3% Asian or Pacific Islander **Most popular recent majors** Education, fashion merchandising, physical therapy **Academic program** Average class size 14, advanced placement, self-designed majors, tutorials, honors program, internships **Contact** Ms. Adrienne Franciosi, Director of Admission, Lasell College, Newton, MA 02166-2709. Telephone: 617-243-2225. Fax: 617-243-2389.

LESLEY COLLEGE
CAMBRIDGE, MASSACHUSETTS

Entrance Moderately difficult **General** Independent, comprehensive, women only **Setting** 5-acre urban campus **Enrollment** 6,166 **Faculty** 14:1 **Application deadline** 3/15 **Freshmen** 75% accepted **Housing** Yes **Tuition** $14,606 **Undergraduates** 6% part-time, 4% Hispanic, 6% black, 3% Asian or Pacific Islander **Most popular recent majors** Education, human services, business administration/commerce/management **Academic program** Average class size 16, advanced placement, summer session, adult/continuing education programs, internships **Contact** Ms. Jane A. Raley, Director of Women's College Admissions, Lesley College, 29 Everett Street, Cambridge, MA 02138-2790. Telephone: 617-349-8800. Fax: 617-349-8150.

MASSACHUSETTS COLLEGE OF ART
BOSTON, MASSACHUSETTS

Entrance Very difficult **General** State-supported, comprehensive, specialized, coed **Setting** 5-acre urban campus **Enrollment** 1,487 **Faculty** 12:1 **Application deadline** 3/1 **Freshmen** 54% accepted **Housing** Yes **Tuition** $3964 **Undergraduates** 59% women, 13% part-time, 30% 25 or older, 0% Native American, 4% Hispanic, 3% black, 5% Asian or Pacific Islander **Most popular recent majors** Painting/drawing, illustration, graphic arts **Academic program** Advanced placement, self-designed majors, summer session, internships **Contact** Ms. Kay Ransdell, Director of Admissions, Massachusetts College of Art, 621 Huntington Avenue, Boston, MA 02115-5882. Telephone: 617-232-1555 Ext. 235. Fax: 617-566-4034 Ext. 261.

MASSACHUSETTS COLLEGE OF PHARMACY AND ALLIED HEALTH SCIENCES
BOSTON, MASSACHUSETTS

Entrance Moderately difficult **General** Independent, coed **Setting** 2-acre urban campus **Enrollment** 1,451 **Faculty** 14:1 **Application deadline** 3/1 **Freshmen** 66% accepted **Housing** Yes **Tuition** $14,508 **Undergraduates** 59% women, 15% part-time, 20% 25 or older, 1% Native American, 13% Hispanic, 4% black, 15% Asian or Pacific Islander **Most popular recent majors** Pharmacy/pharmaceutical sciences, nursing, nuclear medical technology **Academic program** Advanced placement, tutorials, summer session, adult/continuing education programs, internships **Contact** Ms. Joan Monahan, Director of Admissions and Registrar, Massachusetts College of Pharmacy and Allied Health Sciences, 179 Longwood Avenue, Boston, MA 02115-5896. Telephone: 617-732-2850.

MASSACHUSETTS INSTITUTE OF TECHNOLOGY
CAMBRIDGE, MASSACHUSETTS

Entrance Most difficult **General** Independent, coed **Setting** 154-acre urban campus **Enrollment** 9,947 **Faculty** 5:1 **Application deadline** 1/1 **Freshmen** 24% accepted **Housing** Yes **Tuition** $23,100 **Undergraduates** 39% women, 1% part-time, 1% 25 or older, 1% Native American, 10% Hispanic, 6% black, 28% Asian or Pacific Islander **Most popular recent majors** Electrical engineering, computer science, mechanical engineering **Academic program** Advanced placement, accelerated degree program, self-designed majors, tutorials, summer session, internships **Contact** Mr. Michael C. Behnke, Director of Admissions, Massachusetts Institute of Technology, 77 Massachusetts Avenue, Cambridge, MA 02139-4307. Telephone: 617-253-4791. Fax: 617-258-8304.

MASSACHUSETTS MARITIME ACADEMY
BUZZARDS BAY, MASSACHUSETTS

Entrance Moderately difficult **General** State-supported, 4-year, coed **Setting** 55-acre small-town campus **Enrollment** 750 **Faculty** 14:1 **Application deadline** Rolling **Freshmen** 67% accepted **Housing** Yes **Tuition** $3023 **Undergraduates** 10% women, 3% part-time, 9% 25 or older, 0% Native American, 3% Hispanic, 2% black, 2% Asian or Pacific Islander **Most popular recent major** Marine engineering **Academic program** Advanced placement, tutorials, adult/continuing education programs, internships **Contact** Cdr. Keith D. Rabine, Dean of Enrollment Services, Massachusetts Maritime Academy, Buzzards Bay, MA 02532-3400. Telephone: 508-830-5000. Fax: 508-830-5077.

MERRIMACK COLLEGE
NORTH ANDOVER, MASSACHUSETTS

Entrance Moderately difficult **General** Independent Roman Catholic, 4-year, coed **Setting** 220-acre small-town campus **Enrollment** 2,804 **Faculty** 15:1 **Application deadline** 3/1 **Freshmen** 79% accepted **Housing** Yes **Tuition** $14,530 **Undergraduates** 50% women, 35% part-time, 3% 25 or older, 0% Native American, 2% Hispanic, 1% black, 1% Asian or Pacific Islander **Most popular recent majors** Business administration/commerce/management, psychology, biology/biological sciences **Academic program** ESL program, Advanced placement, self-designed majors, tutorials, summer session, adult/continuing education programs, internships **Contact** Ms. MaryLou Retelle, Dean of Admissions and Financial Aid, Merrimack College, North Andover, MA 01845-5800. Telephone: 508-837-5100 Ext. 5120. Fax: 508-837-5222.

MONTSERRAT COLLEGE OF ART
BEVERLY, MASSACHUSETTS

Entrance Moderately difficult **General** Independent, 4-year, specialized, coed **Setting** 10-acre suburban campus **Enrollment** 320 **Faculty** 11:1 **Application deadline** 7/15 **Freshmen** 90% accepted **Housing** Yes **Tuition** $11,675 **Undergraduates** 44% women, 11% part-time, 20% 25 or older, 0% Native American, 3% Hispanic, 2% black, 5% Asian or Pacific Islander **Most popular recent majors** Painting/drawing, graphic arts, illustration **Academic program** Average class size 20, ESL program, advanced placement, self-designed majors, honors program, summer session, internships **Contact** Ms. Carol Lee Conchar, Executive Director of Enrollment Management, Montserrat College of Art, Beverly, MA 01915. Telephone: 508-921-2353. Fax: 508-922-4268.

MOUNT HOLYOKE COLLEGE
SOUTH HADLEY, MASSACHUSETTS

Entrance Very difficult **General** Independent, comprehensive, women only **Setting** 800-acre small-town campus **Enrollment** 1,898 **Faculty** 10:1 **Application deadline** 1/15 **Freshmen** 65% accepted **Housing** Yes **Tuition** $22,340 **Undergraduates** 1% part-time, 5% 25 or older, 1% Native American, 4% Hispanic, 4% black, 8% Asian or Pacific Islander **Most popular recent majors** English, political science/government, biology/biological sciences **Academic program** Advanced placement, accelerated degree program, self-designed majors, tutorials, honors program, adult/continuing education programs, internships **Contact** Ms. Anita Smith, Director of Admissions, Mount Holyoke College, South Hadley, MA 01075-1414. Telephone: 413-538-2023. Fax: 413-538-2409.

NEW ENGLAND COLLEGE OF OPTOMETRY
BOSTON, MASSACHUSETTS

Entrance Moderately difficult **General** Independent, upper-level, specialized, coed **Setting** Urban campus **Enrollment** 416 **Freshmen** 13% accepted **Tuition** $20,659 **Undergraduates** 62% women, 0% part-time, 1% 25 or older, 3% Hispanic, 7% black, 18% Asian or Pacific Islander **Academic program** Internships **Contact** Mr. Lawrence W. Shattuck, Director of Student Recruitment, New England College of Optometry, 424 Beacon Street, Boston, MA 02115-1100. Telephone: 617-236-6210.

NEW ENGLAND CONSERVATORY OF MUSIC
BOSTON, MASSACHUSETTS

Entrance Very difficult **General** Independent, comprehensive, specialized, coed **Setting** Urban campus **Enrollment** 792 **Faculty** 5:1 **Application deadline** 1/3 **Freshmen** 19% accepted **Housing** Yes **Tuition** $18,000 **Undergraduates** 54% women, 1% part-time, 3% 25 or older, 1% Native American, 1% Hispanic, 2% black, 4% Asian or Pacific Islander **Most popular recent majors** Voice, piano/organ, stringed instruments **Academic program** Average class size 20, advanced placement, adult/continuing education programs, internships **Contact** Ms. Allison T. Ball, Dean of Enrollment Services, New England Conservatory of Music, 290 Huntington Avenue, Boston, MA 02115-5000. Telephone: 617-262-1120 Ext. 430.

THE NEW ENGLAND SCHOOL OF ART AND DESIGN AT SUFFOLK UNIVERSITY

BOSTON, MASSACHUSETTS

Entrance Difficulty N/R **General** Independent, 4-year, specialized, coed **Setting** Urban campus **Enrollment** 180 **Freshmen** 80% accepted **Housing** Yes **Tuition** $12,920 **Undergraduates** 55% women, 40% part-time, 55% 25 or older, 1% Native American, 5% Hispanic, 1% black, 5% Asian or Pacific Islander **Contact** Ms. Anne Blevins, Associate Director of Admissions and Placement, The New England School of Art and Design at Suffolk University, 81 Arlington Street, Boston, MA 02116. Telephone: 617-536-0383 Ext. 11. Fax: 617-536-0461.

NICHOLS COLLEGE

DUDLEY, MASSACHUSETTS

Entrance Minimally difficult **General** Independent, comprehensive, coed **Setting** 210-acre rural campus **Enrollment** 1,501 **Faculty** 22:1 **Application deadline** Rolling **Freshmen** 86% accepted **Housing** Yes **Tuition** $11,295 **Undergraduates** 37% women, 44% part-time, 1% 25 or older, 0% Native American, 1% Hispanic, 1% black, 1% Asian or Pacific Islander **Most popular recent majors** Business administration/commerce/management, accounting, marketing/retailing/merchandising **Academic program** Advanced placement, summer session, adult/continuing education programs, internships **Contact** Ms. Louise Sisley, Records Assistant, Nichols College, Dudley, MA 01571. Telephone: 508-943-2055 Ext. 275. Fax: 508-943-9885.

NORTH ADAMS STATE COLLEGE

NORTH ADAMS, MASSACHUSETTS

Entrance Moderately difficult **General** State-supported, comprehensive, coed **Setting** 80-acre small-town campus **Enrollment** 1,745 **Faculty** 15:1 **Application deadline** Rolling **Freshmen** 68% accepted **Housing** Yes **Tuition** $3437 **Undergraduates** 58% women, 14% part-time, 24% 25 or older, 1% Native American, 1% Hispanic, 3% black, 1% Asian or Pacific Islander **Most popular recent majors** English, sociology, psychology **Academic program** Average class size 22, advanced placement, self-designed majors, tutorials, honors program, summer session, internships **Contact** Ms. Denise Richardello, Dean of Enrollment Management, North Adams State College, North Adams, MA 01247-4100. Telephone: 413-662-5410 Ext. 5416. Fax: 413-662-5179.

NORTHEASTERN UNIVERSITY

BOSTON, MASSACHUSETTS

Entrance Moderately difficult **General** Independent, coed **Setting** 57-acre urban campus **Enrollment** 24,579 **Faculty** 11:1 **Application deadline** Rolling **Freshmen** 74% accepted **Housing** Yes **Tuition** $14,157 **Undergraduates** 53% women, 42% part-time, 1% Native American, 4% Hispanic, 7% black, 7% Asian or Pacific Islander **Most popular recent majors** Criminal justice, physical therapy, finance/banking **Academic program** Advanced placement, self-designed majors, tutorials, honors program, summer session, adult/continuing education programs, internships **Contact** Mr. Alan Kines, Dean of Admissions, Northeastern University, 360 Huntington Avenue, Boston, MA 02115-5096. Telephone: 617-373-2200. Fax: 617-373-8780.

PINE MANOR COLLEGE

CHESTNUT HILL, MASSACHUSETTS

Entrance Minimally difficult **General** Independent, comprehensive, women only **Setting** 79-acre suburban campus **Enrollment** 300 **Application deadline** Rolling **Freshmen** 78% accepted **Housing** Yes **Tuition** $10,700 **Undergraduates** 12% part-time, 9% 25 or older, 6% Hispanic, 12% black, 2% Asian or Pacific Islander **Most popular recent majors** Psychology, business administration/commerce/management, communication **Academic program** ESL program, Advanced placement, accelerated degree program, self-designed majors, tutorials, honors program, summer session, adult/continuing education programs, internships **Contact** Ms. Nancy H. Spaulding, Director of Admissions, Pine Manor College, Chestnut Hill, MA 02167-2332. Telephone: 617-731-7104. Fax: 617-731-7199.

RADCLIFFE COLLEGE

SEE HARVARD UNIVERSITY

REGIS COLLEGE

WESTON, MASSACHUSETTS

Entrance Moderately difficult **General** Independent Roman Catholic, comprehensive, women only **Setting** 168-acre small-town campus **Enrollment** 1,401 **Faculty** 10:1 **Application deadline** Rolling **Freshmen** 91% accepted **Housing** Yes **Tuition** $15,250 **Undergraduates** 39% part-time, 10% 25 or older, 1% Native American, 3% Hispanic, 3% black, 4% Asian or Pacific Islander **Most popular recent majors** English, political science/government, communication **Academic program** Advanced placement, self-designed majors, tutorials, honors program, summer session, adult/continuing education programs, internships **Contact** Ms. Valerie L. Brown, Associate Director of Admission, Regis College, Weston, MA 02193-1571. Telephone: 617-768-7100 Ext. 2050. Fax: 617-768-7107.

SAINT JOHN'S SEMINARY COLLEGE OF LIBERAL ARTS
BRIGHTON, MASSACHUSETTS

Entrance Minimally difficult **General** Independent Roman Catholic, 4-year, specialized, men only **Setting** 70-acre urban campus **Enrollment** 33 **Faculty** 4:1 **Application deadline** 8/1 **Freshmen** 67% accepted **Housing** Yes **Tuition** $5200 **Undergraduates** 25% part-time, 25% 25 or older, 0% Native American, 4% Hispanic, 2% black, 4% Asian or Pacific Islander **Academic program** Average class size 10, self-designed majors, tutorials **Contact** Vocation Director, Archdiocese of Boston, Saint John's Seminary College of Liberal Arts, 197 Foster Street, Brighton, MA 02135-4644. Telephone: 617-254-2610.

SALEM STATE COLLEGE
SALEM, MASSACHUSETTS

Entrance Minimally difficult **General** State-supported, comprehensive, coed **Setting** 62-acre small-town campus **Enrollment** 10,132 **Faculty** 20:1 **Application deadline** 3/1 **Freshmen** 78% accepted **Housing** Yes **Tuition** $3408 **Undergraduates** 60% women, 6% part-time, 28% 25 or older, 1% Native American, 4% Hispanic, 4% black, 3% Asian or Pacific Islander **Most popular recent majors** Business administration/commerce/management, education, criminal justice **Academic program** Advanced placement, self-designed majors, tutorials, honors program, summer session, adult/continuing education programs, internships **Contact** Mr. Nate Bryant, Director of Admissions, Salem State College, Salem, MA 01970-5353. Telephone: 508-741-6200.

SCHOOL OF THE MUSEUM OF FINE ARTS
BOSTON, MASSACHUSETTS

Entrance Moderately difficult **General** Independent, comprehensive, specialized, coed **Setting** 14-acre urban campus **Enrollment** 723 **Faculty** 10:1 **Application deadline** Rolling **Freshmen** 70% accepted **Tuition** $15,125 **Undergraduates** 64% women, 12% part-time, 56% 25 or older, 0% Native American, 4% Hispanic, 1% black, 4% Asian or Pacific Islander **Academic program** Self-designed majors, tutorials, summer session, adult/continuing education programs **Contact** Ms. Patricia Barsoumian, Director of Admissions, School of the Museum of Fine Arts, 230 The Fenway, Boston, MA 02115. Telephone: 617-267-1218. Fax: 617-424-6271.

SIMMONS COLLEGE
BOSTON, MASSACHUSETTS

Entrance Moderately difficult **General** Independent, comprehensive, women only **Setting** 12-acre urban campus **Enrollment** 3,740 **Faculty** 10:1 **Application deadline** 2/1 **Freshmen** 69% accepted **Housing** Yes **Tuition** $18,564 **Undergraduates** 35% part-time, 15% 25 or older, 0% Native American, 3% Hispanic, 6% black, 7% Asian or Pacific Islander **Most popular recent majors** Nursing, physical therapy, psychology **Academic program** Advanced placement, accelerated degree program, self-designed majors, tutorials, honors program, summer session, adult/continuing education programs, internships **Contact** Ms. Lyn Fulton John, Assistant Director of Admissions, Simmons College, 300 The Fenway, Boston, MA 02115. Telephone: 617-521-2051. Fax: 617-521-3199.

SIMON'S ROCK COLLEGE OF BARD
GREAT BARRINGTON, MASSACHUSETTS

Entrance Very difficult **General** Independent, 4-year, coed **Setting** 275-acre rural campus **Enrollment** 334 **Faculty** 9:1 **Application deadline** 6/15 **Freshmen** 76% accepted **Housing** Yes **Tuition** $21,550 **Undergraduates** 58% women, 1% part-time, 0% 25 or older, 1% Native American, 2% Hispanic, 4% black, 7% Asian or Pacific Islander **Academic program** Tutorials, adult/continuing education programs, internships **Contact** Ms. Mary King Austin, Director of Admissions, Simon's Rock College of Bard, Great Barrington, MA 01230-9702. Telephone: 413-528-0771 Ext. 317. Fax: 413-528-7334.

SMITH COLLEGE
NORTHAMPTON, MASSACHUSETTS

Entrance Very difficult **General** Independent, comprehensive, women only **Setting** 125-acre urban campus **Enrollment** 2,788 **Faculty** 10:1 **Application deadline** 1/15 **Freshmen** 52% accepted **Housing** Yes **Tuition** $21,512 **Undergraduates** 3% part-time, 9% 25 or older, 1% Native American, 4% Hispanic, 4% black, 11% Asian or Pacific Islander **Most popular recent majors** Political science/government, psychology, economics **Academic program** Advanced placement, accelerated degree program, self-designed majors, tutorials, honors program, adult/continuing education programs, internships **Contact** Ms. Nanci Tessier, Director of Admissions, Smith College, 7 College Lane, Northampton, MA 01063. Telephone: 413-585-2500. Fax: 413-585-2527.

SPRINGFIELD COLLEGE
SPRINGFIELD, MASSACHUSETTS

Entrance Moderately difficult **General** Independent, comprehensive, coed **Setting** 167-acre suburban campus **Enrollment** 2,923 **Faculty** 15:1 **Application deadline** 4/1 **Freshmen** 56% accepted **Housing** Yes **Tuition** $12,700 **Undergraduates** 49% women, 3% part-time, 0% Native American, 1% Hispanic, 6% black, 1% Asian or Pacific Islander **Academic program** Advanced placement, accelerated degree program, honors program, summer session, adult/continuing education programs, internships **Contact** Mr. Frederick Bartlett, Director of Admissions, Springfield College, Springfield, MA 01109-3797. Telephone: 413-748-3136.

STONEHILL COLLEGE
EASTON, MASSACHUSETTS

Entrance Moderately difficult **General** Independent Roman Catholic, 4-year, coed **Setting** 375-acre suburban campus **Enrollment** 2,041 **Faculty** 13:1 **Application deadline** 2/1 **Freshmen** 54% accepted **Housing** Yes **Tuition** $14,856 **Undergraduates** 57% women, 1% part-time, 1% 25 or older, 0% Native American, 1% Hispanic, 2% black, 2% Asian or Pacific Islander **Most popular recent majors** Psychology, criminal justice, biology/biological sciences **Academic program** Average class size 25, advanced placement, self-designed majors, tutorials, honors program, summer session, adult/continuing education programs, internships **Contact** Mr. Brian P. Murphy, Dean of Admissions and Enrollment, Stonehill College, 320 Washington Street, Easton, MA 02357. Telephone: 508-565-1373. Fax: 508-565-1500.

SUFFOLK UNIVERSITY
BOSTON, MASSACHUSETTS

Entrance Moderately difficult **General** Independent, comprehensive, coed **Setting** 2-acre urban campus **Enrollment** 6,401 **Faculty** 12:1 **Application deadline** Rolling **Freshmen** 73% accepted **Housing** Yes **Tuition** $12,920 **Undergraduates** 53% women, 20% part-time, 24% 25 or older, 1% Native American, 4% Hispanic, 6% black, 7% Asian or Pacific Islander **Most popular recent majors** Sociology, finance/banking, accounting **Academic program** Advanced placement, accelerated degree program, tutorials, honors program, summer session, adult/continuing education programs, internships **Contact** Ms. Kathleen Teehun, Director of Undergraduate Admission, Suffolk University, 8 Ashburton Place, Boston, MA 02108-2770. Telephone: 617-573-8460. Fax: 617-742-4291.

TUFTS UNIVERSITY
MEDFORD, MASSACHUSETTS

Entrance Most difficult **General** Independent, coed **Setting** 150-acre suburban campus **Enrollment** 8,183 **Faculty** 13:1 **Application deadline** 1/1 **Freshmen** 31% accepted **Housing** Yes **Tuition** $22,811 **Undergraduates** 52% women, 0% part-time, 5% Hispanic, 4% black, 15% Asian or Pacific Islander **Most popular recent majors** Biology/biological sciences, English, international relations **Academic program** Average class size 25, advanced placement, self-designed majors, tutorials, honors program, summer session, adult/continuing education programs, internships **Contact** Mr. David D. Cuttino, Dean of Undergraduate Admissions, Tufts University, Medford, MA 02155. Telephone: 617-627-3170. Fax: 617-627-3860.

UNIVERSITY OF MASSACHUSETTS AMHERST
AMHERST, MASSACHUSETTS

Entrance Moderately difficult **General** State-supported, coed **Setting** 1,463-acre small-town campus **Enrollment** 23,108 **Faculty** 18:1 **Application deadline** 2/1 **Freshmen** 74% accepted **Housing** Yes **Tuition** $5329 **Undergraduates** 48% women, 5% part-time, 8% 25 or older, 1% Native American, 4% Hispanic, 5% black, 6% Asian or Pacific Islander **Most popular recent majors** Psychology, communication, hotel and restaurant management **Academic program** Average class size 46, advanced placement, self-designed majors, tutorials, honors program, summer session, adult/continuing education programs, internships **Contact** Ms. Arlene Cash, Director of Undergraduate Admissions, University of Massachusetts Amherst, Amherst, MA 01003-0120. Telephone: 413-545-0222.

UNIVERSITY OF MASSACHUSETTS BOSTON
BOSTON, MASSACHUSETTS

Entrance Moderately difficult **General** State-supported, coed **Setting** 177-acre urban campus **Enrollment** 10,216 **Faculty** 16:1 **Application deadline** 3/1 **Freshmen** 66% accepted **Tuition** $4297 **Undergraduates** 56% women, 34% part-time, 55% 25 or older, 1% Native American, 6% Hispanic, 16% black, 10% Asian or Pacific Islander

Most popular recent majors Business administration/commerce/management, nursing, psychology **Academic program** Average class size 25, advanced placement, accelerated degree program, self-designed majors, tutorials, honors program, summer session, adult/continuing education programs, internships **Contact** Office of Admissions Information Service, University of Massachusetts Boston, 100 Morrissey Boulevard, Boston, MA 02125-3393. Telephone: 617-287-6000.

UNIVERSITY OF MASSACHUSETTS DARTMOUTH

NORTH DARTMOUTH, MASSACHUSETTS

Entrance Moderately difficult **General** State-supported, comprehensive, coed **Setting** 710-acre suburban campus **Enrollment** 5,103 **Faculty** 15:1 **Application deadline** Rolling **Freshmen** 67% accepted **Housing** Yes **Tuition** $4151 **Undergraduates** 52% women, 8% part-time, 16% 25 or older, 1% Native American, 2% Hispanic, 2% black, 3% Asian or Pacific Islander **Most popular recent majors** Accounting, humanities, business administration/commerce/management **Academic program** Advanced placement, self-designed majors, tutorials, honors program, summer session, adult/continuing education programs, internships **Contact** Dr. Richard Burke, Interim Director of Admissions, University of Massachusetts Dartmouth, North Dartmouth, MA 02747-2300. Telephone: 508-999-8605. Fax: 508-999-8901.

UNIVERSITY OF MASSACHUSETTS LOWELL

LOWELL, MASSACHUSETTS

Entrance Moderately difficult **General** State-supported, coed **Setting** 100-acre urban campus **Enrollment** 12,731 **Application deadline** Rolling **Freshmen** 82% accepted **Housing** Yes **Tuition** $4422 **Undergraduates** 38% women, 8% part-time, 1% 25 or older, 1% Native American, 3% Hispanic, 3% black, 54% Asian or Pacific Islander **Most popular recent majors** Business administration/commerce/management, criminal justice, electrical engineering **Academic program** Advanced placement, accelerated degree program, honors program, summer session, adult/continuing education programs **Contact** Ms. Rayanne Drouin, Assistant Director of Admissions, University of Massachusetts Lowell, 1 University Avenue, Lowell, MA 01854-2881. Telephone: 508-934-3944.

WELLESLEY COLLEGE

WELLESLEY, MASSACHUSETTS

Entrance Most difficult **General** Independent, 4-year, women only **Setting** 500-acre suburban campus **Enrollment** 2,319 **Faculty** 9:1 **Application deadline** 1/15 **Freshmen** 40% accepted **Housing** Yes **Tuition** $21,662 **Undergraduates** 6% part-time, 2% 25 or older, 1% Native American, 7% Hispanic, 7% black, 30% Asian or Pacific Islander **Most popular recent majors** Psychology, economics, English **Academic program** Advanced placement, accelerated degree program, self-designed majors, honors program, adult/continuing education programs, internships **Contact** Ms. Janet Lavin Rapelye, Dean of Admission, Wellesley College, 240 Green Hall, Wellesley, MA 02181. Telephone: 617-283-2270. Fax: 617-283-3678.

WENTWORTH INSTITUTE OF TECHNOLOGY

BOSTON, MASSACHUSETTS

Entrance Moderately difficult **General** Independent, 4-year, coed **Setting** 35-acre urban campus **Enrollment** 2,264 **Faculty** 18:1 **Application deadline** Rolling **Freshmen** 91% accepted **Housing** Yes **Tuition** $11,500 **Undergraduates** 14% women, 15% part-time, 15% 25 or older, 5% Hispanic, 7% black, 12% Asian or Pacific Islander **Most popular recent majors** Electronics engineering technology, architectural technologies, mechanical engineering technology **Academic program** Advanced placement, accelerated degree program, self-designed majors, summer session **Contact** Ms. Melinda Mitchell, Director of Admissions, Wentworth Institute of Technology, 550 Huntington Avenue, Boston, MA 02115-5998. Telephone: 617-989-4003. Fax: 617-989-4010.

WESTERN NEW ENGLAND COLLEGE

SPRINGFIELD, MASSACHUSETTS

Entrance Moderately difficult **General** Independent, comprehensive, coed **Setting** 185-acre suburban campus **Enrollment** 4,574 **Faculty** 17:1 **Application deadline** Rolling **Freshmen** 77% accepted **Housing** Yes **Tuition** $11,448 **Undergraduates** 37% women, 39% part-time, 36% 25 or older, 0% Native American, 2% Hispanic, 3% black, 2% Asian or Pacific Islander **Most popular recent majors** Criminal justice, accounting, business administration/commerce/management **Academic program** Average class size 24, advanced placement, accelerated degree program, self-designed majors, tutorials, summer session, adult/continuing education programs, internships **Contact** Dr. Charles R. Pollock, Dean of Enrollment

Management, Western New England College, Springfield, MA 01119-2654. Telephone: 413-782-1321. Fax: 413-782-1777.

WESTFIELD STATE COLLEGE
WESTFIELD, MASSACHUSETTS

Entrance Moderately difficult **General** State-supported, comprehensive, coed **Setting** 227-acre small-town campus **Enrollment** 4,878 **Faculty** 19:1 **Application deadline** Rolling **Freshmen** 63% accepted **Housing** Yes **Tuition** $3094 **Undergraduates** 51% women, 21% part-time, 5% 25 or older, 0% Native American, 2% Hispanic, 3% black, 1% Asian or Pacific Islander **Most popular recent majors** Criminal justice, psychology, elementary education **Academic program** Average class size 30, advanced placement, accelerated degree program, tutorials, honors program, summer session, adult/continuing education programs, internships **Contact** Ms. Michelle Mattie, Director of Admission and Financial Aid, Westfield State College, Westfield, MA 01086. Telephone: 413-572-5218 Ext. 218.

WHEATON COLLEGE
NORTON, MASSACHUSETTS

Entrance Moderately difficult **General** Independent, 4-year, coed **Setting** 385-acre small-town campus **Enrollment** 1,350 **Faculty** 13:1 **Application deadline** 2/1 **Freshmen** 75% accepted **Housing** Yes **Tuition** $20,820 **Undergraduates** 66% women, 2% part-time, 1% 25 or older, 1% Native American, 3% Hispanic, 2% black, 4% Asian or Pacific Islander **Most popular recent majors** Psychology, English, sociology **Academic program** Average class size 19, advanced placement, accelerated degree program, self-designed majors, tutorials, honors program, adult/continuing education programs, internships **Contact** Mr. Steven Inzer, Director of Admission, Wheaton College, Norton, MA 02766. Telephone: 508-285-8251. Fax: 508-285-8271.

WHEELOCK COLLEGE
BOSTON, MASSACHUSETTS

Entrance Moderately difficult **General** Independent, comprehensive, primarily women **Setting** 5-acre urban campus **Enrollment** 1,369 **Faculty** 11:1 **Application deadline** 2/15 **Freshmen** 78% accepted **Housing** Yes **Tuition** $15,520 **Undergraduates** 96% women, 12% part-time, 8% 25 or older, 0% Native American, 1% Hispanic, 4% black, 2% Asian or Pacific Islander **Most popular recent majors** Education, social work, child care/child and family studies **Academic program** Advanced placement, honors program, internships **Contact** Ms. Lynne E. Dailey, Dean of Admissions, Wheelock College, 200 The Riverway, Boston, MA 02215. Telephone: 617-734-5200 Ext. 204. Fax: 617-566-7369.

WILLIAMS COLLEGE
WILLIAMSTOWN, MASSACHUSETTS

Entrance Most difficult **General** Independent, comprehensive, coed **Setting** 450-acre small-town campus **Enrollment** 2,138 **Faculty** 11:1 **Application deadline** 1/1 **Freshmen** 24% accepted **Housing** Yes **Tuition** $22,990 **Undergraduates** 49% women, 0% part-time, 1% 25 or older, 1% Native American, 7% Hispanic, 6% black, 10% Asian or Pacific Islander **Most popular recent majors** History, biology/biological sciences, English **Academic program** Advanced placement, accelerated degree program, self-designed majors, tutorials, honors program, internships **Contact** Mr. Thomas H. Parker, Director of Admission, Williams College, PO Box 487, Williamstown, MA 01267. Telephone: 413-597-2211.

WORCESTER POLYTECHNIC INSTITUTE
WORCESTER, MASSACHUSETTS

Entrance Very difficult **General** Independent, coed **Setting** 80-acre suburban campus **Enrollment** 3,648 **Faculty** 12:1 **Application deadline** 2/15 **Freshmen** 82% accepted **Housing** Yes **Tuition** $18,910 **Undergraduates** 21% women, 3% part-time, 3% 25 or older, 1% Native American, 2% Hispanic, 1% black, 6% Asian or Pacific Islander **Most popular recent majors** Mechanical engineering, electrical engineering, computer science **Academic program** Advanced placement, accelerated degree program, self-designed majors, summer session, adult/continuing education programs **Contact** Mr. Robert G. Voss, Executive Director of Admissions and Financial Aid, Worcester Polytechnic Institute, Worcester, MA 01609-2247. Telephone: 508-831-5286. Fax: 508-831-5875.

WORCESTER STATE COLLEGE
WORCESTER, MASSACHUSETTS

Entrance Moderately difficult **General** State-supported, comprehensive, coed **Setting** 58-acre urban campus **Enrollment** 5,369 **Faculty** 16:1 **Application deadline** Rolling **Freshmen** 67% accepted **Housing** Yes **Tuition** $2615 **Undergraduates** 63% women, 42% part-time, 42% 25 or older, 0% Native American, 3% Hispanic, 3% black, 3% Asian or Pacific Islander **Most popular re-**

cent majors Business administration/commerce/management, psychology, occupational therapy **Academic program** Advanced placement, summer session, adult/continuing education programs, internships **Contact** Mr. E. Jay Tierney, Director of Admissions, Worcester State College, 486 Chandler Street, Worcester, MA 01602-2597. Telephone: 508-793-8040.

New Hampshire

COLBY-SAWYER COLLEGE
NEW LONDON, NEW HAMPSHIRE

Entrance Moderately difficult **General** Independent, 4-year, coed **Setting** 196-acre small-town campus **Enrollment** 755 **Faculty** 12:1 **Application deadline** Rolling **Freshmen** 81% accepted **Housing** Yes **Tuition** $16,310 **Undergraduates** 65% women, 4% part-time, 5% 25 or older, 1% Native American, 1% Hispanic, 1% black, 1% Asian or Pacific Islander **Most popular recent majors** Sports medicine, child psychology/child development, business administration/commerce/management **Academic program** Advanced placement, accelerated degree program, self-designed majors, tutorials, honors program, adult/continuing education programs, internships **Contact** Mr. Jeffrey J. Papa, Vice President for Enrollment Management, Colby-Sawyer College, New London, NH 03257-4648. Telephone: 603-526-3700. Fax: 603-526-3452.

COLLEGE FOR LIFELONG LEARNING OF THE UNIVERSITY SYSTEM OF NEW HAMPSHIRE
SEE UNIVERSITY SYSTEM COLLEGE FOR LIFELONG LEARNING

DANIEL WEBSTER COLLEGE
NASHUA, NEW HAMPSHIRE

Entrance Moderately difficult **General** Independent, 4-year, coed **Setting** 50-acre suburban campus **Enrollment** 476 **Faculty** 15:1 **Application deadline** Rolling **Freshmen** 83% accepted **Housing** Yes **Tuition** $13,845 **Undergraduates** 21% women, 6% part-time, 4% 25 or older, 0% Native American, 3% Hispanic, 4% black, 1% Asian or Pacific Islander **Most popular recent majors** Aviation administration, flight training, business administration/commerce/management **Academic program** Average class size 20, advanced placement, summer session, adult/continuing education programs, internships **Contact** Mr. Paul D. LaBarre, Director of Admissions, Daniel Webster College, Nashua, NH 03063-1300. Telephone: 603-577-6603. Fax: 603-577-6001.

DARTMOUTH COLLEGE
HANOVER, NEW HAMPSHIRE

Entrance Most difficult **General** Independent, coed **Setting** 265-acre rural campus **Enrollment** 5,300 **Faculty** 12:1 **Application deadline** 1/1 **Freshmen** 20% accepted **Housing** Yes **Tuition** $23,012 **Undergraduates** 48% women, 0% part-time, 1% 25 or older, 2% Native American, 5% Hispanic, 7% black, 10% Asian or Pacific Islander **Most popular recent majors** Political science/government, history, engineering (general) **Academic program** Average class size 28, advanced placement, accelerated degree program, self-designed majors, tutorials, honors program, summer session **Contact** Mr. Karl M. Furstenberg, Dean of Admissions and Financial Aid, Dartmouth College, 6016 McNutt Hall, Hanover, NH 03755. Telephone: 603-646-2875. Fax: 603-646-1216.

FRANKLIN PIERCE COLLEGE
RINDGE, NEW HAMPSHIRE

Entrance Moderately difficult **General** Independent, 4-year, coed **Setting** 1,000-acre rural campus **Enrollment** 1,327 **Faculty** 15:1 **Application deadline** Rolling **Freshmen** 75% accepted **Housing** Yes **Tuition** $16,170 **Undergraduates** 46% women, 3% part-time, 3% 25 or older, 0% Native American, 2% Hispanic, 4% black, 2% Asian or Pacific Islander **Most popular recent majors** Elementary education, history, communication **Academic program** Average class size 25, advanced placement, accelerated degree program, self-designed majors, tutorials, honors program, summer session, adult/continuing education programs, internships **Contact** Mr. Thomas E. Desrosiers, Director of Admissions, Franklin Pierce College, Rindge, NH 03461-0060. Telephone: 603-899-4050. Fax: 603-899-4372.

KEENE STATE COLLEGE
KEENE, NEW HAMPSHIRE

Entrance Moderately difficult **General** State-supported, comprehensive, coed **Setting** 160-acre small-town campus **Enrollment** 4,021 **Faculty** 20:1 **Application deadline** 3/1 **Freshmen** 76% accepted **Housing** Yes **Tuition** $4340 **Undergraduates** 60% women, 16% part-time, 25% 25 or older, 1% Native American, 1% Hispanic, 1% black, 1% Asian or Pacific Islander **Most popular recent majors** Elementary education, psychology, business administration/commerce/management **Academic program** ESL program, Advanced placement, accelerated degree program, self-designed majors, honors program, summer session, adult/continuing education programs, internships **Contact** Mrs. Kathryn Dodge, Director of Admissions, Keene State College, Keene, NH 03435-1701. Telephone: 603-358-2276. Fax: 603-358-2767.

NEW ENGLAND COLLEGE
HENNIKER, NEW HAMPSHIRE

Entrance Moderately difficult **General** Independent, comprehensive, coed **Setting** 212-acre small-town campus **Enrollment** 800 **Faculty** 12:1 **Application deadline** Rolling **Freshmen** 72% accepted **Housing** Yes **Tuition** $15,784 **Undergraduates** 48% women, 8% part-time, 3% 25 or older, 1% Hispanic, 3% black, 0% Asian or Pacific Islander **Most popular recent majors** Business administration/commerce/management, education, communication **Academic program** Advanced placement, self-designed majors, tutorials, honors program, summer session, adult/continuing education programs, internships **Contact** Mr. Donald Parker, Director of Admission, New England College, Henniker, NH 03242-3293. Telephone: 603-428-2223.

NEW HAMPSHIRE COLLEGE
MANCHESTER, NEW HAMPSHIRE

Entrance Moderately difficult **General** Independent, comprehensive, coed **Setting** 200-acre suburban campus **Enrollment** 5,614 **Faculty** 17:1 **Application deadline** Rolling **Freshmen** 81% accepted **Housing** Yes **Tuition** $12,980 **Undergraduates** 45% women, 1% part-time, 1% 25 or older, 0% Native American, 1% Hispanic, 1% black, 3% Asian or Pacific Islander **Most popular recent majors** Business administration/commerce/management, accounting, sports administration **Academic program** Advanced placement, accelerated degree program, tutorials, honors program, summer session, adult/continuing education programs, internships **Contact** Mr. Brad Poznanski, Director of Admission and Financial Aid, New Hampshire College, 2500 North River Road, Manchester, NH 03106-1045. Telephone: 603-645-9611. Fax: 603-645-9693.

NOTRE DAME COLLEGE
MANCHESTER, NEW HAMPSHIRE

Entrance Moderately difficult **General** Independent Roman Catholic, comprehensive, coed **Setting** 8-acre suburban campus **Enrollment** 1,017 **Faculty** 11:1 **Application deadline** Rolling **Freshmen** 90% accepted **Housing** Yes **Tuition** $11,840 **Undergraduates** 73% women, 30% part-time, 40% 25 or older, 1% Native American, 1% Hispanic, 2% black, 1% Asian or Pacific Islander **Most popular recent major** Interdisciplinary studies **Academic program** Advanced placement, accelerated degree program, summer session, adult/continuing education programs, internships **Contact** Mr. Joseph P. Wagner, Dean of Admissions, Notre Dame College, Manchester, NH 03104-2299. Telephone: 603-669-4298 Ext. 169.

PLYMOUTH STATE COLLEGE OF THE UNIVERSITY SYSTEM OF NEW HAMPSHIRE
PLYMOUTH, NEW HAMPSHIRE

Entrance Moderately difficult **General** State-supported, comprehensive, coed **Setting** 150-acre small-town campus **Enrollment** 4,000 **Faculty** 20:1 **Application deadline** 4/1 **Freshmen** 86% accepted **Housing** Yes **Tuition** $4342 **Undergraduates** 50% women, 15% part-time **Academic program** Advanced placement, accelerated degree program, self-designed majors, honors program, summer session, adult/continuing education programs, internships **Contact** Mr. Eugene Fahey, Director of Admissions, Plymouth State College of the University System of New Hampshire, 17 High Street, Plymouth, NH 03264-1595. Telephone: 603-535-2237. Fax: 603-535-2714.

RIVIER COLLEGE
NASHUA, NEW HAMPSHIRE

Entrance Moderately difficult **General** Independent Roman Catholic, comprehensive, coed **Setting** 60-acre suburban campus **Enrollment** 2,798 **Faculty** 13:1 **Application deadline** Rolling **Freshmen** 78% accepted **Housing** Yes **Tuition** $12,500 **Undergraduates** 83% women, 63% part-time, 43% 25 or older, 1% Native American, 2% Hispanic, 1% black, 2% Asian or Pacific Islander **Most popular recent majors** Business administration/commerce/management, education, behavioral sciences **Academic program** Advanced placement, tutorials, summer session, adult/continuing education programs, internships **Contact** Mr. James Slattery, Director of Admissions, Rivier College, Nashua, NH 03060-5086. Telephone: 603-888-1311 Ext. 8507. Fax: 603-891-1799.

SAINT ANSELM COLLEGE
MANCHESTER, NEW HAMPSHIRE

Entrance Moderately difficult **General** Independent Roman Catholic, 4-year, coed **Setting** 450-acre suburban campus **Enrollment** 1,928 **Faculty** 17:1 **Application deadline** Rolling **Freshmen** 84% accepted **Housing** Yes **Tuition** $15,830 **Undergraduates** 57% women, 1% part-time, 1% 25 or older, 2% Hispanic, 1% black, 1% Asian or

Pacific Islander **Most popular recent majors** Biology/biological sciences, history, English **Academic program** Average class size 22, advanced placement, tutorials, honors program, summer session, internships **Contact** Mr. Donald E. Healy, Director of Admissions, Saint Anselm College, 100 Saint Anselm Drive, Manchester, NH 03102-1310. Telephone: 603-641-7500. Fax: 603-641-7550.

THOMAS MORE COLLEGE OF LIBERAL ARTS
MERRIMACK, NEW HAMPSHIRE

Entrance Moderately difficult **General** Independent, 4-year, coed, affiliated with Roman Catholic Church **Setting** 14-acre small-town campus **Enrollment** 63 **Faculty** 9:1 **Application deadline** Rolling **Freshmen** 84% accepted **Housing** Yes **Tuition** $8700 **Undergraduates** 50% women, 0% part-time, 7% 25 or older, 0% Native American, 1% Hispanic, 0% black, 0% Asian or Pacific Islander **Most popular recent majors** Literature, philosophy, political science/government **Academic program** Average class size 15 **Contact** Mr. Peter O'Connor, Director of Admissions, Thomas More College of Liberal Arts, 6 Manchester Street, Merrimack, NH 03054-4818. Telephone: 603-880-8308. Fax: 603-880-9280.

UNIVERSITY OF NEW HAMPSHIRE
DURHAM, NEW HAMPSHIRE

Entrance Moderately difficult **General** State-supported, coed **Setting** 200-acre small-town campus **Enrollment** 12,454 **Faculty** 18:1 **Application deadline** 2/1 **Freshmen** 77% accepted **Housing** Yes **Tuition** $5889 **Undergraduates** 57% women, 6% part-time, 8% 25 or older, 0% Native American, 1% Hispanic, 1% black, 2% Asian or Pacific Islander **Most popular recent majors** Business administration/commerce/management, English, biology/biological sciences **Academic program** Average class size 47, advanced placement, accelerated degree program, self-designed majors, tutorials, honors program, summer session, adult/continuing education programs, internships **Contact** Mr. James Washington Jr., Director of Admissions, University of New Hampshire, Grant House, 4 Garrison Avenue, Durham, NH 03824. Telephone: 603-862-1360.

UNIVERSITY OF NEW HAMPSHIRE AT MANCHESTER
MANCHESTER, NEW HAMPSHIRE

Entrance Moderately difficult **General** State-supported, 4-year, coed **Setting** 800-acre urban campus **Enrollment** 719 **Faculty** 6:1 **Application deadline** 6/15 **Freshmen** 65% accepted **Tuition** $3920 **Undergraduates** 67% women, 44% part-time, 39% 25 or older, 1% Hispanic, 1% black, 2% Asian or Pacific Islander **Most popular recent majors** Liberal arts/general studies, business administration/commerce/management, psychology **Academic program** Advanced placement, self-designed majors, summer session, adult/continuing education programs, internships **Contact** Ms. Susan Miller, Admissions Secretary, University of New Hampshire at Manchester, 220 Hackett Hill Road, Manchester, NH 03102-8597. Telephone: 603-668-0700 Ext. 250. Fax: 603-623-2745.

UNIVERSITY SYSTEM COLLEGE FOR LIFELONG LEARNING
CONCORD, NEW HAMPSHIRE

Entrance Noncompetitive **General** State and locally supported, 4-year, coed **Setting** Rural campus **Enrollment** 2,187 **Faculty** 12:1 **Application deadline** Rolling **Tuition** $4535 **Undergraduates** 78% women, 73% part-time, 88% 25 or older, 1% Native American, 1% Hispanic, 1% black, 1% Asian or Pacific Islander **Academic program** Average class size 12, advanced placement, accelerated degree program, self-designed majors, tutorials, summer session, adult/continuing education programs **Contact** Ms. Teresa McDonnell, Associate Dean of Learner Services, University System College for Lifelong Learning, Concord, NH 03301. Telephone: 603-228-3000 Ext. 308. Fax: 603-229-0964.

Rhode Island

BROWN UNIVERSITY
PROVIDENCE, RHODE ISLAND

Entrance Most difficult **General** Independent, coed **Setting** 140-acre urban campus **Enrollment** 7,626 **Faculty** 8:1 **Application deadline** 1/1 **Freshmen** 19% accepted **Housing** Yes **Tuition** $23,124 **Undergraduates** 53% women, 6% part-time, 1% 25 or older, 1% Native American, 5% Hispanic, 6% black, 15% Asian or Pacific Islander **Most popular recent majors** Biology/biological sciences, history, psychology **Academic program** Advanced placement, accelerated degree program, self-designed majors, tutorials, honors program, summer session, adult/continuing education programs, internships **Contact** Mr. Michael Goldberger, Director of Admission, Brown University, Box 1876, Providence, RI 02912. Telephone: 401-863-2378. Fax: 401-863-9300.

BRYANT COLLEGE
SMITHFIELD, RHODE ISLAND

Entrance Moderately difficult **General** Independent, comprehensive, coed **Setting** 387-acre suburban campus **Enrollment** 3,332 **Faculty** 18:1 **Application deadline** Rolling **Freshmen** 83% accepted **Housing** Yes **Tuition** $14,800 **Undergraduates** 46% women, 21% part-time, 19% 25 or older, 1% Native American, 2% Hispanic, 2% black, 3% Asian or Pacific Islander **Most popular recent majors** Business administration/commerce/management, accounting, finance/banking **Academic program** Average class size 30, advanced placement, accelerated degree program, tutorials, honors program, summer session, adult/continuing education programs, internships **Contact** Ms. Margaret L. Drugovich, Dean of Admissions, Bryant College, Smithfield, RI 02917-1287. Telephone: 401-232-6100. Fax: 401-232-6741.

JOHNSON & WALES UNIVERSITY
PROVIDENCE, RHODE ISLAND

Entrance Minimally difficult **General** Independent, comprehensive, coed **Setting** 47-acre urban campus **Enrollment** 7,851 **Faculty** 30:1 **Application deadline** Rolling **Freshmen** 86% accepted **Housing** Yes **Tuition** $11,952 **Undergraduates** 47% women, 15% part-time, 11% 25 or older, 0% Native American, 5% Hispanic, 10% black, 2% Asian or Pacific Islander **Most popular recent majors** Culinary arts, hotel and restaurant management, hospitality services **Academic program** Average class size 30, advanced placement, accelerated degree program, honors program, summer session, adult/continuing education programs, internships **Contact** Mr. Kenneth DiSaia, Dean of Admissions, Johnson & Wales University, 8 Abbott Park Place, Providence, RI 02903-3703. Telephone: 401-598-4664 Ext. 2345. Fax: 401-598-1835.

PROVIDENCE COLLEGE
PROVIDENCE, RHODE ISLAND

Entrance Very difficult **General** Independent Roman Catholic, comprehensive, coed **Setting** 105-acre suburban campus **Enrollment** 5,621 **Faculty** 13:1 **Application deadline** 1/15 **Freshmen** 71% accepted **Housing** Yes **Tuition** $16,570 **Undergraduates** 58% women, 30% part-time, 1% 25 or older, 0% Native American, 1% Hispanic, 3% black, 1% Asian or Pacific Islander **Most popular recent majors** Business administration/commerce/management, education, English **Academic program** Average class size 25, advanced placement, self-designed majors, tutorials, honors program, summer session, adult/continuing education programs, internships **Contact** Mr. William DiBrienza, Dean of Admissions and Financial Aid, Providence College, Providence, RI 02918. Telephone: 401-865-2535. Fax: 401-865-2826.

RHODE ISLAND COLLEGE
PROVIDENCE, RHODE ISLAND

Entrance Moderately difficult **General** State-supported, comprehensive, coed **Setting** 170-acre suburban campus **Enrollment** 7,150 **Faculty** 17:1 **Application deadline** 5/1 **Freshmen** 74% accepted **Housing** Yes **Tuition** $3076 **Undergraduates** 66% women, 33% part-time, 30% 25 or older, 1% Native American, 4% Hispanic, 4% black, 2% Asian or Pacific Islander **Most popular recent majors** Education, psychology, nursing **Academic program** Advanced placement, accelerated degree program, self-designed majors, tutorials, honors program, summer session, adult/continuing education programs, internships **Contact** Dr. Holly Shaddian, Interim Director of Admissions, Rhode Island College, Providence, RI 02908-1924. Telephone: 401-456-8234.

RHODE ISLAND SCHOOL OF DESIGN
PROVIDENCE, RHODE ISLAND

Entrance Very difficult **General** Independent, comprehensive, specialized, coed **Setting** 13-acre urban campus **Enrollment** 2,003 **Faculty** 12:1 **Application deadline** 2/15 **Freshmen** 43% accepted **Housing** Yes **Tuition** $19,670 **Undergraduates** 56% women, 0% part-time, 14% 25 or older, 1% Native American, 3% Hispanic, 2% black, 11% Asian or Pacific Islander **Most popular recent majors** Illustration, architecture, graphic arts **Academic program** Advanced placement, tutorials, adult/continuing education programs, internships **Contact** Mr. Edward Newhall, Director of Admissions, Rhode Island School of Design, 2 College Street, Providence, RI 02903-2784. Telephone: 401-454-6300. Fax: 401-454-6309.

ROGER WILLIAMS UNIVERSITY
BRISTOL, RHODE ISLAND

Entrance Moderately difficult **General** Independent, comprehensive, coed **Setting** 130-acre small-town campus **Enrollment** 3,875 **Faculty** 16:1 **Application deadline** Rolling **Freshmen** 92% accepted **Housing** Yes **Tuition** $15,840 **Undergraduates** 46% women, 40% part-time, 40% 25 or older, 1% Native American, 2% Hispanic, 2% black, 2% Asian or Pacific Islander **Most popular recent majors** Architecture, business administration/commerce/management, paralegal studies

Academic program Advanced placement, accelerated degree program, self-designed majors, honors program, summer session, adult/continuing education programs, internships **Contact** Office of Admissions, Roger Williams University, Bristol, RI 02809. Telephone: 401-254-3500.

SALVE REGINA UNIVERSITY
NEWPORT, RHODE ISLAND

Entrance Moderately difficult **General** Independent Roman Catholic, comprehensive, coed **Setting** 65-acre suburban campus **Enrollment** 1,844 **Faculty** 12:1 **Application deadline** Rolling **Freshmen** 88% accepted **Housing** Yes **Tuition** $15,650 **Undergraduates** 66% women, 9% part-time, 9% 25 or older, 0% Native American, 2% Hispanic, 2% black, 1% Asian or Pacific Islander **Most popular recent majors** Business administration/commerce/management, elementary education, nursing **Academic program** Average class size 30, advanced placement, accelerated degree program, tutorials, honors program, summer session, adult/continuing education programs, internships **Contact** Ms. Laura E. McPhie, Dean of Enrollment Services, Salve Regina University, 100 Ochre Point Avenue, Newport, RI 02840-4192. Telephone: 401-847-6650. Fax: 401-848-2823.

UNIVERSITY OF RHODE ISLAND
KINGSTON, RHODE ISLAND

Entrance Moderately difficult **General** State-supported, coed **Setting** 1,200-acre small-town campus **Enrollment** 13,261 **Faculty** 15:1 **Application deadline** 3/1 **Freshmen** 81% accepted **Housing** Yes **Tuition** $4592 **Undergraduates** 55% women, 19% part-time, 19% 25 or older, 1% Native American, 3% Hispanic, 3% black, 3% Asian or Pacific Islander **Most popular recent majors** Psychology, pharmacy/pharmaceutical sciences, human development **Academic program** Advanced placement, accelerated degree program, tutorials, honors program, summer session, adult/continuing education programs, internships **Contact** Ms. Catherine Zeiser, Assistant Dean of Admissions, University of Rhode Island, Kingston, RI 02881. Telephone: 401-874-7100.

Vermont

BENNINGTON COLLEGE
BENNINGTON, VERMONT

Entrance Very difficult **General** Independent, comprehensive, coed **Setting** 550-acre small-town campus **Enrollment** 380 **Faculty** 7:1 **Application deadline** 2/1 **Freshmen** 70% accepted **Housing** Yes **Tuition** $26,400 **Undergraduates** 60% women, 1% part-time, 0% Native American, 1% Hispanic, 6% black, 7% Asian or Pacific Islander **Most popular recent majors** Literature, interdisciplinary studies, theater arts/drama **Academic program** Self-designed majors, tutorials, internships **Contact** Ms. Elena Ruocco Bachrach, Dean of Admissions and the Freshman Year, Bennington College, Bennington, VT 05201-9993. Telephone: 802-442-5401 Ext. 161.

BURLINGTON COLLEGE
BURLINGTON, VERMONT

Entrance Noncompetitive **General** Independent, 4-year, coed **Setting** 1-acre urban campus **Enrollment** 198 **Faculty** 4:1 **Application deadline** Rolling **Freshmen** 100% accepted **Tuition** $8420 **Undergraduates** 60% women, 48% part-time, 75% 25 or older, 3% Native American, 3% Hispanic, 5% black, 1% Asian or Pacific Islander **Most popular recent majors** Psychology, humanities, human services **Academic program** Accelerated degree program, self-designed majors, tutorials, summer session, adult/continuing education programs, internships **Contact** Ms. Nancy Wilson, Director of Admissions, Burlington College, 95 North Avenue, Burlington, VT 05401-2998. Telephone: 802-862-9616 Ext. 32. Fax: 802-658-0071.

CASTLETON STATE COLLEGE
CASTLETON, VERMONT

Entrance Moderately difficult **General** State-supported, comprehensive, coed **Setting** 130-acre rural campus **Enrollment** 1,854 **Application deadline** Rolling **Freshmen** 87% accepted **Housing** Yes **Tuition** $4506 **Undergraduates** 55% women, 18% part-time, 18% 25 or older, 1% Native American, 1% Hispanic, 1% black, 1% Asian or Pacific Islander **Most popular recent majors** Business administration/commerce/management, education, communication **Academic program** Advanced placement, self-designed majors, tutorials, honors program, summer session, adult/continuing education programs, internships **Contact** Ms. Patricia A. Tencza, Director of Admissions, Castleton State College, Castleton, VT 05735. Telephone: 802-468-5611 Ext. 213.

COLLEGE OF ST. JOSEPH
RUTLAND, VERMONT

Entrance Minimally difficult **General** Independent Roman Catholic, comprehensive, coed **Set-**

ting 99-acre small-town campus **Enrollment** 478 **Faculty** 11:1 **Application deadline** Rolling **Freshmen** 93% accepted **Housing** Yes **Tuition** $10,100 **Undergraduates** 66% women, 39% part-time, 40% 25 or older, 1% Native American, 1% Hispanic, 2% black, 1% Asian or Pacific Islander **Academic program** Advanced placement, accelerated degree program, self-designed majors, tutorials, summer session, adult/continuing education programs, internships **Contact** Mr. Steven Soba, Director of Admissions, College of St. Joseph, Rutland, VT 05701-3899. Telephone: 802-773-5900 Ext. 205.

GODDARD COLLEGE
PLAINFIELD, VERMONT

Entrance Moderately difficult **General** Independent, comprehensive, coed **Setting** 250-acre rural campus **Enrollment** 550 **Faculty** 7:1 **Application deadline** Rolling **Freshmen** 72% accepted **Housing** Yes **Tuition** $15,650 **Undergraduates** 53% women, 0% part-time, 20% 25 or older, 1% Native American, 2% Hispanic, 8% black, 0% Asian or Pacific Islander **Most popular recent majors** Creative writing, education, psychology **Academic program** Advanced placement, self-designed majors, tutorials, summer session, adult/continuing education programs, internships **Contact** Ms. Ellen W. Codling, Acting Director of Admissions, Goddard College, Plainfield, VT 05667. Telephone: 802-454-8311 Ext. 257. Fax: 802-454-8017.

GREEN MOUNTAIN COLLEGE
POULTNEY, VERMONT

Entrance Moderately difficult **General** Independent, 4-year, coed, affiliated with United Methodist Church **Setting** 155-acre small-town campus **Enrollment** 585 **Faculty** 14:1 **Application deadline** Rolling **Freshmen** 85% accepted **Housing** Yes **Tuition** $15,140 **Undergraduates** 51% women, 7% part-time, 4% 25 or older, 1% Native American, 1% Hispanic, 2% black, 1% Asian or Pacific Islander **Most popular recent majors** Behavioral sciences, business administration/commerce/management **Academic program** ESL program, Advanced placement, accelerated degree program, self-designed majors, honors program, adult/continuing education programs, internships **Contact** Mr. Peter L. Freyberg, Vice President for Enrollment Services, Green Mountain College, Poultney, VT 05764-1199. Telephone: 802-287-8208. Fax: 802-287-8099.

JOHNSON STATE COLLEGE
JOHNSON, VERMONT

Entrance Moderately difficult **General** State-supported, comprehensive, coed **Setting** 350-acre rural campus **Enrollment** 1,591 **Faculty** 18:1 **Application deadline** Rolling **Freshmen** 88% accepted **Housing** Yes **Tuition** $4516 **Undergraduates** 54% women, 20% part-time, 30% 25 or older, 2% Native American, 1% Hispanic, 1% black, 1% Asian or Pacific Islander **Most popular recent majors** Biology/biological sciences, education, business administration/commerce/management **Academic program** Average class size 16, advanced placement, accelerated degree program, tutorials, summer session, adult/continuing education programs, internships **Contact** Mr. Jonathan H. Henry, Director of Admissions, Johnson State College, RR 2, Box 75, Johnson, VT 05656-9405. Telephone: 802-635-1219.

LYNDON STATE COLLEGE
LYNDONVILLE, VERMONT

Entrance Moderately difficult **General** State-supported, comprehensive, coed **Setting** 175-acre rural campus **Enrollment** 1,137 **Faculty** 17:1 **Application deadline** Rolling **Freshmen** 88% accepted **Housing** Yes **Tuition** $4516 **Undergraduates** 48% women, 10% part-time, 20% 25 or older, 0% Native American, 1% Hispanic, 1% black **Most popular recent majors** Business administration/commerce/management, communication, education **Academic program** Average class size 20, advanced placement, self-designed majors, summer session, adult/continuing education programs, internships **Contact** Mr. Joseph Bellavance Jr., Director of Admissions, Lyndon State College, Lyndonville, VT 05851. Telephone: 802-626-6413.

MARLBORO COLLEGE
MARLBORO, VERMONT

Entrance Moderately difficult **General** Independent, comprehensive, coed **Setting** 350-acre rural campus **Enrollment** 282 **Faculty** 8:1 **Application deadline** Rolling **Freshmen** 72% accepted **Housing** Yes **Tuition** $19,882 **Undergraduates** 54% women, 5% part-time, 12% 25 or older, 1% Native American, 3% Hispanic, 1% black, 2% Asian or Pacific Islander **Academic program** Advanced placement, accelerated degree program, self-designed majors, tutorials, honors program, summer session, internships **Contact** Mr. Wayne R. Wood, Director of Admissions, Marlboro College, Marlboro, VT 05344. Telephone: 802-257-4333 Ext. 237.

MIDDLEBURY COLLEGE
MIDDLEBURY, VERMONT

Entrance Very difficult **General** Independent, comprehensive, coed **Setting** 350-acre small-town campus **Enrollment** 2,097 **Faculty** 11:1 **Application deadline** 12/31 **Freshmen** 28% accepted **Housing** Yes **Tuition** $29,340 **Undergraduates** 50% women **Most popular recent majors** English, psychology, history **Academic program** Advanced placement, self-designed majors, honors program, internships **Contact** Mr. John Hanson, Director of Admissions, Emma Willard House, Middlebury College, Middlebury, VT 05753-6002. Telephone: 802-443-3000 Ext. 5153. Fax: 802-443-2056.

NORWICH UNIVERSITY
NORTHFIELD, VERMONT

Entrance Moderately difficult **General** Independent, comprehensive, coed **Setting** 1,125-acre small-town campus **Enrollment** 2,556 **Faculty** 14:1 **Application deadline** Rolling **Freshmen** 94% accepted **Housing** Yes **Tuition** $14,950 **Undergraduates** 30% women, 6% part-time, 10% 25 or older, 1% Native American, 5% Hispanic, 3% black, 3% Asian or Pacific Islander **Most popular recent majors** Criminal justice, mechanical engineering, business administration/commerce/management **Academic program** Advanced placement, tutorials, honors program, summer session, adult/continuing education programs, internships **Contact** Mr. Frank Griffis, Dean of Admissions, Norwich University, Northfield, VT 05663. Telephone: 802-485-2001. Fax: 802-485-2580.

SAINT MICHAEL'S COLLEGE
COLCHESTER, VERMONT

Entrance Moderately difficult **General** Independent Roman Catholic, comprehensive, coed **Setting** 440-acre small-town campus **Enrollment** 2,641 **Faculty** 14:1 **Application deadline** 2/15 **Freshmen** 62% accepted **Housing** Yes **Tuition** $15,900 **Undergraduates** 55% women, 4% part-time, 6% 25 or older, 0% Native American, 1% Hispanic, 1% black, 1% Asian or Pacific Islander **Most popular recent majors** Psychology, business administration/commerce/management, English **Academic program** Average class size 25, advanced placement, self-designed majors, tutorials, honors program, summer session, adult/continuing education programs, internships **Contact** Mr. Jerry E. Flanagan, Associate Vice President for Admission/Enrollment Management, Saint Michael's College, Colchester, VT 05452. Telephone: 802-654-3000. Fax: 802-654-2591.

SCHOOL FOR INTERNATIONAL TRAINING
BRATTLEBORO, VERMONT

Entrance Moderately difficult **General** Independent, upper-level, coed **Setting** 200-acre small-town campus **Enrollment** 431 **Faculty** 7:1 **Freshmen** 62% accepted **Housing** Yes **Tuition** $12,975 **Undergraduates** 63% women, 0% part-time, 38% 25 or older, 0% Native American, 2% Hispanic, 2% black, 4% Asian or Pacific Islander **Most popular recent majors** International studies, social science **Academic program** Self-designed majors, tutorials, adult/continuing education programs, internships **Contact** Mr. Ed Parker, Undergraduate Admissions Counselor, School for International Training, Brattleboro, VT 05302-0676. Telephone: 802-257-7751. Fax: 802-258-3500.

SOUTHERN VERMONT COLLEGE
BENNINGTON, VERMONT

Entrance Minimally difficult **General** Independent, 4-year, coed **Setting** 371-acre small-town campus **Enrollment** 616 **Faculty** 18:1 **Application deadline** Rolling **Freshmen** 86% accepted **Housing** Yes **Tuition** $11,300 **Undergraduates** 58% women, 39% part-time, 38% 25 or older, 0% Native American, 1% Hispanic, 1% black, 1% Asian or Pacific Islander **Most popular recent majors** Criminal justice, business administration/commerce/management, liberal arts/general studies **Academic program** Average class size 18, ESL program, advanced placement, accelerated degree program, self-designed majors, tutorials, honors program, summer session, adult/continuing education programs, internships **Contact** Ms. Mary Van Arsdale, Director of Admissions, Southern Vermont College, Bennington, VT 05201-2128. Telephone: 802-442-5427 Ext. 138. Fax: 802-447-4695.

TRINITY COLLEGE OF VERMONT
BURLINGTON, VERMONT

Entrance Moderately difficult **General** Independent Roman Catholic, comprehensive, primarily women **Setting** 20-acre suburban campus **Enrollment** 1,042 **Faculty** 11:1 **Application deadline** Rolling **Freshmen** 96% accepted **Housing** Yes **Tuition** $13,420 **Undergraduates** 87% women, 46% part-time, 55% 25 or older, 1% Native American, 1% Hispanic, 1% black, 1% Asian or Pacific Islander **Most popular recent majors** Business administration/commerce/management, psychology, elementary education **Academic program** Advanced placement, self-designed majors, tutorials, summer session, adult/continuing education programs, internships **Contact** Ms. Dorothy

Watson, Director of Admissions, Trinity College of Vermont, Burlington, VT 05401-1470. Telephone: 802-658-0337 Ext. 218. Fax: 802-658-5446.

UNIVERSITY OF VERMONT
BURLINGTON, VERMONT

Entrance Moderately difficult **General** State-supported, coed **Setting** 425-acre small-town campus **Enrollment** 8,929 **Faculty** 13:1 **Application deadline** 2/1 **Freshmen** 75% accepted **Housing** Yes **Tuition** $7530 **Undergraduates** 54% women, 6% part-time, 6% 25 or older, 1% Native American, 1% Hispanic, 1% black, 2% Asian or Pacific Islander **Most popular recent majors** Business administration/commerce/management, political science/government, psychology **Academic program** Advanced placement, self-designed majors, honors program, summer session, internships **Contact** Mr. Robert J. Mansueto, Director of Admissions, University of Vermont, Burlington, VT 05401-3596. Telephone: 802-656-3370. Fax: 802-656-8611.

New York

ADELPHI UNIVERSITY

GARDEN CITY, NEW YORK

Entrance Moderately difficult **General** Independent, coed **Setting** 75-acre suburban campus **Enrollment** 5,969 **Faculty** 12:1 **Application deadline** Rolling **Freshmen** 71% accepted **Housing** Yes **Tuition** $14,000 **Undergraduates** 66% women, 32% part-time, 41% 25 or older, 0% Native American, 7% Hispanic, 16% black, 5% Asian or Pacific Islander **Most popular recent majors** Business administration/commerce/management, nursing, psychology **Academic program** Advanced placement, tutorials, honors program, summer session, internships **Contact** Ms. Esther Goodcuff, Director of Admissions, Adelphi University, Garden City, NY 11530. Telephone: 516-877-3050.

ALBANY COLLEGE OF PHARMACY OF UNION UNIVERSITY

ALBANY, NEW YORK

Entrance Moderately difficult **General** Independent, comprehensive, specialized, coed **Setting** 1-acre urban campus **Enrollment** 722 **Faculty** 19:1 **Application deadline** Rolling **Freshmen** 76% accepted **Housing** Yes **Tuition** $10,713 **Undergraduates** 57% women, 5% part-time, 6% 25 or older, 1% Native American, 1% Hispanic, 1% black, 12% Asian or Pacific Islander **Academic program** Advanced placement, tutorials, summer session, internships **Contact** Mrs. Janis Fisher, Director of Admissions and Registrar, Albany College of Pharmacy of Union University, 106 New Scotland Avenue, Albany, NY 12208-3425. Telephone: 518-445-7221. Fax: 518-445-7202.

ALBERT A. LIST COLLEGE OF JEWISH STUDIES

SEE JEWISH THEOLOGICAL SEMINARY OF AMERICA

ALFRED UNIVERSITY

ALFRED, NEW YORK

Entrance Moderately difficult **General** Independent, coed **Setting** 232-acre rural campus **Enrollment** 2,397 **Faculty** 12:1 **Application deadline** 2/1 **Freshmen** 84% accepted **Housing** Yes **Tuition** $18,972 **Undergraduates** 50% women, 5% part-time, 9% 25 or older, 1% Native American, 3% Hispanic, 4% black, 2% Asian or Pacific Islander **Most popular recent majors** Art/fine arts, business administration/commerce/management, psychology **Academic program** Advanced placement, accelerated degree program, self-designed majors, tutorials, honors program, summer session, adult/continuing education programs, internships **Contact** Ms. Katherine McCarthy, Director of Admissions, Alfred University, Alumni Hall, Alfred, NY 14802-1205. Telephone: 607-871-2115. Fax: 607-871-2198.

ARNOLD & MARIE SCHWARTZ COLLEGE OF PHARMACY AND HEALTH SCIENCES

SEE LONG ISLAND UNIVERSITY, BROOKLYN CAMPUS

AUDREY COHEN COLLEGE

NEW YORK, NEW YORK

Entrance Moderately difficult **General** Independent, comprehensive, coed **Setting** Urban campus **Enrollment** 1,180 **Application deadline** 8/15 **Freshmen** 75% accepted **Tuition** $8860 **Undergraduates** 65% women, 0% part-time, 58% 25 or older, 5% Native American, 23% Hispanic, 58% black, 2% Asian or Pacific Islander **Most popular recent major** Human services **Academic program** Accelerated degree program, tutorials, summer session, adult/continuing education programs, internships **Contact** Ms. Joan M. Miller, Admissions Counselor, Audrey Cohen College, 75 Varick Street, New York, NY 10013. Telephone: 212-343-1234 Ext. 2703. Fax: 212-343-8470.

BARD COLLEGE

ANNANDALE-ON-HUDSON, NEW YORK

Entrance Very difficult **General** Independent, comprehensive, coed **Setting** 600-acre rural campus **Enrollment** 1,244 **Faculty** 9:1 **Application deadline** 1/31 **Freshmen** 54% accepted **Housing** Yes **Tuition** $22,220 **Undergraduates** 52% women, 3% part-time, 1% 25 or older, 1% Native American, 5% Hispanic, 5% black, 4% Asian or Pacific Islander **Most popular recent majors** Social science, art/fine arts, literature **Academic program** Average class size 15, advanced placement, accelerated degree program, self-designed majors, tutorials, adult/continuing education programs, internships **Contact** Ms. Mary Backlund, Director of Admissions, Bard College, Annandale-on-Hudson, NY 12504. Telephone: 914-758-7472.

BARNARD COLLEGE

NEW YORK, NEW YORK

Entrance Most difficult **General** Independent, 4-year, women only **Setting** 4-acre urban campus **Enrollment** 19,000 **Faculty** 12:1 **Application deadline** 1/15 **Freshmen** 46% accepted **Hous-**

ing Yes **Tuition** $20,976 **Undergraduates** 3% part-time, 0% 25 or older, 1% Native American, 5% Hispanic, 4% black, 26% Asian or Pacific Islander **Most popular recent majors** English, psychology, political science/government **Academic program** Advanced placement, accelerated degree program, self-designed majors, tutorials, honors program, internships **Contact** Ms. Doris Davis, Dean of Admissions, Barnard College, 3009 Broadway, New York, NY 10027. Telephone: 212-854-2014. Fax: 212-854-6220.

BARUCH COLLEGE OF THE CITY UNIVERSITY OF NEW YORK
NEW YORK, NEW YORK

Entrance Moderately difficult **General** State and locally supported, coed **Setting** Urban campus **Enrollment** 15,223 **Faculty** 31:1 **Application deadline** 6/15 **Freshmen** 57% accepted **Tuition** $3330 **Undergraduates** 58% women, 38% part-time, 38% 25 or older, 0% Native American, 20% Hispanic, 20% black, 24% Asian or Pacific Islander **Most popular recent majors** Accounting, finance/banking, human resources **Academic program** Advanced placement, self-designed majors, tutorials, honors program, summer session, adult/continuing education programs, internships **Contact** Mr. James F. Murphy, Director of Admissions, Baruch College of the City University of New York, Box H-0720, New York, NY 10010-5585. Telephone: 212-802-2300.

BORICUA COLLEGE
NEW YORK, NEW YORK

Entrance Moderately difficult **General** Independent, comprehensive, coed **Setting** Urban campus **Enrollment** 1,052 **Application deadline** Rolling **Freshmen** 31% accepted **Tuition** $6400 **Undergraduates** 78% women, 0% part-time, 89% 25 or older, 1% Native American, 93% Hispanic, 6% black, 0% Asian or Pacific Islander **Most popular recent majors** Business administration/commerce/management, human services, elementary education **Academic program** Average class size 20, accelerated degree program, honors program, summer session, adult/continuing education programs, internships **Contact** Dr. Alicea Mercedes, Director of Registration and Assessment, Boricua College, 3755 Broadway, New York, NY 10032-1560. Telephone: 212-694-1000.

BROOKLYN COLLEGE OF THE CITY UNIVERSITY OF NEW YORK
BROOKLYN, NEW YORK

Entrance Moderately difficult **General** State and locally supported, comprehensive, coed **Setting** 26-acre urban campus **Enrollment** 13,267 **Faculty** 16:1 **Application deadline** 7/30 **Freshmen** 83% accepted **Tuition** $3413 **Undergraduates** 60% women, 27% part-time, 29% 25 or older, 0% Native American, 11% Hispanic, 26% black, 10% Asian or Pacific Islander **Most popular recent majors** Accounting, elementary education, business administration/commerce/management **Academic program** Advanced placement, honors program, summer session, adult/continuing education programs, internships **Contact** Mr. John Fraire, Director of Admissions, Brooklyn College of the City University of New York, 1602 James Hall, Brooklyn, NY 11210-2889. Telephone: 718-951-5001.

CANISIUS COLLEGE
BUFFALO, NEW YORK

Entrance Moderately difficult **General** Independent Roman Catholic (Jesuit), comprehensive, coed **Setting** 26-acre urban campus **Enrollment** 4,746 **Faculty** 18:1 **Application deadline** Rolling **Freshmen** 84% accepted **Housing** Yes **Tuition** $12,926 **Undergraduates** 47% women, 13% part-time, 11% 25 or older, 1% Native American, 3% Hispanic, 6% black, 2% Asian or Pacific Islander **Most popular recent majors** Psychology, business administration/commerce/management, physical education **Academic program** Average class size 21, advanced placement, self-designed majors, tutorials, honors program, summer session, adult/continuing education programs, internships **Contact** Miss Penelope H. Lips, Director of Admissions, Canisius College, 2001 Main Street, Buffalo, NY 14208-1098. Telephone: 716-888-2200. Fax: 716-888-2525.

CAZENOVIA COLLEGE
CAZENOVIA, NEW YORK

Entrance Minimally difficult **General** Independent, 4-year, coed **Setting** 40-acre small-town campus **Enrollment** 727 **Faculty** 14:1 **Application deadline** Rolling **Freshmen** 86% accepted **Housing** Yes **Tuition** $11,648 **Undergraduates** 65% women, 10% part-time, 6% 25 or older, 1% Native American, 4% Hispanic, 12% black, 1% Asian or Pacific Islander **Most popular recent majors** Liberal arts/general studies, interior design **Academic program** Average class size 20, advanced placement, self-designed majors, tutorials, honors program, summer session, adult/continuing education programs, internships **Contact** Mr. Tim Williams, Dean of Admission and Financial Aid, Cazenovia College, Cazenovia, NY 13035. Telephone: 315-655-8005 Ext. 158. Fax: 315-655-2190.

CENTRAL YESHIVA TOMCHEI TMIMIM-LUBAVITCH
BROOKLYN, NEW YORK

Entrance Difficulty N/R **General** Independent Jewish, comprehensive, specialized, men only **Enrollment** 376 **Housing** Yes **Tuition** $4800 **Contact** Rabbi Joseph Wilmowski, Director of Admissions, Central Yeshiva Tomchei Tmimim-Lubavitch, 841-853 Ocean Parkway, Brooklyn, NY 11230. Telephone: 718-859-7600.

CITY COLLEGE OF THE CITY UNIVERSITY OF NEW YORK
NEW YORK, NEW YORK

Entrance Moderately difficult **General** State and locally supported, coed **Setting** 35-acre urban campus **Enrollment** 12,494 **Faculty** 15:1 **Application deadline** Rolling **Freshmen** 60% accepted **Tuition** $3309 **Undergraduates** 51% women, 33% part-time, 39% 25 or older, 1% Native American, 31% Hispanic, 38% black, 15% Asian or Pacific Islander **Most popular recent majors** Electrical engineering, architecture **Academic program** Advanced placement, self-designed majors, honors program, summer session, adult/continuing education programs, internships **Contact** Ms. Laurie Austin, Director of Admissions, City College of the City University of New York, 160 Convent Avenue, New York, NY 10031-6977. Telephone: 212-650-6977. Fax: 212-650-6417.

CLARKSON UNIVERSITY
POTSDAM, NEW YORK

Entrance Very difficult **General** Independent, coed **Setting** 640-acre small-town campus **Enrollment** 2,670 **Faculty** 16:1 **Application deadline** 3/15 **Housing** Yes **Tuition** $18,593 **Undergraduates** 28% women, 2% part-time, 6% 25 or older, 1% Native American, 2% Hispanic, 2% black, 2% Asian or Pacific Islander **Most popular recent majors** Civil engineering, mechanical engineering, chemical engineering **Academic program** Advanced placement, accelerated degree program, self-designed majors, honors program, summer session **Contact** Mr. Robert Croot, Executive Director of Undergraduate Admission, Clarkson University, Holcroft House, Potsdam, NY 13699. Telephone: 315-268-6463. Fax: 315-268-7647.

COLGATE UNIVERSITY
HAMILTON, NEW YORK

Entrance Very difficult **General** Independent, comprehensive, coed **Setting** 515-acre rural campus **Enrollment** 2,859 **Faculty** 11:1 **Application deadline** 1/15 **Freshmen** 37% accepted **Housing** Yes **Tuition** $22,770 **Undergraduates** 52% women, 1% part-time, 1% 25 or older, 1% Native American, 3% Hispanic, 4% black, 5% Asian or Pacific Islander **Most popular recent majors** English, political science/government, history **Academic program** Average class size 21, advanced placement, self-designed majors, tutorials, honors program **Contact** Ms. Mary F. Hill, Dean of Admission, Colgate University, Hamilton, NY 13346-1386. Telephone: 315-824-7401. Fax: 315-824-7544.

COLLEGE OF AERONAUTICS
FLUSHING, NEW YORK

Entrance Minimally difficult **General** Independent, 4-year, specialized, primarily men **Setting** 6-acre urban campus **Enrollment** 960 **Faculty** 20:1 **Application deadline** Rolling **Freshmen** 52% accepted **Housing** Yes **Tuition** $8240 **Undergraduates** 5% women, 18% part-time, 17% 25 or older, 34% Hispanic, 26% black, 14% Asian or Pacific Islander **Most popular recent majors** Aircraft and missile maintenance, aviation technology **Academic program** Advanced placement, summer session, adult/continuing education programs, internships **Contact** Mr. Vincent J. Montera, Director of Admissions, College of Aeronautics, La Guardia Airport, Flushing, NY 11371. Telephone: 718-429-6600. Fax: 718-429-0256.

COLLEGE OF INSURANCE
NEW YORK, NEW YORK

Entrance Very difficult **General** Independent, comprehensive, coed **Setting** Urban campus **Enrollment** 2,379 **Faculty** 12:1 **Application deadline** 5/1 **Freshmen** 59% accepted **Housing** Yes **Tuition** $13,600 **Undergraduates** 52% women, 32% part-time, 9% Hispanic, 14% black, 9% Asian or Pacific Islander **Most popular recent major** Insurance **Academic program** Advanced placement, summer session, adult/continuing education programs **Contact** Ms. Theresa C. Marro, Director of Admissions, College of Insurance, 101 Murray Street, New York, NY 10007-2165. Telephone: 212-815-9232.

COLLEGE OF MOUNT SAINT VINCENT
RIVERDALE, NEW YORK

Entrance Moderately difficult **General** Independent, comprehensive, coed **Setting** 70-acre suburban campus **Enrollment** 1,500 **Faculty** 12:1 **Application deadline** Rolling **Freshmen** 68% accepted **Housing** Yes **Tuition** $13,580 **Under-**

graduates 70% women, 34% part-time, 25% 25 or older, 0% Native American, 29% Hispanic, 12% black, 10% Asian or Pacific Islander **Most popular recent majors** Nursing, business administration/commerce/management, communication **Academic program** Advanced placement, accelerated degree program, self-designed majors, tutorials, honors program, summer session, adult/continuing education programs, internships **Contact** Mrs. Lenore M. Mott, Dean of Admissions and Financial Aid, College of Mount Saint Vincent, Riverdale, NY 10471-1093. Telephone: 718-405-3268. Fax: 718-549-7945.

COLLEGE OF NEW ROCHELLE
NEW ROCHELLE, NEW YORK

Entrance Moderately difficult **General** Independent, comprehensive, primarily women **Setting** 20-acre suburban campus **Enrollment** 2,698 **Application deadline** Rolling **Freshmen** 65% accepted **Housing** Yes **Tuition** $11,100 **Undergraduates** 97% women, 36% part-time, 13% 25 or older, 1% Native American, 18% Hispanic, 32% black, 6% Asian or Pacific Islander **Most popular recent majors** Psychology, communication, art/fine arts **Academic program** Advanced placement, accelerated degree program, self-designed majors, tutorials, honors program, summer session, adult/continuing education programs, internships **Contact** Mr. John P. Hine Jr., Director of Admission, College of New Rochelle, New Rochelle, NY 10805-2308. Telephone: 914-654-5262. Fax: 914-654-5554.

THE COLLEGE OF SAINT ROSE
ALBANY, NEW YORK

Entrance Moderately difficult **General** Independent, comprehensive, coed **Setting** 22-acre urban campus **Enrollment** 3,857 **Application deadline** 8/15 **Freshmen** 69% accepted **Housing** Yes **Tuition** $11,724 **Undergraduates** 73% women, 35% part-time, 34% 25 or older, 1% Hispanic, 6% black **Academic program** Advanced placement, accelerated degree program, self-designed majors, summer session, adult/continuing education programs, internships **Contact** Ms. Mary O'Donnell, Director of Admissions, The College of Saint Rose, 432 Western Avenue, Albany, NY 12203-1419. Telephone: 518-454-5150.

COLLEGE OF STATEN ISLAND OF THE CITY UNIVERSITY OF NEW YORK
STATEN ISLAND, NEW YORK

Entrance Noncompetitive **General** State and locally supported, comprehensive, coed **Setting** 204-acre urban campus **Enrollment** 12,208 **Faculty** 23:1 **Application deadline** Rolling **Freshmen** 100% accepted **Tuition** $3326 **Undergraduates** 60% women, 46% part-time, 47% 25 or older, 1% Native American, 8% Hispanic, 9% black, 7% Asian or Pacific Islander **Most popular recent majors** Business administration/commerce/management, psychology **Academic program** Advanced placement, self-designed majors, summer session, adult/continuing education programs, internships **Contact** Ms. Castell Burton, Director of Admissions, College of Staten Island of the City University of New York, 2800 Victory Boulevard, Staten Island, NY 10314-6600. Telephone: 718-982-2011. Fax: 718-982-2068.

COLUMBIA COLLEGE
NEW YORK, NEW YORK

Entrance Most difficult **General** Independent, 4-year, coed **Setting** 35-acre urban campus **Enrollment** 19,000 **Faculty** 7:1 **Application deadline** 1/1 **Freshmen** 21% accepted **Housing** Yes **Tuition** $22,650 **Undergraduates** 49% women, 0% part-time, 0% 25 or older, 1% Native American, 8% Hispanic, 9% black, 19% Asian or Pacific Islander **Most popular recent majors** English, history, political science/government **Academic program** Advanced placement, self-designed majors, honors program, summer session **Contact** Director of Admissions, Columbia College, 212 Hamilton Hall, New York, NY 10027. Telephone: 212-854-2522. Fax: 212-854-1209.

COLUMBIA UNIVERSITY, BARNARD COLLEGE
SEE BARNARD COLLEGE

COLUMBIA UNIVERSITY, COLUMBIA COLLEGE
SEE COLUMBIA COLLEGE (NY)

COLUMBIA UNIVERSITY, SCHOOL OF ENGINEERING AND APPLIED SCIENCE
NEW YORK, NEW YORK

Entrance Most difficult **General** Independent, coed **Setting** Urban campus **Enrollment** 19,000 **Application deadline** 1/1 **Freshmen** 45% accepted **Housing** Yes **Tuition** $22,650 **Undergraduates** 24% women, 0% part-time, 0% 25 or older, 0% Native American, 6% Hispanic, 4% black, 44% Asian or Pacific Islander **Most popular recent majors** Computer science, electrical engineering, mechanical engineering **Academic program** Advanced placement, accelerated degree program, tutorials, honors program, summer session, adult/continuing education programs, internships **Contact** Director of Admissions, Columbia

University, School of Engineering and Applied Science, 500 West 120th Street, New York, NY 10027. Telephone: 212-854-2522. Fax: 212-854-1209.

COLUMBIA UNIVERSITY, SCHOOL OF GENERAL STUDIES

NEW YORK, NEW YORK

Entrance Most difficult **General** Independent, 4-year, coed **Setting** 36-acre urban campus **Enrollment** 19,000 **Application deadline** 7/15 **Freshmen** 50% accepted **Housing** Yes **Tuition** $19,594 **Undergraduates** 51% women, 55% part-time, 70% 25 or older, 0% Native American, 10% Hispanic, 9% black, 8% Asian or Pacific Islander **Most popular recent majors** Literature, English, history **Academic program** Advanced placement, accelerated degree program, self-designed majors, summer session, adult/continuing education programs, internships **Contact** Ms. Shirley Bé, Admissions Officer, Columbia University, School of General Studies, 2970 Broadway, New York, NY 10027. Telephone: 212-854-2772.

COLUMBIA UNIVERSITY, SCHOOL OF NURSING

NEW YORK, NEW YORK

Entrance Moderately difficult **General** Independent, upper-level, specialized, primarily women **Setting** Urban campus **Enrollment** 19,000 **Freshmen** 44% accepted **Housing** Yes **Tuition** $20,884 **Undergraduates** 91% women, 38% part-time, 82% 25 or older, 0% Native American, 6% Hispanic, 4% black, 8% Asian or Pacific Islander **Academic program** Advanced placement, summer session, adult/continuing education programs, internships **Contact** Dr. Theresa Doddato, Associate Dean for Student Affairs, Columbia University, School of Nursing, 630 West 168th Street, New York, NY 10032-3702. Telephone: 212-305-5756.

CONCORDIA COLLEGE

BRONXVILLE, NEW YORK

Entrance Moderately difficult **General** Independent Lutheran, 4-year, coed **Setting** 33-acre suburban campus **Enrollment** 556 **Faculty** 13:1 **Application deadline** 3/15 **Freshmen** 85% accepted **Housing** Yes **Tuition** $11,990 **Undergraduates** 55% women, 15% part-time, 18% 25 or older, 0% Native American, 8% Hispanic, 17% black, 6% Asian or Pacific Islander **Most popular recent majors** Education, business administration/commerce/management **Academic program** Advanced placement, accelerated degree program, self-designed majors, honors program, adult/continuing education programs, internships **Contact** Mr. Thomas Weede, Dean of Enrollment Management, Concordia College, Bronxville, NY 10708-1998. Telephone: 914-337-9300 Ext. 2155. Fax: 914-395-4500.

COOPER UNION FOR THE ADVANCEMENT OF SCIENCE AND ART

NEW YORK, NEW YORK

Entrance Most difficult **General** Independent, comprehensive, coed **Setting** Urban campus **Enrollment** 927 **Faculty** 7:1 **Freshmen** 15% accepted **Housing** Yes **Undergraduates** 35% women, 3% part-time, 3% 25 or older, 0% Native American, 11% Hispanic, 5% black, 27% Asian or Pacific Islander **Most popular recent majors** Art/fine arts, architecture, electrical engineering **Academic program** Advanced placement, self-designed majors, tutorials, honors program, summer session, internships **Contact** Mr. Richard Bory, Dean of Admissions and Records, Cooper Union for the Advancement of Science and Art, 30 Cooper Square, New York, NY 10003-7120. Telephone: 212-353-4120. Fax: 212-353-4343.

CORNELL UNIVERSITY

ITHACA, NEW YORK

Entrance Most difficult **General** Independent, coed **Setting** 745-acre small-town campus **Enrollment** 18,849 **Faculty** 9:1 **Application deadline** 1/1 **Freshmen** 33% accepted **Housing** Yes **Tuition** $21,914 **Undergraduates** 47% women, 0% part-time, 3% 25 or older, 1% Native American, 6% Hispanic, 4% black, 17% Asian or Pacific Islander **Most popular recent majors** Biology/biological sciences, economics, hotel and restaurant management **Academic program** Advanced placement, self-designed majors, tutorials, honors program, summer session, internships **Contact** Ms. Nancy Meislahn, Director of Admissions, Cornell University, 410 Thurston Avenue, Ithaca, NY 14850. Telephone: 607-255-5241. Fax: 607-255-0659.

C.W. POST CAMPUS OF LONG ISLAND UNIVERSITY

SEE LONG ISLAND UNIVERSITY, C.W. POST CAMPUS

DAEMEN COLLEGE

AMHERST, NEW YORK

Entrance Minimally difficult **General** Independent, comprehensive, coed **Setting** 39-acre suburban campus **Enrollment** 1,815 **Faculty** 17:1 **Application deadline** Rolling **Freshmen** 75%

accepted **Housing** Yes **Tuition** $10,980 **Undergraduates** 70% women, 27% part-time, 42% 25 or older, 0% Native American, 2% Hispanic, 5% black, 2% Asian or Pacific Islander **Most popular recent majors** Physical therapy, nursing **Academic program** ESL program, Advanced placement, self-designed majors, tutorials, summer session, adult/continuing education programs, internships **Contact** Ms. Maria P. Dillard, Director of Enrollment Management, Daemen College, Amherst, NY 14226-3592. Telephone: 716-839-8225. Fax: 716-839-8516.

DOMINICAN COLLEGE OF BLAUVELT
ORANGEBURG, NEW YORK

Entrance Moderately difficult **General** Independent, comprehensive, coed **Setting** 14-acre suburban campus **Enrollment** 1,811 **Faculty** 12:1 **Application deadline** Rolling **Freshmen** 74% accepted **Housing** Yes **Tuition** $8758 **Undergraduates** 74% women, 60% part-time, 72% 25 or older, 0% Native American, 7% Hispanic, 11% black, 5% Asian or Pacific Islander **Most popular recent majors** Occupational therapy, business administration/commerce/management, nursing **Academic program** Average class size 20, advanced placement, accelerated degree program, honors program, summer session, adult/continuing education programs, internships **Contact** Ms. Colleen M. O'Connor, Director of Admissions, Dominican College of Blauvelt, Orangeburg, NY 10962-1210. Telephone: 914-359-7800 Ext. 271. Fax: 914-359-2313.

DOWLING COLLEGE
OAKDALE, NEW YORK

Entrance Moderately difficult **General** Independent, comprehensive, coed **Setting** 156-acre suburban campus **Enrollment** 6,046 **Faculty** 9:1 **Application deadline** Rolling **Freshmen** 93% accepted **Housing** Yes **Tuition** $12,630 **Undergraduates** 55% women, 76% part-time, 34% 25 or older, 0% Native American, 5% Hispanic, 6% black, 2% Asian or Pacific Islander **Most popular recent majors** Business administration/commerce/management, liberal arts/general studies, education **Academic program** Average class size 17, advanced placement, accelerated degree program, self-designed majors, tutorials, honors program, summer session, internships **Contact** Mrs. Kate Rowe, Director of Admissions, Dowling College, Oakdale, NY 11769-1999. Telephone: 516-244-3030. Fax: 516-563-3827.

D'YOUVILLE COLLEGE
BUFFALO, NEW YORK

Entrance Moderately difficult **General** Independent, comprehensive, coed **Setting** 7-acre urban campus **Enrollment** 1,915 **Faculty** 15:1 **Application deadline** Rolling **Freshmen** 53% accepted **Housing** Yes **Tuition** $10,040 **Undergraduates** 73% women, 27% part-time, 37% 25 or older, 1% Native American, 3% Hispanic, 9% black, 2% Asian or Pacific Islander **Most popular recent majors** Physical therapy, occupational therapy, nursing **Academic program** Average class size 40, advanced placement, tutorials, honors program, summer session, adult/continuing education programs, internships **Contact** Mr. Ronald H. Dannecker, Director of Admissions and Financial Aid, D'Youville College, 320 Porter Avenue, Buffalo, NY 14201-1084. Telephone: 716-881-7600. Fax: 716-881-7790.

EASTMAN SCHOOL OF MUSIC
SEE UNIVERSITY OF ROCHESTER

ELMIRA COLLEGE
ELMIRA, NEW YORK

Entrance Moderately difficult **General** Independent, 4-year, coed **Setting** 42-acre small-town campus **Enrollment** 1,117 **Faculty** 15:1 **Application deadline** 7/15 **Freshmen** 76% accepted **Housing** Yes **Tuition** $19,170 **Undergraduates** 60% women, 0% part-time, 4% 25 or older, 1% Native American, 2% Hispanic, 2% black, 2% Asian or Pacific Islander **Most popular recent majors** Psychology, business administration/commerce/management, elementary education **Academic program** Average class size 20, advanced placement, accelerated degree program, self-designed majors, tutorials, summer session, adult/continuing education programs, internships **Contact** Mr. William S. Neal, Dean of Admissions, Elmira College, Elmira, NY 14901. Telephone: 607-735-1724. Fax: 607-735-1718.

EUGENE LANG COLLEGE, NEW SCHOOL FOR SOCIAL RESEARCH
NEW YORK, NEW YORK

Entrance Moderately difficult **General** Independent, 4-year, coed **Setting** 5-acre urban campus **Enrollment** 5,833 **Faculty** 9:1 **Application deadline** 2/1 **Freshmen** 69% accepted **Housing** Yes **Tuition** $16,920 **Undergraduates** 65% women, 5% part-time, 1% 25 or older, 0% Native American, 11% Hispanic, 9% black, 3% Asian or Pacific Islander **Most popular recent majors** Creative writing, theater arts/drama, interdisciplinary studies **Academic program** Advanced placement, accelerated degree program, self-designed majors, tutorials, summer session, adult/continuing education programs, internships **Contact** Ms. Jennifer Fondiller, Director of Admissions, Eugene Lang College, New School for Social Research, 65 West 11th Street, New York, NY 10011-8601. Telephone: 212-229-5665. Fax: 212-229-5355.

FASHION INSTITUTE OF TECHNOLOGY
NEW YORK, NEW YORK

Entrance Moderately difficult **General** State and locally supported, comprehensive, coed **Setting** 5-acre urban campus **Enrollment** 8,489 **Faculty** 14:1 **Application deadline** Rolling **Freshmen** 50% accepted **Housing** Yes **Tuition** $2710 **Undergraduates** 79% women, 55% part-time, 50% 25 or older, 0% Native American, 14% Hispanic, 12% black, 24% Asian or Pacific Islander **Most popular recent majors** Fashion merchandising, fashion design and technology, advertising **Academic program** Advanced placement, summer session, adult/continuing education programs, internships **Contact** Mr. Jim Pidgeon, Director of Admissions, Fashion Institute of Technology, Seventh Avenue at 27th Street, New York, NY 10001-5992. Telephone: 212-760-7675.

FIVE TOWNS COLLEGE
DIX HILLS, NEW YORK

Entrance Minimally difficult **General** Independent, 4-year, coed **Setting** 34-acre suburban campus **Enrollment** 650 **Faculty** 13:1 **Application deadline** Rolling **Freshmen** 87% accepted **Housing** Yes **Tuition** $8800 **Undergraduates** 39% women, 5% part-time, 18% 25 or older, 0% Native American, 12% Hispanic, 20% black, 3% Asian or Pacific Islander **Most popular recent majors** Business administration/commerce/management, music, music education **Academic program** Advanced placement, tutorials, summer session, internships **Contact** Ms. Jennifer Roemer, Director of Admissions, Five Towns College, 305 North Service Road, Dix Hills, NY 11746-6055. Telephone: 516-424-7000 Ext. 110. Fax: 516-424-7006.

FORDHAM UNIVERSITY
NEW YORK, NEW YORK

Entrance Very difficult **General** Independent Roman Catholic (Jesuit), coed **Setting** 85-acre urban campus **Enrollment** 13,723 **Faculty** 17:1 **Application deadline** 2/1 **Freshmen** 70% accepted **Housing** Yes **Tuition** $16,000 **Undergraduates** 59% women, 23% part-time, 0% Native American, 15% Hispanic, 6% black, 5% Asian or Pacific Islander **Most popular recent majors** Business administration/commerce/management, communication, English **Academic program** Average class size 24, advanced placement, accelerated degree program, self-designed majors, tutorials, honors program, summer session, adult/continuing education programs, internships **Contact** Mr. John W. Buckley, Director of Admissions, Fordham University, East Fordham Road, New York, NY 10458. Telephone: 718-817-4000. Fax: 718-367-9404.

FRIENDS WORLD COLLEGE
SEE LONG ISLAND UNIVERSITY, SOUTHAMPTON COLLEGE, FRIENDS WORLD PROGRAM

HAMILTON COLLEGE
CLINTON, NEW YORK

Entrance Very difficult **General** Independent, 4-year, coed **Setting** 1,200-acre rural campus **Enrollment** 1,715 **Faculty** 10:1 **Application deadline** 1/15 **Freshmen** 44% accepted **Housing** Yes **Tuition** $22,700 **Undergraduates** 47% women, 2% part-time, 1% 25 or older, 1% Native American, 3% Hispanic, 2% black, 3% Asian or Pacific Islander **Most popular recent majors** Economics, English, political science/government **Academic program** Advanced placement, accelerated degree program, self-designed majors, tutorials, adult/continuing education programs, internships **Contact** Mr. Richard M. Fuller, Dean of Admission and Financial Aid, Hamilton College, Clinton, NY 13323-1218. Telephone: 315-859-4421. Fax: 315-859-4457.

HARTWICK COLLEGE
ONEONTA, NEW YORK

Entrance Moderately difficult **General** Independent, 4-year, coed **Setting** 375-acre small-town campus **Enrollment** 1,494 **Faculty** 13:1 **Application deadline** 2/15 **Freshmen** 90% accepted **Housing** Yes **Tuition** $22,235 **Undergraduates** 53% women, 1% part-time, 2% 25 or older, 1% Native American, 4% Hispanic, 5% black, 2% Asian or Pacific Islander **Most popular recent majors** Nursing, biology/biological sciences **Academic program** Advanced placement, accelerated degree program, self-designed majors, tutorials, honors program, internships **Contact** Mrs. Karyl B. Clemens, Dean of Admissions, Hartwick College, Oneonta, NY 13820-4020. Telephone: 607-431-4150. Fax: 607-431-4138.

HILBERT COLLEGE
HAMBURG, NEW YORK

Entrance Minimally difficult **General** Independent, 4-year, coed **Setting** 40-acre small-town campus **Enrollment** 807 **Faculty** 20:1 **Application deadline** 9/1 **Freshmen** 99% accepted **Housing** Yes **Tuition** $9500 **Undergraduates** 67% women, 39% part-time, 51% 25 or older, 1% Native American, 2% Hispanic, 3% black, 0% Asian or Pacific Islander **Most popular recent majors** Criminal justice, business administration/commerce/management, human services **Academic program** ESL program, Advanced placement, tutorials, summer session, internships **Contact** Ms. Beatrice Slick, Director of Admissions, Hilbert College, Hamburg, NY 14075-1597. Telephone: 716-649-7900 Ext. 244. Fax: 716-649-0702.

HOBART AND WILLIAM SMITH COLLEGES
GENEVA, NEW YORK

Entrance Very difficult **General** Independent, 4-year, coed **Setting** 200-acre small-town campus **Enrollment** 1,794 **Faculty** 13:1 **Application deadline** 2/1 **Freshmen** 78% accepted **Housing** Yes **Tuition** $22,380 **Undergraduates** 52% women, 1% part-time, 0% 25 or older, 1% Native American, 4% Hispanic, 5% black, 2% Asian or Pacific Islander **Most popular recent majors** English, economics, interdisciplinary studies **Academic program** Advanced placement, accelerated degree program, self-designed majors, tutorials, honors program, adult/continuing education programs, internships **Contact** Ms. Mara O'Laughlin, Director of Admission, Hobart and William Smith Colleges, Geneva, NY 14456-3397. Telephone: 315-789-3500. Fax: 315-781-5471.

HOFSTRA UNIVERSITY
HEMPSTEAD, NEW YORK

Entrance Moderately difficult **General** Independent, coed **Setting** 238-acre suburban campus **Enrollment** 12,279 **Faculty** 15:1 **Application deadline** Rolling **Freshmen** 88% accepted **Housing** Yes **Tuition** $13,544 **Undergraduates** 53% women, 16% part-time, 11% 25 or older, 1% Native American, 5% Hispanic, 5% black, 5% Asian or Pacific Islander **Most popular recent majors** Psychology, accounting, marketing/retailing/merchandising **Academic program** Advanced placement, accelerated degree program, self-designed majors, tutorials, honors program, summer session, adult/continuing education programs, internships **Contact** Ms. Mary Beth Carey, Dean of Admissions, Hofstra University, Hempstead, NY 11550-1090. Telephone: 516-463-6700. Fax: 516-560-7660.

HOLY TRINITY ORTHODOX SEMINARY
JORDANVILLE, NEW YORK

Entrance Noncompetitive **General** Independent Russian Orthodox, 5-year, specialized, men only **Setting** Rural campus **Enrollment** 39 **Application deadline** 5/1 **Freshmen** 71% accepted **Housing** Yes **Tuition** $1800 **Undergraduates** 0% part-time, 30% 25 or older **Academic program** Average class size 8, accelerated degree program, tutorials **Contact** Very Rev. Abbot Luke, Registrar, Holy Trinity Orthodox Seminary, Jordanville, NY 13361. Telephone: 315-858-0945. Fax: 315-858-0505.

HOUGHTON COLLEGE
HOUGHTON, NEW YORK

Entrance Moderately difficult **General** Independent Wesleyan, 4-year, coed **Setting** 1,300-acre rural campus **Enrollment** 1,249 **Faculty** 15:1 **Application deadline** 3/1 **Freshmen** 77% accepted **Housing** Yes **Tuition** $12,724 **Undergraduates** 64% women, 3% part-time, 7% 25 or older, 1% Native American, 1% Hispanic, 2% black, 1% Asian or Pacific Islander **Most popular recent majors** Elementary education, biology/biological sciences, psychology **Academic program** Advanced placement, tutorials, honors program, summer session, adult/continuing education programs, internships **Contact** Mr. David Mee, Director of Admissions, Houghton College, PO Box 128, Houghton, NY 14744. Telephone: 716-567-9353. Fax: 716-567-9522.

HUNTER COLLEGE OF THE CITY UNIVERSITY OF NEW YORK
NEW YORK, NEW YORK

Entrance Moderately difficult **General** State and locally supported, comprehensive, coed **Setting** Urban campus **Enrollment** 18,250 **Faculty** 18:1 **Application deadline** 1/15 **Freshmen** 41% accepted **Housing** Yes **Tuition** $3329 **Undergraduates** 73% women, 36% part-time, 60% 25 or older, 1% Native American, 25% Hispanic, 22% black, 16% Asian or Pacific Islander **Most popular recent majors** Psychology, sociology, English **Academic program** Advanced placement, self-designed majors, tutorials, honors program, summer session, internships **Contact** Office of Admissions, Hunter College of the City University of New York, 695 Park Avenue, New York, NY 10021-5085. Telephone: 212-772-4490.

IONA COLLEGE
NEW ROCHELLE, NEW YORK

Entrance Moderately difficult **General** Independent, comprehensive, coed **Setting** 35-acre suburban campus **Enrollment** 5,588 **Faculty** 17:1 **Application deadline** 3/15 **Freshmen** 72% accepted **Housing** Yes **Tuition** $13,420 **Undergraduates** 57% women, 27% part-time, 33% 25 or older, 0% Native American, 13% Hispanic, 19% black, 2% Asian or Pacific Islander **Most popular recent majors** Communication, education, accounting **Academic program** Advanced placement, accelerated degree program, honors program, summer session, adult/continuing education programs, internships **Contact** Mr. Tom Delahunt, Director of Undergraduate Admissions, Iona College, New Rochelle, NY 10801-1890. Telephone: 914-633-2502. Fax: 914-633-2096.

ITHACA COLLEGE
ITHACA, NEW YORK

Entrance Moderately difficult **General** Independent, comprehensive, coed **Setting** 600-acre small-town campus **Enrollment** 5,683 **Faculty** 12:1 **Application deadline** 3/1 **Freshmen** 73% accepted **Housing** Yes **Tuition** $16,900 **Undergraduates** 54% women, 1% part-time, 2% 25 or older, 1% Native American, 3% Hispanic, 2% black, 2% Asian or Pacific Islander **Most popular recent majors** Radio and television studies, sociology, physical therapy **Academic program** Average class size 20, advanced placement, accelerated degree program, self-designed majors, honors program, summer session, adult/continuing education programs, internships **Contact** Ms. Paula Mitchell, Director of Admissions, Ithaca College, Ithaca, NY 14850-7020. Telephone: 607-274-3124.

JEWISH THEOLOGICAL SEMINARY OF AMERICA
NEW YORK, NEW YORK

Entrance Very difficult **General** Independent Jewish, coed **Setting** 1-acre urban campus **Enrollment** 560 **Faculty** 5:1 **Application deadline** 2/15 **Freshmen** 80% accepted **Housing** Yes **Tuition** $7490 **Undergraduates** 55% women, 5% part-time, 1% 25 or older, 0% Native American, 1% Hispanic, 0% black, 0% Asian or Pacific Islander **Most popular recent majors** Biblical studies, history, philosophy **Academic program** Advanced placement, self-designed majors, tutorials, honors program, summer session, adult/continuing education programs **Contact** Ms. Marci Harris Blumenthal, Director of Admissions, Jewish Theological Seminary of America, Room 614 Schiff, 3080 Broadway, New York, NY 10027-4649. Telephone: 212-678-8832. Fax: 212-678-8947.

JOHN JAY COLLEGE OF CRIMINAL JUSTICE, THE CITY UNIVERSITY OF NEW YORK
NEW YORK, NEW YORK

Entrance Moderately difficult **General** State and locally supported, comprehensive, coed **Setting** Urban campus **Enrollment** 10,724 **Faculty** 18:1 **Application deadline** Rolling **Tuition** $3309 **Undergraduates** 53% women, 29% part-time, 35% 25 or older, 1% Native American, 34% Hispanic, 29% black, 3% Asian or Pacific Islander **Most popular recent majors** Criminal justice, public administration, forensic sciences **Academic program** Advanced placement, honors program, summer session, internships **Contact** Mr. Donald J. Gray, Acting Dean for Admissions and Registration, John Jay College of Criminal Justice, the City University of New York, 899 Tenth Avenue, New York, NY 10019-1093. Telephone: 212-237-8878.

THE JUILLIARD SCHOOL
NEW YORK, NEW YORK

Entrance Most difficult **General** Independent, comprehensive, coed **Setting** Urban campus **Enrollment** 851 **Faculty** 4:1 **Application deadline** 1/8 **Freshmen** 11% accepted **Housing** Yes **Tuition** $15,000 **Undergraduates** 52% women, 0% part-time, 9% 25 or older, 1% Native American, 5% Hispanic, 8% black, 30% Asian or Pacific Islander **Most popular recent majors** Piano/organ, stringed instruments, dance **Academic program** Accelerated degree program, self-designed majors, tutorials, adult/continuing education programs **Contact** Ms. Mary K. Gray, Director of Admissions, The Juilliard School, 60 Lincoln Center Plaza, New York, NY 10023-6588. Telephone: 212-799-5000 Ext. 223. Fax: 212-724-0263.

KEHILLATH YAKOV RABBINICAL SEMINARY
BROOKLYN, NEW YORK

Entrance Difficulty N/R **General** Independent-religious, comprehensive, men only **Enrollment** 150 **Freshmen** 75% accepted **Tuition** $4000 **Housing** College housing not available. **Financial Aid** 54% applied for aid, 100% of those who applied for aid were judged to have need, 100% of those were aided. Average percent of need met: 65%. Average amount received per student (from all sources): $3000. Required forms: FAFSA. Financial aid deadline: continuous.

KEUKA COLLEGE
KEUKA PARK, NEW YORK

Entrance Moderately difficult **General** Independent, 4-year, coed, affiliated with American Baptist Churches in the U.S.A. **Setting** 173-acre rural campus **Enrollment** 938 **Faculty** 15:1 **Application deadline** Rolling **Freshmen** 81% accepted **Housing** Yes **Tuition** $11,400 **Undergraduates** 75% women, 6% part-time, 17% 25 or older, 0% Native American, 2% Hispanic, 2% black, 1% Asian or Pacific Islander **Most popular recent majors** Occupational therapy, elementary education, business administration/commerce/management **Academic program** Advanced placement, self-designed majors, tutorials, honors program, summer session, adult/continuing education programs, internships **Contact** Mr. Robert J. Iannuzzo, Dean of Admissions and Financial Aid, Keuka College, Keuka Park, NY 14478-0098. Telephone: 315-536-4411 Ext. 5254. Fax: 315-536-5386.

KOL YAAKOV TORAH CENTER
MONSEY, NEW YORK

Entrance Minimally difficult **General** Independent Jewish, comprehensive, specialized, men only **Setting** 3-acre small-town campus **Enrollment** 40 **Application deadline** Rolling **Freshmen** 50% accepted **Housing** Yes **Tuition** $3300 **Undergraduates** 10% part-time, 7% 25 or older, 0% Native American, 0% Hispanic, 0% black, 5% Asian or Pacific Islander **Academic program** Self-designed majors, tutorials, honors program, summer session, adult/continuing education programs **Contact** Mr. Aaron Parry, Assistant Director of Admissions, Kol Yaakov Torah Center, Monsey, NY 10952-2954. Telephone: 914-425-3871.

LABORATORY INSTITUTE OF MERCHANDISING
NEW YORK, NEW YORK

Entrance Minimally difficult **General** Proprietary, 4-year, specialized, coed **Setting** Urban campus **Enrollment** 184 **Faculty** 8:1 **Application deadline** Rolling **Freshmen** 84% accepted **Tuition** $11,450 **Undergraduates** 97% women, 3% part-time, 1% 25 or older, 1% Native American, 16% Hispanic, 23% black, 6% Asian or Pacific Islander **Academic program** Advanced placement, tutorials, summer session, internships **Contact** Mr. Drew Ippolito, Director of Admissions, Laboratory Institute of Merchandising, 12 East 53rd Street, New York, NY 10022-5268. Telephone: 212-752-1530. Fax: 212-832-6708.

LEHMAN COLLEGE OF THE CITY UNIVERSITY OF NEW YORK
BRONX, NEW YORK

Entrance Moderately difficult **General** State and locally supported, comprehensive, coed **Setting** 37-acre urban campus **Enrollment** 9,413 **Faculty** 17:1 **Application deadline** Rolling **Freshmen** 51% accepted **Tuition** $3320 **Undergraduates** 72% women, 43% part-time, 54% 25 or older, 0% Native American, 46% Hispanic, 34% black, 4% Asian or Pacific Islander **Most popular recent majors** Psychology, accounting, nursing **Academic program** Advanced placement, self-designed majors, tutorials, honors program, summer session, adult/continuing education programs, internships **Contact** Mr. Clarence Wilkes, Director of Admissions, Lehman College of the City University of New York, 250 Bedford Park Boulevard West, Bronx, NY 10468-1589. Telephone: 718-960-8706.

LE MOYNE COLLEGE
SYRACUSE, NEW YORK

Entrance Moderately difficult **General** Independent Roman Catholic (Jesuit), comprehensive, coed **Setting** 161-acre suburban campus **Enrollment** 2,713 **Faculty** 13:1 **Application deadline** 3/15 **Freshmen** 79% accepted **Housing** Yes **Tuition** $13,390 **Undergraduates** 60% women, 10% part-time, 14% 25 or older, 1% Native American, 4% Hispanic, 3% black, 1% Asian or Pacific Islander **Most popular recent majors** Accounting, business administration/commerce/management, psychology **Academic program** Average class size 19, advanced placement, accelerated degree program, tutorials, honors program, summer session, adult/continuing education programs, internships **Contact** Mr. Dennis R. DePerro, Dean of Enrollment Management, Le Moyne College, Syracuse, NY 13214-1399. Telephone: 315-445-4707.

LIST COLLEGE OF JEWISH STUDIES
SEE JEWISH THEOLOGICAL SEMINARY OF AMERICA

LONG ISLAND UNIVERSITY, BROOKLYN CAMPUS
BROOKLYN, NEW YORK

Entrance Minimally difficult **General** Independent, comprehensive, coed **Setting** 10-acre urban campus **Enrollment** 8,264 **Application deadline** Rolling **Freshmen** 59% accepted **Housing** Yes **Tuition** $13,596 **Undergraduates** 64%

women, 10% part-time, 33% 25 or older, 1% Native American, 15% Hispanic, 43% black, 11% Asian or Pacific Islander **Most popular recent majors** Pharmacy/pharmaceutical sciences, business administration/commerce/management, nursing **Academic program** Advanced placement, accelerated degree program, self-designed majors, honors program, summer session, adult/continuing education programs, internships **Contact** Mr. Alan B. Chaves, Dean of Admissions, Long Island University, Brooklyn Campus, One University Plaza, Brooklyn, NY 11201-8423. Telephone: 718-488-1011.

LONG ISLAND UNIVERSITY, C.W. POST CAMPUS
BROOKVILLE, NEW YORK

Entrance Moderately difficult **General** Independent, comprehensive, coed **Setting** 305-acre small-town campus **Enrollment** 9,172 **Faculty** 10:1 **Application deadline** Rolling **Freshmen** 76% accepted **Housing** Yes **Tuition** $13,690 **Undergraduates** 64% women, 22% part-time, 24% 25 or older, 2% Native American, 7% Hispanic, 8% black, 4% Asian or Pacific Islander **Most popular recent majors** Liberal arts/general studies, business administration/commerce/management, education **Academic program** Average class size 30, advanced placement, accelerated degree program, self-designed majors, honors program, summer session, adult/continuing education programs, internships **Contact** Ms. Christine Natali, Director of Admissions, Long Island University, C.W. Post Campus, Brookville, NY 11548-1300. Telephone: 516-299-2413.

LONG ISLAND UNIVERSITY, SOUTHAMPTON COLLEGE
SOUTHAMPTON, NEW YORK

Entrance Moderately difficult **General** Independent, comprehensive, coed **Setting** 110-acre rural campus **Enrollment** 1,491 **Faculty** 11:1 **Application deadline** Rolling **Freshmen** 80% accepted **Housing** Yes **Tuition** $13,760 **Undergraduates** 63% women, 10% part-time, 12% 25 or older, 1% Native American, 6% Hispanic, 6% black, 1% Asian or Pacific Islander **Most popular recent majors** Marine biology, art/fine arts, business administration/commerce/management **Academic program** Average class size 25, advanced placement, accelerated degree program, self-designed majors, tutorials, honors program, summer session, adult/continuing education programs, internships **Contact** Ms. Carol Gilbert, Director of Admissions, Long Island University, Southampton College, 239 Montauk Highway, Southampton, NY 11968-9822. Telephone: 516-283-4000 Ext. 200. Fax: 516-283-4081.

LONG ISLAND UNIVERSITY, SOUTHAMPTON COLLEGE, FRIENDS WORLD PROGRAM
SOUTHAMPTON, NEW YORK

Entrance Noncompetitive **General** Independent, 4-year, coed **Setting** 110-acre rural campus **Enrollment** 200 **Faculty** 7:1 **Application deadline** Rolling **Freshmen** 85% accepted **Housing** Yes **Tuition** $13,600 **Undergraduates** 70% women, 3% part-time, 10% 25 or older, 1% Native American, 3% Hispanic, 6% black, 2% Asian or Pacific Islander **Academic program** Average class size 10, advanced placement, accelerated degree program, self-designed majors, tutorials, adult/continuing education programs, internships **Contact** Ms. Susan Kropf, Director of Enrollment, Long Island University, Southampton College, Friends World Program, Southampton, NY 11968. Telephone: 516-287-8466.

MACHZIKEI HADATH RABBINICAL COLLEGE
BROOKLYN, NEW YORK

Entrance Moderately difficult **General** Independent-religious, comprehensive, men only **Enrollment** 150 **Application deadline** Rolling **Freshmen** 88% accepted **Housing** Yes **Tuition** $5200 **Undergraduates** 0% part-time, 0% Native American, 0% Hispanic, 0% black, 0% Asian or Pacific Islander **Contact** Rabbi Abraham M. Lezerowitz, Director of Admissions, Machzikei Hadath Rabbinical College, Brooklyn, NY 11204-1805. Telephone: 718-854-8777.

MANHATTAN COLLEGE
RIVERDALE, NEW YORK

Entrance Moderately difficult **General** Independent, comprehensive, coed, affiliated with Roman Catholic Church **Setting** 50-acre urban campus **Enrollment** 3,076 **Faculty** 14:1 **Application deadline** 3/1 **Freshmen** 77% accepted **Housing** Yes **Tuition** $14,555 **Undergraduates** 45% women, 9% part-time, 8% 25 or older, 0% Native American, 15% Hispanic, 7% black, 7% Asian or Pacific Islander **Most popular recent majors** Marketing/retailing/merchandising, civil engineering, finance/banking **Academic program** Advanced placement, accelerated degree program, tutorials, honors program, summer session, adult/continuing education programs, internships **Contact** Mr. John J. Brennan Jr., Dean of Admissions/Financial Aid, Manhattan College, 4513 Manhattan College Parkway, Riverdale, NY 10471. Telephone: 718-862-7200. Fax: 718-862-8019.

MANHATTAN SCHOOL OF MUSIC
NEW YORK, NEW YORK

Entrance Very difficult **General** Independent, comprehensive, specialized, coed **Setting** 1-acre urban campus **Enrollment** 862 **Faculty** 10:1 **Application deadline** 3/15 **Freshmen** 52% accepted **Housing** Yes **Tuition** $17,980 **Undergraduates** 50% women, 3% part-time, 20% 25 or older, 0% Native American, 3% Hispanic, 5% black, 9% Asian or Pacific Islander **Most popular recent majors** Voice, piano/organ, jazz **Academic program** Average class size 10, advanced placement, tutorials, summer session **Contact** Ms. Lee Cioppa, Director of Admission, Manhattan School of Music, 120 Claremont Avenue, New York, NY 10027-4698. Telephone: 212-749-2802 Ext. 2. Fax: 212-749-5471.

MANHATTANVILLE COLLEGE
PURCHASE, NEW YORK

Entrance Moderately difficult **General** Independent, comprehensive, coed **Setting** 100-acre suburban campus **Enrollment** 1,500 **Application deadline** 3/1 **Freshmen** 75% accepted **Housing** Yes **Tuition** $17,300 **Undergraduates** 67% women, 20% part-time, 4% 25 or older, 1% Native American, 15% Hispanic, 7% black, 7% Asian or Pacific Islander **Most popular recent majors** Economics, business administration/commerce/management, political science/government **Academic program** Advanced placement, accelerated degree program, self-designed majors, tutorials, honors program, summer session, adult/continuing education programs, internships **Contact** Mr. Jose Flores, Director of Admissions, Manhattanville College, Purchase, NY 10577-2132. Telephone: 914-323-5124. Fax: 914-694-1732.

MANNES COLLEGE OF MUSIC, NEW SCHOOL FOR SOCIAL RESEARCH
NEW YORK, NEW YORK

Entrance Very difficult **General** Independent, comprehensive, specialized, coed **Setting** Urban campus **Enrollment** 5,833 **Application deadline** 7/15 **Freshmen** 18% accepted **Housing** Yes **Tuition** $14,805 **Undergraduates** 49% women, 2% part-time, 8% 25 or older, 0% Native American, 3% Hispanic, 2% black, 4% Asian or Pacific Islander **Most popular recent majors** Stringed instruments, voice, piano/organ **Academic program** Accelerated degree program, summer session, adult/continuing education programs **Contact** Ms. Lisa Wright, Director of Admissions and Registration, Mannes College of Music, New School for Social Research, 150 West 85th Street, New York, NY 10024-4402. Telephone: 212-580-0210 Ext. 246. Fax: 212-580-1738.

MARIST COLLEGE
POUGHKEEPSIE, NEW YORK

Entrance Moderately difficult **General** Independent, comprehensive, coed **Setting** 120-acre small-town campus **Enrollment** 4,372 **Faculty** 15:1 **Application deadline** 3/1 **Freshmen** 65% accepted **Housing** Yes **Tuition** $13,098 **Undergraduates** 56% women, 14% part-time, 15% 25 or older, 0% Native American, 5% Hispanic, 5% black, 2% Asian or Pacific Islander **Most popular recent majors** Communication, business administration/commerce/management, psychology **Academic program** Advanced placement, accelerated degree program, tutorials, honors program, summer session, adult/continuing education programs, internships **Contact** Mr. Sean Kaylor, Associate Director of Admissions, Marist College, Poughkeepsie, NY 12601-1387. Telephone: 914-575-3226 Ext. 2441.

MARYMOUNT COLLEGE
TARRYTOWN, NEW YORK

Entrance Moderately difficult **General** Independent, 4-year, primarily women **Setting** 25-acre suburban campus **Enrollment** 947 **Faculty** 12:1 **Application deadline** 4/15 **Freshmen** 84% accepted **Housing** Yes **Tuition** $13,815 **Undergraduates** 94% women, 28% part-time, 47% 25 or older, 14% Hispanic, 16% black, 3% Asian or Pacific Islander **Most popular recent majors** Business administration/commerce/management, education, nutrition **Academic program** ESL program, Advanced placement, self-designed majors, tutorials, honors program, summer session, adult/continuing education programs, internships **Contact** Ms. Christine Richard, Dean of Admissions, Marymount College, 100 Marymount Avenue, Tarrytown, NY 10591-3796. Telephone: 914-332-8295. Fax: 914-332-4956.

MARYMOUNT MANHATTAN COLLEGE
NEW YORK, NEW YORK

Entrance Moderately difficult **General** Independent, 4-year, coed **Setting** 1-acre urban campus **Enrollment** 2,015 **Faculty** 17:1 **Application deadline** Rolling **Freshmen** 79% accepted **Housing** Yes **Tuition** $11,900 **Undergraduates** 82% women, 42% part-time, 45% 25 or older, 1% Native American, 16% Hispanic, 20% black, 7% Asian or Pacific Islander **Most popular recent majors** Business administration/commerce/management, theater arts/drama, psychology **Academic program** Advanced placement, accelerated degree program, tutorials, honors program, summer session, adult/continuing education programs, internships **Contact** Ms. Jocelyn Williams, Associate Director of Admissions, Marymount Manhattan College, 221 East 71st Street, New York, NY 10021. Telephone: 212-517-0555.

MEDAILLE COLLEGE

BUFFALO, NEW YORK

Entrance Minimally difficult **General** Independent, 4-year, coed **Setting** 13-acre urban campus **Enrollment** 878 **Faculty** 17:1 **Application deadline** Rolling **Freshmen** 67% accepted **Housing** Yes **Tuition** $10,470 **Undergraduates** 70% women, 25% part-time, 57% 25 or older, 1% Native American, 2% Hispanic, 14% black, 0% Asian or Pacific Islander **Most popular recent majors** Elementary education, veterinary technology, liberal arts/general studies **Academic program** Average class size 16, advanced placement, accelerated degree program, self-designed majors, tutorials, honors program, summer session, adult/continuing education programs, internships **Contact** Mrs. Jacqueline S. Matheny, Director of Enrollment Management, Medaille College, 18 Agassiz Circle, Buffalo, NY 14214-2695. Telephone: 716-884-3281 Ext. 204. Fax: 716-884-0291.

MEDGAR EVERS COLLEGE OF THE CITY UNIVERSITY OF NEW YORK

BROOKLYN, NEW YORK

Entrance Noncompetitive **General** State and locally supported, 4-year, coed **Setting** 1-acre urban campus **Enrollment** 5,402 **Application deadline** Rolling **Freshmen** 100% accepted **Tuition** $3282 **Undergraduates** 45% part-time, 72% 25 or older, 1% Native American, 2% Hispanic, 90% black, 2% Asian or Pacific Islander **Academic program** Advanced placement, honors program, summer session, adult/continuing education programs, internships **Contact** Ms. Jessica Celestine, Director of Admissions, Medgar Evers College of the City University of New York, 1650 Bedford Avenue, Brooklyn, NY 11225-2298. Telephone: 718-270-6021.

MERCY COLLEGE

DOBBS FERRY, NEW YORK

Entrance Noncompetitive **General** Independent, comprehensive, coed **Setting** 20-acre small-town campus **Enrollment** 7,364 **Faculty** 14:1 **Application deadline** Rolling **Freshmen** 90% accepted **Housing** Yes **Tuition** $7200 **Undergraduates** 70% women, 30% part-time, 58% 25 or older, 1% Native American, 19% Hispanic, 22% black, 6% Asian or Pacific Islander **Most popular recent majors** Business administration/commerce/management, computer science, behavioral sciences **Academic program** ESL program, Advanced placement, accelerated degree program, self-designed majors, honors program, summer session, adult/continuing education programs, internships **Contact** Ms. Joy Colelli, Dean for Admissions, Mercy College, Dobbs Ferry, NY 10522-1189. Telephone: 914-674-7600. Fax: 914-674-7382.

MOLLOY COLLEGE

ROCKVILLE CENTRE, NEW YORK

Entrance Moderately difficult **General** Independent, comprehensive, coed **Setting** 25-acre suburban campus **Enrollment** 2,346 **Faculty** 12:1 **Application deadline** Rolling **Freshmen** 77% accepted **Tuition** $10,304 **Undergraduates** 83% women, 18% part-time, 29% 25 or older, 1% Native American, 5% Hispanic, 13% black, 2% Asian or Pacific Islander **Most popular recent majors** Nursing, social work, psychology **Academic program** Average class size 30, advanced placement, tutorials, summer session, adult/continuing education programs, internships **Contact** Mr. Wayne F. James, Director of Admissions and Freshman Transfer Aid, Molloy College, Rockville Centre, NY 11571-5002. Telephone: 516-678-5000 Ext. 233.

MOUNT SAINT MARY COLLEGE

NEWBURGH, NEW YORK

Entrance Moderately difficult **General** Independent, comprehensive, coed **Setting** 72-acre suburban campus **Enrollment** 1,978 **Faculty** 16:1 **Application deadline** Rolling **Freshmen** 73% accepted **Housing** Yes **Tuition** $9480 **Undergraduates** 68% women, 30% part-time, 35% 25 or older, 0% Native American, 7% Hispanic, 8% black, 1% Asian or Pacific Islander **Most popular recent majors** Business administration/commerce/management, English, accounting **Academic program** Advanced placement, accelerated degree program, self-designed majors, tutorials, honors program, summer session, adult/continuing education programs, internships **Contact** Mr. J. Randall Ognibene, Director of Admissions, Mount Saint Mary College, Newburgh, NY 12550-3494. Telephone: 914-569-3248. Fax: 914-562-6762.

NAZARETH COLLEGE OF ROCHESTER
ROCHESTER, NEW YORK

Entrance Moderately difficult **General** Independent, comprehensive, coed **Setting** 75-acre suburban campus **Enrollment** 2,761 **Faculty** 14:1 **Application deadline** 3/1 **Freshmen** 79% accepted **Housing** Yes **Tuition** $12,966 **Undergraduates** 76% women, 24% part-time, 30% 25 or older, 1% Native American, 3% Hispanic, 4% black, 1% Asian or Pacific Islander **Most popular recent majors** Business administration/commerce/management, psychology, social work **Academic program** Advanced placement, accelerated degree program, honors program, summer session, adult/continuing education programs, internships **Contact** Mr. Thomas K. DaRin, Dean of Admissions, Nazareth College of Rochester, Rochester, NY 14618-3790. Telephone: 716-389-2860. Fax: 716-389-2826.

NEW SCHOOL BACHELOR OF ARTS, NEW SCHOOL FOR SOCIAL RESEARCH
NEW YORK, NEW YORK

Entrance Moderately difficult **General** Independent, upper-level, coed **Setting** Urban campus **Enrollment** 5,833 **Freshmen** 89% accepted **Housing** Yes **Tuition** $13,420 **Undergraduates** 66% women, 58% part-time, 70% 25 or older, 1% Native American, 6% Hispanic, 10% black, 3% Asian or Pacific Islander **Academic program** Advanced placement, self-designed majors, tutorials, summer session, adult/continuing education programs, internships **Contact** Ms. Gerianne Brusati, Director of Educational Advising and Admissions, New School Bachelor of Arts, New School for Social Research, 66 West 12th Street, New York, NY 10011-8603. Telephone: 212-229-5630.

NEW SCHOOL FOR SOCIAL RESEARCH, EUGENE LANG COLLEGE
SEE EUGENE LANG COLLEGE, NEW SCHOOL FOR SOCIAL RESEARCH

NEW SCHOOL FOR SOCIAL RESEARCH, MANNES COLLEGE OF MUSIC
SEE MANNES COLLEGE OF MUSIC, NEW SCHOOL FOR SOCIAL RESEARCH

NEW SCHOOL FOR SOCIAL RESEARCH, PARSONS SCHOOL OF DESIGN
SEE PARSONS SCHOOL OF DESIGN, NEW SCHOOL FOR SOCIAL RESEARCH

NEW YORK INSTITUTE OF TECHNOLOGY
OLD WESTBURY, NEW YORK

Entrance Moderately difficult **General** Independent, comprehensive, coed **Setting** 700-acre suburban campus **Enrollment** 9,396 **Faculty** 18:1 **Application deadline** Rolling **Freshmen** 78% accepted **Housing** Yes **Tuition** $10,630 **Undergraduates** 32% women, 32% part-time, 39% 25 or older, 9% Hispanic, 16% black, 10% Asian or Pacific Islander **Most popular recent majors** Architectural technologies, business administration/commerce/management, communication **Academic program** Average class size 25, advanced placement, accelerated degree program, tutorials, summer session, adult/continuing education programs, internships **Contact** Ms. Doreen Meyer, Director of Financial Aid, New York Institute of Technology, Old Westbury, NY 11568-8000. Telephone: 516-686-7680. Fax: 516-686-7613.

NEW YORK SCHOOL OF INTERIOR DESIGN
NEW YORK, NEW YORK

Entrance Moderately difficult **General** Independent, 4-year, specialized, coed **Setting** Urban campus **Enrollment** 695 **Freshmen** 85% accepted **Tuition** $12,800 **Undergraduates** 86% women, 70% part-time, 62% 25 or older, 1% Native American, 5% Hispanic, 5% black, 8% Asian or Pacific Islander **Academic program** Advanced placement, tutorials, summer session, adult/continuing education programs, internships **Contact** Ms. Jessica Aguayo, Admissions Associate, New York School of Interior Design, 170 East 70th Street, New York, NY 10021-5110. Telephone: 212-472-1500 Ext. 23. Fax: 212-472-3800.

NEW YORK STATE COLLEGE OF CERAMICS
SEE ALFRED UNIVERSITY

NEW YORK UNIVERSITY
NEW YORK, NEW YORK

Entrance Very difficult **General** Independent, coed **Setting** 28-acre urban campus **Enrollment** 36,056 **Faculty** 12:1 **Application deadline** 1/15 **Freshmen** 44% accepted **Housing** Yes **Tuition** $21,730 **Undergraduates** 59% women, 16% part-time, 0% Native American, 8% Hispanic, 10% black, 19% Asian or Pacific Islander **Most popular recent majors** Business administration/commerce/management, theater arts/drama, social science **Academic program** Average class size 25, advanced placement, self-designed majors, tutorials, honors program, summer session, adult/continuing education programs, internships **Contact** Director of Admissions, New York University, 22 Washington Square North, New York, NY 10012-1019. Telephone: 212-998-4500. Fax: 212-995-4902.

NIAGARA UNIVERSITY
NIAGARA FALLS, NEW YORK

Entrance Moderately difficult **General** Independent, comprehensive, coed **Setting** 160-acre suburban campus **Enrollment** 2,935 **Faculty** 15:1 **Application deadline** 8/1 **Freshmen** 81% accepted **Housing** Yes **Tuition** $12,890 **Undergraduates** 61% women, 12% part-time, 17% 25 or older, 1% Native American, 2% Hispanic, 5% black, 1% Asian or Pacific Islander **Most popular recent majors** Business administration/commerce/management, tourism and travel, social science **Academic program** Advanced placement, accelerated degree program, tutorials, honors program, summer session, adult/continuing education programs, internships **Contact** Mrs. Christine M. McDermott, Associate Director of Admissions, Niagara University, Niagara University, NY 14109. Telephone: 716-286-8700 Ext. 8715. Fax: 716-286-8733.

NYACK COLLEGE
NYACK, NEW YORK

Entrance Moderately difficult **General** Independent, comprehensive, coed, affiliated with The Christian and Missionary Alliance **Setting** 102-acre suburban campus **Enrollment** 1,312 **Application deadline** 9/11 **Freshmen** 74% accepted **Housing** Yes **Tuition** $11,100 **Undergraduates** 54% women, 7% part-time, 20% 25 or older, 0% Native American, 15% Hispanic, 16% black, 13% Asian or Pacific Islander **Most popular recent majors** Elementary education, psychology, business administration/commerce/management **Academic program** Average class size 45, advanced placement, summer session, adult/continuing education programs, internships **Contact** Mr. Miguel A. Sanchez, Director of Admissions, Nyack College, Nyack, NY 10960-3698. Telephone: 914-358-1710 Ext. 350. Fax: 914-358-3047.

PACE UNIVERSITY
NEW YORK, NEW YORK

Entrance Moderately difficult **General** Independent, coed **Enrollment** 11,915 **Faculty** 17:1 **Application deadline** 8/15 **Freshmen** 99% accepted **Housing** Yes **Tuition** $13,030 **Undergraduates** 62% women, 25% part-time, 29% 25 or older, 1% Native American, 11% Hispanic, 14% black, 13% Asian or Pacific Islander **Academic program** Advanced placement, accelerated degree program, tutorials, honors program, summer session, adult/continuing education programs, internships **Contact** Mr. Richard Alvarez, Director of Admission for New York City Campus, Pace University, New York, NY 10038. Telephone: 212-346-1225. Fax: 212-346-1040.

PACE UNIVERSITY, PLEASANTVILLE/BRIARCLIFF CAMPUS
SEE PACE UNIVERSITY (NEW YORK CITY)

PACE UNIVERSITY, WHITE PLAINS CAMPUS
SEE PACE UNIVERSITY (NEW YORK CITY)

PARSONS SCHOOL OF DESIGN, NEW SCHOOL FOR SOCIAL RESEARCH
NEW YORK, NEW YORK

Entrance Very difficult **General** Independent, comprehensive, specialized, coed **Setting** 2-acre urban campus **Enrollment** 5,833 **Faculty** 14:1 **Application deadline** Rolling **Freshmen** 49% accepted **Housing** Yes **Tuition** $18,540 **Undergraduates** 69% women, 5% part-time, 17% 25 or older, 0% Native American, 7% Hispanic, 3% black, 15% Asian or Pacific Islander **Most popular recent majors** Fashion design and technology, graphic arts, illustration **Academic program** Advanced placement, summer session, adult/continuing education programs, internships **Contact** Ms. Nadine M. Bourgeois, Director of Admissions, Parsons School of Design, New School for Social Research, 66 Fifth Avenue, New York, NY 10011-8878. Telephone: 212-229-8910. Fax: 212-229-8975.

POLYTECHNIC UNIVERSITY, BROOKLYN CAMPUS
BROOKLYN, NEW YORK

Entrance Very difficult **General** Independent, coed **Setting** 3-acre urban campus **Enrollment** 2,219 **Faculty** 14:1 **Application deadline** Rolling **Freshmen** 72% accepted **Housing** Yes **Tuition** $19,150 **Undergraduates** 19% women, 12% part-time, 19% 25 or older, 1% Native American, 9% Hispanic, 12% black, 32% Asian or Pacific Islander **Most popular recent majors** Electrical engineering, computer science, civil engineering **Academic program** Average class size 25, advanced placement, accelerated degree program, tutorials, honors program, summer session **Contact** Mr. Peter Grant Jordan, Dean of Admissions, Polytechnic University, Brooklyn Campus, Six Metrotech Center, Brooklyn, NY 11201-2990. Telephone: 718-260-3100. Fax: 718-260-3136.

POLYTECHNIC UNIVERSITY, FARMINGDALE CAMPUS

FARMINGDALE, NEW YORK

Entrance Very difficult **General** Independent, coed **Setting** 25-acre suburban campus **Enrollment** 697 **Faculty** 14:1 **Application deadline** Rolling **Freshmen** 83% accepted **Housing** Yes **Tuition** $19,150 **Undergraduates** 12% women, 10% part-time, 10% 25 or older, 0% Native American, 12% Hispanic, 6% black, 14% Asian or Pacific Islander **Most popular recent majors** Electrical engineering, mechanical engineering, civil engineering **Academic program** Average class size 25, advanced placement, accelerated degree program, tutorials, honors program, summer session **Contact** Mr. Steve Kerge, Associate Dean of Admissions, Long Island Center, Polytechnic University, Farmingdale Campus, Farmingdale, NY 11735-3995. Telephone: 516-755-4200. Fax: 516-755-4404.

PRACTICAL BIBLE COLLEGE

BIBLE SCHOOL PARK, NEW YORK

Entrance Minimally difficult **General** Independent-religious, 4-year, specialized, coed **Setting** 22-acre suburban campus **Enrollment** 240 **Faculty** 23:1 **Application deadline** Rolling **Freshmen** 95% accepted **Housing** Yes **Tuition** $5140 **Undergraduates** 42% women, 25% part-time, 39% 25 or older, 1% Native American, 1% Hispanic, 2% black, 1% Asian or Pacific Islander **Academic program** Advanced placement, tutorials, summer session, adult/continuing education programs, internships **Contact** Ms. Nannette Pettyjohn, Admissions Office Assistant, Practical Bible College, Bible School Park, NY 13737-0601. Telephone: 607-729-1581 Ext. 406. Fax: 607-729-2962.

PRATT INSTITUTE

BROOKLYN, NEW YORK

Entrance Moderately difficult **General** Independent, comprehensive, coed **Setting** 25-acre urban campus **Enrollment** 3,363 **Faculty** 10:1 **Application deadline** Rolling **Freshmen** 74% accepted **Housing** Yes **Tuition** $17,151 **Undergraduates** 44% women, 8% part-time, 27% 25 or older, 0% Native American, 9% Hispanic, 9% black, 12% Asian or Pacific Islander **Most popular recent majors** Architecture, art/fine arts **Academic program** Average class size 17, advanced placement, self-designed majors, summer session, internships **Contact** Mr. Joe Korevec, Associate Dean of Admissions, Pratt Institute, DeKalb Hall, 200 Willoughby Avenue, Brooklyn, NY 11205-3899. Telephone: 718-636-3669.

PURCHASE COLLEGE, STATE UNIVERSITY OF NEW YORK

PURCHASE, NEW YORK

Entrance Moderately difficult **General** State-supported, comprehensive, coed **Setting** 550-acre small-town campus **Enrollment** 2,396 **Faculty** 20:1 **Application deadline** Rolling **Freshmen** 54% accepted **Housing** Yes **Tuition** $3879 **Undergraduates** 58% women, 11% part-time, 21% 25 or older, 1% Native American, 10% Hispanic, 10% black, 4% Asian or Pacific Islander **Most popular recent majors** Art/fine arts, literature, liberal arts/general studies **Academic program** Advanced placement, self-designed majors, summer session, adult/continuing education programs, internships **Contact** Ms. Betsy Immergut, Director of Admissions, Purchase College, State University of New York, Purchase, NY 10577-1400. Telephone: 914-251-6300.

QUEENS COLLEGE OF THE CITY UNIVERSITY OF NEW YORK

FLUSHING, NEW YORK

Entrance Moderately difficult **General** State and locally supported, comprehensive, coed **Setting** 76-acre urban campus **Enrollment** 17,073 **Faculty** 19:1 **Application deadline** 1/15 **Freshmen** 61% accepted **Tuition** $3393 **Undergraduates** 61% women, 39% part-time, 25% 25 or older, 0% Native American, 15% Hispanic, 9% black, 16% Asian or Pacific Islander **Most popular recent majors** Accounting, communication, elementary education **Academic program** Advanced placement, accelerated degree program, self-designed majors, tutorials, honors program, summer session, adult/continuing education programs, internships **Contact** Admissions Office, Queens College of the City University of New York, 65-30 Kissena Boulevard, Flushing, NY 11367-1597. Telephone: 718-997-5600.

RABBINICAL ACADEMY MESIVTA RABBI CHAIM BERLIN

BROOKLYN, NEW YORK

Entrance Moderately difficult **General** Independent Jewish, comprehensive, specialized, men only **Enrollment** 375 **Freshmen** 100% accepted **Housing** Yes **Tuition** $4750 **Undergraduates** 0% black **Contact** Mr. Mayer Weinberger, Executive Administrator, Rabbinical Academy Mesivta Rabbi Chaim Berlin, Brooklyn, NY 11230-4715. Telephone: 718-377-0777.

REGENTS COLLEGE

SEE UNIVERSITY OF THE STATE OF NEW YORK, REGENTS COLLEGE

RENSSELAER POLYTECHNIC INSTITUTE

TROY, NEW YORK

Entrance Very difficult **General** Independent, coed **Setting** 260-acre suburban campus **Enrollment** 6,250 **Faculty** 12:1 **Application deadline** 1/1 **Freshmen** 82% accepted **Housing** Yes **Tuition** $20,600 **Undergraduates** 25% women, 0% part-time, 0% Native American, 4% Hispanic, 3% black, 14% Asian or Pacific Islander **Most popular recent majors** Mechanical engineering, electrical engineering, computer science **Academic program** Advanced placement, accelerated degree program, self-designed majors, tutorials, honors program, summer session, adult/continuing education programs, internships **Contact** Ms. Teresa Duffy, Dean of Admissions, Rensselaer Polytechnic Institute, Troy, NY 12180-3590. Telephone: 518-276-6216. Fax: 518-276-4072.

ROBERTS WESLEYAN COLLEGE

ROCHESTER, NEW YORK

Entrance Moderately difficult **General** Independent, comprehensive, coed, affiliated with Free Methodist Church of North America **Setting** 75-acre suburban campus **Enrollment** 1,337 **Faculty** 14:1 **Application deadline** Rolling **Freshmen** 89% accepted **Housing** Yes **Tuition** $12,400 **Undergraduates** 64% women, 10% part-time, 27% 25 or older, 1% Native American, 2% Hispanic, 4% black, 1% Asian or Pacific Islander **Most popular recent majors** Education, nursing, business administration/commerce/management **Academic program** Average class size 45, advanced placement, tutorials, honors program, summer session, adult/continuing education programs, internships **Contact** Miss Linda Kurtz, Director of Admissions, Roberts Wesleyan College, Rochester, NY 14624-1997. Telephone: 716-594-6400. Fax: 716-594-6371.

ROCHESTER INSTITUTE OF TECHNOLOGY

ROCHESTER, NEW YORK

Entrance Moderately difficult **General** Independent, comprehensive, coed **Setting** 1,300-acre suburban campus **Enrollment** 12,933 **Faculty** 13:1 **Application deadline** 7/1 **Freshmen** 76% accepted **Housing** Yes **Tuition** $16,359 **Undergraduates** 34% women, 25% part-time, 29% 25 or older, 1% Native American, 3% Hispanic, 5% black, 5% Asian or Pacific Islander **Most popular recent majors** Engineering (general), engineering technology, art/fine arts **Academic program** Advanced placement, self-designed majors, tutorials, summer session, adult/continuing education programs, internships **Contact** Mr. Daniel Shelley, Director of Admissions, Rochester Institute of Technology, Rochester, NY 14623-5604. Telephone: 716-475-6631. Fax: 716-475-7424.

RUSSELL SAGE COLLEGE

TROY, NEW YORK

Entrance Moderately difficult **General** Independent, 4-year, women only **Setting** 8-acre urban campus **Enrollment** 1,038 **Faculty** 12:1 **Application deadline** 8/1 **Freshmen** 96% accepted **Housing** Yes **Tuition** $14,230 **Undergraduates** 11% part-time, 23% 25 or older, 1% Native American, 3% Hispanic, 5% black, 2% Asian or Pacific Islander **Most popular recent majors** Physical therapy, nursing, occupational therapy **Academic program** Advanced placement, accelerated degree program, self-designed majors, honors program, summer session, adult/continuing education programs, internships **Contact** Ms. Lisa Carr-Tutt, Director of Admissions, Russell Sage College, 45 Ferry Street, Troy, NY 12180-4115. Telephone: 518-270-2217. Fax: 518-271-4545.

ST. BONAVENTURE UNIVERSITY

ST. BONAVENTURE, NEW YORK

Entrance Moderately difficult **General** Independent, comprehensive, coed, affiliated with Roman Catholic Church **Setting** 600-acre small-town campus **Enrollment** 2,723 **Faculty** 17:1 **Application deadline** 3/1 **Freshmen** 90% accepted **Housing** Yes **Tuition** $13,100 **Undergraduates** 52% women, 5% part-time, 4% 25 or older, 0% Native American, 1% Hispanic, 1% black, 1% Asian or Pacific Islander **Most popular recent majors** Accounting, elementary education, communication **Academic program** Advanced placement, accelerated degree program, self-designed majors, tutorials, honors program, summer session, internships **Contact** Mr. Alexander P. Nazemetz, Director of Admissions, St. Bonaventure University, St. Bonaventure, NY 14778-2284. Telephone: 716-375-2400. Fax: 716-375-2005.

ST. FRANCIS COLLEGE

BROOKLYN HEIGHTS, NEW YORK

Entrance Moderately difficult **General** Independent, 4-year, coed **Setting** 1-acre urban campus **Enrollment** 2,077 **Application deadline** Rolling **Freshmen** 84% accepted **Tuition** $7700 **Undergraduates** 60% women, 25% part-time, 24%

25 or older, 17% Hispanic, 24% black, 1% Asian or Pacific Islander **Most popular recent majors** Business administration/commerce/management, liberal arts/general studies, psychology **Academic program** Average class size 25, advanced placement, accelerated degree program, tutorials, honors program, summer session, adult/continuing education programs, internships **Contact** Br. George Larkin, OSF, Dean of Admissions, St. Francis College, 180 Remsen Street, Brooklyn Heights, NY 11201-4398. Telephone: 718-522-2300 Ext. 357. Fax: 718-522-1274.

ST. JOHN FISHER COLLEGE
ROCHESTER, NEW YORK

Entrance Moderately difficult **General** Independent, comprehensive, coed, affiliated with Roman Catholic Church **Setting** 125-acre suburban campus **Enrollment** 2,333 **Faculty** 15:1 **Application deadline** Rolling **Freshmen** 78% accepted **Housing** Yes **Tuition** $12,500 **Undergraduates** 58% women, 20% part-time, 28% 25 or older, 1% Native American, 2% Hispanic, 6% black, 3% Asian or Pacific Islander **Most popular recent majors** Business administration/commerce/management, psychology, accounting **Academic program** Advanced placement, accelerated degree program, self-designed majors, tutorials, honors program, summer session, adult/continuing education programs, internships **Contact** Mr. Gerry Rooney, Dean of Enrollment Management, St. John Fisher College, Rochester, NY 14618-3597. Telephone: 716-385-8064. Fax: 716-385-8386.

ST. JOHN'S UNIVERSITY
JAMAICA, NEW YORK

Entrance Moderately difficult **General** Independent, coed, affiliated with Roman Catholic Church **Setting** 96-acre urban campus **Enrollment** 16,804 **Faculty** 19:1 **Application deadline** Rolling **Freshmen** 87% accepted **Tuition** $12,230 **Undergraduates** 54% women, 29% part-time, 13% 25 or older, 1% Native American, 11% Hispanic, 11% black, 11% Asian or Pacific Islander **Most popular recent majors** Pharmacy/pharmaceutical sciences, accounting, criminal justice **Academic program** Advanced placement, accelerated degree program, tutorials, honors program, summer session, adult/continuing education programs, internships **Contact** Ms. Jeanne Umland, Associate Vice President and Executive Director of Admission, St. John's University, 8000 Utopia Parkway, Jamaica, NY 11439. Telephone: 718-990-6240.

ST. JOSEPH'S COLLEGE, NEW YORK
BROOKLYN, NEW YORK

Entrance Moderately difficult **General** Independent, 4-year, coed **Setting** Urban campus **Enrollment** 1,263 **Faculty** 12:1 **Application deadline** 8/15 **Freshmen** 59% accepted **Tuition** $8326 **Undergraduates** 77% women, 55% part-time, 72% 25 or older, 0% Native American, 8% Hispanic, 37% black, 4% Asian or Pacific Islander **Most popular recent majors** Health services administration, early childhood education **Academic program** Average class size 15, advanced placement, tutorials, honors program, summer session, adult/continuing education programs, internships **Contact** Ms. Elizabeth Hughes, Director of Admissions, St. Joseph's College, New York, 245 Clinton Avenue, Brooklyn, NY 11205-3688. Telephone: 718-636-6868.

ST. JOSEPH'S COLLEGE, SUFFOLK CAMPUS
PATCHOGUE, NEW YORK

Entrance Moderately difficult **General** Independent, comprehensive, coed **Setting** 28-acre small-town campus **Enrollment** 2,593 **Faculty** 13:1 **Application deadline** 8/15 **Freshmen** 74% accepted **Tuition** $8697 **Undergraduates** 70% women, 37% part-time, 49% 25 or older, 1% Native American, 9% Hispanic, 4% black, 1% Asian or Pacific Islander **Most popular recent majors** Elementary education, business administration/commerce/management, accounting **Academic program** Average class size 25, advanced placement, summer session, adult/continuing education programs, internships **Contact** Mrs. Marion E. Salgado, Director of Admissions, St. Joseph's College, Suffolk Campus, Patchogue, NY 11772-2399. Telephone: 516-447-3200 Ext. 3219. Fax: 516-654-1782.

ST. LAWRENCE UNIVERSITY
CANTON, NEW YORK

Entrance Very difficult **General** Independent, comprehensive, coed **Setting** 1,000-acre small-town campus **Enrollment** 2,096 **Faculty** 12:1 **Application deadline** 2/15 **Freshmen** 66% accepted **Housing** Yes **Tuition** $21,425 **Undergraduates** 50% women, 1% part-time, 2% 25 or older, 1% Native American, 2% Hispanic, 2% black, 2% Asian or Pacific Islander **Most popular recent majors** Psychology, economics, political science/government **Academic program** Average class size 15, advanced placement, accelerated degree program, self-designed majors, tutorials, honors program, summer session, internships **Con-**

tact Ms. Kathryn Mullaney, Chair, Admissions Management Team, St. Lawrence University, Canton, NY 13617-1455. Telephone: 315-379-5261. Fax: 315-379-5502.

ST. THOMAS AQUINAS COLLEGE
SPARKILL, NEW YORK

Entrance Moderately difficult **General** Independent, comprehensive, coed **Setting** 46-acre suburban campus **Enrollment** 2,100 **Faculty** 17:1 **Application deadline** Rolling **Freshmen** 71% accepted **Housing** Yes **Tuition** $10,400 **Undergraduates** 60% women, 30% part-time, 19% 25 or older, 1% Native American, 12% Hispanic, 6% black, 4% Asian or Pacific Islander **Most popular recent majors** Education, business administration/commerce/management, psychology **Academic program** Average class size 30, advanced placement, accelerated degree program, honors program, summer session, adult/continuing education programs, internships **Contact** Mr. Joseph L. Chillo, Director of Admissions, St. Thomas Aquinas College, Sparkill, NY 10976. Telephone: 914-398-4100.

SARAH LAWRENCE COLLEGE
BRONXVILLE, NEW YORK

Entrance Very difficult **General** Independent, comprehensive, coed **Setting** 40-acre suburban campus **Enrollment** 1,329 **Faculty** 6:1 **Application deadline** 2/1 **Freshmen** 54% accepted **Housing** Yes **Tuition** $23,076 **Undergraduates** 76% women, 7% part-time, 1% Native American, 5% Hispanic, 7% black, 4% Asian or Pacific Islander **Most popular recent majors** Literature, creative writing, theater arts/drama **Academic program** Advanced placement, self-designed majors, tutorials, adult/continuing education programs, internships **Contact** Mr. Robert M. Kinnally, Dean of Admissions, Sarah Lawrence College, Bronxville, NY 10708. Telephone: 914-395-2510. Fax: 914-395-2668.

SCHOOL OF VISUAL ARTS
NEW YORK, NEW YORK

Entrance Moderately difficult **General** Proprietary, comprehensive, coed **Setting** 1-acre urban campus **Enrollment** 3,047 **Faculty** 9:1 **Application deadline** Rolling **Freshmen** 70% accepted **Housing** Yes **Tuition** $13,890 **Undergraduates** 41% women, 12% part-time, 20% 25 or older, 9% Hispanic, 5% black, 8% Asian or Pacific Islander **Most popular recent majors** Illustration, graphic arts, photography **Academic program** Tutorials, summer session, adult/continuing education programs **Contact** Mr. Richard M. Longo III, Director of Admissions, School of Visual Arts, 209 East 23rd Street, New York, NY 10010-3994. Telephone: 212-592-2100. Fax: 212-725-3584.

SIENA COLLEGE
LOUDONVILLE, NEW YORK

Entrance Moderately difficult **General** Independent Roman Catholic, comprehensive, coed **Setting** 155-acre suburban campus **Enrollment** 3,212 **Faculty** 16:1 **Application deadline** 3/1 **Freshmen** 76% accepted **Housing** Yes **Tuition** $12,710 **Undergraduates** 54% women, 20% part-time, 17% 25 or older, 1% Native American, 2% Hispanic, 2% black, 2% Asian or Pacific Islander **Most popular recent majors** Accounting, marketing/retailing/merchandising, biology/biological sciences **Academic program** Average class size 22, advanced placement, tutorials, honors program, summer session, adult/continuing education programs, internships **Contact** Mr. Edward Jones, Director of Admissions, Siena College, Loudonville, NY 12211-1462. Telephone: 518-783-2423.

SKIDMORE COLLEGE
SARATOGA SPRINGS, NEW YORK

Entrance Very difficult **General** Independent, comprehensive, coed **Setting** 800-acre small-town campus **Enrollment** 2,244 **Faculty** 11:1 **Application deadline** 2/1 **Freshmen** 66% accepted **Housing** Yes **Tuition** $21,988 **Undergraduates** 60% women, 1% part-time, 0% 25 or older, 1% Native American, 5% Hispanic, 2% black, 4% Asian or Pacific Islander **Most popular recent majors** Business administration/commerce/management, English, psychology **Academic program** Advanced placement, accelerated degree program, self-designed majors, tutorials, summer session, internships **Contact** Ms. Mary Lou Bates, Director of Admissions, Skidmore College, Saratoga Springs, NY 12866-1632. Telephone: 518-584-5000 Ext. 2213. Fax: 518-581-7462.

SOUTHAMPTON CAMPUS OF LONG ISLAND UNIVERSITY
SEE LONG ISLAND UNIVERSITY, SOUTHAMPTON COLLEGE

STATE UNIVERSITY OF NEW YORK AT ALBANY
SEE UNIVERSITY AT ALBANY, STATE UNIVERSITY OF NEW YORK

STATE UNIVERSITY OF NEW YORK AT BINGHAMTON

BINGHAMTON, NEW YORK

Entrance Very difficult **General** State-supported, coed **Setting** 606-acre suburban campus **Enrollment** 11,976 **Faculty** 21:1 **Application deadline** 2/15 **Freshmen** 42% accepted **Housing** Yes **Tuition** $4101 **Undergraduates** 53% women, 5% part-time, 8% 25 or older, 1% Native American, 6% Hispanic, 5% black, 14% Asian or Pacific Islander **Most popular recent majors** English, psychology, biology/biological sciences **Academic program** Advanced placement, accelerated degree program, self-designed majors, tutorials, honors program, summer session, adult/continuing education programs, internships **Contact** Mr. Geoffrey D. Gould, Director of Admissions, State University of New York at Binghamton, PO Box 6001, Binghamton, NY 13902-6001. Telephone: 607-777-2171.

STATE UNIVERSITY OF NEW YORK AT BUFFALO

BUFFALO, NEW YORK

Entrance Very difficult **General** State-supported, coed **Setting** 1,350-acre suburban campus **Enrollment** 23,577 **Faculty** 13:1 **Application deadline** Rolling **Freshmen** 71% accepted **Housing** Yes **Tuition** $4340 **Undergraduates** 45% women, 15% part-time, 19% 25 or older, 1% Native American, 3% Hispanic, 7% black, 12% Asian or Pacific Islander **Most popular recent majors** Business administration/commerce/management, social science, psychology **Academic program** Average class size 24, advanced placement, self-designed majors, tutorials, honors program, summer session, adult/continuing education programs, internships **Contact** Mr. Kevin M. Durkin, Director of Admissions, State University of New York at Buffalo, Capen Hall, Room 17, North Campus, Buffalo, NY 14260-1660. Telephone: 716-645-6900. Fax: 716-645-6411.

STATE UNIVERSITY OF NEW YORK AT NEW PALTZ

NEW PALTZ, NEW YORK

Entrance Moderately difficult **General** State-supported, comprehensive, coed **Setting** 216-acre small-town campus **Enrollment** 7,539 **Faculty** 19:1 **Application deadline** 5/1 **Freshmen** 43% accepted **Housing** Yes **Tuition** $3885 **Undergraduates** 62% women, 22% part-time, 29% 25 or older, 1% Native American, 8% Hispanic, 7% black, 5% Asian or Pacific Islander **Most popular recent majors** Elementary education, psychology, business administration/commerce/management **Academic program** Average class size 25, advanced placement, accelerated degree program, self-designed majors, tutorials, honors program, summer session, adult/continuing education programs, internships **Contact** Mr. L. David Eaton, Dean of Admissions and Enrollment Management, State University of New York at New Paltz, New Paltz, NY 12561-2499. Telephone: 914-257-3200. Fax: 914-257-3209.

STATE UNIVERSITY OF NEW YORK AT OSWEGO

OSWEGO, NEW YORK

Entrance Moderately difficult **General** State-supported, comprehensive, coed **Setting** 696-acre small-town campus **Enrollment** 8,264 **Faculty** 22:1 **Application deadline** Rolling **Freshmen** 57% accepted **Housing** Yes **Tuition** $3945 **Undergraduates** 53% women, 15% part-time, 12% 25 or older, 1% Native American, 4% Hispanic, 4% black, 2% Asian or Pacific Islander **Most popular recent majors** Business administration/commerce/management, elementary education, communication **Academic program** Advanced placement, self-designed majors, tutorials, honors program, summer session, adult/continuing education programs, internships **Contact** Dr. Joseph F. Grant Jr., Vice President for Development, Enrollment, and Marketing, State University of New York at Oswego, Oswego, NY 13126. Telephone: 315-341-2250.

STATE UNIVERSITY OF NEW YORK AT STONY BROOK

STONY BROOK, NEW YORK

Entrance Very difficult **General** State-supported, coed **Setting** 1,100-acre small-town campus **Enrollment** 17,309 **Faculty** 17:1 **Application deadline** Rolling **Freshmen** 58% accepted **Housing** Yes **Tuition** $3932 **Undergraduates** 52% women, 11% part-time, 18% 25 or older, 0% Native American, 7% Hispanic, 10% black, 18% Asian or Pacific Islander **Most popular recent majors** Psychology, biology/biological sciences, business administration/commerce/management **Academic program** Advanced placement, self-designed majors, tutorials, honors program, summer session, adult/continuing education programs, internships **Contact** Mrs. Gigi Lamens, Director of Admissions, State University of New York at Stony Brook, Stony Brook, NY 11794. Telephone: 516-632-6868.

STATE UNIVERSITY OF NEW YORK COLLEGE AT BROCKPORT
BROCKPORT, NEW YORK

Entrance Moderately difficult **General** State-supported, comprehensive, coed **Setting** 591-acre small-town campus **Enrollment** 8,723 **Faculty** 21:1 **Application deadline** Rolling **Freshmen** 55% accepted **Housing** Yes **Tuition** $3940 **Undergraduates** 54% women, 18% part-time, 22% 25 or older, 1% Native American, 2% Hispanic, 7% black, 1% Asian or Pacific Islander **Most popular recent majors** Business administration/commerce/management, psychology, criminal justice **Academic program** Advanced placement, accelerated degree program, self-designed majors, honors program, summer session, adult/continuing education programs, internships **Contact** Mr. James R. Cook, Director of Admissions, State University of New York College at Brockport, 350 New Campus Drive, Brockport, NY 14420-2997. Telephone: 716-395-2751. Fax: 716-395-5397.

STATE UNIVERSITY OF NEW YORK COLLEGE AT BUFFALO
BUFFALO, NEW YORK

Entrance Moderately difficult **General** State-supported, comprehensive, coed **Setting** 115-acre urban campus **Enrollment** 11,184 **Faculty** 23:1 **Application deadline** Rolling **Freshmen** 60% accepted **Housing** Yes **Tuition** $3791 **Undergraduates** 56% women, 23% part-time, 29% 25 or older, 1% Native American, 3% Hispanic, 11% black, 2% Asian or Pacific Islander **Most popular recent majors** Business administration/commerce/management, elementary education, criminal justice **Academic program** Advanced placement, tutorials, honors program, summer session, adult/continuing education programs, internships **Contact** Director of Admissions, State University of New York College at Buffalo, 1300 Elmwood Avenue, Buffalo, NY 14222-1095. Telephone: 716-878-4017. Fax: 716-878-6100.

STATE UNIVERSITY OF NEW YORK COLLEGE AT CORTLAND
CORTLAND, NEW YORK

Entrance Moderately difficult **General** State-supported, comprehensive, coed **Setting** 191-acre small-town campus **Enrollment** 6,278 **Faculty** 20:1 **Application deadline** 12/1 **Freshmen** 57% accepted **Housing** Yes **Tuition** $3884 **Undergraduates** 55% women, 4% part-time, 9% 25 or older, 1% Native American, 3% Hispanic, 2% black, 1% Asian or Pacific Islander **Most popular recent majors** Elementary education, physical education, psychology **Academic program** Advanced placement, self-designed majors, tutorials, honors program, summer session, adult/continuing education programs, internships **Contact** Mr. Gradon Avery, Director of Admission, State University of New York College at Cortland, Cortland, NY 13045. Telephone: 607-753-4711. Fax: 607-753-5999.

STATE UNIVERSITY OF NEW YORK COLLEGE AT FREDONIA
FREDONIA, NEW YORK

Entrance Moderately difficult **General** State-supported, comprehensive, coed **Setting** 266-acre small-town campus **Enrollment** 4,556 **Faculty** 21:1 **Application deadline** Rolling **Freshmen** 64% accepted **Housing** Yes **Tuition** $4075 **Undergraduates** 56% women, 5% part-time, 8% 25 or older, 1% Native American, 2% Hispanic, 2% black, 1% Asian or Pacific Islander **Most popular recent majors** Business administration/commerce/management, elementary education, medical technology **Academic program** Advanced placement, accelerated degree program, self-designed majors, tutorials, honors program, summer session, adult/continuing education programs, internships **Contact** Mr. William S. Clark, Director of Admissions, State University of New York College at Fredonia, Fredonia, NY 14063. Telephone: 716-673-3251. Fax: 716-673-3249.

STATE UNIVERSITY OF NEW YORK COLLEGE AT GENESEO
GENESEO, NEW YORK

Entrance Very difficult **General** State-supported, comprehensive, coed **Setting** 220-acre small-town campus **Enrollment** 5,564 **Faculty** 19:1 **Application deadline** 2/15 **Freshmen** 56% accepted **Housing** Yes **Tuition** $4016 **Undergraduates** 64% women, 2% part-time, 4% 25 or older, 1% Native American, 3% Hispanic, 2% black, 6% Asian or Pacific Islander **Most popular recent majors** Education, biology/biological sciences, psychology **Academic program** Average class size 35, advanced placement, tutorials, honors program, summer session, internships **Contact** Mr. Scott Hooker, Interim Director of Admissions, State University of New York College at Geneseo, 1 College Circle, Geneseo, NY 14454-1401. Telephone: 716-245-5571. Fax: 716-245-5005.

STATE UNIVERSITY OF NEW YORK COLLEGE AT OLD WESTBURY
OLD WESTBURY, NEW YORK

Entrance Minimally difficult **General** State-supported, 4-year, coed **Setting** 605-acre suburban campus **Enrollment** 3,790 **Faculty** 16:1 **Application deadline** Rolling **Freshmen** 88% accepted **Housing** Yes **Tuition** $3731 **Undergraduates** 57% women, 26% part-time, 39% 25 or older, 1% Native American, 15% Hispanic, 29% black, 7% Asian or Pacific Islander **Academic program** Average class size 30, advanced placement, tutorials, summer session, internships **Contact** Ms. Olga Dunning, Assistant Director of Admissions, State University of New York College at Old Westbury, PO Box 210, Old Westbury, NY 11568-0210. Telephone: 516-876-3073. Fax: 516-876-3307.

STATE UNIVERSITY OF NEW YORK COLLEGE AT ONEONTA
ONEONTA, NEW YORK

Entrance Moderately difficult **General** State-supported, comprehensive, coed **Setting** 251-acre small-town campus **Enrollment** 5,616 **Faculty** 21:1 **Application deadline** 5/1 **Freshmen** 75% accepted **Housing** Yes **Tuition** $3908 **Undergraduates** 59% women, 8% part-time, 13% 25 or older, 4% Hispanic, 3% black, 1% Asian or Pacific Islander **Most popular recent majors** Education, business economics, psychology **Academic program** Advanced placement, tutorials, honors program, summer session, adult/continuing education programs, internships **Contact** Mr. Roger Sullivan, Director of Admissions, State University of New York College at Oneonta, Alumni Hall 116, Oneonta, NY 13820-4016. Telephone: 607-436-2524. Fax: 607-436-3074.

STATE UNIVERSITY OF NEW YORK COLLEGE AT PLATTSBURGH
PLATTSBURGH, NEW YORK

Entrance Moderately difficult **General** State-supported, comprehensive, coed **Setting** 265-acre small-town campus **Enrollment** 5,624 **Faculty** 21:1 **Application deadline** Rolling **Freshmen** 69% accepted **Housing** Yes **Tuition** $3845 **Undergraduates** 57% women, 5% part-time, 12% 25 or older, 1% Native American, 2% Hispanic, 3% black, 1% Asian or Pacific Islander **Most popular recent majors** Elementary education, nursing, psychology **Academic program** Advanced placement, self-designed majors, honors program, summer session, adult/continuing education programs, internships **Contact** Mr. Richard Higgins, Director of Admissions, State University of New York College at Plattsburgh, Plattsburgh, NY 12901. Telephone: 518-564-2040.

STATE UNIVERSITY OF NEW YORK COLLEGE AT POTSDAM
POTSDAM, NEW YORK

Entrance Moderately difficult **General** State-supported, comprehensive, coed **Setting** 240-acre small-town campus **Enrollment** 4,073 **Faculty** 20:1 **Application deadline** Rolling **Freshmen** 84% accepted **Housing** Yes **Tuition** $3899 **Undergraduates** 56% women, 6% part-time, 11% 25 or older, 1% Native American, 2% Hispanic, 2% black, 1% Asian or Pacific Islander **Most popular recent majors** Education, music education, psychology **Academic program** Average class size 20, advanced placement, self-designed majors, tutorials, honors program, summer session, adult/continuing education programs, internships **Contact** Ms. Karen O'Brien, Director of Admissions and Financial Aid, State University of New York College at Potsdam, Potsdam, NY 13676. Telephone: 315-267-2180. Fax: 315-267-2163.

STATE UNIVERSITY OF NEW YORK COLLEGE AT PURCHASE
SEE PURCHASE COLLEGE, STATE UNIVERSITY OF NEW YORK

STATE UNIVERSITY OF NEW YORK COLLEGE OF ENVIRONMENTAL SCIENCE AND FORESTRY
SYRACUSE, NEW YORK

Entrance Very difficult **General** State-supported, coed **Setting** 12-acre urban campus **Enrollment** 1,740 **Application deadline** Rolling **Freshmen** 37% accepted **Housing** Yes **Tuition** $3413 **Undergraduates** 37% women, 7% part-time, 26% 25 or older, 1% Native American, 2% Hispanic, 3% black, 2% Asian or Pacific Islander **Most popular recent majors** Environmental biology, environmental engineering, environmental sciences **Academic program** Advanced placement, honors program, adult/continuing education programs, internships **Contact** Ms. Susan Sanford, Associate Director of Admissions, State University of New York College of Environmental Science and Forestry, 1 Forestry Drive, Syracuse, NY 13210-2779. Telephone: 315-470-6600. Fax: 315-470-6933.

STATE UNIVERSITY OF NEW YORK EMPIRE STATE COLLEGE
SARATOGA SPRINGS, NEW YORK

Entrance Minimally difficult **General** State-supported, comprehensive, coed **Setting** Small-town campus **Enrollment** 7,123 **Faculty** 18:1 **Application deadline** Rolling **Freshmen** 95% accepted **Tuition** $3545 **Undergraduates** 56% women, 77% part-time, 80% 25 or older, 0% Native American, 5% Hispanic, 11% black, 1% Asian or Pacific Islander **Academic program** Advanced placement, self-designed majors, adult/continuing education programs **Contact** Dr. Martin Thorsland, Director of Admissions and Assessment, State University of New York Empire State College, Saratoga Springs, NY 12866-4391. Telephone: 518-587-2100 Ext. 223.

STATE UNIVERSITY OF NEW YORK HEALTH SCIENCE CENTER AT BROOKLYN
BROOKLYN, NEW YORK

Entrance Moderately difficult **General** State-supported, upper-level, specialized, coed **Setting** Urban campus **Enrollment** 1,604 **Freshmen** 18% accepted **Housing** Yes **Tuition** $3625 **Undergraduates** 84% women, 50% part-time, 46% 25 or older, 0% Native American, 3% Hispanic, 48% black, 3% Asian or Pacific Islander **Academic program** Summer session, adult/continuing education programs, internships **Contact** Ms. Liliana Montano, Director of Admissions, State University of New York Health Science Center at Brooklyn, 450 Clarkson Avenue, Brooklyn, NY 11203-2098. Telephone: 718-270-3013. Fax: 718-270-7592.

STATE UNIVERSITY OF NEW YORK HEALTH SCIENCE CENTER AT SYRACUSE
SYRACUSE, NEW YORK

Entrance Moderately difficult **General** State-supported, coed **Setting** 25-acre urban campus **Enrollment** 1,020 **Faculty** 7:1 **Application deadline** Rolling **Freshmen** 11% accepted **Housing** Yes **Tuition** $3710 **Undergraduates** 66% women, 4% part-time, 2% Native American, 4% Hispanic, 6% black, 4% Asian or Pacific Islander **Most popular recent majors** Respiratory therapy, physical therapy, radiological technology **Academic program** Advanced placement, summer session, internships **Contact** Mrs. Noreen Neitz, Assistant Director of Admissions, State University of New York Health Science Center at Syracuse, 750 East Adams Street, Syracuse, NY 13210-2334. Telephone: 315-464-4570. Fax: 315-464-8823.

STATE UNIVERSITY OF NEW YORK INSTITUTE OF TECHNOLOGY AT UTICA/ROME
UTICA, NEW YORK

Entrance Moderately difficult **General** State-supported, upper-level, coed **Setting** 800-acre suburban campus **Enrollment** 2,317 **Faculty** 19:1 **Freshmen** 82% accepted **Housing** Yes **Tuition** $3939 **Undergraduates** 51% women, 38% part-time, 60% 25 or older, 1% Native American, 2% Hispanic, 5% black, 2% Asian or Pacific Islander **Most popular recent majors** Business administration/commerce/management, nursing, telecommunications **Academic program** Average class size 30, advanced placement, honors program, summer session, adult/continuing education programs, internships **Contact** Mr. Donald Young, Director of Admissions, State University of New York Institute of Technology at Utica/Rome, Utica, NY 13504-3050. Telephone: 315-792-7500. Fax: 315-792-7837.

STATE UNIVERSITY OF NEW YORK MARITIME COLLEGE
THROGS NECK, NEW YORK

Entrance Moderately difficult **General** State-supported, comprehensive, coed **Setting** 56-acre suburban campus **Enrollment** 776 **Faculty** 14:1 **Application deadline** Rolling **Freshmen** 66% accepted **Housing** Yes **Tuition** $4005 **Undergraduates** 10% women, 4% part-time, 11% 25 or older, 1% Native American, 6% Hispanic, 6% black, 5% Asian or Pacific Islander **Most popular recent majors** Business administration/commerce/management, marine engineering, naval architecture **Academic program** Advanced placement, tutorials, summer session, adult/continuing education programs, internships **Contact** Mr. Peter Cooney, Director of Admissions and Financial Aid, State University of New York Maritime College, Throgs Neck, NY 10465. Telephone: 718-409-7220. Fax: 718-409-7392.

STERN COLLEGE FOR WOMEN
SEE YESHIVA UNIVERSITY

SYRACUSE UNIVERSITY
SYRACUSE, NEW YORK

Entrance Very difficult **General** Independent, coed **Setting** 200-acre urban campus **Enrollment** 14,719 **Faculty** 12:1 **Application deadline** 2/1 **Freshmen** 65% accepted **Housing** Yes **Tuition** $18,056 **Undergraduates** 52% women, 1% part-time, 3% 25 or older, 1% Native American,

5% Hispanic, 7% black, 5% Asian or Pacific Islander **Most popular recent majors** Computer information systems, psychology, architecture **Academic program** Average class size 18, advanced placement, accelerated degree program, self-designed majors, tutorials, honors program, summer session, adult/continuing education programs, internships **Contact** Office of Admissions, Syracuse University, 201 Tolley Administration Building, Syracuse, NY 13244-0003. Telephone: 315-443-3611.

SYRACUSE UNIVERSITY, UTICA COLLEGE

SEE UTICA COLLEGE OF SYRACUSE UNIVERSITY

TOURO COLLEGE

NEW YORK, NEW YORK

Entrance Moderately difficult **General** Independent, comprehensive, coed **Setting** Urban campus **Enrollment** 8,876 **Faculty** 11:1 **Application deadline** 5/15 **Freshmen** 64% accepted **Housing** Yes **Tuition** $8980 **Undergraduates** 73% women, 1% part-time, 51% 25 or older, 1% Native American, 14% Hispanic, 15% black, 5% Asian or Pacific Islander **Most popular recent majors** Liberal arts/general studies, business administration/commerce/management, education **Academic program** Advanced placement, accelerated degree program, self-designed majors, tutorials, honors program, summer session, internships **Contact** Ms. Amy Harrison, Director of Admissions, Touro College, 27-33 West 23rd Street, New York, NY 10010. Telephone: 212-463-0400. Fax: 212-779-2344.

UNION COLLEGE

SCHENECTADY, NEW YORK

Entrance Very difficult **General** Independent, comprehensive, coed **Setting** 100-acre suburban campus **Enrollment** 2,335 **Faculty** 11:1 **Application deadline** 2/1 **Freshmen** 55% accepted **Housing** Yes **Tuition** $22,135 **Undergraduates** 47% women, 2% part-time, 0% Native American, 3% Hispanic, 3% black, 6% Asian or Pacific Islander **Most popular recent majors** Psychology, economics, English **Academic program** Advanced placement, accelerated degree program, self-designed majors, tutorials, summer session, adult/continuing education programs **Contact** Mr. Daniel Lundquist, Vice President for Admissions and Financial Aid, Union College, Schenectady, NY 12308-2311. Telephone: 518-388-6112. Fax: 518-388-6986.

UNITED STATES MERCHANT MARINE ACADEMY

KINGS POINT, NEW YORK

Entrance Moderately difficult **General** Federally supported, 4-year, specialized, coed **Setting** 80-acre suburban campus **Enrollment** 950 **Faculty** 11:1 **Application deadline** 3/1 **Freshmen** 58% accepted **Housing** Yes **Tuition** $0 **Undergraduates** 12% women, 0% part-time, 0% 25 or older, 1% Native American, 4% Hispanic, 1% black, 4% Asian or Pacific Islander **Academic program** Tutorials, honors program, internships **Contact** Capt. James M. Skinner, USMS, Director of Admissions, United States Merchant Marine Academy, Kings Point, NY 11024-1699. Telephone: 516-773-5391. Fax: 516-773-5390.

UNITED STATES MILITARY ACADEMY

WEST POINT, NEW YORK

Entrance Most difficult **General** Federally supported, 4-year, coed **Setting** 16,080-acre small-town campus **Enrollment** 4,016 **Faculty** 8:1 **Application deadline** 3/21 **Freshmen** 12% accepted **Housing** Yes **Tuition** $0 **Undergraduates** 13% women, 0% part-time, 0% 25 or older, 1% Native American, 5% Hispanic, 7% black, 6% Asian or Pacific Islander **Most popular recent majors** Mechanical engineering, geography, civil engineering **Academic program** Average class size 15, advanced placement, tutorials, summer session **Contact** Col. Michael C. Jones, Director of Admissions, United States Military Academy, West Point, NY 10996. Telephone: 914-938-4041. Fax: 914-938-3021.

UNIVERSITY AT ALBANY, STATE UNIVERSITY OF NEW YORK

ALBANY, NEW YORK

Entrance Very difficult **General** State-supported, coed **Setting** 560-acre suburban campus **Enrollment** 14,215 **Faculty** 16:1 **Application deadline** Rolling **Freshmen** 65% accepted **Housing** Yes **Tuition** $4130 **Undergraduates** 48% women, 6% part-time, 9% 25 or older, 1% Native American, 7% Hispanic, 8% black, 9% Asian or Pacific Islander **Most popular recent majors** English, psychology, business administration/commerce/management **Academic program** Advanced placement, self-designed majors, tutorials, honors program, summer session, internships **Contact** Dr. Michelleen Treadwell, Director of Admissions, University at Albany, State University of New York, Albany, NY 12222-0001. Telephone: 518-442-5435.

UNIVERSITY OF ROCHESTER
ROCHESTER, NEW YORK

Entrance Very difficult **General** Independent, coed **Setting** 534-acre suburban campus **Enrollment** 8,172 **Faculty** 12:1 **Application deadline** 1/31 **Freshmen** 52% accepted **Housing** Yes **Tuition** $20,080 **Undergraduates** 50% women, 3% part-time, 0% Native American, 5% Hispanic, 8% black, 11% Asian or Pacific Islander **Most popular recent majors** Psychology, political science/government, economics **Academic program** Advanced placement, self-designed majors, honors program, summer session, internships **Contact** Mr. Wayne A. Locust, Director of Admissions, University of Rochester, Meliora Hall, Intercampus Drive, Rochester, NY 14627-0001. Telephone: 716-275-3221. Fax: 716-461-4595.

UNIVERSITY OF THE STATE OF NEW YORK, REGENTS COLLEGE
ALBANY, NEW YORK

Entrance Noncompetitive **General** Independent, 4-year, coed **Setting** Urban campus **Enrollment** 18,432 **Application deadline** Rolling **Undergraduates** 62% women, 100% part-time, 97% 25 or older, 1% Native American, 4% Hispanic, 12% black, 4% Asian or Pacific Islander **Most popular recent majors** Liberal arts/general studies, nursing, business administration/commerce/management **Academic program** Advanced placement, accelerated degree program, self-designed majors, adult/continuing education programs **Contact** Ms. Chari Leader, Dean of Enrollment Management, University of the State of New York, Regents College, 7 Columbia Circle, Albany, NY 12203-5159. Telephone: 518-464-8500. Fax: 518-464-8777.

UTICA COLLEGE OF SYRACUSE UNIVERSITY
UTICA, NEW YORK

Entrance Moderately difficult **General** Independent, 4-year, coed **Setting** 132-acre suburban campus **Enrollment** 1,748 **Faculty** 17:1 **Application deadline** Rolling **Freshmen** 85% accepted **Housing** Yes **Tuition** $14,912 **Undergraduates** 63% women, 17% part-time, 31% 25 or older, 0% Native American, 3% Hispanic, 7% black, 2% Asian or Pacific Islander **Most popular recent majors** Business administration/commerce/management, criminal justice, occupational therapy **Academic program** Average class size 25, advanced placement, accelerated degree program, tutorials, honors program, summer session, adult/continuing education programs, internships **Contact** Ms. Leslie North, Director of Admissions, Utica College of Syracuse University, Utica, NY 13502-4892. Telephone: 315-792-3006. Fax: 315-792-3292.

VASSAR COLLEGE
POUGHKEEPSIE, NEW YORK

Entrance Very difficult **General** Independent, comprehensive, coed **Setting** 1,000-acre suburban campus **Enrollment** 2,330 **Faculty** 11:1 **Application deadline** 1/1 **Freshmen** 48% accepted **Housing** Yes **Tuition** $22,090 **Undergraduates** 62% women, 3% part-time, 4% 25 or older, 1% Native American, 5% Hispanic, 5% black, 9% Asian or Pacific Islander **Most popular recent majors** English, political science/government, psychology **Academic program** Average class size 15, advanced placement, accelerated degree program, self-designed majors, internships **Contact** Mr. Lloyd Peterson, Director of Admissions, Vassar College, Poughkeepsie, NY 12604. Telephone: 914-437-7300. Fax: 914-437-7063.

WADHAMS HALL SEMINARY-COLLEGE
OGDENSBURG, NEW YORK

Entrance Minimally difficult **General** Independent Roman Catholic, 4-year, primarily men **Setting** 208-acre rural campus **Enrollment** 28 **Faculty** 2:1 **Application deadline** Rolling **Freshmen** 82% accepted **Housing** Yes **Tuition** $4900 **Undergraduates** 14% women, 4% part-time, 21% 25 or older, 0% Native American, 0% Hispanic, 0% black, 3% Asian or Pacific Islander **Academic program** Advanced placement **Contact** Rev. Donald A. Robinson, Director of Admissions and Recruitment, Wadhams Hall Seminary-College, Ogdensburg, NY 13669-9308. Telephone: 315-393-4231 Ext. 224. Fax: 315-393-4249.

WAGNER COLLEGE
STATEN ISLAND, NEW YORK

Entrance Moderately difficult **General** Independent, comprehensive, coed **Setting** 105-acre urban campus **Enrollment** 2,002 **Faculty** 16:1 **Application deadline** Rolling **Freshmen** 71% accepted **Housing** Yes **Tuition** $16,000 **Undergraduates** 60% women, 7% part-time, 6% 25 or older, 1% Native American, 5% Hispanic, 6% black, 3% Asian or Pacific Islander **Most popular recent majors** Business administration/commerce/management, nursing, biology/biological sciences **Academic program** Advanced placement, accelerated degree program, self-designed majors, tutorials, honors program, summer session, internships **Contact** Mr. Angelo Araimo, Director of Admissions, Wagner College, 631 Howard Avenue, Staten Island, NY 10301. Telephone: 718-390-3411. Fax: 718-390-3105.

WEBB INSTITUTE
GLEN COVE, NEW YORK

Entrance Most difficult **General** Independent, comprehensive, specialized, primarily men **Setting** 26-acre suburban campus **Enrollment** 93 **Faculty** 8:1 **Application deadline** 2/15 **Freshmen** 45% accepted **Housing** Yes **Tuition** $0 **Undergraduates** 14% women, 0% part-time, 0% 25 or older, 0% Native American, 0% Hispanic, 0% black, 2% Asian or Pacific Islander **Academic program** Average class size 21, internships **Contact** Mr. William G. Murray, Director of Admissions, Webb Institute, Glen Cove, NY 11542-1398. Telephone: 516-671-2213.

WELLS COLLEGE
AURORA, NEW YORK

Entrance Moderately difficult **General** Independent, 4-year, women only **Setting** 360-acre rural campus **Enrollment** 425 **Faculty** 8:1 **Application deadline** 2/15 **Freshmen** 90% accepted **Housing** Yes **Tuition** $17,540 **Undergraduates** 6% part-time, 11% 25 or older, 1% Native American, 5% Hispanic, 6% black, 8% Asian or Pacific Islander **Most popular recent majors** Psychology, English, biology/biological sciences **Academic program** Average class size 12, ESL program, advanced placement, accelerated degree program, self-designed majors, tutorials, adult/continuing education programs, internships **Contact** Ms. Susan Raith Sloan, Director of Admissions, Wells College, Aurora, NY 13026. Telephone: 315-364-3264. Fax: 315-364-3362.

WILLIAM SMITH COLLEGE
SEE HOBART AND WILLIAM SMITH COLLEGES

YESHIVA COLLEGE
SEE YESHIVA UNIVERSITY

YESHIVA KARLIN STOLIN
BROOKLYN, NEW YORK

Entrance Very difficult **General** Independent Jewish, comprehensive, specialized, men only **Setting** Urban campus **Enrollment** 53 **Application deadline** Rolling **Housing** Yes **Tuition** $4200 **Undergraduates** 0% part-time, 0% Hispanic, 0% black **Contact** Mr. Chaim Kugelman, Director of Admissions, Yeshiva Karlin Stolin, 1818 Fifty-fourth Street, Brooklyn, NY 11204. Telephone: 718-232-7800. Fax: 718-331-4833.

YESHIVA UNIVERSITY
NEW YORK, NEW YORK

Entrance Moderately difficult **General** Independent, coed **Setting** Urban campus **Enrollment** 5,246 **Faculty** 9:1 **Application deadline** 2/15 **Freshmen** 84% accepted **Housing** Yes **Tuition** $14,590 **Undergraduates** 43% women, 5% part-time, 1% 25 or older **Most popular recent majors** Psychology, biology/biological sciences, accounting **Academic program** Advanced placement, self-designed majors, tutorials, honors program, summer session, internships **Contact** Mr. Michael Kranzler, Director of Admissions, Yeshiva University, 500 West 185th Street, New York, NY 10033-3201. Telephone: 212-960-5400 Ext. 277. Fax: 212-960-0043.

YORK COLLEGE OF THE CITY UNIVERSITY OF NEW YORK
JAMAICA, NEW YORK

Entrance Noncompetitive **General** State and locally supported, 4-year, coed **Setting** 50-acre urban campus **Enrollment** 6,335 **Application deadline** Rolling **Freshmen** 100% accepted **Tuition** $3292 **Undergraduates** 69% women, 43% part-time, 2% Native American, 14% Hispanic, 52% black, 9% Asian or Pacific Islander **Most popular recent majors** Elementary education, business administration/commerce/management, mathematics **Academic program** Advanced placement, self-designed majors, tutorials, honors program, summer session, adult/continuing education programs, internships **Contact** Ms. Sally Nelson, Director of Admissions, York College of the City University of New York, 94-20 Guy R Brewer Boulevard, Jamaica, NY 11451-0001. Telephone: 718-262-2165.

Alabama

ALABAMA AGRICULTURAL AND MECHANICAL UNIVERSITY

NORMAL, ALABAMA

Entrance Minimally difficult **General** State-supported, coed **Setting** 2,001-acre suburban campus **Enrollment** 5,263 **Faculty** 11:1 **Application deadline** Rolling **Freshmen** 66% accepted **Housing** Yes **Tuition** $2168 **Undergraduates** 52% women, 9% part-time, 7% 25 or older, 91% black **Most popular recent majors** Business administration/commerce/management, computer science, elementary education **Academic program** Average class size 30, advanced placement, accelerated degree program, tutorials, honors program, summer session, adult/continuing education programs, internships **Contact** Mr. James Heyward, Director of Admissions, Alabama Agricultural and Mechanical University, PO Box 908, Normal, AL 35762-1357. Telephone: 205-851-5245. Fax: 205-851-9747.

ALABAMA STATE UNIVERSITY

MONTGOMERY, ALABAMA

Entrance Minimally difficult **General** State-supported, comprehensive, coed **Setting** 114-acre urban campus **Enrollment** 5,554 **Faculty** 19:1 **Application deadline** 8/26 **Freshmen** 68% accepted **Housing** Yes **Tuition** $2030 **Undergraduates** 57% women, 12% part-time, 11% 25 or older, 1% Hispanic, 93% black, 1% Asian or Pacific Islander **Most popular recent majors** Business administration/commerce/management, liberal arts/general studies, education **Academic program** Advanced placement, accelerated degree program, honors program, summer session, adult/continuing education programs, internships **Contact** Mr. Billy Brooks, Director of Admissions and Recruitment, Alabama State University, 915 South Jackson Street, Montgomery, AL 36101-0271. Telephone: 334-229-4291. Fax: 334-269-5879.

ATHENS STATE COLLEGE

ATHENS, ALABAMA

Entrance Noncompetitive **General** State-supported, upper-level, coed **Setting** 45-acre small-town campus **Enrollment** 2,800 **Faculty** 30:1 **Freshmen** 90% accepted **Housing** Yes **Tuition** $2145 **Undergraduates** 61% women, 55% part-time, 68% 25 or older, 1% Native American, 1% Hispanic, 7% black, 1% Asian or Pacific Islander **Most popular recent majors** Education, business administration/commerce/management, computer science **Academic program** Advanced placement, tutorials, summer session, adult/continuing education programs **Contact** Ms. Necedah Henderson, Coordinator of Admissions, Athens State College, Athens, AL 35611-1902. Telephone: 205-233-8217. Fax: 205-233-8164.

AUBURN UNIVERSITY

AUBURN, ALABAMA

Entrance Moderately difficult **General** State-supported, coed **Setting** 1,875-acre small-town campus **Enrollment** 21,778 **Faculty** 16:1 **Application deadline** 9/1 **Freshmen** 89% accepted **Housing** Yes **Tuition** $2565 **Undergraduates** 47% women, 8% part-time, 9% 25 or older, 1% Native American, 1% Hispanic, 6% black, 1% Asian or Pacific Islander **Most popular recent majors** Psychology, civil engineering, business administration/commerce/management **Academic program** Advanced placement, accelerated degree program, honors program, summer session, adult/continuing education programs, internships **Contact** Mr. John Fletcher, Interim Director of Admissions, Auburn University, 202 Mary Martin Hall, Auburn University, AL 36849-0001. Telephone: 334-844-4080.

AUBURN UNIVERSITY AT MONTGOMERY

MONTGOMERY, ALABAMA

Entrance Moderately difficult **General** State-supported, comprehensive, coed **Setting** 500-acre suburban campus **Enrollment** 5,645 **Application deadline** 9/1 **Freshmen** 92% accepted **Housing** Yes **Tuition** $2289 **Undergraduates** 61% women, 33% part-time, 30% 25 or older, 1% Native American, 1% Hispanic, 29% black, 2% Asian or Pacific Islander **Most popular recent majors** Elementary education, nursing, secondary education **Academic program** Average class size 22, advanced placement, accelerated degree program, self-designed majors, tutorials, honors program, summer session, adult/continuing education programs, internships **Contact** Mr. Lee Davis, Director of Admissions, Auburn University at Montgomery, Montgomery, AL 36117-3596. Telephone: 334-244-3611. Fax: 334-244-3762.

BIRMINGHAM-SOUTHERN COLLEGE

BIRMINGHAM, ALABAMA

Entrance Moderately difficult **General** Independent Methodist, comprehensive, coed **Setting** 185-acre urban campus **Enrollment** 1,492 **Faculty** 12:1 **Application deadline** 5/1 **Freshmen** 94% accepted **Housing** Yes **Tuition** $13,960 **Undergraduates** 57% women, 1% part-time, 13% 25 or older, 1% Native American, 1% Hispanic, 14%

black, 3% Asian or Pacific Islander **Most popular recent majors** Business administration/commerce/management, biology/biological sciences, English **Academic program** Average class size 22, advanced placement, accelerated degree program, self-designed majors, tutorials, honors program, summer session, adult/continuing education programs, internships **Contact** Ms. DeeDee Barnes Bruns, Dean of Admission and Financial Aid, Birmingham-Southern College, 900 Arkadelphia Road, Birmingham, AL 35254. Telephone: 205-226-4696. Fax: 205-226-4627.

CONCORDIA COLLEGE
SELMA, ALABAMA

Entrance Noncompetitive **General** Independent Lutheran, 4-year, coed **Setting** 22-acre small-town campus **Enrollment** 476 **Application deadline** 9/2 **Housing** Yes **Tuition** $4600 **Undergraduates** 85% women, 30% part-time, 40% 25 or older, 0% Native American, 0% Hispanic, 96% black **Academic program** Summer session, adult/continuing education programs **Contact** Ms. Gwendolyn Moore, Director of Enrollment Management, Concordia College, Selma, AL 36701. Telephone: 334-874-7143. Fax: 334-875-5755.

FAULKNER UNIVERSITY
MONTGOMERY, ALABAMA

Entrance Moderately difficult **General** Independent, comprehensive, coed, affiliated with Church of Christ **Setting** 75-acre urban campus **Enrollment** 2,376 **Faculty** 16:1 **Application deadline** Rolling **Freshmen** 64% accepted **Housing** Yes **Tuition** $7440 **Undergraduates** 49% women, 25% part-time, 42% 25 or older, 0% Native American, 1% Hispanic, 27% black, 1% Asian or Pacific Islander **Most popular recent majors** Business administration/commerce/management, elementary education, biblical studies **Academic program** Accelerated degree program, tutorials, summer session, adult/continuing education programs, internships **Contact** Mr. Keith Mock, Director of Admissions, Faulkner University, 5345 Atlanta Highway, Montgomery, AL 36109-3398. Telephone: 334-260-6200. Fax: 334-260-6137.

HUNTINGDON COLLEGE
MONTGOMERY, ALABAMA

Entrance Moderately difficult **General** Independent United Methodist, 4-year, coed **Setting** 58-acre suburban campus **Enrollment** 646 **Faculty** 12:1 **Application deadline** Rolling **Freshmen** 83% accepted **Housing** Yes **Tuition** $10,600 **Undergraduates** 60% women, 15% part-time, 12% 25 or older, 1% Native American, 1% Hispanic, 9% black, 1% Asian or Pacific Islander **Most popular recent majors** Business administration/commerce/management, history, psychology **Academic program** Average class size 14, advanced placement, accelerated degree program, self-designed majors, tutorials, honors program, summer session, adult/continuing education programs, internships **Contact** Ms. Suellen Ofe, Vice President of Enrollment Management, Huntingdon College, Montgomery, AL 36106-2148. Telephone: 334-833-4515. Fax: 334-833-4347.

INTERNATIONAL BIBLE COLLEGE
FLORENCE, ALABAMA

Entrance Noncompetitive **General** Independent, 4-year, specialized, coed, affiliated with Church of Christ **Setting** 46-acre small-town campus **Enrollment** 155 **Application deadline** Rolling **Freshmen** 100% accepted **Housing** Yes **Tuition** $5220 **Undergraduates** 36% women, 33% part-time, 68% 25 or older, 2% Native American, 0% Hispanic, 11% black, 0% Asian or Pacific Islander **Academic program** Accelerated degree program, tutorials, summer session, adult/continuing education programs, internships **Contact** Mr. Jim Collins, Director of Enrollment Services, International Bible College, Florence, AL 35630. Telephone: 205-766-6610 Ext. 26.

JACKSONVILLE STATE UNIVERSITY
JACKSONVILLE, ALABAMA

Entrance Minimally difficult **General** State-supported, comprehensive, coed **Setting** 345-acre small-town campus **Enrollment** 7,688 **Faculty** 21:1 **Application deadline** Rolling **Freshmen** 90% accepted **Housing** Yes **Tuition** $2040 **Undergraduates** 55% women, 19% part-time, 25% 25 or older, 0% Native American, 1% Hispanic, 16% black, 1% Asian or Pacific Islander **Most popular recent majors** Education, business administration/commerce/management, computer science **Academic program** Average class size 26, advanced placement, accelerated degree program, tutorials, honors program, summer session, adult/continuing education programs, internships **Contact** Dr. Jerry D. Smith, Dean of Admissions and Records, Jacksonville State University, Jacksonville, AL 36265-9982. Telephone: 205-782-5400. Fax: 205-782-5291.

JUDSON COLLEGE
MARION, ALABAMA

Entrance Moderately difficult **General** Independent Baptist, 4-year, women only **Setting** 80-acre rural campus **Enrollment** 331 **Faculty** 12:1 **Application deadline** Rolling **Freshmen** 78% accepted **Housing** Yes **Tuition** $6700 **Undergraduates** 20% part-time, 20% 25 or older, 0% Native American, 1% Hispanic, 13% black, 0% Asian or Pacific Islander **Most popular recent majors** Biology/biological sciences, education, (pre)medicine sequence **Academic program** Average class size 30, advanced placement, accelerated degree program, tutorials, honors program, summer session, adult/continuing education programs, internships **Contact** Mrs. Charlotte Clements, Director of Admissions, Judson College, PO Box 120, Marion, AL 36756. Telephone: 334-683-5110. Fax: 334-683-5158.

LIVINGSTON UNIVERSITY

SEE UNIVERSITY OF WEST ALABAMA

MILES COLLEGE

BIRMINGHAM, ALABAMA

Entrance Noncompetitive **General** Independent Christian Methodist Episcopal, 4-year, coed **Setting** 35-acre small-town campus **Enrollment** 1,234 **Faculty** 21:1 **Application deadline** Rolling **Freshmen** 100% accepted **Housing** Yes **Tuition** $4150 **Undergraduates** 52% women, 11% part-time, 9% 25 or older, 0% Native American, 1% Hispanic, 99% black, 0% Asian or Pacific Islander **Most popular recent majors** Business administration/commerce/management, elementary education, humanities **Academic program** Accelerated degree program, tutorials, honors program, summer session, adult/continuing education programs, internships **Contact** Ms. Brenda Grant-Smith, Director of Admissions and Recruitment, Miles College, Birmingham, AL 35208. Telephone: 205-929-1657.

OAKWOOD COLLEGE

HUNTSVILLE, ALABAMA

Entrance Minimally difficult **General** Independent Seventh-day Adventist, 4-year, coed **Setting** 1,200-acre campus **Enrollment** 1,666 **Faculty** 12:1 **Application deadline** Rolling **Freshmen** 82% accepted **Housing** Yes **Tuition** $7628 **Undergraduates** 59% women, 16% part-time, 18% 25 or older, 1% Native American, 1% Hispanic, 85% black **Most popular recent majors** Psychology, social work, nursing **Academic program** Average class size 35, advanced placement, accelerated degree program **Contact** Mr. Robert Edwards, Director of Enrollment Management, Oakwood College, Oakwood Road, NW, Huntsville, AL 35810. Telephone: 205-726-7354.

SAMFORD UNIVERSITY

BIRMINGHAM, ALABAMA

Entrance Moderately difficult **General** Independent Baptist, coed **Setting** 280-acre suburban campus **Enrollment** 4,473 **Faculty** 17:1 **Application deadline** Rolling **Freshmen** 88% accepted **Housing** Yes **Tuition** $9432 **Undergraduates** 61% women, 12% part-time, 11% 25 or older, 0% Native American, 1% Hispanic, 5% black, 1% Asian or Pacific Islander **Most popular recent majors** Liberal arts/general studies, business administration/commerce/management **Academic program** Advanced placement, accelerated degree program, self-designed majors, summer session, adult/continuing education programs, internships **Contact** Dr. Don Belcher, Dean of Admissions and Financial Aid, Samford University, Birmingham, AL 35229-0002. Telephone: 205-870-2901. Fax: 205-870-2171.

SOUTHEASTERN BIBLE COLLEGE

BIRMINGHAM, ALABAMA

Entrance Moderately difficult **General** Independent nondenominational, 4-year, coed **Setting** 10-acre suburban campus **Enrollment** 191 **Faculty** 17:1 **Application deadline** Rolling **Freshmen** 88% accepted **Housing** Yes **Tuition** $5040 **Undergraduates** 35% women, 24% part-time, 38% 25 or older, 0% Native American, 0% Hispanic, 10% black, 1% Asian or Pacific Islander **Academic program** Advanced placement, tutorials, summer session, adult/continuing education programs, internships **Contact** Mrs. Jean Judge, Registrar, Southeastern Bible College, Birmingham, AL 35243-4181. Telephone: 205-969-0880 Ext. 208.

SOUTHERN CHRISTIAN UNIVERSITY

MONTGOMERY, ALABAMA

Entrance Minimally difficult **General** Independent, comprehensive, specialized, primarily men, affiliated with Church of Christ **Setting** 9-acre urban campus **Enrollment** 188 **Faculty** 6:1 **Tuition** $7026 **Undergraduates** 10% women, 90% 25 or older, 24% black **Contact** Mr. Mac Adkins, Director of Admissions, Southern Christian University, 1200 Taylor Road, Montgomery, AL 36117. Telephone: 334-277-2277.

SPRING HILL COLLEGE

MOBILE, ALABAMA

Entrance Moderately difficult **General** Independent Roman Catholic (Jesuit), comprehensive, coed **Setting** 500-acre suburban campus **Enrollment** 1,445 **Faculty** 15:1 **Application deadline**

Rolling **Freshmen** 90% accepted **Housing** Yes **Tuition** $13,860 **Undergraduates** 59% women, 23% part-time, 12% 25 or older, 1% Native American, 3% Hispanic, 10% black, 2% Asian or Pacific Islander **Most popular recent majors** Psychology, public relations, business administration/commerce/management **Academic program** Advanced placement, accelerated degree program, self-designed majors, honors program, summer session, adult/continuing education programs, internships **Contact** Mr. Steven Pochard, Dean of Enrollment Management, Spring Hill College, Mobile, AL 36608-1791. Telephone: 334-380-3030. Fax: 334-460-2186.

STILLMAN COLLEGE
TUSCALOOSA, ALABAMA

Entrance Minimally difficult **General** Independent, 4-year, coed, affiliated with Presbyterian Church (U.S.A.) **Setting** 100-acre urban campus **Enrollment** 842 **Faculty** 12:1 **Application deadline** Rolling **Freshmen** 77% accepted **Housing** Yes **Tuition** $5460 **Undergraduates** 67% women, 3% part-time, 6% 25 or older, 0% Native American, 0% Hispanic, 99% black, 0% Asian or Pacific Islander **Most popular recent majors** Business administration/commerce/management, education, biology/biological sciences **Academic program** Advanced placement, accelerated degree program, honors program, summer session, internships **Contact** Mr. Mason Bonner, Enrollment Management Coordinator, Stillman College, PO Drawer 1430, Tuscaloosa, AL 35403-9990. Telephone: 205-366-8817. Fax: 205-366-8996.

TALLADEGA COLLEGE
TALLADEGA, ALABAMA

Entrance Minimally difficult **General** Independent, 4-year, coed **Setting** 135-acre small-town campus **Enrollment** 642 **Faculty** 9:1 **Application deadline** Rolling **Freshmen** 38% accepted **Housing** Yes **Tuition** $5949 **Undergraduates** 65% women, 4% part-time, 5% 25 or older, 0% Native American, 0% Hispanic, 99% black, 0% Asian or Pacific Islander **Most popular recent majors** Biology/biological sciences, business administration/commerce/management, psychology **Academic program** Average class size 36, accelerated degree program, tutorials, honors program, adult/continuing education programs, internships **Contact** Mrs. Floretta J. Dortch, Associate Dean of Enrollment Management, Talladega College, Talladega, AL 35160. Telephone: 205-761-6341. or Telephone: 205-761-6526. Fax: 205-362-2268.

TROY STATE UNIVERSITY
TROY, ALABAMA

Entrance Moderately difficult **General** State-supported, comprehensive, coed **Setting** 500-acre small-town campus **Enrollment** 6,211 **Faculty** 22:1 **Application deadline** Rolling **Freshmen** 78% accepted **Housing** Yes **Tuition** $2175 **Undergraduates** 62% women, 25% part-time, 1% Native American, 1% Hispanic, 20% black, 1% Asian or Pacific Islander **Most popular recent majors** Education, business administration/commerce/management, nursing **Academic program** Advanced placement, accelerated degree program, self-designed majors, honors program, summer session, adult/continuing education programs, internships **Contact** Mr. Jim Hutto, Dean of Enrollment Services, Troy State University, Troy, AL 36082. Telephone: 334-670-3179. Fax: 334-670-3815.

TROY STATE UNIVERSITY DOTHAN
DOTHAN, ALABAMA

Entrance Minimally difficult **General** State-supported, comprehensive, coed **Setting** 250-acre small-town campus **Enrollment** 2,150 **Application deadline** Rolling **Freshmen** 61% accepted **Tuition** $2229 **Undergraduates** 56% women, 58% part-time, 85% 25 or older, 1% Native American, 3% Hispanic, 12% black, 1% Asian or Pacific Islander **Most popular recent majors** Business administration/commerce/management, education, psychology **Academic program** Advanced placement, accelerated degree program, summer session, internships **Contact** Mr. Bob Willis, Director of Admissions, Troy State University Dothan, Dothan, AL 36304-0368. Telephone: 334-983-6556 Ext. 231. Fax: 334-983-6322.

TROY STATE UNIVERSITY MONTGOMERY
MONTGOMERY, ALABAMA

Entrance Noncompetitive **General** State-supported, comprehensive, coed **Setting** Urban campus **Enrollment** 3,360 **Application deadline** Rolling **Freshmen** 94% accepted **Tuition** $2085 **Undergraduates** 59% women, 77% part-time, 70% 25 or older, 0% Native American, 3% Hispanic, 31% black, 1% Asian or Pacific Islander **Most popular recent majors** Computer science, liberal arts/general studies, business administration/commerce/management **Academic program** ESL program, Advanced placement, accelerated degree program, self-designed majors, honors program, summer session, adult/continuing education programs **Contact** Mr. Frank Hrabe, Director of Enrollment Management, Troy State University Montgomery, PO Drawer 4419, Montgomery, AL 36103-4419. Telephone: 334-241-9506.

TUSKEGEE UNIVERSITY
TUSKEGEE, ALABAMA

Entrance Moderately difficult **General** Independent, comprehensive, coed **Setting** 4,390-acre small-town campus **Enrollment** 3,124 **Faculty** 12:1 **Application deadline** 4/15 **Freshmen** 79% accepted **Housing** Yes **Tuition** $8020 **Undergraduates** 58% women, 5% part-time, 1% 25 or older, 3% Hispanic, 92% black **Most popular recent majors** Electrical engineering, business administration/commerce/management, (pre)veterinary medicine sequence **Academic program** Honors program, summer session, internships **Contact** Ms. Carolyn Tippett, Acting Director of Admissions, Tuskegee University, Carnegie Hall, Tuskegee, AL 36088. Telephone: 334-727-8500.

THE UNIVERSITY OF ALABAMA
TUSCALOOSA, ALABAMA

Entrance Moderately difficult **General** State-supported, coed **Setting** 1,000-acre suburban campus **Enrollment** 17,565 **Faculty** 19:1 **Application deadline** 6/1 **Freshmen** 77% accepted **Housing** Yes **Tuition** $2570 **Undergraduates** 53% women, 11% part-time, 6% 25 or older, 1% Native American, 1% Hispanic, 12% black, 1% Asian or Pacific Islander **Most popular recent majors** Marketing/retailing/merchandising, elementary education, accounting **Academic program** Average class size 31, ESL program, advanced placement, accelerated degree program, self-designed majors, tutorials, honors program, summer session, adult/continuing education programs, internships **Contact** Dr. Randall W. Dahl, Director of Admissions, Records and Testing, The University of Alabama, Tuscaloosa, AL 35487. Telephone: 205-348-5666. Fax: 205-348-9046.

THE UNIVERSITY OF ALABAMA AT BIRMINGHAM
BIRMINGHAM, ALABAMA

Entrance Moderately difficult **General** State-supported, coed **Setting** 265-acre urban campus **Enrollment** 15,274 **Faculty** 17:1 **Application deadline** 8/1 **Freshmen** 88% accepted **Housing** Yes **Tuition** $2945 **Undergraduates** 56% women, 37% part-time, 37% 25 or older, 0% Native American, 1% Hispanic, 25% black, 3% Asian or Pacific Islander **Most popular recent majors** Nursing, psychology, biology/biological sciences **Academic program** Advanced placement, accelerated degree program, self-designed majors, tutorials, honors program, summer session, adult/continuing education programs, internships **Contact** Ms. Wendy Troxel, Director of Admissions, The University of Alabama at Birmingham, UAB Station, Birmingham, AL 35294. Telephone: 205-934-8221.

THE UNIVERSITY OF ALABAMA IN HUNTSVILLE
HUNTSVILLE, ALABAMA

Entrance Moderately difficult **General** State-supported, coed **Setting** 337-acre suburban campus **Enrollment** 4,982 **Faculty** 10:1 **Application deadline** 8/15 **Freshmen** 71% accepted **Housing** Yes **Tuition** $2948 **Undergraduates** 51% women, 37% part-time, 34% 25 or older, 2% Native American, 2% Hispanic, 14% black, 4% Asian or Pacific Islander **Most popular recent majors** Nursing, electrical engineering, mechanical engineering **Academic program** Advanced placement, honors program, summer session, adult/continuing education programs, internships **Contact** Ms. Sabrina Williams, Associate Director, Admissions, The University of Alabama in Huntsville, Enrollment Services, Huntsville, AL 35899. Telephone: 205-890-6070. Fax: 205-890-6073.

UNIVERSITY OF MOBILE
MOBILE, ALABAMA

Entrance Moderately difficult **General** Independent Southern Baptist, comprehensive, coed **Setting** 830-acre suburban campus **Enrollment** 2,241 **Faculty** 22:1 **Application deadline** Rolling **Freshmen** 82% accepted **Housing** Yes **Tuition** $7736 **Undergraduates** 65% women, 17% part-time, 30% 25 or older, 1% Native American, 1% Hispanic, 17% black, 1% Asian or Pacific Islander **Most popular recent majors** Nursing, elementary education **Academic program** Average class size 35, advanced placement, accelerated degree program, honors program, summer session, adult/continuing education programs, internships **Contact** Mrs. Kim Leousis, Director of Admissions, University of Mobile, Mobile, AL 36663-0220. Telephone: 334-675-5990 Ext. 290. Fax: 334-675-5446.

UNIVERSITY OF MONTEVALLO
MONTEVALLO, ALABAMA

Entrance Moderately difficult **General** State-supported, comprehensive, coed **Setting** 106-acre small-town campus **Enrollment** 3,206 **Faculty** 19:1 **Application deadline** 8/1 **Freshmen** 76% accepted **Housing** Yes **Tuition** $3180 **Un-**

dergraduates 68% women, 12% part-time, 12% 25 or older, 1% Native American, 0% Hispanic, 11% black, 0% Asian or Pacific Islander **Most popular recent majors** Elementary education, speech pathology and audiology, communication **Academic program** Advanced placement, honors program, summer session, internships **Contact** Mr. Robert A. Doyle, Director of Admissions, University of Montevallo, Montevallo, AL 35115. Telephone: 205-665-6030.

UNIVERSITY OF NORTH ALABAMA
FLORENCE, ALABAMA

Entrance Minimally difficult **General** State-supported, comprehensive, coed **Setting** 125-acre urban campus **Enrollment** 5,529 **Faculty** 23:1 **Application deadline** Rolling **Freshmen** 76% accepted **Housing** Yes **Tuition** $2166 **Undergraduates** 57% women, 15% part-time, 22% 25 or older, 2% Native American, 1% Hispanic, 8% black, 1% Asian or Pacific Islander **Most popular recent majors** Nursing, secondary education, elementary education **Academic program** Advanced placement, tutorials, summer session, adult/continuing education programs **Contact** Mrs. Kim Mauldin, Director of Admissions, University of North Alabama, University Station, Florence, AL 35632-0001. Telephone: 205-760-4680. Fax: 205-760-4644.

UNIVERSITY OF SOUTH ALABAMA
MOBILE, ALABAMA

Entrance Moderately difficult **General** State-supported, coed **Setting** 1,215-acre suburban campus **Enrollment** 12,041 **Faculty** 16:1 **Application deadline** 9/10 **Freshmen** 93% accepted **Housing** Yes **Tuition** $2838 **Undergraduates** 55% women, 27% part-time, 1% Native American, 1% Hispanic, 11% black, 3% Asian or Pacific Islander **Most popular recent majors** Nursing, liberal arts/general studies, finance/banking **Academic program** Advanced placement, accelerated degree program, self-designed majors, summer session, adult/continuing education programs, internships **Contact** Ms. Catherine P. King, Director of Admissions, University of South Alabama, Mobile, AL 36688-0002. Telephone: 334-460-6141. Fax: 334-460-7023.

THE UNIVERSITY OF WEST ALABAMA
LIVINGSTON, ALABAMA

Entrance Minimally difficult **General** State-supported, comprehensive, coed **Setting** 595-acre small-town campus **Enrollment** 2,153 **Faculty** 18:1 **Application deadline** Rolling **Freshmen** 76% accepted **Housing** Yes **Tuition** $2370 **Undergraduates** 56% women, 12% part-time, 22% 25 or older, 1% Native American, 1% Hispanic, 34% black, 1% Asian or Pacific Islander **Most popular recent majors** Elementary education, business administration/commerce/management, physical education **Academic program** Advanced placement, accelerated degree program, honors program, summer session, internships **Contact** Dr. Ervin L. Wood, Dean of Students, The University of West Alabama, Livingston, AL 35470. Telephone: 205-652-9661 Ext. 352.

Arkansas

ARKANSAS STATE UNIVERSITY
JONESBORO, ARKANSAS

Entrance Moderately difficult **General** State-supported, comprehensive, coed **Setting** 800-acre small-town campus **Enrollment** 9,828 **Faculty** 23:1 **Application deadline** Rolling **Freshmen** 87% accepted **Housing** Yes **Tuition** $2290 **Undergraduates** 57% women, 18% part-time, 24% 25 or older, 0% Native American, 1% Hispanic, 10% black, 1% Asian or Pacific Islander **Most popular recent majors** Elementary education, accounting, business administration/commerce/management **Academic program** Average class size 40, advanced placement, accelerated degree program, self-designed majors, tutorials, honors program, summer session, adult/continuing education programs, internships **Contact** Ms. Paula James, Director of Admissions, Arkansas State University, P.O. Box 1630, State University, AR 72467. Telephone: 501-972-3024. Fax: 501-972-3843.

ARKANSAS TECH UNIVERSITY
RUSSELLVILLE, ARKANSAS

Entrance Minimally difficult **General** State-supported, comprehensive, coed **Setting** 517-acre small-town campus **Enrollment** 4,490 **Faculty** 18:1 **Application deadline** 9/15 **Freshmen** 96% accepted **Housing** Yes **Tuition** $2126 **Undergraduates** 57% women, 24% part-time, 28% 25 or older, 1% Native American, 1% Hispanic, 3% black, 1% Asian or Pacific Islander **Most popular recent majors** Elementary education, business administration/commerce/management, nursing **Academic program** Advanced placement, accelerated degree program, tutorials, honors program, summer session, adult/continuing education programs, internships **Contact** Mr. Harold Cornett, Director of Admissions, Arkansas Tech University, Alumni House, Russellville, AR 72801-2222. Telephone: 501-968-0343.

CENTRAL BAPTIST COLLEGE

CONWAY, ARKANSAS

Entrance Minimally difficult **General** Independent Baptist, 4-year, coed **Setting** 11-acre small-town campus **Enrollment** 283 **Faculty** 16:1 **Application deadline** 8/15 **Freshmen** 87% accepted **Housing** Yes **Tuition** $4544 **Undergraduates** 46% women, 12% part-time, 14% 25 or older, 0% Native American, 0% Hispanic, 4% black, 0% Asian or Pacific Islander **Most popular recent majors** Biblical studies, music, religious education **Academic program** Advanced placement, summer session, internships **Contact** Mr. Gary McAllister, Registrar, Central Baptist College, Conway, AR 72032-6470. Telephone: 501-329-6872 Ext. 106.

HARDING UNIVERSITY

SEARCY, ARKANSAS

Entrance Very difficult **General** Independent, comprehensive, coed, affiliated with Church of Christ **Setting** 200-acre small-town campus **Enrollment** 4,081 **Faculty** 16:1 **Application deadline** 7/1 **Freshmen** 64% accepted **Housing** Yes **Tuition** $7712 **Undergraduates** 55% women, 5% part-time, 8% 25 or older, 1% Native American, 1% Hispanic, 3% black, 1% Asian or Pacific Islander **Most popular recent majors** Business administration/commerce/management, elementary education, communication **Academic program** Average class size 34, advanced placement, accelerated degree program, self-designed majors, tutorials, honors program, summer session, adult/continuing education programs, internships **Contact** Mr. Mike Williams, Assistant Vice President of Admissions, Harding University, Searcy, AR 72149-0001. Telephone: 501-279-4407. Fax: 501-279-4865.

HENDERSON STATE UNIVERSITY

ARKADELPHIA, ARKANSAS

Entrance Moderately difficult **General** State-supported, comprehensive, coed **Setting** 132-acre small-town campus **Enrollment** 3,527 **Faculty** 19:1 **Application deadline** Rolling **Freshmen** 94% accepted **Housing** Yes **Tuition** $2166 **Undergraduates** 56% women, 12% part-time, 19% 25 or older, 1% Native American, 1% Hispanic, 16% black, 1% Asian or Pacific Islander **Most popular recent majors** Elementary education, business administration/commerce/management, social science **Academic program** Average class size 30, advanced placement, accelerated degree program, honors program, summer session, internships **Contact** Ms. Vikita Hardwrick, Director of University Relations/Admissions, Henderson State University, Arkadelphia, AR 71999-0001. Telephone: 870-230-5028. Fax: 870-230-5144.

HENDRIX COLLEGE

CONWAY, ARKANSAS

Entrance Moderately difficult **General** Independent United Methodist, 4-year, coed **Setting** 158-acre suburban campus **Enrollment** 982 **Faculty** 12:1 **Application deadline** Rolling **Freshmen** 90% accepted **Housing** Yes **Tuition** $10,435 **Undergraduates** 56% women, 1% 25 or older, 0% Native American, 1% Hispanic, 4% black, 4% Asian or Pacific Islander **Most popular recent majors** Biology/biological sciences, psychology, economics **Academic program** Advanced placement, self-designed majors, tutorials, honors program, internships **Contact** Mr. Rock Jones, Vice President for Enrollment, Hendrix College, Conway, AR 72032. Telephone: 501-450-1362.

JOHN BROWN UNIVERSITY

SILOAM SPRINGS, ARKANSAS

Entrance Moderately difficult **General** Independent nondenominational, comprehensive, coed **Setting** 200-acre small-town campus **Enrollment** 1,379 **Faculty** 16:1 **Application deadline** 3/1 **Freshmen** 68% accepted **Housing** Yes **Tuition** $9120 **Undergraduates** 66% women, 9% part-time, 19% 25 or older, 2% Native American, 1% Hispanic, 1% black, 1% Asian or Pacific Islander **Most popular recent majors** Business administration/commerce/management, elementary education, engineering (general) **Academic program** Average class size 30, advanced placement, tutorials, honors program, adult/continuing education programs, internships **Contact** Mr. Don Crandall, Vice President for Enrollment Management, John Brown University, Siloam Springs, AR 72761-2121. Telephone: 501-524-7150. Fax: 501-524-4196.

LYON COLLEGE

BATESVILLE, ARKANSAS

Entrance Very difficult **General** Independent Presbyterian, 4-year, coed **Setting** 136-acre small-town campus **Enrollment** 559 **Faculty** 11:1 **Application deadline** Rolling **Freshmen** 51% accepted **Housing** Yes **Tuition** $9880 **Undergraduates** 57% women, 17% part-time, 15% 25 or older, 1% Native American, 1% Hispanic, 3% black, 2% Asian or Pacific Islander **Most popular recent majors** Biology/biological sciences, elementary education, chemistry **Academic program** Average class size 20, advanced placement, self-designed majors, tutorials, summer session, adult/continuing education programs **Contact** Ms. Kristine Penix, Associate Director of Admissions, Lyon College, Batesville, AR 72503-2317. Telephone: 501-698-4250. Fax: 501-698-4622.

OUACHITA BAPTIST UNIVERSITY

ARKADELPHIA, ARKANSAS

Entrance Moderately difficult **General** Independent Baptist, 4-year, coed **Setting** 60-acre small-town campus **Enrollment** 1,604 **Faculty** 11:1 **Application deadline** 8/15 **Freshmen** 77% accepted **Housing** Yes **Tuition** $8090 **Undergraduates** 50% women, 4% part-time, 6% 25 or older, 0% Native American, 0% Hispanic, 3% black, 0% Asian or Pacific Islander **Most popular recent major** Education **Academic program** Advanced placement, accelerated degree program, tutorials, honors program, summer session, internships **Contact** Mr. Randy Garner, Director of Admissions Counseling, Ouachita Baptist University, Arkadelphia, AR 71998-0001. Telephone: 501-245-5110. Fax: 501-245-5500.

PHILANDER SMITH COLLEGE

LITTLE ROCK, ARKANSAS

Entrance Noncompetitive **General** Independent United Methodist, 4-year, coed **Setting** 20-acre urban campus **Enrollment** 925 **Application deadline** Rolling **Freshmen** 54% accepted **Housing** Yes **Tuition** $3288 **Undergraduates** 63% women, 18% part-time, 37% 25 or older, 94% black, 4% Asian or Pacific Islander **Most popular recent majors** Business administration/commerce/management, mathematics, biology/biological sciences **Academic program** Average class size 15, tutorials, summer session, internships **Contact** Ms. Beverly Richardson, Dean of Enrollment Management and Records, Philander Smith College, 812 West 13th Street, Little Rock, AR 72202-3799. Telephone: 501-370-5215. Fax: 501-370-5225.

SOUTHERN ARKANSAS UNIVERSITY–MAGNOLIA

MAGNOLIA, ARKANSAS

Entrance Minimally difficult **General** State-supported, comprehensive, coed **Setting** 781-acre small-town campus **Enrollment** 2,592 **Faculty** 18:1 **Application deadline** 8/15 **Freshmen** 98% accepted **Housing** Yes **Tuition** $1896 **Undergraduates** 56% women, 15% part-time, 33% 25 or older, 1% Native American, 1% Hispanic, 22% black, 1% Asian or Pacific Islander **Most popular recent majors** Nursing, elementary education, business administration/commerce/management **Academic program** Average class size 30, advanced placement, accelerated degree program, tutorials, summer session, adult/continuing education programs, internships **Contact** Mr. James E. Whittington, Director of Admissions, Southern Arkansas University–Magnolia, Magnolia, AR 71753. Telephone: 870-235-4040. Fax: 870-235-5005.

UNIVERSITY OF ARKANSAS

FAYETTEVILLE, ARKANSAS

Entrance Moderately difficult **General** State-supported, coed **Setting** 420-acre small-town campus **Enrollment** 14,577 **Faculty** 14:1 **Application deadline** 8/15 **Freshmen** 88% accepted **Housing** Yes **Tuition** $2661 **Undergraduates** 47% women, 14% part-time, 15% 25 or older, 2% Native American, 1% Hispanic, 6% black, 2% Asian or Pacific Islander **Most popular recent majors** Elementary education, accounting, psychology **Academic program** Advanced placement, honors program, summer session, adult/continuing education programs, internships **Contact** Ms. Maribeth Lynes, Director of Undergraduate Recruitment, University of Arkansas, 200 Silas H. Hunt Hall, Fayetteville, AR 72701-1201. Telephone: 501-575-5346. Fax: 501-575-7515.

UNIVERSITY OF ARKANSAS AT LITTLE ROCK

LITTLE ROCK, ARKANSAS

Entrance Minimally difficult **General** State-supported, coed **Setting** 150-acre urban campus **Enrollment** 10,720 **Faculty** 17:1 **Application deadline** Rolling **Freshmen** 74% accepted **Housing** Yes **Tuition** $3026 **Undergraduates** 59% women, 39% part-time, 35% 25 or older, 1% Native American, 1% Hispanic, 21% black, 4% Asian or Pacific Islander **Most popular recent majors** Psychology, biology/biological sciences, nursing **Academic program** Advanced placement, accelerated degree program, self-designed majors, honors program, summer session, adult/continuing education programs, internships **Contact** Office of Admissions and Records, University of Arkansas at Little Rock, 2801 South University Avenue, Little Rock, AR 72204-1099. Telephone: 501-569-3127. Fax: 501-569-8915.

UNIVERSITY OF ARKANSAS AT MONTICELLO

MONTICELLO, ARKANSAS

Entrance Noncompetitive **General** State-supported, comprehensive, coed **Setting** 400-acre small-town campus **Enrollment** 2,124 **Faculty**

20:1 **Application deadline** 8/1 **Freshmen** 98% accepted **Housing** Yes **Tuition** $2040 **Undergraduates** 55% women, 13% part-time, 27% 25 or older, 1% Native American, 1% Hispanic, 19% black, 1% Asian or Pacific Islander **Most popular recent majors** Elementary education, business administration/commerce/management **Academic program** Advanced placement, accelerated degree program, tutorials, summer session **Contact** Mrs. JoBeth Johnson, Director of Admissions, University of Arkansas at Monticello, Monticello, AR 71656. Telephone: 501-460-1026. Fax: 501-460-1321.

UNIVERSITY OF ARKANSAS AT PINE BLUFF
PINE BLUFF, ARKANSAS

Entrance Minimally difficult **General** State-supported, comprehensive, coed **Setting** 327-acre urban campus **Enrollment** 3,242 **Faculty** 18:1 **Application deadline** 8/1 **Freshmen** 98% accepted **Housing** Yes **Tuition** $2046 **Undergraduates** 59% women, 16% part-time, 17% 25 or older, 89% black **Most popular recent majors** Business administration/commerce/management, accounting, computer science **Academic program** Advanced placement, accelerated degree program, tutorials, honors program, summer session, adult/continuing education programs, internships **Contact** Ms. Kwurly M. Floyd, Director of Admissions and Academic Records, University of Arkansas at Pine Bluff, UAPB Box 17, 1200 University Drive, Pine Bluff, AR 71601-2799. Telephone: 501-543-8487.

UNIVERSITY OF ARKANSAS FOR MEDICAL SCIENCES
LITTLE ROCK, ARKANSAS

Entrance Very difficult **General** State-supported, coed **Setting** 5-acre urban campus **Enrollment** 1,851 **Housing** Yes **Tuition** $2208 **Undergraduates** 79% women, 27% part-time, 54% 25 or older, 0% Native American, 1% Hispanic, 13% black, 2% Asian or Pacific Islander **Most popular recent major** Nursing **Contact** Mr. Paul Carter, Assistant to the Vice Chancellor for Academic Affairs, University of Arkansas for Medical Sciences, 4301 West Markham-Slot 601, Little Rock, AR 72205-7199. Telephone: 501-686-5454.

UNIVERSITY OF CENTRAL ARKANSAS
CONWAY, ARKANSAS

Entrance Moderately difficult **General** State-supported, comprehensive, coed **Setting** 262-acre small-town campus **Enrollment** 8,994 **Faculty** 18:1 **Application deadline** Rolling **Freshmen** 93% accepted **Housing** Yes **Tuition** $2692 **Undergraduates** 60% women, 13% part-time, 24% 25 or older, 1% Native American, 1% Hispanic, 12% black, 1% Asian or Pacific Islander **Most popular recent majors** Physical therapy, (pre)medicine sequence, education **Academic program** Average class size 35, advanced placement, accelerated degree program, tutorials, honors program, summer session, internships **Contact** Mr. Joe F. Darling, Director of Admissions, University of Central Arkansas, Conway, AR 72035-0001. Telephone: 501-450-5145. Fax: 501-450-5168.

UNIVERSITY OF THE OZARKS
CLARKSVILLE, ARKANSAS

Entrance Moderately difficult **General** Independent Presbyterian, 4-year, coed **Setting** 56-acre small-town campus **Enrollment** 575 **Faculty** 15:1 **Application deadline** 8/15 **Freshmen** 96% accepted **Housing** Yes **Tuition** $7390 **Undergraduates** 54% women, 10% part-time, 1% Native American, 1% Hispanic, 6% black, 1% Asian or Pacific Islander **Most popular recent majors** Business administration/commerce/management, elementary education, secondary education **Academic program** Advanced placement, summer session **Contact** Mr. James D. Decker, Director of Admissions, University of the Ozarks, Clarksville, AR 72830-2880. Telephone: 501-979-1227. Fax: 501-979-1355.

WILLIAMS BAPTIST COLLEGE
WALNUT RIDGE, ARKANSAS

Entrance Minimally difficult **General** Independent Southern Baptist, 4-year, coed **Setting** 186-acre rural campus **Enrollment** 564 **Faculty** 10:1 **Application deadline** Rolling **Freshmen** 79% accepted **Housing** Yes **Tuition** $5260 **Undergraduates** 55% women, 26% part-time, 20% 25 or older, 0% Native American, 0% Hispanic, 1% black, 0% Asian or Pacific Islander **Most popular recent majors** Elementary education, business administration/commerce/management, psychology **Academic program** Average class size 22, advanced placement, self-designed majors, tutorials, honors program, summer session, adult/continuing education programs, internships **Contact** Ms. Angela Flippo, Director of Admissions, Williams Baptist College, Walnut Ridge, AR 72476. Telephone: 501-886-6741 Ext. 127.

Florida

BARRY UNIVERSITY
MIAMI SHORES, FLORIDA

Entrance Moderately difficult **General** Independent Roman Catholic, comprehensive, coed **Set-**

ting 90-acre suburban campus **Enrollment** 7,016 **Faculty** 14:1 **Application deadline** Rolling **Freshmen** 77% accepted **Housing** Yes **Tuition** $13,550 **Undergraduates** 67% women, 42% part-time, 67% 25 or older, 0% Native American, 27% Hispanic, 17% black, 2% Asian or Pacific Islander **Academic program** Advanced placement, accelerated degree program, tutorials, honors program, summer session, adult/continuing education programs, internships **Contact** Mr. Gregory Miller, Dean of Enrollment Services, Barry University, Miami Shores, FL 33161-6695. Telephone: 305-899-3100. Fax: 305-899-2971.

BETHUNE-COOKMAN COLLEGE
DAYTONA BEACH, FLORIDA

Entrance Minimally difficult **General** Independent Methodist, 4-year, coed **Setting** 60-acre urban campus **Enrollment** 2,335 **Faculty** 16:1 **Application deadline** 7/30 **Freshmen** 84% accepted **Housing** Yes **Tuition** $7280 **Undergraduates** 60% women, 8% part-time, 16% 25 or older, 0% Native American, 1% Hispanic, 93% black, 0% Asian or Pacific Islander **Most popular recent majors** Business administration/commerce/management, elementary education, criminal justice **Academic program** Average class size 24, advanced placement, accelerated degree program, honors program, summer session, adult/continuing education programs, internships **Contact** Ms. Florida Wilson, Assistant Admissions Director, Bethune-Cookman College, 640 Dr. Mary McLeod Bethune Blvd, Daytona Beach, FL 32114-3099. Telephone: 904-255-1401 Ext. 333. Fax: 904-257-5338.

CARIBBEAN CENTER FOR ADVANCED STUDIES/MIAMI INSTITUTE OF PSYCHOLOGY
MIAMI, FLORIDA

Entrance Difficulty N/R **General** Independent, upper-level, specialized, coed **Setting** 2-acre urban campus **Enrollment** 600 **Faculty** 4:1 **Freshmen** 100% accepted **Tuition** $5934 **Undergraduates** 70% women, 87% part-time, 70% 25 or older, 61% Hispanic, 13% black **Academic program** Average class size 6, advanced placement, summer session, adult/continuing education programs, internships **Contact** Ms. Zoraida Seguinot, Recruitment and Outreach, Caribbean Center for Advanced Studies/Miami Institute of Psychology, 8180 NW 36th Street, 2nd Floor, Miami, FL 33166-6653. Telephone: 305-593-1223 Ext. 137.

CLEARWATER CHRISTIAN COLLEGE
CLEARWATER, FLORIDA

Entrance Minimally difficult **General** Independent nondenominational, 4-year, coed **Setting** 50-acre suburban campus **Enrollment** 518 **Faculty** 15:1 **Application deadline** 8/1 **Freshmen** 85% accepted **Housing** Yes **Tuition** $7300 **Undergraduates** 53% women, 7% part-time, 12% 25 or older, 1% Native American, 5% Hispanic, 4% black, 1% Asian or Pacific Islander **Academic program** Advanced placement, summer session, internships **Contact** Mr. Benjamin J. Puckett, Director of Admissions and Placement Services, Clearwater Christian College, Clearwater, FL 34619-4595. Telephone: 813-726-1153 Ext. 228.

ECKERD COLLEGE
ST. PETERSBURG, FLORIDA

Entrance Moderately difficult **General** Independent Presbyterian, 4-year, coed **Setting** 267-acre suburban campus **Enrollment** 1,466 **Faculty** 14:1 **Application deadline** Rolling **Freshmen** 83% accepted **Housing** Yes **Tuition** $17,130 **Undergraduates** 54% women, 2% part-time, 5% 25 or older, 1% Native American, 4% Hispanic, 3% black, 2% Asian or Pacific Islander **Most popular recent majors** Marine sciences, international business, biology/biological sciences **Academic program** Average class size 25, advanced placement, accelerated degree program, self-designed majors, tutorials, honors program, summer session, adult/continuing education programs, internships **Contact** Dr. Richard R. Hallin, Dean of Admissions, Eckerd College, St. Petersburg, FL 33711. Telephone: 813-864-8331. Fax: 813-866-2304.

EDWARD WATERS COLLEGE
JACKSONVILLE, FLORIDA

Entrance Noncompetitive **General** Independent African Methodist Episcopal, 4-year, coed **Setting** 20-acre urban campus **Faculty** 13:1 **Application deadline** Rolling **Freshmen** 100% accepted **Housing** Yes **Tuition** $5760 **Undergraduates** 16% part-time, 0% Native American, 0% Hispanic, 99% black **Most popular recent major** Business administration/commerce/management **Academic program** Self-designed majors, tutorials, honors program, summer session, adult/continuing education programs, internships **Contact** Dr. William Barnes, Interim Registrar, Edward Waters College, 1658 Kings Road, Jacksonville, FL 32209-6199. Telephone: 904-366-2715.

EMBRY-RIDDLE AERONAUTICAL UNIVERSITY
DAYTONA BEACH, FLORIDA

Entrance Moderately difficult **General** Independent, comprehensive, specialized, coed **Setting** 164-acre urban campus **Enrollment** 4,135 **Fac-**

ulty 19:1 **Application deadline** 3/1 **Freshmen** 82% accepted **Housing** Yes **Tuition** $8740 **Undergraduates** 14% women, 10% part-time, 19% 25 or older, 0% Native American, 8% Hispanic, 6% black, 8% Asian or Pacific Islander **Most popular recent majors** Aerospace sciences, aviation administration, aerospace engineering **Academic program** Advanced placement, tutorials, summer session, adult/continuing education programs, internships **Contact** Ms. Carol Cotman Hogan, Director of Admissions, Embry-Riddle Aeronautical University, 600 South Clyde Morris Boulevard, Daytona Beach, FL 32114-3900. Telephone: 904-226-6112. Fax: 904-226-7070.

EMBRY-RIDDLE AERONAUTICAL UNIVERSITY, EXTENDED CAMPUS
DAYTONA BEACH, FLORIDA

Entrance Minimally difficult **General** Independent, comprehensive, specialized, coed **Enrollment** 11,716 **Faculty** 12:1 **Application deadline** Rolling **Freshmen** 79% accepted **Undergraduates** 10% women, 98% part-time, 89% 25 or older, 1% Native American, 6% Hispanic, 8% black, 3% Asian or Pacific Islander **Most popular recent majors** Aerospace sciences, business administration/commerce/management **Academic program** Average class size 10, advanced placement, adult/continuing education programs, internships **Contact** Mrs. Pam Thomas, Director of Admissions, Records and Registration, Embry-Riddle Aeronautical University, Extended Campus, Daytona Beach, FL 32114-3900. Telephone: 904-226-6914.

FLAGLER COLLEGE
ST. AUGUSTINE, FLORIDA

Entrance Moderately difficult **General** Independent, 4-year, coed **Setting** 36-acre small-town campus **Enrollment** 1,526 **Faculty** 21:1 **Application deadline** 3/15 **Freshmen** 61% accepted **Housing** Yes **Tuition** $5760 **Undergraduates** 62% women, 2% part-time, 7% 25 or older, 1% Native American, 3% Hispanic, 1% black, 1% Asian or Pacific Islander **Most popular recent majors** Elementary education, business administration/commerce/management, communication **Academic program** Average class size 24, advanced placement, tutorials, summer session, internships **Contact** Mr. Marc G. Williar, Director of Admissions, Flagler College, PO Box 1027, St. Augustine, FL 32085-1027. Telephone: 904-829-6481 Ext. 220. Fax: 904-826-0094.

FLORIDA AGRICULTURAL AND MECHANICAL UNIVERSITY
TALLAHASSEE, FLORIDA

Entrance Moderately difficult **General** State-supported, coed **Setting** 419-acre urban campus **Enrollment** 10,448 **Faculty** 16:1 **Application deadline** 5/1 **Freshmen** 60% accepted **Housing** Yes **Tuition** $2105 **Undergraduates** 59% women, 18% part-time, 18% 25 or older, 0% Native American, 1% Hispanic, 89% black, 1% Asian or Pacific Islander **Most popular recent majors** Education, business administration/commerce/management **Academic program** Average class size 23, advanced placement, accelerated degree program, honors program, summer session, adult/continuing education programs, internships **Contact** Mrs. Barbara Cox, Deputy Registrar for Admissions, Florida Agricultural and Mechanical University, Office of the University Registrar, Tallahassee, FL 32307. Telephone: 904-599-3796. Fax: 904-561-2428.

FLORIDA ATLANTIC UNIVERSITY
BOCA RATON, FLORIDA

Entrance Moderately difficult **General** State-supported, coed **Setting** 850-acre suburban campus **Enrollment** 18,362 **Faculty** 18:1 **Application deadline** 5/1 **Freshmen** 74% accepted **Housing** Yes **Tuition** $2023 **Undergraduates** 59% women, 55% part-time, 55% 25 or older, 1% Native American, 10% Hispanic, 11% black, 4% Asian or Pacific Islander **Most popular recent majors** Elementary education, biology/biological sciences, accounting **Academic program** Advanced placement, accelerated degree program, self-designed majors, honors program, summer session, adult/continuing education programs, internships **Contact** Mr. Richard Griffin, Director of Admissions, Florida Atlantic University, 777 Glades Road, PO Box 3091, Boca Raton, FL 33431-0991. Telephone: 561-367-3040 Ext. 3031. Fax: 561-367-2758.

FLORIDA BAPTIST THEOLOGICAL COLLEGE
GRACEVILLE, FLORIDA

Entrance Noncompetitive **General** Independent Southern Baptist, 4-year, coed **Setting** 150-acre small-town campus **Enrollment** 529 **Application deadline** Rolling **Housing** Yes **Tuition** $2934 **Undergraduates** 26% women, 17% part-time, 88% 25 or older, 0% Native American, 3% Hispanic, 3% black, 1% Asian or Pacific Islander **Most popular recent majors** Theology, religious education, sacred music **Academic program** Advanced placement, accelerated degree program, summer session, adult/continuing education programs, internships **Contact** Rev. O. Lavan Wilson, Director of Admissions, Florida Baptist Theological College, PO Box 1306, Graceville, FL 32440-3306. Telephone: 904-263-3261 Ext. 62. Fax: 904-263-7506.

FLORIDA BIBLE COLLEGE
MIRAMAR, FLORIDA

Entrance Minimally difficult **General** Independent nondenominational, 4-year, coed **Setting** 10-acre small-town campus **Enrollment** 76 **Faculty** 12:1 **Application deadline** Rolling **Freshmen** 100% accepted **Housing** Yes **Tuition** $4928 **Undergraduates** 49% women, 10% part-time, 15% 25 or older, 5% Hispanic **Most popular recent majors** Biblical studies, elementary education, pastoral studies **Academic program** ESL program, Advanced placement, summer session, internships **Contact** Ms. Marie Brady, Director of Admissions, Florida Bible College, Miramar, FL 33025. Telephone: 954-431-6776 Ext. 210.

FLORIDA CHRISTIAN COLLEGE
KISSIMMEE, FLORIDA

Entrance Minimally difficult **General** Independent, 4-year, specialized, coed, affiliated with Christian Churches and Churches of Christ **Setting** 40-acre small-town campus **Enrollment** 153 **Faculty** 14:1 **Application deadline** 7/15 **Freshmen** 76% accepted **Housing** Yes **Tuition** $5174 **Undergraduates** 41% women, 21% part-time, 29% 25 or older, 0% Native American, 1% Hispanic, 3% black, 0% Asian or Pacific Islander **Academic program** Advanced placement, summer session, adult/continuing education programs, internships **Contact** Dr. Tony Buchanan, Academic Dean, Florida Christian College, Kissimmee, FL 34744-5301. Telephone: 407-847-8966 Ext. 316.

FLORIDA INSTITUTE OF TECHNOLOGY
MELBOURNE, FLORIDA

Entrance Moderately difficult **General** Independent, coed **Setting** 175-acre small-town campus **Enrollment** 4,185 **Faculty** 11:1 **Application deadline** Rolling **Freshmen** 86% accepted **Housing** Yes **Tuition** $15,100 **Undergraduates** 31% women, 9% part-time, 13% 25 or older, 1% Native American, 7% Hispanic, 4% black, 2% Asian or Pacific Islander **Most popular recent majors** Aerospace sciences, electrical engineering, biology/biological sciences **Academic program** Advanced placement, accelerated degree program, tutorials, summer session, adult/continuing education programs, internships **Contact** Ms. Judi Marino, Acting Dean of Admissions, Florida Institute of Technology, Melbourne, FL 32901-6975. Telephone: 407-768-8000 Ext. 8030. Fax: 407-723-9468.

FLORIDA INTERNATIONAL UNIVERSITY
MIAMI, FLORIDA

Entrance Moderately difficult **General** State-supported, coed **Setting** 573-acre urban campus **Enrollment** 24,413 **Faculty** 15:1 **Application deadline** Rolling **Freshmen** 64% accepted **Housing** Yes **Tuition** $2035 **Undergraduates** 57% women, 46% part-time, 33% 25 or older, 0% Native American, 54% Hispanic, 14% black, 4% Asian or Pacific Islander **Most popular recent majors** Psychology, biology/biological sciences, accounting **Academic program** Advanced placement, accelerated degree program, tutorials, honors program, summer session, adult/continuing education programs, internships **Contact** Ms. Carmen Brown, Director of Admissions, Florida International University, University Park, Miami, FL 33199. Telephone: 305-348-3675. Fax: 305-348-3648.

FLORIDA MEMORIAL COLLEGE
MIAMI, FLORIDA

Entrance Noncompetitive **General** Independent, 4-year, coed, affiliated with Baptist Church **Setting** 77-acre suburban campus **Enrollment** 1,457 **Application deadline** 7/1 **Housing** Yes **Tuition** $5850 **Undergraduates** 59% women, 7% part-time, 30% 25 or older, 0% Native American, 20% Hispanic, 80% black **Most popular recent majors** Business administration/commerce/management, computer science **Academic program** Tutorials, honors program, summer session, internships **Contact** Mrs. Peggy Kelley, Director of Admissions and International Student Advisor, Florida Memorial College, Miami, FL 33054. Telephone: 305-626-3750.

FLORIDA METROPOLITAN UNIVERSITY–FORT LAUDERDALE COLLEGE
FORT LAUDERDALE, FLORIDA

Entrance Minimally difficult **General** Proprietary, 4-year, coed **Setting** Suburban campus **Enrollment** 490 **Faculty** 20:1 **Application deadline** Rolling **Freshmen** 78% accepted **Tuition** $4503 **Undergraduates** 60% women, 25% 25 or older, 0% Native American, 20% Hispanic, 30% black, 3% Asian or Pacific Islander **Most popular recent majors** Accounting, paralegal studies, computer programming **Academic program** Advanced placement, accelerated degree program, tutorials, summer session, adult/continuing education programs, internships **Contact** Mr. Terry Nichols, Director of Admissions, Florida Metropolitan University–Fort Lauderdale College, Fort Lauderdale, FL 33304-2522. Telephone: 305-568-1600. Fax: 305-568-2008.

FLORIDA METROPOLITAN UNIVERSITY–ORLANDO COLLEGE, NORTH
ORLANDO, FLORIDA

Entrance Minimally difficult **General** Proprietary, comprehensive, coed **Setting** 1-acre urban campus **Enrollment** 1,375 **Application deadline** Rolling **Freshmen** 89% accepted **Tuition** $4140 **Undergraduates** 50% women, 0% part-time, 32% 25 or older, 1% Native American, 3% Hispanic, 4% black, 2% Asian or Pacific Islander **Most popular recent majors** Business administration/commerce/management, marketing/retailing/merchandising, computer programming **Academic program** Accelerated degree program, self-designed majors, summer session, internships **Contact** Ms. Shana Dyer, Director of Admissions, Florida Metropolitan University–Orlando College, North, 5421 Diplomat Circle, Orlando, FL 32810-5674. Telephone: 407-628-5870 Ext. 12. Fax: 407-628-2616.

FLORIDA METROPOLITAN UNIVERSITY–TAMPA COLLEGE, PINELLAS
CLEARWATER, FLORIDA

Entrance Minimally difficult **General** Proprietary, comprehensive, coed **Setting** 3-acre urban campus **Enrollment** 724 **Faculty** 24:1 **Application deadline** Rolling **Freshmen** 93% accepted **Tuition** $4464 **Undergraduates** 72% women, 1% part-time, 91% 25 or older, 1% Native American, 4% Hispanic, 8% black, 4% Asian or Pacific Islander **Academic program** Average class size 30, advanced placement, accelerated degree program, tutorials, honors program, summer session, adult/continuing education programs, internships **Contact** Mr. Mark Page, Director of Admissions, Florida Metropolitan University–Tampa College, Pinellas, 2471 McMullen Booth Road, Clearwater, FL 34619. Telephone: 813-725-2688 Ext. 52.

FLORIDA METROPOLITAN UNIVERSITY–TAMPA COLLEGE, LAKELAND
LAKELAND, FLORIDA

Entrance Minimally difficult **General** Proprietary, comprehensive, coed **Setting** Suburban campus **Enrollment** 500 **Tuition** $5220 **Undergraduates** 70% women, 5% part-time, 56% 25 or older, 0% Native American, 3% Hispanic, 26% black **Most popular recent majors** Paralegal studies, computer science, accounting **Academic program** Advanced placement, tutorials, summer session, adult/continuing education programs, internships **Contact** Ms. Gerrie Smith, Director of Admissions, Florida Metropolitan University–Tampa College, Lakeland, Lakeland, FL 33801-5907. Telephone: 941-686-1444. Fax: 941-688-9881.

FLORIDA METROPOLITAN UNIVERSITY–TAMPA COLLEGE
TAMPA, FLORIDA

Entrance Minimally difficult **General** Proprietary, comprehensive, coed **Setting** 4-acre urban campus **Enrollment** 1,250 **Faculty** 30:1 **Application deadline** Rolling **Freshmen** 87% accepted **Tuition** $5220 **Undergraduates** 60% women, 3% part-time, 46% 25 or older, 1% Native American, 19% Hispanic, 20% black, 2% Asian or Pacific Islander **Most popular recent majors** Business administration/commerce/management, marketing/retailing/merchandising, accounting **Academic program** Advanced placement, accelerated degree program, self-designed majors, summer session, adult/continuing education programs, internships **Contact** Mr. Foster Thomas, Admissions Coordinator, Florida Metropolitan University–Tampa College, 3319 West Hillsborough Avenue, Tampa, FL 33614-5899. Telephone: 813-879-6000. Fax: 813-871-2483.

FLORIDA METROPOLITAN UNIVERSITY–TAMPA COLLEGE, BRANDON
TAMPA, FLORIDA

Entrance Difficulty N/R **General** Proprietary, comprehensive **Enrollment** 850 **Freshmen** 79% accepted **Undergraduates** 65% women, 2% part-time, 87% 25 or older, 1% Native American, 15% Hispanic, 25% black, 5% Asian or Pacific Islander **Contact** Admissions, Florida Metropolitan University–Tampa College, Brandon, Tampa, FL 33619. Telephone: 813-621-0041.

FLORIDA SOUTHERN COLLEGE
LAKELAND, FLORIDA

Entrance Moderately difficult **General** Independent, comprehensive, coed, affiliated with United Methodist Church **Setting** 100-acre suburban campus **Enrollment** 1,964 **Faculty** 17:1 **Application deadline** 8/1 **Freshmen** 74% accepted **Housing** Yes **Tuition** $10,604 **Undergraduates** 60% women, 15% part-time, 18% 25 or older, 4% Hispanic, 5% black, 1% Asian or Pacific Islander **Most popular recent majors** Business administration/commerce/management, education, biology/biological sciences **Academic program** Average class size 32, advanced placement, summer session, adult/continuing education programs, internships **Contact** Mr. Robert B. Palmer Jr., Vice President and Dean of Enrollment Management, Florida Southern College, Lakeland, FL 33801-5698. Telephone: 941-680-6212. Fax: 941-680-4120.

FLORIDA STATE UNIVERSITY
TALLAHASSEE, FLORIDA

Entrance Very difficult **General** State-supported, coed **Setting** 451-acre suburban campus **Enrollment** 30,264 **Application deadline** 3/3 **Freshmen** 75% accepted **Housing** Yes **Tuition** $1988 **Undergraduates** 55% women, 11% part-time, 13% 25 or older, 1% Native American, 9% Hispanic, 10% black, 3% Asian or Pacific Islander **Most popular recent majors** Biology/biological sciences, criminology, psychology **Academic program** Advanced placement, accelerated degree program, honors program, summer session, adult/continuing education programs, internships **Contact** Mr. John Barnhill, Director of Admissions, Florida State University, Tallahassee, FL 32306-1009. Telephone: 904-644-6200 Ext. 16.

HARID CONSERVATORY
BOCA RATON, FLORIDA

Entrance Most difficult **General** Independent, 4-year, specialized, coed **Setting** 5-acre suburban campus **Enrollment** 50 **Faculty** 2:1 **Application deadline** 3/31 **Tuition** $0 **Undergraduates** 46% women, 0% part-time, 2% 25 or older, 0% Native American, 4% Hispanic, 0% black, 27% Asian or Pacific Islander **Academic program** Average class size 15, advanced placement, tutorials **Contact** Ms. Chantal Prosperi, Administrative Assistant/Admissions, Harid Conservatory, 2285 Potomac Road, Boca Raton, FL 33431. Telephone: 561-997-2677 Ext. 62. Fax: 561-997-8920.

HOBE SOUND BIBLE COLLEGE
HOBE SOUND, FLORIDA

Entrance Noncompetitive **General** Independent nondenominational, 4-year, coed **Setting** 84-acre small-town campus **Enrollment** 118 **Application deadline** Rolling **Freshmen** 97% accepted **Housing** Yes **Tuition** $4140 **Undergraduates** 57% women, 24% part-time, 26% 25 or older, 0% Native American, 1% Hispanic, 1% black, 0% Asian or Pacific Islander **Academic program** Advanced placement, summer session, internships **Contact** Mrs. Ann French, Director of Admissions, Hobe Sound Bible College, PO Box 1065, Hobe Sound, FL 33475-1065. Telephone: 561-546-5534 Ext. 415. Fax: 561-546-9379.

INTERNATIONAL ACADEMY OF MERCHANDISING & DESIGN, INC.
TAMPA, FLORIDA

Entrance Noncompetitive **General** Proprietary, 4-year, coed **Setting** 1-acre urban campus **Enrollment** 500 **Faculty** 12:1 **Application deadline** Rolling **Freshmen** 100% accepted **Tuition** $9270 **Undergraduates** 85% women, 70% part-time, 60% 25 or older, 1% Native American, 15% Hispanic, 10% black, 1% Asian or Pacific Islander **Most popular recent major** Interior design **Academic program** Advanced placement, accelerated degree program, summer session, adult/continuing education programs, internships **Contact** Mr. F. Michael Santoro, President, International Academy of Merchandising & Design, Inc., 5225 Memorial Highway, Tampa, FL 33634-7350. Telephone: 813-881-0007. Fax: 813-881-0008.

INTERNATIONAL COLLEGE
NAPLES, FLORIDA

Entrance Minimally difficult **General** Independent, 4-year, coed **Setting** Suburban campus **Enrollment** 600 **Faculty** 15:1 **Application deadline** Rolling **Freshmen** 91% accepted **Tuition** $6735 **Undergraduates** 77% women, 52% part-time, 82% 25 or older, 0% Native American, 6% Hispanic, 6% black, 0% Asian or Pacific Islander **Academic program** Average class size 18, advanced placement, accelerated degree program, tutorials, summer session, adult/continuing education programs, internships **Contact** Ms. Bunty Cantwell, Director of Enrollment Management, International College, Naples, FL 34112. Telephone: 941-774-4700. Fax: 941-774-4593.

JACKSONVILLE UNIVERSITY
JACKSONVILLE, FLORIDA

Entrance Moderately difficult **General** Independent, comprehensive, coed **Setting** 260-acre suburban campus **Enrollment** 2,321 **Faculty** 14:1 **Application deadline** 8/1 **Freshmen** 71% accepted **Housing** Yes **Tuition** $13,900 **Undergraduates** 55% women, 24% part-time, 1% Native American, 4% Hispanic, 10% black, 2% Asian or Pacific Islander **Most popular recent majors** Business administration/commerce/management, nursing, biology/biological sciences **Academic program** Advanced placement, accelerated degree program, self-designed majors, tutorials, honors program, summer session, adult/continuing education programs, internships **Contact** Dr. Susan Hallenbeck, Director of Admissions, Jacksonville University, Jacksonville, FL 32211-3394. Telephone: 904-745-7000. Fax: 904-745-7012.

JOHNSON & WALES UNIVERSITY

NORTH MIAMI, FLORIDA

Entrance Minimally difficult **General** Independent, 4-year, coed **Setting** 8-acre suburban campus **Enrollment** 875 **Faculty** 22:1 **Application deadline** Rolling **Freshmen** 76% accepted **Housing** Yes **Tuition** $11,952 **Undergraduates** 34% women, 4% part-time, 36% 25 or older, 1% Native American, 23% Hispanic, 17% black, 2% Asian or Pacific Islander **Most popular recent major** Culinary arts **Academic program** Advanced placement, accelerated degree program, tutorials, honors program, summer session, internships **Contact** Ms. Licia Dwyer, Director of Admissions, Johnson & Wales University, 1701 Northeast 127th Street, North Miami, FL 33181. Telephone: 305-892-7600.

JONES COLLEGE

JACKSONVILLE, FLORIDA

Entrance Noncompetitive **General** Independent, 4-year, coed **Setting** 5-acre urban campus **Enrollment** 860 **Faculty** 17:1 **Application deadline** Rolling **Tuition** $4350 **Undergraduates** 73% women, 71% part-time, 65% 25 or older, 0% Native American, 18% Hispanic, 31% black, 2% Asian or Pacific Islander **Most popular recent majors** Business administration/commerce/management, medical assistant technologies **Academic program** Average class size 25, accelerated degree program, self-designed majors, tutorials, summer session, adult/continuing education programs, internships **Contact** Mr. Barry Darden, Director of Development, Jones College, 5353 Arlington Expressway, Jacksonville, FL 32211-5540. Telephone: 904-743-1122 Ext. 115.

LYNN UNIVERSITY

BOCA RATON, FLORIDA

Entrance Minimally difficult **General** Independent, comprehensive, coed **Setting** 123-acre suburban campus **Enrollment** 1,652 **Faculty** 19:1 **Application deadline** 8/15 **Freshmen** 80% accepted **Housing** Yes **Tuition** $16,700 **Undergraduates** 45% women, 24% part-time, 24% 25 or older, 1% Native American, 5% Hispanic, 4% black, 1% Asian or Pacific Islander **Most popular recent majors** Hotel and restaurant management, international business, business administration/commerce/management **Academic program** Advanced placement, honors program, summer session, adult/continuing education programs, internships **Contact** Mr. James P. Sullivan, Director of Admissions, Lynn University, Boca Raton, FL 33431-5598. Telephone: 561-994-0770 Ext. 157. Fax: 561-241-3552.

NEW COLLEGE OF THE UNIVERSITY OF SOUTH FLORIDA

SARASOTA, FLORIDA

Entrance Very difficult **General** State-supported, 4-year, coed **Setting** 140-acre suburban campus **Enrollment** 596 **Faculty** 11:1 **Application deadline** Rolling **Freshmen** 59% accepted **Housing** Yes **Tuition** $2033 **Undergraduates** 54% women, 0% part-time, 5% 25 or older, 0% Native American, 6% Hispanic, 2% black, 6% Asian or Pacific Islander **Most popular recent majors** Psychology, biology/biological sciences, literature **Academic program** Average class size 19, accelerated degree program, self-designed majors, tutorials, honors program, internships **Contact** Ms. Kathleen Killion, Acting Director of Admissions, New College of the University of South Florida, Sarasota, FL 34243-2197. Telephone: 941-359-4269.

NEW WORLD SCHOOL OF THE ARTS

MIAMI, FLORIDA

Entrance Most difficult **General** State-supported, 4-year, coed **Setting** 5-acre urban campus **Enrollment** 375 **Faculty** 4:1 **Tuition** $1350 **Undergraduates** 55% women, 5% part-time, 10% 25 or older, 0% Native American, 40% Hispanic, 12% black, 5% Asian or Pacific Islander **Academic program** Average class size 25, advanced placement, honors program, summer session, internships **Contact** Mr. Robert Stevens, Director of Student Services, New World School of the Arts, 300 NE 2nd Avenue, Miami, FL 33132. Telephone: 305-237-3472.

NORTHWOOD UNIVERSITY, FLORIDA CAMPUS

WEST PALM BEACH, FLORIDA

Entrance Moderately difficult **General** Independent, 4-year, coed **Setting** 90-acre suburban campus **Enrollment** 760 **Faculty** 17:1 **Application deadline** Rolling **Freshmen** 54% accepted **Housing** Yes **Tuition** $10,874 **Undergraduates** 33% women, 7% part-time, 7% 25 or older, 0% Native American, 7% Hispanic, 16% black, 1% Asian or Pacific Islander **Most popular recent majors** Business administration/commerce/management, computer management, accounting **Academic**

program Advanced placement, accelerated degree program, tutorials, honors program, summer session, adult/continuing education programs, internships **Contact** Mr. John M. Letvinchuck, Director of Admissions, Northwood University, Florida Campus, West Palm Beach, FL 33409-2999. Telephone: 561-478-5500. Fax: 561-640-3328.

NOVA SOUTHEASTERN UNIVERSITY
FORT LAUDERDALE, FLORIDA

Entrance Moderately difficult **General** Independent, coed **Setting** 225-acre suburban campus **Enrollment** 14,951 **Faculty** 16:1 **Application deadline** Rolling **Freshmen** 69% accepted **Housing** Yes **Tuition** $10,420 **Undergraduates** 68% women, 41% part-time, 69% 25 or older, 0% Native American, 18% Hispanic, 16% black, 2% Asian or Pacific Islander **Most popular recent majors** Business administration/commerce/management, education, psychology **Academic program** Average class size 15, advanced placement, accelerated degree program, summer session, adult/continuing education programs, internships **Contact** Dr. Jean Lewis, Director of Undergraduate Admissions, Nova Southeastern University, Fort Lauderdale, FL 33314-7721. Telephone: 954-475-7360.

PALM BEACH ATLANTIC COLLEGE
WEST PALM BEACH, FLORIDA

Entrance Moderately difficult **General** Independent nondenominational, comprehensive, coed **Setting** 25-acre urban campus **Enrollment** 1,830 **Faculty** 16:1 **Application deadline** 8/1 **Freshmen** 81% accepted **Housing** Yes **Tuition** $9900 **Undergraduates** 60% women, 10% part-time, 22% 25 or older, 1% Native American, 7% Hispanic, 7% black, 1% Asian or Pacific Islander **Most popular recent majors** Business administration/commerce/management, education, psychology **Academic program** Advanced placement, tutorials, honors program, summer session, adult/continuing education programs, internships **Contact** Mr. Buck James, Dean of Enrollment Services, Palm Beach Atlantic College, 901 South Flagler Dr, PO Box 24708, West Palm Beach, FL 33416-4708. Telephone: 561-803-2100.

RINGLING SCHOOL OF ART AND DESIGN
SARASOTA, FLORIDA

Entrance Moderately difficult **General** Independent, 4-year, specialized, coed **Setting** 35-acre urban campus **Enrollment** 830 **Faculty** 13:1 **Application deadline** Rolling **Freshmen** 42% accepted **Housing** Yes **Tuition** $13,250 **Undergraduates** 40% women, 5% part-time, 25% 25 or older, 1% Native American, 8% Hispanic, 3% black, 5% Asian or Pacific Islander **Most popular recent majors** Illustration, graphic arts **Academic program** Advanced placement, internships **Contact** Mr. James Dean, Dean of Admissions, Ringling School of Art and Design, 2700 North Tamiami Trail, Sarasota, FL 34234-5895. Telephone: 941-351-5100. Fax: 941-359-7517.

ROLLINS COLLEGE
WINTER PARK, FLORIDA

Entrance Very difficult **General** Independent, comprehensive, coed **Setting** 67-acre suburban campus **Enrollment** 3,297 **Faculty** 12:1 **Application deadline** 2/15 **Freshmen** 71% accepted **Housing** Yes **Tuition** $20,010 **Undergraduates** 55% women, 1% part-time, 2% 25 or older, 1% Native American, 8% Hispanic, 3% black, 4% Asian or Pacific Islander **Most popular recent majors** Psychology, economics, English **Academic program** Advanced placement, accelerated degree program, self-designed majors, tutorials, honors program, adult/continuing education programs, internships **Contact** Mr. David Erdmann, Dean of Admissions and Student Financial Planning, Rollins College, Winter Park, FL 32789-4499. Telephone: 407-646-2161. Fax: 407-646-2600.

ST. JOHN VIANNEY COLLEGE SEMINARY
MIAMI, FLORIDA

Entrance Moderately difficult **General** Independent Roman Catholic, 4-year, specialized **Setting** 33-acre urban campus **Enrollment** 44 **Faculty** 3:1 **Application deadline** Rolling **Freshmen** 100% accepted **Housing** Yes **Tuition** $7000 **Undergraduates** 6% part-time, 50% 25 or older, 0% Native American, 32% Hispanic, 9% black, 2% Asian or Pacific Islander **Academic program** Advanced placement, tutorials **Contact** Dr. Zoila L. Diaz, Academic Dean, St. John Vianney College Seminary, 2900 Southwest 87th Avenue, Miami, FL 33165-3244. Telephone: 305-223-4561 Ext. 13.

SAINT LEO COLLEGE
SAINT LEO, FLORIDA

Entrance Moderately difficult **General** Independent Roman Catholic, comprehensive, coed **Setting** 170-acre rural campus **Enrollment** 1,651 **Faculty** 15:1 **Application deadline** 8/1 **Freshmen** 68% accepted **Housing** Yes **Tuition** $10,996 **Undergraduates** 60% women, 42% part-time, 53% 25 or older, 1% Native American, 7% Hispanic, 6% black, 1% Asian or Pacific Islander **Most popular**

recent majors Business administration/commerce/management, education, criminology **Academic program** Advanced placement, accelerated degree program, honors program, summer session, adult/continuing education programs, internships **Contact** Mr. Gary Bracken, Director of Admissions, Saint Leo College, Saint Leo, FL 33574-2008. Telephone: 352-588-8283. Fax: 352-588-8257.

ST. THOMAS UNIVERSITY
MIAMI, FLORIDA

Entrance Moderately difficult **General** Independent Roman Catholic, comprehensive, coed **Setting** 140-acre suburban campus **Enrollment** 2,262 **Faculty** 15:1 **Application deadline** Rolling **Freshmen** 70% accepted **Housing** Yes **Tuition** $11,840 **Undergraduates** 54% women, 13% part-time, 20% 25 or older, 1% Native American, 32% Hispanic, 21% black, 2% Asian or Pacific Islander **Most popular recent majors** Elementary education, business administration/commerce/management, accounting **Academic program** Advanced placement, tutorials, honors program, summer session, adult/continuing education programs, internships **Contact** Mr. Daryl Perry, Associate Director of Admissions, St. Thomas University, Miami, FL 33054-6459. Telephone: 305-628-6546. Fax: 305-628-6591.

SCHILLER INTERNATIONAL UNIVERSITY
DUNEDIN, FLORIDA

Entrance Noncompetitive **General** Independent, comprehensive, coed **Setting** Suburban campus **Enrollment** 266 **Application deadline** Rolling **Housing** Yes **Tuition** $11,750 **Undergraduates** 44% women, 5% part-time, 13% 25 or older **Most popular recent majors** International business, hotel and restaurant management, tourism and travel **Academic program** Advanced placement, accelerated degree program, self-designed majors, tutorials, summer session, adult/continuing education programs, internships **Contact** Mr. Christoph Leibrecht, Director of Admissions, Schiller International University, Dunedin, FL 34698-7532. Telephone: 813-736-5082. Fax: 813-734-0359.

SOUTHEASTERN COLLEGE OF THE ASSEMBLIES OF GOD
LAKELAND, FLORIDA

Entrance Minimally difficult **General** Independent, 4-year, coed, affiliated with Assemblies of God **Setting** 62-acre small-town campus **Enrollment** 1,090 **Faculty** 20:1 **Application deadline** 8/1 **Freshmen** 99% accepted **Housing** Yes **Tuition** $4804 **Undergraduates** 51% women, 6% part-time, 15% 25 or older, 1% Native American, 10% Hispanic, 3% black, 1% Asian or Pacific Islander **Most popular recent majors** Ministries, education, psychology **Academic program** Average class size 55, advanced placement, accelerated degree program, summer session, internships **Contact** Admissions Secretary, Southeastern College of the Assemblies of God, Lakeland, FL 33801-6099. Telephone: 941-667-5011. Fax: 941-667-5200.

STETSON UNIVERSITY
DELAND, FLORIDA

Entrance Moderately difficult **General** Independent, comprehensive, coed **Setting** 150-acre small-town campus **Enrollment** 2,784 **Faculty** 11:1 **Application deadline** 3/15 **Freshmen** 86% accepted **Housing** Yes **Tuition** $15,765 **Undergraduates** 57% women, 4% part-time, 10% 25 or older, 0% Native American, 5% Hispanic, 3% black, 2% Asian or Pacific Islander **Most popular recent majors** Business administration/commerce/management, education, psychology **Academic program** Advanced placement, accelerated degree program, self-designed majors, honors program, summer session, adult/continuing education programs, internships **Contact** Ms. Mary Napier, Dean of Admissions, Stetson University, DeLand, FL 32720-3781. Telephone: 904-822-7100. Fax: 904-822-8832.

TRINITY BAPTIST COLLEGE
JACKSONVILLE, FLORIDA

Entrance Difficulty N/R **General** Independent Baptist, 4-year, coed **Setting** 6-acre urban campus **Enrollment** 310 **Faculty** 11:1 **Housing** Yes **Tuition** $3698 **Undergraduates** 35% women, 12% part-time, 20% 25 or older, 0% Native American, 1% Hispanic, 2% black, 3% Asian or Pacific Islander **Academic program** Average class size 30, ESL program, advanced placement, accelerated degree program, summer session, adult/continuing education programs **Contact** Dr. Gordon Woods, Director of Admissions, Trinity Baptist College, 426 South McDuff Avenue, Jacksonville, FL 32254. Telephone: 904-384-2206 Ext. 125.

TRINITY COLLEGE OF FLORIDA
NEW PORT RICHEY, FLORIDA

Entrance Minimally difficult **General** Independent nondenominational, 4-year, coed **Setting** 20-acre small-town campus **Enrollment** 170 **Faculty** 12:1 **Application deadline** Rolling **Fresh-**

men 91% accepted **Housing** Yes **Tuition** $3470 **Undergraduates** 40% women, 50% part-time, 34% 25 or older, 1% Native American, 6% Hispanic, 7% black, 3% Asian or Pacific Islander **Most popular recent majors** Biblical studies, pastoral studies **Academic program** Advanced placement, tutorials, summer session, internships **Contact** Mr. Bill Morrison, Director of Admissions, Trinity College of Florida, New Port Richey, FL 34655. Telephone: 813-376-6911 Ext. 1216. Fax: 813-376-0781.

TRINITY INTERNATIONAL UNIVERSITY, SOUTH FLORIDA CAMPUS

MIAMI, FLORIDA

Entrance Moderately difficult **General** Independent nondenominational, comprehensive, coed **Setting** 16-acre urban campus **Enrollment** 423 **Faculty** 16:1 **Application deadline** Rolling **Freshmen** 75% accepted **Tuition** $7808 **Undergraduates** 50% women, 18% part-time, 57% 25 or older, 0% Native American, 37% Hispanic, 40% black, 1% Asian or Pacific Islander **Most popular recent majors** Human resources, biblical studies, education **Academic program** Advanced placement, accelerated degree program, summer session, adult/continuing education programs, internships **Contact** Mr. Liam Gillen, Director of Enrollment Services, Trinity International University, South Florida Campus, PO Box 019674, Miami, FL 33101-9674. Telephone: 305-577-4600 Ext. 135.

UNIVERSITY OF CENTRAL FLORIDA

ORLANDO, FLORIDA

Entrance Moderately difficult **General** State-supported, coed **Setting** 1,445-acre suburban campus **Enrollment** 27,278 **Faculty** 17:1 **Application deadline** 7/15 **Freshmen** 69% accepted **Housing** Yes **Tuition** $2025 **Undergraduates** 54% women, 31% part-time, 36% 25 or older, 1% Native American, 10% Hispanic, 6% black, 5% Asian or Pacific Islander **Most popular recent majors** Business administration/commerce/management, elementary education, electrical engineering **Academic program** Advanced placement, accelerated degree program, self-designed majors, honors program, summer session, adult/continuing education programs, internships **Contact** Ms. Susan J. McKinnon, Director of Admissions, University of Central Florida, PO Box 160111, Orlando, FL 32816. Telephone: 407-823-3000. Fax: 407-823-3419.

UNIVERSITY OF FLORIDA

GAINESVILLE, FLORIDA

Entrance Very difficult **General** State-supported, coed **Setting** 2,000-acre suburban campus **Enrollment** 39,932 **Faculty** 17:1 **Application deadline** 2/1 **Freshmen** 59% accepted **Housing** Yes **Tuition** $1928 **Undergraduates** 53% women, 12% part-time, 22% 25 or older, 9% Hispanic, 6% black, 6% Asian or Pacific Islander **Most popular recent majors** Psychology, finance/banking, English **Academic program** Advanced placement, accelerated degree program, self-designed majors, tutorials, honors program, summer session, adult/continuing education programs, internships **Contact** Admissions Office, University of Florida, PO Box 114000, Gainesville, FL 32611-4000. Telephone: 352-392-1365.

UNIVERSITY OF MIAMI

CORAL GABLES, FLORIDA

Entrance Moderately difficult **General** Independent, coed **Setting** 260-acre suburban campus **Enrollment** 13,677 **Faculty** 13:1 **Application deadline** 3/1 **Freshmen** 60% accepted **Housing** Yes **Tuition** $19,513 **Undergraduates** 53% women, 12% part-time, 14% 25 or older, 0% Native American, 28% Hispanic, 11% black, 5% Asian or Pacific Islander **Most popular recent majors** Psychology, biology/biological sciences, nursing **Academic program** Advanced placement, accelerated degree program, self-designed majors, tutorials, honors program, summer session, adult/continuing education programs, internships **Contact** Mr. Edward M. Gillis, Associate Dean of Enrollments, University of Miami, PO Box 248025, Coral Gables, FL 33124. Telephone: 305-284-4323.

UNIVERSITY OF NORTH FLORIDA

JACKSONVILLE, FLORIDA

Entrance Very difficult **General** State-supported, comprehensive, coed **Setting** 1,000-acre urban campus **Enrollment** 10,909 **Faculty** 14:1 **Application deadline** 6/1 **Freshmen** 70% accepted **Housing** Yes **Tuition** $2006 **Undergraduates** 59% women, 52% part-time, 58% 25 or older, 0% Native American, 4% Hispanic, 10% black, 5% Asian or Pacific Islander **Most popular recent majors** Business administration/commerce/management, education, psychology **Academic program** Advanced placement, accelerated degree program, tutorials, honors program, summer session, adult/continuing education programs, internships **Contact** Ms. Mary Bolla, Director of Admissions, University of North Florida, 4567 St Johns Bluff Road South, Jacksonville, FL 32224-2645. Telephone: 904-646-2624.

UNIVERSITY OF SOUTH FLORIDA
TAMPA, FLORIDA

Entrance Moderately difficult **General** State-supported, coed **Setting** 1,913-acre urban campus **Enrollment** 30,938 **Faculty** 23:1 **Application deadline** 5/1 **Freshmen** 67% accepted **Housing** Yes **Tuition** $2086 **Undergraduates** 58% women, 36% part-time, 40% 25 or older, 1% Native American, 9% Hispanic, 10% black, 5% Asian or Pacific Islander **Most popular recent majors** Business administration/commerce/management, education, psychology **Academic program** Average class size 36, advanced placement, accelerated degree program, self-designed majors, honors program, summer session, adult/continuing education programs, internships **Contact** Dr. Mark Rubinstein, Director of Admissions, University of South Florida, 4202 East Fowler Avenue, Tampa, FL 33620-6900. Telephone: 813-974-3350. Fax: 813-974-9689.

UNIVERSITY OF SOUTH FLORIDA, NEW COLLEGE
SEE NEW COLLEGE OF THE UNIVERSITY OF SOUTH FLORIDA

THE UNIVERSITY OF TAMPA
TAMPA, FLORIDA

Entrance Moderately difficult **General** Independent, comprehensive, coed **Setting** 69-acre urban campus **Enrollment** 2,712 **Faculty** 15:1 **Application deadline** Rolling **Freshmen** 77% accepted **Housing** Yes **Tuition** $14,652 **Undergraduates** 58% women, 22% part-time, 32% 25 or older, 1% Native American, 8% Hispanic, 6% black, 2% Asian or Pacific Islander **Most popular recent majors** Business administration/commerce/management, psychology, communication **Academic program** Advanced placement, accelerated degree program, tutorials, honors program, summer session, adult/continuing education programs, internships **Contact** Ms. Barbara P. Strickler, Vice President for Enrollment, The University of Tampa, 401 West Kennedy Boulevard, Tampa, FL 33606-1480. Telephone: 813-253-6211. Fax: 813-254-4955.

UNIVERSITY OF WEST FLORIDA
PENSACOLA, FLORIDA

Entrance Moderately difficult **General** State-supported, comprehensive, coed **Setting** 1,000-acre suburban campus **Enrollment** 8,054 **Faculty** 27:1 **Application deadline** 6/30 **Freshmen** 84% accepted **Housing** Yes **Tuition** $1985 **Undergraduates** 57% women, 44% part-time, 1% Native American, 3% Hispanic, 8% black, 3% Asian or Pacific Islander **Most popular recent majors** Psychology, elementary education, business administration/commerce/management **Academic program** Advanced placement, honors program, summer session, internships **Contact** Ms. Susie Neeley, Director of Admissions, University of West Florida, Pensacola, FL 32514-5750. Telephone: 904-474-2230.

WARNER SOUTHERN COLLEGE
LAKE WALES, FLORIDA

Entrance Minimally difficult **General** Independent, 4-year, coed, affiliated with Church of God **Setting** 320-acre rural campus **Enrollment** 601 **Faculty** 14:1 **Application deadline** Rolling **Freshmen** 56% accepted **Housing** Yes **Tuition** $8220 **Undergraduates** 61% women, 13% part-time, 54% 25 or older, 0% Native American, 5% Hispanic, 14% black **Most popular recent majors** Business administration/commerce/management, elementary education, pastoral studies **Academic program** Advanced placement, accelerated degree program, tutorials, summer session, adult/continuing education programs, internships **Contact** Mr. Jeff Bush, Director of Admissions, Warner Southern College, Lake Wales, FL 33853-8725. Telephone: 941-638-7250 Ext. 7208. Fax: 941-638-1472.

WEBBER COLLEGE
BABSON PARK, FLORIDA

Entrance Moderately difficult **General** Independent, 4-year, specialized, coed **Setting** 110-acre small-town campus **Enrollment** 438 **Faculty** 15:1 **Application deadline** Rolling **Freshmen** 96% accepted **Housing** Yes **Tuition** $7390 **Undergraduates** 44% women, 19% part-time, 26% 25 or older, 0% Native American, 4% Hispanic, 6% black, 1% Asian or Pacific Islander **Most popular recent majors** Business administration/commerce/management, marketing/retailing/merchandising, hotel and restaurant management **Academic program** Advanced placement, accelerated degree program, tutorials, summer session, adult/continuing education programs, internships **Contact** Mr. Steve Jameson, Director of Admissions, Webber College, Babson Park, FL 33827-0096. Telephone: 941-638-2910. Fax: 941-638-2823.

Georgia

AGNES SCOTT COLLEGE

DECATUR, GEORGIA

Entrance Very difficult **General** Independent, comprehensive, women only, affiliated with Presbyterian Church (U.S.A.) **Setting** 100-acre urban campus **Enrollment** 715 **Faculty** 8:1 **Application deadline** 3/1 **Freshmen** 82% accepted **Housing** Yes **Tuition** $14,960 **Undergraduates** 5% part-time, 14% 25 or older, 1% Native American, 2% Hispanic, 16% black, 5% Asian or Pacific Islander **Most popular recent majors** English, biology/biological sciences, psychology **Academic program** Average class size 17, advanced placement, accelerated degree program, self-designed majors, tutorials, summer session, adult/continuing education programs, internships **Contact** Ms. Stephanie Balmer, Director of Admission, Agnes Scott College, 141 East College Avenue, Decatur, GA 30030-3797. Telephone: 404-638-6285. Fax: 404-638-6414.

ALBANY STATE UNIVERSITY

ALBANY, GEORGIA

Entrance Minimally difficult **General** State-supported, comprehensive, coed **Setting** 131-acre urban campus **Enrollment** 3,150 **Faculty** 20:1 **Application deadline** 9/1 **Freshmen** 70% accepted **Housing** Yes **Tuition** $1860 **Undergraduates** 64% women, 20% part-time, 15% 25 or older, 1% Native American, 1% Hispanic, 89% black, 1% Asian or Pacific Islander **Academic program** Advanced placement, tutorials, honors program, summer session, adult/continuing education programs, internships **Contact** Mrs. Patricia Price, Assistant Director of Admissions, Albany State University, 504 College Drive, Albany, GA 31705-2717. Telephone: 912-430-4646.

THE AMERICAN COLLEGE

ATLANTA, GEORGIA

Entrance Noncompetitive **General** Proprietary, comprehensive, coed **Setting** Urban campus **Enrollment** 960 **Faculty** 12:1 **Application deadline** Rolling **Freshmen** 100% accepted **Housing** Yes **Tuition** $9855 **Undergraduates** 82% women, 20% part-time, 8% 25 or older, 4% Hispanic, 16% black, 1% Asian or Pacific Islander **Academic program** Accelerated degree program, summer session, internships **Contact** Ms. Suzanne McBride, Vice President and Director of Admissions, The American College, 3330 Peachtree Road, NE, Atlanta, GA 30326-1019. Telephone: 404-231-9000. Fax: 404-231-1062.

ARMSTRONG ATLANTIC STATE UNIVERSITY

SAVANNAH, GEORGIA

Entrance Minimally difficult **General** State-supported, comprehensive, coed **Setting** 250-acre suburban campus **Enrollment** 5,617 **Faculty** 14:1 **Application deadline** 8/15 **Freshmen** 78% accepted **Housing** Yes **Tuition** $1836 **Undergraduates** 70% women, 36% part-time, 57% 25 or older, 1% Native American, 2% Hispanic, 21% black, 2% Asian or Pacific Islander **Most popular recent majors** Education, nursing, criminal justice **Academic program** Average class size 18, advanced placement, accelerated degree program, tutorials, honors program, summer session, adult/continuing education programs, internships **Contact** Mr. Kim West, Registrar/Director of Admissions, Armstrong Atlantic State University, Savannah, GA 31419-1997. Telephone: 912-927-5275. Fax: 912-921-5462.

ATLANTA CHRISTIAN COLLEGE

EAST POINT, GEORGIA

Entrance Minimally difficult **General** Independent Christian, 4-year, coed **Setting** 52-acre suburban campus **Enrollment** 276 **Faculty** 9:1 **Application deadline** 8/1 **Freshmen** 86% accepted **Housing** Yes **Tuition** $6426 **Undergraduates** 51% women, 14% part-time, 30% 25 or older, 0% Native American, 0% Hispanic, 22% black, 2% Asian or Pacific Islander **Most popular recent majors** Biblical studies, human development, early childhood education **Academic program** Advanced placement, tutorials, summer session, internships **Contact** Ms. Nancy Swartz, Director of Admissions, Atlanta Christian College, East Point, GA 30344-1999. Telephone: 404-761-8861.

ATLANTA COLLEGE OF ART

ATLANTA, GEORGIA

Entrance Moderately difficult **General** Independent, 4-year, specialized, coed **Setting** 6-acre urban campus **Enrollment** 396 **Faculty** 7:1 **Application deadline** Rolling **Freshmen** 86% accepted **Housing** Yes **Tuition** $11,900 **Undergraduates** 47% women, 0% part-time, 0% Native American, 2% Hispanic, 18% black, 3% Asian or Pacific Islander **Most popular recent majors** Commercial art, painting/drawing, photography **Academic program** Advanced placement, self-designed majors, honors program, summer session, adult/continuing education programs, internships **Contact** Ms. Joy E. Martin, Director of Enrollment Management, Atlanta College of Art, 1280 Peachtree Street, NE, Atlanta, GA 30309-3582. Telephone: 404-733-5101. Fax: 404-733-5107.

AUGUSTA STATE UNIVERSITY
AUGUSTA, GEORGIA

Entrance Minimally difficult **General** State-supported, comprehensive, coed **Setting** 72-acre urban campus **Enrollment** 5,561 **Application deadline** 8/15 **Freshmen** 79% accepted **Tuition** $1926 **Undergraduates** 64% women, 34% part-time, 31% 25 or older, 1% Native American, 2% Hispanic, 19% black, 4% Asian or Pacific Islander **Most popular recent majors** Nursing, early childhood education, biology/biological sciences **Academic program** Advanced placement, summer session, adult/continuing education programs, internships **Contact** Mr. Lee Young, Director of Admissions/Assistant Dean for Enrollment Service, Augusta State University, 2500 Walton Way, Augusta, GA 30904-2200. Telephone: 706-737-1632. Fax: 706-737-1777.

BERRY COLLEGE
MOUNT BERRY, GEORGIA

Entrance Moderately difficult **General** Independent, comprehensive, coed **Setting** 28,000-acre small-town campus **Enrollment** 2,085 **Faculty** 15:1 **Application deadline** Rolling **Freshmen** 82% accepted **Housing** Yes **Tuition** $10,210 **Undergraduates** 61% women, 3% part-time, 5% 25 or older, 0% Native American, 1% Hispanic, 2% black, 2% Asian or Pacific Islander **Most popular recent majors** Early childhood education, psychology, middle school education **Academic program** Advanced placement, accelerated degree program, self-designed majors, honors program, summer session, adult/continuing education programs, internships **Contact** Mr. George Gaddie, Dean of Admissions, Berry College, Mount Berry, GA 30149-0159. Telephone: 706-236-2215.

BEULAH HEIGHTS BIBLE COLLEGE
ATLANTA, GEORGIA

Entrance Noncompetitive **General** Independent-religious, 4-year, coed **Setting** 7-acre urban campus **Enrollment** 374 **Faculty** 12:1 **Application deadline** Rolling **Housing** Yes **Tuition** $3620 **Undergraduates** 49% women, 47% part-time, 94% 25 or older, 0% Native American, 0% Hispanic, 71% black, 2% Asian or Pacific Islander **Most popular recent major** Biblical languages **Academic program** Average class size 45, advanced placement, accelerated degree program, summer session, adult/continuing education programs, internships **Contact** Dr. James B. Keiller, Vice President and Academic Dean, Beulah Heights Bible College, 892 Berne Street, SE, Atlanta, GA 30316. Telephone: 404-627-2681. Fax: 404-627-0702.

BRENAU UNIVERSITY
GAINESVILLE, GEORGIA

Entrance Moderately difficult **General** Independent, comprehensive, primarily women **Setting** 50-acre small-town campus **Enrollment** 2,225 **Faculty** 13:1 **Application deadline** Rolling **Freshmen** 74% accepted **Housing** Yes **Tuition** $10,740 **Undergraduates** 97% women, 10% part-time, 22% 25 or older, 1% Native American, 2% Hispanic, 7% black, 1% Asian or Pacific Islander **Most popular recent majors** Education, business administration/commerce/management, nursing **Academic program** Advanced placement, accelerated degree program, self-designed majors, honors program, summer session, internships **Contact** Dr. John D. Upchurch, Director of Admissions, Brenau University, Gainesville, GA 30501-3697. Telephone: 770-534-6100. Fax: 770-534-6114.

BREWTON-PARKER COLLEGE
MT. VERNON, GEORGIA

Entrance Noncompetitive **General** Independent Southern Baptist, 4-year, coed **Setting** 280-acre rural campus **Enrollment** 1,582 **Faculty** 16:1 **Application deadline** Rolling **Freshmen** 99% accepted **Housing** Yes **Tuition** $5520 **Undergraduates** 64% women, 21% part-time, 35% 25 or older, 1% Native American, 1% Hispanic, 15% black, 1% Asian or Pacific Islander **Most popular recent majors** Business administration/commerce/management, education, religious studies **Academic program** Advanced placement, tutorials, honors program, summer session, adult/continuing education programs, internships **Contact** Mrs. Jill O'Neal, Director of Admissions, Brewton-Parker College, Highway 280, Mt. Vernon, GA 30445. Telephone: 912-583-3268. Fax: 912-583-4498.

CLARK ATLANTA UNIVERSITY
ATLANTA, GEORGIA

Entrance Moderately difficult **General** Independent United Methodist, coed **Setting** 113-acre urban campus **Enrollment** 5,798 **Faculty** 16:1 **Application deadline** 3/1 **Freshmen** 70% accepted **Housing** Yes **Tuition** $9348 **Undergraduates** 68% women, 5% part-time, 99% black, 1% Asian or Pacific Islander **Most popular recent majors** Communication, business administration/commerce/management, psychology **Academic program** Average class size 25, advanced placement, accelerated degree program, tutorials, honors program, summer session, adult/continuing education programs, internships **Contact** Office of Admissions, Clark Atlanta University, James P Brawley Dr at Fair St, SW, Atlanta, GA 30314. Telephone: 404-880-8784 Ext. 6650.

CLAYTON COLLEGE & STATE UNIVERSITY
MORROW, GEORGIA

Entrance Minimally difficult **General** State-supported, 4-year, coed **Setting** 163-acre suburban campus **Enrollment** 4,687 **Faculty** 22:1 **Application deadline** 8/15 **Tuition** $1968 **Undergraduates** 65% women, 59% part-time, 37% 25 or older, 0% Native American, 2% Hispanic, 26% black, 2% Asian or Pacific Islander **Most popular recent majors** Business administration/commerce/management, nursing, dental services **Academic program** Average class size 25, advanced placement, tutorials, honors program, summer session, adult/continuing education programs, internships **Contact** Ms. Carol S. Montgomery, Admissions, Clayton College & State University, 5900 North Lee Street, Morrow, GA 30260-0285. Telephone: 770-961-3500. Fax: 770-961-3752.

COLUMBUS STATE UNIVERSITY
COLUMBUS, GEORGIA

Entrance Minimally difficult **General** State-supported, comprehensive, coed **Setting** 132-acre suburban campus **Enrollment** 5,536 **Faculty** 24:1 **Application deadline** 8/30 **Freshmen** 73% accepted **Housing** Yes **Tuition** $1941 **Undergraduates** 61% women, 38% part-time, 36% 25 or older, 3% Hispanic, 23% black, 3% Asian or Pacific Islander **Most popular recent majors** Liberal arts/general studies, criminal justice, elementary education **Academic program** Advanced placement, accelerated degree program, tutorials, summer session, adult/continuing education programs, internships **Contact** Ms. Patty L. Ross, Director of Admissions, Columbus State University, 4225 University Avenue, Columbus, GA 31907-5645. Telephone: 706-568-2035. Fax: 706-568-2462.

COVENANT COLLEGE
LOOKOUT MOUNTAIN, GEORGIA

Entrance Moderately difficult **General** Independent, comprehensive, coed, affiliated with Presbyterian Church in America **Setting** 250-acre suburban campus **Enrollment** 763 **Faculty** 15:1 **Application deadline** Rolling **Freshmen** 98% accepted **Housing** Yes **Tuition** $12,880 **Undergraduates** 57% women, 3% part-time, 1% Hispanic, 2% black, 1% Asian or Pacific Islander **Most popular recent majors** Elementary education, history, interdisciplinary studies **Academic program** Average class size 25, advanced placement, accelerated degree program, tutorials, honors program, summer session, internships **Contact** Mr. Joe Stephens, Director of Admissions, Covenant College, Lookout Mountain, GA 30750. Telephone: 706-820-1560 Ext. 1643.

DEVRY INSTITUTE OF TECHNOLOGY
DECATUR, GEORGIA

Entrance Minimally difficult **General** Proprietary, 4-year, coed **Setting** 21-acre suburban campus **Enrollment** 3,109 **Faculty** 23:1 **Application deadline** Rolling **Freshmen** 68% accepted **Tuition** $6968 **Undergraduates** 36% women, 19% part-time, 48% 25 or older, 0% Native American, 2% Hispanic, 63% black, 2% Asian or Pacific Islander **Most popular recent majors** Computer information systems, electronics engineering technology, electrical and electronics technologies **Academic program** Advanced placement, accelerated degree program, summer session, adult/continuing education programs **Contact** Mr. George Ollennu, Director of Admissions, DeVry Institute of Technology, Decatur, GA 30030-2198. Telephone: 404-292-2645 Ext. 430.

EMMANUEL COLLEGE
FRANKLIN SPRINGS, GEORGIA

Entrance Minimally difficult **General** Independent, 4-year, coed, affiliated with Pentecostal Holiness Church **Setting** 90-acre rural campus **Enrollment** 695 **Faculty** 10:1 **Application deadline** 8/1 **Freshmen** 68% accepted **Housing** Yes **Tuition** $6060 **Undergraduates** 56% women, 10% part-time, 17% 25 or older, 1% Hispanic, 9% black, 1% Asian or Pacific Islander **Most popular recent majors** Biblical studies, early childhood education, business administration/commerce/management **Academic program** Average class size 35, advanced placement, summer session, internships **Contact** Mr. Tim Harrison, Director of Admissions, Emmanuel College, PO Box 129, Franklin Springs, GA 30639-0129. Telephone: 706-245-7226 Ext. 2722.

EMORY UNIVERSITY
ATLANTA, GEORGIA

Entrance Most difficult **General** Independent Methodist, coed **Setting** 631-acre suburban campus **Enrollment** 11,270 **Faculty** 10:1 **Application deadline** 1/15 **Freshmen** 44% accepted **Housing** Yes **Tuition** $21,120 **Undergraduates** 53% women, 2% part-time, 0% 25 or older, 0% Native American, 4% Hispanic, 10% black, 12% Asian or Pacific Islander **Most popular recent**

majors Psychology, biology/biological sciences, political science/government **Academic program** Average class size 35, advanced placement, accelerated degree program, tutorials, honors program, summer session, internships **Contact** Mr. Daniel C. Walls, Dean of Admissions, Emory University, Boisfeuillet Jones Center–Office of Admissions, Atlanta, GA 30322-1100. Telephone: 404-727-6036.

FORT VALLEY STATE UNIVERSITY
FORT VALLEY, GEORGIA

Entrance Minimally difficult **General** State-supported, comprehensive, coed **Setting** 1,307-acre small-town campus **Enrollment** 3,024 **Faculty** 18:1 **Application deadline** 9/1 **Housing** Yes **Tuition** $2157 **Undergraduates** 59% women, 15% part-time, 0% Native American, 1% Hispanic, 93% black, 1% Asian or Pacific Islander **Academic program** Advanced placement, tutorials, honors program, summer session, adult/continuing education programs, internships **Contact** Dr. Mildred P. Hill, Dean of Admissions and Enrollment, Fort Valley State University, Fort Valley, GA 31030-3298. Telephone: 912-825-6307.

GEORGIA BAPTIST COLLEGE OF NURSING
ATLANTA, GEORGIA

Entrance Moderately difficult **General** Independent Baptist, 4-year, specialized, women only **Setting** 20-acre urban campus **Enrollment** 334 **Faculty** 10:1 **Application deadline** 4/15 **Freshmen** 37% accepted **Housing** Yes **Tuition** $7200 **Undergraduates** 10% part-time, 38% 25 or older, 0% Native American, 1% Hispanic, 12% black, 2% Asian or Pacific Islander **Academic program** Advanced placement, tutorials, summer session **Contact** Mrs. Judy Craven, Director of Admissions, Georgia Baptist College of Nursing, 274 Boulevard, NE, Atlanta, GA 30312. Telephone: 404-265-4800.

GEORGIA COLLEGE
MILLEDGEVILLE, GEORGIA

Entrance Moderately difficult **General** State-supported, comprehensive, coed **Setting** 696-acre small-town campus **Enrollment** 5,534 **Application deadline** Rolling **Freshmen** 97% accepted **Housing** Yes **Tuition** $2064 **Undergraduates** 64% women, 23% part-time, 24% 25 or older, 0% Native American, 1% Hispanic, 17% black, 1% Asian or Pacific Islander **Most popular recent majors** Nursing, early childhood education, accounting **Academic program** Advanced placement, accelerated degree program, self-designed majors, honors program, summer session, adult/continuing education programs, internships **Contact** Ms. Maryllis Wolfgang, Director of Admissions, Georgia College, CPO Box 023, Milledgeville, GA 31061. Telephone: 912-453-6285. Fax: 912-453-1914.

GEORGIA INSTITUTE OF TECHNOLOGY
ATLANTA, GEORGIA

Entrance Very difficult **General** State-supported, coed **Setting** 360-acre urban campus **Enrollment** 12,985 **Faculty** 19:1 **Application deadline** 2/1 **Freshmen** 56% accepted **Housing** Yes **Tuition** $2685 **Undergraduates** 28% women, 7% part-time, 6% 25 or older, 1% Native American, 4% Hispanic, 10% black, 12% Asian or Pacific Islander **Most popular recent majors** Electrical engineering, mechanical engineering, industrial engineering **Academic program** Advanced placement, accelerated degree program, self-designed majors, tutorials, honors program, summer session, internships **Contact** Ms. Deborah Smith, Director of Admissions, Georgia Institute of Technology, 225 North Avenue, NW, Atlanta, GA 30332-0320. Telephone: 404-894-4154. Fax: 404-853-9163.

GEORGIA SOUTHERN UNIVERSITY
STATESBORO, GEORGIA

Entrance Moderately difficult **General** State-supported, comprehensive, coed **Setting** 601-acre small-town campus **Enrollment** 14,312 **Faculty** 25:1 **Application deadline** 8/1 **Freshmen** 70% accepted **Housing** Yes **Tuition** $2256 **Undergraduates** 54% women, 8% part-time, 11% 25 or older, 1% Native American, 2% Hispanic, 26% black, 1% Asian or Pacific Islander **Most popular recent majors** Early childhood education, marketing/retailing/merchandising, finance/banking **Academic program** Average class size 30, advanced placement, honors program, summer session, adult/continuing education programs, internships **Contact** Dr. Dale Wasson, Director of Admissions, Georgia Southern University, GSU P.O. Box 8024, Statesboro, GA 30460. Telephone: 912-681-5531. Fax: 912-681-0081.

GEORGIA SOUTHWESTERN STATE UNIVERSITY
AMERICUS, GEORGIA

Entrance Moderately difficult **General** State-supported, comprehensive, coed **Setting** 187-acre small-town campus **Enrollment** 2,522 **Faculty** 15:1 **Application deadline** Rolling **Freshmen** 74% accepted **Housing** Yes **Tuition** $2145 **Undergraduates** 66% women, 27% part-time, 24%

25 or older, 1% Native American, 1% Hispanic, 24% black, 2% Asian or Pacific Islander **Most popular recent majors** Education, business administration/commerce/management, computer science **Academic program** Average class size 22, advanced placement, tutorials, honors program, summer session, adult/continuing education programs, internships **Contact** Mr. Gary Fallis, Director of Admissions, Georgia Southwestern State University, Americus, GA 31709-4693. Telephone: 912-928-1273. Fax: 912-931-2059.

GEORGIA STATE UNIVERSITY
ATLANTA, GEORGIA

Entrance Moderately difficult **General** State-supported, coed **Setting** 24-acre urban campus **Enrollment** 23,410 **Faculty** 14:1 **Application deadline** 7/1 **Freshmen** 70% accepted **Housing** Yes **Tuition** $2673 **Undergraduates** 60% women, 46% part-time, 58% 25 or older, 1% Native American, 2% Hispanic, 17% black, 6% Asian or Pacific Islander **Most popular recent majors** Business administration/commerce/management, mathematics, accounting **Academic program** Advanced placement, accelerated degree program, self-designed majors, tutorials, honors program, summer session, adult/continuing education programs, internships **Contact** Mr. Rob Sheinkopf, Dean of Admissions and Acting Dean for Enrollment Services, Georgia State University, University Plaza, Atlanta, GA 30303-3083. Telephone: 404-651-2365.

KENNESAW STATE UNIVERSITY
KENNESAW, GEORGIA

Entrance Moderately difficult **General** State-supported, comprehensive, coed **Setting** 186-acre suburban campus **Enrollment** 12,537 **Faculty** 27:1 **Application deadline** 8/15 **Freshmen** 86% accepted **Tuition** $2013 **Undergraduates** 61% women, 44% part-time, 42% 25 or older, 1% Native American, 2% Hispanic, 7% black, 2% Asian or Pacific Islander **Academic program** Average class size 27, ESL program, advanced placement, honors program, summer session, adult/continuing education programs, internships **Contact** Ms. Angela Evans, Admissions Counselor, Kennesaw State University, Kennesaw, GA 30144-5591. Telephone: 770-423-6300 Ext. 2001. Fax: 770-423-6541.

LAGRANGE COLLEGE
LAGRANGE, GEORGIA

Entrance Moderately difficult **General** Independent United Methodist, comprehensive, coed **Setting** 120-acre small-town campus **Enrollment** 984 **Faculty** 11:1 **Application deadline** 8/15 **Freshmen** 79% accepted **Housing** Yes **Tuition** $9168 **Undergraduates** 59% women, 35% 25 or older, 0% Native American, 1% Hispanic, 14% black, 1% Asian or Pacific Islander **Academic program** Advanced placement, tutorials, summer session, adult/continuing education programs, internships **Contact** Mr. Philip L. Dodson, Dean of Admissions, LaGrange College, LaGrange, GA 30240-2999. Telephone: 706-812-7260.

LUTHER RICE BIBLE COLLEGE AND SEMINARY
LITHONIA, GEORGIA

Entrance Noncompetitive **General** Independent Baptist, comprehensive, primarily men **Setting** 5-acre urban campus **Enrollment** 1,285 **Faculty** 18:1 **Application deadline** Rolling **Freshmen** 98% accepted **Tuition** $2512 **Undergraduates** 20% women, 85% part-time, 88% 25 or older, 0% Native American, 1% Hispanic, 20% black, 5% Asian or Pacific Islander **Academic program** Adult/continuing education programs **Contact** Dr. Dennis Dieringer, Director of Admissions and Records, Luther Rice Bible College and Seminary, 3038 Evans Mill Road, Lithonia, GA 30038. Telephone: 770-484-1204.

MEDICAL COLLEGE OF GEORGIA
AUGUSTA, GEORGIA

Entrance Moderately difficult **General** State-supported, coed **Setting** 100-acre urban campus **Enrollment** 2,048 **Application deadline** 11/15 **Freshmen** 15% accepted **Housing** Yes **Tuition** $2526 **Undergraduates** 80% women, 10% part-time, 1% Native American, 1% Hispanic, 10% black, 4% Asian or Pacific Islander **Most popular recent majors** Nursing, occupational therapy, physician's assistant studies **Contact** Ms. Elizabeth Griffin, Director of Academic Admissions, Medical College of Georgia, 1120 Fifteenth Street, Augusta, GA 30912-1003. Telephone: 706-721-2725. Fax: 706-721-3461.

MERCER UNIVERSITY
MACON, GEORGIA

Entrance Moderately difficult **General** Independent Baptist, comprehensive, coed **Setting** 130-acre suburban campus **Enrollment** 6,960 **Faculty** 17:1 **Application deadline** Rolling **Freshmen** 88% accepted **Housing** Yes **Tuition** $13,896 **Undergraduates** 56% women, 5% part-time, 10% 25 or older, 1% Native American, 2% Hispanic, 16% black, 5% Asian or Pacific Islander **Most popu-**

lar recent majors Business administration/commerce/management, human services, early childhood education **Academic program** Advanced placement, self-designed majors, tutorials, summer session, adult/continuing education programs, internships **Contact** Director of Admission, Mercer University, 1400 Coleman Avenue, Macon, GA 31207-0003. Telephone: 912-752-2650. Fax: 912-752-2828.

MERCER UNIVERSITY, CECIL B. DAY CAMPUS
ATLANTA, GEORGIA

Entrance Moderately difficult **General** Independent Baptist, upper-level, coed **Setting** 400-acre suburban campus **Enrollment** 1,900 **Faculty** 15:1 **Freshmen** 89% accepted **Tuition** $7650 **Undergraduates** 46% women, 68% part-time, 75% 25 or older, 3% Hispanic, 23% black, 14% Asian or Pacific Islander **Most popular recent majors** Business administration/commerce/management, accounting, computer science **Academic program** Advanced placement, tutorials, summer session, adult/continuing education programs **Contact** Ms. Argy Russell, Director of Admissions, Mercer University, Cecil B. Day Campus, Atlanta, GA 30341-4155. Telephone: 770-986-3134. Fax: 770-986-3135.

MOREHOUSE COLLEGE
ATLANTA, GEORGIA

Entrance Moderately difficult **General** Independent, 4-year, men only **Setting** 61-acre urban campus **Enrollment** 2,926 **Faculty** 17:1 **Application deadline** 2/15 **Freshmen** 68% accepted **Housing** Yes **Tuition** $9724 **Undergraduates** 4% part-time, 98% black **Most popular recent majors** Business administration/commerce/management, engineering (general), biology/biological sciences **Academic program** Advanced placement, tutorials, honors program, summer session, internships **Contact** Mr. André Pattillo, Director of Admissions, Morehouse College, 830 Westview Drive, SW, Atlanta, GA 30314. Telephone: 404-215-2632. Fax: 404-659-6536.

MORRIS BROWN COLLEGE
ATLANTA, GEORGIA

Entrance Minimally difficult **General** Independent, 4-year, coed, affiliated with African Methodist Episcopal Church **Setting** 21-acre urban campus **Enrollment** 2,153 **Faculty** 15:1 **Application deadline** 6/30 **Freshmen** 66% accepted **Housing** Yes **Tuition** $8210 **Undergraduates** 58% women, 3% part-time, 6% 25 or older, 0% Native American, 1% Hispanic, 95% black, 0% Asian or Pacific Islander **Most popular recent majors** Early childhood education, accounting, business administration/commerce/management **Academic program** Average class size 20, accelerated degree program, tutorials, honors program, adult/continuing education programs, internships **Contact** Director of Enrollment Management, Morris Brown College, 643 Martin Luther King Jr Drive, NW, Atlanta, GA 30314-4140. Telephone: 404-220-0152. Fax: 404-220-0267.

NORTH GEORGIA COLLEGE & STATE UNIVERSITY
DAHLONEGA, GEORGIA

Entrance Moderately difficult **General** State-supported, comprehensive, coed **Setting** 140-acre small-town campus **Enrollment** 3,198 **Faculty** 16:1 **Application deadline** 8/15 **Freshmen** 66% accepted **Housing** Yes **Tuition** $2052 **Undergraduates** 63% women, 18% part-time, 1% Native American, 1% Hispanic, 2% black, 1% Asian or Pacific Islander **Most popular recent majors** Criminal justice, education, business administration/commerce/management **Academic program** Average class size 35, advanced placement, honors program, summer session, internships **Contact** Mr. Bill Smith, Director of Recruitment, North Georgia College & State University, Admissions Center, Dahlonega, GA 30533. Telephone: 706-864-1800.

OGLETHORPE UNIVERSITY
ATLANTA, GEORGIA

Entrance Very difficult **General** Independent, comprehensive, coed **Setting** 118-acre suburban campus **Enrollment** 1,227 **Faculty** 12:1 **Application deadline** 8/1 **Freshmen** 77% accepted **Housing** Yes **Tuition** $15,920 **Undergraduates** 58% women, 36% part-time, 6% 25 or older, 1% Native American, 3% Hispanic, 8% black, 4% Asian or Pacific Islander **Most popular recent majors** Business administration/commerce/management, psychology, communication **Academic program** Average class size 22, advanced placement, accelerated degree program, self-designed majors, tutorials, honors program, summer session, adult/continuing education programs, internships **Contact** Mr. Dennis T. Matthews, Associate Dean for Enrollment Management, Oglethorpe University, Atlanta, GA 30319-2797. Telephone: 404-364-8307. Fax: 404-364-8500.

PAINE COLLEGE
AUGUSTA, GEORGIA

Entrance Minimally difficult **General** Independent Methodist, 4-year, coed **Setting** 54-acre urban campus **Enrollment** 915 **Faculty** 13:1 **Application deadline** 8/1 **Freshmen** 63% accepted **Housing** Yes **Tuition** $6910 **Undergraduates** 64% women, 13% part-time, 20% 25 or older, 0% Native American, 1% Hispanic, 96% black, 0% Asian or Pacific Islander **Most popular recent majors** Business administration/commerce/management, sociology, psychology **Academic program** Advanced placement, accelerated degree program, tutorials, honors program, summer session, internships **Contact** Mrs. Ellen C. King, Director of Admission, Paine College, 1235 15th Street, Augusta, GA 30901-3182. Telephone: 706-821-8320. Fax: 706-821-8293.

PIEDMONT COLLEGE
DEMOREST, GEORGIA

Entrance Moderately difficult **General** Independent, comprehensive, coed, affiliated with Congregational Christian Church **Setting** 300-acre rural campus **Enrollment** 1,128 **Faculty** 12:1 **Application deadline** Rolling **Freshmen** 67% accepted **Housing** Yes **Tuition** $7200 **Undergraduates** 63% women, 14% part-time, 48% 25 or older, 1% Native American, 1% Hispanic, 6% black, 1% Asian or Pacific Islander **Most popular recent majors** Business administration/commerce/management, early childhood education, English **Academic program** Average class size 16, advanced placement, accelerated degree program, tutorials, honors program, summer session, adult/continuing education programs, internships **Contact** Mr. James Clement, Director of Admissions, Piedmont College, Demorest, GA 30535-0010. Telephone: 706-776-0103 Ext. 183. Fax: 706-776-2811.

REINHARDT COLLEGE
WALESKA, GEORGIA

Entrance Moderately difficult **General** Independent, 4-year, coed, affiliated with United Methodist Church **Setting** 600-acre rural campus **Enrollment** 959 **Faculty** 18:1 **Application deadline** Rolling **Freshmen** 83% accepted **Housing** Yes **Tuition** $6762 **Undergraduates** 60% women, 16% part-time, 20% 25 or older, 1% Native American, 1% Hispanic, 3% black, 1% Asian or Pacific Islander **Most popular recent majors** Liberal arts/general studies, business administration/commerce/management, science **Academic program** Average class size 18, advanced placement, tutorials, honors program, summer session, adult/continuing education programs, internships **Contact** Mr. Timothy Copeland, Director of Admissions, Reinhardt College, Waleska, GA 30183-0128. Telephone: 770-720-5526. Fax: 770-720-5899.

SAVANNAH COLLEGE OF ART AND DESIGN
SAVANNAH, GEORGIA

Entrance Moderately difficult **General** Independent, comprehensive, specialized, coed **Setting** Urban campus **Enrollment** 3,093 **Faculty** 18:1 **Application deadline** Rolling **Freshmen** 73% accepted **Housing** Yes **Tuition** $12,600 **Undergraduates** 44% women, 11% part-time, 9% 25 or older, 1% Native American, 2% Hispanic, 6% black, 2% Asian or Pacific Islander **Most popular recent majors** Graphic arts, computer graphics, illustration **Academic program** Average class size 20, advanced placement, tutorials, summer session, internships **Contact** Mrs. May Poetter, Vice President of Admissions, Savannah College of Art and Design, PO Box 3146, Savannah, GA 31402. Telephone: 912-238-2483. Fax: 912-238-2436.

SAVANNAH STATE UNIVERSITY
SAVANNAH, GEORGIA

Entrance Minimally difficult **General** State-supported, 4-year, coed **Setting** 165-acre suburban campus **Enrollment** 3,211 **Application deadline** 9/1 **Freshmen** 66% accepted **Housing** Yes **Tuition** $2226 **Undergraduates** 57% women, 15% part-time, 9% 25 or older, 1% Hispanic, 86% black, 2% Asian or Pacific Islander **Academic program** Advanced placement, accelerated degree program, tutorials, summer session, adult/continuing education programs, internships **Contact** Dr. Roy A. Jackson, Director of Admissions, Savannah State University, PO Box 20209, Savannah, GA 31404. Telephone: 912-356-2181. Fax: 912-356-2256.

SHORTER COLLEGE
ROME, GEORGIA

Entrance Moderately difficult **General** Independent Baptist, 4-year, coed **Setting** 155-acre small-town campus **Enrollment** 1,577 **Faculty** 13:1 **Application deadline** Rolling **Freshmen** 75% accepted **Housing** Yes **Tuition** $8260 **Undergraduates** 64% women, 8% part-time, 13% 25 or older, 0% Native American, 1% Hispanic, 3% black, 1% Asian or Pacific Islander **Most popular recent majors** Business administration/commerce/management, psychology, elementary education **Academic program** Average class size 25, advanced placement, accelerated degree program, self-designed majors, tutorials, honors program, summer session, adult/continuing education programs, internships **Contact** Ms. Wendy Sutton, Director of Admissions, Shorter College, Rome, GA 30165-4298. Telephone: 706-233-7319. Fax: 706-236-1515.

SOUTH COLLEGE
SAVANNAH, GEORGIA

Entrance Minimally difficult **General** Proprietary, 4-year, coed **Setting** 5-acre suburban campus **Enrollment** 427 **Faculty** 7:1 **Application deadline** Rolling **Tuition** $5710 **Undergraduates** 83% women, 25% part-time, 68% 25 or older, 0% Native American, 2% Hispanic, 35% black, 1% Asian or Pacific Islander **Most popular recent majors** Medical assistant technologies, paralegal studies, business administration/commerce/management **Academic program** Tutorials, summer session, adult/continuing education programs, internships **Contact** Mr. Robin Manning, Director of Admissions, South College, Savannah, GA 31406-4881. Telephone: 912-651-8100 Ext. 14. Fax: 912-356-1409.

SOUTHERN COLLEGE OF TECHNOLOGY
SEE SOUTHERN POLYTECHNIC STATE UNIVERSITY

SOUTHERN POLYTECHNIC STATE UNIVERSITY
MARIETTA, GEORGIA

Entrance Moderately difficult **General** State-supported, comprehensive, coed **Setting** 200-acre suburban campus **Enrollment** 3,871 **Faculty** 18:1 **Application deadline** 8/31 **Freshmen** 74% accepted **Housing** Yes **Tuition** $1998 **Undergraduates** 17% women, 37% part-time, 42% 25 or older, 1% Native American, 2% Hispanic, 17% black, 5% Asian or Pacific Islander **Most popular recent majors** Electrical engineering technology, civil engineering technology, industrial engineering technology **Academic program** Average class size 25, advanced placement, accelerated degree program, summer session, adult/continuing education programs **Contact** Ms. Virginia A. Head, Director of Admissions, Southern Polytechnic State University, Marietta, GA 30060-2896. Telephone: 770-528-7281.

SPELMAN COLLEGE
ATLANTA, GEORGIA

Entrance Very difficult **General** Independent, 4-year, women only **Setting** 32-acre urban campus **Enrollment** 1,961 **Application deadline** 2/1 **Freshmen** 47% accepted **Housing** Yes **Tuition** $9500 **Undergraduates** 4% part-time, 4% 25 or older, 0% Native American, 0% Hispanic, 98% black, 0% Asian or Pacific Islander **Most popular recent majors** Psychology, economics, English **Academic program** Advanced placement, accelerated degree program, self-designed majors, honors program, adult/continuing education programs, internships **Contact** Ms. Victoria Valle, Director of Admissions and Orientation Services, Spelman College, 350 Spelman Lane, SW, Atlanta, GA 30314-4399. Telephone: 404-681-3643 Ext. 2188. Fax: 404-223-1449.

STATE UNIVERSITY OF WEST GEORGIA
CARROLLTON, GEORGIA

Entrance Minimally difficult **General** State-supported, comprehensive, coed **Setting** 400-acre small-town campus **Enrollment** 8,560 **Faculty** 16:1 **Application deadline** Rolling **Freshmen** 65% accepted **Housing** Yes **Tuition** $1989 **Undergraduates** 61% women, 20% part-time, 21% 25 or older, 0% Native American, 1% Hispanic, 16% black, 1% Asian or Pacific Islander **Most popular recent majors** Early childhood education, nursing, psychology **Academic program** Advanced placement, accelerated degree program, honors program, summer session, adult/continuing education programs, internships **Contact** Dr. Robert Johnson, Director of Admissions, State University of West Georgia, Carrollton, GA 30118. Telephone: 770-836-6416. Fax: 770-836-6720.

THOMAS COLLEGE
THOMASVILLE, GEORGIA

Entrance Noncompetitive **General** Independent, 4-year, coed **Setting** 24-acre small-town campus **Enrollment** 827 **Faculty** 14:1 **Application deadline** Rolling **Freshmen** 100% accepted **Tuition** $5340 **Undergraduates** 68% women, 21% part-time, 44% 25 or older, 1% Native American, 1% Hispanic, 30% black, 1% Asian or Pacific Islander **Most popular recent majors** Education, business administration/commerce/management, liberal arts/general studies **Academic program** Advanced placement, accelerated degree program, tutorials, summer session, adult/continuing education programs, internships **Contact** Ms. Darla Glass, Registrar, Thomas College, Thomasville, GA 31792-7499. Telephone: 912-226-1621 Ext. 20.

TOCCOA FALLS COLLEGE
TOCCOA FALLS, GEORGIA

Entrance Moderately difficult **General** Independent interdenominational, 4-year, coed **Setting** 1,100-acre small-town campus **Enrollment** 892 **Faculty** 18:1 **Application deadline** Rolling **Housing** Yes **Tuition** $7419 **Undergraduates** 54% women, 11% part-time, 1% Hispanic, 3% black, 4% Asian or Pacific Islander **Most popular recent majors** Early childhood education, communication, pastoral studies **Academic program** Average class size 35, advanced placement, accelerated degree program, self-designed majors, tutorials, summer session, adult/continuing education programs, internships **Contact** Mr. Eric Bennett, Assistant Director of Admissions, Toccoa Falls College, Toccoa Falls, GA 30598-1000. Telephone: 706-886-6831 Ext. 5380. Fax: 706-886-6412.

UNIVERSITY OF GEORGIA
ATHENS, GEORGIA

Entrance Moderately difficult **General** State-supported, coed **Setting** 1,601-acre suburban campus **Enrollment** 29,404 **Application deadline** 2/1 **Freshmen** 56% accepted **Housing** Yes **Tuition** $2838 **Undergraduates** 54% women, 11% part-time, 5% 25 or older, 1% Native American, 1% Hispanic, 7% black, 3% Asian or Pacific Islander **Most popular recent majors** English, accounting, political science/government **Academic program** Advanced placement, accelerated degree program, self-designed majors, honors program, summer session, adult/continuing education programs, internships **Contact** Dr. John Albright, Associate Director of Admissions, University of Georgia, Athens, GA 30602. Telephone: 706-542-3000.

VALDOSTA STATE UNIVERSITY
VALDOSTA, GEORGIA

Entrance Minimally difficult **General** State-supported, coed **Setting** 168-acre small-town campus **Enrollment** 9,810 **Faculty** 22:1 **Application deadline** Rolling **Freshmen** 73% accepted **Housing** Yes **Tuition** $1974 **Undergraduates** 61% women, 17% part-time, 22% 25 or older, 1% Native American, 1% Hispanic, 19% black, 1% Asian or Pacific Islander **Most popular recent majors** Biology/biological sciences, business administration/commerce/management, early childhood education **Academic program** Advanced placement, accelerated degree program, tutorials, honors program, summer session, adult/continuing education programs, internships **Contact** Mr. Walter Peacock, Director of Admissions, Valdosta State University, Valdosta, GA 31698. Telephone: 912-333-5791.

WESLEYAN COLLEGE
MACON, GEORGIA

Entrance Moderately difficult **General** Independent United Methodist, comprehensive, women only **Setting** 200-acre suburban campus **Enrollment** 476 **Faculty** 10:1 **Application deadline** Rolling **Freshmen** 95% accepted **Housing** Yes **Tuition** $14,200 **Undergraduates** 10% part-time, 15% 25 or older, 1% Native American, 4% Hispanic, 17% black, 4% Asian or Pacific Islander **Most popular recent majors** Business administration/commerce/management, psychology, English **Academic program** Average class size 27, advanced placement, accelerated degree program, self-designed majors, tutorials, honors program, summer session, adult/continuing education programs, internships **Contact** Ms. Lynne Henderson, Director of Admissions, Wesleyan College, Macon, GA 31210-4462. Telephone: 912-757-5206. Fax: 912-757-4030.

WEST GEORGIA COLLEGE
SEE STATE UNIVERSITY OF WEST GEORGIA

Kentucky

ALICE LLOYD COLLEGE
PIPPA PASSES, KENTUCKY

Entrance Moderately difficult **General** Independent, 4-year, coed **Setting** 175-acre rural campus **Enrollment** 511 **Faculty** 18:1 **Application deadline** 8/1 **Freshmen** 69% accepted **Housing** Yes **Tuition** $440 **Undergraduates** 55% women, 4% part-time, 10% 25 or older, 0% Native American, 0% Hispanic, 0% black, 0% Asian or Pacific Islander **Most popular recent majors** Elementary education, business administration/commerce/management **Academic program** Average class size 30, advanced placement, tutorials **Contact** Mr. Billy C. Melton, Director of Admissions, Alice Lloyd College, Pippa Passes, KY 41844. Telephone: 606-368-2101 Ext. 4404. Fax: 606-368-2125.

ASBURY COLLEGE
WILMORE, KENTUCKY

Entrance Moderately difficult **General** Independent nondenominational, 4-year, coed **Setting** 400-acre small-town campus **Enrollment** 1,167 **Faculty** 14:1 **Application deadline** Rolling **Freshmen** 82% accepted **Housing** Yes **Tuition** $11,225 **Undergraduates** 58% women, 6% part-time, 6% 25 or older, 0% Native American, 1% Hispanic, 1% black, 1% Asian or Pacific Islander **Most popular recent majors** Education, business administration/commerce/management, psychology **Academic program** Average class size 35, advanced placement, tutorials, honors program, summer session, internships **Contact** Mr. Stan F. Wiggam, Dean of Admissions, Asbury College, Wilmore, KY 40390. Telephone: 606-858-3511 Ext. 2142. Fax: 606-858-3921.

BELLARMINE COLLEGE
LOUISVILLE, KENTUCKY

Entrance Moderately difficult **General** Independent Roman Catholic, comprehensive, coed **Setting** 120-acre suburban campus **Enrollment** 2,180 **Faculty** 14:1 **Application deadline** 8/1 **Freshmen** 88% accepted **Housing** Yes **Tuition** $10,970 **Undergraduates** 58% women, 42% part-time, 26% 25 or older, 0% Native American, 1% Hispanic, 3% black, 1% Asian or Pacific Islander **Most popular recent majors** Business administration/commerce/management, accounting, nursing **Academic program** Advanced placement, accelerated degree program, self-designed majors, honors program, summer session, adult/continuing education programs, internships **Contact** Mr. Timothy A. Sturgeon, Associate Dean of Admissions, Bellarmine College, Louisville, KY 40205-0671. Telephone: 502-452-8131. Fax: 502-452-8002.

BEREA COLLEGE
BEREA, KENTUCKY

Entrance Moderately difficult **General** Independent, 4-year, coed **Setting** 140-acre small-town campus **Enrollment** 1,524 **Faculty** 12:1 **Application deadline** Rolling **Freshmen** 31% accepted **Housing** Yes **Tuition** $195 **Undergraduates** 57% women, 4% part-time, 8% 25 or older, 0% Native American, 1% Hispanic, 8% black, 2% Asian or Pacific Islander **Most popular recent major** Business administration/commerce/management **Academic program** Advanced placement, self-designed majors, summer session, internships **Contact** Mr. John S. Cook, Director of Admissions, Berea College, CPO 2344, Berea, KY 40404. Telephone: 606-986-9341 Ext. 5083.

BRESCIA COLLEGE
OWENSBORO, KENTUCKY

Entrance Moderately difficult **General** Independent Roman Catholic, comprehensive, coed **Setting** 6-acre urban campus **Enrollment** 753 **Faculty** 15:1 **Application deadline** Rolling **Freshmen** 82% accepted **Housing** Yes **Tuition** $8648 **Undergraduates** 70% women, 42% part-time, 55% 25 or older, 1% Native American, 1% Hispanic, 3% black, 1% Asian or Pacific Islander **Most popular recent majors** Business administration/commerce/management, speech pathology and audiology, social science **Academic program** Advanced placement, accelerated degree program, self-designed majors, tutorials, honors program, summer session, adult/continuing education programs, internships **Contact** Mr. Sam McNair, Director of Admissions, Brescia College, 717 Frederica Street, Owensboro, KY 42301-3023. Telephone: 502-686-4241 Ext. 241. Fax: 502-686-4266.

CAMPBELLSVILLE UNIVERSITY
CAMPBELLSVILLE, KENTUCKY

Entrance Moderately difficult **General** Independent Southern Baptist, coed **Setting** 60-acre small-town campus **Enrollment** 1,530 **Faculty** 16:1 **Application deadline** Rolling **Freshmen** 66% accepted **Housing** Yes **Tuition** $7302 **Undergraduates** 52% women, 24% part-time, 20% 25 or older, 1% Native American, 1% Hispanic, 8% black, 1% Asian or Pacific Islander **Most popular recent majors** Elementary education, business administration/commerce/management, social science **Academic program** Advanced placement, accelerated degree program, honors program, summer session, adult/continuing education programs, internships **Contact** Mr. R. Trent Argo, Director of Admissions, Campbellsville University, Campbellsville, KY 42718-2799. Telephone: 502-789-5220. Fax: 502-789-5020.

CENTRE COLLEGE
DANVILLE, KENTUCKY

Entrance Very difficult **General** Independent, 4-year, coed **Setting** 100-acre small-town campus **Enrollment** 968 **Faculty** 11:1 **Application deadline** 3/1 **Freshmen** 82% accepted **Housing** Yes **Tuition** $14,600 **Undergraduates** 51% women, 1% part-time, 1% 25 or older, 0% Native American, 1% Hispanic, 2% black, 1% Asian or Pacific Islander **Academic program** Average class size 18, advanced placement, self-designed majors, tutorials, summer session, internships **Contact** Mr. Thomas B. Martin, Dean of Enrollment Management, Centre College, Danville, KY 40422-1394. Telephone: 606-238-5350.

CLEAR CREEK BAPTIST BIBLE COLLEGE
PINEVILLE, KENTUCKY

Entrance Noncompetitive **General** Independent Southern Baptist, 4-year, specialized, primarily men **Setting** 700-acre rural campus **Enrollment** 150 **Faculty** 12:1 **Application deadline** 7/15 **Freshmen** 100% accepted **Housing** Yes **Tuition** $2370 **Undergraduates** 10% women, 5% part-time, 90% 25 or older, 0% Native American, 0% Hispanic, 1% black, 0% Asian or Pacific Islander **Academic program** Tutorials, summer session **Contact** Mr. Jayson Barnett, Director of Financial Aid and Admissions, Clear Creek Baptist Bible College, 300 Clear Creek Road, Pineville, KY 40977-9754. Telephone: 606-337-3196 Ext. 108.

CUMBERLAND COLLEGE
WILLIAMSBURG, KENTUCKY

Entrance Moderately difficult **General** Independent Kentucky Baptist, comprehensive, coed **Setting** 30-acre rural campus **Enrollment** 1,614 **Faculty** 16:1 **Application deadline** Rolling **Freshmen** 64% accepted **Housing** Yes **Tuition** $8430 **Undergraduates** 53% women, 11% part-time, 10% 25 or older, 1% Native American, 1% Hispanic, 3% black, 1% Asian or Pacific Islander **Most popular recent majors** Elementary education, psychology, English **Academic program** Average class size 25, advanced placement, accelerated degree program, self-designed majors, tutorials, honors program, summer session, adult/continuing education programs, internships **Contact** Mrs. Erica Harris, Coordinator of Admissions, Cumberland College, Williamsburg, KY 40769-1372. Telephone: 606-539-4241. Fax: 606-539-4303.

EASTERN KENTUCKY UNIVERSITY
RICHMOND, KENTUCKY

Entrance Noncompetitive **General** State-supported, comprehensive, coed **Setting** 350-acre small-town campus **Enrollment** 16,060 **Faculty** 23:1 **Application deadline** Rolling **Freshmen** 95% accepted **Housing** Yes **Tuition** $2060 **Undergraduates** 57% women, 21% part-time, 29% 25 or older, 1% Native American, 5% Hispanic, 5% black, 1% Asian or Pacific Islander **Most popular recent major** Nursing **Academic program** Advanced placement, accelerated degree program, self-designed majors, honors program, summer session, adult/continuing education programs, internships **Contact** Mr. Les Grigsby, Director of Admissions, Eastern Kentucky University, Richmond, KY 40475-3101. Telephone: 606-622-2106.

GEORGETOWN COLLEGE
GEORGETOWN, KENTUCKY

Entrance Moderately difficult **General** Independent, comprehensive, coed, affiliated with Baptist Church **Setting** 110-acre suburban campus **Enrollment** 1,514 **Faculty** 13:1 **Application deadline** Rolling **Freshmen** 94% accepted **Housing** Yes **Tuition** $10,190 **Undergraduates** 58% women, 5% part-time, 3% 25 or older, 0% Native American, 0% Hispanic, 2% black, 0% Asian or Pacific Islander **Most popular recent majors** Business administration/commerce/management, communication, psychology **Academic program** Average class size 25, advanced placement, accelerated degree program, self-designed majors, tutorials, summer session, internships **Contact** Mr. Michael Konopski, Director of Admissions, Georgetown College, Georgetown, KY 40324-1696. Telephone: 502-863-8009. Fax: 502-868-8891.

KENTUCKY CHRISTIAN COLLEGE
GRAYSON, KENTUCKY

Entrance Moderately difficult **General** Independent, 4-year, coed, affiliated with Christian Churches and Churches of Christ **Setting** 124-acre rural campus **Enrollment** 529 **Faculty** 15:1 **Application deadline** 8/1 **Freshmen** 87% accepted **Housing** Yes **Tuition** $5984 **Undergraduates** 56% women, 4% part-time, 14% 25 or older, 1% Hispanic, 1% black **Most popular recent majors** Ministries, elementary education, business administration/commerce/management **Academic program** Average class size 30, advanced placement, summer session, internships **Contact** Mrs. Sandra Deakins, Director of Admissions, Kentucky Christian College, Grayson, KY 41143-2205. Telephone: 606-474-3266. Fax: 606-474-3155.

KENTUCKY MOUNTAIN BIBLE COLLEGE
VANCLEVE, KENTUCKY

Entrance Minimally difficult **General** Independent interdenominational, 4-year, coed **Setting** Rural campus **Enrollment** 61 **Application deadline** Rolling **Freshmen** 67% accepted **Housing** Yes **Tuition** $3050 **Academic program** Average class size 15, advanced placement, adult/continuing education programs, internships **Contact** Mr. William Angus, Recruiting Officer, Kentucky Mountain Bible College, Vancleve, KY 41385. Telephone: 606-666-5000 Ext. 235.

KENTUCKY STATE UNIVERSITY
FRANKFORT, KENTUCKY

Entrance Minimally difficult **General** State-related, comprehensive, coed **Setting** 485-acre small-town campus **Enrollment** 2,356 **Faculty** 15:1 **Application deadline** Rolling **Freshmen** 63% accepted **Housing** Yes **Tuition** $2050 **Undergraduates** 56% women, 27% part-time, 33% 25 or older, 0% Native American, 0% Hispanic, 53% black, 0% Asian or Pacific Islander **Most popular recent majors** Nursing, business administration/commerce/management, computer science **Academic program** Advanced placement, accelerated degree program, self-designed majors, tutorials, honors program, summer session, adult/

continuing education programs, internships **Contact** Ms. Laronistine Dyson, Interim Associate Director of Admissions II, Kentucky State University, East Main Street, Dept. PG-92, Frankfort, KY 40601. Telephone: 502-227-6000.

KENTUCKY WESLEYAN COLLEGE
OWENSBORO, KENTUCKY

Entrance Moderately difficult **General** Independent Methodist, 4-year, coed **Setting** 52-acre suburban campus **Enrollment** 714 **Faculty** 10:1 **Application deadline** Rolling **Freshmen** 80% accepted **Housing** Yes **Tuition** $9370 **Undergraduates** 56% women, 9% part-time, 13% 25 or older, 0% Native American, 0% Hispanic, 6% black, 0% Asian or Pacific Islander **Most popular recent majors** Nursing, business administration/commerce/management, psychology **Academic program** Average class size 18, advanced placement, self-designed majors, tutorials, summer session, adult/continuing education programs, internships **Contact** Mr. Scott Goplin, Dean of Admission, Kentucky Wesleyan College, Owensboro, KY 42302-1039. Telephone: 502-926-3111 Ext. 145. Fax: 502-926-3196.

LEXINGTON BAPTIST COLLEGE
LEXINGTON, KENTUCKY

Entrance Minimally difficult **General** Independent, 4-year, coed, affiliated with Baptist Church **Setting** Urban campus **Enrollment** 82 **Faculty** 9:1 **Application deadline** Rolling **Freshmen** 100% accepted **Tuition** $3200 **Undergraduates** 52% women, 20% part-time, 0% Native American, 0% Hispanic, 5% black, 0% Asian or Pacific Islander **Academic program** Average class size 15, advanced placement, tutorials, summer session, adult/continuing education programs, internships **Contact** Mr. Robert B. Traeger, Director of Admissions and Records, Lexington Baptist College, 147 Walton Avenue, Lexington, KY 40508. Telephone: 606-252-1130. Fax: 606-252-5649.

LINDSEY WILSON COLLEGE
COLUMBIA, KENTUCKY

Entrance Minimally difficult **General** Independent United Methodist, comprehensive, coed **Setting** 40-acre rural campus **Enrollment** 1,317 **Faculty** 20:1 **Application deadline** Rolling **Freshmen** 72% accepted **Housing** Yes **Tuition** $8280 **Undergraduates** 50% women, 10% part-time, 17% 25 or older, 0% Native American, 0% Hispanic, 9% black, 1% Asian or Pacific Islander **Most popular recent majors** Business administration/commerce/management, elementary education, human services **Academic program** Advanced placement, accelerated degree program, self-designed majors, summer session, adult/continuing education programs **Contact** Mr. Kevin A. Thompson, Vice President of Enrollment, Lindsey Wilson College, 210 Lindsey Wilson Street, Columbia, KY 42728-1298. Telephone: 502-384-8100. Fax: 502-384-8200.

MID-CONTINENT BAPTIST BIBLE COLLEGE
MAYFIELD, KENTUCKY

Entrance Noncompetitive **General** Independent, 4-year, coed, affiliated with Baptist Church **Setting** 60-acre small-town campus **Enrollment** 115 **Faculty** 11:1 **Application deadline** Rolling **Freshmen** 100% accepted **Housing** Yes **Tuition** $3260 **Undergraduates** 24% women, 39% part-time, 61% 25 or older, 0% Hispanic, 5% black, 0% Asian or Pacific Islander **Academic program** Summer session **Contact** Mr. Jerry Muniz, Dean of Students, Mid-Continent Baptist Bible College, Mayfield, KY 42066. Telephone: 502-247-8521.

MIDWAY COLLEGE
MIDWAY, KENTUCKY

Entrance Minimally difficult **General** Independent, 4-year, women only, affiliated with Christian Church (Disciples of Christ) **Setting** 105-acre small-town campus **Enrollment** 930 **Faculty** 14:1 **Application deadline** Rolling **Freshmen** 79% accepted **Housing** Yes **Tuition** $8160 **Undergraduates** 46% part-time, 40% 25 or older, 1% Hispanic, 4% black, 1% Asian or Pacific Islander **Most popular recent majors** Nursing, equestrian studies, business administration/commerce/management **Academic program** Average class size 25, advanced placement, accelerated degree program, self-designed majors, tutorials, summer session, adult/continuing education programs, internships **Contact** Mrs. Karen Britt Statler, Director of Admissions, Midway College, 512 East Stephens Street, Midway, KY 40347-1120. Telephone: 606-846-5345. Fax: 606-846-5349.

MOREHEAD STATE UNIVERSITY
MOREHEAD, KENTUCKY

Entrance Minimally difficult **General** State-supported, comprehensive, coed **Setting** 809-acre small-town campus **Enrollment** 8,344 **Faculty** 20:1 **Application deadline** Rolling **Freshmen** 89% accepted **Housing** Yes **Tuition** $2090 **Undergraduates** 60% women, 14% part-time, 24% 25 or older, 1% Hispanic, 3% black **Most popular recent majors** Elementary education, interdisciplinary studies, biology/biological sciences **Aca-**

demic program Advanced placement, accelerated degree program, self-designed majors, honors program, summer session, adult/continuing education programs, internships **Contact** Mr. Charles Myers, Director of Admissions, Morehead State University, Morehead, KY 40351. Telephone: 606-783-2000. Fax: 606-783-2678.

MURRAY STATE UNIVERSITY

MURRAY, KENTUCKY

Entrance Moderately difficult **General** State-supported, comprehensive, coed **Setting** 238-acre small-town campus **Enrollment** 8,636 **Faculty** 16:1 **Application deadline** Rolling **Freshmen** 66% accepted **Housing** Yes **Tuition** $2120 **Undergraduates** 55% women, 14% part-time, 22% 25 or older, 1% Native American, 1% Hispanic, 6% black, 1% Asian or Pacific Islander **Most popular recent majors** Business administration/commerce/management, education, occupational safety and health **Academic program** Advanced placement, accelerated degree program, honors program, summer session, adult/continuing education programs, internships **Contact** Mrs. Kristi Jackson, Admission Clerk, Murray State University, Murray, KY 42071-0009. Telephone: 502-762-3035. Fax: 502-762-3050.

NORTHERN KENTUCKY UNIVERSITY

HIGHLAND HEIGHTS, KENTUCKY

Entrance Noncompetitive **General** State-supported, comprehensive, coed **Setting** 300-acre suburban campus **Enrollment** 11,505 **Faculty** 17:1 **Application deadline** Rolling **Freshmen** 100% accepted **Housing** Yes **Tuition** $2020 **Undergraduates** 58% women, 37% part-time, 40% 25 or older, 1% Native American, 1% Hispanic, 3% black, 1% Asian or Pacific Islander **Most popular recent majors** Education, nursing, psychology **Academic program** Average class size 26, advanced placement, self-designed majors, honors program, summer session, adult/continuing education programs, internships **Contact** Mrs. Debbie Poweleit, Associate Director of Admissions, Northern Kentucky University, Administrative Center 400, Highland Heights, KY 41099-7010. Telephone: 606-572-5220 Ext. 5154.

PIKEVILLE COLLEGE

PIKEVILLE, KENTUCKY

Entrance Noncompetitive **General** Independent, 4-year, coed, affiliated with Presbyterian Church (U.S.A.) **Setting** 25-acre small-town campus **Enrollment** 824 **Faculty** 15:1 **Application deadline** 9/4 **Freshmen** 100% accepted **Housing** Yes **Tuition** $7000 **Undergraduates** 69% women, 12% part-time, 25% 25 or older, 0% Native American, 0% Hispanic, 2% black, 0% Asian or Pacific Islander **Most popular recent majors** Education, business administration/commerce/management, nursing **Academic program** Average class size 22, accelerated degree program, summer session, adult/continuing education programs, internships **Contact** Dr. John Sanders, Associate Dean of Admissions and Financial Aid, Pikeville College, Pikeville, KY 41501. Telephone: 606-432-9325. Fax: 606-432-9372.

SPALDING UNIVERSITY

LOUISVILLE, KENTUCKY

Entrance Moderately difficult **General** Independent, comprehensive, coed, affiliated with Roman Catholic Church **Setting** 5-acre urban campus **Enrollment** 1,423 **Faculty** 17:1 **Application deadline** 8/15 **Freshmen** 84% accepted **Housing** Yes **Tuition** $10,496 **Undergraduates** 79% women, 35% part-time, 47% 25 or older, 0% Native American, 1% Hispanic, 11% black, 1% Asian or Pacific Islander **Most popular recent majors** Nursing, business administration/commerce/management, education **Academic program** Advanced placement, tutorials, summer session, adult/continuing education programs, internships **Contact** Ms. Dorothy G. Allen, Director of Admission, Spalding University, 851 South Fourth Street, Louisville, KY 40203-2188. Telephone: 502-585-7111 Ext. 225. Fax: 502-585-7158.

SUE BENNETT COLLEGE

LONDON, KENTUCKY

Entrance Noncompetitive **General** Independent, 4-year, coed, affiliated with United Methodist Church **Setting** 48-acre small-town campus **Enrollment** 404 **Faculty** 16:1 **Application deadline** Rolling **Housing** Yes **Tuition** $7780 **Undergraduates** 49% women, 13% part-time, 29% 25 or older, 2% Native American, 1% Hispanic, 6% black, 1% Asian or Pacific Islander **Academic program** Average class size 15, advanced placement, tutorials, summer session, adult/continuing education programs, internships **Contact** Mrs. Pamela Jarrett, Director of Admissions, Sue Bennett College, 151 College Street, London, KY 40741-2400. Telephone: 606-864-2238 Ext. 1113. Fax: 606-864-2238 Ext. 1198.

SULLIVAN COLLEGE

LOUISVILLE, KENTUCKY

Entrance Minimally difficult **General** Proprietary, 4-year, coed **Setting** 10-acre suburban campus **Enrollment** 2,321 **Faculty** 20:1 **Application deadline** 9/30 **Freshmen** 95% accepted **Housing** Yes **Tuition** $8904 **Undergraduates** 66% women, 33% part-time, 50% 25 or older, 15% black **Most popular recent majors** Business administration/commerce/management, culinary arts, paralegal studies **Academic program** Average class size 20, accelerated degree program, summer session, adult/continuing education programs, internships **Contact** Mr. Greg Cawthon, Director of Admissions, Sullivan College, 3101 Bardstown Road, Louisville, KY 40205. Telephone: 502-456-6504 Ext. 330. Fax: 502-454-4880.

THOMAS MORE COLLEGE
CRESTVIEW HILLS, KENTUCKY

Entrance Moderately difficult **General** Independent Roman Catholic, comprehensive, coed **Setting** 120-acre suburban campus **Enrollment** 1,345 **Faculty** 12:1 **Application deadline** 8/15 **Freshmen** 77% accepted **Housing** Yes **Tuition** $11,250 **Undergraduates** 53% women, 43% part-time, 36% 25 or older, 1% Native American, 1% Hispanic, 5% black, 1% Asian or Pacific Islander **Most popular recent majors** Business administration/commerce/management, biology/biological sciences, computer information systems **Academic program** ESL program, Advanced placement, accelerated degree program, self-designed majors, tutorials, honors program, summer session, adult/continuing education programs, internships **Contact** Mr. Robert A. McDermott, Director of Admissions, Thomas More College, Crestview Hills, KY 41017-3495. Telephone: 606-344-3332. Fax: 606-344-3638.

TRANSYLVANIA UNIVERSITY
LEXINGTON, KENTUCKY

Entrance Very difficult **General** Independent, 4-year, coed, affiliated with Christian Church (Disciples of Christ) **Setting** 35-acre urban campus **Enrollment** 979 **Faculty** 14:1 **Application deadline** 3/1 **Freshmen** 91% accepted **Housing** Yes **Tuition** $13,260 **Undergraduates** 54% women, 2% part-time, 3% 25 or older, 0% Native American, 1% Hispanic, 2% black, 3% Asian or Pacific Islander **Most popular recent majors** Business administration/commerce/management, biology/biological sciences, psychology **Academic program** Average class size 25, advanced placement, accelerated degree program, self-designed majors, tutorials, summer session, internships **Contact** Mr. John O. Gaines, Acting Director of Admissions, Transylvania University, 300 North Broadway, Lexington, KY 40508-1797. Telephone: 606-233-8242. Fax: 606-233-8797.

UNION COLLEGE
BARBOURVILLE, KENTUCKY

Entrance Moderately difficult **General** Independent United Methodist, comprehensive, coed **Setting** 110-acre small-town campus **Enrollment** 987 **Faculty** 13:1 **Application deadline** 8/15 **Freshmen** 83% accepted **Housing** Yes **Tuition** $9340 **Undergraduates** 52% women, 12% part-time, 21% 25 or older, 1% Native American, 1% Hispanic, 7% black, 0% Asian or Pacific Islander **Most popular recent majors** Education, business administration/commerce/management, sociology **Academic program** Advanced placement, accelerated degree program, tutorials, honors program, summer session, adult/continuing education programs, internships **Contact** Mrs. Lisa Jordan-Payne, Dean of Admissions, Union College, Barbourville, KY 40906-1499. Telephone: 606-546-1220. Fax: 606-546-1217.

UNIVERSITY OF KENTUCKY
LEXINGTON, KENTUCKY

Entrance Moderately difficult **General** State-supported, coed **Setting** 682-acre urban campus **Enrollment** 23,431 **Faculty** 16:1 **Application deadline** 6/1 **Freshmen** 78% accepted **Housing** Yes **Tuition** $2736 **Undergraduates** 50% women, 14% part-time, 8% 25 or older, 0% Native American, 1% Hispanic, 5% black, 2% Asian or Pacific Islander **Most popular recent majors** Psychology, accounting, marketing/retailing/merchandising **Academic program** Advanced placement, accelerated degree program, self-designed majors, honors program, summer session, adult/continuing education programs, internships **Contact** Mr. Randy Mills, Senior Associate Director of Admissions, University of Kentucky, Lexington, KY 40506-0032. Telephone: 606-257-2000.

UNIVERSITY OF LOUISVILLE
LOUISVILLE, KENTUCKY

Entrance Moderately difficult **General** State-supported, coed **Setting** 169-acre urban campus **Enrollment** 21,020 **Faculty** 12:1 **Application deadline** Rolling **Freshmen** 66% accepted **Housing** Yes **Tuition** $2660 **Undergraduates** 53% women, 35% part-time, 36% 25 or older, 1% Native American, 1% Hispanic, 13% black, 3% Asian or Pacific Islander **Most popular recent majors** Psychology, accounting, communication **Academic program** Advanced placement, accelerated degree program, self-designed majors, honors program, summer session, adult/continuing education programs, internships **Contact** Ms. Lynn Bacon, Director of Admissions for School Relations, University of Louisville, 2301 South Third Street, Louisville, KY 40292-0001. Telephone: 502-852-6531. Fax: 502-588-6685.

WESTERN KENTUCKY UNIVERSITY
BOWLING GREEN, KENTUCKY

Entrance Moderately difficult **General** State-supported, comprehensive, coed **Setting** 223-acre suburban campus **Enrollment** 14,613 **Application deadline** 8/1 **Freshmen** 97% accepted **Housing** Yes **Tuition** $2140 **Undergraduates** 57% women, 21% part-time, 23% 25 or older, 1% Hispanic, 7% black, 1% Asian or Pacific Islander **Most popular recent majors** Elementary education, liberal arts/general studies, nursing **Academic program** Advanced placement, accelerated degree program, self-designed majors, honors program, summer session, adult/continuing education programs, internships **Contact** Dr. Cheryl C. Chambless, Director of Admissions, Western Kentucky University, Potter Hall, Bowling Green, KY 42101-3576. Telephone: 502-745-5422. Fax: 502-745-6133.

Louisiana

AMERICAN COLLEGE OF PREHOSPITAL MEDICINE
NEW ORLEANS, LOUISIANA

Entrance Noncompetitive **General** Proprietary, 4-year, coed **Enrollment** 120 **Faculty** 3:1 **Application deadline** Rolling **Freshmen** 100% accepted **Undergraduates** 20% women, 100% part-time, 90% 25 or older, 2% Native American, 2% Hispanic, 0% black, 1% Asian or Pacific Islander **Contact** Dr. Richard A. Clinchy, Chairman/CEO, American College of Prehospital Medicine, New Orleans, LA 70130-1135. Telephone: 504-561-6543.

CENTENARY COLLEGE OF LOUISIANA
SHREVEPORT, LOUISIANA

Entrance Moderately difficult **General** Independent United Methodist, comprehensive, coed **Setting** 65-acre suburban campus **Enrollment** 971 **Faculty** 10:1 **Application deadline** 3/1 **Freshmen** 83% accepted **Housing** Yes **Tuition** $11,400 **Undergraduates** 57% women, 3% part-time, 5% 25 or older, 1% Native American, 1% Hispanic, 6% black, 2% Asian or Pacific Islander **Most popular recent majors** Business administration/commerce/management, biology/biological sciences, education **Academic program** Advanced placement, accelerated degree program, self-designed majors, tutorials, honors program, summer session, adult/continuing education programs, internships **Contact** Mr. Joel R. Wincowski, Dean of Enrollment Management, Centenary College of Louisiana, Shreveport, LA 71134-1188. Telephone: 318-869-5131.

DILLARD UNIVERSITY
NEW ORLEANS, LOUISIANA

Entrance Moderately difficult **General** Independent interdenominational, 4-year, coed **Setting** 46-acre urban campus **Enrollment** 1,563 **Faculty** 15:1 **Application deadline** 7/15 **Freshmen** 90% accepted **Housing** Yes **Tuition** $8000 **Undergraduates** 74% women, 2% part-time, 3% 25 or older, 99% black **Most popular recent majors** Business administration/commerce/management, communication, nursing **Academic program** Average class size 30, advanced placement, accelerated degree program, honors program, summer session, internships **Contact** Mr. Darrin Q. Rankin, Director, Enrollment Management and Admissions, Dillard University, 2601 Gentilly Boulevard, New Orleans, LA 70122-3097. Telephone: 504-286-4670. Fax: 504-286-4895.

GRAMBLING STATE UNIVERSITY
GRAMBLING, LOUISIANA

Entrance Noncompetitive **General** State-supported, comprehensive, coed **Setting** 340-acre small-town campus **Enrollment** 8,000 **Application deadline** 7/15 **Freshmen** 74% accepted **Housing** Yes **Tuition** $2088 **Undergraduates** 59% women, 9% part-time, 16% 25 or older, 0% Native American, 1% Hispanic, 95% black, 1% Asian or Pacific Islander **Most popular recent majors** Criminal justice, business administration/commerce/management, computer information systems **Academic program** Advanced placement, honors program, summer session, adult/continuing education programs, internships **Contact** Mr. Martin Lemelle, Head Recruiter/Admission Officer, Grambling State University, Grambling, LA 71245. Telephone: 318-274-3395. Fax: 318-274-2777.

GRANTHAM COLLEGE OF ENGINEERING
SLIDELL, LOUISIANA

Entrance Noncompetitive **General** Proprietary, 4-year, primarily men **Enrollment** 1,430 **Application deadline** Rolling **Undergraduates** 6% women, 100% part-time, 96% 25 or older **Most**

popular recent majors Electronics engineering technology, computer technologies, computer science **Academic program** Advanced placement, accelerated degree program, adult/continuing education programs **Contact** Mr. Philip Grantham, Director of Student Services, Grantham College of Engineering, PO Box 5700, Slidell, LA 70460-6815. Telephone: 504-649-4191. Fax: 504-649-4183.

LOUISIANA COLLEGE
PINEVILLE, LOUISIANA

Entrance Moderately difficult **General** Independent Southern Baptist, 4-year, coed **Setting** 81-acre small-town campus **Enrollment** 959 **Faculty** 15:1 **Application deadline** 8/1 **Freshmen** 78% accepted **Housing** Yes **Tuition** $6763 **Undergraduates** 60% women, 13% part-time, 22% 25 or older, 1% Native American, 1% Hispanic, 7% black, 1% Asian or Pacific Islander **Most popular recent majors** Business administration/commerce/management, nursing, education **Academic program** Average class size 25, advanced placement, accelerated degree program, self-designed majors, tutorials, honors program, summer session, adult/continuing education programs, internships **Contact** Ms. Karin Gregorczyk, Director of Admissions, Louisiana College, Box 560, Pineville, LA 71359-0001. Telephone: 318-487-7259. Fax: 318-487-7191.

LOUISIANA STATE UNIVERSITY AND AGRICULTURAL AND MECHANICAL COLLEGE
BATON ROUGE, LOUISIANA

Entrance Moderately difficult **General** State-supported, coed **Setting** 2,000-acre urban campus **Enrollment** 26,842 **Faculty** 18:1 **Application deadline** 6/1 **Freshmen** 81% accepted **Housing** Yes **Tuition** $2711 **Undergraduates** 51% women, 16% part-time, 17% 25 or older, 1% Native American, 3% Hispanic, 9% black, 4% Asian or Pacific Islander **Most popular recent majors** Liberal arts/general studies, psychology, accounting **Academic program** Average class size 29, advanced placement, honors program, summer session, adult/continuing education programs, internships **Contact** Ms. Lisa Harris, Dean of Admissions, Louisiana State University and Agricultural and Mechanical College, Baton Rouge, LA 70803-3103. Telephone: 504-388-1175.

LOUISIANA STATE UNIVERSITY IN SHREVEPORT
SHREVEPORT, LOUISIANA

Entrance Noncompetitive **General** State-supported, comprehensive, coed **Setting** 200-acre urban campus **Enrollment** 3,945 **Faculty** 18:1 **Application deadline** 8/5 **Freshmen** 99% accepted **Tuition** $2080 **Undergraduates** 60% women, 39% part-time, 39% 25 or older, 1% Native American, 1% Hispanic, 15% black, 2% Asian or Pacific Islander **Most popular recent majors** Psychology, elementary education, accounting **Academic program** Average class size 30, advanced placement, accelerated degree program, self-designed majors, tutorials, honors program, summer session, adult/continuing education programs, internships **Contact** Ms. Sylvia Booras, Assistant Director of Admissions, Louisiana State University in Shreveport, One University Place, Shreveport, LA 71115-2399. Telephone: 318-797-5057. Fax: 318-797-5286.

LOUISIANA STATE UNIVERSITY MEDICAL CENTER
NEW ORLEANS, LOUISIANA

Entrance Very difficult **General** State-supported, coed **Setting** Urban campus **Enrollment** 2,965 **Housing** Yes **Tuition** $1845 **Undergraduates** 78% women, 12% part-time, 24% 25 or older, 1% Native American, 4% Hispanic, 6% black, 4% Asian or Pacific Islander **Academic program** Advanced placement, summer session **Contact** Mr. Edmund A. Vidacovich, Registrar, Louisiana State University Medical Center, 433 Bolivar Street, New Orleans, LA 70112-2223. Telephone: 504-568-4829.

LOUISIANA TECH UNIVERSITY
RUSTON, LOUISIANA

Entrance Moderately difficult **General** State-supported, coed **Setting** 235-acre small-town campus **Enrollment** 9,313 **Faculty** 25:1 **Application deadline** Rolling **Freshmen** 98% accepted **Housing** Yes **Tuition** $2452 **Undergraduates** 48% women, 21% part-time, 25% 25 or older, 0% Native American, 1% Hispanic, 13% black, 1% Asian or Pacific Islander **Most popular recent majors** Nursing, aviation technology, marketing/retailing/merchandising **Academic program** ESL program, Advanced placement, tutorials, honors program, summer session, adult/continuing education programs, internships **Contact** Mrs. Jan Albritton, Director of Admissions, Louisiana Tech University, Ruston, LA 71272. Telephone: 318-257-3036.

LOYOLA UNIVERSITY NEW ORLEANS
NEW ORLEANS, LOUISIANA

Entrance Moderately difficult **General** Independent Roman Catholic (Jesuit), comprehensive, coed **Setting** 26-acre urban campus **Enrollment** 5,203 **Faculty** 9:1 **Application deadline** Rolling **Freshmen** 88% accepted **Housing** Yes **Tuition** $13,266 **Undergraduates** 62% women, 22% part-time, 25% 25 or older, 1% Native American, 12% Hispanic, 14% black, 4% Asian or Pacific Islander **Most popular recent majors** Communication, psychology, accounting **Academic program** Average class size 23, advanced placement, accelerated degree program, self-designed majors, tutorials, honors program, summer session, adult/continuing education programs, internships **Contact** Ms. Nan Massingill, Director of Admissions, Loyola University New Orleans, 6363 Saint Charles Avenue, New Orleans, LA 70118-6195. Telephone: 504-865-3240. Fax: 504-865-3383.

MCNEESE STATE UNIVERSITY
LAKE CHARLES, LOUISIANA

Entrance Noncompetitive **General** State-supported, comprehensive, coed **Setting** 580-acre suburban campus **Enrollment** 8,059 **Faculty** 26:1 **Application deadline** 7/15 **Freshmen** 99% accepted **Housing** Yes **Tuition** $2012 **Undergraduates** 58% women, 19% part-time, 32% 25 or older, 0% Native American, 1% Hispanic, 16% black, 1% Asian or Pacific Islander **Most popular recent majors** Business administration/commerce/management, education, nursing **Academic program** Advanced placement, accelerated degree program, summer session, adult/continuing education programs, internships **Contact** Ms. Kathy Bond, Admissions Counselor, McNeese State University, PO Box 92495, Lake Charles, LA 70609-2495. Telephone: 318-475-5148.

NEW ORLEANS BAPTIST THEOLOGICAL SEMINARY
NEW ORLEANS, LOUISIANA

Entrance Minimally difficult **General** Independent Southern Baptist, comprehensive, specialized, coed **Setting** 81-acre suburban campus **Enrollment** 1,822 **Application deadline** 8/9 **Freshmen** 90% accepted **Housing** Yes **Tuition** $1900 **Undergraduates** 35% women, 40% part-time, 100% 25 or older, 3% black **Academic program** Summer session, adult/continuing education programs, internships **Contact** Dr. Paul E. Gregoire Jr., Registrar/Director of Admissions, New Orleans Baptist Theological Seminary, 3939 Gentilly Boulevard, New Orleans, LA 70126-4858. Telephone: 504-282-4455 Ext. 3632.

NICHOLLS STATE UNIVERSITY
THIBODAUX, LOUISIANA

Entrance Noncompetitive **General** State-supported, comprehensive, coed **Setting** 210-acre small-town campus **Enrollment** 7,210 **Faculty** 18:1 **Application deadline** Rolling **Freshmen** 92% accepted **Housing** Yes **Tuition** $2016 **Undergraduates** 60% women, 21% part-time, 31% 25 or older, 1% Native American, 1% Hispanic, 14% black, 1% Asian or Pacific Islander **Most popular recent majors** Liberal arts/general studies, nursing, elementary education **Academic program** Average class size 30, advanced placement, accelerated degree program, tutorials, summer session, adult/continuing education programs, internships **Contact** Mr. John A. Williamson, Director of Admissions, Nicholls State University, PO Box 2009-NSU, Thibodaux, LA 70310. Telephone: 504-448-4145. Fax: 504-448-4929.

NORTHEAST LOUISIANA UNIVERSITY
MONROE, LOUISIANA

Entrance Noncompetitive **General** State-supported, comprehensive, coed **Setting** 238-acre urban campus **Enrollment** 11,116 **Faculty** 19:1 **Application deadline** Rolling **Freshmen** 96% accepted **Housing** Yes **Tuition** $1932 **Undergraduates** 60% women, 15% part-time, 23% 25 or older, 1% Native American, 1% Hispanic, 22% black, 3% Asian or Pacific Islander **Most popular recent majors** Pharmacy/pharmaceutical sciences, liberal arts/general studies, nursing **Academic program** Advanced placement, accelerated degree program, honors program, summer session, adult/continuing education programs, internships **Contact** Mr. Don Weems, Director of Admissions, Northeast Louisiana University, Monroe, LA 71209-0001. Telephone: 318-342-5252.

NORTHWESTERN STATE UNIVERSITY OF LOUISIANA
NATCHITOCHES, LOUISIANA

Entrance Noncompetitive **General** State-supported, comprehensive, coed **Setting** 1,000-acre small-town campus **Enrollment** 9,037 **Faculty** 32:1 **Application deadline** Rolling **Freshmen** 99% accepted **Housing** Yes **Tuition** $2059 **Undergraduates** 64% women, 24% part-time, 32% 25 or older, 2% Native American, 2% Hispanic, 22% black, 1% Asian or Pacific Islander **Most popular recent majors** Nursing, business administration/commerce/management, education **Academic program** Average class size 33, advanced placement, honors program, summer session, adult/continuing education programs, internships **Contact** Mr. Chris Maggio, Director of Recruiting and Admissions, Northwestern State University of Louisiana, Natchitoches, LA 71497. Telephone: 318-357-4503.

OUR LADY OF HOLY CROSS COLLEGE
NEW ORLEANS, LOUISIANA

Entrance Minimally difficult **General** Independent Roman Catholic, comprehensive, coed **Setting** 40-acre suburban campus **Enrollment** 1,316 **Faculty** 23:1 **Application deadline** Rolling **Freshmen** 99% accepted **Tuition** $5580 **Undergraduates** 60% women, 45% part-time, 50% 25 or older, 3% Native American, 3% Hispanic, 26% black, 2% Asian or Pacific Islander **Most popular recent majors** Nursing, business education, education **Academic program** Advanced placement, summer session, adult/continuing education programs, internships **Contact** Ms. Kristine Hatfield, Director of Student Affairs and Admissions, Our Lady of Holy Cross College, New Orleans, LA 70131-7399. Telephone: 504-394-7744 Ext. 185.

SAINT JOSEPH SEMINARY COLLEGE
SAINT BENEDICT, LOUISIANA

Entrance Minimally difficult **General** Independent Roman Catholic, 4-year, primarily men **Setting** 1,300-acre rural campus **Enrollment** 62 **Faculty** 2:1 **Application deadline** Rolling **Freshmen** 100% accepted **Housing** Yes **Tuition** $5780 **Undergraduates** 0% part-time, 39% 25 or older, 0% Native American, 0% Hispanic, 5% black, 23% Asian or Pacific Islander **Academic program** Advanced placement, adult/continuing education programs **Contact** Mr. Thomas A. Siegrist, Registrar/Director of Admissions, Saint Joseph Seminary College, Saint Benedict, LA 70457. Telephone: 504-892-1800 Ext. 29.

SOUTHEASTERN LOUISIANA UNIVERSITY
HAMMOND, LOUISIANA

Entrance Noncompetitive **General** State-supported, comprehensive, coed **Setting** 365-acre small-town campus **Enrollment** 14,592 **Application deadline** 7/15 **Housing** Yes **Tuition** $2055 **Undergraduates** 61% women, 18% part-time, 25% 25 or older, 1% Native American, 1% Hispanic, 1% black, 1% Asian or Pacific Islander **Most popular recent majors** Business administration/commerce/management, education, nursing **Academic program** Advanced placement, self-designed majors, honors program, summer session, adult/continuing education programs, internships **Contact** Mr. Stephen C. Soutullo, Director of Enrollment Services, Southeastern Louisiana University, SLU 752, Hammond, LA 70402. Telephone: 504-549-2066. Fax: 504-549-5095.

SOUTHERN UNIVERSITY AND AGRICULTURAL AND MECHANICAL COLLEGE
BATON ROUGE, LOUISIANA

Entrance Noncompetitive **General** State-supported, comprehensive, coed **Setting** 512-acre suburban campus **Enrollment** 9,800 **Faculty** 16:1 **Application deadline** 7/1 **Freshmen** 100% accepted **Housing** Yes **Tuition** $2068 **Undergraduates** 57% women, 8% part-time, 1% Native American, 1% Hispanic, 96% black, 2% Asian or Pacific Islander **Most popular recent majors** Engineering (general), business administration/commerce/management, nursing **Academic program** Self-designed majors, honors program, summer session, adult/continuing education programs **Contact** Mr. Wayne Broomfield, Director of Admissions, Southern University and Agricultural and Mechanical College, Baton Rouge, LA 70813. Telephone: 504-771-2430.

SOUTHERN UNIVERSITY AT NEW ORLEANS
NEW ORLEANS, LOUISIANA

Entrance Noncompetitive **General** State-supported, comprehensive, coed **Setting** 17-acre campus **Enrollment** 4,500 **Application deadline** 7/1 **Freshmen** 100% accepted **Tuition** $1662 **Undergraduates** 67% women, 20% part-time, 50% 25 or older, 1% Native American, 1% Hispanic, 87% black, 1% Asian or Pacific Islander **Most popular recent majors** Business administration/commerce/management, elementary education, criminal justice **Academic program** Adult/continuing education programs **Contact** Dr. Melvin Hodges, Registrar/Director of Admissions, Southern University at New Orleans, New Orleans, LA 70126-1009. Telephone: 504-286-5314.

TULANE UNIVERSITY
NEW ORLEANS, LOUISIANA

Entrance Very difficult **General** Independent, coed **Setting** 110-acre urban campus **Enrollment** 11,246 **Faculty** 10:1 **Application deadline** 1/15 **Freshmen** 76% accepted **Housing** Yes **Tuition** $22,066 **Undergraduates** 50% women, 23% part-time, 15% 25 or older, 1% Native American, 5% Hispanic, 10% black, 5% Asian or Pacific Islander **Most popular recent majors** Biology/biological sciences, English, psychology **Academic program** Advanced placement, accelerated degree program, self-designed majors, tutorials, honors program, summer session, adult/continuing education programs, internships **Contact** Mr. Richard Whiteside, Dean of Admission and Enrollment Management, Tulane University, 6823 St Charles Avenue, New Orleans, LA 70118-5669. Telephone: 504-865-5731. Fax: 504-862-8715.

UNIVERSITY OF NEW ORLEANS
NEW ORLEANS, LOUISIANA

Entrance Moderately difficult **General** State-supported, coed **Setting** 345-acre urban campus **Enrollment** 15,665 **Faculty** 16:1 **Application deadline** 8/19 **Freshmen** 89% accepted **Housing** Yes **Tuition** $2362 **Undergraduates** 56% women, 31% part-time, 31% 25 or older, 1% Native American, 6% Hispanic, 18% black, 4% Asian or Pacific Islander **Most popular recent majors** Interdisciplinary studies, elementary education, accounting **Academic program** Advanced placement, self-designed majors, honors program, summer session, adult/continuing education programs, internships **Contact** Ms. Roslyn Sheley, Director of Admissions, University of New Orleans, Lake Front, New Orleans, LA 70148. Telephone: 504-280-6595.

UNIVERSITY OF SOUTHWESTERN LOUISIANA
LAFAYETTE, LOUISIANA

Entrance Noncompetitive **General** State-supported, coed **Setting** 1,375-acre urban campus **Enrollment** 16,742 **Faculty** 23:1 **Application deadline** Rolling **Freshmen** 99% accepted **Housing** Yes **Tuition** $1897 **Undergraduates** 57% women, 22% part-time, 29% 25 or older, 1% Native American, 1% Hispanic, 20% black, 1% Asian or Pacific Islander **Academic program** Advanced placement, accelerated degree program, self-designed majors, tutorials, honors program, summer session, adult/continuing education programs, internships **Contact** Mr. Leroy Broussard Jr., Director of Admissions, University of Southwestern Louisiana, 104 University Circle, Lafayette, LA 70504. Telephone: 318-482-6473.

XAVIER UNIVERSITY OF LOUISIANA
NEW ORLEANS, LOUISIANA

Entrance Moderately difficult **General** Independent Roman Catholic, comprehensive, coed **Setting** 23-acre urban campus **Enrollment** 3,526 **Faculty** 14:1 **Application deadline** 3/1 **Freshmen** 88% accepted **Housing** Yes **Tuition** $8215 **Undergraduates** 70% women, 2% part-time, 13% 25 or older, 0% Native American, 1% Hispanic, 96% black, 1% Asian or Pacific Islander **Most popular recent majors** Biology/biological sciences, business administration/commerce/management **Academic program** Advanced placement, tutorials, honors program, summer session, adult/continuing education programs, internships **Contact** Mr. Winston Brown, Dean of Admissions, Xavier University of Louisiana, 7325 Palmetto Street, New Orleans, LA 70125. Telephone: 504-483-7388.

Mississippi

ALCORN STATE UNIVERSITY
LORMAN, MISSISSIPPI

Entrance Minimally difficult **General** State-supported, comprehensive, coed **Setting** 1,700-acre rural campus **Enrollment** 3,073 **Faculty** 15:1 **Application deadline** 8/15 **Freshmen** 36% accepted **Housing** Yes **Tuition** $2429 **Undergraduates** 62% women, 9% part-time, 0% Native American, 0% Hispanic, 95% black, 0% Asian or Pacific Islander **Most popular recent majors** Business administration/commerce/management, agronomy/soil and crop sciences, computer science **Academic program** Advanced placement, accelerated degree program, honors program, summer session **Contact** Mr. Emmanuel Barnes, Director of Admissions, Alcorn State University, Lorman, MS 39096-9402. Telephone: 601-877-6147.

BELHAVEN COLLEGE
JACKSON, MISSISSIPPI

Entrance Moderately difficult **General** Independent Presbyterian, comprehensive, coed **Setting** 42-acre urban campus **Enrollment** 1,256 **Faculty** 14:1 **Application deadline** Rolling **Freshmen** 77% accepted **Housing** Yes **Tuition** $9370 **Undergraduates** 60% women, 24% part-time, 51% 25 or older, 0% Native American, 0% Hispanic, 19% black, 1% Asian or Pacific Islander **Most popular recent majors** Business administration/commerce/management, biology/biological sciences, accounting **Academic program** Average class size 25, advanced placement, accelerated degree program, tutorials, honors program, summer session, adult/continuing education programs, internships **Contact** Ms. Linda Phillips, Director of Enrollment Services/Financial Aid, Belhaven College, 1500 Peachtree Street, Jackson, MS 39202-1789. Telephone: 601-968-5940. Fax: 601-968-9998.

BLUE MOUNTAIN COLLEGE
BLUE MOUNTAIN, MISSISSIPPI

Entrance Minimally difficult **General** Independent Southern Baptist, 4-year, primarily women

Setting 44-acre rural campus **Enrollment** 420 **Faculty** 14:1 **Application deadline** Rolling **Freshmen** 100% accepted **Housing** Yes **Tuition** $4640 **Undergraduates** 83% women, 31% part-time, 42% 25 or older, 0% Native American, 1% Hispanic, 10% black, 1% Asian or Pacific Islander **Most popular recent majors** Education, ministries **Academic program** Advanced placement, accelerated degree program, honors program, summer session, internships **Contact** Ms. Charlotte Lewis, Director of Admissions, Blue Mountain College, PO Box 126BMC, Blue Mountain, MS 38610-9509. Telephone: 601-685-4161.

DELTA STATE UNIVERSITY
CLEVELAND, MISSISSIPPI

Entrance Minimally difficult **General** State-supported, comprehensive, coed **Setting** 274-acre small-town campus **Enrollment** 3,860 **Faculty** 14:1 **Application deadline** Rolling **Freshmen** 97% accepted **Housing** Yes **Tuition** $2334 **Undergraduates** 60% women, 14% part-time, 20% 25 or older, 27% black, 1% Asian or Pacific Islander **Most popular recent majors** Business administration/commerce/management, elementary education, nursing **Academic program** Advanced placement, accelerated degree program, tutorials, summer session, adult/continuing education programs, internships **Contact** Ms. Debbie Heslep, Coordinator of Admissions, Delta State University, Kethley 107, Cleveland, MS 38733-0001. Telephone: 601-846-4018. Fax: 601-846-4016.

JACKSON STATE UNIVERSITY
JACKSON, MISSISSIPPI

Entrance Minimally difficult **General** State-supported, coed **Setting** 128-acre urban campus **Enrollment** 6,218 **Faculty** 17:1 **Application deadline** 8/1 **Freshmen** 55% accepted **Housing** Yes **Tuition** $2380 **Undergraduates** 58% women, 12% part-time, 13% 25 or older, 0% Native American, 0% Hispanic, 94% black, 1% Asian or Pacific Islander **Most popular recent majors** Business administration/commerce/management, computer science, biology/biological sciences **Academic program** Advanced placement, accelerated degree program, tutorials, honors program, summer session, adult/continuing education programs, internships **Contact** Mrs. Linda Rush, Admissions Counselor, Jackson State University, PO Box 17330, 1400 John R. Lynch Street, Jackson, MS 39217. Telephone: 601-968-2911.

MAGNOLIA BIBLE COLLEGE
KOSCIUSKO, MISSISSIPPI

Entrance Noncompetitive **General** Independent, 4-year, specialized, primarily men, affiliated with Church of Christ **Setting** 5-acre small-town campus **Enrollment** 70 **Faculty** 5:1 **Application deadline** 8/31 **Freshmen** 100% accepted **Housing** Yes **Tuition** $4020 **Undergraduates** 23% women, 31% part-time, 93% 25 or older, 1% Native American, 0% Hispanic, 18% black, 81% Asian or Pacific Islander **Academic program** Summer session **Contact** Mr. Allen Coker, Director of Admissions, Magnolia Bible College, Kosciusko, MS 39090-1109. Telephone: 601-289-2896.

MILLSAPS COLLEGE
JACKSON, MISSISSIPPI

Entrance Moderately difficult **General** Independent United Methodist, comprehensive, coed **Setting** 100-acre urban campus **Enrollment** 1,377 **Faculty** 13:1 **Application deadline** 3/1 **Freshmen** 78% accepted **Housing** Yes **Tuition** $13,612 **Undergraduates** 52% women, 7% part-time, 10% 25 or older, 1% Native American, 1% Hispanic, 6% black, 3% Asian or Pacific Islander **Most popular recent majors** Biology/biological sciences, English, business administration/commerce/management **Academic program** Average class size 20, advanced placement, tutorials, honors program, summer session, adult/continuing education programs, internships **Contact** Ms. Florence W. Hines, Director of Admissions, Millsaps College, 1701 North State Street, Jackson, MS 39210-0001. Telephone: 601-974-1050. Fax: 601-974-1059.

MISSISSIPPI COLLEGE
CLINTON, MISSISSIPPI

Entrance Moderately difficult **General** Independent Southern Baptist, comprehensive, coed **Setting** 320-acre small-town campus **Enrollment** 3,321 **Faculty** 12:1 **Application deadline** Rolling **Freshmen** 85% accepted **Housing** Yes **Tuition** $7650 **Undergraduates** 58% women, 23% part-time, 44% 25 or older, 1% Native American, 1% Hispanic, 14% black, 1% Asian or Pacific Islander **Most popular recent majors** Business administration/commerce/management, elementary education, nursing **Academic program** Average class size 25, advanced placement, accelerated degree program, honors program, summer session, adult/continuing education programs, internships **Contact** Dr. Jim Turcotte, Director of Admissions, Mississippi College, PO Box 4203, Clinton, MS 39058. Telephone: 601-925-3240. Fax: 601-925-3804.

MISSISSIPPI STATE UNIVERSITY
MISSISSIPPI STATE, MISSISSIPPI

Entrance Moderately difficult **General** State-supported, coed **Setting** 4,200-acre small-town campus **Enrollment** 14,064 **Faculty** 17:1 **Application deadline** 7/26 **Freshmen** 83% accepted **Housing** Yes **Tuition** $2731 **Undergraduates** 42% women, 12% part-time, 20% 25 or older, 1% Native American, 1% Hispanic, 16% black, 1% Asian or Pacific Islander **Most popular recent majors** Elementary education, business administration/commerce/management, marketing/retailing/merchandising **Academic program** Advanced placement, accelerated degree program, honors program, summer session, adult/continuing education programs, internships **Contact** Mr. Jerry Inmon, Director of Admissions, Mississippi State University, PO Box 5268, Mississippi State, MS 39762. Telephone: 601-325-2224.

MISSISSIPPI UNIVERSITY FOR WOMEN
COLUMBUS, MISSISSIPPI

Entrance Moderately difficult **General** State-supported, comprehensive, primarily women **Setting** 110-acre small-town campus **Enrollment** 3,278 **Faculty** 17:1 **Application deadline** 9/6 **Freshmen** 74% accepted **Housing** Yes **Tuition** $2284 **Undergraduates** 82% women, 38% part-time, 43% 25 or older, 1% Native American, 1% Hispanic, 27% black, 1% Asian or Pacific Islander **Most popular recent majors** Nursing, elementary education, business administration/commerce/management **Academic program** Advanced placement, accelerated degree program, tutorials, honors program, summer session, adult/continuing education programs, internships **Contact** Ms. Melanie Freeman, Director of Admissions, Mississippi University for Women, PO Box 1613, Columbus, MS 39701-9998. Telephone: 601-329-7106. Fax: 601-241-7481.

MISSISSIPPI VALLEY STATE UNIVERSITY
ITTA BENA, MISSISSIPPI

Entrance Minimally difficult **General** State-supported, comprehensive, coed **Setting** 450-acre small-town campus **Enrollment** 2,200 **Faculty** 18:1 **Application deadline** Rolling **Freshmen** 25% accepted **Housing** Yes **Tuition** $2353 **Undergraduates** 55% women, 7% part-time, 9% 25 or older, 1% Hispanic, 99% black, 1% Asian or Pacific Islander **Most popular recent majors** Criminal justice, business administration/commerce/management, social work **Academic program** Tutorials, honors program, summer session, adult/continuing education programs, internships **Contact** Mrs. Maxine B. Rush, Director of Admissions and Recruitment, Mississippi Valley State University, Itta Bena, MS 38941-1400. Telephone: 601-254-3344.

RUST COLLEGE
HOLLY SPRINGS, MISSISSIPPI

Entrance Moderately difficult **General** Independent United Methodist, 4-year, coed **Setting** 126-acre rural campus **Enrollment** 937 **Faculty** 18:1 **Application deadline** Rolling **Freshmen** 50% accepted **Housing** Yes **Tuition** $5025 **Undergraduates** 54% women, 9% part-time, 15% 25 or older, 94% black **Most popular recent majors** Business administration/commerce/management, social work, communication **Academic program** Accelerated degree program, honors program, summer session, adult/continuing education programs, internships **Contact** Miss Joann Scott, Director of Admissions, Rust College, 150 East Rust Avenue, Holly Springs, MS 38635-2328. Telephone: 601-252-8000 Ext. 4068. Fax: 601-252-6107.

SOUTHEASTERN BAPTIST COLLEGE
LAUREL, MISSISSIPPI

Entrance Noncompetitive **General** Independent Baptist, 4-year, coed **Setting** 23-acre small-town campus **Enrollment** 69 **Faculty** 6:1 **Application deadline** Rolling **Freshmen** 100% accepted **Housing** Yes **Tuition** $2220 **Undergraduates** 32% women, 55% part-time, 65% 25 or older, 0% Native American, 0% Hispanic, 13% black, 0% Asian or Pacific Islander **Academic program** Advanced placement, summer session, adult/continuing education programs **Contact** Mrs. Emma Bond, Director of Admissions, Southeastern Baptist College, Laurel, MS 39440-1096. Telephone: 601-426-6346.

TOUGALOO COLLEGE
TOUGALOO, MISSISSIPPI

Entrance Minimally difficult **General** Independent interdenominational, 4-year, coed **Setting** 509-acre suburban campus **Enrollment** 982 **Faculty** 12:1 **Application deadline** Rolling **Freshmen** 50% accepted **Housing** Yes **Tuition** $6160 **Undergraduates** 68% women, 4% part-time, 6% 25 or older, 100% black, 0% Asian or Pacific Islander **Most popular recent majors** Economics, psychology, biology/biological sciences **Academic program** Accelerated degree program, self-designed majors, honors program, adult/continuing education programs, internships **Contact** Ms. Cynthia Hewitt, Data Entry Specialist, Tougaloo College, Tougaloo, MS 39174. Telephone: 601-977-7768. Fax: 601-977-7739.

UNIVERSITY OF MISSISSIPPI
OXFORD, MISSISSIPPI

Entrance Moderately difficult **General** State-supported, coed **Setting** 2,500-acre small-town campus **Enrollment** 10,280 **Application deadline** 7/26 **Freshmen** 78% accepted **Housing** Yes **Tuition** $2631 **Undergraduates** 53% women, 7% part-time, 10% 25 or older, 0% Native American, 1% Hispanic, 10% black, 1% Asian or Pacific Islander **Most popular recent majors** Business administration/commerce/management, English, psychology **Academic program** Advanced placement, accelerated degree program, honors program, summer session, adult/continuing education programs, internships **Contact** Mr. Beckett Howorth, Director of Admissions and Records, University of Mississippi, University, MS 38677. Telephone: 601-232-7226. Fax: 601-232-5986.

UNIVERSITY OF MISSISSIPPI MEDICAL CENTER
JACKSON, MISSISSIPPI

Entrance Moderately difficult **General** State-supported, upper-level, coed **Setting** 164-acre urban campus **Enrollment** 1,806 **Faculty** 5:1 **Freshmen** 27% accepted **Housing** Yes **Tuition** $2106 **Undergraduates** 79% women, 7% part-time, 35% 25 or older, 0% Native American, 0% Hispanic, 12% black, 1% Asian or Pacific Islander **Most popular recent majors** Nursing, physical therapy, occupational therapy **Academic program** Summer session, internships **Contact** Dr. Billy M. Bishop, Director of Student Services and Records, University of Mississippi Medical Center, 2500 North State Street, Jackson, MS 39216-4505. Telephone: 601-984-1080. Fax: 601-984-1080.

UNIVERSITY OF SOUTHERN MISSISSIPPI
HATTIESBURG, MISSISSIPPI

Entrance Moderately difficult **General** State-supported, coed **Setting** 1,090-acre suburban campus **Enrollment** 12,497 **Faculty** 21:1 **Application deadline** Rolling **Freshmen** 72% accepted **Housing** Yes **Tuition** $2518 **Undergraduates** 58% women, 11% part-time, 23% 25 or older, 1% Native American, 1% Hispanic, 21% black, 2% Asian or Pacific Islander **Most popular recent majors** Elementary education, nursing, psychology **Academic program** Advanced placement, accelerated degree program, tutorials, honors program, summer session, adult/continuing education programs **Contact** Dr. Bucky Wesley, Director of Recruiting and Orientation, University of Southern Mississippi, Hattiesburg, MS 39406-5001. Telephone: 601-266-5000.

WESLEY COLLEGE
FLORENCE, MISSISSIPPI

Entrance Noncompetitive **General** Independent-religious, 4-year, coed **Setting** 40-acre small-town campus **Enrollment** 87 **Application deadline** Rolling **Freshmen** 79% accepted **Housing** Yes **Tuition** $2200 **Undergraduates** 44% women, 12% part-time, 54% 25 or older, 1% Native American, 5% Hispanic, 24% black, 1% Asian or Pacific Islander **Academic program** Advanced placement, summer session, adult/continuing education programs, internships **Contact** Ms. Janelle Bond, Admissions Assistant, Wesley College, Florence, MS 39073-1070. Telephone: 601-845-2265.

WILLIAM CAREY COLLEGE
HATTIESBURG, MISSISSIPPI

Entrance Moderately difficult **General** Independent Southern Baptist, comprehensive, coed **Setting** 64-acre small-town campus **Enrollment** 2,254 **Faculty** 17:1 **Application deadline** Rolling **Freshmen** 52% accepted **Housing** Yes **Tuition** $6624 **Undergraduates** 66% women, 25% part-time, 46% 25 or older, 1% Native American, 1% Hispanic, 24% black, 2% Asian or Pacific Islander **Academic program** Accelerated degree program, honors program, summer session, adult/continuing education programs **Contact** Mr. Scott Hilton, Director of Admissions, William Carey College, Hattiesburg, MS 39401-5499. Telephone: 601-582-5051 Ext. 103. Fax: 601-582-6454.

North Carolina

APPALACHIAN STATE UNIVERSITY
BOONE, NORTH CAROLINA

Entrance Moderately difficult **General** State-supported, comprehensive, coed **Setting** 255-acre small-town campus **Enrollment** 11,909 **Faculty** 15:1 **Application deadline** 4/15 **Freshmen** 61% accepted **Housing** Yes **Tuition** $1814 **Undergraduates** 51% women, 7% part-time, 10% 25 or older, 0% Native American, 1% Hispanic, 3% black, 1% Asian or Pacific Islander **Most popular recent majors** Business administration/commerce/management, communication, elementary education **Academic program** Advanced placement, accelerated degree program, self-designed majors, honors program, summer session, adult/continuing education programs, internships **Contact** Mr. Joe Watts, Director of Admissions/

Enrollment Services, Appalachian State University, Boone, NC 28608. Telephone: 704-262-2120. Fax: 704-262-3296.

BARBER-SCOTIA COLLEGE
CONCORD, NORTH CAROLINA

Entrance Noncompetitive **General** Independent, 4-year, coed, affiliated with Presbyterian Church (U.S.A.) **Setting** 23-acre small-town campus **Enrollment** 435 **Faculty** 14:1 **Application deadline** Rolling **Housing** Yes **Tuition** $5594 **Undergraduates** 50% women, 3% part-time, 0% Native American, 0% Hispanic, 99% black, 0% Asian or Pacific Islander **Most popular recent majors** Sociology, business administration/commerce/management, biology/biological sciences **Academic program** Advanced placement, honors program, summer session, internships **Contact** Mr. Grady Deese, Director of Admissions, Barber-Scotia College, 145 Cabarrus Avenue, West, Concord, NC 28025-5187. Telephone: 704-789-2902. Fax: 704-784-3817.

BARTON COLLEGE
WILSON, NORTH CAROLINA

Entrance Minimally difficult **General** Independent, 4-year, coed, affiliated with Christian Church (Disciples of Christ) **Setting** 62-acre small-town campus **Enrollment** 1,295 **Faculty** 12:1 **Application deadline** Rolling **Freshmen** 97% accepted **Housing** Yes **Tuition** $8984 **Undergraduates** 64% women, 26% part-time, 32% 25 or older, 1% Native American, 1% Hispanic, 13% black, 1% Asian or Pacific Islander **Most popular recent majors** Business administration/commerce/management, nursing, education **Academic program** Advanced placement, accelerated degree program, tutorials, honors program, summer session, adult/continuing education programs, internships **Contact** Mr. Anthony Britt, Director of Admissions, Barton College, Wilson, NC 27893. Telephone: 919-399-6314. Fax: 919-237-1620.

BELMONT ABBEY COLLEGE
BELMONT, NORTH CAROLINA

Entrance Moderately difficult **General** Independent Roman Catholic, comprehensive, coed **Setting** 650-acre small-town campus **Enrollment** 959 **Faculty** 16:1 **Application deadline** 8/15 **Freshmen** 83% accepted **Housing** Yes **Tuition** $11,034 **Undergraduates** 53% women, 12% part-time, 26% 25 or older, 1% Native American, 2% Hispanic, 5% black, 2% Asian or Pacific Islander **Most popular recent majors** Business administration/commerce/management, education, accounting **Academic program** Average class size 18, advanced placement, accelerated degree program, honors program, summer session, adult/continuing education programs, internships **Contact** Mr. Denis Stokes, Vice President of Enrollment Management, Belmont Abbey College, Belmont, NC 28012. Telephone: 704-825-6665. Fax: 704-825-6670.

BENNETT COLLEGE
GREENSBORO, NORTH CAROLINA

Entrance Moderately difficult **General** Independent United Methodist, 4-year, women only **Setting** 55-acre urban campus **Enrollment** 550 **Faculty** 11:1 **Application deadline** Rolling **Freshmen** 70% accepted **Housing** Yes **Tuition** $7615 **Undergraduates** 2% part-time, 6% 25 or older, 99% black **Most popular recent majors** Interdisciplinary studies, biology/biological sciences, business administration/commerce/management **Academic program** Self-designed majors, tutorials, honors program, summer session, internships **Contact** Dr. Tiajuana Mosby, Vice President of Student Development, Bennett College, 900 East Washington Street, Greensboro, NC 27401-3239. Telephone: 910-370-8624.

CAMPBELL UNIVERSITY
BUIES CREEK, NORTH CAROLINA

Entrance Moderately difficult **General** Independent Baptist, coed **Setting** 850-acre rural campus **Enrollment** 6,920 **Faculty** 18:1 **Application deadline** Rolling **Freshmen** 60% accepted **Housing** Yes **Tuition** $10,003 **Undergraduates** 57% women, 10% part-time, 18% 25 or older, 1% Native American, 3% Hispanic, 8% black, 5% Asian or Pacific Islander **Most popular recent majors** Business administration/commerce/management, (pre)law sequence, communication **Academic program** Average class size 25, advanced placement, accelerated degree program, honors program, summer session, adult/continuing education programs, internships **Contact** Mr. Herbert V. Kerner Jr., Dean of Admissions, Financial Aid, and Veterans Affairs, Campbell University, Buies Creek, NC 27506. Telephone: 910-893-1291. Fax: 910-893-9274.

CATAWBA COLLEGE
SALISBURY, NORTH CAROLINA

Entrance Moderately difficult **General** Independent, comprehensive, coed, affiliated with United Church of Christ **Setting** 210-acre small-town campus **Enrollment** 1,178 **Faculty** 15:1 **Application deadline** Rolling **Freshmen** 84% accepted **Housing** Yes **Tuition** $11,352 **Undergraduates**

50% women, 6% part-time, 17% 25 or older, 0% Native American, 1% Hispanic, 10% black, 1% Asian or Pacific Islander **Most popular recent majors** Business administration/commerce/management, education, communication **Academic program** Average class size 20, advanced placement, self-designed majors, tutorials, honors program, summer session, adult/continuing education programs, internships **Contact** Mr. Robert W. Bennett, Dean of Admissions, Catawba College, Salisbury, NC 28144-2488. Telephone: 704-637-4402.

CHOWAN COLLEGE
MURFREESBORO, NORTH CAROLINA

Entrance Minimally difficult **General** Independent Baptist, 4-year, coed **Setting** 300-acre rural campus **Enrollment** 746 **Faculty** 12:1 **Application deadline** Rolling **Freshmen** 80% accepted **Housing** Yes **Tuition** $10,760 **Undergraduates** 46% women, 3% part-time, 10% 25 or older, 1% Native American, 2% Hispanic, 18% black, 1% Asian or Pacific Islander **Most popular recent majors** Business administration/commerce/management, physical education, printing technologies **Academic program** Average class size 25, advanced placement, self-designed majors, summer session, internships **Contact** Mrs. Austine O. Evans, Vice President for Enrollment Management, Chowan College, Murfreesboro, NC 27855. Telephone: 919-398-1236. Fax: 919-398-1190.

DAVIDSON COLLEGE
DAVIDSON, NORTH CAROLINA

Entrance Very difficult **General** Independent Presbyterian, 4-year, coed **Setting** 464-acre small-town campus **Enrollment** 1,613 **Faculty** 12:1 **Application deadline** 1/15 **Freshmen** 37% accepted **Housing** Yes **Tuition** $20,595 **Undergraduates** 49% women, 0% part-time, 1% 25 or older, 1% Native American, 2% Hispanic, 4% black, 3% Asian or Pacific Islander **Most popular recent majors** History, English, biology/biological sciences **Academic program** Advanced placement, self-designed majors, tutorials, honors program **Contact** Dr. Nancy J. Cable, Dean of Admission and Financial Aid, Davidson College, Davidson, NC 28036-1719. Telephone: 704-892-2231. Fax: 704-892-2016.

DUKE UNIVERSITY
DURHAM, NORTH CAROLINA

Entrance Most difficult **General** Independent, coed, affiliated with United Methodist Church **Setting** 8,500-acre suburban campus **Enrollment** 11,589 **Faculty** 10:1 **Application deadline** 1/2 **Freshmen** 32% accepted **Housing** Yes **Tuition** $22,073 **Undergraduates** 49% women, 1% part-time, 2% 25 or older, 1% Native American, 4% Hispanic, 8% black, 12% Asian or Pacific Islander **Most popular recent majors** Biology/biological sciences, psychology, history **Academic program** Advanced placement, accelerated degree program, self-designed majors, tutorials, honors program, summer session, adult/continuing education programs, internships **Contact** Mr. Christoph Guttentag, Director of Admissions, Duke University, Durham, NC 27708-0586. Telephone: 919-684-3214. Fax: 919-681-8941.

EAST CAROLINA UNIVERSITY
GREENVILLE, NORTH CAROLINA

Entrance Moderately difficult **General** State-supported, coed **Setting** 465-acre urban campus **Enrollment** 16,805 **Faculty** 19:1 **Application deadline** 3/15 **Freshmen** 77% accepted **Housing** Yes **Tuition** $1752 **Undergraduates** 58% women, 12% part-time, 16% 25 or older, 1% Native American, 1% Hispanic, 11% black, 1% Asian or Pacific Islander **Most popular recent majors** Business administration/commerce/management, nursing, elementary education **Academic program** Advanced placement, accelerated degree program, tutorials, honors program, summer session, adult/continuing education programs, internships **Contact** Dr. Thomas Powell Jr., Director of Admissions, East Carolina University, East Fifth Street, Greenville, NC 27858-4353. Telephone: 919-328-6640. Fax: 919-328-4232.

EAST COAST BIBLE COLLEGE
CHARLOTTE, NORTH CAROLINA

Entrance Minimally difficult **General** Independent, 4-year, coed, affiliated with Church of God **Setting** 100-acre urban campus **Enrollment** 182 **Faculty** 10:1 **Application deadline** Rolling **Freshmen** 95% accepted **Housing** Yes **Tuition** $5180 **Undergraduates** 47% women, 25% part-time, 60% 25 or older, 1% Native American, 2% Hispanic, 13% black **Academic program** Advanced placement, summer session, internships **Contact** Mrs. Linda P. Allen, Registrar, East Coast Bible College, 6900 Wilkinson Boulevard, Charlotte, NC 28214. Telephone: 704-394-2307. Fax: 704-393-3689.

ELIZABETH CITY STATE UNIVERSITY
ELIZABETH CITY, NORTH CAROLINA

Entrance Moderately difficult **General** State-supported, 4-year, coed **Setting** 125-acre small-town campus **Enrollment** 2,000 **Faculty** 16:1

Application deadline 8/1 **Freshmen** 79% accepted **Housing** Yes **Tuition** $1720 **Undergraduates** 62% women, 7% part-time, 21% 25 or older, 1% Native American, 1% Hispanic, 74% black, 1% Asian or Pacific Islander **Most popular recent majors** Business administration/commerce/management, computer science, criminal justice **Academic program** Advanced placement, honors program, summer session, adult/continuing education programs, internships **Contact** Mr. Leon Rouson, Interim Director of Admissions, Elizabeth City State University, PO Box 901 ECSU, Elizabeth City, NC 27909-7806. Telephone: 919-335-3305.

ELON COLLEGE
ELON COLLEGE, NORTH CAROLINA

Entrance Moderately difficult **General** Independent, comprehensive, coed, affiliated with United Church of Christ **Setting** 330-acre suburban campus **Enrollment** 3,588 **Faculty** 17:1 **Application deadline** Rolling **Freshmen** 70% accepted **Housing** Yes **Tuition** $11,542 **Undergraduates** 57% women, 5% part-time, 1% 25 or older, 0% Native American, 1% Hispanic, 6% black, 1% Asian or Pacific Islander **Most popular recent majors** Business administration/commerce/management, communication, education **Academic program** Advanced placement, accelerated degree program, self-designed majors, tutorials, honors program, summer session, internships **Contact** Mrs. Nan P. Perkins, Dean of Admissions and Financial Planning, Elon College, 2700 Campus Box, Elon College, NC 27244. Telephone: 910-584-2370. Fax: 910-538-3986.

FAYETTEVILLE STATE UNIVERSITY
FAYETTEVILLE, NORTH CAROLINA

Entrance Minimally difficult **General** State-supported, comprehensive, coed **Setting** 156-acre urban campus **Enrollment** 3,951 **Faculty** 16:1 **Application deadline** Rolling **Freshmen** 88% accepted **Housing** Yes **Tuition** $1662 **Undergraduates** 63% women, 17% part-time, 35% 25 or older, 1% Native American, 3% Hispanic, 72% black, 2% Asian or Pacific Islander **Most popular recent majors** Business administration/commerce/management, elementary education, psychology **Academic program** Average class size 20, accelerated degree program, honors program, summer session, adult/continuing education programs **Contact** Mr. Charles Darlington, Director of Enrollment Management, Fayetteville State University, 1200 Murchison Road, Fayetteville, NC 28301-4298. Telephone: 910-486-1371. Fax: 910-486-6024.

GARDNER-WEBB UNIVERSITY
BOILING SPRINGS, NORTH CAROLINA

Entrance Moderately difficult **General** Independent Baptist, comprehensive, coed **Setting** 200-acre small-town campus **Enrollment** 2,739 **Faculty** 16:1 **Application deadline** Rolling **Freshmen** 88% accepted **Housing** Yes **Tuition** $9620 **Undergraduates** 60% women, 16% part-time, 36% 25 or older, 0% Native American, 0% Hispanic, 12% black, 1% Asian or Pacific Islander **Most popular recent majors** Business administration/commerce/management, education, biology/biological sciences **Academic program** Advanced placement, accelerated degree program, honors program, summer session, adult/continuing education programs, internships **Contact** Mr. Ray McKay Hardee, Dean of Admissions, Gardner-Webb University, PO Box 817, Boiling Springs, NC 28017. Telephone: 704-434-2361. Fax: 704-434-6246.

GREENSBORO COLLEGE
GREENSBORO, NORTH CAROLINA

Entrance Moderately difficult **General** Independent United Methodist, 4-year, coed **Setting** 40-acre urban campus **Enrollment** 1,023 **Faculty** 10:1 **Application deadline** Rolling **Freshmen** 78% accepted **Housing** Yes **Tuition** $9990 **Undergraduates** 61% women, 20% part-time, 28% 25 or older, 1% Native American, 1% Hispanic, 13% black, 1% Asian or Pacific Islander **Most popular recent majors** Education, business administration/commerce/management, biology/biological sciences **Academic program** Average class size 22, advanced placement, accelerated degree program, self-designed majors, tutorials, honors program, summer session, adult/continuing education programs, internships **Contact** Mr. Randy Doss, Dean of Admissions, Greensboro College, 815 West Market Street, Greensboro, NC 27401-1875. Telephone: 910-272-7102 Ext. 211. Fax: 910-271-6634.

GUILFORD COLLEGE
GREENSBORO, NORTH CAROLINA

Entrance Moderately difficult **General** Independent, 4-year, coed, affiliated with Society of Friends **Setting** 340-acre suburban campus **Enrollment** 1,071 **Faculty** 14:1 **Application deadline** 2/1 **Freshmen** 85% accepted **Housing** Yes **Tuition** $14,750 **Undergraduates** 51% women, 1% part-time, 1% 25 or older, 1% Native American, 2% Hispanic, 6% black, 2% Asian or Pacific Islander **Most popular recent majors** Psychology, English, business administration/commerce/management **Academic program** Advanced placement, accelerated degree program, self-designed majors, tutorials, honors program, summer session, adult/continuing education programs, internships **Contact** Mr. Alton Newell, Dean of Admission, Guilford College, Greensboro, NC 27410-4173. Telephone: 910-316-2100. Fax: 910-316-2954.

HERITAGE BIBLE COLLEGE
DUNN, NORTH CAROLINA

Entrance Difficulty N/R **General** Independent Pentecostal Free Will Baptist, 4-year, specialized, coed **Setting** 82-acre small-town campus **Enrollment** 93 **Housing** Yes **Tuition** $2850 **Undergraduates** 39% women, 37% part-time, 71% 25 or older, 0% Native American, 0% Hispanic, 25% black, 1% Asian or Pacific Islander **Academic program** Average class size 25, summer session, adult/continuing education programs, internships **Contact** Dr. Herbert F. Carter, Academic Dean, Heritage Bible College, PO Box 1628, Dunn, NC 28335. Telephone: 910-892-4268. Fax: 910-891-1660.

HIGH POINT UNIVERSITY
HIGH POINT, NORTH CAROLINA

Entrance Moderately difficult **General** Independent United Methodist, comprehensive, coed **Setting** 77-acre suburban campus **Enrollment** 2,596 **Faculty** 15:1 **Application deadline** Rolling **Freshmen** 84% accepted **Housing** Yes **Tuition** $10,420 **Undergraduates** 61% women, 13% part-time, 21% 25 or older, 1% Native American, 1% Hispanic, 11% black, 1% Asian or Pacific Islander **Most popular recent majors** Business administration/commerce/management, accounting, elementary education **Academic program** Average class size 20, advanced placement, accelerated degree program, self-designed majors, tutorials, honors program, summer session, adult/continuing education programs, internships **Contact** Mr. James L. Schlimmer, Dean of Admissions, High Point University, High Point, NC 27262-3598. Telephone: 910-841-9216. Fax: 910-841-5123.

JOHNSON C. SMITH UNIVERSITY
CHARLOTTE, NORTH CAROLINA

Entrance Minimally difficult **General** Independent, 4-year, coed **Setting** 105-acre urban campus **Enrollment** 1,427 **Faculty** 17:1 **Application deadline** 8/1 **Freshmen** 61% accepted **Housing** Yes **Tuition** $8469 **Undergraduates** 58% women, 6% part-time, 6% 25 or older, 100% black **Most popular recent majors** Business administration/commerce/management, communication, computer science **Academic program** Advanced placement, accelerated degree program, tutorials, honors program, summer session, internships **Contact** Ms. Treva Norman, Vice President for Student Affairs, Johnson C. Smith University, 100-300 Beatties Ford Road, Charlotte, NC 28216. Telephone: 704-378-1010.

JOHN WESLEY COLLEGE
HIGH POINT, NORTH CAROLINA

Entrance Minimally difficult **General** Independent interdenominational, 4-year, coed **Setting** 24-acre urban campus **Enrollment** 161 **Faculty** 11:1 **Application deadline** 8/1 **Freshmen** 94% accepted **Housing** Yes **Tuition** $4840 **Undergraduates** 49% women, 20% part-time, 78% 25 or older, 0% Native American, 0% Hispanic, 8% black, 0% Asian or Pacific Islander **Most popular recent majors** Pastoral studies, biblical studies, psychology **Academic program** Advanced placement, summer session, adult/continuing education programs, internships **Contact** Ms. Gwen W. Armstrong, Director of Admissions, John Wesley College, 2314 North Centennial Street, High Point, NC 27265-3197. Telephone: 910-889-2262 Ext. 127.

LEES-MCRAE COLLEGE
BANNER ELK, NORTH CAROLINA

Entrance Minimally difficult **General** Independent, 4-year, coed, affiliated with Presbyterian Church (U.S.A.) **Setting** 400-acre rural campus **Enrollment** 453 **Faculty** 14:1 **Application deadline** 8/1 **Freshmen** 78% accepted **Housing** Yes **Tuition** $10,130 **Undergraduates** 43% women, 6% part-time, 7% 25 or older, 2% Native American, 2% Hispanic, 4% black, 1% Asian or Pacific Islander **Most popular recent majors** Business administration/commerce/management, education, theater arts/drama **Academic program** Average class size 30, advanced placement, accelerated degree program, self-designed majors, tutorials, honors program, summer session, adult/continuing education programs, internships **Contact** Dr. Tim C. Bailey, Dean of Admissions and Financial Aid, Lees-McRae College, PO Box 128, Banner Elk, NC 28604-0128. Telephone: 704-898-8723. Fax: 704-898-8814.

LENOIR-RHYNE COLLEGE
HICKORY, NORTH CAROLINA

Entrance Moderately difficult **General** Independent Lutheran, comprehensive, coed **Setting** 100-acre small-town campus **Enrollment** 1,579 **Fac-**

ulty 11:1 **Application deadline** Rolling **Freshmen** 86% accepted **Housing** Yes **Tuition** $12,036 **Undergraduates** 63% women, 13% part-time, 27% 25 or older, 1% Native American, 1% Hispanic, 5% black, 1% Asian or Pacific Islander **Most popular recent majors** Nursing, business administration/commerce/management, education **Academic program** Average class size 23, advanced placement, accelerated degree program, self-designed majors, honors program, summer session, adult/continuing education programs, internships **Contact** Mr. Tim Jackson, Director of Admissions, Lenoir-Rhyne College, Hickory, NC 28603. Telephone: 704-328-7300 Ext. 300. Fax: 704-328-7338.

LIVINGSTONE COLLEGE
SALISBURY, NORTH CAROLINA

Entrance Minimally difficult **General** Independent, 4-year, coed, affiliated with African Methodist Episcopal Zion Church **Setting** 272-acre small-town campus **Enrollment** 689 **Faculty** 15:1 **Application deadline** Rolling **Freshmen** 62% accepted **Housing** Yes **Tuition** $6900 **Undergraduates** 44% women, 3% part-time, 11% 25 or older, 0% Native American, 1% Hispanic, 98% black, 1% Asian or Pacific Islander **Most popular recent majors** Business administration/commerce/management, education, computer science **Academic program** Summer session, internships **Contact** Ms. Diedre Stewart, Assistant Director of Admissions, Livingstone College, Salisbury, NC 28144-5298. Telephone: 704-638-5502.

MARS HILL COLLEGE
MARS HILL, NORTH CAROLINA

Entrance Minimally difficult **General** Independent Baptist, 4-year, coed **Setting** 180-acre small-town campus **Enrollment** 1,050 **Faculty** 13:1 **Application deadline** Rolling **Freshmen** 87% accepted **Housing** Yes **Tuition** $8900 **Undergraduates** 50% women, 2% part-time, 23% 25 or older, 1% Native American, 1% Hispanic, 6% black, 1% Asian or Pacific Islander **Most popular recent majors** Recreation and leisure services, education, business administration/commerce/management **Academic program** Advanced placement, accelerated degree program, tutorials, honors program, summer session, adult/continuing education programs, internships **Contact** Mr. Rick Hinshaw, Dean of Admissions and Financial Aid, Mars Hill College, Mars Hill, NC 28754. Telephone: 704-689-1201. Fax: 704-689-1474.

MEREDITH COLLEGE
RALEIGH, NORTH CAROLINA

Entrance Moderately difficult **General** Independent, comprehensive, women only, affiliated with Baptist Church **Setting** 225-acre urban campus **Enrollment** 2,574 **Faculty** 16:1 **Application deadline** 2/15 **Freshmen** 88% accepted **Housing** Yes **Tuition** $8490 **Undergraduates** 16% part-time, 22% 25 or older, 1% Native American, 1% Hispanic, 5% black, 1% Asian or Pacific Islander **Most popular recent majors** Business administration/commerce/management, psychology, child psychology/child development **Academic program** Average class size 22, advanced placement, accelerated degree program, self-designed majors, tutorials, honors program, summer session, adult/continuing education programs, internships **Contact** Ms. Vanessa Goodman Barnes, Assistant Director of Admissions, Meredith College, 3800 Hillsborough Street, Raleigh, NC 27607-5298. Telephone: 919-829-8581 Ext. 8110. Fax: 919-829-2348.

METHODIST COLLEGE
FAYETTEVILLE, NORTH CAROLINA

Entrance Moderately difficult **General** Independent United Methodist, 4-year, coed **Setting** 600-acre suburban campus **Enrollment** 1,736 **Faculty** 17:1 **Application deadline** Rolling **Freshmen** 69% accepted **Housing** Yes **Tuition** $11,250 **Undergraduates** 50% women, 28% part-time, 35% 25 or older, 1% Native American, 4% Hispanic, 18% black, 2% Asian or Pacific Islander **Most popular recent majors** Business administration/commerce/management, education, sociology **Academic program** Advanced placement, accelerated degree program, honors program, summer session, adult/continuing education programs, internships **Contact** Mr. J. Alan Coheley, Vice President of Enrollment Services, Methodist College, Fayetteville, NC 28311-1420. Telephone: 910-630-7027. Fax: 910-630-2123.

MONTREAT COLLEGE
MONTREAT, NORTH CAROLINA

Entrance Moderately difficult **General** Independent Presbyterian, comprehensive, coed **Setting** 100-acre small-town campus **Enrollment** 1,000 **Application deadline** 8/20 **Freshmen** 89% accepted **Housing** Yes **Tuition** $10,042 **Undergraduates** 52% women, 1% part-time, 64% 25 or older, 1% Native American, 1% Hispanic, 12% black, 1% Asian or Pacific Islander **Most popular recent majors** Business administration/commerce/management, environmental sciences, religious studies **Academic program** Advanced placement, adult/continuing education programs, internships **Contact** Mr. Willie Mangum, Director of Admissions, Montreat College, Montreat, NC 28757-1267. Telephone: 704-669-8012 Ext. 3784. Fax: 704-669-0120.

MOUNT OLIVE COLLEGE
MOUNT OLIVE, NORTH CAROLINA

Entrance Minimally difficult **General** Independent Free Will Baptist, 4-year, coed **Setting** 123-acre small-town campus **Enrollment** 1,341 **Faculty** 15:1 **Application deadline** Rolling **Freshmen** 90% accepted **Housing** Yes **Tuition** $8490 **Undergraduates** 49% women, 44% part-time, 52% 25 or older, 1% Native American, 1% Hispanic, 20% black, 1% Asian or Pacific Islander **Most popular recent majors** Business administration/commerce/management, psychology, recreation and leisure services **Academic program** Advanced placement, accelerated degree program, tutorials, honors program, summer session, adult/continuing education programs, internships **Contact** Mr. Tim Woodard, Director of Admissions, Mount Olive College, Mount Olive, NC 28365. Telephone: 919-658-2502 Ext. 3009. Fax: 919-658-8934.

NORTH CAROLINA AGRICULTURAL AND TECHNICAL STATE UNIVERSITY
GREENSBORO, NORTH CAROLINA

Entrance Moderately difficult **General** State-supported, coed **Setting** 181-acre urban campus **Enrollment** 7,533 **Faculty** 15:1 **Application deadline** 6/1 **Freshmen** 65% accepted **Housing** Yes **Tuition** $1596 **Undergraduates** 52% women, 10% part-time, 15% 25 or older, 1% Native American, 1% Hispanic, 92% black, 1% Asian or Pacific Islander **Most popular recent majors** Nursing, electrical engineering, accounting **Academic program** Average class size 24, ESL program, advanced placement, tutorials, honors program, summer session, adult/continuing education programs, internships **Contact** Mr. John Smith, Director of Admissions, North Carolina Agricultural and Technical State University, 1601 East Market Street, Greensboro, NC 27411. Telephone: 910-334-7946. Fax: 910-334-7136.

NORTH CAROLINA CENTRAL UNIVERSITY
DURHAM, NORTH CAROLINA

Entrance Minimally difficult **General** State-supported, comprehensive, coed **Setting** 103-acre urban campus **Enrollment** 5,400 **Application deadline** 7/1 **Freshmen** 69% accepted **Housing** Yes **Tuition** $1788 **Undergraduates** 64% women, 18% part-time, 24% 25 or older, 0% Native American, 1% Hispanic, 92% black, 0% Asian or Pacific Islander **Most popular recent majors** Political science/government, business administration/commerce/management, law enforcement/police sciences **Academic program** Advanced placement, tutorials, honors program, summer session, adult/continuing education programs, internships **Contact** Ms. Nancy R. Rowland, Director of Admissions, North Carolina Central University, 1801 Fayetteville Street, Durham, NC 27707-3129. Telephone: 919-560-6326.

NORTH CAROLINA SCHOOL OF THE ARTS
WINSTON-SALEM, NORTH CAROLINA

Entrance Very difficult **General** State-supported, comprehensive, coed **Setting** 57-acre urban campus **Enrollment** 716 **Faculty** 9:1 **Application deadline** Rolling **Freshmen** 41% accepted **Housing** Yes **Tuition** $2229 **Undergraduates** 40% women, 1% part-time, 10% 25 or older, 1% Native American, 3% Hispanic, 7% black, 2% Asian or Pacific Islander **Most popular recent major** Music **Academic program** Tutorials **Contact** Ms. Carol J. Palm, Director of Admissions, North Carolina School of the Arts, 200 Waughtown Street, PO Box 12189, Winston-Salem, NC 27117-2189. Telephone: 910-770-3291.

NORTH CAROLINA STATE UNIVERSITY
RALEIGH, NORTH CAROLINA

Entrance Very difficult **General** State-supported, coed **Setting** 1,623-acre suburban campus **Enrollment** 27,169 **Faculty** 14:1 **Application deadline** 2/1 **Freshmen** 66% accepted **Housing** Yes **Tuition** $2200 **Undergraduates** 43% women, 9% part-time, 9% 25 or older, 1% Native American, 2% Hispanic, 9% black, 4% Asian or Pacific Islander **Most popular recent majors** Business administration/commerce/management, electrical engineering, mechanical engineering **Academic program** Average class size 34, advanced placement, self-designed majors, tutorials, honors program, summer session, adult/continuing education programs, internships **Contact** Dr. George R. Dixon, Vice Provost and Director of Admissions, North Carolina State University, Box 7103, 112 Peele Hall, Raleigh, NC 27695. Telephone: 919-515-2434. Fax: 919-515-5039.

NORTH CAROLINA WESLEYAN COLLEGE
ROCKY MOUNT, NORTH CAROLINA

Entrance Moderately difficult **General** Independent, 4-year, coed, affiliated with United Methodist Church **Setting** 200-acre suburban campus **Enrollment** 610 **Faculty** 14:1 **Application deadline** Rolling **Freshmen** 81% accepted **Housing** Yes **Tuition** $7430 **Undergraduates** 52% women, 9% part-time, 1% Native American, 2% Hispanic, 19% black, 1% Asian or Pacific Islander **Most popular recent majors** Business administration/commerce/management, computer information systems **Academic program** Advanced placement, tutorials, honors program, summer session, adult/continuing education programs, internships **Contact** Ms. Patricia Cerjan, Vice President of Admissions and Financial Aid, North Carolina Wesleyan College, Rocky Mount, NC 27804-8677. Telephone: 919-985-5200. Fax: 919-985-5295.

PEMBROKE STATE UNIVERSITY

SEE UNIVERSITY OF NORTH CAROLINA AT PEMBROKE

PFEIFFER UNIVERSITY

MISENHEIMER, NORTH CAROLINA

Entrance Minimally difficult **General** Independent United Methodist, comprehensive, coed **Setting** 300-acre rural campus **Enrollment** 1,534 **Faculty** 16:1 **Application deadline** Rolling **Freshmen** 81% accepted **Housing** Yes **Tuition** $9816 **Undergraduates** 53% women, 12% part-time, 27% 25 or older, 1% Native American, 1% Hispanic, 15% black, 1% Asian or Pacific Islander **Most popular recent majors** Business administration/commerce/management, criminal justice, sports medicine **Academic program** Advanced placement, accelerated degree program, tutorials, summer session, internships **Contact** Ms. Elsie Lowder, Director of Admissions, Pfeiffer University, Misenheimer, NC 28109-0960. Telephone: 704-463-1360 Ext. 2067. Fax: 704-463-1363.

PIEDMONT BIBLE COLLEGE

WINSTON-SALEM, NORTH CAROLINA

Entrance Noncompetitive **General** Independent Baptist, comprehensive, coed **Setting** 12-acre urban campus **Enrollment** 270 **Faculty** 13:1 **Application deadline** Rolling **Freshmen** 94% accepted **Housing** Yes **Tuition** $5250 **Undergraduates** 41% women, 26% part-time, 36% 25 or older, 0% Native American, 0% Hispanic, 5% black, 1% Asian or Pacific Islander **Most popular recent majors** Aviation technology, elementary education, biblical studies **Academic program** Advanced placement, summer session, adult/continuing education programs, internships **Contact** Mr. Darryl McConnell, Director of Admissions, Piedmont Bible College, 716 Franklin Street, Winston-Salem, NC 27101-5197. Telephone: 910-725-8344 Ext. 231. Fax: 910-725-5522.

QUEENS COLLEGE

CHARLOTTE, NORTH CAROLINA

Entrance Moderately difficult **General** Independent Presbyterian, comprehensive, coed **Setting** 25-acre suburban campus **Enrollment** 1,564 **Faculty** 12:1 **Application deadline** Rolling **Freshmen** 76% accepted **Housing** Yes **Tuition** $12,980 **Undergraduates** 80% women, 42% part-time, 35% 25 or older, 1% Native American, 2% Hispanic, 14% black, 2% Asian or Pacific Islander **Most popular recent majors** Business administration/commerce/management, nursing, communication **Academic program** Average class size 18, advanced placement, honors program, summer session, adult/continuing education programs, internships **Contact** Ms. Eileen T. Dills, Dean of Admissions, Queens College, Charlotte, NC 28274-0002. Telephone: 704-337-2212. Fax: 704-337-2403.

ROANOKE BIBLE COLLEGE

ELIZABETH CITY, NORTH CAROLINA

Entrance Minimally difficult **General** Independent Christian, 4-year, specialized, coed **Setting** 19-acre small-town campus **Enrollment** 161 **Faculty** 12:1 **Application deadline** 8/1 **Freshmen** 98% accepted **Housing** Yes **Tuition** $5020 **Undergraduates** 51% women, 26% part-time, 29% 25 or older, 0% Native American, 0% Hispanic, 13% black, 0% Asian or Pacific Islander **Academic program** Advanced placement, internships **Contact** Mr. Garrett Lewis, Vice President for Student Affairs, Roanoke Bible College, Elizabeth City, NC 27909-3926. Telephone: 919-338-5191 Ext. 205. Fax: 919-338-0801.

ST. ANDREWS PRESBYTERIAN COLLEGE

LAURINBURG, NORTH CAROLINA

Entrance Moderately difficult **General** Independent Presbyterian, 4-year, coed **Setting** 600-acre small-town campus **Enrollment** 662 **Faculty** 12:1 **Application deadline** Rolling **Freshmen** 84% accepted **Housing** Yes **Tuition** $12,182 **Undergraduates** 56% women, 15% part-time, 10% 25 or older, 1% Native American, 1% Hispanic, 8% black, 1% Asian or Pacific Islander **Most popular recent majors** Business administration/commerce/management, education, physical education **Academic program** Advanced placement, accelerated degree program, self-designed majors, tutorials, honors program, summer session, adult/continuing education programs, internships

Contact Ms. Anne Todd, Director of Admissions, St. Andrews Presbyterian College, Laurinburg, NC 28352-5598. Telephone: 910-277-5000. Fax: 910-277-5087.

SAINT AUGUSTINE'S COLLEGE

RALEIGH, NORTH CAROLINA

Entrance Minimally difficult **General** Independent Episcopal, 4-year, coed **Setting** 110-acre urban campus **Enrollment** 1,584 **Faculty** 21:1 **Application deadline** 8/10 **Freshmen** 39% accepted **Housing** Yes **Tuition** $6560 **Undergraduates** 54% women, 6% part-time, 9% 25 or older, 97% black **Most popular recent majors** Business administration/commerce/management, computer science, communication **Academic program** Honors program, summer session, adult/continuing education programs, internships **Contact** Mr. Wanzo Hendrix, Director of Admissions, Saint Augustine's College, 1315 Oakwood Avenue, Raleigh, NC 27610-2298. Telephone: 919-516-4016. Fax: 919-834-6473.

SALEM COLLEGE

WINSTON-SALEM, NORTH CAROLINA

Entrance Moderately difficult **General** Independent Moravian, comprehensive, primarily women **Setting** 57-acre small-town campus **Enrollment** 903 **Faculty** 12:1 **Application deadline** Rolling **Freshmen** 87% accepted **Housing** Yes **Tuition** $12,415 **Undergraduates** 98% women, 22% part-time, 36% 25 or older, 1% Native American, 1% Hispanic, 13% black, 1% Asian or Pacific Islander **Most popular recent majors** Business administration/commerce/management, communication, interior design **Academic program** Advanced placement, self-designed majors, honors program, summer session, adult/continuing education programs, internships **Contact** Ms. Katherine Knapp Watts, Dean of Admissions and Financial Aid, Salem College, Winston-Salem, NC 27108-0548. Telephone: 910-721-2621. Fax: 910-724-7102.

SHAW UNIVERSITY

RALEIGH, NORTH CAROLINA

Entrance Minimally difficult **General** Independent Baptist, 4-year, coed **Setting** 18-acre urban campus **Enrollment** 2,262 **Faculty** 14:1 **Application deadline** 8/10 **Freshmen** 75% accepted **Housing** Yes **Tuition** $6304 **Undergraduates** 59% women, 8% part-time, 30% 25 or older, 96% black, 1% Asian or Pacific Islander **Most popular recent majors** Business administration/commerce/management, social science, criminal justice **Academic program** Advanced placement, summer session, adult/continuing education programs, internships **Contact** Mr. Keith Smith, Director of Admissions and Recruitment, Shaw University, 118 East South Street, Raleigh, NC 27601-2399. Telephone: 919-546-8275. Fax: 919-546-8301.

UNIVERSITY OF NORTH CAROLINA AT ASHEVILLE

ASHEVILLE, NORTH CAROLINA

Entrance Moderately difficult **General** State-supported, comprehensive, coed **Setting** 265-acre suburban campus **Enrollment** 3,092 **Faculty** 12:1 **Application deadline** 4/15 **Freshmen** 60% accepted **Housing** Yes **Tuition** $1842 **Undergraduates** 57% women, 28% part-time, 35% 25 or older, 0% Native American, 2% Hispanic, 4% black, 2% Asian or Pacific Islander **Most popular recent majors** Business administration/commerce/management, psychology, biology/biological sciences **Academic program** Average class size 23, advanced placement, accelerated degree program, self-designed majors, honors program, summer session, adult/continuing education programs, internships **Contact** Mr. John White, Director of Admissions, University of North Carolina at Asheville, University Heights, Asheville, NC 28804-3299. Telephone: 704-251-6481. Fax: 704-251-6841.

THE UNIVERSITY OF NORTH CAROLINA AT CHAPEL HILL

CHAPEL HILL, NORTH CAROLINA

Entrance Very difficult **General** State-supported, coed **Setting** 789-acre suburban campus **Enrollment** 24,141 **Application deadline** 1/15 **Freshmen** 38% accepted **Housing** Yes **Tuition** $2165 **Undergraduates** 60% women, 6% part-time, 6% 25 or older, 1% Native American, 1% Hispanic, 10% black, 5% Asian or Pacific Islander **Most popular recent majors** Biology/biological sciences, business administration/commerce/management, psychology **Academic program** Advanced placement, accelerated degree program, self-designed majors, honors program, summer session, adult/continuing education programs, internships **Contact** Dr. James Walters, Associate Provost/Director of Undergraduate Admissions, The University of North Carolina at Chapel Hill, Chapel Hill, NC 27599. Telephone: 919-966-3621.

UNIVERSITY OF NORTH CAROLINA AT CHARLOTTE
CHARLOTTE, NORTH CAROLINA

Entrance Moderately difficult **General** State-supported, coed **Setting** 1,000-acre urban campus **Enrollment** 15,795 **Faculty** 16:1 **Application deadline** 7/1 **Freshmen** 72% accepted **Housing** Yes **Tuition** $1718 **Undergraduates** 52% women, 26% part-time, 28% 25 or older, 1% Native American, 1% Hispanic, 16% black, 4% Asian or Pacific Islander **Most popular recent majors** Psychology, English, criminal justice **Academic program** Average class size 37, advanced placement, tutorials, honors program, summer session, adult/continuing education programs, internships **Contact** Mr. Craig Fulton, Director of Admissions, University of North Carolina at Charlotte, 9201 University City Boulevard, Charlotte, NC 28223-0001. Telephone: 704-547-2213.

UNIVERSITY OF NORTH CAROLINA AT GREENSBORO
GREENSBORO, NORTH CAROLINA

Entrance Moderately difficult **General** State-supported, coed **Setting** 190-acre urban campus **Enrollment** 12,323 **Faculty** 15:1 **Application deadline** 8/1 **Freshmen** 80% accepted **Housing** Yes **Tuition** $2021 **Undergraduates** 66% women, 19% part-time, 27% 25 or older, 1% Native American, 1% Hispanic, 15% black, 2% Asian or Pacific Islander **Most popular recent majors** Business administration/commerce/management, nursing, psychology **Academic program** Advanced placement, accelerated degree program, self-designed majors, tutorials, honors program, summer session, adult/continuing education programs, internships **Contact** Ms. Rachel M. Hendrickson, Director of Admissions, University of North Carolina at Greensboro, 1000 Spring Garden Street, Greensboro, NC 27412-0001. Telephone: 910-334-5243. Fax: 910-334-5932.

UNIVERSITY OF NORTH CAROLINA AT PEMBROKE
PEMBROKE, NORTH CAROLINA

Entrance Moderately difficult **General** State-supported, comprehensive, coed **Setting** 108-acre rural campus **Enrollment** 3,006 **Faculty** 18:1 **Application deadline** 7/15 **Freshmen** 91% accepted **Housing** Yes **Tuition** $1510 **Undergraduates** 60% women, 20% part-time, 41% 25 or older, 25% Native American, 1% Hispanic, 14% black, 1% Asian or Pacific Islander **Most popular recent majors** Education, business administration/commerce/management, sociology **Academic program** Average class size 20, advanced placement, accelerated degree program, tutorials, honors program, summer session, adult/continuing education programs, internships **Contact** Ms. Jacqueline Clark, Director of Admissions, University of North Carolina at Pembroke, Pembroke, NC 28372-1510. Telephone: 910-521-6262.

UNIVERSITY OF NORTH CAROLINA AT WILMINGTON
WILMINGTON, NORTH CAROLINA

Entrance Moderately difficult **General** State-supported, comprehensive, coed **Setting** 650-acre urban campus **Enrollment** 9,077 **Faculty** 16:1 **Application deadline** Rolling **Freshmen** 63% accepted **Housing** Yes **Tuition** $1748 **Undergraduates** 60% women, 16% part-time, 16% 25 or older, 1% Native American, 1% Hispanic, 6% black, 1% Asian or Pacific Islander **Most popular recent majors** Psychology, marine biology, English **Academic program** Average class size 30, advanced placement, accelerated degree program, honors program, summer session, adult/continuing education programs, internships **Contact** Mr. Ronald E. Whittaker, Director of Admissions and Registrar, University of North Carolina at Wilmington, 601 South College Road, Wilmington, NC 28403-3201. Telephone: 910-962-3243. Fax: 910-962-3038.

WAKE FOREST UNIVERSITY
WINSTON-SALEM, NORTH CAROLINA

Entrance Very difficult **General** Independent, coed **Setting** 350-acre suburban campus **Enrollment** 5,910 **Faculty** 12:1 **Application deadline** 1/15 **Freshmen** 42% accepted **Housing** Yes **Tuition** $16,300 **Undergraduates** 50% women, 2% part-time, 1% 25 or older, 1% Native American, 1% Hispanic, 8% black **Most popular recent majors** Business administration/commerce/management, biology/biological sciences, psychology **Academic program** Advanced placement, accelerated degree program, self-designed majors, honors program, summer session, internships **Contact** Mr. William G. Starling, Director of Admissions, Wake Forest University, PO Box 7305, Winston-Salem, NC 27109. Telephone: 910-759-5201.

WARREN WILSON COLLEGE
ASHEVILLE, NORTH CAROLINA

Entrance Moderately difficult **General** Independent, comprehensive, coed, affiliated with Presbyterian Church (U.S.A.) **Setting** 1,100-acre small-town campus **Enrollment** 655 **Faculty** 11:1 **Application deadline** 3/15 **Freshmen** 86% accepted **Housing** Yes **Tuition** $12,500 **Undergraduates** 59% women, 1% part-time, 3% 25 or older, 1% Native American, 4% Hispanic, 3% black, 5% Asian or Pacific Islander **Most popular recent majors** Environmental studies, biology/biological sciences, English **Academic program** Average class size 17, advanced placement, accelerated degree program, self-designed majors, tutorials, honors program, internships **Contact** Mr. Richard Blomgren, Dean of Admission, Warren Wilson College, Asheville, NC 28815-9000. Telephone: 704-298-3325 Ext. 246. Fax: 704-298-1440.

WESTERN CAROLINA UNIVERSITY
CULLOWHEE, NORTH CAROLINA

Entrance Moderately difficult **General** State-supported, comprehensive, coed **Setting** 260-acre rural campus **Enrollment** 6,511 **Faculty** 18:1 **Application deadline** 8/1 **Freshmen** 85% accepted **Housing** Yes **Tuition** $1839 **Undergraduates** 51% women, 10% part-time, 16% 25 or older, 2% Native American, 1% Hispanic, 4% black, 1% Asian or Pacific Islander **Most popular recent majors** Criminal justice, marketing/retailing/merchandising, nursing **Academic program** Advanced placement, accelerated degree program, honors program, summer session, adult/continuing education programs, internships **Contact** Mr. Doyle Bickers, Director of Admissions, Western Carolina University, Cullowhee, NC 28723. Telephone: 704-227-7317.

WINGATE UNIVERSITY
WINGATE, NORTH CAROLINA

Entrance Moderately difficult **General** Independent Baptist, comprehensive, coed **Setting** 330-acre small-town campus **Enrollment** 1,275 **Faculty** 13:1 **Application deadline** 8/1 **Freshmen** 79% accepted **Housing** Yes **Tuition** $11,690 **Undergraduates** 48% women, 8% part-time, 9% 25 or older, 1% Native American, 1% Hispanic, 10% black, 1% Asian or Pacific Islander **Most popular recent majors** Business administration/commerce/management, communication, education **Academic program** Average class size 20, advanced placement, accelerated degree program, tutorials, honors program, summer session, adult/continuing education programs, internships **Contact** Mr. Walter P. Crutchfield III, Dean of Admissions, Wingate University, Wingate, NC 28174. Telephone: 704-233-8000.

WINSTON-SALEM STATE UNIVERSITY
WINSTON-SALEM, NORTH CAROLINA

Entrance Minimally difficult **General** State-supported, 4-year, coed **Setting** 92-acre urban campus **Enrollment** 2,781 **Faculty** 19:1 **Application deadline** Rolling **Freshmen** 61% accepted **Housing** Yes **Tuition** $1552 **Undergraduates** 66% women, 24% part-time, 29% 25 or older, 0% Native American, 1% Hispanic, 79% black, 1% Asian or Pacific Islander **Most popular recent majors** Physical therapy, business administration/commerce/management, nursing **Academic program** Advanced placement, accelerated degree program, honors program, summer session, adult/continuing education programs, internships **Contact** Mr. Van C. Wilson, Director of Admissions, Winston-Salem State University, 601 Martin Luther King Jr Drive, Winston-Salem, NC 27110-0003. Telephone: 910-750-2070. Fax: 910-750-2079.

South Carolina

ALLEN UNIVERSITY
COLUMBIA, SOUTH CAROLINA

Entrance Noncompetitive **General** Independent African Methodist Episcopal, 4-year, coed **Setting** Suburban campus **Enrollment** 281 **Faculty** 6:1 **Application deadline** Rolling **Freshmen** 100% accepted **Housing** Yes **Tuition** $4750 **Undergraduates** 41% women, 2% part-time, 2% 25 or older, 0% Native American, 100% black **Most popular recent majors** Business administration/commerce/management, social work, education **Contact** Mr. Chris Vaughn, Director of Admissions, Allen University, 1530 Harden Street, Columbia, SC 29204-1085. Telephone: 803-376-5735.

ANDERSON COLLEGE
ANDERSON, SOUTH CAROLINA

Entrance Minimally difficult **General** Independent Baptist, 4-year, coed **Setting** 44-acre small-town campus **Enrollment** 900 **Faculty** 15:1 **Application deadline** 7/15 **Freshmen** 81% accepted **Housing** Yes **Tuition** $9475 **Undergraduates** 54% women, 28% part-time, 25% 25 or older, 0% Native American, 0% Hispanic, 13% black, 0% Asian or Pacific Islander **Most popular recent majors** Business administration/commerce/management, physical education, art/fine arts **Academic program** Advanced placement, tutorials, honors program, summer session, adult/continuing education programs, internships **Contact** Ms. Pam Bryant, Director of Admissions, Anderson College, Anderson, SC 29621-4035. Telephone: 864-231-2030. Fax: 864-231-2004.

BENEDICT COLLEGE
COLUMBIA, SOUTH CAROLINA

Entrance Noncompetitive **General** Independent Baptist, 4-year, coed **Setting** 20-acre urban campus **Enrollment** 2,138 **Faculty** 17:1 **Application deadline** Rolling **Housing** Yes **Tuition** $6820 **Undergraduates** 46% women, 5% part-time, 17% 25 or older, 99% black **Most popular recent majors** Business administration/commerce/management, criminal justice, social work **Academic program** Advanced placement, honors program, summer session, adult/continuing education programs, internships **Contact** Dr. Marcia Conston, Associate Vice President, Institutional Effectiveness, Benedict College, P.O. Box 98, Columbia, SC 29204. Telephone: 803-253-5526. Fax: 803-253-5167.

CHARLESTON SOUTHERN UNIVERSITY
CHARLESTON, SOUTH CAROLINA

Entrance Moderately difficult **General** Independent Baptist, comprehensive, coed **Setting** 350-acre suburban campus **Enrollment** 2,329 **Faculty** 18:1 **Application deadline** Rolling **Freshmen** 89% accepted **Housing** Yes **Tuition** $9248 **Undergraduates** 56% women, 33% part-time, 38% 25 or older, 0% Native American, 1% Hispanic, 18% black, 1% Asian or Pacific Islander **Most popular recent majors** Business administration/commerce/management, education, psychology **Academic program** Advanced placement, accelerated degree program, summer session, internships **Contact** Mrs. Debbie Williamson, Director of Enrollment Management, Charleston Southern University, Charleston, SC 29423-8087. Telephone: 803-863-7050.

THE CITADEL, THE MILITARY COLLEGE OF SOUTH CAROLINA
CHARLESTON, SOUTH CAROLINA

Entrance Moderately difficult **General** State-supported, comprehensive, coed **Setting** 130-acre urban campus **Enrollment** 4,319 **Faculty** 13:1 **Application deadline** 7/1 **Freshmen** 86% accepted **Housing** Yes **Tuition** $4329 **Undergraduates** 1% women, 4% part-time, 6% 25 or older, 0% Native American, 2% Hispanic, 7% black, 2% Asian or Pacific Islander **Most popular recent majors** Business administration/commerce/management, political science/government, civil engineering **Academic program** Advanced placement, honors program, summer session, adult/continuing education programs, internships **Contact** Lt. Col. Steven Klein, Dean of Enrollment Management, The Citadel, The Military College of South Carolina, 171 Moultrie Street, Charleston, SC 29409. Telephone: 803-953-5230. Fax: 803-953-7630.

CLAFLIN COLLEGE
ORANGEBURG, SOUTH CAROLINA

Entrance Minimally difficult **General** Independent United Methodist, 4-year, coed **Setting** 32-acre small-town campus **Enrollment** 979 **Faculty** 15:1 **Application deadline** Rolling **Freshmen** 57% accepted **Housing** Yes **Tuition** $5580 **Undergraduates** 60% women, 5% part-time, 3% 25 or older, 98% black **Academic program** ESL program, Advanced placement, honors program, summer session, internships **Contact** Mr. George Lee, Director of Admission and Records, Claflin College, Orangeburg, SC 29115. Telephone: 803-534-2710 Ext. 339.

CLEMSON UNIVERSITY
CLEMSON, SOUTH CAROLINA

Entrance Moderately difficult **General** State-supported, coed **Setting** 1,400-acre small-town campus **Enrollment** 16,537 **Faculty** 16:1 **Application deadline** 5/1 **Freshmen** 78% accepted **Housing** Yes **Tuition** $3392 **Undergraduates** 45% women, 7% part-time, 3% 25 or older, 1% Native American, 1% Hispanic, 8% black, 1% Asian or Pacific Islander **Most popular recent majors** Nursing, business administration/commerce/management, accounting **Academic program** Advanced placement, accelerated degree program, honors program, summer session, internships **Contact** Dr. Michael Heintze, Director of Admissions, Clemson University, 105 Sikes Hall, PO Box 345124, Clemson, SC 29634. Telephone: 864-656-2287. Fax: 864-656-2464.

COASTAL CAROLINA UNIVERSITY
CONWAY, SOUTH CAROLINA

Entrance Moderately difficult **General** State-supported, comprehensive, coed **Setting** 244-acre suburban campus **Enrollment** 4,477 **Faculty** 18:1 **Application deadline** 8/15 **Freshmen** 75% accepted **Housing** Yes **Tuition** $3170 **Undergraduates** 57% women, 21% part-time, 25% 25 or older, 1% Native American, 1% Hispanic, 9% black, 1% Asian or Pacific Islander **Most popular recent majors** Marine sciences, elementary education, business administration/commerce/management **Academic program** Advanced placement, accelerated degree program, self-designed majors, honors program, summer session, adult/continuing education programs, internships **Contact** Mr. Timothy J. McCormick, Director of Admissions, Coastal Carolina University, Conway, SC 29528-6054. Telephone: 803-349-2026. Fax: 803-349-2127.

COKER COLLEGE
HARTSVILLE, SOUTH CAROLINA

Entrance Moderately difficult **General** Independent, 4-year, coed **Setting** 30-acre small-town campus **Enrollment** 666 **Faculty** 10:1 **Application deadline** Rolling **Freshmen** 70% accepted **Housing** Yes **Tuition** $13,400 **Undergraduates** 60% women, 7% part-time, 54% 25 or older, 1% Native American, 1% Hispanic, 22% black, 1% Asian or Pacific Islander **Most popular recent majors** Business administration/commerce/management, elementary education, social science **Academic program** Advanced placement, accelerated degree program, self-designed majors, tutorials, honors program, summer session, adult/continuing education programs, internships **Contact** Dr. Stephen B. Terry, Vice President for Enrollment Management, Coker College, Hartsville, SC 29550. Telephone: 803-383-8050. Fax: 803-383-8095.

COLLEGE OF CHARLESTON
CHARLESTON, SOUTH CAROLINA

Entrance Moderately difficult **General** State-supported, 4-year, coed **Setting** 52-acre urban campus **Enrollment** 11,053 **Faculty** 18:1 **Application deadline** 7/1 **Freshmen** 73% accepted **Housing** Yes **Tuition** $3290 **Undergraduates** 62% women, 13% part-time, 15% 25 or older, 0% Native American, 1% Hispanic, 8% black, 2% Asian or Pacific Islander **Most popular recent majors** Business administration/commerce/management, psychology, elementary education **Academic program** Average class size 26, advanced placement, accelerated degree program, tutorials, honors program, summer session, adult/continuing education programs, internships **Contact** Mr. Donald Burkard, Dean of Admissions, College of Charleston, 66 George Street, Charleston, SC 29424-0002. Telephone: 803-953-5670.

COLUMBIA COLLEGE
COLUMBIA, SOUTH CAROLINA

Entrance Moderately difficult **General** Independent United Methodist, comprehensive, women only **Setting** 33-acre suburban campus **Enrollment** 1,321 **Faculty** 14:1 **Application deadline** Rolling **Freshmen** 81% accepted **Housing** Yes **Tuition** $11,595 **Undergraduates** 14% part-time, 27% 25 or older, 0% Native American, 1% Hispanic, 29% black, 1% Asian or Pacific Islander **Most popular recent majors** Education, business administration/commerce/management **Academic program** Average class size 22, advanced placement, accelerated degree program, self-designed majors, honors program, summer session, adult/continuing education programs, internships **Contact** Mr. J. Joseph Mitchell, Dean of Enrollment Management, Columbia College, Columbia, SC 29203-5998. Telephone: 803-786-3871. Fax: 803-786-3674.

COLUMBIA INTERNATIONAL UNIVERSITY
COLUMBIA, SOUTH CAROLINA

Entrance Minimally difficult **General** Independent nondenominational, comprehensive, coed **Setting** 450-acre suburban campus **Enrollment** 1,032 **Faculty** 15:1 **Application deadline** Rolling **Freshmen** 85% accepted **Housing** Yes **Tuition** $7891 **Undergraduates** 46% women, 12% part-time, 35% 25 or older, 1% Native American, 1% Hispanic, 5% black, 1% Asian or Pacific Islander **Academic program** Advanced placement, accelerated degree program, summer session, internships **Contact** Mr. Frank J. Bedell, Director of Recruitment, Columbia International University, Columbia, SC 29230-3122. Telephone: 803-754-4100 Ext. 3024. Fax: 803-787-4209.

CONVERSE COLLEGE
SPARTANBURG, SOUTH CAROLINA

Entrance Moderately difficult **General** Independent, comprehensive, women only **Setting** 70-acre urban campus **Enrollment** 1,250 **Faculty** 9:1 **Application deadline** 8/1 **Freshmen** 92% accepted **Housing** Yes **Tuition** $14,445 **Undergraduates** 16% part-time, 11% 25 or older, 0% Native American, 1% Hispanic, 4% black, 1% Asian or Pacific Islander **Most popular recent majors** Education, art/fine arts, business administration/commerce/management **Academic program** Advanced placement, accelerated degree program, honors program, summer session, adult/continuing education programs, internships **Contact** Mr. John F. Fluke, Vice President for Enrollment, Converse College, 580 East Main, Spartanburg, SC 29302-0006. Telephone: 864-596-9040. Fax: 864-596-9158.

ERSKINE COLLEGE
DUE WEST, SOUTH CAROLINA

Entrance Moderately difficult **General** Independent, 4-year, coed, affiliated with Associate Reformed Presbyterian Church **Setting** 85-acre rural campus **Enrollment** 536 **Faculty** 13:1 **Application deadline** Rolling **Freshmen** 86% accepted **Housing** Yes **Tuition** $13,807 **Undergraduates**

59% women, 1% part-time, 1% 25 or older, 1% Hispanic, 5% black, 1% Asian or Pacific Islander **Most popular recent majors** Business administration/commerce/management, elementary education, chemistry **Academic program** Average class size 20, advanced placement, accelerated degree program, tutorials, summer session, internships **Contact** Mrs. Dot Carter, Director of Admissions and Financial Aid, Erskine College, PO Box 176, Due West, SC 29639. Telephone: 864-379-8830. Fax: 864-379-8759.

FRANCIS MARION UNIVERSITY
FLORENCE, SOUTH CAROLINA

Entrance Moderately difficult **General** State-supported, comprehensive, coed **Setting** 309-acre rural campus **Enrollment** 3,722 **Faculty** 19:1 **Application deadline** Rolling **Freshmen** 70% accepted **Housing** Yes **Tuition** $3360 **Undergraduates** 55% women, 15% part-time, 15% 25 or older, 1% Native American, 1% Hispanic, 25% black, 1% Asian or Pacific Islander **Most popular recent majors** Business administration/commerce/management, biology/biological sciences **Academic program** Advanced placement, accelerated degree program, tutorials, honors program, summer session, adult/continuing education programs, internships **Contact** Mr. Mark Sandy, Director of Admissions, Francis Marion University, Florence, SC 29501-0547. Telephone: 803-661-1231. Fax: 803-661-1219.

FURMAN UNIVERSITY
GREENVILLE, SOUTH CAROLINA

Entrance Very difficult **General** Independent, comprehensive, coed **Setting** 750-acre suburban campus **Enrollment** 2,734 **Faculty** 12:1 **Application deadline** 2/1 **Freshmen** 80% accepted **Housing** Yes **Tuition** $16,419 **Undergraduates** 55% women, 5% part-time, 1% 25 or older, 0% Native American, 1% Hispanic, 4% black, 2% Asian or Pacific Islander **Most popular recent majors** Biology/biological sciences, political science/government, business administration/commerce/management **Academic program** Advanced placement, accelerated degree program, self-designed majors, tutorials, summer session, adult/continuing education programs, internships **Contact** Mr. J. Carey Thompson, Director of Admissions, Furman University, Greenville, SC 29613-0688. Telephone: 864-294-2034. Fax: 864-294-3127.

JOHNSON & WALES UNIVERSITY
CHARLESTON, SOUTH CAROLINA

Entrance Minimally difficult **General** Independent, 4-year, coed **Setting** Urban campus **Enrollment** 1,246 **Faculty** 27:1 **Application deadline** Rolling **Freshmen** 86% accepted **Housing** Yes **Tuition** $10,836 **Undergraduates** 39% women, 3% part-time, 22% 25 or older, 0% Native American, 1% Hispanic, 14% black, 1% Asian or Pacific Islander **Most popular recent majors** Culinary arts, food services management, hotel and restaurant management **Academic program** Average class size 30, accelerated degree program, summer session, adult/continuing education programs, internships **Contact** Ms. Mary Hovis, Director of Admissions, Johnson & Wales University, PCC Box 1409, 701 East Bay Street, Charleston, SC 29403. Telephone: 803-727-3000.

LANDER UNIVERSITY
GREENWOOD, SOUTH CAROLINA

Entrance Moderately difficult **General** State-supported, comprehensive, coed **Setting** 100-acre small-town campus **Enrollment** 2,722 **Faculty** 16:1 **Application deadline** Rolling **Freshmen** 89% accepted **Housing** Yes **Tuition** $3600 **Undergraduates** 62% women, 18% part-time, 26% 25 or older, 0% Native American, 1% Hispanic, 20% black, 1% Asian or Pacific Islander **Most popular recent majors** Business administration/commerce/management, education, nursing **Academic program** Advanced placement, accelerated degree program, self-designed majors, honors program, summer session, adult/continuing education programs, internships **Contact** Ms. Whitney T. Marcengill, Associate Director of Admissions, Lander University, Greenwood, SC 29649-2099. Telephone: 864-388-8307. Fax: 864-388-8125.

LIMESTONE COLLEGE
GAFFNEY, SOUTH CAROLINA

Entrance Minimally difficult **General** Independent, 4-year, coed **Setting** 115-acre small-town campus **Enrollment** 366 **Faculty** 11:1 **Application deadline** Rolling **Freshmen** 76% accepted **Housing** Yes **Tuition** $8600 **Undergraduates** 48% women, 5% part-time, 0% 25 or older, 0% Native American, 0% Hispanic, 18% black, 1% Asian or Pacific Islander **Most popular recent majors** Business administration/commerce/management, education, music **Academic program** Average class size 20, ESL program, advanced placement, accelerated degree program, self-designed majors, tutorials, honors program, summer session, adult/continuing education programs, internships **Contact** Dr. Charles Cunning, Vice President for Academic Affairs, Limestone College, Gaffney, SC 29340-3798. Telephone: 803-489-7151 Ext. 540. Fax: 803-487-8706.

MEDICAL UNIVERSITY OF SOUTH CAROLINA
CHARLESTON, SOUTH CAROLINA

Entrance Very difficult **General** State-supported, upper-level, coed **Setting** 55-acre urban campus **Enrollment** 2,334 **Faculty** 11:1 **Freshmen** 52% accepted **Tuition** $3522 **Undergraduates** 73% women, 13% part-time, 60% 25 or older, 1% Native American, 1% Hispanic, 8% black, 3% Asian or Pacific Islander **Most popular recent majors** Health science, nursing, pharmacy/pharmaceutical sciences **Academic program** Advanced placement, internships **Contact** Ms. Wanda L. Taylor, University Director of Admissions, Medical University of South Carolina, 171 Ashley Avenue, Charleston, SC 29425-0002. Telephone: 803-792-5396. Fax: 803-792-3764.

MORRIS COLLEGE
SUMTER, SOUTH CAROLINA

Entrance Minimally difficult **General** Independent, 4-year, coed, affiliated with Baptist Educational and Missionary Convention of South Carolina **Setting** 34-acre small-town campus **Enrollment** 911 **Faculty** 16:1 **Application deadline** Rolling **Freshmen** 87% accepted **Housing** Yes **Tuition** $5105 **Undergraduates** 64% women, 3% part-time, 10% 25 or older, 0% Native American, 0% Hispanic, 100% black, 0% Asian or Pacific Islander **Most popular recent majors** Business administration/commerce/management, sociology, elementary education **Academic program** Accelerated degree program, honors program, summer session, internships **Contact** Mrs. Queen W. Spann, Director of Admissions and Records, Morris College, Sumter, SC 29150-3599. Telephone: 803-775-9371 Ext. 225. Fax: 803-773-3687.

NEWBERRY COLLEGE
NEWBERRY, SOUTH CAROLINA

Entrance Moderately difficult **General** Independent Lutheran, 4-year, coed **Setting** 60-acre small-town campus **Enrollment** 700 **Faculty** 11:1 **Application deadline** Rolling **Freshmen** 89% accepted **Housing** Yes **Tuition** $12,326 **Undergraduates** 47% women, 7% part-time, 0% Native American, 1% Hispanic, 17% black, 1% Asian or Pacific Islander **Most popular recent majors** Business administration/commerce/management, physical education, sociology **Academic program** Average class size 15, advanced placement, accelerated degree program, tutorials, honors program, summer session, internships **Contact** Mr. Stephen Cloniger, Vice President for Enrollment Management, Newberry College, Newberry, SC 29108-2197. Telephone: 803-321-5127.

NORTH GREENVILLE COLLEGE
TIGERVILLE, SOUTH CAROLINA

Entrance Minimally difficult **General** Independent Southern Baptist, 4-year, coed **Setting** 500-acre rural campus **Enrollment** 942 **Faculty** 15:1 **Application deadline** 8/27 **Freshmen** 91% accepted **Housing** Yes **Tuition** $6900 **Undergraduates** 39% women, 12% part-time, 15% 25 or older, 0% Native American, 1% Hispanic, 15% black, 0% Asian or Pacific Islander **Academic program** Average class size 25, advanced placement, accelerated degree program, self-designed majors, tutorials, honors program, summer session, internships **Contact** Mr. Buddy Freeman, Executive Director of Admissions, North Greenville College, Tigerville, SC 29688-1892. Telephone: 864-977-7052. Fax: 864-977-7021.

PRESBYTERIAN COLLEGE
CLINTON, SOUTH CAROLINA

Entrance Very difficult **General** Independent Presbyterian, 4-year, coed **Setting** 215-acre small-town campus **Enrollment** 1,153 **Faculty** 13:1 **Application deadline** 4/1 **Freshmen** 82% accepted **Housing** Yes **Tuition** $14,806 **Undergraduates** 50% women, 3% part-time, 1% 25 or older, 1% Native American, 1% Hispanic, 3% black, 1% Asian or Pacific Islander **Most popular recent majors** Business administration/commerce/management, education, biology/biological sciences **Academic program** Average class size 21, advanced placement, accelerated degree program, tutorials, honors program, summer session, internships **Contact** Mr. Eddie G. Rogers, Associate Director of Admissions, Presbyterian College, South Broad Street, Clinton, SC 29325. Telephone: 864-833-8228. Fax: 864-833-8481.

SOUTH CAROLINA STATE UNIVERSITY
ORANGEBURG, SOUTH CAROLINA

Entrance Minimally difficult **General** State-supported, comprehensive, coed **Setting** 160-acre small-town campus **Enrollment** 4,993 **Application deadline** 7/31 **Freshmen** 59% accepted **Housing** Yes **Tuition** $2924 **Undergraduates** 58% women, 10% part-time, 12% 25 or older, 0% Native American, 0% Hispanic, 96% black, 1% Asian or Pacific Islander **Most popular recent majors** Business administration/commerce/management, electrical engineering technology **Academic program** Advanced placement, honors program, summer session, adult/continuing education programs, internships **Contact** Ms. Dorothy Brown, Director of Admissions, South Carolina State University, Orangeburg, SC 29117-0001. Telephone: 803-536-7185 Ext. 8407.

SOUTHERN WESLEYAN UNIVERSITY
CENTRAL, SOUTH CAROLINA

Entrance Minimally difficult **General** Independent, comprehensive, coed, affiliated with Wesleyan Church **Setting** 230-acre small-town campus **Enrollment** 1,298 **Faculty** 14:1 **Application deadline** 8/10 **Freshmen** 42% accepted **Housing** Yes **Tuition** $10,180 **Undergraduates** 58% women, 3% part-time, 66% 25 or older, 1% Native American, 1% Hispanic, 17% black, 1% Asian or Pacific Islander **Most popular recent majors** Business administration/commerce/management, education, psychology **Academic program** Advanced placement, accelerated degree program, tutorials, honors program, summer session, adult/continuing education programs, internships **Contact** Mr. Charles Mealy, Dean of Enrollment Management, Southern Wesleyan University, Central, SC 29630-1020. Telephone: 864-639-2453 Ext. 327. Fax: 864-639-0826.

UNIVERSITY OF SOUTH CAROLINA
COLUMBIA, SOUTH CAROLINA

Entrance Moderately difficult **General** State-supported, coed **Setting** 242-acre urban campus **Enrollment** 25,489 **Faculty** 17:1 **Application deadline** Rolling **Freshmen** 78% accepted **Housing** Yes **Tuition** $3434 **Undergraduates** 55% women, 21% part-time, 20% 25 or older, 1% Native American, 1% Hispanic, 19% black, 3% Asian or Pacific Islander **Academic program** Advanced placement, accelerated degree program, self-designed majors, honors program, summer session, adult/continuing education programs, internships **Contact** Ms. Terry L. Davis, Director of Admissions, University of South Carolina, Columbia, SC 29208. Telephone: 803-777-7700.

UNIVERSITY OF SOUTH CAROLINA–AIKEN
AIKEN, SOUTH CAROLINA

Entrance Minimally difficult **General** State-supported, comprehensive, coed **Setting** 144-acre small-town campus **Enrollment** 3,027 **Faculty** 12:1 **Application deadline** 8/1 **Freshmen** 77% accepted **Housing** Yes **Tuition** $3014 **Undergraduates** 65% women, 38% part-time, 37% 25 or older, 1% Native American, 1% Hispanic, 18% black, 1% Asian or Pacific Islander **Most popular recent majors** Business administration/commerce/management, education, nursing **Academic program** Advanced placement, accelerated degree program, self-designed majors, tutorials, honors program, summer session, adult/continuing education programs **Contact** Mr. Randy R. Duckett, Director of Admissions, University of South Carolina–Aiken, Aiken, SC 29801-6309. Telephone: 803-648-6851. Fax: 803-641-3362.

UNIVERSITY OF SOUTH CAROLINA–SPARTANBURG
SPARTANBURG, SOUTH CAROLINA

Entrance Moderately difficult **General** State-supported, comprehensive, coed **Setting** 298-acre urban campus **Enrollment** 3,549 **Faculty** 16:1 **Application deadline** 8/15 **Freshmen** 61% accepted **Tuition** $3014 **Undergraduates** 63% women, 30% part-time, 32% 25 or older, 0% Native American, 1% Hispanic, 16% black, 2% Asian or Pacific Islander **Most popular recent majors** Business administration/commerce/management, psychology, nursing **Academic program** Average class size 19, advanced placement, accelerated degree program, self-designed majors, tutorials, summer session, adult/continuing education programs, internships **Contact** Ms. Donette Stewart, Director of Admissions, University of South Carolina–Spartanburg, 800 University Way, Spartanburg, SC 29303-4932. Telephone: 864-503-5280.

VOORHEES COLLEGE
DENMARK, SOUTH CAROLINA

Entrance Minimally difficult **General** Independent Episcopal, 4-year, coed **Setting** 350-acre rural campus **Enrollment** 800 **Faculty** 20:1 **Application deadline** Rolling **Freshmen** 67% accepted **Housing** Yes **Tuition** $4784 **Undergraduates** 53% women, 1% part-time, 10% 25 or older, 1% Hispanic, 97% black, 1% Asian or Pacific Islander **Most popular recent majors** Sociology, criminal justice, business administration/commerce/management **Academic program** Advanced placement, honors program, summer session, adult/continuing education programs, internships **Contact** Mrs. Roe B. W. Kemp, Director of Admissions, Records, and Registration, Voorhees College, Denmark, SC 29042. Telephone: 803-793-3351 Ext. 7302. Fax: 803-793-4584.

WINTHROP UNIVERSITY
ROCK HILL, SOUTH CAROLINA

Entrance Moderately difficult **General** State-supported, comprehensive, coed **Setting** 418-acre small-town campus **Enrollment** 5,402 **Faculty** 17:1 **Application deadline** 5/1 **Freshmen** 87% accepted **Housing** Yes **Tuition** $3918 **Undergraduates** 68% women, 14% part-time, 15% 25 or older, 0% Native American, 1% Hispanic, 22% black, 1% Asian or Pacific Islander **Most popular recent majors** Business administration/

commerce/management, psychology, special education **Academic program** Advanced placement, tutorials, honors program, summer session, adult/continuing education programs, internships **Contact** Ms. Deborah Barber, Director of Admissions, Winthrop University, Rock Hill, SC 29733. Telephone: 803-323-2191. Fax: 803-323-2137.

WOFFORD COLLEGE
SPARTANBURG, SOUTH CAROLINA

Entrance Very difficult **General** Independent, 4-year, coed, affiliated with United Methodist Church **Setting** 140-acre urban campus **Enrollment** 1,115 **Faculty** 13:1 **Application deadline** 2/1 **Freshmen** 89% accepted **Housing** Yes **Tuition** $15,390 **Undergraduates** 46% women, 4% part-time, 2% 25 or older, 0% Native American, 1% Hispanic, 6% black, 1% Asian or Pacific Islander **Most popular recent majors** Biology/biological sciences, English, business economics **Academic program** Average class size 21, advanced placement, accelerated degree program, self-designed majors, tutorials, summer session, internships **Contact** Mr. Brand Stille, Director of Admissions, Wofford College, 429 North Church Street, Spartanburg, SC 29303-3663. Telephone: 864-597-4130. Fax: 864-597-4149.

Tennessee

AMERICAN BAPTIST COLLEGE OF AMERICAN BAPTIST THEOLOGICAL SEMINARY
NASHVILLE, TENNESSEE

Entrance Noncompetitive **General** Independent Baptist, 4-year, coed **Setting** 52-acre urban campus **Enrollment** 125 **Application deadline** 7/1 **Housing** Yes **Tuition** $2530 **Undergraduates** 25% women, 10% part-time, 85% 25 or older, 98% black **Academic program** Accelerated degree program, self-designed majors, summer session, adult/continuing education programs **Contact** Ms. Theresa Chandler, Director of Admissions, American Baptist College of American Baptist Theological Seminary, 1800 Baptist World Center Drive, Nashville, TN 37207. Telephone: 615-228-7877 Ext. 35.

AMERICAN TECHNICAL INSTITUTE
BRUNSWICK, TENNESSEE

Entrance Moderately difficult **General** Independent, 4-year, specialized, primarily men **Setting** Small-town campus **Enrollment** 450 **Faculty** 20:1 **Undergraduates** 10% women, 100% part-time, 2% black **Academic program** Advanced placement **Contact** Dr. D. R. Brady, Dean of Admissions and Special Programs, American Technical Institute, Brunswick, TN 38014-0009. Telephone: 901-685-2000. Fax: 901-685-2099.

AUSTIN PEAY STATE UNIVERSITY
CLARKSVILLE, TENNESSEE

Entrance Moderately difficult **General** State-supported, comprehensive, coed **Setting** 200-acre suburban campus **Enrollment** 8,187 **Faculty** 18:1 **Application deadline** 7/27 **Freshmen** 74% accepted **Housing** Yes **Tuition** $2280 **Undergraduates** 55% women, 40% part-time, 37% 25 or older, 1% Native American, 4% Hispanic, 17% black, 2% Asian or Pacific Islander **Most popular recent majors** Elementary education, business administration/commerce/management, nursing **Academic program** Average class size 20, advanced placement, accelerated degree program, tutorials, honors program, summer session, adult/continuing education programs, internships **Contact** Mr. Charles McCorkle, Director of Admissions, Austin Peay State University, PO Box 4548, Clarksville, TN 37044-0001. Telephone: 615-648-7661.

BELMONT UNIVERSITY
NASHVILLE, TENNESSEE

Entrance Moderately difficult **General** Independent Baptist, comprehensive, coed **Setting** 34-acre urban campus **Enrollment** 2,926 **Faculty** 14:1 **Application deadline** 8/1 **Freshmen** 77% accepted **Housing** Yes **Tuition** $10,300 **Undergraduates** 60% women, 17% part-time, 22% 25 or older, 0% Native American, 1% Hispanic, 3% black, 1% Asian or Pacific Islander **Most popular recent majors** Music business, business administration/commerce/management, nursing **Academic program** Average class size 15, advanced placement, accelerated degree program, tutorials, honors program, summer session, adult/continuing education programs, internships **Contact** Dr. Kathryn Baugher, Dean of Admissions, Belmont University, 1900 Belmont Boulevard, Nashville, TN 37212-3757. Telephone: 615-385-6785.

BETHEL COLLEGE
MCKENZIE, TENNESSEE

Entrance Minimally difficult **General** Independent Cumberland Presbyterian, comprehensive, coed **Setting** 100-acre small-town campus **Enrollment** 558 **Application deadline** 8/10 **Fresh-**

men 77% accepted **Housing** Yes **Tuition** $7240 **Undergraduates** 50% women, 8% part-time, 21% 25 or older, 0% Native American, 1% Hispanic, 13% black, 1% Asian or Pacific Islander **Most popular recent majors** Education, business administration/commerce/management **Academic program** Advanced placement, accelerated degree program, self-designed majors, tutorials, honors program, summer session, adult/continuing education programs, internships **Contact** Ms. Suzanne Teel, Co-Director of Admissions, Bethel College, McKenzie, TN 38201. Telephone: 901-352-4030.

BRYAN COLLEGE
DAYTON, TENNESSEE

Entrance Moderately difficult **General** Independent interdenominational, 4-year, coed **Setting** 100-acre small-town campus **Enrollment** 455 **Faculty** 14:1 **Application deadline** Rolling **Freshmen** 64% accepted **Housing** Yes **Tuition** $10,000 **Undergraduates** 57% women, 5% part-time, 4% 25 or older, 0% Native American, 1% Hispanic, 1% black, 1% Asian or Pacific Islander **Most popular recent majors** Education, business administration/commerce/management, biology/biological sciences **Academic program** Advanced placement, tutorials, honors program, summer session, adult/continuing education programs, internships **Contact** Mr. Ronald Petitte, Registrar, Bryan College, PO Box 7000, Dayton, TN 37321-7000. Telephone: 423-775-2041 Ext. 236. Fax: 423-775-7330.

CARSON-NEWMAN COLLEGE
JEFFERSON CITY, TENNESSEE

Entrance Moderately difficult **General** Independent Southern Baptist, comprehensive, coed **Setting** 100-acre small-town campus **Enrollment** 2,265 **Faculty** 13:1 **Application deadline** 8/1 **Freshmen** 86% accepted **Housing** Yes **Tuition** $9990 **Undergraduates** 58% women, 11% part-time, 21% 25 or older, 0% Native American, 1% Hispanic, 5% black, 2% Asian or Pacific Islander **Most popular recent majors** Education, biology/biological sciences, business administration/commerce/management **Academic program** Average class size 16, advanced placement, accelerated degree program, self-designed majors, honors program, summer session, adult/continuing education programs, internships **Contact** Mrs. Sheryl M. Gray, Director of Undergraduate Admissions, Carson-Newman College, PO Box 72025, Jefferson City, TN 37760. Telephone: 423-471-3223. Fax: 423-471-3502.

CHRISTIAN BROTHERS UNIVERSITY
MEMPHIS, TENNESSEE

Entrance Moderately difficult **General** Independent Roman Catholic, comprehensive, coed **Setting** 70-acre urban campus **Enrollment** 1,785 **Faculty** 16:1 **Application deadline** 7/1 **Freshmen** 84% accepted **Housing** Yes **Tuition** $11,930 **Undergraduates** 51% women, 13% part-time, 7% 25 or older, 2% Hispanic, 17% black, 3% Asian or Pacific Islander **Most popular recent majors** Accounting, psychology, biology/biological sciences **Academic program** Average class size 25, advanced placement, accelerated degree program, tutorials, honors program, summer session, internships **Contact** Mr. Michael Daush, Dean of Admissions, Christian Brothers University, 650 East Parkway South, Memphis, TN 38104-5581. Telephone: 901-322-3205 Ext. 210. Fax: 901-321-3202.

CRICHTON COLLEGE
MEMPHIS, TENNESSEE

Entrance Minimally difficult **General** Independent, 4-year, coed **Setting** Urban campus **Enrollment** 560 **Faculty** 13:1 **Application deadline** 8/31 **Housing** Yes **Tuition** $6360 **Undergraduates** 56% women, 30% part-time, 57% 25 or older, 1% Native American, 1% Hispanic, 27% black, 1% Asian or Pacific Islander **Most popular recent majors** Education, biblical studies, psychology **Academic program** Advanced placement, summer session, adult/continuing education programs, internships **Contact** Mr. Barry Mooney, Vice President of Enrollment Management, Crichton College, 6655 Winchester Road, PO Box 757830, Memphis, TN 38115. Telephone: 901-367-3888.

CUMBERLAND UNIVERSITY
LEBANON, TENNESSEE

Entrance Moderately difficult **General** Independent, comprehensive, coed **Setting** 44-acre small-town campus **Enrollment** 1,062 **Faculty** 12:1 **Application deadline** Rolling **Freshmen** 80% accepted **Housing** Yes **Tuition** $8190 **Undergraduates** 55% women, 28% part-time, 36% 25 or older, 0% Native American, 2% Hispanic, 7% black, 1% Asian or Pacific Islander **Most popular recent majors** Business administration/commerce/management, education, nursing **Academic program** Advanced placement, self-designed majors, tutorials, honors program, summer session, adult/continuing education programs, internships **Contact** Ms. Lana Suite, Director of Admissions and

Financial Aid, Cumberland University, Lebanon, TN 37087-3554. Telephone: 615-444-2562. Fax: 615-444-2569.

DAVID LIPSCOMB UNIVERSITY
NASHVILLE, TENNESSEE

Entrance Moderately difficult **General** Independent, comprehensive, coed, affiliated with Church of Christ **Setting** 65-acre urban campus **Enrollment** 2,543 **Faculty** 18:1 **Application deadline** Rolling **Freshmen** 89% accepted **Housing** Yes **Tuition** $9313 **Undergraduates** 56% women, 15% part-time, 15% 25 or older, 1% Hispanic, 4% black, 2% Asian or Pacific Islander **Most popular recent majors** Business administration/commerce/management, education, history **Academic program** Average class size 30, advanced placement, accelerated degree program, self-designed majors, tutorials, honors program, summer session, adult/continuing education programs, internships **Contact** Mrs. Cyndi Butler, Director of Admissions, David Lipscomb University, 3901 Granny White Pike, Nashville, TN 37204-3951. Telephone: 615-269-1000 Ext. 1776. Fax: 615-269-1804.

EAST TENNESSEE STATE UNIVERSITY
JOHNSON CITY, TENNESSEE

Entrance Moderately difficult **General** State-supported, coed **Setting** 366-acre small-town campus **Enrollment** 11,859 **Faculty** 19:1 **Application deadline** Rolling **Freshmen** 84% accepted **Housing** Yes **Tuition** $2100 **Undergraduates** 58% women, 20% part-time, 32% 25 or older, 1% Native American, 1% Hispanic, 4% black, 1% Asian or Pacific Islander **Most popular recent majors** Nursing, criminal justice, engineering technology **Academic program** Advanced placement, accelerated degree program, tutorials, honors program, summer session, adult/continuing education programs, internships **Contact** Mr. Mike Pitts, Director of Admissions, East Tennessee State University, PO Box 70731, ETSU, Johnson City, TN 37614-0734. Telephone: 423-439-6861. Fax: 423-439-7156.

FISK UNIVERSITY
NASHVILLE, TENNESSEE

Entrance Moderately difficult **General** Independent, comprehensive, coed, affiliated with United Church of Christ **Setting** 40-acre urban campus **Enrollment** 900 **Faculty** 14:1 **Application deadline** 6/15 **Freshmen** 81% accepted **Housing** Yes **Tuition** $7750 **Undergraduates** 72% women, 1% part-time, 5% 25 or older, 1% Native American, 1% Hispanic, 98% black, 0% Asian or Pacific Islander **Most popular recent majors** Business administration/commerce/management, chemistry, psychology **Academic program** Advanced placement, self-designed majors, honors program, internships **Contact** Mr. Derrick W. Dowell Jr., Director of Admissions, Fisk University, 1000 17th Avenue North, Nashville, TN 37208-3051. Telephone: 615-329-8665.

FREED-HARDEMAN UNIVERSITY
HENDERSON, TENNESSEE

Entrance Moderately difficult **General** Independent, comprehensive, coed, affiliated with Church of Christ **Setting** 96-acre rural campus **Enrollment** 1,564 **Faculty** 20:1 **Application deadline** Rolling **Freshmen** 68% accepted **Housing** Yes **Tuition** $7524 **Undergraduates** 53% women, 5% part-time, 11% 25 or older, 1% Hispanic, 4% black, 1% Asian or Pacific Islander **Most popular recent majors** Business administration/commerce/management, education, biblical studies **Academic program** Advanced placement, accelerated degree program, self-designed majors, honors program, summer session, adult/continuing education programs, internships **Contact** Mr. Wayne Scott, Director of Admissions, Freed-Hardeman University, Henderson, TN 38340-2399. Telephone: 901-989-6651. Fax: 901-989-6775.

FREE WILL BAPTIST BIBLE COLLEGE
NASHVILLE, TENNESSEE

Entrance Noncompetitive **General** Independent Free Will Baptist, 4-year, coed **Setting** 10-acre suburban campus **Enrollment** 340 **Faculty** 10:1 **Application deadline** Rolling **Freshmen** 100% accepted **Housing** Yes **Tuition** $5215 **Undergraduates** 46% women, 14% part-time, 7% 25 or older, 1% Native American, 0% Hispanic, 0% black, 1% Asian or Pacific Islander **Most popular recent majors** Business administration/commerce/management, education, pastoral studies **Academic program** Advanced placement, self-designed majors, summer session, internships **Contact** Dr. Charles E. Hampton, Registrar/Chairman of Department of General Education, Free Will Baptist Bible College, Nashville, TN 37205-2498. Telephone: 615-383-1340 Ext. 2233. Fax: 615-269-6028.

JOHNSON BIBLE COLLEGE
KNOXVILLE, TENNESSEE

Entrance Minimally difficult **General** Independent, comprehensive, coed, affiliated with Christian Churches and Churches of Christ **Setting** 50-acre rural campus **Enrollment** 460 **Faculty** 15:1 **Application deadline** Rolling **Freshmen** 79% accepted **Housing** Yes **Tuition** $5000 **Undergraduates** 47% women, 9% part-time, 17% 25 or older, 1% Native American, 1% Hispanic, 2% black, 1% Asian or Pacific Islander **Academic program** Average class size 45, advanced placement, tutorials, summer session, internships **Contact** Mr. Larry Green, Director of Admissions, Johnson Bible College, Knoxville, TN 37998. Telephone: 423-573-4517 Ext. 2346.

KING COLLEGE
BRISTOL, TENNESSEE

Entrance Moderately difficult **General** Independent, 4-year, coed, affiliated with Presbyterian Church (U.S.A.) **Setting** 135-acre suburban campus **Enrollment** 589 **Faculty** 15:1 **Application deadline** Rolling **Freshmen** 85% accepted **Housing** Yes **Tuition** $10,550 **Undergraduates** 58% women, 4% part-time, 9% 25 or older, 0% Native American, 1% Hispanic, 1% black, 1% Asian or Pacific Islander **Most popular recent majors** Behavioral sciences, economics, psychology **Academic program** Advanced placement, self-designed majors, summer session, internships **Contact** Mr. Roger Kieffer, Vice President for Enrollment, King College, Bristol, TN 37620-2699. Telephone: 423-652-4861. Fax: 423-968-4456.

KNOXVILLE COLLEGE
KNOXVILLE, TENNESSEE

Entrance Noncompetitive **General** Independent Presbyterian, 4-year, coed **Setting** 39-acre campus **Enrollment** 433 **Faculty** 17:1 **Application deadline** Rolling **Housing** Yes **Tuition** $5792 **Undergraduates** 45% women, 2% part-time, 1% Native American, 1% Hispanic, 96% black **Most popular recent majors** Business administration/commerce/management, psychology, computer science **Academic program** Honors program, internships **Contact** Ms. Carol Scott, Director of Admissions, Knoxville College, Knoxville, TN 37921-4799. Telephone: 423-524-6525. Fax: 423-524-6686.

LAMBUTH UNIVERSITY
JACKSON, TENNESSEE

Entrance Moderately difficult **General** Independent United Methodist, 4-year, coed **Setting** 50-acre urban campus **Enrollment** 1,036 **Faculty** 19:1 **Application deadline** Rolling **Freshmen** 65% accepted **Housing** Yes **Tuition** $6194 **Undergraduates** 55% women, 14% part-time, 26% 25 or older, 1% Native American, 1% Hispanic, 13% black, 1% Asian or Pacific Islander **Most popular recent majors** Business administration/commerce/management, education, communication **Academic program** Average class size 25, advanced placement, accelerated degree program, self-designed majors, tutorials, summer session, adult/continuing education programs, internships **Contact** Mrs. Nancy M. Callis, Director of Admissions, Lambuth University, 705 Lambuth Boulevard, Jackson, TN 38301. Telephone: 901-425-3223. Fax: 901-988-4600.

LANE COLLEGE
JACKSON, TENNESSEE

Entrance Minimally difficult **General** Independent, 4-year, coed, affiliated with Christian Methodist Episcopal Church **Setting** 17-acre suburban campus **Enrollment** 664 **Faculty** 16:1 **Application deadline** Rolling **Freshmen** 76% accepted **Housing** Yes **Tuition** $5400 **Undergraduates** 50% women, 2% part-time, 7% 25 or older, 0% Native American, 0% Hispanic, 100% black **Most popular recent majors** Business administration/commerce/management, sociology **Academic program** Advanced placement, tutorials, honors program, summer session, internships **Contact** Ms. E. R. Maddox, Director of Admissions, Lane College, 545 Lane Avenue, Jackson, TN 38301-4598. Telephone: 901-426-7532.

LEE COLLEGE
CLEVELAND, TENNESSEE

Entrance Minimally difficult **General** Independent, 4-year, coed, affiliated with Church of God **Setting** 45-acre small-town campus **Enrollment** 2,477 **Application deadline** Rolling **Freshmen** 80% accepted **Housing** Yes **Tuition** $5372 **Undergraduates** 50% women, 7% part-time, 16% 25 or older, 1% Native American, 5% Hispanic, 2% black, 1% Asian or Pacific Islander **Most popular recent majors** Human development, biology/biological sciences, business administration/commerce/management **Academic program** Advanced placement, honors program, summer session, adult/continuing education programs, internships **Contact** Ms. Michele Bowman, Admissions Coordinator, Lee College, Cleveland, TN 37311-4475. Telephone: 423-478-7316. Fax: 423-478-7499.

LEMOYNE-OWEN COLLEGE
MEMPHIS, TENNESSEE

Entrance Minimally difficult **General** Independent, comprehensive, coed, affiliated with United

Church of Christ **Setting** 15-acre urban campus **Enrollment** 1,104 **Faculty** 12:1 **Application deadline** 8/1 **Freshmen** 87% accepted **Housing** Yes **Tuition** $6300 **Undergraduates** 70% women, 14% part-time, 43% 25 or older, 0% Native American, 0% Hispanic, 97% black, 0% Asian or Pacific Islander **Most popular recent majors** Business administration/commerce/management, biology/biological sciences, education **Academic program** ESL program, Advanced placement, accelerated degree program, self-designed majors, tutorials, honors program, summer session, adult/continuing education programs, internships **Contact** Mr. Alex Dancy, Assistant Director Admissions/Recruitment, LeMoyne-Owen College, 807 Walker Avenue, Memphis, TN 38126-6595. Telephone: 901-942-7302 Ext. 214. Fax: 901-942-6272.

LINCOLN MEMORIAL UNIVERSITY
HARROGATE, TENNESSEE

Entrance Moderately difficult **General** Independent, comprehensive, coed **Setting** 990-acre small-town campus **Enrollment** 2,003 **Faculty** 13:1 **Application deadline** Rolling **Freshmen** 78% accepted **Housing** Yes **Tuition** $7350 **Undergraduates** 72% women, 37% part-time, 24% 25 or older, 3% black **Most popular recent major** Elementary education **Academic program** Advanced placement, accelerated degree program, tutorials, honors program, summer session, adult/continuing education programs **Contact** Mr. Conrad Daniels, Dean of Admissions and Recruitment, Lincoln Memorial University, Harrogate, TN 37752-1901. Telephone: 423-869-6280.

LIPSCOMB UNIVERSITY
SEE DAVID LIPSCOMB UNIVERSITY

MARTIN METHODIST COLLEGE
PULASKI, TENNESSEE

Entrance Minimally difficult **General** Independent United Methodist, 4-year, coed **Setting** 6-acre small-town campus **Enrollment** 535 **Faculty** 13:1 **Application deadline** 8/30 **Freshmen** 100% accepted **Housing** Yes **Tuition** $6900 **Undergraduates** 55% women, 23% part-time, 10% 25 or older, 0% Native American, 1% Hispanic, 8% black **Most popular recent majors** Business administration/commerce/management, early childhood education, physical education **Academic program** Advanced placement, self-designed majors, summer session, adult/continuing education programs **Contact** Mr. Robby Shelton, Director of Admissions and Enrollment Management, Martin Methodist College, Pulaski, TN 38478-2716. Telephone: 615-363-9807. Fax: 615-363-9818.

MARYVILLE COLLEGE
MARYVILLE, TENNESSEE

Entrance Moderately difficult **General** Independent Presbyterian, 4-year, coed **Setting** 350-acre suburban campus **Enrollment** 927 **Faculty** 13:1 **Application deadline** 3/1 **Freshmen** 75% accepted **Housing** Yes **Tuition** $14,425 **Undergraduates** 54% women, 10% part-time, 14% 25 or older, 1% Native American, 1% Hispanic, 5% black, 1% Asian or Pacific Islander **Most popular recent majors** Biology/biological sciences, business administration/commerce/management, elementary education **Academic program** Advanced placement, self-designed majors, tutorials, honors program, summer session, adult/continuing education programs, internships **Contact** Ms. Donna Davis, Vice President of Admissions and Enrollment, Maryville College, 502 East Lamar Alexander Parkway, Maryville, TN 37804-5907. Telephone: 423-981-8092. Fax: 423-983-0581.

MEMPHIS COLLEGE OF ART
MEMPHIS, TENNESSEE

Entrance Moderately difficult **General** Independent, comprehensive, specialized, coed **Setting** 200-acre urban campus **Enrollment** 291 **Application deadline** Rolling **Freshmen** 98% accepted **Housing** Yes **Tuition** $10,950 **Undergraduates** 41% women, 8% part-time, 19% 25 or older, 1% Native American, 2% Hispanic, 16% black, 2% Asian or Pacific Islander **Academic program** Average class size 25, advanced placement, tutorials, summer session, adult/continuing education programs, internships **Contact** Ms. Susan Miller, Director of Admissions, Memphis College of Art, Overton Park, 1930 Poplar Avenue, Memphis, TN 38104-2764. Telephone: 901-726-4085 Ext. 30. Fax: 901-726-9371.

MIDDLE TENNESSEE STATE UNIVERSITY
MURFREESBORO, TENNESSEE

Entrance Moderately difficult **General** State-supported, coed **Setting** 500-acre urban campus **Enrollment** 17,924 **Faculty** 20:1 **Application deadline** Rolling **Freshmen** 69% accepted **Housing** Yes **Tuition** $2126 **Undergraduates** 54% women, 20% part-time, 27% 25 or older, 1% Native American, 1% Hispanic, 10% black, 1% Asian or Pacific Islander **Most popular recent majors** Business administration/commerce/management, communication **Academic program** Advanced placement, accelerated degree program, self-designed majors, tutorials, honors program, summer session, adult/continuing education programs, internships **Contact** Ms. Lynn Palmer, Director of Admissions, Middle Tennessee State University, Murfreesboro, TN 37132. Telephone: 615-898-2111.

MILLIGAN COLLEGE

MILLIGAN COLLEGE, TENNESSEE

Entrance Moderately difficult **General** Independent Christian, comprehensive, coed **Setting** 145-acre suburban campus **Enrollment** 836 **Faculty** 14:1 **Application deadline** Rolling **Freshmen** 95% accepted **Housing** Yes **Tuition** $10,260 **Undergraduates** 60% women, 9% part-time, 20% 25 or older, 1% Native American, 1% Hispanic, 2% black, 1% Asian or Pacific Islander **Most popular recent majors** Nursing, business administration/commerce/management, education **Academic program** Advanced placement, accelerated degree program, tutorials, summer session, adult/continuing education programs, internships **Contact** Mr. Michael A. Johnson, Director of Admissions, Milligan College, PO Box 210, Milligan College, TN 37682. Telephone: 423-461-8730. Fax: 423-461-8960.

O'MORE COLLEGE OF DESIGN

FRANKLIN, TENNESSEE

Entrance Minimally difficult **General** Independent, 4-year, primarily women **Setting** 6-acre small-town campus **Enrollment** 151 **Faculty** 7:1 **Application deadline** 8/1 **Freshmen** 65% accepted **Tuition** $7955 **Undergraduates** 85% women, 20% part-time, 35% 25 or older, 0% Native American, 1% Hispanic, 5% black, 2% Asian or Pacific Islander **Most popular recent majors** Interior design, graphic arts **Academic program** Summer session, internships **Contact** Mr. Thomas L. Campbell, Registrar and Director of Admissions, O'More College of Design, Franklin, TN 37064-2816. Telephone: 615-794-4254.

RHODES COLLEGE

MEMPHIS, TENNESSEE

Entrance Very difficult **General** Independent Presbyterian, comprehensive, coed **Setting** 100-acre suburban campus **Enrollment** 1,425 **Faculty** 12:1 **Application deadline** 2/1 **Freshmen** 75% accepted **Housing** Yes **Tuition** $17,518 **Undergraduates** 55% women, 3% part-time, 2% 25 or older, 0% Native American, 1% Hispanic, 3% black, 4% Asian or Pacific Islander **Most popular recent majors** Biology/biological sciences, English, business administration/commerce/management **Academic program** Average class size 18, advanced placement, accelerated degree program, self-designed majors, tutorials, honors program, summer session, internships **Contact** Mr. David J. Wottle, Dean of Admissions and Financial Aid, Rhodes College, 2000 North Parkway, Memphis, TN 38112-1690. Telephone: 901-843-3700. Fax: 901-843-3719.

SOUTHERN ADVENTIST UNIVERSITY

COLLEGEDALE, TENNESSEE

Entrance Moderately difficult **General** Independent Seventh-day Adventist, comprehensive, coed **Setting** 1,000-acre small-town campus **Enrollment** 1,650 **Faculty** 13:1 **Application deadline** Rolling **Freshmen** 98% accepted **Housing** Yes **Tuition** $9736 **Undergraduates** 56% women, 21% part-time, 16% 25 or older, 0% Native American, 8% Hispanic, 4% black, 6% Asian or Pacific Islander **Most popular recent majors** Nursing, business administration/commerce/management, biology/biological sciences **Academic program** Advanced placement, accelerated degree program, tutorials, honors program, summer session, adult/continuing education programs, internships **Contact** Dr. Ronald M. Barrow, Vice President for Admissions and College Relations, Southern Adventist University, Collegedale, TN 37315-0370. Telephone: 423-238-2843. Fax: 423-238-3005.

TENNESSEE STATE UNIVERSITY

NASHVILLE, TENNESSEE

Entrance Minimally difficult **General** State-supported, comprehensive, coed **Setting** 450-acre urban campus **Enrollment** 8,643 **Application deadline** 8/1 **Freshmen** 67% accepted **Housing** Yes **Tuition** $2118 **Undergraduates** 61% women, 20% part-time, 39% 25 or older, 1% Native American, 1% Hispanic, 75% black, 1% Asian or Pacific Islander **Most popular recent majors** Nursing, elementary education, business administration/commerce/management **Academic program** Average class size 35, accelerated degree program, honors program, summer session, adult/continuing education programs, internships **Contact** Mr. John Cade, Dean of Admissions and Records, Tennessee State University, 3500 John A Merritt Boulevard, Nashville, TN 37209-1561. Telephone: 615-963-5101. Fax: 615-963-5108.

TENNESSEE TECHNOLOGICAL UNIVERSITY

COOKEVILLE, TENNESSEE

Entrance Moderately difficult **General** State-supported, coed **Setting** 235-acre small-town campus **Enrollment** 8,173 **Faculty** 18:1 **Application**

deadline Rolling **Freshmen** 90% accepted **Housing** Yes **Tuition** $2298 **Undergraduates** 47% women, 14% part-time, 20% 25 or older, 1% Native American, 1% Hispanic, 3% black, 2% Asian or Pacific Islander **Most popular recent majors** Mechanical engineering, business administration/commerce/management, elementary education **Academic program** Advanced placement, accelerated degree program, honors program, summer session, adult/continuing education programs **Contact** Mr. Jim Rose, Associate Vice President for Enrollment and Records, Tennessee Technological University, TTU Box 5006, Cookeville, TN 38505. Telephone: 615-372-3888. Fax: 615-372-6250.

TENNESSEE TEMPLE UNIVERSITY
CHATTANOOGA, TENNESSEE

Entrance Minimally difficult **General** Independent Baptist, comprehensive, coed **Setting** 55-acre urban campus **Enrollment** 541 **Faculty** 11:1 **Application deadline** 8/20 **Freshmen** 100% accepted **Housing** Yes **Tuition** $6270 **Undergraduates** 53% women, 10% part-time, 25% 25 or older, 1% Hispanic, 2% black **Academic program** Advanced placement, tutorials, honors program, summer session, adult/continuing education programs, internships **Contact** Mr. Dick Costner, Registrar, Tennessee Temple University, 1815 Union Avenue, Chattanooga, TN 37404-3587. Telephone: 423-493-4373. Fax: 423-493-4497.

TENNESSEE WESLEYAN COLLEGE
ATHENS, TENNESSEE

Entrance Moderately difficult **General** Independent United Methodist, 4-year, coed **Setting** 40-acre small-town campus **Enrollment** 738 **Faculty** 9:1 **Application deadline** Rolling **Freshmen** 90% accepted **Housing** Yes **Tuition** $6600 **Undergraduates** 63% women, 34% part-time, 34% 25 or older, 7% black **Most popular recent majors** Business administration/commerce/management, education, interdisciplinary studies **Academic program** Advanced placement, accelerated degree program, self-designed majors, honors program, summer session, adult/continuing education programs, internships **Contact** Mr. John Head, Director of Admission, Tennessee Wesleyan College, PO Box 40, Athens, TN 37371-0040. Telephone: 423-745-7504.

TREVECCA NAZARENE UNIVERSITY
NASHVILLE, TENNESSEE

Entrance Noncompetitive **General** Independent Nazarene, comprehensive, coed **Setting** 80-acre urban campus **Enrollment** 1,547 **Faculty** 14:1 **Application deadline** Rolling **Freshmen** 100% accepted **Housing** Yes **Tuition** $9090 **Undergraduates** 56% women, 20% part-time, 38% 25 or older, 2% Hispanic, 7% black **Most popular recent majors** Business administration/commerce/management, early childhood education, physician's assistant studies **Academic program** Advanced placement, accelerated degree program, summer session, adult/continuing education programs, internships **Contact** Mr. Jan R. Forman, Dean of Enrollment Services, Trevecca Nazarene University, 333 Murfreesboro Road, Nashville, TN 37210-2834. Telephone: 615-248-1343. Fax: 615-248-7728.

TUSCULUM COLLEGE
GREENEVILLE, TENNESSEE

Entrance Moderately difficult **General** Independent Presbyterian, comprehensive, coed **Setting** 140-acre small-town campus **Enrollment** 1,516 **Faculty** 13:1 **Application deadline** Rolling **Freshmen** 76% accepted **Housing** Yes **Tuition** $11,150 **Undergraduates** 62% women, 3% part-time, 0% Native American, 1% Hispanic, 6% black, 0% Asian or Pacific Islander **Most popular recent majors** Business administration/commerce/management, elementary education, psychology **Academic program** Average class size 14, advanced placement, self-designed majors, tutorials, summer session, adult/continuing education programs, internships **Contact** Mr. Dan Hall, Director of Admissions, Tusculum College, PO Box 5047, Greeneville, TN 37743-9997. Telephone: 423-636-7312. Fax: 423-638-7166.

UNION UNIVERSITY
JACKSON, TENNESSEE

Entrance Moderately difficult **General** Independent Southern Baptist, comprehensive, coed **Setting** 290-acre small-town campus **Enrollment** 1,975 **Faculty** 13:1 **Application deadline** 2/1 **Freshmen** 80% accepted **Housing** Yes **Tuition** $8180 **Undergraduates** 63% women, 13% part-time, 0% Native American, 0% Hispanic, 4% black, 0% Asian or Pacific Islander **Most popular recent majors** Nursing, education, business administration/commerce/management **Academic program** Average class size 23, advanced placement, accelerated degree program, tutorials, honors program, summer session, adult/continuing education programs, internships **Contact** Mr. Carroll Griffin, Director of Admissions, Union University, Jackson, TN 38305. Telephone: 901-661-5000. Fax: 901-661-5187.

THE UNIVERSITY OF MEMPHIS
MEMPHIS, TENNESSEE

Entrance Moderately difficult **General** State-supported, coed **Setting** 1,100-acre urban campus **Enrollment** 19,271 **Faculty** 20:1 **Application deadline** 8/1 **Freshmen** 70% accepted **Housing** Yes **Tuition** $2412 **Undergraduates** 57% women, 28% part-time, 19% 25 or older, 1% Hispanic, 27% black, 3% Asian or Pacific Islander **Most popular recent majors** Finance/banking, accounting, business administration/commerce/management **Academic program** Average class size 25, advanced placement, accelerated degree program, self-designed majors, honors program, summer session, adult/continuing education programs, internships **Contact** Mr. David Wallace, Director of Admissions, The University of Memphis, Memphis, TN 38152. Telephone: 901-678-2101. Fax: 901-678-3299.

UNIVERSITY OF TENNESSEE AT CHATTANOOGA
CHATTANOOGA, TENNESSEE

Entrance Moderately difficult **General** State-supported, comprehensive, coed **Setting** 101-acre urban campus **Enrollment** 8,296 **Faculty** 17:1 **Application deadline** Rolling **Freshmen** 53% accepted **Housing** Yes **Tuition** $2200 **Undergraduates** 56% women, 23% part-time, 27% 25 or older, 1% Native American, 1% Hispanic, 13% black, 3% Asian or Pacific Islander **Most popular recent majors** Business administration/commerce/management, secondary education, nursing **Academic program** Average class size 23, advanced placement, accelerated degree program, honors program, summer session, adult/continuing education programs, internships **Contact** Ms. Patsy Reynolds, Director of Admissions, University of Tennessee at Chattanooga, 615 McCallie Avenue, Chattanooga, TN 37403-2598. Telephone: 423-755-4662.

THE UNIVERSITY OF TENNESSEE AT MARTIN
MARTIN, TENNESSEE

Entrance Moderately difficult **General** State-supported, comprehensive, coed **Setting** 250-acre small-town campus **Enrollment** 5,491 **Faculty** 14:1 **Application deadline** Rolling **Freshmen** 97% accepted **Housing** Yes **Tuition** $2240 **Undergraduates** 57% women, 13% part-time, 24% 25 or older, 1% Native American, 1% Hispanic, 14% black, 1% Asian or Pacific Islander **Most popular recent majors** Marketing/retailing/merchandising, health education, accounting **Academic program** Advanced placement, accelerated degree program, self-designed majors, tutorials, honors program, summer session, adult/continuing education programs, internships **Contact** Ms. Judy Rayburn, Director of Admission, The University of Tennessee at Martin, Martin, TN 38238-1000. Telephone: 901-587-7032. Fax: 901-587-7029.

UNIVERSITY OF TENNESSEE, KNOXVILLE
KNOXVILLE, TENNESSEE

Entrance Moderately difficult **General** State-supported, coed **Setting** 511-acre urban campus **Enrollment** 25,517 **Faculty** 17:1 **Application deadline** 7/1 **Freshmen** 75% accepted **Housing** Yes **Tuition** $2576 **Undergraduates** 50% women, 14% part-time, 18% 25 or older, 1% Native American, 1% Hispanic, 5% black, 3% Asian or Pacific Islander **Most popular recent majors** Psychology, English, accounting **Academic program** Advanced placement, accelerated degree program, self-designed majors, tutorials, honors program, summer session, adult/continuing education programs, internships **Contact** Dr. Gordon Stanley, Director of Admissions, University of Tennessee, Knoxville, Knoxville, TN 37996. Telephone: 423-974-2184.

UNIVERSITY OF TENNESSEE, MEMPHIS
MEMPHIS, TENNESSEE

Entrance Very difficult **General** State-supported, upper-level, coed **Setting** 55-acre urban campus **Enrollment** 2,092 **Housing** Yes **Tuition** $1824 **Undergraduates** 83% women, 3% part-time, 44% 25 or older, 2% Hispanic, 14% black, 5% Asian or Pacific Islander **Most popular recent majors** Physical therapy, dental services, occupational therapy **Academic program** Advanced placement, adult/continuing education programs **Contact** Ms. June Peoples, Director of Admissions, University of Tennessee, Memphis, 800 Madison Avenue, Memphis, TN 38163-0002. Telephone: 901-448-5560. Fax: 901-448-7585.

UNIVERSITY OF THE SOUTH
SEWANEE, TENNESSEE

Entrance Very difficult **General** Independent Episcopal, comprehensive, coed **Setting** 10,000-acre small-town campus **Enrollment** 1,346 **Faculty** 11:1 **Application deadline** 2/1 **Freshmen** 66% accepted **Housing** Yes **Tuition** $17,730 **Undergraduates** 51% women, 2% part-time, 0% 25 or older, 0% Native American, 1% Hispanic, 2% black, 1% Asian or Pacific Islander **Most popular recent majors** English, history, psychology **Academic program** Advanced placement, accelerated degree program, self-designed majors, tutorials, honors program, summer session, internships **Contact** Mr. Robert M. Hedrick, Director of Admission, University of the South, Sewanee, TN 37383-1000. Telephone: 615-598-1238. Fax: 615-598-1667.

VANDERBILT UNIVERSITY
NASHVILLE, TENNESSEE

Entrance Very difficult **General** Independent, coed **Setting** 330-acre urban campus **Enrollment** 10,253 **Faculty** 8:1 **Application deadline** 1/15 **Freshmen** 60% accepted **Housing** Yes **Tuition** $21,478 **Undergraduates** 48% women, 1% part-time, 1% 25 or older, 0% Native American, 3% Hispanic, 4% black, 8% Asian or Pacific Islander **Most popular recent majors** Psychology, human development, economics **Academic program** Average class size 24, advanced placement, accelerated degree program, self-designed majors, tutorials, honors program, summer session, internships **Contact** Ms. Terry Cowdrey, Acting Dean of Undergraduate Admissions, Vanderbilt University, 2305 West End Avenue, Nashville, TN 37203-1700. Telephone: 615-322-2561.

Texas

ABILENE CHRISTIAN UNIVERSITY
ABILENE, TEXAS

Entrance Moderately difficult **General** Independent, comprehensive, coed, affiliated with Church of Christ **Setting** 208-acre suburban campus **Enrollment** 4,397 **Faculty** 19:1 **Application deadline** Rolling **Freshmen** 52% accepted **Housing** Yes **Tuition** $9752 **Undergraduates** 53% women, 12% part-time, 12% 25 or older, 1% Native American, 5% Hispanic, 5% black, 3% Asian or Pacific Islander **Most popular recent majors** Elementary education, biology/biological sciences, nursing **Academic program** Average class size 25, advanced placement, accelerated degree program, self-designed majors, tutorials, honors program, summer session, adult/continuing education programs, internships **Contact** Mr. Don King, Director of Admissions, Abilene Christian University, ACU Box 29000, Abilene, TX 79699. Telephone: 915-674-2650.

AMBER UNIVERSITY
GARLAND, TEXAS

Entrance Minimally difficult **General** Independent nondenominational, upper-level, coed **Setting** 5-acre suburban campus **Enrollment** 1,610 **Freshmen** 99% accepted **Tuition** $4025 **Undergraduates** 58% women, 72% part-time, 98% 25 or older, 1% Native American, 5% Hispanic, 20% black, 1% Asian or Pacific Islander **Most popular recent majors** Management information systems, human resources, human development **Academic program** Self-designed majors, summer session, adult/continuing education programs, internships **Contact** Ms. Judy George, Director for Admissions and Records, Amber University, Garland, TX 75041-5595. Telephone: 972-279-6511 Ext. 130.

ANGELO STATE UNIVERSITY
SAN ANGELO, TEXAS

Entrance Moderately difficult **General** State-supported, comprehensive, coed **Setting** 268-acre urban campus **Enrollment** 6,200 **Faculty** 25:1 **Application deadline** 8/1 **Freshmen** 71% accepted **Housing** Yes **Tuition** $2006 **Undergraduates** 55% women, 28% part-time, 27% 25 or older, 1% Native American, 17% Hispanic, 4% black, 1% Asian or Pacific Islander **Most popular recent majors** Education, nursing, business administration/commerce/management **Academic program** Advanced placement, accelerated degree program, summer session, adult/continuing education programs **Contact** Mr. Manuel R. Lujan, Dean of Admissions/Registrar, Angelo State University, 2601 West Avenue N, San Angelo, TX 76909. Telephone: 915-942-2042.

ARLINGTON BAPTIST COLLEGE
ARLINGTON, TEXAS

Entrance Noncompetitive **General** Independent Baptist, 4-year, coed **Setting** 32-acre urban campus **Enrollment** 198 **Application deadline** Rolling **Freshmen** 100% accepted **Housing** Yes **Tuition** $2810 **Undergraduates** 42% women, 16% part-time, 25% 25 or older, 0% Native American, 3% Hispanic, 4% black, 1% Asian or Pacific Islander **Most popular recent majors** Liberal arts/general studies, biblical studies, education **Academic program** Advanced placement, accelerated degree program, summer session, internships **Contact** Br. Danny Moody, Director of Institutional Advancement, Arlington Baptist College, 3001 West Division, Arlington, TX 76012-3425. Telephone: 817-461-8741 Ext. 103. Fax: 817-274-1138.

AUSTIN COLLEGE
SHERMAN, TEXAS

Entrance Very difficult **General** Independent Presbyterian, comprehensive, coed **Setting** 60-

acre suburban campus **Enrollment** 1,149 **Faculty** 13:1 **Application deadline** Rolling **Freshmen** 79% accepted **Housing** Yes **Tuition** $13,560 **Undergraduates** 54% women, 2% part-time, 3% 25 or older, 1% Native American, 8% Hispanic, 3% black, 7% Asian or Pacific Islander **Most popular recent majors** Psychology, biology/biological sciences, business administration/commerce/management **Academic program** Average class size 25, advanced placement, accelerated degree program, self-designed majors, tutorials, honors program, summer session, adult/continuing education programs, internships **Contact** Mr. Jonathan Stroud, Vice President for Institutional Enrollment, Austin College, Sherman, TX 75090-4440. Telephone: 903-813-3000. Fax: 903-813-3198.

BAPTIST MISSIONARY ASSOCIATION THEOLOGICAL SEMINARY
JACKSONVILLE, TEXAS

Entrance Noncompetitive **General** Independent Baptist, comprehensive, specialized, primarily men **Setting** 17-acre small-town campus **Enrollment** 61 **Faculty** 8:1 **Application deadline** 7/17 **Freshmen** 100% accepted **Housing** Yes **Tuition** $1980 **Undergraduates** 16% women, 80% part-time, 97% 25 or older, 0% Native American, 3% Hispanic, 10% black, 0% Asian or Pacific Islander **Academic program** Summer session, adult/continuing education programs, internships **Contact** Dr. Wilbur K. Benningfield, Dean/Registrar, Baptist Missionary Association Theological Seminary, 1530 East Pine Street, Jacksonville, TX 75766-5407. Telephone: 903-586-2501.

BAYLOR COLLEGE OF DENTISTRY
DALLAS, TEXAS

Entrance Moderately difficult **General** State-supported, upper-level, specialized, coed **Setting** 1-acre urban campus **Enrollment** 503 **Freshmen** 31% accepted **Tuition** $6380 **Undergraduates** 99% women, 0% part-time, 25% 25 or older, 0% Native American, 1% Hispanic, 1% black, 5% Asian or Pacific Islander **Academic program** Summer session **Contact** Dr. Jack Long, Director of Admissions and Academic Records, Baylor College of Dentistry, 3302 Gaston Avenue, PO Box 660677, Dallas, TX 75266-0677. Telephone: 214-828-8230.

BAYLOR UNIVERSITY
WACO, TEXAS

Entrance Moderately difficult **General** Independent Baptist, coed **Setting** 432-acre urban campus **Enrollment** 12,391 **Faculty** 17:1 **Application deadline** Rolling **Freshmen** 88% accepted **Housing** Yes **Tuition** $9428 **Undergraduates** 56% women, 4% part-time, 5% 25 or older, 1% Native American, 8% Hispanic, 5% black, 5% Asian or Pacific Islander **Academic program** Advanced placement, accelerated degree program, self-designed majors, honors program, summer session, adult/continuing education programs, internships **Contact** Ms. Teri Tippit, Director of Recruitment, Baylor University, PO Box 97056, Waco, TX 76798. Telephone: 817-755-3435.

CONCORDIA UNIVERSITY AT AUSTIN
AUSTIN, TEXAS

Entrance Moderately difficult **General** Independent, 4-year, coed, affiliated with Lutheran Church–Missouri Synod **Setting** 20-acre urban campus **Enrollment** 723 **Faculty** 11:1 **Application deadline** 8/1 **Freshmen** 96% accepted **Housing** Yes **Tuition** $9400 **Undergraduates** 62% women, 23% part-time, 37% 25 or older, 1% Native American, 10% Hispanic, 7% black, 1% Asian or Pacific Islander **Most popular recent majors** Business administration/commerce/management, elementary education, communication **Academic program** Advanced placement, tutorials, summer session, adult/continuing education programs, internships **Contact** Ms. Rachel Meissner, Associate Director of Admissions, Concordia University at Austin, 3400 Interstate 35 North, Austin, TX 78705-2799. Telephone: 512-452-7661. Fax: 512-459-8517.

THE CRISWELL COLLEGE
DALLAS, TEXAS

Entrance Minimally difficult **General** Independent Baptist, comprehensive, specialized, coed **Setting** 1-acre urban campus **Enrollment** 442 **Faculty** 20:1 **Application deadline** 8/15 **Freshmen** 85% accepted **Tuition** $3250 **Undergraduates** 23% women, 56% part-time, 73% 25 or older, 1% Native American, 8% Hispanic, 21% black, 8% Asian or Pacific Islander **Most popular recent major** Biblical studies **Academic program** Summer session, internships **Contact** Mr. Rich Grimm, Vice President for Enrollment Services, The Criswell College, 4010 Gaston Avenue, Dallas, TX 75246-1537. Telephone: 214-821-5433 Ext. 1302. Fax: 214-818-1310.

DALLAS BAPTIST UNIVERSITY
DALLAS, TEXAS

Entrance Moderately difficult **General** Independent Southern Baptist, comprehensive, coed **Setting** 200-acre urban campus **Enrollment** 3,283 **Faculty** 14:1 **Application deadline** Rolling **Fresh-**

men 88% accepted **Housing** Yes **Tuition** $7440 **Undergraduates** 54% women, 62% part-time, 67% 25 or older, 1% Native American, 6% Hispanic, 16% black, 5% Asian or Pacific Islander **Most popular recent majors** Business administration/commerce/ management, education, music **Academic program** Advanced placement, summer session, adult/ continuing education programs, internships **Contact** Mr. Aaron T. Vann, Director of Admissions, Dallas Baptist University, 3000 Mountain Creek Parkway, Dallas, TX 75211-9299. Telephone: 214-333-5360. Fax: 214-333-5447.

DALLAS CHRISTIAN COLLEGE
DALLAS, TEXAS

Entrance Minimally difficult **General** Independent, 4-year, coed, affiliated with Christian Churches and Churches of Christ **Setting** 22-acre urban campus **Enrollment** 240 **Faculty** 15:1 **Application deadline** Rolling **Freshmen** 88% accepted **Housing** Yes **Tuition** $3840 **Undergraduates** 39% women, 1% part-time, 61% 25 or older, 1% Native American, 4% Hispanic, 15% black, 1% Asian or Pacific Islander **Academic program** Advanced placement, tutorials, summer session, adult/ continuing education programs, internships **Contact** Mr. Michael Frisbie, Director of Student Recruitment, Dallas Christian College, 2700 Christian Parkway, Dallas, TX 75234-7299. Telephone: 972-241-3371 Ext. 123. Fax: 972-241-8021.

DEVRY INSTITUTE OF TECHNOLOGY
IRVING, TEXAS

Entrance Minimally difficult **General** Proprietary, 4-year, coed **Setting** 13-acre suburban campus **Enrollment** 2,419 **Faculty** 18:1 **Application deadline** Rolling **Freshmen** 73% accepted **Tuition** $6968 **Undergraduates** 23% women, 35% part-time, 56% 25 or older, 1% Native American, 15% Hispanic, 26% black, 6% Asian or Pacific Islander **Most popular recent majors** Computer information systems, electronics engineering technology, electrical and electronics technologies **Academic program** Advanced placement, accelerated degree program, summer session, adult/continuing education programs **Contact** Mr. Daniel Millan, Director of Admissions, DeVry Institute of Technology, Irving, TX 75063-2440. Telephone: 972-929-5770.

EAST TEXAS BAPTIST UNIVERSITY
MARSHALL, TEXAS

Entrance Moderately difficult **General** Independent Baptist, comprehensive, coed **Setting** 193-acre small-town campus **Enrollment** 1,222 **Faculty** 16:1 **Application deadline** Rolling **Freshmen** 85% accepted **Housing** Yes **Tuition** $7110 **Undergraduates** 61% women, 10% part-time, 27% 25 or older, 0% Native American, 2% Hispanic, 10% black, 1% Asian or Pacific Islander **Most popular recent majors** Education, business administration/ commerce/management, behavioral sciences **Academic program** Advanced placement, accelerated degree program, tutorials, honors program, summer session, adult/continuing education programs, internships **Contact** Mr. David Howard, Director of Admissions, East Texas Baptist University, Marshall, TX 75670-1498. Telephone: 903-935-7963 Ext. 225. Fax: 903-935-3447.

EAST TEXAS STATE UNIVERSITY AT TEXARKANA
SEE TEXAS A&M UNIVERSITY–TEXARKANA

HARDIN-SIMMONS UNIVERSITY
ABILENE, TEXAS

Entrance Moderately difficult **General** Independent Baptist, comprehensive, coed **Setting** 40-acre urban campus **Enrollment** 2,279 **Faculty** 11:1 **Application deadline** Rolling **Freshmen** 88% accepted **Housing** Yes **Tuition** $8380 **Undergraduates** 51% women, 14% part-time, 13% 25 or older, 1% Native American, 7% Hispanic, 4% black, 1% Asian or Pacific Islander **Most popular recent majors** Education, psychology, nursing **Academic program** Average class size 20, advanced placement, accelerated degree program, tutorials, summer session, adult/continuing education programs, internships **Contact** Mrs. Laura Moore, Director of Admissions, Hardin-Simmons University, Box 16050, Abilene, TX 79698-0001. Telephone: 915-670-1206. Fax: 915-670-1527.

HOUSTON BAPTIST UNIVERSITY
HOUSTON, TEXAS

Entrance Moderately difficult **General** Independent Baptist, comprehensive, coed **Setting** 158-acre urban campus **Enrollment** 2,243 **Faculty** 18:1 **Application deadline** Rolling **Freshmen** 76% accepted **Housing** Yes **Tuition** $8535 **Undergraduates** 65% women, 22% part-time, 31% 25 or older, 0% Native American, 12% Hispanic, 14% black, 19% Asian or Pacific Islander **Most popular recent majors** (pre)medicine sequence, business administration/commerce/management, nursing **Academic program** Advanced placement, summer session, adult/continuing education programs, internships **Contact** Dr. Jerry Ford, Director of Admissions, Houston Baptist University, 7502 Fondren Road, Houston, TX 77074-3298. Telephone: 713-995-3211. Fax: 713-995-3217.

HOWARD PAYNE UNIVERSITY
BROWNWOOD, TEXAS

Entrance Minimally difficult **General** Independent Southern Baptist, 4-year, coed **Setting** 30-acre small-town campus **Enrollment** 1,468 **Faculty** 16:1 **Application deadline** Rolling **Freshmen** 92% accepted **Housing** Yes **Tuition** $6450 **Undergraduates** 49% women, 17% part-time, 16% 25 or older, 0% Native American, 9% Hispanic, 6% black, 2% Asian or Pacific Islander **Most popular recent majors** Education, business administration/commerce/management, biology/biological sciences **Academic program** Average class size 20, ESL program, advanced placement, self-designed majors, honors program, summer session, adult/continuing education programs, internships **Contact** Ms. Cheryl Mangrum, Coordinator of Admission Services, Howard Payne University, Brownwood, TX 76801-2715. Telephone: 915-649-8027. Fax: 915-649-8901.

HUSTON-TILLOTSON COLLEGE
AUSTIN, TEXAS

Entrance Moderately difficult **General** Independent-religious, 4-year, coed **Setting** 23-acre urban campus **Enrollment** 701 **Faculty** 15:1 **Application deadline** 5/1 **Freshmen** 87% accepted **Housing** Yes **Tuition** $6030 **Undergraduates** 55% women, 18% part-time, 25% 25 or older, 0% Native American, 8% Hispanic, 78% black, 3% Asian or Pacific Islander **Most popular recent majors** Business administration/commerce/management, accounting, communication **Academic program** Advanced placement, accelerated degree program, summer session, internships **Contact** Mr. Donnie J. Scott, Director of Admissions, Huston-Tillotson College, 900 Chicon Street, Austin, TX 78702-2795. Telephone: 512-505-3027. Fax: 512-474-0762.

ICI UNIVERSITY
IRVING, TEXAS

Entrance Noncompetitive **General** Independent, comprehensive, specialized, coed, affiliated with Assemblies of God **Setting** 6-acre suburban campus **Enrollment** 8,628 **Faculty** 30:1 **Undergraduates** 30% women, 50% part-time, 70% 25 or older **Academic program** ESL program, Advanced placement, accelerated degree program, tutorials, honors program, adult/continuing education programs **Contact** Dr. Mark Barcliff, Associate Dean of Student Services, ICI University, Irving, TX 75063-2631. Telephone: 972-751-1111 Ext. 8211. Fax: 972-714-8185.

INCARNATE WORD COLLEGE
SEE UNIVERSITY OF THE INCARNATE WORD

INSTITUTE FOR CHRISTIAN STUDIES
AUSTIN, TEXAS

Entrance Moderately difficult **General** Independent, upper-level, specialized, coed, affiliated with Church of Christ **Setting** Urban campus **Enrollment** 54 **Freshmen** 92% accepted **Housing** Yes **Tuition** $920 **Undergraduates** 26% women, 48% part-time, 65% 25 or older, 0% Native American, 9% Hispanic, 4% black, 0% Asian or Pacific Islander **Academic program** Average class size 12, advanced placement, tutorials, summer session, adult/continuing education programs, internships **Contact** Mrs. Cindy Lippe, Director of Admissions and Registrar, Institute for Christian Studies, 1909 University Avenue, Austin, TX 78705-5610. Telephone: 512-476-2772.

JARVIS CHRISTIAN COLLEGE
HAWKINS, TEXAS

Entrance Minimally difficult **General** Independent, 4-year, coed, affiliated with Christian Church (Disciples of Christ) **Setting** 465-acre rural campus **Enrollment** 557 **Application deadline** Rolling **Freshmen** 90% accepted **Housing** Yes **Tuition** $6694 **Undergraduates** 54% women, 4% 25 or older, 0% Native American, 0% Hispanic, 98% black, 0% Asian or Pacific Islander **Most popular recent majors** Mathematics, sociology **Academic program** Advanced placement, tutorials, honors program, internships **Contact** Ms. Serena Sentell, Admissions Counselor, Jarvis Christian College, PO Drawer G, Hawkins, TX 75765-9989. Telephone: 903-769-5700. Fax: 903-769-4842.

LAMAR UNIVERSITY
BEAUMONT, TEXAS

Entrance Minimally difficult **General** State-supported, coed **Setting** 200-acre suburban campus **Enrollment** 8,418 **Faculty** 20:1 **Application deadline** 8/1 **Freshmen** 82% accepted **Housing** Yes **Tuition** $1796 **Undergraduates** 57% women, 38% part-time, 39% 25 or older, 1% Native American, 4% Hispanic, 16% black, 3% Asian or Pacific Islander **Most popular recent majors** Interdisciplinary studies, electrical engineering, criminal justice **Academic program** Advanced placement, accelerated degree program, self-designed majors, honors program, summer session, adult/continuing education programs, internships **Contact** Ms. Melissa Chesser, Director of

Recruitment, Lamar University, Beaumont, TX 77710. Telephone: 409-880-8888. Fax: 409-880-8463.

LETOURNEAU UNIVERSITY
LONGVIEW, TEXAS

Entrance Moderately difficult **General** Independent nondenominational, comprehensive, coed **Setting** 162-acre suburban campus **Enrollment** 2,059 **Faculty** 15:1 **Application deadline** 8/15 **Freshmen** 50% accepted **Housing** Yes **Tuition** $10,220 **Undergraduates** 39% women, 7% part-time, 56% 25 or older, 1% Native American, 4% Hispanic, 7% black, 2% Asian or Pacific Islander **Most popular recent majors** Aviation technology, mechanical engineering, electrical engineering **Academic program** Average class size 24, advanced placement, summer session, adult/continuing education programs, internships **Contact** Mr. Howard Wilson, Director of Admissions, LeTourneau University, Longview, TX 75607-7001. Telephone: 903-233-3400 Ext. 240. Fax: 903-233-3411.

LUBBOCK CHRISTIAN UNIVERSITY
LUBBOCK, TEXAS

Entrance Noncompetitive **General** Independent, comprehensive, coed, affiliated with Church of Christ **Setting** 120-acre suburban campus **Enrollment** 1,232 **Faculty** 15:1 **Application deadline** Rolling **Freshmen** 96% accepted **Housing** Yes **Tuition** $8578 **Undergraduates** 57% women, 17% part-time, 25% 25 or older, 1% Native American, 7% Hispanic, 5% black, 1% Asian or Pacific Islander **Most popular recent majors** Education, business administration/commerce/management **Academic program** Advanced placement, accelerated degree program, self-designed majors, summer session, internships **Contact** Office of Admissions, Lubbock Christian University, Lubbock, TX 79407-2099. Telephone: 806-796-8800 Ext. 260. Fax: 806-796-8917.

MCMURRY UNIVERSITY
ABILENE, TEXAS

Entrance Moderately difficult **General** Independent United Methodist, 4-year, coed **Setting** 41-acre urban campus **Enrollment** 1,400 **Faculty** 13:1 **Application deadline** 8/15 **Freshmen** 69% accepted **Housing** Yes **Tuition** $8587 **Undergraduates** 48% women, 31% part-time, 31% 25 or older, 1% Native American, 10% Hispanic, 9% black, 1% Asian or Pacific Islander **Most popular recent majors** Education, business administration/commerce/management, sociology **Academic program** Average class size 28, advanced placement, tutorials, honors program, summer session, internships **Contact** Mr. L. Russell Watjen, Vice President, Enrollment Management and Student Relations, McMurry University, Box 947, Abilene, TX 79697. Telephone: 915-691-6370. Fax: 915-691-6599.

MIDWESTERN STATE UNIVERSITY
WICHITA FALLS, TEXAS

Entrance Minimally difficult **General** State-supported, comprehensive, coed **Setting** 172-acre urban campus **Enrollment** 5,643 **Faculty** 20:1 **Application deadline** 8/7 **Freshmen** 77% accepted **Housing** Yes **Tuition** $2091 **Undergraduates** 56% women, 33% part-time, 39% 25 or older, 1% Native American, 6% Hispanic, 6% black, 2% Asian or Pacific Islander **Most popular recent majors** Business administration/commerce/management, nursing **Academic program** ESL program, Advanced placement, accelerated degree program, honors program, summer session, adult/continuing education programs, internships **Contact** Ms. Billye Tims, Registrar and Director of Admissions, Midwestern State University, 3410 Taft Boulevard, Wichita Falls, TX 76308-2096. Telephone: 817-689-4321. Fax: 817-689-4672.

NORTHWOOD UNIVERSITY, TEXAS CAMPUS
CEDAR HILL, TEXAS

Entrance Minimally difficult **General** Independent, 4-year, coed **Setting** 350-acre small-town campus **Enrollment** 354 **Faculty** 17:1 **Application deadline** 9/1 **Freshmen** 76% accepted **Housing** Yes **Tuition** $10,839 **Undergraduates** 42% women, 2% part-time, 5% 25 or older, 2% Native American, 21% Hispanic, 15% black, 3% Asian or Pacific Islander **Academic program** Average class size 30, advanced placement, honors program, summer session, adult/continuing education programs, internships **Contact** Mr. James R. Hickerson, Director of Admissions, Northwood University, Texas Campus, Cedar Hill, TX 75104-1204. Telephone: 972-291-1541. Fax: 972-291-3824.

OUR LADY OF THE LAKE UNIVERSITY OF SAN ANTONIO
SAN ANTONIO, TEXAS

Entrance Moderately difficult **General** Independent Roman Catholic, comprehensive, coed **Setting** 75-acre urban campus **Enrollment** 3,468 **Faculty** 16:1 **Application deadline** Rolling **Freshmen** 74% accepted **Housing** Yes **Tuition** $10,354 **Undergraduates** 75% women, 49% part-time, 56% 25 or older, 0% Native American, 58% Hispanic, 8%

black, 1% Asian or Pacific Islander **Most popular recent majors** Business administration/commerce/management, computer information systems, psychology **Academic program** Advanced placement, accelerated degree program, tutorials, summer session, adult/continuing education programs, internships **Contact** Ms. Debbie Hamilton, Director of Admissions, Our Lady of the Lake University of San Antonio, 411 Southwest 24th Street, San Antonio, TX 78207-4689. Telephone: 210-434-6711 Ext. 314. Fax: 210-436-0824.

PAUL QUINN COLLEGE
DALLAS, TEXAS

Entrance Moderately difficult **General** Independent African Methodist Episcopal, 4-year, coed **Setting** 132-acre suburban campus **Enrollment** 700 **Faculty** 20:1 **Application deadline** 6/1 **Freshmen** 72% accepted **Housing** Yes **Tuition** $4685 **Undergraduates** 60% women, 12% part-time, 20% 25 or older, 15% Hispanic, 85% black **Most popular recent majors** Education, business administration/commerce/management, (pre)medicine sequence **Academic program** Average class size 30, advanced placement, accelerated degree program, honors program, summer session, adult/continuing education programs, internships **Contact** Mr. Ralph Spencer, Director of Admissions, Paul Quinn College, Dallas, TX 75241-4331. Telephone: 214-302-3520. Fax: 214-302-3559.

PRAIRIE VIEW A&M UNIVERSITY
PRAIRIE VIEW, TEXAS

Entrance Moderately difficult **General** State-supported, comprehensive, coed **Setting** 1,440-acre small-town campus **Enrollment** 5,999 **Faculty** 20:1 **Application deadline** Rolling **Freshmen** 90% accepted **Housing** Yes **Tuition** $1900 **Undergraduates** 54% women, 10% part-time, 25% 25 or older, 0% Native American, 2% Hispanic, 86% black, 2% Asian or Pacific Islander **Academic program** Advanced placement, accelerated degree program, honors program, summer session, internships **Contact** Mr. Samuel Montgomery, Director of Admissions and Records, Prairie View A&M University, PO Box 3089, Prairie View, TX 77446-0188. Telephone: 409-857-2626. Fax: 409-857-2699.

RICE UNIVERSITY
HOUSTON, TEXAS

Entrance Most difficult **General** Independent, coed **Setting** 300-acre urban campus **Enrollment** 4,225 **Faculty** 9:1 **Application deadline** 1/2 **Freshmen** 25% accepted **Housing** Yes **Tuition** $11,905 **Undergraduates** 46% women, 0% part-time, 1% 25 or older, 1% Native American, 11% Hispanic, 7% black, 15% Asian or Pacific Islander **Most popular recent majors** Political science/government, English, history **Academic program** Advanced placement, accelerated degree program, self-designed majors, tutorials, honors program, summer session, internships **Contact** Ms. Julie M. Browning, Director of Admissions, Rice University, MS 17, Houston, TX 77005. Telephone: 713-527-4036.

ST. EDWARD'S UNIVERSITY
AUSTIN, TEXAS

Entrance Moderately difficult **General** Independent Roman Catholic, comprehensive, coed **Setting** 180-acre urban campus **Enrollment** 3,082 **Faculty** 15:1 **Application deadline** Rolling **Freshmen** 77% accepted **Housing** Yes **Tuition** $10,400 **Undergraduates** 60% women, 32% part-time, 17% 25 or older, 1% Native American, 25% Hispanic, 5% black, 3% Asian or Pacific Islander **Most popular recent majors** Criminal justice, psychology, marketing/retailing/merchandising **Academic program** Average class size 25, advanced placement, accelerated degree program, tutorials, honors program, summer session, adult/continuing education programs, internships **Contact** Ms. Megan Murphy, Director of Admissions, St. Edward's University, 3001 South Congress Avenue, Austin, TX 78704-6489. Telephone: 512-448-8500. Fax: 512-448-8492.

ST. MARY'S UNIVERSITY OF SAN ANTONIO
SAN ANTONIO, TEXAS

Entrance Moderately difficult **General** Independent Roman Catholic, comprehensive, coed **Setting** 135-acre urban campus **Enrollment** 4,096 **Faculty** 18:1 **Application deadline** 8/15 **Freshmen** 87% accepted **Housing** Yes **Tuition** $10,608 **Undergraduates** 55% women, 14% part-time, 17% 25 or older, 1% Native American, 64% Hispanic, 3% black, 2% Asian or Pacific Islander **Most popular recent majors** Biology/biological sciences, accounting, international business **Academic program** Advanced placement, accelerated degree program, tutorials, honors program, summer session, adult/continuing education programs, internships **Contact** Mr. Richard Castillo, Director of Admissions, St. Mary's University of San Antonio, 1 Camino Santa Maria, San Antonio, TX 78228-8503. Telephone: 210-436-3126. Fax: 210-431-6742.

SAM HOUSTON STATE UNIVERSITY
HUNTSVILLE, TEXAS

Entrance Moderately difficult **General** State-supported, comprehensive, coed **Setting** 2,143-acre small-town campus **Enrollment** 12,564 **Faculty** 21:1 **Application deadline** Rolling **Freshmen** 84% accepted **Housing** Yes **Tuition** $1982 **Undergraduates** 54% women, 19% part-time, 19% 25 or older, 0% Native American, 8% Hispanic, 12% black, 1% Asian or Pacific Islander **Academic program** Advanced placement, accelerated degree program, honors program, summer session, adult/continuing education programs, internships **Contact** Ms. Joey Chandler, Director of Admissions and Recruitment, Sam Houston State University, Huntsville, TX 77341-2448. Telephone: 409-294-1056.

SCHREINER COLLEGE
KERRVILLE, TEXAS

Entrance Moderately difficult **General** Independent Presbyterian, 4-year, coed **Setting** 175-acre small-town campus **Enrollment** 675 **Faculty** 13:1 **Application deadline** Rolling **Freshmen** 80% accepted **Housing** Yes **Tuition** $10,135 **Undergraduates** 56% women, 17% part-time, 26% 25 or older, 0% Native American, 15% Hispanic, 3% black, 1% Asian or Pacific Islander **Most popular recent majors** Business administration/commerce/management, mathematics, psychology **Academic program** Advanced placement, self-designed majors, tutorials, honors program, summer session, internships **Contact** Mr. Todd Brown, Director of Admission and Financial Aid, Schreiner College, Kerrville, TX 78028-5697. Telephone: 210-896-5411 Ext. 225. Fax: 210-896-3232.

SOUTHERN METHODIST UNIVERSITY
DALLAS, TEXAS

Entrance Moderately difficult **General** Independent, coed, affiliated with United Methodist Church **Setting** 163-acre suburban campus **Enrollment** 9,464 **Faculty** 12:1 **Application deadline** 4/1 **Freshmen** 90% accepted **Housing** Yes **Tuition** $19,190 **Undergraduates** 54% women, 7% part-time, 8% 25 or older, 1% Native American, 9% Hispanic, 6% black, 6% Asian or Pacific Islander **Most popular recent majors** Finance/banking, psychology, advertising **Academic program** Advanced placement, self-designed majors, tutorials, honors program, summer session, adult/continuing education programs, internships **Contact** Mr. Ron W. Moss, Director of Admission and Enrollment Management, Southern Methodist University, Dallas, TX 75275. Telephone: 214-768-2058.

SOUTHWESTERN ADVENTIST UNIVERSITY
KEENE, TEXAS

Entrance Noncompetitive **General** Independent Seventh-day Adventist, comprehensive, coed **Setting** 150-acre rural campus **Enrollment** 1,030 **Faculty** 14:1 **Application deadline** Rolling **Freshmen** 99% accepted **Housing** Yes **Tuition** $8500 **Undergraduates** 58% women, 28% part-time, 36% 25 or older, 1% Native American, 14% Hispanic, 10% black, 5% Asian or Pacific Islander **Academic program** Accelerated degree program, self-designed majors, tutorials, honors program, summer session, internships **Contact** Mrs. Flavia Illingworth, Admissions Counselor, Southwestern Adventist University, PO Box 567, Keene, TX 76059. Telephone: 817-645-3921 Ext. 252. Fax: 817-556-4744.

SOUTHWESTERN ASSEMBLIES OF GOD UNIVERSITY
WAXAHACHIE, TEXAS

Entrance Noncompetitive **General** Independent, 4-year, coed, affiliated with Assemblies of God **Setting** 70-acre small-town campus **Enrollment** 1,142 **Faculty** 29:1 **Application deadline** Rolling **Freshmen** 80% accepted **Housing** Yes **Tuition** $4402 **Undergraduates** 47% women, 24% part-time, 40% 25 or older, 1% Native American, 11% Hispanic, 2% black, 1% Asian or Pacific Islander **Most popular recent majors** Pastoral studies, business administration/commerce/management, religious education **Academic program** Advanced placement, summer session, adult/continuing education programs, internships **Contact** Mr. Greg Dufrene, Registrar, Southwestern Assemblies of God University, Waxahachie, TX 75165-2342. Telephone: 214-937-4010 Ext. 114.

SOUTHWESTERN CHRISTIAN COLLEGE
TERRELL, TEXAS

Entrance Noncompetitive **General** Independent, 4-year, coed, affiliated with Church of Christ **Setting** 25-acre small-town campus **Enrollment** 198 **Application deadline** 7/15 **Freshmen** 90% accepted **Housing** Yes **Tuition** $5150 **Undergraduates** 49% women, 13% part-time, 14% 25 or older, 0% Native American, 4% Hispanic, 84% black, 0% Asian or Pacific Islander **Most popular recent majors** Business administration/commerce/management, religious studies, liberal arts/general studies **Contact** Admissions Department, Southwestern Christian College, Terrell, TX 75160-0010. Telephone: 214-524-3341.

SOUTHWESTERN UNIVERSITY
GEORGETOWN, TEXAS

Entrance Very difficult **General** Independent Methodist, 4-year, coed **Setting** 500-acre suburban campus **Enrollment** 1,226 **Faculty** 11:1 **Application deadline** 2/15 **Freshmen** 79% accepted **Housing** Yes **Tuition** $14,000 **Undergraduates** 58% women, 4% part-time, 3% 25 or older, 1% Native American, 11% Hispanic, 3% black, 5% Asian or Pacific Islander **Most popular recent majors** Psychology, biology/biological sciences, business administration/commerce/management **Academic program** Advanced placement, accelerated degree program, self-designed majors, tutorials, honors program, summer session, internships **Contact** Mr. John W. Lind, Vice President for Enrollment Management, Southwestern University, Georgetown, TX 78626. Telephone: 512-863-1200. Fax: 512-863-9601.

SOUTHWEST TEXAS STATE UNIVERSITY
SAN MARCOS, TEXAS

Entrance Moderately difficult **General** State-supported, comprehensive, coed **Setting** 423-acre small-town campus **Enrollment** 20,776 **Faculty** 26:1 **Application deadline** 7/1 **Freshmen** 68% accepted **Housing** Yes **Tuition** $2698 **Undergraduates** 54% women, 22% part-time, 24% 25 or older, 1% Native American, 18% Hispanic, 5% black, 2% Asian or Pacific Islander **Most popular recent majors** Elementary education, accounting, business administration/commerce/management **Academic program** Advanced placement, accelerated degree program, tutorials, honors program, summer session, internships **Contact** Mr. Fernando Yarrito, Director of Admissions, Southwest Texas State University, Admissions and Visitors Center, San Marcos, TX 78666. Telephone: 512-245-2364 Ext. 2803. Fax: 512-245-8044.

STEPHEN F. AUSTIN STATE UNIVERSITY
NACOGDOCHES, TEXAS

Entrance Moderately difficult **General** State-supported, comprehensive, coed **Setting** 400-acre small-town campus **Enrollment** 11,671 **Faculty** 19:1 **Application deadline** Rolling **Freshmen** 71% accepted **Housing** Yes **Tuition** $1513 **Undergraduates** 53% women, 19% part-time, 23% 25 or older, 1% Native American, 4% Hispanic, 6% black, 1% Asian or Pacific Islander **Most popular recent majors** Interdisciplinary studies, marketing/retailing/merchandising, physical fitness/exercise science **Academic program** Average class size 28, advanced placement, accelerated degree program, self-designed majors, tutorials, honors program, summer session, adult/continuing education programs, internships **Contact** Mr. Roger Bilow, Director of Admission, Stephen F. Austin State University, Nacogdoches, TX 75962. Telephone: 409-468-2504. Fax: 409-468-3849.

SUL ROSS STATE UNIVERSITY
ALPINE, TEXAS

Entrance Noncompetitive **General** State-supported, comprehensive, coed **Setting** 640-acre small-town campus **Enrollment** 2,458 **Faculty** 16:1 **Application deadline** Rolling **Freshmen** 83% accepted **Housing** Yes **Tuition** $1680 **Undergraduates** 46% women, 11% part-time, 24% 25 or older, 1% Native American, 41% Hispanic, 5% black, 0% Asian or Pacific Islander **Most popular recent majors** Animal sciences, elementary education, business administration/commerce/management **Academic program** Honors program, summer session, internships **Contact** Mr. Robert Cullins, Dean of Admissions and Records, Sul Ross State University, Box C-2, Alpine, TX 79832. Telephone: 915-837-8052. Fax: 915-837-8046.

TARLETON STATE UNIVERSITY
STEPHENVILLE, TEXAS

Entrance Moderately difficult **General** State-supported, comprehensive, coed **Setting** 165-acre small-town campus **Enrollment** 6,369 **Faculty** 20:1 **Application deadline** 8/1 **Freshmen** 74% accepted **Housing** Yes **Tuition** $2464 **Undergraduates** 52% women, 6% part-time, 21% 25 or older, 1% Native American, 5% Hispanic, 3% black, 1% Asian or Pacific Islander **Most popular recent majors** Interdisciplinary studies, physical fitness/exercise science, agricultural education **Academic program** Advanced placement, accelerated degree program, honors program, summer session, adult/continuing education programs, internships **Contact** Ms. Gail Mayfield, Director of Admissions, Tarleton State University, Stephenville, TX 76402. Telephone: 817-968-9125. Fax: 817-968-9389.

TEXAS A&M INTERNATIONAL UNIVERSITY
LAREDO, TEXAS

Entrance Moderately difficult **General** State-supported, comprehensive, coed **Setting** 300-acre urban campus **Enrollment** 2,510 **Application deadline** 7/1 **Freshmen** 96% accepted **Tuition** $2101 **Undergraduates** 63% women, 44% part-time, 44% 25 or older, 0% Native American, 92% Hispanic, 1% black, 1% Asian or Pacific Islander **Most popular recent majors** Interdisciplinary studies, accounting, criminal justice **Academic program** Average class size 21, advanced placement, summer session **Contact** Ms. Betty L. Momayez, Director of Enrollment Management and School Relations, Texas A&M International University, 5201 University Boulevard, Laredo, TX 78041-1999. Telephone: 210-326-2270.

TEXAS A&M UNIVERSITY
COLLEGE STATION, TEXAS

Entrance Moderately difficult **General** State-supported, coed **Setting** 5,142-acre suburban campus **Enrollment** 41,892 **Faculty** 27:1 **Application deadline** 3/1 **Freshmen** 69% accepted **Housing** Yes **Tuition** $2738 **Undergraduates** 45% women, 13% part-time, 4% 25 or older, 0% Native American, 10% Hispanic, 3% black, 4% Asian or Pacific Islander **Most popular recent majors** Psychology, management information systems, accounting **Academic program** Advanced placement, accelerated degree program, tutorials, honors program, summer session, internships **Contact** Mr. Gary R. Engelgau, Executive Director of Admissions and Records, Texas A&M University, 217 John J. Koldus Building, College Station, TX 77843-1265. Telephone: 409-845-3741.

TEXAS A&M UNIVERSITY AT GALVESTON
GALVESTON, TEXAS

Entrance Moderately difficult **General** State-supported, 4-year, specialized, coed **Setting** 100-acre suburban campus **Enrollment** 1,203 **Faculty** 15:1 **Application deadline** Rolling **Freshmen** 86% accepted **Housing** Yes **Tuition** $2681 **Undergraduates** 49% women, 17% part-time, 18% 25 or older, 1% Native American, 9% Hispanic, 1% black, 2% Asian or Pacific Islander **Most popular recent majors** Marine biology, marine sciences, marine engineering **Academic program** Advanced placement, accelerated degree program, summer session **Contact** Ms. Donna Lang, Registrar, Texas A&M University at Galveston, PO Box 1675, Galveston, TX 77553-1675. Telephone: 409-740-4415. Fax: 409-740-4709.

TEXAS A&M UNIVERSITY–COMMERCE
COMMERCE, TEXAS

Entrance Moderately difficult **General** State-supported, coed **Setting** 140-acre small-town campus **Enrollment** 7,546 **Application deadline** 8/1 **Freshmen** 67% accepted **Housing** Yes **Tuition** $2288 **Undergraduates** 56% women, 13% part-time, 52% 25 or older, 1% Native American, 4% Hispanic, 14% black, 1% Asian or Pacific Islander **Most popular recent majors** Education, business administration/commerce/management, computer science **Academic program** Advanced placement, accelerated degree program, tutorials, honors program, summer session, adult/continuing education programs, internships **Contact** Mr. Randy McDonald, Director of School Relations, Texas A&M University–Commerce, Commerce, TX 75429-3011. Telephone: 903-886-5072. Fax: 903-886-5888.

TEXAS A&M UNIVERSITY–CORPUS CHRISTI
CORPUS CHRISTI, TEXAS

Entrance Moderately difficult **General** State-supported, comprehensive, coed **Setting** 240-acre suburban campus **Enrollment** 5,671 **Faculty** 14:1 **Application deadline** 7/1 **Freshmen** 78% accepted **Housing** Yes **Tuition** $2395 **Undergraduates** 62% women, 45% part-time, 54% 25 or older, 1% Native American, 35% Hispanic, 2% black, 2% Asian or Pacific Islander **Most popular recent majors** Psychology, interdisciplinary studies, criminal justice **Academic program** Advanced placement, tutorials, summer session, internships **Contact** Ms. Margaret Dechant, Director of Admissions, Texas A&M University–Corpus Christi, 6300 Ocean Drive, Corpus Christi, TX 78412-5503. Telephone: 512-994-2414. Fax: 512-994-5887.

TEXAS A&M UNIVERSITY–KINGSVILLE
KINGSVILLE, TEXAS

Entrance Moderately difficult **General** State-supported, coed **Setting** 255-acre small-town campus **Enrollment** 6,113 **Application deadline** Rolling **Freshmen** 83% accepted **Housing** Yes **Tuition** $1772 **Undergraduates** 49% women, 18% part-time, 32% 25 or older, 60% Hispanic, 4% black, 1% Asian or Pacific Islander **Most popular recent majors** Education, accounting, business administration/commerce/management **Academic program** ESL program, Advanced placement, accelerated degree program, tutorials, summer session, adult/continuing education programs, internships **Contact** Mr. Joe Estrada, Registrar/Admissions Director, Texas A&M University–Kingsville, Kingsville, TX 78363. Telephone: 512-593-2811. or Telephone: 512-593-2315.

TEXAS A&M UNIVERSITY–TEXARKANA
TEXARKANA, TEXAS

Entrance Noncompetitive **General** State-supported, upper-level, coed **Setting** 1-acre small-town campus **Enrollment** 1,187 **Faculty** 19:1 **Freshmen** 100% accepted **Tuition** $2048 **Undergraduates** 68% women, 66% part-time, 65%

25 or older, 1% Native American, 0% Hispanic, 10% black, 0% Asian or Pacific Islander **Academic program** Self-designed majors, summer session **Contact** Mrs. Sandra Rogers, Director of Academic and Student Services, Texas A&M University–Texarkana, Texarkana, TX 75505-5518. Telephone: 903-838-6514 Ext. 227. Fax: 903-832-8890.

TEXAS CHIROPRACTIC COLLEGE

PASADENA, TEXAS

Entrance Difficulty N/R **General** Independent, upper-level, specialized, coed **Setting** 18-acre suburban campus **Enrollment** 560 **Freshmen** 83% accepted **Tuition** $13,200 **Undergraduates** 25% women, 1% Native American, 9% Hispanic, 7% black, 14% Asian or Pacific Islander **Contact** Mr. Robert Cooper, Director of Admissions, Texas Chiropractic College, Pasadena, TX 77505-1699. Telephone: 713-998-6017.

TEXAS CHRISTIAN UNIVERSITY

FORT WORTH, TEXAS

Entrance Moderately difficult **General** Independent, coed, affiliated with Christian Church (Disciples of Christ) **Setting** 237-acre suburban campus **Enrollment** 6,961 **Faculty** 15:1 **Application deadline** 2/15 **Freshmen** 74% accepted **Housing** Yes **Tuition** $11,380 **Undergraduates** 59% women, 10% part-time, 11% 25 or older, 1% Native American, 6% Hispanic, 5% black, 3% Asian or Pacific Islander **Most popular recent majors** Nursing, psychology, marketing/retailing/merchandising **Academic program** Average class size 26, advanced placement, accelerated degree program, self-designed majors, tutorials, honors program, summer session, adult/continuing education programs, internships **Contact** Ms. Sandra J. Ware, Interim Dean of Admissions, Texas Christian University, Fort Worth, TX 76129-0002. Telephone: 817-921-7490. Fax: 817-921-7333.

TEXAS LUTHERAN UNIVERSITY

SEGUIN, TEXAS

Entrance Moderately difficult **General** Independent, 4-year, coed, affiliated with Evangelical Lutheran Church **Setting** 161-acre small-town campus **Enrollment** 1,234 **Faculty** 13:1 **Application deadline** Rolling **Freshmen** 81% accepted **Housing** Yes **Tuition** $10,370 **Undergraduates** 61% women, 29% part-time, 8% 25 or older, 1% Native American, 14% Hispanic, 4% black, 1% Asian or Pacific Islander **Most popular recent major** Business administration/commerce/management **Academic program** Advanced placement, accelerated degree program, tutorials, honors program, summer session, adult/continuing education programs, internships **Contact** Mr. E. Norman Jones, Vice President for Enrollment Services, Texas Lutheran University, 1000 West Court Street, Seguin, TX 78155-5999. Telephone: 210-372-8050. Fax: 210-372-8091.

TEXAS SOUTHERN UNIVERSITY

HOUSTON, TEXAS

Entrance Noncompetitive **General** State-supported, coed **Setting** 147-acre urban campus **Enrollment** 9,518 **Faculty** 16:1 **Application deadline** 8/10 **Freshmen** 100% accepted **Housing** Yes **Tuition** $2064 **Undergraduates** 61% women, 27% part-time, 34% 25 or older, 1% Native American, 2% Hispanic, 88% black, 2% Asian or Pacific Islander **Most popular recent majors** Business administration/commerce/management, law enforcement/police sciences, criminal justice **Academic program** Accelerated degree program, honors program, summer session, adult/continuing education programs **Contact** Ms. Georgia Cooley, Coordinator of Recruitment, Texas Southern University, 3100 Cleburne, Houston, TX 77004-4598. Telephone: 713-313-7474. Fax: 713-527-7842.

TEXAS TECH UNIVERSITY

LUBBOCK, TEXAS

Entrance Moderately difficult **General** State-supported, coed **Setting** 1,839-acre urban campus **Enrollment** 24,717 **Faculty** 18:1 **Application deadline** Rolling **Freshmen** 80% accepted **Housing** Yes **Tuition** $2326 **Undergraduates** 46% women, 12% part-time, 11% 25 or older, 0% Native American, 11% Hispanic, 3% black, 2% Asian or Pacific Islander **Most popular recent majors** Business administration/commerce/management, engineering technology, education **Academic program** Advanced placement, accelerated degree program, self-designed majors, tutorials, honors program, summer session, adult/continuing education programs, internships **Contact** Mrs. Judy Stocking, Administrative Secretary for New Student Relations, Texas Tech University, Box 45005, Lubbock, TX 79409-5005. Telephone: 806-742-1482. Fax: 806-742-0980.

TEXAS WESLEYAN UNIVERSITY

FORT WORTH, TEXAS

Entrance Moderately difficult **General** Independent United Methodist, comprehensive, coed **Setting** 74-acre urban campus **Enrollment** 2,966 **Faculty** 15:1 **Application deadline** Rolling

Freshmen 79% accepted **Housing** Yes **Tuition** $7600 **Undergraduates** 65% women, 32% part-time, 60% 25 or older, 2% Native American, 10% Hispanic, 13% black, 2% Asian or Pacific Islander **Most popular recent majors** Business administration/commerce/management, education, psychology **Academic program** Advanced placement, accelerated degree program, tutorials, summer session, adult/continuing education programs, internships **Contact** Ms. Stephanie Lewis-Boatner, Director of Freshman Admissions, Texas Wesleyan University, 1201 Wesleyan, Fort Worth, TX 76105-1536. Telephone: 817-531-4422. Fax: 817-531-4231.

TEXAS WOMAN'S UNIVERSITY
DENTON, TEXAS

Entrance Minimally difficult **General** State-supported, primarily women **Setting** 270-acre suburban campus **Enrollment** 9,788 **Application deadline** 7/15 **Freshmen** 79% accepted **Housing** Yes **Tuition** $1929 **Undergraduates** 94% women, 34% part-time, 47% 25 or older, 1% Native American, 9% Hispanic, 15% black, 4% Asian or Pacific Islander **Most popular recent majors** Nursing, interdisciplinary studies, occupational therapy **Academic program** Advanced placement, accelerated degree program, tutorials, honors program, summer session, adult/continuing education programs, internships **Contact** Ms. Cynthia Johnson, Director of Undergraduate Admissions, Texas Woman's University, PO Box 425679, Denton, TX 76201-0909. Telephone: 817-898-3040. Fax: 817-898-3198.

TRINITY UNIVERSITY
SAN ANTONIO, TEXAS

Entrance Very difficult **General** Independent, comprehensive, coed, affiliated with Presbyterian Church **Setting** 113-acre urban campus **Enrollment** 2,495 **Faculty** 11:1 **Application deadline** 2/1 **Freshmen** 79% accepted **Housing** Yes **Tuition** $13,644 **Undergraduates** 51% women, 5% part-time, 1% 25 or older, 1% Native American, 9% Hispanic, 2% black, 9% Asian or Pacific Islander **Most popular recent majors** Business administration/commerce/management, biology/biological sciences, English **Academic program** Average class size 20, advanced placement, accelerated degree program, tutorials, summer session, internships **Contact** Dr. George Boyd, Director of Admissions, Trinity University, 715 Stadium Drive, San Antonio, TX 78212-7200. Telephone: 210-736-7207.

UNIVERSITY OF CENTRAL TEXAS
KILLEEN, TEXAS

Entrance Noncompetitive **General** Independent, upper-level, coed **Setting** 545-acre small-town campus **Enrollment** 1,039 **Faculty** 21:1 **Freshmen** 100% accepted **Housing** Yes **Tuition** $3204 **Undergraduates** 53% women, 61% part-time, 84% 25 or older, 1% Native American, 8% Hispanic, 24% black, 4% Asian or Pacific Islander **Most popular recent majors** Business administration/commerce/management, aviation technology, psychology **Academic program** Self-designed majors, summer session, internships **Contact** Ms. Pat Moran, Admissions Advisor, University of Central Texas, Killeen, TX 76540-1416. Telephone: 817-526-8262 Ext. 251.

UNIVERSITY OF DALLAS
IRVING, TEXAS

Entrance Very difficult **General** Independent Roman Catholic, coed **Setting** 750-acre suburban campus **Enrollment** 2,771 **Faculty** 13:1 **Application deadline** 3/1 **Freshmen** 89% accepted **Housing** Yes **Tuition** $12,144 **Undergraduates** 63% women, 8% part-time, 10% 25 or older, 0% Native American, 14% Hispanic, 2% black, 6% Asian or Pacific Islander **Most popular recent majors** Biology/biological sciences, English, political science/government **Academic program** Average class size 20, advanced placement, accelerated degree program, self-designed majors, tutorials, summer session, adult/continuing education programs, internships **Contact** Mr. Fred Zuker, Dean of Admissions and Financial Aid, University of Dallas, Irving, TX 75062-4799. Telephone: 214-721-5266. Fax: 214-721-5017.

UNIVERSITY OF HOUSTON
HOUSTON, TEXAS

Entrance Moderately difficult **General** State-supported, coed **Setting** 557-acre urban campus **Enrollment** 30,774 **Faculty** 18:1 **Application deadline** 7/1 **Freshmen** 62% accepted **Housing** Yes **Tuition** $2389 **Undergraduates** 52% women, 31% part-time, 30% 25 or older, 1% Native American, 17% Hispanic, 12% black, 18% Asian or Pacific Islander **Most popular recent majors** Business administration/commerce/management, engineering (general), biology/biological sciences **Academic program** Average class size 53, advanced placement, accelerated degree program, honors program, summer session, adult/continuing education programs, internships **Contact** Mr. Ed Apodacq, Associate Vice President of Enrollment Services, University of Houston, 4800 Calhoun, Houston, TX 77204-2161. Telephone: 713-743-9565.

UNIVERSITY OF HOUSTON–CLEAR LAKE
HOUSTON, TEXAS

Entrance Minimally difficult **General** State-supported, upper-level, coed **Setting** 487-acre suburban campus **Enrollment** 6,968 **Faculty** 17:1 **Freshmen** 100% accepted **Tuition** $2088 **Undergraduates** 62% women, 56% part-time, 66% 25 or older, 1% Native American, 10% Hispanic, 5% black, 6% Asian or Pacific Islander **Most popular recent majors** Business administration/commerce/management, interdisciplinary studies, behavioral sciences **Academic program** Average class size 35, accelerated degree program, self-designed majors, tutorials, summer session, internships **Contact** Ms. Darella L. Banks, Executive Director of Enrollment Services, University of Houston–Clear Lake, 2700 Bay Area Boulevard, Box 13, Houston, TX 77058-1098. Telephone: 281-283-2517. Fax: 281-283-2530.

UNIVERSITY OF HOUSTON–DOWNTOWN
HOUSTON, TEXAS

Entrance Noncompetitive **General** State-supported, 4-year, coed **Setting** 20-acre urban campus **Enrollment** 7,947 **Application deadline** 8/15 **Freshmen** 100% accepted **Tuition** $1977 **Undergraduates** 54% women, 54% part-time, 52% 25 or older, 1% Native American, 31% Hispanic, 25% black, 11% Asian or Pacific Islander **Most popular recent majors** Criminal justice, interdisciplinary studies, accounting **Academic program** Advanced placement, accelerated degree program, self-designed majors, summer session, adult/continuing education programs, internships **Contact** Dr. Ann McDonald, Executive Director of Enrollment Services/Student Affairs, University of Houston–Downtown, One Main Street, Houston, TX 77002-1001. Telephone: 713-221-8100. Fax: 713-221-8157.

UNIVERSITY OF HOUSTON–VICTORIA
VICTORIA, TEXAS

Entrance Minimally difficult **General** State-supported, upper-level, coed **Setting** Small-town campus **Enrollment** 1,809 **Freshmen** 85% accepted **Tuition** $2148 **Undergraduates** 13% Hispanic, 3% black **Contact** Mr. Richard Phillips, Director of Enrollment Management, University of Houston–Victoria, 2302-C Red River, Victoria, TX 77901-4450. Telephone: 512-576-3151.

UNIVERSITY OF MARY HARDIN-BAYLOR
BELTON, TEXAS

Entrance Minimally difficult **General** Independent Southern Baptist, comprehensive, coed **Setting** 100-acre small-town campus **Enrollment** 2,265 **Faculty** 17:1 **Application deadline** Rolling **Freshmen** 71% accepted **Housing** Yes **Tuition** $6524 **Undergraduates** 67% women, 22% part-time, 35% 25 or older, 1% Native American, 8% Hispanic, 7% black, 2% Asian or Pacific Islander **Most popular recent majors** Education, business administration/commerce/management, nursing **Academic program** Advanced placement, accelerated degree program, honors program, summer session, adult/continuing education programs **Contact** Ms. Diane Stanford, Assistant Director of Admissions, University of Mary Hardin-Baylor, Belton, TX 76513. Telephone: 817-939-8642. Fax: 817-939-4235.

UNIVERSITY OF NORTH TEXAS
DENTON, TEXAS

Entrance Moderately difficult **General** State-supported, coed **Setting** 456-acre urban campus **Enrollment** 24,957 **Faculty** 20:1 **Application deadline** 6/15 **Freshmen** 76% accepted **Housing** Yes **Tuition** $2187 **Undergraduates** 52% women, 32% part-time, 14% 25 or older, 1% Native American, 7% Hispanic, 8% black, 3% Asian or Pacific Islander **Most popular recent majors** Biology/biological sciences, psychology, accounting **Academic program** Advanced placement, accelerated degree program, self-designed majors, tutorials, honors program, summer session, internships **Contact** Ms. Marcilla Collinsworth, Director of Admissions, University of North Texas, Box 13797, Denton, TX 76203-6737. Telephone: 817-565-3921. Fax: 817-565-2408.

UNIVERSITY OF ST. THOMAS
HOUSTON, TEXAS

Entrance Moderately difficult **General** Independent Roman Catholic, comprehensive, coed **Setting** 20-acre urban campus **Enrollment** 2,504 **Faculty** 9:1 **Application deadline** Rolling **Freshmen** 83% accepted **Housing** Yes **Tuition** $11,070 **Undergraduates** 66% women, 26% part-time, 35% 25 or older, 1% Native American, 24% Hispanic, 7% black, 10% Asian or Pacific Islander **Most popular recent majors** Psychology, biology/biological sciences, business administration/commerce/management **Academic program** Advanced placement, accelerated degree program, self-designed majors, tutorials, honors program, summer session, adult/continuing education programs, internships **Con-**

tact Mrs. Elsie Biron, Director of Admissions, University of St. Thomas, 3800 Montrose Boulevard, Houston, TX 77006-4694. Telephone: 713-525-3500. Fax: 713-525-3558.

THE UNIVERSITY OF TEXAS AT ARLINGTON

ARLINGTON, TEXAS

Entrance Moderately difficult **General** State-supported, coed **Setting** 395-acre suburban campus **Enrollment** 20,544 **Application deadline** 8/1 **Freshmen** 88% accepted **Housing** Yes **Tuition** $2571 **Undergraduates** 51% women, 42% part-time, 41% 25 or older, 1% Native American, 9% Hispanic, 10% black, 11% Asian or Pacific Islander **Most popular recent majors** Interdisciplinary studies, business administration/commerce/management, accounting **Academic program** Advanced placement, honors program, summer session, adult/continuing education programs **Contact** Ms. Norma Coppage, Associate Director of Admissions, The University of Texas at Arlington, Arlington, TX 76019-0407. Telephone: 817-272-2225. Fax: 817-272-3435.

THE UNIVERSITY OF TEXAS AT AUSTIN

AUSTIN, TEXAS

Entrance Very difficult **General** State-supported, coed **Setting** 350-acre urban campus **Enrollment** 48,008 **Faculty** 19:1 **Application deadline** 2/1 **Freshmen** 61% accepted **Housing** Yes **Tuition** $2866 **Undergraduates** 49% women, 13% part-time, 11% 25 or older, 1% Native American, 15% Hispanic, 4% black, 13% Asian or Pacific Islander **Academic program** Advanced placement, accelerated degree program, self-designed majors, honors program, summer session, adult/continuing education programs, internships **Contact** Ms. Shirley F. Binder, Director of Admissions, The University of Texas at Austin, Austin, TX 78712. Telephone: 512-475-7399.

THE UNIVERSITY OF TEXAS AT BROWNSVILLE

BROWNSVILLE, TEXAS

Entrance Noncompetitive **General** State-supported, upper-level, coed **Setting** 65-acre urban campus **Enrollment** 2,752 **Freshmen** 95% accepted **Tuition** $1988 **Undergraduates** 63% women, 48% part-time, 56% 25 or older, 1% Native American, 82% Hispanic, 1% black, 1% Asian or Pacific Islander **Academic program** Advanced placement, summer session **Contact** Mr. Ernesto Garcia, Director of Enrollment, The University of Texas at Brownsville, 80 Fort Brown, Brownsville, TX 78520-4991. Telephone: 210-544-8254. Fax: 210-544-8832.

THE UNIVERSITY OF TEXAS AT DALLAS

RICHARDSON, TEXAS

Entrance Very difficult **General** State-supported, coed **Setting** 455-acre suburban campus **Enrollment** 9,378 **Faculty** 20:1 **Application deadline** 8/1 **Freshmen** 74% accepted **Housing** Yes **Tuition** $2788 **Undergraduates** 50% women, 48% part-time, 49% 25 or older, 1% Native American, 7% Hispanic, 6% black, 12% Asian or Pacific Islander **Most popular recent majors** Business administration/commerce/management, interdisciplinary studies, accounting **Academic program** ESL program, Advanced placement, accelerated degree program, self-designed majors, tutorials, summer session, adult/continuing education programs, internships **Contact** Admissions Office, The University of Texas at Dallas, PO Box 830688 Mail Station MC18, Richardson, TX 75083-0688. Telephone: 972-883-2341. Fax: 972-883-2599.

THE UNIVERSITY OF TEXAS AT EL PASO

EL PASO, TEXAS

Entrance Minimally difficult **General** State-supported, coed **Setting** 360-acre urban campus **Enrollment** 15,386 **Faculty** 17:1 **Application deadline** 7/1 **Freshmen** 79% accepted **Housing** Yes **Tuition** $2236 **Undergraduates** 54% women, 34% part-time, 29% 25 or older, 1% Native American, 68% Hispanic, 3% black, 2% Asian or Pacific Islander **Most popular recent majors** Interdisciplinary studies, criminal justice, psychology **Academic program** Advanced placement, accelerated degree program, tutorials, honors program, summer session, adult/continuing education programs, internships **Contact** Ms. Diana Guerrero, Director of Admissions, The University of Texas at El Paso, 500 West University Avenue, El Paso, TX 79968-0001. Telephone: 915-747-5588. Fax: 915-747-5122.

THE UNIVERSITY OF TEXAS AT SAN ANTONIO

SAN ANTONIO, TEXAS

Entrance Moderately difficult **General** State-supported, comprehensive, coed **Setting** 600-acre suburban campus **Enrollment** 17,547 **Faculty** 22:1 **Application deadline** 7/1 **Freshmen** 80% accepted **Housing** Yes **Tuition** $2684 **Undergraduates** 53% women, 36% part-time, 41% 25 or older, 1% Native American, 37% Hispanic, 4% black, 1% Asian or Pacific Islander **Most popular recent majors** Accounting, business administration/commerce/management, interdisciplinary studies **Academic program** Advanced placement, accelerated degree program, tutorials, honors program, summer session, internships **Contact** Ms. Sandy Speed, Associate Director of Admissions, The University of Texas at San Antonio, San Antonio, TX 78249. Telephone: 210-691-4530.

THE UNIVERSITY OF TEXAS AT TYLER

TYLER, TEXAS

Entrance Difficulty N/R **General** State-supported, upper-level, coed **Setting** 200-acre urban campus **Enrollment** 3,789 **Faculty** 10:1 **Freshmen** 86% accepted **Housing** Yes **Tuition** $1784 **Undergraduates** 65% women, 49% part-time, 59% 25 or older, 1% Native American, 1% Hispanic, 7% black, 1% Asian or Pacific Islander **Academic program** Self-designed majors, honors program, summer session, adult/continuing education programs **Contact** Ms. Martha Wheat, Director of Admissions and Student Records, The University of Texas at Tyler, 3900 University Boulevard, Tyler, TX 75799-0001. Telephone: 903-566-7201.

THE UNIVERSITY OF TEXAS HEALTH SCIENCE CENTER AT SAN ANTONIO

SAN ANTONIO, TEXAS

Entrance Moderately difficult **General** State-supported, upper-level, specialized, coed **Setting** 100-acre suburban campus **Enrollment** 2,721 **Faculty** 6:1 **Tuition** $1280 **Undergraduates** 65% women, 14% part-time, 75% 25 or older, 1% Native American, 18% Hispanic, 6% black, 5% Asian or Pacific Islander **Academic program** Summer session, adult/continuing education programs **Contact** Mr. James Peak, Registrar, The University of Texas Health Science Center at San Antonio, San Antonio, TX 78284-6200. Telephone: 210-567-2629. Fax: 210-567-2685.

THE UNIVERSITY OF TEXAS–HOUSTON HEALTH SCIENCE CENTER

HOUSTON, TEXAS

Entrance Moderately difficult **General** State-supported, upper-level, coed **Setting** Urban campus **Enrollment** 3,111 **Freshmen** 17% accepted **Housing** Yes **Tuition** $1659 **Undergraduates** 86% women, 28% part-time, 67% 25 or older, 0% Native American, 10% Hispanic, 9% black, 15% Asian or Pacific Islander **Academic program** Summer session, adult/continuing education programs **Contact** Mr. Robert Jenkins, Assistant Registrar/Admissions, The University of Texas–Houston Health Science Center, PO Box 20036, Houston, TX 77225-0036. Telephone: 713-500-3333 Ext. 2203. Fax: 713-500-3356.

THE UNIVERSITY OF TEXAS MEDICAL BRANCH AT GALVESTON

GALVESTON, TEXAS

Entrance Most difficult **General** State-supported, upper-level, coed **Setting** 82-acre small-town campus **Enrollment** 2,204 **Faculty** 7:1 **Freshmen** 33% accepted **Housing** Yes **Tuition** $1290 **Undergraduates** 74% women, 17% part-time, 62% 25 or older, 1% Native American, 15% Hispanic, 6% black, 10% Asian or Pacific Islander **Academic program** Advanced placement, summer session, internships **Contact** Mr. Curt Coonrod, Director of Admissions, The University of Texas Medical Branch at Galveston, 1.212 Ashbel Smith, Galveston, TX 77555-1305. Telephone: 409-772-1215. Fax: 409-772-5056.

THE UNIVERSITY OF TEXAS OF THE PERMIAN BASIN

ODESSA, TEXAS

Entrance Moderately difficult **General** State-supported, comprehensive, coed **Setting** 600-acre urban campus **Enrollment** 2,193 **Faculty** 16:1 **Application deadline** 8/1 **Freshmen** 89% accepted **Housing** Yes **Tuition** $1920 **Undergraduates** 65% women, 43% part-time, 75% 25 or older, 22% Hispanic, 4% black, 1% Asian or Pacific Islander **Most popular recent majors** History, accounting, psychology **Academic program** Advanced placement, summer session, internships **Contact** Ms. Vicki Gomez, Director of Admissions, The University of Texas of the Permian Basin, 4901 East University, Odessa, TX 79762-0001. Telephone: 915-552-2605. Fax: 915-552-2374.

THE UNIVERSITY OF TEXAS–PAN AMERICAN

EDINBURG, TEXAS

Entrance Noncompetitive **General** State-supported, comprehensive, coed **Setting** 200-acre rural campus **Enrollment** 12,692 **Faculty** 27:1 **Application deadline** 7/15 **Freshmen** 100% accepted **Housing** Yes **Tuition** $1973 **Undergraduates** 58% women, 41% part-time, 26% 25 or older, 1% Native American, 87% Hispanic, 1% black, 1% Asian or Pacific Islander **Most popular recent majors** Business administration/commerce/management, elementary education, criminal justice **Academic program** Accelerated degree program, honors program, summer session, adult/continuing education programs, internships **Contact** Mr. David Zuniga, Director of Admissions, The University of Texas–Pan American, Edinburg, TX 78539-2999. Telephone: 210-381-2201.

THE UNIVERSITY OF TEXAS SOUTHWESTERN MEDICAL CENTER AT DALLAS
DALLAS, TEXAS

Entrance Difficulty N/R **General** State-supported, upper-level, coed **Setting** 98-acre urban campus **Enrollment** 1,714 **Faculty** 4:1 **Freshmen** 47% accepted **Tuition** $1393 **Undergraduates** 74% women, 32% part-time, 71% 25 or older, 0% Native American, 5% Hispanic, 9% black, 7% Asian or Pacific Islander **Most popular recent majors** Physical therapy, physician's assistant studies **Academic program** Advanced placement, internships **Contact** Ms. Laura Jarnagin, Assistant to the Registrar, The University of Texas Southwestern Medical Center at Dallas, 5323 Harry Hines Boulevard, Dallas, TX 75235-9002. Telephone: 214-648-3606. Fax: 214-648-3289.

UNIVERSITY OF THE INCARNATE WORD
SAN ANTONIO, TEXAS

Entrance Moderately difficult **General** Independent Roman Catholic, comprehensive, coed **Setting** 200-acre urban campus **Enrollment** 3,287 **Faculty** 14:1 **Application deadline** Rolling **Freshmen** 80% accepted **Housing** Yes **Tuition** $10,335 **Undergraduates** 70% women, 39% part-time, 33% 25 or older, 1% Native American, 58% Hispanic, 6% black, 1% Asian or Pacific Islander **Most popular recent majors** Business administration/commerce/management, nursing, education **Academic program** Average class size 16, advanced placement, accelerated degree program, tutorials, summer session, adult/continuing education programs, internships **Contact** Mr. Brian F. Dalton, Dean of Enrollment, University of the Incarnate Word, 4301 Broadway, San Antonio, TX 78209-6397. Telephone: 210-829-6005. Fax: 210-829-3921.

WAYLAND BAPTIST UNIVERSITY
PLAINVIEW, TEXAS

Entrance Minimally difficult **General** Independent Baptist, comprehensive, coed **Setting** 80-acre small-town campus **Enrollment** 4,009 **Faculty** 15:1 **Application deadline** Rolling **Freshmen** 99% accepted **Housing** Yes **Tuition** $6200 **Undergraduates** 41% women, 79% part-time, 74% 25 or older, 1% Native American, 13% Hispanic, 13% black, 2% Asian or Pacific Islander **Most popular recent majors** Business administration/commerce/management, education, human services **Academic program** Average class size 25, advanced placement, accelerated degree program, tutorials, honors program, summer session, adult/continuing education programs, internships **Contact** Mr. Claude Lusk, Director of Student Admissions, Wayland Baptist University, Plainview, TX 79072-6998. Telephone: 806-296-4709.

WEST TEXAS A&M UNIVERSITY
CANYON, TEXAS

Entrance Moderately difficult **General** State-supported, comprehensive, coed **Setting** 128-acre small-town campus **Enrollment** 6,482 **Faculty** 25:1 **Application deadline** 8/16 **Freshmen** 82% accepted **Housing** Yes **Tuition** $1854 **Undergraduates** 53% women, 22% part-time, 22% 25 or older, 1% Native American, 11% Hispanic, 2% black, 1% Asian or Pacific Islander **Most popular recent majors** Interdisciplinary studies, nursing, business administration/commerce/management **Academic program** Average class size 25, advanced placement, accelerated degree program, self-designed majors, honors program, summer session, adult/continuing education programs, internships **Contact** Ms. Lila Vars, Director of Admissions, West Texas A&M University, WT Box 907, Canyon, TX 79016-0001. Telephone: 806-656-2020.

WILEY COLLEGE
MARSHALL, TEXAS

Entrance Noncompetitive **General** Independent, 4-year, coed, affiliated with United Methodist Church **Setting** 58-acre small-town campus **Enrollment** 508 **Application deadline** 8/1 **Freshmen** 97% accepted **Housing** Yes **Tuition** $4556 **Undergraduates** 60% women, 5% part-time, 18% 25 or older, 0% Native American, 1% Hispanic, 99% black, 0% Asian or Pacific Islander **Most popular recent majors** Elementary education, hotel and restaurant management, biology/biological sciences **Academic program** Self-designed majors, summer session, adult/continuing education programs **Contact** Mr. Frederick Pryor Jr., Director of Admissions, Wiley College, Marshall, TX 75670-5199. Telephone: 903-927-3311. Fax: 903-938-8100.

Alaska

ALASKA BIBLE COLLEGE

GLENNALLEN, ALASKA

Entrance Minimally difficult **General** Independent nondenominational, 4-year, coed **Setting** 80-acre rural campus **Enrollment** 34 **Faculty** 6:1 **Application deadline** 8/1 **Freshmen** 77% accepted **Housing** Yes **Tuition** $3790 **Undergraduates** 38% women, 33% part-time, 47% 25 or older, 9% Native American, 0% Hispanic, 0% black, 0% Asian or Pacific Islander **Most popular recent majors** Religious education, pastoral studies **Academic program** Average class size 15, advanced placement, self-designed majors, internships **Contact** Ms. Connie Riedman, Admissions Officer, Alaska Bible College, Box 289, Glennallen, AK 99588-0289. Telephone: 907-822-3201. Fax: 907-822-5027.

ALASKA PACIFIC UNIVERSITY

ANCHORAGE, ALASKA

Entrance Minimally difficult **General** Independent-religious, comprehensive, coed **Setting** 170-acre suburban campus **Enrollment** 450 **Faculty** 9:1 **Application deadline** 2/1 **Freshmen** 52% accepted **Housing** Yes **Tuition** $8480 **Undergraduates** 64% women, 21% part-time, 56% 25 or older, 12% Native American, 3% Hispanic, 6% black, 4% Asian or Pacific Islander **Most popular recent majors** Business administration/commerce/management, elementary education, environmental sciences **Academic program** Average class size 12, ESL program, advanced placement, accelerated degree program, self-designed majors, tutorials, summer session, adult/continuing education programs, internships **Contact** Mr. Michael Mills, Director of Admissions, Alaska Pacific University, Anchorage, AK 99508-4672. Telephone: 907-564-8248.

SHELDON JACKSON COLLEGE

SITKA, ALASKA

Entrance Noncompetitive **General** Independent, 4-year, coed, affiliated with Presbyterian Church (U.S.A.) **Setting** 320-acre small-town campus **Enrollment** 223 **Faculty** 11:1 **Application deadline** Rolling **Freshmen** 100% accepted **Housing** Yes **Tuition** $9300 **Undergraduates** 51% women, 15% part-time, 40% 25 or older, 25% Native American, 1% Hispanic, 1% black, 1% Asian or Pacific Islander **Most popular recent majors** Natural resource management, fish and game management, education **Academic program** Average class size 10, advanced placement, self-designed majors, tutorials, internships **Contact** Mr. John Schafer, Dean of Enrollment, Sheldon Jackson College, Sitka, AK 99835-7699. Telephone: 907-747-5221. Fax: 907-747-5212.

UNIVERSITY OF ALASKA ANCHORAGE

ANCHORAGE, ALASKA

Entrance Noncompetitive **General** State-supported, comprehensive, coed **Setting** 428-acre urban campus **Enrollment** 13,049 **Faculty** 29:1 **Application deadline** Rolling **Freshmen** 81% accepted **Housing** Yes **Tuition** $2293 **Undergraduates** 60% women, 59% part-time, 62% 25 or older, 7% Native American, 4% Hispanic, 6% black, 4% Asian or Pacific Islander **Most popular recent majors** Accounting, elementary education, psychology **Academic program** Advanced placement, self-designed majors, tutorials, summer session, adult/continuing education programs, internships **Contact** Ms. Linda Berg Smith, Associate Vice Chancellor for Enrollment Services, University of Alaska Anchorage, Administration Building, Room 176, Anchorage, AK 99508-8060. Telephone: 907-786-1480. Fax: 907-786-4888.

UNIVERSITY OF ALASKA FAIRBANKS

FAIRBANKS, ALASKA

Entrance Moderately difficult **General** State-supported, coed **Setting** 2,250-acre small-town campus **Enrollment** 5,197 **Application deadline** 8/1 **Freshmen** 79% accepted **Housing** Yes **Tuition** $2470 **Undergraduates** 57% women, 47% part-time, 57% 25 or older, 15% Native American, 2% Hispanic, 2% black, 2% Asian or Pacific Islander **Most popular recent majors** Education, business administration/commerce/management, accounting **Academic program** Advanced placement, accelerated degree program, self-designed majors, tutorials, honors program, summer session, adult/continuing education programs **Contact** Ms. Nancy Dix, Admissions Counselor, University of Alaska Fairbanks, PO Box 757480, Fairbanks, AK 99775-7480. Telephone: 907-474-7822. Fax: 907-474-5379.

UNIVERSITY OF ALASKA SOUTHEAST

JUNEAU, ALASKA

Entrance Noncompetitive **General** State-supported, comprehensive, coed **Setting** 198-acre small-town campus **Enrollment** 2,944 **Faculty** 15:1 **Application deadline** Rolling **Freshmen** 88% accepted **Housing** Yes **Tuition** $2164 **Undergraduates** 60% women, 87% part-time, 56% 25 or older, 12% Native American, 1% Hispanic, 1% black, 4% Asian or Pacific Islander **Most popu-**

lar recent majors Education, business administration/commerce/management **Academic program** Average class size 20, advanced placement, self-designed majors, tutorials, summer session, adult/continuing education programs, internships **Contact** Mr. Greg Wagner, Director of Admissions, University of Alaska Southeast, Juneau, AK 99801-8625. Telephone: 907-465-6239. Fax: 907-465-6239.

Arizona

AMERICAN INDIAN COLLEGE OF THE ASSEMBLIES OF GOD, INC.

PHOENIX, ARIZONA

Entrance Minimally difficult **General** Independent, 4-year, coed, affiliated with Assemblies of God **Setting** 10-acre urban campus **Enrollment** 106 **Application deadline** 8/15 **Freshmen** 96% accepted **Housing** Yes **Tuition** $3280 **Undergraduates** 59% women, 13% part-time, 36% 25 or older, 65% Native American, 11% Hispanic, 2% Asian or Pacific Islander **Academic program** Internships **Contact** Mr. Peter Cordova, Director of Admissions, American Indian College of the Assemblies of God, Inc., 10020 North Fifteenth Avenue, Phoenix, AZ 85021-2199. Telephone: 602-944-3335 Ext. 232.

ARIZONA COLLEGE OF THE BIBLE

PHOENIX, ARIZONA

Entrance Minimally difficult **General** Independent-religious, 4-year, specialized, coed **Setting** 7-acre urban campus **Enrollment** 106 **Faculty** 10:1 **Application deadline** 8/5 **Freshmen** 83% accepted **Housing** Yes **Tuition** $5886 **Undergraduates** 34% women, 38% part-time, 39% 25 or older, 3% Native American, 4% Hispanic, 7% black, 6% Asian or Pacific Islander **Academic program** Summer session, adult/continuing education programs, internships **Contact** Dr. John Bechtle, Academic Dean, Arizona College of the Bible, 1718 West Maryland Avenue, Phoenix, AZ 85015. Telephone: 602-242-6400 Ext. 307. Fax: 602-864-8183.

ARIZONA STATE UNIVERSITY

TEMPE, ARIZONA

Entrance Moderately difficult **General** State-supported, coed **Setting** 814-acre suburban campus **Enrollment** 38,664 **Faculty** 17:1 **Application deadline** Rolling **Freshmen** 78% accepted **Housing** Yes **Tuition** $2059 **Undergraduates** 51% women, 21% part-time, 26% 25 or older, 2% Native American, 10% Hispanic, 3% black, 4% Asian or Pacific Islander **Most popular recent majors** Business administration/commerce/management, psychology, elementary education **Academic program** Advanced placement, accelerated degree program, honors program, summer session, adult/continuing education programs, internships **Contact** Mr. Timothy J. Desch, Interim Director of Undergraduate Admissions, Arizona State University, Box 870112, Tempe, AZ 85287. Telephone: 602-965-7788.

ARIZONA STATE UNIVERSITY WEST

PHOENIX, ARIZONA

Entrance Moderately difficult **General** State-supported, upper-level, coed **Setting** 300-acre urban campus **Enrollment** 3,898 **Faculty** 12:1 **Freshmen** 91% accepted **Tuition** $1988 **Undergraduates** 65% women, 55% part-time, 69% 25 or older, 1% Native American, 11% Hispanic, 3% black, 3% Asian or Pacific Islander **Most popular recent majors** Elementary education, business administration/commerce/management, communication **Academic program** Self-designed majors, tutorials, honors program, summer session, adult/continuing education programs, internships **Contact** Mr. Tom Cabot, Director of Enrollment Services/Registrar, Arizona State University West, 4701 West Thunderbird Road, PO Box 37100, Phoenix, AZ 85069-7100. Telephone: 602-543-8123.

CAD INSTITUTE

SEE UNIVERSITY OF ADVANCING COMPUTER TECHNOLOGY

DEVRY INSTITUTE OF TECHNOLOGY

PHOENIX, ARIZONA

Entrance Minimally difficult **General** Proprietary, 4-year, coed **Setting** 18-acre urban campus **Enrollment** 2,862 **Faculty** 34:1 **Application deadline** Rolling **Freshmen** 73% accepted **Tuition** $6968 **Undergraduates** 21% women, 20% part-time, 42% 25 or older, 4% Native American, 11% Hispanic, 5% black, 6% Asian or Pacific Islander **Most popular recent majors** Electronics engineering technology, computer information systems, electrical and electronics technologies **Academic program** Advanced placement, accelerated degree program, summer session, adult/continuing education programs **Contact** Mr. Kim Galetti, Director of Admissions, DeVry Institute of Technology, 2149 West Dunlap Avenue, Phoenix, AZ 85021-2995. Telephone: 602-870-9201 Ext. 451.

EMBRY-RIDDLE AERONAUTICAL UNIVERSITY
PRESCOTT, ARIZONA

Entrance Moderately difficult **General** Independent, 4-year, specialized, coed **Setting** 510-acre small-town campus **Enrollment** 1,435 **Faculty** 17:1 **Application deadline** Rolling **Freshmen** 91% accepted **Housing** Yes **Tuition** $8740 **Undergraduates** 16% women, 8% part-time, 14% 25 or older, 1% Native American, 5% Hispanic, 2% black, 7% Asian or Pacific Islander **Most popular recent majors** Aerospace sciences, aerospace engineering, aviation administration **Academic program** Average class size 24, advanced placement, tutorials, summer session, adult/continuing education programs, internships **Contact** Mr. Terry E. Whittum, Director of Enrollment Management, Embry-Riddle Aeronautical University, Prescott, AZ 86301-3720. Telephone: 520-708-3728 Ext. 857.

GRAND CANYON UNIVERSITY
PHOENIX, ARIZONA

Entrance Moderately difficult **General** Independent Southern Baptist, comprehensive, coed **Setting** 70-acre suburban campus **Enrollment** 2,119 **Faculty** 16:1 **Application deadline** 8/15 **Freshmen** 99% accepted **Housing** Yes **Tuition** $8946 **Undergraduates** 62% women, 24% part-time, 35% 25 or older, 2% Native American, 6% Hispanic, 4% black, 2% Asian or Pacific Islander **Most popular recent majors** Elementary education, nursing, psychology **Academic program** Advanced placement, accelerated degree program, honors program, summer session, adult/continuing education programs, internships **Contact** Mr. Carl Tichenor, Director of Admissions, Grand Canyon University, Phoenix, AZ 85017-3030. Telephone: 602-589-2855. Fax: 602-589-2895.

INTERNATIONAL BAPTIST COLLEGE
TEMPE, ARIZONA

Entrance Difficulty N/R **General** Independent Baptist, comprehensive **Housing** Yes **Tuition** $3540 **Contact** Dr. Stanley Bushey, Director of Admissions, International Baptist College, Tempe, AZ 85282. Telephone: 602-878-7070. Fax: 602-838-5432.

NORTHERN ARIZONA UNIVERSITY
FLAGSTAFF, ARIZONA

Entrance Moderately difficult **General** State-supported, coed **Setting** 730-acre small-town campus **Enrollment** 19,605 **Faculty** 22:1 **Application deadline** 7/15 **Freshmen** 84% accepted **Housing** Yes **Tuition** $2060 **Undergraduates** 56% women, 15% part-time, 26% 25 or older, 7% Native American, 9% Hispanic, 1% black, 2% Asian or Pacific Islander **Most popular recent majors** Business administration/commerce/management, education, psychology **Academic program** Advanced placement, accelerated degree program, tutorials, honors program, summer session, internships **Contact** Ms. Molly Carder, Director of Admissions, Northern Arizona University, PO Box 4084, Flagstaff, AZ 86011. Telephone: 520-523-5511.

PRESCOTT COLLEGE, ADULT DEGREE PROGRAM
PRESCOTT, ARIZONA

Entrance Moderately difficult **General** Independent, upper-level, coed **Setting** 4-acre small-town campus **Enrollment** 331 **Freshmen** 63% accepted **Tuition** $6600 **Undergraduates** 74% women, 12% part-time, 90% 25 or older, 5% Native American, 14% Hispanic, 2% black, 3% Asian or Pacific Islander **Most popular recent majors** Education, human services, business administration/commerce/management **Academic program** Advanced placement, self-designed majors, tutorials, summer session, adult/continuing education programs, internships **Contact** Ms. Mary Ellen Hale, ADP Admissions Counselor, Prescott College, Adult Degree Program, 220 Grove Avenue, Prescott, AZ 86301-2990. Telephone: 520-776-7116. Fax: 520-776-5151.

PRESCOTT COLLEGE CENTER FOR INTER-TRIBAL STUDIES
PRESCOTT, ARIZONA

Entrance Noncompetitive **General** Independent, upper-level, specialized, coed **Setting** Small-town campus **Enrollment** 52 **Freshmen** 100% accepted **Tuition** $6600 **Undergraduates** 76% women, 1% part-time, 100% 25 or older, 92% Native American, 0% Hispanic, 0% black, 0% Asian or Pacific Islander **Most popular recent majors** Elementary education, bilingual/bicultural education, secondary education **Academic program** Self-designed majors, tutorials, summer session, adult/continuing education programs, internships **Contact** Ms. Karen Winings, Admissions Counselor, Prescott College Center for Inter-Tribal Studies, Prescott, AZ 86301-2990. Telephone: 520-776-5189. Fax: 520-776-5137.

PRESCOTT COLLEGE, RESIDENT DEGREE PROGRAM
PRESCOTT, ARIZONA

Entrance Moderately difficult **General** Independent, comprehensive, coed **Setting** Small-town campus **Enrollment** 398 **Faculty** 9:1 **Application deadline** 2/1 **Freshmen** 74% accepted **Tuition** $11,283 **Undergraduates** 50% women, 7% part-time, 17% 25 or older, 0% Native American, 0% Hispanic, 0% black, 1% Asian or Pacific Islander **Most popular recent majors** Environmental studies, interdisciplinary studies, humanities **Academic program** Advanced placement, accelerated degree program, self-designed majors, tutorials, summer session, adult/continuing education programs, internships **Contact** Ms. Shari Sterling, Director of RDP Admissions, Prescott College, Resident Degree Program, Prescott, AZ 86301-2990. Telephone: 520-776-5180. Fax: 520-776-5137.

SOUTHWESTERN COLLEGE
PHOENIX, ARIZONA

Entrance Minimally difficult **General** Independent Conservative Baptist, 4-year, coed **Setting** 17-acre urban campus **Enrollment** 185 **Faculty** 16:1 **Application deadline** 8/15 **Freshmen** 80% accepted **Housing** Yes **Tuition** $6300 **Undergraduates** 54% women, 14% part-time, 36% 25 or older, 0% Native American, 5% Hispanic, 0% black, 0% Asian or Pacific Islander **Most popular recent majors** Ministries, elementary education, pastoral studies **Academic program** Advanced placement, accelerated degree program, summer session, adult/continuing education programs, internships **Contact** Mrs. Nancy Jones, Admissions Counselor, Southwestern College, 2625 East Cactus Road, Phoenix, AZ 85032-7097. Telephone: 602-992-6101.

UNIVERSITY OF ADVANCING COMPUTER TECHNOLOGY
PHOENIX, ARIZONA

Entrance Difficulty N/R **General** Proprietary, 4-year, coed **Setting** Urban campus **Enrollment** 750 **Undergraduates** 0% part-time **Academic program** Accelerated degree program **Contact** Mr. Dominic Pistillo, President, University of Advancing Computer Technology, 4100 East Broadway Road, Suite 180, Phoenix, AZ 85040. Telephone: 602-437-0405.

UNIVERSITY OF ARIZONA
TUCSON, ARIZONA

Entrance Moderately difficult **General** State-supported, coed **Setting** 347-acre urban campus **Enrollment** 33,504 **Application deadline** 4/1 **Freshmen** 84% accepted **Housing** Yes **Tuition** $2060 **Undergraduates** 51% women, 19% part-time, 19% 25 or older, 2% Native American, 15% Hispanic, 3% black, 6% Asian or Pacific Islander **Most popular recent majors** Psychology, political science/government, elementary education **Academic program** Advanced placement, self-designed majors, tutorials, honors program, summer session, adult/continuing education programs, internships **Contact** Ms. Lori Goldman, Interim Director of Admissions, University of Arizona, Tucson, AZ 85721. Telephone: 520-621-3237. Fax: 520-621-9799.

UNIVERSITY OF PHOENIX
PHOENIX, ARIZONA

Entrance Noncompetitive **General** Proprietary, comprehensive, coed **Setting** Urban campus **Enrollment** 31,000 **Application deadline** Rolling **Freshmen** 99% accepted **Tuition** $8400 **Undergraduates** 57% women, 0% part-time, 87% 25 or older, 1% Native American, 12% Hispanic, 10% black, 2% Asian or Pacific Islander **Most popular recent majors** Business administration/commerce/management, accounting, computer information systems **Academic program** Advanced placement, accelerated degree program, adult/continuing education programs **Contact** Ms. Nina Omelchenko, Vice President of University Services, University of Phoenix, 4615 East Elwood St, PO Box 52069, Phoenix, AZ 85072-2069. Telephone: 602-966-9577 Ext. 1712.

WESTERN INTERNATIONAL UNIVERSITY
PHOENIX, ARIZONA

Entrance Moderately difficult **General** Proprietary, comprehensive, coed **Setting** 4-acre urban campus **Enrollment** 1,200 **Faculty** 15:1 **Application deadline** Rolling **Freshmen** 18% accepted **Tuition** $5280 **Undergraduates** 43% women, 0% part-time, 90% 25 or older, 1% Native American, 12% Hispanic, 7% black, 5% Asian or Pacific Islander **Most popular recent majors** Computer information systems, business administration/commerce/management, accounting **Academic program** Advanced placement, accelerated degree program, summer session, adult/continuing education programs **Contact** Ms. Jo Arney, Director of Student Services, Western International University, 9215 North Black Canyon Highway, Phoenix, AZ 85021-2718. Telephone: 602-943-2311 Ext. 139.

California

ACADEMY OF ART COLLEGE
SAN FRANCISCO, CALIFORNIA

Entrance Noncompetitive **General** Proprietary, comprehensive, specialized, coed **Setting** 3-acre urban campus **Enrollment** 4,568 **Faculty** 20:1 **Application deadline** Rolling **Housing** Yes **Tuition** $14,910 **Undergraduates** 44% women, 32% part-time, 27% 25 or older, 1% Native American, 11% Hispanic, 6% black, 20% Asian or Pacific Islander **Most popular recent majors** Graphic arts, illustration, interior design **Academic program** Tutorials, summer session, adult/continuing education programs, internships **Contact** Ms. Cynthia Donnelly, Director of Pre-Admissions, Academy of Art College, 79 New Montgomery Street, San Francisco, CA 94105-3410. Telephone: 415-274-2222. Fax: 415-546-9737.

THE ADVERTISING ARTS COLLEGE
SAN DIEGO, CALIFORNIA

Entrance Minimally difficult **General** Proprietary, 4-year, coed **Setting** Urban campus **Enrollment** 300 **Faculty** 12:1 **Application deadline** Rolling **Freshmen** 85% accepted **Tuition** $8650 **Undergraduates** 60% women, 0% part-time, 10% 25 or older, 1% Native American, 35% Hispanic, 2% black, 20% Asian or Pacific Islander **Most popular recent majors** Advertising, computer graphics, graphic arts **Academic program** Average class size 31, internships **Contact** Ms. Tracy Myers, Vice President and Director of Admissions, The Advertising Arts College, 10025 Mesa Rim Road, San Diego, CA 92121. Telephone: 619-546-0602.

THE AMERICAN COLLEGE
LOS ANGELES, CALIFORNIA

Entrance Noncompetitive **General** Proprietary, comprehensive, coed **Setting** Urban campus **Enrollment** 450 **Faculty** 10:1 **Application deadline** Rolling **Freshmen** 100% accepted **Housing** Yes **Tuition** $11,250 **Undergraduates** 68% women, 5% part-time, 3% 25 or older, 1% Native American, 5% Hispanic, 5% black, 1% Asian or Pacific Islander **Academic program** Accelerated degree program, summer session, internships **Contact** Ms. Laurie Nalepa, Director of Admissions, The American College, 1651 Westwood Boulevard, Los Angeles, CA 90024-5603. Telephone: 310-470-2000 Ext. 32. Fax: 310-477-8640.

ANTIOCH SOUTHERN CALIFORNIA/LOS ANGELES
MARINA DEL REY, CALIFORNIA

Entrance Moderately difficult **General** Independent, upper-level, coed **Setting** 1-acre urban campus **Enrollment** 552 **Faculty** 6:1 **Freshmen** 91% accepted **Tuition** $9600 **Undergraduates** 79% women, 51% part-time, 93% 25 or older, 2% Native American, 7% Hispanic, 8% black, 4% Asian or Pacific Islander **Academic program** Average class size 8, advanced placement, accelerated degree program, self-designed majors, tutorials, summer session, adult/continuing education programs, internships **Contact** Ms. Mehee Hyun, Director of Admissions, Antioch Southern California/Los Angeles, 13274 Fiji Way, Marina del Rey, CA 90292-7090. Telephone: 310-578-1080 Ext. 101. Fax: 310-822-4824.

ANTIOCH SOUTHERN CALIFORNIA/SANTA BARBARA
SANTA BARBARA, CALIFORNIA

Entrance Minimally difficult **General** Independent, upper-level, coed **Setting** Small-town campus **Enrollment** 232 **Freshmen** 100% accepted **Tuition** $8850 **Undergraduates** 80% women, 63% part-time, 95% 25 or older, 1% Native American, 6% Hispanic, 2% black, 2% Asian or Pacific Islander **Academic program** Average class size 15, accelerated degree program, self-designed majors, tutorials, summer session, adult/continuing education programs, internships **Contact** Ms. Linda Ferro, Admissions Coordinator, Antioch Southern California/Santa Barbara, Santa Barbara, CA 93101-1580. Telephone: 805-962-8179 Ext. 113. Fax: 805-962-4786.

ARMSTRONG UNIVERSITY
RICHMOND, CALIFORNIA

Entrance Moderately difficult **General** Independent, comprehensive, coed **Setting** Urban campus **Enrollment** 156 **Faculty** 3:1 **Application deadline** Rolling **Freshmen** 52% accepted **Tuition** $5985 **Undergraduates** 47% women, 6% part-time, 45% 25 or older, 3% black, 3% Asian or Pacific Islander **Most popular recent majors** International business, business administration/commerce/management, finance/banking **Academic program** Average class size 5, advanced placement, accelerated degree program, tutorials, summer session **Contact** Ms. Ziba Mahdavi, Dean of Students, Armstrong University, 3254 Pierce Street, Richmond, CA 94804. Telephone: 510-848-7902. Fax: 510-848-9438.

ART CENTER COLLEGE OF DESIGN
PASADENA, CALIFORNIA

Entrance Very difficult **General** Independent, comprehensive, specialized, coed **Setting** 175-acre suburban campus **Enrollment** 1,477 **Faculty** 5:1 **Application deadline** Rolling **Freshmen** 44% accepted **Tuition** $16,200 **Undergraduates** 36% women, 0% part-time, 39% 25 or older, 1% Native American, 8% Hispanic, 2% black,

27% Asian or Pacific Islander **Most popular recent majors** Illustration, graphic arts, industrial design **Academic program** Average class size 20, advanced placement, accelerated degree program, tutorials, summer session, adult/continuing education programs **Contact** Ms. Kit Baron, Vice President, Student Services, Art Center College of Design, Pasadena, CA 91103-1999. Telephone: 818-396-2373. Fax: 818-405-9104.

ART INSTITUTE OF SOUTHERN CALIFORNIA
LAGUNA BEACH, CALIFORNIA

Entrance Moderately difficult **General** Independent, 4-year, specialized, coed **Setting** Small-town campus **Enrollment** 181 **Faculty** 5:1 **Application deadline** Rolling **Freshmen** 73% accepted **Tuition** $10,900 **Undergraduates** 55% women, 31% part-time, 35% 25 or older, 2% Native American, 4% Hispanic, 2% black, 14% Asian or Pacific Islander **Most popular recent major** Art/fine arts **Academic program** Average class size 12, advanced placement, tutorials, summer session, adult/continuing education programs, internships **Contact** Mr. Anthony Padilla, Director of Admissions, Art Institute of Southern California, 2222 Laguna Canyon Road, Laguna Beach, CA 92651-1136. Telephone: 714-497-3309. Fax: 714-497-4399.

AZUSA PACIFIC UNIVERSITY
AZUSA, CALIFORNIA

Entrance Moderately difficult **General** Independent nondenominational, comprehensive, coed **Setting** 60-acre small-town campus **Enrollment** 4,547 **Faculty** 15:1 **Application deadline** 7/15 **Freshmen** 87% accepted **Housing** Yes **Tuition** $13,607 **Undergraduates** 60% women, 5% part-time, 1% Native American, 11% Hispanic, 4% black, 7% Asian or Pacific Islander **Most popular recent majors** Liberal arts/general studies, business administration/commerce/management, nursing **Academic program** Advanced placement, accelerated degree program, honors program, summer session, adult/continuing education programs, internships **Contact** Mrs. Deana Porterfield, Dean of Admissions, Azusa Pacific University, Azusa, CA 91702-7000. Telephone: 818-812-3016.

BETHANY COLLEGE OF THE ASSEMBLIES OF GOD
SCOTTS VALLEY, CALIFORNIA

Entrance Minimally difficult **General** Independent, comprehensive, coed, affiliated with Assemblies of God **Setting** 40-acre small-town campus **Enrollment** 699 **Faculty** 20:1 **Application deadline** 7/1 **Freshmen** 95% accepted **Housing** Yes **Tuition** $8670 **Undergraduates** 59% women, 18% part-time, 48% 25 or older, 2% Native American, 9% Hispanic, 3% black, 4% Asian or Pacific Islander **Most popular recent majors** Ministries, education, psychology **Academic program** Advanced placement, summer session, adult/continuing education programs, internships **Contact** Ms. Jennifer Bowman, Director of Admissions, Bethany College of the Assemblies of God, Scotts Valley, CA 95066-2820. Telephone: 408-438-3800 Ext. 1400. Fax: 408-438-4517.

BIOLA UNIVERSITY
LA MIRADA, CALIFORNIA

Entrance Moderately difficult **General** Independent interdenominational, coed **Setting** 95-acre suburban campus **Enrollment** 3,039 **Faculty** 19:1 **Application deadline** 6/1 **Freshmen** 55% accepted **Housing** Yes **Tuition** $14,286 **Undergraduates** 62% women, 5% part-time, 1% Native American, 9% Hispanic, 2% black, 12% Asian or Pacific Islander **Most popular recent majors** Business administration/commerce/management, communication, psychology **Academic program** Advanced placement, accelerated degree program, tutorials, honors program, summer session, adult/continuing education programs, internships **Contact** Mr. Greg Vaughan, Director of Admissions, Biola University, La Mirada, CA 90639-0001. Telephone: 562-903-4727. Fax: 562-903-4709.

BROOKS INSTITUTE OF PHOTOGRAPHY
SANTA BARBARA, CALIFORNIA

Entrance Moderately difficult **General** Proprietary, comprehensive, specialized, coed **Setting** 25-acre suburban campus **Enrollment** 351 **Faculty** 14:1 **Application deadline** Rolling **Freshmen** 39% accepted **Tuition** $14,910 **Undergraduates** 40% women, 5% part-time, 50% 25 or older **Academic program** Average class size 21, advanced placement, accelerated degree program, adult/continuing education programs, internships **Contact** Ms. Inge B. Kautzmann, Director of Admissions, Brooks Institute of Photography, Santa Barbara, CA 93108-2399. Telephone: 805-966-3888 Ext. 217. Fax: 805-564-1475.

CALIFORNIA BAPTIST COLLEGE
RIVERSIDE, CALIFORNIA

Entrance Minimally difficult **General** Independent Southern Baptist, comprehensive, coed **Setting** 60-acre suburban campus **Enrollment** 2,687 **Faculty** 16:1 **Application deadline** Rolling

Freshmen 91% accepted **Housing** Yes **Tuition** $8236 **Undergraduates** 57% women, 5% part-time, 1% Native American, 10% Hispanic, 6% black, 5% Asian or Pacific Islander **Most popular recent majors** Business administration/commerce/management, psychology, education **Academic program** Average class size 16, advanced placement, accelerated degree program, tutorials, honors program, summer session, adult/continuing education programs, internships **Contact** Mr. Phillip T. Martinez, Director of Admissions, California Baptist College, Riverside, CA 92504-3206. Telephone: 909-343-4212.

CALIFORNIA COLLEGE FOR HEALTH SCIENCES
NATIONAL CITY, CALIFORNIA

Entrance Noncompetitive **General** Proprietary, comprehensive, coed **Setting** 2-acre urban campus **Enrollment** 9,100 **Application deadline** Rolling **Undergraduates** 75% women, 100% part-time, 85% 25 or older, 10% Hispanic, 10% black, 10% Asian or Pacific Islander **Most popular recent majors** Respiratory therapy, health science, health services administration **Academic program** Accelerated degree program, internships **Contact** Ms. Gina Echito, Registrar, Director of Admissions and Records, California College for Health Sciences, 222 West 24th Street, National City, CA 91950-6605. Telephone: 619-477-4800 Ext. 320. Fax: 619-477-4360.

CALIFORNIA COLLEGE OF ARTS AND CRAFTS
SAN FRANCISCO, CALIFORNIA

Entrance Moderately difficult **General** Independent, comprehensive, specialized, coed **Setting** 4-acre urban campus **Enrollment** 1,056 **Faculty** 10:1 **Application deadline** Rolling **Freshmen** 69% accepted **Housing** Yes **Tuition** $15,052 **Undergraduates** 57% women, 9% part-time, 48% 25 or older, 1% Native American, 7% Hispanic, 4% black, 13% Asian or Pacific Islander **Most popular recent majors** Graphic arts, architecture, painting/drawing **Academic program** Average class size 15, advanced placement, self-designed majors, summer session, internships **Contact** Ms. Sheri Sivin McKenzie, Director of Enrollment Services, California College of Arts and Crafts, 450 Irwin St at 16th and Wisconsin, San Francisco, CA 94107. Telephone: 415-703-9523. Fax: 415-703-9539.

CALIFORNIA INSTITUTE OF TECHNOLOGY
PASADENA, CALIFORNIA

Entrance Most difficult **General** Independent, coed **Setting** 124-acre suburban campus **Enrollment** 1,902 **Faculty** 3:1 **Application deadline** 1/1 **Freshmen** 26% accepted **Housing** Yes **Tuition** $18,811 **Undergraduates** 26% women, 0% part-time, 0% 25 or older, 0% Native American, 5% Hispanic, 1% black, 28% Asian or Pacific Islander **Most popular recent majors** Engineering and applied sciences, physics, biology/biological sciences **Academic program** Average class size 13, self-designed majors, tutorials, internships **Contact** Ms. Charlene Liebau, Director of Admissions, California Institute of Technology, Pasadena, CA 91125-0001. Telephone: 818-395-6341. Fax: 818-683-3026.

CALIFORNIA INSTITUTE OF THE ARTS
VALENCIA, CALIFORNIA

Entrance Very difficult **General** Independent, comprehensive, coed **Setting** 60-acre suburban campus **Enrollment** 1,125 **Faculty** 8:1 **Application deadline** 2/1 **Freshmen** 39% accepted **Housing** Yes **Tuition** $17,315 **Undergraduates** 40% women, 0% part-time, 15% 25 or older, 1% Native American, 8% Hispanic, 5% black, 7% Asian or Pacific Islander **Academic program** Advanced placement, self-designed majors, tutorials, honors program, internships **Contact** Mr. Kenneth Young, Director of Admissions, California Institute of the Arts, Valencia, CA 91355-2340. Telephone: 805-255-1050 Ext. 7863.

CALIFORNIA LUTHERAN UNIVERSITY
THOUSAND OAKS, CALIFORNIA

Entrance Moderately difficult **General** Independent Lutheran, comprehensive, coed **Setting** 290-acre suburban campus **Enrollment** 2,457 **Faculty** 13:1 **Application deadline** 6/1 **Freshmen** 76% accepted **Housing** Yes **Tuition** $14,780 **Undergraduates** 55% women, 19% part-time, 32% 25 or older, 1% Native American, 14% Hispanic, 3% black, 4% Asian or Pacific Islander **Most popular recent majors** Business administration/commerce/management, liberal arts/general studies, communication **Academic program** Advanced placement, accelerated degree program, self-designed majors, tutorials, summer session, adult/continuing education programs, internships **Contact** Mr. Marc Meredith, Director of Admissions, California Lutheran University, Thousand Oaks, CA 91360-2787. Telephone: 805-493-3135. Fax: 805-493-3114.

CALIFORNIA MARITIME ACADEMY
VALLEJO, CALIFORNIA

Entrance Moderately difficult **General** State-supported, 4-year, primarily men **Setting** 67-acre suburban campus **Enrollment** 400 **Faculty** 14:1 **Application deadline** 7/1 **Freshmen** 54% accepted **Housing** Yes **Tuition** $3812 **Undergraduates** 11% women, 31% 25 or older, 2% Native American, 7% Hispanic, 4% black, 17% Asian or Pacific Islander **Academic program** Advanced placement, tutorials, summer session, internships **Contact** Ms. Bonita A. Roznos, Director of Admissions and Outreach, California Maritime Academy, P.O. Box 1392, Vallejo, CA 94590-0644. Telephone: 707-648-4222. Fax: 707-648-4204.

CALIFORNIA POLYTECHNIC STATE UNIVERSITY, SAN LUIS OBISPO

SAN LUIS OBISPO, CALIFORNIA

Entrance Moderately difficult **General** State-supported, comprehensive, coed **Setting** 6,000-acre small-town campus **Enrollment** 17,000 **Faculty** 19:1 **Application deadline** 11/30 **Freshmen** 58% accepted **Housing** Yes **Tuition** $2244 **Undergraduates** 43% women, 8% part-time, 13% 25 or older, 2% Native American, 14% Hispanic, 2% black, 13% Asian or Pacific Islander **Most popular recent majors** Business administration/commerce/management, agricultural business, mechanical engineering **Academic program** Average class size 35, advanced placement, summer session, internships **Contact** Mr. James Maraviglia, Director of Admissions and Evaluations, California Polytechnic State University, San Luis Obispo, San Luis Obispo, CA 93407. Telephone: 805-756-2311.

CALIFORNIA STATE POLYTECHNIC UNIVERSITY, POMONA

POMONA, CALIFORNIA

Entrance Moderately difficult **General** State-supported, comprehensive, coed **Setting** 1,400-acre urban campus **Enrollment** 16,803 **Faculty** 19:1 **Application deadline** Rolling **Freshmen** 60% accepted **Housing** Yes **Tuition** $1923 **Undergraduates** 42% women, 24% part-time, 24% 25 or older, 1% Native American, 21% Hispanic, 4% black, 29% Asian or Pacific Islander **Most popular recent majors** Computer information systems, electronics engineering, marketing/retailing/merchandising **Academic program** Advanced placement, accelerated degree program, summer session, adult/continuing education programs, internships **Contact** Ms. Rose M. Smith, Associate Director of Admissions, California State Polytechnic University, Pomona, 3801 West Temple Avenue, Pomona, CA 91768-2557. Telephone: 909-869-2000.

CALIFORNIA STATE UNIVERSITY, BAKERSFIELD

BAKERSFIELD, CALIFORNIA

Entrance Moderately difficult **General** State-supported, comprehensive, coed **Setting** 575-acre urban campus **Enrollment** 5,435 **Faculty** 19:1 **Application deadline** 9/23 **Freshmen** 68% accepted **Housing** Yes **Tuition** $1965 **Undergraduates** 62% women, 24% part-time, 37% 25 or older, 2% Native American, 29% Hispanic, 7% black, 8% Asian or Pacific Islander **Most popular recent majors** Education, business administration/commerce/management **Academic program** Advanced placement, accelerated degree program, self-designed majors, honors program, summer session, adult/continuing education programs, internships **Contact** Dr. Homer S. Montalvo, Associate Dean of Admissions and Records, California State University, Bakersfield, 9001 Stockdale Highway, Bakersfield, CA 93311-1022. Telephone: 805-664-2160.

CALIFORNIA STATE UNIVERSITY, CHICO

CHICO, CALIFORNIA

Entrance Moderately difficult **General** State-supported, comprehensive, coed **Setting** 119-acre small-town campus **Enrollment** 13,919 **Faculty** 19:1 **Application deadline** Rolling **Freshmen** 83% accepted **Housing** Yes **Tuition** $2075 **Undergraduates** 51% women, 11% part-time, 27% 25 or older, 2% Native American, 10% Hispanic, 3% black, 5% Asian or Pacific Islander **Most popular recent majors** Business administration/commerce/management, liberal arts/general studies, psychology **Academic program** Average class size 24, advanced placement, self-designed majors, tutorials, honors program, summer session, adult/continuing education programs, internships **Contact** Ms. Linda MacMichael, Director of Admissions, California State University, Chico, Chico, CA 95929-0722. Telephone: 916-898-4879. Fax: 916-898-6456.

CALIFORNIA STATE UNIVERSITY, DOMINGUEZ HILLS

CARSON, CALIFORNIA

Entrance Moderately difficult **General** State-supported, comprehensive, coed **Setting** 350-acre urban campus **Enrollment** 10,400 **Application deadline** Rolling **Freshmen** 76% accepted **Housing** Yes **Tuition** $1821 **Undergraduates** 65% women, 43% part-time, 50% 25 or older, 1% Native American, 32% Hispanic, 34% black, 12% Asian or Pacific Islander **Most popular recent major** Business administration/commerce/management **Academic program** Advanced placement, self-designed majors, honors program, summer session, adult/continuing education programs, internships **Contact** Information Center, California State University, Dominguez Hills, 1000 East Victoria Street, Carson, CA 90747-0001. Telephone: 310-516-3696.

CALIFORNIA STATE UNIVERSITY, FRESNO

FRESNO, CALIFORNIA

Entrance Moderately difficult **General** State-supported, comprehensive, coed **Setting** 1,410-acre urban campus **Enrollment** 17,213 **Faculty** 18:1 **Application deadline** 5/15 **Freshmen** 71% accepted **Housing** Yes **Tuition** $1806 **Undergraduates** 54% women, 8% part-time, 29% 25 or older, 1% Native American, 28% Hispanic, 6% black, 11% Asian or Pacific Islander **Most popular recent majors** Business administration/commerce/management, early childhood education, criminology **Academic program** Advanced placement, accelerated degree program, self-designed majors, summer session, adult/continuing education programs, internships **Contact** Mr. Joseph Marshall, Associate Vice President of Enrollment Services, California State University, Fresno, 5241 North Maple Avenue, Fresno, CA 93740. Telephone: 209-278-2261. Fax: 209-278-4812.

CALIFORNIA STATE UNIVERSITY, FULLERTON

FULLERTON, CALIFORNIA

Entrance Moderately difficult **General** State-supported, comprehensive, coed **Setting** 225-acre suburban campus **Enrollment** 24,040 **Faculty** 22:1 **Application deadline** Rolling **Freshmen** 84% accepted **Housing** Yes **Tuition** $1947 **Undergraduates** 56% women, 33% part-time, 30% 25 or older, 1% Native American, 18% Hispanic, 3% black, 18% Asian or Pacific Islander **Most popular recent majors** Communication, finance/banking, child psychology/child development **Academic program** Advanced placement, accelerated degree program, self-designed majors, honors program, summer session, adult/continuing education programs, internships **Contact** Ms. Nancy Dority, Admissions Director, California State University, Fullerton, PO Box 34080, Fullerton, CA 92634-9480. Telephone: 714-773-2370.

CALIFORNIA STATE UNIVERSITY, HAYWARD

HAYWARD, CALIFORNIA

Entrance Moderately difficult **General** State-supported, comprehensive, coed **Setting** 343-acre suburban campus **Enrollment** 12,734 **Application deadline** 9/12 **Freshmen** 82% accepted **Housing** Yes **Tuition** $1815 **Undergraduates** 62% women, 27% part-time, 35% 25 or older, 1% Native American, 13% Hispanic, 14% black, 31% Asian or Pacific Islander **Most popular recent majors** Business administration/commerce/management, liberal arts/general studies, computer science **Academic program** ESL program, Advanced placement, accelerated degree program, self-designed majors, honors program, summer session, adult/continuing education programs, internships **Contact** Dr. Maria DeAnda-Ramos, Director of Admissions and Outreach, California State University, Hayward, Hayward, CA 94542-3000. Telephone: 510-885-3828 Ext. f.

CALIFORNIA STATE UNIVERSITY, LONG BEACH

LONG BEACH, CALIFORNIA

Entrance Moderately difficult **General** State-supported, comprehensive, coed **Setting** 320-acre suburban campus **Enrollment** 27,431 **Faculty** 20:1 **Application deadline** 11/30 **Freshmen** 83% accepted **Housing** Yes **Tuition** $1864 **Undergraduates** 55% women, 28% part-time, 30% 25 or older, 1% Native American, 20% Hispanic, 8% black, 25% Asian or Pacific Islander **Academic program** Advanced placement, self-designed majors, tutorials, honors program, summer session, adult/continuing education programs, internships **Contact** Mr. Thomas Enders, Director of Enrollment Services, California State University, Long Beach, Long Beach, CA 90840-0119. Telephone: 562-985-4641.

CALIFORNIA STATE UNIVERSITY, LOS ANGELES

LOS ANGELES, CALIFORNIA

Entrance Moderately difficult **General** State-supported, comprehensive, coed **Setting** 173-acre urban campus **Enrollment** 18,849 **Faculty** 19:1 **Application deadline** 6/15 **Freshmen** 53% accepted **Housing** Yes **Tuition** $1754 **Undergraduates** 59% women, 31% part-time, 40% 25 or older, 1% Native American, 44% Hispanic, 9% black, 25% Asian or Pacific Islander **Most popular recent majors** Finance/banking, child psychology/child development, accounting **Academic program** ESL program, Advanced placement, accelerated degree program, self-designed majors, honors program, summer session, adult/continuing education programs **Contact** Mr. George Bachmann, Associate Director of Admissions and University Outreach, California State University, Los Angeles, 5151 State University Drive, Los Angeles, CA 90032-8530. Telephone: 213-343-3131.

CALIFORNIA STATE UNIVERSITY, NORTHRIDGE

NORTHRIDGE, CALIFORNIA

Entrance Moderately difficult **General** State-supported, comprehensive, coed **Setting** 353-acre urban campus **Enrollment** 25,020 **Application deadline** 11/30 **Freshmen** 79% accepted **Housing** Yes **Tuition** $1980 **Undergraduates** 55% women, 31% part-time, 31% 25 or older, 1% Native American, 21% Hispanic, 8% black, 13% Asian or Pacific Islander **Most popular recent majors** Business administration/commerce/management, psychology, liberal arts/general studies **Academic program** Advanced placement, accelerated degree program, self-designed majors, honors program, summer session, adult/continuing education programs **Contact** Ms. Mary Baxton, Associate Director of Admissions and Records, California State University, Northridge, 18111 Nordhoff Street, Northridge, CA 91330. Telephone: 818-677-3777. Fax: 818-677-3766.

CALIFORNIA STATE UNIVERSITY, SACRAMENTO

SACRAMENTO, CALIFORNIA

Entrance Moderately difficult **General** State-supported, comprehensive, coed **Setting** 288-acre urban campus **Enrollment** 23,420 **Application deadline** 5/1 **Freshmen** 53% accepted **Housing** Yes **Tuition** $1982 **Undergraduates** 54% women, 27% part-time, 35% 25 or older, 1% Native American, 12% Hispanic, 6% black, 15% Asian or Pacific Islander **Most popular recent majors** Business administration/commerce/management, liberal arts/general studies, engineering (general) **Academic program** Average class size 30, advanced placement, self-designed majors, tutorials, summer session, internships **Contact** Ms. Doris Tormes, Director of University Outreach Services, California State University, Sacramento, 6000 J Street, Sacramento, CA 95819-6048. Telephone: 916-278-7362.

CALIFORNIA STATE UNIVERSITY, SAN BERNARDINO

SAN BERNARDINO, CALIFORNIA

Entrance Moderately difficult **General** State-supported, comprehensive, coed **Setting** 430-acre suburban campus **Enrollment** 12,153 **Faculty** 19:1 **Application deadline** Rolling **Freshmen** 70% accepted **Housing** Yes **Tuition** $1896 **Undergraduates** 59% women, 34% part-time, 38% 25 or older, 1% Native American, 20% Hispanic, 9% black, 8% Asian or Pacific Islander **Most popular recent majors** Business administration/commerce/management, humanities, social science **Academic program** Advanced placement, self-designed majors, honors program, summer session, adult/continuing education programs **Contact** Mrs. Cheryl Smith, Associate Vice President for Enrollment Services, California State University, San Bernardino, 5500 University Parkway, San Bernardino, CA 92407-2397. Telephone: 909-880-5188.

CALIFORNIA STATE UNIVERSITY, SAN MARCOS

SAN MARCOS, CALIFORNIA

Entrance Moderately difficult **General** State-supported, comprehensive, coed **Setting** 302-acre suburban campus **Enrollment** 3,841 **Application deadline** Rolling **Freshmen** 79% accepted **Housing** Yes **Tuition** $1720 **Undergraduates** 63% women, 51% part-time, 52% 25 or older, 2% Native American, 16% Hispanic, 4% black, 8% Asian or Pacific Islander **Academic program** Advanced placement, self-designed majors, honors program, summer session, internships **Contact** Mr. Richard Riehl, Executive Director of Enrollment Services, California State University, San Marcos, San Marcos, CA 92096. Telephone: 619-750-4810. Fax: 619-750-4030.

CALIFORNIA STATE UNIVERSITY, STANISLAUS

TURLOCK, CALIFORNIA

Entrance Moderately difficult **General** State-supported, comprehensive, coed **Setting** 220-acre small-town campus **Enrollment** 6,100 **Faculty** 18:1 **Application deadline** 7/31 **Freshmen** 95% accepted **Housing** Yes **Tuition** $1915 **Undergraduates** 79% women, 24% part-time, 39% 25 or older, 2% Native American, 22% Hispanic, 4% black, 10% Asian or Pacific Islander **Most popular recent majors** Liberal arts/general studies, business administration/commerce/management, psychology **Academic program** Advanced placement, accelerated degree program, self-designed majors, tutorials, honors program, summer session, adult/continuing education programs, internships **Contact** Admissions Office, California State University, Stanislaus, Turlock, CA 95382. Telephone: 209-667-3070. Fax: 209-667-3333.

CHAPMAN UNIVERSITY
ORANGE, CALIFORNIA

Entrance Moderately difficult **General** Independent, comprehensive, coed, affiliated with Christian Church (Disciples of Christ) **Setting** 40-acre suburban campus **Enrollment** 3,673 **Faculty** 11:1 **Application deadline** 3/1 **Freshmen** 76% accepted **Housing** Yes **Tuition** $18,750 **Undergraduates** 56% women, 8% part-time, 20% 25 or older, 1% Native American, 14% Hispanic, 6% black, 8% Asian or Pacific Islander **Most popular recent majors** Communication, business administration/commerce/management, liberal arts/general studies **Academic program** Advanced placement, accelerated degree program, self-designed majors, tutorials, honors program, summer session, adult/continuing education programs, internships **Contact** Mr. Michael Drummy, Director of Admissions, Chapman University, Orange, CA 92866. Telephone: 714-997-6711.

CHARLES R. DREW UNIVERSITY OF MEDICINE AND SCIENCE
LOS ANGELES, CALIFORNIA

Entrance Moderately difficult **General** Independent, comprehensive, specialized, coed **Enrollment** 320 **Application deadline** 2/28 **Freshmen** 20% accepted **Tuition** $6850 **Contact** Dr. Theodore Miller, Associate Dean for Student Affairs, Charles R. Drew University of Medicine and Science, Los Angeles, CA 90059. Telephone: 213-563-4987.

CHRISTIAN HERITAGE COLLEGE
EL CAJON, CALIFORNIA

Entrance Moderately difficult **General** Independent nondenominational, 4-year, coed **Setting** 32-acre suburban campus **Enrollment** 555 **Faculty** 15:1 **Application deadline** Rolling **Freshmen** 97% accepted **Housing** Yes **Tuition** $9600 **Undergraduates** 58% women, 10% part-time, 46% 25 or older, 1% Native American, 7% Hispanic, 6% black, 4% Asian or Pacific Islander **Most popular recent majors** Business administration/commerce/management, psychology, elementary education **Academic program** Average class size 25, advanced placement, self-designed majors, tutorials, summer session, adult/continuing education programs, internships **Contact** Mr. Paul Berry, Vice President of Enrollment Management/Registrar, Christian Heritage College, El Cajon, CA 92019-1157. Telephone: 619-441-2200.

CLAREMONT MCKENNA COLLEGE
CLAREMONT, CALIFORNIA

Entrance Very difficult **General** Independent, 4-year, coed **Setting** 50-acre small-town campus **Enrollment** 954 **Faculty** 9:1 **Application deadline** 1/15 **Freshmen** 29% accepted **Housing** Yes **Tuition** $19,020 **Undergraduates** 44% women, 1% part-time, 1% 25 or older, 1% Native American, 11% Hispanic, 4% black, 20% Asian or Pacific Islander **Most popular recent majors** Economics, political science/government, psychology **Academic program** Advanced placement, accelerated degree program, self-designed majors, tutorials, honors program, internships **Contact** Mr. Richard C. Vos, Vice President/Dean of Admission and Financial Aid, Claremont McKenna College, Claremont, CA 91711. Telephone: 909-621-8088.

COGSWELL POLYTECHNICAL COLLEGE
SUNNYVALE, CALIFORNIA

Entrance Moderately difficult **General** Independent, 4-year, coed **Setting** 2-acre suburban campus **Enrollment** 458 **Faculty** 10:1 **Application deadline** Rolling **Freshmen** 95% accepted **Tuition** $7360 **Undergraduates** 10% women, 64% part-time, 50% 25 or older, 0% Native American, 10% Hispanic, 3% black, 35% Asian or Pacific Islander **Most popular recent majors** Computer graphics, musical instrument technology, electronics engineering technology **Academic program** Average class size 14, advanced placement, accelerated degree program, self-designed majors, tutorials, honors program, summer session, adult/continuing education programs, internships **Contact** Dr. James T. Thompson, President, Cogswell Polytechnical College, Sunnyvale, CA 94089-1299. Telephone: 408-541-0100 Ext. 103. Fax: 408-747-0764.

COLEMAN COLLEGE
LA MESA, CALIFORNIA

Entrance Moderately difficult **General** Independent, comprehensive, coed **Setting** Suburban campus **Enrollment** 930 **Faculty** 15:1 **Application deadline** Rolling **Freshmen** 51% accepted **Tuition** $9000 **Undergraduates** 25% women, 10% part-time, 68% 25 or older, 1% Native American, 9% Hispanic, 8% black, 9% Asian or Pacific Islander **Most popular recent majors** Information science, computer technologies, secretarial studies/office management **Academic program** Accelerated degree program, summer session **Contact** Admissions Department, Coleman College, 7380 Parkway Drive, La Mesa, CA 91942-1532. Telephone: 619-465-3990. Fax: 619-465-0162.

COLLEGE OF NOTRE DAME
BELMONT, CALIFORNIA

Entrance Moderately difficult **General** Independent Roman Catholic, comprehensive, coed **Setting** 80-acre suburban campus **Enrollment** 1,743 **Faculty** 10:1 **Application deadline** 6/1 **Freshmen** 82% accepted **Housing** Yes **Tuition** $14,976 **Undergraduates** 73% women, 37% part-time, 48% 25 or older, 0% Native American, 16% Hispanic, 7% black, 13% Asian or Pacific Islander **Most popular recent majors** Business administration/commerce/management, psychology, liberal arts/general studies **Academic program** Average class size 15, advanced placement, accelerated degree program, self-designed majors, tutorials, summer session, adult/continuing education programs, internships **Contact** Dr. Gregory Smith, Director of Admission, College of Notre Dame, Belmont, CA 94002-1997. Telephone: 415-508-3607. Fax: 415-637-0493.

COLUMBIA COLLEGE–HOLLYWOOD
HOLLYWOOD, CALIFORNIA

Entrance Minimally difficult **General** Independent, 4-year, coed **Setting** 1-acre urban campus **Enrollment** 234 **Application deadline** Rolling **Freshmen** 95% accepted **Tuition** $6705 **Undergraduates** 23% women, 0% part-time, 35% 25 or older, 1% Native American, 6% Hispanic, 6% black, 4% Asian or Pacific Islander **Academic program** Accelerated degree program, summer session, adult/continuing education programs **Contact** Ms. Natasha Kobrinsky, Student Affairs Officer, Columbia College–Hollywood, 925 North La Brea Avenue, Hollywood, CA 90038-2392. Telephone: 213-851-0550. Fax: 213-851-6401.

CONCORDIA UNIVERSITY
IRVINE, CALIFORNIA

Entrance Moderately difficult **General** Independent, comprehensive, coed, affiliated with Lutheran Church–Missouri Synod **Setting** 70-acre suburban campus **Enrollment** 1,027 **Faculty** 18:1 **Application deadline** Rolling **Freshmen** 83% accepted **Housing** Yes **Tuition** $13,800 **Undergraduates** 63% women, 12% part-time, 10% 25 or older, 1% Native American, 8% Hispanic, 4% black, 8% Asian or Pacific Islander **Most popular recent majors** Education, business administration/commerce/management, behavioral sciences **Academic program** Average class size 20, advanced placement, self-designed majors, honors program, summer session, adult/continuing education programs, internships **Contact** Mr. W. Stan Meyer, Vice President of Enrollment Services, Concordia University, Irvine, CA 92612-3299. Telephone: 714-854-8002 Ext. 108. Fax: 714-854-6854.

DESIGN INSTITUTE OF SAN DIEGO
SAN DIEGO, CALIFORNIA

Entrance Noncompetitive **General** Proprietary, 4-year, specialized, coed **Setting** Urban campus **Enrollment** 215 **Faculty** 11:1 **Application deadline** Rolling **Freshmen** 84% accepted **Tuition** $9200 **Undergraduates** 90% women, 28% part-time, 70% 25 or older, 9% Hispanic, 1% black, 5% Asian or Pacific Islander **Academic program** Internships **Contact** Ms. Paula Parrish, Director of Admissions, Design Institute of San Diego, 8555 Commerce Avenue, San Diego, CA 92121-2685. Telephone: 619-566-1200. Fax: 619-4DESIGN.

DEVRY INSTITUTE OF TECHNOLOGY
LONG BEACH, CALIFORNIA

Entrance Minimally difficult **General** Proprietary, 4-year, coed **Setting** Urban campus **Enrollment** 1,366 **Faculty** 18:1 **Application deadline** Rolling **Freshmen** 74% accepted **Tuition** $6968 **Undergraduates** 25% women, 22% part-time, 48% 25 or older, 1% Native American, 23% Hispanic, 16% black, 18% Asian or Pacific Islander **Most popular recent majors** Computer information systems, electrical and electronics technologies, telecommunications **Academic program** Advanced placement, summer session **Contact** Ms. Elaine Francisco, Director of Admissions, DeVry Institute of Technology, 3880 Kilroy Airport Way, Long Beach, CA 90806. Telephone: 310-427-4162.

DEVRY INSTITUTE OF TECHNOLOGY
POMONA, CALIFORNIA

Entrance Minimally difficult **General** Proprietary, 4-year, coed **Setting** 15-acre urban campus **Enrollment** 3,037 **Faculty** 26:1 **Application deadline** Rolling **Freshmen** 76% accepted **Tuition** $6968 **Undergraduates** 23% women, 24% part-time, 48% 25 or older, 0% Native American, 22% Hispanic, 9% black, 14% Asian or Pacific Islander **Most popular recent majors** Telecommunications, computer information systems, electrical and electronics technologies **Academic program** Advanced placement, accelerated degree program, summer session, adult/continuing education programs **Contact** Mr. Keith Paridy, Director of Admissions, DeVry Institute of Technology, 901 Corporate Center Drive, Pomona, CA 91768-2642. Telephone: 909-622-9800.

DOMINICAN COLLEGE OF SAN RAFAEL
SAN RAFAEL, CALIFORNIA

Entrance Moderately difficult **General** Independent Roman Catholic, comprehensive, coed **Setting** 80-acre suburban campus **Enrollment** 1,417 **Faculty** 12:1 **Application deadline** Rolling **Freshmen** 81% accepted **Housing** Yes **Tuition** $15,424 **Undergraduates** 80% women, 41% part-time, 67% 25 or older, 1% Native American, 10% Hispanic, 6% black, 12% Asian or Pacific Islander **Most popular recent majors** Nursing, psychology, business administration/commerce/management **Academic program** Advanced placement, self-designed majors, tutorials, honors program, summer session, adult/continuing education programs, internships **Contact** Mr. Allen Gallaway, Director of Freshman Admissions, Dominican College of San Rafael, San Rafael, CA 94901-2298. Telephone: 415-485-3204. Fax: 415-485-3214.

DOMINICAN SCHOOL OF PHILOSOPHY AND THEOLOGY
BERKELEY, CALIFORNIA

Entrance Moderately difficult **General** Independent Roman Catholic, upper-level, specialized, coed **Setting** Urban campus **Enrollment** 93 **Faculty** 5:1 **Freshmen** 100% accepted **Housing** Yes **Tuition** $7130 **Undergraduates** 22% part-time, 100% 25 or older, 0% Native American, 22% Hispanic, 0% black, 0% Asian or Pacific Islander **Academic program** Tutorials **Contact** Ms. Cheryl A. Trainor, Director of Admissions and Registrar, Dominican School of Philosophy and Theology, 2401 Ridge Road, Berkeley, CA 94709-1295. Telephone: 510-883-2085.

FRESNO PACIFIC UNIVERSITY
FRESNO, CALIFORNIA

Entrance Moderately difficult **General** Independent, comprehensive, coed, affiliated with Mennonite Brethren Church **Setting** 42-acre suburban campus **Enrollment** 1,000 **Faculty** 15:1 **Application deadline** Rolling **Freshmen** 78% accepted **Housing** Yes **Tuition** $11,936 **Undergraduates** 65% women, 4% part-time, 32% 25 or older, 2% Native American, 14% Hispanic, 3% black, 3% Asian or Pacific Islander **Most popular recent majors** Business administration/commerce/management, liberal arts/general studies, social science **Academic program** Advanced placement, self-designed majors, summer session, adult/continuing education programs, internships **Contact** Mr. Cary Templeton, Director of Admissions, Fresno Pacific University, Fresno, CA 93702-4709. Telephone: 209-453-2030. Fax: 209-453-2007.

GOLDEN GATE UNIVERSITY
SAN FRANCISCO, CALIFORNIA

Entrance Moderately difficult **General** Independent, coed **Setting** Urban campus **Enrollment** 6,119 **Application deadline** Rolling **Freshmen** 91% accepted **Tuition** $7680 **Undergraduates** 57% women, 75% part-time, 71% 25 or older, 1% Native American, 7% Hispanic, 7% black, 14% Asian or Pacific Islander **Most popular recent majors** Business administration/commerce/management, human resources, accounting **Academic program** Advanced placement, accelerated degree program, summer session, adult/continuing education programs, internships **Contact** Mr. Archie Porter, Vice President Enrollment Services, Golden Gate University, 536 Mission Street, San Francisco, CA 94105-2968. Telephone: 415-442-7800. Fax: 415-442-7857.

HARVEY MUDD COLLEGE
CLAREMONT, CALIFORNIA

Entrance Most difficult **General** Independent, comprehensive, coed **Setting** 33-acre suburban campus **Enrollment** 648 **Faculty** 8:1 **Application deadline** 1/15 **Freshmen** 46% accepted **Housing** Yes **Tuition** $20,325 **Undergraduates** 25% women, 0% part-time, 1% 25 or older, 1% Native American, 5% Hispanic, 1% black, 22% Asian or Pacific Islander **Most popular recent majors** Engineering (general), computer science, chemistry **Academic program** Advanced placement, self-designed majors, tutorials **Contact** Ms. Patricia Coleman, Dean of Admission, Harvey Mudd College, Claremont, CA 91711-5994. Telephone: 909-621-8011.

HOLY NAMES COLLEGE
OAKLAND, CALIFORNIA

Entrance Moderately difficult **General** Independent Roman Catholic, comprehensive, coed **Setting** 60-acre urban campus **Enrollment** 923 **Faculty** 6:1 **Application deadline** 8/1 **Freshmen** 70% accepted **Housing** Yes **Tuition** $13,870 **Undergraduates** 80% women, 60% part-time, 25% 25 or older, 1% Native American, 9% Hispanic, 28% black, 8% Asian or Pacific Islander **Most popular recent majors** Nursing, business administration/commerce/management, human services **Academic program** Advanced placement, self-designed majors, honors program, summer session, adult/continuing education programs, internships **Contact** Ms. Joanne Lopez-Hayden, Director of Admissions, Holy Names College, 3500 Mountain Boulevard, Oakland, CA 94619-1699. Telephone: 510-436-1321. Fax: 510-436-1199.

HOPE INTERNATIONAL UNIVERSITY
FULLERTON, CALIFORNIA

Entrance Minimally difficult **General** Independent, comprehensive, coed, affiliated with Christian Churches and Churches of Christ **Setting** 16-acre suburban campus **Enrollment** 841 **Faculty** 16:1 **Application deadline** 7/1 **Freshmen** 90% accepted **Housing** Yes **Tuition** $9265 **Undergraduates** 50% women, 17% part-time, 35% 25 or older, 1% Native American, 12% Hispanic, 1% black, 4% Asian or Pacific Islander **Most popular recent majors** Ministries, elementary education, psychology **Academic program** Advanced placement, accelerated degree program, self-designed majors, honors program, summer session, adult/continuing education programs, internships **Contact** Admissions Office, Hope International University, Fullerton, CA 92631-3138. Telephone: 714-879-3901. Fax: 714-526-0231.

HUMBOLDT STATE UNIVERSITY
ARCATA, CALIFORNIA

Entrance Moderately difficult **General** State-supported, comprehensive, coed **Setting** 161-acre rural campus **Enrollment** 7,686 **Faculty** 17:1 **Application deadline** 11/30 **Freshmen** 76% accepted **Housing** Yes **Tuition** $1926 **Undergraduates** 51% women, 9% part-time, 32% 25 or older, 3% Native American, 8% Hispanic, 2% black, 4% Asian or Pacific Islander **Most popular recent majors** Biology/biological sciences, elementary education, business administration/commerce/management **Academic program** Advanced placement, accelerated degree program, self-designed majors, tutorials, summer session, adult/continuing education programs, internships **Contact** Office of Admissions and School Relations, Humboldt State University, Arcata, CA 95521-8299. Telephone: 707-826-4402. Fax: 707-826-6194.

HUMPHREYS COLLEGE
STOCKTON, CALIFORNIA

Entrance Noncompetitive **General** Independent, comprehensive, coed **Setting** 10-acre suburban campus **Enrollment** 1,083 **Faculty** 11:1 **Application deadline** Rolling **Freshmen** 96% accepted **Housing** Yes **Tuition** $6258 **Undergraduates** 85% women, 36% part-time, 70% 25 or older, 1% Native American, 17% Hispanic, 7% black, 4% Asian or Pacific Islander **Most popular recent majors** Court reporting, paralegal studies, business administration/commerce/management **Academic program** Average class size 15, advanced placement, accelerated degree program, self-designed majors, tutorials, summer session, adult/continuing education programs, internships **Contact** Mrs. Pamela Knapp, Admission Counselor, Humphreys College, Stockton, CA 95207-3896. Telephone: 209-478-0800. Fax: 209-478-8721.

JOHN F. KENNEDY UNIVERSITY
ORINDA, CALIFORNIA

Entrance Noncompetitive **General** Independent, comprehensive, coed **Setting** 14-acre suburban campus **Enrollment** 1,859 **Tuition** $9252 **Undergraduates** 81% women, 89% part-time, 93% 25 or older, 3% Native American, 5% Hispanic, 5% black, 3% Asian or Pacific Islander **Academic program** Advanced placement, self-designed majors, summer session, adult/continuing education programs **Contact** Admissions and Records Office, John F. Kennedy University, Orinda, CA 94563-2689. Telephone: 510-258-2213. Fax: 510-254-6964.

LA SIERRA UNIVERSITY
RIVERSIDE, CALIFORNIA

Entrance Minimally difficult **General** Independent Seventh-day Adventist, comprehensive, coed **Setting** 630-acre suburban campus **Enrollment** 1,607 **Faculty** 13:1 **Application deadline** Rolling **Freshmen** 76% accepted **Housing** Yes **Tuition** $13,905 **Undergraduates** 53% women, 9% part-time, 12% 25 or older, 1% Native American, 22% Hispanic, 5% black, 31% Asian or Pacific Islander **Most popular recent majors** Business administration/commerce/management, biology/biological sciences, elementary education **Academic program** Average class size 20, advanced placement, accelerated degree program, self-designed majors, tutorials, honors program, summer session, adult/continuing education programs, internships **Contact** Mr. Cyril Connelly, Director of Enrollment Services, La Sierra University, Riverside, CA 92515. Telephone: 909-785-2118. Fax: 909-785-2901.

LEE COLLEGE AT THE UNIVERSITY OF JUDAISM
SEE UNIVERSITY OF JUDAISM

LIFE BIBLE COLLEGE
SAN DIMAS, CALIFORNIA

Entrance Minimally difficult **General** Independent, 4-year, specialized, coed, affiliated with International Church of the Foursquare Gospel **Setting** 9-acre suburban campus **Enrollment** 411 **Faculty** 16:1 **Application deadline** 7/15 **Freshmen** 91% accepted **Housing** Yes **Tuition** $4880 **Undergraduates** 48% women, 25% part-time, 25% 25 or older, 8% Hispanic, 3% black, 4% Asian or Pacific Islander **Academic program** Advanced placement, summer session, internships **Contact** Ms. Linda Hibdon, Director of Admissions, LIFE Bible College, San Dimas, CA 91773-3298. Telephone: 909-599-5433 Ext. 310.

LINCOLN UNIVERSITY
SAN FRANCISCO, CALIFORNIA

Entrance Minimally difficult **General** Independent, comprehensive, coed **Setting** 2-acre urban campus **Enrollment** 369 **Application deadline** 8/31 **Freshmen** 92% accepted **Tuition** $5245 **Undergraduates** 28% women, 0% part-time, 58% 25 or older, 0% Native American, 1% Hispanic, 0% black, 1% Asian or Pacific Islander **Most popular recent majors** Business administration/commerce/management, computer science **Academic program** Average class size 20, advanced placement, tutorials, summer session, internships **Contact** Ms. Vivian Xu, Admissions Officer, Lincoln University, 281 Masonic Avenue, San Francisco, CA 94118-4498. Telephone: 415-221-1212 Ext. 115. Fax: 415-387-9730.

LOMA LINDA UNIVERSITY
LOMA LINDA, CALIFORNIA

Entrance Difficulty N/R **General** Independent Seventh-day Adventist, coed **Setting** Small-town campus **Enrollment** 3,308 **Housing** Yes **Tuition** $11,970 **Undergraduates** 71% women, 20% part-time, 2% black **Contact** Dr. Tony Valenzuela, Director of Marketing, Loma Linda University, Loma Linda, CA 92350. Telephone: 909-824-4792.

LOUISE SALINGER ACADEMY OF FASHION
SAN FRANCISCO, CALIFORNIA

Entrance Moderately difficult **General** Independent, 4-year, specialized, coed **Setting** Urban campus **Enrollment** 200 **Faculty** 15:1 **Application deadline** Rolling **Freshmen** 89% accepted **Tuition** $12,540 **Undergraduates** 70% women, 40% part-time, 50% 25 or older, 0% Native American, 3% Hispanic, 6% black, 23% Asian or Pacific Islander **Most popular recent majors** Fashion design and technology, fashion merchandising **Academic program** Accelerated degree program, tutorials, summer session **Contact** Mr. Joe Herschelle, Director of Admissions, Louise Salinger Academy of Fashion, 101 Jessie Street, San Francisco, CA 94105-3507. Telephone: 415-974-6666. Fax: 415-982-0113.

LOYOLA MARYMOUNT UNIVERSITY
LOS ANGELES, CALIFORNIA

Entrance Moderately difficult **General** Independent Roman Catholic, comprehensive, coed **Setting** 128-acre suburban campus **Enrollment** 6,729 **Faculty** 14:1 **Application deadline** 2/1 **Freshmen** 66% accepted **Housing** Yes **Tuition** $16,495 **Undergraduates** 57% women, 7% part-time, 8% 25 or older, 1% Native American, 21% Hispanic, 8% black, 14% Asian or Pacific Islander **Most popular recent majors** Business administration/commerce/management, communication, psychology **Academic program** Average class size 20, advanced placement, accelerated degree program, self-designed majors, tutorials, honors program, summer session, adult/continuing education programs, internships **Contact** Mr. Matthew X. Fissinger, Director of Admissions, Loyola Marymount University, Los Angeles, CA 90045-8350. Telephone: 310-338-2750. Fax: 310-338-2797.

THE MASTER'S COLLEGE AND SEMINARY
SANTA CLARITA, CALIFORNIA

Entrance Moderately difficult **General** Independent nondenominational, coed **Setting** 100-acre suburban campus **Enrollment** 793 **Application deadline** Rolling **Freshmen** 73% accepted **Housing** Yes **Tuition** $12,180 **Undergraduates** 53% women, 7% part-time, 9% 25 or older, 1% Native American, 4% Hispanic, 2% black, 3% Asian or Pacific Islander **Most popular recent majors** Biblical studies, liberal arts/general studies, business administration/commerce/management **Academic program** Advanced placement, accelerated degree program, tutorials, summer session, adult/continuing education programs, internships **Contact** Mr. Yaphet Peterson, Director of Enrollment, The Master's College and Seminary, Santa Clarita, CA 91321-1200. Telephone: 805-259-3540 Ext. 368. Fax: 805-254-1998.

MENLO COLLEGE
ATHERTON, CALIFORNIA

Entrance Minimally difficult **General** Independent, 4-year, coed **Setting** Small-town campus **Enrollment** 516 **Faculty** 20:1 **Application deadline** Rolling **Freshmen** 91% accepted **Housing** Yes **Tuition** $16,180 **Undergraduates** 39% women, 4% part-time, 20% 25 or older, 0% Native American, 9% Hispanic, 7% black, 15% Asian or

Pacific Islander **Most popular recent majors** Business administration/commerce/management, communication **Academic program** Average class size 20, advanced placement, accelerated degree program, tutorials, honors program, summer session, adult/continuing education programs, internships **Contact** Mr. Guy R. Adams, Vice President of Admissions, Menlo College, Atherton, CA 94027-4301. Telephone: 415-688-3761. Fax: 415-617-2395.

MILLS COLLEGE
OAKLAND, CALIFORNIA

Entrance Moderately difficult **General** Independent, comprehensive, women only **Setting** 135-acre urban campus **Enrollment** 1,182 **Faculty** 12:1 **Application deadline** Rolling **Freshmen** 84% accepted **Housing** Yes **Tuition** $16,522 **Undergraduates** 8% part-time, 28% 25 or older, 1% Native American, 7% Hispanic, 8% black, 10% Asian or Pacific Islander **Most popular recent majors** English, political, legal, and economic analysis, communication **Academic program** Advanced placement, accelerated degree program, self-designed majors, tutorials, adult/continuing education programs, internships **Contact** Ms. Jean Flaherty, Dean of Admission and Enrollment Planning, Mills College, 5000 MacArthur Boulevard, Oakland, CA 94613-1000. Telephone: 510-430-2135. Fax: 510-430-3314.

MONTEREY INSTITUTE OF INTERNATIONAL STUDIES
MONTEREY, CALIFORNIA

Entrance Moderately difficult **General** Independent, upper-level, coed **Setting** 5-acre small-town campus **Enrollment** 721 **Freshmen** 72% accepted **Tuition** $17,245 **Undergraduates** 55% women, 1% part-time, 25% 25 or older, 0% Native American, 5% Hispanic, 2% black, 5% Asian or Pacific Islander **Academic program** Honors program, summer session, internships **Contact** Ms. Jane Roberts, Admissions Officer, Monterey Institute of International Studies, Monterey, CA 93940-2691. Telephone: 408-647-4124.

MOUNT ST. MARY'S COLLEGE
LOS ANGELES, CALIFORNIA

Entrance Moderately difficult **General** Independent Roman Catholic, comprehensive, primarily women **Setting** 71-acre suburban campus **Enrollment** 1,411 **Faculty** 12:1 **Application deadline** Rolling **Freshmen** 63% accepted **Housing** Yes **Tuition** $15,216 **Undergraduates** 97% women, 5% part-time, 20% 25 or older, 1% Native American, 35% Hispanic, 7% black, 24% Asian or Pacific Islander **Most popular recent majors** Nursing, liberal arts/general studies, business administration/commerce/management **Academic program** Advanced placement, self-designed majors, tutorials, honors program, summer session, adult/continuing education programs, internships **Contact** Ms. Katy Murphy, Executive Director of Admissions and Financial Aid, Mount St. Mary's College, Los Angeles, CA 90049-1597. Telephone: 310-476-2237 Ext. 516. Fax: 310-476-9296.

MUSICIANS INSTITUTE
HOLLYWOOD, CALIFORNIA

Entrance Minimally difficult **General** Proprietary, 4-year, specialized, coed **Application deadline** Rolling **Tuition** $12,000 **Contact** Mr. Steve Lunn, Admissions Representative, Musicians Institute, Hollywood, CA 90028. Telephone: 213-462-1384 Ext. 156.

THE NATIONAL HISPANIC UNIVERSITY
SAN JOSE, CALIFORNIA

Entrance Minimally difficult **General** Independent, 4-year, coed **Setting** 1-acre urban campus **Enrollment** 300 **Faculty** 10:1 **Application deadline** 8/15 **Freshmen** 82% accepted **Tuition** $3875 **Undergraduates** 65% women, 70% part-time, 40% 25 or older, 0% Native American, 90% Hispanic, 5% black, 2% Asian or Pacific Islander **Academic program** Average class size 10, advanced placement, accelerated degree program, tutorials, summer session, adult/continuing education programs, internships **Contact** Ms. Leticia Vallejo, Director of Admissions, The National Hispanic University, 14271 Story Road, San Jose, CA 95127-3823. Telephone: 408-254-6900 Ext. 17.

NATIONAL UNIVERSITY
LA JOLLA, CALIFORNIA

Entrance Noncompetitive **General** Independent, comprehensive, coed **Setting** 15-acre urban campus **Application deadline** Rolling **Freshmen** 100% accepted **Tuition** $6660 **Undergraduates** 49% women, 56% part-time, 86% 25 or older, 1% Native American, 12% Hispanic, 11% black, 8% Asian or Pacific Islander **Most popular recent majors** Business administration/commerce/management, computer science, psychology **Academic program** Advanced placement, accelerated degree program, summer session, adult/continuing education programs **Contact** Admission Department, National University, 11255 North Torrey Pines Road, La Jolla, CA 92037-1011. Telephone: 619-563-7100. Fax: 619-563-7395.

NEW COLLEGE OF CALIFORNIA
SAN FRANCISCO, CALIFORNIA

Entrance Noncompetitive **General** Independent, comprehensive, coed **Setting** Urban campus **Enrollment** 1,600 **Application deadline** Rolling **Freshmen** 90% accepted **Tuition** $8376 **Undergraduates** 55% women, 25% part-time, 50% 25 or older, 8% Native American, 10% Hispanic, 18% black, 2% Asian or Pacific Islander **Academic program** ESL program, Advanced placement, accelerated degree program, self-designed majors, tutorials, internships **Contact** Ms. Colleen O'Neal, Interim Director of Admissions, New College of California, 50 Fell Street, San Francisco, CA 94102-5206. Telephone: 415-437-3460 Ext. 381. Fax: 415-626-5541.

NEWSCHOOL OF ARCHITECTURE
SAN DIEGO, CALIFORNIA

Entrance Minimally difficult **General** Proprietary, comprehensive, coed **Setting** Urban campus **Enrollment** 93 **Faculty** 10:1 **Application deadline** 8/15 **Freshmen** 33% accepted **Housing** Yes **Tuition** $10,080 **Undergraduates** 30% women, 10% part-time, 65% 25 or older, 0% Native American, 30% Hispanic, 10% black, 10% Asian or Pacific Islander **Most popular recent majors** Architecture, graphic arts, architectural technologies **Academic program** Advanced placement, tutorials, summer session, adult/continuing education programs, internships **Contact** Ms. Katie Gent, Director of Admissions, Newschool of Architecture, 1249 F Street, San Diego, CA 92101-6634. Telephone: 619-235-4100 Ext. 112.

NORTHROP-RICE AVIATION INSTITUTE OF TECHNOLOGY
INGLEWOOD, CALIFORNIA

Entrance Noncompetitive **General** Proprietary, comprehensive, specialized, primarily men **Setting** Urban campus **Enrollment** 220 **Application deadline** Rolling **Freshmen** 99% accepted **Tuition** $11,583 **Contact** Mr. Bill Robinson, Director of Admissions, Northrop-Rice Aviation Institute of Technology, 8911 Aviation Boulevard, Inglewood, CA 90301-2904. Telephone: 310-337-4444.

OCCIDENTAL COLLEGE
LOS ANGELES, CALIFORNIA

Entrance Very difficult **General** Independent, comprehensive, coed **Setting** 136-acre urban campus **Enrollment** 1,534 **Faculty** 10:1 **Application deadline** 1/15 **Freshmen** 73% accepted **Housing** Yes **Tuition** $19,974 **Undergraduates** 57% women, 2% part-time, 3% 25 or older, 1% Native American, 21% Hispanic, 7% black, 19% Asian or Pacific Islander **Most popular recent majors** Psychology, English, biology/biological sciences **Academic program** Advanced placement, accelerated degree program, self-designed majors, tutorials, honors program, summer session, internships **Contact** Ms. Amy Abrams, Director of Admissions, Occidental College, 1600 Campus Road, Los Angeles, CA 90041-3392. Telephone: 213-259-2700. Fax: 213-259-2958.

OTIS COLLEGE OF ART AND DESIGN
LOS ANGELES, CALIFORNIA

Entrance Moderately difficult **General** Independent, comprehensive, specialized, coed **Setting** 5-acre urban campus **Enrollment** 771 **Application deadline** Rolling **Freshmen** 71% accepted **Tuition** $15,350 **Undergraduates** 60% women, 30% 25 or older, 1% Native American, 17% Hispanic, 5% black, 27% Asian or Pacific Islander **Academic program** Average class size 25, advanced placement, self-designed majors, tutorials, summer session, adult/continuing education programs, internships **Contact** Mr. Michael Fuller, Director of Admissions, Otis College of Art and Design, 9045 Lincoln Boulevard, Los Angeles, CA 90045-9785. Telephone: 310-665-6800. Fax: 310-665-6805.

PACIFIC CHRISTIAN COLLEGE
SEE HOPE INTERNATIONAL UNIVERSITY

PACIFIC OAKS COLLEGE
PASADENA, CALIFORNIA

Entrance Noncompetitive **General** Independent, upper-level, coed **Setting** 2-acre small-town campus **Enrollment** 600 **Tuition** $12,305 **Undergraduates** 95% women, 61% part-time, 90% 25 or older, 1% Native American, 8% Hispanic, 11% black, 5% Asian or Pacific Islander **Academic program** Average class size 24, summer session, adult/continuing education programs, internships **Contact** Ms. Marsha Franker, Director of Admissions, Pacific Oaks College, Pasadena, CA 91103. Telephone: 818-397-1349.

PACIFIC STATES UNIVERSITY
LOS ANGELES, CALIFORNIA

Entrance Difficulty N/R **General** Independent, comprehensive, coed **Setting** 1-acre urban campus **Enrollment** 100 **Faculty** 5:1 **Freshmen** 100% accepted **Tuition** $7425 **Undergraduates**

50% women, 5% part-time, 5% Asian or Pacific Islander **Academic program** Accelerated degree program, self-designed majors, tutorials, adult/continuing education programs **Contact** Ms. Jill Currey, Admissions Officer, Pacific States University, 1516 South Western Avenue, Los Angeles, CA 90006. Telephone: 213-731-2383.

PACIFIC UNION COLLEGE
ANGWIN, CALIFORNIA

Entrance Moderately difficult **General** Independent Seventh-day Adventist, comprehensive, coed **Setting** 200-acre rural campus **Enrollment** 1,544 **Faculty** 13:1 **Application deadline** Rolling **Freshmen** 67% accepted **Housing** Yes **Tuition** $13,530 **Undergraduates** 55% women, 10% part-time, 17% 25 or older, 1% Native American, 9% Hispanic, 3% black, 17% Asian or Pacific Islander **Most popular recent majors** Nursing, business administration/commerce/management, behavioral sciences **Academic program** Advanced placement, accelerated degree program, self-designed majors, honors program, summer session, adult/continuing education programs, internships **Contact** Mr. Al Trace, Director of Enrollment Services, Pacific Union College, Angwin, CA 94508. Telephone: 707-965-6336.

PATTEN COLLEGE
OAKLAND, CALIFORNIA

Entrance Noncompetitive **General** Independent interdenominational, 4-year, coed **Setting** 5-acre urban campus **Enrollment** 627 **Faculty** 13:1 **Application deadline** 7/15 **Freshmen** 91% accepted **Housing** Yes **Tuition** $7008 **Undergraduates** 41% women, 64% part-time, 58% 25 or older, 1% Native American, 7% Hispanic, 42% black, 23% Asian or Pacific Islander **Most popular recent majors** Pastoral studies, liberal arts/general studies, business administration/commerce/management **Academic program** Average class size 15, advanced placement, accelerated degree program, tutorials, summer session, adult/continuing education programs, internships **Contact** Mrs. Sharon Barta, Director of Admissions, Patten College, 2433 Coolidge Avenue, Oakland, CA 94601-2699. Telephone: 510-533-8300 Ext. 265. Fax: 510-534-8564.

PEPPERDINE UNIVERSITY
MALIBU, CALIFORNIA

Entrance Very difficult **General** Independent, coed, affiliated with Church of Christ **Setting** 830-acre small-town campus **Enrollment** 7,896 **Faculty** 13:1 **Application deadline** 2/1 **Freshmen** 81% accepted **Housing** Yes **Tuition** $20,210 **Undergraduates** 57% women, 5% part-time, 4% 25 or older, 1% Native American, 8% Hispanic, 3% black, 7% Asian or Pacific Islander **Most popular recent majors** Business administration/commerce/management, communication, international studies **Academic program** Advanced placement, accelerated degree program, self-designed majors, tutorials, honors program, summer session, internships **Contact** Mr. Paul Long, Dean of Admission, Pepperdine University, Malibu, CA 90263-0001. Telephone: 310-456-4392. Fax: 310-456-4861.

PITZER COLLEGE
CLAREMONT, CALIFORNIA

Entrance Very difficult **General** Independent, 4-year, coed **Setting** 35-acre suburban campus **Enrollment** 869 **Faculty** 9:1 **Application deadline** 2/1 **Freshmen** 76% accepted **Housing** Yes **Tuition** $21,880 **Undergraduates** 51% women, 10% part-time, 1% Native American, 10% Hispanic, 5% black, 11% Asian or Pacific Islander **Most popular recent majors** Psychology, sociology, anthropology **Academic program** Advanced placement, self-designed majors, tutorials, honors program, adult/continuing education programs, internships **Contact** Dr. Willam D. Tingley, Vice President for Admission and Financial Aid, Pitzer College, 1050 North Mills Avenue, Claremont, CA 91711-6101. Telephone: 909-621-8129. Fax: 909-621-8770.

POINT LOMA NAZARENE COLLEGE
SAN DIEGO, CALIFORNIA

Entrance Moderately difficult **General** Independent Nazarene, comprehensive, coed **Setting** 88-acre suburban campus **Enrollment** 2,491 **Faculty** 15:1 **Application deadline** 8/1 **Freshmen** 91% accepted **Housing** Yes **Tuition** $12,464 **Undergraduates** 61% women, 8% part-time, 10% 25 or older, 1% Native American, 7% Hispanic, 1% black, 4% Asian or Pacific Islander **Most popular recent majors** Liberal arts/general studies, nursing, business administration/commerce/management **Academic program** Average class size 25, advanced placement, accelerated degree program, tutorials, honors program, summer session, internships **Contact** Mr. Bill Young, Executive Director for Enrollment Services, Point Loma Nazarene College, San Diego, CA 92106-2899. Telephone: 619-849-2225. Fax: 619-849-2579.

POMONA COLLEGE
CLAREMONT, CALIFORNIA

Entrance Most difficult **General** Independent, 4-year, coed **Setting** 140-acre suburban campus

Enrollment 1,420 **Faculty** 9:1 **Application deadline** 1/1 **Freshmen** 34% accepted **Housing** Yes **Tuition** $20,680 **Undergraduates** 48% women, 0% part-time, 1% 25 or older, 1% Native American, 12% Hispanic, 4% black, 20% Asian or Pacific Islander **Most popular recent majors** Economics, psychology, chemistry **Academic program** Advanced placement, self-designed majors, internships **Contact** Mr. Bruce Poch, Dean of Admissions, Pomona College, Claremont, CA 91711. Telephone: 909-621-8134. Fax: 909-621-8403.

ST. JOHN'S SEMINARY COLLEGE
CAMARILLO, CALIFORNIA

Entrance Moderately difficult **General** Independent Roman Catholic, 4-year, men only **Setting** 100-acre suburban campus **Enrollment** 66 **Faculty** 3:1 **Application deadline** 7/15 **Freshmen** 100% accepted **Housing** Yes **Tuition** $7080 **Undergraduates** 0% part-time, 37% 25 or older, 0% Native American, 41% Hispanic, 0% black, 35% Asian or Pacific Islander **Most popular recent majors** Philosophy, theology **Academic program** Advanced placement, tutorials **Contact** Rev. Gary Landry, CM, Director of Admissions, St. John's Seminary College, Camarillo, CA 93012-2599. Telephone: 805-482-4697 Ext. 206. Fax: 805-987-5097.

SAINT MARY'S COLLEGE OF CALIFORNIA
MORAGA, CALIFORNIA

Entrance Moderately difficult **General** Independent Roman Catholic, comprehensive, coed **Setting** 440-acre suburban campus **Enrollment** 4,204 **Faculty** 14:1 **Application deadline** 2/1 **Freshmen** 89% accepted **Housing** Yes **Tuition** $15,998 **Undergraduates** 55% women, 2% part-time, 5% 25 or older, 1% Native American, 15% Hispanic, 4% black, 11% Asian or Pacific Islander **Most popular recent majors** Business administration/commerce/management, psychology, communication **Academic program** Average class size 20, advanced placement, self-designed majors, tutorials, honors program, adult/continuing education programs, internships **Contact** Ms. Jennifer Wong, Director of Admissions, Saint Mary's College of California, PO Box 4800, Moraga, CA 94575. Telephone: 510-631-4224. Fax: 510-376-7193.

SAMUEL MERRITT COLLEGE
OAKLAND, CALIFORNIA

Entrance Moderately difficult **General** Independent, comprehensive, coed **Setting** 1-acre urban campus **Enrollment** 677 **Faculty** 7:1 **Application deadline** Rolling **Freshmen** 67% accepted **Housing** Yes **Tuition** $14,625 **Undergraduates** 90% women, 9% part-time, 59% 25 or older, 2% Native American, 6% Hispanic, 6% black, 17% Asian or Pacific Islander **Academic program** Advanced placement, accelerated degree program, tutorials, summer session, internships **Contact** Office of Admissions, Samuel Merritt College, 370 Hawthorne Avenue, Oakland, CA 94609-3108. Telephone: 510-869-6576.

SAN DIEGO STATE UNIVERSITY
SAN DIEGO, CALIFORNIA

Entrance Moderately difficult **General** State-supported, coed **Setting** 300-acre urban campus **Enrollment** 29,331 **Faculty** 13:1 **Application deadline** Rolling **Freshmen** 82% accepted **Housing** Yes **Tuition** $1932 **Undergraduates** 55% women, 18% part-time, 37% 25 or older, 1% Native American, 18% Hispanic, 5% black, 14% Asian or Pacific Islander **Most popular recent majors** Business administration/commerce/management, psychology, biology/biological sciences **Academic program** Advanced placement, accelerated degree program, self-designed majors, tutorials, honors program, summer session, adult/continuing education programs, internships **Contact** Admissions and Records Office, San Diego State University, 5500 Campanile Drive, San Diego, CA 92182-0771. Telephone: 619-594-6871.

SAN FRANCISCO ART INSTITUTE
SAN FRANCISCO, CALIFORNIA

Entrance Moderately difficult **General** Independent, comprehensive, specialized, coed **Setting** 3-acre urban campus **Enrollment** 681 **Faculty** 9:1 **Application deadline** Rolling **Freshmen** 70% accepted **Tuition** $17,400 **Undergraduates** 49% women, 21% part-time, 80% 25 or older, 1% Native American, 7% Hispanic, 2% black, 6% Asian or Pacific Islander **Most popular recent majors** Painting/drawing, photography, film studies **Academic program** Average class size 20, advanced placement, self-designed majors, tutorials, honors program, summer session, adult/continuing education programs, internships **Contact** Mr. Tim Robison, Vice President of Enrollment Services, San Francisco Art Institute, 800 Chestnut Street, San Francisco, CA 94133-2299. Telephone: 415-771-7020.

SAN FRANCISCO CONSERVATORY OF MUSIC
SAN FRANCISCO, CALIFORNIA

Entrance Moderately difficult **General** Independent, comprehensive, specialized, coed **Setting**

2-acre urban campus **Enrollment** 270 **Faculty** 7:1 **Application deadline** 3/1 **Freshmen** 67% accepted **Tuition** $16,550 **Undergraduates** 53% women, 3% part-time, 17% 25 or older, 0% Native American, 5% Hispanic, 1% black, 20% Asian or Pacific Islander **Most popular recent majors** Piano/organ, voice, stringed instruments **Academic program** Average class size 10, advanced placement, accelerated degree program **Contact** Ms. Joan Gordon, Admissions Officer, San Francisco Conservatory of Music, 1201 Ortega Street, San Francisco, CA 94122-4411. Telephone: 415-759-3431. Fax: 415-759-3499.

SAN FRANCISCO STATE UNIVERSITY
SAN FRANCISCO, CALIFORNIA

Entrance Moderately difficult **General** State-supported, comprehensive, coed **Setting** 90-acre urban campus **Enrollment** 27,420 **Faculty** 21:1 **Application deadline** 11/30 **Freshmen** 72% accepted **Housing** Yes **Tuition** $1982 **Undergraduates** 58% women, 30% part-time, 35% 25 or older, 1% Native American, 13% Hispanic, 8% black, 26% Asian or Pacific Islander **Most popular recent majors** Accounting, liberal arts/general studies, business administration/commerce/management **Academic program** Advanced placement, accelerated degree program, self-designed majors, honors program, summer session, adult/continuing education programs **Contact** Admissions Office, San Francisco State University, 1600 Holloway Avenue, San Francisco, CA 94132-1722. Telephone: 415-338-7238. Fax: 415-338-7196.

SAN JOSE CHRISTIAN COLLEGE
SAN JOSE, CALIFORNIA

Entrance Noncompetitive **General** Independent nondenominational, 4-year, coed **Setting** 9-acre urban campus **Enrollment** 338 **Faculty** 12:1 **Application deadline** 8/1 **Freshmen** 100% accepted **Housing** Yes **Tuition** $7014 **Undergraduates** 37% women, 41% part-time, 63% 25 or older, 1% Native American, 6% Hispanic, 4% black, 2% Asian or Pacific Islander **Most popular recent majors** Biblical studies, pastoral studies, education **Academic program** Advanced placement, summer session, internships **Contact** Mrs. Karen Lambrechtsen, Director of Admissions, San Jose Christian College, PO Box 1090, San Jose, CA 95108. Telephone: 408-293-9058. Fax: 408-293-7352.

SAN JOSE STATE UNIVERSITY
SAN JOSE, CALIFORNIA

Entrance Moderately difficult **General** State-supported, comprehensive, coed **Setting** 104-acre urban campus **Enrollment** 25,874 **Faculty** 18:1 **Application deadline** Rolling **Freshmen** 78% accepted **Housing** Yes **Tuition** $2017 **Undergraduates** 51% women, 31% part-time, 41% 25 or older, 1% Native American, 15% Hispanic, 5% black, 28% Asian or Pacific Islander **Most popular recent majors** Accounting, marketing/retailing/merchandising, art/fine arts **Academic program** Advanced placement, accelerated degree program, self-designed majors, honors program, summer session, adult/continuing education programs, internships **Contact** Mr. Leon Washington, Associate Vice President for Student Enrollment, San Jose State University, One Washington Square, San Jose, CA 95192-0009. Telephone: 408-924-2000.

SANTA CLARA UNIVERSITY
SANTA CLARA, CALIFORNIA

Entrance Moderately difficult **General** Independent Roman Catholic (Jesuit), comprehensive, coed **Setting** 104-acre suburban campus **Enrollment** 7,863 **Faculty** 10:1 **Application deadline** 1/15 **Freshmen** 74% accepted **Housing** Yes **Tuition** $16,635 **Undergraduates** 53% women, 3% part-time, 5% 25 or older, 1% Native American, 14% Hispanic, 3% black, 22% Asian or Pacific Islander **Most popular recent majors** Finance/banking, psychology, political science/government **Academic program** Average class size 31, advanced placement, self-designed majors, tutorials, honors program, summer session, adult/continuing education programs, internships **Contact** Ms. Charlene Aguilar, Director of Undergraduate Admissions, Santa Clara University, Santa Clara, CA 95053-0001. Telephone: 408-554-4700. Fax: 408-554-5255.

SCRIPPS COLLEGE
CLAREMONT, CALIFORNIA

Entrance Very difficult **General** Independent, 4-year, women only **Setting** 30-acre suburban campus **Enrollment** 704 **Faculty** 11:1 **Application deadline** 2/1 **Freshmen** 77% accepted **Housing** Yes **Tuition** $19,480 **Undergraduates** 2% part-time, 3% 25 or older, 0% Native American, 7% Hispanic, 3% black, 21% Asian or Pacific Islander **Most popular recent majors** English, psychology, international relations **Academic program** Advanced placement, self-designed majors, tutorials, honors program, internships **Contact** Ms. Patricia F. Goldsmith, Dean of Admission and Financial Aid, Scripps College, 1030 Columbia Avenue, Claremont, CA 91711-3948. Telephone: 909-621-8149. Fax: 909-621-8323.

SHASTA BIBLE COLLEGE
REDDING, CALIFORNIA

Entrance Difficulty N/R **General** Independent nondenominational, 4-year **Enrollment** 175 **Housing** Yes **Tuition** $3430 **Contact** Mr. George Gunn, Director of Admissions, Shasta Bible College, Redding, CA 96002. Telephone: 916-221-4275.

SIMPSON COLLEGE
REDDING, CALIFORNIA

Entrance Moderately difficult **General** Independent, comprehensive, coed, affiliated with The Christian and Missionary Alliance **Setting** 60-acre suburban campus **Enrollment** 1,169 **Faculty** 20:1 **Application deadline** Rolling **Freshmen** 71% accepted **Housing** Yes **Tuition** $9110 **Undergraduates** 58% women, 3% part-time, 1% Native American, 5% Hispanic, 1% black, 6% Asian or Pacific Islander **Most popular recent majors** Liberal arts/general studies, business administration/commerce/management, psychology **Academic program** Average class size 26, advanced placement, self-designed majors, tutorials, summer session, adult/continuing education programs, internships **Contact** Mrs. Beth Spencer, Administrative Assistant to Vice President for Enrollment, Simpson College, Redding, CA 96003-8606. Telephone: 916-224-5606 Ext. 2602. Fax: 916-224-5627.

SONOMA STATE UNIVERSITY
ROHNERT PARK, CALIFORNIA

Entrance Moderately difficult **General** State-supported, comprehensive, coed **Setting** 220-acre small-town campus **Enrollment** 6,999 **Faculty** 19:1 **Application deadline** 1/30 **Freshmen** 83% accepted **Housing** Yes **Tuition** $2130 **Undergraduates** 61% women, 18% part-time, 30% 25 or older, 1% Native American, 10% Hispanic, 4% black, 6% Asian or Pacific Islander **Most popular recent majors** Business administration/commerce/management, psychology, liberal arts/general studies **Academic program** Advanced placement, self-designed majors, tutorials, summer session, adult/continuing education programs, internships **Contact** Ms. Sarah Boldt, Data Coordinator, Sonoma State University, Rohnert Park, CA 94928-3609. Telephone: 707-664-2322.

SOUTHERN CALIFORNIA COLLEGE
COSTA MESA, CALIFORNIA

Entrance Moderately difficult **General** Independent, comprehensive, coed, affiliated with Assemblies of God **Setting** 38-acre suburban campus **Enrollment** 1,226 **Faculty** 16:1 **Application deadline** Rolling **Freshmen** 89% accepted **Housing** Yes **Tuition** $11,848 **Undergraduates** 57% women, 8% part-time, 20% 25 or older, 1% Native American, 10% Hispanic, 2% black, 4% Asian or Pacific Islander **Most popular recent majors** Religious studies, business administration/commerce/management **Academic program** Advanced placement, accelerated degree program, summer session, adult/continuing education programs, internships **Contact** Mr. Virgil Zeigler, Associate Director of Admissions, Southern California College, Costa Mesa, CA 92626-6597. Telephone: 714-556-3610 Ext. 219. Fax: 714-668-6194.

SOUTHERN CALIFORNIA INSTITUTE OF ARCHITECTURE
LOS ANGELES, CALIFORNIA

Entrance Moderately difficult **General** Independent, comprehensive, specialized, coed **Setting** Urban campus **Enrollment** 430 **Faculty** 15:1 **Application deadline** Rolling **Freshmen** 65% accepted **Tuition** $13,990 **Undergraduates** 23% women, 2% part-time, 42% 25 or older, 1% Native American, 10% Hispanic, 2% black, 34% Asian or Pacific Islander **Academic program** Advanced placement, summer session, internships **Contact** Ms. Debra Abel, Director of Admissions, Southern California Institute of Architecture, 5454 Beethoven Street, Los Angeles, CA 90066-7017. Telephone: 310-574-3625. Fax: 310-829-7518.

STANFORD UNIVERSITY
STANFORD, CALIFORNIA

Entrance Most difficult **General** Independent, coed **Setting** 8,180-acre suburban campus **Enrollment** 13,811 **Faculty** 10:1 **Application deadline** 12/15 **Freshmen** 16% accepted **Housing** Yes **Tuition** $21,389 **Undergraduates** 50% women, 0% part-time, 2% Native American, 11% Hispanic, 8% black, 24% Asian or Pacific Islander **Most popular recent majors** Engineering (general), economics **Academic program** Advanced placement, accelerated degree program, self-designed majors, tutorials, honors program, summer session, adult/continuing education programs, internships **Contact** Mr. John Bunnell, Associate Dean of Admissions, Stanford University, Stanford, CA 94305-9991. Telephone: 415-723-2091. Fax: 415-725-2846.

THOMAS AQUINAS COLLEGE
SANTA PAULA, CALIFORNIA

Entrance Very difficult **General** Independent Roman Catholic, 4-year, coed **Setting** 159-acre rural campus **Enrollment** 223 **Faculty** 10:1 **Application deadline** Rolling **Freshmen** 81% accepted **Housing** Yes **Tuition** $13,900 **Undergraduates** 43% women, 0% part-time, 11% 25 or older, 1% Native American, 6% Hispanic, 0% black, 2% Asian or Pacific Islander **Academic program** Average class size 15 **Contact** Mr. Thomas J. Susanka Jr., Director of Admissions, Thomas Aquinas College, Santa Paula, CA 93060-9980. Telephone: 805-525-4417 Ext. 359. Fax: 805-525-0620.

UNITED STATES INTERNATIONAL UNIVERSITY
SAN DIEGO, CALIFORNIA

Entrance Moderately difficult **General** Independent, coed **Setting** 200-acre suburban campus **Enrollment** 1,873 **Application deadline** Rolling **Freshmen** 71% accepted **Housing** Yes **Tuition** $11,745 **Undergraduates** 55% women, 12% part-time, 30% 25 or older, 1% Native American, 13% Hispanic, 5% black, 7% Asian or Pacific Islander **Most popular recent majors** International business, psychology **Academic program** ESL program, Advanced placement, accelerated degree program, honors program, summer session, adult/continuing education programs, internships **Contact** Ms. Darla J. Wilson, Director of Admissions, United States International University, San Diego, CA 92131-1799. Telephone: 619-635-4772. Fax: 619-635-4739.

UNIVERSITY OF CALIFORNIA, BERKELEY
BERKELEY, CALIFORNIA

Entrance Very difficult **General** State-supported, coed **Setting** 1,232-acre urban campus **Enrollment** 29,630 **Faculty** 17:1 **Application deadline** 11/30 **Freshmen** 36% accepted **Housing** Yes **Tuition** $4355 **Undergraduates** 48% women, 0% part-time, 1% Native American, 13% Hispanic, 6% black, 40% Asian or Pacific Islander **Most popular recent majors** English, molecular biology, political science/government **Academic program** Advanced placement, accelerated degree program, self-designed majors, tutorials, honors program, summer session, adult/continuing education programs, internships **Contact** Office of Undergraduate Admission, University of California, Berkeley, Berkeley, CA 94720-5800. Telephone: 510-642-3175. Fax: 510-642-7333.

UNIVERSITY OF CALIFORNIA, DAVIS
DAVIS, CALIFORNIA

Entrance Very difficult **General** State-supported, coed **Setting** 5,993-acre suburban campus **Enrollment** 23,931 **Faculty** 14:1 **Application deadline** 11/30 **Freshmen** 74% accepted **Housing** Yes **Tuition** $4234 **Undergraduates** 53% women, 2% part-time, 8% 25 or older, 1% Native American, 11% Hispanic, 3% black, 34% Asian or Pacific Islander **Most popular recent majors** Psychology, biology/biological sciences, international relations **Academic program** Advanced placement, self-designed majors, tutorials, honors program, summer session, adult/continuing education programs, internships **Contact** Dr. Gary Tudor, Director of Undergraduate Admissions, University of California, Davis, Davis, CA 95616. Telephone: 916-752-2971.

UNIVERSITY OF CALIFORNIA, IRVINE
IRVINE, CALIFORNIA

Entrance Moderately difficult **General** State-supported, coed **Setting** 1,489-acre suburban campus **Enrollment** 17,281 **Faculty** 19:1 **Application deadline** 11/30 **Freshmen** 73% accepted **Housing** Yes **Tuition** $4050 **Undergraduates** 53% women, 6% part-time, 8% 25 or older, 1% Native American, 13% Hispanic, 3% black, 50% Asian or Pacific Islander **Most popular recent majors** Biology/biological sciences, economics, English **Academic program** Advanced placement, accelerated degree program, honors program, summer session, adult/continuing education programs, internships **Contact** Ms. Susan Wilbur, Director of Admissions, University of California, Irvine, Irvine, CA 92697. Telephone: 714-824-6703.

UNIVERSITY OF CALIFORNIA, LOS ANGELES
LOS ANGELES, CALIFORNIA

Entrance Very difficult **General** State-supported, coed **Setting** 419-acre urban campus **Enrollment** 34,935 **Faculty** 17:1 **Application deadline** 11/30 **Freshmen** 39% accepted **Housing** Yes **Tuition** $4050 **Undergraduates** 52% women, 0% part-time, 9% 25 or older, 1% Native American, 18% Hispanic, 6% black, 40% Asian or Pacific Islander **Most popular recent majors** Biology/biological sciences, psychology, economics **Academic program** Advanced placement, self-designed majors, honors program, summer session, adult/continuing education programs, internships **Contact** Dr. Rae Lee Siporin, Director of Undergraduate Admissions, University of California, Los Angeles, 405 Hilgard Avenue, Los Angeles, CA 90095. Telephone: 310-825-3101.

UNIVERSITY OF CALIFORNIA, RIVERSIDE
RIVERSIDE, CALIFORNIA

Entrance Very difficult **General** State-supported, coed **Setting** 1,200-acre suburban campus **Enrollment** 9,063 **Faculty** 18:1 **Application deadline** 11/30 **Freshmen** 78% accepted **Housing** Yes **Tuition** $4126 **Undergraduates** 52% women, 2% part-time, 9% 25 or older, 1% Native American, 18% Hispanic, 5% black, 39% Asian or Pacific Islander **Most popular recent majors** Business administration/commerce/management, biology/biological sciences, psychology **Academic program** ESL program, Advanced placement, accelerated degree program, self-designed majors, tutorials, honors program, summer session, adult/continuing education programs, internships **Contact** Ms. Laurie Nelson, Associate Admissions Officer, University of California, Riverside, Riverside, CA 92521-0102. Telephone: 909-787-3411.

UNIVERSITY OF CALIFORNIA, SAN DIEGO

LA JOLLA, CALIFORNIA

Entrance Very difficult **General** State-supported, coed **Setting** 1,976-acre suburban campus **Enrollment** 18,119 **Faculty** 10:1 **Application deadline** 11/30 **Freshmen** 50% accepted **Housing** Yes **Tuition** $4200 **Undergraduates** 50% women, 1% part-time, 9% 25 or older, 1% Native American, 11% Hispanic, 2% black, 27% Asian or Pacific Islander **Most popular recent majors** Biology/biological sciences, psychology, political science/government **Academic program** ESL program, Advanced placement, accelerated degree program, self-designed majors, tutorials, honors program, summer session, adult/continuing education programs, internships **Contact** Mr. Tim Johnston, Acting Director of Student Outreach and Recruitment, University of California, San Diego, La Jolla, CA 92093-5003. Telephone: 619-534-4831.

UNIVERSITY OF CALIFORNIA, SANTA BARBARA

SANTA BARBARA, CALIFORNIA

Entrance Very difficult **General** State-supported, coed **Setting** 989-acre suburban campus **Enrollment** 18,531 **Faculty** 19:1 **Application deadline** 11/30 **Freshmen** 78% accepted **Housing** Yes **Tuition** $4105 **Undergraduates** 53% women, 4% part-time, 6% 25 or older, 1% Native American, 13% Hispanic, 3% black, 17% Asian or Pacific Islander **Most popular recent majors** Business economics, biology/biological sciences, psychology **Academic program** Advanced placement, accelerated degree program, self-designed majors, honors program, summer session, internships **Contact** Mr. William Villa, Director of Admissions/Relations with Schools, University of California, Santa Barbara, Santa Barbara, CA 93106. Telephone: 805-893-2485.

UNIVERSITY OF CALIFORNIA, SANTA CRUZ

SANTA CRUZ, CALIFORNIA

Entrance Very difficult **General** State-supported, coed **Setting** 2,000-acre small-town campus **Enrollment** 10,215 **Faculty** 19:1 **Application deadline** 11/30 **Freshmen** 83% accepted **Housing** Yes **Tuition** $4181 **Undergraduates** 60% women, 2% part-time, 10% 25 or older, 1% Native American, 17% Hispanic, 4% black, 14% Asian or Pacific Islander **Most popular recent majors** Biology/biological sciences, psychology, literature **Academic program** Average class size 20, advanced placement, self-designed majors, tutorials, summer session, internships **Contact** Mr. J. Michael Thompson, Director of Admissions, University of California, Santa Cruz, Admissions Office, Cook House, Santa Cruz, CA 95064. Telephone: 408-459-5453. Fax: 408-459-4452.

UNIVERSITY OF JUDAISM

LOS ANGELES, CALIFORNIA

Entrance Moderately difficult **General** Independent Jewish, comprehensive, coed **Setting** 28-acre suburban campus **Enrollment** 179 **Faculty** 6:1 **Application deadline** 1/31 **Freshmen** 81% accepted **Housing** Yes **Tuition** $14,400 **Undergraduates** 61% women, 9% part-time, 33% 25 or older, 1% Hispanic, 1% black, 1% Asian or Pacific Islander **Most popular recent majors** Psychology, literature, Judaic studies **Academic program** Advanced placement, accelerated degree program, self-designed majors, honors program, summer session, adult/continuing education programs, internships **Contact** Mr. Richard Scaffidi, Director of Undergraduate Admissions, University of Judaism, Los Angeles, CA 90077-1599. Telephone: 310-476-9777 Ext. 250. Fax: 310-471-1278.

UNIVERSITY OF LA VERNE

LA VERNE, CALIFORNIA

Entrance Moderately difficult **General** Independent, coed **Setting** 26-acre suburban campus **Enrollment** 2,965 **Faculty** 15:1 **Application deadline** Rolling **Freshmen** 74% accepted **Housing** Yes **Tuition** $14,710 **Undergraduates** 58% women, 5% part-time, 1% Native American, 32% Hispanic, 12% black, 11% Asian or Pacific Islander **Most popular recent majors** Business administration/commerce/management, communication, physical education **Academic program** Advanced placement, accelerated degree program, self-designed majors, tutorials, honors program, summer session, adult/continuing education programs, internships **Contact** Mr. Douglas Wible, Director of Admissions, University of La Verne, La Verne, CA 91750-4443. Telephone: 909-593-3511 Ext. 4026. Fax: 909-593-0965.

UNIVERSITY OF REDLANDS
REDLANDS, CALIFORNIA

Entrance Moderately difficult **General** Independent, comprehensive, coed **Setting** 140-acre small-town campus **Enrollment** 3,584 **Faculty** 12:1 **Application deadline** 3/1 **Freshmen** 83% accepted **Housing** Yes **Tuition** $18,545 **Undergraduates** 51% women, 5% part-time, 1% 25 or older, 1% Native American, 14% Hispanic, 4% black, 8% Asian or Pacific Islander **Most popular recent majors** Liberal arts/general studies, social science, business administration/commerce/management **Academic program** Average class size 12, advanced placement, self-designed majors, tutorials, honors program, adult/continuing education programs, internships **Contact** Mr. Paul Driscoll, Dean of Admissions, University of Redlands, Redlands, CA 92373-0999. Telephone: 909-335-4074. Fax: 909-335-4089.

UNIVERSITY OF SAN DIEGO
SAN DIEGO, CALIFORNIA

Entrance Moderately difficult **General** Independent Roman Catholic, coed **Setting** 180-acre urban campus **Enrollment** 6,603 **Faculty** 18:1 **Application deadline** 1/15 **Freshmen** 70% accepted **Housing** Yes **Tuition** $15,780 **Undergraduates** 56% women, 4% part-time, 9% 25 or older, 1% Native American, 15% Hispanic, 3% black, 9% Asian or Pacific Islander **Most popular recent majors** Business administration/commerce/management, political science/government, psychology **Academic program** Average class size 22, advanced placement, tutorials, honors program, summer session, adult/continuing education programs, internships **Contact** Mr. Warren Muller, Director of Undergraduate Admissions, University of San Diego, 5998 Alcala Park, San Diego, CA 92110-2492. Telephone: 619-260-4506.

UNIVERSITY OF SAN FRANCISCO
SAN FRANCISCO, CALIFORNIA

Entrance Moderately difficult **General** Independent Roman Catholic (Jesuit), coed **Setting** 55-acre urban campus **Enrollment** 7,888 **Application deadline** 2/15 **Freshmen** 77% accepted **Housing** Yes **Tuition** $15,950 **Undergraduates** 64% women, 7% part-time, 14% 25 or older, 1% Native American, 10% Hispanic, 4% black, 24% Asian or Pacific Islander **Most popular recent majors** Business administration/commerce/management, nursing, communication **Academic program** Average class size 27, advanced placement, accelerated degree program, self-designed majors, honors program, summer session, adult/continuing education programs, internships **Contact** Dr. William Henley, Director of Admissions, University of San Francisco, 2130 Fulton Street, San Francisco, CA 94117-1080. Telephone: 415-422-6563. Fax: 415-422-2217.

UNIVERSITY OF SOUTHERN CALIFORNIA
LOS ANGELES, CALIFORNIA

Entrance Moderately difficult **General** Independent, coed **Setting** 150-acre urban campus **Enrollment** 27,558 **Faculty** 14:1 **Application deadline** 2/1 **Freshmen** 72% accepted **Housing** Yes **Tuition** $19,516 **Undergraduates** 48% women, 9% part-time, 11% 25 or older, 1% Native American, 14% Hispanic, 7% black, 23% Asian or Pacific Islander **Most popular recent majors** Business administration/commerce/management, communication, political science/government **Academic program** Advanced placement, accelerated degree program, self-designed majors, tutorials, honors program, summer session, internships **Contact** Mr. Duncan Murdoch, Director of Admissions, University of Southern California, University Park Campus, Los Angeles, CA 90089-0911. Telephone: 213-740-1111. Fax: 213-740-6364.

UNIVERSITY OF THE PACIFIC
STOCKTON, CALIFORNIA

Entrance Moderately difficult **General** Independent, coed **Setting** 175-acre suburban campus **Enrollment** 4,785 **Faculty** 15:1 **Application deadline** 3/1 **Freshmen** 85% accepted **Housing** Yes **Tuition** $18,800 **Undergraduates** 55% women, 5% part-time, 5% 25 or older, 1% Native American, 8% Hispanic, 4% black, 23% Asian or Pacific Islander **Most popular recent majors** Liberal arts/general studies, pharmacy/pharmaceutical sciences, business administration/commerce/management **Academic program** Average class size 25, advanced placement, accelerated degree program, self-designed majors, tutorials, honors program, summer session, adult/continuing education programs, internships **Contact** Mr. Edward Schoenberg, Dean of Enrollment Services, University of the Pacific, Stockton, CA 95211-0197. Telephone: 209-946-2211. Fax: 209-946-2413.

UNIVERSITY OF WEST LOS ANGELES
INGLEWOOD, CALIFORNIA

Entrance Minimally difficult **General** Independent, upper-level, specialized, coed **Setting** 2-acre suburban campus **Faculty** 12:1 **Tuition** $5335 **Undergraduates** 68% women, 80% part-time, 90% 25 or older, 1% Native American, 9% Hispanic, 24% black, 5% Asian or Pacific Islander **Academic program** Adult/continuing education programs, internships **Contact** Mr. Joel Abend, Director of Admissions, University of West Los Angeles, Inglewood, CA 90301-2902. Telephone: 310-342-5200 Ext. 287. Fax: 310-313-2124.

WESTERN STATE UNIVERSITY COLLEGE OF LAW OF SAN DIEGO
SEE THOMAS JEFFERSON SCHOOL OF LAW

WESTMONT COLLEGE
SANTA BARBARA, CALIFORNIA

Entrance Moderately difficult **General** Independent interdenominational, 4-year, coed **Setting** 133-acre suburban campus **Enrollment** 1,320 **Faculty** 14:1 **Application deadline** 3/1 **Freshmen** 86% accepted **Housing** Yes **Tuition** $17,998 **Undergraduates** 60% women, 0% part-time, 2% 25 or older, 1% Native American, 5% Hispanic, 1% black, 4% Asian or Pacific Islander **Most popular recent majors** Biology/biological sciences, business economics, English **Academic program** Advanced placement, accelerated degree program, self-designed majors, tutorials, honors program, summer session, internships **Contact** Mr. David Morley, Dean of Admissions, Westmont College, Santa Barbara, CA 93108-1099. Telephone: 805-565-6200. Fax: 805-565-6234.

WHITTIER COLLEGE
WHITTIER, CALIFORNIA

Entrance Moderately difficult **General** Independent, comprehensive, coed **Setting** 95-acre suburban campus **Enrollment** 2,165 **Faculty** 13:1 **Application deadline** Rolling **Freshmen** 70% accepted **Housing** Yes **Tuition** $18,634 **Undergraduates** 56% women, 2% part-time, 6% 25 or older, 1% Native American, 31% Hispanic, 5% black, 10% Asian or Pacific Islander **Most popular recent majors** Business administration/commerce/management, English, biology/biological sciences **Academic program** Advanced placement, accelerated degree program, self-designed majors, tutorials, honors program, summer session, adult/continuing education programs, internships **Contact** Mr. Doug Locker, Director of Admission, Whittier College, Whittier, CA 90608-0634. Telephone: 310-907-4238.

WOODBURY UNIVERSITY
BURBANK, CALIFORNIA

Entrance Moderately difficult **General** Independent, comprehensive, coed **Setting** 23-acre suburban campus **Enrollment** 1,132 **Faculty** 14:1 **Application deadline** Rolling **Freshmen** 79% accepted **Housing** Yes **Tuition** $15,170 **Undergraduates** 55% women, 23% part-time, 34% 25 or older, 1% Native American, 29% Hispanic, 6% black, 18% Asian or Pacific Islander **Most popular recent majors** Business administration/commerce/management, interior design, architecture **Academic program** Average class size 16, ESL program, advanced placement, accelerated degree program, tutorials, summer session, adult/continuing education programs, internships **Contact** Mr. Pat Contrades, Director of Admission, Woodbury University, 7500 Glenoaks Boulevard, Burbank, CA 91510-7846. Telephone: 818-767-0888. Fax: 818-504-9320.

YESHIVA OHR ELCHONON CHABAD/WEST COAST TALMUDICAL SEMINARY
LOS ANGELES, CALIFORNIA

Entrance Moderately difficult **General** Independent Jewish, 4-year, specialized, men only **Setting** 4-acre urban campus **Enrollment** 46 **Faculty** 8:1 **Application deadline** Rolling **Freshmen** 64% accepted **Housing** Yes **Tuition** $4600 **Undergraduates** 0% part-time, 0% 25 or older, 0% Native American, 0% black **Academic program** Average class size 10, tutorials, honors program, summer session, adult/continuing education programs, internships **Contact** Rabbi Joseph Schneerson, Director of Student Financial Aid, Yeshiva Ohr Elchonon Chabad/West Coast Talmudical Seminary, 7215 Waring Avenue, Los Angeles, CA 90046-7660. Telephone: 213-937-3763.

Colorado

ADAMS STATE COLLEGE
ALAMOSA, COLORADO

Entrance Moderately difficult **General** State-supported, comprehensive, coed **Setting** 90-acre small-town campus **Enrollment** 2,444 **Faculty** 18:1 **Application deadline** 8/1 **Freshmen** 86% accepted **Housing** Yes **Tuition** $1958 **Undergraduates** 57% women, 14% part-time, 24% 25 or older, 2% Native American, 27% Hispanic, 2% black, 1% Asian or Pacific Islander **Most popular**

recent majors Biology/biological sciences, business administration/commerce/management, education **Academic program** Average class size 45, advanced placement, accelerated degree program, self-designed majors, tutorials, summer session, adult/continuing education programs **Contact** Mr. Gary C. Pierson, Director of Admissions, Adams State College, Alamosa, CO 81102. Telephone: 719-587-7712. Fax: 719-587-7522.

BETH-EL COLLEGE OF NURSING AND HEALTH SCIENCES

COLORADO SPRINGS, COLORADO

Entrance Moderately difficult **General** City-supported, comprehensive, specialized, primarily women **Setting** 1-acre urban campus **Enrollment** 439 **Faculty** 10:1 **Application deadline** 2/15 **Tuition** $3851 **Undergraduates** 91% women, 66% part-time, 80% 25 or older, 1% Native American, 4% Hispanic, 2% black, 3% Asian or Pacific Islander **Academic program** Average class size 45, summer session, adult/continuing education programs **Contact** Mrs. Marilyn J. Atwood, Director of Student Affairs, Beth-El College of Nursing and Health Sciences, 2790 North Academy Blvd, Suite 200, Colorado Springs, CO 80917-5399. Telephone: 719-475-5170.

COLORADO CHRISTIAN UNIVERSITY

LAKEWOOD, COLORADO

Entrance Moderately difficult **General** Independent interdenominational, comprehensive, coed **Setting** 26-acre suburban campus **Enrollment** 3,006 **Faculty** 17:1 **Application deadline** 8/15 **Freshmen** 89% accepted **Housing** Yes **Tuition** $10,010 **Undergraduates** 58% women, 16% part-time, 72% 25 or older, 1% Native American, 4% Hispanic, 6% black, 2% Asian or Pacific Islander **Most popular recent majors** Business administration/commerce/management, computer information systems, elementary education **Academic program** Advanced placement, accelerated degree program, self-designed majors, tutorials, honors program, summer session, adult/continuing education programs, internships **Contact** Ms. Martha Heffernan, Admissions Office Manager, Colorado Christian University, Lakewood, CO 80226-7499. Telephone: 303-202-0100 Ext. 165. Fax: 303-238-2191.

THE COLORADO COLLEGE

COLORADO SPRINGS, COLORADO

Entrance Very difficult **General** Independent, 4-year, coed **Setting** 90-acre suburban campus **Enrollment** 2,099 **Faculty** 12:1 **Application deadline** 1/15 **Freshmen** 58% accepted **Housing** Yes **Tuition** $19,980 **Undergraduates** 54% women, 0% part-time, 1% 25 or older, 1% Native American, 6% Hispanic, 2% black, 3% Asian or Pacific Islander **Most popular recent majors** English, biology/biological sciences, economics **Academic program** Advanced placement, self-designed majors, tutorials, honors program, summer session **Contact** Mr. Terrance K. Swenson, Dean of Admission and Financial Aid, The Colorado College, Colorado Springs, CO 80903-3294. Telephone: 719-389-6344. Fax: 719-389-6816.

COLORADO SCHOOL OF MINES

GOLDEN, COLORADO

Entrance Very difficult **General** State-supported, coed **Setting** 307-acre small-town campus **Enrollment** 3,203 **Faculty** 14:1 **Application deadline** 6/1 **Freshmen** 87% accepted **Housing** Yes **Tuition** $5069 **Undergraduates** 24% women, 3% part-time, 2% 25 or older, 1% Native American, 7% Hispanic, 1% black, 5% Asian or Pacific Islander **Most popular recent majors** Engineering (general), chemical engineering, computer science **Academic program** Advanced placement, accelerated degree program, honors program, summer session, adult/continuing education programs **Contact** Mr. Bill Young, Director of Enrollment Management, Colorado School of Mines, Golden, CO 80401-1887. Telephone: 303-273-3227. Fax: 303-273-3509.

COLORADO STATE UNIVERSITY

FORT COLLINS, COLORADO

Entrance Very difficult **General** State-supported, coed **Setting** 666-acre urban campus **Enrollment** 21,970 **Faculty** 22:1 **Application deadline** 7/1 **Freshmen** 77% accepted **Housing** Yes **Tuition** $2983 **Undergraduates** 51% women, 12% part-time, 16% 25 or older, 1% Native American, 5% Hispanic, 2% black, 3% Asian or Pacific Islander **Most popular recent majors** Business administration/commerce/management, liberal arts/general studies, physical fitness/exercise science **Academic program** Advanced placement, accelerated degree program, self-designed majors, tutorials, honors program, summer session, adult/continuing education programs, internships **Contact** Ms. Mary Ontiveros, Director of Admissions, Colorado State University, Spruce Hall, Fort Collins, CO 80523-0015. Telephone: 970-491-6909. Fax: 970-491-7799.

COLORADO TECHNICAL UNIVERSITY

COLORADO SPRINGS, COLORADO

Entrance Moderately difficult **General** Proprietary, comprehensive, coed **Setting** 14-acre suburban campus **Enrollment** 1,521 **Faculty** 14:1 **Application deadline** Rolling **Freshmen** 92% accepted **Tuition** $6468 **Undergraduates** 21% women, 64% part-time, 71% 25 or older, 1% Native American, 5% Hispanic, 7% black, 3% Asian or Pacific Islander **Most popular recent majors** Computer science, electronics engineering technology, electrical engineering **Academic program** Average class size 26, advanced placement, accelerated degree program, tutorials, honors program, summer session, adult/continuing education programs, internships **Contact** Mr. John Richardson, Undergraduate Admissions Advisor, Colorado Technical University, 4435 North Chestnut Street, Colorado Springs, CO 80907-3896. Telephone: 719-598-0200. Fax: 719-598-3740.

DENVER INSTITUTE OF TECHNOLOGY
DENVER, COLORADO

Entrance Moderately difficult **General** Proprietary, 4-year, coed **Setting** 11-acre suburban campus **Enrollment** 950 **Faculty** 20:1 **Application deadline** Rolling **Freshmen** 92% accepted **Undergraduates** 35% women, 33% 25 or older, 2% Native American, 18% Hispanic, 5% black, 2% Asian or Pacific Islander **Academic program** Advanced placement, accelerated degree program, tutorials, summer session, internships **Contact** Mr. Richard A. Rodman, Director of Admissions, Denver Institute of Technology, 7350 North Broadway, Denver, CO 80221-3653. Telephone: 303-650-5050 Ext. 360. Fax: 303-426-4647.

DENVER TECHNICAL COLLEGE
DENVER, COLORADO

Entrance Moderately difficult **General** Proprietary, comprehensive, coed **Setting** 1-acre urban campus **Enrollment** 1,500 **Application deadline** Rolling **Freshmen** 70% accepted **Undergraduates** 49% women, 10% part-time, 60% 25 or older, 1% Native American, 4% Hispanic, 11% black, 1% Asian or Pacific Islander **Academic program** Accelerated degree program, tutorials, honors program, summer session, adult/continuing education programs, internships **Contact** Mr. Raul Valdes-Pages, Chief Operating Officer, Denver Technical College, 925 South Niagara Street, Denver, CO 80224-1658. Telephone: 303-329-3000.

FORT LEWIS COLLEGE
DURANGO, COLORADO

Entrance Moderately difficult **General** State-supported, 4-year, coed **Setting** 350-acre small-town campus **Enrollment** 4,600 **Faculty** 21:1 **Application deadline** 7/15 **Freshmen** 73% accepted **Housing** Yes **Tuition** $2050 **Undergraduates** 48% women, 11% part-time, 20% 25 or older, 12% Native American, 5% Hispanic, 1% black, 1% Asian or Pacific Islander **Most popular recent majors** Business administration/commerce/management, humanities, English **Academic program** Average class size 20, advanced placement, accelerated degree program, self-designed majors, tutorials, honors program, summer session, adult/continuing education programs, internships **Contact** Mr. Harlan Steinle, Vice President of Admission, Fort Lewis College, Durango, CO 81301-3999. Telephone: 970-247-7184. Fax: 970-247-7179.

MESA STATE COLLEGE
GRAND JUNCTION, COLORADO

Entrance Minimally difficult **General** State-supported, 4-year, coed **Setting** 42-acre small-town campus **Enrollment** 4,724 **Faculty** 20:1 **Application deadline** 8/15 **Freshmen** 88% accepted **Housing** Yes **Tuition** $1986 **Undergraduates** 56% women, 20% part-time, 34% 25 or older, 1% Native American, 8% Hispanic, 1% black, 1% Asian or Pacific Islander **Most popular recent majors** Business administration/commerce/management, liberal arts/general studies, nursing **Academic program** ESL program, Advanced placement, accelerated degree program, self-designed majors, honors program, summer session, adult/continuing education programs, internships **Contact** Mr. Paul Jones, Director of Admissions, Mesa State College, P.O. Box 2647, Grand Junction, CO 81502-2647. Telephone: 970-248-1376. Fax: 970-248-1973.

METROPOLITAN STATE COLLEGE OF DENVER
DENVER, COLORADO

Entrance Minimally difficult **General** State-supported, 4-year, coed **Setting** 171-acre urban campus **Enrollment** 17,177 **Faculty** 19:1 **Application deadline** 7/21 **Freshmen** 83% accepted **Tuition** $2093 **Undergraduates** 56% women, 46% part-time, 49% 25 or older, 1% Native American, 12% Hispanic, 6% black, 4% Asian or Pacific Islander **Most popular recent majors** Accounting, business administration/commerce/management, psychology **Academic program** Advanced placement, accelerated degree program, self-designed majors, tutorials, honors program, summer session, adult/continuing education programs, internships **Contact** Mr. Thomas R. Gray, Assistant Dean of Admissions and Records, Metropolitan State College of Denver, PO Box 173362, Denver, CO 80217-3362. Telephone: 303-556-3058.

THE NAROPA INSTITUTE
BOULDER, COLORADO

Entrance Moderately difficult **General** Independent, upper-level, coed **Setting** 4-acre urban campus **Enrollment** 700 **Freshmen** 95% accepted **Tuition** $11,358 **Undergraduates** 61% women, 30% part-time, 69% 25 or older, 1% Native American, 1% Hispanic, 1% black, 3% Asian or Pacific Islander **Most popular recent majors** Psychology, environmental studies, early childhood education **Academic program** Average class size 10, advanced placement, self-designed majors, tutorials, summer session, adult/continuing education programs, internships **Contact** Ms. Marta Shoman, Director of Admissions, The Naropa Institute, 2130 Arapahoe Avenue, Boulder, CO 80302-6697. Telephone: 303-444-0202 Ext. 514. Fax: 303-444-0410.

NATIONAL COLLEGE
COLORADO SPRINGS, COLORADO

Entrance Noncompetitive **General** Proprietary, 4-year, coed **Setting** 1-acre suburban campus **Enrollment** 350 **Faculty** 13:1 **Application deadline** Rolling **Freshmen** 100% accepted **Tuition** $7995 **Undergraduates** 56% women, 56% part-time, 98% 25 or older **Most popular recent majors** Business administration/commerce/management, accounting, computer information systems **Academic program** Accelerated degree program, tutorials, summer session, adult/continuing education programs, internships **Contact** Mr. Nathan Larson, Director of Admissions, National College, Colorado Springs, CO 80909. Telephone: 719-471-4205.

NATIONAL COLLEGE
DENVER, COLORADO

Entrance Noncompetitive **General** Proprietary, 4-year, coed **Setting** Urban campus **Enrollment** 350 **Application deadline** Rolling **Freshmen** 100% accepted **Tuition** $8400 **Undergraduates** 60% women, 50% part-time, 85% 25 or older, 5% Hispanic, 5% black **Most popular recent major** Business administration/commerce/management **Academic program** Advanced placement, accelerated degree program, tutorials, summer session, adult/continuing education programs **Contact** Ms. Leigh Ann Sutherland, Director of Admissions, National College, 1325 South Colorado Blvd, Suite 100, Denver, CO 80222. Telephone: 303-758-6700.

NAZARENE BIBLE COLLEGE
COLORADO SPRINGS, COLORADO

Entrance Noncompetitive **General** Independent, 4-year, specialized, coed, affiliated with Church of the Nazarene **Setting** 64-acre urban campus **Enrollment** 426 **Faculty** 14:1 **Application deadline** 8/31 **Freshmen** 100% accepted **Tuition** $5055 **Undergraduates** 34% women, 41% part-time, 82% 25 or older, 0% Native American, 1% Hispanic, 6% black, 1% Asian or Pacific Islander **Most popular recent major** Biblical studies **Academic program** Summer session, internships **Contact** Rev. J. Fred Shepard, Director of Admissions/Public Relations, Nazarene Bible College, 1111 Academy Park Loop, Colorado Springs, CO 80916. Telephone: 719-596-5110 Ext. 167. Fax: 719-550-9437.

REGIS UNIVERSITY
DENVER, COLORADO

Entrance Moderately difficult **General** Independent Roman Catholic (Jesuit), comprehensive, coed **Setting** 90-acre suburban campus **Enrollment** 7,039 **Faculty** 16:1 **Application deadline** 8/15 **Freshmen** 89% accepted **Housing** Yes **Tuition** $14,970 **Undergraduates** 56% women, 5% part-time, 11% 25 or older, 1% Native American, 9% Hispanic, 2% black, 3% Asian or Pacific Islander **Most popular recent majors** Nursing, business administration/commerce/management, communication **Academic program** Advanced placement, accelerated degree program, self-designed majors, tutorials, honors program, summer session, adult/continuing education programs, internships **Contact** Ms. Penny Dempsey St. John, Director of Admissions, Regis University, Denver, CO 80221-1099. Telephone: 303-458-4900. Fax: 303-964-5534.

ROCKY MOUNTAIN COLLEGE OF ART & DESIGN
DENVER, COLORADO

Entrance Moderately difficult **General** Proprietary, 4-year, specialized, coed **Setting** 1-acre urban campus **Enrollment** 459 **Faculty** 18:1 **Application deadline** Rolling **Freshmen** 72% accepted **Tuition** $6840 **Undergraduates** 55% women, 15% part-time, 35% 25 or older, 2% Native American, 10% Hispanic, 5% black, 3% Asian or Pacific Islander **Most popular recent majors** Graphic arts, illustration, painting/drawing **Aca-**

demic program Average class size 18, advanced placement, summer session, internships **Contact** Mr. Rex Whisman, Admissions Director, Rocky Mountain College of Art & Design, 6875 East Evans Avenue, Denver, CO 80224-2329. Telephone: 303-753-6046. Fax: 303-759-4970.

UNITED STATES AIR FORCE ACADEMY
COLORADO SPRINGS, COLORADO

Entrance Most difficult **General** Federally supported, 4-year, coed **Setting** 18,000-acre suburban campus **Enrollment** 4,308 **Faculty** 8:1 **Application deadline** 1/31 **Freshmen** 18% accepted **Housing** Yes **Tuition** $0 **Undergraduates** 16% women, 0% part-time, 0% 25 or older, 1% Native American, 7% Hispanic, 5% black, 5% Asian or Pacific Islander **Most popular recent majors** Business administration/commerce/management, biology/biological sciences, civil engineering **Academic program** Average class size 18, advanced placement, self-designed majors, tutorials, summer session, internships **Contact** Mr. Rolland Stoneman, Associate Director of Admissions/Selections, United States Air Force Academy, HQ USAFA/RR 2304 Cadet Drive, Suite 200, USAF Academy, CO 80840-5025. Telephone: 719-333-2520. Fax: 719-333-3012.

UNIVERSITY OF COLORADO AT BOULDER
BOULDER, COLORADO

Entrance Moderately difficult **General** State-supported, coed **Setting** 600-acre suburban campus **Enrollment** 24,622 **Faculty** 14:1 **Application deadline** 2/15 **Freshmen** 80% accepted **Housing** Yes **Tuition** $2939 **Undergraduates** 47% women, 7% part-time, 11% 25 or older, 1% Native American, 5% Hispanic, 2% black, 6% Asian or Pacific Islander **Most popular recent majors** Psychology, English, environmental biology **Academic program** Advanced placement, accelerated degree program, self-designed majors, tutorials, honors program, summer session, adult/continuing education programs, internships **Contact** Admissions Counselor, University of Colorado at Boulder, Campus Box 30, Boulder, CO 80309-0030. Telephone: 303-492-6301. Fax: 303-492-7115.

UNIVERSITY OF COLORADO AT COLORADO SPRINGS
COLORADO SPRINGS, COLORADO

Entrance Moderately difficult **General** State-supported, comprehensive, coed **Setting** 400-acre suburban campus **Enrollment** 5,840 **Faculty** 13:1 **Application deadline** 7/1 **Freshmen** 76% accepted **Housing** Yes **Tuition** $2510 **Undergraduates** 57% women, 36% part-time, 42% 25 or older, 1% Native American, 9% Hispanic, 4% black, 4% Asian or Pacific Islander **Most popular recent majors** Business administration/commerce/management, psychology, communication **Academic program** Average class size 25, advanced placement, accelerated degree program, summer session, adult/continuing education programs, internships **Contact** Mr. James Tidwell, Assistant Admissions Director, University of Colorado at Colorado Springs, Colorado Springs, CO 80933-7150. Telephone: 719-262-3383.

UNIVERSITY OF COLORADO AT DENVER
DENVER, COLORADO

Entrance Moderately difficult **General** State-supported, coed **Setting** 171-acre urban campus **Enrollment** 10,844 **Application deadline** 7/22 **Freshmen** 75% accepted **Tuition** $2204 **Undergraduates** 52% women, 41% part-time, 47% 25 or older, 1% Native American, 16% Hispanic, 3% black, 14% Asian or Pacific Islander **Most popular recent majors** Business administration/commerce/management, psychology, biology/biological sciences **Academic program** Advanced placement, accelerated degree program, self-designed majors, tutorials, honors program, summer session, adult/continuing education programs, internships **Contact** Ms. Alice Holman, Associate Director of Admissions, University of Colorado at Denver, PO Box 173364, Denver, CO 80217-3364. Telephone: 303-556-2275.

UNIVERSITY OF COLORADO HEALTH SCIENCES CENTER
DENVER, COLORADO

Entrance Moderately difficult **General** State-supported, upper-level, coed **Setting** 40-acre urban campus **Enrollment** 2,156 **Freshmen** 28% accepted **Tuition** $3071 **Undergraduates** 74% women, 3% part-time, 1% Native American, 9% Hispanic, 4% black, 16% Asian or Pacific Islander **Most popular recent majors** Pharmacy/pharmaceutical sciences, nursing **Academic program** Advanced placement, summer session, adult/continuing education programs, internships **Contact** Dr. David P. Sorenson, Director of Admissions, University of Colorado Health Sciences Center, 4200 East Ninth Avenue, Denver, CO 80262. Telephone: 303-315-7676. Fax: 303-315-3358.

UNIVERSITY OF DENVER
DENVER, COLORADO

Entrance Moderately difficult **General** Independent, coed **Setting** 125-acre suburban campus **En-**

rollment 8,714 **Faculty** 13:1 **Application deadline** Rolling **Freshmen** 94% accepted **Housing** Yes **Tuition** $17,886 **Undergraduates** 52% women, 4% part-time, 9% 25 or older, 1% Native American, 6% Hispanic, 3% black, 6% Asian or Pacific Islander **Most popular recent majors** Biology/biological sciences, communication, marketing/retailing/merchandising **Academic program** Average class size 20, advanced placement, accelerated degree program, self-designed majors, tutorials, honors program, summer session, adult/continuing education programs, internships **Contact** Mr. Morris Price, Associate Dean of Admission, University of Denver, Denver, CO 80208. Telephone: 303-871-3373. Fax: 303-871-3301.

UNIVERSITY OF NORTHERN COLORADO
GREELEY, COLORADO

Entrance Moderately difficult **General** State-supported, coed **Setting** 240-acre suburban campus **Enrollment** 10,306 **Faculty** 21:1 **Application deadline** Rolling **Freshmen** 79% accepted **Housing** Yes **Tuition** $2596 **Undergraduates** 59% women, 8% part-time, 12% 25 or older, 1% Native American, 8% Hispanic, 3% black, 4% Asian or Pacific Islander **Most popular recent majors** Business administration/commerce/management, physical education, social science **Academic program** Average class size 42, advanced placement, accelerated degree program, self-designed majors, honors program, summer session, adult/continuing education programs, internships **Contact** Mr. Gary O. Gullickson, Director of Admissions, University of Northern Colorado, Greeley, CO 80639. Telephone: 970-351-2881.

UNIVERSITY OF SOUTHERN COLORADO
PUEBLO, COLORADO

Entrance Moderately difficult **General** State-supported, comprehensive, coed **Setting** 275-acre suburban campus **Enrollment** 4,109 **Faculty** 17:1 **Application deadline** Rolling **Freshmen** 85% accepted **Housing** Yes **Tuition** $2191 **Undergraduates** 53% women, 20% part-time, 36% 25 or older, 1% Native American, 25% Hispanic, 3% black, 1% Asian or Pacific Islander **Most popular recent majors** Business administration/commerce/management, communication, biology/biological sciences **Academic program** Advanced placement, accelerated degree program, tutorials, honors program, summer session, adult/continuing education programs, internships **Contact** Ms. Christie Kangas, Director of Admissions, University of Southern Colorado, Pueblo, CO 81001-4901. Telephone: 719-549-2461. Fax: 719-549-2419.

WESTERN STATE COLLEGE OF COLORADO
GUNNISON, COLORADO

Entrance Moderately difficult **General** State-supported, 4-year, coed **Setting** 381-acre small-town campus **Enrollment** 2,534 **Faculty** 20:1 **Application deadline** Rolling **Freshmen** 87% accepted **Housing** Yes **Tuition** $2152 **Undergraduates** 40% women, 6% part-time, 14% 25 or older, 1% Native American, 4% Hispanic, 1% black, 1% Asian or Pacific Islander **Most popular recent majors** Business administration/commerce/management, physical fitness/exercise science, sociology **Academic program** Advanced placement, accelerated degree program, self-designed majors, honors program, summer session, adult/continuing education programs, internships **Contact** Ms. Sara Axelson, Director of Admissions, Western State College of Colorado, Gunnison, CO 81231. Telephone: 970-943-2119. Fax: 970-943-7069.

Hawaii

BRIGHAM YOUNG UNIVERSITY–HAWAII CAMPUS
LAIE, OAHU, HAWAII

Entrance Moderately difficult **General** Independent Latter-day Saints, 4-year, coed **Setting** 60-acre small-town campus **Enrollment** 2,287 **Faculty** 16:1 **Application deadline** 3/31 **Freshmen** 70% accepted **Housing** Yes **Tuition** $2665 **Undergraduates** 62% women, 6% part-time, 22% 25 or older, 1% Native American, 2% Hispanic, 1% black, 54% Asian or Pacific Islander **Most popular recent majors** Business administration/commerce/management, accounting, education **Academic program** Average class size 25, advanced placement, accelerated degree program, honors program, summer session, adult/continuing education programs, internships **Contact** Dr. David Settle, Assistant Dean for Admissions and Records, Brigham Young University–Hawaii Campus, Laie, Oahu, HI 96762-1294. Telephone: 808-293-3738.

CHAMINADE UNIVERSITY OF HONOLULU
HONOLULU, HAWAII

Entrance Moderately difficult **General** Independent Roman Catholic, comprehensive, coed **Setting** 62-acre urban campus **Enrollment** 2,674

Faculty 16:1 **Application deadline** Rolling **Freshmen** 95% accepted **Housing** Yes **Tuition** $10,850 **Undergraduates** 54% women, 11% part-time, 5% 25 or older, 1% Native American, 1% Hispanic, 3% black, 54% Asian or Pacific Islander **Most popular recent majors** Criminal justice, biology/biological sciences, behavioral sciences **Academic program** Advanced placement, honors program, summer session, adult/continuing education programs, internships **Contact** Office of Admissions, Chaminade University of Honolulu, 3140 Waialae Avenue, Honolulu, HI 96816-1578. Telephone: 808-735-4735. Fax: 808-739-4647.

HAWAII PACIFIC UNIVERSITY
HONOLULU, HAWAII

Entrance Moderately difficult **General** Independent, comprehensive, coed **Setting** 135-acre urban campus **Enrollment** 8,270 **Faculty** 20:1 **Application deadline** Rolling **Freshmen** 77% accepted **Housing** Yes **Tuition** $7500 **Undergraduates** 51% women, 38% part-time, 36% 25 or older, 1% Native American, 4% Hispanic, 7% black, 22% Asian or Pacific Islander **Most popular recent majors** Business administration/commerce/management, computer science, tourism and travel **Academic program** Average class size 22, ESL program, advanced placement, accelerated degree program, self-designed majors, tutorials, honors program, summer session, adult/continuing education programs, internships **Contact** Mr. Scott Stensrud, Director of Admissions, Hawaii Pacific University, 1164 Bishop Street, Honolulu, HI 96813-2785. Telephone: 808-544-0238. Fax: 808-544-1136.

INTERNATIONAL COLLEGE AND GRADUATE SCHOOL
HONOLULU, HAWAII

Entrance Difficulty N/R **General** Independent interdenominational, upper-level, specialized **Enrollment** 225 **Freshmen** 86% accepted **Tuition** $3640 **Contact** Mr. Jon Rawlings, Director of Admissions, International College and Graduate School, Honolulu, HI 96817. Telephone: 808-595-4247. Fax: 808-595-4779.

UNIVERSITY OF HAWAII AT HILO
HILO, HAWAII

Entrance Moderately difficult **General** State-supported, 4-year, coed **Setting** 115-acre small-town campus **Enrollment** 2,870 **Faculty** 11:1 **Application deadline** 5/15 **Freshmen** 62% accepted **Housing** Yes **Tuition** $1322 **Undergraduates** 59% women, 25% part-time, 41% 25 or older, 19% Native American, 2% Hispanic, 1% black, 35% Asian or Pacific Islander **Most popular recent majors** Business administration/commerce/management, psychology, English **Academic program** Advanced placement, accelerated degree program, self-designed majors, tutorials, honors program, summer session, adult/continuing education programs, internships **Contact** Mr. James West, UH Student Services Specialist III, University of Hawaii at Hilo, Hilo, HI 96720-4091. Telephone: 808-974-7315.

UNIVERSITY OF HAWAII AT MANOA
HONOLULU, HAWAII

Entrance Moderately difficult **General** State-supported, coed **Setting** 300-acre urban campus **Enrollment** 17,023 **Faculty** 14:1 **Application deadline** 5/1 **Freshmen** 64% accepted **Housing** Yes **Tuition** $2950 **Undergraduates** 54% women, 18% part-time, 20% 25 or older, 1% Native American, 1% Hispanic, 1% black, 72% Asian or Pacific Islander **Most popular recent majors** Psychology, elementary education, business administration/commerce/management **Academic program** Average class size 25, advanced placement, self-designed majors, tutorials, honors program, summer session, adult/continuing education programs, internships **Contact** Dr. David Robb, Director of Admissions and Records, University of Hawaii at Manoa, 2444 Dole Street, Honolulu, HI 96822. Telephone: 808-956-8975.

UNIVERSITY OF HAWAII–WEST OAHU
PEARL CITY, HAWAII

Entrance Moderately difficult **General** State-supported, upper-level, coed **Setting** Small-town campus **Enrollment** 644 **Freshmen** 70% accepted **Tuition** $1762 **Undergraduates** 63% women, 62% part-time, 76% 25 or older, 0% Native American, 2% Hispanic, 1% black, 43% Asian or Pacific Islander **Most popular recent majors** Business administration/commerce/management, psychology, public administration **Academic program** Self-designed majors, tutorials, summer session, internships **Contact** Ms. Stella Ho-McGinnes, Dean of Student Services, University of Hawaii-West Oahu, Pearl City, HI 96782-3366. Telephone: 808-453-6565.

Idaho

ALBERTSON COLLEGE OF IDAHO
CALDWELL, IDAHO

Entrance Moderately difficult **General** Independent, 4-year, coed **Setting** 43-acre small-town campus **Enrollment** 651 **Faculty** 11:1 **Application deadline** 6/1 **Freshmen** 86% accepted **Housing** Yes **Tuition** $15,365 **Undergraduates** 55% women, 6% part-time, 0% Native American, 2% Hispanic, 0% black, 2% Asian or Pacific Islander **Most popular recent majors** Business administration/commerce/management, history, biology/biological sciences **Academic program** Average class size 16, advanced placement, accelerated degree program, self-designed majors, tutorials, honors program, adult/continuing education programs, internships **Contact** Mr. Dennis P. Bergvall, Dean of Admissions, Albertson College of Idaho, Caldwell, ID 83605-4494. Telephone: 208-459-5305. Fax: 208-454-2077.

BOISE BIBLE COLLEGE
BOISE, IDAHO

Entrance Noncompetitive **General** Independent nondenominational, 4-year, specialized, coed **Setting** 17-acre suburban campus **Enrollment** 113 **Faculty** 14:1 **Application deadline** Rolling **Freshmen** 100% accepted **Housing** Yes **Tuition** $4340 **Undergraduates** 38% women, 18% part-time, 19% 25 or older, 0% Native American, 1% Hispanic, 1% black, 0% Asian or Pacific Islander **Most popular recent majors** Ministries, biblical studies, sacred music **Academic program** Average class size 30, advanced placement, internships **Contact** Mr. Randy Bourne, Registrar/Director of Admissions, Boise Bible College, Boise, ID 83714-1220. Telephone: 208-376-7731 Ext. 11.

BOISE STATE UNIVERSITY
BOISE, IDAHO

Entrance Minimally difficult **General** State-supported, comprehensive, coed **Setting** 130-acre urban campus **Enrollment** 15,137 **Faculty** 18:1 **Application deadline** 7/23 **Freshmen** 90% accepted **Housing** Yes **Tuition** $2294 **Undergraduates** 57% women, 45% part-time, 50% 25 or older, 1% Native American, 4% Hispanic, 1% black, 1% Asian or Pacific Islander **Most popular recent majors** Elementary education, accounting, marketing/retailing/merchandising **Academic program** Average class size 40, advanced placement, self-designed majors, honors program, summer session, adult/continuing education programs, internships **Contact** Mr. Stephen Spafford, Dean of Admissions, Boise State University, 1910 University Drive, Boise, ID 83725-0399. Telephone: 208-385-1177.

IDAHO STATE UNIVERSITY
POCATELLO, IDAHO

Entrance Minimally difficult **General** State-supported, coed **Setting** 274-acre small-town campus **Enrollment** 12,154 **Faculty** 18:1 **Application deadline** 8/1 **Freshmen** 88% accepted **Housing** Yes **Tuition** $1726 **Undergraduates** 56% women, 25% part-time, 41% 25 or older, 2% Native American, 3% Hispanic, 1% black, 1% Asian or Pacific Islander **Most popular recent majors** Business administration/commerce/management, elementary education, secondary education **Academic program** Advanced placement, self-designed majors, honors program, summer session, adult/continuing education programs, internships **Contact** Ms. Bessie Katsulometes, Associate Director of Enrollment Planning/Academic Services, Idaho State University, PO Box 8054, Pocatello, ID 83209. Telephone: 208-236-3277. Fax: 208-236-4314.

LEWIS-CLARK STATE COLLEGE
LEWISTON, IDAHO

Entrance Minimally difficult **General** State-supported, 4-year, coed **Setting** 44-acre rural campus **Enrollment** 2,978 **Faculty** 16:1 **Application deadline** Rolling **Freshmen** 99% accepted **Housing** Yes **Tuition** $1868 **Undergraduates** 60% women, 32% part-time, 40% 25 or older, 4% Native American, 1% Hispanic, 1% black, 1% Asian or Pacific Islander **Most popular recent majors** Business administration/commerce/management, education, nursing **Academic program** Advanced placement, accelerated degree program, self-designed majors, tutorials, honors program, summer session, adult/continuing education programs, internships **Contact** Mrs. Christine Licht, Assistant Director of Admissions, Lewis-Clark State College, Lewiston, ID 83501-2698. Telephone: 208-799-2210. Fax: 208-799-2831.

NORTHWEST NAZARENE COLLEGE
NAMPA, IDAHO

Entrance Moderately difficult **General** Independent, comprehensive, coed, affiliated with Church of the Nazarene **Setting** 65-acre small-town campus **Enrollment** 1,201 **Faculty** 11:1 **Application deadline** 9/19 **Freshmen** 41% accepted **Housing** Yes **Tuition** $12,138 **Undergraduates** 56% women, 6% part-time, 7% 25 or older, 1% Native American, 2% Hispanic, 1% black, 1% Asian or Pacific Islander **Most popular recent majors** Elementary education, business administration/commerce/management, social science **Academic program** Advanced placement, accelerated degree program, self-designed majors, tutorials, honors program, summer session, internships **Contact** Mr. Barry Swanson, Director of

Enrollment Management, Northwest Nazarene College, Nampa, ID 83686-5897. Telephone: 208-467-8773.

UNIVERSITY OF IDAHO
MOSCOW, IDAHO

Entrance Moderately difficult **General** State-supported, coed **Setting** 1,450-acre small-town campus **Enrollment** 11,727 **Faculty** 17:1 **Application deadline** 8/1 **Freshmen** 85% accepted **Housing** Yes **Tuition** $1942 **Undergraduates** 43% women, 10% part-time, 24% 25 or older, 1% Native American, 2% Hispanic, 1% black, 2% Asian or Pacific Islander **Most popular recent majors** Communication, engineering (general), biology/biological sciences **Academic program** Average class size 28, advanced placement, accelerated degree program, self-designed majors, honors program, summer session, adult/continuing education programs, internships **Contact** Mr. Dan Davenport, Director of Admissions, University of Idaho, Moscow, ID 83844. Telephone: 208-885-6326. Fax: 208-885-5752.

Montana

CARROLL COLLEGE
HELENA, MONTANA

Entrance Moderately difficult **General** Independent Roman Catholic, 4-year, coed **Setting** 64-acre small-town campus **Enrollment** 1,352 **Faculty** 11:1 **Application deadline** 6/1 **Freshmen** 94% accepted **Housing** Yes **Tuition** $11,316 **Undergraduates** 62% women, 17% part-time, 24% 25 or older, 2% Native American, 1% Hispanic, 1% black, 1% Asian or Pacific Islander **Most popular recent majors** Business administration/commerce/management, biology/biological sciences, nursing **Academic program** Average class size 25, advanced placement, accelerated degree program, self-designed majors, tutorials, honors program, summer session, adult/continuing education programs, internships **Contact** Ms. Candace A. Cain, Director of Admission, Carroll College, Helena, MT 59625-0002. Telephone: 406-447-4384.

COLLEGE OF GREAT FALLS
SEE UNIVERSITY OF GREAT FALLS

MONTANA STATE UNIVERSITY–BILLINGS
BILLINGS, MONTANA

Entrance Moderately difficult **General** State-supported, comprehensive, coed **Setting** 92-acre urban campus **Enrollment** 4,006 **Faculty** 20:1 **Application deadline** 7/1 **Housing** Yes **Tuition** $2388 **Undergraduates** 63% women, 25% part-time, 36% 25 or older, 5% Native American, 2% Hispanic, 1% black, 1% Asian or Pacific Islander **Most popular recent majors** Elementary education, secondary education, business administration/commerce/management **Academic program** Advanced placement, accelerated degree program, tutorials, honors program, summer session, adult/continuing education programs, internships **Contact** Ms. Karen Everett, Admissions/Records Registrar, Montana State University–Billings, 1500 North 30th Street, Billings, MT 59101-9984. Telephone: 406-657-2158. Fax: 406-657-2302.

MONTANA STATE UNIVERSITY–BOZEMAN
BOZEMAN, MONTANA

Entrance Moderately difficult **General** State-supported, coed **Setting** 1,170-acre small-town campus **Enrollment** 11,611 **Faculty** 18:1 **Application deadline** 7/1 **Freshmen** 75% accepted **Housing** Yes **Tuition** $2504 **Undergraduates** 44% women, 13% part-time, 19% 25 or older, 2% Native American, 1% Hispanic, 1% black, 1% Asian or Pacific Islander **Most popular recent majors** Business administration/commerce/management, nursing, education **Academic program** Average class size 47, advanced placement, accelerated degree program, self-designed majors, honors program, summer session, adult/continuing education programs, internships **Contact** Ms. Rhonda Russell, Director of New Student Services, Montana State University–Bozeman, 120 Hamilton Hall, Bozeman, MT 59717. Telephone: 406-994-2452.

MONTANA STATE UNIVERSITY–NORTHERN
HAVRE, MONTANA

Entrance Moderately difficult **General** State-supported, comprehensive, coed **Setting** 105-acre small-town campus **Enrollment** 1,702 **Faculty** 19:1 **Application deadline** Rolling **Housing** Yes **Tuition** $2350 **Undergraduates** 55% women, 25% part-time, 47% 25 or older, 8% Native American, 1% Hispanic, 1% black, 1% Asian or Pacific Islander **Most popular recent majors** Education, business administration/commerce/management, nursing **Academic program** Advanced placement, tutorials, honors program, summer session, adult/continuing education programs, internships **Contact** Ms. Rosalie Spinler, Director of Admissions, Montana State University–Northern, Havre, MT 59501-7751. Telephone: 406-265-3704. Fax: 406-265-3777.

MONTANA TECH OF THE UNIVERSITY OF MONTANA
BUTTE, MONTANA

Entrance Moderately difficult **General** State-supported, comprehensive, coed **Setting** 56-acre small-town campus **Enrollment** 1,860 **Faculty** 16:1 **Application deadline** 7/1 **Freshmen** 83% accepted **Housing** Yes **Tuition** $2373 **Undergraduates** 40% women, 21% part-time, 34% 25 or older, 1% Native American, 1% Hispanic, 1% black, 1% Asian or Pacific Islander **Most popular recent majors** Environmental engineering, computer science, engineering sciences **Academic program** Average class size 30, advanced placement, tutorials, summer session, adult/continuing education programs, internships **Contact** Ms. Monica Bruning, Director of Admissions, Montana Tech of The University of Montana, 1300 West Park Street, Butte, MT 59701-8997. Telephone: 406-496-4178. Fax: 406-496-4710.

ROCKY MOUNTAIN COLLEGE
BILLINGS, MONTANA

Entrance Moderately difficult **General** Independent interdenominational, 4-year, coed **Setting** 60-acre suburban campus **Enrollment** 744 **Faculty** 15:1 **Application deadline** Rolling **Freshmen** 99% accepted **Housing** Yes **Tuition** $10,599 **Undergraduates** 53% women, 13% part-time, 29% 25 or older, 6% Native American, 2% Hispanic, 1% black, 1% Asian or Pacific Islander **Most popular recent majors** Business administration/commerce/management, education, psychology **Academic program** Average class size 15, advanced placement, accelerated degree program, self-designed majors, tutorials, honors program, summer session, adult/continuing education programs, internships **Contact** Mr. Craig Gould, Director of Admissions, Rocky Mountain College, Billings, MT 59102-1796. Telephone: 406-657-1026. Fax: 406-259-9751.

UNIVERSITY OF GREAT FALLS
GREAT FALLS, MONTANA

Entrance Noncompetitive **General** Independent Roman Catholic, comprehensive, coed **Setting** 40-acre urban campus **Enrollment** 1,291 **Faculty** 15:1 **Application deadline** Rolling **Freshmen** 100% accepted **Housing** Yes **Tuition** $8100 **Undergraduates** 67% women, 38% part-time, 73% 25 or older, 9% Native American, 1% Hispanic, 1% black, 2% Asian or Pacific Islander **Most popular recent majors** Criminal justice, human services, education **Academic program** Advanced placement, accelerated degree program, summer session, adult/continuing education programs, internships **Contact** Ms. Audrey Thompson, Director of Admissions and Records, University of Great Falls, 1301 Twentieth Street South, Great Falls, MT 59405. Telephone: 406-761-8210 Ext. 260.

THE UNIVERSITY OF MONTANA–MISSOULA
MISSOULA, MONTANA

Entrance Moderately difficult **General** State-supported, coed **Setting** 220-acre urban campus **Enrollment** 11,886 **Faculty** 19:1 **Application deadline** 7/1 **Freshmen** 83% accepted **Housing** Yes **Tuition** $2229 **Undergraduates** 51% women, 18% part-time, 24% 25 or older, 3% Native American, 1% Hispanic, 1% black, 1% Asian or Pacific Islander **Most popular recent majors** Business administration/commerce/management, education, forestry **Academic program** Average class size 50, advanced placement, tutorials, honors program, summer session, adult/continuing education programs, internships **Contact** Office of New Student Services, The University of Montana–Missoula, Missoula, MT 59812-0002. Telephone: 406-243-6266.

WESTERN MONTANA COLLEGE OF THE UNIVERSITY OF MONTANA
DILLON, MONTANA

Entrance Moderately difficult **General** State-supported, 4-year, coed **Setting** 36-acre small-town campus **Enrollment** 1,115 **Faculty** 20:1 **Application deadline** Rolling **Freshmen** 95% accepted **Housing** Yes **Tuition** $2326 **Undergraduates** 56% women, 15% part-time, 20% 25 or older, 1% Native American, 0% Hispanic, 2% black **Most popular recent majors** Elementary education, liberal arts/general studies, physical education **Academic program** Average class size 40, advanced placement, accelerated degree program, self-designed majors, tutorials, honors program, summer session, adult/continuing education programs, internships **Contact** Ms. Kay Leum, Director of Admissions and New Student Services, Western Montana College of The University of Montana, Dillon, MT 59725-3598. Telephone: 406-683-7331. Fax: 406-683-7493.

Nevada

MORRISON COLLEGE
RENO, NEVADA

Entrance Noncompetitive **General** Proprietary, 4-year, coed **Setting** 2-acre urban campus **Enrollment** 290 **Faculty** 10:1 **Undergraduates** 60%

women, 30% part-time, 74% 25 or older, 3% Native American, 4% Hispanic, 4% black, 4% Asian or Pacific Islander **Most popular recent majors** Accounting, paralegal studies, computer information systems **Academic program** Accelerated degree program, tutorials, summer session, adult/continuing education programs, internships **Contact** Ms. Rose Hoffert, Director of Admissions, Morrison College, 140 Washington Street, Reno, NV 89503-5600. Telephone: 702-323-4145. Fax: 702-323-8495.

SIERRA NEVADA COLLEGE
INCLINE VILLAGE, NEVADA

Entrance Moderately difficult **General** Independent, 4-year, coed **Setting** 20-acre small-town campus **Enrollment** 600 **Faculty** 12:1 **Application deadline** Rolling **Freshmen** 97% accepted **Housing** Yes **Tuition** $9450 **Undergraduates** 38% women, 29% part-time, 20% 25 or older, 0% Native American, 1% Hispanic, 0% black, 0% Asian or Pacific Islander **Most popular recent majors** Business administration/commerce/management, hotel and restaurant management, humanities **Academic program** Advanced placement, accelerated degree program, tutorials, summer session, adult/continuing education programs, internships **Contact** Mr. Sam Drury, Admissions Counselor, Sierra Nevada College, Incline Village, NV 89450-4269. Telephone: 702-831-1314 Ext. 3103.

UNIVERSITY OF NEVADA, LAS VEGAS
LAS VEGAS, NEVADA

Entrance Moderately difficult **General** State-supported, coed **Setting** 335-acre urban campus **Enrollment** 19,682 **Faculty** 21:1 **Application deadline** 8/15 **Freshmen** 85% accepted **Housing** Yes **Tuition** $2045 **Undergraduates** 52% women, 45% part-time, 50% 25 or older, 1% Native American, 8% Hispanic, 8% black, 4% Asian or Pacific Islander **Most popular recent majors** Hotel and restaurant management, business administration/commerce/management, accounting **Academic program** Advanced placement, accelerated degree program, self-designed majors, honors program, summer session, adult/continuing education programs, internships **Contact** Mr. John Witter, Associate Director of Admissions, University of Nevada, Las Vegas, 4505 Maryland Parkway, Las Vegas, NV 89154-1021. Telephone: 702-895-3443.

UNIVERSITY OF NEVADA, RENO
RENO, NEVADA

Entrance Moderately difficult **General** State-supported, coed **Setting** 200-acre urban campus **Enrollment** 11,652 **Application deadline** 3/1 **Freshmen** 86% accepted **Housing** Yes **Tuition** $2242 **Undergraduates** 52% women, 27% part-time, 26% 25 or older, 1% Native American, 5% Hispanic, 2% black, 6% Asian or Pacific Islander **Most popular recent majors** Education, psychology, criminal justice **Academic program** Advanced placement, tutorials, honors program, summer session, adult/continuing education programs, internships **Contact** Dr. Melissa N. Choroszy, Associate Dean of Records and Enrollment Services, University of Nevada, Reno, Reno, NV 89557. Telephone: 702-784-6865.

New Mexico

COLLEGE OF SANTA FE
SANTA FE, NEW MEXICO

Entrance Moderately difficult **General** Independent, comprehensive, coed **Setting** 98-acre suburban campus **Enrollment** 1,469 **Faculty** 14:1 **Application deadline** Rolling **Freshmen** 80% accepted **Housing** Yes **Tuition** $13,240 **Undergraduates** 64% women, 35% part-time, 17% 25 or older, 3% Native American, 27% Hispanic, 3% black, 1% Asian or Pacific Islander **Most popular recent majors** Film and video production, education, business administration/commerce/management **Academic program** Average class size 16, ESL program, advanced placement, self-designed majors, tutorials, summer session, adult/continuing education programs, internships **Contact** Mr. Dale Reinhart, Director of Admissions, College of Santa Fe, 1600 Saint Michael's Drive, Santa Fe, NM 87505-7634. Telephone: 505-473-6133. Fax: 505-473-6127.

COLLEGE OF THE SOUTHWEST
HOBBS, NEW MEXICO

Entrance Moderately difficult **General** Independent, comprehensive, coed **Setting** 162-acre small-town campus **Enrollment** 538 **Faculty** 8:1 **Application deadline** Rolling **Freshmen** 41% accepted **Housing** Yes **Tuition** $4430 **Undergraduates** 73% women, 36% part-time, 61% 25 or older, 1% Native American, 22% Hispanic, 2% black **Most popular recent majors** Education, business education, psychology **Academic program** Average class size 20, advanced placement, accelerated degree program, tutorials, summer session, adult/continuing education programs, internships **Contact** Mr. Jamie Hodgins, Director of Admissions, College of the Southwest, Hobbs, NM 88240-9129. Telephone: 505-392-6561.

EASTERN NEW MEXICO UNIVERSITY
PORTALES, NEW MEXICO

Entrance Minimally difficult **General** State-supported, comprehensive, coed **Setting** 240-acre rural campus **Enrollment** 3,617 **Application deadline** Rolling **Freshmen** 99% accepted **Housing** Yes **Tuition** $1654 **Undergraduates** 56% women, 19% part-time, 28% 25 or older, 2% Native American, 22% Hispanic, 4% black, 1% Asian or Pacific Islander **Most popular recent majors** Education, sociology, liberal arts/general studies **Academic program** Advanced placement, accelerated degree program, self-designed majors, honors program, summer session, adult/continuing education programs, internships **Contact** Mr. Larry Fuqua, Director of Admissions, Eastern New Mexico University, Station #5 ENMU, Portales, NM 88130. Telephone: 505-562-2178.

NATIONAL COLLEGE
ALBUQUERQUE, NEW MEXICO

Entrance Noncompetitive **General** Proprietary, 4-year, coed **Setting** Suburban campus **Enrollment** 294 **Application deadline** Rolling **Tuition** $8210 **Undergraduates Most popular recent majors** Business administration/commerce/management, computer information systems, accounting **Academic program** Accelerated degree program, tutorials, internships **Contact** Ms. Nancy Pointer, Educational Consultant, National College, Albuquerque, NM 87110. Telephone: 505-265-7517. Fax: 505-265-7542.

NAZARENE INDIAN BIBLE COLLEGE
ALBUQUERQUE, NEW MEXICO

Entrance Moderately difficult **General** Independent, 4-year, coed, affiliated with Church of the Nazarene **Setting** Suburban campus **Enrollment** 46 **Application deadline** Rolling **Freshmen** 80% accepted **Housing** Yes **Tuition** $4170 **Contact** Ms. Yolanda Vielle, Acting Registrar, Nazarene Indian Bible College, Albuquerque, NM 87105. Telephone: 505-877-0240.

NEW MEXICO HIGHLANDS UNIVERSITY
LAS VEGAS, NEW MEXICO

Entrance Minimally difficult **General** State-supported, comprehensive, coed **Setting** 120-acre small-town campus **Enrollment** 2,751 **Faculty** 20:1 **Application deadline** Rolling **Freshmen** 91% accepted **Housing** Yes **Tuition** $1662 **Undergraduates** 54% women, 13% part-time, 26% 25 or older, 5% Native American, 70% Hispanic, 3% black, 1% Asian or Pacific Islander **Most popular recent majors** Business administration/commerce/management, elementary education, social work **Academic program** Average class size 30, advanced placement, accelerated degree program, tutorials, honors program, summer session, internships **Contact** Mr. Larry Cruz, Director of Student Recruitment, New Mexico Highlands University, Las Vegas, NM 87701. Telephone: 505-454-3256. Fax: 505-454-3311.

NEW MEXICO INSTITUTE OF MINING AND TECHNOLOGY
SOCORRO, NEW MEXICO

Entrance Moderately difficult **General** State-supported, coed **Setting** 320-acre small-town campus **Enrollment** 1,461 **Faculty** 11:1 **Application deadline** 8/1 **Freshmen** 77% accepted **Housing** Yes **Tuition** $2074 **Undergraduates** 36% women, 20% part-time, 30% 25 or older, 3% Native American, 20% Hispanic, 1% black, 3% Asian or Pacific Islander **Most popular recent majors** Electrical engineering, environmental engineering, mathematics **Academic program** Average class size 23, advanced placement, self-designed majors, tutorials, summer session, adult/continuing education programs, internships **Contact** Ms. Melissa Jaramillo-Fleming, Director of Admissions, New Mexico Institute of Mining and Technology, Socorro, NM 87801. Telephone: 505-835-5424. Fax: 505-835-5989.

NEW MEXICO STATE UNIVERSITY
LAS CRUCES, NEW MEXICO

Entrance Moderately difficult **General** State-supported, coed **Setting** 5,800-acre suburban campus **Enrollment** 14,748 **Application deadline** 8/14 **Freshmen** 80% accepted **Housing** Yes **Tuition** $2196 **Undergraduates** 51% women, 25% part-time, 27% 25 or older, 3% Native American, 37% Hispanic, 2% black, 1% Asian or Pacific Islander **Most popular recent majors** Marketing/retailing/merchandising, electrical engineering technology, education **Academic program** Advanced placement, accelerated degree program, self-designed majors, honors program, summer session, adult/continuing education programs, internships **Contact** Ms. Angela Mora, Director of Admissions, New Mexico State University, Box 30001, Department 3A, Las Cruces, NM 88003-8001. Telephone: 505-646-3121.

ST. JOHN'S COLLEGE
SANTA FE, NEW MEXICO

Entrance Moderately difficult **General** Independent, comprehensive, coed **Setting** 250-acre small-town campus **Enrollment** 472 **Faculty** 8:1 **Application deadline** Rolling **Freshmen** 81% accepted **Housing** Yes **Tuition** $19,700 **Undergraduates** 47% women, 2% part-time, 8% 25 or older, 1% Native American, 5% Hispanic, 1% black, 3% Asian or Pacific Islander **Academic program** Average class size 17, tutorials **Contact** Mr. Larry Clendenin, Director of Admissions, St. John's College, Santa Fe, NM 87501-4599. Telephone: 505-984-6060.

UNIVERSITY OF NEW MEXICO
ALBUQUERQUE, NEW MEXICO

Entrance Moderately difficult **General** State-supported, coed **Setting** 625-acre urban campus **Enrollment** 23,617 **Application deadline** 7/20 **Freshmen** 74% accepted **Housing** Yes **Tuition** $2165 **Undergraduates** 57% women, 28% part-time, 36% 25 or older, 5% Native American, 29% Hispanic, 3% black, 3% Asian or Pacific Islander **Most popular recent majors** Liberal arts/general studies, elementary education, nursing **Academic program** Advanced placement, self-designed majors, honors program, summer session, adult/continuing education programs, internships **Contact** Ms. Cynthia Stuart, Director of Admissions, University of New Mexico, Albuquerque, NM 87131-2039. Telephone: 505-277-2446.

WESTERN NEW MEXICO UNIVERSITY
SILVER CITY, NEW MEXICO

Entrance Noncompetitive **General** State-supported, comprehensive, coed **Setting** 83-acre rural campus **Enrollment** 2,533 **Faculty** 16:1 **Application deadline** 8/15 **Freshmen** 100% accepted **Housing** Yes **Tuition** $1711 **Undergraduates** 62% women, 36% part-time, 46% 25 or older, 2% Native American, 42% Hispanic, 2% black, 1% Asian or Pacific Islander **Most popular recent majors** Education, business administration/commerce/management, social science **Academic program** Advanced placement, accelerated degree program, self-designed majors, tutorials, summer session, adult/continuing education programs, internships **Contact** Mr. Michael Alecksen, Director of Admissions, Western New Mexico University, College Avenue, Silver City, NM 88062-0680. Telephone: 505-538-6106. Fax: 505-538-6155.

Oregon

BASSIST COLLEGE
PORTLAND, OREGON

Entrance Minimally difficult **General** Proprietary, 4-year, coed **Setting** 1-acre urban campus **Enrollment** 101 **Faculty** 8:1 **Application deadline** 9/1 **Freshmen** 100% accepted **Housing** Yes **Tuition** $8990 **Undergraduates** 86% women, 14% part-time, 40% 25 or older, 0% Native American, 7% Hispanic, 3% black, 7% Asian or Pacific Islander **Most popular recent majors** Interior design, fashion design and technology **Academic program** Accelerated degree program, tutorials, summer session, internships **Contact** Ms. Kelly Alston, Director of Admissions, Bassist College, 2000 Southwest Fifth Avenue, Portland, OR 97201-4907. Telephone: 503-228-6528. Fax: 503-228-4227.

CASCADE COLLEGE
PORTLAND, OREGON

Entrance Noncompetitive **General** Independent, 4-year, coed, affiliated with Church of Christ **Setting** 13-acre urban campus **Enrollment** 255 **Faculty** 17:1 **Application deadline** Rolling **Freshmen** 99% accepted **Housing** Yes **Tuition** $7550 **Undergraduates** 50% women, 2% part-time, 1% Native American, 2% Hispanic, 7% black, 2% Asian or Pacific Islander **Most popular recent majors** Liberal arts/general studies, biblical studies **Academic program** Average class size 30, advanced placement, accelerated degree program, tutorials, summer session, internships **Contact** Ms. Mary Horton, Director of Admissions, Cascade College, 9101 East Burnside Street, Portland, OR 97216-1515. Telephone: 503-257-1202.

CONCORDIA UNIVERSITY
PORTLAND, OREGON

Entrance Minimally difficult **General** Independent, comprehensive, coed, affiliated with Lutheran Church–Missouri Synod **Setting** 13-acre urban campus **Enrollment** 1,020 **Faculty** 18:1 **Application deadline** Rolling **Freshmen** 88% accepted **Housing** Yes **Tuition** $11,030 **Undergraduates** 57% women, 21% part-time, 50% 25 or older, 1% Native American, 2% Hispanic, 4% black, 2% Asian or Pacific Islander **Most popular recent majors** Education, business administration/commerce/management, health services administration **Academic program** Advanced placement, accelerated degree program, self-designed majors, tutorials, summer session, adult/continuing education programs, internships **Contact** Mr. Peter Johnson, Director of Admissions, Concordia University, 2811 Northeast Holman, Portland, OR 97211-6099. Telephone: 503-280-8501. Fax: 503-280-8531.

EASTERN OREGON UNIVERSITY
LA GRANDE, OREGON

Entrance Moderately difficult **General** State-supported, comprehensive, coed **Setting** 121-acre rural campus **Enrollment** 1,876 **Faculty** 14:1 **Application deadline** 8/1 **Freshmen** 61% accepted **Housing** Yes **Tuition** $3011 **Undergraduates** 52% women, 11% part-time, 24% 25 or older, 2% Native American, 4% Hispanic, 1% black, 3% Asian or Pacific Islander **Most popular recent majors** Education, business economics, biology/biological sciences **Academic program** Advanced placement, accelerated degree program, self-designed majors, tutorials, summer session, adult/continuing education programs, internships **Contact** Ms. Terral Schut, Director of Admissions and New Student Programs, Eastern Oregon University, La Grande, OR 97850-2899. Telephone: 541-962-3393. Fax: 541-962-3418.

EUGENE BIBLE COLLEGE
EUGENE, OREGON

Entrance Minimally difficult **General** Independent, 4-year, specialized, coed, affiliated with Open Bible Standard Churches **Setting** 40-acre suburban campus **Enrollment** 250 **Faculty** 14:1 **Application deadline** 9/1 **Freshmen** 88% accepted **Housing** Yes **Tuition** $4977 **Undergraduates** 47% women, 24% part-time, 28% 25 or older, 1% Native American, 4% Hispanic, 5% black, 3% Asian or Pacific Islander **Academic program** Summer session, internships **Contact** Mr. Trent Combs, Director of Admissions, Eugene Bible College, Eugene, OR 97405-1194. Telephone: 541-485-1780 Ext. 35. Fax: 541-343-5801.

GEORGE FOX UNIVERSITY
NEWBERG, OREGON

Entrance Moderately difficult **General** Independent Friends, coed **Setting** 73-acre small-town campus **Enrollment** 2,188 **Faculty** 16:1 **Application deadline** 6/1 **Freshmen** 87% accepted **Housing** Yes **Tuition** $15,520 **Undergraduates** 61% women, 3% part-time, 18% 25 or older, 1% Native American, 2% Hispanic, 1% black, 3% Asian or Pacific Islander **Most popular recent majors** Education, business administration/commerce/management, biology/biological sciences **Academic program** Average class size 25, advanced placement, accelerated degree program, self-designed majors, tutorials, honors program, adult/continuing education programs, internships **Contact** Mr. Jeff Rickey, Dean of Admissions, George Fox University, Newberg, OR 97132-2697. Telephone: 503-538-8383 Ext. 2240. Fax: 503-538-7234.

LEWIS & CLARK COLLEGE
PORTLAND, OREGON

Entrance Very difficult **General** Independent, comprehensive, coed **Setting** 115-acre suburban campus **Enrollment** 3,074 **Faculty** 13:1 **Application deadline** 2/1 **Freshmen** 68% accepted **Housing** Yes **Tuition** $18,530 **Undergraduates** 56% women, 2% part-time, 2% 25 or older, 1% Native American, 3% Hispanic, 1% black, 10% Asian or Pacific Islander **Most popular recent majors** International studies, psychology, biology/biological sciences **Academic program** Average class size 20, advanced placement, accelerated degree program, self-designed majors, tutorials, honors program, summer session, internships **Contact** Mr. Michael Sexton, Dean of Admissions, Lewis & Clark College, Portland, OR 97219-7899. Telephone: 503-768-7040. Fax: 503-768-7055.

LINFIELD COLLEGE
MCMINNVILLE, OREGON

Entrance Moderately difficult **General** Independent American Baptist, 4-year, coed **Setting** 110-acre small-town campus **Enrollment** 1,594 **Faculty** 15:1 **Application deadline** 2/15 **Freshmen** 88% accepted **Housing** Yes **Tuition** $16,013 **Undergraduates** 55% women, 5% part-time, 4% 25 or older, 1% Native American, 2% Hispanic, 1% black, 5% Asian or Pacific Islander **Most popular recent majors** Business administration/commerce/management, elementary education, biology/biological sciences **Academic program** Advanced placement, accelerated degree program, honors program, summer session, adult/continuing education programs, internships **Contact** Mr. Ernie Sandlin, Director of Admissions, Linfield College, McMinnville, OR 97128-6894. Telephone: 503-434-2213. Fax: 503-434-2472.

MARYLHURST COLLEGE
MARYLHURST, OREGON

Entrance Noncompetitive **General** Independent Roman Catholic, comprehensive, coed **Setting** 73-acre suburban campus **Enrollment** 1,228 **Faculty** 10:1 **Application deadline** Rolling **Freshmen** 100% accepted **Housing** Yes **Tuition** $9960 **Undergraduates** 76% women, 72% part-time, 89% 25 or older, 2% Native American, 2% Hispanic, 3% black, 2% Asian or Pacific Islander **Most popular recent majors** Business administration/commerce/management, communication, social science **Academic program** Average class size 15, advanced placement, accelerated degree program, self-designed majors, tutorials, summer session, adult/continuing education programs, internships **Contact** Mr. John Rolston, Registrar, Marylhurst College, Marylhurst, OR 97036-0261. Telephone: 503-636-8141 Ext. 3316. Fax: 503-636-9526.

MOUNT ANGEL SEMINARY
SAINT BENEDICT, OREGON

Entrance Moderately difficult **General** Independent Roman Catholic, comprehensive, men only **Setting** 75-acre rural campus **Enrollment** 144 **Faculty** 3:1 **Application deadline** 7/15 **Freshmen** 73% accepted **Housing** Yes **Tuition** $8400 **Undergraduates** 0% part-time, 60% 25 or older, 0% Native American, 20% Hispanic, 0% black, 16% Asian or Pacific Islander **Most popular recent majors** Philosophy, liberal arts/general studies **Academic program** Advanced placement, adult/continuing education programs **Contact** Fr. Odo Recker, OSB, Registrar/Admissions Officer, Mount Angel Seminary, Saint Benedict, OR 97373. Telephone: 503-845-3951.

MULTNOMAH BIBLE COLLEGE AND BIBLICAL SEMINARY
PORTLAND, OREGON

Entrance Moderately difficult **General** Independent interdenominational, comprehensive, specialized, coed **Setting** 17-acre urban campus **Enrollment** 750 **Application deadline** 7/15 **Freshmen** 77% accepted **Housing** Yes **Tuition** $7590 **Undergraduates** 44% women, 12% part-time, 24% 25 or older, 1% Native American, 2% Hispanic, 1% black, 2% Asian or Pacific Islander **Academic program** Advanced placement, summer session, adult/continuing education programs, internships **Contact** Miss Joyce L. Kehoe, Director of Admissions and Registrar, Multnomah Bible College and Biblical Seminary, 8435 Northeast Glisan Street, Portland, OR 97220-5898. Telephone: 503-255-0332 Ext. 371. Fax: 503-254-1268.

NORTHWEST CHRISTIAN COLLEGE
EUGENE, OREGON

Entrance Minimally difficult **General** Independent interdenominational, comprehensive, coed **Setting** 10-acre urban campus **Enrollment** 408 **Faculty** 15:1 **Application deadline** Rolling **Freshmen** 97% accepted **Housing** Yes **Tuition** $11,074 **Undergraduates** 71% women, 20% part-time, 6% 25 or older, 1% Native American, 1% Hispanic, 1% black, 1% Asian or Pacific Islander **Most popular recent majors** Communication, business administration/commerce/management, education **Academic program** Average class size 20, advanced placement, self-designed majors, tutorials, adult/continuing education programs, internships **Contact** Ms. Christie McDonald, Director of Community Relations, Northwest Christian College, 828 East 11th Avenue, Eugene, OR 97401-3727. Telephone: 541-343-1641 Ext. 45.

OREGON COLLEGE OF ART AND CRAFT
PORTLAND, OREGON

Entrance Minimally difficult **General** Independent, 4-year, specialized, coed **Setting** 7-acre urban campus **Enrollment** 91 **Faculty** 5:1 **Freshmen** 92% accepted **Tuition** $12,990 **Undergraduates** 74% women, 62% part-time, 62% 25 or older, 2% Native American, 0% Hispanic, 0% black, 5% Asian or Pacific Islander **Most popular recent majors** Art/fine arts, ceramic art and design **Academic program** Advanced placement, tutorials **Contact** Ms. Jennifer Green, Director of Admissions, Oregon College of Art and Craft, 8245 Southwest Barnes Road, Portland, OR 97225. Telephone: 503-297-5544. Fax: 503-297-9651.

OREGON HEALTH SCIENCES UNIVERSITY
PORTLAND, OREGON

Entrance Moderately difficult **General** State-related, upper-level, specialized, coed **Setting** 116-acre urban campus **Enrollment** 1,812 **Housing** Yes **Tuition** $3336 **Undergraduates** 86% women, 27% part-time, 48% 25 or older, 1% Native American, 3% Hispanic, 2% black, 9% Asian or Pacific Islander **Academic program** Advanced placement, summer session **Contact** Ms. Victoria Souza, Registrar and Director of Financial Aid, Oregon Health Sciences University, 3181 SW Sam Jackson Park Road, Portland, OR 97201-3098. Telephone: 503-494-7800.

OREGON INSTITUTE OF TECHNOLOGY
KLAMATH FALLS, OREGON

Entrance Moderately difficult **General** State-supported, comprehensive, coed **Setting** 173-acre small-town campus **Enrollment** 2,339 **Faculty** 12:1 **Application deadline** 6/1 **Freshmen** 63% accepted **Housing** Yes **Tuition** $3144 **Undergraduates** 42% women, 34% part-time, 42% 25 or older, 3% Native American, 3% Hispanic, 1% black, 5% Asian or Pacific Islander **Most popular recent majors** Radiological technology, civil engineering technology, electronics engineering technology **Academic program** Average class size 25, advanced placement, tutorials, summer session, adult/continuing education programs, internships **Contact** Mrs. Barbara Kratochvil, Director of Admissions, Oregon Institute of Technology, Klamath Falls, OR 97601-8801. Telephone: 541-885-1150. Fax: 541-885-1115.

OREGON SCHOOL OF ART AND CRAFT

SEE OREGON COLLEGE OF ART AND CRAFT

OREGON STATE UNIVERSITY

CORVALLIS, OREGON

Entrance Moderately difficult **General** State-supported, coed **Setting** 530-acre small-town campus **Enrollment** 13,784 **Faculty** 8:1 **Application deadline** 3/1 **Freshmen** 89% accepted **Housing** Yes **Tuition** $3510 **Undergraduates** 45% women, 9% part-time, 12% 25 or older, 2% Native American, 3% Hispanic, 1% black, 8% Asian or Pacific Islander **Most popular recent majors** Business administration/commerce/management, mechanical engineering, communication **Academic program** Advanced placement, self-designed majors, tutorials, honors program, summer session, internships **Contact** Ms. Michele Sandlin, Associate Director of Processing, Oregon State University, Corvallis, OR 97331. Telephone: 541-737-4411. Fax: 541-737-6157.

PACIFIC NORTHWEST COLLEGE OF ART

PORTLAND, OREGON

Entrance Minimally difficult **General** Independent, 4-year, specialized, coed **Setting** Urban campus **Enrollment** 257 **Application deadline** 8/1 **Freshmen** 79% accepted **Tuition** $10,732 **Undergraduates** 56% women, 12% part-time, 59% 25 or older, 2% Native American, 2% Hispanic, 2% black, 2% Asian or Pacific Islander **Most popular recent majors** Painting/drawing, sculpture, graphic arts **Academic program** Advanced placement, self-designed majors, adult/continuing education programs, internships **Contact** Ms. Pearl Fisher, Admission Counselor, Pacific Northwest College of Art, 1219 SW Park Avenue, PO Box 2725, Portland, OR 97208-2725. Telephone: 503-226-0462. Fax: 503-226-4842.

PACIFIC UNIVERSITY

FOREST GROVE, OREGON

Entrance Moderately difficult **General** Independent, comprehensive, coed **Setting** 55-acre small-town campus **Enrollment** 1,750 **Faculty** 14:1 **Application deadline** 2/15 **Freshmen** 85% accepted **Housing** Yes **Tuition** $16,220 **Undergraduates** 57% women, 8% part-time, 5% 25 or older, 1% Native American, 2% Hispanic, 1% black, 12% Asian or Pacific Islander **Most popular recent majors** Business administration/commerce/management, modern languages, biology/biological sciences **Academic program** Average class size 20, advanced placement, accelerated degree program, self-designed majors, tutorials, honors program, summer session, internships **Contact** Ms. Beth Woodward, Director of Undergraduate Admissions, Pacific University, Forest Grove, OR 97116-1797. Telephone: 503-359-2218. Fax: 503-359-2242.

PORTLAND STATE UNIVERSITY

PORTLAND, OREGON

Entrance Minimally difficult **General** State-supported, coed **Setting** 36-acre urban campus **Enrollment** 14,768 **Faculty** 18:1 **Application deadline** 6/1 **Freshmen** 86% accepted **Housing** Yes **Tuition** $3180 **Undergraduates** 52% women, 39% part-time, 45% 25 or older, 1% Native American, 3% Hispanic, 3% black, 10% Asian or Pacific Islander **Most popular recent majors** Accounting, business administration/commerce/management, psychology **Academic program** Average class size 16, advanced placement, accelerated degree program, self-designed majors, tutorials, honors program, summer session, adult/continuing education programs, internships **Contact** Ms. Agnes A. Hoffman, Director of Admissions and Records, Portland State University, PO Box 751, Portland, OR 97207-0751. Telephone: 503-725-3511. Fax: 503-725-4882.

REED COLLEGE

PORTLAND, OREGON

Entrance Very difficult **General** Independent, comprehensive, coed **Setting** 98-acre suburban campus **Enrollment** 1,325 **Faculty** 10:1 **Application deadline** 2/1 **Freshmen** 76% accepted **Housing** Yes **Tuition** $22,340 **Undergraduates** 53% women, 3% part-time, 2% 25 or older, 1% Native American, 4% Hispanic, 1% black, 9% Asian or Pacific Islander **Most popular recent majors** Biology/biological sciences, history, English **Academic program** Advanced placement, accelerated degree program, self-designed majors, tutorials **Contact** Dr. Jon W. Rivenburg, Acting Dean of Admission, Reed College, Portland, OR 97202-8199. Telephone: 503-777-7511.

SOUTHERN OREGON UNIVERSITY

ASHLAND, OREGON

Entrance Moderately difficult **General** State-supported, comprehensive, coed **Setting** 175-

acre small-town campus **Enrollment** 4,247 **Faculty** 18:1 **Application deadline** Rolling **Freshmen** 77% accepted **Housing** Yes **Tuition** $3147 **Undergraduates** 54% women, 21% part-time, 25% 25 or older, 2% Native American, 3% Hispanic, 1% black, 3% Asian or Pacific Islander **Most popular recent majors** Psychology, interdisciplinary studies, English **Academic program** Advanced placement, accelerated degree program, self-designed majors, honors program, summer session, adult/continuing education programs **Contact** Mr. Allen H. Blaszak, Director of Admissions and Records, Southern Oregon University, Ashland, OR 97520. Telephone: 541-552-6411. Fax: 541-552-6329.

UNIVERSITY OF OREGON
EUGENE, OREGON

Entrance Moderately difficult **General** State-supported, coed **Setting** 250-acre urban campus **Enrollment** 17,269 **Faculty** 19:1 **Application deadline** 3/1 **Freshmen** 90% accepted **Housing** Yes **Tuition** $3540 **Undergraduates** 52% women, 13% part-time, 10% 25 or older, 1% Native American, 3% Hispanic, 2% black, 7% Asian or Pacific Islander **Most popular recent majors** Business administration/commerce/management, psychology, journalism **Academic program** Advanced placement, accelerated degree program, self-designed majors, tutorials, honors program, summer session, adult/continuing education programs, internships **Contact** Ms. Martha Pitts, Director of Admissions, University of Oregon, Eugene, OR 97403. Telephone: 541-346-3201. Fax: 541-346-5815.

UNIVERSITY OF PORTLAND
PORTLAND, OREGON

Entrance Moderately difficult **General** Independent Roman Catholic, comprehensive, coed **Setting** 125-acre suburban campus **Enrollment** 2,639 **Faculty** 14:1 **Application deadline** Rolling **Freshmen** 92% accepted **Housing** Yes **Tuition** $15,520 **Undergraduates** 55% women, 5% part-time, 13% 25 or older, 1% Native American, 2% Hispanic, 1% black, 5% Asian or Pacific Islander **Most popular recent majors** Nursing, business administration/commerce/management, education **Academic program** Average class size 25, advanced placement, accelerated degree program, self-designed majors, tutorials, honors program, summer session, adult/continuing education programs, internships **Contact** Mr. Daniel B. Reilly, Director of Admissions, University of Portland, Portland, OR 97203-5798. Telephone: 503-283-7147.

WARNER PACIFIC COLLEGE
PORTLAND, OREGON

Entrance Moderately difficult **General** Independent, comprehensive, coed, affiliated with Church of God **Setting** 15-acre urban campus **Enrollment** 601 **Faculty** 16:1 **Application deadline** Rolling **Freshmen** 89% accepted **Housing** Yes **Tuition** $10,382 **Undergraduates** 61% women, 28% part-time, 40% 25 or older, 1% Native American, 2% Hispanic, 4% black, 6% Asian or Pacific Islander **Most popular recent majors** Education, business administration/commerce/management, human development **Academic program** Average class size 25, advanced placement, self-designed majors, tutorials, honors program, summer session, adult/continuing education programs, internships **Contact** Mr. William D. Stenberg, Dean of Admissions, Warner Pacific College, 2219 Southeast 68th Avenue, Portland, OR 97215-4099. Telephone: 503-788-7495.

WESTERN BAPTIST COLLEGE
SALEM, OREGON

Entrance Moderately difficult **General** Independent-religious, 4-year, coed **Setting** 107-acre suburban campus **Enrollment** 720 **Faculty** 12:1 **Application deadline** Rolling **Freshmen** 91% accepted **Housing** Yes **Tuition** $12,350 **Undergraduates** 59% women, 22% part-time, 25% 25 or older, 2% Native American, 2% Hispanic, 1% black, 1% Asian or Pacific Islander **Most popular recent majors** Business administration/commerce/management, education, psychology **Academic program** Advanced placement, honors program, summer session, adult/continuing education programs, internships **Contact** Mr. Daren Milionis, Director of Admissions, Western Baptist College, Salem, OR 97301-9392. Telephone: 503-375-7005. Fax: 503-585-4316.

WESTERN OREGON UNIVERSITY
MONMOUTH, OREGON

Entrance Moderately difficult **General** State-supported, comprehensive, coed **Setting** 134-acre rural campus **Enrollment** 4,030 **Faculty** 15:1 **Application deadline** Rolling **Freshmen** 56% accepted **Housing** Yes **Tuition** $3153 **Undergraduates** 58% women, 9% part-time, 23% 25 or older, 2% Native American, 4% Hispanic, 1% black, 5% Asian or Pacific Islander **Academic program** Advanced placement, accelerated degree program, self-designed majors, tutorials, honors program, summer session, adult/continuing education programs, internships **Contact** Ms. Alison

Marshall, Director of Admissions, Western Oregon University, Monmouth, OR 97361. Telephone: 503-838-8211.

WESTERN STATES CHIROPRACTIC COLLEGE
PORTLAND, OREGON

Entrance Moderately difficult **General** Independent, upper-level, specialized, coed **Setting** 22-acre suburban campus **Enrollment** 489 **Faculty** 10:1 **Tuition** $13,455 **Undergraduates** 33% women, 0% part-time, 95% 25 or older, 1% Native American, 2% Hispanic, 1% black, 3% Asian or Pacific Islander **Academic program** Summer session **Contact** Mr. Jack Roberts, Dean of Enrollment Services, Western States Chiropractic College, Portland, OR 97230-3099. Telephone: 503-251-5734. Fax: 503-251-5723.

WILLAMETTE UNIVERSITY
SALEM, OREGON

Entrance Very difficult **General** Independent United Methodist, comprehensive, coed **Setting** 72-acre urban campus **Enrollment** 2,501 **Faculty** 11:1 **Application deadline** 2/1 **Freshmen** 74% accepted **Housing** Yes **Tuition** $20,290 **Undergraduates** 57% women, 3% part-time, 5% 25 or older, 1% Native American, 4% Hispanic, 1% black, 6% Asian or Pacific Islander **Most popular recent majors** Economics, psychology, biology/biological sciences **Academic program** Average class size 15, advanced placement, accelerated degree program, self-designed majors, tutorials, internships **Contact** Mr. James M. Sumner, Dean of Admissions, Willamette University, 900 State Street, Salem, OR 97301-3931. Telephone: 503-370-6303. Fax: 503-375-5363.

Utah

BRIGHAM YOUNG UNIVERSITY
PROVO, UTAH

Entrance Moderately difficult **General** Independent, coed, affiliated with Church of Jesus Christ of Latter-day Saints **Setting** 638-acre suburban campus **Enrollment** 30,563 **Faculty** 29:1 **Application deadline** 2/15 **Freshmen** 77% accepted **Housing** Yes **Tuition** $2630 **Undergraduates** 48% women, 4% part-time, 17% 25 or older, 1% Native American, 3% Hispanic, 1% black, 3% Asian or Pacific Islander **Most popular recent majors** Business administration/commerce/management, elementary education, zoology **Academic program** Average class size 43, advanced placement, accelerated degree program, honors program, summer session, adult/continuing education programs, internships **Contact** Mr. Erlend D. Peterson, Dean of Admissions and Records, Brigham Young University, Provo, UT 84602-1001. Telephone: 801-378-2539.

SOUTHERN UTAH UNIVERSITY
CEDAR CITY, UTAH

Entrance Moderately difficult **General** State-supported, comprehensive, coed **Setting** 113-acre small-town campus **Enrollment** 5,640 **Faculty** 24:1 **Application deadline** 7/1 **Freshmen** 99% accepted **Housing** Yes **Tuition** $1854 **Undergraduates** 57% women, 25% part-time, 29% 25 or older, 1% Native American, 1% Hispanic, 1% black, 3% Asian or Pacific Islander **Most popular recent majors** Elementary education, business administration/commerce/management, biology/biological sciences **Academic program** ESL program, Advanced placement, accelerated degree program, self-designed majors, summer session, adult/continuing education programs, internships **Contact** Mr. Dale S. Orton, Director of Admissions, Southern Utah University, 351 West Center Street, Cedar City, UT 84720-2498. Telephone: 801-586-7740.

UNIVERSITY OF UTAH
SALT LAKE CITY, UTAH

Entrance Moderately difficult **General** State-supported, coed **Setting** 1,500-acre urban campus **Enrollment** 24,930 **Faculty** 23:1 **Application deadline** 7/1 **Freshmen** 91% accepted **Housing** Yes **Tuition** $2601 **Undergraduates** 46% women, 32% part-time, 32% 25 or older, 1% Native American, 3% Hispanic, 1% black, 3% Asian or Pacific Islander **Most popular recent majors** Sociology, psychology, political science/government **Academic program** Average class size 61, advanced placement, accelerated degree program, self-designed majors, tutorials, honors program, summer session, adult/continuing education programs, internships **Contact** Ms. Suzanne Espinoza, Director of High School Services, University of Utah, 250 South Student Services Building, Salt Lake City, UT 84112. Telephone: 801-581-8761. Fax: 801-585-3034.

UTAH STATE UNIVERSITY
LOGAN, UTAH

Entrance Moderately difficult **General** State-supported, coed **Setting** 456-acre urban campus **Enrollment** 20,808 **Faculty** 22:1 **Application deadline** 7/1 **Freshmen** 99% accepted **Housing** Yes **Tuition** $2175 **Undergraduates** 53% women,

32% part-time, 24% 25 or older, 1% Native American, 2% Hispanic, 1% black, 1% Asian or Pacific Islander **Most popular recent majors** Elementary education, family services, accounting **Academic program** Advanced placement, accelerated degree program, self-designed majors, honors program, summer session, adult/continuing education programs, internships **Contact** Mr. Lynn Poulsen, Director of Admissions, Utah State University, University Hill, Logan, UT 84322. Telephone: 801-797-1107.

WEBER STATE UNIVERSITY
OGDEN, UTAH

Entrance Moderately difficult **General** State-supported, comprehensive, coed **Setting** 422-acre urban campus **Enrollment** 13,906 **Faculty** 19:1 **Application deadline** Rolling **Housing** Yes **Tuition** $1935 **Undergraduates** 53% women, 39% part-time, 38% 25 or older, 1% Native American, 3% Hispanic, 1% black, 2% Asian or Pacific Islander **Most popular recent majors** Nursing, education, business administration/commerce/management **Academic program** Advanced placement, accelerated degree program, self-designed majors, tutorials, honors program, summer session, adult/continuing education programs, internships **Contact** Ms. Kristen Olsen, Admissions Advisor, Weber State University, 1001 University Circle, Ogden, UT 84408-1001. Telephone: 801-626-6050. Fax: 801-626-6747.

WESTMINSTER COLLEGE OF SALT LAKE CITY
SALT LAKE CITY, UTAH

Entrance Moderately difficult **General** Independent, comprehensive, coed **Setting** 27-acre suburban campus **Enrollment** 1,922 **Faculty** 11:1 **Application deadline** Rolling **Freshmen** 91% accepted **Housing** Yes **Tuition** $11,246 **Undergraduates** 64% women, 33% part-time, 44% 25 or older, 1% Native American, 3% Hispanic, 1% black, 2% Asian or Pacific Islander **Most popular recent majors** Nursing, business administration/commerce/management, psychology **Academic program** Average class size 16, advanced placement, self-designed majors, tutorials, honors program, summer session, internships **Contact** Mr. Philip J. Alletto, V.P., Student Development and Enrollment Management, Westminster College of Salt Lake City, Salt Lake City, UT 84105-3697. Telephone: 801-488-4200. Fax: 801-466-6916.

Washington

ANTIOCH UNIVERSITY SEATTLE
SEATTLE, WASHINGTON

Entrance Noncompetitive **General** Independent, upper-level, coed **Setting** Urban campus **Enrollment** 740 **Application deadline** 9/15 **Freshmen** 82% accepted **Tuition** $9075 **Undergraduates** 74% women, 58% part-time, 95% 25 or older, 2% Native American, 0% Hispanic, 5% black, 3% Asian or Pacific Islander **Academic program** Advanced placement, accelerated degree program, self-designed majors, summer session, adult/continuing education programs **Contact** Ms. Vicki Tolbert, Admissions Officer, Antioch University Seattle, 2607 Second Avenue, Seattle, WA 98121-1211. Telephone: 206-441-5352 Ext. 12.

BASTYR UNIVERSITY
BOTHELL, WASHINGTON

Entrance Moderately difficult **General** Independent, upper-level, specialized, coed **Setting** 50-acre suburban campus **Enrollment** 555 **Faculty** 12:1 **Freshmen** 81% accepted **Housing** Yes **Tuition** $7875 **Undergraduates** 84% women, 33% part-time, 80% 25 or older, 2% Native American, 1% Hispanic, 2% black, 1% Asian or Pacific Islander **Academic program** Advanced placement, internships **Contact** Ms. Sandra Lane, Associate Director of Admissions, Bastyr University, Bothell, WA 98011. Telephone: 206-523-9585 Ext. 111.

CENTRAL WASHINGTON UNIVERSITY
ELLENSBURG, WASHINGTON

Entrance Moderately difficult **General** State-supported, comprehensive, coed **Setting** 380-acre small-town campus **Enrollment** 8,569 **Faculty** 20:1 **Application deadline** 3/1 **Freshmen** 77% accepted **Housing** Yes **Tuition** $2826 **Undergraduates** 52% women, 9% part-time, 23% 25 or older, 2% Native American, 4% Hispanic, 2% black, 4% Asian or Pacific Islander **Most popular recent majors** Business administration/commerce/management, accounting, elementary education **Academic program** Advanced placement, accelerated degree program, self-designed majors, tutorials, honors program, summer session, adult/continuing education programs, internships **Contact** Mr. William Swain, Director of Admissions and Academic Advising Services, Central Washington University, Mitchell Hall, Ellensburg, WA 98926-7567. Telephone: 509-963-1200. Fax: 509-963-3022.

CITY UNIVERSITY
BELLEVUE, WASHINGTON

Entrance Noncompetitive **General** Independent, comprehensive, coed **Setting** Suburban campus **Enrollment** 12,875 **Application deadline** Rolling **Freshmen** 100% accepted **Tuition** $2925 **Undergraduates** 59% women, 86% 25 or older, 1% Native American, 2% Hispanic, 3% black, 2% Asian or Pacific Islander **Most popular recent majors** Business administration/commerce/management, accounting, liberal arts/general studies **Academic program** Advanced placement, accelerated degree program, honors program, summer session, adult/continuing education programs, internships **Contact** Mr. Nabil El-Khatib, Vice President of Admissions and Student Affairs, City University, 919 SW Grady Way, Renton, WA 98055. Telephone: 206-637-1010.

COGSWELL COLLEGE NORTH
SEE HENRY COGSWELL COLLEGE

CORNISH COLLEGE OF THE ARTS
SEATTLE, WASHINGTON

Entrance Moderately difficult **General** Independent, 4-year, coed **Setting** 4-acre urban campus **Enrollment** 640 **Faculty** 4:1 **Application deadline** 8/15 **Freshmen** 79% accepted **Tuition** $10,990 **Undergraduates** 54% women, 8% part-time, 34% 25 or older, 2% Native American, 3% Hispanic, 2% black, 5% Asian or Pacific Islander **Most popular recent majors** Graphic arts, art/fine arts, music **Academic program** Average class size 25, advanced placement, summer session, internships **Contact** Ms. Sharron Starling, Associate Director of Admissions, Cornish College of the Arts, 710 East Roy Street, Seattle, WA 98102-4696. Telephone: 206-323-1400 Ext. 208.

DOMINION COLLEGE
SEATTLE, WASHINGTON

Entrance Moderately difficult **General** Independent, 4-year, coed **Setting** Urban campus **Enrollment** 54 **Application deadline** Rolling **Freshmen** 80% accepted **Tuition** $5200 **Undergraduates** 50% women, 2% Native American, 9% Hispanic, 11% black, 2% Asian or Pacific Islander **Academic program** Average class size 10, advanced placement, tutorials, summer session **Contact** Ms. Natalie Ellington, Dean, Enrollment Management, Dominion College, PO Box 98947, Seattle, WA 98198. Telephone: 206-870-3554. Fax: 206-870-3553.

EASTERN WASHINGTON UNIVERSITY
CHENEY, WASHINGTON

Entrance Moderately difficult **General** State-supported, comprehensive, coed **Setting** 335-acre small-town campus **Enrollment** 7,589 **Faculty** 16:1 **Application deadline** 7/1 **Freshmen** 90% accepted **Housing** Yes **Tuition** $2526 **Undergraduates** 58% women, 7% part-time, 39% 25 or older, 2% Native American, 4% Hispanic, 2% black, 3% Asian or Pacific Islander **Most popular recent majors** Business administration/commerce/management, reading education, liberal arts/general studies **Academic program** Advanced placement, accelerated degree program, self-designed majors, tutorials, honors program, summer session, internships **Contact** Mr. Keith Flamer, Director of Admissions, Eastern Washington University, EWU MS-148, Cheney, WA 99004-2431. Telephone: 509-359-6058. Fax: 509-359-6927.

THE EVERGREEN STATE COLLEGE
OLYMPIA, WASHINGTON

Entrance Moderately difficult **General** State-supported, comprehensive, coed **Setting** 1,000-acre small-town campus **Enrollment** 3,714 **Faculty** 24:1 **Application deadline** 3/1 **Freshmen** 88% accepted **Housing** Yes **Tuition** $2643 **Undergraduates** 57% women, 13% part-time, 38% 25 or older, 4% Native American, 4% Hispanic, 4% black, 4% Asian or Pacific Islander **Most popular recent majors** Human services, environmental studies, public affairs and policy studies **Academic program** Advanced placement, self-designed majors, tutorials, summer session, internships **Contact** Ms. Christine Licht, Senior Admissions Officer, The Evergreen State College, Olympia, WA 98505. Telephone: 360-866-6000 Ext. 6170. Fax: 360-866-6680.

GONZAGA UNIVERSITY
SPOKANE, WASHINGTON

Entrance Moderately difficult **General** Independent Roman Catholic, comprehensive, coed **Setting** 94-acre urban campus **Enrollment** 4,479 **Faculty** 20:1 **Application deadline** 4/1 **Freshmen** 82% accepted **Housing** Yes **Tuition** $15,350 **Undergraduates** 55% women, 10% part-time, 46% 25 or older, 2% Native American, 4% Hispanic, 1% black, 6% Asian or Pacific Islander **Academic program** Advanced placement, accelerated degree program, self-designed majors, honors program, summer session, adult/continuing education programs, internships **Contact** Mr. Philip Ballinger, Dean of Admissions, Gonzaga University, Spokane, WA 99258. Telephone: 509-328-4220 Ext. 3172.

HENRY COGSWELL COLLEGE
EVERETT, WASHINGTON

Entrance Noncompetitive **General** Independent, 4-year, coed **Setting** 1-acre urban campus **Enrollment** 170 **Faculty** 7:1 **Application deadline** 5/1 **Freshmen** 100% accepted **Tuition** $9360 **Undergraduates** 10% women, 93% part-time, 98% 25 or older, 0% Native American, 2% Hispanic, 2% black, 11% Asian or Pacific Islander **Most popular recent majors** Mechanical engineering technology, electrical engineering, computer science **Academic program** Advanced placement, tutorials, summer session, adult/continuing education programs **Contact** Mrs. Jacqueline B. Juras, Director of Admissions and Registrar, Henry Cogswell College, 2802 Wetmore Avenue, Suite 100, Everett, WA 98201. Telephone: 206-258-3351.

HERITAGE COLLEGE
TOPPENISH, WASHINGTON

Entrance Noncompetitive **General** Independent, comprehensive, coed **Setting** 10-acre rural campus **Enrollment** 1,187 **Application deadline** Rolling **Tuition** $6470 **Undergraduates** 73% women, 44% part-time, 79% 25 or older, 19% Native American, 30% Hispanic, 1% black, 1% Asian or Pacific Islander **Most popular recent majors** Elementary education, social science, business administration/commerce/management **Academic program** Advanced placement, self-designed majors, tutorials, summer session, adult/continuing education programs, internships **Contact** Ms. Tangee Hyde, Director of Recruitment, Heritage College, 3240 Fort Road, Toppenish, WA 98948-9599. Telephone: 509-865-2244 Ext. 2001. Fax: 509-865-4469.

THE LEADERSHIP INSTITUTE OF SEATTLE
BELLEVUE, WASHINGTON

Entrance Difficulty N/R **General** Independent, upper-level, coed **Setting** Suburban campus **Enrollment** 385 **Faculty** 14:1 **Housing** Yes **Tuition** $10,288 **Undergraduates** 83% women, 2% part-time, 97% 25 or older, 3% Native American, 7% black **Academic program** Advanced placement, internships **Contact** Mr. Don Werner, Director of Undergraduate Admissions, The Leadership Institute of Seattle, 1450 114th Avenue SE, Suite 230, Bellevue, WA 98004-6934. Telephone: 206-635-1187 Ext. 254.

LUTHERAN BIBLE INSTITUTE OF SEATTLE
ISSAQUAH, WASHINGTON

Entrance Minimally difficult **General** Independent Lutheran, 4-year, specialized, coed **Setting** 46-acre suburban campus **Enrollment** 167 **Faculty** 13:1 **Application deadline** 8/15 **Freshmen** 48% accepted **Housing** Yes **Tuition** $5310 **Undergraduates** 50% women, 13% part-time, 31% 25 or older, 0% Native American, 4% Hispanic, 1% black, 5% Asian or Pacific Islander **Most popular recent majors** Biblical studies, ministries, religious education **Academic program** Advanced placement, adult/continuing education programs, internships **Contact** Ms. Sigrid Cutler, Admission Representative, Lutheran Bible Institute of Seattle, Issaquah, WA 98029-9299. Telephone: 206-392-0400 Ext. 279. Fax: 206-392-0404.

NORTHWEST COLLEGE OF ART
POULSBO, WASHINGTON

Entrance Moderately difficult **General** Proprietary, 4-year, specialized, coed **Setting** 46-acre small-town campus **Faculty** 5:1 **Application deadline** 7/15 **Tuition** $7600 **Undergraduates** 58% women, 10% part-time, 30% 25 or older, 0% Native American, 1% Hispanic, 5% black, 1% Asian or Pacific Islander **Most popular recent majors** Commercial art, interior design, art/fine arts **Academic program** Accelerated degree program, tutorials, summer session, internships **Contact** Mrs. Jessica Jalbert Kempf, Registrar, Northwest College of Art, Poulsbo, WA 98370. Telephone: 360-779-9993. Fax: 360-779-9933.

NORTHWEST COLLEGE OF THE ASSEMBLIES OF GOD
KIRKLAND, WASHINGTON

Entrance Moderately difficult **General** Independent, 4-year, coed, affiliated with Assemblies of God **Setting** 63-acre suburban campus **Enrollment** 802 **Faculty** 18:1 **Application deadline** 8/1 **Freshmen** 98% accepted **Housing** Yes **Tuition** $8940 **Undergraduates** 55% women, 5% part-time, 18% 25 or older, 1% Native American, 4% Hispanic, 2% black, 5% Asian or Pacific Islander **Most popular recent majors** Pastoral studies, behavioral sciences, elementary education **Academic program** Average class size 24, advanced placement, accelerated degree program, self-designed majors, summer session, adult/continuing education programs, internships **Contact** Dr. Calvin L. White, Director of Enrollment Services, Northwest College of the Assemblies of God, PO Box 579, Kirkland, WA 98083-0579. Telephone: 206-889-5231. Fax: 206-827-0148.

PACIFIC LUTHERAN UNIVERSITY
TACOMA, WASHINGTON

Entrance Moderately difficult **General** Independent, comprehensive, coed, affiliated with Evangelical Lutheran Church in America **Setting** 126-acre suburban campus **Enrollment** 3,463 **Faculty** 13:1 **Application deadline** Rolling **Freshmen** 96% accepted **Housing** Yes **Tuition** $15,136 **Undergraduates** 61% women, 9% part-time, 20% 25 or older, 1% Native American, 2% Hispanic, 2% black, 6% Asian or Pacific Islander **Most popular recent majors** Business administration/commerce/management, education, nursing **Academic program** Advanced placement, accelerated degree program, self-designed majors, tutorials, honors program, summer session, adult/continuing education programs, internships **Contact** Dr. Laura J. Polcyn, Dean of Admissions, Pacific Lutheran University, Tacoma, WA 98447. Telephone: 253-535-7158. Fax: 253-535-8320.

PUGET SOUND CHRISTIAN COLLEGE
EDMONDS, WASHINGTON

Entrance Minimally difficult **General** Independent Christian, 4-year, coed **Setting** 4-acre suburban campus **Enrollment** 166 **Faculty** 15:1 **Application deadline** 9/15 **Freshmen** 74% accepted **Housing** Yes **Tuition** $6075 **Undergraduates** 46% women, 10% part-time, 39% 25 or older, 1% Native American, 4% Hispanic, 4% black, 1% Asian or Pacific Islander **Most popular recent majors** Ministries, religious education **Academic program** Advanced placement, adult/continuing education programs, internships **Contact** Ms. Delores Scarbrough, Registrar, Puget Sound Christian College, Edmonds, WA 98020-3171. Telephone: 206-775-8686 Ext. 211.

SAINT MARTIN'S COLLEGE
LACEY, WASHINGTON

Entrance Moderately difficult **General** Independent Roman Catholic, comprehensive, coed **Setting** 380-acre suburban campus **Enrollment** 958 **Faculty** 12:1 **Application deadline** 8/1 **Freshmen** 65% accepted **Housing** Yes **Tuition** $13,120 **Undergraduates** 64% women, 30% part-time, 65% 25 or older, 1% Native American, 5% Hispanic, 4% black, 7% Asian or Pacific Islander **Most popular recent majors** Education, business administration/commerce/management **Academic program** Advanced placement, accelerated degree program, tutorials, summer session, adult/continuing education programs, internships **Contact** Mr. Ronald Noborikawa, Director of Admissions, Saint Martin's College, Lacey, WA 98503-7500. Telephone: 360-438-4311. Fax: 360-459-4124.

SEATTLE PACIFIC UNIVERSITY
SEATTLE, WASHINGTON

Entrance Moderately difficult **General** Independent Free Methodist, comprehensive, coed **Setting** 35-acre urban campus **Enrollment** 3,293 **Faculty** 15:1 **Application deadline** 9/1 **Freshmen** 91% accepted **Housing** Yes **Tuition** $14,130 **Undergraduates** 64% women, 19% part-time, 19% 25 or older, 1% Native American, 2% Hispanic, 2% black, 5% Asian or Pacific Islander **Most popular recent majors** Education, nursing **Academic program** Advanced placement, self-designed majors, tutorials, honors program, summer session, adult/continuing education programs, internships **Contact** Ms. Ruth Adams, Registrar, Seattle Pacific University, 3307 Third Avenue West, Seattle, WA 98119-1997. Telephone: 206-281-2021.

SEATTLE UNIVERSITY
SEATTLE, WASHINGTON

Entrance Moderately difficult **General** Independent Roman Catholic, comprehensive, coed **Setting** 46-acre urban campus **Enrollment** 5,990 **Faculty** 14:1 **Application deadline** 3/1 **Freshmen** 91% accepted **Housing** Yes **Tuition** $14,805 **Undergraduates** 58% women, 16% part-time, 28% 25 or older, 1% Native American, 3% Hispanic, 4% black, 19% Asian or Pacific Islander **Most popular recent majors** Business administration/commerce/management, psychology, engineering and applied sciences **Academic program** Advanced placement, accelerated degree program, tutorials, honors program, summer session, adult/continuing education programs, internships **Contact** Mr. Michael K. McKeon, Dean of Admissions, Seattle University, Broadway and Madison, Seattle, WA 98122. Telephone: 206-296-5800. Fax: 206-296-5656.

UNIVERSITY OF PUGET SOUND
TACOMA, WASHINGTON

Entrance Very difficult **General** Independent, comprehensive, coed **Setting** 97-acre suburban campus **Enrollment** 3,039 **Faculty** 12:1 **Application deadline** 2/1 **Freshmen** 82% accepted **Housing** Yes **Tuition** $18,940 **Undergraduates** 59% women, 5% part-time, 6% 25 or older, 1% Native American, 3% Hispanic, 2% black, 10% Asian or Pacific Islander **Most popular recent majors** Biology/biological sciences, English, political science/government **Academic program** Average class size 24, advanced placement, tutorials, honors program, summer session, adult/continuing education programs, internships **Contact** Dr. George H. Mills, Vice President for Enrollment, University of Puget Sound, Tacoma, WA 98416-0005. Telephone: 206-756-3211. Fax: 206-756-3500.

UNIVERSITY OF WASHINGTON
SEATTLE, WASHINGTON

Entrance Moderately difficult **General** State-supported, coed **Setting** 703-acre urban campus **Enrollment** 34,368 **Faculty** 9:1 **Application deadline** 2/1 **Freshmen** 69% accepted **Housing** Yes **Tuition** $3366 **Undergraduates** 51% women, 18% part-time, 21% 25 or older, 1% Native American, 4% Hispanic, 3% black, 22% Asian or Pacific Islander **Academic program** Average class size 31, advanced placement, accelerated degree program, self-designed majors, honors program, summer session, adult/continuing education programs, internships **Contact** Ms. Stephanie Preston, Assistant Director of Admissions, University of Washington, Office of Admissions, Seattle, WA 98195. Telephone: 206-543-9686.

WALLA WALLA COLLEGE
COLLEGE PLACE, WASHINGTON

Entrance Moderately difficult **General** Independent Seventh-day Adventist, comprehensive, coed **Setting** 77-acre small-town campus **Enrollment** 1,763 **Faculty** 12:1 **Application deadline** Rolling **Housing** Yes **Tuition** $12,693 **Undergraduates** 49% women, 14% part-time, 14% 25 or older, 1% Native American, 5% Hispanic, 1% black, 4% Asian or Pacific Islander **Most popular recent majors** Engineering (general), nursing, business administration/commerce/management **Academic program** Average class size 30, advanced placement, accelerated degree program, self-designed majors, tutorials, honors program, summer session, internships **Contact** Mr. Dallas Weis, Director of Admissions, Walla Walla College, College Place, WA 99324-1198. Telephone: 509-527-2327. Fax: 509-527-2397.

WASHINGTON STATE UNIVERSITY
PULLMAN, WASHINGTON

Entrance Moderately difficult **General** State-supported, coed **Setting** 620-acre rural campus **Enrollment** 20,121 **Faculty** 12:1 **Application deadline** 5/1 **Freshmen** 89% accepted **Housing** Yes **Tuition** $3270 **Undergraduates** 50% women, 11% part-time, 17% 25 or older, 2% Native American, 3% Hispanic, 2% black, 5% Asian or Pacific Islander **Most popular recent majors** Business administration/commerce/management, communication, social science **Academic program** Advanced placement, honors program, summer session, adult/continuing education programs, internships **Contact** Ms. Terese M. Flynn, Director of Admissions, Washington State University, Office of Admissions, PO Box 641067, Pullman, WA 99164-1067. Telephone: 509-335-5586.

WESTERN WASHINGTON UNIVERSITY
BELLINGHAM, WASHINGTON

Entrance Moderately difficult **General** State-supported, comprehensive, coed **Setting** 223-acre small-town campus **Enrollment** 11,039 **Faculty** 21:1 **Application deadline** 3/1 **Freshmen** 83% accepted **Housing** Yes **Tuition** $2940 **Undergraduates** 56% women, 5% part-time, 12% 25 or older, 2% Native American, 3% Hispanic, 2% black, 7% Asian or Pacific Islander **Most popular recent majors** Business administration/commerce/management, English **Academic program** Advanced placement, accelerated degree program, self-designed majors, tutorials, honors program, summer session, adult/continuing education programs, internships **Contact** Ms. Karen Copetas, Director of Admissions, Western Washington University, Bellingham, WA 98225-9009. Telephone: 360-650-3440 Ext. 3443.

WHITMAN COLLEGE
WALLA WALLA, WASHINGTON

Entrance Very difficult **General** Independent, 4-year, coed **Setting** 55-acre small-town campus **Enrollment** 1,309 **Faculty** 11:1 **Application deadline** 2/1 **Freshmen** 54% accepted **Housing** Yes **Tuition** $19,756 **Undergraduates** 54% women, 3% part-time, 2% 25 or older, 1% Native American, 2% Hispanic, 2% black, 7% Asian or Pacific Islander **Most popular recent majors** History, psychology, English **Academic program** Advanced placement, accelerated degree program, self-designed majors, tutorials, honors program, internships **Contact** Mr. John Bogley, Dean of Admission and Financial Aid, Whitman College, Walla Walla, WA 99362-2083. Telephone: 509-527-5176. Fax: 509-527-4967.

WHITWORTH COLLEGE
SPOKANE, WASHINGTON

Entrance Very difficult **General** Independent Presbyterian, comprehensive, coed **Setting** 200-acre suburban campus **Enrollment** 2,026 **Faculty** 16:1 **Application deadline** 3/1 **Freshmen** 85% accepted **Housing** Yes **Tuition** $14,424 **Undergraduates** 59% women, 10% part-time, 15% 25 or older, 1% Native American, 2% Hispanic, 1% black, 6% Asian or Pacific Islander **Most popular recent majors** Elementary education, business administration/commerce/management, history **Academic program** Average class size 27, advanced placement, self-designed majors, tutorials, summer session, adult/continuing education programs, internships **Contact** Mr. Ken Moyer, Director of Admissions, Whitworth College, Spokane, WA 99251-0001. Telephone: 509-466-3212. Fax: 509-466-3773.

Wyoming

UNIVERSITY OF WYOMING

LARAMIE, WYOMING

Entrance Moderately difficult **General** State-supported, coed **Setting** 785-acre small-town campus **Enrollment** 11,251 **Faculty** 15:1 **Application deadline** 8/10 **Freshmen** 96% accepted **Housing** Yes **Tuition** $2326 **Undergraduates** 51% women, 14% part-time, 24% 25 or older, 1% Native American, 5% Hispanic, 1% black, 1% Asian or Pacific Islander **Most popular recent majors** Elementary education, psychology, nursing **Academic program** Advanced placement, self-designed majors, tutorials, honors program, summer session, adult/continuing education programs, internships **Contact** Mr. James T. Mansfield, Director of Admissions, University of Wyoming, Box 3435, Laramie, WY 82071. Telephone: 307-766-5160. Fax: 307-766-4042.

INTERNATIONAL

This section contains quick-reference profiles of selected international colleges and universities that hold U.S. accreditation. The profiles cover such items as background information, entrance difficulty, academic programs, and contact information. The data in each of these profiles, collected from fall 1996 to spring 1997, come solely from Peterson's Annual Survey of Undergraduate Institutions, which was sent to deans or admissions officers at each institution. The profiles are arranged alphabetically.

France

THE AMERICAN UNIVERSITY OF PARIS

PARIS, FRANCE

Entrance Moderately difficult **General** Independent, 4-year, coed **Setting** Urban campus **Enrollment** 800 **Faculty** 13:1 **Application deadline** 5/1 **Freshmen** 86% accepted **Tuition** $17,106 **Undergraduates** 58% women, 10% part-time **Most popular recent majors** International business, international relations, art history **Academic program** Advanced placement, tutorials, honors program, summer session, adult/continuing education programs, internships **Contact** Ms. Candace McLaughlin, New York Office, The American University of Paris, 31 Avenue Bosquet, New York, NY 10017. Telephone: 212-983-1414. Fax: 212-983-0444.

United Kingdom

RICHMOND, THE AMERICAN INTERNATIONAL UNIVERSITY IN LONDON

RICHMOND, SURREY, UNITED KINGDOM

Entrance Moderately difficult **General** Independent, comprehensive, coed **Setting** 5-acre urban campus **Enrollment** 1,200 **Faculty** 12:1 **Application deadline** Rolling **Freshmen** 85% accepted **Housing** Yes **Tuition** $13,380 **Undergraduates** 50% women **Most popular recent major** International business **Academic program** Advanced placement, tutorials, honors program, summer session, internships **Contact** Mr. Brian E. Davis, Director of United States Admissions, Richmond, The American International University in London, 19 Bay State Road, Boston, MA 02215. Telephone: 617-954-9942. Fax: 617-236-4703.

DESCRIPTIONS

The full-page descriptions in this section provide a broad overview of some of the colleges and universities profiled in the previous section. These descriptions are offered to help give students a better sense of the individuality of each institution, in terms that include mission statements, campus environments, and academic programs. The absence from this section of any college or university does not constitute an editorial decision on the part of Peterson's. In essence, this section is an open forum for colleges and universities, on a voluntary basis, to communicate their particular messages to prospective college students.

The descriptions are arranged alphabetically by the official name of the institution. See the directory on pages 357–358 for a listing of the schools included.

DIRECTORY

Academy of Art College
Adrian College
Albany College of Pharmacy of Union University
Alfred University
Allegheny College
Allegheny University of the Health Sciences
Alma College
American University of Paris
Aquinas College
Art Institute of Boston
Atlanta College of Art
Audrey Cohen College
Ball State University
Bay Path College
Belmont University
Beloit College
Benedictine University
Bethel College
Bloomfield College
Bowie State University
Brevard College
California College of Arts and Crafts
California State Polytechnic University, Pomona
Calvin College
Campbell University
Capitol College
Carroll College
Carson-Newman College
The Catholic University of America
Cedar Crest College
Chaminade University of Honolulu
Chestnut Hill College
Claremont McKenna College
Clarion University of Pennsylvania
Clarkson College
Cleary College
Cogswell Polytechnical College
Colby-Sawyer College
College of Aeronautics
College of Saint Benedict/Saint John's University
The College of Wooster
Columbia College
Columbia University, School of General Studies
Cumberland College
Daniel Webster College
David Lipscomb University
Drexel University
Earlham College
Eastern College
Eastern Mennonite University
Elmira College
Embry-Riddle Aeronautical University
Fairmont State College
Ferris State University
Ferrum College
Fitchburg State College
Five Towns College
Florida Institute of Technology
Gardner-Webb University
George Fox University
Georgian Court College
Glenville State College
GMI Engineering & Management Institute
Golden Gate University
Gonzaga University
Gordon College
Goucher College
Grace College
Grove City College
Hampshire College
Hardin-Simmons University
Haverford College
Hawaii Pacific University
Hofstra University
Immaculata College
Ithaca College
Johnson State College
Kent State University
Kentucky Wesleyan College
LaGrange College
Le Moyne College
Limestone College
Loyola University Chicago
Loyola University New Orleans
Luther College
Lynchburg College
Maharishi University of Management
Maine College of Art
Maine Maritime Academy
Manhattan College
Marian College of Fond du Lac
Marietta College
Marymount University
Massachusetts College of Pharmacy and Allied Health Sciences
Mercyhurst College
Meredith College
Midland Lutheran College
Mills College
Minneapolis College of Art and Design
Missouri Southern State College
Montclair State University
Montreat College
Morgan State University

Mount Ida College
National American University
Newbury College
New York School of Interior Design
New York University
Niagara University
Northeastern University
North Georgia College & State University
Northwood University
Nova Southeastern University
Ohio University
Olivet College
Otis College of Art and Design
Pace University
Pacific Lutheran University
Point Park College
Providence College
Randolph-Macon Woman's College
Reed College
Regis University
Rensselaer Polytechnic Institute
The Richard Stockton College of New Jersey
Richmond College, The American International University in London
Rider University
Ripon College
Rochester Institute of Technology
Rosemont College
St. Ambrose University
St. Andrews Presbyterian College
St. John's University
Saint Joseph College
Saint Leo College
St. Mary's College of Maryland
Saint Peter's College
St. Thomas University
Saint Vincent College
Schiller International University
Seton Hill College
Shimer College
Shorter College
Simmons College
Simpson College
Slippery Rock University of Pennsylvania
Southern California College
Southern Connecticut State University
Southern Vermont College
Southwest Texas State University
Springfield College
State University of New York at Binghamton
State University of New York at Buffalo School of Engineering and Applied Sciences
State University of New York College at Brockport
State University of New York College at Oneonta
Stephens College
Suomi College
Sweet Briar College
Thiel College
Tulane University
United States International University
United States Military Academy
University at Albany, State University of New York
The University of Alabama in Huntsville
The University of Alabama
University of Maryland, College Park
University of Massachusetts Amherst
University of Massachusetts Boston
University of Montevallo
University of Oregon
University of Pittsburgh at Johnstown
University of San Diego
The University of Tampa
University of the Incarnate Word
Valparaiso University
Vanderbilt University
Warren Wilson College
Washington College
Webber College
Wells College
Wentworth Institute of Technology
West Chester University of Pennsylvania
Western Illinois University
Western Maryland College
Western Michigan University
Western Montana College of The University of Montana
Westminster College
William Paterson University of New Jersey
Winthrop University
Woodbury University

ACADEMY OF ART COLLEGE
SAN FRANCISCO, CALIFORNIA

The College

In 1929, Academy of Art College founder Richard S. Stephens, who was the advertising creative director of *Sunset* magazine, acted on his belief that "aspiring artists and designers, given proper instruction, hard work, and dedication, can learn the skills needed to become successful professionals." His new school of advertising art consisted of 46 students meeting in one room on San Francisco's Kearny Street. The instructors, who were professional artists, brought "real-world" problems, situations, solutions, and practical experience to the students. Thus was born the school's unofficial philosophy by the founder: Hire today's best practicing professionals to teach the art and design professionals of tomorrow. At that time, advertising consisted primarily of illustrations, photos, and copy. Consequently, it became necessary to teach beginning students the fundamentals of drawing, painting, color, light, and photography as well as layout and typography. Today the Academy of Art College is the largest private art and design school in the nation and has an enrollment of more than 5,800 students from nearly every country in the world. One third of the student body is made up of international students. The Academy has thirteen buildings that house classrooms, studios, galleries, and dormitories. The students, who are admitted through an open enrollment policy (there is no portfolio requirement since the severe cutback in high school art classes), aspire to earn either a B.F.A. or an M.F.A. degree in one of twenty-five different majors and concentrations.

Academic Program

First-year students must complete six foundation courses and English. Only Drawing Principles and Color/Design Principles are taken by all majors. The other four foundation courses are related specifically to the student's major to prepare them to begin intense focus courses in their field by the sophomore year. All major courses of study are structured so that the student builds upon skills learned the previous semester and advances to the next level of technical or creative proficiency. Some related major courses may be taken concurrently. Each course is worth 3 credit units. A total of 132 credit units must be completed to earn a Bachelor of Fine Arts degree. They consist of 18 units of foundations courses, 60 units in the major, 12 units of art electives, and 42 units of liberal arts/art history courses. Liberal arts courses teach practical applications for forging a professional career in art and design. International students who come from countries where English is not the primary language may have up to 9 units of mandatory ESL classes, as determined by English language proficiency testing. Students meet with department directors at least once during the academic year to have their progress assessed. Portfolios are reviewed before the junior year to determine if a student has progressed sufficiently to continue study at the Academy.

Financial Aid

The Academy offers financial aid packages consisting of grants, loans, and work-study to eligible students with a demonstrated need. Low-interest loans are available to all eligible students, regardless of need. As financial aid programs, procedures, and eligibility requirements change frequently, applicants should contact the Financial Aid Office for current requirements at 79 New Montgomery Street, 3rd Floor, San Francisco, California 94105.

Application and Information

Further information and a catalog may be obtained by contacting:

Academy of Art College Admissions Department
79 New Montgomery Street
San Francisco, California 94105

Telephone: 415-274-2222
800-544-ARTS (toll-free)
Fax: 415-284-9743
Web site: http://www.academyart.edu

ADRIAN COLLEGE
ADRIAN, MICHIGAN

The College
Adrian College, chartered in 1859, is a private liberal arts college affiliated with the United Methodist Church. Recognized for providing high-quality education by the *New York Times* and *U.S. News & World Report,* Adrian is characterized by teaching excellence and individual treatment of students. The College's mission is to maintain a learning environment that stimulates individual growth and academic excellence. To fulfill this mission, the College is committed to fostering creativity, encouraging ethical values and the pursuit of truth, and helping students develop the necessary skills to lead satisfying lives and careers within a global society. Currently, students come from over thirty-five states, but most come from the surrounding Midwest states of Michigan, Indiana, and Ohio. The international student population is currently represented by Japan, Kenya, Taiwan, Croatia, Liberia, Saudi Arabia, Thailand, Northern Ireland, Russia, France, and South Korea.

Academic Program
Distribution requirements are designed to emphasize liberal education through a broad understanding of the liberal arts and have been established in several liberal arts areas (arts, humanities, social sciences, natural and physical sciences, and cross-cultural perspective) and in basic skill areas that indicate education proficiency (communication, linguistics, and physical development). All students must complete at least one course in religion or philosophy and at least one 4-hour laboratory science course. Students must also declare their major during their sophomore year. Successful completion of a minimum of 124 semester hours, with at least 30 hours at the most advanced level, is needed to obtain a baccalaureate degree. Up to 60 semester hours may be earned through nontraditional credit programs such as CLEP, PEP, LLE, Advanced Placement, and others.

Financial Aid
Approximately 85 percent of the student body receives some form of financial aid through scholarships, grants, loans, and campus employment. The College also participates in all applicable Michigan aid programs, as well as the Federal Work-Study, Federal Pell Grant, and Federal Supplemental Educational Opportunity Grant (FSEOG) programs. The Federal Perkins Loan, Federal Stafford Student Loan, TERI Supplemental Loan, and Federal Parent Loan (PLUS) programs are also available. A number of part-time positions are available for those who wish to work on campus while earning applicable financial assistance. For those with a demonstrated record of high academic ability, merit-based scholarship assistance is available. To be considered for any financial assistance, a student must complete the Adrian College Application for Admission and Financial Aid. Need-based assistance is determined once parents and students complete the Free Application for Federal Student Aid (FAFSA) form, which is used to conduct a need analysis for the student. The FAFSA may be obtained from most high school counselors or directly from the Adrian College Office of Financial Aid.

Application and Information
A nonrefundable fee of $20 must be submitted with an application for admission. Application can be made anytime following the completion of the junior year of high school. Students are usually notified of the admission decision within two weeks after the application file is complete. Campus visits are strongly encouraged but not required.

For more information about Adrian College or to schedule a campus visit, students should contact:

Office of Admissions
Adrian College
110 South Madison Street
Adrian, Michigan 49221-2575

Telephone: 517-265-5161
800-877-2246 (toll-free)
E-mail: admission@adrian.adrian.edu

ALBANY COLLEGE OF PHARMACY OF UNION UNIVERSITY
ALBANY, NEW YORK

The College

When students choose the Albany College of Pharmacy (ACP), they choose a style, a philosophy, and a way of life, as well as an education that, if properly applied, will be a source of satisfaction, personal growth, and livelihood. ACP offers excellent academic preparation in the profession of pharmacy. Its small size and methods of personal instruction give students an opportunity to grow and discover their greatest potential. Throughout its history, the school's concern has always been to provide a professional challenge—in the classroom and in the laboratory—and a personal challenge, fostering independence, responsibility, and self-awareness. Founded in 1881 as the Department of Pharmacy of Union University, the Albany College of Pharmacy was the vision of Archibald McClure, president of an Albany pharmaceutical firm. He conceived the plan of educating professional pharmacists in a formal academic environment. The plan emphasizes the necessity of a strong foundation in the basic sciences. Today, the pharmacy professional is an active participant in the health-care system; he or she spends a significant amount of time interacting with and counseling patients. ACP has been engaged in the education of the pharmacist for more than 110 years. The Alumni Hall offers a full range of facilities to all noncommuting freshmen. Each furnished one- or two-bedroom apartment has its own living room, kitchen, and bathroom. Housing for noncommuting upperclass students is available in homes and apartments in the surrounding areas.

Academic Program

ACP has a long tradition of preparing students for careers in the health-care field. Graduates follow a wide variety of career paths. Students are required to take a core program that emphasizes a three-year concentration in math and science, including courses in biology, chemistry, physics, and calculus, as well as required courses in English and other liberal arts subjects. The B.S. in pharmacy program is a five-year program. Students choose from more than fifty courses offered at ACP. Students earning grades of 4 or better on Advanced Placement examinations may receive college credit. To earn the B.S./M.S., students must take 36 graduate course credits. The program requires five years of study including summers. Graduates of the ACP/Union College health systems management curriculum are exceptionally well prepared to meet the demands of an increasingly complex health-care system. Their extensive pharmacy education is augmented by training in health statistics, computers, and the behavior and management of organizations and personnel. Applications for the program may be obtained from ACP. New York State law requires that a pharmacist complete a six-month internship and pass a licensing examination before practicing in the state.

Financial Aid

Need-based scholarships; low-interest, long-term loans; Federal Supplemental Educational Opportunity Grants; and work-study awards are available to all students who are judged to have need of financial assistance. More than 85 percent of ACP students receive some form of aid, ranging from loans to a combination of loans, grants, and part-time employment.

Application and Information

Applicants for the freshman year should complete the application and submit it to the director of admissions. An official secondary school transcript must be sent from the applicant's high school. The majority of admission decisions are made by February 15.

For further information, prospective students should contact:

Janis Fisher
Director of Admissions
Albany College of Pharmacy of Union University
106 New Scotland Avenue
Albany, New York 12208
Telephone: 518-445-7221

ALFRED UNIVERSITY
ALFRED, NEW YORK

The University
Alfred University is a residential institution of 2,500 graduate and undergraduate students, located 70 miles south of Rochester, between the Finger Lakes region and the Allegheny Mountains in western New York State. Alfred is composed of the privately endowed Colleges of Business, Liberal Arts and Sciences, and Engineering and Professional Studies, as well as the publicly supported New York State College of Ceramics, which comprises the School of Art and Design and the School of Ceramic Engineering and Sciences. With men and women nearly equal in number, the University's 2,000 undergraduates include representatives from forty-three U.S. states and territories as well as from twenty different nations. Students participate in and support AU athletics events, which are held on the Merrill Field omniturf or in McLane Center. Students participate in more than seventy campus clubs and organizations, such as the American Ceramic Society, Forest People, Jazz Ensemble, Karate Club, and Ski Club.

Academic Program
Candidates are required to complete 124 semester hours for the B.A. from the College of Liberal Arts and Sciences, 120 for the B.S. from the College of Business, 125 for the B.S. from the College of Engineering and Professional Studies, 137 for the B.S. from the School of Ceramic Engineering and Sciences, and 128 for the B.F.A. from the School of Art and Design. To encourage students with strong ability and initiative, the University recognizes the Advanced Placement and International Baccalaureate programs. In addition, the University offers its own challenge examination program for students already enrolled. The honors program is available to students enrolled in any major at the University.

Financial Aid
In 1995–96, University-funded aid provided more than $10 million to undergraduate students. For private-sector programs, 90 percent of freshmen received some form of financial assistance, and for the New York State College of Ceramics, 76 percent of freshmen received assistance. Aid administered by the University usually consists of a combination of scholarships or grants-in-aid, loans, and part-time work. Students may be eligible for financial assistance under the Federal Pell Grant, Federal Supplemental Educational Opportunity Grant, Federal Perkins Loan, and Federal Work-Study programs. New York State residents may be eligible for aid under the Tuition Assistance Program. The University sponsors National Merit Scholarships, departmental talent awards, and Presidential, Southern Tier, Junior Achievement, and transfer scholarships.

Application and Information
Candidates must submit a completed Alfred University application form or the Common Application form, SAT I or ACT results, a letter of recommendation, and a $40 application fee. Students who bring their completed application and essay with them when they visit campus will receive a $40 application fee waiver. They must also have their high school guidance office send a copy of their transcript. Applicants to the School of Art and Design must submit a portfolio of their work, normally fifteen to twenty slides. The application and portfolio deadline under the early decision plan is December 1, with notification by December 15. The application deadline for regular admission is February 1, with notification by early March. The portfolio deadline for regular admission is February 15. Transfer applicants should file an application by August 1 for September admission or December 1 for January admission. Applications and inquiries should be addressed to:

Katherine McCarthy
Director of Admissions
Alumni Hall
Alfred University
Saxon Drive
Alfred, New York 14802

Telephone: 607-871-2115
800-541-9229 (toll-free)
Fax: 607-871-2198
E-mail: admwww@bigvax.alfred.edu

ALLEGHENY COLLEGE
MEADVILLE, PENNSYLVANIA

The College

Founded on America's western frontier in 1815, Allegheny is a classical, selective college of the liberal arts and sciences. Although highly regarded as a preprofessional school, its impact on students transcends preparation for careers. Allegheny not only develops in its students such essential skills as writing, critical thinking, and problem solving but also fosters a capacity for lifelong learning, the ability to manage everyday affairs, responsible citizenship, social skills, and values. While nonsectarian in outlook and practice, Allegheny has been affiliated with the United Methodist Church since 1833. The 1,800 students come from forty states and twenty other countries. Five percent are members of minority groups and three fourths reside on campus. On-campus residence is required of freshmen and sophomores and optional for other students, but it is guaranteed for all four years for all who seek it. Faculty members describe Allegheny students as active and hardworking. Seventy percent come from the highest fifth of their high school class, 1 in 3 was president of a student organization, and 80 percent were active in volunteer service groups. At Allegheny, students sustain more than 100 clubs, committees, and organizations in drama, dance, vocal and instrumental music, publications, radio, religious life, politics, social service, professional and multicultural interest areas, and the governance of student life. Intramural athletics involve three fourths of the students, and the varsity program is one of the best in NCAA Division III. Of the twenty teams for men and women, about half are nationally ranked each year.

Academic Program

Allegheny ensures that students develop wholeness across the divisions of knowledge (arts and humanities, social sciences, and natural sciences) as well as expertise in one or more fields. Each student must complete thirty-two semester courses; the major may require eight to twelve courses, including a junior seminar and the distinctive Senior Project, while the remainder are electives and Liberal Studies Program courses. The innovative Liberal Studies Program includes a freshman seminar, with a strong advising component; a sophomore writing course; and some in-depth study in a subject outside the division of the major. Writing proficiency is emphasized throughout the Allegheny years: it is a central objective of the freshman seminar; it is developed further in the sophomore writing course, after students have mastered some college-level material; and it must be demonstrated in all other courses.

Financial Aid

A large number of merit-based scholarships are awarded annually, making the College more affordable even to families who do not qualify for need-based financial aid. Also, scholarships, grants, loans, and campus employment are awarded to students who need assistance to meet College expenses. The Free Application for Federal Student Aid (FAFSA), which establish an applicant's eligibility for virtually all institutional, state, and federal assistance, must be submitted by February 15. Notices about the receipt of financial aid are sent to students shortly after their acceptance by the College. Nine out of ten students receive some form of financial aid.

Application and Information

The application for admission should be submitted by February 15 (November 15 to January 15 for early decision), and the SAT I or ACT test results should be forwarded to the College by each candidate. Applicants for early decision are notified on a rolling basis between December 15 and January 31. Regular applicants are informed of the admission decision by April 1.

Office of Admissions
Allegheny College
Meadville, Pennsylvania 16335-3902

Telephone: 814-332-4351
800-521-5293 (toll-free)
E-mail: admiss@admin.alleg.edu
Web site: http://www.alleg.edu

ALLEGHENY UNIVERSITY OF THE HEALTH SCIENCES, SCHOOL OF HEALTH PROFESSIONS
PHILADELPHIA, PENNSYLVANIA

The University and The School

Allegheny University of the Health Sciences (AUHS) is an academic health center that includes more than 4,000 faculty members and 3,100 students in its MCP•Hahnemann School of Medicine, School of Health Professions, School of Nursing, and School of Public Health and grants degrees from the associate through the doctorate in more than forty programs. It has a rich combined heritage spanning two centuries of health-care education. Hahnemann University was founded in 1848, while Medical College of Pennsylvania was founded in 1850. In 1993, the two schools consolidated into one institution, Medical College of Pennsylvania and Hahnemann University, which was given its present name in June 1996. With campuses in Philadelphia and Pittsburgh, the University is the academic anchor of Allegheny Health, Education and Research Foundation (AHERF), a statewide health-care system. As a private, nonprofit academic health center, AUHS is dedicated to teaching, learning, healing the sick, and conserving health. The University is accredited by the Middle States Association of Colleges and Schools. The University is not affiliated with Allegheny College, Meadville, Pennsylvania.

Academic Program

Candidates for graduation must have fulfilled all course requirements in the major curriculum prescribed by the program director. Associate degree candidates must have completed course work equivalent to a minimum of 60 semester hours with a minimum cumulative grade point average of 2.0 on a 4.0 scale. In addition, the following distributional requirements must be met: 3 semester hours each of social sciences, humanities, and natural sciences and 6 semester hours of English (6 semester hours in college-level composition, 6 semester hours in combined college-level composition and literature, or 3 semester hours in college-level composition and 3 semester hours in literature). Bachelor's degree candidates must have completed course work equivalent to a minimum of 120 semester hours with a minimum cumulative grade point average of 2.0. In addition, the following distributional requirements must be met: 3 semester hours each of mathematics/statistics and computer science; 6 semester hours each of humanities and natural sciences; 6 semester hours of English (see above); and 12 semester hours of social sciences (3 semester hours of health administration and management may be selected in lieu of 3 semester hours of a social science at the program director's discretion).

Financial Aid

AUHS awards funds to students from loan programs and numerous scholarship and grant programs. Awards are based on financial need, with the neediest students funded first. Some scholarship funds are awarded to students based on both financial need and academic merit. Students must complete the Free Application for Federal Student Aid (FAFSA) forms to be considered for any aid from the University.

Application and Information

AUHS has a rolling admissions policy, except for the following programs: addictions counseling sciences and mental health technology—application deadline June 1, supporting credentials deadline July 15; cardiovascular perfusion technology—application and credentials due January 1; humanities and sciences—application July 15, supporting credentials August 15; physical therapist assistant studies—fall semester application January 31, supporting credentials February 28, spring semester application August 31, supporting credentials September 30; physician assistant studies, fall 1998—application and credentials due October 1, 1997. Admission information and material can be requested from:

University Office of Admissions and Recruitment
Allegheny University of the Health Services
School of Health Professions
Broad and Vine, Mail Stop 472
Philadelphia, Pennsylvania 19102-1192

Telephone: 215-762-8288
Web site: http://www.allegheny.edu

ALMA COLLEGE
ALMA, MICHIGAN

The College

Regarded as one of the nation's best liberal arts colleges, Alma College is in its second century of superior education and professional distinction. Founded by Presbyterians in 1886, Alma remains a private liberal arts institution committed to a values-oriented style of education. In a time when many professionals find that their technical training is already out of date, Alma's graduates are entering the job market with an education that will always serve them. Alma's academic philosophy, rooted in the liberal arts tradition and providing a broad educational base with flexible, innovative course work, has earned Alma a Phi Beta Kappa chapter. Classes are small—the average size is 22—enabling students to do more than just listen. Students enjoy the rigorous academic atmosphere; 86 percent of the faculty hold the highest degree in their field.

Academic Program

The College operates on a 4-4-1 calendar—two 4-month terms in the fall and winter and one 1-month term in the spring. During the spring term, there are opportunities for international study as well as for on-campus instruction and research. In keeping with Alma's philosophy of educating the whole person, the College requires that all students complete liberal arts courses spanning the humanities, the natural sciences, and the social sciences. The B.A. and B.S. degree programs require the completion of 136 credits; the B.F.A. and B.M. degree programs, 148 credits. Highly qualified students are challenged by Alma's honors program, featuring a specially designed freshman course that explores the methods of communication used in the liberal arts disciplines. The honors concept extends throughout the four years at Alma.

Financial Aid

At Alma, students can achieve scholarship recognition regardless of need on the basis of outstanding scholastic achievement. Several academically competitive scholarship programs provide awards for eligible students, including a full tuition scholarship for National Merit Finalists. The College also offers performance scholarships in recognition of individual talent, as well as grants, loans, and deferred-payment plans. Up to 400 campus and community jobs are filled by Alma students yearly. To apply for aid, students are required only to file the Free Application for Federal Student Aid (FAFSA) in January of the year of prospective enrollment at Alma.

Application and Information

Students may apply at any time after completing their junior year of high school. Freshman applicants should send the completed application for admission along with a $20 nonrefundable application fee, high school transcripts, and ACT or SAT I scores. Students are required to submit a recommendation from their high school guidance counselor. Early decision applications are due by November 1. Transfer students should submit transcripts from all colleges and high schools attended, the completed application for admission, a $20 nonrefundable application fee, a financial aid transcript, and a Transfer Recommendation Form from the last college attended. Applications are handled on a rolling basis; students should hear about admission decisions within three weeks after sending an application and records. Alma College's nondiscrimination policy includes age, color, creed, gender, national origin, physical ability, race, religion, and sexual orientation.

All records and forms should be mailed to:

Admissions Office
Alma College
Alma, Michigan 48801-1599

Telephone: 800-321-ALMA (toll-free)
E-mail: admissions@alma.edu
Web site: http://www.alma.edu

AMERICAN UNIVERSITY OF PARIS
PARIS, FRANCE

The University

The American University of Paris is an independent four-year institution that was founded in Paris more than a quarter of a century ago. It serves as a major center of American higher education, bringing together the strengths of an American curriculum and curricular flexibility, its privileged location in one of the great cities of Europe, an international student body, and its immediate access to important cultural events and intellectual currents. The University seeks to educate its students to understand the complexities of an interdependent world. The student body numbers 1,000. Thirty-six percent are American, 12 percent are French, and 52 percent are from eighty different countries. Student mobility to and from other U.S. institutions is ensured because the University is accredited by the Middle States Association of Colleges and Schools. American in its structures, academic policies, and educational philosophy, the University offers degree programs with a strong comparative thrust and the opportunity to work with a well-credentialed, multinational faculty—all in the context of the extraordinary city of Paris.

Academic Program

The degree programs of the American University of Paris reflect its international character. Each major area of study has been selected and developed to bring together the best of an American curriculum and the extraordinary resources of Paris and Europe. In addition to the University's basic distribution requirements, all students are required to complete two years of French. (French is not a prerequisite for admission.) A minimum of 120 credit hours is needed for graduation. Special programs include independent study, cross-registration with the Université de Paris–La Sorbonne, and English as a second language for students whose primary language is not English. The University operates on a semester basis; the academic year is complemented by a six-week summer session (June–July), which is preceded by a three-week intersession (total-immersion French is offered at this time). The summer programs feature an outstanding cultural program and excursions to Normandy, Burgundy, Champagne, and the Loire Valley.

Financial Aid

The University offers a financial aid program that supplements the ability of each family to contribute to the total educational cost. A reasonable family contribution and grants from non-University sources are deducted from the full cost of tuition and other expenses as established by the University. An award that will assist the student in meeting costs is then determined. Financial aid awards from the University vary depending on the individual's need and the availability of resources. These awards consist of a tuition reduction and/or work-study. Typically, an award ranges from $1090 to $7000 in tuition reduction; work-study amounts to a maximum of $1600 per academic year. Eligibility for student loans is determined on the basis of the Financial Aid PROFILE of the College Scholarship Service and the Free Application for Federal Student Aid.

Application and Information

An application for admission and further information may be obtained by contacting the American University of Paris at either its U.S. address (for residents of the United States and Canada) or its Paris address.

U.S. Office
American University of Paris
60 East 42nd Street, Suite 1463
New York, New York 10017

Telephone: 212-983-1414
Fax: 212-983-0444

Office of Admissions
American University of Paris
31, avenue Bosquet
75007 Paris
France

Telephone: 33-1-40-62-07-20
Fax: 33-1-47-05-34-32
E-mail: admissions@aup.fr
Web site: http://www.aup.fr

AQUINAS COLLEGE
GRAND RAPIDS, MICHIGAN

The College

Founded by the Dominican Sisters of Grand Rapids in 1922, Aquinas has a Catholic heritage and a Christian tradition. The Dominican tradition of working and serving remains alive at Aquinas. It is lived out by Aquinas students who volunteer their time and talents in the Grand Rapids community and by those who travel to places such as Oaxaca, Mexico; Appalachia, Kentucky; or any of a dozen other service learning project sites. Aquinas, a coeducational liberal arts college, offers an approach to learning and living that teaches students unlimited ways of seeing the world. That is why every Aquinas student enrolls in the humanities program, a two-semester exploration of the best that has been thought, written, composed, and painted. And as students find their way in the world of thought, the core curriculum in natural science ensures that they discover the workings of the physical world as well. The College's curriculum, with its more than forty majors and cognates, is designed to provide students with both breadth and depth and to foster a thirst for knowledge and truth and a spirit of intellectual dialogue and inquiry. Arriving from places as near as Grand Rapids, Chicago, and Detroit and as far as India and China, the 2,493 students include 1,235 full-time, 716 part-time, and 479 graduate students. The Insignis program at Aquinas encourages students of exceptional academic ability to participate in social and intellectual activities such as lectures and receptions for visiting scholars and trips to places of cultural interest. Aquinas offers more than thirty student organizations, ranging from intramural teams and departmental clubs to a wide variety of musical groups, student publications, and service organizations.

Academic Program

In addition to their major and minor fields of study, students take an integrated skills course called Inquiry and Expression. This course spans the entire freshman year and has an emphasis on writing integrated with reading critically, oral communication skills, critical thinking, library/electronic research methods, computer utilization, and basic quantitative reasoning. The thematic content is American Pluralism: The Individual in a Diverse America. Sophomores take a yearlong course in the humanities. As juniors they are required to take 3 hours in Religious Dimensions of Human Existence, with a choice among three categories: Scripture, Catholic/Christian Thought, or Contemporary Religious Experience. The senior year includes a capstone course called Global Perspective. Students are also required to be proficient in a second language through the 201 level. There also is a distribution plan in the general education plan covering The Individual in a Global Community; Myth, Mind, Body, and Spirit; Natural World; Artistic and Creative Studies; and Quantitative Reasoning and Technology. Aquinas also accepts credit through CLEP and Advanced Placement.

Financial Aid

Aquinas College awards both merit-based financial assistance and traditional need-based assistance to qualified students. The Spectrum Scholarship Program was developed to recognize students' achievements in academics, leadership, and service. More than 50 percent of entering freshmen receive some form of financial assistance. The College administers the traditional grant and loan programs, including Federal Stafford Student Loans and Federal PLUS loans. Athletic grants are also available. The College participates in the Academic Management Services Plan and provides the Aquinas College Multiple Payment Plan. These plans assist students in paying costs over a period of time. To apply for financial assistance, students must complete the Free Application for Federal Student Aid (FAFSA).

Application and Information

For further information, interested students should contact:

Tom Mikowski
Director of Admissions
Aquinas College
1607 Robinson Road, SE
Grand Rapids, Michigan 49506

Telephone: 616-732-4460
800-678-9593 (toll-free)

ART INSTITUTE OF BOSTON
BOSTON, MASSACHUSETTS

The Institute

Founded in 1912, the Art Institute of Boston (AIB), the city's only independent college of art, today offers degree, diploma, and continuing education programs in design, fine arts, illustration/animation, and photography. AIB's typical student is intrigued by the visual image and directs his or her energies and talent toward making successful and effective art, whether it be fine art or commercial art. The Art Institute of Boston's programs are studio intensive, integrating liberal arts courses that broaden students' intellectual and artistic perceptions. Classes are taught by a faculty drawn from the front ranks of New England's artistic, educational, and business communities. AIB's classes are small, generally containing fewer than 15 students per class, which allows for much individual attention. The school has a total of 461 full- and part-time students from thirty-three states and twenty countries. Projects and assignments are demanding, but the atmosphere is informal and friendly, and students have many opportunities to develop close ties with other students and with members of the faculty and staff.

Academic Program

In the first year, foundation courses for art majors and photography majors familiarize students with the language of visual communication, develop and sharpen their technical skills, and explore the cultural, historical, and social forces that shape and define our world. The foundation year is a major first step in discovering and developing talents, skills, and interests. Advanced programs are directed at training students to become contributing members of the art community. Work is directly related to achieving students' professional goals. Internships during the senior year provide first-hand experience in their prospective fields. Credit-hour requirements range from 124 to 128, depending on the particular program. Generally, students earn 30 credits each year, 15 per semester. The academic calendar consists of fall, spring, and summer semesters, and credit courses are offered during the day and evening year-round.

Financial Aid

AIB maintains an active financial aid program that awards loans and part-time jobs. More than 70 percent of AIB's students receive aid each year. Awards are made on the basis of need as determined by the College Scholarship Service and the United States Department of Education, which analyze all the financial resources of the student. The Financial Aid Office's goal is to help students meet established needs through a combination of Federal Pell Grants, Federal Stafford Student Loans, Federal Work-Study, other federal grants, scholarships, and state programs. Various merit-based and need-based scholarships are available. The Art Institute of Boston administers more than $1.7 million in scholarships, financial aid, and loans for students each year. The application deadline for merit scholarships is February 20, 1998; the deadline is March 13 for need-based awards.

Application and Information

Admission decisions are made on a rolling basis. Applications are reviewed as they are received, and the applicant can expect a decision within three weeks of having completed the application. To ensure a place in the desired program and in order to meet application deadlines for financial aid, students are encouraged to apply as early as possible. The complete application consists of an application form with essay and fee, transcript(s) of grades, an interview, and a portfolio. Transfer and international students are encouraged to apply. For further information, students should contact:

Diana Arcadipone
Dean of Admissions
Art Institute of Boston
700 Beacon Street
Boston, Massachusetts 02215-2598
Telephone: 617-262-1223
800-773-0494 (toll-free from New England states, New York, and Pennsylvania)
E-mail: admissions@aiboston.edu
Web site: http://www.aiboston.edu

ATLANTA COLLEGE OF ART
ATLANTA, GEORGIA

The College

The Atlanta College of Art provides an educational environment for the career-minded student with a talent and passion for art or design. Founded in 1928, the College is an accredited institutional member of the National Association of Schools of Art and Design and the Commission on Colleges of the Southern Association of Colleges and Schools. Approximately 425 students from thirty-one states and more than twenty-four countries compose a highly charged, creative community that nurtures the development of educated, effective, and successful professionals in the visual arts. The Atlanta College of Art is a founding member of the Woodruff Arts Center, the focus of the cultural life of the region, which completed a $15-million pre-Olympic renovation project, thus expanding the studio, library, and office space of the College. As the only art college in the United States that shares its campus with three other arts organizations—the High Museum of Art, the Alliance Theater, and the Atlanta Symphony Orchestra—the College is able to offer students access to a variety of art forms and resources on a working and thriving campus.

Academic Program

The College's first-year Foundation Program combines visual studies courses, which emphasize visual thinking and problem solving, with courses in drawing and liberal arts as well as work in a studio area of choice. In the sophomore year, students develop their own course of study with a faculty adviser, either electing an established major or designing their own individualized major program. During the course of study, studio work is combined with courses in art history and criticism, English, literature, philosophy, psychology, anthropology, sociology, science, and math in a ratio of 2:1.

Financial Aid

The Atlanta College of Art offers extensive financial assistance to students, combining institutional funds with funds from federal and state grant and loan programs. Each year, need-based grants, loans, and work-study jobs are awarded to students who apply for financial assistance using the College Scholarship Service Financial Aid PROFILE and the Free Application of Federal Student Aid. While the priority deadline for applying for financial aid is March 15, awards are made on a first-come, first-served basis. The College also offers merit scholarships to both entering students and returning students. The Presidential Scholarship is awarded on the basis of the excellence of the portfolio and scholastic achievement. The School of Excellence award is given in recognition of the high quality of the student's high school or two-year college art program and the students' achievement in that program. The Dean's Scholarship is awarded on the basis of ACT or SAT I scores. Georgia residents are eligible for the Georgia Tuition Equalization Grant and the Hope Scholarship program.

Application and Information

Beginning in October, the portfolios and academic credentials of applicants are reviewed. Students are admitted to the College on a rolling basis, and an admission decision is made by the admission staff and faculty Admissions Committee as soon as the applicant file is complete. While there is no official deadline for submission of an application, students are encouraged to apply early for priority consideration as space in both housing and classes is limited.

For an application and more information, students should contact:

John A. Farkas
Director of Enrollment Management
Atlanta College of Art
Woodruff Arts Center
1280 Peachtree Street, NE
Atlanta, Georgia 30309

Telephone: 404-733-5100
800-832-2104 (toll-free)

AUDREY COHEN COLLEGE
NEW YORK, NEW YORK

The College

Founded in 1964, Audrey Cohen College offers the student a unique Purpose Centered System of Education, a design developed by the College. (The curriculum and its components are registered with the U.S. Patent Office.) This system examines the global, information- and service-centered economy, which employs more than 80 percent of the American work force, and responds to the questions: What must professionals be able to do, and how can they prepare for demanding and changing roles? Audrey Cohen College alone has reinvented higher education to reflect the needs of this economy. Its graduates pursue careers in such areas as banking, community affairs, corrections, early childhood education, public policy, counseling, finance, government, health and human resources, personnel administration, social work, and law. If they choose, students are able to work full-time while pursuing their studies full-time, the latter being a College requirement. This becomes possible because of the strong educational relationships the College develops with students' employers.

Academic Program

In both the School for Human Services and the School for Business, each semester of study is organized around a major Purpose, which research has shown to be critical for professional life in a global, information- and service-centered economy. One of the undergraduate Purposes is "Developing Professional Relationships," another is "Effective Supervision," a third is "Managing Human Resources," and so on. There are eight Purposes in each of the programs. Five courses (whose names remain constant) define how each Purpose is viewed holistically. These are Purpose, Values and Ethics, Self and Others, Systems, and Skills. The theory examined in those classes is different for each of the Purposes. Incorporated into the curriculum are the social and behavioral sciences, the humanities, and professional studies, among others. They are fused into a transdisciplinary model. Simultaneous to attending classes, each semester students must show, at their work site or at an internship, how they have taken theory from all five courses and used it to address an organizational need related to their Purpose. The College terms this taking Constructive Action and awards credit upon its successful completion. In each class, the professor incorporates material covered in other classes within that specific Purpose, thus ensuring the holistic, action-centered education that exemplifies the College.

Financial Aid

Audrey Cohen College participates in the federally administered Federal Pell Grant, Federal Stafford Student Loan, and Federal PLUS loan programs and in the Tuition Assistance Program (TAP), sponsored and administered by New York State for its state residents. The College also has limited resources under two other federal financial aid programs: the Federal Supplemental Educational Opportunity Grant Program and the Federal Work-Study Program. In addition, the College has its own scholarship program.

Application and Information

All applicants must complete and return the application with a $20 application fee, take the Test of Adult Basic Education (TABE) at the College, have a personal interview with an admission counselor, submit two letters of reference, provide official transcripts from each educational institution previously attended, and submit proof of immunization against measles, mumps, and rubella. Each applicant is also required to write an essay during the admission testing process. Applicants are informed of decisions as soon as all application materials have been received and evaluated.

For additional information, students should contact:

Admissions Office
Audrey Cohen College
75 Varick Street
New York, New York 10013

Telephone: 212-343-1234 Ext. 5001
Fax: 212-343-8470
Web site: http://www.audrey-cohen.edu

BALL STATE UNIVERSITY
MUNCIE, INDIANA

The University

Ball State University was founded as a state institution in 1918, but its antecedents date from the late nineteenth century when the Ball family, prominent industrialists, purchased and donated to the state of Indiana the campus and buildings of the Muncie Normal Institute. In 1922 the Board of Trustees gave the school the name of Ball Teachers College, and in 1929 the school became Ball State Teachers College. In 1965 the Indiana General Assembly renamed the institution Ball State University in recognition of its phenomenal growth in enrollment, in physical facilities, and in the variety and quality of its educational programs and services. The fifty-eight buildings on the 955-acre campus reflect the changing architectural styles of the twentieth century. There are more than 300 student organizations that provide extracurricular activities. These include leadership programs, departmental organizations, honorary societies, music groups, religious organizations, fraternities, sororities, governing groups, special interest organizations, and service groups. The University Health Service staff members offer health education, provide care in cases of acute illness and injury while a student is in attendance, and serve as medical advisers for the University.

Academic Program

Undergraduate programs combine general studies with majors and minors. Most degrees require 126 semester hours, at least a 2.0 grade point average, and the last year in residence. The academic calendar consists of fall and spring semesters and two summer terms. The Honors College, a four-year University-wide program featuring special course offerings, colloquia, seminars, and independent study, is especially designed to challenge the talented student. University College is organized to provide support services to students undecided about their majors. The Learning Center is structured to meet the needs of certain recent Indiana high school graduates, GED awardees, veterans, and students whose past academic records indicate underpreparedness in basic skills. The University, recognizing that there are other ways to obtain an education than through regular enrollment in a class, grants a maximum of 63 credit hours through any combination of credit for successful scores on Advanced Placement tests or College-Level Examination Program tests, credit for military service, credit by departmental examination, and credit by departmental authorization.

Financial Aid

Through a program of scholarships, grants, loans, and employment, Ball State's Office of Scholarships and Financial Aid provides aid for deserving students. The Free Application for Federal Student Aid, obtainable from a high school guidance counselor, should be filed no later than March 1.

Application and Information

High school students should complete an application in the fall of their senior year. Application materials must be submitted by March 1 for priority consideration for the autumn semester and by December 1 for the spring semester. Requests for appointments and information should be addressed to:

Director of Admissions
Ball State University
Muncie, Indiana 47306

Telephone: 317-285-8300
E-mail: askus@wp.bsu.edu
visitus@wp.bsu.edu
Web site: http://www.bsu.edu/cover.html

BAY PATH COLLEGE
LONGMEADOW, MASSACHUSETTS

The College

Founded in 1897, Bay Path College today offers baccalaureate and associate degrees. As a professional college for women, Bay Path's philosophy of education focuses on the total development of the individual and encourages self-understanding and the realization of each student's full potential. In an atmosphere combining traditional values with contemporary education, students are prepared for successful interaction with others, both professionally and personally. The College's Career Services Center assists graduates who seek immediate employment; this service is available to them throughout their lives at no cost. In recent years, 95 to 98 percent of Bay Path's students have obtained jobs upon graduation. Bay Path is a member of the College Entrance Examination Board, the Association of Independent Colleges and Universities in Massachusetts, the College Board, the National Association of College Admission Counselors, the National Association of Independent Colleges and Universities, and the Women's College Coalition.

Academic Program

Bay Path's programs prepare women either for entry into the career world or for continued studies. A minimum of 60 credits must be completed successfully to earn an associate degree, and a minimum of 120 credits are required for a baccalaureate. The general education requirements are intended to provide students with a foundation for learning in the humanities and fine arts, mathematics, and the natural and social sciences, regardless of their choice of major. The courses are all directed toward fulfilling the College's mission. All of the course offerings incorporate one or more of the three themes of the College's vision statement, Bay Path 2001: leadership, communication, and technology. Internships are an integral part of many programs, and students are placed with professionals in local businesses for on-the-job experience. Bay Path interns work in law firms, hotels, retail stores, travel agencies, decorating firms, insurance companies, airline offices, cruise lines, social service agencies, correctional facilities, schools, and hospitals.

Financial Aid

Bay Path is keenly interested in admitting talented women who are serious about their education, and it encourages such students to apply regardless of their financial means. Scholarships, grants, loans, and employment opportunities are available. Bay Path has a commitment to continue to aid qualified students who receive aid in their freshman year; every effort is made to maintain or increase the funding level to enable these students to graduate. Approximately 85 percent of current Bay Path students receive some form of financial aid. Financial aid applicants are reviewed beginning on December 15.

Application and Information

The College follows a rolling admissions policy and encourages students to apply early. Notification of decision is generally within two weeks of receiving the completed application and accompanying materials. The candidate reply is due by May 1. For September enrollment, December 1 is the application deadline recommended for early decision consideration, with notification by December 15. The candidate reply is due by May 1. The application, application fee, and all credentials must be received before the admission process can begin. The completed application should be sent to the Office of Admissions, together with a $25 nonrefundable application fee or fee-waiver request.

For application forms and additional information, students should contact:

Dean of Enrollment Services
Bay Path College
588 Longmeadow Street
Longmeadow, Massachusetts 01106
Telephone: 413-567-0621
800-782-7284 (toll-free outside 413 area code)
Fax: 413-567-0501
E-mail: admiss@baypath.edu

BELMONT ABBEY COLLEGE
BELMONT, NORTH CAROLINA

The College

The most notable characteristics of Belmont Abbey College are its warmth and friendliness. Its origins in Christian tradition are exemplified in the lives of the monks and staff members who belong to the community of Belmont Abbey. The strong family nature of the community directly influences the campus and classroom atmosphere. Because the College is small, students know the faculty and administration, and the development of lifelong friendships is common. Residence life gives the student opportunities to develop both social and academic ideals. The sense of community is featured in both the academic and social aspects of the College. The student body of approximately 1,000 men and women represents twenty-five states and sixteen countries. This diversity adds a valuable dimension to the student's educational experience. The College is coeducational, and approximately 50 percent of the students live on campus. Cars are permitted for all.

Academic Program

The academic program is built on a distinctive core curriculum that responds to the diverse nature and needs of the traditional-age student. The core reflects over 100 years of commitment to liberal arts, Catholic, and Benedictine values and emphasizes faith, truth, social justice, the place of the individual in community, international studies, and the use of primary sources in the pursuit of knowledge. A cumulative average of at least C (2.0 on a 4.0 scale) is required for graduation. The Adult Degree Program and Weekend College serve students who need to attend college in a program outside the traditional day school program. Students in the Adult Degree Program attend classes three nights each week. Students can earn up to 12 semester hours of credit (this is considered full-time), making them eligible to apply for federal, state, and institutional financial aid. Students in the Weekend College attend classes Friday night and Saturday and can earn up to 12 semester hours of credit.

Financial Aid

College-administered aid comes from the full range of federal programs—Federal Pell Grants and Federal Supplemental Educational Opportunity Grants, Federal Work-Study awards, Federal Perkins Loans, and Federal Stafford Student Loans. North Carolina students have access to state grant funds administered by the College. Tuition is reduced by $900 per year for all siblings after the first one is enrolled full-time and paying full tuition. Scholarships based on academic promise are granted each year. About 80 percent of all students receive College aid in some form. All applicants for aid must file the Free Application for Federal Student Aid (FAFSA) of the College Scholarship Service with the Financial Aid Office at Belmont Abbey College by March 15. The two criteria for receiving aid are financial need and academic promise. Numerous companies throughout the region have employees in Belmont Abbey College's Adult Degree Program. Many of these companies provide some form of tuition reimbursement. Belmont Abbey offers a tuition deferment program for students eligible for employer reimbursement.

Application and Information

An application, together with a $25 nonrefundable application fee, may be submitted for either the fall or spring semester; the deadlines are August 15 and December 31, respectively, but early application is advised. Notification of acceptance is given on a rolling basis upon completion of application data. A $300 tuition and room-reservation deposit for boarding students or a $100 tuition deposit for commuting students is due thirty days after the notice of acceptance is received.

For further information, prospective students should contact:

Office of Admissions
Belmont Abbey College
Belmont, North Carolina 28012

Telephone: 704-825-6665
800-523-2355 (toll-free)
Fax: 704-825-6670

BELOIT COLLEGE
BELOIT, WISCONSIN

The College

Beloit College was founded in 1846 by Yale graduates who wanted to bring to the West the solid classical tradition they had experienced. Today, Beloit is a private, national, liberal arts college whose focus is great teaching with an interdisciplinary, international, and experiential emphasis. Beloit's student body is 11 percent international, is racially diverse (1 in 6 is non-Caucasian), includes a number of religious orientations, and represents a wide range of socioeconomic backgrounds. New students quickly become part of this active and diverse environment through First Year Initiatives (FYI), an innovative program that places first-year students in an interdisciplinary seminar taught by an experienced professor or staff member. These seminars begin the first day new students arrive on campus and provide an academic class, a social base, and a two-year faculty adviser to assist students in their adjustment to Beloit.

Academic Program

Beloit's academic calendar consists of two 14-week semesters with one-week mid-term breaks. Students are required to complete either a double major or a major with an interdisciplinary minor or teaching certification. In addition, Beloit's open core curriculum requires two classes from each of the three academic divisions, plus an interdisciplinary requirement and a writing requirement. Thirty-one units are required for graduation, each unit representing the equivalent of a course of study involving 4 hours of class time a week per semester. Submission of a comprehensive academic plan (CAP) is also required in the sophomore year. Sophomore students work with their faculty advisers to define academic and personal goals, including completion of graduation requirements and declaration of major, and develop a plan for accomplishing them. A CAP allows students to shape their time at Beloit and ensure they will reach their goals.

Financial Aid

Beloit College has a need-blind admissions policy and is committed to making the Beloit experience affordable to all qualified students. The financial aid program recognizes two criteria—scholastic ability and financial need—that may qualify students for awards. During the 1996–97 academic year about three quarters of Beloit College students received financial assistance through grants, loans, or work-study employment. The average need-based grant for first year students was $9843. The College also awards merit scholarships.

Application and Information

Beloit has modified rolling admissions, so students may apply at any time. For priority consideration, both in admissions and in financial aid, however, students should file their applications by February 1. Students who do apply by this date will be mailed notification by March 1. Early decision applications are due December 1, with notification December 15. Transfer applications for the fall term are due by May 1, for the spring term by December 1. Notification for transfer applications is rolling. For further information, students should contact:

Admissions Office
Beloit College
700 College Street
Beloit, Wisconsin 53511

Telephone: 608-363-2500
800-356-0751 (toll-free)
Fax: 608-363-2075
E-mail: admiss@beloit.edu
Web site: http://www.beloit.edu

BENEDICTINE UNIVERSITY
LISLE, ILLINOIS

The University

Benedictine University was founded in 1887 as St. Procopius College. One hundred ten years later, the University remains committed to providing a high-quality, Catholic, liberal education for men and women. The undergraduate enrollment is 1,600 students. Most are from the Chicago area and suburbs or other parts of Illinois, although other states and other countries are represented. The student body comprises students of diverse ages, religions, races, and national origins. Forty-seven percent of the full-time students reside on campus. Benedictine University is situated on a rolling, tree-covered 108-acre campus of ten major buildings with air-conditioned classrooms and modern, well-equipped laboratories. All of the residence halls are comfortable and spacious and have access to the Internet. Other features include a scenic campus pond, spacious and well-kept athletic fields, and a student center with dining halls, a game room, lounges, bookstore, and meeting rooms. Aside from varsity and intramural athletic programs, a variety of organizations exist, including a newspaper, an orchestra, jazz groups, an African-American Student Union, an Indian Student Union, the Coalition of Latin American Students, campus ministry, a drama club, and various other extracurricular and academic organizations.

Academic Program

For graduation, a student must earn at least 120 semester hours, at least half of which must be completed at a four-year regionally accredited college, and at least the final 45 semester hours must be completed at Benedictine University. The University makes selective exceptions to the normal academic residency requirement of 45 semester hours for adults who are eligible for the Degree Completion Program. Eligibility is limited to those who have nearly completed their undergraduate studies, but who, for reasons of employment, career change, or family situation, found it necessary to interrupt their studies. The Second Major Program is designed for people who already have a degree in one area and would like to gain expertise in another. This program allows the student to concentrate on courses that will fulfill the requirements of a second major. The student receives a certificate upon completion. Each year, a select number of talented and motivated prospective students are invited to participate in the Scholars Program. The program is designed to enhance the college experience by developing students' international awareness and strengthening their leadership ability.

Financial Aid

In 1996–97, Benedictine University freshmen received assistance totaling $2.2 million from sources that included loans, scholarships/grants, tuition remission, and employment opportunities. Almost 89 percent of the freshman class participated, receiving an average package of $9338. Benedictine University has dedicated more than $4 million of the annual budget to providing grants and scholarships to students, including scholarships for study in the humanities and a separate scholarship program designed to attract and serve members of minority groups. Students who wish to apply for aid must complete the Free Application for Federal Student Aid (FAFSA), the Benedictine University application for financial aid, and the Benedictine University application for admission.

Application and Information

Applications are reviewed on a rolling basis. Students are encouraged to apply for admission at any time after completing their junior year of high school. Transfer students may apply for admission during their last semester or quarter before anticipated transfer to Benedictine University. Earlier applications are encouraged. For further information, students should contact:

Office of Admissions
Benedictine University
5700 College Road
Lisle, Illinois 60532-0900

Telephone: 630-829-6300
E-mail: admissions@ben.edu
Web site: http://www.ben.edu

BETHEL COLLEGE
ST. PAUL, MINNESOTA

The College
Bethel College began its four-year Christian liberal arts program in 1945 but traces its roots to Bethel Theological Seminary, founded in 1871. Bethel is operated as a ministry of the Baptist General Conference. The College encourages growth and learning in a distinctly Christian environment, continually striving to help students discover and develop the skills God has given them. Bethel's 2,039 students represent a wide range of national and international cultures and more than thirty denominations. The campus, built in the 1970s, is the newest among Minnesota colleges. Versatile buildings are centers for the sciences, humanities, physical education, learning resources, and fine arts.

Academic Program
General education classes are grouped around the following themes: Bible and theology, Western heritage, world citizenship, self-understanding, science and technology, and health and wholeness. In addition, in order to graduate, all Bethel students must demonstrate competence in mathematics, writing, speaking, and computing. Bethel College follows a 4-1-4 academic calendar, consisting of two 15-week semesters and a 3-week Interim in January. A full-time academic load for each semester is 12 to 18 credits. To graduate, a student must complete a minimum of 122 credits with a cumulative grade point average of at least 2.0 and a minimum 2.25 grade point average in his or her major. Also required are 50 credits of general education. Bethel awards advanced placement in recognition of learning that has been achieved apart from a college classroom situation. A maximum of 30 advanced placement credits can be applied toward a degree program. Students may also individualize their academic program through directed studies with faculty members and through academic internships with off-campus institutions.

Financial Aid
Bethel College strives to make it financially possible for every qualified student to attend. Each year, nearly 90 percent of the students receive some kind of financial aid, including scholarships, grants, loans, and assistance in the form of on-campus employment. Students who wish to be considered for financial aid must first be admitted to the College and then submit a Family Financial Statement (FFS). Bethel's priority deadline is April 15 of each year. Students who have completed and mailed all necessary forms by this date receive first consideration.

Application and Information
Students wishing to apply for admission to Bethel must send the following: a completed Bethel application form with a $20 nonrefundable application fee; test scores from the PSAT, SAT I, or ACT; transcripts of all course work completed at the high school and college levels; and references from a pastor and an adult friend or employer. Admission decisions are made on a rolling basis. Although there is no deadline, applicants for fall admission are encouraged to complete their files before May 1. For further information about specific Bethel programs and campus visit opportunities, students should contact:

Office of Admissions
Bethel College
3900 Bethel Drive
St. Paul, Minnesota 55112

Telephone: 612-638-6242
800-255-8706 Ext. 6242 (toll-free)
Fax: 612-635-1490
E-mail: bcoll-admit@bethel.edu
Web site: http://www.bethel.edu

BLOOMFIELD COLLEGE
BLOOMFIELD, NEW JERSEY

The College
Founded in 1868, Bloomfield College is an independent four-year coeducational college that offers programs in the liberal arts and sciences, creative arts and technology, and professional studies, which include accounting, business administration, computer information systems, criminal justice, materials management, nursing, prechiropractic, and the sciences. Bloomfield is accredited by the Middle States Association of Colleges and Schools, and the nursing program is accredited by the National League for Nursing. The College is chartered by the state of New Jersey, and its academic programs are approved by the New Jersey Commission on Higher Education. The accounting program is a Registered Accounting Curriculum for Public Accountancy in the State of New Jersey and meets the state's educational requirements for candidates applying to sit for the CPA examination. The College is affiliated with the Presbyterian Church (U.S.A.) through the Synod of the Northeast and is a member of the Association of Presbyterian Colleges and Universities.

Academic Program
Degree candidacy requires the successful completion of at least 33 course units; a full course unit is equivalent to 4 semester hours. A minimum of 16 course units must be completed at an advanced level. Five categories of courses are offered at the College: all-College required courses, general education courses, courses required for the major, elective courses in the major, and unrestricted electives. Course requirements for the degree vary among majors. The prechiropractic program is a sequence of courses preparing the student for study for the Doctor of Chiropractic (D.C.) degree. The student may either complete graduation requirements for a bachelor's degree or transfer from Bloomfield College directly into a D.C. program after three years. Other special programs available at Bloomfield College include a B.S./RN Transfer Program for nursing students who already have a two-year degree; the Educational Opportunity Fund Program, a state-funded program of educational and special services for disadvantaged students; English as a second language; an honors program; a program, under the auspices of the division of creative arts and technology, in circus performing, in which students join a troupe; Weekend College, a complete degree program for adults that is offered on alternate weekends; and various internship programs.

Financial Aid
In 1996–97, Bloomfield College students received more than $11 million in scholarships and financial aid, with more than 85 percent of the full-time day student population receiving some form of financial assistance. Academic scholarships are administered by the Office of Admission; athletic scholarships are administered by the athletics department. College, state, and federal programs, such as grants, loans, and work-study, are administered by the Financial Aid Office.

Application and Information
All applicants are encouraged to visit the College to discuss their academic and career plans with an admission counselor. Applicants may also spend a day on campus attending classes and talking with students, faculty members, and administrators about academic programs and student activities as well as the issues of admission and financial assistance. Recommended application deadlines are May 15 for the fall semester, December 15 for the spring semester, and May 15 for the summer session. Applications received after these dates are considered on a space-available basis. For further information, students may contact:

George P. Lynes II, Dean of Admission
Bloomfield College
1 Park Place
Bloomfield, New Jersey 07003

Telephone: 201-748-9000 Ext. 230
800-848-4555 (toll-free)
Fax: 201-748-0916

BOWIE STATE UNIVERSITY
BOWIE, MARYLAND

The University

Bowie State University began as a normal school in the city of Baltimore in 1865, and it has evolved over the years into a four-year, coeducational, liberal arts institution. It is currently situated on a beautiful 312-acre campus in Prince Georges County, Maryland, and offers both graduate and undergraduate programs of study. In 1988, Bowie State achieved university status. The University is accredited by the Middle States Association of Colleges and Schools and approved by the Maryland State Department of Education.

Academic Program

Academic offerings can be divided into four main areas: humanities, science and mathematics, social sciences, and education. To receive a bachelor's degree, a student must earn a minimum of 120 semester hours with a cumulative grade point average of 2.0 or better. Students who enter through the University College of Excellence (UCE) are provided the opportunity to complete the General Studies Program, acquire lifelong learning skills for a competitive world, and make a successful transition into their junior year. General studies requirements include communication skills, 9 hours; humanities, 9 hours; social sciences, 18 hours; science and mathematics, 9 hours; and physical education, 2 hours. Students must also pass the test of Proficiency in the English Language and must take the national standardized test in their major area. The Honors Program is designed for students with outstanding academic records and potential and provides a special educational opportunity for young adults with exceptional talent. The Special Services Project is a federally funded program designed to retain and graduate first-generation, low-income, and disabled students who have been admitted to Bowie State University. Through the Cooperative Education Program, a student may choose either the alternate or parallel programs of study and work in business, industry, government, or a social-service agency. This program is open to Bowie State students who have completed at least one academic year with a minimum cumulative grade point average of 2.0. The University participates in the College-Level Examination Program (CLEP), administered by the Educational Testing Service for the College Board, and in the Defense Activity for Non-Traditional Education Support (DANTES) program. Through all of these programs, qualified students may receive up to 30 credit hours toward their degree. Two-year and three-year scholarships are available.

Financial Aid

Federal Pell Grants, Supplemental Grants, Work-Study, Perkins Loans, and Direct Loans are available. University scholarships, tuition waivers, and diversity grants are awarded. Most awards are based on need. Merit scholarships could be offered to students with cumulative grade point averages of at least 3.0 and minimum recentered SAT I scores of 1050. Full-tuition awards are possible for out-of-state students who have a minimum cumulative grade point average of 3.3 and a minimum recentered SAT I score of 1130. More than 85 percent of all undergraduate students receive some form of financial aid. Scholarships and assistantships are offered through the Model Institutions for Excellence Program for Science, Engineering, and Mathematics. Deadlines are May 1 for the fall semester and November 15 for the spring semester.

Application and Information

The application deadline is April 1 for the fall semester and November 1 for spring. For an application form, students should contact:

Director of Enrollment, Recruitment and Registration
Bowie State University
Bowie, Maryland 20715-9465

Telephone: 301-464-6570
410-880-4100 Ext. 6570 (from the Baltimore-Columbia area)

BREVARD COLLEGE
BREVARD, NORTH CAROLINA

The College

Founded in 1853, Brevard is a church-related, coeducational liberal arts college that offers innovative four-year and two-year curriculums, with specialties in music, art, environmental studies, wilderness leadership, and other interdisciplinary majors, on a beautiful mountain campus near Asheville, North Carolina. The College's low student-faculty ratio of 8:1, covenant that binds faculty and students in a nurturing community of learning, rich cultural offerings, numerous opportunities for student leadership, nationally competitive athletic programs, and incomparable access to national parks, forest, wilderness areas and white-water recreational rivers make Brevard distinctive. Inspired by its setting among the world's oldest mountains and founded upon the principles of the Christian faith, Brevard College has the purpose of educating students in the tradition of the liberal arts and in the spirit of love and service. The College's faculty and staff, academic and cocurricular programs, financial resources, and support services are devoted to providing an educational climate that fosters respect for learning and beauty, creativity and hard work, tolerance and personal integrity, intellect and love of knowledge, and vigorous activity and spiritual reflection.

Academic Program

The core liberal arts curriculum of the College requires each student to build a strong base in languages and literature, religion, humanities, mathematics and analytical reasoning, history, natural and social sciences, fine arts, and environmental studies. Students are exposed to several other cultures and make a significant investment in volunteer work in the community. The curriculum utilizes classroom studies in the Pisgah National Forest, Davidson and French Broad River ecosystems, Great Smoky Mountain National Park, and the Cradle of Forestry in America, which is designated as a National Historic Site. Programs in music and art afford talented students excellent educational and performance opportunities at the College as well as in such off-campus settings as the famed Brevard Music Center, the Brevard Chamber Orchestra, and the Asheville Art Museum. Consistent with the philosophy of the College, various courses at Brevard College use service as a learning component to enhance the classroom environment. Coordination of the student's service experience is performed by the Center for Service Learning, which works with students to prepare transcripts detailing their cocurricular accomplishments.

Financial Aid

Opportunities for student financial aid are available to every student who can show financial need, superior academic achievement, or talent in athletics, art, drama, or music. All students desiring financial aid must submit the Free Application for Federal Student Aid (FAFSA). The College annually awards more than $200,000 in merit scholarships to select students who display academic excellence, unselfish character, and leadership potential as Brevard Scholars. These students participate in a variety of enriched intellectual, cultural, and leadership programs and work closely with distinguished professors who serve both as advisers and program directors. The Angier B. Duke Scholarships, awarded only by Brevard College and Duke University, are the premier scholarships among more than eighty Brevard Scholars Awards made each year.

Application and Information

Students must submit an application for admission, a recommendation from the guidance counselor on the form provided by the Office of Admissions, official SAT I or ACT scores, and an official high school transcript. Students are advised of the admission decision as soon as all required application materials are received. In addition, Brevard College requires a medical history and a physical examination of each applicant prior to enrollment to the College.

For more information, students should contact:

Dean of Admissions
Brevard College
400 North Broad Street
Brevard, North Carolina 28712

Telephone: 704-884-8300
Fax: 704-884-3790
E-mail: admissions@brevard.edu

CALIFORNIA COLLEGE OF ARTS AND CRAFTS
OAKLAND AND SAN FRANCISCO, CALIFORNIA

The College
The California College of Arts and Crafts was founded in 1907 with a new approach to art schooling—to offer a higher education for artists that includes training not only in the traditional fine arts but also in design and architecture. In the ensuing years, the College has maintained and expanded its commitment to provide as wide a range of art education as possible within the context of a small, private four-year college. The current undergraduate enrollment is about 1,100 men and women. The College comprises two campuses, in San Francisco and Oakland. The San Francisco campus houses the architecture and design programs in a spectacular light-filled building located in the heart of the city's design district. The Oakland campus features a blend of Victorian and modern structures in a four-acre garden setting. CCAC is accredited by the Western Association of Schools and Colleges and the National Association of Schools of Art and Design. The interior design program is accredited by the Foundation for Interior Design Education Research, and the architecture program is accredited by the National Architectural Accrediting Board.

Academic Program
The Bachelor of Fine Arts degree requires the completion of a minimum of 126 semester units, of which 75 must be in studio work and 51 must be in humanities and sciences. All undergraduates at CCAC begin in a foundation—or core—program designed to orient them to a variety of two- and three-dimensional art and design media as well as to strengthen their communication skills and refine and develop their knowledge of history. Students select a major after completing this program. The Bachelor of Architecture, a five-year degree program, requires the completion of a minimum of 162 units, including the one-semester core program with an orientation to two-dimensional and three-dimensional media and a nine-semester major program. Upon completion of the core program, a student's portfolio is developed and reviewed for approval for further study in the program.

Financial Aid
Scholarships, grants, loans, and work-study awards are available for students on the basis of merit and financial need. Students applying for aid in 1997–98 should submit the Free Application for Federal Student Aid (FAFSA) to the Federal Student Aid Processing Agency by March 2. Students should also submit all additional documents required by CCAC by March 2 for priority consideration. CCAC continues to fund students after the priority deadline as long as funds remain available. Applications for Federal Pell Grants and Federal Direct Student Loans may be submitted throughout the school year. CCAC is approved for veterans attending under the Veterans Administration Educational Benefits Program. Approximately 65 percent of students attending CCAC during the 1996–97 year received some type of financial aid. CCAC also offers an extended interest-free payment plan.

Application and Information
CCAC has a rolling admissions deadline. Applications received by the priority filing dates of March 2 for fall admission and October 1 for spring will be given first consideration for registration, housing, and financial aid opportunities. The application fee is $30. Persons who wish to take one or more individual classes may register as nondegree students on a space-available basis and receive College credit for courses completed. For undergraduate application forms, current College bulletins, or any additional information, students should contact:

Director of Enrollment Services
California College of Arts and Crafts
450 Irwin Street
San Francisco, California 94107
Telephone: 800-447-1ART (toll-free)

CALIFORNIA STATE POLYTECHNIC UNIVERSITY, POMONA

POMONA, CALIFORNIA

The University

California State Polytechnic University, Pomona (Cal Poly Pomona) sits on 1,400 acres and is located 35 miles from downtown Los Angeles. Perhaps the most unique of the California State University campuses, it was originally the Arabian horse ranch of cereal magnate W. K. Kellogg. Thousands of people from around the world travel to the ranch for the Sunday horse shows, which began in 1927 and continue today. Now, thousands of students from throughout California, the United States, and the world come to Cal Poly Pomona for its practical education, which places an emphasis on students. Although Cal Poly Pomona's campus is large, it has the feel of a small, private college. Most buildings are within easy walking distance of each other, and the campus sits in a small valley surrounded by hills; these factors contribute to the strong sense of community. Most classrooms seat fewer than 50 students, and the student-faculty ratio is 18:1. Residence halls accommodate approximately 1,200 students in single, super-single, double, and triple rooms, often in academic major, special interest, or lifestyle theme areas. "Learn by doing" is the University's motto, and the curriculum features hands-on education in sixty undergraduate majors in eight schools and colleges.

Academic Program

Classes are offered in four 11-week quarters. Candidates for Bachelor of Arts degrees must earn at least 186 quarter units. The Bachelor of Science degree requires at least 198 quarter units. A graduation writing requirement exists for all baccalaureate degrees. Currently, the Bachelor of Architecture degree is impacted and open only to California residents. Cal Poly Pomona offers early admission for academically talented high school students, Air Force and Army Reserve Officers Training Corps, a California Pre-Doctoral Program, CSU International Programs and Cal Poly Pomona Study Abroad, an Educational Opportunity Program, the Faculty Student Mentoring Program, a National Student Exchange, a Teacher Aide Path to Teaching, University Equity Programs, and other special programs. The Transfer Center works closely with students considering transferring. The University features special centers such as the innovative Center for Regenerative Studies, which allows students to study and live in a sustainable environment community; the W. K. Kellogg Arabian Horse Center, a modern horse breeding, training, and show facility; the Equine Research Center, which specializes in the research of equine nutrition, physiology, parasitology, immunology, and management of all horse breeds; the Apparel Technology and Research Center; and the Center for Turf, Irrigation, and Landscape Technology.

Financial Aid

Though the cost of attending Cal Poly Pomona is less than many of the CSU campuses, the University is cognizant of the need for broad financial aid, which is received by approximately half of the student body. The priority application period is January 1 through March 2 for the following fall, and students must submit a Free Application for Federal Student Aid (FAFSA). Aid comes through grants, loans, scholarships, and work-study. Merit-based scholarships, which require individual application, are available. Interested students should call (909-869-3700) or e-mail (finaid@csupomona.edu) the financial aid office.

Application and Information

Cal Poly Pomona begins accepting applications for the following fall on November 1 of the preceding year. The application fee is $55, but waivers may be granted. The University encourages students to apply on-line over the Internet, with no downloading required. Students can access Cal Poly Pomona's home page (http://www.csupomona.edu) on the World Wide Web. For further information, students should contact:

Student Outreach Recruitment
3801 West Temple Avenue
Pomona, California 91768

Telephone: 909-869-3210

CALVIN COLLEGE
GRAND RAPIDS, MICHIGAN

The College

Calvin College is dedicated to relating the Christian faith to the whole learning process; this view affects every area of campus life from the content of each course to volunteer service and life in the residence halls. Calvin is one of the nation's largest and most respected evangelical Christian colleges. Calvin maintains a strong affiliation with the Christian Reformed Church, and students from more than sixty other church denominations across North America and the world also choose Calvin for its extensive curriculum and Christian emphasis. Calvin is deeply committed to being a genuinely diverse community and is taking deliberate steps to increase opportunities for women, members of minority groups, and the disabled. Students are challenged not only to obtain a fine education and career preparation but also to live examined lives of commitment and service.

Academic Program

Calvin College maintains a high commitment to a liberal arts curriculum as an integral avenue to assist students to understand God's world and their place in it. Typically, students take four courses each semester and one course during the Interim. Graduation requires the successful completion of 124 semester hours, including courses taken in three Interims; the designated liberal arts core; at least two writing enriched courses (part of Calvin's Writing Across the Curriculum Program); and an approved program of concentration. Core curriculum requirements include foreign language, history, literature and arts, mathematics, natural sciences, philosophy, physical education, religion, social sciences, and written and spoken rhetoric. Some requirements can be satisfied by advanced high school work in foreign language, literature, mathematics, and natural sciences. Qualified students can earn course exemption and/or credit by completing college-level work in high school or by examination. Satisfactory scores on Advanced Placement (AP), International Baccalaureate (I.B.), and/or CLEP exams are also accepted.

Financial Aid

Sixty percent of the students receive need-based financial aid; demonstrated need is the most important criterion in determining eligibility. Students wishing to be considered for financial aid must be admitted to the College and must submit the Free Application for Federal Student Aid (FAFSA) and Calvin's Supplemental Application for Financial Aid. February 15 is the suggested filing deadline for maximum consideration. Financial awards to eligible applicants consist of state and federal grants, loans, Federal Work-Study funds, and institutional grants and scholarships. Part-time employment is available on campus, and placement preference is given to needy students. The College also helps students to find and maintain off-campus employment and runs a job transportation service that gets them safely to and from their jobs for a minimal fee.

Application and Information

Applicants must submit a completed application form, a high school or college transcript, results of either the ACT or SAT I, and an educational recommendation completed by a teacher or counselor. Admission decisions are made on a rolling basis beginning in mid-October. Applicants for fall admission are urged to complete their file before February 1, although there is no deadline as long as space remains in the entering class. Campus visits are strongly recommended, although not required. Students and parents are welcome to visit at any time that is convenient for them. The "Fridays at Calvin" campus visit program also provides an excellent opportunity to experience life at Calvin firsthand. For more information about Calvin or about visiting the campus, students should contact:

Admissions Office
Calvin College
3201 Burton Street, SE
Grand Rapids, Michigan 49546

Telephone: 800-688-0122 (toll-free in North America)
Fax: 616-957-8550
E-mail: admissions@calvin.edu
Web site: http://www.calvin.edu

CAMPBELL UNIVERSITY
BUIES CREEK, NORTH CAROLINA

The University

Founded in 1887, Campbell University has had the distinction of being North Carolina's second-largest private undergraduate institution. Graduate programs were established, and in 1979 the name of the institution was changed from Campbell College to Campbell University. Its current enrollment is more than 7,800 students. In an average year, the student body comes from about ninety North Carolina counties, fifty states, and forty-six countries. Sixty-six percent of the students come from North Carolina. Although it is owned by the Baptist State Convention of North Carolina, the University is nonsectarian. Approximately 60 percent of its students are Baptist, but young people of twenty-two other faiths complete its student body. It is concerned with maintaining, for living and learning, an environment consistent with Christian ideals.

Academic Program

The curriculum of Campbell University is designed to meet individual needs and interests. During the first two years, students follow a general course of study, the General College Curriculum, to broaden their backgrounds in the basic fields of knowledge. By the end of the sophomore year, they should have selected a major subject for specialized study during the final two years. Basic curriculum requirements for the first two years in semester hours are English, 12; social studies, 6; natural science, 8; religion, 6; music, art appreciation, or drama, 3; foreign language, up to 9, depending on high school credits and the program of study; and health and physical education, 3. Candidates for a bachelor's degree must earn a minimum of 128 credits, including the 3 in health and physical education, while maintaining at least a C average in academic course work; must complete a minimum of 32 semester hours in the departmental major at Campbell; and must average C or better in all courses required for the major. Candidates for the Associate in Arts degree must complete 64 semester hours of work and have at least a 2.0 GPA on all work required for graduation and at least a 2.0 GPA on 80 percent of all work attempted. The University calendar enables students to complete first-semester course work and examinations before Christmas vacation and end the spring session by the middle of May. Campbell offers the nation's first undergraduate program in trust management and since 1968 has been training prospective trust officers for the banks and trust companies of the region. Campbell also sponsors the Southeastern Trust School, a summer institute for trust officers.

Financial Aid

Campbell University has private and institutional scholarships, federal grants, loans, and Federal Work-Study Program awards. Loans are available through the Federal Stafford Student Loan Program and the Federal Perkins Loan Program. Needs analysis forms (Free Application for Federal Student Aid) are available January 1 and are due in the Financial Aid Office by March 15 if the applicant wishes to be considered for a maximum award. Eighty-five percent of the student body received $36 million in financial assistance in 1996–97. All assistance is offered without regard to race, creed, or national origin.

Application and Information

An application for admission, accompanied by a $15 nonrefundable application fee, must be filed. When all records are on file, the Admissions Committee notifies the student of its decision. Application forms and further information may be requested from:

Office of Admissions
Campbell University
P.O. Box 546
Buies Creek, North Carolina 27506

Telephone: 910-893-1320
910-893-1415 (international)
800-334-4111 (toll-free)
Web site: http://www.campbell.edu/CUIndex.html

CAPITOL COLLEGE
LAUREL, MARYLAND

The College

Capitol College, a private coeducational college, provides practical educational experiences that enable graduates to advance, manage, and communicate changes in the information age. Chartered in 1964, Capitol College offers degree programs in engineering, engineering technology, communications, and management. Career development is an integral aspect of the College's mission, and graduates are in great demand by business and industry. The College is accredited by the Commission of Higher Education of the Middle States Association of Colleges and Schools. The Bachelor of Science and Associate in Applied Science degree programs in computer engineering technology and electronics engineering technology and the Bachelor of Science degree program in telecommunications engineering technology are accredited by the Technology Accreditation Commission of the Accreditation Board for Engineering and Technology (TAC/ABET). The Bachelor of Science in electrical engineering is accredited by the Engineering Accreditation Commission of the Accreditation Board of Engineering and Technology (EAC/ABET).

Academic Program

At Capitol College, learning is centered both in and out of the classroom. Professors are available on a one-on-one basis outside of the classroom, and tutors and lab aides are available for additional assistance. The College's cooperative education program gives students the opportunity to obtain paid education work experience to supplement their academic program. In the engineering and technology curricula, students reinforce their classroom lectures with assigned laboratory projects. Each department has its own sequence requirements for graduation. To earn a bachelor's degree, students must complete between 123 and 137 semester credit hours. To earn an associate degree, students must complete between 64 and 67 semester credit hours. In each degree program, students must complete a core of courses, including mathematics, sciences, humanities, and social sciences. The average course load is 15 credits per semester. Advanced standing can be earned through Advanced Placement (AP) and College-Level Examination Program (CLEP) tests. Credits can also be earned through institutional validation examinations. Established to complement a student's academic program and to broaden his or her educational experience, the Cooperative Education Program arranges for paid work experience, prior to graduation, in jobs related to a student's major. Once hired, a student may work full- or part-time while enrolled at the College.

Financial Aid

Capitol College maintains an extensive program of financial aid to assist students who need help in financing their education. Aid is available in the form of loans, grants, scholarships, and employment programs. Awards are based on financial need and/or academic ability. All students who wish to apply for aid must submit the Free Application for Federal Student Aid (FAFSA). Students are encouraged to contact the director of financial aid at the College for assistance and for information about institutional scholarships.

Application and Information

An application is considered when the student's file is complete, including a $25 application fee, the required test scores, and transcripts from each school attended. Application forms are available from the Office of Admissions. Capitol College maintains a rolling admission policy, and applicants are notified of the admission decision within one month of the completion of their file. To receive full consideration for financial aid and housing, students are encouraged to apply by April 1. For more information, students should contact:

Anthony G. Miller
Director of Admissions
Capitol College
11301 Springfield Road
Laurel, Maryland 20708

Telephone: 301-953-3200 (from Washington, D.C.)
410-792-8800 (from Baltimore)
800-950-1992 (toll-free outside the Baltimore–Washington, D.C., area)

CARROLL COLLEGE
HELENA, MONTANA

The College

Carroll College was founded in 1909, when Bishop John Patrick Carroll and William Howard Taft, the twenty-seventh president of the United States, laid the cornerstone of St. Charles Hall. Bishop Carroll envisioned a college that would emphasize students' intellectual, spiritual, imaginative, moral, personal, and social development. In September 1910, Mount Saint Charles College opened its doors for classes, and the first college student graduated in 1916. In 1932, the school's name was changed to Carroll College in honor of its founder. Since then, Carroll has progressively expanded its programs, facilities, and reputation for academic excellence. Today, Carroll is known for its nationally recognized programs, an award-winning faculty, and its talented student body. As a Catholic college, Carroll is dedicated to the principles of Christianity and welcomes everyone. Carroll College is accredited by the Northwest Association of Schools and Colleges and holds membership in the National Association of Independent Colleges and Universities, the American Council on Education, the Council of Independent Colleges, the Association of Catholic Colleges and Universities, and the Western Independent Colleges fund.

Academic Program

As a liberal arts college, Carroll emphasizes an education that prepares students for their chosen career and other areas of life. All students attend classes in the arts, sciences, humanities, and social sciences for at least four of their eight semesters at Carroll. This comprehensive learning curriculum gives students a broad educational background for the future in addition to the skills they need for a competitive edge in the job market. For students seeking an international experience, Carroll offers study-abroad programs in several countries around the world. Students who enjoy academic challenge may apply to the Honors Scholars Program, a special humanities curriculum that emphasizes the development of scholarship, personal character, and community service. Adult continuing education courses are offered throughout the year, and a special summer schedule of courses is open at all students.

Financial Aid

In the 1996–97 academic year, Carroll awarded more than $8 million to 85 percent of its incoming freshmen and 78 percent of its other students in the form of College-sponsored scholarships, federal work-study, and student loan programs, including Federal Pell Grants, Federal Perkins Loans, Federal Stafford Student Loans, PLUS loans for parents, State Student Incentive Grants, and Federal Supplemental Educational Opportunity Grants. More information on Carroll scholarships is available through the Office of Admission. To be considered for scholarships, a student must be accepted for admission by March 1. Carroll requires interested students to submit the Free Application for Federal Student Aid (FAFSA), available from a high school counselor, as early as possible. This ensures that students are awarded all of the aid for which they qualify.

Application and Information

Carroll operates on a rolling admission policy. Within two weeks of submission of all materials, candidates are notified of acceptance, conditional acceptance, or denial by Carroll's Office of Admission. Students should note that late submission of materials may jeopardize their financial aid awards. For an application form or further information about Carroll College's people and programs, financial aid and scholarships, student activities, or residential life, students should contact:

Director of Admission
Carroll College
1601 North Benton Avenue
Helena, Montana 59625-0002

Telephone: 406-447-4384
800-99-ADMIT (toll-free)
E-mail: enroll@carroll.edu

CARSON-NEWMAN COLLEGE
JEFFERSON CITY, TENNESSEE

The College
Founded in 1851, Carson-Newman is a private liberal arts college affiliated with the Tennessee Baptist Convention. The College has an enrollment of 2,050 undergraduate and 200 graduate students. The average class size is 16 students, and the male-female ratio is 1:1. Each fall Carson-Newman enrolls approximately 450 freshmen and 150 transfers. While Carson-Newman students come primarily from the Southeastern states, forty-one states are represented.

Academic Program
All baccalaureate degrees require completion of 128 semester hours. Students must complete 51 semester hours in general education requirements and a total of 36 semester hours at junior/senior level. Specific course requirements vary depending on major and degree program. Honors courses, independent study, and internships are available to students who qualify. Advanced credit is available for students who achieve required scores on AP exams, CLEP tests, and C-N departmental examinations.

Financial Aid
Carson-Newman allocates thousands of dollars each year to help supplement the resources of families. Financial aid awards are tailored to meet students' economic needs. Carson-Newman participates in all state and federal aid programs and awards aid based on demonstrated need as documented by a need analysis form, such as the Free Application for Federal Student Aid (FAFSA). Carson-Newman also awards academic scholarships based on achievement. Deadline for filing financial aid forms is April 1.

Application and Information
Applicants must submit an application for admission, official transcripts, and a nonrefundable $25 application fee. Admission decisions are made on a rolling basis, and students are notified within two weeks of receipt of all required documents. Application deadline is May 1 for fall semester, December 1 for spring semester. Applicants who wish to be considered for full-tuition scholarships must apply by December 31. For additional information, students should contact:

Office of Undergraduate Admissions
Carson-Newman College
Jefferson City, Tennessee 37760

Telephone: 615-471-3223
800-678-9061 (toll-free)
E-mail: sgray@cncadm.cn.edu

CATHOLIC UNIVERSITY OF AMERICA
WASHINGTON, D.C.

The University

The Catholic University of America (CUA) offers an outstanding collegiate experience, with challenging undergraduate programs based in the liberal arts. CUA is the national university of the Catholic Church and the only higher education institution established by the U.S. Catholic bishops. Founded as a graduate institution more than a century ago, CUA introduced undergraduate education in 1904. The University today serves 6,000 students, including 2,400 undergraduates, from all 50 states and more than 100 other countries. Students from all religious traditions are welcome. While the University maintains a small-college atmosphere with a student-faculty ratio of 10:1, CUA is a major research institution. The University's Washington, D.C., location enriches student life. Cultural, scientific, and political resources are minutes away by Metrorail, a modern mass transit system that stops adjacent to campus. With housing guaranteed for four years, the majority of undergraduates live on campus in thirteen residence halls.

Academic Program

Engineering, nursing, music, and architecture students follow study courses that provide professional training integrated with a broad range of academic disciplines. Students in the School of Arts and Sciences undertake a major course of study within a liberal arts curriculum that encompasses the humanities, languages and literature, philosophy, the social sciences, mathematics and natural sciences, and religion. Most majors require the satisfactory completion of forty courses that are 3 credits each for graduation. Certain majors under the Bachelor of Science degree may require additional credits. In addition to the major, students may complete a minor course sequence by utilizing the elective courses included in the undergraduate program.

Financial Aid

CUA administers two separate and distinct financial assistance programs: merit scholarships and need-based financial aid. The University offers financial aid to students based on need as demonstrated by the Free Application for Federal Student Aid (FAFSA) and the Institutional Aid Form, which can be found in the CUA admissions application. The College Scholarship Service's Financial Aid PROFILE is required. Loans, work-study, and University grants are available. Candidates who complete the admission application process before February 15 of their senior year of secondary school are considered for academic scholarships and receive priority for financial aid. CUA has a need-blind admissions policy and makes admission decisions without regard to financial aid status.

Application and Information

Admissions decisions are made on a rolling basis. Applicants for early action scholarship awards must apply by November 15 and will be notified by December 15. Regular action scholarship awards and financial aid decisions will be made shortly after the February 15 deadline. Candidates for freshman admission must submit CUA's secondary school report, high school transcripts, scores on the SAT I or ACT, and a $50 application fee. CUA accepts transfer applicants each semester. Transfer candidates should request applications for transfer admission from the Office of Admissions and Financial Aid. In addition to the high school records and SAT I or ACT scores, transfer students must furnish transcripts from the school the students are attending (a minimum 2.8 GPA is recommended). Transfer applicants are notified of their status on a rolling basis and at least one month prior to the opening of the semester for which they are applying for admission. Transfer students are guaranteed on-campus housing. Financial aid is awarded on the same basis as for freshman students.

Dean of Admissions and Financial Aid
Catholic University of America
Washington, D.C. 20064

Telephone: 202-319-5305
800-673-2772 (toll-free)
Fax: 202-319-6533
E-mail: cua-admissions@cua.edu
Web site: http://www.cua.edu

CEDAR CREST COLLEGE
ALLENTOWN, PENNSYLVANIA

The College

Since its founding in 1867 as an independent liberal arts college for women, Cedar Crest has educated women for leadership in a changing world. Of the approximately 1,700 students who come to the College annually from twenty-six states and twenty other countries, 892 are full-time undergraduates. The 12:1 student-faculty ratio provides for small classes, individual advising, and independent work in an environment that emphasizes interdisciplinary, values-oriented education. The Honor Philosophy is the most compelling statement of each student's rights and responsibilities for her own academic and cocurricular performance. Cedar Crest's health science programs, including genetic engineering, nuclear medicine, nursing, and nutrition, generate the largest student enrollment. Business and psychology generate the next largest enrollments. The genetic engineering major was the first such program at a women's college and the second at an undergraduate institution. In fall 1997, majors in neuroscience and environmental science will be added and a new science, health, and art building will open, doubling the space for student research.

Academic Program

Self-designed majors, double majors, minors, independent study programs, and individual and group research projects support serious concentration at the undergraduate level. Working with her adviser, each student designs a program of study that meets the 120-credit College (nursing: 126 credits) and major requirements as well as her personal interests and professional goals. The College's curriculum is structured to provide course work in the areas that define a liberal arts education: a knowledge-based curriculum with Basic Composition and Construction of Knowledge taught in a computer classroom environment, Analytical Thinking, Scientific Literacy (The Human Agenda, The Environment), a departmentally determined mathematics requirement, and electives constitute the freshman-year program. The Sophomore Seminar integrates applied ethics and service-learning opportunities. Acquisition of Knowledge courses are selected in four categories: The Study of Humankind, The Study of Written Texts, The Study of Creativity and Creativity in Practice, and Global Issues and Distinct Cultures.

Financial Aid

Cedar Crest offers a generous program of scholarships based on academic achievement and financial need, including scholarships, grants, loans, and employment. Federal funds available are Federal Pell Grants, Federal Supplemental Educational Opportunity Grants, Federal Perkins Loans, Federal Work-Study Program awards, and Nursing Student Loans. The size of an award varies with need. More than 80 percent of the students at Cedar Crest receive aid. Students applying for financial aid should file the Free Application for Federal Student Aid (FAFSA). Outstanding international students may also qualify for financial aid.

Application and Information

Students need to submit the application form, an official transcript of the secondary school record, examination results from the SAT I or ACT, and a personal essay. Cedar Crest has a rolling admission policy; applications are reviewed on a continuing basis. Students are encouraged to apply early in their senior year of high school. Admission is awarded for the fall or spring semester. Transfer students applying to Cedar Crest must fulfill all of the requirements stated above. They must also submit official transcripts and a catalog from each college previously attended. International students must complete the international student application form; students educated in non-English-speaking countries must also submit TOEFL examination scores.

An application form, the College catalog, financial aid forms, and additional information may be obtained by contacting:

Vice President for Enrollment Management
Cedar Crest College
100 College Drive
Allentown, Pennsylvania 18104-6196

Telephone: 800-360-1222 (toll-free)
Fax: 610-606-4647
E-mail: cccadmis@cedarcrest.edu
Web site: http://www.cedarcrest.edu

CHAMINADE UNIVERSITY OF HONOLULU
HONOLULU, HAWAII

The University

Chaminade University of Honolulu, a private, coeducational institution, was established in 1955 by the Society of Mary (Marianists). A major goal of the University is to educate and train students for leadership both within Chaminade and in communities beyond the campus. The University also has two sister universities on the mainland: the University of Dayton in Dayton, Ohio, and St. Mary's University in San Antonio, Texas.

Academic Program

Undergraduate study is structured into four parts: practice in basic skills, liberal arts course work that provides a general education, intensive study in a chosen field of concentration (the major), and elective courses outside the major field to complement general and specialized knowledge. All baccalaureate degrees require a minimum of 124 credit hours of course work with a minimum of 45 hours in upper-division courses. All appropriate courses at Chaminade require writing assignments from students. The Chaminade Leadership Institute offers courses and workshops on leadership issues and skills. The Institute for Religion and Social Change aims at a multicultural, multireligious interpretation of tradition and change, offering programs and conferences in an interfaith context that engage students in a search for more effective participation in their own development and in the decision-making processes affecting their lives. Students who complete the Chaminade Leadership Program, a series of leadership conferences of varying subject matter and format, graduate with leadership distinction. A Developmental Skills Program is available for students who need to improve skills in reading, writing, and mathematics. Chaminade cooperates with two major programs that enable students to receive college credit prior to admission. These two programs, Advanced Placement and College-Level Examination Program, are sponsored by the College Board.

Financial Aid

Those with a high school GPA between 3.5 and 4.0 are eligible for a $5000 yearly scholarship; between 3.0 and 3.49, a $4500 yearly scholarship; between 2.5 and 2.99, a $3500 yearly grant; and between 2.25 to 2.49, a $3000 yearly grant. The Hawaii Grant for new full-time day session students from Hawaii is $1500 per semester. Scholarships and grants, available to regular full-time undergraduate students, are renewable for four years and are awarded without regard to financial need. Students may obtain only one of the Chaminade scholarships or grants. A tuition discount of 20 percent is offered to additional family members when one member of the family is paying full-time tuition.

Application and Information

Chaminade University has a rolling admission process. As soon as all required information is received by the Admission Office, the application is reviewed by an application committee. Students are notified of the committee's decision usually within three to four weeks. Applications are accepted throughout the year. A $50 fee is payable upon application. All students desiring housing must file an application along with a $300 deposit applicable to the total cost per semester. Space and placement are not guaranteed without this deposit. A housing damage deposit of $100 is also required. Evidence of health insurance coverage from a U.S. insurer is required of all dormitory residents and international students. To ensure full consideration for scholarships or grants, students are urged to complete the appropriate application by April 1. Award notices are mailed by April 30. Inquiries and application materials should be sent to:

Admission Office
Chaminade University
3140 Waialae Avenue
Honolulu, Hawaii 96816

Telephone: 808-735-4735
800-735-3733 (toll-free from the mainland; collect from neighboring islands)
Fax: 808-739-4647

CHESTNUT HILL COLLEGE
PHILADELPHIA, PENNSYLVANIA

The College

Chestnut Hill College is a four-year Catholic liberal arts college for women. Founded in 1924 by the Sisters of St. Joseph, it is situated on a 45-acre campus overlooking Wissahickon Creek. Conscious of women's roles in society, Chestnut Hill College has chosen to remain a women's college at the traditional-age undergraduate level. Students come from sixteen states, thirteen countries, and every imaginable background. There are 404 full-time undergraduate women in the day programs and 350 part-time undergraduate men and women. When it comes to student activities, students enthusiastically engage in thirty clubs and organizations and participate in everything from aerobics and horseback riding to golf and street hockey. The College has NCAA Division III teams for intercollegiate competition in basketball, field hockey, lacrosse, softball, tennis, and volleyball.

Academic Program

As a liberal arts college, CHC offers courses of study that provide the student with a broad background in the fine arts and humanities, a knowledge of science, and a keen awareness of the social problems of the day, as well as intensive, in-depth study in a major field. CHC confers a B.S. or B.A. degree to students who earn 120 semester hours of credit and satisfy specific requirements set by the faculty. Distribution requirements are as follows: 11 semester hours in natural sciences (8 hours of which must be in a laboratory science), 9 semester hours in social sciences, and 21 semester hours in the humanities. In addition to these 41 hours of credit, every student must take 6 semester hours of religious studies, 6 hours beyond the elementary level in a classical or modern foreign language, and 3 hours in a writing course (unless exempted by the English department). As many as 45 of the 120 semester hours may be within the major area. Each year selected freshmen and sophomores are invited into an interdepartmental honors program that challenges intellectual initiative and provides the opportunity for independent study and seminar discussion. Sophomores of high scholastic standing are invited by their major departments to engage in a program of independent study during their junior and senior years.

Financial Aid

Financial aid is available in the form of academic scholarships, guaranteed loans, work-study programs, federal grants, and Chestnut Hill College grants. Most of these are based on financial need and are awarded in financial aid packages that combine various forms of aid and are tailored to each student's need. More than 75 percent of CHC students receive financial aid to meet college costs. All applicants for aid should file a copy of the Free Application for Federal Student Aid (FAFSA). Full tuition scholarships are awarded each year strictly on the basis of achievement. Students should submit a completed application, the application essay, SAT I or ACT scores, a high school transcript, and letters of recommendation from a principal or guidance counselor and a teacher before January 15. An interview is also required for those students wishing to be considered for Presidential Scholarships. The interview may be in person or by phone.

Application and Information

Applications are processed on a rolling admission system. To arrange an interview or to obtain more detailed information about the academic program, students should contact:

Annabell Smith
Director of Admissions
Chestnut Hill College
9601 Germantown Avenue
Philadelphia, Pennsylvania 19118-2695

Telephone: 215-248-7001
800-248-0052 (toll-free)

CLAREMONT MCKENNA COLLEGE
CLAREMONT, CALIFORNIA

The College

Founded in 1946 as the third undergraduate college in the cluster of the Claremont Colleges, Claremont McKenna College occupies a unique place among American colleges. Through a grounding in the traditional liberal arts, CMC's purpose is to educate future leaders in business, the professions, and public affairs. Claremont McKenna College is one of six institutions—five undergraduate colleges and a graduate school—that constitute the Claremont Colleges. The others are Harvey Mudd College, Pitzer College, Pomona College, Scripps College, and the Claremont Graduate School. The current undergraduate enrollment at CMC is 954 (543 men and 411 women). Students come from thirty-nine states and twenty-one countries. Claremont supports a wide variety of cultural events—concerts, plays, lectures, conferences, art exhibits, and films—and the Claremont Colleges cooperate to provide organized extracurricular activities. There are intercollegiate athletics programs, a four-college chorus, a five-college theater program, a five-college weekly newsmagazine, a five-college orchestra, and five-college forensics. The sports teams compete in the Southern California Intercollegiate Athletic Conference (SCIAC). The men's teams, known as the Stags, compete in baseball, basketball, cross-country, football, golf, soccer, swimming/diving, tennis, track, and water polo. Women's teams, known as the Athenas, compete in basketball, cross-country, golf, soccer, softball, swimming/diving, tennis, track, volleyball, and water polo.

Academic Program

Students must satisfactorily complete thirty-two semester courses, including general education and major requirements, in order to graduate. In addition, students must complete a third semester of a foreign language and a Questions of Civilization course. Depending on the department, credit or advanced placement, or both, may be granted for college courses taken while in high school and for scores of 4 or 5 on Advanced Placement tests. By intercollegiate agreement, CMC students may take courses not offered at Claremont McKenna at any of the Claremont Colleges. Up to one third of a student's courses may be taken at the other Claremont Colleges. CMC operates on an early semester calendar, beginning the first week in September and ending in mid-May.

Financial Aid

Financial aid is awarded in the form of grants (nonrepayable gift aid), student loans, and part-time employment. Grants range from $1000 to $20,000 per year and average $12,500; loans for entering freshmen average $3000 per year. The total amount of aid a student is awarded is based on need. The College offers twenty-five McKenna Achievement Awards to members of each entering freshman class. These awards are valued at $5000 or $3000 each and are renewable for each of the four years, provided the student earns at least a B average. To be considered for one of these awards, a student usually must rank among the top 5 percent in his or her high school class and earn a score of more than 650 on both the mathematical and verbal portions of the SAT I. Candidates must also have excellent school recommendations and strong extracurricular involvement and must have filed a completed application by January 1.

Application and Information

Application materials must be received by November 15 from applicants seeking early decision, November 1 for midyear entrance, and January 15 for those seeking entrance in the fall.

Further information is available from:

Richard C. Vos
Dean of Admission and Financial Aid
Claremont McKenna College
890 Columbia Avenue
Claremont, California 91711-6425

Telephone: 909-621-8088

CLARION UNIVERSITY OF PENNSYLVANIA
CLARION, PENNSYLVANIA

The University

Clarion University of Pennsylvania is fully accredited by the Middle States Association of Colleges and Schools. It was founded in 1867 and is one of fourteen state-owned institutions of higher education in Pennsylvania. Its programs in education are accredited by the National Council for Accreditation of Teacher Education and the National Academy of Early Childhood Programs, and its chemistry program is approved by the American Chemical Society. The University is a member of the American Assembly of Collegiate Schools of Business, the American Association of Colleges for Teacher Education, and the American Association of State Colleges and Universities and is an Educational Associate of the Institute of International Education. The Bachelor and Associate of Science in Nursing degree programs have the accreditation of the National League for Nursing. Clarion's graduate program in library science is accredited by the prestigious American Library Association, and its graduate program in speech pathology and audiology is accredited by the Education Standards Board of the American Speech-Language-Hearing Association. The legal business studies program at the Venango campus is approved by the American Bar Association. The occupational therapy assistant program, also at the Venango campus, was recently granted developing program status by the American Occupational Therapy Association.

Academic Program

A philosophy of liberal education at Clarion allows students to become intellectually well rounded while specializing in one field. The flexibility of the academic program also enables students to have dual majors if they so desire. In most cases, students must complete 128 credits to earn a bachelor's degree and 64 credits to earn an associate degree, but requirements vary according to the specific program. An honors program for high-achieving students is offered. In addition to this program, scholastic excellence may also be recognized through awards and admission to honorary societies. The school year is on a semester basis. Entering students may apply for college credit through Advanced Placement programs, by examination, or by courses taught directly in selected high schools by Clarion University faculty members.

Financial Aid

Clarion University participates in three campus-based federal aid programs: the Federal Perkins Loan, Federal Work-Study, and Federal Supplemental Educational Opportunity Grant programs. The institution also participates in the Federal Pell Grant and Federal Stafford Student Loan programs. Students who are residents of Pennsylvania are potentially eligible for grants and loans through the Pennsylvania Higher Education Assistance Agency (PHEAA) program. In addition, numerous academic scholarships are available to qualified students attending Clarion University. All aid applicants must file the Free Application for Federal Student Aid (FAFSA). For further information, applicants should contact the University's financial aid director at 814-226-2315.

Application and Information

Continuous evaluation is the admission policy at Clarion. Students may apply for early admission, regular admission, or admission under the student development and academic support program. Qualified applicants may receive an acceptance offer one year in advance without being required to respond until the spring of their senior year in high school. Campus visits are welcome, and appointments should be arranged between 9 a.m. and 4 p.m., Monday through Friday, and on some Saturdays. On-campus visitation days, which parents and prospective students are encouraged to attend, are conducted throughout the year. Application forms and additional information may be obtained by contacting:

Office of Admissions
Clarion University of Pennsylvania
840 Wood Street
Clarion, Pennsylvania 16214

Telephone: 814-226-2306
800-672-7171 (toll-free in Pennsylvania)
Web site: http://www.clarion.edu
http://www.petersons.com

CLARKSON COLLEGE
OMAHA, NEBRASKA

The College

Clarkson College is a regionally accredited private institution, with exceptional programs for nursing, radiography and medical imaging, occupational therapy assistant and physical therapist assistant studies, business, and health-care management. The College offers the personal qualities of a small institution and the technological advantages found within a larger educational environment. Founded in 1888, it was the first school of nursing in Nebraska and the thirty-fifth in the nation and was approved to grant academic degrees in 1984. The baccalaureate and master's programs in nursing and the associate allied health programs have professional accreditation. The current Clarkson enrollment of 570 students consists of individuals of diverse ages and ethnic and cultural backgrounds. The College's Distance Education programs enroll more than 150 students. Student support resources at the College are exceptional. Professional staff members in the offices of admissions, financial aid, counseling, housing, and activities are readily available to assist students. Both faculty and staff members are committed to providing the support services needed to ensure that students grow and learn to the maximum of their abilities. The Clarkson Student Nurses' Association, Clarkson Radiography Student Association, Clarkson Physical Therapist Assistant Student Association, and Student Occupational Therapy Association are voluntary organizations for students desiring involvement in preprofessional activities.

Academic Program

The goal of Clarkson College is to prepare individuals to be competent in the technical aspects of their profession and educated with the intellectual skills developed with liberal arts courses. The curriculum is supported by courses in the liberal arts and sciences and combines knowledge of course content with the development of intellectual and clinical competencies. Each student's curriculum plan reflects the individual's needs and interest. Although degree requirements remain constant, the scheduling of courses within the curriculum may be individualized. The flexibility of the programs permits full-time or part-time enrollment. Candidates for the baccalaureate degree must complete 128 semester hours of course work, including 60 hours of general education and support courses. Advanced placement into the curriculum beyond the beginning of the freshman year is accomplished through transfer of credits or credit by examination and other means. The associate degree program requirements also include a general education component. All courses are offered each semester.

Financial Aid

In 1996–97, the College awarded financial aid to approximately 85 percent of its undergraduate students. Scholarships, grants, loans, and work-study are available to meet the individual financial needs of students who qualify. Scholarships are awarded to outstanding applicants. Students are required to submit the completed Free Application for Federal Student Aid (FAFSA) or the Renewal Application as well as the Clarkson College Financial Aid Information Form for eligibility for all forms of aid.

Application and Information

The enrollment policy of Clarkson College allows potential students to apply anytime during the year. A completed application form, accompanied by the application fee, an official high school transcript or certification of successful completion of the General Educational Development test (GED) (when no high school diploma is available), and ACT or SAT I scores should be submitted when seeking admission. Students with previous postsecondary course work should also submit an official transcript from each institution of higher education attended. For additional information, students should contact:

Enrollment Services
Clarkson College
101 South 42nd Street
Omaha, Nebraska 68131-2739

Telephone: 402-552-3041
800-647-5500 (toll-free)
E-mail: admiss@clrkcol.crhsnet.edu

CLEARY COLLEGE
HOWELL AND YPSILANTI, MICHIGAN

The College

Cleary College is a private four-year college of business with a 113-year history as a baccalaureate institution of higher education. Cleary College operates from two campuses in Michigan. The Livingston Campus, situated on 27 wooded acres east of Howell, Michigan, is a growing community featuring a historic downtown area. Future expansion plans for the Livingston Campus include a new library/student center building and conference center for use by the College and the local community. The Washtenaw Campus, located on 21 acres within the Ypsilanti business district, houses the Bonisteel Library and the Knostman Tax Library. Future plans for the Washtenaw Campus call for construction in 1998 of a new state-of-the-art campus on current College property. The new campus will feature a more flexible arrangement of classrooms and meeting areas as well as the computer, satellite, and telecommunications technology needed by today's students. Cleary College enrolls approximately 900 students, all of whom commute. The College maintains no residence halls. Cleary students are focused on a business career, and most students work while completing their degrees—either on their own or as part of an internship or degree program requirement. Cleary College emphasizes practical application of business theory and enjoys an excellent reputation among area employers for preparing graduates who succeed in the workplace. In addition to the traditional on-campus offerings, Cleary College also provides a one-year bachelor's degree completion program at six locations throughout southeast Michigan.

Academic Program

Cleary programs are intended for the serious student who has a clear goal to complete the B.B.A. and is motivated to apply energy to reach that goal. Emphasis is placed on providing a learning environment that fosters a mastery of current business theory and technology and the application of these skills to real-life business situations. Cleary strives to graduate students who know exactly what to do in their jobs, have the skills to do it well, and as a result are successful and able to make important contributions to their communities.

Financial Aid

More than 60 percent of students receive some form of financial assistance. Cleary participates in state and federal financial aid programs and accepts the Free Application for Federal Student Aid (FAFSA). Some of the programs include the Federal Pell Grant, Federal SEOG, Federal College Work-Study program, Federal Stafford Loan, and Michigan Tuition Grant. In addition, a number of Cleary scholarships and grants are available, including the McKenny Scholarship, the PR Cleary Scholarship, the Rosin Canton Community Grant, the President's Scholarship, and the Morse B. Barker Scholarship.

Application and Information

Quarters begin in September, January, March, and June. Applications are accepted all year and must be submitted with a $25 nonrefundable application fee payable to Cleary College in the form of a check or money order. Application to the Direct Degree and Gateway Programs is recommended at least eight weeks prior to the start of the term.

Additional information and application materials are available from:

Office of Admissions
Cleary College
Washtenaw Campus
2170 Washtenaw Avenue
Ypsilanti, Michigan 48197

Telephone: 800-686-1883 (toll-free)

Office of Admissions
Cleary College
Livingston Campus
3750 Cleary College Drive
Howell, Michigan 48843

Telephone: 800-589-1979 (toll-free)

COGSWELL POLYTECHNICAL COLLEGE
SUNNYVALE, CALIFORNIA

The College

Established in San Francisco in 1887 as a private, independent institution, Cogswell has developed new programs over the years to meet the emerging needs of technology industries. In 1985, the College moved from San Francisco to Cupertino. In 1994, the College moved to a permanent campus in Sunnyvale to be in proximity to the many technology companies located there. The College operates a day and evening class schedule, enabling students already working to complete their degree requirements. The student body of 400 brings together men and women of diverse ages, nationalities, and backgrounds who share a strong career orientation, a desire to make things function as designed, and a willingness to work together to achieve goals. Faculty members work closely with all students, enabling them to learn both the concepts and skills needed in technology. The independent study program for fire service professionals, Open Learning for the Fire Service, currently has 125 registered students. Membership is available in clubs that are the student affiliates of the Institute of Electrical and Electronics Engineers (IEEE), the American Society of Mechanical Engineers (ASME), the Society of Automotive Engineers (SAE), the Audio Engineering Society (AES), the Society of Motion Picture and Television Engineers (SMPTE), and the Music and Entertainment Industry Educators Association (MEIEA). Cogswell College is accredited by the Senior Commission of the Western Association of Schools and Colleges. The electronics and mechanical engineering technology programs are also accredited by the Technology Accreditation Commission of the Accreditation Board for Engineering and Technology.

Academic Program

Cogswell College has a trimester system, and the courses of study are carefully designed to provide a student with the theory and practical skills needed in technology industries. Students begin taking courses in their chosen area from the first trimester they enroll. General studies and communication courses round out each year and place technology in its human context. In keeping with Cogswell's practical approach to education, a senior project is required. Students originate an idea and then design, build, and demonstrate it for faculty members and other students. The associate degree requires 65 semester units. The Bachelor of Science in Engineering Technology and the Bachelor of Science in Software Engineering require 130 semester units each. The Bachelor of Science in Electrical Engineering degree requires 127 semester units and includes concentrations in computer, mechanical, music, and software engineering. The Bachelor of Arts in Computer and Video Imaging requires 124 semester units.

Financial Aid

To enable students from diverse economic backgrounds to attend Cogswell, the Financial Aid Office helps students put together an aid package based on their need. In addition to federal and state loans and grants, qualified students may also receive aid from the Cogswell College Scholarship fund and many private scholarships unique to Cogswell. The College has jobs available on campus for work-study students. All programs are approved for veterans' training. The state of California grants (Cal Grants) have an application deadline of March 2 for the following academic year. All other aid may be requested throughout the year. For more information or to set up an appointment to discuss particular needs, students should contact the Financial Aid Office.

Application and Information

For additional information and an application for admission, students should contact:

Admissions Office
Cogswell Polytechnical College
1175 Bordeaux Drive
Sunnyvale, California 94089-1299

Telephone: 408-541-0100
800-264-7955 (toll-free)
E-mail: admissions@cogswell.edu
Web site: http://www.cogswell.edu

COLBY–SAWYER COLLEGE
NEW LONDON, NEW HAMPSHIRE

The College
Colby-Sawyer College, a coeducational, residential, undergraduate college founded in 1837, evolved from the New England academy tradition and has been engaged in higher education since 1928. The College provides programs of study that innovatively integrate the liberal arts and sciences with professional preparation. The College is accredited by the New England Association of Schools and Colleges, and professional programs also carry the appropriate accreditations. Colby-Sawyer has received recognition as one of the top colleges in its category.

Academic Program
Colby-Sawyer College faculty and staff are excellent at working with students who are undecided on a major and are highly qualified to help students explore their values, talents, and academic and career interests. Through a carefully crafted program offered by the Harrington Center for Career Development, all students are encouraged throughout their four years of study to continue to clarify their interests and goals and to gain practical experiences through student employment, internships, and voluntary service to the community. Internships are a key element in career development. Colby-Sawyer has an impressive roster of internship opportunities available, and through the internship experience, students often receive their first offer of a permanent position. During the internship, students have an opportunity to work directly with professionals in their field of study while developing valuable contacts who can serve as references and career mentors. Organizations that have recently accepted Colby-Sawyer interns include Merrill Lynch, Continental Cable, Beth Israel Hospital, Blue Cross/Blue Shield, Harvard University Athletic Department, the Buffalo Bisons, the Currier Gallery of Art, the Basketball Hall of Fame, the Olympic Regional Development Authority, Channel 7 (Boston), the Appalachian Mountain Club, and CNN.

Financial Aid
Through its Financial Aid Program, Colby-Sawyer encourages the attendance of students from a variety of ethnic and cultural backgrounds, economic levels, and geographic regions. Seventy-seven percent of the students currently receive some form of financial assistance, and Colby-Sawyer provides more than $3.5 million a year in grant assistance to its students. Both need-based and merit awards are available, including recently established merit awards for outstanding academic achievement or student leadership. Merit awards are also available for students with special talents in art, music, or creative writing and for those students who have been significantly involved in community service. Applicants who wish to be considered for merit awards must submit all required admissions materials by February 1. Each applicant for need-based aid must submit the Free Application for Federal Student Aid (FAFSA) and the Colby-Sawyer Application for Financial Aid. Priority will be given to students who complete and postmark all forms on or before the March 1 deadline. A modest amount of financial assistance is available for international students.

Application and Information
Colby-Sawyer receives and considers applications throughout the year. Beginning in December, applications are reviewed as soon as they become complete, and candidates are notified as soon as the admissions decision is finalized. A completed application includes a transcript of the candidate's high school work (including first-quarter grades for the senior year), SAT I or ACT scores, two letters of recommendation (one from a teacher and one from a guidance professional), a personal statement, and a $40 nonrefundable application fee. Application forms and additional information may be obtained by contacting:

Office of Admissions
Colby-Sawyer College
100 Main Street
New London, New Hampshire 03257
Telephone: 603-526-3700
800-272-1015 (toll-free)
Fax: 603-526-3452
E-mail: csadmiss@colby-sawyer.edu
Web site: http://www.colby-sawyer.edu

COLLEGE OF AERONAUTICS
FLUSHING, NEW YORK

The College

The College of Aeronautics is a private, independent technical college that is chartered by the Board of Regents of the State of New York and is accredited by the Middle States Association of Colleges and Schools. Undergraduate enrollment is approximately 1,000 students. This includes full-time, part-time, day, and evening students. Founded in 1932, the College has enjoyed much success in the preparation, through education, of individuals who seek careers in the world of aeronautical technologies. The educational experiences offered by the College are designed to develop both a high degree of technical competence and a sense of personal responsibility—essential characteristics of the engineering technician. The College, located in the heart of East Coast aviation, air transportation, and electronics industries, offers many opportunities for liaison with airlines, private aviation, and aircraft and electronics manufacturers. The College of Aeronautics is exceptional in that it emphasizes hands-on technical courses, which are given through a number of laboratory exercises and projects. The practical education provided by the College makes its graduates highly desirable candidates for employment. The Career Development Office offers access to the aviation/aerospace industry. Many of the College's graduates have made important contributions to aeronautical developments through the years, and many hold prestigious positions in the industry today.

Academic Program

A 60-credit arts and science core is the common thread in all of the Bachelor of Science programs. The B.T. program in maintenance requires the completion of 134 credits of study; the B.T. in maintenance management requires 136 credits. The A.O.S. degree requires the completion of 92½ credits of study. A.A.S. degree programs require the completion of 64 to 110 credits of study and are easily transferred to the bachelor degree programs. The College of Aeronautics offers many different degree options in five primary areas of study: aeronautical engineering technology (pre-engineering), aircraft operations, avionics (aircraft electronics), computerized design, and maintenance.

Financial Aid

Eighty percent of the students receive financial aid. The maximum amount of financial aid awarded to a freshman is $7000; the average amount awarded is $3300. Financial aid is available in the form of Federal Pell Grant and New York State TAP (Tuition Assistance Program) Grant awards, the FSEOG (Federal Supplemental Educational Opportunity Grant), the Federal Stafford Student Loan, and the Federal Perkins Loan.

Application and Information

The director of admissions and the counseling staff are available to advise applicants and their parents and to provide up-to-date information and materials for high school guidance counselors.

For further details, interested persons should contact:

Office of Admissions
College of Aeronautics
LaGuardia Airport
Flushing, New York 11371

Telephone: 718-429-6600 Ext. 102
800-776-2376 (toll-free)

E-mail: pro@aero.edu

COLLEGE OF SAINT BENEDICT/SAINT JOHN'S UNIVERSITY
ST. JOSEPH AND COLLEGEVILLE, MINNESOTA

The College and The University

The College of Saint Benedict (CSB) and Saint John's University (SJU) are private, residential, liberal arts institutions. CSB for women was founded in 1887; SJU for men was founded in 1857. The Carnegie Foundation for the Advancement of Teaching and *U.S. News & World Report* rank CSB and SJU as two of only five Catholic colleges nationwide included in the selective national liberal arts category. The two institutions offer a common curriculum, class schedule, and social and cultural programming. Women and men students attend classes and utilize the services and facilities at both campuses. Each campus, however, addresses the unique needs of the adult development of its students—including gender-specific issues—through residential life programming and activities. The sponsoring communities of Benedictine women and men continue the centuries-old tradition of a balanced education addressing the developmental needs of mind, body, and spirit. While they are Catholic institutions, CSB and SJU welcome students and faculty members of all faith backgrounds and preferences.

Academic Program

The faculties of CSB and SJU jointly offer an innovative core curriculum. First-year students participate in a yearlong symposium, limited to 8 men and 8 women, which focuses on the development of oral and written communication skills along with proficiency in a variety of reading styles. Seniors participate in a seminar in which they integrate moral and ethical decision making with contemporary issues. An honors program of challenging interdisciplinary and major course work that approaches topics beyond the general curriculum is available to selected students. The core also requires proficiency in a foreign language, discussion, writing, and mathematics. Each academic major is set in the context of the liberal arts, thereby providing the appropriate preparation either for career entry or for graduate or professional study.

Financial Aid

Assistance for financing an education at CSB and SJU is identified as scholarships for students with excellent academic and leadership records and as grants, employment, and loans for students from low- and middle-income families who demonstrate a need for assistance in paying for college. About 75 percent of the students currently attending the colleges receive financial assistance, many under both (non-need and need) categories. Students interested in applying for grants, employment, and loans should complete the Free Application for Federal Student Aid (FAFSA). The colleges participate in state and federal financial aid programs such as the Federal Pell Grant, Federal Work-Study, and Federal Stafford Student Loan programs. In addition, the colleges offer generous financial assistance from their own funds to assist students.

Application and Information

Offers of admission are granted on a rolling basis, and applicants should expect to be notified within three weeks of the receipt of their completed application. CSB and SJU are members of the Common Application and also accept Apply!, College Connector, CollegeLink, and Peterson's Universal applications. Students are encouraged to visit the campuses for a tour and to meet with an admission counselor. Appointments should be made at least five days in advance. Application forms and additional information may be obtained by writing or calling:

Admission Office
College of Saint Benedict (for women)
37 South College Avenue
St. Joseph, Minnesota 56374-2099
Telephone: 800-544-1489 (toll-free)
Fax: 320-363-5010
E-mail: admissions@csbsju.edu
Web site: http://www.csbsju.edu/index.html

Admission Office
Saint John's University (for men)
P.O. Box 7155
Collegeville, Minnesota 56321-7155
Telephone: 800-245-6467 (toll-free)
Fax: 320-363-3206
E-mail: admissions@csbsju.edu
Web site: http://www.csbsju.edu/index.html

THE COLLEGE OF WOOSTER
WOOSTER, OHIO

The College
One of the first coeducational colleges in the country, the College of Wooster was founded in 1866 by Presbyterians who wanted to do "their proper part in the great work of educating those who are to mold society and give shape to all its institutions." Today it is a fully independent, privately endowed liberal arts college with a rich tradition of academic excellence. That tradition defines student life at Wooster, beginning with the First-Year Seminar in Critical Inquiry and culminating in the Independent Study program. The Student Activities Board organizes dances, concerts, films, trips, and many other activities. An arts and crafts program, the music and theater departments, and local social clubs also contribute to the activities on campus. The student entertainment center (The Underground) hosts live bands for dancing, miniconcerts, and folksingers and sometimes serves as a dinner theater.

Academic Program
Wooster's academic program is designed to provide a liberal education that prepares undergraduates for a lifetime of intellectual adventure, allows them to develop harmoniously and independently, and helps them meet new situations as they arise. To be eligible for a Bachelor of Arts degree, a student must successfully complete thirty-two courses, including three courses of Independent Study. An overall grade point average of at least 2.0 (on a 4.0 scale) is required for graduation. Students may receive credit for work done at other colleges and for scores of 4 or better on the Advanced Placement tests offered by the College Board. Courses are graded A–D or No Credit unless the student exercises an option to take certain courses on a Satisfactory/No Credit basis.

Financial Aid
Almost all financial assistance is awarded on the basis of need, as determined by the Free Application for Federal Student Aid (FAFSA). Aid is allocated when students are admitted to the College. Financial assistance information and forms should be requested at the time of application. Applications for aid should be submitted by March 1. Merit aid is available on a competitive basis. The College Scholar program offers five awards of $15,000 each per year, based on a competitive examination. Additional awards of $8000 each per year are available. Selected entering students receive academic and achievement awards independent of the College Scholars program. Synod of the Covenant scholarships for Presbyterian communicants are available, as are Scottish Arts awards. The Clarence B. Allen Scholarship program awards up to four scholarships of $15,000 a year to entering African-American students with a demonstrated record of academic achievement and promise of continued success in college. The Arthur Holly Compton Scholarships are awarded to students who demonstrate unusual aptitude for Wooster's program of Independent Study. Compton Scholarships are awarded for $7000 and $14,000 annually. Music scholarships of $6000 each are awarded to entering first-year students based on auditions in voice or on an instrument. A 15-minute performance of works representing several styles of music is required. Theater scholarships of $6000 each are awarded on a competitive basis. An audition is required. Byron E. Morris Scholarships of up to $6000 are awarded to students who have a demonstrated record of achievement in their school or community in the areas of volunteer/community service or leadership.

Application and Information
Dean of Admissions
The College of Wooster
Wooster, Ohio 44691

Telephone: 330-263-2000 Ext. 2270 or 2323
800-877-9905 (toll-free)

Fax: 330-263-2621
Web site: http://www.wooster.edu

COLUMBIA COLLEGE
CHICAGO, ILLINOIS

The College

Columbia College was established during the World Colombian Exposition of 1890. Its original emphasis on communication arts expanded to include media arts, applied and fine arts, theatrical and performing arts, and management and marketing arts. The foundations of a Columbia College education continue to include small class sizes that ensure close interaction with a faculty of working professionals who bring the working world into the classroom, abundant internship opportunities with major employers in the Chicago marketplace, and outstanding professional facilities to foster learning by doing. All students are encouraged to begin course work in their chosen fields immediately, allowing them four full years in which to master their craft and build professional portfolios, audition tapes, résumés, and clip books. The College provides a sound liberal arts background for the developing artist or communicator and supports a student's employment goals through a full range of career services. Columbia College's enrollment of approximately 8,000 students is drawn from the city of Chicago and its suburbs, from across the United States, and from thirty-six other countries. Creative students who enjoy a supportive but challenging environment thrive at Columbia. Outside the classroom, students participate in activities that include the College's student newspaper, radio station, cable television soap opera, three theaters, dance center, photography and art museums, and film and video festival. Many of the twenty-eight student clubs on campus are linked to an academic discipline and offer students opportunities to expand their social and professional networking experiences.

Academic Program

The College supports creative and integrated approaches to education and encourages interdisciplinary study. The Bachelor of Arts degree is awarded to students who successfully complete 124 semester hours of study; 48 of these hours are distributed among courses in the humanities, science, English composition, literature, mathematics, social sciences, and computer applications. Columbia continues to expand its extensive internship program. Because of the College's location, students can intern with major employers in Chicago's marketplace. From fashion merchandising to film and photography, from computer graphics to illustration, Chicago provides professional settings, classrooms, and employers for Columbia students. The Career Services office offers a full range of services designed to help students launch their careers. Services include career counseling; seminars on interviewing, résumé writing, and job search strategies; internships; placement assistance; job fairs; and alumni activities and assistance.

Financial Aid

Columbia College makes every effort to help students seek out and obtain financial assistance, and it also provides information for students seeking part-time employment. In addition, Columbia offers institution-based scholarships such as Presidential Scholarships for freshmen, scholarships for transfer students, academic excellence awards, housing grants, Fischetti Scholarships for outstanding Columbia journalism students, and Weisman Scholarships for special communications-related projects. The Financial Aid Office administers federal and state grant and loan programs. Part-time jobs are available in technical, clerical, secretarial, and food service areas. Appropriate application forms for financial aid are provided by the Financial Aid Office and are mailed to students who request them.

Application and Information

Applications are accepted on a continuing basis. Applicants must submit an application for admission, a writing sample, proof of high school graduation (GED or equivalent preparation is accepted), and transcripts of previous college work, if any. Applicants are asked to submit a nonrefundable $25 acceptance fee at the time they are notified of acceptance. For more information, students should contact:

Terry Miller
Director of Admissions Recruitment
Columbia College
600 South Michigan Avenue
Chicago, Illinois 60605

Telephone: 312-663-1600 Ext. 5130
E-mail: admissions@colum.edu

COLUMBIA UNIVERSITY, SCHOOL OF GENERAL STUDIES
NEW YORK, NEW YORK

The University and The School

The School of General Studies is the liberal arts division of Columbia University for adult men and women whose education after high school has been interrupted or postponed by at least one year. Students may study full- or part-time. The School has more than 1,000 undergraduate degree candidates and about 300 postbaccalaureate premedical students. In addition to its bachelor's degree program, the School of General Studies offers combined undergraduate/graduate degree programs with Columbia's Schools of Social Work, International and Public Affairs, Law, Business, and Dental and Oral Surgery, as well as with Teachers College, the College of Physicians and Surgeons, and the Juilliard School.

Academic Program

Requirements for the bachelor's degree comprise three elements: (1) core requirements, intended to develop in students the ability to write and communicate clearly; to understand the modes of thought that characterize the humanities, the social sciences, and the sciences; to gain some familiarity with central cultural ideas through literature, fine arts, and music; and to acquire a working proficiency in a foreign language; (2) major requirements, designed to give students sustained and coherent exposure to a particular discipline in an area of strong intellectual interest; and (3) elective courses, in which students pursue particular interests and skills for their own sake or for their relationship to future professional or personal objectives. Students are required to complete a minimum of 124 points for the bachelor's degree; 64 of these may be in transfer credit, but at least 60 points (including the last 30 points) must be completed at Columbia. In addition to the usual graduation honors (cum laude, magna cum laude, and summa cum laude), honors programs for superior students are available in sixteen of the School's twenty-nine departments.

Financial Aid

The School of General Studies awards financial aid based upon need and academic ability. Approximately 60 percent of General Studies degree candidates receive some form of financial aid, including Federal Pell Grants, New York State TAP Grants, Federal Stafford and unsubsidized Stafford Loans, Federal Perkins Loans, General Studies Scholarships, and Federal College Work-Study Program awards. Application deadlines are July 15 for the autumn 1997 semester and November 15 for the spring 1998 semester.

Application and Information

Application deadlines are July 15 for the autumn semester and November 15 for the spring semester. The School holds information sessions in the fall and spring for prospective applicants. Applicants from countries outside the U.S. are urged to apply by August 1 for the spring semester and March 15 for the autumn semester. Applications are reviewed as they are completed, and applicants are notified of decisions shortly thereafter. For more information, students should contact:

Office of Admissions and Financial Aid
School of General Studies
408 Lewisohn Hall
2970 Broadway
Columbia University, Mail Code 4101
New York, New York 10027

Telephone: 212-854-2772
E-mail: gs-admit@columbia.edu

CUMBERLAND COLLEGE
WILLIAMSBURG, KENTUCKY

The College

For more than 100 years, Cumberland College has been committed to providing a superior education in an exceptional Christian atmosphere at an affordable cost. Emphasis is placed on the growth of the individual student. The College strives to instill in students the desire to be agents of change in the world and to use knowledge for the benefit of others as well as themselves. Cumberland is a four-year, coed liberal arts college offering a broad curriculum with over forty programs of undergraduate study from which to choose. A graduate program leading to the Master of Arts in Education is also offered. The student body consists of 1,600 students representing twenty-eight states and eighteen countries. Most students live on campus in the College's eight residence halls. Each hall is supervised by a director assisted by student staff members. Students benefit from such special services as the Counseling and Career Development Center, Center for Leadership Studies, Student Health Center, Counseling Office, Academic Resource Center, and free tutorial assistance. Cumberland College is accredited by the Commission on Colleges of the Southern Association of Colleges and Schools.

Academic Program

Cumberland seeks to provide academic specialization within the broad framework of a liberal arts education. To supplement the in-depth knowledge acquired within each major, 45 semester hours of general studies from the areas of Christian faith and values, cultural and aesthetic values, the English language, humanities, leadership and community service, natural and mathematical sciences, physical education, and social sciences are required. Students must earn 128 semester hours to graduate with a bachelor's degree. Students may receive credit for successful scores on the Advanced Placement examinations of the College Board, the College-Level Examination Program (CLEP), and special departmental tests. Through the honors program, highly qualified students have the opportunity to undertake advanced independent study.

Financial Aid

Cumberland sponsors a large financial aid program that coordinates money from federal, state, private, and College sources. Last year, 85 percent of Cumberland students shared over $8.5 million in aid. To apply for financial aid, it is necessary to complete the Free Application for Federal Student Aid (FAFSA). For further information about financial aid opportunities, students should contact the director of financial aid at 800-532-0828. Applications made by March 15 are given priority for the fall semester. Numerous scholarships and leadership grants are available.

Application and Information

Applicants for admission should contact the admissions office for an application form and return the completed form to the College, along with the appropriate application fee. Applicants should also have official transcripts of all high school and college work sent to the College, along with a copy of the ACT or SAT I scores. Each student is notified regarding official admission within ten working days after the application procedure has been completed. Students accepted for admission must submit the required enrollment deposit.

Additional information may be obtained by contacting:

Office of Admissions
Cumberland College
Williamsburg, Kentucky 40769

Telephone: 606-549-2200 Ext. 4241
800-343-1609 (toll-free)
E-mail: admiss@cc.cumber.edu.us

DANIEL WEBSTER COLLEGE
NASHUA, NEW HAMPSHIRE

The College

Daniel Webster College is committed to the success of its students and alumni. The College's updated curriculums of aviation, business, computer sciences, and engineering help prepare students to become tomorrow's industry leaders. Originally founded as the New England Aeronautical Institute, Daniel Webster College is accredited by the New England Association of Schools and Colleges, is a member of the New Hampshire College and University Council, and holds Federal Aviation Administration Air Agency Certification PSE 15-21 as an approved pilot school. The College operates its training courses under Part 141 and Part 61 of the FAA regulations. Students at Daniel Webster College represent twenty-four states and sixteen countries.

Academic Program

The College operates on a semester system. Curricula are designed to provide the highest quality in educational opportunities. Independent study, a customized internship program, and advanced placement programs are available for students who meet the criteria. The Aviation Division reorganized the professional flight training program in 1982 and has augmented its curriculum by introducing glider and aerobatic flight. Students can qualify for the private single engine, private glider, instrument, commercial, multiengine, and instructor ratings. A student instructor internship is available to qualified juniors and seniors. Air Force ROTC is offered.

Financial Aid

The College makes every effort to assist students in developing financial strategies to help pay for their education. Currently, 86 percent of the students receive some kind of financial aid. Eligibility is determined by an analysis of the Free Application for Federal Student Aid (FAFSA). The FAFSA may be obtained through high school guidance offices. DWC offers four-year renewable merit scholarships to students who exhibit high academic achievement as evidenced by high school GPA and test scores. In addition to providing aid through its own scholarship and work program, the College administers both federal and local financial aid programs. More information is available by writing to the director of financial assistance.

Application and Information

The application fee is $35. The College operates on a rolling admission basis, and students are notified within two weeks after their file is complete. Interested students are urged to arrange a campus visit while the College is in session. For further information, students should contact:

Office of Admissions
Daniel Webster College
Twenty University Drive
Nashua, New Hampshire 03063-1300
Telephone: 603-577-6600
800-325-6876 (toll-free)
Fax: 603-577-6001

DAVID LIPSCOMB UNIVERSITY
NASHVILLE, TENNESSEE

The University

David Lipscomb University is a private, coeducational university of liberal arts and sciences in Nashville, Tennessee, that offers bachelor's and master's degrees. Since its inception, Lipscomb has been dedicated to the concept of academic excellence. Established in 1891, the University is associated with the Churches of Christ and is committed to providing for its students the finest liberal arts education in a Christian environment. Lipscomb's 2,500 students represent forty-one states and twenty-nine countries.

Academic Program

Lipscomb requires that students complete general education courses in Bible, communication, humanities, mathematics, natural and social sciences, and physical education. Each student must also satisfy a writing requirement. All degree-seeking candidates must complete a minimum of 132 semester hours of work with a minimum grade point average of 2.0 overall, 2.0 in the major, and 2.0 in the minor. The academic year is on a traditional semester calendar. Lipscomb University is accredited by the Commission on Colleges of the Southern Association of Colleges and Schools (1866 Southern Lane, Decatur, Georgia 30033-4097; telephone 404-679-4500) to award bachelor's and master's degrees. Professional accreditations have been awarded by the National Association of Schools of Music, the Council on Social Work Education, and the Association of Collegiate Business Schools and Programs. The professional chemistry major has been approved by the Committee on Professional Education of the American Chemical Society. Advanced placement examinations such as AP and CLEP may be used to establish a maximum credit of 30 semester hours. An Honors Program provides superior students with opportunities for unusual intellectual challenge and growth. Admittance to the Honors Program requires a score of 27 or higher on the ACT or 1210 or higher on the SAT I as well as a high school class ranking in the top 10 percent.

Financial Aid

The University annually awards approximately $8 million in all types of financial assistance. More than 70 percent of the students receive some form of financial aid. Assistance is based on merit and/or need; awards range from $400 to $10,000 per year. Need is determined by filing a Free Application for Federal Student Aid (FAFSA). Lipscomb provides aid through institutional scholarships and grants; through the Federal Pell Grant, Federal Supplemental Educational Opportunity Grant, and state grants; through the Federal Perkins Loan, Federal Stafford Student Loan, and Federal Parent Loan for Undergraduate Students (PLUS); and through Federal Work-Study and University employment. Information on these and other programs can be obtained through the Office of Student Aid Services.

Application and Information

Tours are given Monday through Friday at 11 a.m. and 2 p.m. Prospective students are encouraged to spend a night in a residence hall, attend classes, and meet with faculty and students. Guest suites are provided for prospective students. Arrangements must be made in advance through the Office of Admissions. Priority consideration is given to applicants who submit an application and all supporting materials by November 15. Those who apply by November 15 are notified by January 1. Students whose applications are received after the November 15 deadline will be notified by May 1. Accompanying the application must be a $35 fee, an official high school transcript, results from the ACT Assessment or the SAT I, and two recommendations. It is highly recommended that application be made by January 1 for priority consideration in admission, financial aid, and awarding of scholarships. For further information, students may contact:

Cyndi R. Butler
Director of Admissions
David Lipscomb University
3901 Granny White Pike
Nashville, Tennessee 37204-3951

Telephone: 615-269-1776
800-333-4358 Ext. 1776 (toll-free)
E-mail: admissions@dlu.edu

DREXEL UNIVERSITY
PHILADELPHIA, PENNSYLVANIA

The University

Drexel is a private, nonsectarian, coeducational university that has maintained a reputation for academic excellence since its founding in 1891. Its academic programs offer students practical preparation for graduate school and a variety of careers. Full-time, paid professional experience through Drexel's cooperative education program is a vital part of a Drexel education. Students gain professional experience in jobs related to their career interests by alternating classroom study with periods of employment in business, industry, and government. More than 1,700 employers from nineteen states and eleven other countries participate in this program. Another distinctive element is the University's microcomputer requirement, through which all undergraduates participate in a computer-enhanced education.

Academic Program

Among Drexel's distinguishing features are its microcomputer requirement and Drexel Co-op: "The Ultimate Internship." These features, combined with rigorous academic programs, provide an education that enables students to bridge the gap between academic studies and the working world. The computer, integral to course work in all disciplines, is a tool that furthers the student's academic reach. The co-op/internship program generates a two-way educational force: academic knowledge finds concrete form in the workplace, while personal growth and experiential learning on the job enrich the academic experience. All undergraduates are prepared for full-time professional internships through Drexel's cooperative education program. With the new flexible degree programs, studies in engineering, information systems, and commerce and engineering, as well as science programs in the College of Arts and Sciences, are designed to be completed in four or five years, including eighteen months of co-op experience. Design arts programs require four years to complete and include six months of co-op. Business, humanities, and social science programs offer both four-year and five-year co-op/internship options.

Financial Aid

Approximately 87 percent of all freshmen receive financial aid. The aid package may contain academic, athletic, or performing arts scholarships; grants; loans; or part-time employment. Federal programs are also included. All students applying for aid must submit the Free Application for Federal Student Aid by May 1. Notification of incoming freshmen and transfer students begins about March 1. Drexel offers a unique achievement-based award, the A. J. Drexel Scholarship, to all qualified incoming freshmen and transfer students. With an annual award value of up to $8000, the A. J. Drexel Scholarship is renewable on a yearly basis, provided the student maintains a 3.0 grade point average and full-time status. Criteria include a strong academic record and involvement in extracurricular and community service activities.

Application and Information

Application forms with complete instructions for admission and financial aid and the appropriate college prospectus may be obtained by writing to the address given below. Each application must be accompanied by a nonrefundable application fee of $35; however, the fee may be waived in cases of extreme hardship if requested by the secondary school or if the student visits the campus. Applications for regular full-time undergraduate status are accepted throughout the senior year. Drexel subscribes to the College Board's Candidates Reply Date of May 1. Transfer students should apply at least three months before the beginning of the term in which they wish to enroll.

Office of Undergraduate Admissions
Drexel University
3141 Chestnut Streets
Philadelphia, Pennsylvania 19104

Telephone: 800-2-DREXEL (toll-free)
Web site: http://www.drexel.edu

EARLHAM COLLEGE
RICHMOND, INDIANA

The College
Earlham College, founded in 1847 by the Society of Friends, is an independent, liberal arts college. Earlham enrolls approximately 1,050 students—550 women and 500 men—representing forty-six states and eighteen countries. Eighty percent of Earlham's students are from outside Indiana, and 50 percent come from at least 500 miles away. Students are of many races, religious backgrounds, economic levels, and ethnic traditions. Earlham believes that a strong liberal arts education is the best intellectual preparation for a satisfying and successful life. Graduates have distinguished themselves in careers in science, medicine, law, business, higher education, and social and humanitarian service.

Academic Program
Earlham introduces students to concepts and methods of inquiry in the humanities, social sciences, natural sciences, fine arts, and foreign languages through a program of subject area requirements, stressing both broad exposure and personal flexibility in course scheduling. An interdisciplinary humanities program provides a common intellectual experience for all students in their first year. Students gain an in-depth understanding of one or more disciplines in their major area of academic concentration. An academic major usually consists of eight to ten courses in one department, a senior research project or seminar, and a departmental comprehensive examination. Earlham grants credit for Advanced Placement examinations and higher-level International Baccalaureate subjects. Students may also receive credit for independent studies and academic internships.

Financial Aid
Most financial aid is awarded on the basis of demonstrated need; more than 50 percent of Earlham's students receive financial assistance. Earlham usually meets the full need of all accepted students with a combination of Earlham Alumni Scholarships, endowed scholarships, loans, federal and state grants, and campus work. Students must file both the Free Application for Federal Student Aid (FAFSA) and a special Earlham form. Scholarships are awarded without regard to financial need and recognize achievement in all areas of the liberal arts. The Carleton B. Edwards scholarship is available for students planning to major in chemistry. Earlham also offers scholarships through the National Merit Scholarship Corporation. Special scholarships are available to members of the Society of Friends and students who will enhance the diversity of the student body. There are scholarships and limited financial aid for international students (non-U.S. citizens).

Application and Information
Earlham offers several admission options: the early decision deadline is December 1 (notification by December 15); the early action deadline is January 15 (notification by February 1); the regular decision deadline is February 15 (notification by April 2); and the transfer deadline is April 1. International students (non-U.S. citizens) should apply by March 1. Applications are accepted after these deadline dates as long as places remain in the entering class. Students who submit applications after April 1 are notified of the admission decision approximately two weeks after their application is complete.

Students wishing additional information or materials on Earlham College should contact:

Office of Admissions
Earlham College
Richmond, Indiana 47374

Telephone: 765-983-1600
800-EARLHAM (toll-free)
Fax: 765-983-1560
E-mail: admission@earlham.edu
Web site: http://admis.earlham.edu/

EASTERN COLLEGE
ST. DAVIDS, PENNSYLVANIA

The College

Eastern College brings a special purpose to its mission as a Christian institution of higher education. The College wants to produce world Christians, capable of confronting injustice and indifference with the character, competence, and commitment Eastern has helped them develop. First and foremost, Eastern remains true to its biblical heritage. The power of the prophetic Word and the Lordship of Jesus Christ provide the context for the College's theological position. The College is sure of its Christian stand, and this encourages it to strengthen its faith by confronting serious contemporary issues. Neither narrow-minded nor staid, the College affirms and embraces Christians whose doctrinal positions may be broader or more restrictive. As a result, those at the College can actively pursue the full dynamic of an abundant Christian life and take an obedient walk with Him. In addition, the academic process revolves around a curriculum that emphasizes foundational skills as well as the understanding and application of knowledge in an increasingly complex society. Classroom experience is intellectually rigorous. A creative core curriculum builds on basic truths and continually challenges the potential of an expanding mind. Practical experience is generated through an extensive internship program as well as through relationships with established ministries like Young Life, Youth for Christ, foreign missions, and Christian outreach programs. The academic climate is enhanced through the presence of graduate programs. Knowledge, ultimately, is written as indelibly on the heart as it is on the mind. Justice and a will obedient to the Lord result from such an academic experience.

Academic Program

In the core curriculum, students take courses designed to fulfill the basic mission of Eastern: to provide biblical foundations to which all learning and action can be related, to ensure acquisition of certain basic skills, and to broaden the student's view of the world. Courses in the breadth area of the core are planned and taught in such a way that central themes of the Christian faith are integrated into the course content. The Fixed Core includes courses such as justice and diversity in a pluralistic society and science, technology, and values.

Financial Aid

Eastern is committed to providing education to qualified students regardless of their means. The financial aid program offers scholarships, grants, loans, and employment. The College utilizes the Pennsylvania Higher Education Assistance Agency (PHEAA) for needs analysis forms processing. The student is required to complete the Free Application for Federal Student Aid (FAFSA) to determine financial aid eligibility. Overall, the College views financial assistance to students as a cooperative investment. If parents contribute to the maximum of their ability and if the student contributes his or her fair share through earnings and personal savings, the College attempts to complete the partnership. In addition, estimates of financial aid eligibility may be obtained from the Financial Aid Office whether or not the student is an applicant. Non-need academic scholarships ranging from $500 to $5000 are available. These scholarships are awarded on the basis of SAT I or ACT scores and high school class rank information. Music leadership and church-matching grants are other college-based grant programs that are available.

Application and Information

Applications are accepted until the beginning of each term. Admission decisions are made within 48 hours of receipt of all materials.

Mark Seymour
Executive Director of Enrollment Management
Eastern College
St. Davids, Pennsylvania 19087-3696

Telephone: 610-341-5967

EASTERN MENNONITE UNIVERSITY
HARRISONBURG, VIRGINIA

The University

Eastern Mennonite, a private Christian university founded in 1917, provides a high-quality liberal arts education that emphasizes spiritual growth and cross-cultural awareness. The nurturing environment of EMU's student-oriented campus not only prepares students for a wide variety of careers but also challenges students to answer Christ's call to a life of witness, service, and peacemaking. The undergraduate experience is enriched by the recent addition of graduate programs in conflict transformation, counseling, and education. The University also has a seminary. EMU is accredited by the Southern Association of Colleges and Schools. In addition, the nursing, teacher education, and social work programs are accredited by their specialty organizations at the national level.

Academic Program

The academic calendar consists of two 15-week semesters from late August to late April. The baccalaureate degree requires 128 semester hours. All students complete a major, the Global Village general education curriculum, and electives. The Global Village curriculum is a sequence of courses consisting of 49 semester hours distributed as follows: faith (11), humanities (9), cross-cultural studies (9), math/natural science (9), social science (3), writing (3), speech (2), physical education (2), and the first-year experience (1). Associate degrees require 64 semester hours of general education requirements, a concentration in a major, and electives. Thirty semester hours are needed to complete a certificate. Cross-cultural studies take students to another culture for a semester or a three- to nine-week summer session. An honors program provides academic challenges and leadership opportunities for a select group of students through faculty mentoring, seminars, research opportunities, and special projects. Seven honors students are selected from each first-year class. Other special academic opportunities include credit by examination and extension credit for special programs with outside organizations.

Financial Aid

More than 90 percent of EMU students receive financial aid. Scholarships include those given for academic achievement and an award of $1000 given to new first-year students who are children of alumni. Other grant aid, given to meet financial need, includes federal aid, endowed scholarships, foundation grants, and aid from the operating budget. Admission is need-blind. In addition, students with financial need may obtain federal loans or participate in the work-study program. Virginia residents receive the Virginia Tuition Assistance Grant, regardless of need, which amounts to $2000 or more annually. If students receive grants from their churches, EMU matches up to $500 per year. No application is needed for academic scholarships except for honors awards. Students applying for need-based aid must complete the Free Application for Federal Student Aid (FAFSA). Applications should be completed by February 15.

Application and Information

The freshman application priority filing date is March 1. The final filing date is August 1. The application deadline for transfer applicants is thirty days prior to the start of the term for both fall and spring. Notification of admission is sent on a rolling basis. Inquiries and application materials should be sent to:

Ellen B. Miller
Director of Admissions
Eastern Mennonite University
Harrisonburg, Virginia 22801

Telephone: 800-368-2665 (toll-free)
Fax: 540-432-4444
E-mail: admiss@emu.edu
Web site: http://www.emu.edu

ELMIRA COLLEGE
ELMIRA, NEW YORK

The College

Elmira College is a small, independent college that is recognized for its emphasis on education of high quality in the liberal arts and preprofessional preparation. One of the oldest colleges in the United States, Elmira was founded in 1855. The College has always produced graduates interested in both community service and successful careers. Friendliness, personal attention, strong college spirit, and support for learning beyond the classroom help to make Elmira a special place. Elmira College is one of only 250 colleges in the nation to be granted a chapter of the prestigious Phi Beta Kappa honor society. The full-time undergraduate enrollment is about 1,125 men and women. The students at Elmira represent more than twenty-seven states, primarily those in the Northeast, with the highest representation coming from New York, New Jersey, Massachusetts, Connecticut, and Pennsylvania. Ninety-five percent of the full-time undergraduates live in College residence halls.

Academic Program

The College's calendar is composed of two 12-week terms followed by a 6-week spring term. Students enroll for four subjects during the 12-week terms, completing the first term by mid-December and the second during the first week of April. The 6-week term, from mid-April through May, may be devoted to a particular project involving travel, internship, research, or independent study. Students are required to participate in internships in order to gain practical and meaningful experience related to their program of study. Credit is awarded for these projects. Special opportunities for outstanding students include participation in eight national honorary societies on campus and a chance to assist faculty members in teaching and research. The College also offers an accelerated three-year graduation option for outstanding students. Army and Air Force ROTC are available.

Financial Aid

Financial aid is available for both freshmen and transfer students. Awards are based upon the Free Application for Federal Student Aid (FAFSA) and Financial Aid PROFILE as well as the student's academic potential. Types of aid include grants, scholarships, federal loans, Elmira College loans, and work opportunities. In addition, superior students may apply for non-need Elmira College Honors Scholarships. For 1996–97, the average freshman aid package (including all types of aid) amounted to more than $13,000. Transfer students applying for financial aid must submit a financial aid transcript from all colleges previously attended, whether or not they received financial aid. About 80 percent of the full-time undergraduates receive financial aid.

Application and Information

For further information, applicants should contact:

Dean of Admissions
Elmira College
Elmira, New York 14901
Telephone: 800-935-6472 (toll-free)

EMBRY-RIDDLE AERONAUTICAL UNIVERSITY
PRESCOTT, ARIZONA

The University

Students at Embry-Riddle Aeronautical University-Arizona (ERAU-AZ) receive a comprehensive, technical, and applied education geared toward designing the next generation of aviation and aerospace vehicles and the systems that support them. Embry-Riddle's reputation is based upon its leadership role in aviation education as well as its commitment to a strong academic preparation and learning environment. Embry-Riddle is a private, independent, four-year university and is accredited by the Commission on Colleges of the Southern Association of Colleges and Schools. Students share a love of aviation and a special motivation to succeed and become experts in their field. The coed (16 percent female) student population of 1,450 undergraduates comes from fifty-four states and territories and more than twenty other countries. Eight percent of the students are international. There are more than forty student clubs and organizations, five professional associations, four fraternities and two sororities, four sports clubs, and thirty-five intramural sports. The NAIA wrestling team, women's volleyball team, and the intercollegiate flight team compete with other regional and national universities. The extended Embry-Riddle family consists of 12,000 students and 34,000 alumni. The ERAU Daytona Beach, Florida, campus, with 4,000 undergraduate and 200 graduate students, offers additional resources. At Extended Campus Centers around the U.S. and the world, 5,000 undergraduate and 1,200 graduate students find ERAU's programs geared toward the needs of adult and part-time learners.

Academic Program

The undergraduate academic preparation provides a strong foundation for all students, whether or not they choose a career in aviation. Each major is a combination of general education, specialized aviation focus, and applied technology. The general education component consists of courses in communication skills, social sciences/humanities, mathematics, computer science, and physical science. Along with the major, students may opt to select a minor from the following fields: airline management, airport management, air transportation studies, aviation business administration, aviation safety, computer applications, computer science, humanities, mathematics, and psychology. Army and Air Force Reserve Officer Training Corps (ROTC) courses are also available to all Embry-Riddle students and may lead to a position as a commissioned officer. Through additional participation in internships and cooperative education (co-op) arrangements, ERAU-AZ students gain valuable work experience. The Student Success Center offers the college success course, orientation programs, academic advisement and counseling, and tutoring and supplemental instruction. In the Career Placement and Co-Op Services Office, students find assistance through job fairs, resume preparation and referral, job bank and interviews, and the careers library.

Financial Aid

Students and their families find many sources of aid available to assist with paying the costs of a private university; more than 70 percent of students receive financial assistance. Embry-Riddle participates in all national and state assistance programs. The completion of the Department of Education's Free Application for Federal Student Aid (FAFSA) forms assures students consideration for these funds. In addition, ERAU-AZ provides assistance in the form of on-campus jobs, academic scholarships, veterans' educational benefits, and ROTC room and board stipends.

Application and Information

A virtual tour of ERAU-AZ is available on the World Wide Web at http://www.erau.edu. For additional information, including information on campus visits, and application forms, students may contact:

Terry E. Whittum
Director of Admissions and Enrollment Management
3200 Willow Creek Road
Prescott, Arizona 86301

Telephone: 520-708-6600
800-888-ERAU (toll-free)
E-mail: admit@pr.erau.edu

FAIRMONT STATE COLLEGE
FAIRMONT, WEST VIRGINIA

The College

Fairmont State College (FSC) is the largest state-supported four-year college in West Virginia, with an enrollment of 6,500 students. Founded in 1867, the College is located in the north-central portion of the state in the city of Fairmont, West Virginia. In addition to the main campus, which includes thirteen major buildings, classes are also offered at the FSC Robert C. Byrd National Aerospace Education Center in Bridgeport, as well as at the Clarksburg campus. The College also has satellite facilities reaching across the north-central region of West Virginia.

Academic Program

Fairmont State College offers 126 program areas in the following divisions: business and economics; education/health, physical education, recreation, and safety; fine arts; language and literature; science, mathematics, and health careers; social science; and technology and family and consumer sciences. Special degrees such as the Regents Bachelor of Arts degree offer nontraditional approaches for individual career or personal requirements. Certificate programs are designed to provide basic skills or increased proficiency in specific occupational areas. Preprofessional studies are designed to prepare students for a wide variety of professional programs beyond a four-year degree. The first steps toward a Caribbean classroom were taken by the College in fall 1994, when 2.2 acres of oceanfront land in Costa Rica were donated by a local physician. The College plans to develop a Costa Rican field station for tropical studies in the areas of natural sciences, social sciences, and educational-recreational programs.

Financial Aid

About 53 percent of Fairmont State College students receive some form of financial aid. Guidelines and forms for West Virginia and out-of-state residents are available from high school guidance counselors or FSC's Financial Aid Office.

Application and Information

Campus tours are available Monday through Friday by appointment. Fairmont State College also sponsors a Saturday Campus Visitation Day once each fall and spring semester. For more information or to schedule a tour, students should contact:

Office of Student Affairs
Fairmont State College
1201 Locust Avenue
Fairmont, West Virginia 26554

Telephone: 304-367-4216
800-641-5678 (toll-free)
304-367-4141 (admissions and records)
304-367-4213 (financial aid)
304-367-4216 (housing)
304-367-4000 (campus operator)
304-623-5721 (Clarksburg Center)
304-842-8300 (Aviation Center)

FERRIS STATE UNIVERSITY
BIG RAPIDS, MICHIGAN

The University

Ferris State University (FSU) is Michigan's foremost professional and technical university, providing career-oriented education to nearly 10,000 students. Accredited by the North Central Association of Colleges and Schools, the University offers nearly 100 programs through the Colleges of Allied Health Sciences, Arts and Sciences, Business, Education, Pharmacy, Technology, and the Michigan College of Optometry. These offerings lead to bachelor's and associate degrees and certificates; master's degrees in accountancy, computer information systems management, and career and technical education; and doctorates in optometry and pharmacy. Services available to Ferris students include academic and personal counseling, tutoring, the collegiate skills program, aptitude and CLEP testing, career study classes, career planning and placement, and a variety of programs and seminars on crime prevention, safety, and substance abuse prevention and education. In addition to an extensive academic support system characterized by close student-faculty interaction, Ferris also offers positive cocurricular experiences to help students grow socially and culturally as well as academically. Students may choose to participate in any of more than 100 student organizations, including an extensive intramural program, twelve varsity sports, and theater and musical activities, as well as many social and academic fraternities and sororities that are open to students majoring in any field.

Academic Program

Ferris is dedicated to the ideal of blending career-oriented professional training with a solid base of general education. While major programs of study provide graduates with the skills and knowledge required to enter a chosen career, general education provides graduates with the academic skills, analytic flexibility, and broad base of knowledge required for continued learning, performance, and advancement in their personal and professional lives. Ferris currently is on the semester system, and the minimum requirement for a baccalaureate degree is 120 semester hours. The average program requires between 120 and 130 semester hours. The minimum number of hours required for an associate degree is 60. The University's academic year begins in August and ends in early May.

Financial Aid

Approximately 70 percent of Ferris students receive some type of financial aid through federal, state, and University programs. In 1996–97, student financial aid included more than $40 million in scholarships, grants, loans, work-study, or a combination of these. The Free Application for Federal Student Aid (FAFSA) must be submitted by April 1 to receive priority consideration for need-based financial aid. The University also provides merit-based scholarships in recognition of superior academic performance and residence-based scholarships for students living on campus who maintain high academic grades. The Woodbridge N. Ferris Scholarship Program offers competitive awards ranging from $1200 to $6000 per year to those who qualify. The Residential Life Scholarship offers $2000 per year for entering students who live in a residence hall on campus, have a 3.2 or better high school GPA, and have a minimum score of 21 on the ACT. Information and counseling are available from the office of scholarships and financial aid (telephone: 616-592-2110 or 800-940-4-AID, toll-free).

Application and Information

Admission applications may be obtained from high school or college counselors or by contacting:

Admissions Office
Ferris State University
420 Oak Street, PRK 101
Big Rapids, Michigan 49307-2020

Telephone: 616-592-2100
800-4FERRIS (toll-free)
E-mail: admissions@act01.ferris.edu

FERRUM COLLEGE
FERRUM, VIRGINIA

The College

Ferrum College is a four-year, independent, coeducational college situated on a 700-acre wooded campus in the foothills of southcentral Virginia's Blue Ridge Mountains. Ferrum is a self-contained community; 79 percent of the student body lives on campus, and many faculty members live on or near campus and are closely involved in campus life. Founded in 1913 by the United Methodist Church, Ferrum is a comprehensive liberal arts college accredited by the Southern Association of Colleges and Schools. Ferrum's student body of about 1,100 (56 percent men, 44 percent women) is a diverse group; while the largest contingent comes from Virginia, twenty-four other states and more than a dozen other countries are also represented. Ferrum's curriculum provides solid career preparation that includes rigorous academics, a strong experiential learning component, and a practical, broad-based, "real-life" emphasis. Ferrum students take what they learn in the classroom and apply it in the community through internships, volunteer opportunities, and fieldwork.

Academic Program

Ferrum College's comprehensive approach to higher education provides the benefits of liberal arts education with solid, practical career preparation. To graduate, students must complete 127 semester hours of academic work, meet the appropriate distribution and major/minor requirements, and achieve a cumulative grade point average of at least 2.0. Internships are required for programs such as environmental science, agriculture, teacher education, social work, recreation and leisure, and sports medicine and strongly recommended for many others, reflecting the College's belief in the value of hands-on learning. Ferrum students can also do volunteer work, join student government and/or the residence life staff, or work on campus in jobs ranging from student trainers to ropes course facilitators to public relations interns. The College's innovative teacher education program is a single multisemester course designed to encourage participants to develop a personal philosophy of education. Students receive more than 500 hours of teacher training over the course of the program and can become certified at the elementary, middle school, and/or secondary levels.

Financial Aid

In 1996–97, 95 percent of Ferrum students were offered some form of financial assistance. For the 76 percent of students receiving need-based aid, the average financial aid package totaled $10,006, or 67 percent of total costs for the year. A comprehensive assistance program includes campus jobs, scholarships, grants, and loans. A typical package consists of 58 percent scholarships and grants, 30 percent low-interest loans, and 12 percent campus-based jobs. Ferrum College is one of a small group of colleges nationwide that offers a unique financial aid opportunity known as the Bonner Scholars Program, which gives qualified students a chance to receive scholarship funds and to become involved in various service projects. The Free Application for Federal Student Aid (FAFSA) and forms concerning grants and scholarships are sent to all applicants and should be completed and submitted no later than April 1 for priority consideration. Virginia residents are eligible for grants under the Tuition Assistance Grant (TAG) Program, and out-of-state students receive a comparable TAG offered by the College.

Application and Information

Applicants should submit a completed application (available on request from the Admissions Office), a high school transcript (and a college transcript, if applicable), and scores from the SAT I or ACT. Further information may be obtained by contacting:

Director of Admissions
Spilman House
Ferrum College
Ferrum, Virginia 24088-9009

Telephone: 800-868-9797 (toll-free)
540-365-4614 (TDD)
E-mail: admissions@ferrum.edu
Web site: http://www.ferrum.edu

FITCHBURG STATE COLLEGE
FITCHBURG, MASSACHUSETTS

The College

Fitchburg State College is a liberal arts institution where career-oriented and professional education programs thrive. Under the leadership of its new president, Dr. Michael Riccards, Fitchburg State has undertaken a number of major initiatives. The College now offers a three-year baccalaureate program, more internship opportunities, a substantially increased Merit Scholarship program, and a guarantee that its graduates will be qualified for jobs in their fields. The College is investing in new technologies in every curriculum to assure that Fitchburg State continues to place more than 85 percent of its graduates in their chosen professions. Fitchburg State's excellent academic reputation and graduate placement can be attributed to a nationally recognized faculty and a commitment to teaching that is unparalleled in Massachusetts. The College serves 3,000 students in its day division and another 4,000 students in its evening and graduate programs. The average class size is 25, and the overall student-teacher ratio remains low at 15:1. There are numerous and varied opportunities for student leadership through the Student Government Association, the Athletic Council, the All-College Committee, the Campus Center Advisory Committee, the Residence Hall Councils, publications, and student-faculty-administration committees. Three student publications offer creative opportunities—the *Strobe,* a weekly newspaper; the *Scrimshaw,* a literary magazine; and the *Saxifrage,* the College yearbook. A number of special interest clubs are open to all students. Several sororities and fraternities contribute to the social and recreational life of the campus. Hundreds of popular and well-attended activities take place during the year, including films, lectures, concerts, seminars, coffeehouses, pub entertainment, recreational tournaments, performing arts series, and visual arts exhibits. In addition to the bachelor's degrees listed below, Fitchburg State confers the Master of Arts in Teaching (M.A.T.), the Master of Education (M.Ed.) in several disciplines, and the Master of Science (M.S.) in communications media, computer science, counseling, and management. Several Certificate of Advanced Graduate Studies (C.A.G.S.) programs are available as well.

Academic Program

The College operates on a two-semester basis. The first semester begins in early September and ends in mid-December, and the second semester begins in mid-January and ends in mid-May. The curriculum has a strong liberal arts and sciences requirement, providing a strong foundation for either further academic study or a career. Students may obtain practical experience through volunteer placement in social agencies, government offices, and businesses related to their interests. Some major programs require an extensive supervised practicum to complete degree requirements. For education majors, a broad spectrum of student-teaching experiences is available. The four-year honors program, for students with excellent high school records, culminates in a senior thesis or project.

Financial Aid

Many sources of financial aid are available to Fitchburg State students. The College participates in federal and state programs, including the Federal Direct Student Loan Program. Packages consisting of grants, loans, work-study awards, and scholarships are given to students demonstrating financial need. Financial aid applications for the fall semester must be completed by the preceding March 30 to be given priority consideration.

Application and Information

Acceptance of qualified applicants begins in January and proceeds on a rolling basis until all available spaces are taken. Students should apply by April 1 for the fall semester and by December 1 for the spring semester. For further information, students should contact:

Director of Admissions
Fitchburg State College
Fitchburg, Massachusetts 01420

Telephone: 508-665-3144
800-705-9692 (toll-free)
Fax: 508-665-4540
E-mail: admissions@fsc.edu

FIVE TOWNS COLLEGE
DIX HILLS, NEW YORK

The College

Founded in 1972 by a group of educators and community leaders who wished to provide students with an alternative to the large university atmosphere, Five Towns College is a nonsectarian, coeducational institution that places its emphasis on the student as an individual. As an institution of higher learning that offers both two-year and four-year degree programs, the College is the only school on Long Island with the authority to offer the prestigious Bachelor of Music degree (Mus.B.).

Academic Program

The music education program is designed for students interested in a career as a teacher of music in a public or private school (K–12). Music majors are required to complete at least 40 credits with a minimum grade point average of 3.0 before admission to the music education program. The audio recording technology concentration is designed to provide students with the tools needed to succeed as professional engineers and producers in the recording industry. The music business concentration is designed for students interested in a career in music-related business fields such as the recorded music industry. The composition/songwriting concentration provides professional training for students who intend to pursue careers as composers, arrangers, and songwriters. The performance concentration is designed for students planning to pursue careers as professional performers. The video music concentration provides professional training in music scoring and compositional techniques and in the artistic and technical skills required for the creation of video music. To earn a Bachelor of Music degree, a student must complete 128 credits. Distribution of credits varies according to degree and concentration sought.

Financial Aid

The annual tuition at Five Towns College is among the lowest of all the private colleges in the region. Nevertheless, the institution is aware of the financial constraints facing college students and their families. Approximately 65 percent of all students on campus receive some form of financial aid. Need-based federal, state, and institutional funds are available to qualified students and include grants, loans, and on-campus work-study arrangements. Merit-based scholarships, not based on financial need, are also available in all subject areas. Scholarships are available for transfer students. Prospective students are urged to contact the Five Towns College Financial Aid Office for specific details and information.

Application and Information

Students must apply to either the two-year associate degree programs or the four-year baccalaureate degree programs. While admission into any of the associate degree programs has been classified as minimally difficult, admission into the Bachelor of Music program is contingent upon passing an audition demonstrating skill in performance on a major instrument or vocally. Bachelor of Music degree applicants are also required to take written and aural examinations in harmony, sight-singing, and ear training in order to demonstrate talent, well-developed musicianship, and artistic sensibilities. An interview is required. Students are accepted on a rolling admission basis and are notified shortly after all required documents have been filed with the admissions office. New students may begin their studies at the start of either the fall semester or the spring semester. There is an application fee of $25. For further information, students should contact:

Coordinator of Admissions
Five Towns College
305 North Service Road
Dix Hills, New York 11746-6055
Telephone: 516-424-7000 Ext. 110

FLORIDA INSTITUTE OF TECHNOLOGY
MELBOURNE, FLORIDA

The Institute

Florida Institute of Technology was founded in 1958 for the purpose of offering science and engineering courses to specialists working on the space program at Cape Canaveral. The primary aim of the university has been to keep abreast of current and anticipated needs in the developing fields of high technology. This philosophy is reflected in Florida Tech's response to the nation's growing need for qualified specialists trained in the fields of science and engineering. Other degree programs offered at Florida Tech (aviation, business administration, psychology, and business and technical communication) give the university a well-rounded approach to higher education. There are more than 4,100 graduate and undergraduate students currently enrolled at Florida Tech. Men's intercollegiate sports are baseball, basketball, crew, cross-country, soccer, and tennis. Women's sports are basketball, crew, cross-country, softball, and volleyball. There are seven national fraternities, two national sororities, and one local sorority. Student chapters of professional and social organizations include the American Institute of Aeronautics and Astronautics, Society of Physics Students, and Blue Key National Honor Fraternity. Student services include the Campus Ministry, Counseling Center, Veterans Administration Office, Placement and Cooperative Education Office, Health Service, Individual Learning Center, and Freshman Counseling.

Academic Program

Programs in the pure sciences prepare the student for graduate or professional work. Practical aspects of computer science and engineering can be combined with management science for the business minded, and a wide variety of programs are available for the environmentalist. Baccalaureate programs are completely outlined for each discipline; opportunity for diversification is provided by the technical and humanities electives offered during the junior and senior years. In the School of Aeronautics, the bachelor's programs provide a strong business or science background in the first two years and concentrate on specialized knowledge in the aviation industry during the final two years. Students can select from five accredited aviation bachelor's degrees, including aviation management, aeronautical science, and aviation computer science. Flight training is an integral part of the aviation management and aeronautical science programs, but both can be completed without flight. Flight students earn their FAA commercial, instrument, and multiengine flight certificates and can earn their instructor, air taxi, and airline transport pilot ratings and the flight dispatcher certificate. Students at Florida Tech may qualify for advanced placement through chemistry and mathematics examinations administered by the university. Transfer students desiring credit by examination should petition the appropriate department. Advanced credit is awarded for Advanced Placement (AP) exams and higher-level International Baccalaureate subjects.

Financial Aid

Awards are based on academic promise, need, college costs, and the availability of funds. Approximately 75 percent of the university's students receive grants, scholarships, loans, and employment, either in a single award or in various combinations. Several kinds of monthly installment plans are available for tuition and other expenses. The application deadline for financial aid is February 1 for incoming freshmen and March 15 for all other students. Inquiries should be sent to the director of financial aid. Students eligible for Veterans Administration benefits may contact the VA representative on the Melbourne campus.

Application and Information

The university encourages applicants from every social, ethnic, racial, and religious background. Florida Tech practices a rolling admission policy. The application fee is $35. Completed applications, high school and college transcripts, and standardized test results should be sent to the office below. For further information, students may contact:

Office of Admissions
Florida Institute of Technology
150 West University Boulevard
Melbourne, Florida 32901-6988

Telephone: 407-768-8000 Ext. 8030
800-888-4348 (toll-free)
E-mail: admissions@fit.edu

GARDNER–WEBB UNIVERSITY
BOILING SPRINGS, NORTH CAROLINA

The University
Gardner-Webb University was founded in 1905 as a private high school by a group of Baptist associations. It became a junior college in 1928, was renamed Gardner-Webb College in 1942 in honor of former governor O. Max Gardner, and became a fully accredited senior college in 1971. Gardner-Webb moved to University status in 1993. Its origins are obviously deep in Christian tradition, which is exemplified in the lives of staff and faculty members. The cosmopolitan student body (more than 2,740 men and women, of whom nearly 2,200 are undergraduates) represents twenty-one states and nine other countries and gives an added, valuable dimension to a student's educational experience. About 75 percent of the students live on campus. The Program for the Blind at Gardner-Webb University has been developed to allow students with visual handicaps to receive a liberal arts education. Special support services and job opportunities are provided for every entering student who is visually impaired. The Degree Program for the Deaf provides interpreters, note takers, and tutors skilled in sign language so that hearing-impaired students have full access to all University programs.

Academic Program
The total program is marked by flexibility for the student but encourages, through active faculty advisement, choosing a substantial course of study. Elements of the humanities, the social and physical sciences, and mathematics or related disciplines must be taken. A typical bachelor's degree program requires 128 semester hours for graduation: 40 to 52 in the core (humanities and social and physical sciences), 30 in the major, 42 to 58 in supporting subjects, and 12 to 28 in complementary or free electives. Requirements for science curricula vary somewhat. The associate degree requires the completion of 64 semester hours. A cumulative average of C (2.0 on a 4.0 scale) or better is required for graduation. Gardner-Webb grants advanced placement and credit on the basis of the College-Level Examination Program (CLEP) or Advanced Placement (AP) tests of the College Board.

Financial Aid
Prospective applicants with financial need should contact the financial aid director early in their senior year of high school for a financial need estimate. Applications received after April 1 can be considered only in terms of available funds. An applicant must be accepted for admission before being awarded aid. Students must file the Free Application for Federal Student Aid (FAFSA). Scholarships and other types of aid include academic awards, Christian service awards, endowed scholarships, and annual scholarships. There are several Gardner-Webb loan funds. The University also administers aid from the full range of federal programs: Federal Pell Grants, Federal Work-Study Program awards, Federal Perkins Loans, and federally guaranteed Federal Stafford Student and Federal PLUS loans. North Carolina students have access to state grant funds administered by the University. Scholarships based on academic promise are also granted each year. Of all students, 79 percent receive aid in some form. The two criteria for receiving financial aid are financial need and academic promise.

Application and Information
Applications, together with a nonrefundable $20 application fee, may be submitted for either semester. Early application is advised. Notification of the admission decision is given on a rolling basis upon receipt of all application data. A $150 room deposit for boarding students is due thirty days after acceptance and is refundable until May 1. A $50 deposit is required of commuting students.

For further information, students should contact:
Director of Admissions
Gardner-Webb University
Boiling Springs, North Carolina 28017

Telephone: 704-434-4GWU
800-253-6472 (toll-free)

GEORGE FOX UNIVERSITY
NEWBERG, OREGON

The University
George Fox University was founded 106 years ago by the Society of Friends (Quakers) with the purpose of providing students a challenging academic atmosphere and a commitment to Christian faith. From a modest beginning of 15 students in 1891, George Fox has grown to an enrollment of 2,050 students from thirteen countries. Students find George Fox to be a place where the integration of spiritual and intellectual challenge takes place in a friendly, caring environment. This tradition of integration has been recognized by the Templeton Foundation by naming George Fox University to the honor roll of character-building colleges. National recognition for academic reputation has also been given by *U.S. News & World Report.* Seventy-five percent of George Fox students live in campus residence halls, suites, and apartments. Opportunities for extracurricular involvement are available in music, drama, journalism, student government, radio, clubs, and athletics. George Fox is a member of the NAIA (but is moving to NCAA Division III) and competes in six men's sports (baseball, basketball, cross-country, soccer, tennis, and track) and seven women's sports (basketball, cross-country, soccer, softball, tennis, track, and volleyball). A number of intramural sports are also available. Regular chapel services bring the campus community together in worship. Students have the opportunity to put their faith into action on volunteer mission trips and during community outreach activities. In addition to its undergraduate degrees, George Fox confers the Master of Business Administration, Master of Education, Master of Arts in Teaching, Master of Christian Service, and Doctor of Psychology degrees, and seven master's degrees through Western Evangelical Seminary, a graduate school of George Fox University.

Academic Program
The academic year at George Fox University is divided into two semesters of fifteen weeks. In addition to the two semesters, the University sponsors a three-week May Term. For graduation, students are required to earn 126 credit hours, including 54 general education and 42 upper-division credits. Students may reduce the number of required courses and add flexibility to their undergraduate years with credit earned through Advanced Placement, the College-Level Examination Program, and credit by examination. An innovative program called "Computers Across the Curriculum" expands the computer literacy of students. The University issues every incoming freshman a Macintosh computer for school and personal use. The computer becomes the property of the student upon graduation. To meet the needs of this program, the University has a full-service computer store, a campus network, and a CD-ROM computer center on campus. George Fox demonstrates its commitment to freshmen by providing a Freshman Seminar Program to assist students as they integrate themselves into the academic and social life of the University community.

Financial Aid
George Fox maintains that every qualified student should be able to attend the university of his or her choice without letting limited finances stand in the way. To this end, federal, state, and institutional need-based funds are available, as are merit awards in academics, music, and drama. About 87 percent of all students receive financial aid.

Application and Information
For additional information, students should contact:

Office of Admissions
George Fox University
Newberg, Oregon 97132-2697

Telephone: 503-538-8383 Ext. 2240
E-mail: admissions@georgefox.edu

GEORGIAN COURT COLLEGE
LAKEWOOD, NEW JERSEY

The College

Georgian Court College, founded by the Sisters of Mercy of New Jersey, began in 1908 as a liberal arts college for young women. The current undergraduate enrollment in the women's college is 1,114. In 1976, the College expanded to include a Graduate School of Education. In 1979, the coeducational Undergraduate Evening Division was established to provide both men and women the means to pursue a baccalaureate degree while being involved in full- or part-time employment; it now enrolls 549 students. Both resident and commuting students participate in a wide variety of activities, including numerous cultural and social functions. There are also forty-five cultural, educational, honorary, and service-oriented clubs and organizations. Women's intercollegiate competition is offered in basketball, cross-country, soccer, and softball.

Academic Program

Successful completion of 132 credit hours is required for a B.A., B.F.A., B.S., or B.S.W. degree. With departmental approval, students may elect a second major. All students must complete general education requirements, which are designed to provide the breadth essential for complete development of the truly liberally educated person. Internships, externships, and practicums are offered in most majors, and independent studies are available in many.

Financial Aid

Georgian Court College has endeavored to keep the cost of attending an independent college affordable. A large percentage of its students receive financial assistance. Financial aid consists of all scholarships, grants, loans, or campus jobs offered to the applicant to help meet education-related expenses. Eligible students may be aided through a combination of these items, called a financial aid package. Georgian Court offers both need-based and no-need financial aid. For example, some scholarships are granted on the basis of a superior academic record, College Board and ACT scores, and financial need; other scholarships are based on academic excellence only. Athletics grants of variable amounts are available to students who qualify for admission and demonstrate the ability to participate in the sports program while advancing their college career. Georgian Court financial aid is usually available for U.S. citizens and eligible noncitizens. The College also participates in the New Jersey Educational Opportunity Fund program. In order to be considered for any financial aid, all students must submit a Georgian Court financial aid form to the Financial Aid Office. All applicants must also submit the Free Application for Federal Student Aid (FAFSA). The data are evaluated by the Financial Aid Committee, beginning February 15. An award letter and acceptance statement are then sent to students who qualify for aid, indicating the assistance provided to meet the student's financial need.

Application and Information

To apply for admission, regular freshman applicants should send an application, high school transcript, and nonrefundable $30 application fee. Transfer students should submit an application, the fee, and transcripts from high school and all colleges attended. Freshman applicants are urged to file an application as early as possible in their senior year of high school. Freshman and transfer applications must be received by August 1 for the fall semester and by January 1 for the spring semester. The College has a rolling admissions policy; however, transfer and freshman applications should be received by August 1 for the fall semester and December 15 for the spring semester for the best course selection.

Nancy G. Hazelgrove
Director of Admissions
Georgian Court College
900 Lakewood Avenue
Lakewood, New Jersey 08701

Telephone: 908-364-2200 Ext. 760
800-458-8422 (toll-free)
Fax: 908-364-4442
E-mail: admissions-ugrad@georgian.edu
Web site: http://www.georgian.edu

GLENVILLE STATE COLLEGE
GLENVILLE, WEST VIRGINIA

The College

Glenville State College was founded in 1872 and is a part of the state college system of West Virginia. The enrollment generally falls within the 2,200–2,500 range, with slightly more women than men. The College is located in the beautiful hill country of central West Virginia, overlooking the town of Glenville, and the campus is nestled in a magnificent grove of maples. Most students are from West Virginia, but more and more out-of-state students are being attracted to this tranquil, rural setting. Interstate Highway 79 passes within 15 miles of the campus. There are ten major buildings on campus, including Pickens Hall, which houses women in Scott and Williams wings and men in Wagner wing, and Louis Bennett Hall for men, which is situated in the center of the campus. Affiliated with the NCAA Division II and formerly with the NAIA Division I, Glenville has a strong athletic program for both men and women and has been in the national championships of the NAIA in basketball, bowling, football, and golf. An intramural program is also available, and the College has a football stadium with an all-weather track. In addition, many extracurricular activities are offered on campus throughout the year.

Academic Program

In accordance with the stated objectives of Glenville State College, candidates for all baccalaureate degrees must complete a program of general studies. The common program for all degrees covers the areas of the humanities, science and mathematics, the social sciences, and physical education. The traditional grading system is used at Glenville, with an optional credit/no-credit system for electives in the upper division. The College operates on the two-semester system and also has two summer terms of 4½ weeks' duration. The unit of credit is the semester hour, which represents the equivalent of 1 hour of recitation a week during a semester of seventeen weeks. Laboratory courses require additional time.

Financial Aid

Glenville State College provides financial assistance for qualified students in the form of scholarships, workships, and loans. Scholarships and workships are awarded on the basis of achievement and need. Usually they will not be given to a student whose high school average is below 3.0, and no student may receive or continue a workship if his or her overall grade point average is below 2.0.

Application and Information

Candidates applying under the above guidelines must submit a completed application for admission, their ACT or SAT I scores, a copy of their high school transcript, and proof of measles and rubella vaccinations to the Office of Admissions. Transfer students must submit transcripts from all colleges attended. International students must submit a TOEFL score of at least 450. All correspondence concerning admissions and all credentials in support of an application must be on file at least thirty days prior to the opening of a semester. The College uses a rolling admissions procedure, and students are notified of the admission decision soon after their completed application has been received.

For an application form and additional information, students should contact:

Office of Records and Enrollment Management
Glenville State College
Glenville, West Virginia 26351

Telephone: 304-462-7361
Fax: 304-462-8619
E-mail: cottrill@wvngsc.wvnet.edu
Web site: http://www.glenville.wvnet.edu

GMI ENGINEERING & MANAGEMENT INSTITUTE
FLINT, MICHIGAN

The Institute

GMI, America's "co-op college," has a unique partnership that offers students, business, and industry an opportunity found at no other undergraduate college in America. GMI, a five-year cooperative engineering, management, science, and math college, is the only institution that assists incoming freshmen to be selected by companies for cooperative employment, a process GMI initiates for all accepted students. GMI successfully integrates the practical aspects of the workplace into the world of higher education through its more than 550 corporate partners, corporations, and agencies located throughout the United States, Canada, and selected countries. GMI's corporate partners represent most major industrial groups; many are recognized as worldwide leaders in business innovation and manufacturing technology. These corporations share a commitment to "grow their own" engineers and managers by employing exceptionally talented young men and women in one of the ten GMI baccalaureate degree programs. GMI's corporate partners invest in students' futures by providing a five-year program of progressive work experience that exposes them to processes, products, corporate culture, and the technology necessary to compete in tomorrow's business environment. Founded in 1919, GMI is a private college enrolling 2,400 undergraduate students. The Institute is accredited by the North Central Association of Colleges and Schools.

Academic Program

Although each curriculum at GMI has its own sequence requirements, 180 credit hours are generally required, including thesis credit hours. The five-year program involves nine semesters of cooperative and academic work and a tenth semester of thesis preparation. Students alternate between twelve-week periods of academic study on the campus in Flint and twelve-week periods of related work experience with their corporate employer. The academic year consists of two 12-week academic terms at GMI and two 12-week terms of paid work experience. A typical GMI cooperative student who works both terms of his or her freshman year earns, on the average, $8900 per year before taxes.

Financial Aid

One of the many advantages of attending GMI is the opportunity for students to earn a salary during work terms. This "ultimate scholarship" covers part of the cost of a GMI education and supplements the family contribution and the standard forms of need-based financial aid. Students who live at home during work experience periods are able to contribute a greater proportion of earnings directly to educational expenses. About 70 percent of GMI students are able to live at home during work terms. The typical range of co-op earnings over the five-year program is $40,000 to $65,000. GMI offers all the traditional forms of financial aid, both need- and merit-based. Michigan residents often are recipients of the Michigan Competitive Scholarship. Students who wish to apply for financial aid should complete the Free Application for Federal Student Aid (FAFSA) and request that a copy of the analysis be sent to GMI (GMI's code number is 1246). Aid is given as grants, scholarships, loans, and work-study awards.

Application and Information

Prospective freshmen are encouraged to file their application early in their senior year. Transfer students can apply any time after successful completion of 30 credits. Applications are accepted all year long; however, early application greatly increases visibility for early employment possibilities in the co-op search process. The application fee is $25.

Admissions Office
GMI Engineering & Management Institute
1700 West Third Avenue
Flint, Michigan 48504-4898

Telephone: 810-762-7865
800-955-4464 (toll-free in the United States and Canada)
E-mail: admissions@gmi.edu
Web site: http://www.gmi.edu

GOLDEN GATE UNIVERSITY
SAN FRANCISCO, CALIFORNIA

The University

Golden Gate University (GGU), whose origins in San Francisco trace to 1853, is a private, nonprofit institution of higher learning accredited by the Western Association of Schools and Colleges. The University has a combined day and evening enrollment of approximately 7,000 students and offers undergraduate and graduate degrees through the doctoral level. GGU students are mature and highly motivated, and many are employed full- or part-time. Many applicants seeking admission on the basis of their high school records have had several years of work or military experience since high school graduation. Approximately 59 percent of the undergraduate students are women.

Academic Program

Golden Gate University is dedicated to the belief that personally and socially useful higher education requires a combination of professional and liberal studies and a balance of theoretical training and responsible participation in society. Class sizes are limited to ensure opportunities for student-faculty interaction and discussion, and class schedules are arranged to serve both full-time day students and those who wish to combine their academic studies with full- or part-time work. For this purpose, the University offers its undergraduate programs in both the day and the evening, enabling students to attend morning classes on a full-time basis and work in the afternoon or to work during the day and attend evening classes. Through the University's Cooperative Education and Internship Program, students may arrange to pursue their degree by alternating terms of full-time study and full-time work or by working part-time concurrently with their studies. The University's undergraduate curricula are sharply focused on various professional specializations within the general areas of management, public administration accounting, and computer information systems. GGU was one of the first colleges or universities in the nation to institute the trimester system, which enables students to make accelerated progress toward attainment of their educational goals. The completion of 123 units is required for a bachelor's degree. Midterm examinations are given in most courses, and final examinations are given in all courses. A student may take one course per term on a credit/no credit basis, provided that the course is not required and not in the major field of study.

Financial Aid

Financial assistance is available for students who could not attend the University without it. Aid is provided through federal, state, and University loan, grant, and work-study programs. A number of scholarships are available for entering students. Students with Veterans Administration education benefits may use them at Golden Gate University.

Application and Information

An undergraduate applicant seeking admission as a degree candidate must file an application with a nonrefundable application fee of $50 ($65 for international applicants) and submit official transcripts of all high school and previous college work. The University has a rolling admissions policy, but international students and all students applying for financial aid must apply by November 1 for spring admission, July 1 for fall admission, and March 1 for the summer.

Application forms and further information may be obtained from:

Enrollment Services
Golden Gate University
536 Mission Street
San Francisco, California 94105-2968

Telephone: 415-442-7800
800-448-4968 (toll-free)
Fax: 415-442-7807
E-mail: info@ggu.edu
Web site: http://www.ggu.edu

GONZAGA UNIVERSITY
SPOKANE, WASHINGTON

The University

Gonzaga, founded in 1887, is an independent, comprehensive university with a distinguished background in the Catholic, Jesuit, and humanistic tradition. Gonzaga emphasizes the moral and ethical implications of learning, living, and working in today's global society. Through the University Core Curriculum, each student develops a strong liberal arts foundation, which many alumni cite as a most valuable asset. In addition, students specialize in any of more than fifty academic majors. Gonzaga enrolls approximately 5,000 students, of whom about 2,900 are undergraduates. About 40 percent of the students come from Washington State, with forty-six other states and forty-six other countries also represented. In addition to its undergraduate colleges and schools, Gonzaga University has a Graduate School that includes more than twenty master's programs and a doctoral program in Educational Leadership, a School of Law, and the Saint Michael's Institute, which prepares Jesuit scholastics for the priesthood.

Academic Program

Gonzaga University believes that it is necessary for all students, regardless of their chosen major or profession, to achieve an education that goes beyond specialization. Therefore, all students attending Gonzaga receive a strong liberal arts background as well as depth in their major. The Core Curriculum is a very important component of the 128 semester units a student must earn for graduation. The Honors Program challenges special achievers with an integrated curriculum compatible with any major and most double majors. The program requires a separate application. Gonzaga also offers a Dual Enrollment Program that gives qualified Spokane-area high school seniors an opportunity to enroll in classes at the University. Credits earned through the Washington State Running Start Program or International Baccalaureate (IB) program are accepted on a class-by-class basis. College credit is given for certain test scores in most Advanced Placement (AP) subjects.

Financial Aid

Gonzaga University offers many different types of financial aid to qualified students, including scholarships, Federal Pell Grants, Federal Supplemental Educational Opportunity Grants, work-study jobs, Federal Perkins Loans, Federal Stafford Student Loans, and on- and off-campus employment. In order to apply for financial aid awards, a student must first be accepted by the University and must see that the Free Application for Federal Student Aid (FAFSA) is submitted by February 1. After this date, awards are made on a funds-available basis. Approximately 85 percent of the students at Gonzaga receive some sort of financial assistance.

Application and Information

Gonzaga University's priority deadline for admissions applications is March 1. The final deadline is April 1 for freshmen and July 1 for transfer students. Applicants are notified of the admission decision within four weeks of receipt of a completed application (application form, transcripts, test scores, letters of recommendation, an essay, and a list of awards and activities). It is recommended that all students applying for financial aid for the fall semester submit their application materials by March 1. All requests for further information or materials should be addressed to:

Dean of Admission
Gonzaga University
Spokane, Washington 99258-0102

Telephone: 800-322-2584 (toll-free)
E-mail: ballinger@gu.gonzaga.edu
Web site: http://www.gonzaga.edu/

GORDON COLLEGE
WENHAM, MASSACHUSETTS

The College
Gordon College is a traditional New England liberal arts college with a difference. Founded in 1889 as a missionary training institute, the College today offers the solid liberal arts foundation that distinguishes the best of New England's small colleges. What sets Gordon apart from other New England colleges is that the liberal arts and sciences are taught from a Christian perspective. There is also a commitment to a multicultural approach to learning that reflects the diversity of the world.

Academic Program
The four-year baccalaureate degree program is conducted within the context of a semester academic calendar, and the academic year is divided into two 15-week semesters. Sixteen semester hours per term constitute a normal registration, and courses normally carry 4 semester hours of credit. Graduation requirements include a minimum of 128 semester hours of credit, 32 of which must be taken at Gordon, the last 16 in residence; a grade point average of 2.0 or above; fulfillment of the liberal arts core curriculum; and fulfillment of the course requirements specified for the major, with no fewer than 16 semester hours in the major earned at Gordon. The Kenneth L. Pike Honors Program provides exceptional students with an opportunity to design a flexible, individualized academic program. To enter the Pike program, a student must have completed at least one term at Gordon and have a cumulative grade point average of at least 3.5. Gordon accepts a limited amount of credit validated by the College-Level Examination Program (CLEP). Students may also take placement tests in writing and/or foreign languages to determine whether they may waive, respectively, the basic writing requirement and/or one or more of the foreign language courses.

Financial Aid
Students who demonstrate financial need normally receive a combination of grants, loans, and student employment opportunities. Students applying for financial aid must complete the Financial Aid PROFILE of the College Scholarship Service and a Gordon College application for financial aid. Nearly 80 percent of Gordon students receive financial aid, which includes federal, state, private, and institutional awards. The A. J. Gordon Scholarship Program awards approximately twenty-five $8000 scholarships per year to incoming freshmen who show promise of leadership and academic achievement. There is a separate application that requires a prearranged visit to campus on one of the special A. J. Gordon Scholarship days.

Application and Information
Regular admission is on a rolling basis; the application deadline for early decision is December 1. For further information, students may contact:

Pamela B. Lazarakis
Dean of Admissions
Gordon College
Wenham, Massachusetts 01984-9988
Telephone: 800-343-1379 (toll-free)

GOUCHER COLLEGE
BALTIMORE, MARYLAND

The College

Since its inception in 1885, Goucher College has maintained a reputation for academic excellence and a tradition of high quality combined with flexibility. The past few decades have seen many changes in academic programs, governance, and social regulations, during which time Goucher has held fast to its commitment to a superior liberal arts education designed to help students achieve their fullest potential. The 1,100 undergraduates enrolled come from all parts of the United States and several other countries; they represent diverse backgrounds, interests, and points of view. Goucher confers a Bachelor of Arts degree; a postbaccalaureate, premedical certificate; and postbaccalaureate teaching certification. There is also a B.A./B.S. dual-degree program in science and engineering with Johns Hopkins University. In collaboration with the Sheppard Pratt National Center for Human Development, the College confers a Master of Education, with specializations in education of at-risk students, middle school education, urban education, school improvement leadership, and school mediation. Two master's programs include a Master of Teaching and a limited-residency Master of Arts in historic preservation. Athletic facilities include a 50,000-square-foot Sports and Recreation Center, the Welsh gymnasium, and the von Borries swimming pool. The sports center features a field house, sauna, wellness laboratory, weight-training room, squash and racquetball courts, lockers, and offices. There are two dance studios, 4 miles of wooded riding and jogging trails, six tennis courts, riding rings, and stables. Goucher belongs to NCAA Division III. Varsity sports for men are basketball, cross-country, lacrosse, soccer, swimming, and tennis. Women's varsity sports are basketball, cross-country, field hockey, lacrosse, soccer, swimming, tennis, and volleyball. The College competes on a coeducational basis in equestrian sports.

Academic Program

The core curriculum is the foundation for a Goucher education. Recently revised, the core retains Goucher's tradition of academic rigor while becoming more relevant to a changing world. There is a strong emphasis on both interdisciplinary study and the development of a global perspective. Requirements include a demonstrated proficiency in a foreign language, English composition, and computer technology, along with courses in the arts, natural sciences, humanities, social sciences, and mathematics. The computer proficiency requirement gives students a basic familiarity with computers, their applications, and their languages—an increasingly important tool both in business and in academe. All freshmen take the semester-long Freshman Colloquium. Taught in small sections, the course integrates humanities and social sciences perspectives. There is an interdisciplinary honors program in addition to honors courses in each department. The Goucher degree requires 120 semester hours of credit. The departmental major consists of at least 30 credits (about ten courses); the double major requires 60 credits. The 5-credit off-campus requirement reflects the College's belief in balancing classroom theory with real-world experience and may take the form of an internship, a period of study abroad, or an independent project. Goucher's calendar is based on the semester system.

Financial Aid

In an average year, more than half of Goucher's students receive some form of aid; 45 percent are awarded grants, ranging from $400 to the total cost of the education. The average financial aid award is more than $11,000. Goucher participates in the Federal Work-Study Program and helps students benefit from Federal Supplemental Educational Opportunity Grants, Federal Pell Grants, Federal Perkins Loans, Federal Stafford Student Loans, and College loans. Goucher also offers a competitive merit award program.

Application and Information

Director of Admissions
Goucher College
1021 Dulaney Valley Road
Baltimore, Maryland 21204-2794

Telephone: 410-337-6100
800-GOUCHER (toll-free)

GRACE COLLEGE
WINONA LAKE, INDIANA

The College

Grace College is a Christian undergraduate college of arts and sciences founded in 1948 and affiliated with the Fellowship of Grace Brethren Churches, a conservative evangelical denomination. Grace College attracts students from a variety of conservative evangelical backgrounds and from around the United States and several other countries. The College offers an environment and academic program that are conservative in theology and progressive in spirit and that emphasize three qualities for students as they reach adulthood—mature Christian character, academic and career competence, and a heart for service to mankind. Enrollment at Grace College is 725, providing an ideal atmosphere in which students can learn, grow, and develop lasting friendships.

Academic Program

The requirements for the bachelor's degree include the successful completion of one major (36–56 semester hours) and one minor (20–28 semester hours) area of concentration in addition to the specified program of general education courses. Students are required to complete a total of 124 semester hours of course work. Through the January session (Winterim) offered each year, students have an opportunity to take courses off campus as well as to take courses at Grace that are not generally offered during the regular school year. Grace College operates on a two-semester calendar and offers three summer sessions in addition to Winterim. Advanced Placement (AP) and College-Level Examination Program (CLEP) test scores are considered for college credit and advanced placement.

Financial Aid

The College offers extensive financial assistance to qualified students. Most students receive some sort of financial assistance—in the form of a scholarship, grant, loan, or campus employment—to help pay college costs. The average amount of financial aid awarded to a Grace College student totals $4800 per year. To be considered for financial assistance at Grace College, students must submit the Free Application for Federal Student Aid (FAFSA). Students may receive Federal Pell Grants, Federal Perkins Loans, and Federal Supplemental Educational Opportunity Grants. In addition, students may be eligible for Federal Work-Study Program awards. The FAFSA should be on file by March 1 for priority consideration. To renew financial aid, students must refile the FAFSA each year.

Application and Information

Students may apply for admission to any semester. Applications are accepted on a rolling basis until January 1 for the spring term and August 1 for the fall term. There is a $20 nonrefundable application fee. Interested students and their parents are encouraged to visit the campus and to arrange for an interview at that time in order to get a clear picture of Grace College. Arrangements can be made for housing and meals for applicants by contacting the Grace Visitor Center. Catalogs, application forms, a video presentation about the campus, and additional information may be obtained from the address below.

Grace College
200 Seminary Drive
Winona Lake, Indiana 46590

Telephone: 800-54-GRACE (toll-free nationwide)

GROVE CITY COLLEGE
GROVE CITY, PENNSYLVANIA

The College

While the College has changed to meet the needs of the society it serves, its basic philosophy has remained unchanged since its founding in 1876. It is a Christian liberal arts and sciences institution of ideal size and dedicated to the principle of providing the highest-quality education at the lowest possible cost. Wishing to remain truly independent and to retain its distinctive qualities as a private school governed by private citizens (trustees), it is one of the very few colleges in the country that does not accept any state or federal monies. Affiliated with the Presbyterian Church (U.S.A.) but not narrowly denominational, the College believes that to be well educated a student should be exposed to the central ideas of the Judeo-Christian tradition. A 20-minute chapel program offered Tuesday and Thursday mornings, along with a Sunday evening worship service, challenge students in their faith. Sixteen chapel services per semester are required out of forty opportunities. Religious organizations and activities exist to provide fellowship and spiritual growth.

Academic Program

The general education requirements provide all students with a high level of cultural literacy and communication skills. They include 38–50 semester hours of courses with emphases in the humanities, social sciences, and natural sciences and in quantitative and logical reasoning, as well as a language requirement for nonengineering and science majors. Degree candidates must also complete the requirements in their field of concentration, physical education, electives, and convocation. To graduate, a student must have completed 128 semester hours (136 in engineering) plus 4 convocation credits. About 80 percent of those entering as freshmen stay and receive a diploma.

Financial Aid

Because the College's tuition charges are low, every student, in effect, receives significant financial assistance. More than 30 percent of the freshmen receive additional aid from GCC. Students applying for financial assistance must complete the Free Application for Federal Student Aid. Job opportunities are available both on and off campus.

Application and Information

A regular admission applicant should take the SAT I or ACT by October or November of the senior year in high school. The application should include scores on the SAT I (preferred) or the ACT, a high school transcript, references, a recommendation from the student's principal or counselor, and a nonrefundable application fee of $25. An application may be submitted after the eleventh grade. An early decision applicant should take the entrance test in the eleventh grade, visit the College for an interview, and submit the application by November 15; notification of the admission decision is mailed on December 15. Approved early decision applicants must accept by January 15 and submit a nonrefundable deposit of $200. Applicants seeking regular decision must submit the completed application and supporting documents by February 15 of their senior year. Notification of the admission decision is mailed on March 15. Students who are offered admission should reply as soon as possible, but no later than May 1, and include a nonrefundable deposit of $150. Applications received after February 15 will be considered as space permits. The College receives five applications for every freshman vacancy. Additional information may be obtained from:

Jeffrey C. Mincey
Director of Admissions
Grove City College
100 Campus Drive
Grove City, Pennsylvania 16127-2104

Telephone: 412-458-2100
Fax: 412-458-3395
E-mail: admissions@gcc.edu
Web site: http://www.gcc.edu

HAMPSHIRE COLLEGE
AMHERST, MASSACHUSETTS

The College

Hampshire College was founded in 1965 through the cooperative efforts of educators at Amherst, Mount Holyoke, and Smith colleges and the University of Massachusetts. Individualized programs of study, close collaboration between faculty and students, multidisciplinary learning, and an emphasis on independent research and creative work have been the foundation of Hampshire's program since its opening in 1970.

Academic Program

Students complete three divisions of study, rather than the traditional freshman–senior sequence. In Division I, Basic Studies, students explore their interests by taking courses and pursuing research or creative projects in each of Hampshire's four schools. In Division II, the Concentration, they gain mastery of their chosen field through continued course work and independent study and internships or study in other countries. In Division III, Advanced Studies, students complete a major academic or creative project—a written thesis, artistic exhibition or performance, or scientific experiment. Finally, every student must engage in community service sometime during his or her Hampshire career. Students at Hampshire receive extensive written evaluation of their work instead of traditional letter or number grades. Passage from one division to the next is marked by a final meeting in which a faculty committee reviews the student's activities and accomplishments.

Financial Aid

Hampshire has developed a generous financial aid program, which awards more than $8.5 million in grant aid annually. To be considered for an award, applicants must demonstrate financial need and submit all required materials by the stated deadline. Financial aid for international students is competitive, with maximum awards covering only up to tuition. Financial aid packages consist of income from on-campus employment (work-study), student loans, and grant assistance. Hampshire also offers a limited number of scholarships based on academic merit. The Harold F. Johnson Scholarship, named for the College's founding benefactor, provides renewable grants ranging from $5000 to $7500 to entering students who have demonstrated outstanding academic achievement. Talented students who are members of minority groups may receive Arturo Schomburg Scholarships of $7500 per year that are renewable for three years. Students wishing to apply for financial aid at Hampshire College must do so at the same time they apply for admission. Any student applying for financial aid must complete the Hampshire financial aid application, a PROFILE application, a Separated/Divorced Parent Statement (if applicable), and the Free Application for Federal Student Aid (FAFSA). Applicants register to receive a customized PROFILE application from the College Scholarship Service (CSS) and return the completed PROFILE application to them.

Application and Information

Applications for September admission are due February 1 for first-year students and March 1 for transfer students. Notification is sent out on April 1; accepted students must respond to Hampshire's offer of admission by May 1, the standard Candidates Reply Date. Students who wish to apply for Early Decision must submit their application materials no later than November 15; notification is mailed December 15. Applications for February admission are due November 15, and notification follows on December 15. Applications from international students are accepted for fall entry only and are due February 1 for first-year and transfer students. Hampshire offers a nonbinding Early Action Plan, with applications due January 1 and notification sent on January 21. Early Action Plan students have until May 1 to notify Hampshire of their intention to enroll. Under its Early Entrance Plan, Hampshire admits a limited number of high school juniors who show exceptional academic ability and personal maturity. An interview is required. For complete information and application materials, students should contact:

Director of Admissions
Hampshire College
Amherst, Massachusetts 01002-5001

Telephone: 413-582-5471
E-mail: admissions@hamp.hampshire.edu

HARDIN–SIMMONS UNIVERSITY
ABILENE, TEXAS

The University

Established in 1891, Hardin-Simmons University (HSU) is rich in tradition and heritage. The University has been affiliated with the Baptist General Convention of Texas since 1941 and is a leading institution of higher education. HSU has approximately 2,300 students (half men, half women) from thirty-seven states and eleven countries. Throughout the years, the University's graduates have assumed places of responsibility in business, religion, education, the professions, politics, music, art, and science. The major University divisions are the College of Arts and Sciences, the Graduate School, the Irvin School of Education, the Logsdon School of Theology, the School of Business and Finance, the School of Music, and the School of Nursing. The University competes as a member of the American Southwest Conference and NCAA Division III. The University's Mabee Athletic Complex, besides serving as home for the Cowboy basketball team, houses an aerobics facility, Nautilus equipment, racquetball courts, classrooms, offices, and the HSU Athletic Hall of Fame. Other athletics facilities include an indoor and an outdoor pool, six Brunswick bowling lanes, a lighted track and intramural field, The John Hunter Field for baseball, Sandefer Field House, and the Shelton Stadium for football and soccer. Varsity sports at HSU include baseball, basketball, and football for men; basketball and volleyball for women; and golf, soccer, and tennis for men and women. The University and its programs are fully accredited by the Southern Association of Colleges and Schools, National Association of Schools of Music, National League for Nursing, Texas Education Agency, Council on Social Work Education, and Board of Nurse Examiners for the State of Texas. Hardin-Simmons also holds membership in the American Association of Colleges for Teacher Education, American Assembly of Collegiate Schools of Business, American Council on Education, American Mathematical Society, Association of Southern Baptist Colleges and Schools, Association of Texas Colleges and Universities, Mathematical Association of America, and Texas Association of Schools of Art. Alumnae of the University are approved for membership in the American Association of University Women.

Academic Program

The University seeks to promote a thorough education in a nurturing Christian environment on campus so that each student has an opportunity to do his or her best at all times. A faculty adviser from the student's major field of study is assigned to give assistance in planning the student's course of study. Counseling is always available. Students are encouraged to assume the responsibility for meeting their advisers and to feel free to take problems of any nature to them, to the counselor to students, or to someone in the Family Psychology Center on campus. The semester hour is the unit of course credit at Hardin-Simmons. At least 124 hours are required for all undergraduate degrees. Students who wish to take course work without reference to the degree requirements are unclassified students; however, all students are urged to work toward meeting the requirements of a degree.

Financial Aid

Numerous financial aid programs are available. The University has funds for student employment, scholarships, and grants and also participates in the Federal Perkins Loan, Federal Pell Grant, Federal Supplemental Educational Opportunity Grant, Federal Work-Study, and Federal Stafford Student Loan programs and the Tuition Equalization Grant Program for Texas students. There are also special incentives for dependents of Baptist denominational workers and for licensed Baptist ministers. There is no financial assistance available for international students.

Application and Information

For more information, students should contact:

Office of Enrollment Services
Hardin-Simmons University
Box 16050
Abilene, Texas 79698-6050

Telephone: 915-670-1206
800-568-2692 (toll-free)

HAVERFORD COLLEGE
HAVERFORD, PENNSYLVANIA

The College

Haverford is the first college established by members of the Society of Friends (Quakers). Founded in 1833, Haverford has chosen to remain small, undergraduate, and residential to carry out its educational philosophy and to maintain a strong sense of community. An Honor Code is created and directed by students and is an important element of the Haverford community. The Honor Code allows students to directly confront academic and social issues in a spirit of cooperation and mutual respect. Haverford's 1,100 students represent forty-five states, Puerto Rico, the District of Columbia, and twenty countries. Nineteen percent of the students are students of color, while an additional 4 percent are international students.

Academic Program

Students plan their programs using established guidelines and with the help of faculty advisers. They must have at least three courses in each of the divisions of the College: humanities, social science, and natural science. In addition, they must fulfill requirements in foreign language, social justice, writing, and quantitative course work. Flexibility in the curriculum allows opportunities for independent study, foreign study, and noncollegiate academic study. Majors are selected at the end of the sophomore year. Normally, students take four courses a semester and thirty-two courses over four years. However, scheduling is flexible, and students may arrange programs to meet individual needs, including six-semester, seven-semester, and five-year programs. Credit is given on the basis of AP (Advanced Placement) examinations, A-Level examinations, and International Baccalaureate Higher Level examinations.

Financial Aid

The College has an extensive financial aid program. Approximately 36 percent of Haverford's students receive College grant aid. Candidates for Haverford College funded aid must file the Financial Aid PROFILE with the College Scholarship Service, along with the FAFSA. Applicants may register for the PROFILE by completing a short form, available from their local high school guidance office, and sending it to the College Scholarship Service. Regular decision students should complete the PROFILE registration process by January 2, so the College Scholarship Service can send the form and have students complete it by the January 31 deadline. The FAFSA is also available from high school guidance offices and must also be filed by January 31. Early decision candidates should complete the PROFILE registration process by October 15 and file the PROFILE form with the College Scholarship Service by November 15. Further details are given in the leaflet "Financial Aid at Haverford," which is included in the admission application booklet. Haverford's College Scholarship Service PROFILE code number is 2289, and the FAFSA code number is 003274.

Application and Information

The application deadlines for admission are November 15 for early decision candidates, January 15 for regular decision candidates, and March 31 for transfer candidates. Haverford also accepts the Common Application, which is available in school guidance offices. The admission office is open from 9 a.m. to 5 p.m. on weekdays (8:30 a.m. to 4:30 p.m. from June to August) and, during the fall, from 9 a.m. to noon on Saturday. For more information or to arrange an interview or tour appointment, students should contact:

Office of Admission
Haverford College
370 Lancaster Avenue
Haverford, Pennsylvania 19041-1392

Telephone: 610-896-1350
Fax: 610-896-1338
E-mail: admitme@haverford.edu
Web site: http://www.haverford.edu

HAWAII PACIFIC UNIVERSITY
HONOLULU, HAWAII

The University

Hawaii Pacific University is an independent, coeducational, career-oriented comprehensive university with a foundation in the liberal arts. Undergraduate and graduate degrees are offered in close to fifty different areas. Hawaii Pacific prides itself on maintaining small class size (averaging 25) and individual attention to students. Students at HPU come from every state in the union and more than eighty countries around the world. The diversity of the student body stimulates learning about other cultures firsthand, both in and out of the classroom. There is no majority population at HPU. Students are encouraged to examine the values, customs, traditions, and principles of others to gain a clearer understanding of their own perspectives. HPU students develop friendships with students from throughout the United States and the world, important connections for success in the global economy of the twenty-first century. The Housing Office at HPU offers many services and options for students. Residence halls with cafeteria service are available on the Windward campus, while University-sponsored apartments are available in the Waikiki area for those seeking more independent living arrangements.

Academic Program

The baccalaureate student must complete at least 124 semester hours of credit. Forty-five of these credits provide the student with a strong foundation in the liberal arts, with the remaining credits comprised of appropriate upper-division classes in the student's major and related areas. The academic year operates on a modified 4-1-4 semester system, featuring a five-week winter intersession. The University also offers extensive summer sessions. A student can earn up to 15 semester credits during the summer. By attending these supplemental sessions, a student may complete the baccalaureate degree program in three years. A five-year B.S.B.A./M.B.A. program is also available.

Financial Aid

The University provides financial aid for qualified students through institutional, state, and federal aid programs. Approximately 50 percent of the University's students receive financial aid. Among the forms of aid available are Federal Perkins Loans, Federal Stafford Student Loans, Guaranteed Parental Loans, Federal Pell Grants, and Federal Supplemental Educational Opportunity Grants. To apply for aid, students must submit the Free Application for Federal Student Aid (FAFSA). The FAFSA may be submitted at any time, but the priority deadline is March 1.

Application and Information

Candidates are notified of admission decisions on a rolling basis, usually within two weeks of receipt of application materials. Early entrance and deferred entrance are available. HPU accepts the Common Application form.

For further information and for application materials, students should contact:

Office of Admissions
Hawaii Pacific University
1164 Bishop Street, Suite 200
Honolulu, Hawaii 96813

Telephone: 808-544-0238
800-669-4724 (toll-free)
Fax: 808-544-1136
E-mail: admissions@hpu.edu
Web site: http://www.hpu.edu/

HOFSTRA UNIVERSITY
HEMPSTEAD, NEW YORK

The University

Hofstra University is traditional, contemporary, and innovative. As universities go, Hofstra is young, but the extraordinary vigor and growth shown in the brief span of its life have marked it as an educational phenomenon. The University offers the student with ability a good education and unusual opportunities for choice. In many fields, special facilities—clinics, Hofstra's Television Institute, the radio station, a reading center, and a playhouse—enrich the curriculum. Hofstra's philosophy is to provide a strong foundation in the liberal arts and sciences. The University's ultimate goal for its students is "the pursuit of knowledge, understanding, and wisdom upon which a good life can be built." The extracurricular program is full and varied. As a result of the Program for the Higher Education of the Disabled, 100 percent of the facilities on campus are accessible, and necessary services are provided for wheelchair-bound and other disabled students who meet all academic requirements for admission.

Academic Program

The requirement for the B.A. degree is 124 semester hours, of which 94 must be in liberal arts and 30 in free electives. Successful completion of at least 124 semester hours with a quality point average of 2.0 or better is required for graduation. For the major, each academic department defines the special pattern of required and suggested study that suits its discipline. Beyond this major requirement, five general requirements in humanities, natural sciences, social sciences, English, and foreign languages must be fulfilled. A candidate for graduation with the degree of B.B.A. must successfully complete at least 125 semester hours with a quality point average of 2.0 or better, completing at least 62 hours in liberal arts subjects (humanities, mathematics, natural sciences, and social sciences), 30 hours in general business courses (accounting, business law, quantitative methods, business writing, finance, and general business), and all major and additional requirements as listed under the department of specialization. Each of the scientific-technical programs leading to the B.S. degree requires a total of 124 to 134 semester hours, of which approximately half must be in liberal arts courses exclusive of those offered by the academic department of major specialization.

Financial Aid

Financial aid options range from scholarships through assistance grants to loans and part-time jobs. About 75 percent of all students receive financial help, and almost 65 percent work to earn part of their expenses. Scholarships average $3825 per year; loans average $2625 per year. Hofstra subscribes to the principles of the College Scholarship Service in determining the amount of awards. Federal funds include Federal Perkins Loans, Federal Pell and Federal Supplemental Educational Opportunity grants, and Federal Work-Study Program awards. To be considered for financial aid, completed financial aid applications and credentials (including the Free Application for Federal Student Aid) should be received on or before March 1.

Application and Information

Freshman applicants must submit the application, a $40 application fee, the high school transcript, test scores, and a guidance counselor's recommendation. Transfer students must submit an application, the application fee, high school and college transcripts, and test scores (if fewer than 24 semester hours were attempted at the previous college). For additional information, students should contact:

Dean of Admissions
Hofstra University
Hempstead, New York 11550

Telephone: 516-463-6700
800-HOFSTRA (toll-free)
Fax: 516-560-7660
E-mail: hofstra@hofstra.edu

IMMACULATA COLLEGE
IMMACULATA, PENNSYLVANIA

The College

Immaculata is a Catholic liberal arts college for women of all faiths that offers a friendly, individualized education with excellence as its ultimate goal. The College was founded in 1920 and has since grown to enroll 2,000 students in both undergraduate and graduate programs. The main building, Villa Maria Hall, is of neo-Renaissance architecture in gray stone with a red tile roof. The other thirteen major campus buildings are likewise gray stone with red tile roofs, unifying the aesthetic appearance of the campus. Approximately 400 traditional-age women attend the day division, with 85 percent of them living in campus housing. The evening division includes both graduate and undergraduate programs that are open to both men and women, most of whom commute. Traditional-age students represent fifteen states and twenty-six countries, giving the campus both ethnic and geographic diversity. Eleven percent of the traditional-age students are members of minority groups. Resident students live in four dormitory buildings containing both double and single rooms. Both resident and nonresident students participate in more than thirty student clubs and organizations that represent interests in athletics, student government, academic disciplines, community action, music, dance, theater, and student publications. Graduate degrees offered include the Master of Arts in cultural and linguistic diversity, counseling psychology, educational leadership administration, music therapy, and nutrition education. Doctoral degrees are offered in clinical psychology and education administration.

Academic Program

Two factors are emphasized in the educational program at Immaculata: a comprehensive liberal arts background and a major field of concentration that prepares students to begin a career or to attend graduate school. Degrees in all majors require 126 credits. This number includes 54 credits in a liberal arts core, which is required of all students. The honors program, an option for gifted students, offers an array of courses designed to give those who participate a special involvement in the learning process.

Financial Aid

Financial aid is available in the form of scholarships, grants, loans, and part-time campus employment through the resources of Immaculata, federal and state governments, and private endowments. Presidential and Immaculata scholarships are awarded for academic excellence. Approximately 90 percent of the students receive some form of aid, and all students who demonstrate need are offered financial aid packages. Beginning March 1, the College sends financial aid packages to accepted students as their files are completed.

Application and Information

Applications are accepted from prospective freshmen and transfer students until May 1 for the fall semester and until December 1 for the spring semester. Decisions are made on a rolling basis three to four weeks after an applicant's file is complete. All admission credentials should be sent to the address below. For further information, students should contact:

Director of Admission
Immaculata College
PO Box 642
Immaculata, Pennsylvania 19345-0901

Telephone: 610-647-4400 Ext. 3015
888-777-2780 (toll-free)
Fax: 610-251-1668
E-mail: admission@immaculata.edu
Web site: http://www.immaculata.edu

ITHACA COLLEGE
ITHACA, NEW YORK

The College

Coeducational and nonsectarian since its founding in 1892, Ithaca College enrolls approximately 5,800 students—about 2,600 men and 3,200 women. The College community is a multicultural one; virtually every state is represented in the student population, as are sixty-seven other countries. Students come to Ithaca because of its comprehensive program, a blend of preprofessional training and liberal arts education. The program is offered in five schools: the School of Humanities and Sciences (2,050 students), School of Business (450 students), Roy H. Park School of Communications (1,200 students), School of Health Sciences and Human Performance (1,400 students), and School of Music (450 students). There are approximately 250 graduate students. Among undergraduate comprehensive and liberal arts institutions in the United States, Ithaca College ranks in the top 8 percent in the number of graduates who have gone on to complete doctoral degrees. Ninety-five percent of first-year graduates are employed or are full-time graduate students.

Academic Program

Each degree offered requires a minimum of 120 semester hours and a specified number of liberal arts credits. Minors, academic concentrations, and numerous teacher certification programs are available. Exceptionally qualified applicants to the School of Humanities and Sciences will be invited to apply to the honors program, an intensive four-year program of interdisciplinary seminars. The writing center offers programs to students who need assistance in any stage of the writing process, and Academic Computing and Client Services aids students in the use of personal and College computers. The Gerontology Institute provides opportunities for students to work with the elderly in a variety of community settings. The Center for Teacher Education serves to coordinate the twenty-five courses of study leading to a teaching certificate.

Financial Aid

Financial aid, which totals approximately $65 million from all sources, is extended to 75 percent of Ithaca students and is based on need. To apply for financial aid, students should check the proper space on the College's admission application, and if seeking federal aid, submit the Free Application for Federal Student Aid (FAFSA) by February 1 with the U.S. Department of Education at the address indicated on the form. Early decision and physical therapy candidates should follow the time line outlined under the Application and Information section below. All accepted applicants are considered for merit aid in recognition of their academic and personal achievement. Programs providing grants and loans include the Federal Work-Study, Federal Pell Grant, Federal Perkins Loan, Federal Stafford Student Loan, and Federal Supplemental Educational Opportunity Grant.

Application and Information

Application should be made no later than March 1; applicants are notified by April 15 and must confirm their enrollment by May 1. There is a $40 application fee. All students seeking federal aid should submit the FAFSA by February 1 with the U.S. Department of Education at the address indicated on the form. Early decision candidates should also file the College Scholarship Service PROFILE application by November 1, with all supporting materials received by November 15; applicants are notified by December 18 and must confirm their enrollment by February 1. Admission to the physical therapy program is through the early decision program only, and candidates follow the same time line. For additional information and application forms, students should contact:

Paula J. Mitchell
Director of Admission
Office of Admission
Ithaca College
100 Job Hall
Ithaca, New York 14850-7020

Telephone: 800-429-4274 (toll-free)
607-274-3124
Fax: 607-274-1900
Web site: http://www.ithaca.edu

JOHNSON STATE COLLEGE
JOHNSON, VERMONT

The College

Founded in 1828, Johnson State College served as a school for the training of teachers until the 1960s, when it expanded into the liberal arts and the sciences. The current enrollment is more than 1,600 men and women. The College is accredited by the New England Association of Schools and Colleges and is approved by the Vermont State Board of Higher Education. At the graduate level, the College offers the Master of Arts in Education degree in administration and supervision, early childhood education, elementary curricula, reading and language arts, special education of the gifted and talented, and special education of the handicapped; the Master of Arts in counseling; and the Master of Fine Arts in studio arts. More than thirty clubs and organizations provide a variety of student activities. These include *Basement Medicine* (the student newspaper), the Dance Ensemble, the Theater Club, the radio station (WJSC-FM), the Jazz Ensemble, the College Concert Band, and the Outing, Cycling, Astronomy, and International clubs. Varsity athletic competition is available for women in basketball, cross-country running, Nordic and Alpine skiing, soccer, softball, and tennis and for men in basketball, cross-country running, lacrosse, Nordic and Alpine skiing, soccer, and tennis. Many intramural and club sports, including indoor soccer, hockey, lacrosse, rugby, swimming, and volleyball, are also available.

Academic Program

The Johnson State curriculum provides students with a general liberal arts background and the opportunity for career preparation in a specific area. All students in four-year programs are required to complete at least 120 credit hours in the selected program of study. Those studying for the associate degree must complete at least 62 semester hours of credit in the selected program of study. Students may transfer internally from two-year to four-year programs. Transfer credit is awarded for courses in which a grade of C– or above was earned. Johnson State College accepts all credit earned for an awarded associate degree from an accredited college.

Financial Aid

Sixty-seven percent of Johnson's students receive financial assistance from federal, state, College, or other sources. Grants, loans, and work-study jobs are available for qualified students. Applicants for financial aid should file the Free Application for Federal Student Aid (FAFSA) by March 1 of the year preceding anticipated enrollment. All financial aid awards are based on need. The College offers renewable academic scholarships for both freshmen and transfers. Special scholarships are also available.

Application and Information

The College has a rolling admission policy and processes applications throughout the year. However, high school students seeking fall enrollment are encouraged to apply early in their senior year. The College admits first-year and transfer students regardless of their state of residence. Notification dates are also rolling. Students may enter at the beginning of the fall or spring semester. The student's application file is complete when the following items have been received: a completed application form, a $30 nonrefundable application fee, a transcript from the high school and any colleges previously attended, a writing sample, standardized test scores, and a reference from a teacher, a college adviser, or an employer. An enrollment deposit of $200 is required by May 1 or within two weeks of notification of acceptance if the applicant applies after May 1.

For application forms and further information, students should contact:

Jonathan H. Henry
Director of Admissions
Johnson State College
Johnson, Vermont 05656

Telephone: 802-635-1219
800-635-2356 (toll-free)
Fax: 802-635-1230
E-mail: jscapply@badger.jsc.vsc.edu

KENT STATE UNIVERSITY
KENT, OHIO

The University

Chartered in 1910, the University provides more than 170 fields of study in a wide range of undergraduate and graduate credit and noncredit programs. Two-year associate degree programs are offered through seven regional campuses in Ashtabula, Geauga, Stark, Trumbull, and Tuscarawas counties and in the cities of Salem and East Liverpool.

Academic Program

Kent State University's colleges and schools all maintain separate academic programs; completion of 39 credits of liberal education course work is a University requirement for all students. The number of credit hours required for graduation varies but is generally 129 semester hours. Credits can be transferred from previous college work satisfactorily completed or earned through work taken at one of Kent State University's regional campuses. Credit by examination is available. Generally, to earn a degree, students must earn at least 32 semester hours in residence. The Honors College offers four-year programs of undergraduate study with concurrent enrollment in one of the University's degree-granting programs. In addition, the Honors College offers advanced placement credit, early admission to high school students, and specialized academic advising. Its Experimental and Integrative Studies Division offers nontraditional learning experiences for the students and faculty of the entire University community.

Financial Aid

To be considered for financial aid awards, students must be admitted to the University and must submit the Free Application for Federal Student Aid (FAFSA). Ohio students should also check the Ohio Instructional Grant (OIG) box on the FAFSA if they are interested in being considered. Students planning to attend the fall semester as freshmen should apply for financial aid after January 1 and before April 1 of the same year. In order to meet the April 1 priority deadline, it is recommended that all financial aid forms be completed and mailed no later than February 15. Applications received after April 1 will be considered, but sufficient funds to assist all late applicants may be lacking. Additional information and forms are available from the Office of Student Financial Aid, 103 Michael Schwartz Center. Kent State University's Honors College awards merit scholarships to selected individuals who have the potential for superior scholarly and creative work at the University as determined by academic performance and creative artist competitions. For additional information, students should write to the Dean, Honors College, P.O. Box 5190. The Office of Student Financial Aid also administers numerous private scholarships, including the President's Scholarship for out-of-state students, the President's Grant for out-of-state students who are children of alumni, and various departmental scholarships. Kent also administers the Oscar Ritchie Memorial Scholarship competition for qualified high school juniors who are members of underrepresented minority groups, including African Americans, Hispanics, and Native Americans. Kent initiated the Founders Scholarship Program for academically talented freshmen entering the University in the fall. Qualified students are invited to campus to participate in an examination and meetings with faculty members. Scholarships range from full tuition, fees, room, and board to partial scholarships of varying amounts.

Application and Information

Application forms are available from the Office of Admissions upon request. A $30 nonrefundable application fee is required. Application early in the senior year helps ensure priority consideration for fall registration, residence hall preference, and financial aid. The application deadline is March 15.

Office of Admissions
Kent State University
P.O. Box 5190
Kent, Ohio 44242-0001

Telephone: 330-672-2444
800-988-KENT (toll-free)

KENTUCKY WESLEYAN COLLEGE
OWENSBORO, KENTUCKY

The College
The tradition of high-quality teaching and a talent for translating a liberal arts education into usable and useful service have long been hallmarks of Kentucky Wesleyan College (KWC). Founded by the United Methodist Church in 1858, the College's mission is to prepare leaders for the twenty-first century through a coordinated and integrated liberal arts education. To fulfill its mission, Kentucky Wesleyan offers Leadership KWC, a nationally recognized leadership program established with an $800,000 grant from the W. K. Kellogg Foundation. Liberal arts course work forms the basis of Leadership KWC and represents the College's belief that a solid liberal arts education provides the communication, problem-solving, and creative-thinking skills necessary for tomorrow's leaders. Students may choose to participate in Leadership XXI, a more extensive cocurricular leadership program that involves leadership courses, community service, leadership workshops, campus activity participation, and a senior thesis or project.

Academic Program
There are three academic divisions in the Kentucky Wesleyan College curriculum: the Natural Sciences, the Humanities and Fine Arts, and the Social Sciences. The requirements for the degrees of Bachelor of Science and Bachelor of Arts are based on the principle of a broad distribution of studies among the representative fields of human culture and a concentration of studies in a specific field. In most cases, 128 semester hours are required to obtain a bachelor's degree. Students have the opportunity to develop and carry out individual programs of studies related to their particular vocational or professional goal through the Interdisciplinary Studies (IDS) Program. Kentucky Wesleyan operates on a semester calendar with classes from late August to mid-December and from mid-January to mid-May.

Financial Aid
Kentucky Wesleyan participates in all federal student aid programs and is committed to helping each student meet his or her demonstrated financial need. No student should hesitate to apply for admission due to financial reasons. Kentucky Wesleyan awards more than $6.2 million each year in financial aid to eligible students. Kentucky residents may qualify for Kentucky Higher Education Assistance Authority Grants. In addition to federal and state financial aid programs, Kentucky Wesleyan invests more than $2.6 million annually in scholarships and grants for its students. Students who demonstrate a strong record of leadership in their school, church, place of employment, or community are encouraged to apply for Stanley Reed Leadership Awards. These awards range from $2000 to $4000 and are renewable annually (applications are available from the Office of Admission). For maximum financial aid consideration, students are requested to submit the Free Application for Federal Student Aid (FAFSA) and the Kentucky Wesleyan College Financial Aid Application by March 1. Kentucky Wesleyan is need-blind in its admission process.

Application and Information
The Office of Admission is open from 8 a.m. to 5 p.m., Monday through Friday, and on Saturday by appointment. Interested students are encouraged to visit the campus during one of the College's weekend open houses in the fall and winter or by individual appointment during the week. Students who wish to stay on campus overnight are welcome to do so at no charge. Students may apply for admission after completing their junior year. Applications are evaluated on a rolling basis, and students can expect to be notified of a decision within two weeks of completing their application for admission. To arrange a campus visit or request application materials, students should contact:

Office of Admission
Kentucky Wesleyan College
3000 Frederica Street
Box 1039
Owensboro, Kentucky 42302-1039

Telephone: 502-926-3111
800-999-0592 (toll free)
E-mail: admission@kwc.edu

LAGRANGE COLLEGE
LAGRANGE, GEORGIA

The College

Founded in 1831, LaGrange College is the oldest private college in Georgia. Affiliated with the United Methodist Church, LaGrange College seeks to admit any qualified student. With an enrollment of approximately 1,000 men and women and only 17 students in the average classroom, LaGrange College provides a challenging and supportive academic environment. Students live in college residence halls that provide 24-hour access to the College's fiber-optic computer network. This network provides continuous access to the Internet and the World Wide Web and also WordPerfect, Lotus 1-2-3, e-mail, computer games, and the on-line files of the College library. In addition to computer network access, each room is also outfitted with central air-conditioning, cable television, and local telephone service. The College is fully accredited by the Commission on Colleges of the Southern Association of Colleges and Schools as well as the University Senate of the United Methodist Church.

Academic Program

Each program of study contains a substantial general education component and extensive specified course work in the discipline in which the student has selected a major. Ninety-five quarter hours of general education courses are required for all bachelor's degrees. Most majors require an additional 100 quarter hours of credit beyond the general education curriculum. Students may be eligible for credit and/or exemption in certain areas through the Advanced Placement (AP) tests or the College-Level Examination Program (CLEP).

Financial Aid

As a private college, LaGrange is committed to helping meet the difference between the funds any student has available and the cost of attending LaGrange College. More than 80 percent of LaGrange students receive some combination of financial awards. These awards may include grants, loans, scholarships, and employment opportunities. Federal financial aid and institutional funds are available to all students who qualify. The state of Georgia provides additional funding for Georgia residents. All Georgia residents who enroll as full-time students receive the Georgia Tuition Equalization Grant in the amount of $1000 per year. The HOPE Scholarship, which totals $3000 per year, is awarded to all Georgia residents who have graduated from high school since 1996 with a B average and who enter as freshmen. Georgia residents who do not qualify for the HOPE Scholarship as freshmen may be able to obtain the HOPE Scholarship by maintaining a 3.0 grade point average through the freshman and sophomore years. Academic scholarships that range from $1000 to $4000 are also awarded. All accepted students are considered for scholarships; a separate application is not required. In 1995–96, all financial aid applicants were awarded financial aid. The average award totaled $9245 for the year.

Application and Information

Applications for admission are evaluated on a rolling basis and should be submitted at least one month prior to the beginning of the quarter in which entrance is desired. Applicants can expect to receive notification within two to three weeks of the date that all documents are submitted. Weekday campus visits are encouraged, and appointments can be arranged by contacting the Admission Office. For additional information, students should contact:

Office of Admission
LaGrange College
601 Broad Street
LaGrange, Georgia 30240

Telephone: 706-812-7260
Fax: 706-812-7348
E-mail: pdodson@mentor.lgc.peachnet.edu
Web site: http://www.lgc.peachnet.edu

LE MOYNE COLLEGE
SYRACUSE, NEW YORK

The College

Le Moyne College is a four-year Jesuit college of approximately 1,770 undergraduate students that uniquely balances a comprehensive liberal arts education with preparation for specific career paths or graduate study. Founded by the Society of Jesus in 1946, Le Moyne is the second-youngest of the twenty-eight Jesuit colleges and universities in the United States. The campus environment is one of a closely knit community. Le Moyne's personal approach to education is reflected in the quality of contact between students and faculty members. A wide range of student-directed activities, athletics, clubs, and service organizations complement the academic experience. Intramural sports are very popular with Le Moyne students, and approximately 60 percent of the students participate. Le Moyne also has sixteen NCAA intercollegiate teams (eight for men and eight for women). Approximately 74 percent of students live in residence halls and town houses on campus, and 26 percent of students live locally with their families. The Residence Hall Councils and the Le Moyne Student Programming Board organize many campus activities, including concerts, dances, a weekly film series, student talent programs, and special lectures as well as off-campus trips and skiing excursions.

Academic Program

While each major department has its own sequence requirements for the minimum 120 credit hours needed for the Le Moyne degree, the College is convinced that there is a fundamental intellectual discipline that should characterize the graduate of a superior liberal arts college. Le Moyne's core curriculum provides this foundation by including studies of English language and literature, philosophy, history, religious studies, science, mathematics, and social sciences. For exceptional students, Le Moyne offers an integral honors program that includes an interdisciplinary humanities sequence as well as departmental honors courses. Le Moyne also offers a part-time course of study during evening hours through its Center for Continuous Learning.

Financial Aid

Financial aid is offered to 95 percent of Le Moyne's students through scholarships, grants, loans, and work-study assignments, and the College meets 90 percent of the aggregate student need. Le Moyne offers a generous program of merit-based academic and athletic scholarships as well as financial aid based on a student's need and academic promise. Federal funds are available through the Federal Pell Grant, Federal Work-Study, Federal Supplemental Educational Opportunity Grant, and Federal Perkins Loan programs. A student's eligibility for need-based financial aid is determined from both the Free Application for Federal Student Aid (FAFSA) and the Le Moyne Financial Aid Application Form. It is recommended that these forms be mailed by February 1.

Application and Information

The Admission Committee reviews applications and mails decisions on a rolling admission cycle beginning January 1. The priority deadline for applications is March 1; all students who wish to be considered for academic non-need scholarships should have a completed application on file in the Office of Admission before this date. Students who wish to be considered under the early decision program must have a completed application submitted by December 1. Early decision applicants will by notified by December 15. Transfer students are encouraged to apply before May 1 for the fall semester and December 1 for the spring semester. A fun-filled two-day orientation program takes place in mid-summer.

David M. Pirani
Director of Admission
Le Moyne College
Syracuse, New York 13214-1399

Telephone: 315-445-4300
800-333-4733 Ext. 4300 (toll-free)

LIMESTONE COLLEGE
GAFFNEY, SOUTH CAROLINA

The College

Founded in 1845, Limestone is a fully accredited, private, coeducational liberal arts college. The College maintains a small student body (enrollment 350) and a well-qualified faculty in order to create an atmosphere in which each student will develop intellectually, physically, and socially. The College endeavors to help students prepare for a satisfying, useful life through the development of meaningful leisure-time activities, effective communication skills, responsible decision-making abilities, and lifelong aspirations. In addition to its programs on campus, Limestone offers several of its academic majors in an accelerated evening and Saturday format (Block Program) at several locations throughout South Carolina. These programs are intended primarily for working adults. Extracurricular activities play a vital part in the development of all students at Limestone College. Among these activities are intercollegiate athletics in men's baseball, basketball, golf, lacrosse, soccer, and tennis and in women's basketball, lacrosse, soccer, softball, tennis, and volleyball. Students who are interested in music have the opportunity to participate in several instrumental and choral ensembles. The classrooms, library, laboratories, auditorium, bookstore, post office, and administrative offices are housed in buildings that border the central and circular drives, making each easily accessible to the others. The back campus has a plaza of four dormitories, and a cafeteria is located nearby.

Academic Program

The course of study leading to the B.A., B.S., or A.A. degree consists of four elements: requirements in communication and quantitative skills; a general liberal arts program, involving five different subject groups; courses in the major; and appropriate electives. The baccalaureate degree programs require the completion of a minimum of 120 semester hours. Advanced placement and credit are given for scores of 3 or higher on the Advanced Placement examinations of the College Board. An honors program involving special courses, seminars, and lectures is available for exceptional students. Admission to this program is contingent upon outstanding high school grades and scores on the Scholastic Assessment Test (SAT I) of the College Board, the completion of a special application, and an interview. Almost 10 percent of all Limestone students are enrolled in this rigorous academic program. A Program for Alternative Learning Styles (PALS) is available for qualified students with certified learning disabilities who might not otherwise succeed at the college level.

Financial Aid

Limestone College endeavors to meet the financial need of any qualified student through scholarships, grants, loans, work-study opportunities, or a combination of these. Limestone offers merit scholarships to students with outstanding academic, leadership, or athletic abilities as well as to those who have exceptional talents in such areas as art and music. More than 90 percent of Limestone College students receive some type of financial aid. Because institutional financial aid is limited, students are urged to submit their applications for admission and financial aid as early as possible.

Application and Information

Completed application forms for admission and for financial aid should be sent to the director of admissions at Limestone College. It is recommended that applications be submitted by May 1. Any admission applications received after that date are considered on a space-available basis. The College practices a rolling admissions policy. As soon as the application, high school transcript, and test scores have been received, the applicant is notified of his or her status. Upon acceptance, a student is required to submit a $100 deposit.

Director of Admissions
Limestone College
1115 College Drive
Gaffney, South Carolina 29340

Telephone: 864-488-4554
800-795-7151 (toll-free)
Fax: 864-487-8706

LOYOLA UNIVERSITY CHICAGO
CHICAGO, ILLINOIS

The University
Loyola University Chicago is the most comprehensive Jesuit university in the United States and has one of the largest endowments of all Catholic universities in the country. Founded in 1870 by priests of the Society of Jesus, Loyola continues the Jesuit commitment to education, which is well-grounded in the liberal arts and traditionally based on excellent teaching. Loyola attracts students from all fifty states and seventy-four other countries to its eleven schools, colleges, and institutes: the Stritch School of Medicine, the School of Law, the College of Arts and Sciences, the School of Business Administration, the Niehoff School of Nursing, the School of Education, the School of Social Work, the Graduate School, the Institute of Pastoral Studies, the Institute of Human Resources and Industrial Relations, and Mundelein College. Each year, Loyola enrolls 1,100 freshmen and 500 transfer students. The University seeks to provide an environment that will enhance the social and spiritual growth of students. More than 140 student organizations, including fifteen national fraternities and sororities, and extensive recreational sports programs and facilities are provided.

Academic Program
Jesuit educators believe that a solid foundation in the liberal arts and sciences is essential for students entering all professions. Loyola's Core Curriculum is designed to give students this foundation. The core requirements vary by college but usually include courses in literature, expressive arts, history, social sciences, mathematical and natural sciences, philosophy, and theology. Most majors require 128 semester hours for graduation. Exceptionally well qualified students may apply to the Honors Program. Students may receive credit through the Advanced Placement Program (AP Program) tests, the International Baccalaureate (I.B.), and certain College-Level Examination Program (CLEP) tests are accepted.

Financial Aid
Loyola attempts to meet the financial need of as many students as possible. Seventy-eight percent of Loyola students receive some form of aid, including University-funded scholarships and grants, federal and state grants, work-study, and loans. Students are encouraged to file the Free Application for Federal Student Aid (FAFSA) and the College Scholarship Service PROFILE Form by mid-February in order to receive consideration for all types of aid. Merit scholarships are awarded to entering freshmen who have outstanding academic records. Presidential, Damen, and Loyola scholarships are awarded to students who rank at the top of their high school graduating class and score well on the ACT or SAT I. Scholarship amounts for these programs are $5000–$10,000 per year. These awards are renewable for up to three years. Other scholarships available include competitive awards for students admitted to the Honors Program and students from Jesuit/BVM/Sisters of Christian Charity high schools, theater scholarships (awarded by audition), and debate, leadership, nursing, and public accounting awards. Transfer students who have completed 30 hours of college credit with an outstanding record of academic achievement may receive a Transfer Academic Scholarship. These awards are renewable for up to three years.

Application and Information
Applicants are notified of the admission decision three to four weeks after the application, supporting credentials, secondary school counselor recommendation, and $25 application fee are received. Prospective students are encouraged to visit the campus. The Undergraduate Admission Office encourages students to schedule individual appointments and campus tours or to participate in one of the many campus programs offered throughout the year. To obtain an application and further information and to arrange a visit, students should contact:

Undergraduate Admission Office
Loyola University Chicago
820 North Michigan Avenue
Chicago, Illinois 60611

Telephone: 312-915-6500
800-262-2373 (toll-free)
E-mail: admission@luc.edu
Web site: http://www.luc.edu/

LOYOLA UNIVERSITY NEW ORLEANS
NEW ORLEANS, LOUISIANA

The University

Founded by the Jesuits in 1912, Loyola University's more than 35,000 graduates have excelled in innumerable professional fields for more than eighty years. Loyola students represent fifty states and fifty-nine countries. More than 47 percent of the students permanently reside outside Louisiana, and 34 percent belong to minority groups. Loyola's 20-acre main campus and 4-acre Broadway campus are located in the historic uptown area of New Orleans and are hubs of student activity. The Joseph A. Butt, S. J., College of Business Administration is fully accredited at both the undergraduate and graduate levels by the American Assembly of Collegiate Schools of Business and houses the Mildred Soule and Clarence A. Lengendre Chair in Business Ethics.

Academic Program

Once enrolled at Loyola, students are introduced to the Common Curriculum, designed to give them a well-rounded preparation in their major field of concentration as well as the ability to understand and reflect on disciplines allied to or outside their major. The curriculum is divided into four categories: major, minor, Common Curriculum, and elective courses. Students must meet the requirements of their degree program as specified by their particular college; the minimum four-year program requires 128 hours. Common Curriculum courses include seven introductory courses in English composition, math, science, philosophy, religion, literature, and history and nine upper-division courses in humanities, social science, and natural science. Through the Early Scholars/Early Artists Program, academically gifted and artistically talented local high school sophomores, juniors, and seniors may participate in challenging college courses and earn academic credit. (Interested students should contact the Office of Admissions for more information.) The College of Arts and Sciences also requires a minimum of one year of study in a modern foreign language. The honors program and independent studies provide special opportunities for qualified students.

Financial Aid

Loyola University's endowment provides money for financial aid in addition to that provided by federal funding. Assistance in the forms of scholarships, loans, work-study program awards, and grants is awarded on the basis of academic achievement and need. More than 450 scholarships are awarded annually to students with competitive grades and test scores. To compete for one of the scholarships, students must have a GPA of at least 3.2 and competitive standardized test scores. Offers of financial aid are not made until after admission. Notifications of awards are sent within four weeks of the receipt of completed financial aid applications. Awards of need-based financial aid packages are made on a first-come, first-served basis.

Application and Information

Interested students are encouraged to contact:

Office of Admissions
Loyola University
6363 St. Charles Avenue, Box 18
New Orleans, Louisiana 70118

Telephone: 504-865-3240
800-4-LOYOLA (toll-free)
Fax: 504-865-3383
Web site: http://www.loyno.edu

LUTHER COLLEGE
DECORAH, IOWA

The College

As an academic community, the students and faculty of Luther College are committed to liberal learning in the arts and sciences. Founded in 1861 by Norwegian immigrants, Luther is a college of the Evangelical Lutheran Church in America. Most students live on campus in the seven residence halls. Eighty-four percent of the 2,409 students come from Iowa, Minnesota, Wisconsin, and Illinois. All together, thirty-eight states and forty-eight other nations are represented in the student body. Throughout the year, the College provides a stimulating cultural and educational atmosphere by bringing distinguished public figures, theater groups, musicians, and educators to the campus.

Academic Program

Luther operates on a 4-1-4 academic calendar. The first semester runs from September to December, followed by a 3-week January Term and the second semester, which runs from February to May. Two 4-week summer sessions are offered, one in June and the other in July. Each candidate is required to complete satisfactorily a total of 128 semester hours of credit with a C average or better. At least 76 of the required 128 semester hours must be earned outside the major discipline. Each senior writes a research paper in his or her major. Students are required to complete the following number of semester hours of credit in designated areas: 12 of Paideia, an interdisciplinary course; 9 of religion/philosophy; 8 of natural science (4 of which may be in mathematics); 8 of social science; 3–9 of foreign language or culture (proficiency based); 3 of fine arts; and 2 of physical education. Demonstration of competency in mathematics is required. Advanced placement and credit by examination are available. A qualified student may develop an interdisciplinary major in consultation with a faculty adviser.

Financial Aid

More than 80 percent of all Luther students receive some financial aid in the form of grants, such as the Federal Pell Grant; scholarships from Luther and other sources; loans; and jobs on campus. Luther awards Regents and Presidential scholarships to applicants demonstrating superior academic achievement. The amount of aid given is determined by the College's analysis of the Free Application for Federal Student Aid. The priority deadline for a financial aid application is March 1 each year. Students receive notification of financial aid awards after their acceptance for admission.

Application and Information

An application, SAT I or ACT scores, an educator's reference, a transcript of previous academic work, and a $20 application fee are required for admission. On-campus interviews are recommended but not required. For more information about Luther, students should contact:

Admissions Office
Luther College
Decorah, Iowa 52101-1042

Telephone: 319-387-1287
800-458-8437 (toll-free)
Fax: 319-387-2159
319-387-1060 (international)
E-mail: admissions@luther.edu (admissions)
lutherfa@luther.edu (financial planning)
lundsony@luther.edu (international)
Web site: http://www.luther.edu

LYNCHBURG COLLEGE
LYNCHBURG, VIRGINIA

The College

Lynchburg College is a fully accredited, coeducational, nonsectarian liberal arts college related to the Christian Church (Disciples of Christ). The College is committed to the principle that every individual is of infinite worth, and it endeavors to provide a program of liberal education consistent with the needs of contemporary society. It draws its undergraduate student body of 1,517 men and women from thirty-one states and fifteen countries. There are service (Cardinal Key) and honor (Phi Kappa Phi) organizations, more than 40 clubs, five fraternities, and three sororities, as well as opportunities to participate in dramatic productions, student publications, religious activities, and musical performances. The varsity athletics program is widely diversified and includes baseball, basketball, cross-country, equestrian sports, golf, indoor and outdoor track and field, lacrosse, soccer, and tennis for men and basketball, cross-country, equestrian sports, field hockey, lacrosse, soccer, softball, tennis, track, and volleyball for women.

Academic Program

To be eligible for a degree, a student must complete at least 124 semester hours of college-level academic work. In addition, a degree candidate must have a grade point average of at least 2.0 on all work undertaken, plus an average of at least 2.0 on all work undertaken in the major field. The curriculum at Lynchburg College is divided into two general areas; some additional hours are available for students to explore course work in free elective areas of their choice. The first of the two areas of study consists of General Education Requirements (GERs) selected from the broad disciplines of world literature, fine arts, philosophy, religious studies, mathematics, history, social science, laboratory science, foreign languages, and health and movement science. The second of the two general areas is the major. The College offers forty-four majors, ranging from education and business to the sciences and the humanities, as well as eleven preprofessional programs. Outstanding students may be selected to participate in the College's Westover Honors Program. An Advanced Placement Scholars Program permits some students to enter with advanced standing, credit, or both. Credit is also awarded on the basis of satisfactory scores on the CLEP subject exams.

Financial Aid

Lynchburg College administers a financial aid budget of more than $12 million. These resources are awarded to students as a result of meritorious achievement and/or demonstrated need. Lynchburg College offers academic and achievement scholarships averaging $8500 that are based on performance and accomplishments at the high school or community college level. These awards are renewable each year until the student graduates, as long as the recipient maintains a qualifying minimum academic average each year. Free early aid estimates are available for students. To determine eligibility for need-based financial aid, the student should complete the Free Application for Federal Student Aid (FAFSA), which may be obtained at most high schools and at Lynchburg College. The FAFSA results will determine the student's eligibility for federally funded grants and loans and other support such as work-study opportunities. In addition, students from Virginia are eligible to apply for the Virginia Tuition Assistance grant.

Application and Information

Early decision admission applications must be received by November 15; notification of acceptance will be made by December 15. All other applications are processed on a rolling admissions basis. Applicants will be notified of the status of their application within two weeks of the date their application file is completed. For information, students should contact:

Dr. David G. Behrs, Vice President for Enrollment Management
Lynchburg College
1501 Lakeside Drive
Lynchburg, Virginia 24501

Telephone: 804-522-8300
800-426-8101 (toll-free)
Fax: 804-522-0653

MAHARISHI UNIVERSITY OF MANAGEMENT
FAIRFIELD, IOWA

The University

Maharishi University of Management (Maharishi International University 1971–95) was founded in 1971 by Maharishi Mahesh Yogi to make education complete so that every student may enjoy great success and fulfillment in life. It is accredited at the bachelor's, master's, and doctoral levels by the North Central Association of Colleges and Schools. The University is respected for its academic excellence in education, its healthy and harmonious environment, and its high quality of student life. It is unique in adding to traditional education systematic programs for students to develop their full potential. They make rapid progress not only in academic achievement, but also in developing their creativity, intelligence, and radiant good health. Academic excellence means that students study with outstanding faculty members, including internationally recognized scholars and researchers who hold degrees from such universities as Oxford, Harvard, Stanford, Princeton, Yale, and Massachusetts Institute of Technology. Students enjoy their studies even more as the result of learning systematic programs, including the Transcendental Meditation program, which expands the "container" of knowledge—the mind—to increase their learning capacity, broaden their comprehension, unfold their full creative potential, and acquire more and more knowledge. Students come to study at Maharishi University of Management from almost every state and more than ninety countries. Whether students major in the arts, sciences, or humanities, in business, engineering, or computer science, they learn to apply knowledge to practical, professional values. University graduates are successful in careers in business, education, the arts, and the sciences and have been engaged by many leading corporations, including IBM, Citibank, AT&T Bell Laboratories, Ford Motor Company, Xerox, Motorola, Apple Computer, Hewlett-Packard, American Express, and Union Bank of Switzerland. Students get a head start in their careers through internship opportunities with high-technology companies based in Fairfield that have offices nationwide and even worldwide.

Academic Program

Students study one course at a time through the "block system," which allows them to go more deeply into each subject and retain more knowledge with greater ease and enjoyment. They enjoy a learning experience that gives them the wholeness of knowledge in every class—faculty members relate every part of each discipline students study to the whole of the discipline and the whole to the deepest level of the student's own intelligence. This approach makes learning personally relevant—students feel at home with all knowledge. First-year undergraduate students explore more than twenty disciplines in light of the interdisciplinary principles of the Science of Creative Intelligence, a new discipline that connects each branch of knowledge to the whole tree of knowledge. Through these first-year core courses, students become thoroughly prepared to choose their major fields of study.

Financial Aid

The financial aid priority filing date is April 15, and the deadline for fall admission is July 15. Notification of awards is given on a rolling basis. Filing a Free Application for Federal Student Aid (FAFSA) is required. Federal Work-Study, Federal Pell Grant, FSEOG, Federal Stafford Student Loan, and Federal Perkins Loan programs are available, as are state grants, loans, and/or work-study. The University also provides institutional funds for grants and loans and both merit- and need-based scholarships.

Application and Information

For more information, students should contact:

Brad Mylett, Director of Admissions
Maharishi University of Management
Fairfield, Iowa 52557

Telephone: 515-472-1110
E-mail: admissions@mum.edu
Web site: http://www.mum.edu

MAINE COLLEGE OF ART
PORTLAND, MAINE

The College

Maine College of Art (MECA) is northern New England's only professional four-year college of art and design offering the Bachelor of Fine Arts degree in eight studio majors. Founded in 1882, the College is a fully accredited, independent college with an enrollment of approximately 300 students who come from New England and throughout the United States as well as other countries. In 1992, the school changed its name from Portland School of Art to Maine College of Art. The College has earned a reputation for an intimate learning atmosphere with a low student-faculty ratio of 10:1. Its unparalleled location combines many cultural activities with a superb natural environment, and its accomplished faculty members, who are often found working alongside their students, are uniquely dedicated to the students' goals.

Academic Program

The structured four-year B.F.A. degree curriculum develops students' abilities in perception, organization, and expression and increases their self-understanding, oral and written skills, and sense of personal place in human thought and cultural accomplishment. The academic year consists of two 15-week semesters. A comprehensive Thesis Exhibition of work accomplished during the fourth year in the student's major area is shown at the end of the school year. Maine College of Art is noted for its strong two-year foundation program in drawing and two- and three-dimensional design, which precedes study in the major. The mastery of these fundamentals permits students to devote the greater part of their time in the second two years to the major. Throughout the four years, art history and liberal arts studies are critical elements of the educational program. Such knowledge fosters and enriches ideas for the artist's work. The program is designed to equip students with the skills, visual insights, self-confidence, and self-discipline traditionally associated with the professional artist or designer. An exchange program with Bowdoin College, located 20 miles north of Portland, allows full-time students at Maine College of Art to take academic courses at Bowdoin College at no additional tuition charge. The College belongs to the Greater Portland Alliance of Colleges and Universities, which allows exchanges for credit at five different area institutions. Prior to taking such courses, interested students must fulfill their English composition and art history survey requirements at Maine College of Art and must have the approval of the appropriate department head. The College offers a summer Early College Program for high school students, which bears college credit. Scholarships for the high school Early College Program are available. Maine College of Art's year-round Continuing Studies Program offers credit courses in a variety of disciplines for adults. Classes for students in grades 4–12 are offered on Saturdays during the academic year as well as on weekdays in the summer.

Financial Aid

Maine College of Art offers a wide range of financial aid programs and services to assist students and families with paying for college. The College participates in all federal and state financial aid programs and also offers a significant amount of institutional grant and scholarship funding. Alternative loan programs based on student and/or family credit are available to supplement traditional forms of financial aid. The deadline for preferential consideration of financial aid requests is March 1.

Application and Information

A complete packet of materials may be obtained by contacting:

Admissions Office
Maine College of Art
97 Spring Street
Portland, Maine 04101

Telephone: 207-775-3052
800-639-4808 (toll-free)
E-mail: admsns@meca.edu
Web site: http://www.meca.edu/gdmeca

MAINE MARITIME ACADEMY
CASTINE, MAINE

The Academy

Maine Maritime Academy (MMA) offers a unique learning experience and a tradition of seafaring education. The hands-on, practical application of classroom instruction is found in all academic areas. Established in 1941 with an inaugural class of 28, the Academy had as its mission the provision of a comprehensive course of instruction and professional training to prepare graduates to become licensed officers in the U.S. Merchant Marines or commissioned officers in the U.S. Navy or Coast Guard. Today, Maine Maritime has expanded on its initial mission. With additional academic offerings and degrees, modern buildings, sophisticated labs and simulators, and assorted training vessels, Maine Maritime has become one of the most progressive maritime training colleges in North America. Experiential learning is a cornerstone of a Maine Maritime education. Every academic program requires its students to participate in major-specific cooperatives or internships during their enrollment. In addition to the practical hands-on experience they receive, students are given an opportunity to visit many countries throughout the world. A full program of student activities, clubs, and intramural and varsity athletics is offered.

Academic Program

The academic year is structured in the traditional two-semester academic format, with most students participating in either cruises, co-ops, or internships during the spring or summer months. All marine engineering and nautical science programs lead to qualification for an unlimited U.S. Coast Guard license. For these programs, students are required to do three 60-day at-sea training cruises aboard the college's training ship, *State of Maine,* as well as aboard commercial merchant ships. Students in the international business and logistics, ocean studies, and power engineering technology majors perform summer internships in their field of study as well. Like the other programs, the marina management and small-vessel operations majors provide similar work experiences, but the number required depends on whether a student is enrolled in the associate or bachelor's degree program. Small-vessel operations graduates qualify to take the U.S. Coast Guard license exam for 200-ton mate, near coastal waters. Maine Maritime has a Naval Reserve Officers' Training Corps (NROTC) program on campus.

Financial Aid

Maine Maritime participates in the Federal Work-Study, Federal Perkins Loan, and Federal Supplemental Educational Opportunity Grant programs and is an eligible institution for the federally insured Federal Stafford Student Loan, Federal Pell Grant, and veterans' programs. The college also has other campus-based loan and scholarship programs available to its students. To apply for financial aid, students must complete the Free Application for Federal Student Aid (FAFSA) and send it in after January 1 (but not later than April 15) of the year of desired entry. In addition to need-based financial aid, qualified students in each entering class receive Federal Student Incentive Payments of $3000 per year. The NROTC Scholarship Program offers the following benefits: all tuition paid, all books furnished, a monthly subsistence allowance during the school year, and a substantial uniform allowance.

Application and Information

Application should be made as early as possible in the senior year of secondary school and no later than June 1. The college uses an early decision process if a completed file is received by December 20. Otherwise, a rolling admissions system is used, and decisions are reached when an applicant's materials are received and evaluated. For information and applications, students should contact:

Director of Admissions
Maine Maritime Academy
Pleasant Street
Castine, Maine 04420

Telephone: 800-464-6565 (toll-free in Maine)
800-227-8465 (toll-free outside Maine)
Web site: http://www.mainemaritime.edu

MANHATTAN COLLEGE
RIVERDALE, NEW YORK

The College

Manhattan College was founded by the Brothers of the Christian Schools in 1853 and chartered by the state of New York in 1863. Traditionally a private men's college, in 1964 it began a student-faculty exchange program with the College of Mount Saint Vincent. Manhattan became fully coeducational in 1973. The College has an enrollment of more than 3,200, of whom 2,600 are undergraduates. Approximately 82 percent of Manhattan's students come from New York State; 17.3 percent represent thirty-nine other states and the remainder represent fifty other countries. Approximately 1,500 housing units are available, consisting of on-campus residence halls and off-campus apartments. About 55 percent of the students reside on campus. Manhattan offers seventy extracurricular organizations and five student publications and fields twenty varsity and club sports teams. Of Manhattan's 40,000 living alumni, more than 18,000 work in the New York City area. Manhattan graduates are prominent leaders in business, government, education, the arts, the sciences, and engineering.

Academic Program

The core curriculum in the School of Arts and School of Science studies some of the vital works of humankind, explores new ideas, examines the meaning of scientific experimentation, and encourages a student to develop his or her thinking and leadership abilities. The major programs offer advanced work in specific humanistic and scientific disciplines and opportunities to work on research projects in collaboration with faculty scholars. In the School of Engineering, all engineering students follow a common core curriculum during the first two years and choose a major at the beginning of the junior year. Each curriculum includes a generous selection of courses in basic sciences, the engineering sciences, humanistic studies, and mathematics. The School of Business prepares students for positions of executive responsibility in business, government, and nonprofit organizations. The business curriculum is based on a strong commitment to liberal education and is well balanced between professional business courses, humanities, sciences, and social sciences. The particular objectives of the School of Education are to prepare young men and women for the teaching profession and to encourage future educational leadership in creative teaching, guidance, administration, curriculum development, and special programs for gifted, exceptional, and underprivileged young people.

Financial Aid

Manhattan grants or administers financial assistance in the form of tuition awards to students on the basis of need and/or ability. Need is evaluated through the FAFSA. In addition to a general scholarship fund, Manhattan offers endowed scholarships, special-category scholarships and grants, student athletic grants, Federal Pell Grants, Federal Supplemental Educational Opportunity Grants, student loans, Federal Work-Study Program awards, and New York State financial assistance. A total of 1,500 students receive financial aid from Manhattan College, and approximately 89 percent receive financial aid from government or private agencies.

Application and Information

Application forms are furnished by the Admission Center on request. The Common Application Form, which is available in many high school guidance offices, may also be used. After supplying the information required, students must send the application for admission to the Admission Center at Manhattan College. The high school report and the student evaluation and transcript must be submitted by the high school guidance counselor. This should be done after six terms of high school or right after the seventh term. The final date for filing applications is March 1 for admission the following fall and February 1 for financial aid applications. A nonrefundable application fee of $25 is required.

William J. Bisset
Dean of Admissions and Financial Aid
Manhattan College
Riverdale, New York 10471

Telephone: 718-862-7200
800-MC2-XCEL (toll-free)
E-mail: admit@manhattan.edu

MARIAN COLLEGE OF FOND DU LAC
FOND DU LAC, WISCONSIN

The College

Marian College is a Catholic coeducational liberal arts college whose first commitment is to the education of the whole person. Founded in 1936 by the Sisters of Saint Agnes as a school for teacher education, Marian now offers more than thirty major fields of study. The warm and friendly environment of the campus supports faculty, administration, and students. A strong liberal arts foundation gives students the values and ethics that they will need throughout their lives. There are approximately 1,900 undergraduate students at Marian, and an additional 600 are pursuing a Master of Arts in education. Students at Marian can be involved in many social organizations and clubs on campus, including Greek organizations. Marian participates in the NAIA and NCAA Division III athletic programs and offers men's intercollegiate baseball, basketball, golf, hockey, soccer, and tennis. Women's intercollegiate sports are basketball, soccer, softball, tennis, and volleyball. Two modern residence halls and a town house village are available for Marian students on a first-come, first-served basis. With enrollment growing, a complex of apartment-style housing, the Courtyard Village, was constructed, adding an element of style and excitement to Marian's beautiful 50-acre campus.

Academic Program

All programs are based upon common general requirements. All students, regardless of their specific degree program, must successfully complete 48 credits in liberal arts, complete at least one major program, and have taken at least 128 hours of credit with a minimum average of 2 grade points for each credit hour. The senior year, or at least the last 32 credit hours, must have been completed in residence at Marian College. Credit is awarded for CLEP subject and general examinations according to the current criteria and policies of Marian College. Details may be obtained from the assistant dean of academic affairs.

Financial Aid

The Marian College Financial Aid Office coordinates an active program of financial assistance for students. Aid is based on need and/or academic merit. The principle sources of aid include the Federal Pell Grant Program, the Federal Work-Study Program, and Marian Assistance. Academic scholarships, including the Presidential Scholarship ($5000), the Naber Leadership Award ($3000), and the Trustee and Regional Awards, are available to entering students and are renewable.

Application and Information

For additional information regarding the application process or for other information, students may contact:

Carol Reichenberger
Vice President for Enrollment Services
Marian College of Fond du Lac
45 South National Avenue
Fond du Lac, Wisconsin 54935

Telephone: 414-923-7650
800-2-MARIAN (toll-free)
E-mail: admit@mariancoll.edu
Web site: http://www.mariancol

MARIETTA COLLEGE
MARIETTA, OHIO

The College

Founded in 1835, Marietta College traces its roots to the Muskingum Academy, which was founded in 1797 as the first institution of higher learning in the Northwest Territory. Marietta's chapter of Phi Beta Kappa was the sixteenth in the nation, showing the College's early dedication to scholarship. Women were first admitted in 1897. About half of Marietta's 1,300 students come from a variety of states along the Eastern Seaboard, the South, and the Midwest; the rest come primarily from Ohio, the surrounding states, and nine other countries. Situated on 120 acres within a block of downtown Marietta, the College has a number of academic and extracurricular facilities. Recent additions to the campus include the Andrews Student Center (1993); the McDonough Leadership Center, home to the most comprehensive program in leadership studies in the country; the McKinney Media Center, which houses two radio stations, a cable television station, and an award-winning student newspaper; a pedestrian mall that enhances the central campus; a Cardiovascular Fitness Center; new sports medicine facilities; and the Chuck McCoy Athletic Facility (1993), which houses lacrosse, football, women's soccer and softball, athletic offices, weight rooms, and meeting rooms.

Academic Program

Marietta students are known for both their breadth and depth of study. Freshmen take a special first-year program that begins with the College Experience Seminar and includes courses in composition (English 101), oral presentation (Speech 101), and mathematics. Every student also completes a liberal arts core of sequence courses in the humanities, social sciences, science, and the fine arts. Seniors complete a Senior Capstone, the culmination of advanced study in their majors. There is an honors program for students who are prepared for and desire an extra challenge and who wish to graduate with honors.

Financial Aid

It is expected that both students and parents will contribute toward the cost of the student's education to the fullest extent of their ability. About 70 percent of current Marietta students receive financial aid based on need. A number of merit-based scholarships are available in addition to funds allocated through College grants and federal and state sources. Members of the entering freshman class receive academic merit scholarships for three different levels of achievement. Students with a minimum GPA of 3.75, a minimum score of 30 on the ACT, or a minimum score of 1350 on the SAT I receive a Trustees scholarship valued at $12,000. Students with a GPA of 3.5, a score of 27 on the ACT, or a score of 1200 on the SAT I receive a President's scholarship valued at $7000. Finally, those students with a GPA of 3.25, a score of 25 on the ACT, or a score of 1150 on the SAT I receive a Dean's scholarship valued at $3500. A Fine Arts Scholarship is awarded annually to winners of an art, music, and drama competition. Numerous work-study jobs are available to students in many campus departments.

Application and Information

Students should apply early in their senior year of high school to guarantee a place in the fall. Marietta operates on a rolling admission plan, and students are notified of acceptance after all application materials are complete. Students applying for financial aid should apply before March 1 of their senior year to be considered for merit scholarships.

To receive information about Marietta or to apply for admission, students should contact:

Office of Admission
Marietta College
Marietta, Ohio 45750-4005

Telephone: 800-331-7896 (toll-free)
E-mail: admit@mcnet.marietta.edu
Web site: http://www.marietta.edu

MARYMOUNT UNIVERSITY
ARLINGTON, VIRGINIA

The University

Marymount University is a comprehensive, coeducational Catholic institution, founded in 1950. Marymount emphasizes excellence in teaching, attention to the individual, and values and ethics across the curriculum. Marymount offers thirty-seven undergraduate majors and twenty-four graduate degree programs through the Schools of Arts and Sciences, Business Administration, Education and Human Services, and Nursing.

Academic Program

Undergraduate degrees require completion of an internship in the chosen field in addition to all necessary course work in the major and a required core of liberal arts courses. This balancing of academics and hands-on, practical experience is a cornerstone of Marymount's commitment to providing students with a well-rounded education. High-quality academics, ethics across the curriculum, and a focus on service complete the solid foundation Marymount provides students. The Honors Program offers especially challenging courses for the strongest students.

Financial Aid

Marymount participates in all federal and state aid programs. To be considered for aid, students must file the Free Application for Federal Student Aid (FAFSA) with the College Scholarship Service and Marymount's financial aid application with the University's Financial Aid Office. Approximately 80 percent of full-time undergraduate students receive aid in the form of scholarships, grants, loans, work-study awards, or on-campus employment. Academic scholarships are available for freshmen and are renewable each year.

Application and Information

High school students seeking admission are advised to apply early during their senior year. They should submit an application, a nonrefundable fee of $35, a high school transcript, SAT I or ACT scores, evidence of expected graduation from an accredited high school, and a recommendation from a high school counselor or an appropriate school official. Those who have attended another college or university must submit the application, $35 fee, test scores, evidence of high school graduation, transcripts of college-level study, and a recommendation from the Dean of Students at the previous institution. The University has a rolling admission policy and notifies applicants soon after the application process is completed and the Admissions Committee has acted on the application. An application form, a catalog, curriculum brochures, and other information may be obtained by contacting:

Dean of Admissions
Marymount University
2807 North Glebe Road
Arlington, Virginia 22207-4299

Telephone: 703-284-1500
800-548-7638 (toll-free)
E-mail: admissions@marymount.edu
Web site: http://www.marymount.edu

MASSACHUSETTS COLLEGE OF PHARMACY AND ALLIED HEALTH SCIENCES
BOSTON, MASSACHUSETTS

The College

Founded in 1823, the Massachusetts College of Pharmacy and Allied Health Sciences (MCP/AHS) is well into its second century as the nation's second-oldest school of pharmacy. One of only a few that remain private and independent, the College has the distinct advantage of quickly responding to change. That flexibility has allowed the College to expand its mission and programs over time to include nursing and the allied health sciences. With its distinguished history and an international reputation, the Massachusetts College of Pharmacy and Allied Health Sciences is helping to redefine the roles of pharmacists, nurses, and allied health professionals in health-care delivery. The College's unique programs integrate theoretical and applied knowledge in the health professions with general education in the arts and sciences, so that graduates may become enlightened citizens as well as competent practitioners. The curriculum at MCP/AHS is designed to develop active thinkers and learners who are prepared for changing professions and a complex world. A core of liberal arts and sciences courses, or "science building blocks," are built into all bachelor's degree programs. Developed by scholars and working professionals, these courses are often custom-tailored to give students practical information and valuable insights into today's health-care concerns.

Academic Program

Students in each of the undergraduate programs begin their studies in the basic sciences, humanities, and social sciences. First-year classes include two semesters of English, math, biology, and chemistry. Students pursuing an Associate in Science degree begin advanced course work in their chosen majors in their second year while also participating in the clinical setting. After completing basic science courses, Bachelor of Science degree candidates progress to advanced courses in chemistry, psychology, pharmaceutics, and pharmacology. Students are also required to complete professional development courses such as interpersonal communications, ethics, and law courses. In addition, students must complete 12 semester hours of elective courses in the humanities, social sciences, and behavioral sciences, as well as 12 semester hours of general elective course work. A significant aspect of every student's education at MCP/AHS is the application of theoretical knowledge in a clinical setting. For example, pharmacy students are required to participate in three externships during their fifth-year of study—a hospital pharmacy externship, a clinical clerkship, and one in an ambulatory health-care practice setting.

Financial Aid

Financial aid is based solely on need and the assistance available. A combination of various forms of aid is usually offered to meet the established needs of each qualified student. Equal consideration is given to applications from in-state and out-of-state students and transfers. The College administers Federal Work-Study Program awards, Health Professions Student Loans, Federal Pell Grants, Federal Supplemental Educational Opportunity Grants, and Federal Perkins Loans as well as in-house scholarships. The priority deadline for application is April 1, and notification is made on a rolling basis. Approximately 75 percent of the students at the College receive financial aid.

Application and Information

For application forms or information, students should contact:

Director for Admission
Massachusetts College of Pharmacy
and Allied Health Sciences
179 Longwood Avenue
Boston, Massachusetts 02115

Telephone: 617-732-2850
800-225-5506 (toll-free outside Massachusetts)
Fax: 617-732-2801

MERCYHURST COLLEGE
ERIE, PENNSYLVANIA

The College

Mercyhurst College is a distinctive Catholic liberal arts college with excellent programs in the arts and sciences, professional preparation, and technology. Founded in 1926 by the Sisters of Mercy, Mercyhurst College is a fully accredited, primarily undergraduate, four-year institution for men and women. Located on an 84-acre campus in Glenwood Hills, in Erie, Pennsylvania, Mercyhurst currently enrolls over 2,700 students in liberal arts and career programs. At Mercyhurst College, small classes enable the faculty to give maximum attention to each student. At the same time, students are challenged to develop and grow through active participation in the classroom. The belief at Mercyhurst is that given various academic programs of high quality and a personal atmosphere in which to pursue them, students will receive meaningful preparation, whether it be for further studies, a career, or living a wholesome life. Mercyhurst has intercollegiate sports programs in baseball, basketball, crew, cross-country running, women's field hockey, football, golf, hockey, lacrosse, soccer, softball, tennis, and volleyball. Students can participate in over twenty clubs, intramural sports, the student government, publications, theater, and the campus ministry. At the heart of student life are the residence halls, the bookstore, and the student union.

Academic Program

In keeping with a renewed emphasis on the liberal arts, in 1990–91, Mercyhurst adopted new core requirements, which include a select, limited number of courses, primarily from the liberal arts disciplines, that are designed to furnish students with a broad base of skills and liberalizing knowledge. In addition to completing the core program, students must complete a major. Graduation requirements for the Bachelor of Arts degree are 126 credits; for the Bachelor of Music degree, 128 credits; and for the Bachelor of Science degree, 120 credits. The Associate of Science degree requires that a minimum of 60 credits be successfully completed. Mercyhurst College offers an honors program, cooperative education, a contract major, independent/tutorial study, and off-campus study. Students may earn credit or advanced placement through challenge examinations, life experience, Advanced Placement tests, and CLEP tests.

Financial Aid

Eighty-five percent of Mercyhurst's students receive financial aid. Academic scholarships include valedictorian/salutatorian scholarships (up to full tuition), and Egan Honor Scholarships ($1000–$4500). Special institutional grants include Presidential Service Grants ($200–$2000), athletic grants ($200 to full tuition), D'Angelo Music Scholarships ($500 to full tuition), and institutional employment grants (up to $1000). Programs of special interest include the Mercyhurst Family Plan, Mercyhurst three-year degree program, and prepayment discounts. Government aid programs include Federal Pell Grants, state grants and loans, Federal Supplemental Educational Opportunity Grants, Federal Stafford Student Loans, Federal Perkins Loans, Federal PLUS loans, and Federal Work-Study employment. The Mercyhurst College financial aid application must be filed by every student seeking any type of financial assistance through the College, whether merit- or need-based. The preferential filing deadline is March 15 of each academic year.

Application and Information

Mercyhurst College follows a rolling admission policy. Students must file a completed application form, along with a $25 nonrefundable application fee, and arrange with the high school and/or other appropriate educational institutions to have a complete transcript and SAT I or ACT scores mailed to the Admissions Office.

For additional information about Mercyhurst College, students should contact:

Matthew Whelan, Director of Admissions
Mercyhurst College
Glenwood Hills
Erie, Pennsylvania 16546

Telephone: 814-824-2202
800-825-1926 (toll-free)
E-mail: mwhelan@paradise.mercy.edu

MEREDITH COLLEGE
RALEIGH, NORTH CAROLINA

The College

Meredith College, founded in 1891 by North Carolina Baptists to provide excellence in education for women, is today the largest private women's college in the Southeast. The College emphasizes the liberal arts, career preparation, and personal development. Meredith students develop confidence, knowledge, and a global perspective that will prepare them for the challenges of the twenty-first century. Approximately 2,050 undergraduate degree candidates choose from more than thirty major fields. Students may also complete a teacher licensure program, preprofessional preparation in medicine and law, or experiential learning through internships and cooperative education in such settings as the state legislature or Research Triangle Park. Meredith students enjoy a faculty-student ratio of 1:16. The faculty is dedicated to teaching and advising and to challenging the students to meet their academic and personal goals. Undergraduate students pursue programs leading to Bachelor of Arts, Science, and Music degrees; the College also offers Master of Business Administration, Master of Education, and Master of Music degrees. College programs are accredited by the Southern Association of Colleges and Schools, the National Council for the Accreditation of Teacher Education, the Council on Social Work Education, the Foundation for Interior Design Education and Research (FIDER), and the National Association of Schools of Music. Meredith is one of only two private colleges in the state selected to host the North Carolina Teaching Fellows Program.

Academic Program

To achieve breadth in her education, each student must fulfill general education requirements in humanities and arts, social and behavioral sciences, mathematics and natural sciences, and health and physical education. By the end of the sophomore year, she declares a major and begins to study her chosen field in depth. She may round out her program by completing a second major, a minor or a concentration, a teacher education program, an experiential learning component (an internship, co-op, or field work), a study-abroad program, or various other options.

Financial Aid

Meredith's financial aid program is designed to meet a high percentage of the analyzed need of the student. Approximately 46 percent of undergraduate students receive need-based assistance; when competitive scholarships and state entitlement grants are added, approximately 97 percent of Meredith students receive some form of financial assistance. The Free Application for Federal Student Aid (FAFSA) and a Meredith financial aid application are used to determine eligibility for need-based federal, state, and institutional funds that include grants and scholarships, loans, and work-study. A freshman candidate may also file special application forms for the competitive scholarships that recognize students for superior academic ability and talent in art, music, or interior design. A North Carolina Teaching Fellow who is selected for Meredith's program may use her scholarship at the College and will have other gift assistance coordinated to match the stipend provided by the state.

Application and Information

An application for admission should be sent to the Office of Admissions along with a nonrefundable $25 processing fee (or acceptable fee-waiver request). The student is responsible for requesting that her official high school transcript, SAT I or ACT scores, and recommendations be sent to the admissions office. A transfer student must file an official transcript from each postsecondary institution attended.

For additional information and for planning a campus visit, students should contact:

Office of Admissions
Meredith College
3800 Hillsborough Street
Raleigh, North Carolina 27607-5298

Telephone: 919-829-8581
800-MEREDITH (toll-free)
Fax: 919-829-2348
E-mail: admissions@meredith.edu
Web site: http://www.meredith.edu/Meredith

MIDLAND LUTHERAN COLLEGE
FREMONT, NEBRASKA

The College
Midland Lutheran College is committed to providing a value-based education that prepares students for success in a variety of careers. While the College is related to the Evangelical Lutheran Church in America, it actively seeks and celebrates religious diversity. Students represent the full range of the Judeo-Christian tradition. Midland's 1,062 men and women come from twenty-three states and seven countries. With a 15:1 student-faculty ratio, the College emphasizes close relationships between teachers and students. Faculty members at Midland make teaching and advising a priority, keeping generous office hours and making themselves available at home during evenings and weekends. Students at Midland receive the close attention that makes for a satisfying college career. Midland balances a fine liberal arts tradition with a forward-looking commitment to achievement in vocation. Upperclass students have the option of living off campus in homes or apartments in the community. Either way, students are integrated into the academic and cocurricular life of the campus.

Academic Program
Midland seeks to provide every student with the breadth of study important to a liberal arts education. All students are required to take the yearlong interdisciplinary humanities course, Odyssey in the Human Spirit. The award-winning Odyssey is taught by a team of humanities professors who present major themes in Western cultural heritage through the study of individual personalities. Students in the course also learn basic research and writing skills. Students meet general education requirements in seven general education areas. By taking courses in each of these areas, students are exposed to a variety of disciplines and ways of thinking. These courses become the foundation for more specialized learning in the student's academic career. Midland operates under the 4-1-4 academic calendar. The fall and spring semesters are separated by the one-month Interterm in January.

Financial Aid
More than 90 percent of Midland's students receive financial assistance. The deadline for application is May 1, but awards are made on a rolling basis. Applications received prior to the May 1 deadline receive priority examination. Midland requires that students complete the College's own financial aid application along with the Free Application for Federal Student Aid (FAFSA). Students must be accepted for admission before financial aid can be awarded. Scholarships are awarded on the basis of academic achievement and special abilities in athletics, music, art, and drama. Scholarship assistance may range from $500 to $5000 per year. Lutheran students are automatically eligible for a $500 Lutheran Student Award. In addition, funded scholarships ranging from $100 to $1000 provide assistance for students in a variety of areas. Federally funded programs provide assistance to students in the form of Federal Pell Grants, Federal Supplemental Educational Opportunity Grants, Federal Stafford Student Loans, Federal Perkins Loans, and a variety of other kinds of aid. Midland is committed to providing adequate sources of financial aid for deserving students.

Application and Information
Students are encouraged to apply as early as possible to Midland. Applications are reviewed on a rolling basis, and students are notified of acceptance as soon as possible after all of their application materials are received. Along with a completed Midland application form and a $20 application fee, students should submit ACT scores and a copy of their high school transcript. Transfer students should also submit copies of transcripts from all colleges or universities attended. For more information, students should contact:

Roland R. Kahnk
Vice President for Enrollment Services
Midland Lutheran College
900 North Clarkson
Fremont, Nebraska 68025

Telephone: 402-721-5480 (call collect)
800-642-8382 (toll-free in Nebraska)

MILLS COLLEGE
OAKLAND, CALIFORNIA

The College

Mills is the only women's college among the many fine educational institutions in the San Francisco Bay Area. Founded in 1852 as the first women's college west of the Rockies, it is committed to remaining a women's college because it believes that such an environment offers women special advantages in preparing for new roles and responsibilities. A small, liberal arts college, Mills enrolls about 800 undergraduate women and 300 graduate women and men. The faculty is equally divided between women and men, and the ratio of students to faculty is approximately 12:1. The College has remained small because ideas and enthusiasm are more readily transmitted in a community of this size. Classes are normally small; 85 percent contain 20 or fewer students. Faculty members observe each person's work closely, encouraging high performance and offering individual instruction when appropriate.

Academic Program

To earn a Mills B.A., students must take thirty-four semester courses (usually four courses each semester). Grading is traditional, and a pass-fail option is available outside the major. First-year students take interdisciplinary seminars on such topics as Science and Pseudoscience, Tribal Cultures in Fact and Fiction, and Music and the Written Word. Students are also expected to choose two courses from each of four areas (natural sciences and mathematics, social sciences, humanities, and fine arts), a one-semester multicultural or cross-cultural course, and one course that heavily stresses writing skills. They also must choose at least half their courses from outside their major field. Students complete their chosen major with a senior project or thesis. A comprehensive program in mathematics and computer science offers basic grounding in mathematics for women who have had insufficient high school preparation but need math skills for their prospective careers.

Financial Aid

Awards are primarily need-based, although academic merit is also considered for certain awards. Scholarship grants range from $200 to $16,000 per year. Mills makes a special effort to provide financial aid to members of minority groups who demonstrate need. Financial aid applicants are expected to apply for assistance from appropriate outside sources, such as the National Merit Scholarship, Federal Pell Grant, and California State Grant programs. Loans may be obtained by most students, and 45 percent of undergraduates are offered campus work opportunities; some students take off-campus jobs. All freshman and transfer candidates who are California residents must file the Free Application for Federal Student Aid (FAFSA) to be considered for all types of government aid and must also file the Cal Grant GPA Verification Form. Students who seek Mills scholarship funds must also file the Mills Financial Aid Form. Priority is given to applicants who meet the published deadlines.

Application and Information

Because Mills uses a rolling admission plan, domestic candidates may file their applications at any time up to August 1 for fall entrance or November 1 for spring entrance. However, international students, merit scholarship applicants, and all other financial aid applicants must apply by February 15 for subsequent fall entrance or November 1 for spring entrance. Students who want to be considered for a California State Grant for spring semester must apply by the previous March 2 deadline. Financial aid is awarded on a first-come, first-served basis, starting with those who meet the February 15 deadline. Financial aid awards are made after admission decisions.

For more information, students should contact:

Jean Flaherty
Dean of Admission and Enrollment Planning
Mills College
5000 MacArthur Boulevard
Oakland, California 94613

Telephone: 510-430-2135
800-87-MILLS (toll-free)
Fax: 510-430-3314
E-mail: admission@mills.edu
Web site: http://www.mills.edu

MINNEAPOLIS COLLEGE OF ART AND DESIGN
MINNEAPOLIS, MINNESOTA

The College

In addition to its regular academic program, the College offers evening, Saturday, and summer school classes and art-related films, lectures, performances, and conferences through the Continuing Studies Office. The MCAD Gallery hosts exhibitions during the academic year, providing students with an excellent opportunity to view the work of important contemporary artists and designers. As part of a visiting artists program, nationally prominent artists, designers, and critics visit the campus for varying periods of time to teach, lecture, and work with students and faculty.

Academic Program

In order to be awarded the B.S. degree, students are required to complete 120 semester credits, 36 of which concentrate in courses relating to visualization (e.g., communication theory and marketing: history, strategies, forms and perceptions, media analysis, hypermedia), and 21 credits, which are taken within MCAD's studio offerings. Students are also required to participate in a community-related project, an externship or study abroad program, and a senior project/exhibit. This degree program offers preprofessional training in visual persuasion and information techniques applicable to the fields of advertising/marketing, science/technology, entertainment, education, and corporate communications. The B.F.A. program requires students to complete 120 semester credits. Twelve of these are in the first-year Foundation Studies program, 39 are in the liberal arts area, and 69 are in the studio. The goals of the first-year Foundation Studies Program are to develop a student's ability to integrate verbal and visual communication skills and enhance personal expression while preparing for the major areas of study. Course work within the various majors provides students with a solid foundation in craftsmanship and offers both technical and conceptual information. Complementing work in the studio courses, the Liberal Arts Division offers study in history, criticism, literature, philosophy, religion, and the social and behavioral sciences.

Financial Aid

More than 72 percent of the College student body receive financial aid to meet education costs. Financial aid administered by the College comes from federal, state, and private sources and includes Federal Pell Grants, Federal Stafford Student Loans, Federal Supplemental Educational Opportunity Grants, Federal Perkins Loans, and Minnesota State Scholarships and Grants-in-Aid. College-controlled aid includes a variety of College grants, scholarships, and work-study contracts. Aid from private sources is also available. To qualify, applicants must submit the Free Application for Federal Student Aid (FAFSA).

Application and Information

For a College catalog and an application form, students should write to the following address:

Admissions Office
Minneapolis College of Art and Design
2501 Stevens Avenue South
Minneapolis, Minnesota 55404

Telephone: 612-874-3760
800-874-6223 (toll-free)
Fax: 612-874-3711
E-mail: admissions@mn.mcad.edu
Web site: http://www.mcad.edu/

MISSOURI SOUTHERN STATE COLLEGE
JOPLIN, MISSOURI

The College

Missouri Southern State College specializes in undergraduate university education with an international perspective. Since its inception as a junior college in 1937 and its evolution into a public four-year institution in 1967, the College has focused on classroom teaching, resulting in a tradition of small classes and close, personal interaction between faculty members and approximately 5,500 students. This approach is maintained through a 16:1 student-teacher ratio. Southern's faculty members come from all over the world, with degrees from prestigious universities and professional experience in the disciplines they teach. Because students cannot learn everything they need to know while in college, Southern stresses two important elements: developing the ability to learn on one's own and learning to conceptualize, solve problems, manipulate thoughts and patterns, and work cooperatively. Those elements, coupled with an international emphasis, enable Southern's graduates to compete successfully in the rapidly changing world. In 1995, the Missouri General Assembly enhanced the College's mission through House Bill 442, directing the institution to "develop such academic support programs and public service activities it deems necessary and appropriate to establish international or global education as a distinctive theme of its mission." The centerpiece of the global emphasis is the Institute of International Studies, which coordinates all international programs and activities, including a pervasive global dimension in all curricula, study-abroad opportunities for faculty and students, internships abroad for students, and expanded foreign language offerings.

Academic Program

Because graduates may change occupations and careers several times during their working lives, all students pursuing a degree complete the core curriculum, a series of courses carefully designed to instill certain lifelong thinking and learning skills. Core courses emphasize critical thinking, problem-solving, and communications skills; a general understanding of scientific and artistic aspects of this culture; and the ability to function in a global society through knowledge and understanding of other cultures. In both the core and major studies, writing skills and computer literacy are developed, and an international perspective is stressed in every possible course. The baccalaureate degree requires 51 credit hours of the core and a total of 128 hours; the Associate of Arts degree requires a total of 64 hours, with 42 hours from the core; and the Associate of Science degree requires 64 hours, with 26 hours from the core curriculum.

Financial Aid

A wide variety of financial aid options assist students with college costs. Federal programs include the Federal Pell Grant, Federal Supplemental Educational Opportunity Grant, Federal Work-Study Program, Federal Perkins Loan, and Federal Stafford Student Loan, among others. Several state programs aid prospective teachers and students with high academic standing. In addition, the College provides a wide range of scholarships, performing awards, and student employment. Special scholarships are available for qualified junior college transfer students, and out-of-state tuition waivers are offered to students in a designated surrounding area.

Application and Information

The College has a rolling application deadline, and students may apply any time during their senior year of high school. There is a $15 nonrefundable application fee. Information on specific academic areas and other College programs is readily available from the Admission Office and on-line by contacting:

Admission Office
Missouri Southern State College
3950 East Newman Road
Joplin, Missouri 64801-1595

Telephone: 417-625-9378
800-606-MSSC (6772) (toll-free)
Fax: 417-659-4429
E-mail: admis@vm.mssc.edu
Web site: http://www.mssc.edu

MONTCLAIR STATE UNIVERSITY
UPPER MONTCLAIR, NEW JERSEY

The University

Founded in 1908 as a normal school oriented to the education of future teachers, Montclair State has evolved into a four-year comprehensive public teaching university that offers a broad range of educational and cultural opportunities. Montclair State comprises five schools (the School of Business, School of the Arts, College of Humanities and Social Sciences, College of Science and Mathematics, and College of Education and Human Services) and a Division of Graduate Studies and confers degrees in forty-four undergraduate majors and thirty-three graduate majors. Through its diverse programs and services, Montclair State seeks to develop educated men and women who are inquiring, creative, and responsible contributors to society. Montclair State has been designated a Center of Excellence in the fine and performing arts in northern New Jersey. It is accredited by the Middle States Association of Colleges and Schools, and its teacher education, administrative, and school service personnel programs are approved by the National Council for Accreditation of Teacher Education. The total enrollment was 13,035 in fall 1996; 5,971 women and 3,670 men were enrolled as undergraduates. The majority of students are from New Jersey, and approximately 80 percent commute. The remainder live in campus dormitories or apartments or in University-approved off-campus housing. Approximately 70 percent belong to student organizations. Some of the organizations that are involved in student life are the College Life Union Board, which is responsible for coordinating all social, cultural, educational, and recreational student programs; the Intercollegiate Athletic Council, which provides men and women of all the schools with the opportunity to participate in many varsity sports; and the Student Intramural and Leisure Council, which runs one of the country's few student-controlled intramural programs.

Academic Program

Successful completion of a minimum of 128 semester hours is necessary for graduation. Course requirements include general education (34–58 semester hours), comprising communication, humanities and the arts, pure and applied sciences, social and behavioral sciences, a physical education requirement, and a multicultural awareness requirement; courses in the major field of study in arts and sciences programs (a minimum of 33–82 semester hours); and electives (12–37 semester hours). Montclair State also offers undergraduate degrees through the Second Careers Program (for students over 25 years of age) and the Weekend College.

Financial Aid

Four major types of financial aid programs are available at Montclair State: loans, grants, scholarships, and employment. Within each of these categories, funding may be available through federal, state, and/or institutional sources. State aid programs include Tuition Aid Grants, Educational Opportunity Fund Grants, Bloustein Distinguished Scholars awards, Public Tuition Benefits awards, and N.J. CLASS loans. Federal sources of aid include Federal Pell Grants, Federal Supplemental Educational Opportunity Grants, Federal Perkins Loans, Federal Work-Study, Federal Stafford Student Loans, Federal PLUS loans, and programs for veterans. Approximately 75 percent of undergraduates receive financial aid. Students should contact the Financial Aid Office regarding application materials and deadline dates.

Application and Information

Applicants must submit a completed application form, a nonrefundable application fee of $40, a copy of their official high school transcript, and copies of their SAT I or ACT scores. Admission decisions are announced on a rolling basis until all spaces are filled.

For application forms and additional admission information, students should contact:

Office of Admissions
Montclair State University
Upper Montclair, New Jersey 07043-1624
Telephone: 800-331-9205 (toll-free)

MONTREAT COLLEGE
MONTREAT, NORTH CAROLINA

The College

Montreat is a four-year Christian liberal arts college affiliated with the Presbyterian Church (USA). At Montreat College, a student's experience is enhanced by an education of value, grounded in a strong liberal arts core, taught by outstanding Christian faculty, and prized by today's employers and graduate schools. Students benefit from Montreat's small classes where their opinions matter, and they grow through one-on-one interaction with professors and classmates. Studies challenge them to integrate faith and learning while considering subjects in ways never thought possible. Hands-on experiences in the majors (internships, field studies, mission programs, community service, and independent research) enable students to gain practical career and life preparation. In a diverse and multicultural environment, students learn how to investigate the unfamiliar, think critically, and communicate and clarify their ideas. In the process, they develop the skills, personal values, and faith to take their place in the world with confidence. Montreat College welcomes students of many denominations and cultural backgrounds, including students from all corners of the world. The distinct spirit of community goes beyond the faculty, staff, and students and extends to visiting Christian conference members and residents of the neighboring towns of Montreat and Black Mountain, as well as to the "cottagers" who vacation there throughout the seasons.

Academic Program

Upon enrollment, students are assigned a faculty adviser to assist them in clarifying their educational objectives and meeting the requirements for graduation. Students and faculty advisers work together in arranging a program of study leading to graduation. Graduation requirements are a minimum of 126 semester hours, cumulative quality point average of at least 2.0, completion of the general education core requirements, 33 semester hours in 300-level or above courses, completion of all major requirements, a grade of C or better in courses needed for the major or minor, and completion of at least 31 semester hours at Montreat College. Students interested in careers in medicine, law, criminology, and other professional areas are reminded that the best preparation, according to graduate school advisers in these areas, is a solid liberal arts degree program such as that found at Montreat College.

Financial Aid

Through generous financial aid and scholarship packages, deserving students receive the quality academics of a private college at a modest cost. Each year, more than 85 percent of Montreat students receive some form of financial aid. Working individually with each student, the College awards financial aid packages that include scholarships, grants, loans, and work-study jobs. Scholarships are also made available to transfer students. All students must submit the Free Application for Federal Student Aid (FAFSA) and the Montreat College Application for Scholarship and Financial Assistance. To drastically reduce processing time, the FAFSA can be electronically submitted by the College to the federal government for students who have applied, been accepted, and submitted a $100 deposit. For more information, students should call the Financial Aid Office at 800-545-4656 (toll-free).

Application and Information

Students are required to submit a formal application accompanied by a $15 application fee. The common application is accepted. An official transcript of high school credits must be submitted directly from the high school to the College Office of Admissions. SAT I/ACT verification is also required. Montreat College's school code is 005423.

For more information, students should write or call:

Office of Admissions
Montreat College
P.O. Box 1267
Montreat, North Carolina 28757

Telephone: 704-669-8012 Ext. 3781
800-622-6968 (toll-free)
Fax: 704-669-0120
E-mail: admissions@montreat.edu

MORGAN STATE UNIVERSITY
BALTIMORE, MARYLAND

The University

Morgan State University, a coeducational institution, is located in a residential section of Baltimore, Maryland. The University offers both graduate and undergraduate programs of study. At the graduate level, the University offers the Master of Arts degree in African-American studies, economics, English, history, international studies, mathematics, music, sociology, and teaching. The Master of Business Administration is offered in accounting, finance, international management, management, and marketing. The Master of Science degree is offered in educational administration and supervision, elementary and middle school education, engineering, science, and transportation. Professional degrees are offered in architecture, city and regional planning, and landscape architecture. The Doctor of Education degree is offered in mathematics education, science education, and urban educational leadership. In addition, the Doctor of Philosophy degree is offered in history, and the Doctor of Engineering degree is offered in civil, electrical, and industrial engineering. The institution was chartered in 1867 and was built on its present site in 1890. From 1867 to 1890, it was known as the Centenary Biblical Institute; from 1890 to 1938 as Morgan College; and from 1938 to 1975 as Morgan State College. In 1975, the college became Morgan State University. The University is a member institution of several consortia, including the National Student Exchange, a consortium of twenty-two state colleges and universities across the country.

Academic Program

Students admitted to Morgan to study for a Bachelor of Arts or Bachelor of Science degree are generally expected to adhere to the accepted standards of higher education. Honors programs, independent study, and cooperative education programs are available in most areas. For those students requiring special placement and/or special assistance, support services and programs are provided. To earn a bachelor's degree, students must generally complete a minimum of 120 semester hours, depending on the program. Engineering students should expect to earn 135 semester hours to qualify for the degree. Through the Continuing Studies Program, students can pursue an education outside traditional daytime classwork. Students in the program include part-time students, as well as many full-time students who have been away from a formal educational experience for two or more years and want to pursue courses for personal fulfillment or career advancement. Morgan State's Weekend University is designed for working adults and others who are unable to attend weekday classes. Classes are scheduled on Friday evenings and Saturdays, providing students the opportunity to earn a bachelor's degree in accounting, business administration, social work, or telecommunications in approximately five to six years.

Financial Aid

Scholarships, loans, and campus employment are available, and awards are made on the basis of student merit and financial need. Information on these as well as on Federal Pell Grants, other federal grants, and Federal Work-Study awards may be obtained by contacting the Financial Aid Office.

Application and Information

Morgan State University does not discriminate against applicants because of race, sex, religion, or nationality. Applications for August entrance should be submitted no later than April 15; those for January entrance should be submitted no later than December 1. Applications to Morgan State University are accepted as far as the facilities will permit. Transfer students must submit a transcript from every college previously attended. A limited number of out-of-state and international students may be accepted. All application forms must be accompanied by a $25 application fee and should be forwarded to:

The Office of Admissions
Morgan State University
Cold Spring Lane and Hillen Road
Baltimore, Maryland 21239

Telephone: 410-319-3000

MOUNT IDA COLLEGE
NEWTON CENTRE, MASSACHUSETTS

The College

Founded in 1899, Mount Ida has become one of the Northeast's most innovative postsecondary institutions. All freshman students begin in Mount Ida's renowned Junior College Division, which features eight schools that offer 37 two- and three-year associate degree programs. After earning an associate degree, students may choose to enter employment or to continue in one of the Mount Ida Senior College Division's two-year bachelor's degree programs. The associate degree guarantees that a student may enter the junior year of at least one Mount Ida bachelor's degree program. This flexible system allows students to exercise educational options one step at a time as they gain knowledge and experience. Approximately 2,000 full-time students are enrolled at Mount Ida. Ninety percent of these students represent New England, New York, New Jersey, and Pennsylvania. More than 800 men and women reside in five College dormitories, three of which are coed, one of which is all female, and one of which is all male. Mount Ida's beautiful 85-acre campus was once an elegant country estate. Academic, administrative, and residential buildings are surrounded by playing fields, ponds, and wooded areas in a comfortable, self-contained environment. At Mount Ida College, where each student is known by name and recognized as an individual, students find it easy to become involved. Students are encouraged to start new positive groups on campus that will enrich the College community. Campus organizations and clubs reflect the diversity of the student body and afford wonderful opportunities for creative expression and leadership development.

Academic Program

The Senior College Division's bachelor's degree programs are designed for students who have completed associate degree programs at Mount Ida or at other accredited institutions and choose to continue study to earn a baccalaureate degree. The liberal studies program accepts all credits earned by associate degree graduates or 60 credits earned by students during the first two years of college, regardless of course content, provided that a quality point average (QPA) of at least 2.0 has been achieved. The senior-year core curriculum includes interdisciplinary courses covering liberal arts, humanities, and sciences in addition to an independent study project. Students entering any other senior college program must have their transcripts evaluated on a course-by-course basis to determine what they will earn in transfer credit. Every effort is made to allow maximum credit transfer. The College operates on a semester calendar.

Financial Aid

Mount Ida supplements federal, state, and private funding with a substantial commitment of College funds. As a result, about 70 percent of Mount Ida's students received financial assistance during the academic year 1996–97. Grants, scholarships, campus employment, and loans are utilized to enable students to afford the College's opportunities. Mount Ida does not have a financial aid application deadline.

Application and Information

Mount Ida uses a rolling admission policy, so there is no deadline for the submission of applications. Applications are considered as long as there is space in the desired program of study. Applicants are notified within three to four weeks after all credentials have been received. All correspondence should be directed to:

Judith A. Kaufman, Dean of Admissions or
Harold C. Duvall, Dean of Enrollment Management
Mount Ida College
777 Dedham Street
Newton Centre, Massachusetts 02159

Telephone: 617-928-4553
617-928-4535
Fax: 617-928-4760
World Wide Web: http://www.mountida.edu

NATIONAL AMERICAN UNIVERSITY
RAPID CITY, SOUTH DAKOTA

The University

The mission of National American University is to provide career education to students of diverse backgrounds, interests, and abilities. National American University is a private, multicampus institution of higher education committed to building a learning partnership with students by creating a challenging and effective educational environment. National American University offers educational programs that are responsive to the career interests and objectives of its students and to the needs of employers, government, and society. In 1941, National American University established its first campus in Rapid City, South Dakota. The school geared its programs toward a business administration curriculum. The curricular offerings have since expanded to include a variety of high-demand majors such as paralegal studies, medical assisting, health information technology, and veterinary technology. National American University is accredited by the Commission on Institutions of Higher Education of the North Central Association of Colleges and Schools.

Academic Program

In order to obtain a Bachelor of Science degree, students are required to complete all capstone courses with a minimum grade of C, finish with a minimum 2.0 grade point average overall in the major core, and complete 192 quarter hours of credit, with the final 48 coming in residence at National American University. National American University accepts credits earned through the University-Level Examination Program (CLEP), the Defense Activity for Non-Traditional Education Support (DANTES), and ACT PEP. Also, the school has its own credit-by-examination program. Certification exams can be taken on site at the National American University Prometric Testing Centers at either the Rapid City or Sioux Falls campuses. The school observes a quarter calendar year with classes beginning in early September and concluding in May.

Financial Aid

National American University realizes that financing higher education is a major concern, and the financial aid staff works with students on financing. The University provides assistance in the form of grants, scholarships, work-study, and low-interest loan programs through federal, state, and local sources. When applying for federal student aid, the information reported is used in a formula established by the U.S. Congress that calculates Expected Family Contribution (EFC). This is an amount that students and their families are expected to contribute toward education. The EFC determines the student's eligibility for federal financial aid programs. Merit-based academic and athletic scholarships are also available to qualified new and continuing students. In addition, many National American University students work part-time while attending the University.

Application and Information

To apply for admission, an application for admission must be completed and mailed or personally delivered to the director of admissions. Application materials may be obtained and arrangements may be made for visiting the University through the Admissions Office. The application for admission form must be submitted along with a $25 application fee. A letter of acceptance is mailed as soon as possible. If the applicant is not accepted, the application fee is refunded. Early application is to the student's advantage if University housing (in a Rapid City location), financial aid, and/or part-time employment are desired. For applications or more information, students should contact:

Director of Admissions
National American University
321 Kansas City Street
Rapid City, South Dakota 57701

Telephone: 605-394-4827
800-843-8892 (toll-free)

NEWBURY COLLEGE
BROOKLINE, MASSACHUSETTS

The College

Newbury College is a private coeducational college that offers a four-year degree program in selected areas as well as a host of two-year associate degree programs. Nearly 1,000 men and women are currently enrolled as full-time day students, and the total College enrollment is near 5,400. Approximately 40 percent of the College's day students come from states other than Massachusetts. The College provides housing for men and women on campus. Residence halls differ in age and design, providing a variety of styles. Approximately 28 percent of the day students live in the College's residence halls. Founded in 1962, Newbury College has grown and changed dramatically in the past thirty-five years. However, its educational philosophy remains the same: to prepare graduates to succeed in their chosen career. All of the College's regionally accredited academic programs feature hands-on training to sharpen job skills. The College is accredited by the New England Association of Schools and Colleges. In addition, the American Physical Therapy Association and the American Medical Association Joint Review Committee for Respiratory Therapy Education have granted accreditation to the physical therapist assistant and respiratory care programs. The interior design program is accredited by the Foundation for Interior Design and Education Research (FIDER).

Academic Program

Working with an adviser, students plan their course of study around a prescribed major core. Program requirements establish a framework that includes intensive study in the major area where hands-on training is stressed as well as course work in general education. By fulfilling the general education requirements and selecting courses outside the major, students receive a well-rounded education. At least 120 credit hours, usually five courses per semester, are required for graduation in most bachelor degree programs. At least 60 credit hours are required for the associate degree.Clinical affiliations/internships are an integral part of the health professions programs. Students in the culinary arts and in most other programs also participate in internships and affiliations, which provide them with on-the-job experience in their chosen field.

Financial Aid

It is the College's hope that all qualified and motivated students have the opportunity to pursue a college degree. To this end, Newbury endeavors to meet the financial needs of all students. A brochure describing financial planning, scholarships, grant aid, and loan programs may be obtained from the Financial Aid Office. The College also sponsors several academically based scholarship programs. These include the Presidential Scholarships and the Newbury College Recognition Scholarships, which are awarded on the basis of a student's academic record, extracurricular activities, and motivation to succeed. Applications for these programs will be given to interested students together with admission applications.

Application and Information

Applications for admission should be filed well in advance of the proposed entrance date, especially if the applicant intends to seek financial aid. However, students submitting applications as late as August or September may be considered for admission if there is still space available in the entering freshman class. A nonrefundable application fee of $30 must accompany the application for all day-school applicants. In addition, international students should submit an affidavit of financial support.

For more information, students should contact:

Director of Admission
Newbury College
Admission Center
129 Fisher Avenue
Brookline, Massachusetts 02146

Telephone: 617-730-7007
800-NEWBURY (toll-free)
E-mail: info@newbury.edu

NEW YORK SCHOOL OF INTERIOR DESIGN
NEW YORK, NEW YORK

The School

The New York School of Interior Design (NYSID) is an independent, coeducational, nonprofit college accredited by NASAD. It was established in 1916 by architect Sherrill Whiton and chartered by the Board of Regents of the University of the State of New York in 1924. The college is specifically designed for those who wish to pursue a career in one or more of the various fields of interior design. The college's location and its programs provide students with a physical introduction to the world of the interior designer. The area's professional design studios, art and antique shops, showrooms, and museums are all an exciting part of the "campus."

Academic Program

The New York School of Interior Design devotes all of its resources to providing a comprehensive education in interior design. The various academic programs compose an integrated curriculum covering interior design concepts; history of art, architecture, interiors, and furniture; technical and communication skills, materials and methods, philosophy and theory; and professional design procedures and design problem solving. The Basic Interior Design Program consists of a 24-credit required sequence of basic courses in which all of the School's students are enrolled. These courses provide a general, cultural, and professional introduction to the field of interior design. For most students, completion of the Basic Interior Design Program serves as the foundation for matriculation into the degree programs. The A.A.S. degree program provides the background in technical skills and visual sensitivity necessary for the development of design ability. Of the 66 credits required to earn the associate degree, 52 are in design and 14 are in the liberal arts. In the Bachelor of Fine Arts degree program, studies focus on the development of a broad array of technical skills, conceptual analysis, creative problem solving, and relevant cultural developments. In addition to the design and professional courses, students are required to take liberal arts courses in art, antiques, and architectural history.

Financial Aid

The New York School of Interior Design is concerned about students with limited financial resources and makes every attempt to provide assistance. Several institutional scholarships are available for students who meet the criteria. Students are encouraged to apply for the New York State Tuition Assistance Program (TAP—for New York State residents only), the Federal Pell Grant, and Federal Education Loans. In addition, because of the college's location and its close relationship with the interior design industry, its job placement counselor is very effective in helping students find part-time employment.

Application and Information

Admission decisions are made on a rolling basis; it is recommended that applications be submitted at least eight weeks prior to the start of the first semester for which the student applies. Applicants are notified of the Admission Committee's decision by mail shortly after all required documents have been received and visual requirements fulfilled. Inquiries and applications should be directed to:

Director of Admissions
New York School of Interior Design
170 East 70th Street
New York, New York 10021

Telephone: 212-472-1500 Ext. 23
800-336-9743 (toll-free)
Fax: 212-472-1867

NEW YORK UNIVERSITY
NEW YORK, NEW YORK

The University

New York University (NYU) was founded in 1831 by Albert Gallatin, secretary of the treasury under Thomas Jefferson; he believed that the place for a university was not in "the seclusion of cloistered halls but in the throbbing heart of a great city." NYU draws top students from every state and more than 120 countries. The distinguished academic atmosphere attracts the teachers, and the teachers and the atmosphere together attract the students who are capable of benefiting from both. Within three years of graduation, 80 percent of NYU's students go on to postbaccalaureate work. Of those who apply for admission to medical and dental schools, 80 percent are accepted (the national average is 40 percent). The faculty includes world-famous scholars, researchers, and artists, among them Nobel laureates, winners of the Pulitzer Prize, and members of the National Science Foundation. NYU is a member of the prestigious Association of American Universities. A study sponsored by the National Science Foundation placed NYU among the top four universities in the country in the number of "leading intellectuals" on the faculty. Full professors teach on both the graduate and undergraduate levels. Seven undergraduate divisions provide extensive offerings in a wide range of subjects: more than 2,500 courses in 160 major fields are available to NYU's full-time undergraduates. The average class size is under 30, and the faculty-student ratio is 1:12—benefits generally associated with a much smaller institution.

Academic Program

Requirements for graduation vary among departments and schools. A liberal arts core curriculum is an integral part of all areas of concentration. The baccalaureate degree requires completion of at least 128 credits. The University calendar is organized on the traditional semester system, including two 6-week summer sessions. Some divisions offer part-time programs during the day and evening and on weekends.

Financial Aid

Financial aid at NYU comes from many sources. All students are encouraged to apply for financial assistance or one of NYU's innovative financing plans. Sixty-six percent of NYU's undergraduates receive financial assistance. Each year more than 1,600 entering freshmen are awarded scholarships based on academic promise and/or financial need. The University may offer a package of aid that includes scholarships or grants, loans, or work-study programs. NYU requires the submission of the Free Application for Federal Student Aid (FAFSA). The deadline for filing this financial aid form is February 15 for the fall semester and November 1 for the spring semester.

Application and Information

For entrance in the fall term, the application for admission—including all supporting credentials—must be received by November 15 (early decision freshman candidates), January 15 (freshmen), or April 1 (transfer students). For entrance in the spring term, the application materials must be received by December 1 for both freshman and transfer candidates. For entrance in the summer, the application materials should be received by April 15 for both freshman and transfer candidates. Applications for admission received after these dates are considered only if space remains. Official notification of fall admission is made on April 1 and on a rolling basis thereafter. A campus tour or an appointment for an information session can be arranged by calling 212-998-4524.

Office of Undergraduate Admissions
New York University
22 Washington Square North
New York, New York 10011

Telephone: 212-998-4500
Web site: http://www.nyu.edu

NIAGARA UNIVERSITY
NIAGARA UNIVERSITY, NEW YORK

The University
Niagara University (NU), founded in 1856, is a private, independent university rooted in a Catholic and Vincentian tradition. The suburban 160-acre campus combines the old and new; both ivy-covered buildings and modern architectural structures are among its twenty-seven buildings. DeVeaux, a 50-acre satellite campus, is located a mile from the main campus. The DeVeaux Campus provides Niagara students with additional athletic facilities. The University is easily accessible from every major city in the eastern and midwestern United States via the New York State Thruway, Buffalo International Airport, and rail and bus service. There are more than 2,200 undergraduate and 644 graduate students enrolled at Niagara. Of the total enrollment, approximately 58 percent live on campus. A large percentage of students take advantage of the more than seventy extracurricular and cocurricular activities offered. Volunteer work in the community is popular among the students and enhances community relations.

Academic Program
Niagara University's curricula enable students to pursue their academic preferences and to complete courses that lead to proficiency in other academic areas. Courses that have been conventionally considered upper-division courses are available to all students. This provides students with the opportunity to avoid introductory and survey courses and permits motivated students to take advantage of more challenging courses early in their collegiate career. The honors program provides special academic opportunities that stimulate, encourage, and challenge participants. In addition, an accelerated three-year degree program is offered to qualified students. Students pursuing a bachelor's degree must complete a total of 40 or 42 course units (120 or 126 hours) to meet graduation requirements. Niagara grants credit for successful scores on the Advanced Placement tests, College-Level Examination Program tests, and College Proficiency Examinations. Internships, research, independent study, and cooperative education are available in many academic programs. An Army ROTC program is also offered. The University operates on a two-semester plan (fall and spring). A comprehensive summer session offers a diversity of courses. NU is fully accredited by the Middle States Association of Colleges and Schools. Its programs in the respective areas are accredited by the National League for Nursing, the National Council for Accreditation of Teacher Education, the Council on Social Work Education, and the American Chemical Society; the travel, hotel, and restaurant administration program is accredited by the Commission for Programs in Hospitality Administration.

Financial Aid
Ninety-one percent of the enrolled students at NU receive a financial aid package averaging $11,700 per year. They receive assistance in the form of merit scholarships, loans, grants, or campus employment. Students seeking financial aid should file the Free Application for Federal Student Aid (FAFSA). New York State residents should also file a Tuition Assistance Program (TAP) application.

Application and Information
Niagara operates on a rolling admission basis and adheres to the College Board Candidates Reply Date. A visit to the campus is encouraged, and overnight accommodations in a residence hall are available. Information on all aspects of the University can be obtained by contacting the Admissions Office.

George C. Pachter
Dean of Admissions
639 Bailo Hall
Niagara University
Niagara University, New York 14109-2011

Telephone: 716-286-8700
800-462-2111 (toll-free)
Fax: 716-286-8710
E-mail: admissions@niagara.edu
Web site: http://www.niagara.edu

NORTHEASTERN UNIVERSITY
BOSTON, MASSACHUSETTS

The University

Located at the center of Boston's thriving educational and cultural life, Northeastern University is dedicated to excellence in research and scholarship and is committed to responding to individual and community educational needs. Since its founding in 1898, Northeastern has pioneered a wide range of educational programs and services for students of all ages. The current undergraduate enrollment is 11,387 full-time and 8,393 part-time students.

Academic Program

A University-wide honors program gives students opportunities to participate in enriched educational experiences, such as honors equivalents of required academic courses and interdisciplinary colloquia. The Cooperative Education Program enables students to gain practical experience in the work place while helping to finance their education. The Ujima Scholars Program is an academic support program designed to assist students of color who have demonstrated an ability to succeed in college but need additional academic assistance, particularly during their first year. Such students must enroll in a credit-offering reading and study skills course, attend tutorial sessions and group meetings, complete profile assessments, and participate in career/vocational workshops, individual counseling, and academic advising and scheduling sessions. NUPRIME, a program designed to aid African-Americans, Hispanic-Americans, and Native Americans, is offered through the College of Engineering. Credit may be awarded through the Advanced Placement or College-Level Examination programs. Support services for students with disabilities include orientation, special registration, counseling, housing, textbooks on tape, modified testing, readers, interpreters, notetakers, auxiliary aids, adaptive physical education, physical and speech therapy, sign-language classes, and scribes.

Financial Aid

By coordinating the resources of the University and various public and private scholarship programs, the Office of Student Financial Services was able to provide more than $87 million to more than 8,055 students last year. Approximately 73 percent of the freshman class received financial assistance from University-based sources, and another 14 percent received aid through the Federal Stafford Student Loan Program. In addition, the University's cooperative plan enables students to earn income that offsets a portion of their college expenses after their freshman year. Financial aid is based on need and academic promise and may consist of a grant, a loan, part-time employment, or any combination of these three. To apply, students must file a Free Application for Federal Student Aid (FAFSA) and a PROFILE form with the College Scholarship Service by March 1. Students who are accepted by March 1 have priority in receiving funds.

Application and Information

Under Northeastern's rolling admission plan, candidates may apply and be accepted at the point in their secondary school careers where there is sufficient evidence that they can profit from University study. Applications completed by March 1 will secure a decision in time for the May 1 Candidates Reply Date (applies to fall quarter freshman applicants only). Junior-year and deferred admissions are available, and students who have successfully completed study at other accredited institutions are eligible for advanced standing. Freshmen may enroll in all programs in September and, depending on the availability of courses, in January, April, and June. Transfer students in most programs may apply for entrance at the beginning of each quarter. Personal interviews are recommended but not required. Campus tours and group information sessions are held daily, and open house programs are scheduled throughout the year.

Office of Undergraduate Admissions
Northeastern University
360 Huntington Avenue
Boston, Massachusetts 02115

Telephone: 617-373-2200 (voice)
617-373-3100 (TTY)
E-mail: undergrad-admissions@neu.edu

NORTH GEORGIA COLLEGE & STATE UNIVERSITY
The Military College of Georgia
DAHLONEGA, GEORGIA

The College
Originally named North Georgia Agricultural College, the institution was established in 1873 as a land-grant school of agriculture and mechanical arts, particularly mining engineering. The school was renamed North Georgia College in summer 1929 and North Georgia College & State University (NGCSU) in fall 1996. NGCSU is a member of the University System of Georgia. Today, approximately 20 percent of the student body choose to be in NGCSU's nationally prominent ROTC program, which is administered by the U.S. Army. In fact, NGCSU is the only public, coeducational, liberal arts, military school in the country. NGCSU is unique in that it serves as a military college for its Corps of Cadets and as a liberal arts academic institution for all its students. Women have been fully qualified members of the Corps of Cadets since 1973. The Corps of Cadets comprises approximately 20 percent of the student body and 40 percent of the resident population. All male resident students are required to be members of the Corps of Cadets. Membership in the Corps is optional for women and commuter students. North Georgia College & State University offers varied programs of study leading to degrees at the associate, bachelor's, and master's level. The preprofessional programs have reputations as being among the finest in the area, and recently renovated labs and classroom facilities have enhanced the quality of these programs. Dual-degree programs in cooperation with the Georgia Institute of Technology and Clemson University prepare students for careers in engineering, computer science, and business.

Academic Program
North Georgia requires all students to complete core curriculum requirements. The core curriculum consists of 20 quarter hours of English and humanities, 20 quarter hours of science and mathematics (including a 10-hour sequence in a laboratory science), 20 quarter hours of social science, and 30 quarter hours of course work related to the major, such as computer science and modern language. The minimum requirement for a degree is 185 quarter hours, including 18 hours of military science for members of the Corps of Cadets. All students must complete an additional 6 quarter hours of physical education. The state of Georgia requires all graduates to meet U.S. and Georgia history and U.S. and Georgia Constitution requirements. These are met upon completion of the core curriculum. All students must also pass the Regents' Test of Reading and Writing before graduating. Participation in the Honors Program is limited to 20 freshman each year. In addition to completing approximately 30 hours of the required honors-only course work, honors students participate in numerous on- and off-campus enrichment programs, such as field trips and faculty mentoring opportunities. Completion of a senior research paper is required of all Honors Program participants.

Financial Aid
Of those students who apply for financial assistance, more than 80 percent receive financial aid. Aid is available through a combination of scholarships, grants, loans, and campus employment. Among the federal funds available are grants, student loans, Federal Work-Study, and ROTC scholarships. Georgia residents who participate in the Corps of Cadets receive $500 per quarter, provided they maintain a cumulative average of 2.0. Nonresidents who participate in the Corps of Cadets may have their out-of-state tuition waived if they maintain a cumulative average of 2.0.

Application and Information
Director of Admissions
North Georgia College & State University
Dahlonega, Georgia 30597
Telephone: 706-864-1800
800-498-9581 (toll-free)
Fax: 706-864-1478
E-mail: tdavis@nugget.ngc.peachnet.edu
Web site: http://www.ngc.peachnet.edu

NORTHWOOD UNIVERSITY
MIDLAND, MICHIGAN; CEDAR HILL, TEXAS; AND WEST PALM BEACH, FLORIDA

The University

Northwood University was founded in 1959 by Dr. Arthur E. Turner and Dr. R. Gary Stauffer, who had decided that the liberal arts approach to business did not really expose students to the wealth of opportunities the world of work had to offer. Established originally in Alma, Michigan, the school moved to Midland in 1961. The Texas campus was opened in 1966. Other recent expansions include the Florida campus in West Palm Beach and the Northwood University Margaret Chase Smith Library Center in Skowhegan, Maine. The University has extension centers in Mt. Clemens, Michigan; New Orleans, Louisiana; Dallas, Texas; and Washington, D.C. Northwood University also coordinates an external degree program in Michigan, Florida, Louisiana, Indiana, Texas, and Kentucky, which enables highly motivated students to earn their degree while working full-time. Even though Northwood's campuses are in different locations, with students coming from more than forty states and many countries, all have one goal in common: the preservation and promotion of the American free enterprise work ethic. Students come to Northwood to develop entry-level skills for management positions in business and industry.

Academic Program

Northwood University's programs have been designed to prepare men and women for specific career goals. The courses for the major (approximately 30 percent of the total requirements) are reinforced by classes in general business (30 percent) and the humanities (40 percent). Associate degree candidates are required to complete 90 term hours with a minimum GPA of 2.0. Bachelor's degree candidates must complete 180 term hours with a minimum GPA of 2.0. Northwood's terms last ten weeks. The fall term runs from September through November, the winter term from December through February, and the spring term from March through May. In addition, the college offers three 3-week summer sessions. Northwood believes strongly in the free enterprise system and, accordingly, has designed its curriculum to reflect this belief. All students must satisfactorily complete core courses in accounting, business law, economics, management, and marketing. No matter what the ultimate career goal of a student may be, he or she will have acquired a set of basic skills as preparation for the productive world of work. This academic program, however, does not prohibit students from appreciating the arts. Northwood strongly promotes the interrelationship between the business and art worlds by providing on- and off-campus voluntary programs.

Financial Aid

Students should file the Free Application for Federal Student Aid (FAFSA). Available aid includes Federal Pell Grants, Federal Supplemental Educational Opportunity Grants, state and institutional grants and scholarships, Federal Stafford Student Loans, loans for parents, Federal Perkins Loans, and Federal Work-Study awards. Approximately 70 percent of students receive some type of financial aid.

Application and Information

There is no deadline for submitting applications for freshman-year admission. Transfer students are admitted year-round. For more information, students should contact the appropriate campus:

Director of Admissions
Northwood University
3225 Cook Road
Midland, Michigan 48640
Telephone: 800-457-7878 (toll-free)

Director of Admissions
Northwood University
P.O. Box 58
Cedar Hill, Texas 75104
Telephone: 214-291-1541
800-927-9663 (toll-free)

Director of Admissions
Northwood University
2600 North Military Trail
West Palm Beach, Florida 33409
Telephone: 800-458-8325 (toll-free)

NOVA SOUTHEASTERN UNIVERSITY
FORT LAUDERDALE, FLORIDA

The University

Nova Southeastern University is the largest independent or non-tax-supported university in the state of Florida. Based upon annual expenditures, it is among the 100 largest independent colleges and universities in this country. Nova Southeastern University is an independent, nonsectarian, nonprofit, and racially nondiscriminatory university. It is accredited by the Southern Association of Colleges and Schools. Unusual among institutions of higher education, NSU is a university for all ages: the University School for children, numerous undergraduate and graduate degree programs in a variety of fields, and nondegree continuing education programs are all available at Nova Southeastern. The traditional population in the undergraduate program is approximately 1,000 students. Since its beginning, the University has been distinguished by its uncommon programs, which provide alternative choices in forms of education, and by its research, which is aimed at finding solutions to problems of immediate concern to mankind.

Academic Program

The undergraduate program for Nova Southeastern's daytime population combines a core curriculum with a set of majors designed to prepare students for work in graduate school or a professional career. The general education program assumes that the most appropriate learning experience is intensive and focused on issues, thinking skills, and communication and computation, rather than focused simply on disciplinary content. General education courses, therefore, are interdisciplinary in their approach to content and integrate lectures, student-based discussions, films, speakers, and research and field experiences into the curriculum. Other Nova Southeastern University programs are organized for the adult working population. Courses are offered in the evenings and on weekends at the main campus, as well as at off-campus locations convenient to students. Most students are employed and have passed the traditional age of undergraduates; many have families. Credits may be awarded for prior learning experiences after a student's application for such credit has been approved by a faculty committee. Additional credit may be earned through PEP and CLEP general and subject examinations. Credit toward a degree may also be transferred from regionally accredited institutions.

Financial Aid

Nova Southeastern University offers a comprehensive program of financial aid to assist students in meeting their educational expenses. Financial aid is available to help cover direct educational costs, such as tuition, fees, books, and supplies, as well as indirect costs, such as food, clothing, and transportation. The following forms of financial aid are available to qualified undergraduate students: Federal Pell Grants, Federal Supplemental Educational Opportunity Grants, Florida Student Assistance Grants, Florida Academic Scholars Fund awards, Florida Tuition Vouchers, Federal Stafford Student Loans, Federal Perkins Loans, Federal PLUS loans, Federal Work-Study awards, and Florida College Career Work Experience Program awards. In addition, many academic scholarships are available. Deferred-payment plans and veterans' benefits are also offered. Applicants for financial aid are required to submit the Free Application for Federal Student Aid (FAFSA) in order to be considered for all campus-based aid programs. Students who apply before April 1 are given priority consideration for funds; however, applications are accepted all year.

Application and Information

The application should be submitted with a nonrefundable $25 application fee. There is no closing date for applications for the fall term. Applicants are notified of the admission decision on a rolling basis. Deferred admission is available. For further information, prospective applicants are invited to contact:

Office of Undergraduate Admissions
Nova Southeastern University
3301 College Avenue
Fort Lauderdale, Florida 33314

Telephone: 954-475-7360
954-475-7340 (for adult programs)
800-338-4723 Ext. 7360 (toll-free)
E-mail: ncsinfo@polaris.acast.nova.edu

OHIO UNIVERSITY
ATHENS, OHIO

The University

Chartered in 1804, Ohio University symbolizes America's early commitment to higher education. About 19,140 students (16,271 at the undergraduate level and 2,872 at the graduate level) study at Ohio University, and visitors frequently comment that it does not seem as large as they expected it would. Eighty-nine percent of the students are Ohio residents, while 11 percent are from out of state, of which 2 percent are international students from approximately 100 countries. Because the University is located in a small town, most extracurricular activities take place on campus. More than 335 student organizations are registered with the University, and each student tends to get involved in at least one group. About 36 percent of the students take part in intramural sports, and University-sponsored plays, art exhibits, and recitals are quite popular. Sororities and fraternities are the choice of about 14 percent of the student body. Campus recreational facilities include an indoor Olympic-size pool, an ice rink, a fitness center, lighted intramural fields and tennis courts, a nine-hole golf course, and a jogging-bicycling path that partially encircles the campus. A $26-million student recreation center opened in January 1996.

Academic Program

All undergraduate students at Ohio University must complete a core curriculum structured in three tiers. Tier One consists of English composition and mathematics competency-based courses as well as a junior-level English course. Tier Two is made up of 30 quarter hours of work selected from five areas: applied sciences, social sciences, natural sciences, humanities, and Third World cultures. Taken during the senior year, Tier Three is a synthesis course that combines learning from different disciplines. All bachelor's degree programs at Ohio University require 192 quarter hours for graduation. The Honors Tutorial College, the University's excellent honors program, gives students the chance to learn in tutorial settings. The program is limited to 40 freshmen each year, and many honors students earn their degree in three years. Both Army and Air Force ROTC programs are offered.

Financial Aid

Ohio University awards financial aid from federally funded and state-funded programs as well as from privately funded sources. All types of aid fall within two categories: need-based and merit-based assistance. Awards are made based on demonstration of financial need, special merit, or both. Seventy-two percent of Ohio University's undergraduate students receive some form of financial assistance. The University requires all students applying for need-based assistance to complete the Free Application for Federal Student Aid (FAFSA). Freshman scholarships range in value from $750 to full tuition. Scholarships for upperclass students are offered as well. Generally, upperclass students with a grade point average of at least 3.4 are eligible to apply for scholarship assistance.

Application and Information

The deadline for admission to the fall term for freshman applicants is February 1; for transfer students entering in the fall, it is June 1. Some programs reserve the right to close admission before the deadline. Admission decisions are made on a rolling basis beginning in October and continue until all applications received by the deadline have been processed. Applicants are notified of admission status within four weeks after receipt of all application materials.

Inquiries should be made to:

Office of Admissions
Ohio University
Chubb Hall 120
Athens, Ohio 45701-2979

Telephone: 614-593-4100
Fax: 614-593-0560
Web site: http://www.ohiou.edu/

OLIVET COLLEGE
OLIVET, MICHIGAN

The College

Olivet College was founded in 1844 as the first college in the country, by charter, to be open to all persons regardless of race or gender. Today's students come from twenty-nine states and ten countries and represent most major faiths, races, ethnicities, and economic backgrounds. The College enrolls approximately 800 students. Olivet College recently completed a comprehensive review of its educational philosophy and programs to ensure that students acquire the skills needed to succeed in a changing world, both in a career and in a life. An intentional focus on individual and social responsibility, on character as well as competence, and on service as well as career is the cornerstone of the Olivet Plan. The distinctive vision of Olivet College is to provide an education for individual and social responsibility. The Olivet Plan gives students the skills essential for success in a highly competitive marketplace. The Olivet Plan teaches lessons in character and responsibility. These are essential traits for realizing full potential both as individuals and as a society. Olivet graduates develop a solid goal orientation, interpersonal and small group skills, critical thinking skills, clear communication skills, global awareness, an understanding of others with diverse backgrounds, strong ethical and moral character, and an ethic of responsibility for oneself and for others that they demonstrate to employers and graduate schools.

Academic Program

Olivet operates on a modified semester system. Fall semester runs from September through December. Spring semester runs from January through mid-May and includes an intensive learning term (ILT). During the ILT, students may concentrate their attention on completing a single course of special interest in approximately three weeks. Most classes meet only twice a week. Wednesdays are reserved for activities such as service learning, portfolio assessment, and learning communities. At the heart of the Olivet Plan are five key groups of educational outcomes. These outcomes define skills that all students must acquire prior to graduation, whatever their academic majors or career aspirations. Educational outcomes include communicating, reasoning, working together, and individual and social responsibility. Key elements of the Olivet Plan include a portfolio assessment program, the first-year experience, a general education program, required service learning experience, learning communities, the academic major, and senior experience. Celebrating both the wealth of human diversity and the bond of human similarity is a theme that runs throughout all elements of the Olivet Plan.

Financial Aid

Olivet College is the only college in the nation to make civic responsibility and demonstrable community service the keystone of its entire scholarship program. The College has earmarked up to $1 million for 1996 and up to $10 million over the next four years for scholarships for students with a history of service to others. Community Responsibility Scholarships, valued at up to $6000 per year, are an integral part of the College's implementation of its new vision—education for individual and social responsibility.

Application and Information

Prospective students, parents, and counselors are encouraged to visit Olivet to talk with admission representatives, tour the facilities, and meet with students and faculty members. For additional information, students should contact:

Director of Admissions
Olivet College
Olivet, Michigan 49076

Telephone: 616-749-7635
800-456-7189 (toll-free)
E-mail: admissions@olivetnet.edu
Web site: http://www.olivetnet.edu

OTIS COLLEGE OF ART AND DESIGN
LOS ANGELES, CALIFORNIA

The College

In the coming century, artists and designers will be central in a new economic order. Their efforts will provide an important competitive edge—good design in everything from products to clothing, from information to the spaces where people live and work. Through the twentieth century, Otis has evolved as a trend-setting leader in art and design education. A dynamic future awaits the new generation of artists and designers seeking a traditional education coupled with advanced technical training. The Goldsmith campus in Los Angeles' Westchester district has been designed as the realization of the dreams of Otis' working faculty members and dedicated administrators. Otis is an artist's art school, where the spaces are designed specifically for the activities that happen in them. These spaces allow the artist's maximum potential for creativity to emerge in a comprehensive educational setting inclusive of the newest and most advanced facilities and equipment.

Academic Program

The Foundation Year helps new students to master a broad spectrum of studio skills and gives a comprehensive introduction to the liberal arts and sciences. A Foundation Honors Course is an additional challenge for qualified students in English and art history. The primary goal of both the Fine Art and Design Departments is to prepare students in each major for a professional career. While intensive studio classes form the core of the Otis experience, courses in the liberal arts and sciences, art history, and criticism ensure that students acquire the broad-based education the College feels is necessary for a successful life. Other special features include professional internships in the fine arts and design and a written thesis component for most seniors.

Financial Aid

Otis is proud to award scholarships to more than one half of its students. In addition, aid from other sources, such as the state and federal governments, provides aid monies to more than 60 percent of the student body. Students must complete the Free Application for Federal Student Aid (FAFSA) and the Otis Supplemental Financial Aid Application. Applicants for fall admission are encouraged to file on or before the March 2 deadline; applicants for January admission should submit all forms before December 1. California residents are encouraged to file the Cal Grant GPA Verification Form and Application before the March 2 deadline. The FAFSA and Supplemental Application may be submitted after these priority dates, but aid will be awarded on a first-come, first-served basis according to availability. All aid is based on artistic and academic merit and a student's financial need as determined by the College Scholarship Service.

Application and Information

Applicants must complete the Otis Application for Admission and attach the nonrefundable application fee (a $40 check or money order made payable to Otis). High school transcripts should be sent to the Otis Office of Admissions. Students with previous college experience should have those transcripts forwarded as well. Applicants currently in high school must submit either SAT I or ACT scores. Letters of recommendation are encouraged, but they are not required. Additional requirements include a portfolio and an essay describing the student's decision to become an artist or designer. Students are encouraged to visit the Otis campus. The portfolio may be presented in person. Students should call the Office of Admissions to arrange an interview. Students who are unable to present their work in person should mail all materials to the Office of Admissions within three weeks of their application.

Michael Fuller
Director of Admissions
Office of Admissions
Otis College of Art and Design
9045 Lincoln Boulevard
Los Angeles, California 90045-9785

Telephone: 310-665-6800 (Los Angeles residents)
800-527-OTIS (toll-free)

PACE UNIVERSITY
NEW YORK CITY AND PLEASANTVILLE, NEW YORK

The University
Pace University was founded in 1906 by two brothers, Homer and Charles Pace. The vision they had in 1906 is reflected in Pace's motto: "Opportunitas." Pace provides a remarkable array of learning, living, and working opportunities to all students. More than 100 majors and 3,000 courses of study are offered in the following five undergraduate schools: the Dyson College of Arts and Sciences, the Lubin School of Business, the School of Computer Science and Information Systems, the School of Education, and the Lienhard School of Nursing. There are many activities and clubs to choose from, including the Black Students Organization, the Chinese Club, the Caribbean Students Association, student government associations, fraternities, sororities, two campus newspapers, two literary magazines, two yearbooks, two campus radio stations, and intercollegiate baseball, basketball, cross-country running, equestrian sports, football, lacrosse, softball, tennis, and volleyball. In 1996–97, approximately 9,480 undergraduate students were enrolled at Pace. The student body is diversified, with students coming from across the United States and from more than sixty-one countries.

Academic Program
The pattern of study at Pace University emphasizes the breadth of the core curriculum and involves taking prerequisites in the first two years and major courses plus electives in the junior and senior years. Selective academic programs in the University are preparatory to professional training in dentistry, law, medicine, and veterinary science. The University honors program is designed to foster the intellectual life of outstanding students by enabling them to take greater responsibility and initiative in their academic work. Honors advisers assist students through individual advising. The Open Curriculum privilege permits an honors program member to choose courses in arts and sciences with a greater degree of freedom. The Independent Study Program encourages qualified students to undertake research and study to a depth beyond the normal course requirements. Pace participates in the Advanced Placement Program of the College Board. The Cooperative Education Program offers qualified students the opportunity to gain experience in their field while earning a four-year degree. Students can choose full-time, part-time, or summer schedules, working in an area directly related to their major course of study. It is recommended that admission to the program take place during the first year at the University.

Financial Aid
Financial aid is available through scholarships, institutional grants-in-aid, athletic scholarships, Federal Pell Grants, Federal Supplemental Educational Opportunity Grants, Federal Perkins Loans, Federal Stafford Student Loans, New York State Tuition Assistance Program awards (as well as awards from other states' incentive grant programs), Federal Work-Study awards, federal nursing scholarships and loans, and Law Enforcement Education Program awards. Further information on these programs may be obtained by contacting the Office of Financial Aid at the appropriate campus.

Application and Information
Requests for application forms and information for both the Pleasantville and New York City campuses should be addressed to the Student Information Center at the following address.

Student Information Center
Pace University
1 Pace Plaza
New York City, New York 10038

Telephone: 800-874-7223
Fax: 212-346-1821
E-mail: infoctr@ny027.wan.pace.edu
Web site: http://www.pace.edu

PACIFIC LUTHERAN UNIVERSITY
TACOMA, WASHINGTON

The University

Three characteristics make prospective students enthusiastic about Pacific Lutheran University (PLU). The first is academic distinction, documented nationally in *U.S. News & World Report* and *Peterson's Competitive Colleges.* The second is the personality of the University community, which makes a difference in determining the type of student, professor, or employee who chooses to become associated with PLU. Each knows that the University's objectives reflect Christian principles and ideals, a willingness to help and serve, and a sensitivity to the welfare, happiness, and personal integrity of others. The third most alluring feature of the University is its geographic location, which is one of the most beautiful natural environments in the country. Founded in 1890 by Scandinavian Lutheran pioneers, PLU retains pride in its heritage while seeking cultural diversity to stimulate exchange and broaden understanding. A private university owned by the Evangelical Lutheran Church in America, PLU offers many opportunities for expressing and deepening Christian faith. At the same time, many forms of self-expression enrich a campus devoted to the development of knowledgeable, thoughtful, responsible, and dedicated citizens. The University's 3,463 students represent thirty-eight states and thirty-two countries. Multiethnic and international students represent about 15 percent of the campus population.

Academic Program

PLU operates on a 4-1-4 calendar, with two 14-week semesters bridged by a 4-week January term. Three 4-week summer sessions are often used by full-time students to accelerate their college career. All degree-seeking students, regardless of major, may choose one of two core curriculums. Core I (distributive core) requires nine courses in each of the following areas: arts and literature, natural sciences and mathematics, philosophy, religious studies, and social sciences. Core II (integrated studies program) requires completion of seven interdisciplinary classes that explore the theme "The Dynamics of Change." The nationally regarded core emphasizes the interrelationships among all fields of knowledge. Most courses provide 4 semester hours of credit, with 128 semester hours required for graduation. The January term provides a variety of traditional and nontraditional courses, on and off campus, across the country and around the world.

Financial Aid

The Free Application for Federal Student Aid (FAFSA) is used to determine a student's financial need for the awarding of scholarships, grants, and loans. More than $35 million in financial aid is distributed annually to nearly 85 percent of PLU students. The average financial aid package totals more than $12,000. Most awards are made in midspring for the following academic year. Students may find employment on or off campus with the assistance of the Center for Careers and Employment.

Application and Information

Application for admission may be made by submitting a PLU application, which is available from the Admissions Office; a $35 nonrefundable fee; transcripts of high school credits at least through the junior year as well as those of any college course work; SAT I or ACT test scores; a completed essay form; and recommendations from 2 qualified people, such as principals, teachers, counselors, and pastors. Applicants seeking financial aid must submit the FAFSA to the Federal Processing Agent by January 31 for maximum consideration.

Laura Polcyn, Dean
Office of Admissions
Pacific Lutheran University
Tacoma, Washington 98447

Telephone: 800-274-6758 (toll-free)
Fax: 206-535-8320 (As of April 15, area code is 253.)

POINT PARK COLLEGE
PITTSBURGH, PENNSYLVANIA

The College

Point Park College, founded in 1960, has undergone a vigorous development and is accredited by the Middle States Association of Colleges and Schools. Enrollment has grown to 2,200, and the number of majors available now totals more than thirty, including a Master of Arts degree program in journalism and communications and an international M.B.A. In addition to those for the performing arts, internship programs have been developed with local broadcasting stations, area hospitals, and the management and technical training programs of such corporate giants as Westinghouse, USX, and PPG Industries. Clubs associated with specific majors, fraternities, sororities, the Point Park College Singers, and the Student Activities Center are a few of the organizations that students may join.

Academic Program

Point Park is an innovative institution. Its philosophy is not one of molding the student into some predetermined pattern but one of meeting and adapting to individual requirements within the framework of a sound humanistic education. This commitment is reflected in programs that, while providing for the expansion of mind and spirit that the liberal arts alone can give, places strong emphasis on developing career skills. Thus, all degree programs, with the exception of the B.F.A. programs, include a core curriculum requirement of 42 credit hours. The core curriculum includes choices in the humanities as well as in the social, behavioral, and natural sciences. With the approval of their guidance offices, high school students may take courses at Point Park for full college credit. The College grants advanced standing on the basis of the College Board's Advanced Placement tests, the CLEP examinations, and educational experiences in the armed forces. In addition, the College has long-standing experience in meeting the needs of transfer students.

Financial Aid

Point Park makes a sincere effort to ensure that each student who desires to attend is able to do so. Accordingly, the College administers a generous program of financial aid, including Federal Work-Study awards and Point Park, Federal Pell, and Federal Supplemental Educational Opportunity grants. The College administers loans under the Federal Perkins Loan Program and the Federal Stafford Student Loan Program. Academic, talent, and athletic scholarships are also available for all students, including transfer students. Applicants for financial aid must demonstrate financial need and show evidence of academic promise or achievement. To apply, students must submit a completed College application form. All students must submit applications for federal, state, and Point Park financial aid through the Pennsylvania Higher Education Assistance Agency (PHEAA).

Application and Information

Applications for the fall semester are taken on a rolling basis; however, students are urged to apply early in their senior year of secondary school. Early application is particularly important for students desiring residence hall accommodations and financial aid. Applications from freshman and transfer candidates are also considered for the spring semester and should be filed by December 15. The College requires each freshman applicant to submit an application, a nonrefundable $20 fee, SAT I or ACT scores, and an official high school transcript. Transfer applicants must also submit official transcripts from all colleges attended.

Application forms and additional information may be obtained by writing to:

Office of Admissions
Point Park College
201 Wood Street
Pittsburgh, Pennsylvania 15222

Telephone: 412-392-3430
800-321-0129 (toll-free)
Fax: 412-391-1980
Web site: http://www.ppc.edu

PROVIDENCE COLLEGE
PROVIDENCE, RHODE ISLAND

The College

Conducted under the auspices of the Order of Preachers of the Province of St. Joseph, commonly known as the Dominicans, Providence College (PC) was established in 1917. Originally a college for men, it became coeducational in 1971. The College's full-time undergraduate enrollment of more than 3,500 is equally divided between men and women. Approximately 1,680 students live in nine residential halls, and an additional 900 upperclass students are housed in one of the five College apartment complexes. The remainder of the students live in apartments directly off campus or commute from home. The modern Slavin Center, as the nucleus of student social, cultural, and recreational activity, provides numerous facilities; they include lounges, club offices, a post office, a convenience store, a bank, a bookstore/gift shop, a sports pub, a minimall, the Office of Student Services, and offices for the Student Congress, the Board of Programmers, student publications, the Counseling and Placement Center, and the chaplain. The Peterson Recreation Center is the site of intramural athletic activities on campus, in which more than 80 percent of the students participate.

Academic Program

The primary objective of Providence College is to further the intellectual development of its students through the disciplines of the sciences and the humanities. The liberal education provided by the College gives students the chance to increase their ability to formulate their thoughts and communicate them to others, evaluate their varied experiences, and achieve insight into the past, present, and future of civilization. The College is concerned about preparing students to become intelligent, productive, and responsible citizens in a democratic society. The College's programs are also designed to help students discover their particular aptitude and prepare them to undertake specialized studies leading to careers. Students are required to complete a total of 116 credit hours in the core curriculum, in a selected major, and in electives. The College participates in the Advanced Placement Program administered by the College Board. Students who demonstrate superior performance (a score of 4 or 5) on any of the Advanced Placement examinations are considered for advanced placement and standing in the area of study in which they qualify. PC operates on a two-semester calendar. Fall-semester classes begin in early September and spring-semester classes begin in mid-January.

Financial Aid

Providence College's financial aid is distributed on the basis of demonstrated need and the student's ability to benefit from the educational opportunity the assistance offers. To apply for financial aid, candidates must submit both a College Scholarship Service PROFILE application and the Free Application for Federal Student Aid (FAFSA) by February 1. Upon final determination of students' need, the Office of Financial Aid constructs aid packages consisting of work, loan, and grant assistance in accordance with federal regulations, the availability of funds, and institutional policy as approved by the College's Financial Aid Advisory Committee. Sources of financial aid include Federal Work-Study awards, Federal Perkins Loans, Federal Pell Grants, Federal Supplemental Educational Opportunity Grants (FSEOG), Providence College grants-in-aid, Providence College Achievement Scholarships, and Merit Scholarships.

Application and Information

The deadlines for receiving applications for the September term are January 15 for regular applicants and March 15 for transfer students. Early action applicants must file an application by November 15. The deadlines for receiving applications for the January term are November 1 for regular applicants and December 1 for transfer students. Further information may be obtained by contacting:

Dean of Admissions
Providence College
549 River Avenue
Providence, Rhode Island 02918-0001

Telephone: 401-865-2535
Fax: 401-865-2826

RANDOLPH–MACON WOMAN'S COLLEGE
LYNCHBURG, VIRGINIA

The College
Randolph-Macon (R-MWC) was the first women's college to be accredited by the Southern Association of Colleges and Schools and the first southern women's college to be granted a Phi Beta Kappa charter. Academic excellence through the liberal arts and an emphasis on individual learning continue to be Randolph-Macon's top priorities. The College's enduring commitment to women's education has fostered strong programs in career development and in alumnae networking. There are six residence halls on the 100-acre campus, housing 85 percent of the students. The College's location near the Blue Ridge Mountains provides ample recreational opportunities, and proximity to neighboring men's colleges and major universities enhances the social life on and off campus. To supplement the academic program and student activities, the College brings noted speakers, performers, and artists to the campus. In addition, various concerts, plays, films, and exhibitions are presented throughout the year.

Academic Program
Randolph-Macon's academic program offers the student both flexibility and choice. Through consultation with her faculty adviser, each student develops a four-year plan to integrate academic interests with career planning, leadership, and volunteer activities. The academic requirements encourage students to pursue a well-rounded curriculum in the liberal arts. A student selects courses from at least four different departments during each of her first two semesters at the College. At least 124 semester hours of credit are required for both the A.B. and B.S. degrees, including a minimum of 24 hours and no more than 62 hours in the major field. The College operates on a traditional semester system, with self-scheduled exams given before the December vacation and at the end of the second semester in May. R-MWC provides maximum opportunity for independent study and research.

Financial Aid
Randolph-Macon Woman's College encourages students of all socioeconomic backgrounds to apply for admission regardless of their family's current financial status. A generous financial assistance program provides 98.62 percent of the student body with some form of assistance, including merit-based scholarships and need-based grants. Applicants for financial aid must file the Free Application for Federal Student Aid (FAFSA) and the R-MWC Application for Financial Aid by March 1. The usual aid package consists of a grant-in-aid, a loan, and campus employment. Funds are available through the Federal Perkins Loan, the Federal Stafford Student Loan, the Federal Pell Grant, the Federal Supplemental Educational Opportunity Grant, and the Federal Work-Study programs, as well as through the College's own endowment. Honor scholarships, based on academic achievement, are awarded to incoming freshmen under the R-MWC Distinguished Scholar Program. No separate application is required, but in order to be considered for top scholarships, students must submit the application for admission by January 15.

Application and Information
Early decision candidates should apply by November 15 of the senior year in secondary school and will receive notification from the College about December 15. Candidates for general admission must apply by March 1 in order to receive preferential consideration; they will receive notification at the time their files are complete, beginning in late January. A $25 application fee must accompany the application for admission, but this fee may be waived in cases of hardship at the request of the student and the recommendation of her high school counselor. Randolph-Macon also participates in the College Board test fee waiver program. For more information, students should contact:

Director of Admissions
Randolph-Macon Woman's College
2500 Rivermont Avenue
Lynchburg, Virginia 24503

Telephone: 804-947-8100
800-745-7692 (toll-free)
E-mail: admissions@rmwc.edu
Web site: http://www.rmwc.edu

REED COLLEGE
PORTLAND, OREGON

The College

For its 1,200 students and 125 faculty members, Reed College is foremost an intellectual community. Since its founding in 1909, Reed has attracted students with a high degree of self-discipline and a genuine enthusiasm for academic work and intellectual challenge. Reed attracts a geographically diversified student body: four fifths of Reed's students come from outside the Northwest, with more than 20 percent from the Northeast and 5 percent from outside the United States. Campus social opportunities are open to all, with no closed clubs or organizations and no sororities or fraternities. Community life is full of activity and variety, with more than fifty student organizations. Club sports are competitive in a number of areas, but Reed is a college where varsity sports have always been viewed with skepticism. Fitness and development of lifelong skills take precedence over competition.

Academic Program

Hallmarks of academic life at Reed include the demanding, small group conference method of teaching and its reliance on active student participation, a de-emphasis of grades, a yearlong interdisciplinary humanities program, and an integrated academic program that balances the breadth of traditional course content and distribution requirements with flexibility in designing an in-depth senior thesis. Learning and the development of skills in preparation for a life of learning take precedence over the mere memorization of facts. In addition to fulfilling the requirements for the major, taking the humanities course, and writing the senior thesis, students must satisfy a distributional requirement, consisting of two core classes from each of the following academic divisions: literature, philosophy, and the arts; history, social sciences, and psychology; the natural sciences; and math, foreign language, logic, and linguistics.

Financial Aid

Nearly half of Reed students receive financial assistance from the College. A full need-based financial aid program makes Reed accessible to students from a wide range of economic backgrounds. The College guarantees to meet the full demonstrated need of all continuing students in good academic standing. In addition, during their first two semesters, approximately 50 percent of the freshmen and transfer students receive financial assistance equal to their demonstrated need. Admission decisions are separate from financial aid procedures, and students are admitted regardless of ability to pay. Reed's own funds are the primary source of grants to students. The College budgeted more than $7.5 million for this purpose in 1996–97, with individual awards ranging from $750 to $24,360. Reed also administers federal grants and a variety of other awards. Federally subsidized loans and Perkins Loans are available, along with campus employment and work-study programs. The size of a financial aid award is based upon analysis of the student's need. The financial aid program includes grants, loans, and work opportunities.

Application and Information

The Office of Admission is open from 8:30 a.m. until 5 p.m. (Pacific time) all year, except for major holidays. For further information or to arrange a campus tour, overnight stay, information session, or interview, students should call or write:

Office of Admission
Reed College
3203 SE Woodstock Boulevard
Portland, Oregon 97202-8199

Telephone: 503-777-7511
800-547-4750 (toll-free)
Fax: 503-777-7553
E-mail: admission@reed.edu
Web site: http://www.reed.edu

REGIS COLLEGE
WESTON, MASSACHUSETTS

The College
Regis College, a leading Catholic liberal arts and sciences college, is committed to the education of women. Rooted in a strong tradition of academic excellence, Regis College was founded in 1927 by the Sisters of St. Joseph. The College offers challenging academic programs, professional internships, opportunities for developing leadership talents, and a social environment conducive to acquiring friendships that will last a lifetime. The focus of Regis College is on the development of the whole person, enabling students to become educated in all aspects of human behavior: intellectual, spiritual, occupational, social, physical, and emotional. While many of the College's 1,202 undergraduates and 200 graduate students are New England residents, other students are from several different states, Puerto Rico, and seventeen countries, including Argentina, China, Colombia, Germany, Honduras, Japan, Kenya, Thailand, and Venezuela. The multicultural student body offers a diversity that is shared and celebrated on the Regis College campus through programs and activities. A vital part of the Regis College experience is student involvement in activities outside the classroom.

Academic Program
Completion of thirty-eight courses is required to earn the bachelor's degree. All bachelor's degree programs include an eleven-course liberal arts core curriculum, an academic major of concentrated study, and elective courses chosen according to the student's interests. The eleven-course core curriculum consists of courses in the following areas: natural sciences, social sciences, English composition, foreign language, religious studies, and humanities. To fulfill departmental requirements, students must complete from nine to twelve courses in their major field of study. For graduation with Departmental Honors, students are required to complete a two-course sequence of independent study culminating in a written thesis, which must be orally defended, and maintain averages of at least 3.0 overall and 3.3 in their major field.

Financial Aid
Regis sponsors financial aid through federally funded grants, loans, and work-study awards and also provides scholarships from College operating funds. To apply for any scholarship or financial aid program, applicants should submit the Free Application for Federal Student Aid and the CSS Financial Aid PROFILE form. All financial aid applicants are also required to forward a complete copy of their parents' federal income tax return. Students who request scholarships or other financial aid through Regis College are informed of the College's financial aid award decision between March 1 and April 30. Seventy-five percent of all Regis students receive scholarships and financial assistance through federal and College funds. Regis College offers merit scholarships for first-year and transfer students in recognition of academic performance, community service, and leadership abilities. All accepted candidates are considered for the merit scholarships. There are three levels of merit scholarships, $8000, $5000, and $2000, all renewable for four years, provided appropriate GPAs are achieved. These scholarships are awarded on a competitive basis.

Application and Information
An applicant for admission registers by completing the application form, available upon request from the Admissions Office, and returning it with the $30 application fee. Regis College operates on a rolling admission basis; students will hear from the Admissions Office regarding their status within one month of receipt of completed applications. Students are encouraged to visit the campus for interviews and guided tours. For more information and an application for admission, students should contact:

Director of Admission
Regis College
235 Wellesley Street
Weston, Massachusetts 02193-1571

Telephone: 617-768-7100
800-456-1820 (toll-free)

RENSSELAER POLYTECHNIC INSTITUTE
TROY, NEW YORK

The Institute

Rensselaer Polytechnic Institute was founded in 1824 by Stephen Van Rensselaer "for the purpose of instructing persons in the application of science to the common purposes of life." Nearly two centuries later, Rensselaer is still pursuing that original mission and has become one of the world's most outstanding technological universities. Today, Rensselaer is composed of five separate but closely aligned schools: the Schools of Architecture, Engineering, Humanities and Social Sciences, and Science and the Lally School of Management and Technology. It offers more than 100 programs at the bachelor's, master's, and doctoral levels and a growing array of on-campus as well as satellite-transmitted courses in continuing education. Rensselaer has long had a tradition of cross-disciplinary, real-world, industry-oriented research and education, which is reflected in its Incubator Center, Technology Park, and its well-known research centers in such fields as design and manufacturing, integrated electronics, polymer processing, interactive learning, and science and technology policy. Rensselaer has strong and deep ties to a broad range of firms, including large multinational companies such as IBM, AT&T, Intel, Lockheed Martin, and GE; fast-growing entrepreneurial companies such as Arrow International Inc. and MapInfo; consumer-oriented companies such as Procter & Gamble, Bugle Boy, and Pepsi-Cola; consulting firms such as Andersen Consulting and Ernst & Young; and a growing array of firms in the financial services sector such as Salomon Brothers and Merrill Lynch. Rensselaer has a total of 6,300 students—4,150 undergraduate and 2,150 graduate students. One of the Institute's strengths is the diversity of its student body. Rensselaer students come from all fifty states as well as the District of Columbia, Puerto Rico, the Virgin Islands, and more than seventy countries around the world.

Academic Program

While each school has its own sequence requirements, the following minimums apply to all students: 124 credit hours and a 1.8 quality point average in total courses; 24 credit hours in physical, life, and engineering sciences; 24 in humanities and social sciences; 30 in a selected discipline; and 24 in electives. The Undergraduate Research Program offers hands-on experience to students in hundreds of areas. Any full-time undergraduate, from the first year on, can participate for credit or pay during the academic year or the summer. A cooperative education program with industry provides a study-work experience for students who wish to add practical experience to their academic study. The study-work schedule is such that students graduate in the class with whom they matriculated. A cooperative venture with forty-four liberal arts colleges permits undergraduates at those colleges to transfer to Rensselaer under a number of options and to earn dual degrees—the Bachelor of Arts from the first college and the Bachelor of Science or a master's degree from Rensselaer. Air Force, Army, and Naval/Marine ROTC programs are available on an elective basis.

Financial Aid

Most applicants accepted into the freshman class who have financial need are offered assistance. A great many Rensselaer students receive such aid under a comprehensive program of scholarships, loans, and part-time employment that provides assistance ranging from $100 to $24,000 per year. Among federal funds available are student loans, Federal Work-Study Program awards, and ROTC scholarships.

Application and Information

Dean of Undergraduate Admissions
Rensselaer Polytechnic Institute
Troy, New York 12180

Telephone: 518-276-6216
Fax: 518-276-4072
E-mail: admissions@rpi.edu
Web site: http://www.rpi.edu/dept/admissions/www

THE RICHARD STOCKTON COLLEGE OF NEW JERSEY
POMONA, NEW JERSEY

The College
The Richard Stockton College of New Jersey is an undergraduate college of arts, sciences, and professional studies within the New Jersey System of Higher Education. Named for Richard Stockton, one of the New Jersey signers of the Declaration of Independence, the College was authorized by the passage of the state's 1968 bond referendum for higher education and accepted its charter class in 1971. The College is accredited by the Commission on Higher Education of the Middle States Association of Colleges and Schools. As a college of the New Jersey System of Higher Education, Stockton offers programs that are approved by the State Board of Higher Education. The Environmental Health Program is accredited by the National Environmental Health Science and Protection Accreditation Council; the Social Work Program has been accredited by the Council on Social Work Education; the teacher education sequence has been approved by the New Jersey Department of Education and the National Association of State Directors of Teacher Education and Certification; the Nursing Program has been accredited by the National League for Nursing and is approved by the New Jersey Board of Nursing; and the Chemistry Program has been accredited by the American Chemical Society. In addition to its bachelor's degrees, the College offers several graduate programs: a Master of Physical Therapy, a Master of Business Studies (concentrations in accounting, international business, marketing, and management), a Master of Occupational Therapy, a Master of Instructional Technology; and a Master of Nursing (speciality for adult health practitioner).

Academic Program
To earn a baccalaureate degree at Stockton, a student must satisfactorily complete a minimum of 128 semester credits. Degree programs include a combination of general studies and program (major field) studies. The Bachelor of Arts student must earn a total of 64 credits in general studies; the Bachelor of Science student must earn 48. General studies courses are broad cross-disciplinary courses designed to introduce students to all major areas of the curriculum and to the broadly applicable intellectual skills necessary for success in college. Students must select some courses from each major curricular area. The only specifically required courses within general studies are the basic studies courses (up to three), from which students may be exempted on the basis of diagnostic testing. The Bachelor of Arts student must earn a total of 64 credits in program studies; the Bachelor of Science student must earn 80. Program studies (major field) requirements are carefully structured and emphasize sequences of specific courses. Students at Stockton have special opportunities to influence what and how they learn by participating in the major decisions that shape their academic lives. The main avenue of participation is the preceptorial system, which enables students to work, on a personalized basis, with an assigned faculty-staff preceptor in the planning and evaluation of individualized courses of study and in the exploration of various career alternatives.

Financial Aid
Financial aid is available in the form of scholarships, grants, loans, and jobs. Aid is awarded both on a competitive (merit) basis and according to need. Students seeking financial aid must file the Free Application for Federal Student Aid (FAFSA) by March 1. This form is used by the College in evaluating all applications for financial aid.

Application and Information
For more information or application forms, students should contact:

Dean of Enrollment Management
The Richard Stockton College of New Jersey
Jim Leeds Road
Pomona, New Jersey 08240-0195

Telephone: 609-652-4261
E-mail: admissions@pollux.stockton.edu

RICHMOND COLLEGE, THE AMERICAN INTERNATIONAL UNIVERSITY IN LONDON
LONDON, ENGLAND

The University

Richmond College, The American International University in London, prepares men and women to serve with purpose and generosity in an interdependent and multicultural world. Richmond offers a strong academic program with many choices of fields of study, an exceptional faculty, superb campus life, and fellow students from all over the world. Accredited by the Commission on Higher Education of the Middle States Association of Colleges and Schools, a regional accrediting body recognized by the U.S. Department of Education, the University's undergraduate and graduate degrees are designated by the United Kingdom's Department for Education. The University is a comprehensive American liberal arts and professional university. In addition to the undergraduate degree programs described below, Richmond offers a Master of Arts in art history, a Master of Business Administration (M.B.A.), and a Master of Science in systems engineering and management. Small classes, averaging 18 students, enable students to receive personal attention from professors in a supportive environment. The curriculum and academic advising system are structured to enable students to choose courses that provide broad knowledge, relevant skills, and an understanding of the world's many cultures and nations.

Academic Program

In order to graduate with a B.A., students must earn a minimum of 120 credits. Usually this means taking a full load for four years, or eight semesters. Within these 120 credits, students must complete all course requirements for their majors. Students must also meet the University's Language Proficiency and General Education requirements. In addition, valuable work experience for credit is offered through the International Internship and Career Apprenticeship programs. Recent placements have been at the International Herald Tribune, General Electric, The House of Commons, CNN, the United Nations, Lloyds Bank, the Museum of London, and Sony Music Corporation. Credit is also awarded for Advanced Placement tests (6 credits for each subject grade of 3, 4, or 5); a grade of A, B, or C on the "A" Level exams is awarded 9 credits (6 for D or E). Credit is also awarded for the International Baccalaureate, the Baccalauréat de l'Enseignement du Second Degré (France), the Abitur/Reifzuegnis (Germany), the Diploma di Maturità (Italy), and the School Leaving Diploma (Denmark, Finland, Norway, and Sweden).

Financial Aid

Forty to fifty new academic achievement scholarships averaging $2500 are awarded annually to students of high academic ability who also demonstrate financial need. Financial aid for U.S. citizens includes Federal Stafford Student Loans and Federal PLUS loans. All U.S. citizens must file the Free Application for Federal Student Aid (FAFSA) to qualify. Students should contact the admissions office for details regarding application procedures for scholarships and financial aid.

Application and Information

An application for admission and further information may be obtained by contacting the appropriate admissions office.

Applicants residing in the United States should contact:

Director of U.S. Admissions
U.S. Office of Admissions
Richmond College
19 Bay State Road
Boston, Massachusetts 02215

Telephone: 617-954-9942
Fax: 617-236-4703
E-mail: enroll@richmond.ac.uk
Web site: http://www.richmond.ac.uk

Applicants residing in all other countries should contact:

Director of Admissions
Office of Admissions
Richmond College
Queens Road, Richmond
Surrey TW10 6JP
England

Telephone: 181-332-9000
Fax: 181-332-1596
E-mail: enroll@richmond.ac.uk
Web site: http://www.richmond.ac.uk

RIDER UNIVERSITY
LAWRENCEVILLE, NEW JERSEY

The University

Rider University is a private, nonsectarian, coeducational institution operating under the control of a Board of Trustees. Rider was founded as the Trenton Business College in 1865. The name was changed to Rider College shortly after the turn of the century. Four separate schools were established within the college in 1962: the Schools of Business Administration, Education, Liberal Arts and Science, and Continuing Studies. Since then, the Schools of Business Administration and Education have each added a division of graduate studies, and the latter has become the School of Education and Human Services. In 1992, Rider College merged with Westminster Choir College. In April 1994, Rider College officially became Rider University. Rider University is located on a 353-acre campus that contains large open areas and thirty-eight modern buildings constructed within the past twenty-five years. Approximately 70 percent of the 2,750 undergraduates live in University residence halls or in fraternities or sororities on the campus. Entering students and returning students are guaranteed housing on the campus provided that they meet the stated deadlines for submission of housing applications and deposits.

Academic Program

Rider University operates on the semester system. Each College requires a minimum of 120 semester hours of credit for graduation; the last 30 semester hours of credit must be earned at Rider University. The College of Business Administration requires that a student earn at least 45 semester hours, including the last 30, at Rider University.

Financial Aid

Most financial aid is based upon demonstrated financial need. Students and their parents are required to file the Free Application for Federal Student Aid (FAFSA) prior to March 1 to be considered for financial assistance administered by Rider University. The University maintains a need-blind admission policy and attempts to meet the full financial need of all eligible applicants. Entering students are eligible for consideration for Federal Pell Grants, Federal Supplemental Educational Opportunity Grants, Federal Work-Study awards, Federal Perkins Loans, New Jersey Tuition Aid Grants, New Jersey Distinguished Scholar Scholarships, and Rider University grants, Trustee Scholarships, Alumni Scholarships, and other forms of institutional aid. Rider University offers four merit-based scholarship programs for qualified applicants. These scholarships, the Presidential, Diversity, Dean's, and Transfer scholarships, are for up to $10,000 and are renewable for up to four years of study if the student maintains the minimum grade point average specified by the Scholarship Committee. Rider also offers two full-tuition actors scholarships.

Application and Information

Rider University works on a rolling admissions basis, but encourages applications for the fall semester to be submitted by February 15 if the student wishes to obtain housing on the campus. Applications for the spring semester should be submitted by December 15. The application fee of $35 should be included with the application. Students will be notified of the admission decision in approximately 3 to 4 weeks, in accordance with the rolling admission policy. Transfer applicants receive the same priority for admission, housing, and financial aid as freshman applicants.

Interested students are encouraged to contact:

Director of Admissions
Rider University
2083 Lawrenceville Road
Lawrenceville, New Jersey 08648-3099

Telephone: 609-896-5042
800-257-9026 (toll-free)
E-mail: admissions@rider.edu
Web site: http://www.rider.edu

RIPON COLLEGE
RIPON, WISCONSIN

The College
Founded in 1851, Ripon is a distinctive small college of 800 men and women. In all departments, the curriculum emphasizes writing, critical thinking, and analytical skills and encourages students to gain a working familiarity with all the methods of learning that are central to each division of the liberal arts and sciences. Students come from forty states and nineteen countries. They are friendly individuals who actively support one another in their academic and extracurricular endeavors. Students take pride in their excellent relationship with professors, who take on the role of personal and professional mentor, both inside the classroom and out. By the time students graduate, they will have participated in extensive research projects, gained valuable internship experience, made presentations to their classmates, debated ideas in the classroom, and developed the capacity to handle new challenges with confidence.

Academic Program
Each student must fulfill certain requirements for graduation, including courses in behavioral and social sciences, English, fine arts, foreign languages, global studies, humanities, natural sciences, and physical education. College Board SAT II: Subject Tests, Advanced Placement exams, and International Baccalaureate credits may be used to satisfy some graduation requirements. In choosing a major, usually by the second semester of the sophomore year, each student works closely with his or her adviser to develop a program of concentrated study. While pursuing a major, a student elects courses from other disciplines, thereby contributing to the breadth and strength of his or her liberal arts education. To qualify for a Bachelor of Arts degree, students must earn 124 credit hours, have at least a 2.0 grade point average, complete the required courses with passing grades, and meet the requirements for a major in the field of their choice. All work must be taken at Ripon.

Financial Aid
Ripon College endeavors to provide financial aid for all eligible students to the extent of their need, as determined from the Free Application for Federal Student Aid (FAFSA). Financial aid is generally given in the form of a package, which may include a scholarship or grant, a work grant, and a loan. Assistance ranges from $100 to full cost; 80 percent of Ripon's students receive some form of aid. Ripon also offers a number of honor scholarships ranging from $500 to $17,000 per year. These awards are given to the most promising high school seniors and transfer students accepted for admission.

Application and Information
An early decision admission plan is provided for students who have selected Ripon as their first-choice college. The deadline for early decision application is December 1, and notification of the admission decision is made by December 15. Candidates following the regular admission timetable are strongly encouraged to apply by March 15. Applications may be submitted later, but preference is given to students who apply by the suggested deadline. Notices of admission decisions are sent out beginning in the last week of January and every two weeks thereafter. Application forms, the secondary school transcript, and SAT I or ACT results should be filed as early in the senior year as possible. Ripon's application form is available via the Ripon College Web site below. Students seeking financial aid and scholarships should be sure that all records and the FAFSA are received by the College no later than April 1. Ripon also participates in the Common Application program. Transfer students and international applicants are welcome. For further information, students should contact:

Dean of Admission
Ripon College
300 Seward Street
P.O. Box 248
Ripon, Wisconsin 54971

Telephone: 800-94-RIPON (toll-free)
E-mail: adminfo@mac.ripon.edu
Web site: http://www.ripon.edu

ROCHESTER INSTITUTE OF TECHNOLOGY
ROCHESTER, NEW YORK

The Institute

Rochester Institute of Technology was founded in 1829 and has always had a strong orientation toward professional and technological career training. The more than 8,000 full-time undergraduates currently enrolled come from fifty states and eighty countries; 35 percent are women. Many graduates move directly into the careers for which their RIT education has prepared them. A variety of graduate degree programs are offered, including the nation's first and only Ph.D. program in imaging science.

Academic Program

Students entering RIT enroll directly in the college and academic program of their choice; specialization is spread over the duration of their study. Approximately one third of the program of each professional curriculum consists of general education courses in the humanities, sciences, and social sciences. An integral part of the degree requirements in the Colleges of Business, Engineering, and Science and in the Departments of Computer Science; Information Technology; Engineering Technology; Food, Hotel, and Travel Management; and Printing Management and Sciences is the cooperative education program. In this program, the student alternates quarters of study with quarters of paid work experience in business or industry during the upper-division years. This is not only invaluable experience but also a way of meeting the expenses of these years. The cooperative program is offered as an option in several other academic departments. Field experience is integrated with academic programs in the areas of criminal justice and social work. A number of RIT's programs are unusual baccalaureate degree offerings. Among these are the programs of the School for American Crafts; programs in biotechnology, imaging science, international business, microelectronic engineering, nuclear medicine technology, packaging, photography, physician assistant studies, printing, software engineering, and telecommunications; and the programs of the National Technical Institute for the Deaf. Air Force and Army ROTC programs are available on campus. A Naval ROTC program is offered jointly with the University of Rochester.

Financial Aid

Approximately 70 percent of the full-time undergraduates receive some form of financial aid: Institute scholarships; regional, alumni, or industry-supported scholarships; and state and federal government grants. A variety of loans and part-time work positions are also available. The FAFSA must be submitted by March 15. Giving full recognition to scholarship apart from financial need, RIT awards a number of academic scholarships based on grades, test scores, and activities. Freshmen applying by February 1 and transfers applying as juniors by February 15 are considered for these scholarships.

Application and Information

An application, a nonrefundable processing fee of $40 (payable to Rochester Institute of Technology), official transcripts of all high school or college records, and (for prospective freshmen) SAT I or ACT scores should be forwarded to RIT. Freshman applicants for entry in the fall quarter who provide all required materials by March 1 receive admission notification by March 15. Prospective freshmen who apply after March 1 and all transfer students are notified of the admission decision by mail on a rolling basis four to six weeks after their application is complete. RIT also offers an early decision plan, whereby prospective freshmen must have their completed application with all supporting credentials on file in the Admissions Office by December 15 to receive notification by January 15.

For application forms, students should contact:

Director of Admissions
Rochester Institute of Technology
60 Lomb Memorial Drive
Rochester, New York 14623-5604

Telephone: 716-475-6631
Fax: 716-475-7424
E-mail: admissions@rit.edu
Web site: http://www.rit.edu

ROSEMONT COLLEGE
ROSEMONT, PENNSYLVANIA

The College

Founded in 1921, Rosemont College is a residential liberal arts college for undergraduate women. In addition, it offers a nonresidence undergraduate Accelerated Degree Program for both women and men. The College also provides coeducational graduate degrees and professional studies programs. The M.A., M.Ed., and an accelerated M.S. in management are offered. Founded in the Catholic tradition, Rosemont welcomes individuals of all backgrounds and beliefs. A strong academic program and a commitment to women's education and achievement have long been hallmarks of a Rosemont education. With an enrollment of more than 500 women, Rosemont is a friendly and personal community that both supports and challenges students. Rosemont endeavors to prepare women to be active and responsible members of society. Life at Rosemont is characterized by attention to the development of the personal, social, moral, cultural, and intellectual strengths that help women meet the challenges of modern life. Rosemont urges women to assess individual strengths and interests to develop the competence and determination necessary to achieve success. The close community atmosphere of the College lends to the development of the individual. For example, the 8:1 student-faculty ratio provides individual attention both in and out of the classroom and promotes lively discussion and conversation. Rosemont College firmly believes in the liberal arts education. A solid foundation in a variety of different fields of study provides the Rosemont student with an all-encompassing background to create a well-rounded individual.

Academic Program

To earn a Rosemont degree, each candidate must complete 117 credits (120 credits for the B.F.A. and the B.S. in business). In addition to the requirements of a major concentration, all students must complete the general requirements. The general requirements, or core curriculum, focus on the fields of study closely associated with traditional liberal arts and sciences curricula: writing, literature, foreign language, philosophy, religious studies, history, mathematics, natural science, social science, and art. During their senior year, all students must successfully complete a comprehensive exam exhibiting competency in their declared major. Rosemont offers programs granting certification in the following teaching areas: elementary education, secondary education, art education, and special education with a concentration in hearing impaired. In addition, Rosemont has a cooperative program in education with nearby Eastern College that allows students to obtain certification in early childhood education. Rosemont freshmen participate in a comprehensive advising program called Freshman Colloquia. These colloquia are special vehicles for beginning and deepening a relationship with Rosemont. It is an improved system of advising that reaches beyond mere counseling in course selection.

Financial Aid

More than 70 percent of all Rosemont students receive some form of financial aid. Financial aid includes scholarships, grants, loans, and work-study awards. Most financial packages are a combination of various forms of aid. To apply for aid, students are required to submit the Free Application for Federal Student Aid (FAFSA) by March 1.

Application and Information

Applications are accepted on a rolling basis. Those interested in scholarships should apply no later than February 15. To arrange for an interview and a tour, or to receive additional information, students should contact:

Karin E. Storms
Interim Director of Admissions
Rosemont College
1400 Montgomery Avenue
Rosemont, Pennsylvania 19010-1699

Telephone: 610-526-2966
800-331-0708 (toll-free)

ST. AMBROSE UNIVERSITY
DAVENPORT, IOWA

The University

St. Ambrose offers all the resources needed for a successful college experience as well as a successful future. The student body of 2,600 (52 percent women, 48 percent men) consists of people differing in age and background. Founded in 1882, the University was named for St. Ambrose, the fourth-century saint and bishop of Milan, who was a doctor, scholar, author, orator, and teacher. Extracurricular learning opportunities are available through a student newspaper, a campus radio station, cable TV facilities, athletic programs for men and women, honor societies, professional societies, clubs, and other organizations. St. Ambrose is a nonprofit educational institution that admits academically qualified students of any race, color, age, sex, religion, or national origin, without regard to any physical handicap, to all the rights, privileges, programs, and activities generally available to students at the University. It does not discriminate on the basis of race, color, sex, religion, national origin, or physical handicap in administration of any of its educational policies or programs, including admissions, financial aid, and athletics. It is also an equal opportunity employer. The school is authorized under federal law to enroll nonimmigrant alien students.

Academic Program

St. Ambrose is committed to combining the liberal arts with career preparation. The liberal arts component in each student's program consists of courses in six major divisions: arts, languages and literature, natural sciences, philosophy and theology, physical education, and social sciences and/or economics. To be eligible for graduation, students must maintain an average grade of at least C (2.0) and must complete a minimum of 120 semester credits (usually forty courses) in the Bachelor of Arts, Bachelor of Science (but 135 semester credits for the Bachelor of Science in Industrial Engineering degree program), Bachelor of Arts in Special Studies, and Bachelor of Elected Studies degree programs or 136 semester credits in the Bachelor of Music and Bachelor of Music Education degree programs. Credit is given for the CLEP general examination in English with essay. The foreign language/intercultural-understanding requirement may be waived for students who have completed 1 unit of a foreign language in high school or at the college level. Students must demonstrate competence in public oral communication and in mathematics. Credit for nonclassroom learning is awarded through CLEP or through assessment by individual departments of the University.

Financial Aid

Federal, state, and University financial aid programs; scholarships, loans, grants, work-study and cooperative programs; and University employment opportunities are available. Federal programs include the Federal Pell Grant, Federal Supplemental Educational Opportunity Grant, Federal Work-Study, and Federal Perkins Loan programs. State programs are the Iowa Scholarship, Iowa PLUS Loan, and Iowa Tuition Grant programs. Most opportunities for University employment are in the Library and Learning Center, the Division of Arts, and the Physical Education Center. The priority deadline for financial aid applications is March 15 for the following fall semester. In addition to submitting an application for admission, applicants for financial aid must submit the Free Application for Federal Student Aid (FAFSA); this form is available in the offices of high school counselors or in the St. Ambrose University Financial Aid Office.

Application and Information

The completed application for admission, a $25 nonrefundable application fee, high school transcripts or equivalent credentials, and test scores should be sent to the dean of admissions. For more information or to arrange a campus visit, students should contact:

Patrick O'Connor
Dean of Admissions
St. Ambrose University
518 West Locust Street
Davenport, Iowa 52803

Telephone: 319-333-6300
800-383-2627 (toll-free)

ST. ANDREWS PRESBYTERIAN COLLEGE
LAURINBURG, NORTH CAROLINA

The College

A small private college, St. Andrews is affiliated with the Presbyterian Church (U.S.A.) and welcomes students of all beliefs who are seeking a strong, relevant, and broad liberal arts education grounded in such hands-on, practical experience as internships and study-abroad programs. It is this blending of theory and practice that attracts the 720 students (389 women and 331 men) and that has allowed graduates to succeed through the changing times since the College was founded in 1958 with the merging of two older institutions with histories dating back to 1896. St. Andrews students come from across the United States and from thirty countries and pursue active community involvement to the same extent as their academic studies. Among its twenty majors, St. Andrews offers two distinctive programs of study, both among the first in the nation and both pilot programs for others: therapeutic riding and international business.

Academic Program

In addition to a choice of twenty majors, St. Andrews students have the opportunity to work closely with their advisers to design a liberal arts thematic major that best fits their academic and career goals. All students take SAGE (St. Andrews General Education), which has been designed not only to impart the essential skills of critical thinking, reading, and writing but also to explore centuries of human accomplishment and to formulate action-based values from their studies. A total of 120 credits is required for the baccalaureate degree.

Financial Aid

The financial aid program combines merit-based assistance with traditional need-based assistance. St. Andrews is committed to making the cost of education affordable for all families. Nearly 80 percent of all St. Andrews students receive some type of financial assistance. The College administers traditional federal and state programs, including the Federal Pell Grant, Federal Stafford Student Loan, Federal Perkins Loan, and Federal PLUS Loan, as well as the North Carolina Legislative Tuition Grant for North Carolina students and the Founders' Heritage Grant for students in the seven-county area surrounding Laurinburg. Campus employment is available. To apply for assistance, students must complete a Free Application for Federal Student Aid (FAFSA). Many students also request a scholarship application from St. Andrews.

Application and Information

For more information, students should contact:

Dean of Admissions and Student Financial Planning
St. Andrews Presbyterian College
1700 Dogwood Mile
Laurinburg, North Carolina 28352

Telephone: 800-763-0198 (toll-free)
Fax: 910-277-5087
E-mail: admissions@sapc.edu
Web site: http://www.sapc.edu

ST. JOHN'S UNIVERSITY
JAMAICA AND STATEN ISLAND, NEW YORK, AND ROME, ITALY

The University

St. John's University has been a leading urban institution of higher learning since its inception. Founded by the Vincentian Fathers in 1870, it is the largest Catholic university in the nation. The University has developed from a one-building campus in Brooklyn to a three-campus institution with a 95.5-acre campus in Hillcrest, Queens; a 16.5-acre campus in Grymes Hill, Staten Island; and a campus in Rome, Italy. The Queens campus comprises the College of Liberal Arts and Sciences, the College of Business Administration, the School of Education and Human Services, the College of Pharmacy and Allied Health Professions, St. Vincent's College, and Metropolitan College. The Staten Island campus comprises Notre Dame College, the College of Business Administration, and St. Vincent's College. The Rome, Italy, campus comprises the College of Business Administration's M.B.A. program.

Academic Program

To graduate, students in the College of Liberal Arts and Sciences and Notre Dame College must complete a minimum of 126 semester hours for the B.A., 126 semester hours for the B.S., or 144 semester hours for the B.F.A.; in the School of Education and Human Services, 126–39 semester hours; and in the College of Business Administration, 130–34 semester hours. In the College of Pharmacy and Allied Health Professions, students in the pharmacy program must complete a minimum of 168 semester hours; those in the physician assistant program, 134 semester hours; those in the toxicology or pathologist assistant program, 133 semester hours; and those in the medical technology program, 132 semester hours. All students must fulfill the core requirements for their college in addition to completing the major sequence and free-elective groupings. Nine credits in theology and 9 credits in philosophy must be completed for any baccalaureate degree. Students in the A.A. degree programs must complete a minimum of 60 semester hours. Seven A.S. degree programs require the completion of a minimum of 60 semester hours; the Associate in Science in business (accounting option) requires at least 62 semester hours.

Financial Aid

During the 1996–97 academic year, more than 13,000 St. John's University students received in excess of $110 million in financial assistance through scholarships, loans, grants, and work-study programs. At St. John's University, financial aid is primarily awarded on the basis of financial need. Students are encouraged to file the Free Application for Federal Student Aid as the major financial aid application no later than March 1.

Application and Information

To apply, students must submit an official high school transcript, official scores on the SAT I or ACT, and a completed and signed application for admission. Transfer students are encouraged to apply and form a large contingent of the undergraduate population. Transfer students must arrange to have all records of previous high school and college work forwarded to the Admissions Office. On-campus interviews for informational purposes are conducted through the Office of Admissions. The University operates under a procedure of rolling admissions, with the exception of the B.S. pharmacy degree program, which has a February 1 deadline. For further information students should contact:

Office of Admissions
St. John's University
8000 Utopia Parkway
Jamaica, New York 11439

Telephone: 718-990-6114
800-232-4SJU (toll-free)
Fax: 718-990-1677

Office of Admissions
St. John's University
300 Howard Avenue
Staten Island, New York 10301

Telephone: 718-390-4500
800-232-4SJU (toll-free)
Fax: 718-816-4520

SAINT JOSEPH COLLEGE
WEST HARTFORD, CONNECTICUT

The College

For more than sixty years, Saint Joseph College (SJC) has been combining excellence in liberal arts with professional education for women. Founded in 1932 by the Sisters of Mercy, the original women's college has expanded to include a coeducational graduate school and an innovative weekend baccalaureate program for men and women. In partnership with each other, these units of the College offer a diverse student population unmatched opportunities to excel—intellectually, socially, and ethically. There are 918 undergraduates in the Women's College, where faculty members and students have high mutual expectations and strive to maximize each person's potential. The College is a community that promotes the growth of the whole person in a caring environment that encourages strong ethical values, personal integrity, and a sense of responsibility to the needs of society. Women lead every organization, from the Business Society and Student Government to Campus Ministry and Intercultural Affairs. They edit the journals; lead the choirs, dance, and drama groups; and captain every athletic team. Students also serve with faculty members and administrators on all major committees, from strategic planning to Web site development to the Administrative Council—a small group of top advisers to the President. SJC has eleven Georgian brick buildings, including four residence halls, which are arranged around two tree-lined quadrangles on an 84-acre campus. Approximately 50 percent of the full-time Women's College students live on campus. Special student services include career planning, alumnae mentors, internship placement, counseling, health services, academic advisement, and a campus ministry team. Saint Joseph College alumnae have considerable impact on the welfare of their communities. They are leaders in many fields, including aerospace research, business, medicine, education, social work, environmental science, law, and politics. Recent graduates enjoy successful careers in business, industry, government, nonprofit organizations, education, health care, human services, and the arts.

Academic Program

Each student must complete a minimum of 120 credits to obtain a baccalaureate degree, and 53 of those credits should be distributed among the general education/liberal arts courses at the College. The study of a foreign language is recommended. An academic adviser assists each student in planning her program of study. An honors program is available. Students may design their own major or may develop an interdisciplinary major or minor around a particular theme or problem related to their special talents, personal interests, or career goals.

Financial Aid

A highly effective and aggressive program of financial aid demonstrates Saint Joseph College's strong commitment to helping students obtain a high-quality private college education. In 1996–97, more than 80 percent of the College's full-time undergraduate students received some form of financial aid, including loans, work-study awards, grants, and scholarships.

Application and Information

The Committee on Admissions recommends that application for freshman admission be made early in the first semester of the senior year in secondary school. All applications must be completed by May 1. Candidates for financial aid should complete the admission procedure by February 15. A nonrefundable $35 fee must be sent to the director of admissions with the application. Transfer applicants for the spring semester must apply by December 1; applicants for the fall semester, by July 1. However, transfer candidates who wish to apply for financial aid must complete the admission procedure by June 1. For further information about undergraduate programs, students should contact:

Mary C. Demo
Director of Undergraduate Admissions
Saint Joseph College
1678 Asylum Avenue
West Hartford, Connecticut 06117
Telephone: 860-232-4571 Ext. 216
800-285-6565 (toll-free)
Fax: 860-233-5695
E-mail: admissions@mercy.sjc.edu

SAINT LEO COLLEGE
SAINT LEO, FLORIDA

The College
Saint Leo College is a four-year private college affiliated with the Catholic Church. Founded in 1889 by the Order of Saint Benedict, Saint Leo has grown to an enrollment of 1,000 students on the main campus and 7,000 students in extension programs located on eleven military bases stretching from Virginia to Key West. Saint Leo offers its students a personalized education through its dedicated faculty and staff. Students can participate in the nationally recognized honors program and the more than forty different clubs and organizations on campus, including national fraternities and sororities. Saint Leo competes in NCAA Division II sports for men in baseball, basketball, soccer, and tennis and for women in basketball, fast-pitch softball, tennis, and volleyball. Students can also participate in a variety of intramurals as well as sailing. Saint Leo is committed to giving its students an education that prepares them for the future. The goal of the College is to develop the whole person both academically and personally through the Catholic tradition. Saint Leo College is accredited by the Commission on Colleges of the Southern Association of Colleges and Schools to award the associate and bachelor's degrees. Saint Leo College's program in social work is accredited by the Commission on Accreditation of the Council on Social Work Education (BSW level). Saint Leo College has Teacher Education Program approval by the state of Florida Department of Education.

Academic Program
The candidate for a baccalaureate degree gains a broad exposure to a liberal arts education through completion of general College requirements. These requirements consist of a total of fifteen courses in English, fine arts, religious studies, philosophy, science, math, social science, humanities, and computer science. These studies form a basic foundation for the various majors. The courses are usually taken during the freshman and sophomore years. The total number of credit hours required for completion of a bachelor's degree is 124. Students usually acquire these credits over a four-year period. All programs require a minimum 2.0 (C) grade point average for graduation. Saint Leo has designed an academic program to help freshmen adjust to college life. Included in this program is Freshman Studies, which continues through the first semester of the freshman year. All freshmen are also assigned faculty advisers who act as mentors from the first day the students arrive on campus. Students also have the opportunity to receive credit by examination. If a student is able to demonstrate course content mastery for any course listed in the catalog, up to 40 hours of standardized testing credit will be granted toward graduation. Information about credit by examination is available in the Records Office.

Financial Aid
Financial aid is available in the form of scholarships, grants, and loans both federally funded and given through the College. Financial aid is allocated on the basis of need as determined by the federal government from the financial information provided on the Free Application for Federal Student Aid (FAFSA). On-campus jobs are available for students, with priority given to students with demonstrated financial need.

Application and Information
Additional information and application forms can be obtained by contacting the Admissions Office.

Bonnie L. Black
Director of Admissions
Saint Leo College
P.O. Box 2008
Saint Leo, Florida 33574

Telephone: 352-588-8283
Fax: 352-588-8257
E-mail: admissions@saintleo.edu

ST. MARY'S COLLEGE OF MARYLAND
ST. MARY'S CITY, MARYLAND

The College

St. Mary's is a public, state-supported, coeducational college dedicated to providing an excellent liberal arts education. There are 588 men and 765 women enrolled full-time, and 1,030 of these students live on campus. Part-time enrollment is 212 students. St. Mary's combines the educational and personal advantages of a small private college with the affordability of a public institution. Active learning and the development of critical thinking are encouraged in the discussion-oriented format made possible by modest class size. Student leadership in academic, cultural, and social spheres is aided by the community atmosphere; opportunities are greater than at larger schools, and involvement is easier. The College recently received a sizable building grant, which was used for the construction of town house–style residence halls, the renovation of existing dorms, and the construction of a library. A new science building was completed in fall 1993. The campus covers 275 acres, including riverfront, open space, and woodland. The College is accredited by the Middle States Association of Colleges and Schools and the National Association of Schools of Music.

Academic Program

The course of study at the College provides both diversity and depth, leading to a broad understanding of the liberal arts and a specific competence in at least one major field. A limited number of exceptional students may be invited to participate in the honors program. All students must complete requirements for their major field of study and the general education requirements, which total 50–52 semester hours. The general education requirements are designed to develop skills in communication and analysis, acquaint students with the heritage of Western civilization, confront students with the forces and insights that are shaping the modern world, and promote the capacity for integration and synthesis of knowledge. History students can take advantage of the College's location on the site of colonial St. Mary's City, Maryland's first state capital. Many experts consider this area to contain the most abundant and earliest undisturbed artifacts of any American seventeenth-century town. St. Mary's College offers several courses in aquatic biology as an option within the major program in biology. The College's location on the St. Mary's River, a tributary of the Potomac near the mouth of the Chesapeake Bay, is ideal for the study of estuarine ecology. A strong music program provides advanced training in composition and piano performance and the impetus for a jazz ensemble, a percussion ensemble, a choir, a chamber vocal group, and a chamber orchestra for classical performances. Students may receive credit for high scores on the Advanced Placement Program examinations. Independent study for credit is possible in every major, allowing students to investigate subjects not covered in normal course offerings. Also available is the opportunity for students to design their own majors.

Financial Aid

The Office of Financial Aid provides advice and assistance to students in need of financial aid and joins other College offices in awarding scholarships and loans and in offering part-time employment under the work-study program. Several full scholarships are awarded to Maryland residents on a merit basis, and other scholarships, loans, and grants for students are awarded on the basis of ability and need as determined by the federal government's Free Application for Federal Student Aid, which should be filed no later than March 1.

Application and Information

An application form, financial aid information, and other materials are available by contacting:

Director of Admissions
St. Mary's College of Maryland
St. Mary's City, Maryland 20686

Telephone: 301-862-0200
800-492-7181 (toll-free)
Fax: 301-862-0906
E-mail: admissions@honors.smcm.edu

SAINT PETER'S COLLEGE
JERSEY CITY, NEW JERSEY

The College

Chartered in 1872, Saint Peter's College is an independent, coeducational, liberal arts college in the Jesuit tradition. SPC's main campus has an undergraduate enrollment of 2,388 full-time day students and also offers evening and Saturday sessions to undergraduate and graduate adult learners. The College is accredited by the Middle States Association of Colleges and Schools. Individual programs are accredited by the National League for Nursing, the National Association of State Directors of Teacher Education and Certification, and the American Chemical Society.

Academic Program

All students complete a core curriculum requirement consisting of at least 69 credits, distributed as follows: 3 credits each of composition and fine arts; 6 credits each of literature, a modern language, history, social sciences, philosophy, and theology; 6 to 8 credits of mathematics; 9 credits of natural science; and 12 credits of core electives (including one course in ethical values). The College recognizes the Advanced Placement (AP) Program and generally offers credit for scores of 3 or better. Credit is awarded through the College-Level Examination Program (CLEP) tests, provided that the minimum required score is obtained.

Financial Aid

Saint Peter's College admits students regardless of financial status. Eighty-seven percent of SPC students receive financial assistance, and the average package is $10,500 for commuting students and $12,500 for resident students. The only form required is the Free Application for Federal Student Aid (FAFSA). It is recommended that students file the FAFSA by April 15 for fullest consideration of all federal, state, and institutional sources available. Federal sources include Federal Pell Grants, Federal Supplemental Educational Opportunity Grants (FSEOG), the Federal Work-Study Program (FWS), Federal Stafford Student Loans, and Parent Loans for Undergraduate Students (PLUS). New Jersey state sources include Tuition Aid Grants (TAG) and the Educational Opportunity Fund (EOF). All applications for admission and FAFSAs are reviewed for academic scholarships, incentive awards, athletic scholarships, and residential and need-based grants. Students should call the Office of Student Financial Aid (201-915-9308 or 9309) for more information.

Application and Information

Students are encouraged to submit their applications in the fall of their senior year of high school. The Admissions Committee prefers that candidates apply before May 1; however, admission is given on a rolling basis. Students who wish to be considered for an academic scholarship must apply by March 1. When a student's complete application and records are on file, they will be reviewed by the committee. Students are ordinarily notified of the admission decision within two weeks of receipt of the complete admission file, which must include the completed application form, including a personal statement, a high school transcript with official SAT I scores, recommendations, and a $30 application fee ($40 for transfer students). Transfer students must submit official copies of all college transcripts and their application fee by December 1 for admission to the spring semester and before August 1 for admission to the fall semester. To complete their admission file, international students should submit the results of the Test of English as a Foreign Language (TOEFL) or the equivalent, all official documents of education, and an affidavit of financial support as well as the completed application form, including a personal statement, and $40 application fee. International students are encouraged to apply before March 1 for the fall term and before October 1 for the spring term.

For more information, students should contact:

Office of Admissions
Saint Peter's College
2641 Kennedy Boulevard
Jersey City, New Jersey 07306-5944

Telephone: 201-915-9213
Fax: 201-432-5860
E-mail: admissions@spcvxa.spc.edu
World Wide Web: http://www.spc.edu

ST. THOMAS UNIVERSITY
MIAMI, FLORIDA

The University

Founded in 1961 by the Augustinian Order of Villanova, Pennsylvania, at the invitation of the late Most Reverend Coleman F. Carroll, the Archbishop of Miami, St. Thomas University has grown from an institution with an initial enrollment of 45 students to become one of Florida's most comprehensive Catholic coeducational universities, with more than 2,500 students in all programs of study. The University is sponsored by the Archdiocese of Miami and is accredited by the Southern Association of Colleges and Schools.

Academic Program

To receive a bachelor's degree, students must complete at least 120 semester credits with a minimum grade point average of 2.0 overall and an average of at least 2.25 in their academic major; 30 of the last 36 semester credit hours must be earned and at least half of a student's academic major courses must be taken at St. Thomas University. All students must fulfill the general core education requirements of 57 semester credits, which include courses in English, humanities/foreign language, history, social science, mathematics/physical science, philosophy, and religious studies.

Financial Aid

University scholarships and grants, along with federally funded scholarships, grants, loans, and work-study awards, are allocated in a financial aid package according to a student's financial need. Currently, about 85 percent of the University's students receive financial aid. Of all financial aid recipients, 65 percent receive University scholarships and grants. To be eligible for any scholarship or financial aid program, an applicant should complete the University's financial aid application and file a Free Application for Federal Student Aid (FAFSA) with the Department of Education. The filing deadline for University financial aid funds is April 1. Applicants should indicate affirmatively on the FAFSA that their information may be forwarded from the U.S. Department of Education in order to be considered for any state grants for which they may be eligible. The application deadline for need-based state financial aid programs is April 15. Florida applicants who have resided in Florida for the prior twelve consecutive months are eligible to be awarded a Florida Resident Access Grant to attend a private four-year college or university in Florida. The funds for the Florida Resident Grant Program are dependent upon yearly appropriations from the Florida legislature. These funds are outright grants and are not based on financial need.

Application and Information

To facilitate the admission and financial aid processes, students should submit applications during the fall or winter of their senior year in high school and have all supporting material forwarded directly to the University's Undergraduate Admissions Office. Application for entrance as a resident student for the fall semester should be filed by May 15; for entrance as a commuting student, by August 1. Application for the spring semester should be made by December 15. The University operates with a policy of rolling admissions; beginning December 15, applicants for the fall semester are notified of the admission decision within a three-week period provided that all appropriate information has been received. The University adheres to the College Board's Candidates Reply Date of May 1 and does not require a tuition deposit or a room reservation deposit until May 1 in order to allow students ample opportunity to select the college or university of their choice. Dormitory space, however, is limited and is assigned in the order that room reservation deposits are received. For further information, students should contact:

Office of Admissions
St. Thomas University
16400 Northwest 32nd Avenue
Miami, Florida 33054

Telephone: 305-628-6546
800-367-9006 (toll-free in Florida)
800-367-9010 (toll-free outside Florida)

SAINT VINCENT COLLEGE
LATROBE, PENNSYLVANIA

The College

Saint Vincent College provides a liberal arts and sciences education. Since its founding in 1846, it has chosen to remain a small college, emphasizing a stable, hospitable, and personal learning atmosphere patterned after the style of life and educational ideals of the Benedictine order, which has been engaged in education for fifteen centuries. The participation of Benedictine monks in teaching, counseling, and administering the College helps foster a spirit emphasizing the responsibility to live, study, and work together in mutual support. The enrollment design for 1,200 enables all students to participate actively in classes, organizations, and activities. Approximately 800 students live in five residence halls on campus.

Academic Program

The curricula are designed around a basic liberal arts core in which a specific career orientation is placed in the context of broader human values. The core program includes the study of literature, philosophy, social sciences, laboratory sciences, mathematics, theology, and foreign language. For graduation, students must complete a minimum of 124 credits and achieve a minimum quality point average of 2.0. The Scholar Program offers students of superior achievement the opportunity to participate in an honors program.

Financial Aid

The financial aid program at Saint Vincent College is designed both to help students who find it difficult or impossible to attend college without some financial assistance and to acknowledge students who have exemplary achievements. The College offers a comprehensive program of financial aid in the form of scholarships, grants, loans, deferred-payment plans, part-time employment, work-study awards, cooperative education, internships, and federal and state financial assistance. Most financial aid is awarded on the basis of need, as determined by the Free Application for Federal Student Aid (FAFSA). Approximately 90 percent of the students who apply for aid receive some form of financial assistance; awards range from $250 to $8000 per year. Merit scholarships are awarded on the basis of demonstrated academic talent or leadership potential. Several scholarships are also available on a competitive basis in biology/chemistry, computer science, economics/business, mathematics, and music. These scholarships are valued at $1000 to $2000 per year each and are renewable each succeeding year if the student continues to qualify.

Application and Information

Saint Vincent College has a rolling admission policy, and an applicant is notified of the decision of the Committee on Admission soon after all credentials have been received. An applicant for the freshman class should submit the following to the Office of Admission and Financial Aid: a completed application form, a $25 application fee, official scores on the SAT I or American College Testing's ACT examination, and an official secondary school transcript, sent directly to Saint Vincent College by the guidance office at the secondary school of graduation. An applicant who is transferring from another postsecondary school should submit the following to the Office of Admission and Financial Aid: a completed application form with a $25 application fee; official transcripts, sent directly to Saint Vincent College from the postsecondary schools attended; a catalog that describes the courses listed on each postsecondary school transcript; and a secondary school transcript, sent directly to Saint Vincent College from the student's secondary school. Acceptance depends upon the applicant's academic achievement and personal history at the postsecondary schools attended. The secondary school record is requested as background information for academic counseling. For further information, applicants should contact:

Office of Admission and Financial Aid
Saint Vincent College
Latrobe, Pennsylvania 15650-2690

Telephone: 412-537-4540 (during office hours, 8:30 a.m. to 4:30 p.m)
412-532-6600 (after office hours)

E-mail: info@stvincent.edu
Web site: http://www.stvincent.edu

SCHILLER INTERNATIONAL UNIVERSITY
DUNEDIN, FLORIDA

The University

Schiller International University (SIU) was founded in 1964. Although originally intended for American students, the University soon attracted men and women from other nations and is now an international, coeducational four-year institution with eight locations in six countries and alumni from more than 130 countries. SIU prepares students for careers in business and management, multinational organizations, government agencies, academic institutions, and the social services as well as for further study. Through enrollment in both practical and theoretical courses and through discussions with instructors and classmates with multicultural backgrounds, students gain firsthand knowledge of business and cultural relations among the peoples of the world. In addition, SIU students have the unique opportunity to transfer between SIU campuses, without losing any credits, while continuing their chosen program of study. The language of instruction at all campuses is English. The current enrollment is 1,755 students. SIU students are housed in University residence halls, with selected host families, or in private rooms or apartments. Schiller International University is an accredited member of the Accrediting Council for Independent Colleges and Schools, which is recognized by the United States Department of Education as a national institutional accrediting agency.

Academic Program

The academic emphasis at Schiller International University is on international business, international relations and diplomacy, international hotel and tourism management, and languages. The Collegium Palatinum, a division of the University, offers intensive language programs in German, French, and Spanish and in English as a foreign language (EFL) at the Language Institutes located on various campuses. EFL courses are offered at all SIU campuses. Regular University courses in German, French, Spanish, and English are also offered, although not all languages are available at every campus. An associate degree program requires 62 credits; a bachelor's degree program requires 124 credits. An average grade of C (2.0) or higher is required for all programs. Each credit reflects 15 academic hours of classroom work; typical courses earn 3–4 credits. Classes run during two 15-week semesters and a 7-week summer session in a manner similar to that at most universities in the United States.

Financial Aid

SIU grants two kinds of financial aid: academic scholarships (for 200 students) and University service (work-study) grants. Total aid will not exceed one half of the tuition. Students are encouraged to seek assistance through private or government loan and scholarship programs before applying to the University. Eligible students may apply for a Federal Stafford Student Loan (U.S. citizens only) or a Canada Student Loan (Canadian citizens only). Applications for financial aid must be received by March 31 for the following academic year.

Application and Information

Applications are handled individually and without regard to race, sex, religion, national or ethnic origin, or country of citizenship. Because SIU operates on a rolling admissions system, applicants are advised of their admission status soon after all application materials (a completed application form and official transcripts of all secondary-level education and, for transfer applicants, all college-level study) and the $35 application fee have been received. For application forms or further information, students should contact the appropriate campus below.

Schiller International University
Admissions Office
Royal Waterloo House
51-55 Waterloo Road
London, SE1 8TX
England

Telephone: 71 928 8484
Fax: 71 620 1226

Schiller International University
Admissions Office
453 Edgewater Drive
Dunedin, Florida 34698-4964
U.S.A.

Telephone: 813-736-5082
800-336-4133 (toll-free within the U.S. only)
Fax: 813-734-0359
E-mail: study@campus.schiller.edu

SETON HILL COLLEGE
GREENSBURG, PENNSYLVANIA

The College

In 1918, the Sisters of Charity founded Seton Hill College to help women open new doors through the power of education. Since that time, Seton Hill has been recognized as a leader in liberal arts education. Today, Seton Hill College is ranked by *U.S. News & World Report* as one of the top three best buys and one of the top ten for academic reputation among northern liberal arts colleges. Seton Hill College is situated in the Laurel Highlands, an area of southwestern Pennsylvania known for its beautiful scenery and wealth of outdoor activities such as skiing, cycling, hiking, and white-water rafting. Recreational opportunities include an on-campus Internet café, lectures, and theater productions, as well as College-sponsored trips to Pittsburgh for cultural and sports events. Seton Hill has varsity teams in basketball, cross-country, equestrian competition, soccer, softball, tennis, and volleyball, plus a variety of intramural teams. At the graduate level, Seton Hill grants the Master of Arts degree in art therapy, elementary education, and special education.

Academic Program

Seton Hill offers forty-two majors in eighteen departments, with the opportunity to self-design a major, all enhanced by the College's award-winning core curriculum. Special programs are available for students who are undecided about their major. The Seton Hill College Honors Program is available for students who have distinguished themselves academically in high school. Students hoping to one day own a business may be interested in Seton Hill College's National Education Center for Women in Business. The center is the first organization of its kind in the United States to offer courses in business ownership and entrepreneurial activities to students in any major.

Financial Aid

Seton Hill College's Financial Aid Office works with each student to develop an aid package from the wide variety of scholarships, grants, loans, and work-study programs available. Seton Hill offers Presidential Scholarships valued from $3000 to $6200, which are automatically awarded to students who rank in the top 10 percent, 20 percent, or 30 percent of their high school class and meet the admission criteria. In addition, art, music, theater, biology, chemistry, math, and athletic scholarships are awarded based on merit.

Application and Information

Seton Hill College has a rolling admissions policy. Decisions of the Admissions Committee are rendered shortly after all application materials have been submitted. The first-time freshman applicant should submit a completed application form, a $30 nonrefundable application fee, an official secondary school transcript that includes the applicant's rank and cumulative grade point average, and official score reports from either the SAT I of the College Board or American College Testing's ACT. For more information, students should contact:

Office of Admissions
Seton Hill College
Seton Hill Drive
Greensburg, Pennsylvania 15601-1599

Telephone: 412-838-4255
800-826-6234 (toll-free)
Fax: 412-830-4611
E-mail: admit@setonhill.edu
World Wide Web: http://www.setonhill.edu

SHIMER COLLEGE
WAUKEGAN, ILLINOIS

The College
Shimer College, a distinctive four-year liberal arts institution, is one of a handful of schools with an integrated curriculum based upon the reading of original source materials, sometimes called great books. Shimer's classes are small (fewer than 12 students) and utilize the process of discussion and shared inquiry. It is the mission of the College to teach people how—not what—to think and to develop the skills of clear expression and analytical reasoning. The College believes that education is more than the mere transmittal of knowledge or the imparting of vocational skills. Specifically, Shimer is dedicated to the following principles: that the educational process must be intellectually stimulating and challenging; that the classroom should foster clarity in thought, speech, and writing; that a liberal arts education facilitates the formation of enlightened attitudes, concerns, and values; that the College exists to nurture the critical and creative abilities inherent in each student; and that students must develop skills that will enable them to succeed in whatever profession they choose. Shimer provides an education for life by promoting the classical aim of education—freedom—through an exploration of the relationships among all branches of knowledge. The College is dedicated to the concept of integrative studies, the interweaving of clusters of knowledge. Shimer College maintains more than 140 years of history, tradition, academic excellence, and the highest ideal of the liberal arts education, which is the insistence that education is a process and a lifelong pursuit.

Academic Program
The initial contact a student has with a subject of study is through the writings of the original great thinkers in the humanities, social sciences, and natural sciences. These works have been the basis of formal education for centuries and have been studied by the great scholars of all periods. Students are asked to place these works in their historical context and then to consider their relevance to contemporary life and thought. Shimer College has developed a curriculum and way of teaching that require a rigorous educational process. It consists of course sequences in four areas of study: the humanities, natural sciences, social sciences, and integrative studies. For either the B.A. or B.S. degree, 125 credit hours are required. These hours are as follows for the B.A.: 30 in basic studies, 30 in area studies, 25 in integrative studies, and 40 in the concentration and electives. Teaching is accomplished by shared inquiry. The discussion method used, often called the Socratic method, has an ancient precedent described in the writings of Plato in the fourth century B.C. Students gain the sound habits of thinking and of learning to ask the right questions. The method encourages students to become actively involved in their own education. The excitement of genuine dialogue generates self-knowledge and shared insight. Shimer classes are small to facilitate discussion and shared inquiry for all present.

Financial Aid
More than 90 percent of the students at Shimer receive some financial assistance in the form of scholarships, grants, loans, or work-study jobs.

Application and Information
Shimer admissions decisions are made on a rolling basis. As soon as all necessary application materials have been received, a decision is made and the candidate is notified. Students are advised to apply as early as possible to secure maximum financial aid. For more information, students should contact:

Office of Admissions
Shimer College
P.O. Box 500
Waukegan, Illinois 60070-0500

Telephone: 847-623-8400
800-215-7173 (toll-free)
E-mail: shimer.edu@juno.com
Web site: http://www.shimer.edu/shimer

SHORTER COLLEGE
ROME, GEORGIA

The College
Since 1873, Shorter College has been combining academic excellence with caring Christian commitment. The College was established through the generosity of a Baptist layman, Alfred Shorter, and the vision of his pastor. They led a group of northwestern Georgia Baptists in founding the school, originally named Cherokee Baptist Female College. The name was changed to Shorter Female College in 1878 and to Shorter College in 1923. The College became coeducational in 1951. Shorter's enrollment of 1,572 includes students in both traditional semester programs and in innovative continuous programs for working adults. Approximately 800 of these students are located on the main campus in Rome, Georgia. Semester students come from all parts of the United States and from other countries around the world. Affiliated with the Georgia Baptist Convention, the College carries forth its Christian heritage by holding weekly chapel services. The campus minister works with the director of religious activities to provide a wide range of opportunities for spiritual growth.

Academic Program
Shorter is accredited by the Southern Association of Colleges and Schools and the National Association of Schools of Music and strives to provide an academic environment of high quality. Small classes (freshman lecture courses average 20 students) taught by dedicated and highly qualified professors (93 percent of freshman lecture courses are taught by full-time faculty, 24 percent by full professors) ensure that each student receives an education that is both challenging and personally rewarding. For any degree, a candidate must have earned a minimum of 126 semester hours; some degrees require a greater number of hours. As part of the orientation program at the beginning of the fall semester, each new student is assigned to one of several small orientation groups that assist the student in adjusting to college life; the student is also assigned to an academic adviser who assists in the selection and scheduling of courses. The academic calendar is divided into two semesters from September to May, with a third semester offered during the summer.

Financial Aid
Shorter College offers aid through each of the five federal programs: the Federal Pell Grant, Federal Supplemental Educational Opportunity Grant, Federal Work-Study, Federal Perkins Loan, and Federal Stafford Student Loan. Full-time students who are Georgia residents are eligible to receive the Georgia Tuition Equalization Grant and the HOPE Scholarship; those having extreme need may apply for the Georgia Student Incentive Grant. Scholarships are offered for achievement in academics, music, art, theater, and athletics. Awards range from $500 to full tuition. Academic scholarships are renewable each year, provided the student maintains at least the required grade point average. Special grants and scholarships are available to students who plan to enter church-related vocations, who are members of churches in the Georgia Baptist Convention, or who are dependents of employees of a Southern Baptist church, institution, or agency. One hundred percent of all full-time Shorter students receive some form of financial aid.

Application and Information
Shorter accepts students on a rolling basis. Campus visits are highly recommended and are designed to be informative, affording students and parents opportunities to voice questions about student life, housing, financial aid, and academic departments. Students and their families are encouraged to return to campus for one of four planned Visitation Weekends.

Director of Admissions
Shorter College
315 Shorter Avenue
Box 7
Rome, Georgia 30165-4298

Telephone: 706-233-7319
800-868-6980 Ext. 7319 (toll-free in southeastern states and Washington, D.C.)
Fax: 706-233-7224
E-mail: admissions@shorter.edu
Web site: http://www.shorter.edu

SIMMONS COLLEGE
BOSTON, MASSACHUSETTS

The College

Simmons College was founded in 1899 by John Simmons, a Boston businessman, who believed that women were entitled to an education that would prepare them to assume meaningful careers. Since it opened its doors in 1902, Simmons has provided a combination of liberal arts education and professional preparation that has enabled women to succeed in achieving their personal and professional goals. This educational concept is as valid—or even more so—for students today as it was at its inception. In every program, students receive the benefits of a broad-based liberal arts education strengthened by direct experience in their area of concentration, gained through an internship or independent study. Simmons students graduate with a strong sense of direction and confidence in their abilities.

Academic Program

Simmons College seeks to provide its students with a liberal arts education in combination with professional study. The approach to education is flexible, and the curriculum allows each student to develop a program suited to her individual interests and career goals. Students must complete a minimum of 128 semester hours before being graduated. To fulfill the requirements of the basic plan of study, students must demonstrate competence in math and foreign language, complete background courses in the liberal arts and sciences, complete the courses required for the selected major, participate in independent study, and round out their program with appropriate electives. The liberal arts and sciences requirement constitutes 40 semester hours of course work, and the major requires 20 to 40 semester hours, depending on the program. The independent learning requirement constitutes a minimum of 8 and a maximum of 16 semester hours. Independent study is an important component of the Simmons educational program, as it emphasizes student initiative and planning and enables the student to acquire direct professional experience. The requirement may be fulfilled through internships, fieldwork, independent study, and an integrative seminar.

Financial Aid

Simmons makes its educational opportunities available to as many capable, promising students as possible. Applications for financial aid are welcome from students who cannot meet their college expenses without assistance. Approximately 69 percent of Simmons students receive financial aid. Financial aid packages offered by the College consist of federal, state, and institutional grants, loans, and work opportunities. To apply for financial aid, students must complete two forms: the Simmons financial aid application and the Free Application for Federal Student Aid (FAFSA). Freshmen are encouraged to mail the FAFSA by January 15, using estimated information if necessary, in order to meet the priority deadline of February 1. The deadline for transfers is April 1.

Application and Information

To apply, students should submit the Simmons application or the Common Application, along with the $35 fee and all supporting credentials. There are two early decision deadlines: November 15 (notification by December 15) and January 1 (notification by February 1). The deadline for freshman applicants is February 1. Transfer students are evaluated on a rolling basis; the preferred filing date for applications is April 1. Students applying for the semester beginning in January should apply by December 1.

Students are encouraged to visit the College in order to have a campus tour, meet the faculty, attend a class, or have an interview. The Admission Office should be contacted for further information.

Office of Admission
Simmons College
300 The Fenway
Boston, Massachusetts 02115

Telephone: 617-521-2051
800-345-8468 (toll-free)
Fax: 617-521-3190

SIMPSON COLLEGE
INDIANOLA, IOWA

The College
Simpson College was founded in 1860. The institution was named Simpson College to honor Bishop Matthew Simpson (1811–1884), one of the best-known and most influential religious leaders of his day. The College is coeducational; although it is affiliated with the United Methodist Church, it is nonsectarian in spirit and accepts students without regard to race, color, creed, national origin, religion, sex, age, or disability. Students may participate in student government, publications, music, theater, and social groups. Simpson competes in eighteen intercollegiate sports and has an extensive intramural program for both men and women. Men's and women's athletics at Simpson are governed by the NCAA. Simpson also has chapters of three national fraternities, one local fraternity, and four national sororities.

Academic Program
Simpson operates on a 4-4-1 academic calendar. The first semester starts in late August and ends in mid-December; the second semester starts in mid-January and ends in late April. A three-week session takes place during the month of May. New students are assigned faculty advisers who aid them in constructing academically sound majors. Students must participate in one May Term class or program for each year of full-time study or its equivalent at Simpson College. All students must complete the requirements of the Cornerstone Studies in liberal arts and competencies in foreign language, math, and writing. To earn the Bachelor of Arts degree, students may take no more than 42 hours in the major department, excluding May Term programs, and 84 hours in the division of the major, including May Term programs. Also, at least 128 semester hours of course work must be accumulated with a grade point average of C (2.0) or better. For a Bachelor of Music degree, the same requirements apply, except that 84 hours must be earned in the major, excluding May Terms, and the candidate is limited to 12 additional hours in the division of fine arts. Also, at least 132 hours of course work must be completed with a cumulative grade point average of C (2.0) or better.

Financial Aid
Simpson College seeks to make it financially possible for qualified students to experience the advantages of a college education. Generous gifts from alumni, trustees, and friends of the College, in addition to state and federal programs of student aid, make this opportunity possible. Simpson offers financial aid on both a need and no-need basis. Need is determined by filing the Free Application for Federal Student Aid. Awards may equal the cost of education if grants, scholarships, and loans provided through various funds are combined. Simpson also has funds available through the federally sponsored Federal Work-Study Program. Financial aid granted on a no-need basis includes academic scholarships, which are awarded on the basis of prior academic records, and talent scholarships, which are available in theater, music, and art. The talent scholarships are determined by audition/portfolio.

Application and Information
Simpson's rolling admission policy allows prospective students flexibility; however, early application is recommended. Transfer and foreign students are welcome. Students are encouraged to visit the campus.

General information, catalogs, application forms, and financial aid forms are available by contacting:

Office of Admissions
Simpson College
701 North "C" Street
Indianola, Iowa 50125

Telephone: 515-961-1624
800-362-2454 (toll-free)
E-mail: admiss@simpson.edu
World Wide Web: http://www.simpson.edu

SLIPPERY ROCK UNIVERSITY OF PENNSYLVANIA
SLIPPERY ROCK, PENNSYLVANIA

The University

In 1889, the citizens of the borough of Slippery Rock founded the college and gave it their town's picturesque name. In 1983, the school became Slippery Rock University of Pennsylvania. The University is a state-owned, multipurpose institution. Its academic divisions include the Colleges of Arts and Sciences, Education, Health and Human Services, Graduate Studies and Research, and Information Science and Business Administration. Of the total University enrollment of 7,300 students, most come from Pennsylvania; more than 200 students are from sixty-five countries. More than 150 social, honorary, and special interest clubs exist for student participation. Because of the University's excellent facilities and the spaciousness of the campus, intercollegiate and intramural sports for both men and women are very popular. Free counseling and tutorial services are available to all students. Trained specialists are also available to provide services for students with physical disabilities. A unique Do-It-Yourself Career Laboratory allows students to browse through pamphlets and booklets and to use films and tapes about different careers. A placement service is offered to students seeking employment part-time or after graduation. The University's placement record is 94 percent.

Academic Program

Two semesters make up the regular University calendar; the first semester ends before Christmas break. The summer term is divided into two 5-week sessions, a 3-week session, and a 7-week evening session. A minimum of 128 hours, 42–55 of which are in the core curriculum, and a minimum grade point average of 2.0 are required for graduation. To assist eligible students who are underprepared for college, the University sponsors the University Enrichment Program. Students who are admitted under this program enter in the fall semester and are given the necessary support services to provide them with the best opportunity for success. Interested students may participate in the Army Reserve Officers' Training Corps program on campus. Completion of the ROTC program can result in a student's commissioning as an officer in the U.S. Army Reserve or National Guard upon graduation.

Financial Aid

About 80 percent of the University's students receive some sort of financial aid. Slippery Rock participates in five college-based federal aid programs: the Federal Perkins Loan, Federal Stafford Student Loan, Federal PLUS Loan, Federal Work-Study, and Federal Supplemental Educational Opportunity Grant programs. Federal Pell Grants are also available. Pennsylvania students are potentially eligible for Pennsylvania Higher Education Assistance Agency (PHEAA) grants and scholarships. Job opportunities are available on the campus but are limited in the community. Students interested in financial aid should contact the financial aid director at the University as soon as they apply for admission.

Application and Information

There is no application fee required to be considered for admission. The student's high school transcript and scores from either the ACT or SAT I are required. While the ACT is strongly recommended, the SAT I is acceptable. In addition to filing the application form, transfer students must submit transcripts of all previous college work. The recommended deadline for applying for admission is May 1, but applications are accepted on a limited basis after that time. Calls and on-campus interviews are highly recommended.

For additional information on admission and any other aspect of the University, students should contact:

Director of Admissions
Slippery Rock University
Slippery Rock, Pennsylvania 16057-1326

Telephone: 412-738-2015
800-SRU-9111 (toll-free)

SOUTHERN CALIFORNIA COLLEGE
COSTA MESA, CALIFORNIA

The College

Southern California College (SCC) is a Christian liberal arts college that offers a four-year Bachelor of Arts degree in twenty-six majors, Master of Arts degrees in religion and education, and a Master of Theological Studies degree. Founded in 1920, SCC is owned by the Southern California District of the Assemblies of God. Regional accreditation and membership in the Western Association of Schools and Colleges were granted in 1964. In 1967, the College received recognition and approval of its teaching credential program from the California State Board of Education. Southern California College is committed to an education of high quality that integrates the Christian faith with learning and living. With 1,200 students, SCC is large enough to be diverse and challenging, but small enough to be a caring Christian community. Students come from more than twenty denominational backgrounds, every region of the United States, and many countries. A high percentage of those who apply for graduate school after graduation are accepted.

Academic Program

Southern California College offers an exceptional academic program. Since SCC is a teaching college, there are no graduate assistants teaching courses. Because the College is committed to a liberal arts education, each student is required to take 55 credits in general education classes, including studies in humanities and fine arts, natural sciences and mathematics, religion, social science, and professional studies. A minimum of 124 credits is required for graduation. Students are encouraged to take a practicum or internship to gain practical experience in their particular field. Because of SCC's advantageous southern California location, the opportunities for internships in nearly any professional field are virtually limitless. Also, SCC offers a number of courses that include travel to other parts of the country and, sometimes, the world. The academic year is run on a semester system, one in the fall and one in the spring. Summer sessions are also offered.

Financial Aid

SCC has put together a financial aid program that coordinates federal, state, and institutional aid to enable students to pursue a liberal arts education. The program includes the Federal Pell Grant, the Federal Supplemental Educational Opportunity Grant, the Federal Perkins Loan, California Grant A and B, the California Stafford Loan, and various SCC grants and scholarships. Students who have a grade point average of 3.2 or higher are eligible for academic scholarships that cover up to 50 percent of the cost of tuition. A total of $9 million in financial aid is awarded annually to qualified SCC students. In order to receive any financial assistance, a student must apply first for admission and then to the Student Financial Services Office. The priority deadline for financial aid applications is March 2. Campus jobs make it possible for many students to earn varying amounts and involve a number of job categories. In addition to the campus employment program, growing industrial centers in Costa Mesa, Irvine, and Newport Beach afford students excellent job opportunities.

Application and Information

Admission decisions are made on a rolling basis; applications received earliest in the year are considered first. The application deadline is July 31 for the fall semester and December 31 for the spring semester. For further information, students should contact:

Dean for Enrollment Management
Southern California College
55 Fair Drive
Costa Mesa, California 92626

Telephone: 714-556-3610 Ext. 217
800-SCC-6279 (toll-free)

SOUTHERN CONNECTICUT STATE UNIVERSITY
NEW HAVEN, CONNECTICUT

The University
Founded in 1893, Southern Connecticut State University is located on a 168-acre campus in New Haven, a city renowned for its academic and cultural advantages. During its long history, Southern has grown in diversity and excellence. Today, Southern offers bachelor's and master's degrees and sixth-year diplomas in more than 150 areas of study, providing its students with a challenging variety of academic, professional, and personal opportunities. Southern is part of the Connecticut State University System. The student body represents the full spectrum of ethnic and socioeconomic groups. Although most students come from Connecticut, Southern students also represent more than thirty states and forty countries. There are approximately 12,000 students enrolled, about 8,000 of whom are undergraduates. Of the 5,500 full-time undergraduates, 2,000 live on campus in twelve modern residence halls and town houses.

Academic Program
The University operates on a two-semester calendar. Southern also offers two 5-week sessions during the summer and a 3-week intersession program each January. Throughout its history, Southern has held fast to the conviction that the best education stresses the liberal arts and sciences. To ensure all students a chance to acquire such an education, Southern has designed a strong yet flexible program that underscores the basics while encouraging individual choice and self-expression. All baccalaureate degree candidates are required to complete a minimum of 122 hours of credit. Majors consist of at least 30 prescribed hours of credit in one specific, approved field. Degree candidates must also fulfill the All-University Requirements, a common core of courses ranging from 41 to 54 credits in liberal studies.

Financial Aid
The Financial Aid Office coordinates a number of programs. These programs, which include grants and scholarships, long-term low-interest loans, and part-time student employment, are based on the demonstrated financial need of students and their families. The University offers the Federal Perkins Loan, the Federal Pell Grant, the Federal Supplemental Educational Opportunity Grant, the Federal Stafford Student Loan, the Federal PLUS loan, and the Federal Work-Study Program. Southern also provides assistance through alumni scholarships. More than 40 percent of Southern's undergraduates receive some form of financial aid. Students interested in applying for assistance must complete the Free Application for Federal Student Aid (FAFSA) and send it to the central processor so that it is received by March 15. The Financial Aid Office also requires students to submit additional forms, including a University financial aid application. All required forms have deadlines and are available at the Financial Aid Office.

Application and Information
Candidates for admission should apply by May of their senior year in high school. The Admissions Office mails its first notice of acceptance on December 1, and early applicants have priority for housing and financial aid. Applicants must submit previous academic records, including a complete transcript of high school grades and rank in class; an admission application; a $40 nonrefundable fee; a written recommendation from the high school principal, a teacher, or a guidance counselor; and an official copy of the SAT I report. To request application forms and further information, students should contact:

Sharon Brennan
Director of Admissions
Southern Connecticut State University
131 Farnham Avenue
New Haven, Connecticut 06515-1355

Telephone: 203-392-5644
800-448-0661 (toll-free)

SOUTHERN VERMONT COLLEGE
BENNINGTON, VERMONT

The College

Southern Vermont College's philosophy begins with a deep belief in the potential of every individual. Thomas Jefferson's concept of "an aristocracy of achievement arising out of a democracy of opportunity" is attained by keeping Southern Vermont College accessible to all students, including those with financial and academic needs, who are serious about improving their lives through higher education. A student-teacher ratio of 18:1 and small classes allow for maximum interaction. Special academic options include an honors program, internships, and independent studies. Southern Vermont College is accredited by the New England Association of Schools and Colleges. Southern Vermont has intercollegiate sports with teams competing at the NCAA Division III level. The College is a member of the East Coast Athletic Conference (ECAC) as well.

Academic Program

The academic programs at Southern Vermont College challenge students to think independently and creatively. The blend of career skills and the liberal arts provides the depth of learning necessary to succeed in the workplace and throughout life. Bachelor's degree candidates must successfully complete 120 semester hours of credit in the selected program of study; those studying for the associate degree must complete 60 semester hours of credit. Every associate degree student completes the following courses to acquire a solid background in the liberal arts: effective speaking, English composition (two courses), college math, biological world or physical world, history, cultural arts, and sociology. In addition to these core courses, bachelor degree students must complete the following liberal arts courses: cultural arts, economics, environmental issues, government, history, philosophy, psychology, introduction to computers, and both physical world and biological world. Credit will be transferred from all accredited colleges and universities. Transfer credits are applied to fulfill degree requirements if the grade earned was C- or better. Students may transfer up to 45 credits for the associate degree and up to 90 credits for the bachelor's degree. Through the College's life experience program, credits may be awarded for life and work experience. The academic year consists of fall and spring semesters and a variety of summer sessions that last from four to twelve weeks.

Financial Aid

Southern Vermont College is committed to meeting the demonstrated financial needs of students who are unable to meet college costs with their own or their families' earnings, savings, or assets. In order to be considered for aid, a student must file the Free Application for Federal Student Aid (FAFSA). The College participates in a variety of federal, state, and local financial aid programs, including the Federal Pell Grant, Federal Supplemental Opportunity Educational Grant, and Federal Work-Study programs; various student loan programs; state grant programs; and the Southern Vermont College scholarship programs. Of first-year students, 86 percent receive some form of financial aid; 73 percent of all students receive aid. Total financial aid for all students is more than $3.6 million, of which 51 percent is from grants. Students are encouraged to research state, community, and private organizations for additional funding sources.

Application and Information

Southern Vermont College follows a rolling admission policy. To be considered for admission, students must submit a completed application form with a $25 fee; an official transcript from their high school and any colleges previously attended; at least two recommendations from teachers, guidance counselors, employers, or civic officials; and a 300-word essay. While a tour and interview are not required at Southern Vermont, students are encouraged to visit the campus and meet with an admissions counselor. For more information about SVC, students should contact:

Admissions Office
Southern Vermont College
Monument Avenue
Bennington, Vermont 05201

Telephone: 800-378-2782 (toll-free)

SOUTHWEST TEXAS STATE UNIVERSITY
SAN MARCOS, TEXAS

The University

Southwest Texas State University is a comprehensive public university committed to providing an intellectually stimulating and socially diverse climate for its graduate and undergraduate students. SWT is dedicated to effective teaching and the advancement of knowledge and artistic expression. Serving approximately 21,000 students, SWT is the seventh-largest public university in the state. Chartered in 1899, SWT's original mission was to prepare Texas public school teachers. It became renowned for carrying out this mission, but today it does far more. The school has grown to become a major multipurpose university offering programs in the Schools of Applied Arts and Technology, Business, Fine Arts and Communication, Health Professions, Education, Liberal Arts, and Science and in the Graduate School. SWT is proud of its most famous alumnus, Lyndon Baines Johnson, the thirty-sixth president of the United States. LBJ remains the only U.S. president to have graduated from a Texas college.

Academic Program

SWT operates on a two-semester calendar system with the fall semester beginning in late August and the spring semester in mid-January. SWT also offers two 5-week summer sessions. Students may earn college credit hours through the University's credit-by-examination program (AP, CLEP, and departmental exams). The Honors Program offers interdisciplinary courses as part of a five-course requirement, which includes the honors thesis, for graduation in the program. Class size is limited to 17 students. Air Force and Army ROTC programs are also offered. At SWT, all students are required to complete a 52- to 55-hour general studies curriculum that serves as the common foundation for all majors. The purpose of the general studies curriculum is to help students acquire the fundamental skills and cultural background that are the marks of an educated person. The requirement for a bachelor's degree is the successful completion of approximately 128 to 136 semester hours, depending on the degree plan.

Financial Aid

SWT provides financial aid in the form of scholarships, grants, loans, and employment. Most aid, except for scholarships, is based upon individual need and eligibility. Scholarships are merit-based gifts. The scholarship deadline is February 1. To ensure timely processing of financial aid applications, the data from the Free Application for Federal Student Aid (FAFSA) from the federal processing center must be received by SWT by April 1. Approximately 58 percent of SWT students receive financial assistance. For applications and materials, students should write directly to the Office of Student Financial Aid, 601 University Drive, San Marcos, Texas 78666-4602.

Application and Information

Applicants with completed files are notified of admission on a rolling basis beginning October 1 for the fall semester. To apply for admission, students need to submit a $25 application fee, an official high school transcript verifying class rank, and an SAT I or ACT test score. Transfer students need to submit an official college transcript from each school attended. Application forms and credentials must be filed by the following deadlines: fall semester, July 1; spring semester, December 1; summer semester I, May 1; and summer semester II, June 15.

To request an application or additional information, students should contact:

Office of Admission
Southwest Texas State University
429 North Guadalupe
San Marcos, Texas 78666-5709

Telephone: 512-245-2364
E-mail: admissions@swt.edu
Web site: http://www.swt.edu

SPRINGFIELD COLLEGE
SPRINGFIELD, MASSACHUSETTS

The College

Originally founded as a school for training students for service in the YMCA, Springfield College has entered its second century of preparing talented young men and women for careers in the human helping professions. Just a few years after opening its doors to the first eighteen students in 1885, Springfield College could boast an international reputation as a pioneer in teaching and scholarship related to physical education, wellness, and the training of YMCA executives. Today, with a coed undergraduate and graduate body of 3,550, Springfield College is proud of its reputation in these fields and throughout the human helping professions. Participation in cocurricular activities forms an integral part of the Springfield College experience. Clubs range from drama, music, dance, and publications to professional interest groups and community service organizations. More than 90 percent of the student body turns out for participation in an extensive intramural sports program, and more than 30 percent participate in intercollegiate athletics. Women's sports include basketball, cross-country, field hockey, gymnastics, lacrosse, soccer, softball, swimming, tennis, track, and volleyball. Men participate in baseball, basketball, cross-country, football, golf, gymnastics, lacrosse, soccer, swimming, tennis, track, volleyball, and wrestling. On-campus housing is guaranteed for four years, and students have the option of living in either a coeducational or a single-sex dormitory. After the junior year, students may elect to live in off-campus housing.

Academic Program

Humanics, the philosophy that has inspired Springfield College from its beginning, calls for educating the whole person—spirit, mind, and body. Undergraduate education at Springfield College is designed to promote an understanding of how these different aspects of ourselves work together in preparation for a life of service to others. In the classroom, the humanics approach translates to a careful balance of theory and practice—the daily application of an education that connects people to people. The College has a two-semester academic calendar. In order to successfully complete the Springfield experience, students are required to accumulate a minimum of 130 credits toward graduation. These credits comprise major requirements, elective courses, and the All-College Requirements (which include studies in English, philosophy, social science, health, and natural science). Qualified students may also earn credit through the Advanced Placement Program and the College-Level Examination Program administered by the College Board.

Financial Aid

Students who feel they do not have sufficient funds to pay for the total cost of their education are encouraged to apply for financial aid in the form of grants, loans, and student employment. All financial aid offered by Springfield College is based on need, intellectual promise, leadership, and character. Students who submit the Free Application for Federal Student Aid (FAFSA) and the College Scholarship Service Financial Aid PROFILE by April 1 are given full consideration for aid. Students not eligible for financial aid may still be considered for institutional employment.

Application and Information

Springfield College's rolling admission program allows applicants to go into review with the Admissions Committee immediately upon completion of the application process. The deadline for submission of applications for the freshman class is April 1; however, students applying for the programs in physical therapy and athletic training must submit an application prior to January 15. Students applying for the physician assistant program must submit an application prior to February 1. Transfer students must file an application before June 1.

Application forms and further information may be obtained by contacting:

Office of Admissions
Box M
Springfield College
Springfield, Massachusetts 01109
Telephone: 413-748-3136

STATE UNIVERSITY OF NEW YORK AT BINGHAMTON
BINGHAMTON, NEW YORK

The University

At Binghamton University, the values of a liberal arts education are central to the college experience. Harpur College of Arts and Sciences, the original component of the University, is well known for its innovative liberal arts program. In 1965, the college was redesignated the State University of New York at Binghamton, one of four university centers in the State University of New York System authorized to award the Ph.D. Harpur retains its identity within the University, serving as the nucleus of an evolving complex of graduate and professional schools. The Thomas J. Watson School of Engineering and Applied Science enrolls undergraduate and graduate students. The School of Management, the Decker School of Nursing, and the School of Education and Human Development offer both undergraduate and graduate programs and have maintained the liberal arts at the core of their programs to ensure students a broad general education.

Academic Program

To qualify for a B.A. or B.S. from Harpur, students must complete a minimum of 31½ courses, or 126 credits; fulfill a foreign language requirement; and complete both general education and all-college distribution requirements as well as the requirements for the chosen major. The distribution requirement consists of 2 courses in the Division of Humanities (including fine arts), 2 courses in the Division of Science and Mathematics, 2 courses in the Division of Social Sciences, an additional 4 courses taken outside the offerings of the division of the student's major, and 1 half-course (two semesters) in physical education. Students must also fulfill an expository writing requirement and a diversity requirement. Independent and interdisciplinary study can be arranged. Honors programs and minors are available in most departments. A number of courses may be taken for credit in other schools of the University.

Financial Aid

Aid is available through the Federal Pell Grant, Federal Work-Study, Federal Supplemental Educational Opportunity Grant, Federal Direct Loan, and Federal Perkins Loan programs; Tuition Assistance Program (TAP) awards (for New York State residents only); and the University's own financial aid funds. The Binghamton University Foundation underwrites a merit-based University Scholarship Program and offers other limited need- and merit-based scholarships. Students not eligible for Federal Work-Study funds can find jobs both on and off campus. More than $30 million in financial aid was disbursed to Binghamton students in 1995–96; 65 percent of undergraduates received some form of financial assistance. Candidates for financial aid should complete the Free Application for Federal Student Aid. New York residents should also complete the New York State Tuition Assistance Program application. The deadlines for submission of these forms are March 1 for fall admission and November 15 for spring admission.

Application and Information

Application forms are available in all New York State schools and community colleges. Nonresidents of the state may obtain an application form from the admission office. It is suggested that students file an application by mid-January for freshman admission and March for transfers, although deadlines may vary for each undergraduate school. Admission decisions are announced on a rolling basis, starting in March and ending in April, in time for students to adhere to the Candidates' Reply Date of May 1. An early decision plan is available for prospective students who wish to enroll as freshmen in the autumn term. The deadline for filing an application for early decision is November 1; admission decisions are announced by January 1.

Office of Undergraduate Admissions
Binghamton University
P.O. Box 6001
Binghamton, New York 13902-6001

Telephone: 607-777-2171
E-mail: admit@binghamton.edu

STATE UNIVERSITY OF NEW YORK AT BUFFALO
BUFFALO, NEW YORK

The University
The State University of New York at Buffalo, founded in 1846 as the University of Buffalo, is today the largest single unit and most comprehensive undergraduate and graduate center of the State University, enrolling about 25,000 students (about 18,375 attending full-time). There are 1,900 undergraduate students in the School of Engineering and Applied Sciences. The merger in 1962 with the State University System signaled a period of dramatic development. The University offers ninety-three undergraduate, 112 master's, ninety-eight doctoral, and six professional programs.

Academic Program
To graduate, a student is required to complete 128 semester hours. In all engineering programs, students normally complete 64 semester hours by the end of their sophomore year. Included in the 64 semester hours is a required core curriculum that all Bachelor of Science candidates are expected to take during the first two years. Usually in the sophomore year, students specialize in an area by selecting a major and fulfilling departmental requirements in their field of interest. Each engineering area varies in the required number of technical courses. Students should consult the program or department office for the most recent information. Upon admission, each entering student meets with an adviser whose functions are to aid the student in identifying educational goals, to provide information concerning academic programs and procedures, and to help the student plan a program by selecting courses commensurate with his or her background, interests, and vocational goals. The adviser also helps the student to identify and explore any problem areas and, when necessary, refers the student to services on or off campus. Upon entering a field of concentration, a student is assigned a faculty adviser in the field.

Financial Aid
The University at Buffalo participates in all New York State and federal financial aid programs, including the Tuition Assistance Program (available only to New York State residents) and the Federal Pell Grant, Federal Work-Study, Federal Stafford Student Loan, and Federal Perkins Loan programs. Interested students must complete the Free Application for Federal Student Aid in early March. All inquiries concerning financial aid should be addressed to the Office of Financial Aid, Hayes C, State University of New York at Buffalo. Prospective University students should not wait for an admission decision before applying for financial aid. Further information is available in all New York State high schools and may also be obtained by calling the Office of Financial Aid at 716-829-3724.

Application and Information
Students are urged to submit their applications as early as possible. All applications for admission to the fall term (first semester) that are received by the Processing Center before January 5 will receive full and equal consideration for admission in September. Applications received after January 5 will be considered on a space-available basis. Applications for admission to the spring term (second semester) should be completed before December 1. Tours of the School of Engineering and Applied Sciences are available by appointment most Fridays at 9:30 a.m. or by arrangement. Students should contact the School at 716-645-2774 for further information. The e-mail address is meryan@ubvms.cc.buffalo.edu for those who prefer to use it.

Application forms are available in all New York State high schools. For additional information about either freshman studies or the transfer program, students should address requests to:

Office of Admissions
17 Capen Hall
State University of New York at Buffalo
Box 601660
Buffalo, New York 14260-1660

Telephone: 716-645-6900

STATE UNIVERSITY OF NEW YORK COLLEGE AT BROCKPORT

BROCKPORT, NEW YORK

The College

SUNY Brockport cherishes its rise to prominence in higher education. Founded in 1835 as the Brockport Collegiate Institute, it became a normal school for teachers in 1867. The comprehensive college of arts and sciences found at Brockport today represents a 130-year tradition of providing education of the highest quality. The College is committed to serving the citizens of New York, including the large, diverse student population, whose varying interests and needs reflect the complex challenges of contemporary society. Most of its 6,800 undergraduate students come from New York State, 11 percent are members of minority groups, and 1 percent are international students. There are 2,400 students living in various types of campus residence halls, including coed, special option housing for freshmen and transfers. SUNY Brockport also offers a Weekend College option as well as a range of courses at the MetroCenter, a satellite facility located in Rochester, and at more than fifteen other sites in the region.

Academic Program

SUNY Brockport's educational programs strengthen, develop, and enrich the intellectual and social abilities of its students, who must complete a minimum of 120 credits in an approved program with a minimum earned academic average of 2.0 (C). Included in the 120 credits are an academic major program and a general education program of courses in composition and quantitative skills, computer literacy, contemporary issues, fine arts, humanities, natural sciences and mathematics, perspectives on women, and social sciences. Freshmen are required to take an Academic Planning Seminar (APS), which introduces them to the academic rigors and opportunities of college life and assists them in planning an individual program of study that relates to their academic, personal, and career goals. SUNY Brockport awards transfer credit for course work done at other regionally accredited colleges and universities prior to matriculation. Students may earn credit by examination, AP or CLEP, for courses offered by the College. Freshmen with outstanding high school academic records may enroll in the honors program, which includes an honors version of APS and a parallel honors general education program.

Financial Aid

Approximately 84 percent of SUNY Brockport's students receive some form of financial aid. The College participates in the Federal Pell Grant, Federal Supplemental Educational Opportunity Grant, Federal Direct Student Loan, Federal Perkins Loan, Nursing Loans, and Federal Work-Study programs. New York State residents may qualify for Tuition Assistance Program awards, State University Supplemental Tuition Assistance, Assistance for Part-time Study, and Educational Opportunity Grants. Special state scholarships are available for veterans and children of deceased or disabled veterans. The Office of Financial Aid assists students in identifying applicable programs and prepares estimated financial aid packages for all newly accepted students prior to the payment of any advance fees. The Student Employment Office arranges part-time work for students on and off the campus. Numerous campus-controlled scholarships are also available, including twenty-five Alumni Association Awards. The Free Application for Federal Student Aid (FAFSA) is required of all aid applicants.

Application and Information

Students may apply for fall or spring on a rolling admission basis. Accepted applicants may also attend summer sessions. Application forms are available from the Admissions Office or from guidance offices in all New York State high schools and all SUNY two-year and four-year colleges. Students should apply by January 15 for the fall semester and by December 1 for the spring semester.

Director of Admissions
State University of New York College at Brockport
350 New Campus Drive
Brockport, New York 14420-2915

Telephone: 716-395-2751
Web site: http://www.brockport.edu

STATE UNIVERSITY OF NEW YORK COLLEGE AT ONEONTA
ONEONTA, NEW YORK

The College
A comprehensive college of arts and sciences in the SUNY system, the College at Oneonta strives to develop students to their full potential both academically and personally. With the largest library collection in its sector of SUNY, excellent computer facilities, and strong advisement and support programs, Oneonta provides students a solid academic foundation for careers or graduate study. Varied residence life programs and outstanding volunteer service and internship arrangements offer students vast opportunities for personal development. The College's Center for Social Responsibility and Community, established through a $500,000 Kellogg Foundation grant, actively develops and coordinates community service opportunities for students. Career planning and placement services assist students in preparing for careers and securing employment after graduation. Established as a state normal school in 1889, Oneonta was a founding college of the SUNY system in 1948. Though more than 90 percent of Oneonta students are state residents, the College attracts many out-of-state and international students. The College's 5,000 undergraduates represent a medley of cultures, backgrounds, ages, and experiences. Approximately half of Oneonta's students live in the thirteen on-campus residence halls, which have full-time professional directors and staffs of resident advisers. Residence life options include special interest areas.

Academic Program
Oneonta's academic program has three primary components: a general education requirement, specialized in-depth study in a major, and free electives. The newly designed 36-hour general education requirement includes courses in perspectives on nature and mathematics, on society and human behavior, on human value and expression and integrative perspectives, as well as courses that develop thinking, problem-solving, and communication skills. In their major, students complete 30–60 hours of course work on their way to the 122 hours required for graduation. Transfer applications are encouraged, and students may transfer up to 66 credits from two-year colleges or 77 credits from four-year institutions. Degree credits may be earned through proficiency examinations, course challenges, and assessment of prior learning. Students must declare a major by their junior year. A strong academic advisement program provides assistance in choosing curriculums and planning the academic year, which is divided into two 15-week semesters with optional summer sessions.

Financial Aid
Approximately 80 percent of Oneonta's full-time undergraduate students receive financial aid through federal, state, and local programs, including the Federal Pell Grant Program, Federal Supplemental Educational Opportunity Grants, Federal Perkins Loans, Federal Family Educational Loan Program, Federal Work-Study Program, on-campus part-time employment, and College scholarships. To be eligible for financial assistance, students must submit the Free Application for Federal Student Aid to the College as early as possible. Through a concerted effort to expand scholarship opportunities, the College now offers more than 120 scholarship awards. Information about scholarships is available through the Admissions or Financial Aid Offices.

Application and Information
The College at Oneonta uses the standard SUNY application, available in most high school guidance offices or from the College's Admissions Office. Applications are accepted year-round and are evaluated on a rolling basis. For fall semester admission, freshman applicants should submit all materials by February 1; transfer applicants should submit materials by June 1. For more information, students should contact:

Director of Admissions
State University of New York College at Oneonta
Oneonta, New York 13820

Telephone: 607-436-2524
800-SUNY-123 (toll-free)
Fax: 607-436-3074
E-mail: admissions@oneonta.edu
Web site: http://www.oneonta.edu

STEPHENS COLLEGE
COLUMBIA, MISSOURI

The College

The second-oldest women's college in the country, Stephens College was founded in 1833. Nearly 1,000 young women, representing forty-three states and five countries, enrich Stephens with their varied talents, interests, and backgrounds. As students at this private four-year college, these women enjoy a spacious 244-acre campus that is located in the heart of Columbia and adjacent to the University of Missouri. In addition to participating in an academic exchange with the University of Missouri, Stephens' national sororities plan many activities with the fraternities, including Greek Week. Stephens students may choose to join one of twelve honorary societies on campus, including Psi Chi, Alpha Epsilon Rho, and Mortar Board, or become involved in student government. Leadership experience is emphasized in all aspects of life at Stephens. Stephens has five residence halls, which provide much of the focus for campus activity. The Searcy House Plan offers special opportunities for intellectual and personal growth to a select group of 60 freshmen each year. Since it began more than twenty-five years ago as an experiment funded by the Ford Foundation, the Searcy program has served as a model for similar living/learning communities in colleges and universities across the nation. Fashioned after Searcy, the Prunty Science House Plan is also available to a limited number of Stephens students who wish to explore the fields of math, science, and technology.

Academic Program

The B.A. degree may be completed in three to four years. Students pursue depth of study in an academic area, breadth in liberal arts study, and elective course work with guidance from faculty advisers. Academic departments require internships in an area of interest and often provide opportunities for research projects in field settings. Students in the bachelor's degree programs, either B.A., B.F.A., or B.S., must complete the residence requirement of fourteen sessions. All five sessions of the academic year may count toward the requirement. Students also must demonstrate the ability to write proper English or pass as many as three courses in English composition, must demonstrate math competence through examination or by earning credit in basic math courses, and must complete at least twelve courses at an advanced level (including five in the major).

Financial Aid

Approximately 75 percent of the student body receive some form of assistance through scholarships, grants, loans, or employment. Stephens participates in the Federal Pell Grant, Federal Supplemental Educational Opportunity Grant, Federal Perkins Loan, Federal Stafford Student Loan, and Federal Work-Study programs. Missouri residents are encouraged to apply for aid under the Missouri Student Grant Program. The Free Application for Federal Student Aid (FAFSA) is required for financial aid consideration. Applications for financial aid should be received by March 15. Stephens also offers a financial aid estimate service.

Application and Information

Candidates for admission should submit the application with the $25 application fee and arrange to have transcripts and recommendations mailed to the director of admission. Upon receipt of the application, any additional material is mailed to the student. Qualified students are accepted on a rolling admission basis upon receipt of all necessary credentials.

Office of Admission
Campus Box 2121
Stephens College
Columbia, Missouri 65215
Telephone: 573-876-7207
800-876-7207 (toll-free)
Fax: 573-876-7237
E-mail: apply@sc.stephens.edu (for U.S. students)
usa@sc.stephens.edu (for international students)
Gopher: gopher://gopher.stephens.edu
Web site: http://www.stephens.edu

SUOMI COLLEGE
HANCOCK, MICHIGAN

The College
Founded by Finnish immigrants in 1896, Suomi College is the only private college in Michigan's Upper Peninsula. It is one of only twenty-eight colleges in the United States that are affiliated with the Evangelical Lutheran Church in America and remains the only college founded by Finns in the United States. Suomi College provides a college education in a Christian environment but is nonsectarian in its instruction, counseling, and campus religious services. Suomi College offers programs in liberal education, career education, talent development, and continuing/lifelong learning. The College currently services approximately 350 students. With a student-teacher ratio of 15:1, students have access to individualized help and support. The student body represents at least twelve states and six countries. Diversity is welcomed at Suomi, and the college currently has a 12 percent minority representation and a 6 percent international representation.

Academic Program
Graduation from Suomi College at the associate level requires students to have earned a cumulative grade point average of at least 2.0, have completed at least 60 semester hours (at least 30 semester hours at the College), and have completed a program approved by the College. To earn a bachelor's degree students must complete a minimum of 129 semester hours. As a liberal arts college, Suomi believes that the attainment of certain skills is essential to leading an aware, productive, healthy, and satisfying life. The College, therefore, requires a core curriculum, approved by MACRAO, for both the A.A. and B.A. degrees. Within the core curriculum areas, students have an element of choice. Many programs offer the opportunity to gain work experience and to put classroom knowledge into practice through internships. Depending on the program, 1 to 6 credits can be earned. Students who believe they have already learned the content of a course may request an examination for credit. A maximum of 16 hours of credit may be earned in this fashion and applied toward degree requirements. Students may also earn credits through advanced placement.

Financial Aid
Approximately 92 percent of Suomi students receive financial aid. This aid includes grants, scholarships, loans, and on-campus employment (work-study). All students are encouraged to apply for aid. Last year, in addition to federal, state, and private aid, Suomi awarded more than $800,000 in need- and merit-based institutional grants. This institutional aid is awarded not only to students from low-income families, but also to students from middle- and upper-middle–income families. All accepted students are considered for federally and Suomi-funded assistance. Michigan residents may apply for state-funded programs. Students must submit the Free Application for Federal Student Aid (FAFSA) by May 1 to receive priority consideration for need-based aid. Michigan residents are urged to submit these forms by February 15 to maximize consideration for state-funded aid.

Application and Information
While applications are accepted on a rolling basis, May 30 is the priority filing date. Those students interested in the nursing program are encouraged to apply by early March, since the nursing class for the next year is chosen in mid-March. Students should submit all materials for their files as soon as possible. Admission decisions are made within ten working days upon completion of the student's file. For an application or further information on programs or financial aid, students should contact:

Suomi College Admissions
601 Quincy Street
Hancock, Michigan 49930-1882

Telephone: 906-487-7274
800-682-7604 (toll-free)

SWEET BRIAR COLLEGE
SWEET BRIAR, VIRGINIA

The College

Sweet Briar College, the first women's college to establish a prelaw chapter of Phi Alpha Delta Law Fraternity, is consistently ranked as one of the top colleges for women in the nation. Its academic reputation, beautiful location, and attention to the individual attract smart women who want to excel. The College's focus on women allows students, in full partnership with the faculty, to fulfill their promise as scholars and develop leadership skills. Students work one-on-one with faculty members and visiting scholars and engage in meaningful research. Classes are small, averaging 12 students. The four-year Honors Program is nationally recognized for its innovative partnering of interdisciplinary academic and cocurricular programs. The College has a wide geographic, ethnic, and socioeconomic representation. About 600 women from more than forty states and twenty countries are enrolled at Sweet Briar's Virginia campus; another 150 students are enrolled in Sweet Briar's coed Junior Year in France and Junior Year in Spain. Social, recreational, and cocurricular events are coordinated with neighboring colleges. Students play an active role in campus organizations, including honor societies, community service groups, student newspaper, drama and dance clubs, radio club, and singing groups. Varsity athletes compete in NCAA Division III field hockey, lacrosse, riding, soccer, swimming, tennis, and volleyball.

Academic Program

Sweet Briar's academic program supports its mission to prepare women to be active, responsible members of a world community by integrating the liberal arts and sciences with opportunities for internships, campus and community leadership, and career planning. Students complete courses in English, literature or the arts, science, foreign language, non-Western studies, social sciences, humanities, and physical education. Independent studies, available at all levels, and seminars are included in most majors, and a culminating senior course or exercise is required in all majors. Sweet Briar has a chapter of Phi Beta Kappa and offers an honors program that provides an opportunity to take special tutorials and seminars and to do a yearlong research project culminating in an honors thesis on an original topic. Sweet Briar's 4-1-4 calendar, with fall, winter, and spring terms, allows students to participate in intensive courses, independent research projects, or internships on campus or throughout the world during the one-month winter term.

Financial Aid

A family's financial circumstances do not limit a student's choices at Sweet Briar because of the College's generous financial aid program. About 60 percent of students receive need-based aid, including grants, loans, and work-study awards. Academic merit awards are available, including the Founders', Commonwealth, Betty Bean Black, and Sweet Briar scholarships. Several other academic, merit, and leadership awards are also available.

Application and Information

Scholarship candidates should apply by January 15, and regular candidates should apply by February 15 of the senior year. Early decision applications are due by December 1 of the senior year, and notifications are sent December 15; the reservation deposit is due January 15. Transfer applications for the sophomore and junior classes are due by July 1. A completed application includes a transcript of the candidate's school work, scores on the required tests, recommendations from the guidance counselor and a teacher, and essays written by the candidate (on the form provided by the College). Sweet Briar also accepts the Common Application and the CollegeLink application. All materials should be sent to the address given below; information may be requested from the same office.

Dean of Admissions
Sweet Briar College
Sweet Briar, Virginia 24595

Telephone: 804-381-6142
800-381-6142 (toll-free)
Fax: 804-381-6152
E-mail: admissions@sbc.edu
Web site: http://www.sbc.edu

THIEL COLLEGE
GREENVILLE, PENNSYLVANIA

The College

Thiel College was founded in 1866 as one of the first coeducational institutions of higher education in the United States. Located in Greenville, Pennsylvania, in the northwestern corner of the commonwealth, Thiel has become known for the quality of its educational offerings and its blending of liberal arts cutting-edge technology and experiential learning through extensive cooperative education and internship opportunities. Affiliated with the Evangelical Lutheran Church in America, the College enrolls just over 1,000 women and men. Most students come from Pennsylvania, Ohio, and the Middle Atlantic States. Seven percent of the students are members of minority groups, and 3 percent are from fourteen other countries.

Academic Program

The Bachelor of Arts degree programs and the Bachelor of Science in Nursing degree program require a minimum of 124 credits for graduation. The Associate of Arts degree programs require a minimum of 64 credits for graduation. All majors must complete liberal arts integrative requirements as well as core and elective courses. Advanced Placement (AP) and CLEP examination scores are welcome from students entering Thiel. Courses taken at other colleges while students are still in high school are accepted for consideration provided that the grade earned is a C or better (on a 4.0 scale). The Honors Program is offered to outstanding students and provides students with the opportunity to develop special projects, interests, and activities; to meet with visiting artists, scholars, and public figures; and to work closely with professors and other members of the College community. Thiel College follows a two-semester system. Classes typically start near Labor Day in August or September and end in mid-December. Second-term classes begin in mid-January and continue through mid-May. Summer session classes are also offered.

Financial Aid

Thiel College participates in all federal financial aid. Students are encouraged to check with state agencies as well as with local, community, civic, industrial, and church-related groups for additional funding sources. Students are encouraged to file the Free Application for Federal Student Aid (FAFSA) as early as possible after January 1 of their senior year. Award notifications are mailed beginning in late January and continue until funding is exhausted. Admission decisions are non-need-based. Thiel College awards its institutional funds after consideration of academic achievement, special talents and skills, and financial need. Thiel maintains an extensive grant, loan, scholarship, and college work program. In 1997–98, $4.6 million was awarded to students from institutional resources, and 95 percent of students received funding through a combination of federal, state, local, and Thiel resources.

Application and Information

Thiel begins to consider applicants in late September each year for the following fall. Decisions are made on a rolling basis, and applicants are notified within ten days of the completion of an application packet. Applications should be received no later than August 1 for the fall term and December 1 for the spring term. For inquiries and requests for information, students should contact:

Thiel College Admissions Office
75 College Avenue
Greenville, Pennsylvania 16125

Telephone: 412-589-2345
800-248-4435 (toll-free)
Fax: 412-589-2013

TULANE UNIVERSITY
NEW ORLEANS, LOUISIANA

The University

One of a handful of national independent universities in the South, Tulane was founded in 1834 as the Medical College of Louisiana and reorganized as Tulane in 1884. The University is comprehensive by nature, with more than 11,000 students enrolled in eleven schools and colleges ranging from the liberal arts and sciences through a full spectrum of professional schools: law, medicine, business, engineering, architecture, social work, and public health and tropical medicine. Students participate in more than 200 campus organizations. About 1 student in 3 joins a fraternity or sorority; 2 in 3 play intramural or intercollegiate club sports, and more than 500 participate in Tulane's community volunteer organization. Tulane fields sixteen NCAA Division I sports, competing in the newly formed Conference USA.

Academic Program

The Paul Tulane College (for men) and Sophie Newcomb College (for women) offer programs leading to the B.A., B.S., and B.F.A. degrees. In Tulane's coordinate college structure, men and women attend classes together, Newcomb and Tulane share a faculty and a curriculum, and most residence halls are coeducational. The School of Engineering emphasizes design, research, and laboratory experimentation for its Bachelor of Science degree programs in biomedical, chemical, civil, computer, electrical, environmental, and mechanical engineering as well as computer science. The School of Architecture takes advantage of its location in New Orleans, a fascinating living architecture laboratory, where some 250 students are enrolled in the five-year Bachelor of Architecture program. The A. B. Freeman School of Business offers majors in accounting, finance, general business, management, and marketing, leading to the Bachelor of Science in Management degree.

Financial Aid

The University operates a comprehensive aid program; more than half of the students receive some form of financial aid. The average financial aid package (through scholarships, federal grants, loans, and work-study jobs) was about $20,000 for 1996–97. Need, determined by family financial information on the Free Application for Federal Student Aid and the PROFILE from the College Scholarship Service, establishes the appropriate amount of assistance. Merit, based on academic record, determines the proportion of Tulane-funded scholarships in the aid package. The University offers assistance to applicants who demonstrate financial need, and 96 percent of financial aid offers include scholarships or grants. If financial need continues and the student has an acceptable academic record, aid extends through the normal period of undergraduate study. Deans' Honor Scholarships are offered each year to approximately 100 freshmen and cover tuition for the undergraduate career; other merit scholarships, including those for middle-income students, are also available. Tulane also gives at least thirty National Merit Scholarships to National Merit Finalists who have named Tulane as their first-choice college. Tulane offers creative financing options for families that do not qualify for traditional aid but need assistance in meeting costs.

Application and Information

Applications should be submitted by January 15 for admission to the fall semester; admission notification is made no later than April 1. Deans' Honor Scholarship applicants must apply by December 1 and are notified by February 20. Early action candidates should have all credentials on file by November 1 for notification by December 15. Candidates for admission have until May 1 to respond to the University's offer, and housing is required for freshmen. The application fee is $35.

Richard Whiteside
Dean of Admission and Enrollment Management
Tulane University
6823 St. Charles Avenue
New Orleans, Louisiana 70118-5680

Telephone: 504-865-5731
800-873-9283 (toll-free)
Fax: 504-862-8715
E-mail: undergrad.admission@tulane.edu
Web site: http://www.tulane.edu/Admission

UNITED STATES INTERNATIONAL UNIVERSITY
SAN DIEGO, CALIFORNIA

The University
An international focus is an integral part of all degree programs at United States International University (USIU). The University has a 160-acre campus in San Diego and campuses in Nairobi and Mexico City. Founded in 1952 as California Western University, USIU offers a chance to learn from a globally oriented faculty and to study with fellow students from more than eighty countries. The University's mission is to promote the discovery and application of knowledge, the acquisition of skills, and the development of intellect and character in a manner that prepares students to contribute effectively and ethically as citizens of a changing and increasingly technological world.

Academic Program
USIU has a College of Business Administration and a College of Arts and Sciences. Within the College of Business Administration are the programs in business and management and hotel, restaurant, and tourism management. Within the College of Arts and Sciences are programs in education, psychology and family studies, and liberal and interdisciplinary studies. Students' programs are planned in conjunction with academic advisers, using suggested lists of courses as guides. Diverse instructional methods include lectures, seminars, small group discussions, case analyses, simulations, experiential situations, and internships. The opportunity to engage in closely supervised independent study is offered as a supplement to structured classes.

Financial Aid
USIU offers financial assistance to eligible domestic and international students. Merit scholarships are awarded to undergraduates with a 3.0 cumulative GPA or above. Both international and domestic students may be eligible to receive scholarships of up to 60 percent in tuition costs, or a total of $6867. Assistance is provided by federal, state, and University funds and is offered in the form of scholarships, grants, part-time employment, and long-term loans. Applications submitted by March 2 receive priority consideration for funds; a student whose application is received later is awarded funds based on the availability of aid.

Application and Information
Freshman and transfer applicants may be admitted to any quarter. Applications and supportive data should be on file in the Office of Admissions at least thirty days prior to the quarter for which the applicant desires admission. Later applications are processed as quickly as possible on a space-available basis. The completed application form, a nonrefundable $40 application fee, and supporting documents should be sent to:

Office of Admissions
United States International University
10455 Pomerado Road
San Diego, California 92131

Telephone: 619-635-4772
Fax: 619-635-4739
E-mail: usiu_adm@usiu.edu
Web site: http://www.usiu.edu

UNITED STATES MILITARY ACADEMY
WEST POINT, NEW YORK

The Academy

The United States Military Academy, the nation's oldest service academy, offers young men and women one of the most highly respected, quality education programs in the nation. The Military Academy has, since its founding in 1802, provided the broad college education demanded by the military profession while maintaining a degree of academic specialization comparable to that of civilian universities. The Military Academy provides its graduates with a solid foundation for intellectual and moral/ethical growth that is essential for successfully handling high-level responsibilities in national service. When students enter West Point, they are also beginning a profession. Upon graduation, cadets are commissioned as second lieutenants in the U.S. Army and are normally required to serve on active duty for at least five years. Cadets compete annually for Rhodes, Olmsted, Marshall, and Daedalian scholarships and for National Science Foundation, Truman, and Hertz graduate fellowships. West Pointers who remain in the Army are normally selected to attend civilian graduate schools in the United States or abroad between their fourth and tenth years of service. The Academy develops the nation's future Army leaders by immersing cadets in programs of academic, military, and physical development. Each of these programs is rooted in principles of ethical-moral development, epitomized by the Academy motto, "Duty, Honor, Country." The honor code prohibits cadets from lying, cheating, stealing, or tolerating those who do. The code is a source of pride and mutual trust essential in the profession of arms. In addition to academic and military education, cadets participate in athletic and extracurricular activities.

Academic Program

The academic program at the United States Military Academy provides cadets with a broad background in the arts and sciences and prepares them for future graduate study. The total curriculum is designed to develop essential character, competence, and intellectual ability in an officer. The core curriculum is the foundation of the academic program and provides a background in mathematics, physical science, engineering, humanities, behavioral science, and social science. The core curriculum, consisting of thirty-one courses, represents the essential broad base of knowledge necessary for success as a commissioned officer and supports the subsequent choice of an elected area of academic concentration. Classes at West Point are small, averaging 12 to 18 cadets per section. They receive individual attention, and tutorial sessions are available upon request. Advanced and honors courses are available to cadets having exceptional ability. All cadets study military science and receive classroom instruction in the principles of small-unit tactics and leadership during a two-week intersession between the first and second semesters. Concentrated summer field training provides each cadet with the opportunity to learn and practice individual military skills and to apply the principles of tactics and leadership studied in the classroom.

Financial Aid

There are no financial aid programs because expenses are paid by the U.S. government. Scholarship awards may be used by candidates to offset the cost of the initial deposit.

Application and Information

Prospective candidates should write to Admissions, stating their interest in the Military Academy. Each applicant will be sent a Precandidate Questionnaire and prospectus, which outlines the West Point entrance requirements. All applicants are encouraged to start a candidate file at West Point at the end of their junior year or as soon thereafter as possible. This allows for early completion of all candidate file requirements.

Director of Admissions
United States Military Academy
606 Thayer Road
West Point, New York 10996-1797

Telephone: 914-938-4041
Web site: http://www.usma.edu/Admissions

UNIVERSITY AT ALBANY, STATE UNIVERSITY OF NEW YORK
ALBANY, NEW YORK

The University

Designated as a University Center of the State University of New York, the University at Albany has a broad mission of undergraduate and graduate education, research, and service. More than 16,000 students, including 11,000 undergraduate students, are enrolled in the University's eight schools and colleges: arts and sciences, business, education, criminal justice, public affairs, information science and policy, social welfare, and public health. With nearly 200 University-recognized social and professional clubs and activities, Albany offers numerous opportunities for leadership development. Albany has taken a new step by upgrading its athletic teams to NCAA Division II status and joining the New England Collegiate Conference.

Academic Program

To earn the bachelor's degree, a student must complete a minimum of 120 credits, satisfy major requirements, complete a minor or a double major, and satisfy any special program requirements. General education requirements specify that students must complete 6 credits of approved course work in each of three categories: natural sciences, social sciences, and humanities and the arts. Students must satisfactorily complete two writing-intensive courses and a 3-credit course in cultural and historical perspectives and human diversity. Albany's Presidential Scholars Program considers only the top students admitted to the freshman class. There has been a fourfold increase in Presidential Scholars over the past three years, attesting to the rising quality of incoming freshman classes. Presidential Scholars must have at least a 91 high school average and outstanding standardized test scores. Frederick Douglass Scholars, chosen from Presidential Scholars, have demonstrated high academic achievement and are from underrepresented groups. Presidential Scholars, Frederick Douglass Scholars, and students who complete a semester or more at the University at Albany with an average of 3.5 or higher are invited to enter the General Education Honors Program. Albany operates on the semester system. The fall term begins in late August or early September and ends in mid-December, and the spring term begins the third week of January and continues until mid-May. A summer program offers both day and evening classes.

Financial Aid

Merit scholarships are available to high-achieving students. The Office of Financial Aid administers all undergraduate financial assistance, including Federal Work-Study Program employment, Federal Perkins Loans, Federal Supplemental Educational Opportunity Grants, New York Equality of Opportunity Grants, Alumni Scholarships, Federal Pell Grants, Federal Stafford Student Loans, New York Tuition Assistance Program awards, and New York Regents Scholarships. General part-time employment is available both on and off the campus. Aid awarded to students through the Office of Financial Aid is based on demonstrated financial need as determined by the Free Application for Federal Student Aid (FAFSA).

Application and Information

Students may apply for fall, spring, or summer admission. Application forms are available in New York State high schools and all SUNY two- and four-year colleges. To receive full consideration, students should apply by February 15 for the fall term and by November 15 for the spring. Notification is on a rolling basis. All new students are required to deposit $150 against fees in advance of registration. Those planning to live in residence halls must deposit $125 against residence charges.

For further information, students should contact:

Director of Admissions
University at Albany, State University of New York
1400 Washington Avenue
Albany, New York 12222

Telephone: 518-442-5435
E-mail: ugadmit@safnet.albany.edu
World Wide Web: http://www.albany.edu/

UNIVERSITY OF ALABAMA IN HUNTSVILLE
HUNTSVILLE, ALABAMA

The University

The University of Alabama in Huntsville occupies a 350-acre suburban campus and a 10-acre campus located in the city's downtown medical district. Offering courses since 1950 and established as an autonomous campus of the University of Alabama System in 1968, UAH has the following academic and professional colleges and schools: the College of Administrative Science, College of Liberal Arts, College of Science, College of Engineering, College of Nursing, School of Graduate Studies, several research centers and service institutes, and a Division of Continuing Education. The University's current enrollment exceeds 7,000. The degree programs at the University of Alabama in Huntsville are administered by the Colleges of Administrative Science, Engineering, Liberal Arts, Nursing, and Science and the School of Graduate Studies. The School of Graduate Studies awards the master's degree in biological science, chemistry, computer science, electrical and computer engineering, English, history, industrial and systems engineering, management, mathematics and statistics, mechanical engineering, nursing, operations research, physics, psychology, and public affairs. The Doctor of Philosophy degree is awarded in applied mathematics, computer science, electrical and computer engineering, industrial and systems engineering, materials science, mechanical engineering, and physics. The University provides on-campus residence facilities for single students, handicapped students, and married students in an ultramodern residence hall as well as in apartment units.

Academic Program

The University of Alabama in Huntsville is a campus of the University of Alabama System. It is a teaching and research institution dedicated to excellence in the promotion of the intellectual, technological, and economic enhancement of the state, region, and nation. The academic year consists of two 14-week semesters plus two 6-week summer terms and one 10-week summer term. Academic advising is available to students in the Academic Advisement Center, in advising offices in the Colleges of Nursing, Engineering, and Administrative Science, and in the department in which a major has been declared. Special advising is provided in the professional areas of law and medicine, and career counseling is available through the Office of Career Services.

Financial Aid

During the 1996–97 academic year, approximately 3,000 students received in excess of $15 million in student aid funds through the University and through Federal Stafford Student Loans from commercial banks. Financial assistance includes loans, scholarships, part-time employment, and such federal programs as the Federal Pell Grant, Federal Supplemental Educational Opportunity Grant, Federal Work-Study, and Federal Perkins Loan, in addition to the Federal Stafford Student Loan. Applications for financial aid are accepted at any time, but those received by April 1 for the following academic year are given priority. UAH uses the U.S. Department of Education Free Application for Federal Student Aid to determine financial need.

Application and Information

Applications for admission are accepted as early as one year prior to the anticipated date of enrollment. A nonrefundable $20 application fee is charged. For an application form and more information, students should contact:

Office of Admissions
University of Alabama in Huntsville
University Center
Huntsville, Alabama 35899

Telephone: 205-890-6070
800-UAH-CALL (toll-free)
E-mail: admitme@email.uah.edu

THE UNIVERSITY OF ALABAMA
TUSCALOOSA, ALABAMA

The University

With more than 275 degree programs, the University of Alabama is the state's capstone institution of education and a renowned center of education in the Southeast. Strength in teaching is matched by public service and strong research, through which faculty members have made significant advances in magnetic information storage, improving health services for Alabama's rural communities, and aquatic biology and wetlands research.

Academic Program

The University operates on an early-semester system of two 16-week semesters, a 3-week Interim Term in May, and two 5-week summer sessions. The normal full-time academic load for undergraduates is 15–18 hours per semester. To qualify for a degree, students must earn a minimum of 128 semester hours and have an overall academic average of at least C and an average of C or better in all work attempted in the major. One fourth of the total number of semester hours required for the degree must be earned in residence, including 9 of the last 18 hours earned before graduation. Any school or college of the University may specify work in the major or minor fields that must be taken in residence. All students must demonstrate satisfactory ability in English. Up to 45 semester hours of credit can be obtained through satisfactory scores on the College-Level Examination Program (CLEP), the College Board's Advanced Placement, or International Baccalaureate examinations. The University also offers credit programs in Air Force and Army ROTC, which provide a well-developed curriculum in military leadership training. The University's Army ROTC program is one of the largest of its kind in the country.

Financial Aid

In recent years, the University has awarded approximately $57 million in financial aid (including $43 million in loans) annually to more than 8,200 qualified students. Financial assistance includes more than 750 different scholarships awarded for scholastic merit and (in most cases) financial need, part-time employment on campus, and federally funded Federal Perkins Loans, Federal Pell Grants, Federal Stafford Student Loans, and Federal Work-Study awards. Applications for financial aid are accepted at any time, but those received by March 1 for the following academic year are given priority. All financial aid is awarded on an annual basis; a new application must be filed each year.

Application and Information

Applications for admission are accepted as early as one year prior to the anticipated date of enrollment. A medical history and proof of measles immunization must be submitted prior to enrollment in classes. Required medical examination forms are provided by the University upon notification of admission. A nonrefundable $25 application fee is charged; no application fee waivers are granted. For an application and more information, students should contact:

Office of Undergraduate Admissions
The University of Alabama
Box 870132
Tuscaloosa, Alabama 35487-0132

Telephone: 205-348-5666
800-933-BAMA (toll-free in the continental United States)
E-mail: uaadmit@ua1vm.ua.edu

UNIVERSITY OF MARYLAND COLLEGE PARK
COLLEGE PARK, MARYLAND

The University

The University of Maryland at College Park dates back to 1856. As the flagship institution of the eleven-campus University of Maryland system, College Park serves as the state's premier institution for teaching and research. Located on 1,580 acres of land, the University is a coeducational public institution serving 21,167 full-time and 3,362 part-time undergraduates with a full-time faculty of 1,500. About 7,700 students are enrolled in the graduate school. The University encourages diversity in campus activities and sponsors more than 275 clubs, organizations, and religious groups. It provides twenty-five intramural sports for men and women, in addition to Atlantic Coast Conference Division I athletics in fifteen sports for men and women. About 70 percent of Maryland's undergraduate students are state residents, and 34 percent are students of color. The average freshman is 19 years old; the average full-time undergraduate is 21. The University provides both single-sex (with visiting privileges) and coed housing for about 8,000 of its undergraduates. In addition, nearly 12 percent of the students live in fraternity and sorority houses located next to the campus.

Academic Program

The University of Maryland operates on a semester system. Undergraduates must complete a minimum of 46 credit hours of core requirements in addition to course work in their major program and elective courses. Although each major program is unique, generally 30 to 35 credit hours are earned in major fields, and 120 credits are needed to graduate. AP, IB, and CLEP credit is granted. Maryland's honors program includes 1,200 students and consists of small classes and interactive discussions in a wide range of subject matter. College Park Scholars, a living/learning program for academically talented students, offers an innovative mixture of academic and social activities. Many departments offer individual honors programs, and more than forty honor societies have chapters on campus. An Air Force ROTC program exists at College Park. The fall semester begins just after Labor Day and concludes in mid-December. The spring semester begins in mid-January and concludes in mid-May. Two summer sessions are offered annually.

Financial Aid

Financial aid is available through scholarships, grants, loans, and work-study employment. Merit scholarships include the Banneker-Key and Regents full scholarships as well as President's and Dean's partial scholarships. Sixty-one percent of students receive some kind of financial aid. The average amounts of aid awarded to freshmen are $3757 for a scholarship/grant, $4650 for a loan, and $1312 for a work contract. Maryland belongs to the College Scholarship Service. The Free Application for Federal Student Aid (FAFSA) should be submitted by February 15 prior to planned fall or spring enrollment.

Application and Information

Applications for the fall semester must be accompanied by a $45 fee and must be received by February 15. Students are encouraged to apply by December 1, however, to be fully considered for early notification, programs for academically talented students, and scholarships. Applications for the spring semester are due by December 15. Freshmen (excluding architecture students) may begin studies during the spring semester.

For further information, students should contact:

Office of Undergraduate Admissions
University of Maryland at College Park
College Park, Maryland 20742-5235

Telephone: 301-314-8385
800-422-5867 (toll-free)
E-mail: um-admit@uga.umd.edu
World Wide Web: http://www.uga.umd.edu

UNIVERSITY OF MASSACHUSETTS AMHERST
AMHERST, MASSACHUSETTS

The University

The University of Massachusetts was founded in 1863 under the Morrill Land-Grant Act as Massachusetts Agricultural College. It formally opened in 1867 with 56 students, 4 faculty members, and four buildings. After slow, steady growth through the first half of the twentieth century, the University experienced an explosive period of growth during the 1960s, which saw the student population triple (from 6,000 to 18,000), while the size of the faculty, operating budget, and library holdings quadrupled. It is now a large, public, major research university, enrolling more than 18,000 undergraduates (about equally divided between men and women) and offering eighty-eight bachelor's degree programs and six associate degree programs at the undergraduate level as well as seventy-two master's programs and fifty-two doctoral programs. The University's size enables it to offer a great diversity and choice of academic programs, housing arrangements, and extracurricular involvements. In addition, students can enroll with no extra charge in courses at Amherst, Hampshire, Mount Holyoke, and Smith Colleges through the Five College Consortium.

Academic Program

The academic calendar includes a fall and a spring semester separated by a monthlong vacation or winter session from Christmas to late January. Summer school is also available. Students seeking a bachelor's degree must successfully complete a minimum of 120 credit hours (128 to 136 for engineering majors), including general education courses. Students also select a specific major, constituting specialized, intensive study in one discipline or in an approved interdisciplinary area. In addition, there are more than twenty nonmajor curricular programs (for example, aerospace studies, African studies, film studies, linguistics, military science, and statistics). A variety of special academic programs are also offered: a University honors program, area studies programs, legal studies, women's studies, and the Inquiry Program. Residential colleges, the Learning Resource Center, the Committee for the Collegiate Education of Black and Other Minority Students, the Bilingual Collegiate Program, the United Asia Learning Resource Center, and the Minority Engineering Program provide other special academic opportunities. Options are available for honors study, independent study, credit by examination, and advanced placement. The Division of Continuing Education serves nonmatriculated students.

Financial Aid

Financial aid is based on need and is offered to students who cannot, through their own and/or their parents' reasonable efforts, meet the full cost of a college education. Aid consists of scholarships and grants, self-help loans, and work-study employment. Students applying for financial aid are automatically considered for every University-administered program for which they are eligible. The basic financial aid application form required of all applicants is the Free Application for Federal Student Aid (FAFSA). The financial aid need-based resources available total more than $70 million for all types of aid. More than half of the students receive some support from the Financial Aid Office. Students should check with their guidance counselor for the most current financial aid information.

Application and Information

For application forms and further information, students should contact:

Office of Undergraduate Admissions
University Admissions Center
University of Massachusetts
Box 30120
Amherst, Massachusetts 01003-0120

Telephone: 413-545-0222
Fax: 413-545-4312
E-mail: amh.admis@dpc.umassp.edu
Web site: http://www.umass.edu

UNIVERSITY OF MASSACHUSETTS BOSTON
BOSTON, MASSACHUSETTS

The University

The University of Massachusetts Boston was founded in 1964 by the state legislature to provide the opportunity for superior undergraduate and graduate education at a moderate cost at a public urban campus located in the capital city of Boston. With more than 13,000 commuting students in its undergraduate, graduate, and continuing education programs, UMass Boston is the second largest campus of the University of Massachusetts system. The University of Massachusetts Boston is a community of scholars who take pride in academic excellence, diversity, research, and service. The fabric of academic research and scholarship is tightly woven into the public and community service needs of Boston and the modern urban center. More than seventy-five student organizations provide opportunities for cocurricular and extracurricular activities. University institutes provide scholarly research and public-service activities that focus on environmental issues, labor studies, gerontology, international programs, women in politics, the study of war and social consequences, and public policy. Further research is conducted on African-American, Asian, and Latino community issues, along with other concerns of the public interest that are particularly indigenous to urban areas.

Academic Program

The academic calendar runs from early September through the end of May. There is also a one month optional winter session in January and summer school in June, July, and August. Matriculating students may choose to attend on a full- or part-time basis and may adjust their schedules from semester to semester. A minimum of 30 credits must be earned at UMass Boston as a residency requirement for graduation. For the College of Arts and Sciences, 120 credits are required to graduate. The general education curriculum comprises three elements: the distribution requirement, the core curriculum requirement, and the writing requirement. In addition, requirements of the major must be fulfilled. The College offers an Honors Program and an Individual Major Program. For the College of Management, the 120 credit undergraduate program leads to a B.S. degree in management. By fulfilling the general education, management, and elective course work requirements, graduates receive a liberal arts foundation and the theoretical, technical, and functional training to succeed in the business world. The College of Nursing's B.S. program in nursing requires 123 credits, with a liberal arts foundation and intensive study of 63 credits in the principles and practices of nursing. The program in human performance and fitness prepares graduates for the technical aspects of a professional discipline with a foundation in liberal arts and an optional teacher training component.

Financial Aid

Financial aid is based on need and/or merit. Applicants complete the Free Application for Federal Student Aid (FAFSA) and should apply when they apply for admission. Need-based aid is awarded to students who cannot, through their own and/or their parents reasonable efforts, meet the full cost of a college education. Aid consists of scholarships and grants, self-help loans, and work-study employment. Students are automatically considered for every University-administered program for which they are eligible. Nearly 70 percent of the student body received financial aid awards that totaled more than $40 million last year.

Application and Information

For an undergraduate viewbook and application for admission, students should contact:

Admissions Information Service
University of Massachusetts Boston
100 Morrissey Boulevard
Boston, Massachusetts 02125-3393

Telephone: 617-287-6000
617-287-6010 (TTY/TDD)
Fax: 617-265-7173
E-mail: bos.admis@umassp.edu
Web site: http://www.umb.edu

UNIVERSITY OF MONTEVALLO
MONTEVALLO, ALABAMA

The University
The University was founded in 1896 when the town of Montevallo was selected to be the site of a state school. It became known as Alabama College and in 1969 the name was changed to the University of Montevallo to reflect the growth in both enrollment and programs. In order to achieve and maintain high-quality programs, UM is committed to the attainment of national accreditation for all of its undergraduate programs where such recognition is available and appropriate. Montevallo is accredited by the Commission on Colleges of the Southern Association of Colleges and Schools. A variety of social and recreational opportunities are available. Campus activities such as Greek sponsored events, movies, theater productions, concerts, and athletic and other events are regularly scheduled. Students may also participate in more than 100 campus organizations, including national fraternities and sororities, intramural and intercollegiate athletics, clubs, and service and religious organizations. In fall 1996, the enrollment was 3,206, representing twenty-two states and twenty-nine other countries.

Academic Program
Students fulfill the core requirements in general education to qualify for undergraduate degrees. Courses in English, science, mathematics, the arts, and languages introduce students to a broad spectrum of knowledge and experiences designed to develop the mind, emotions, spirit, and the body. A candidate for a degree must have a minimum of 130 semester hours of credit distributed according to curriculum requirements, 260 grade points, and a minimum cumulative grade point average of 2.0 (on a 4.0 scale) on all study attempted. The honors program is designed to provide students of high ability with opportunities for intellectual, cultural, and social enrichment. CLEP, Advanced Placement tests, correspondence credits, and military credit may be applied toward a degree.

Financial Aid
The University administers a comprehensive program of financial assistance. Federal, state, and University funds are combined to provide students with the scholarship, work-study, loan, and grant aid for which they qualify. Financial aid is meant to supplement students' resources and is not intended to be their only support. In 1996–97, 65 percent of students received some form of financial aid. The process for awarding need-based financial aid usually begins in February for the subsequent academic year. The final date for applying for financial aid is August 1. Awards are made on a first-come, first-served basis, and preference is given to applicants with exceptional financial need. Early application is encouraged to ensure consideration for the preferred type of assistance. Montevallo uses the Free Application for Federal Student Aid (FAFSA). Every fall, the University publishes a brochure that includes information regarding available financial aid and scholarships. To request the brochure, students should contact the Student Financial Services Office, Station 6050, University of Montevallo, Montevallo, Alabama 35115-6000.

Application and Information
The application deadline is August 1. All applications must be accompanied by the required $25 processing fee. Prospective students are encouraged to apply early to take advantage of scholarship and housing options. Once an applicant has submitted all required information, an admissions decision is made immediately.

For more information or an application packet, students should contact:

Office of Admissions
Station 6030 Palmer Hall
University of Montevallo
Montevallo, Alabama 35115-6000

Telephone: 205-665-6030
800-292-4349 (toll-free)
E-mail: admissions@um.montevallo.edu
World Wide Web: http://www.montevallo.edu/
http://www.petersons.com/sites/796770si.html

UNIVERSITY OF OREGON
EUGENE, OREGON

The University

The University of Oregon (UO) is recognized nationally and internationally as a research university committed to liberal arts and sciences education as well as professional preparation. For fall 1996, 13,874 undergraduates enrolled at the UO. More than 12 percent are students from minority groups, and more than 1,600 international students from ninety-five countries comprise 10 percent of the student body. Students have opportunities to participate in many clubs on campus, including political and environmental groups, professional organizations, cultural heritage organizations, religious groups, and service programs. The University is a member of the Pac-10 Conference (NCAA Division I) and sponsors eight women's teams and seven men's teams.

Academic Program

Regardless of their major, students are required to complete general requirements. Students spend about one third of their academic career on each of the general requirements, major requirements, and electives or requirements for completing a minor or a second major. One hundred eighty quarter credits are required for a Bachelor of Arts, Bachelor of Education, Bachelor of Music, or Bachelor of Science degree; 220 quarter credits are required for a Bachelor of Fine Arts (B.F.A.) or Bachelor of Landscape Architecture (B.L.A.) degree. The Bachelor of Interior Architecture (B.I.Arch.) degree requires 225 quarter credits, and the Bachelor of Architecture (B.Arch.) degree requires 231 quarter credits. The Robert D. Clark Honors College offers academically motivated students the advantages of a small liberal arts college combined with the rich resources of a large research university. The Honors College provides courses in the humanities, social sciences, and sciences, substituting for the group requirements other UO students must meet for graduation.

Financial Aid

Financial aid is available in the form of grants, loans, and/or work-study. To qualify, students must file the Free Application for Federal Student Aid (FAFSA). To be considered for financial aid at the UO, students must have applied for admission to the University and should indicate the UO as one of their first six choices. The UO awards financial aid based on individual need. Scholarships are awarded through the University, academic departments, and private sources. The general University scholarship application is due by February 1. For information on financial aid or scholarships and applications, students should contact the Office of Student Financial Aid, 1278 University of Oregon, 800-760-6953 (toll-free). For those seeking employment on or off campus, the Office of Student Employment offers several services for students who qualify for work-study as well as for those who do not qualify.

Application and Information

Applicants must submit an application with a $50 nonrefundable application fee, transcripts from each high school and/or college or university attended, and, for freshmen, scores from either the SAT I or the ACT examination. Students may apply any time after October 15 for the following academic year. The freshman application deadline is March 1. The transfer application deadline is May 15. Students planning to enter programs in architecture, fine and applied arts, interior architecture, landscape architecture, music, or the Clark Honors College should inquire directly to the appropriate department or to the Office of Admissions for early deadlines. A campus visit is the best way to decide whether the University of Oregon is right for a student. For information and an application, students should write or call:

Office of Admissions
1217 University of Oregon
Eugene, Oregon 97403-1217

Telephone: 541-346-3201
800-BE-A-DUCK (toll-free in Oregon)

UNIVERSITY OF PITTSBURGH AT JOHNSTOWN
JOHNSTOWN, PENNSYLVANIA

The University

Founded in 1927 as one of the first regional campuses of a major university in the United States, Pitt-Johnstown is a four-year, degree-granting, fully accredited, coeducational, residential undergraduate college of the University of Pittsburgh. With 2,600 well-qualified full-time students and a suburban campus of striking beauty, Pitt-Johnstown combines the strong academic reputation and outstanding resources of a major research university with the personal appeal of a smaller college. There are thirty-one campus buildings, including a library, student union, sports center, performing arts center, and chapel, in addition to a 40-acre nature preserve and outdoor recreation areas. The college has five different styles of housing, including residence halls, small-group lodges, apartments, and a new state-of-the-art living/learning center. An aquatic center includes a weight room and exercise rooms.

Academic Program

Pitt-Johnstown seeks to provide contemporary, innovative academic programs that combine the practical concerns of career orientation with the spirit of inquiry and the traditional goals of higher education. Practical experience of all types is encouraged, including campus activities, community service, media work, and research projects. The Freshman Seminar series introduces freshmen to rigorous intellectual work through small-group elective seminars. Students who show extra potential receive special advising, registration privileges, and scholarships through the President's Scholars Program. Students may complete preliminary requirements for upper-division programs that require relocation to the Pittsburgh campus, including requirements for programs in pharmacy and other health-related areas. In some programs, guaranteed admission is offered to qualified students.

Financial Aid

More than 80 percent of all Pitt-Johnstown students receive some form of financial assistance. In addition to the Pennsylvania Higher Education Assistance Agency (PHEAA) state grant, the Federal Pell Grant, and the Federal Stafford Student Loan, a variety of loans, grants, scholarships, and student-employment positions are awarded through the University. Applicants for all types of financial aid must submit the Free Application for Federal Student Aid by April 1 prior to the academic year for which assistance is requested.

Application and Information

High school graduates and transfer students must file an application, with a $35 fee, on forms provided by the school. The candidate is notified as soon as action is taken on the application.

Office of Admissions
157 Blackington Hall
University of Pittsburgh at Johnstown
Johnstown, Pennsylvania 15904

Telephone: 814-269-7050
800-765-4875 (toll-free)
Web site: http://info.pitt.edu/~upjweb

UNIVERSITY OF SAN DIEGO
SAN DIEGO, CALIFORNIA

The University
Known for its firm commitment to the liberal arts, the University of San Diego has created academic programs providing students with skills necessary to grow and advance personally and professionally. Both independent and Catholic, the University places a special emphasis on the exploration of human values. The students who share in the life at USD and contribute to its growth are a diverse group representing all fifty states and more than thirty-five countries. There are currently 4,000 undergraduates out of a total University enrollment of 6,100 students. Numerous campus activities are available to students, including social and cultural events, informal parties, special interest groups and clubs, and intercollegiate and intramural sports. There are also more than sixty student-controlled clubs and organizations, including nationally affiliated fraternities and sororities, national honor societies, and service organizations.

Academic Program
All of USD's programs are built solidly on the liberal arts, developing critical thinking skills through an emphasis on fundamental disciplines, written and oral communication, and an understanding of the past. USD gives special attention to the exploration of human and spiritual values, the interrelations of knowledge, and the development of an international perspective. The honors program at the University gives promising students the opportunity for both independent academic research and intensive exchange of ideas with other honors students. Selection of students to the program is made primarily on the basis of past academic achievement. College credit may be granted for Advanced Placement courses taken in secondary schools when the classes are completed with scores of 3, 4, or 5 on the appropriate Advanced Placement tests given by the College Board (a score of 4 or 5 must be attained for English credit). A number of subject examinations of the College-Level Examination Program (CLEP) have been approved by the University faculty, and in certain specified areas students may qualify for college credit by satisfactory performance on the CLEP tests.

Financial Aid
The primary purpose of the financial aid program at USD is to provide financial assistance to students who, without such aid, would be unable to attend the University. Each financial aid package is individually designed to meet a student's need, as indicated by the Free Application for Federal Student Aid (FAFSA) and the USD Financial Aid Application (USDFAA). Fifty percent of the students receive aid consisting of scholarships, grants, loans, and campus employment in packages ranging from $200 to $20,000 per academic year. A job placement center is available to students wishing to find off-campus employment. In addition, the University offers academic and leadership scholarships, which are not dependent on need.

Application and Information
Application for admission is made through the Undergraduate Admissions Office. Forms should be completed and filed, together with a transcript of credits, as early as possible and no later than January 15. Upon receipt of all necessary materials, each application is reviewed. Candidates are notified of acceptance by April 15. USD observes the Candidates Reply Date (May 1) set by the College Board and requests accepted applicants to notify the University of their intentions by that date.

For additional information about the University of San Diego, students should contact:

Director of Undergraduate Admissions
University of San Diego
5998 Alcalá Park
San Diego, California 92110

Telephone: 619-260-4506
800-248-4873 (toll-free)
Fax: 619-260-6836

UNIVERSITY OF TAMPA
TAMPA, FLORIDA

The University

The University of Tampa is a private comprehensive university that offers challenging learning experiences in two colleges: the College of Liberal Arts and Sciences and the College of Business. Together, they offer hundreds of courses in more than fifty fields of study. In both colleges, students work with experts in their fields, and there is a shared belief in the value of a liberal arts–centered education, practical work experience, and the ability to communicate effectively, all of which are trademarks of a University of Tampa education. Situated on a self-contained, beautiful, parklike campus on the Hillsborough River, the University is just two blocks from downtown Tampa. At the center of campus is Plant Hall, once a luxurious 511-room hotel for the rich and famous. Its ornate Victorian gingerbread and Moorish minarets, domes, and cupolas still remain a symbol of the city and one of the finest examples of Moorish architecture in the Western Hemisphere. Although Plant Hall receives most of the attention, the campus has thirty-seven other buildings, including a student union, a well-equipped library, art galleries, state-of-the-art science labs, a computer resource center, a television studio, a theater, seven residence halls, and complete athletic facilities. Both coed and single-sex residence halls have mostly double rooms and suites with private baths. Representing forty-eight states and seventy-seven countries, 2,700 students, including 1,700 full-time undergraduates, are enrolled at the University.

Academic Program

The curriculum is designed to give students a broad academic and cultural background as well as concentrated study in a major. The "Baccalaureate Experience" begins with a special freshman seminar program designed to help students assess their skills and research their interests. Students unsure about their major or what they want to do when they graduate may participate in a special Gateways program during the freshman year. During the first two years, students pursue an integrated core program of thirteen courses consisting of two in English, one in math, one in computer science, two in natural sciences, three in social science, and three in humanities. Prior to graduation, students are also required to take three writing-intensive courses, one course that deals with non-Western/Third World concerns, and an international/global awareness course. Students receive advanced placement by earning acceptable scores on Advanced Placement exams, the College-Level Examination Program tests, or by completing the International Baccalaureate Diploma. As much as one year's credit may be awarded.

Financial Aid

A high-quality, private education at the University of Tampa is not as difficult to finance as students may think. Each family's situation is evaluated individually for need-based assistance. Academic achievements, leadership potential, athletic skills, and other special talents are recognized, regardless of need. Army and Air Force ROTC scholarships are also available. The Free Application for Federal Student Aid (FAFSA) is required to determine eligibility for need-based funds. Florida residents should complete the FAFSA no later than April 30 for state grants. Early estimates of aid are available.

Application and Information

High school students may request an application after the end of their junior year. Requests for application forms, catalogs, and other information should be directed to:

University of Tampa
Office of Admissions
401 West Kennedy Boulevard
Tampa, Florida 33606-1490

Telephone: 813-253-6228
800-733-4773 (toll-free)
Fax: 813-254-4955
E-mail: bstrickler@alpha.utampa.edu

UNIVERSITY OF THE INCARNATE WORD
SAN ANTONIO, TEXAS

The University

Consistently rated among the top liberal arts colleges in the Southwest, the University of the Incarnate Word welcomes the interest of prospective students seeking a challenging and diverse small Catholic college atmosphere. Founded in 1881 as Incarnate Word College by the Sisters of Charity of the Incarnate Word, the school achieved university status in 1996. The University has a population of 3,278 students, with 2,731 students seeking baccalaureate degrees in forty majors and 556 students seeking master's degrees in fifteen programs. There are more than thirty different clubs and organizations on campus, including fraternities and sororities, honors organizations, *The Logos* campus newspaper, a yearbook, and theater and musical ensembles. The University of the Incarnate Word is fully accredited by the Southern Association of Colleges and Schools, Texas Education Agency, the Council of Baccalaureate and Higher Degree Programs of the National League for Nursing, the Committee on Accreditation of Allied Health Education (CAAHE), the American Dietetic Association, and the Joint Review Committee on Educational Programs in Nuclear Medicine. The University is affiliated with the American Association of Colleges for Teacher Education, Association of Collegiate Business Programs, Association of Texas Colleges and Universities, Association of Texas Graduate Schools, and the National Catholic Education Association. The University of the Incarnate Word is an equal opportunity institution and an Affirmative Action employer.

Academic Program

To receive any degree from the University of the Incarnate Word, a student must fulfill the requirements of the University's core curriculum in addition to course work specific to the major. The core is composed of 67 hours of course work in rhetoric, literature and arts, foreign language, wellness development, mathematics and natural science, philosophy and religion, history and behavioral sciences, computer literacy, and the integration of knowledge (capstone). Students must complete 30 hours of community service to receive their diploma. The Bachelor of Arts degree entails 128 hours of specified course work; the Bachelor of Business Administration requires 133 hours; the Bachelor of Music specifies 137 hours; the Bachelor of Science in Nursing requires 136 hours; and the Bachelor of Science specifies 133 hours. Academic credit is granted to students who achieve a score of 3 or higher on the College Board Advanced Placement examination. The University routinely administers examinations in the College-Level Examination Program (CLEP) for credit purposes.

Financial Aid

Approximately 78 percent of all UIW students receive financial assistance. The University awards Presidential/Academic, Performance/Visual Arts, and Athletic scholarships, none of which are need-based. Presidential/Academic scholarships are awarded based on high school grade point average and SAT/ACT test scores. All other forms of financial assistance are awarded based on financial need as determined by the Free Application for Federal Student Aid (FAFSA). Other federal/state/institutional financial assistance awarded includes the Federal Pell Grant, Federal Supplemental Educational Opportunity Grant, Texas Equalization Grant, UIW Grant, Federal Perkins Loan, Federal Subsidized and Unsubsidized Stafford Loans, Federal Parent Loan, Texas College Access Loan, Federal Work-Study, Texas Work-Study, and Institutional Employment.

Application and Information

Applications for admission are accepted on a rolling basis, although students are advised to submit them before April 1 as this is the priority deadline for financial assistance. A complete application file will be processed within one week. Application materials and further information on the University of the Incarnate Word may be obtained by contacting:

Director of Admissions
University of the Incarnate Word
4301 Broadway
San Antonio, Texas 78209

Telephone: 210-829-6005
800-749-WORD (toll-free)
Fax: 210-829-3921

VALPARAISO UNIVERSITY
VALPARAISO, INDIANA

The University

Valparaiso University was founded in 1859 by citizens of Valparaiso, Indiana, but its recent history dates from 1925, when it was purchased by the Lutheran University Association. VU is one of the nation's largest Lutheran-affiliated universities, yet it remains independent and is open to individuals of all faiths. The University's 3,500 students represent most states and more than fifty countries; 70 percent come from outside of Indiana. Approximately 150 extracurricular and cocurricular programs are open to all, including the campus radio station, Pre-Medical Society, International Student Association, and various NCAA Division I intercollegiate and intramural sports teams for men and women.

Academic Program

Valparaiso University has a long tradition of combining professional colleges and vocational programs with a strong commitment to the values and broadening experiences of the liberal arts. Programs are structured to provide a solid base for exploration in various fields, while offering students the freedom to develop depth in a specific interest. This philosophy is extended through the upper division, where students have three options in completing a degree: an individual plan of study involving the major and complementary courses from related fields of study, the election of a second academic major in addition to the first, or a special minor in connection with the major. The University participates in the Advanced Placement Program, the College-Level Examination Program, and the International Baccalaureate Program. In addition, Valparaiso provides its own placement testing in several academic areas. All departments of the University offer opportunities for honors work through independent study, seminars, and research. Christ College, the honors college of Valparaiso, has a well-established but continuously evolving program designed to challenge gifted students. Christ College students enroll concurrently in any other VU college.

Financial Aid

Eighty percent of Valparaiso's students receive financial aid totaling more than $36 million. The University attempts to make up the difference between the cost of attending Valparaiso and the amount a family can afford, as determined by the Free Application for Federal Student Aid (FAFSA). VU aid is available in the form of scholarships, grants, loans, and campus employment, and often the aid is a package of these awards. Students are also encouraged to apply for the federal government's Federal Pell Grant, Federal Perkins Loan, and Federal Supplemental Educational Opportunity Grant, state scholarships where applicable, and the various private grants and scholarships that are available. Early application is recommended for VU assistance, since the awarding of aid begins in February of the year of enrollment.

Application and Information

An applicant must complete a formal University admission application to be considered for admission. In addition, VU requires a high school transcript (complete through the junior year), ACT or SAT I scores, and college transcripts (when applicable). Under certain conditions (e.g., when ACT or SAT I scores would not be available early enough for full admission and financial aid action), scores on the PSAT, along with the high school transcript, may be sufficient for preliminary admission consideration. VU's rolling admission procedure means that candidates are notified of a decision shortly after all necessary credentials have been received. For scholarship consideration, May 1 is the deadline for the admission application. Information and application forms for admission and financial aid may be obtained from:

Office of Admissions
Valparaiso University
Valparaiso, Indiana 46383-6493

Telephone: 219-464-5011
888-GO-VALPO (toll-free)
Fax: 219-464-6898
E-mail: undergrad_admissions@valpo.edu
Web site: http://www.valpo.edu

VANDERBILT UNIVERSITY
NASHVILLE, TENNESSEE

The University

When Commodore Cornelius Vanderbilt gave a million dollars to build and endow Vanderbilt University in 1873, he did so with the wish that it would "contribute to strengthening the ties which should exist between all sections of our common country." Today, Vanderbilt more than fulfills the Commodore's hope. It is one of a handful of selective universities of medium size. Vanderbilt is a university where students from many regions, many backgrounds, and many disciplines come together for multidisciplinary study and research. A recent entering class of 1,545 students came from fifty states and thirty-two countries.

Academic Program

Students apply directly to one of the four schools that offer undergraduate programs: the College of Arts and Science, the School of Engineering, Peabody College (education and human development), or the Blair School of Music. Students in the College of Arts and Science plan their early studies under the College Program in Liberal Education. This plan is designed to give students a broad general background and bring them into contact with a variety of disciplines, subjects, and modes of thought that are essential to a broadly educated person. The Blair School of Music offers the Bachelor of Music in composition/theory, musical arts, and performance. Instruction is available in every instrument of the orchestra as well as piano, organ, saxophone, guitar, and voice. The School of Engineering offers a century-long tradition of educating engineers for practice in industry, government, consulting, or teaching and research. Peabody College offers degree programs leading to teacher certification and to careers in other areas of education, child development, cognitive studies, and human and organizational development.

Financial Aid

About 54 percent of the University's undergraduate students receive some type of financial aid. Need-based aid is awarded according to the evaluation of the College Scholarship Service's PROFILE and the FAFSA. Vanderbilt provides assistance through Federal Pell Grants, Federal Supplemental Educational Opportunity Grants, state grants, University scholarships, Federal Stafford Student Loans, institutional loans, Federal Perkins Loans, and Federal Work-Study employment. Information on these and other programs can be obtained from the Office of Student Financial Aid, 2309 West End Avenue, Vanderbilt University, Nashville, Tennessee 37203-1725. A limited number of honor scholarships based on academic merit or, at the Blair School of Music, on performance audition are available. In addition, the Ingram Scholarship Program is designed for students who have shown exemplary initiative in the area of community service. The Fred Russell-Grantland Rice Scholarship is awarded to a College of Arts and Science applicant who has demonstrated superior skills in sportswriting.

Application and Information

Students whose first choice is Vanderbilt may apply under the early decision plan. Applications and all supporting materials must be submitted by November 1; notification is made by December 15. The priority deadline for applying under the regular decision plan is January 15. Personal auditions are scheduled in December, January, and February at the Blair School of Music. Vanderbilt accepts applications after January 15, provided that space is available. Students are informed of the admission decision by April 1. Students seeking transfer admission must submit an application and all supporting materials no later than February 1 for fall semester admission and no later than November 15 for spring semester admission.

Office of Undergraduate Admissions
Vanderbilt University
2305 West End Avenue
Nashville, Tennessee 37203-1725

Telephone: 615-322-2561
E-mail: admissions@vanderbilt.edu
Web site: http://www.vanderbilt.edu/Admissions

WARREN WILSON COLLEGE
ASHEVILLE, NORTH CAROLINA

The College
Since its founding in 1894, Warren Wilson College has educated students with a unique triad of a strong liberal arts program, work for the College, and service to those in need, which makes Warren Wilson unlike any other college. The academic program features a first-rate faculty that does all of the teaching and frequently participates in research with students. Fifteen majors are offered, with a commitment to quality in each program. Each student works 15 hours a week at a job that is essential to running the school. Service is also integral to the College's way of thinking. Students must provide at least 20 hours of service each year to someone off campus.

Academic Program
The goal of the degree program at Warren Wilson College is the completion of three well-designed areas of study. First, students are expected to complete a core of required courses based on the theme "ways of knowing." Second, students must develop a strength in one or more disciplines. A minimum of 128 semester hours is required for the baccalaureate degree, including the core plus major hours. Finally, a student must demonstrate the ability to work effectively with others by participation in a work-and-service program. There is a required freshman seminar designed to provide new students the opportunity to explore various fields. A senior seminar, designed as a capstone experience, is required, as is a senior letter to evaluate the student's college experiences. All Warren Wilson students must demonstrate competence in writing and mathematics either through testing or by completing core courses. Each semester in the academic calendar is broken into two 8-week terms. A student traditionally takes only two courses per term (3 or 4 credit hours per course), with 12 hours per semester considered the minimum for full-time-student status. There are two honors programs at Warren Wilson. One is in English and the other is in the Division of Natural Sciences, where honors can be earned in biology, chemistry, environmental studies, and mathematics.

Financial Aid
Warren Wilson offers a comprehensive financial aid program that seeks to enroll students from all economic backgrounds. This is accomplished through a combination of work, loans, grants, entitlements, and scholarships to students who complete their file prior to May. Students and their families should file the FAFSA and the Warren Wilson Financial Aid Application to be considered for all possible funds.

Application and Information
An application form and further information may be obtained by contacting:

Office of Admission
Warren Wilson College
701 Warren Wilson Road
Asheville, North Carolina 28815-9000

Telephone: 800-934-3536 (toll-free)
E-mail: admit@warren-wilson.edu

WASHINGTON COLLEGE
CHESTERTOWN, MARYLAND

The College

Founded in 1782, Washington College is the tenth-oldest college in the United States. Today, the College is one of the few nationally recognized selective liberal arts institutions with an enrollment of fewer than 1,100 students. Although most students come from the Northeast, international students and students from other regions of the country are enrolled in numbers sufficient to add geographic diversity to the student body.

Academic Program

General education requirements include two freshman seminars, two sophomore seminars, and eight semester courses chosen from the following categories: social science, natural science, the humanities, and formal studies (mathematics, computer science, music theory, logic, and foreign languages). Candidates for a degree must satisfactorily complete thirty-two semester courses and must fulfill the senior obligation (for example, a comprehensive examination or thesis). Washington College offers a nationally renowned creative writing program and awards the prestigious Sophie Kerr Prize every year to the graduating senior who shows the most promise for a career in literary endeavors. Successful scores (4 or 5) on Advanced Placement examinations can provide exemption from distribution requirements. With the aid of a faculty adviser, students can construct their own major fields of study in some areas or pursue independent study for course credit.

Financial Aid

Washington College offers financial assistance to approximately 80 percent of its student body. Awards are based on need and academic performance. Financial aid includes scholarships, grants, loans, and jobs. The College participates in the Federal Perkins Loan Program, the Federal Stafford Student Loan Program, and the Federal Work-Study Program. Federal Pell Grants and Federal Supplemental Educational Opportunity Grants are applicable to Washington College. In addition, financial assistance from the Maryland scholarship program and other state programs can be applied to expenses at the College. Members of the National Honor Society and Cum Laude Society who are admitted to Washington College are awarded $40,000 academic scholarships ($10,000 annually for four years). Other academic scholarships ranging in value from $2500 to $10,000 are offered without regard to financial need. To be eligible for financial assistance, applicants should file the FAFSA and the CSS PROFILE by February 15. An application for admission, with all supporting credentials, should be received by February 15 to establish eligibility. Students interested in Federal Pell Grant assistance or in-state scholarship programs must apply directly to the program concerned.

Application and Information

The application, a $35 fee, the high school transcript (and college transcript, for transfer applicants), scores on the SAT I or ACT, and two teacher recommendations are required. Applications for early decision must be received by November 15, and candidates are notified of the admission decision by December 15. For regular admission, forms must be submitted prior to February 15. Regular-decision candidates are notified of the admission decision on a rolling basis between January 15 and April 1. Applicants for financial assistance must complete the procedures outlined under Financial Aid. Further information and application forms are available from:

Office of Admissions
Washington College
300 Washington Avenue
Chestertown, Maryland 21620-1197

Telephone: 410-778-7700
800-422-1782 (toll-free)
E-mail: adm.off@washcoll.edu
Web site: http://www.washcoll.edu

WEBBER COLLEGE
BABSON PARK, FLORIDA

The College

Webber College was founded in 1927 by Roger Babson, who was an internationally known economist in the early 1900s. The four-year independent coeducational college is located on a beautiful 110-acre campus along the shoreline of Lake Caloosa, 45 minutes from Disney World, Cypress Gardens, and many other attractions. Webber is accredited by the Southern Association of Colleges and Schools. Built on a strong tradition that sets it apart, the College exemplifies integrity, high standards, and achievement. Webber College provides an environment that encourages success through academic excellence and hard work. The College offers intercollegiate sports in basketball, cross-country, golf, soccer, and tennis for men and in basketball, cross-country, soccer, softball, tennis, and volleyball for women. Among the wide variety of social organizations and clubs are a national fraternity, a glee club, a student government association, an international club, Green Key ambassadors, a culture club, a travel-hospitality club, and athletic boosters.

Academic Program

The College requires the completion of 61 credit hours for the Associate of Science degree and 122 credit hours for the Bachelor of Science degree with a minimum grade point average of 2.0. Students in the Bachelor of Science degree program are required to complete 30 hours in the area of concentration, 30 hours in the business core, 41 hours in the general education core, and 21 hours of tailored electives. Students in the Associate of Science degree program are required to complete 21 hours in the business core, 19 hours in the general education core, and 21 hours in the area of concentration and tailored electives. Credit is awarded for successful scores on Advanced Placement (AP) tests and College-Level Examination Program (CLEP) general tests.

Financial Aid

The Student Financial Aid Department offers students its counsel and assistance in meeting their educational expenses. Aid is awarded on the basis of an applicant's need, academic performance, and promise. Approximately 70 percent of the students at Webber College receive financial assistance. To demonstrate need, applicants are required to file the Free Application for Federal Student Aid (FAFSA). Various types of aid, such as scholarships, grants, loans, and Federal Work-Study awards, are used to meet student needs. A limited number of no-need scholarships are available; these awards are based on academic performance, on community and college service, or on athletic ability in basketball, tennis, volleyball, golf, soccer, softball, and cross-country. Applicants for aid must reapply each year. Webber College participates in the Federal Perkins Loan, Federal Supplemental Educational Opportunity Grant, and Federal Work-Study programs. All applicants are expected to apply for any entitlement grant for which they are eligible, such as the Federal Pell Grant; Florida residents must apply for a Florida Student Assistance Grant and the Florida Tuition Voucher Program. Federal Stafford Student Loans are also available. Financial aid applicants should submit their requests and forms before April 1 in order to be eligible for certain financial aid programs.

Application and Information

An application is ready for consideration by the Admissions Committee when it has been received with a $35 application fee, the required test scores and references, and transcripts from each school attended. The College uses a system of rolling admissions. It is recommended that applications be submitted as early as possible, since on-campus housing is limited. (Freshmen are required to live in the dormitory unless they reside with a parent, guardian, or spouse.) For application forms, catalogs, and additional information, students should contact:

Director of Admissions
Webber College
1201 Alternate 27 South
P.O. Box 96
Babson Park, Florida 33827-9990

Telephone: 941-638-1431

WELLS COLLEGE
AURORA, NEW YORK

The College
Wells College, founded in 1868, is proud to be the second institution in the country to award the baccalaureate degree to women. Its founder, Henry Wells, who built his fortune with the creation of the Wells Fargo Express, believed that women would play a vital role in the future of America. What truly distinguishes Wells from other colleges and universities is that it dares to be small. With an enrollment of 400 students, Wells students do not sit quietly among rows of neatly lined desks; instead, they join their classmates and professors around seminar tables where they are expected to contribute their ideas. Wells faculty members are graduates of many of the country's top universities, and 96 percent hold a Ph.D. or equivalent degree. They are widely published and respected in their fields, but teaching is their first priority.

Academic Program
The academic philosophy at Wells is firmly rooted in the liberal arts. The College is organized into four academic divisions: the humanities, natural and mathematical sciences, social sciences, and the arts, but faculty members in all divisions work together to produce a curriculum that recognizes connections between subject areas and fits many pieces together, just as they fit together in life. Students at Wells take one course in common during their first and second years. The purpose of the core curriculum is to give every student a shared academic experience. The first-year course, 21st Century Issues, addresses issues that will become increasingly important in the future. Readings and discussions bring these issues into focus through many different lenses: cultural, historical, psychological, sociological, artistic, and scientific. Students become familiar with academic and campus resources through writing assignments and become active participants in College life through required attendance at plays, concerts, and other campus events.

Financial Aid
Approximately 80 percent of Wells students receive financial aid packaged in the form of grants, scholarships, and loans.

Application and Information
Applications should be received early in the senior year of high school and not later than February 15 of the year in which entrance is desired. Applications from early action candidates must be received by December 15. Transfer applications are reviewed on a rolling basis. Transfer students are eligible for merit scholarships and financial aid. A campus visit is highly recommended for prospective students. Typically, the visit includes a guided tour of the Wells College campus and facilities, overnight accommodations in the residence halls, a personal interview, and the option of attending classes. Appointments with faculty and financial aid representatives are also available.

For more information about Wells College or to schedule a campus visit, students should contact:

Admissions Office
Wells College
Aurora, New York 13026

Telephone: 800-952-9355 (toll-free)
E-mail: admissions@wells.edu

WENTWORTH INSTITUTE OF TECHNOLOGY
BOSTON, MASSACHUSETTS

The Institute

Wentworth Institute of Technology was founded in 1904 to provide education in the mechanical arts. Today, it is one of the nation's leading technical institutes, offering study in a variety of disciplines. Wentworth has a current undergraduate day enrollment of 2,288 men and women and graduates more engineering technicians and technologists each year than any other college in the United States. The technical education acquired at Wentworth enables graduates to assume creative and responsible careers in business and industry. Wentworth is located on a 35-acre campus on Huntington Avenue in Boston.

Academic Program

At Wentworth Institute of Technology, college-level study in technological fundamentals and principles is combined with appropriate laboratory, field, and studio experience. Students apply theory to practical problems, and they acquire skills and techniques by using, operating, and controlling equipment and instruments peculiar to their area of specialization. In addition, study in the social sciences and humanities provides a balanced understanding of the world in which graduates work. Wentworth's programs of study are more practical than theoretical in approach, and the Institute's academic requirements demand extensive time and effort. During the first two years of study in a degree program at Wentworth, students lay the foundation for more advanced study in the third and fourth (and fifth, where applicable) years. While nearly all majors allow continuous study from the freshman through the senior year, the architecture major requires a petition for readmission to the baccalaureate program during the sophomore year. All bachelor's degree programs are conducted as cooperative (co-op) education programs: upon entering their third year, students alternate semesters of academic study at Wentworth with semester-long periods of employment in industry. Two semesters of co-op employment are required; one additional (summer) semester of co-op is optional.

Financial Aid

Scholarships are available to students who demonstrate need and academic promise. Merit scholarships are also available. Wentworth also provides federal and state financial assistance, such as Federal Pell and Federal Supplemental Educational Opportunity Grants, Federal Perkins Loans, Federal Work-Study awards, Gilbert Matching Grants, and Massachusetts No-Interest Loans to students with financial need in accordance with federal and state guidelines. Wentworth has been chosen to participate in the Federal Direct Lending program. As a result, students are eligible to borrow under the Federal Direct Stafford Loan program and parents may borrow under the Federal Direct PLUS program. Individuals participating in these programs borrow money directly from the federal government rather than through lending institutions. In addition to these need-based programs, Wentworth also participates in the MassPlan loan program through the Massachusetts Educational Financing Authority and the TERI program through The Educational Resources Institute. To apply for financial aid, new students should complete the Free Application for Federal Student Aid (FAFSA) by March 1. Applications received after this date will be considered as funds allow.

Application and Information

Students are admitted to Wentworth for September and January enrollment. The priority application deadline for the fall semester is June 1; for the spring, the deadline is December 1. Notification of admission is made on a rolling basis. An application form, an application fee of $30, transcripts from the secondary school and any colleges previously attended, and SAT I scores should be sent to:

Admissions Office
Wentworth Institute of Technology
550 Huntington Avenue
Boston, Massachusetts 02115

Telephone: 617-989-4000
800-556-0610 (toll-free)
Fax: 617-989-4010
E-mail: admissions@wit.edu

WEST CHESTER UNIVERSITY OF PENNSYLVANIA
WEST CHESTER, PENNSYLVANIA

The University

West Chester University is the second largest of the fourteen institutions in the Pennsylvania State System of Higher Education and the third largest university in the Philadelphia metropolitan area. Officially founded in 1871, the University traces its heritage to the West Chester Academy, which existed from 1812 to 1869. The University's 385-acre campus has well-maintained facilities, including eight modern residence halls and garden-style apartments. In keeping with West Chester's rich heritage, the University's Quadrangle buildings, part of the original campus, are on the National Register of Historic Places. While the University attracts the majority of its students from Pennsylvania, New Jersey, and Delaware, it also enrolls many students from other areas across the United States and from more than fifty countries. The University's commitment to expand its continuing education offerings has resulted in increased numbers of nontraditional students. The undergraduate enrollment is 7,696 men and women full-time and 1,726 part-time. Each year, the University community schedules an impressive series of events, including programs with well-known musicians, authors, political figures, and others. Numerous campus groups in music, theater, athletics, and other activities, as well as clubs, fraternities, sororities, service organizations, and honor societies, provide students with the opportunity to participate in a full range of programs. The University offers twenty-three intercollegiate sports and thirteen club sports for men and women. In addition to the facilities in the health and physical education complex, the University has a field house and a gymnasium for varsity sports.

Academic Program

West Chester University is a comprehensive, multipurpose institution now in its second century. The University comprises the College of Arts and Sciences, the School of Business and Public Affairs, the School of Education, the School of Health Sciences, and the School of Music. It operates on a two-semester basis; summer sessions are available. An honors program is available to qualified students for both upper and lower division study; internships and field experiences, self-designed majors, and independent study are also offered. A variety of credit-by-examination programs are available on campus.

Financial Aid

The financial aid available to students includes work-study programs, grants, loans, special awards, and scholarships. A limited number of Merit Scholarships are awarded based on the student's academic standing and accomplishments in high school. Students who qualify will be invited to apply. About 50 percent of all West Chester University students receive some form of aid.

Application and Information

Students are admitted for the fall or spring semester. Applicants for the fall semester are urged to begin the application procedure at the start of their senior year of secondary school. Applicants for the spring semester should apply by December 1. International students are encouraged to apply by May 1 for the fall semester and August 1 for the spring semester. The University operates on a modified rolling admission policy; applicants with the best qualifications are given priority, and their applications are processed expeditiously. Students are encouraged to visit WCU's campus. To arrange a visit or to attend an information session, students may call the Office of Admissions; for updated information or directions, they may check the University's World Wide Web site. Additional information and required forms are available from:

Office of Admissions
Emil H. Messikomer Hall
West Chester University of Pennsylvania
100 West Rosedale Avenue
West Chester, Pennsylvania 19383

Telephone: 610-436-3411
E-mail: ugadmiss@wcupa.edu
Web site: http://www.wcupa.edu

WESTERN ILLINOIS UNIVERSITY
MACOMB, ILLINOIS

The University

The campus of Western Illinois University (WIU) extends over 1,050 acres and includes fifty-three buildings. The residence halls on campus provide for a variety of lifestyles and house 4,800 of the approximately 12,100 students at the University. More than 260 student organizations offer a variety of cocurricular activities to supplement formal classroom education. Cultural programs reflecting both local and national interests are on the calendar several evenings each week. Intercollegiate and intramural athletic programs are available for both women and men. The current undergraduate enrollment is about 9,600 students. Although the majority of students are from Illinois, forty-two other states and fifty-three countries are represented in the student body. Career placement services are offered to graduating students and graduates. Nearly 93 percent of the graduates who register with the job placement office are placed in desirable positions.

Academic Program

It is the philosophy of the University that a broad general education should be an integral part of every degree program. Thus, approximately one third of the degree requirements involve study and the development of fundamental skills in the arts and sciences. The remainder of the program is devoted to either a comprehensive major or a major/minor plus general electives. Credit is awarded for acceptable scores on CLEP general and subject examinations and on the College Board's Advanced Placement examinations in English, foreign languages, history, and mathematics. Proficiency examinations are administered on campus through specific departments. Special educational opportunities for students with high aptitude and superior ability are offered in all colleges at WIU through the honors program. Western offers a four-year and a two-year program in the study of military science through Army ROTC. Successful completion of the program and requirements for the baccalaureate degree leads to a commission as a second lieutenant in the Army.

Financial Aid

During the 1996–97 academic year, approximately 8,700 WIU undergraduate students received financial aid from funds totaling $38 million. Prospective students are urged to apply for the Federal Pell Grant and, if they are Illinois residents, the Illinois Student Assistance Commission Grant. Western also participates in the Federal Perkins Loan, Federal Work-Study, and Federal Supplemental Educational Opportunity Grant programs. Loans and grants are made and work-study jobs are assigned on the basis of calculated financial need, which is determined by the Free Application for Federal Student Aid (FAFSA). The information on the FAFSA must reflect the current income of the applicant's parents, as reported to the Internal Revenue Service. The statement should therefore not be completed until after January 1 of the applicant's senior year in high school. Many student jobs are available in such areas as secretarial work, food service, and building and grounds maintenance. WIU awards talent grants and academic scholarships. Talent grants are offered in men's and women's athletics, music, art, theater, and debate. Students who rank in the upper 15 percent of their class and have an ACT Assessment composite score of at least 28 are eligible to apply for an academic scholarship, which does not require proof of need. Applications for financial aid may be obtained from the Financial Aid Office after December 1 of the student's senior year in high school.

Application and Information

Application forms and admission materials may be secured by contacting:

Admissions Office
Sherman Hall 115
Western Illinois University
1 University Circle
Macomb, Illinois 61455-1390

Telephone: 309-298-3157

WESTERN MARYLAND COLLEGE
WESTMINSTER, MARYLAND

The College
Western Maryland College (WMC) provides an ideal location for learning that brings together students from twenty-three states and nineteen countries. Western Maryland was one of the first coeducational colleges in the nation and has been both innovative and independent since its founding in 1867. The tradition of liberal arts studies rests comfortably at Western Maryland, which has exemplary teaching, both at the undergraduate and graduate levels, as its central mission. Faculty members are engaged in research and professional writing, are involved at the highest levels of their respective professions, and are sought after as consultants in many spheres, but their primary mission is teaching. The enrollment of 1,200 undergraduates enables WMC to care about students in a personal way, to provide individual guidance, and to be responsive to the needs of students. A flexible liberal arts curriculum stresses the ability to think critically and creatively, to act humanely and responsibly, and to be expressive. WMC is fully accredited by the Middle States Association of Colleges and Secondary Schools and is listed as one of the selective national liberal arts colleges by the Carnegie Foundation for the Advancement of Teaching. WMC is internationally recognized for its graduate program in training teachers for the deaf.

Academic Program
WMC's flexible curriculum enables students to acquire a broad base of knowledge in the areas of humanities, natural sciences and mathematics, and social sciences and to pursue in-depth learning in one or more of the sixty fields of study. The program links wide-ranging educational experiences with strong career preparation through an extensive internship program. A total of 128 credit hours is required for graduation. First-year–student seminars provide students with a unique opportunity to become better prepared for many facets of college life. Limited to 15 students, these courses on a variety of topics emphasize important skills—writing, oral presentation, study skills, critical thinking, and time management.

Financial Aid
WMC supports a program of financial aid to eligible students on the basis of both need and merit. Nearly 80 percent of WMC students receive financial assistance. Students who have been accepted by the College and can demonstrate financial need as required by the federal government may be eligible for assistance in the form of scholarships, grants, loans, and opportunities for student employment. Typically an award is a package of these four resources, tailored to the student's needs. Academic scholarships covering partial to full tuition are available for qualified students based on their academic record, SAT I or ACT scores, and extracurricular involvement. First-year students should apply by February 1; transfer scholarships are competitive, and preference is given to students who apply before March 15. The College also offers partial and full ROTC scholarships. To apply, students should file the Free Application for Federal Student Aid (FAFSA) with the federal processor and apply for admission to WMC. Students also must submit a WMC financial aid application, which is available upon request.

Application and Information
Deadlines for receiving completed applications are December 1 for early action, February 1 for academic scholarship consideration, and March 15 for regular admission. Applications from transfer students are accepted through the summer. Complete applications, along with a $30 nonrefundable application fee, should be sent to:

M. Martha O'Connell, Director of Admissions
Western Maryland College
2 College Hill
Westminster, Maryland 21157-4390

Telephone: 410-857-2230
800-638-5005 (Voice/TDD) (toll-free)
E-mail: admissio@ns1.wmc.car.md.us
Web site: http://www.wmdc.edu

WESTERN MICHIGAN UNIVERSITY
KALAMAZOO, MICHIGAN

The University

Western Michigan University is one of the nation's outstanding centers of learning, making a world of difference in an environment of academic excellence. *U.S. News & World Report* has ranked the University "in the major leagues of American higher education" as one of the country's 229 top national universities. WMU is a member of the National Association of State Universities and Land-Grant Colleges, which includes 186 of the nation's most prestigious public universities. WMU is counted among Michigan's top four universities in both size and the complexity and variety of its offerings. Yet WMU has successfully retained the friendliness and personal attention usually associated with much smaller institutions. Its student-faculty ratio is a comfortable 17:1. Only eighty-five of its 4,000 classes have more than 100 students. With 25,699 students, WMU is the fourth-largest university in Michigan and among the nation's sixty largest universities. Members of minority groups represent 10 percent of total enrollment; international students represent 7 percent. About 5,500 students live in twenty-two residence halls that provide a variety of living arrangements. Founded in 1903, WMU has six degree-granting colleges—Arts and Sciences, the Haworth College of Business, Education, Engineering and Applied Sciences, Fine Arts, and Health and Human Services—as well as the Lee Honors College. The University offers 241 academic programs, nearly 160 of them at the undergraduate level.

Academic Program

WMU offers undergraduate students a rich blend of academic majors and minors, as well as its new general education program. This new program assures that students graduate with proficiencies and perspectives they need to succeed in the next century. The University Curriculum Program is for students who are undecided about a major and wish to explore WMU's academic offerings. Last fall, 1,700 students enrolled in the University Curriculum Program, which won a national award for outstanding academic advising. The Lee Honors College provides undergraduates with a unique living/learning environment offering the intimacy of a small college with the resources of a major university.

Financial Aid

Last year, more than 18,000 students received financial assistance totaling over $90 million. There are three basic types of financial aid: merit-based programs, need-based programs, and student employment. Merit-based programs include the Medallion Scholarship Program, the University's most honored scholarships for entering freshmen. Awards range from $4800 to $25,000 over four years. Other scholarships and awards include the $16,000 Higher Education Incentive Scholarships (HEIS), the Army ROTC awards, the Award for National Merit Scholarships, and many other sponsored and departmental scholarships for new and currently enrolled students. Merit-based scholarships also are available to community college transfer students, ranging in value from $500 to $6000. Need-based loans, grants, college work-study, and other aid options are provided for students who demonstrate particular financial need. To be considered, students should complete the Free Application for Federal Student Aid. The student employment option reflects research indicating that students who work part-time are more likely to graduate than students who do not work at all. About 40 percent of WMU's students work while in school, and more than 2,000 jobs are offered through the college work-study program.

Application and Information

For an application or additional information, students should contact:

Office of Admissions and Orientation
Western Michigan University
Kalamazoo, Michigan 49008–5720

Telephone: 616-387–2000
800-400-4WMU (toll-free)
Web site: http://www.wmich.edu

WESTERN MONTANA COLLEGE OF THE UNIVERSITY OF MONTANA
DILLON, MONTANA

The College
Western Montana College of the University of Montana is a small, public, four-year college originally established in 1893 in beautiful southwestern Montana. Western nurtures scholarship, creativity, lifelong learning, and high standards. The intimate size of Western's campus provides accessibility to all aspects of academic and extracurricular life. Currently enrolling an average of 1,100 students, Western specializes in providing individual attention, personalized caring and commitment, and hands-on classroom experiences using state-of-the-art technology. All classes are taught by professors, not graduate students, and the average class size is 20 or fewer. The 34-acre campus is small, friendly, and beautiful, and the sixteen major buildings are easily accessible. Athletics are an important part of campus life at Western Montana College. One in every 5 Western students participates in a sport. Western is affiliated with the National Association of Intercollegiate Athletics and participates in the Frontier Conference. Varsity sports are offered for women in basketball, rodeo, and volleyball. Men compete in basketball, football, and rodeo. Western is affiliated with the University of Montana, which also has four-year campuses in Missoula and Butte and a two-year campus in Helena.

Academic Programs
Each graduate of any associate or baccalaureate degree is expected to have demonstrated competency in both oral and written communication as applied to the particular major and minor fields. The foundation of the general education requirements is oral and written communication. Between 37 and 40 general education credits are required for all four-year degree programs. The baccalaureate degree is conferred upon completion of the proper curriculum, with a minimum of 120 semester credits and with an overall (institutional plus transfer) scholastic average of at least 2.0. Some baccalaureate degrees may require a higher cumulative grade point average. The Western Montana College Honors Program is designed to offer enrichment and challenge to a small number of students who are chosen to participate. Classes in the Honors Program are thematically based interdisciplinary seminars that emphasize independent research. Students who successfully complete a sequence of honors classes throughout their college career are designated Honors Graduates. Some honors classes may be substituted for general education requirements. Western operates on the semester system. Each academic year has fifteen-week fall and spring semesters, four-week courses during May interim, and six-week courses during the summer. Continuing education offers evening and weekend workshops throughout the academic year.

Financial Aid
More than 60 percent of Western Montana College students receive some form of financial assistance while working toward a degree. The more than $2.5 million awarded includes scholarships, grants, loans, and work-study opportunities. Applicants must submit the Free Application for Federal Student Aid and the Western Montana College Financial Aid Application by March 1. Job opportunities are available both on campus and in the Dillon community.

Application and Information
Western Montana College has a rolling admission policy. Students are informed of acceptance two weeks after their admission files have been completed. The Admissions and New Student Services Office is open Monday through Friday, 8 a.m. to 5 p.m. Visitors are welcome to contact the office to schedule a campus tour, obtain admission materials, or meet with an admissions representative. For further information, students should contact:

Admissions and New Student Services
Western Montana College of The University of Montana
710 South Atlantic
Dillon, Montana 59725-3598

Telephone: 406-683–7331
800-WMC-MONT (toll-free)
Fax: 406–683–7493
E-mail: k_leum@wmc.edu
Web site: http://www.wmc.edu

WESTMINSTER COLLEGE
NEW WILMINGTON, PENNSYLVANIA

The College

Westminster College is an independent, coeducational liberal arts college related to the Presbyterian Church (U.S.A.). Throughout its long history, Westminster has been characterized by academic excellence and a reputation for offering a fine educational program within the framework of the Christian tradition. The curriculum stresses a values-oriented approach to learning. The College provides many programs to augment the academic and social life of the academic community, including lectures, dramatic productions, art exhibitions, concerts, symposia, dances, films, and other activities. Students may choose to participate in a wide variety of groups and activities, such as dramatics, publications, volunteer and social service teams, athletics, religious groups, musical groups, radio and television stations, fraternities and sororities, honoraries, and special interest groups. The total enrollment is 1,450. A natatorium and physical education and fitness center are included among Westminster's major buildings, and athletics are carefully integrated into the overall educational program. A full range of intercollegiate and intramural sports for men and women gives each student the opportunity to participate at the level of his or her interest and ability. Westminster is nationally known for the fine records of its teams in intercollegiate athletics. In 1994, Westminster celebrated its 100th year of varsity football by winning the NAIA Division II National Championship.

Academic Program

The liberal arts degree offered by Westminster College reflects the diversity and depth of the classical education and the practicality of its application. Good writing and speaking skills are emphasized, and science and philosophy become a part of life at Westminster. Course requirements for graduation vary according to the major fields, but all-College requirements include courses in writing, communication, religion, computer science, foreign language, and physical education as well as courses from categories covering the humanities, fine arts, social sciences, natural sciences, and literature. Double majors, minors, and individual interdisciplinary programs are possible. Westminster operates on a two-term academic year. The fall term runs from September through December, and the spring term runs from January through May. Every four years since 1936, in conjunction with the Presidential election year, Westminster has held a Mock National Political Convention (for the party out of office) in which more than three fourths of the students have participated, naming their own "candidate."

Financial Aid

About 80 percent of Westminster's students receive some sort of financial aid. Scholarships, Federal Stafford Student Loans, grants, and campus employment are offered to students who have financial need. The student's eligibility for financial aid is determined by the Free Application for Federal Student Aid form. Also, non-need scholarships of up to 50 percent of tuition are awarded to students of high academic ability; these are renewable each year if the student maintains good academic standing. Activity grants in music, theater, and sports are also available. Information is available through the dean of admissions or director of financial aid.

Application and Information

A completed application with the $20 application fee may be submitted anytime after the student's junior year in secondary school. The student should also see that the required SAT I or ACT scores and a high school transcript are sent to the College. The transcript should include grades from the ninth grade through the eleventh grade. For application forms and further information, students should contact:

Dean of Admissions
Westminster College
New Wilmington, Pennsylvania 16172

Telephone: 412-946-7100

WILLIAM PATERSON UNIVERSITY OF NEW JERSEY
WAYNE, NEW JERSEY

The University

Since its founding in 1855, William Paterson University has grown into a comprehensive state institution whose programs reflect the area's need for challenging, affordable educational options. Ideally midsized (the total enrollment is 8,941, of whom 7,570 are degree-seeking undergraduates), William Paterson offers a wider variety of academic programs than smaller colleges, yet provides students with a more personalized atmosphere than larger institutions. Social, cultural, and recreational activities complement the academic programs. The University has eighteen intercollegiate sports teams, nine for men and nine for women, including successful NCAA teams in men's baseball and women's softball.

Academic Program

Students must complete a minimum of 128 credits to earn a baccalaureate degree. Degree programs include a 60-credit general education requirement, 30–60 credits in a major, and 20–40 in elective courses. (In specialized degree programs, such as the B.F.A. and the B.M., general education and major course requirements may differ.) Students uncertain of which career path to follow may take advantage of advisement and counseling programs. In addition, the general education requirements enable students to take up to 60 credits before declaring a major, so that they can acquire a basic understanding of all major fields of knowledge before having to choose a specific area. Diagnostic testing and career seminars, provided by the Career Services Office, also ensure that students receive the guidance necessary to make wise course selections and career decisions. William Paterson offers a variety of special programs. Honors programs are designed for those ambitious and well-qualified students who want to add a challenging dimension to their major. Currently, there are two honors programs—in biopsychology and humanities. Students who have completed the premedical program in the School of Science and Health have consistently been accepted by American medical schools during the last ten years. Students who successfully complete Advanced Placement tests and/or College-Level Examination Program tests may receive credit for acceptable scores. In addition, credit may be awarded for military training and experience. William Paterson University operates on a two-semester and two-summer-session system.

Financial Aid

Financial aid is available through a number of federal and state grant, loan, scholarship, and work-study programs. To apply for need-based aid, students must file the Free Application for Federal Student Aid (FAFSA) with the United States Department of Education by the priority date of April 1. In addition, both the University and the Alumni Association award a number of competitive scholarships, based solely on academic merit, to entering freshmen. They are the Scholarships for Academic Excellence, scholarships for African-American and Hispanic students, and the Trustee Scholarships. Academic Achievement Scholarships are awarded only on a competitive basis to continuing students.

Application and Information

Application forms and transcripts from candidates for freshman status must be received by May 1 for fall admission and November 1 for spring admission. Transfer students, readmitted students, and students seeking a second bachelor's degree must submit their materials by May 1 and November 1 for fall and spring entry, respectively. However, the University closes the application process earlier when the number of new and continuing students strains its ability to provide effective programs and services. A $35 application fee is required. Applications are reviewed on a rolling basis. Campus tours are available during the fall and spring semesters on Friday afternoon at 1:30 p.m. when classes are in session. For additional information and application forms for admission or scholarships, students should contact:

Office of Admissions
William Paterson University of New Jersey
Wayne, New Jersey 07470

Telephone: 973-720-2125
888-4WILPAT (toll-free)

WINTHROP UNIVERSITY
ROCK HILL, SOUTH CAROLINA

The University

Winthrop University, founded in 1886, has been an educational leader in South Carolina for more than a century. Winthrop's distinctive mission is to offer challenging academic programs to a high-achieving, culturally diverse, and socially responsible student body of more than 5,400 students. Thirty-seven states and forty-seven other countries are represented in Winthrop's undergraduate and graduate population. More than 100 campus organizations offer outlets for special interests or talents and provide opportunities to hone leadership skills and build confidence and interpersonal skills. In addition, students enjoy recreational sports and NCAA Division I intercollegiate competition in men's and women's basketball, cross-country, golf, indoor and outdoor track, and tennis; women's softball and volleyball; and men's baseball and soccer. Winthrop's students also benefit from Dinkins Student Union (DSU), the University's activities board. Named the number one programming board in the nation for the past two years, DSU schedules a broad array of fun and interesting entertainment, including bands, comedians, lecturers, and novelty acts for student enjoyment.

Academic Program

The University is fully accredited by the Southern Association of Colleges and Schools. Additional national accreditation of individual programs sets the University apart from its peers and assures Winthrop students of a top-notch curriculum taught by qualified faculty members using the best available resources. A strong liberal arts core provides the foundation for Winthrop's undergraduate and graduate degree programs offered in the four academic divisions: the Colleges of Arts and Sciences, Business, Education, and Visual and Performing Arts. A minimum of 124 credits is required for a baccalaureate degree, with a specified number of general education, major-specific, and elective hours for each degree. Special student programs include the Honors and Freshman Honors Programs; the Critical Issues Symposium for freshmen; cooperative education and internships; PACE for academically gifted African-American students; New Start for adult learners; Leadership Winthrop; and Peer Mentoring, a first-year support program.

Financial Aid

At Winthrop, 60 percent of all students receive some form of financial assistance. The University offers more than 300 scholarships to high-achieving freshmen with strong high school records and SAT or ACT scores. The scholarships range from $1500 to full tuition and board. The completed admissions application also serves as the application for academic scholarships. Additional scholarships are available to talented students in the visual and performing arts as well as in all of Winthrop's sixteen intercollegiate sports. Winthrop's financial aid packages, which are processed in the Financial Resource Center, can include grants, loans, or student employment. Students should complete the Free Application for Federal Student Aid (FAFSA) and the Winthrop institutional aid form as soon as possible after January 1 of their senior year. Families often take advantage of the Winthrop Payment Plan, which divides each semester's costs into four convenient payments. For more information, please contact the Financial Resource Center at 803-323-2189 or by e-mail at wufrc@winthrop.edu.

Application and Information

The following admission credentials should be submitted by applicants: a completed application for admission, the $35 application fee, an official high school transcript or graduate equivalency diploma, and official results of the SAT I or ACT. Transfer applicants must submit transcripts from all colleges previously attended. Application deadlines are May 1 for fall enrollment and January 1 for spring enrollment. Applications are reviewed on a rolling basis. For more information, students should contact:

Winthrop University
Office of Admissions
Rock Hill, South Carolina 29733

Telephone: 803-323-2191
800-763-0230 (toll-free)
E-mail: admissions@winthrop.edu
Web site: http://www.winthrop.edu

WOODBURY UNIVERSITY
BURBANK, CALIFORNIA

The University

Woodbury University offers students practical, applied education; high academic standards; and small classes. The University is an accredited, independent, nonprofit, coeducational, nonsectarian institution. Students attend Woodbury because of its specialization in the areas of architecture, business, computers, professional design, and social science. Also offered is a Master of Business Administration program. The carefully designed curricula at Woodbury give students hands-on experience in their majors in addition to an effective general education. Woodbury maintains small classes to ensure individual student attention. The University presents a variety of opportunities for all students to join cultural, social, and professional organizations, both on and off campus. The Office of Student Services at Woodbury helps meet students' needs through career planning and job placement workshops; educational, cultural, social, and recreational programs; the sponsorship of various student groups; and special services for international students. The career services office provides Woodbury students and alumni with lifetime employment assistance. Woodbury's 22-acre campus in Burbank provides students with such on-campus amenities as a swimming pool, gymnasium, campus lounge, residence halls, an athletic field, and food services, all situated on beautifully landscaped grounds. Founded in 1884, Woodbury's primary mission is to provide programs requisite for success and leadership and to encourage each person's creativity. The University is accredited by the Senior Commission of the Western Association of Schools and Colleges and is approved by the Postsecondary Commission, California Department of Education. The Interior Design Program is accredited by the Foundation for Interior Design Education Research. The Architecture Program is accredited by the National Architectural Accrediting Board.

Academic Program

The academic programs at Woodbury are designed to provide students with the higher education necessary for success and leadership in their chosen fields. The principal emphasis is on relevance of subject matter and personalized instruction, complemented by a strong focus on general education. The academic calendar is based on the semester system. The number of elective units varies depending on the major. To encourage the achievement of academic excellence, Woodbury University recognizes students who demonstrate the initiative and sense of responsibility to excel. Such superior performance is recognized with special awards.

Financial Aid

Assisting students who lack adequate financial resources to attend Woodbury is a primary concern of the University. Various sources of financial aid are available to help meet education costs. Eligible students generally are awarded a financial aid package consisting of a combination of available funds. Financial aid for eligible U.S. citizens and permanent residents includes Federal Pell Grants, California Grants A and B for California residents, Federal Family Educational Loans, veterans' educational benefits, Federal Supplemental Educational Opportunity Grants, Federal Work-Study awards, Federal Perkins Loans, local scholarships, and Woodbury grants. The University offers financial aid and counseling, as well as part-time employment and full-time placement services. Classes are scheduled to permit students to work part-time, usually in the area of their major interest, so that they may not only meet financial needs but also gain excellent experience.

Application and Information

Applications are accepted throughout the year for entrance in any term. Freshman applicants are encouraged to apply before the priority date, March 1. The priority application date for transfer students is April 15. Students should direct all materials and inquiries to the Office of Admission at the address below.

Office of Admission
Woodbury University
7500 Glenoaks Boulevard
Burbank, California 91510-7846

Telephone: 818-767-0888
E-mail: admissions@vaxb.woodbury.edu

APPENDIXES

APPENDIX 1

Returning to School: A Guide for Adult Students

by Sandra Cook, Ph.D., Director, University Advising Center, San Diego State University

Many adults think about returning to school for a long time without taking any action. One purpose of this article is to help the "thinkers" finally make some decisions by examining what is keeping them from action. Another purpose is to describe not only some of the difficulties and obstacles that adult students may face when returning to school but also tactics for coping with them.

If you have been thinking about going back to college, believing you are the only person your age contemplating college, you should know that approximately six million adult students are currently enrolled in higher education institutions. This number represents 45 percent of total higher education enrollments. And the majority of adult students are enrolled at two-year colleges.

There are many reasons why adult students choose to attend a two-year college. Studies have shown that the three most important criteria that adult students consider when choosing a college are location, cost, and availability of the major or program desired. Most two-year colleges are public institutions that serve a geographic district, making them readily accessible to the community. Costs at most two-year colleges are far less than at other types of higher education institutions. For many students who plan to pursue a bachelor's degree, completing their first two years of college at a community college is an affordable means to that end. If you are interested in an academic program that will transfer to a four-year institution, most two-year colleges offer the "general education" courses that compose most freshman and sophomore years. If you are interested in a vocational or technical program, two-year colleges excel in providing this type of training.

Uncertainty, Choice, and Support

There are three different "stages" in the process of adults returning to school. The first stage is uncertainty. Do I really want to go back to school? What will my friends or family think? Can I compete with those 18-year-old whiz kids? Am I too old? The second stage is choice. Once the decision to return has been made, you must choose where you will attend. There are many criteria to use in making this decision. The third stage is support. You have just added another role to your already-too-busy life. There are, however, strategies that will help you accomplish your goals—perhaps not without struggle but with grace and humor. Let's look at each of these stages.

Uncertainty

Why are you thinking about returning to school? Is it to:

- fulfill a dream that had to be delayed?
- become more educationally well rounded?
- fill an intellectual void in your life?

These reasons focus on *personal growth*.
If you are returning to school to:

- meet people and make friends
- attain and enjoy higher social status and prestige among friends, relatives, and associates
- understand/study a cultural heritage, or
- have a medium in which to exchange ideas,

you are interested in *social and cultural opportunities*.
If you are like most adult students, you want to:

- qualify for a new occupation
- enter or reenter the job market
- increase earnings potential, or
- qualify for a more challenging position in the same field of work.

You are seeking *career growth*.

Understanding the reasons why you want to go back to school is an important step in setting your educational goals and will help you to establish some criteria in selecting a college. However, don't delay your decision because you haven't been able to clearly define your motives.

Many times these aren't clear until you have already begun the process, and they may change as you move through your college experience.

Assuming that you agree that additional education will be of benefit to you, what is it that keeps you from returning to school? You may have a litany of excuses running through your mind:

- I don't have time.
- I can't afford it.
- I'm too old to learn.
- My friends will think I'm crazy.
- The teachers will be younger than me.
- My family can't survive without me to take care of them every minute.
- I'll be X years old when I finish.
- I'm afraid.
- I don't know what to expect.

And that is just what these are—excuses. You can make school, like anything else in your life, a priority or not. If you really want to return, you can. The more you understand your motivation for returning to school and the more you understand what excuses are keeping you from taking action, the easier your task will be.

If you think you don't have time: The best way to decide how attending class and studying can fit into your schedule is to keep track of what you do with your time each day for several weeks. Completing a standard time-management grid (each day is plotted out by the half hour) is helpful for visualizing how your time is spent. For each 3-credit-hour class you take, you will need to find 3 hours for class plus 6 to 9 hours for reading-studying-library time. This study time should be spaced evenly throughout the week, not loaded up on one day. It is not possible to learn or retain the material that way. When you examine your grid, see where there are activities that could be replaced with school and study time. You may decide to give up your bowling league or some time in front of the TV. Try not to give up sleeping, and don't cut out every moment of free time. There are also a number of smaller ways to divert time to school. Here are some suggestions that have come from adults who have returned to school:

- Enroll in a time-management workshop. It helps you rethink how you use your time.
- Don't think you have to take more than one course at a time. You may eventually want to work up to taking more, but consider starting with one. (It's more than you're taking now!)

- If you have a family, start assigning those household chores that you usually do to them—and don't redo what they do.
- Use your lunch hour or commuting time for reading.

If you think you can't afford it: As mentioned earlier, two-year colleges are extremely affordable. If you cannot afford the tuition, look into the various financial aid options. Most federal and state funds are available to full- and part-time students. Loans are also available. While many people prefer not to accumulate a debt for school, these same people will think nothing of taking out a loan to buy a car. After five or six years, which is the better investment? Adult students who work should look into whether their company has a tuition-reimbursement policy. There are also an increasing number of private scholarships, available through foundations, service organizations, and clubs, that are focused on adult learners. Your public library and a college financial aid adviser are two excellent sources for reference materials regarding financial aid.

If you think you are too old to learn: This is pure myth. A number of studies have shown that adult learners perform as well as or better than traditional-age students.

If you are afraid your friends will think you're crazy: Who cares? Maybe they will, maybe they won't. Usually they will admire your courage and be just a little jealous of your ambition (although they'll never tell you that). Follow your dreams, not theirs.

If you are concerned because the teachers or students will be younger than you: Don't be. The age differences that may be apparent in other settings evaporate in the classroom. If anything, an adult in the classroom strikes fear into the hearts of some 18-year-olds because adults have been known to be prepared, ask questions, be truly motivated, and be there to learn!

If you think your family will have a difficult time surviving while you are in school: If you have done everything for them up to now, they might struggle. Consider this an opportunity to help them become independent, more self-sufficient people. Your family can only make you feel guilty if you let them. You are not abandoning them; you are becoming an educational role model. When you are happy and working toward your goals, everyone benefits. Admittedly, it sometimes takes time for them to realize this. For single parents there are schools that have begun to offer support groups, child care, and cooperative babysitting.

If you're appalled at the thought of being X years old when you graduate in Y years: How old will you be in Y years if you don't go back to school?

If you are afraid or don't know what to expect: Know that these are natural feelings when one encounters any new situation. Adult students find that their fears usually dissipate once they begin classes. Fear of trying is usually the biggest roadblock to the reentry process.

No doubt you have dreamed up a few more reasons for not making the decision to return to school. Keep in mind that what you are doing is making up excuses, and you are using these excuses to release you from the obligation to make a decision about your life. The thought of returning to college can be scary. Anytime anyone ventures into unknown territory there is a risk, but taking risks is a necessary component of personal and professional growth. It is your life, and you alone are responsible for making the decisions that determine its course. Education is an investment in your future.

Choice

Once you have decided to go back to school, your next task is to decide where to go. If your educational goals are well defined (e.g., you want to pursue a degree in order to change careers), then your task is a bit easier. But even if your educational goals are still evolving, don't deter your return. Many students who enter higher education with a specific major in mind change that major at least once.

Most students who attend a public two-year college choose the community college in the district in which they live. This is generally the closest and least expensive option if the school offers the programs you want. If you are planning to begin your education at a two-year college and then transfer to a four-year school, there are distinct advantages to choosing your four-year school early. Many community and four-year colleges have "articulation" agreements that designate what credits from the two-year school will transfer to the four-year college and how. Some four-year institutions accept an associate degree as equivalent to the freshman and sophomore years regardless of the courses you have taken. Some four-year schools accept two-year college work only on a course-by-course basis. If you can identify which school you will transfer to, you can know in advance exactly how your two-year credits will apply. This can prevent an unexpected loss of credit or time. You can use the strategies outlined below not only to help you choose your two-year college but also to help you identify early which four-year school you will transfer to.

Each institution of higher education is distinctive. Your goal in choosing a college is to come up with the best student-institution fit—matching your needs with the offerings and characteristics of the school. The first step in choosing a college is to determine what criteria are most important to you in attaining your educational goals. Location, cost, and program availability are the three main factors that influenced an adult student's college choice. In considering location, don't forget that some colleges have conveniently located branch campuses. In considering cost, remember to explore your financial aid options before ruling out an institution because of its tuition. Program availability should include not only the major in which you are interested but also whether classes in that major are available when you can take them.

Some additional considerations beyond location, cost, and programs are:

- Does the school have a commitment to adult students and offer appropriate services such as child care, tutoring, and advising?
- Are classes offered when you can take them?
- Are there academic options for adults such as credit for life or work experience, credit by examination (including CLEP and PEP), credit for military service, or accelerated programs?
- Is the faculty sensitive to the needs of adult learners?

Once you determine which criteria are vital in your choice of an institution, you can begin to narrow your choices. There are myriad ways for you to locate the information you desire. This guide and others, including *Peterson's Guide to Four-Year Colleges,* are excellent sources of information. Many urban newspapers publish a "School Guide" several times a year in which colleges and universities advertise to an adult student market. In addition, schools themselves publish catalogs, class schedules, and promotional materials that contain much of the information you need, and they are yours for the asking. Many colleges sponsor information sessions and open houses that allow you to visit the campus and ask questions. An appointment with an adviser is a good way to assess the fit between you and the institution. Be sure to bring your questions with you to your interview.

Support

Once you have made the decision to return to school and have chosen the institution that best meets your needs, take some additional steps to ensure your success during your crucial first semester. Take advantage of institutional support and build some social support systems of your own. Here are some ways of doing just that:

- Plan to participate in any orientation programs. These serve the threefold purpose of providing you with a great deal of important information, familiarizing you with the campus and its facilities, and giving you the opportunity to meet and begin networking with other students.
- Take steps to deal with any academic weaknesses. Take mathematics and writing placement tests if you have reason to believe you may need some extra help in these areas. It is not uncommon for adult students to need a math refresher course or a program to help alleviate math anxiety. Ignoring a weakness won't make it go away.
- Look into adult reentry programs. Many institutions offer study-skills, textbook-reading, test-taking, and time-management workshops to help adult students.
- Build new support networks by joining an adult student organization, making a point of meeting other adult students through workshops, or actively seeking out a "study buddy" in each class—that invaluable friend who shares and understands your experience.
- You can incorporate your new status as "student" into your family life. Doing your homework with your children at a designated "homework time" is a valuable family activity and reinforces the importance of education.
- Make sure you take a reasonable course load in your first semester. It is far better to have some extra time on your hands and succeed magnificently than to spend the entire semester on the brink of a breakdown. Also, whenever possible, try to focus your first courses not only on requirements but also in areas of personal interest.
- Faculty, advisers, and student affairs personnel are there to help you during difficult times—let them.

After completing your first semester, you will probably look back in wonder at why you thought going back to school was so imposing. Certainly it's not without its occasional exasperations. But, as with life, keeping things in perspective and maintaining your sense of humor make the difference between just coping and succeeding brilliantly.

APPENDIX 2

What You Need to Know About Two-Year Colleges

by David R. Pierce President,
American Association of Community Colleges

Two-year colleges are often called the people's colleges. With their open-door policy (admission is open to those with a high school diploma or its equivalent), two-year colleges continue to provide access to higher education for millions of Americans who otherwise might not continue their education. Two-year colleges serve students of all ages, races, and ethnicities. Many students who attend two-year colleges enroll on a part-time basis while at the same time fulfilling other employment and family commitments.

Two-year colleges are also often called community colleges, though some are still known as technical or junior colleges. The American Association of Community Colleges (AACC) defines them as regionally accredited, postsecondary institutions at which the associate degree is the highest credential awarded (the bachelor's degree is the usual credential received from a four-year college). Under this definition the term two-year college includes public, independent, and proprietary colleges that offer comprehensive, technical, transfer, and continuing education or specialized curriculums.

Today there are approximately 1,200 two-year colleges in the United States. They enroll almost 6 million for-credit students, over 40 percent of all students taking college courses for credit. Nearly 55 percent of all freshmen taking courses for college credit for the first time enroll in two-year colleges.

Important Factors in a Two-Year College Education

Two-year colleges provide the very best quality teaching and learning experiences. Students come to two-year colleges to pursue their own goals, follow their own aptitudes, become productive and self-reliant human beings, and gain new knowledge.

Four key characteristics describe most two-year colleges:

- First, they are community-based institutions that establish linkages and partnerships with high schools, community groups, and employers. They deliver high-quality programs at times and places convenient to students.
- Second, they are cost effective. Annual tuition and fees at two-year colleges average approximately half those at public four-year colleges and one eighth of those at private four-year institutions. In addition, since most two-year colleges are community based and generally close to their students' homes, students at these colleges usually save room, board, and transportation expenses.
- Third, they provide a caring environment, with faculty who are expert instructors, known for excellent teaching and for meeting students at the point of their individual needs, regardless of age, sex, race, current job status, or previous academic preparation. Most two-year colleges offer a full range of counseling and career services designed to help students make the most of their educational opportunities.
- Fourth, many offer comprehensive programs, including liberal arts transfer curriculums that provide the first two years leading to a baccalaureate degree; occupational-technical programs that prepare students for employment or assist those already employed to upgrade their skills; developmental education programs that help students improve their basic academic skills and obtain the competence and attitudes necessary for lifelong learning; and adult and life-span education courses that respond to individual and community, social, intellectual, and recreational interests.

Above all, two-year colleges pride themselves on providing high-quality education. Degree requirements are established to ensure that students acquire the knowledge and skills necessary to continue for a baccalaureate degree at a four-year college or to compete in the work force. Two-year colleges offer the associate degree as well as certificates in specific programs that require varying amounts of study.

Getting to Know Your Two-Year College

One important way to determine the quality of your two-year college is to check its accreditation. The colleges included in the list following this section all meet certain accreditation criteria. Once you have established that a college is appropriately accredited, find out as much as you can about the courses and programs it has to offer. Much of that information can be found in this book or in materials the college provides. However, the best way to learn about your college is to visit in person.

During a visit, be prepared to ask a lot of questions. Talk to students, faculty members, administrators, and counselors about the college and its programs. Ask about available certificates and associate degrees. Inquire about the academic fields in which you are interested. Don't be shy. Do what you can to dig below the surface. Ask about the transfer rate to four-year colleges. If a college emphasizes student services, find out what particular assistance is offered, such as educational or career guidance. Colleges are eager to provide you with the information you need to make informed decisions.

Two-Year Colleges Can Save You Money

If you are able to live at home while you attend college, you will certainly save money on room and board, but it does cost something to commute. Many two-year colleges now provide instruction through cable television or public broadcast stations or through home study courses that can save both time and money. Look into all your options, and be sure to add up all the costs of attending various colleges before deciding which is the least expensive.

Financial Aid

Many students who attend two-year colleges are eligible for different types of financial aid, including Federal Pell Grants, student loans, and on-campus jobs. Your high school counselor or the financial aid officer at a two-year college will be able to help you. You must apply for financial aid months in advance, so find out early what assistance is available to you. Many two-year colleges are able to help students who make a last-minute decision to attend college, either through short-term loans or emergency grants. Nevertheless, if you are considering college and feel you might need financial aid, it is best to find out as much as you can as early as you can.

Working and Going to School

Many two-year college students maintain full-time or part-time employment while they earn their degrees. Over the past decades, more and more students have attended two-year colleges on a part-time basis while continuing to fulfill family and employment responsibilities. To meet the needs of their students, most two-year colleges offer classes at night or on weekends.

Of course, the length of time it takes to obtain an associate degree depends on the course load students take: the fewer credits they take per term, the longer it takes to earn a degree. Many colleges award credit through examination or for experience gained through relevant outside activities. This can save a great deal of time and enable students to satisfy credit requirements while they are still working. Find out what options are available at each college in which you are interested. You may discover it will take less time to earn a degree than you first thought.

Preparation for Transfer

About 40 percent of students who attend two-year colleges transfer to four-year colleges and universities, and studies show they do as well academically as the students who entered the four-year institutions as freshmen. Most two-year colleges have agreements with nearby four-year institutions to make transfer of credits easier. If you are thinking of transferring, be sure to meet with a counselor or faculty adviser before choosing your courses. You will want to map out a course of study with transfer in mind. Make sure you find out the credit-transfer requirements of the four-year institutions you might want to attend.

New Career Opportunities

Two-year colleges realize that many entering students are not sure about the area they want to major in or pursue as a career. Often students discover fields and careers they didn't know existed. Two-year colleges have the resources to help students identify areas of career interest and set realistic goals.

Two-year colleges are leaders in providing occupational and technical education. About half the students who take courses for credit at two-year colleges do so to prepare for employment or to acquire or upgrade skills for their current job. If you know you want a career in a particular field, a counselor or faculty adviser will be able to discuss job opportunities in that field and help you map out your course of study.

In addition, since two-year colleges have close ties to their communities, they are in constant communication with individuals in business and industry, union officials, public leaders, and other concerned citizens. Two-year colleges work with these groups to develop training, research, and other programs that help students prepare for the world of work. For example, some two-year colleges have partnerships that provide specialized training programs with local business and industry. Some also provide the academic portion of apprenticeship training. Be sure to examine all the career-preparation opportunities offered by the colleges in which you are interested.

Attending a Two-Year College in Another Area

Although many two-year colleges serve a specific county or district, they are committed (to the extent of their ability) to the goal of equal educational opportunity without regard to economic status, race, creed, color, sex, or national origin. Independent two-year colleges recruit from a much broader geographical area, including the whole country.

Although some two-year colleges do provide housing for their students, most do not. However, even if on-campus housing is not available, most colleges do have housing referral services.

Advantages at a Glance

A Caring Environment. Faculty members at two-year colleges are known for their excellent teaching and for meeting students at the point of their individual needs.

Convenience and Accessibility. Most two-year colleges are community based, making higher education accessible for all qualified citizens in their service district.

Moderate Cost. Two-year colleges are generally quite affordable.

Variety of Associate Degree Programs. College transfer, occupational-technical fields, and lifelong learning are usually included as two-year college programs.

Community Partnerships. Because of their vital link with the community, many two-year colleges establish arrangements with local agencies and employers that provide job opportunities and experience for students both before and after they graduate.

Of course, these are generalizations. There is tremendous variety among two-year colleges, and you would be well-advised to do careful research about the offerings and environment at each college you are considering. Try to visit at least one two-year college as you investigate postsecondary education. You may find—as over 50 percent of all beginning freshmen have—that a two-year college offers you the excellent and affordable education you are looking for.

TWO-YEAR COLLEGES

The Middle Atlantic States

Delaware

Delaware Technical & Community College, Jack F. Owens Campus *Georgetown*
Delaware Technical & Community College, Stanton/Wilmington Campus *Newark*
Delaware Technical & Community College, Terry Campus *Dover*

Maryland

Allegany College of Maryland *Cumberland*
Anne Arundel Community College *Arnold*
Baltimore City Community College *Baltimore*
Baltimore International College *Baltimore*
Carroll Community College *Westminster*
Catonsville Community College *Catonsville*
Cecil Community College *North East*
Charles County Community College *La Plata*
Chesapeake College *Wye Mills*
Dundalk Community College *Baltimore*
Essex Community College *Baltimore*
Frederick Community College *Frederick*
Garrett Community College *McHenry*
Hagerstown Business College *Hagerstown*
Hagerstown Junior College *Hagerstown*
Harford Community College *Bel Air*
Howard Community College *Columbia*
Maryland College of Art and Design *Silver Spring*
Montgomery College–Germantown Campus *Germantown*
Montgomery College–Rockville Campus *Rockville*
Montgomery College–Takoma Park Campus *Takoma Park*
Prince George's Community College *Largo*
Wor-Wic Community College *Salisbury*

New Jersey

Assumption College for Sisters *Mendham*
Atlantic Community College *Mays Landing*
Bergen Community College *Paramus*
Berkeley College *West Paterson*
Brookdale Community College *Lincroft*
Burlington County College *Pemberton*
Camden County College *Blackwood*
County College of Morris *Randolph*
Cumberland County College *Vineland*
DeVry Institute *North Brunswick*
Essex County College *Newark*
Fairleigh Dickinson University, Edward Williams College *Hackensack*
Gloucester County College *Sewell*
Hudson County Community College *Jersey City*
Katharine Gibbs School *Montclair*
Mercer County Community College *Trenton*
Middlesex County College *Edison*
Ocean County College *Toms River*
Passaic County Community College *Paterson*
Raritan Valley Community College *Somerville*
Salem Community College *Carneys Point*
Sussex County Community College *Newton*
Union County College *Cranford*
Warren County Community College *Washington*

Pennsylvania

Allentown Business School *Allentown*
Antonelli Institute *Erdenheim*
The Art Institute of Philadelphia *Philadelphia*
The Art Institute of Pittsburgh *Pittsburgh*
Berean Institute *Philadelphia*
Bradley Academy for the Visual Arts *York*
Bucks County Community College *Newtown*
Butler County Community College *Butler*
Cambria-Rowe Business College *Johnstown*
Central Pennsylvania Business School *Summerdale*
CHI Institute *Southampton*
CHI Institute, RETS Campus *Broomall*
Churchman Business School *Easton*
Community College of Allegheny County *Pittsburgh*
Community College of Beaver County *Monaca*
Community College of Philadelphia *Philadelphia*
Dean Institute of Technology *Pittsburgh*
Delaware County Community College *Media*

DuBois Business College *DuBois*
Duff's Business Institute *Pittsburgh*
Electronic Institutes *Middletown*
Electronic Institutes *Pittsburgh*
Erie Business Center, Main *Erie*
Erie Business Center South *New Castle*
Harcum College *Bryn Mawr*
Harrisburg Area Community College *Harrisburg*
Hussian School of Art *Philadelphia*
ICM School of Business & Medical Careers *Pittsburgh*
ICS Center for Degree Studies *Scranton*
Johnson Technical Institute *Scranton*
Keystone College *La Plume*
Lackawanna Junior College *Scranton*
Lansdale School of Business *North Wales*
Lehigh Carbon Community College *Schnecksville*
Lincoln Technical Institute *Allentown*
Lincoln Technical Institute *Philadelphia*
Luzerne County Community College *Nanticoke*
Manor Junior College *Jenkintown*
McCann School of Business *Mahanoy City*
Median School of Allied Health Careers *Pittsburgh*
Montgomery County Community College *Blue Bell*
Newport Business Institute *Lower Burrell*
Newport Business Institute *Williamsport*
Northampton County Area Community College *Bethlehem*
Peirce College *Philadelphia*
Penn Commercial, Inc. *Washington*
Pennco Tech *Bristol*
Pennsylvania College of Technology *Williamsport*
Pennsylvania Institute of Technology *Media*
Pennsylvania State University Beaver Campus of the Commonwealth College *Monaca*
Pennsylvania State University Delaware County Campus of the Commonwealth College *Media*
Pennsylvania State University DuBois Campus of the Commonwealth College *DuBois*
Pennsylvania State University Fayette Campus of the Commonwealth College *Uniontown*
Pennsylvania State University Hazleton Campus of the Commonwealth College *Hazleton*
Pennsylvania State University McKeesport Campus of the Commonwealth College *McKeesport*
Pennsylvania State University Mont Alto Campus of the Commonwealth College *Mont Alto*
Pennsylvania State University New Kensington Campus of the Commonwealth College *New Kensington*
Pennsylvania State University Shenango Campus of the Commonwealth College *Sharon*
Pennsylvania State University Wilkes-Barre Campus of the Commonwealth College *Lehman*
Pennsylvania State University Worthington Scranton Campus of the Commonwealth College *Dunmore*
Pennsylvania State University York Campus of the Commonwealth College *York*
Pittsburgh Institute of Aeronautics *Pittsburgh*
Pittsburgh Institute of Mortuary Science, Incorporated *Pittsburgh*
Pittsburgh Technical Institute *Pittsburgh*
Reading Area Community College *Reading*
Remington Education Center–Vale Campus *Blairsville*
Thaddeus Stevens State School of Technology *Lancaster*
Thompson Institute *Harrisburg*
Triangle Tech, Inc. *Pittsburgh*
Triangle Tech, Inc.–DuBois School *DuBois*
Triangle Tech, Inc.–Erie School *Erie*
Triangle Tech, Inc.–Greensburg Center *Greensburg*
University of Pittsburgh–Titusville *Titusville*
Valley Forge Military College *Wayne*
Welder Training and Testing Institute *Allentown*
Westmoreland County Community College *Youngwood*
The Williamson Free School of Mechanical Trades *Media*

Virginia

Blue Ridge Community College *Weyers Cave*
Central Virginia Community College *Lynchburg*
Commonwealth College, Hampton *Hampton*
Commonwealth College, Richmond *Richmond*
Commonwealth College, Virginia Beach *Virginia Beach*
Dabney S. Lancaster Community College *Clifton Forge*
Danville Community College *Danville*
Eastern Shore Community College *Melfa*
ECPI College of Computer Technology *Roanoke*
ECPI College of Technology *Hampton*
ECPI College of Technology *Virginia Beach*
ECPI Computer Institute *Richmond*
Germanna Community College *Locust Grove*
ITT Technical Institute *Norfolk*
Johnson & Wales University *Norfolk*
John Tyler Community College *Chester*
J. Sargeant Reynolds Community College *Richmond*
Lord Fairfax Community College *Middletown*
Mountain Empire Community College *Big Stone Gap*
National Business College *Bluefield*
National Business College *Bristol*
National Business College *Charlottesville*

National Business College *Danville*
National Business College *Harrisonburg*
National Business College *Lynchburg*
National Business College *Martinsville*
National Business College *Salem*
New River Community College *Dublin*
Northern Virginia Community College *Annandale*
Patrick Henry Community College *Martinsville*
Paul D. Camp Community College *Franklin*
Piedmont Virginia Community College *Charlottesville*
Rappahannock Community College *Glenns*
Richard Bland College of the College of William and Mary *Petersburg*
Southside Virginia Community College *Alberta*
Southwest Virginia Community College *Richlands*
Thomas Nelson Community College *Hampton*
Tidewater Community College *Portsmouth*
Virginia Highlands Community College *Abingdon*
Virginia Western Community College *Roanoke*
Wytheville Community College *Wytheville*

West Virginia

Huntington Junior College of Business *Huntington*
National Institute of Technology *Cross Lanes*
Ohio Valley College *Parkersburg*
Potomac State College of West Virginia University *Keyser*
Southern West Virginia Community and Technical College *Mount Gay*
Webster College *Fairmont*
West Virginia Career College *Charleston*
West Virginia Career College *Morgantown*
West Virginia Northern Community College *Wheeling*
West Virginia University at Parkersburg *Parkersburg*

The Midwest

Illinois

American Academy of Art *Chicago*
Belleville Area College *Belleville*
Black Hawk College *Kewanee*
Black Hawk College *Moline*
Carl Sandburg College *Galesburg*
Chicago College of Commerce *Chicago*
City Colleges of Chicago, Harold Washington College *Chicago*
City Colleges of Chicago, Harry S Truman College *Chicago*
City Colleges of Chicago, Kennedy-King College *Chicago*
City Colleges of Chicago, Malcolm X College *Chicago*
City Colleges of Chicago, Olive-Harvey College *Chicago*
City Colleges of Chicago, Richard J. Daley College *Chicago*
City Colleges of Chicago, Wilbur Wright College *Chicago*
College of DuPage *Glen Ellyn*
College of Lake County *Grayslake*
Danville Area Community College *Danville*
Elgin Community College *Elgin*
Gem City College *Quincy*
Heartland Community College *Bloomington*
Highland Community College *Freeport*
Illinois Central College *East Peoria*
Illinois Eastern Community Colleges, Frontier Community College *Fairfield*
Illinois Eastern Community Colleges, Lincoln Trail College *Robinson*
Illinois Eastern Community Colleges, Olney Central College *Olney*
Illinois Eastern Community Colleges, Wabash Valley College *Mount Carmel*
Illinois Valley Community College *Oglesby*
ITT Technical Institute *Hoffman Estates*
ITT Technical Institute *Matteson*
John A. Logan College *Carterville*
John Wood Community College *Quincy*
Joliet Junior College *Joliet*
Kankakee Community College *Kankakee*
Kaskaskia College *Centralia*
Kishwaukee College *Malta*
Lake Land College *Mattoon*
Lewis and Clark Community College *Godfrey*
Lexington College *Chicago*
Lincoln College *Lincoln*
Lincoln College *Normal*
Lincoln Land Community College *Springfield*
MacCormac College *Chicago*
McHenry County College *Crystal Lake*
Metropolitan Community College *East St. Louis*
Midstate College *Peoria*
Moraine Valley Community College *Palos Hills*
Morrison Institute of Technology *Morrison*
Morton College *Cicero*
Northwestern Business College *Chicago*
Oakton Community College *Des Plaines*
Parkland College *Champaign*
Prairie State College *Chicago Heights*
Rend Lake College *Ina*
Richland Community College *Decatur*
Rock Valley College *Rockford*
Saint Augustine College *Chicago*
Sauk Valley Community College *Dixon*
Shawnee Community College *Ullin*
Southeastern Illinois College *Harrisburg*
South Suburban College *South Holland*
Spoon River College *Canton*
Springfield College in Illinois *Springfield*

Triton College *River Grove*
Waubonsee Community College *Sugar Grove*
William Rainey Harper College *Palatine*

Indiana

Ancilla College *Donaldson*
Commonwealth Business College *Merrillville*
Commonwealth Business College *Michigan City*
Holy Cross College *Notre Dame*
Indiana Business College *Indianapolis*
International Business College *Fort Wayne*
ITT Technical Institute *Fort Wayne*
ITT Technical Institute *Indianapolis*
ITT Technical Institute *Newburgh*
Ivy Tech State College–Central Indiana *Indianapolis*
Ivy Tech State College–Columbus *Columbus*
Ivy Tech State College–Eastcentral *Muncie*
Ivy Tech State College–Kokomo *Kokomo*
Ivy Tech State College–Lafayette *Lafayette*
Ivy Tech State College–Northcentral *South Bend*
Ivy Tech State College–Northeast *Fort Wayne*
Ivy Tech State College–Northwest *Gary*
Ivy Tech State College–Southcentral *Sellersburg*
Ivy Tech State College–Southeast *Madison*
Ivy Tech State College–Southwest *Evansville*
Ivy Tech State College–Wabash Valley *Terre Haute*
Ivy Tech State College–Whitewater *Richmond*
Lincoln Technical Institute *Indianapolis*
Lutheran College of Health Professions *Fort Wayne*
Michiana College *South Bend*
Mid-America College of Funeral Service *Jeffersonville*
Vincennes University *Vincennes*
Vincennes University Jasper Campus *Jasper*

Iowa

American Institute of Business *Des Moines*
American Institute of Commerce *Davenport*
Clinton Community College *Clinton*
Des Moines Area Community College *Ankeny*
Ellsworth Community College *Iowa Falls*
Hamilton College *Cedar Rapids*
Hawkeye Community College *Waterloo*
Indian Hills Community College *Ottumwa*
Iowa Central Community College *Fort Dodge*
Iowa Lakes Community College *Estherville*
Iowa Western Community College *Council Bluffs*
Kirkwood Community College *Cedar Rapids*
Marshalltown Community College *Marshalltown*
Muscatine Community College *Muscatine*
Northeast Iowa Community College, Calmar Campus *Calmar*
Northeast Iowa Community College, Peosta Campus *Peosta*
North Iowa Area Community College *Mason City*
Northwest Iowa Community College *Sheldon*
Scott Community College *Bettendorf*
Southeastern Community College, North Campus *West Burlington*
Southeastern Community College, South Campus *Keokuk*
Southwestern Community College *Creston*
Waldorf College *Forest City*
Western Iowa Tech Community College *Sioux City*

Kansas

Allen County Community College *Iola*
Barton County Community College *Great Bend*
The Brown Mackie College *Salina*
The Brown Mackie College–Olathe Campus *Olathe*
Butler County Community College *El Dorado*
Central College *McPherson*
Cloud County Community College *Concordia*
Coffeyville Community College *Coffeyville*
Colby Community College *Colby*
Cowley County Community College and Vocational-Technical School *Arkansas City*
Dodge City Community College *Dodge City*
Donnelly College *Kansas City*
Fort Scott Community College *Fort Scott*
Garden City Community College *Garden City*
Haskell Indian Nations University *Lawrence*
Hesston College *Hesston*
Highland Community College *Highland*
Hutchinson Community College and Area Vocational School *Hutchinson*
Independence Community College *Independence*
Johnson County Community College *Overland Park*
Kansas City Kansas Community College *Kansas City*
Labette Community College *Parsons*
Neosho County Community College *Chanute*
Pratt Community College and Area Vocational School *Pratt*
Seward County Community College *Liberal*

Michigan

Alpena Community College *Alpena*
Baker College of Jackson *Jackson*
Bay de Noc Community College *Escanaba*
Bay Mills Community College *Brimley*
Charles Stewart Mott Community College *Flint*
Delta College *University Center*
Glen Oaks Community College *Centreville*
Gogebic Community College *Ironwood*

Grand Rapids Community College *Grand Rapids*
Great Lakes Junior College of Business *Saginaw*
Henry Ford Community College *Dearborn*
Jackson Community College *Jackson*
Kalamazoo Valley Community College *Kalamazoo*
Kellogg Community College *Battle Creek*
Kirtland Community College *Roscommon*
Lake Michigan College *Benton Harbor*
Lansing Community College *Lansing*
Lewis College of Business *Detroit*
Macomb Community College *Warren*
Mid Michigan Community College *Harrison*
Monroe County Community College *Monroe*
Montcalm Community College *Sidney*
Muskegon Community College *Muskegon*
North Central Michigan College *Petoskey*
Northwestern Michigan College *Traverse City*
Oakland Community College *Bloomfield Hills*
St. Clair County Community College *Port Huron*
Schoolcraft College *Livonia*
Southwestern Michigan College *Dowagiac*
Suomi College *Hancock*
Washtenaw Community College *Ann Arbor*
Wayne County Community College *Detroit*
West Shore Community College *Scottville*

Minnesota

Alexandria Technical College *Alexandria*
Anoka-Ramsey Community College *Coon Rapids*
Art Institute of Minnesota *Minneapolis*
Bethany Lutheran College *Mankato*
Brown Institute *Minneapolis*
Central Lakes College *Brainerd*
Century Community and Technical College *White Bear Lake*
College of St. Catherine–Minneapolis *Minneapolis*
Dunwoody Institute *Minneapolis*
Fergus Falls Community College *Fergus Falls*
Fond du Lac Tribal and Community College *Cloquet*
Hennepin Technical College *Brooklyn Park*
Hibbing Community College *Hibbing*
Inver Hills Community College *Inver Grove Heights*
Itasca Community College *Grand Rapids*
Lakeland Medical-Dental Academy *Minneapolis*
Medical Institute of Minnesota *Bloomington*
Mesabi Range Community and Technical College *Virginia*
Minneapolis Community and Technical College *Minneapolis*
Minnesota West Community and Technical College–Granite Falls Campus *Granite Falls*
Minnesota West Community and Technical College–Jackson Campus *Jackson*
Minnesota West Community and Technical College–Pipestone Campus *Pipestone*
Minnesota West Community and Technical College–Worthington Campus *Worthington*
NEI College of Technology *Columbia Heights*
Normandale Community College *Bloomington*
North Hennepin Community College *Minneapolis*
Northland Community and Technical College *Thief River Falls*
Northwest Technical College *Bemidji*
Northwest Technical Institute *Eden Prairie*
Pine Technical College *Pine City*
Rainy River Community College *International Falls*
Rasmussen College Eagan *Eagan*
Rasmussen College Mankato *Mankato*
Rasmussen College Minnetonka *Minnetonka*
Rasmussen College St. Cloud *St. Cloud*
Red Wing/Winona Technical College *Winona*
Ridgewater College *Willmar*
Riverland Community College *Austin*
Rochester Community and Technical College *Rochester*
St. Cloud Technical College *St. Cloud*
St. Paul Technical College *St. Paul*
South Central Technical College *North Mankato*
Vermilion Community College *Ely*

Missouri

Cottey College *Nevada*
Crowder College *Neosho*
East Central College *Union*
ITT Technical Institute *Earth City*
Jefferson College *Hillsboro*
Kemper Military School and College *Boonville*
Longview Community College *Lee's Summit*
Maple Woods Community College *Kansas City*
Mineral Area College *Park Hills*
Moberly Area Community College *Moberly*
North Central Missouri College *Trenton*
Ozarks Technical Community College *Springfield*
Penn Valley Community College *Kansas City*
Ranken Technical College *St. Louis*
Saint Charles County Community College *St. Peters*
St. Louis Community College at Florissant Valley *St. Louis*
St. Louis Community College at Forest Park *St. Louis*
St. Louis Community College at Meramec *Kirkwood*
Sanford-Brown College *Des Peres*
Sanford-Brown College *Hazelwood*
Sanford-Brown College *North Kansas City*
Sanford-Brown College *St. Charles*

Southwest Missouri State University-West Plains *West Plains*
Springfield College *Springfield*
State Fair Community College *Sedalia*
Three Rivers Community College *Poplar Bluff*
Wentworth Military Academy and Junior CollegeLexington

Nebraska

Central Community College-Grand Island Campus *Grand Island*
Central Community College-Hastings Campus *Hastings*
Central Community College-Platte Campus *Columbus*
Grand Island College *Grand Island*
ITT Technical Institute *Omaha*
Lincoln School of Commerce *Lincoln*
McCook Community College *McCook*
Metropolitan Community College *Omaha*
Mid-Plains Community College *North Platte*
Nebraska College of Business *Omaha*
Nebraska College of Technical Agriculture *Curtis*
Nebraska Indian Community College *Macy*
Northeast Community College *Norfolk*
Omaha College of Health Careers *Omaha*
Southeast Community College, Beatrice Campus *Beatrice*
Southeast Community College, Lincoln Campus *Lincoln*
Southeast Community College, Milford Campus *Milford*
Western Nebraska Community College *Scottsbluff*

North Dakota

Bismarck State College *Bismarck*
Cankdeska Cikana Community College *Fort Totten*
Fort Berthold Community College *New Town*
Minot State University-Bottineau *Bottineau*
North Dakota State College of Science *Wahpeton*
Sitting Bull College *Fort Yates*
Turtle Mountain Community College *Belcourt*
United Tribes Technical College *Bismarck*
University of North Dakota-Lake Region *Devils Lake*
University of North Dakota-Williston *Williston*

Ohio

Antonelli College *Cincinnati*
Belmont Technical College *St. Clairsville*
Bowling Green State University-Firelands College *Huron*
Bradford School *Columbus*
Bryant and Stratton College *Parma*
Bryant and Stratton College *Richmond Heights*
Central Ohio Technical College *Newark*
Chatfield College *St. Martin*
Cincinnati State Technical and Community College *Cincinnati*
Clark State Community College *Springfield*
Cleveland Institute of Electronics *Cleveland*
Columbus State Community College *Columbus*
Cuyahoga Community College, Eastern Campus *Highland Hills*
Cuyahoga Community College, Metropolitan Campus *Cleveland*
Cuyahoga Community College, Western Campus *Parma*
Davis College *Toledo*
Edison State Community College *Piqua*
ETI Technical College of Niles *Niles*
Hocking College *Nelsonville*
ITT Technical Institute *Dayton*
ITT Technical Institute *Youngstown*
Jefferson Community College *Steubenville*
Kent State University, Ashtabula Campus *Ashtabula*
Kent State University, East Liverpool Campus *East Liverpool*
Kent State University, Geauga Campus *Burton*
Kent State University, Salem Campus *Salem*
Kent State University, Stark Campus *Canton*
Kent State University, Trumbull Campus *Warren*
Kent State University, Tuscarawas Campus *New Philadelphia*
Kettering College of Medical Arts *Kettering*
Lakeland Community College *Kirtland*
Lima Technical College *Lima*
Lorain County Community College *Elyria*
Marion Technical College *Marion*
Mercy College of Northwest Ohio *Toledo*
Miami-Jacobs College *Dayton*
Miami University-Hamilton Campus *Hamilton*
Miami University-Middletown Campus *Middletown*
Muskingum Area Technical College *Zanesville*
North Central Technical College *Mansfield*
Northwestern College *Lima*
Northwest State Community College *Archbold*
Ohio Institute of Photography and Technology *Dayton*
Ohio State University Agricultural Technical Institute *Wooster*
Ohio University-Southern Campus *Ironton*
Owens Community College *Findlay*
Owens Community College *Toledo*
Professional Skills Institute *Toledo*
RETS Tech Center *Centerville*
Sawyer College of Business *Cleveland Heights*
Sawyer College of Business *Cleveland*
Sinclair Community College *Dayton*

Southern Ohio College, Cincinnati Campus *Cincinnati*
Southern Ohio College, Northeast Campus *Akron*
Southern State Community College *Hillsboro*
Southwestern College of Business *Cincinnati*
Southwestern College of Business *Cincinnati*
Southwestern College of Business *Dayton*
Southwestern College of Business *Middletown*
Stark State College of Technology *Canton*
Terra State Community College *Fremont*
The University of Akron-Wayne College *Orrville*
University of Cincinnati Clermont College *Batavia*
University of Cincinnati Raymond Walters College *Cincinnati*
Virginia Marti College of Fashion and Art *Lakewood*
Washington State Community College *Marietta*
West Side Institute of Technology *Cleveland*
Wright State University, Lake Campus *Celina*

Oklahoma

Bacone College *Muskogee*
Carl Albert State College *Poteau*
Connors State College *Warner*
Eastern Oklahoma State College *Wilburton*
Murray State College *Tishomingo*
Northeastern Oklahoma Agricultural and Mechanical College *Miami*
Northern Oklahoma College *Tonkawa*
Oklahoma City Community College *Oklahoma City*
Oklahoma State University, Oklahoma City *Oklahoma City*
Oklahoma State University, Okmulgee *Okmulgee*
Redlands Community College *El Reno*
Rogers University *Claremore*
Rose State College *Midwest City*
St. Gregory's College *Shawnee*
Seminole State College *Seminole*
Southwestern Oklahoma State University at Sayre *Sayre*
Spartan School of Aeronautics *Tulsa*
Tulsa Community College *Tulsa*
Western Oklahoma State College *Altus*

South Dakota

Central Indian Bible College *Mobridge*
Kilian Community College *Sioux Falls*
Lake Area Technical Institute *Watertown*
Mitchell Technical Institute *Mitchell*
Nettleton Career College *Sioux Falls*
Sisseton-Wahpeton Community College *Sisseton*
Southeast Technical Institute *Sioux Falls*
Western Dakota Technical Institute *Rapid City*

Wisconsin

Blackhawk Technical College *Janesville*
Chippewa Valley Technical College *Eau Claire*
Fox Valley Technical College *Appleton*
Gateway Technical College *Kenosha*
Herzing College of Technology *Madison*
ITT Technical Institute *Greenfield*
Lac Courte Oreilles Ojibwa Community College *Hayward*
Lakeshore Technical College *Cleveland*
Madison Area Technical College *Madison*
Madison Junior College of Business *Madison*
Mid-State Technical College *Wisconsin Rapids*
Milwaukee Area Technical College *Milwaukee*
Moraine Park Technical College *Fond du Lac*
Nicolet Area Technical College *Rhinelander*
Northcentral Technical College *Wausau*
Northeast Wisconsin Technical College *Green Bay*
Southwest Wisconsin Technical College *Fennimore*
Stratton College *Milwaukee*
University of Wisconsin Center-Baraboo/Sauk County *Baraboo*
University of Wisconsin Center-Barron County *Rice Lake*
University of Wisconsin Center-Fond du Lac *Fond du Lac*
University of Wisconsin Center-Fox Valley *Menasha*
University of Wisconsin Center-Manitowoc County *Manitowoc*
University of Wisconsin Center-Marathon County *Wausau*
University of Wisconsin Center-Marinette County *Marinette*
University of Wisconsin Center-Marshfield/Wood County *Marshfield*
University of Wisconsin Center-Richland *Richland Center*
University of Wisconsin Center-Rock County *Janesville*
University of Wisconsin Center-Sheboygan County *Sheboygan*
University of Wisconsin Center-Washington County *West Bend*
University of Wisconsin Center-Waukesha County *Waukesha*
Waukesha County Technical College *Pewaukee*
Western Wisconsin Technical College *La Crosse*
Wisconsin Indianhead Technical College, Ashland Campus *Ashland*
Wisconsin Indianhead Technical College, New Richmond Campus *New Richmond*
Wisconsin Indianhead Technical College, Rice Lake Campus *Rice Lake*
Wisconsin Indianhead Technical College, Superior Campus *Superior*

New England

Connecticut

Asnuntuck Community-Technical College *Enfield*
Briarwood College *Southington*
Capital Community Technical College *Hartford*
Gateway Community-Technical College *New Haven*
Gibbs College *Norwalk*
Housatonic Community-Technical College *Bridgeport*
Manchester Community-Technical College *Manchester*
Middlesex Community-Technical College *Middletown*
Mitchell College *New London*
Naugatuck Valley Community-Technical CollegeWaterbury
Northwestern Connecticut Community-Technical College *Winsted*
Norwalk Community-Technical College *Norwalk*
Quinebaug Valley Community-Technical College *Danielson*
St. Vincent's College *Bridgeport*
Swiss Hospitality Institute *Cesar Ritz Washington*
Three Rivers Community-Technical College *Norwich*
Tunxis Community Technical College *Farmington*

Maine

Andover College *Portland*
Beal College *Bangor*
Casco Bay College *Portland*
Central Maine Medical Center School of Nursing *Lewiston*
Central Maine Technical College *Auburn*
Eastern Maine Technical College *Bangor*
Kennebec Valley Technical College *Fairfield*
Mid-State College *Auburn*
Northern Maine Technical College *Presque Isle*
Southern Maine Technical College *South Portland*
University of Maine at Augusta *Augusta*
Washington County Technical College *Calais*
York County Technical College *Wells*

Massachusetts

Aquinas College at Milton *Milton*
Aquinas College at Newton *Newton*
Baptist Bible College East *Boston*
Bay State College *Boston*
Berkshire Community College *Pittsfield*
Bristol Community College *Fall River*
Bunker Hill Community College *Boston*
Burdett School *Boston*
Cape Cod Community College *West Barnstable*
Dean College *Franklin*
Essex Agricultural and Technical Institute *Hathorne*
Fisher College *Boston*
Franklin Institute of Boston *Boston*
Greenfield Community College *Greenfield*
Holyoke Community College *Holyoke*
ITT Technical Institute *Framingham*
Katharine Gibbs School *Boston*
Labouré College *Boston*
Marian Court College *Swampscott*
Massachusetts Bay Community College *Wellesley Hills*
Massasoit Community College *Brockton*
Middlesex Community College *Bedford*
Mount Ida College *Newton Centre*
Mount Wachusett Community College *Gardner*
Newbury College *Brookline*
The New England Banking Institute *Boston*
Northern Essex Community College *Haverhill*
North Shore Community College *Danvers*
Quincy College *Quincy*
Quinsigamond Community College *Worcester*
Roxbury Community College *Roxbury Crossing*
St. Hyacinth College and Seminary *Granby*
Springfield Technical Community College *Springfield*

New Hampshire

Castle College *Windham*
Hesser College *Manchester*
McIntosh College *Dover*
New Hampshire Community Technical College, Berlin/Laconia *Berlin*
New Hampshire Community Technical College, Manchester/Stratham *Manchester*
New Hampshire Community Technical College, Nashua/Claremont *Nashua*
New Hampshire Technical Institute *Concord*
White Pines College *Chester*

Rhode Island

Community College of Rhode Island *Warwick*
New England Institute of Technology *Warwick*

Vermont

Champlain College *Burlington*
Community College of Vermont *Waterbury*
Landmark College *Putney*
New England Culinary Institute *Montpelier*
Sterling College *Craftsbury Common*
Vermont Technical College *Randolph Center*
Woodbury College *Montpelier*

New York

Adirondack Community College *Queensbury*
American Academy McAllister Institute of Funeral Service *New York*
American Academy of Dramatic Arts *New York*
Berkeley College *New York*
Berkeley College *White Plains*
Borough of Manhattan Community College of the City University of New York *New York*
Bramson ORT Technical Institute *Forest Hills*
Briarcliffe College *Bethpage*
Bronx Community College of the City University of New York *Bronx*
Broome Community College *Binghamton*
Bryant and Stratton Business Institute *Albany*
Bryant and Stratton Business Institute *Buffalo*
Bryant and Stratton Business Institute *Lackawanna*
Bryant and Stratton Business Institute *Liverpool*
Bryant and Stratton Business Institute *Rochester*
Bryant and Stratton Business Institute *Rochester*
Bryant and Stratton Business Institute *Syracuse*
Bryant and Stratton Business Institute, Eastern Hills Campus *Clarence*
Catholic Medical Center of Brooklyn and Queens School of Nursing *Fresh Meadows*
Cayuga County Community College *Auburn*
Central City Business Institute *Syracuse*
Clinton Community College *Plattsburgh*
Cochran School of Nursing *Yonkers*
Columbia-Greene Community College *Hudson*
Corning Community College *Corning*
Culinary Institute of America *Hyde Park*
Dutchess Community College *Poughkeepsie*
Erie Community College, City Campus *Buffalo*
Erie Community College, North Campus *Williamsville*
Erie Community College, South Campus *Orchard Park*
Eugenio María de Hostos Community College of the City University of New York *Bronx*
Finger Lakes Community College *Canandaigua*
Fiorello H. LaGuardia Community College of the City University of New York *Long Island City*
Fulton-Montgomery Community College *Johnstown*
Genesee Community College *Batavia*
Helene Fuld College of Nursing of North General Hospital *New York*
Herkimer County Community College *Herkimer*
Hudson Valley Community College *Troy*
Institute of Design and Construction *Brooklyn*
Interboro Institute *New York*
Jamestown Business College *Jamestown*
Jamestown Community College *Jamestown*
Jefferson Community College *Watertown*
Katharine Gibbs School *Melville*
Katharine Gibbs School *New York*
Kingsborough Community College of the City University of New York *Brooklyn*
Long Island College Hospital School of Nursing *Brooklyn*
Maria College *Albany*
Mater Dei College *Ogdensburg*
Mohawk Valley Community College *Utica*
Monroe College *Bronx*
Monroe College *New Rochelle*
Monroe Community College *Rochester*
Nassau Community College *Garden City*
The New Center College for Wholistic Health Education and Research *Syosset*
New York City Technical College of the City University of New York *Brooklyn*
Niagara County Community College *Sanborn*
North Country Community College *Saranac Lake*
Olean Business Institute *Olean*
Onondaga Community College *Syracuse*
Orange County Community College *Middletown*
Paul Smith's College of Arts and Sciences *Paul Smiths*
Phillips Beth Israel School of Nursing *New York*
Plaza Business Institute *Jackson Heights*
Queensborough Community College of the City University of New York *Bayside*
Rochester Business Institute *Rochester*
Rockland Community College *Suffern*
Sage Junior College of Albany *Albany*
Schenectady County Community College *Schenectady*
Simmons Institute of Funeral Service *Syracuse*
State University of New York at Farmingdale *Farmingdale*
State University of New York College of Agriculture and Technology at Cobleskill *Cobleskill*
State University of New York College of Agriculture and Technology at Morrisville *Morrisville*
State University of New York College of Environmental Science & Forestry, Ranger School *Wanakena*
State University of New York College of Technology at Alfred *Alfred*
State University of New York College of Technology at Canton *Canton*
State University of New York College of Technology at Delhi *Delhi*
Stenotype Academy *New York*
Suffolk County Community College–Ammerman Campus *Selden*
Suffolk County Community College–Eastern Campus *Riverhead*
Suffolk County Community College–Western Campus *Brentwood*
Sullivan County Community College *Loch Sheldrake*
Taylor Business Institute *New York*

Technical Career Institutes *New York*
Tompkins Cortland Community College *Dryden*
Trocaire College *Buffalo*
Ulster County Community College *Stone Ridge*
Utica School of Commerce *Utica*
Villa Maria College of Buffalo *Buffalo*
Westchester Business Institute *White Plains*
Westchester Community College *Valhalla*
Wood Tobe-Coburn School *New York*

The South

Alabama

Alabama Aviation and Technical College *Ozark*
Alabama Southern Community College *Monroeville*
Bessemer State Technical College *Bessemer*
Bevill State Community College *Sumiton*
Bishop State Community College *Mobile*
Central Alabama Community College *Alexander City*
Chattahoochee Valley State Community College *Phenix City*
Community College of the Air Force *Maxwell AFB*
Douglas MacArthur State Technical College *Opp*
Draughons Junior College *Montgomery*
Enterprise State Junior College *Enterprise*
Gadsden State Community College *Gadsden*
George Corley Wallace State Community CollegeSelma
George C. Wallace State Community College *Dothan*
Harry M. Ayers State Technical College *Anniston*
Herzing College of Business and Technology *Birmingham*
ITT Technical Institute *Birmingham*
James H. Faulkner State Community College *Bay Minette*
Jefferson Davis Community College *Brewton*
Jefferson State Community College *Birmingham*
J. F. Drake State Technical College *Huntsville*
John C. Calhoun State Community College *Decatur*
John M. Patterson State Technical College *Montgomery*
Lawson State Community College *Birmingham*
Lurleen B. Wallace State Junior College *Andalusia*
Marion Military Institute *Marion*
Northeast Alabama Community College *Rainsville*
Northwest-Shoals Community College *Muscle Shoals*
Reid State Technical College *Evergreen*
Shelton State Community College *Tuscaloosa*
Snead State Community College *Boaz*
Southern Union State Community College *Wadley*
Trenholm State Technical College *Montgomery*
UAB Walker College *Jasper*
Virginia College at Birmingham *Birmingham*
Virginia College at Huntsville *Huntsville*
Wallace State Community College *Hanceville*

Arkansas

Arkansas State University-Beebe Branch *Beebe*
Black River Technical College *Pocahontas*
Cossatot Technical College *DeQueen*
East Arkansas Community College *Forrest City*
Garland County Community College *Hot Springs*
ITT Technical Institute *Little Rock*
Mid-South Community College *West Memphis*
Mississippi County Community College *Blytheville*
North Arkansas College *Harrison*
NorthWest Arkansas Community College *Bentonville*
Ouachita Technical College *Malvern*
Ozarka Technical College *Melbourne*
Petit Jean Technical College *Morrilton*
Phillips Community College of the University of Arkansas *Helena*
Pulaski Technical College *North Little Rock*
Rich Mountain Community College *Mena*
Shorter College *North Little Rock*
South Arkansas Community College *El Dorado*
Southeast Arkansas Technical College *Pine Bluff*
Southern Arkansas University Tech *Camden*
University of Arkansas Community College at Hope *Hope*
Westark Community College *Fort Smith*

Florida

American Flyers College *Fort Lauderdale*
The Art Institute of Fort Lauderdale *Fort Lauderdale*
ATI Health Education Center *Miami*
Brevard Community College *Cocoa*
Broward Community College *Fort Lauderdale*
Central Florida Community College *Ocala*
Chipola Junior College *Marianna*
Daytona Beach Community College *Daytona Beach*
Edison Community College *Fort Myers*
Education America-Tampa Technical Institute Campus *Tampa*
Flagler Career Institute *Jacksonville*
Florida College *Temple Terrace*
Florida Community College at Jacksonville *Jacksonville*
Florida Hospital College of Health Sciences *Orlando*
Florida Keys Community College *Key West*

Florida National College *Hialeah*
Full Sail Center for the Recording Arts *Winter Park*
Gulf Coast Community College *Panama City*
Hillsborough Community College *Tampa*
Indian River Community College *Fort Pierce*
Institute of Career Education *West Palm Beach*
International Fine Arts College *Miami*
ITT Technical Institute *Fort Lauderdale*
ITT Technical Institute *Jacksonville*
ITT Technical Institute *Tampa*
Keiser College of Technology *Daytona Beach*
Keiser College of Technology *Fort Lauderdale*
Keiser College of Technology *Melbourne*
Keiser College of Technology *Sarasota*
Keiser College of Technology *Tallahassee*
Lake City Community College *Lake City*
Lake-Sumter Community College *Leesburg*
Manatee Community College *Bradenton*
Miami-Dade Community College *Miami*
National Institute for Paralegal Arts and Sciences *Boca Raton*
New England Institute of Technology and Florida Culinary Institute *West Palm Beach*
North Florida Community College *Madison*
Okaloosa-Walton Community College *Niceville*
Palm Beach Community College *Lake Worth*
Pasco-Hernando Community College *Dade City*
Pensacola Junior College *Pensacola*
Peoples College *Kissimmee*
Polk Community College *Winter Haven*
Prospect Hall *Hollywood*
St. Johns River Community College *Palatka*
St. Petersburg Junior College *St. Petersburg*
Santa Fe Community College *Gainesville*
Seminole Community College *Sanford*
South College *West Palm Beach*
Southern College *Orlando*
South Florida Community College *Avon Park*
Southwest Florida College of Business *Fort Myers*
Tallahassee Community College *Tallahassee*
Valencia Community College *Orlando*
Webster College *Holiday*
Webster College *Ocala*

Georgia

Abraham Baldwin Agricultural College *Tifton*
Andrew College *Cuthbert*
The Art Institute of Atlanta *Atlanta*
Athens Area Technical Institute *Athens*
Atlanta Metropolitan College *Atlanta*
Augusta Technical Institute *Augusta*
Bainbridge College *Bainbridge*
Bauder College *Atlanta*
Carroll Technical Institute *Carrollton*
Chattahoochee Technical Institute *Marietta*
Coastal Georgia Community College *Brunswick*
Columbus Technical Institute *Columbus*
Dalton College *Dalton*
Darton College *Albany*
DeKalb College *Decatur*
DeKalb Technical Institute *Clarkston*
East Georgia College *Swainsboro*
Emory University, Oxford College *Oxford*
Floyd College *Rome*
Gainesville College *Gainesville*
Georgia Military College *Milledgeville*
Gordon College *Barnesville*
Griffin Technical Institute *Griffin*
Gupton-Jones College of Funeral Service *Decatur*
Gwinnett Technical Institute *Lawrenceville*
Herzing College of Business and Technology *Atlanta*
Macon College *Macon*
Macon Technical Institute *Macon*
Meadows College of Business *Columbus*
Middle Georgia College *Cochran*
Savannah Technical Institute *Savannah*
South Georgia College *Douglas*
Thomas Technical Institute *Thomasville*
Truett-McConnell College *Cleveland*
Walker Technical Institute *Rock Springs*
Waycross College *Waycross*
Young Harris College *Young Harris*

Kentucky

Draughons Junior College *Bowling Green*
Fugazzi College *Lexington*
Institute of Electronic Technology *Paducah*
ITT Technical Institute *Louisville*
Kentucky College of Business *Danville*
Kentucky College of Business *Florence*
Kentucky College of Business *Lexington*
Kentucky College of Business *Louisville*
Kentucky College of Business *Pikeville*
Kentucky College of Business *Richmond*
Louisville Technical Institute *Louisville*
Owensboro Community College *Owensboro*
Owensboro Junior College of Business *Owensboro*
RETS Electronic Institute *Louisville*
St. Catharine College *St. Catharine*
Southern Ohio College, Northern Kentucky Campus *Fort Mitchell*
Spencerian College *Louisville*
University of Kentucky, Ashland Community College *Ashland*
University of Kentucky, Elizabethtown Community College *Elizabethtown*
University of Kentucky, Hazard Community College *Hazard*
University of Kentucky, Henderson Community College *Henderson*
University of Kentucky, Hopkinsville Community College *Hopkinsville*

University of Kentucky, Jefferson Community College *Louisville*
University of Kentucky, Lexington Community College *Lexington*
University of Kentucky, Madisonville Community College *Madisonville*
University of Kentucky, Maysville Community College *Maysville*
University of Kentucky, Paducah Community College *Paducah*
University of Kentucky, Prestonsburg Community College *Prestonsburg*
University of Kentucky, Somerset Community College *Somerset*
University of Kentucky, Southeast Community College *Cumberland*

Louisiana

Bossier Parish Community College *Bossier City*
Cumberland School of Technology *Baton Rouge*
Delgado Community College *New Orleans*
Elaine P. Nunez Community College *Chalmette*
Louisiana State University at Alexandria *Alexandria*
Louisiana State University at Eunice *Eunice*
Our Lady of the Lake College *Baton Rouge*
Southern University at Shreveport–Bossier City Campus *Shreveport*

Mississippi

Coahoma Community College *Clarksdale*
Copiah-Lincoln Community College *Wesson*
Copiah-Lincoln Community College–Natchez Campus *Natchez*
East Central Community College *Decatur*
East Mississippi Community College *Scooba*
Hinds Community College *Raymond*
Holmes Community College *Goodman*
Itawamba Community College *Fulton*
Jones County Junior College *Ellisville*
Mary Holmes College *West Point*
Meridian Community College *Meridian*
Mississippi Delta Community College *Moorhead*
Mississippi Gulf Coast Community College *Perkinston*
Northeast Mississippi Community College *Booneville*
Northwest Mississippi Community College *Senatobia*
Pearl River Community College *Poplarville*
Southwest Mississippi Community College *Summit*
Wood College *Mathiston*

North Carolina

Alamance Community College *Graham*
Anson Community College *Polkton*
Asheville-Buncombe Technical Community College *Asheville*
Beaufort County Community College *Washington*
Bladen Community College *Dublin*
Blue Ridge Community College *Flat Rock*
Brevard College *Brevard*
Brunswick Community College *Supply*
Cabarrus College of Health Sciences *Concord*
Caldwell Community College and Technical Institute *Hudson*
Cape Fear Community College *Wilmington*
Carolinas College of Health Sciences *Charlotte*
Carteret Community College *Morehead City*
Catawba Valley Community College *Hickory*
Cecils Junior College of Business *Asheville*
Central Carolina Community College *Sanford*
Central Piedmont Community College *Charlotte*
Cleveland Community College *Shelby*
Coastal Carolina Community College *Jacksonville*
College of The Albemarle *Elizabeth City*
Craven Community College *New Bern*
Davidson County Community College *Lexington*
Durham Technical Community College *Durham*
Edgecombe Community College *Tarboro*
Fayetteville Technical Community College *Fayetteville*
Forsyth Technical Community College *Winston-Salem*
Gaston College *Dallas*
Guilford Technical Community College *Jamestown*
Halifax Community College *Weldon*
Haywood Community College *Clyde*
Isothermal Community College *Spindale*
James Sprunt Community College *Kenansville*
Johnston Community College *Smithfield*
Lenoir Community College *Kinston*
Louisburg College *Louisburg*
Martin Community College *Williamston*
Mayland Community College *Spruce Pine*
McDowell Technical Community College *Marion*
Mitchell Community College *Statesville*
Montgomery Community College *Troy*
Nash Community College *Rocky Mount*
Pamlico Community College *Grantsboro*
Peace College *Raleigh*
Piedmont Community College *Roxboro*
Pitt Community College *Greenville*
Randolph Community College *Asheboro*
Richmond Community College *Hamlet*
Roanoke-Chowan Community College *Ahoskie*
Robeson Community College *Lumberton*
Rockingham Community College *Wentworth*
Rowan-Cabarrus Community College *Salisbury*
Sampson Community College *Clinton*
Sandhills Community College *Pinehurst*

Southeastern Baptist Theological Seminary *Wake Forest*
Southeastern Community College *Whiteville*
Southwestern Community College *Sylva*
Stanly Community College *Albemarle*
Surry Community College *Dobson*
Tri-County Community College *Murphy*
Vance-Granville Community College *Henderson*
Wake Technical Community College *Raleigh*
Wayne Community College *Goldsboro*
Western Piedmont Community College *Morganton*
Wilkes Community College *Wilkesboro*
Wilson Technical Community College *Wilson*

South Carolina

Aiken Technical College *Aiken*
Central Carolina Technical College *Sumter*
Chesterfield-Marlboro Technical College *Cheraw*
Columbia Junior College *Columbia*
Denmark Technical College *Denmark*
Florence-Darlington Technical College *Florence*
Forrest Junior College *Anderson*
Greenville Technical College *Greenville*
Horry-Georgetown Technical College *Conway*
Midlands Technical College *Columbia*
Nielsen Electronics Institute *Charleston*
Orangeburg-Calhoun Technical College *Orangeburg*
Piedmont Technical College *Greenwood*
Spartanburg Methodist College *Spartanburg*
Spartanburg Technical College *Spartanburg*
Technical College of the Lowcountry *Beaufort*
Tri-County Technical College *Pendleton*
Trident Technical College *Charleston*
University of South Carolina at Beaufort *Beaufort*
University of South Carolina at Lancaster *Lancaster*
University of South Carolina at Sumter *Sumter*
University of South Carolina at Union *Union*
University of South Carolina Salkehatchie Regional Campus *Allendale*
Williamsburg Technical College *Kingstree*
York Technical College *Rock Hill*

Tennessee

American Academy of Nutrition, College of Nutrition *Knoxville*
Aquinas College *Nashville*
Chattanooga State Technical Community CollegeChattanooga
Cleveland State Community College *Cleveland*
Columbia State Community College *Columbia*
Cumberland School of Technology *Cookeville*
Draughons Junior College *Clarksville*
Draughons Junior College *Nashville*
Dyersburg State Community College *Dyersburg*
Fugazzi College *Nashville*
Hiwassee College *Madisonville*
ITT Technical Institute *Knoxville*
ITT Technical Institute *Memphis*
ITT Technical Institute *Nashville*
Jackson State Community College *Jackson*
John A. Gupton College *Nashville*
Knoxville Business College *Knoxville*
Mid-America Baptist Theological Seminary *Germantown*
Motlow State Community College *Tullahoma*
Nashville State Technical Institute *Nashville*
Northeast State Technical Community College *Blountville*
Pellissippi State Technical Community CollegeKnoxville
Roane State Community College *Harriman*
Shelby State Community College *Memphis*
State Technical Institute at Memphis *Memphis*
Tennessee Institute of Electronics *Knoxville*
Volunteer State Community College *Gallatin*
Walters State Community College *Morristown*
Watkins Institute College of Art and Design *Nashville*

Texas

Alvin Community College *Alvin*
Amarillo College *Amarillo*
Angelina College *Lufkin*
The Art Institute of Dallas *Dallas*
The Art Institute of Houston *Houston*
Austin Community College *Austin*
Bee County College *Beeville*
Blinn College *Brenham*
Brazosport College *Lake Jackson*
Brookhaven College *Farmers Branch*
Cedar Valley College *Lancaster*
Central Texas College *Killeen*
Cisco Junior College *Cisco*
Clarendon College *Clarendon*
The College of Saint Thomas More *Fort Worth*
College of the Mainland *Texas City*
Collin County Community College *McKinney*
Commonwealth Institute of Funeral Service *Houston*
Computer Career Center *El Paso*
Dallas Institute of Funeral Service *Dallas*
Del Mar College *Corpus Christi*
Eastfield College *Mesquite*
El Centro College *Dallas*
El Paso Community College *El Paso*
Frank Phillips College *Borger*
Galveston College *Galveston*
Grayson County College *Denison*
Hill College of the Hill Junior College District *Hillsboro*
Houston Community College System *Houston*
Howard College *Big Spring*

ITT Technical Institute *Arlington*
ITT Technical Institute *Austin*
ITT Technical Institute *Garland*
ITT Technical Institute *Houston*
ITT Technical Institute *Houston*
ITT Technical Institute *San Antonio*
Jacksonville College *Jacksonville*
KD Studio *Dallas*
Kilgore College *Kilgore*
Kingwood College *Kingwood*
Lamar University-Orange *Orange*
Lamar University-Port Arthur *Port Arthur*
Laredo Community College *Laredo*
Lee College *Baytown*
Lon Morris College *Jacksonville*
McLennan Community College *Waco*
Midland College *Midland*
Miss Wade's Fashion Merchandising College *Dallas*
Montgomery College *Conroe*
Mountain View College *Dallas*
Navarro College *Corsicana*
North Central Texas College *Gainesville*
Northeast Texas Community College *Mount Pleasant*
North Harris College *Houston*
North Lake College *Irving*
Odessa College *Odessa*
Palo Alto College *San Antonio*
Panola College *Carthage*
Paris Junior College *Paris*
Ranger College *Ranger*
Richland College *Dallas*
St. Philip's College *San Antonio*
San Antonio College *San Antonio*
San Jacinto College-Central Campus *Pasadena*
San Jacinto College-North Campus *Houston*
San Jacinto College-South Campus *Houston*
South Plains College *Levelland*
South Texas Community College *McAllen*
Southwest Texas Junior College *Uvalde*
Tarrant County Junior College *Fort Worth*
Temple College *Temple*
Texarkana College *Texarkana*
Texas Southmost College *Brownsville*
Texas State Technical College *Sweetwater*
Texas State Technical College-Harlingen *Harlingen*
Texas State Technical College-Waco/Marshall Campus *Waco*
Tomball College *Tomball*
Trinity Valley Community College *Athens*
Tyler Junior College *Tyler*
Vernon Regional Junior College *Vernon*
Victoria College *Victoria*
Weatherford College *Weatherford*
Western Texas College *Snyder*
Wharton County Junior College *Wharton*

The West

Alaska

Charter College *Anchorage*
University of Alaska Anchorage, Kenai Peninsula College *Soldotna*
University of Alaska Anchorage, Kodiak College *Kodiak*
University of Alaska Anchorage, Matanuska-Susitna College *Palmer*
University of Alaska, Prince William Sound Community College *Valdez*
University of Alaska Southeast, Ketchikan Campus *Ketchikan*
University of Alaska Southeast, Sitka Campus *Sitka*

Arizona

Academy of Business College *Phoenix*
Apollo College-Phoenix, Inc. *Phoenix*
Apollo College-Tri-City, Inc. *Mesa*
Apollo College-Tucson, Inc. *Tucson*
Apollo College-Westside, Inc. *Phoenix*
Arizona Western College *Yuma*
The Art Institute of Phoenix *Phoenix*
Central Arizona College *Coolidge*
Chandler-Gilbert Community College *Chandler*
Chaparral College *Tucson*
Cochise College *Douglas*
Cochise College *Sierra Vista*
Coconino County Community College *Flagstaff*
Eastern Arizona College *Thatcher*
Gateway Community College *Phoenix*
Glendale Community College *Glendale*
ITT Technical Institute *Phoenix*
ITT Technical Institute *Tucson*
Lamson Junior College *Tempe*
Mesa Community College *Mesa*
Mohave Community College *Kingman*
Navajo Community College *Tsaile*
Northland Pioneer College *Holbrook*
Paradise Valley Community College *Phoenix*
Paralegal Institute, Inc. *Phoenix*
Phoenix College *Phoenix*
Pima Community College *Tucson*
Pima Medical Institute *Mesa*
Pima Medical Institute *Tucson*
Rio Salado College *Tempe*
Scottsdale Community College *Scottsdale*
South Mountain Community College *Phoenix*
Yavapai College *Prescott*

California

Allan Hancock College *Santa Maria*
American Academy of Dramatic Arts/West *Pasadena*
American River College *Sacramento*
Antelope Valley College *Lancaster*

Bakersfield College *Bakersfield*
Barstow College *Barstow*
Brooks College *Long Beach*
Butte College *Oroville*
Cabrillo College *Aptos*
Cañada College *Redwood City*
Cerritos College *Norwalk*
Cerro Coso Community College *Ridgecrest*
Chabot College *Hayward*
Chaffey College *Rancho Cucamonga*
Citrus College *Glendora*
City College of San Francisco *San Francisco*
Coastline Community College *Fountain Valley*
College of Alameda *Alameda*
College of Marin *Kentfield*
College of Oceaneering *Wilmington*
College of San Mateo *San Mateo*
College of the Canyons *Santa Clarita*
College of the Desert *Palm Desert*
College of the Redwoods *Eureka*
College of the Sequoias *Visalia*
College of the Siskiyous *Weed*
Columbia College *Sonora*
Compton Community College *Compton*
Contra Costa College *San Pablo*
Cosumnes River College *Sacramento*
Crafton Hills College *Yucaipa*
Cuesta College *San Luis Obispo*
Cuyamaca College *El Cajon*
Cypress College *Cypress*
De Anza College *Cupertino*
Deep Springs College *Deep Springs*
Diablo Valley College *Pleasant Hill*
Don Bosco Technical Institute *Rosemead*
D-Q University *Davis*
East Los Angeles College *Monterey Park*
El Camino College *Torrance*
Evergreen Valley College *San Jose*
Fashion Institute of Design and Merchandising, Costa Mesa *Costa Mesa*
Fashion Institute of Design and Merchandising, Los Angeles Campus *Los Angeles*
Fashion Institute of Design and Merchandising, San Diego Campus *San Diego*
Fashion Institute of Design and Merchandising, San Francisco Campus *San Francisco*
Feather River Community College District *Quincy*
Foothill College *Los Altos Hills*
Fresno City College *Fresno*
Fullerton College *Fullerton*
Gavilan College *Gilroy*
Glendale Community College *Glendale*
Golden West College *Huntington Beach*
Grossmont College *El Cajon*
Hartnell College *Salinas*
Heald College, School of Business *Concord*
Heald College, School of Business *Hayward*
Heald College, School of Business *Oakland*
Heald College, School of Business *Rancho Cordova*
Heald College, School of Business *Salinas*
Heald College, School of Business *San Francisco*
Heald College, School of Business *San Jose*
Heald College, School of Business *Santa Rosa*
Heald College, School of Business *Stockton*
Heald College, School of Technology *Hayward*
Heald College, School of Technology *Martinez*
Heald College, School of Technology *Milpitas*
Heald College, School of Technology *Sacramento*
Heald College, School of Technology *San Francisco*
Heald College, Schools of Business and Technology *Fresno*
Imperial Valley College *Imperial*
Irvine Valley College *Irvine*
ITT Technical Institute *Anaheim*
ITT Technical Institute *Carson*
ITT Technical Institute *Oxnard*
ITT Technical Institute *Sacramento*
ITT Technical Institute *San Bernardino*
ITT Technical Institute *San Diego*
ITT Technical Institute *Sylmar*
ITT Technical Institute *West Covina*
Kelsey Jenney College *San Diego*
Kings River Community College *Reedley*
Lake Tahoe Community College *South Lake Tahoe*
Laney College *Oakland*
Las Positas College *Livermore*
Lassen College *Susanville*
Long Beach City College *Long Beach*
Los Angeles City College *Los Angeles*
Los Angeles County Medical Center School for Nursing *Los Angeles*
Los Angeles Harbor College *Wilmington*
Los Angeles Mission College *Sylmar*
Los Angeles Pierce College *Woodland Hills*
Los Angeles Southwest College *Los Angeles*
Los Angeles Trade-Technical College *Los Angeles*
Los Angeles Valley College *Van Nuys*
Los Medanos College *Pittsburg*
Maric College of Medical Careers *San Diego*
Marymount College, Palos Verdes, California *Rancho Palos Verdes*
Mendocino College *Ukiah*
Merced College *Merced*
Merritt College *Oakland*
MiraCosta College *Oceanside*
Mission College *Santa Clara*
Modesto Junior College *Modesto*
Monterey Peninsula College *Monterey*
Moorpark College *Moorpark*
Mt. San Antonio College *Walnut*
Mt. San Jacinto College *San Jacinto*
Napa Valley College *Napa*

Ohlone College *Fremont*
Orange Coast College *Costa Mesa*
Oxnard College *Oxnard*
Palomar College *San Marcos*
Palo Verde College *Blythe*
Pasadena City College *Pasadena*
Porterville College *Porterville*
Queen of the Holy Rosary College *Mission San Jose*
Rancho Santiago College *Santa Ana*
Rio Hondo College *Whittier*
Riverside Community College *Riverside*
Sacramento City College *Sacramento*
Saddleback College *Mission Viejo*
Salvation Army College for Officer Training *Rancho Palos Verdes*
San Bernardino Valley College *San Bernardino*
San Diego City College *San Diego*
San Diego Mesa College *San Diego*
San Diego Miramar College *San Diego*
San Francisco College of Mortuary Science *San Francisco*
San Joaquin Delta College *Stockton*
San Joaquin Valley College *Visalia*
San Jose City College *San Jose*
Santa Barbara City College *Santa Barbara*
Santa Monica College *Santa Monica*
Santa Rosa Junior College *Santa Rosa*
Shasta College *Redding*
Sierra College *Rocklin*
Skyline College *San Bruno*
Solano Community College *Suisun City*
Southwestern College *Chula Vista*
Taft College *Taft*
Ventura College *Ventura*
Victor Valley College *Victorville*
Vista Community College *Berkeley*
West Hills Community College *Coalinga*
West Los Angeles College *Culver City*
West Valley College *Saratoga*
Yuba College *Marysville*

Colorado

Aims Community College *Greeley*
Arapahoe Community College *Littleton*
Bel-Rea Institute of Animal Technology *Denver*
Blair College *Colorado Springs*
The Colorado Institute of Art *Denver*
Colorado Mountain College *Glenwood Springs*
Colorado Mountain College, Alpine Campus *Steamboat Springs*
Colorado Mountain College, Timberline Campus *Leadville*
Colorado Northwestern Community College *Rangely*
Community College of Aurora *Aurora*
Community College of Denver *Denver*
Denver Automotive and Diesel College *Denver*
Front Range Community College *Westminster*
ITT Technical Institute *Aurora*
Johnson & Wales University *Vail*
Lamar Community College *Lamar*
Morgan Community College *Fort Morgan*
Northeastern Junior College *Sterling*
Otero Junior College *La Junta*
Parks College *Denver*
Pikes Peak Community College *Colorado Springs*
Pima Medical Institute *Denver*
PPI Health Careers School *Colorado Springs*
Pueblo Community College *Pueblo*
Red Rocks Community College *Lakewood*
Trinidad State Junior College *Trinidad*

Hawaii

Hawaii Tokai International College *Honolulu*
Heald College, Schools of Business and Technology *Honolulu*
University of Hawaii–Hawaii Community College *Hilo*
University of Hawaii–Honolulu Community College *Honolulu*
University of Hawaii–Kapiolani Community College *Honolulu*
University of Hawaii–Kauai Community College *Lihue*
University of Hawaii–Leeward Community College *Pearl City*
University of Hawaii–Maui Community College *Kahului*
University of Hawaii–Windward Community College *Kaneohe*

Idaho

College of Southern Idaho *Twin Falls*
Eastern Idaho Technical College *Idaho Falls*
ITT Technical Institute *Boise*
North Idaho College *Coeur d'Alene*
Ricks College *Rexburg*

Montana

Blackfeet Community College *Browning*
Dawson Community College *Glendive*
Dull Knife Memorial College *Lame Deer*
Flathead Valley Community College *Kalispell*
Fort Belknap College *Harlem*
Fort Peck Community College *Poplar*
Helena College of Technology of The University of Montana *Helena*
Little Big Horn College *Crow Agency*
Miles Community College *Miles City*
Montana State University College of Technology–Great Falls *Great Falls*
Salish Kootenai College *Pablo*
Stone Child College *Box Elder*

Nevada

Community College of Southern Nevada *North Las Vegas*
Great Basin College *Elko*
Truckee Meadows Community College *Reno*
Western Nevada Community College *Carson City*

New Mexico

Albuquerque Technical Vocational Institute *Albuquerque*
Clovis Community College *Clovis*
Doña Ana Branch Community College *Las Cruces*
Eastern New Mexico University-Roswell *Roswell*
Institute of American Indian Arts *Santa Fe*
Luna Vocational Technical Institute *Las Vegas*
New Mexico Junior College *Hobbs*
New Mexico Military Institute *Roswell*
New Mexico State University-Alamogordo *Alamogordo*
New Mexico State University-Carlsbad *Carlsbad*
New Mexico State University-Grants *Grants*
Northern New Mexico Community College *Espaola*
Parks College *Albuquerque*
Pima Medical Institute *Albuquerque*
San Juan College *Farmington*
Santa Fe Community College *Santa Fe*
Southwestern Indian Polytechnic Institute *Albuquerque*
University of New Mexico-Gallup Branch *Gallup*
University of New Mexico-Los Alamos Branch *Los Alamos*
University of New Mexico-Valencia Campus *Los Lunas*

Oregon

Blue Mountain Community College *Pendleton*
Central Oregon Community College *Bend*
Chemeketa Community College *Salem*
Clackamas Community College *Oregon City*
Clatsop Community College *Astoria*
ITT Technical Institute *Portland*
Lane Community College *Eugene*
Linn-Benton Community College *Albany*
Mt. Hood Community College *Gresham*
Portland Community College *Portland*
Rogue Community College *Grants Pass*
Southwestern Oregon Community College *Coos Bay*
Treasure Valley Community College *Ontario*
Umpqua Community College *Roseburg*

Utah

College of Eastern Utah *Price*
Dixie College *St. George*
ITT Technical Institute *Murray*
LDS Business College *Salt Lake City*
Mountain West College *Salt Lake City*
Salt Lake Community College *Salt Lake City*
Snow College *Ephraim*
Stevens Henager College *Ogden*
Utah Valley State College *Orem*

Washington

The Art Institute of Seattle *Seattle*
Bellevue Community College *Bellevue*
Big Bend Community College *Moses Lake*
Centralia College *Centralia*
Clark College *Vancouver*
Columbia Basin College *Pasco*
Edmonds Community College *Lynnwood*
Everett Community College *Everett*
Grays Harbor College *Aberdeen*
Green River Community College *Auburn*
Highline Community College *Des Moines*
ITT Technical Institute *Seattle*
ITT Technical Institute *Spokane*
Lake Washington Technical College *Kirkland*
Lower Columbia College *Longview*
North Seattle Community College *Seattle*
Northwest Indian College *Bellingham*
Olympic College *Bremerton*
Peninsula College *Port Angeles*
Pierce College *Lakewood*
Pima Medical Institute *Seattle*
Renton Technical College *Renton*
Seattle Central Community College *Seattle*
Shoreline Community College *Seattle*
Skagit Valley College *Mount Vernon*
South Puget Sound Community College *Olympia*
South Seattle Community College *Seattle*
Spokane Community College *Spokane*
Spokane Falls Community College *Spokane*
Tacoma Community College *Tacoma*
Walla Walla Community College *Walla Walla*
Wenatchee Valley College *Wenatchee*
Whatcom Community College *Bellingham*
Yakima Valley Community College *Yakima*

Wyoming

Casper College *Casper*
Central Wyoming College *Riverton*
Eastern Wyoming College *Torrington*
Laramie County Community College *Cheyenne*
Northwest College *Powell*
Sheridan College *Sheridan*
Western Wyoming Community College *Rock Springs*
Wyoming Technical Institute *Laramie*

INDEX OF COLLEGES AND UNIVERSITIES

DeVry Institute of Technology, Chicago, IL 77

DeVry Institute of Technology, Chicago, IL 77

NOTES

NOTES

NOTES

NOTES

NOTES